Markets with cash and/or futures price histories

The following commodities are available on Knight-Ridder's DataPak. Please specify which market(s) you are interested in when you call.

Aluminum	Gold	Potatoes
Barley	Heating Oil	Rapeseed (Canola)
Broilers	Hides and Leather	Rice
Butter	Hogs	Rubber
Cattle and Calves	Knight-Ridder CRB	Rye
Cheese	Futures Index	Silk
Cocoa	Interest Rates, U.S.	Silver
Coconut Oil and Copra	Interest Rates, Worldwide	Soybean Meal
Coffee	Iron and Steel	Soybean Oil
Copper	Lard	Soybeans
Corn	Lead	Stock Index Futures, U.S.
Corn Oil	Lumber and Plywood	Stock Index Futures,
Cotton	Mercury	Worldwide
Cottonseed and Products	Milk	Sugar
Currencies	Nickel	Tallow and Greases
Eggs	Oats	Tin
Fertilizers (Nitrogen,	Oranges and Orange Juice	Wheat and Flour
Phosphate and Potash)	Palm Oil	Wool
Flaxseed and Linseed Oil	Petroleum	Zinc
Gas	Platinum-Group Metals	
Gasoline	Pork Bellies	

To order your DataPak on disk, or for more information, call a Customer Service Representative today. Phone toll-free:

800-526-DATA, ext. 9005

When you call, remember to ask about our CD-ROM product, InfoTech. All historical CRB Yearbook information and price histories are available on a single CD-ROM!

THE CRB COMMODITY YEARBOOK
1995

Knight-Ridder Financial/
Commodity Research Bureau

John Wiley & Sons, Inc.
New York • Chichester • Brisbane • Toronto • Singapore

Printed in the United States of America
10 9 8 7 6 5 4 3 2 1

Knight-Ridder Financial Commodity Research Bureau
30 South Wacker Drive, Suite 1820
Chicago, IL 60606
(312) 454-1801/(800) 621-5271

SUBSCRIPTION NOTICE

This Wiley product is updated on a quarterly basis with supplements to reflect important changes in the subject matter.
It is available as a stand-alone edition or as a subscription service
with three supplements (Fall, Winter, and Summer). These
seasonal supplements will contain updated charts, tables,
and graphs, as well as new data and price information. This
includes supply and demand data, production/consumption
figures, and trading highlights.

If you purchased this product this year and wish to receive
next year's main volume and supplement service, please send
your name, company name (if applicable), address, and the
title of the product to:

Supplement Department
John Wiley & Sons, Inc.
One Wiley Drive
Somerset, NJ 08875
1-800-225-5945

For customers outside the United States, please contact
the Wiley office nearest you:

Professional & Reference Division
John Wiley & Sons, Ltd.
22 Worcester Road
Rexdale, Ontario M9W 1L, Canada
(416) 675-3580
1-800-263-1590 in Canada
John Wiley & Sons, Ltd.
Baffins Lane
Chicester, West Sussex PO19 1UD, United Kingdom
(44) (243) 779777

Professional, Reference and Trade Division
Jacaranda Wiley Ltd.
PO Box 174
Ryde, NSW 2113, Australia
(02) 805-1100

TABLE OF CONTENTS

3T

ACKNOWLEDGMENTS

The editors wish to thank the following for source material:

Aluminum Association
American Bureau of Metal Statistics
American Gas Association
American Iron and Steel Institute
American Metal Market
American Paper and Pulp Association
American Petroleum Institute
Atomic Industrial Forum Inc.
Chicago Board of Trade
Chicago Mercantile Exchange
Citrus Associates of the N.Y. Cotton Exchange
Coffee, Sugar & Cocoa Exchange
Commodity Exchange, N.Y.
Commodity Futures Trading Commission
Edison Electric Institute
F.W. Dodge Corp.
Federal Power Commission
Federal Reserve Board
Florida Department of Citrus
Futures Industry Association
General Services Administration
Gill & Duffus Ltd.
Gold Fields Mineral Services Ltd.
Handy & Harman
International Cotton Advisory Committee
International Monetary Market (Chicago)
International Rubber Study Group
International Tea Committee
Johnson Matthey Ltd.
The Journal of Commerce
Kansas City Board of Trade
Leather Industries of America Inc.
London Metal Exchange
MidAmerica Commodity Exchange

Minneapolis Grain Exchange
National Coffee Association of U.S.A., Inc.
New York Cotton Exchange
New York Futures Exchange
New York Mercantile Exchange
Newsprint Service Bureau
Nuclear Exchange Corp.
Nuclear Regulatory Commission
Oil World
Organization for Economic Co-operation
  and Development
Portland Cement Association
Random Lengths
Rubber Manufacturers Association
Shell Briefing Service
The Silver Institute
Society of the Plastics Industry Inc.
Tea Council Inc.
Textile Economics Bureau Inc.
Textile Organon
U.N. Conference on Trade and Development
U.N. Food and Agriculture Organization
U.S. Bureau of Mines
U.S. Department of Agriculture
U.S. Department of Commerce
U.S. Department of Energy
U.S. Department of the Interior
U.S. Department of Labor
U.S. Department of the Treasury
The Wall Street Journal
Winnipeg Commodity Exchange
Wool Services Co.
Zinc Institute

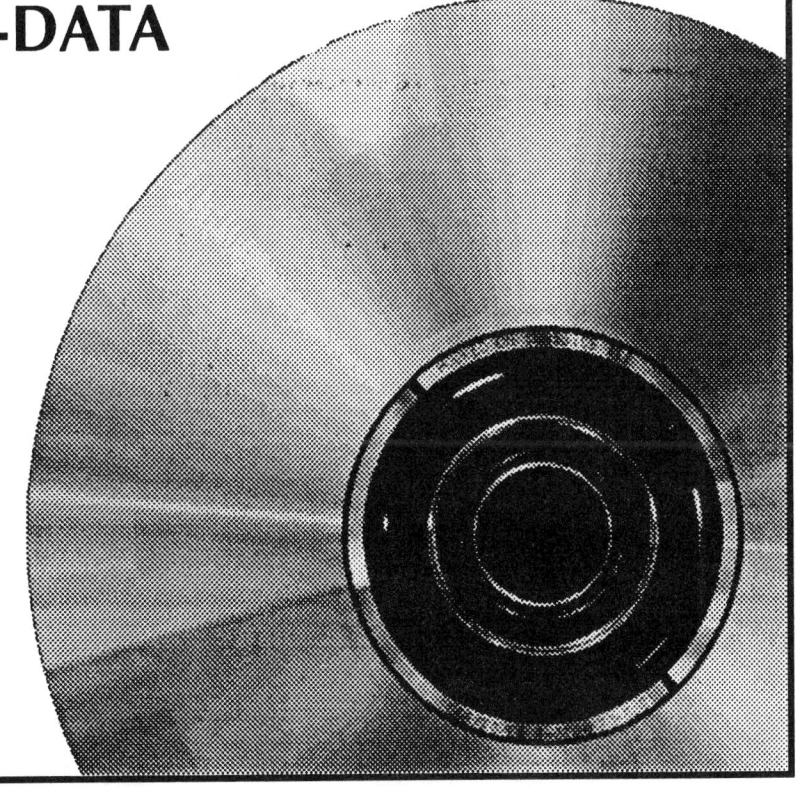

THE COMMODITY PRICE TREND

In 1994, the Knight-Ridder Commodity Research Bureau's Futures Price Index rose for the second consecutive year. The December 30, 1994 closing value of 236.64 was 10.33 higher, or 4.56 percent above the December 31, 1993 level. Unlike 1993, when all seven sub-index groups advanced, 1994's gain was almost exclusively a result of the 51.3 percent rise in the imported group. Also contributing to the year-on-year gain was a 9.9 percent rise in the industrial components.

Four of the seven sub-index groups declined in 1994, although only two groups lost significant ground. The largest drop was in the livestock components, 15.7 percent, followed by the grains, losing 12.4 percent.

Three of the seven sub-index groups, oilseeds, precious metals and the miscellaneous index, showed almost no annual change, finishing the year within 1 percent of the previous year's closing values.

Grains and Oilseeds

The 12.4 percent decline in the grain sub-index was primarily due to the 25 percent drop in corn prices in 1994. The price decline was a result of U.S. farmers producing a record 10 billion bushels of corn, up dramatically from the previous year's flood and drought damaged crop.

A 6 percent shortfall in world wheat production, compared to the previous year, contributed to a 6 percent rise in U.S. wheat prices in 1994. Lower output from Australia, Russia and the United States contributed to the price rise.

Although soybean and soybean meal prices plummeted 22.7 percent and 24.8 percent, respectively, worldwide demand for vegetable oils allowed the oilseed index to only decline an unnoticeable 0.4 percent. Replenished stock levels of soybean oil suggest 1995 will not see the disparity in price movements between soybeans and their products that 1994 did.

Imported

The startling rise of 51.3 percent in the imported sub-index pales in comparison to the 136 percent gain in coffee prices in 1994. A severe freeze in Brazil was the catalyst for the bull market in coffee, but production shortfalls were also attributable to farmer dissatisfaction with low world prices in the early 1990's and the resultant loss of coffee tree population. A new five year agreement among the members of the International Coffee Organization is likely to stabilize prices and increase coffee tree plantings, resulting in larger production in the coming years.

Sugar prices rose 40.8 percent last year, the strength reflecting larger imports by China and lower production in Cuba and Europe.

Cocoa prices gained 11.8 percent in 1994, in spite of anticipated record world production of 2.55 million metric tons.

Industrials

The industrial sub-index advanced 9.9 percent in 1994 led by gains in copper, cotton and crude oil. Lumber prices, which had ended 1993 at record levels, dropped 34.6 percent in 1994.

Strong growth in the U.S. economy and a significant drawdown in stock levels contributed to a 59.2 percent increase in copper prices last year, the strongest component in the group.

Increased worldwide demand and fears of a shortfall in carryover stocks pushed cotton prices to 90¢ by year end, a 33.1 percent increase from the 1993 ending price.

Low global oil stocks, steady OPEC production and the worldwide economic rebound all helped contribute to a 25.3 percent gain in crude oil prices last year.

Livestock

The livestock sub-index was the big loser in 1994, dropping 15.8 percent. Lower hog and pork belly prices, down 13.2 and 27.6 percent respectively, were primarily responsible for the decline. The continuing expansion of large commercial hog operations led to a record market hog inventory in 1994 and prospects of an even larger herd in 1995.

Cattle prices declined a negligible 1.0 percent for the year.

Precious Metals

The precious metals sub-index rose a barely noticeable 0.48 percent in 1994 as small losses in gold and silver were not quite enough to offset a 5.0 percent increase in platinum prices. Strengthening economies and low interest rates led to an increase in auto sales. Usage in catalytic converters accounts for the principal disappearance of platinum.

Miscellaneous

Increasing per capita consumption of orange juice offset the second largest Florida orange crop on record and led to an unnoticeable 1.0 percent drop in the miscellaneous sub-index.

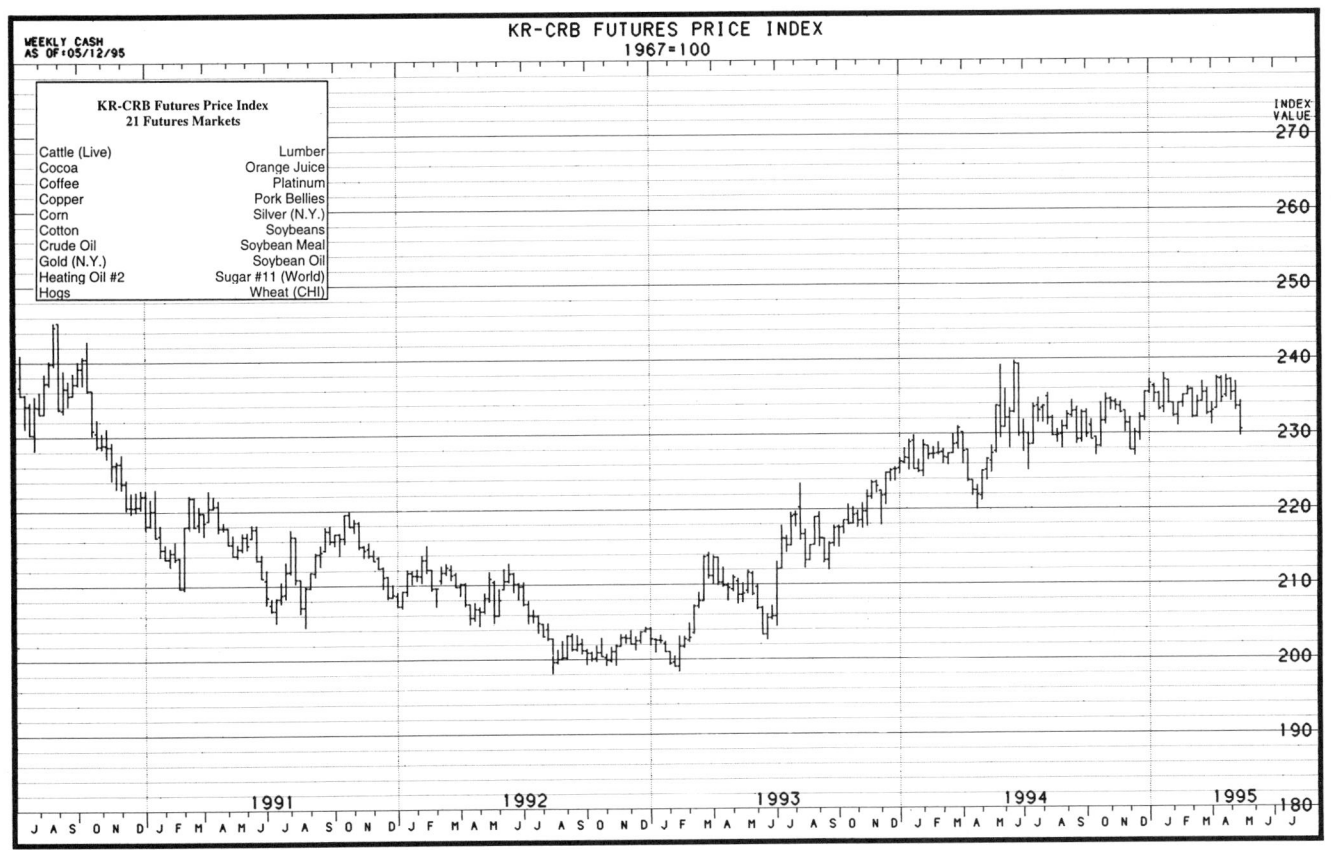

Monthly Knight-Ridder CRB Futures Price Index   High, Low & Close 1967 = 100

Year		Jan.	Feb.	Mar.	Apr.	May	June	July	Aug.	Sept.	Oct.	Nov.	Dec.	Range
1986	High	231.1	216.6	216.5	213.5	216.1	205.7	203.7	207.1	212.3	213.4	213.3	212.0	231.1
	Low	219.9	209.9	209.4	203.0	205.5	201.6	196.9	201.0	208.2	209.7	208.4	207.5	196.9
	Close	219.9	209.9	209.6	213.5	205.5	201.6	200.1	207.1	210.9	211.3	210.7	209.1	----
1987	High	213.9	213.7	210.1	221.7	235.6	234.6	227.8	226.8	227.3	232.7	237.1	234.7	237.1
	Low	208.3	204.2	205.7	209.4	222.6	223.1	220.7	222.4	223.5	222.7	221.1	227.5	204.2
	Close	212.6	205.4	208.7	221.7	224.9	225.9	225.9	223.0	223.8	223.4	234.6	232.5	----
1988	High	239.3	232.9	233.5	236.0	248.4	270.5	265.8	251.0	248.6	246.5	247.0	252.8	270.5
	Low	230.4	224.3	224.5	232.7	232.5	249.8	242.0	243.7	237.1	237.6	236.0	244.1	224.3
	Close	230.4	225.7	233.0	234.4	248.4	265.1	246.2	246.2	238.8	243.9	244.9	251.8	----
1989	High	251.6	243.3	248.1	244.6	242.8	235.4	237.0	225.5	226.8	228.1	231.7	229.9	251.6
	Low	241.1	236.6	241.7	237.7	229.4	227.9	221.2	221.5	222.9	223.0	226.0	225.6	221.2
	Close	242.4	243.2	242.1	238.0	229.4	234.4	221.2	225.5	226.8	225.7	228.8	229.9	----
1990	High	235.1	236.3	239.0	245.8	247.8	241.2	240.0	244.7	239.8	242.0	231.1	223.8	247.8
	Low	228.8	229.9	234.2	238.4	241.5	233.8	230.3	233.1	234.9	228.6	223.2	220.1	220.1
	Close	229.9	234.6	238.2	245.8	241.5	236.9	235.0	233.7	239.2	229.8	223.3	222.6	----
1991	High	222.8	215.6	221.8	222.2	217.0	217.7	214.1	216.5	217.6	219.8	218.6	213.9	222.8
	Low	214.1	209.7	217.3	216.2	214.1	208.4	205.9	204.7	211.9	216.2	213.3	207.2	204.7
	Close	214.1	215.6	218.5	216.2	215.4	208.4	214.1	211.8	215.6	218.2	213.3	208.1	----
1992	High	212.2	215.3	212.9	210.3	211.7	212.9	209.1	204.9	203.5	202.9	203.6	204.3	215.3
	Low	206.9	207.2	208.6	204.5	204.9	208.0	203.0	198.2	199.3	199.1	199.2	201.2	198.2
	Close	211.2	209.6	209.8	204.8	208.0	209.3	203.1	201.0	200.4	199.9	203.1	202.8	----
1993	High	203.2	204.9	214.3	213.9	211.8	210.0	219.7	223.5	217.8	220.6	223.8	226.8	226.8
	Low	199.3	198.4	203.4	207.8	207.4	202.6	207.2	212.1	211.9	216.6	217.4	218.4	198.4
	Close	199.5	202.9	212.5	210.9	208.7	207.1	219.3	217.2	216.1	218.4	218.0	226.3	----
1994	High	229.8	229.2	231.0	227.8	239.2	239.7	234.7	235.4	234.4	235.2	234.7	237.2	239.7
	Low	226.2	225.7	227.4	227.8	225.2	235.9	230.4	228.0	228.6	227.0	228.8	227.0	225.2
	Close	225.6	227.6	227.7	225.0	235.5	230.4	233.7	231.9	229.9	233.3	229.2	236.6	----

Source: Knight-Ridder Financial

KR-CRB FUTURES PRICE INDEX
1967=100

INDEX
VALUE

340
330
320
310
300
290
280
270
260
250
240
230
220
210
200
190
180
170
160
150
140
130
120
110
100

KR-CRB Futures Price Index
21 Futures Markets

Cattle (Live)	Lumber
Cocoa	Orange Juice
Coffee	Platinum
Copper	Pork Bellies
Corn	Silver (N.Y.)
Cotton	Soybeans
Crude Oil	Soybean Meal
Gold (N.Y.)	Soybean Oil
Heating Oil #2	Sugar #11 (World)
Hogs	Wheat (CHI)

'73 '74 '75 '76 '77 '78 '79 '80 '81 '82 '83 '84 '85 '86 '87 '88 '89 '90 '91 '92 '93 '94 '95

8T

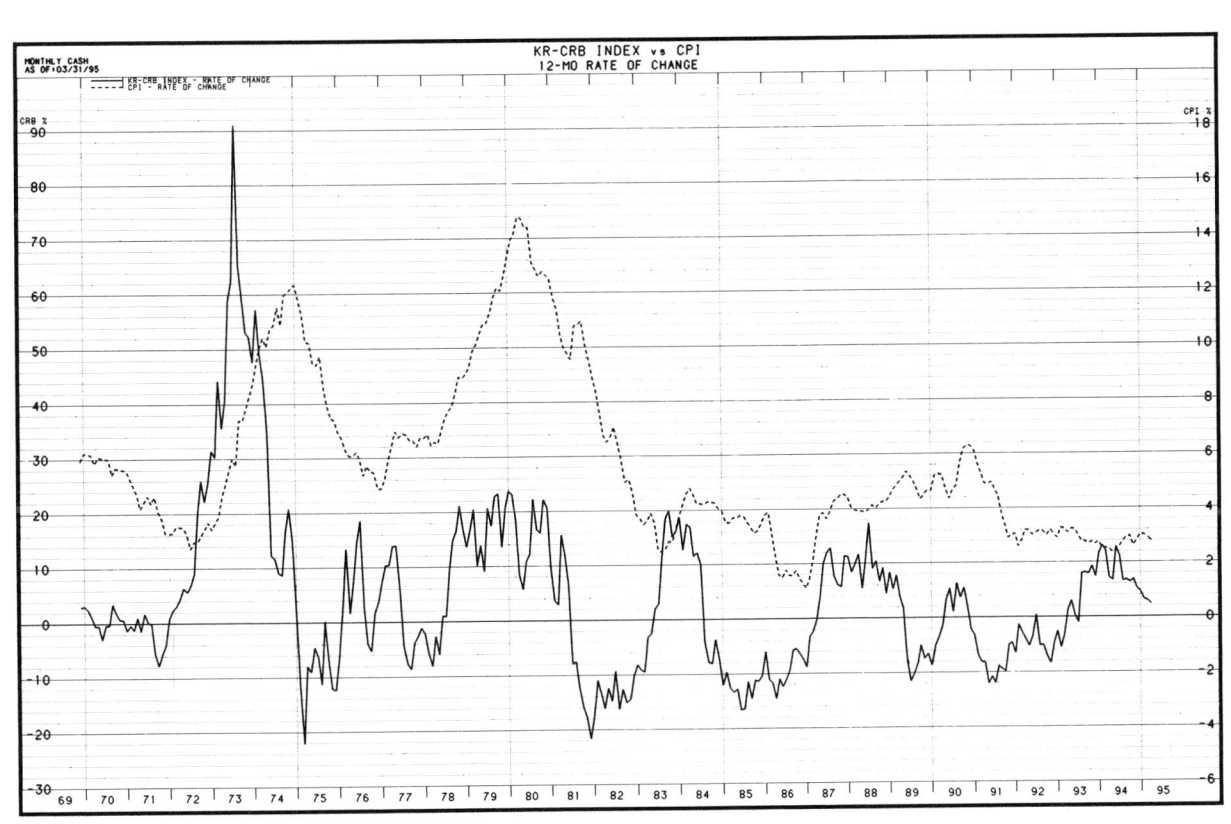

KR-CRB INDICES 1967=100 vs CPI 1982=100

MONTHLY CASH
AS OF 04/30/95

KR-CRB FUTURES PRICE INDEX
KR-CRB (BLS) SPOT PRICE INDEX
CONSUMER PRICE INDEX 82-84=100

INDEX
VALUE

KR-CRB (BLS) Commodity Price Index
23 Spot Markets

Burlap	Rubber
Butter	Soybean Oil
Cocoa	Steel Scrap
Copper Scrap	Steers
Corn	Sugar
Cotton	Tallow
Hides	Tin
Hogs	Wheat (MPLS)
Lard	Wheat (KC)
Lead	Wool Tops
Print Cloth	Zinc
Rosin	

KR-CRB Futures Price Index
21 Futures Markets

Cattle (Live)	Lumber
Cocoa	Orange Juice
Coffee	Platinum
Copper	Pork Bellies
Corn	Silver (N.Y.)
Cotton	Soybeans
Crude Oil	Soybean Meal
Gold (N.Y.)	Soybean Oil
Heating Oil #2	Sugar #11 (World)
Hogs	Wheat (CHI)

73 74 75 76 77 78 79 80 81 82 83 84 85 86 87 88 89 90 91 92 93 94 95

KR-CRB INDEX vs CPI
12-MO RATE OF CHANGE

MONTHLY CASH
AS OF 03/31/95

KR-CRB INDEX - RATE OF CHANGE
CPI - RATE OF CHANGE

CRB %   CPI %

69 70 71 72 73 74 75 76 77 78 79 80 81 82 83 84 85 86 87 88 89 90 91 92 93 94 95

9T

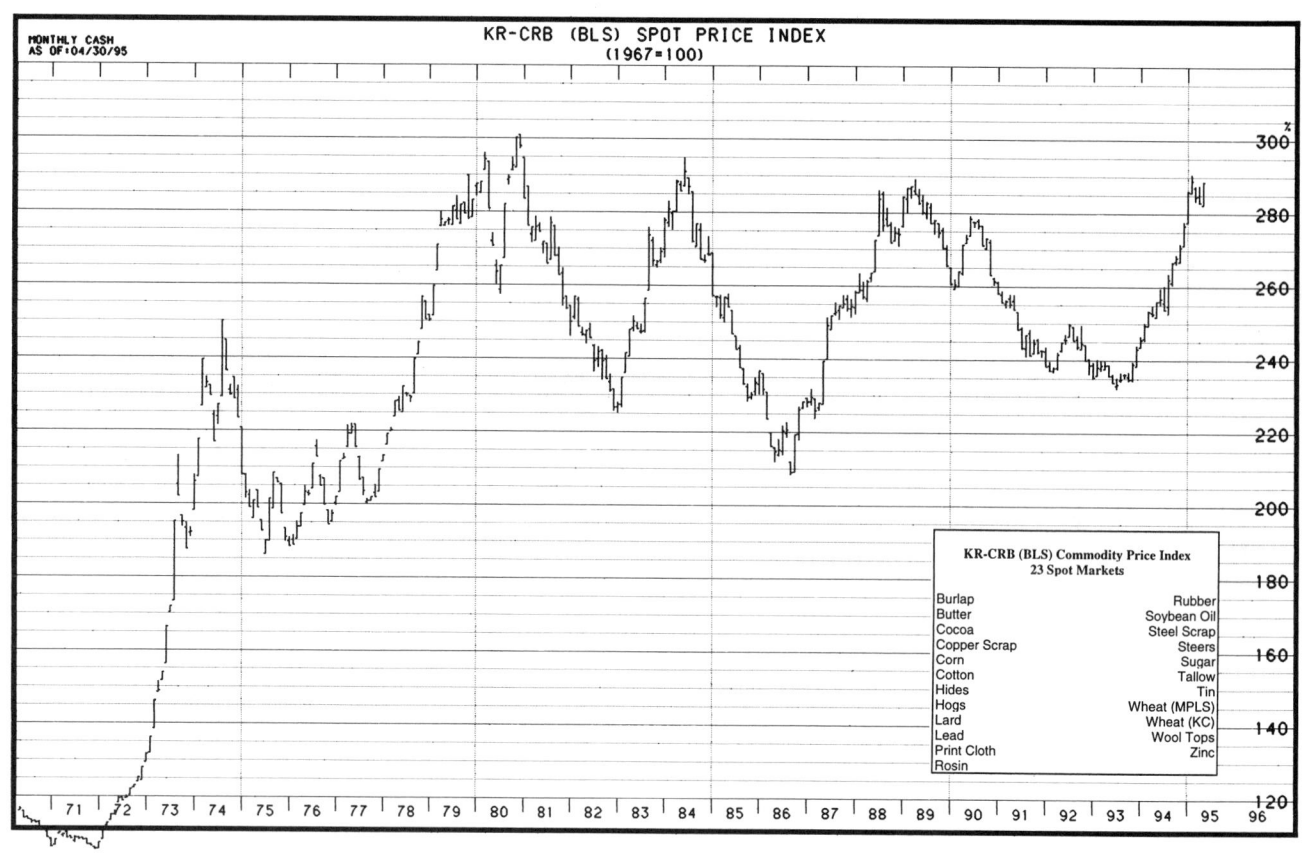

KR-CRB (BLS) SPOT PRICE INDEX
(1967=100)

MONTHLY CASH
AS OF:04/30/95

KR-CRB (BLS) Commodity Price Index
23 Spot Markets

Burlap	Rubber
Butter	Soybean Oil
Cocoa	Steel Scrap
Copper Scrap	Steers
Corn	Sugar
Cotton	Tallow
Hides	Tin
Hogs	Wheat (MPLS)
Lard	Wheat (KC)
Lead	Wool Tops
Print Cloth	Zinc
Rosin	

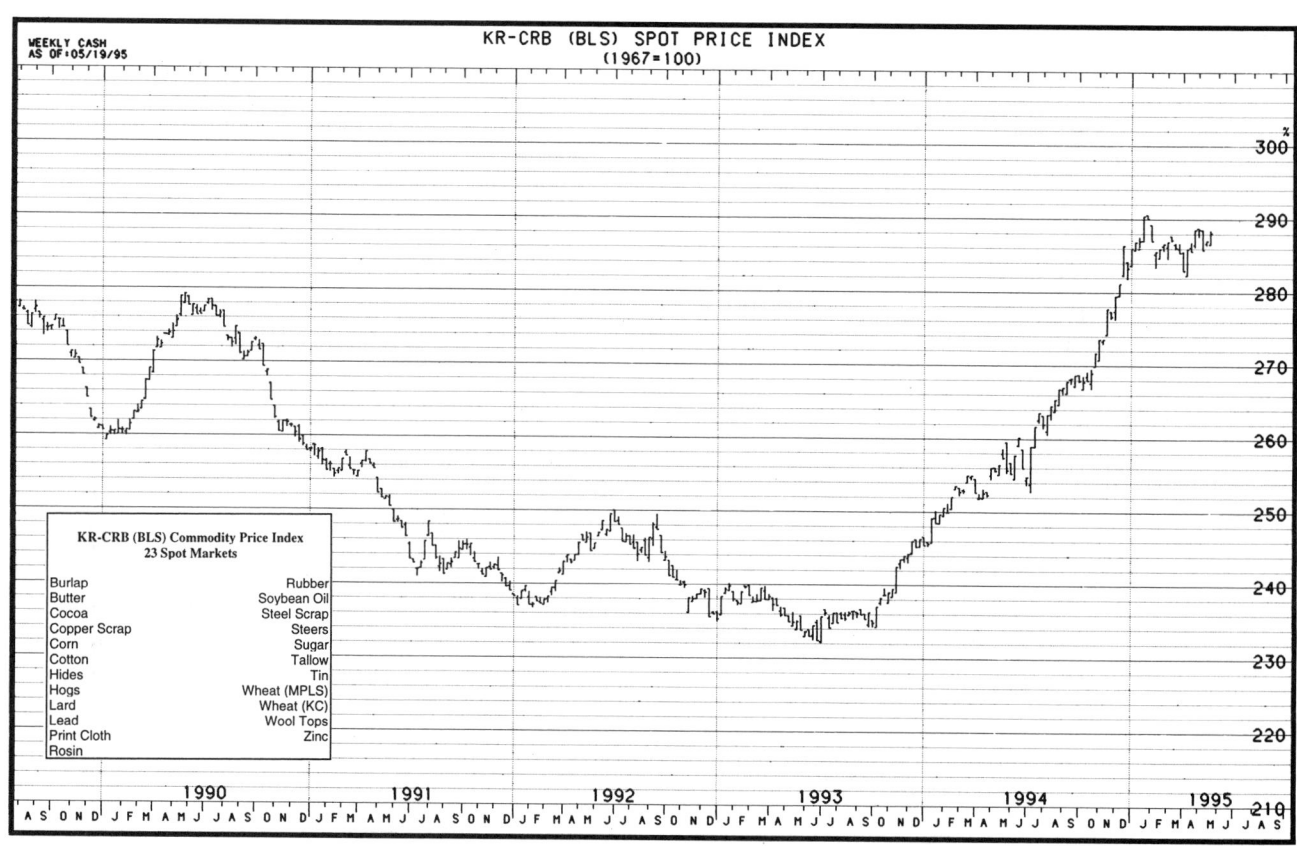

KR-CRB (BLS) SPOT PRICE INDEX
(1967=100)

WEEKLY CASH
AS OF:05/19/95

KR-CRB (BLS) Commodity Price Index
23 Spot Markets

Burlap	Rubber
Butter	Soybean Oil
Cocoa	Steel Scrap
Copper Scrap	Steers
Corn	Sugar
Cotton	Tallow
Hides	Tin
Hogs	Wheat (MPLS)
Lard	Wheat (KC)
Lead	Wool Tops
Print Cloth	Zinc
Rosin	

10T

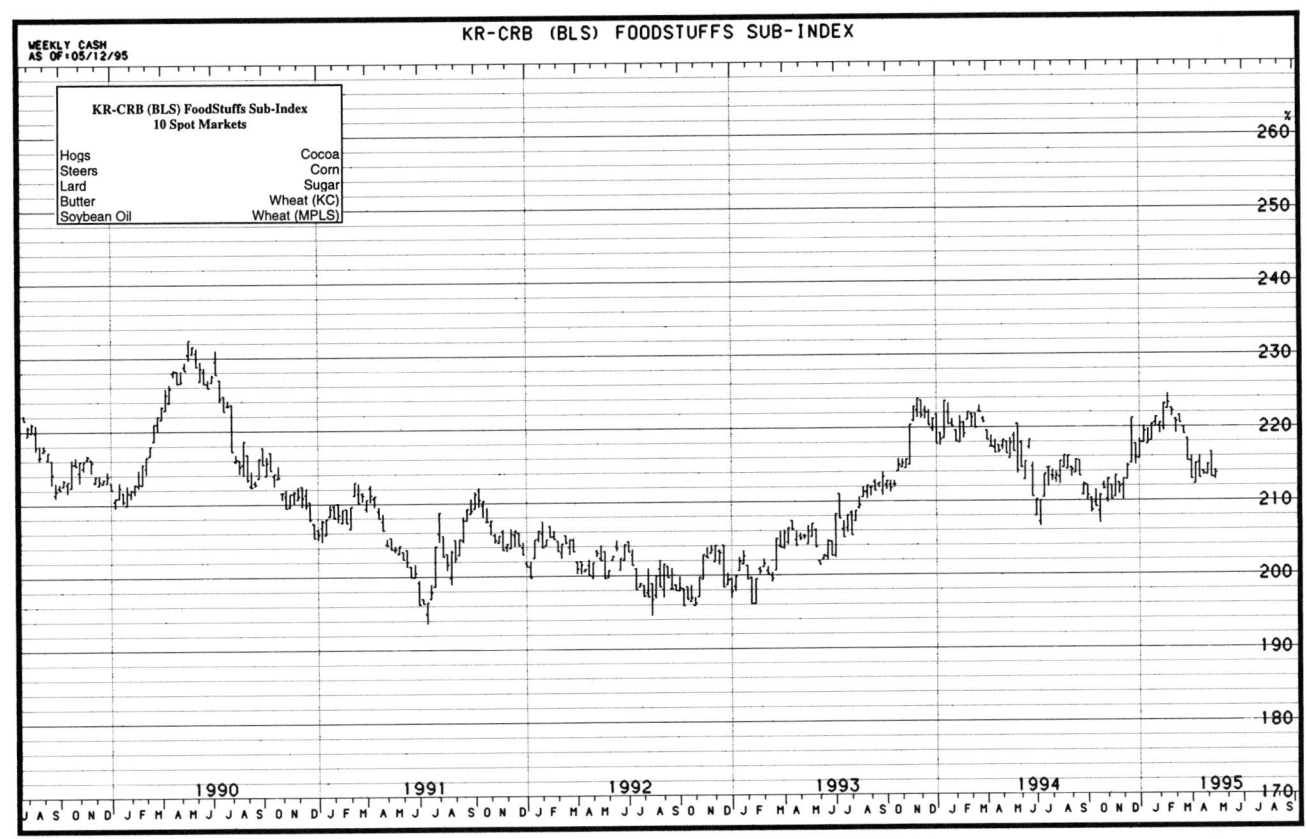

KR-CRB (BLS) FOODSTUFFS SUB-INDEX

WEEKLY CASH
AS OF:05/12/95

KR-CRB (BLS) FoodStuffs Sub-Index
10 Spot Markets

Hogs	Cocoa
Steers	Corn
Lard	Sugar
Butter	Wheat (KC)
Soybean Oil	Wheat (MPLS)

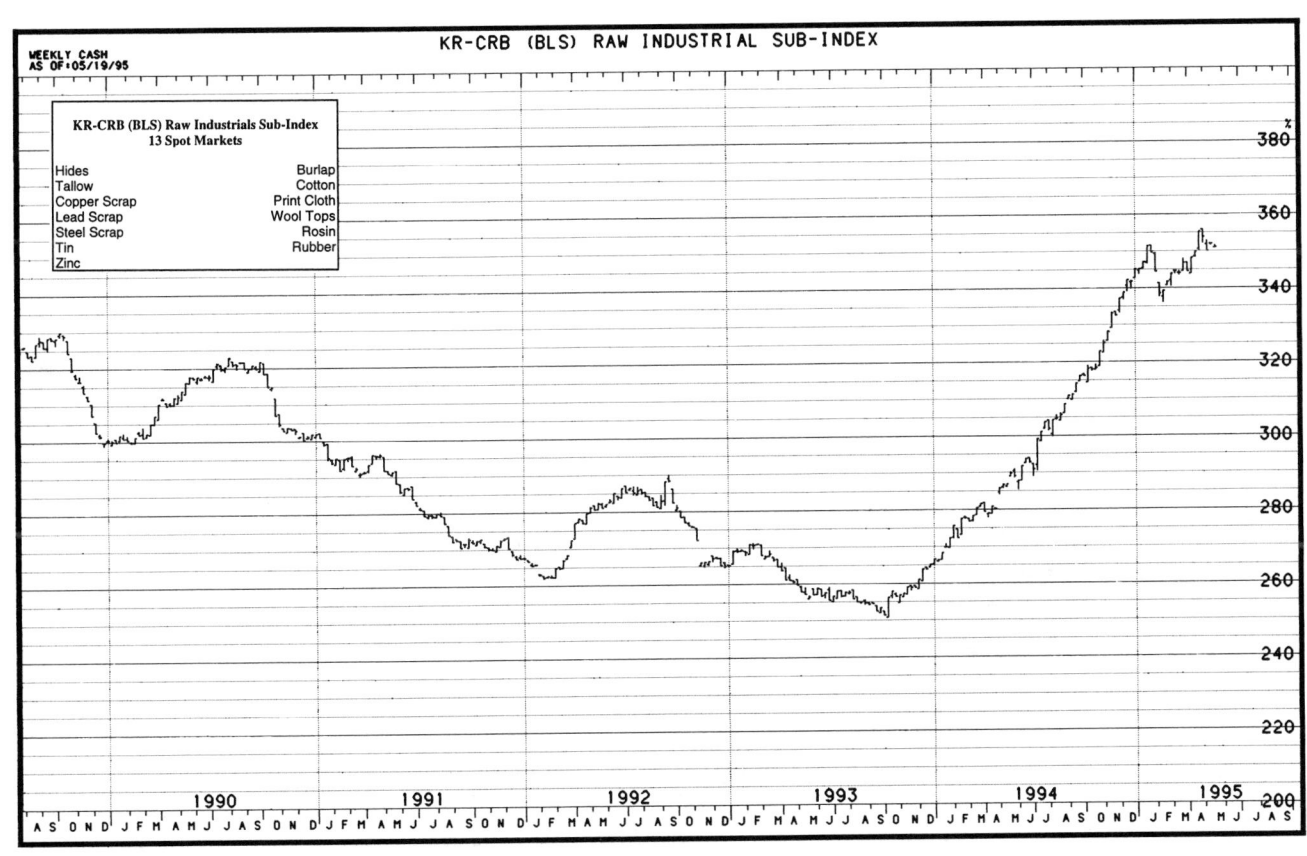

KR-CRB (BLS) RAW INDUSTRIAL SUB-INDEX

WEEKLY CASH
AS OF:05/19/95

KR-CRB (BLS) Raw Industrials Sub-Index
13 Spot Markets

Hides	Burlap
Tallow	Cotton
Copper Scrap	Print Cloth
Lead Scrap	Wool Tops
Steel Scrap	Rosin
Tin	Rubber
Zinc	

11T

KR-CRB IMPORTED SUB-INDEX
(1967=100)

WEEKLY CASH
AS OF:05/19/95

KR-CRB Imported Sub-Index
4 Futures Markets

Cocoa   Sugar
Coffee

KR-CRB INDUSTRIAL SUB-INDEX
(1967=100)

WEEKLY CASH
AS OF:05/19/95

KR-CRB Industrials Sub-Index
6 Futures Markets

Cotton   Lumber
Copper   Platinum
Crude Oil   Silver

12T

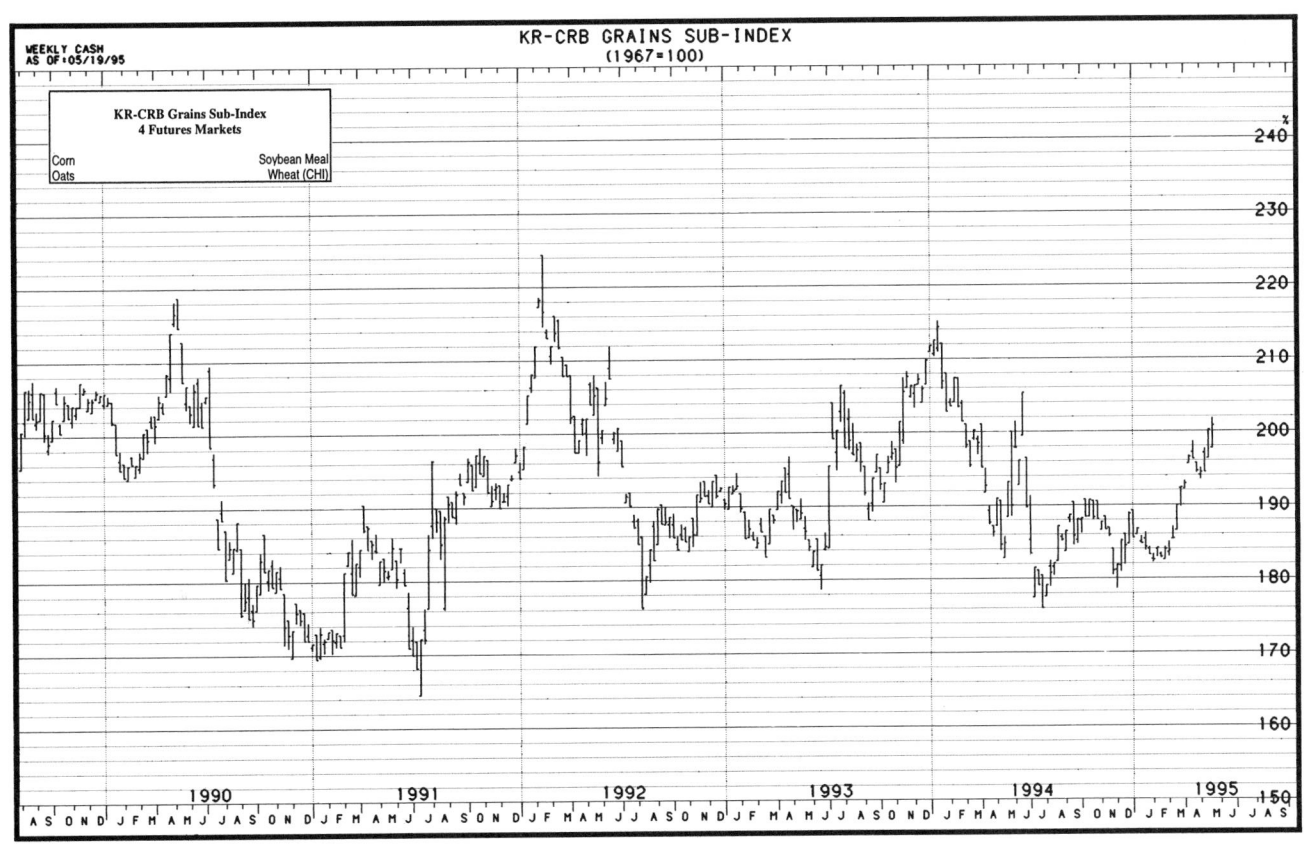

KR-CRB GRAINS SUB-INDEX
(1967=100)

WEEKLY CASH
AS OF :05/19/95

KR-CRB Grains Sub-Index
4 Futures Markets

Corn   Soybean Meal
Oats   Wheat (CHI)

KR-CRB OILSEEDS SUB-INDEX
(1967=100)

WEEKLY CASH
AS OF :05/19/95

KR-CRB Oilseeds Sub-Index
3 Futures Markets

Flaxseed   Soybean Oil
Canola

13T

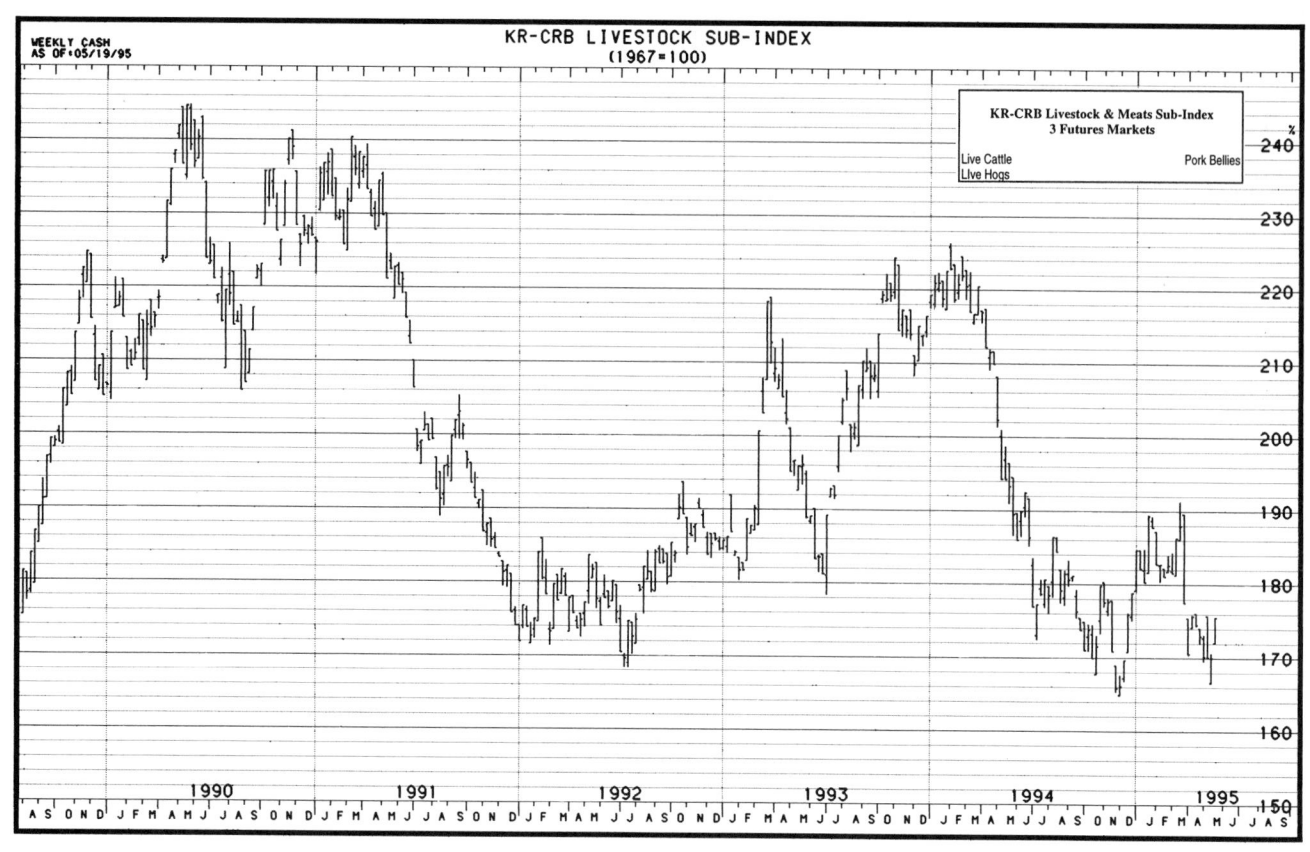

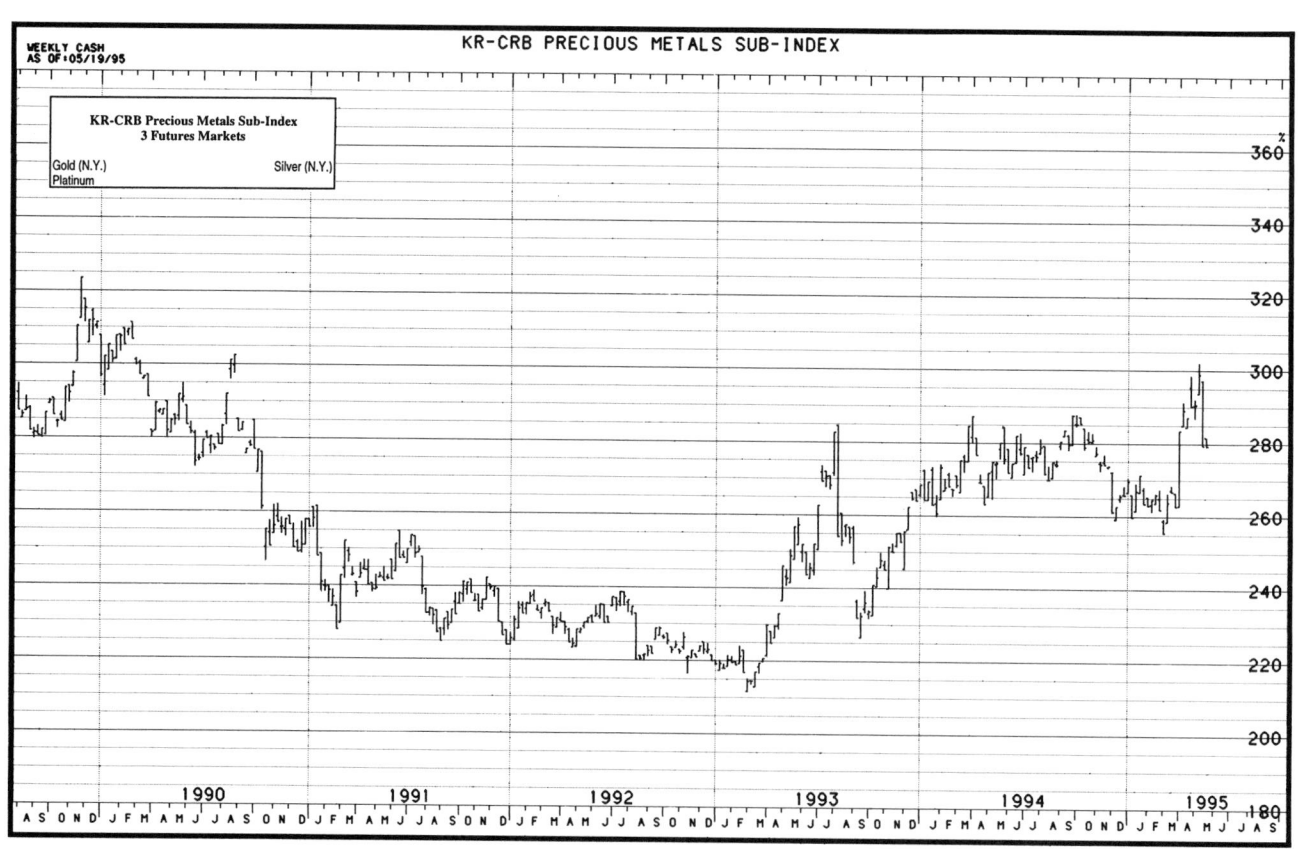

14T

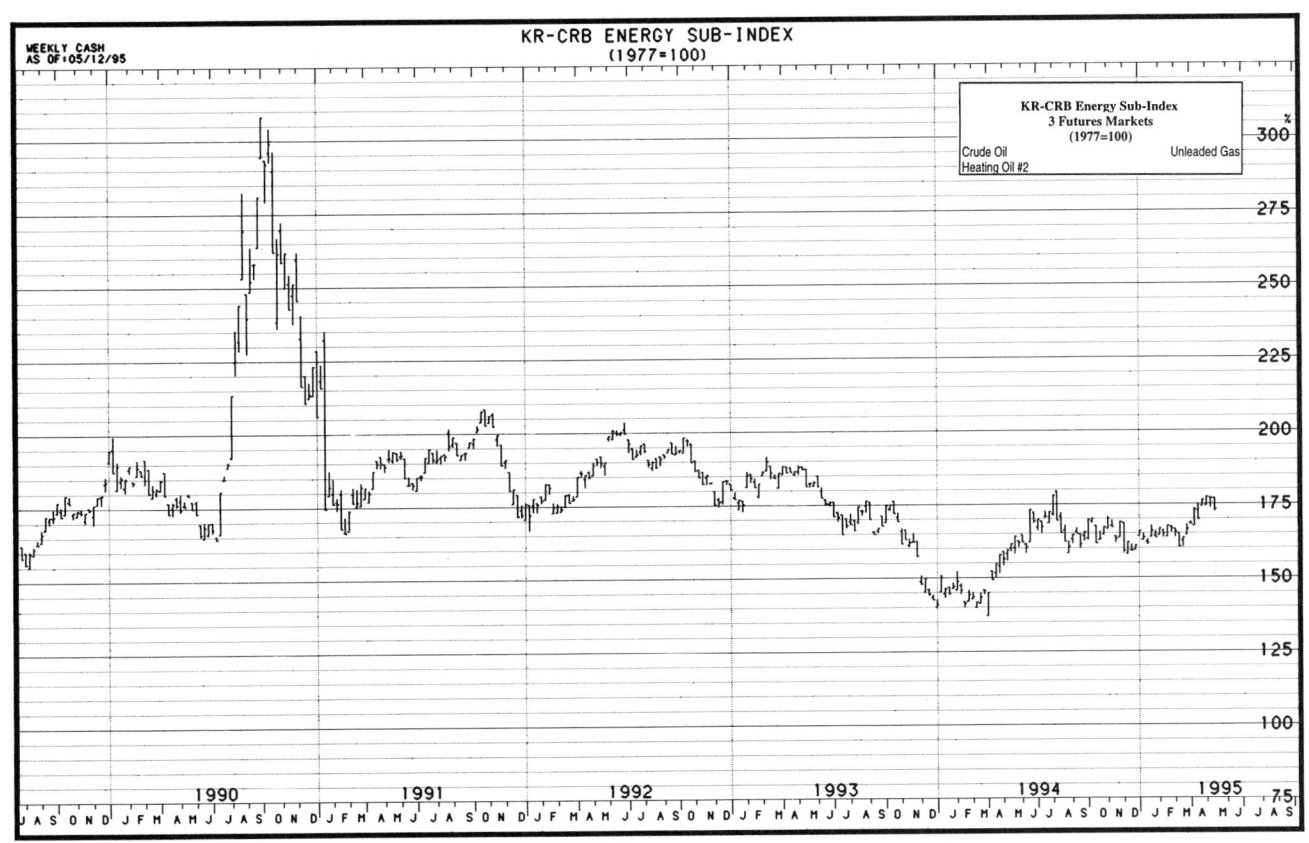

KR-CRB ENERGY SUB-INDEX
(1977=100)

WEEKLY CASH
AS OF 05/12/95

KR-CRB Energy Sub-Index
3 Futures Markets
(1977=100)

Crude Oil   Unleaded Gas
Heating Oil #2

%
300
275
250
225
200
175
150
125
100
75

1990 1991 1992 1993 1994 1995

J A S O N D J F M A M J J A S O N D J F M A M J J A S O N D J F M A M J J A S O N D J F M A M J J A S O N D J F M A M J J A S

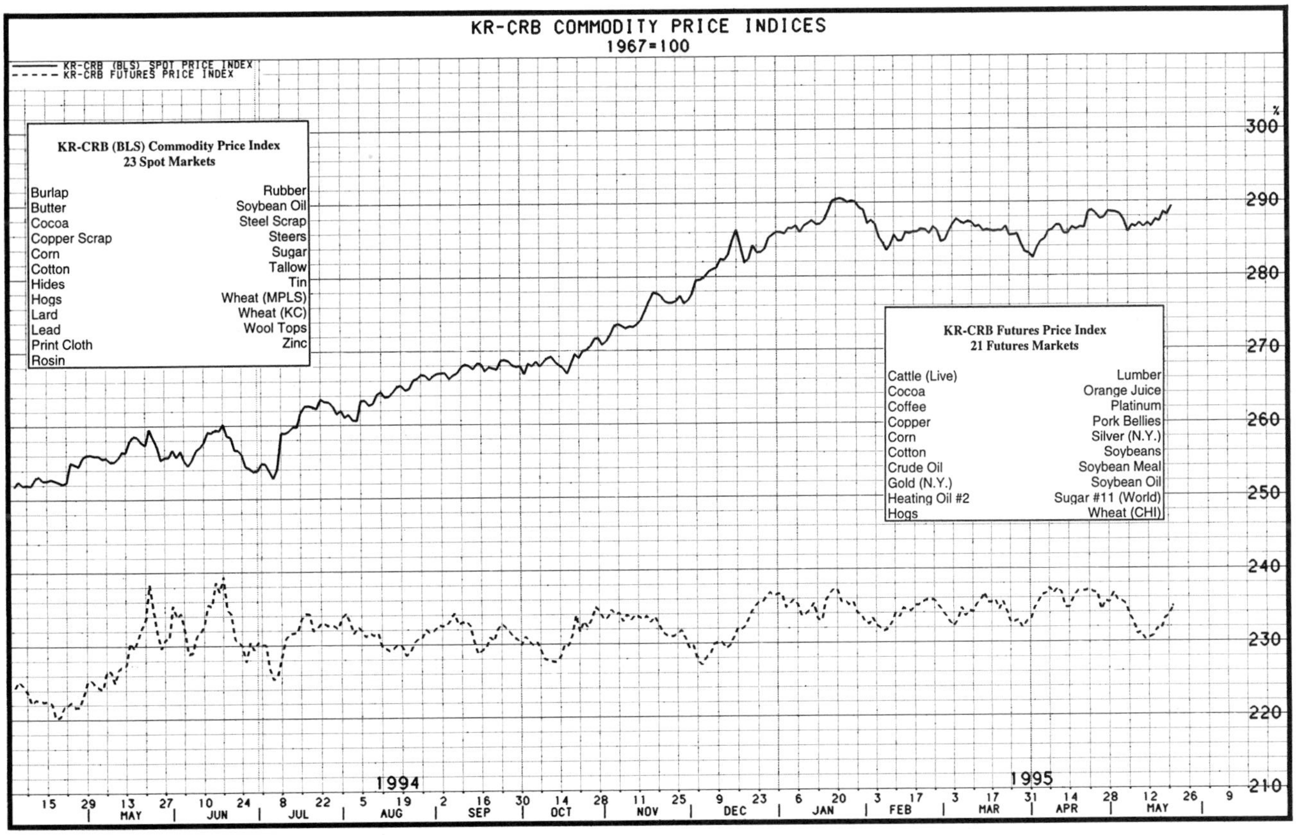

KR-CRB COMMODITY PRICE INDICES
1967=100

—— KR-CRB (BLS) SPOT PRICE INDEX
- - - KR-CRB FUTURES PRICE INDEX

KR-CRB (BLS) Commodity Price Index
23 Spot Markets

Burlap	Rubber
Butter	Soybean Oil
Cocoa	Steel Scrap
Copper Scrap	Steers
Corn	Sugar
Cotton	Tallow
Hides	Tin
Hogs	Wheat (MPLS)
Lard	Wheat (KC)
Lead	Wool Tops
Print Cloth	Zinc
Rosin	

KR-CRB Futures Price Index
21 Futures Markets

Cattle (Live)	Lumber
Cocoa	Orange Juice
Coffee	Platinum
Copper	Pork Bellies
Corn	Silver (N.Y.)
Cotton	Soybeans
Crude Oil	Soybean Meal
Gold (N.Y.)	Soybean Oil
Heating Oil #2	Sugar #11 (World)
Hogs	Wheat (CHI)

%
300
290
280
270
260
250
240
230
220
210

1994   1995

15   29   13   27   10   24   8   22   5   19   2   16   30   14   28   11   25   9   23   6   20   3   17   3   17   31   14   28   12   26   9
MAY   JUN   JUL   AUG   SEP   OCT   NOV   DEC   JAN   FEB   MAR   APR   MAY

15T

WHY 3% OF ALL TRADERS MAKE 100% OF THE PROFITS

by Laurence Connors and Blake Hayward

Why do individuals such as George Soros, Bruce Kovnar and Monroe Trout make millions of dollars year in and year out while 97% of all traders consistently lose? We believe it's because of two reasons. First, these traders have proven trading strategies that allow them to consistently profit from the markets and second, they have a survival of the fittest trading mentality.

In our book, *Investment Secrets of a Hedge Fund Manager*, we list the four components we believe make up the survival of the fittest mentality. They are: commitment, a daily approach that differs from the herd's, an unshakable belief system, and guts. Let's now look at each of these components individually.

Commitment

Success in trading is no different than success in anything else. Unless you are willing to commit yourself 100% to the game, you will never succeed.

Dan Gable worked out seven days a week for six years in his quest for an Olympic gold medal in wrestling. Vince Lombardi worked 18 hours a day and slept in his office most nights during the football season. In the book *Market Wizards,* Marty Schwartz said he worked 14 hours per day. Hedge fund manager Mark Strome, whose fund appreciated more than 130 percent in 1993, works 15 hours per day, seven days a week. It would be insane to train a few hours a week and attempt to wrestle Dan Gable, or coach against Vince Lombardi, but that's exactly the approach most traders take when they compete against the likes of Strome and Schwartz.

Commitment to becoming a successful trader means working at it seven days a week. Unfortunately, this will only put you at best in the same league as a lot of other traders.

A Daily Approach That Is Different From the Herd's

All successful traders do their own thing. This means they have created trading methodologies which separate them from the horde of traders who lose.

Examples of this are the trading approaches of Market Wizards, Linde Rashke and Gil Blake. Both of these individuals consistently outperform 99.9 percent of all money managers and they do it with unconventional approaches to the markets.

Linda Rashke's strategy is to trade the markets utilizing a 3 to 5 day swing trading approach. The basic concept behind her trading is markets tend to go through short-term cycles every 3 to 5 days. She combines this approach with a combination of pattern recognition and short-term oscillators she has created. While most money managers and commodity trading advisors are wrapped up in the political implications of international events, Linda cares only about her swing trading. In 1993, while the average money manager returned 8 percent to his or her client, and most CTAs averaged even less, Linda's accounts appreciated over 100 percent. Ask Linda what she thinks the markets will do over the next year and she will probably shrug her shoulders. Ask the average money manager or CTA what he or she thinks and you will probably get a twenty minute dissertation, which has a 50 percent chance of being wrong. Linda has a proven methodology that consistently makes money on a daily basis, whereas the average manager and trader does not.

Another market wizard who utilizes a different approach to the markets is Gil Blake. Unlike the average money manager who analyzes crop reports, economic data, etc., Gil trades mutual funds for one to four day periods. Sound ridiculous? His average annual return for 12 years is 45 percent! His worst year was in 1984 when he was up only 24 percent. Over a 139 month period he made money 134 months! Gil Blake succeeds because he utilizes an approach that is completely unique. Like Linda Rashke, he has achieved superior gains using unconventional means.

Now, compare the above two strategies to the approaches used by most traders. Instead of implementing a proven trading methodology, the average trader's strategy is based on the recommendations of the latest "expert" interviewed on CNBC, the advise of some guru quoted by *The Wall Street Journal*, the latest "can't miss" pick of the day of his broker, or the recommendation of a $99.00 per year newsletter he subscribes to. Instead of waiting for the correct moment to trade a historically proven strategy, the losing trader will jump into the fracas and let the chips fall where they may.

Successful traders have daily plans that work consistently over a period of time. Their trading methodologies work in bull markets, bear markets and sideways markets. Successful traders are not swayed by experts on television, analysts in newspapers, brokers with hot tips or gurus who sell newsletters. Each morning, successful traders have the war won before the battle begins. Losing traders do not!

An Unshakable Belief System

One reason successful traders won the war before the battle is fought is because they have an unshakable belief in their trading plans. This stems from a combination of three factors: 1) the results they have achieved from back-testing their strategies, 2) the results they achieved from actual trading, and 3) the knowledge that they can make their strategies even better. This belief system allows them to maintain control during draw-down periods. They know that these draw downs are a part of trading that must be tolerated because eventually their overall returns will be in the plus column.

Guts

The final component of the survival of the fittest is guts. It takes guts to be able to take a loss. Most traders are unsuccessful because they do not have the fortitude to accept the fact that they are wrong. Instead of taking a small loss when a trade moves against them, they go into a period of denial and hope their position reverses. This unfortunately leads to larger losses, which only hurts the traders even more. Successful traders have a predetermined stop, which, if triggered, is small enough not to cause much overall damage. These successful traders have the guts to admit they are wrong and move forward to the next trade.

All combined, the four traits listed above require an enormous amount of self-discipline. This discipline,

however, can and will be rewarded when harnessed properly.

Combining the four characteristics of successful traders will take you half way toward the goal of consistent profitable trading. Knowing what strategies work will take you the rest of the way. Here is a strategy that has been quite successful for us.

News Reversals ™

News Reversals are one of our most profitable strategies. The profits from this strategy come quickly and are potentially large.

News Reversals occur when a commodity gaps higher on bullish news, or gaps lower on bearish news, and then reverses.

Let's look at a hypothetical situation in the cotton market. After the market closes, a crop report is released that indicates a shortage of cotton--this is bullish for cotton prices. Analysts and experts make very positive statements about the report. A buying frenzy is created before the opening, causing prices to gap higher. This gap opening creates a short-term overbought condition. Prices, instead of moving higher as expected, begin moving lower. This selling begets further selling. Commercials come into the market to lock into the prices that are higher than yesterday. Short sellers begin to smell blood and push prices even lower. The speculators, who believed prices could only go higher, begin to panic. A full-blown sell-off occurs and prices head much lower. The trading strategy to exploit this scenario can make an individual a great deal of money in a short period of time.

Here are the rules you should follow to maximize our News Reversals strategy:

Rule #1: You must wait for an extremely bullish or bearish event to occur while the market is closed. This could be a crop report, livestock report, economic report, weather report, etc.

Rule #2: The market must gap open above or below the previous day's high or low for a signal to occur.

Rule #3: On openings that gap higher, place a sell stop one tick below the previous day's high. On openings that gap lower, place a buy stop one tick above the previous day's low.

Rule #4: After you are filled, place a stop at the morning's opening price. As prices move in your favor, the stop should be adjusted to lock-in profits.

The following example and chart will help illustrate this strategy:

January 12, 1995 - After the close on January 11, the U.S.D.A. announced the sale of 546,000 metric tons of U.S. winter wheat to China. The U.S.D.A. also raised its final estimate of U.S. wheat exports in 1995 to 34.7 million tons, up from the previous month's estimate of 34.02 million tons. On top of this bullish news, two hours before the opening, the U.S.D.A. also reported that U.S. farmers planted less winter wheat than previously expected.

(1) March wheat opened at $3.91, a gap of four cents above the previous day's high. (2) A sell stop was placed at $3.86 3/4, one tick below the previous day's high. Wheat reached its daily high within the first 15 minutes of trading and began to drift lower. (3) Our sell order was executed at $3.86 3/4 late in the day. (4) A protective stop was placed at $3.91, the morning's opening. The sell-off took wheat as low as $3.81, and as low as $3.77 the following day.

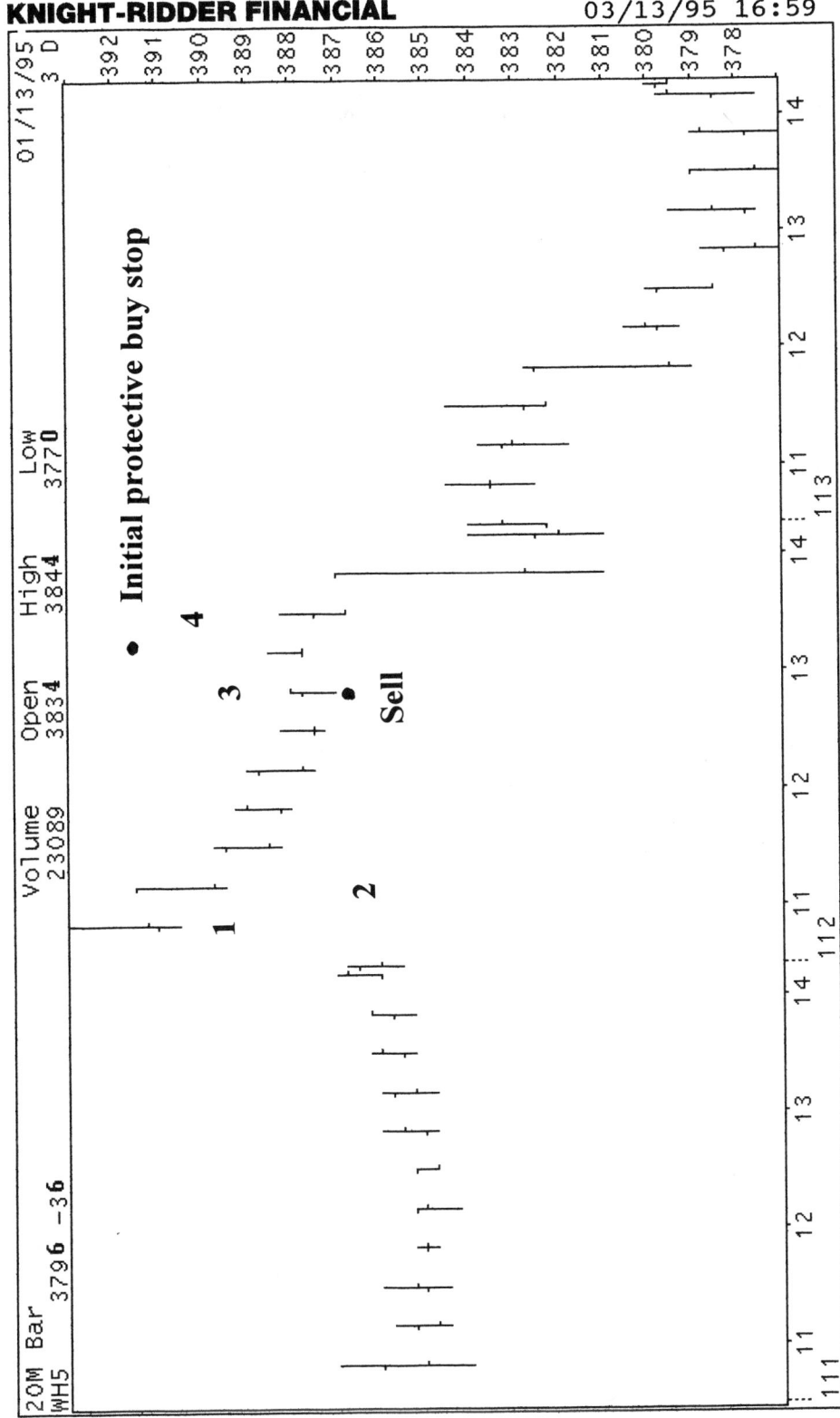

Why does this strategy consistently work? We believe it is because of three reasons. 1) You are identifying the time when the herd mentality has miscalculated the effect of a news story. 2) You are patiently waiting for the gap opening to reverse. This allows you to climb aboard after the reversal has developed instead of guessing if it is going to develop. 3) You are using excellent money management controls. You have a protective stop at the day's opening, and, therefore, any losses will be small.

In summary, the best advice we can give you is make a commitment to study the markets. Create unique trading strategies that work and combine them with solid money management techniques. These are the stepping stones to joining the three percent who consistently win the battle.

*   *   *

Laurence Connors is President of Connors, Bassett & Associates, an investment management firm, and managing partner of Oceanview Financial Research, Inc., a financial markets research firm, both located in Malibu, California. Larry has recently co-authored with Blake Hayward a new book on futures trading entitled Investment Secrets of a Hedge Fund Manager - Exploiting the Herd Mentality of the Financial Markets (Probus Publishing, 1995)

Blake Hayward is a managing partner with Connors, Bassett and Associates and a managing partner of Oceanview Financial Research, Inc. Blake has created a number of computer based trading strategies utilized by traders today.

Both Larry Connors and Blake Hayward can be reached at 310-589-2655.

READING "PRICE TOPS"

by John Knaggs

A comparison of patterns created by Price, the Relative Strength and Directional Movement Indexes.

A Technical Analysis study of the relationships and patterns created between Price and mathematical trading tools such as The Relative Strength & Directional Movement Indices can help you catalog nuances in the behavior of price and these trading tools into an event model, which when applied to future price events will help you recognize and gauge the timing for the climax of a price trend. You'll become alert early to a decaying buy-side trend, and be able to gauge the relative price level and timing for taking buy side profits and testing positions for a trend reversal.

Space here precludes an in-depth explanation of the construction of these mathematical trading tools, for that I must refer you to Mr. Wilder's original work.[1] My purpose here is to highlight how these indexes respond to buy side price behavior as it tops, and point out key visual patterns and relationships that can be used in the future to help you gauge the health of a buying trend.

The Relative Strength Index (R.S.I.) is a Momentum Oscillator and is displayed on the charts as a composite where the R.S.I. for the High, Low, and Close for each day are individually plotted. Inclusion of the R.S.I. for the High and Low adds to the usefulness of the visual patterns that this momentum oscillator paints, and makes the R.S.I. a very strong technical tool.

The Directional Movement Index (D.M.I.) measures and displays individually the Buy Side and Sell Side components of price action. Buying pressure is visible in the +DI 14 (Plus Directional Index), and selling pressure in the -DI 14 (Minus Directional Index). The Average Directional Index, or A.D.X., shows the resultant of these two components as an average. The A.D.X. displays the strength of trending in price; it moves upward when price is trending strongly either to the buy side or the sell side. The A.D.X. is commonly referred to by technical services, so you may be familiar with it. You will discover here how its strength is enhanced by using it in conjunction with its underlying components, the +DI 14 and -DI 14. Both the R.S.I. and the D.M.I. are computed on a 14 day cycle so they run in synch with one another for maximum usefulness as comparative tools.

I've included three detail charts which display characteristic topping action by price and these two indexes, the insets in the small charts show the relationship to the life of the contract in each case.

Principle elements to identify on the example charts.

Price:

A. A Buy Side Trend in Price, characterized by higher highs.
B. One or more small sell side events in price which precede an overall price top; corrections and consolidations which are followed by additional buy side legs in price.

Relative Strength Index:

C. A flat or down sloping trend in the peaks of the R.S.I. for the high daily price. This creates a gradually declining overhead resistance zone in divergence to the price trend. Successive new daily high prices create values in the R.S.I. for the high that probe upward into this declining resistance zone. Once at least one correction and consolidation of price has transpired within the buy side progress of the trend (element B) you will generally have established overall high levels of the R.S.I. for the high. You can then study subsequent buy side legs for indications of new highs in price which are not accompanied by new overall highs in the R.S.I. for the high. As this occurs the divergence in trend between price and the R.S.I. becomes visible.

---

[1] Welles Wilder, Jr., New Concepts in Technical Trading Systems, Trend Research, Greensboro, NC, 1978.

D. When a trend divergence condition becomes evident look for a climaxing event in the R.S.I. for the high which is characterized by a shallow slope, this can give a hint at the potential for a trend reversing day.

Experience with the examples here and other buying climaxes for which you have charts will help you recognize nuances in the overall pattern of the R.S.I. for the high, and help you use these events as opportunities to establish new positions to test the sell side for a potential new trend. If a correction and consolidation begins to occur, hinting at another buy side leg, the testing positions are exited and the resulting buy side continuation is studied as it in turn tops out.

Directional Movement Index - Average Directional Index:

E. An upward move in the Average Directional Index (A.D.X.) which accompanies the initial stages of the rise in price as the Buy Side Price Trend is established. This upward A.D.X. movement is very sensitive to small selling corrections in the buy side price trend. Whether the A.D.X. continues upward to new high levels as price consolidations occur and price resumes its upward climb is an indication about the strength of the buying trend.

F. Note this upward A.D.X. resumption to new highs in Chart Example No. 1 as a response to a crisp short duration correction and consolidation in price, this pattern is an example of a solid trend in price. Compare this A.D.X. behavior after an initial correction and consolidation in price to post price consolidation A.D.X. activity in Example Nos. 2 and 3 (G).

G. Secondary upward A.D.X. movements which accompany buy side price resumption. These should be accompanied by new overall highs in price if they are to be assessed as possible rises into the climax of the price trend.

H. Chart Example No. 3 shows an upward A.D.X. resumption which is not accompanied by new overall highs in price (U). Clearly in this case overall buy side trending of price was not yet at an end. It's a good idea to have the mental requirement at this point in the development of a buy side price event, that upward resumption by the A.D.X. be accompanied by overall new highs in price when you are studying price action for topping indications. As you develop a model of expected "Topping" events, keep it simple and clearly defined, this can help you avoid becoming confused.

Directional Movement Index - Minus Directional Index or -DI14:

I. The -DI14 develops a pattern of support beneath it as the overall buy side price trend proceeds and runs out of steam. A comparison of the patterns of support developing in the -DI14 with patterns of upward stalling by the R.S.I. of the high as it climbs into overhead resistance will provide useful clues as to the timing for establishing positions to test an expected new selling price trend.

J. The climaxing pattern (circled) of the -DI14 as it sinks into its own support, can play itself out over a very few days as in Example Nos. 1 and 3, or over a number of days as in Example No. 2.

K. Characteristically, the -DI14 will develop its shallowest slope (L) a day or two after the shallow rise of the R.S.I. for the high into overhead resistance (D). This is the case in each of the examples here. This may help you make the decision to trade, in hindsight, on the day or days following the one on which the R.S.I. for the high has given its hints at potential price topping action. Nuances like this that help to confirm or corroborate indications hinted at by another trading index become a world of help in making trading decisions in an environment which is confusing and difficult to assess.

The +DI14 is also displayed on the charts: it has the ability to display support of a similar nature when prices are trending downward in a selling climax, thus it is not of primary use in our current study of topping price structure.

No two price events are the same, but the patterns developed by the mathematical trading indexes have these elements within them. Once the visual qualities of the elements are associated in your mind with climaxing price patterns, even if the overall price pattern diverges markedly from known examples, by using these visual cues you will be able to sense the top, interpret the health of the trend, and gauge its climax. Naturally, the greater the number of topping patterns studied, the greater will be your understanding and sense of confidence as a new one unfolds.

As you become familiar with the elements discussed here, and others that you discover yourself, assemble them into a model or pattern of expected events to be used as a template to apply to future trading events. You will find such tools to be a great help in sensing the rhythm and timing of a future price climax.

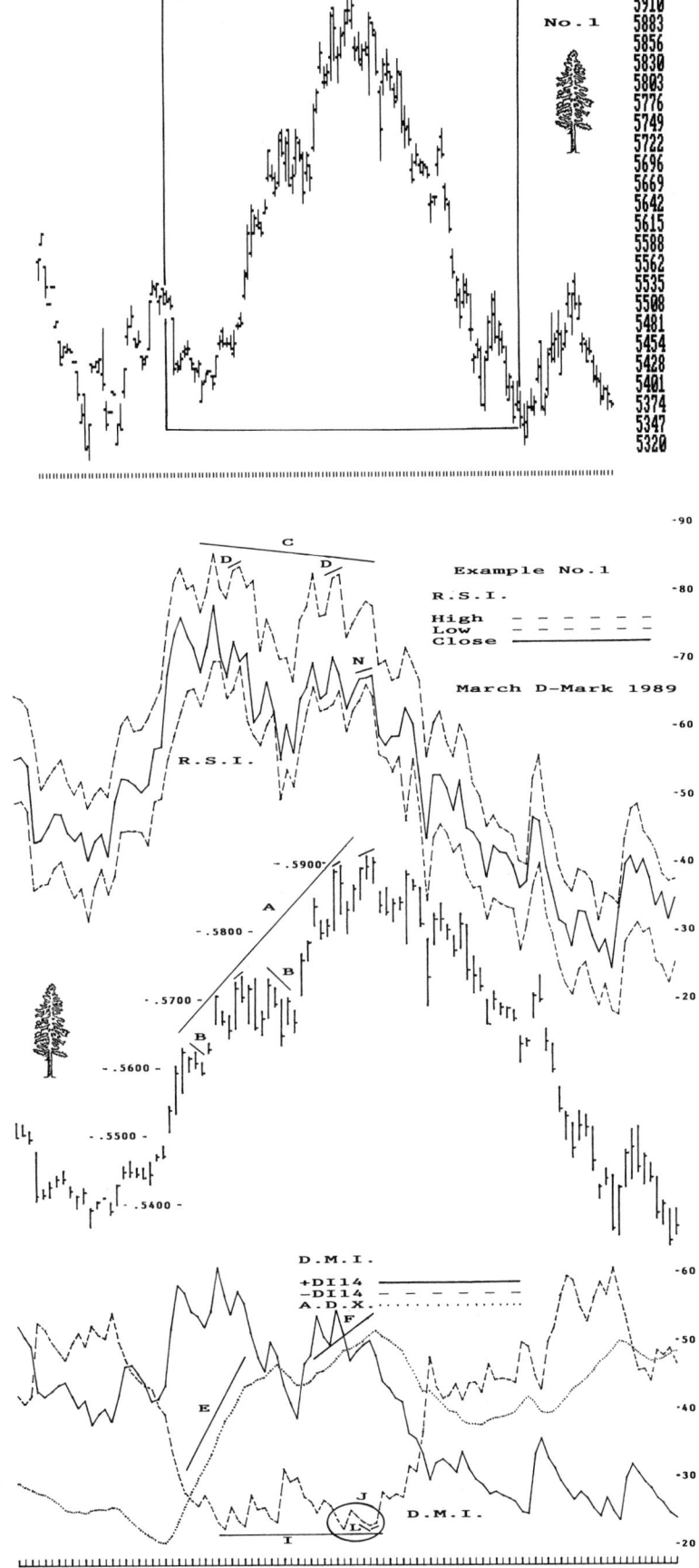

Example One: March D-Mark, 1989

Example One, the 1989 March D-Mark, is my current best example for this type of price topping action, a strong clearly defined buy side trend, a crisp short duration correction, followed by a price acceleration into a topping formation which gives good technical clues that the trend is drying up.

I suggest that you refresh by noting the descriptions associated with the various lettered events, (A) through (L) on the chart, so they become well planted in your mind.

Notable Events:

D. The first occurrence of this shallow upside R.S.I. indication that near term momentum is drying up happens in prelude to the clearly defined correction. The second happens in prelude to an overall top. A ruler will help you see that this second (D) was followed by one last rise in price.

L. The ruler will also help you see that the last shallow failure of the -DI14 into its own rising support zone (L) had not yet occurred as the R.S.I. for the high was defining its second (D) indication. The A.D.X. was still rising at this point.

Resist trading without pattern completion, be stingy about acting until price generated index patterns fill in the required model events. Conversely, when defining your model, keep your expectations simple and clearly defined so they can be applied with a minimum of confusion.

Recap: A second (D) R.S.I. indication, without an (L) -DI14 completion, and a still rising A.D.X.; what could help make the climax of this topping event come into focus?

N. Indication (D) is generated by the R.S.I. for the high price of the day, the middle solid line in the R.S.I. complex is that of the close. Note the two day shallow rise (N) in the R.S.I. for the close. Compare this rise to that of (D) and put it in your mind that it carried on for two trading sessions. Use your ruler and line up the index events with that second struggling day of (N) and its marginally higher close.

At this point you've had the second (D), you've had the two days (N), and your ruler shows that the minus DI14 (L) is turning slightly up in a manner that makes the pattern complete. Except for a still rising A.D.X., the elements have filled in the model.

As you use and develop experience with this kind of technical information you will gain a sense as to when the indications have filled the model conditions--when it's time to place testing trades. Nothing can keep you from groaning as you pick up the phone to place a selling order five minutes before the close on the second day (N) after you

have done an intra-day chart analysis. Price has been rising methodically for weeks and all you have to indicate that it might be over are the technical tools on your charts. Life gets no better, it's not easy, it may not even be fun, but it is astonishing the next morning when prices are down strongly for the "OPEN," and are unable to trade up and fill the gap during the trading session. With experience gained by regular use, and a few successful trades that are technically driven, you will learn to trust and utilize the hints and indications that these valuable mathematical chart tools provide.

Example Two (next page) has a more protracted top, the corrections are entrenched, and the consolidation of the elements that combine to make up the sell side signal environment take longer to evolve.

Go over the (A) through (L) principle elements and develop the psychology of the trading environment mentally for yourself.

Notable Events:

D. Again, the first (D) gives a clue to the near term potential of a correction, while the third hints at yet another opportunity to test the sell side. Put your attention on the middle (D) and note how it resides within a slightly broader pattern (O). You will see this pattern time and again, and need to be able to recognize it as it unfolds.

Look at the range and close of day (P), a narrow range day slightly higher than the previous session, which has a markedly wider range. As well, day (P) has its close in the middle of its range and well up from the previous close. This does not fit the profile of a reversing day. Had you established a new selling position intra-day on the basis of the (D) indication you would have had ample time during the trading session to discover this and offset. This pattern (O) does not always result in a correction like this one or (Q) in Example No. 3. It might turn out to be a final top, but it's important that you at least recognize the potential for a correction and be ready for it.

Using your ruler, compare how the A.D.X. responds to each successive rise in price (G). The lower highs in the A.D.X., (R) as price makes new highs, helps to highlight the fact that price is running out of steam.

Notice how the -DI14 signal pattern (J) plays itself out over some 20 trading sessions before the pattern completes itself (L). In this case (L) is marginally lower than the previous point (S) within the (I) rising support zone.

The third (D) would have been difficult to interpret as the trading signal, a two day price pattern is not enough to give one a sense of confidence. However, the next day (T), a narrow range day at the bottom

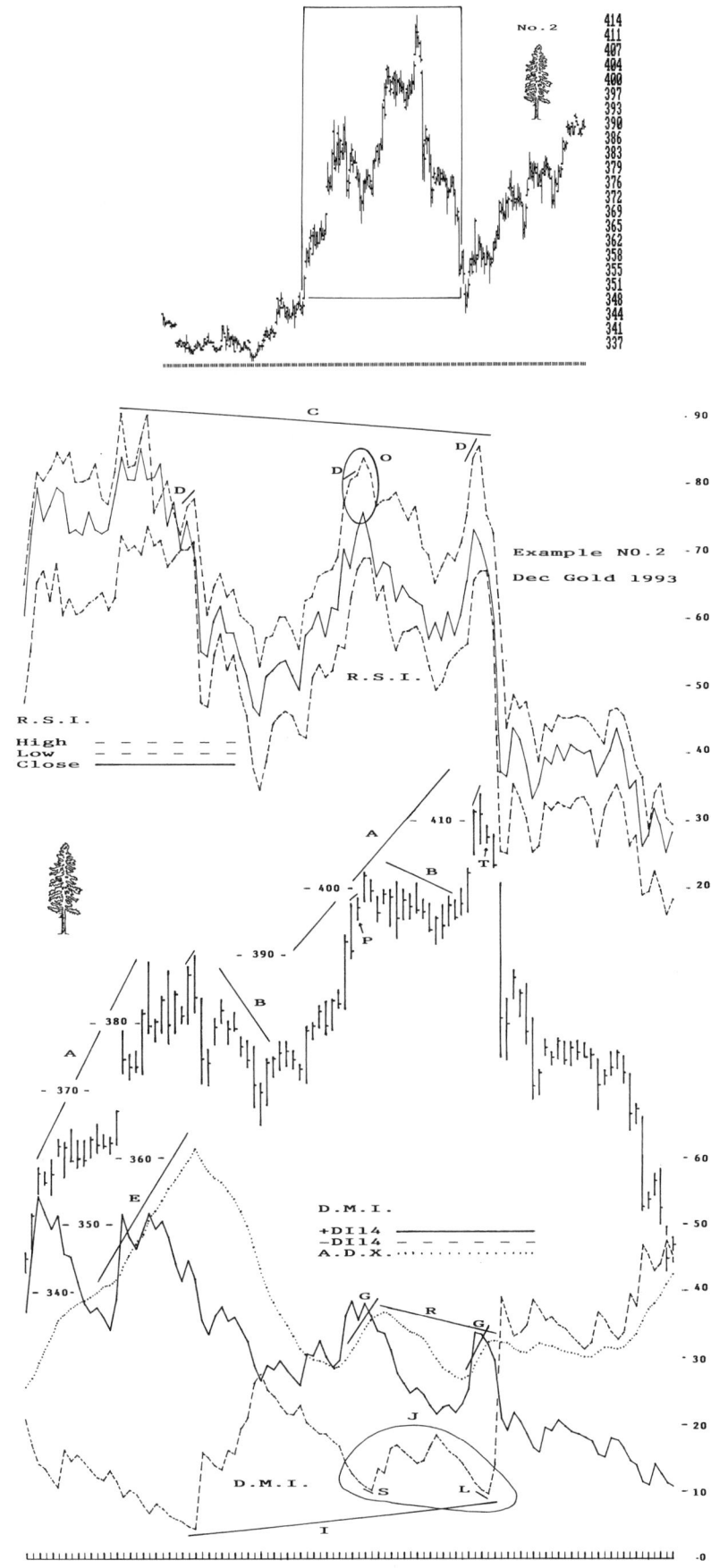

Example Two: December Gold, 1993

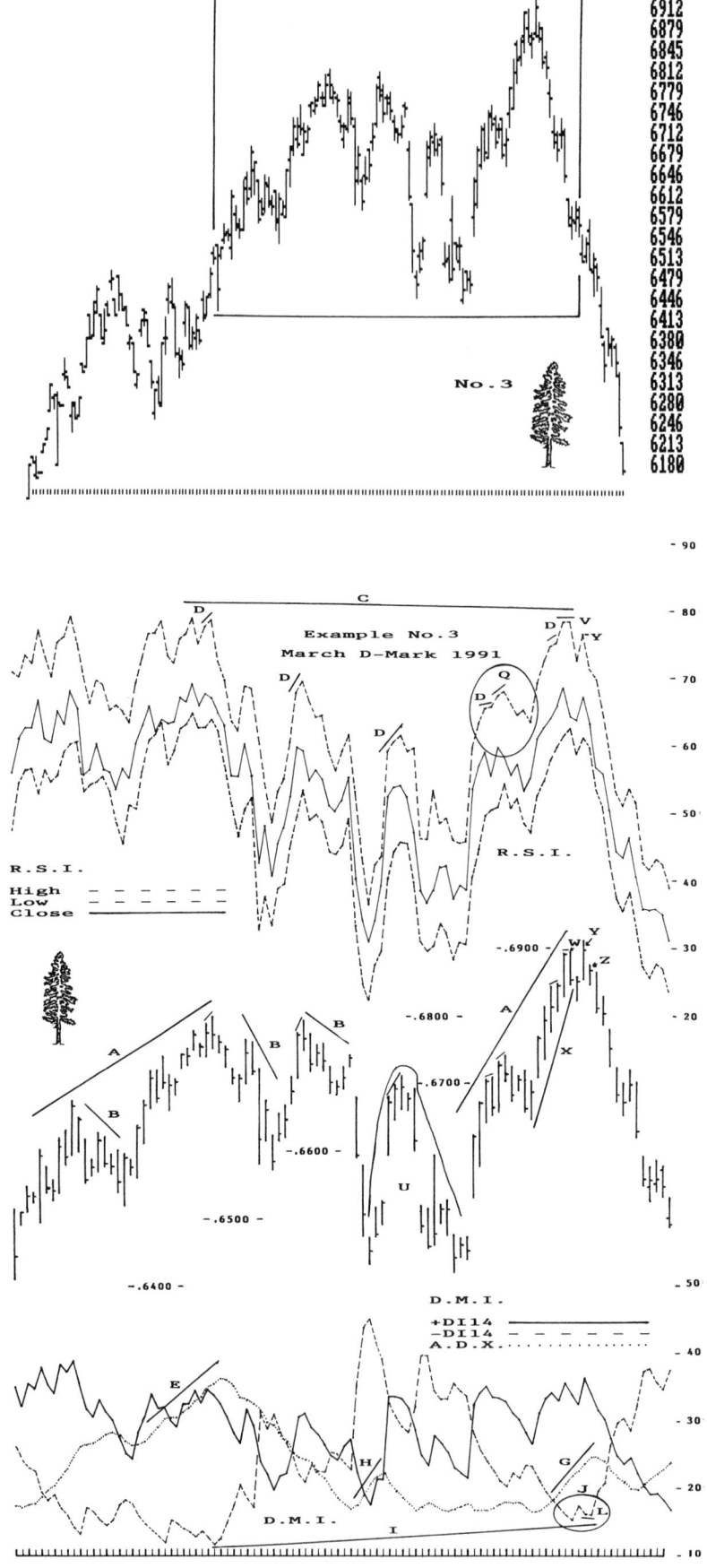

Example Three: March Deutsche Mark, 1991

of the previous range generated the shallow (L) which helped to complete the pattern in the -DI14.

Lastly, note how the third (D), testing into overhead R.S.I. resistance, rises above the (O) R.S.I. crest but not above the highs created initially by the R.S.I. for the high. It's not uncommon to see multiple tests into overhead resistance, in fact it's rather to be expected. Look for an ultimate climaxing test to rise very close to that initial high R.S.I. level.

Not an easy example to trade in reality, but one that effectively displays the pattern elements.

Example Three has a top which is interrupted by price event (U). Short term internal price events can obscure the progress of a trend, they make it imperative that you keep your eye on the larger overall patterns that are playing themselves out.

Go over the primary elements (A) through (L).

Look at all the (D)'s that afford the opportunity of selling tests. Use your ruler and study the resulting selling trends conjecturing how you might have handled each.

Note the height of each of these (D)'s in relation to the initial highs created by the R.S.I. for the high. Again, only the final formation came up to that initial high level. Confidence in the overall pattern doesn't really coalesce unless these initial high R.S.I. levels are actually tested.

Note the flat top (V) that forms the last R.S.I. peak and the day (W) that created it. If the selling pressure on a signal day like (W) cannot press downward through the bottom of the buy side channel (X), it should be expected that price will again test the near term highs, as happened in example Nos. 1 and 3.

On day (Y) as new high prices are made, the R.S.I. spikes to a level below (V), giving us a new high in price unconfirmed by a new high in the R.S.I. An event like this should alert you to study the next sessions price action for a very near term trend change.

Once again, the shallow downside (L) of the -DI14 did not occur until (Z), the day after new highs in price (Y) had been made, thus giving you a hindsight, or day later opportunity, to discover that the signal had formed up.

Lastly, compare the R.S.I. event Q (circled) with the form of the final R.S.I. crest and carefully catalog the similar sequential internal events. You will see comparable cresting R.S.I. patterns in the future. Now you can recognize them and use them to advantage.

Comments:

You can see that the A.D.X. has its own piece of information to display in indicating the health of the trend. The addition of the -DI14 gives you a way to more accurately sense the timing for the end of a trend.

These three rather clearly defined examples provide a primer for reading tops using the R.S.I. and D.M.I., comparing them with charts of other topping price events will broaden your experience base. If you use other trading indices, a comparison of patterns at key development points in price structure should be of interest.

Trading is an imperfect world, but using pattern elements coded into simply defined models can help you make informed trading judgments that can be applied to categories of price events such as this price topping exercise. Price pattern variations within the "Topping" category can differ widely and the model elements will still apply, allowing you to transfer experience from past examples to one of most current concern.

Other technical tools, such as Volume and Open Interest, should be included in your analysis to add accuracy and depth to your understanding of a specific price event. Also, it's always a comfort to have a pair of short term moving averages on line to help you see potential price extremes as price oscillates above and below them.

Respect the job that charts and technical analysis can do for you. Keep in mind that fresh supply/demand events can enter a market at any time. Keep your analysis agile so you can constantly incorporate these new pressures. The technical structure of price plays itself out enough of the time that careful and disciplined technical traders will be amply rewarded.

By having historical sample charts of Tops, Bottoms, Corrections, etc., you will have a way to visualize the potential end of a currently unfolding price event. You will also discover many variations on the patterns you are working with and be able to recognize and utilize them even when they become obscured by transitory short term price events. You can then be ready when that last tired action of price completes the picture. Other traders have gone to sleep, lulled by relatively quiet price action and/or their inability to sense the changing character of the trading environment. Your intra-day index analysis will keep you alert, and quietly hint at support or resistance and an opportunity for the vigilant.

John Knaggs, principal of Evergreen Trading, has been working with Price and Trading Index charts for over twenty years. He maintains a library of reference charts and offers a Custom Large Format Chart Service for disciplined chart traders. He can be reached at PO Box 7615, Santa Rosa, CA. 95407; 707-575-6719.

*   *   *

NEURAL NETS, THE MARKET AND YOU. . . . A PRIMER

By Tom J. Schwartz

Introduction

Today, there is at least $5 billion under computer management in which neural nets are a prime component in the trading or management program. What are these methods called neural nets and what do they do? How good are they? What are the perils and pitfalls, and how can I learn and use them in my trading activities? The successful human trader is the existence proof that neural nets may be used to trade successfully, but as with any advanced technology they must be applied with knowledge and caution.

This article will answer many of these questions. It will discuss technical issues such as data collection, preprocessing, algorithm selection, post processing and hybrid systems. Now, the good news--and bad news. The good news is this: many of the technical analysis methods, and your knowledge of the market you trade in, will be of significant value in using this technology. In addition, we will focus on off-the-shelf software that runs inside PC versions of Excel, so that you won't need to become a neural net rocket scientist. Now the bad news: you will need to learn something about neural nets.

Neural nets can be viewed as biologically motivated statistical analysis. The human brain has evolved over millions of years and is particularly adept at pattern recognition of naturally occurring phenomena. For instance, you can recognize a lion in your peripheral vision in less than . 1 second. Don't you wish you could recognize the beginning of a bear market as quickly? Unfortunately, stock market graphs are not naturally occurring phenomena, and mere humans need at lot of help in recognizing patterns and performing time series predictions. This facility is known as associative memory, in that the brain learns to associate a given input or set of inputs with an outcome. i. e. See lion (input), fight or flight (output).

In the beginning there were statistics which, when applied in the early 1960's, gave the trader an edge. Then, as compute power proliferated, the quality of that edge deteriorated and traders looked for a new edge. The first electronic neural nets were built in 1950, however, they were not very powerful (for reasons to be explained later). By the early 1980's, they had reappeared in much more robust forms and began to attract the interest of various investment houses. In the early 1990's, several firms had started to announce the use of neural nets in portfolio management. The most significant of these was Fidelity, which claimed to have $3 billion under neural net management.

Neural Net History and Technology

The first useful neural nets were developed by Dr. B. Widrow and Dr. A. Hoff of Stanford University in the late 1950's. A diagram is shown in Figure 1 (next page). This basic form of neural net is known as a two layer Perceptron. It has two states--learn and recall (predict). To "learn," the neural net needs a set of cases or examples. Each case will consist of a set of know inputs and one or more known outputs. For instance, the inputs could be high, low, open and close. The known output could be: did the stock close up or down for the following day. Typically, the cases are divided into three categories. 85% of the cases will go in the training set, 10% of the cases will go in the testing set, and the remaining 5% go to the validation set

In the learn mode, each of the case inputs is multiplied by an associated weight (W1, W2, W3 and W4 in the diagram) which can be any number between positive infinity and negative infinity. The results of all inputs are then summed by the neuron or processing element, PE1, and threshold, (greater or less than a predetermined number--in this case it is 5) and compared with the known or desired output. If there is a difference between the neural net output and the known output, then a "learning law" is used to adjust the weights of the net so as to move the net's output closer to the known output. This process continues time and again, for the entire training set of examples, until the net meets a given tolerance for accuracy. This is called net convergence. For our example, let's assume that a 0 output is a sell signal, and an output of 1 is a buy signal.

After convergence, we then present the testing data set to the net while it is in recall mode. In recall mode, the net performs as described above except that there is no weight adjustment. Hopefully, the overall error of the testing set is within 10% of the training set error. If this is the case, then the validation set is run with its error being the specified error for the net. In the event that the error of the testing set is more than 10%, then one might do some neural net engineering (discussed later) to improve the overall error of the net. The reader should be aware that this training and testing methodology is very rigorous and is

Figure 1. Two Layer Perceptron

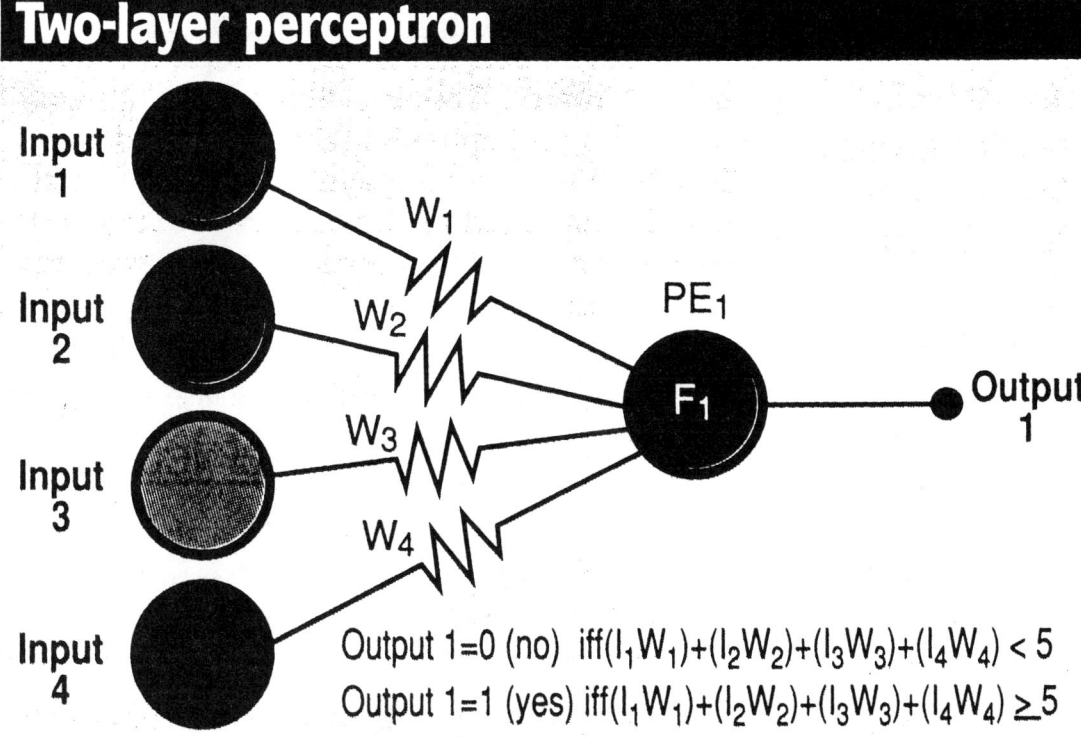

Two-layer perceptron

Input 1

Input 2

Input 3

Input 4

W_1

W_2

W_3

W_4

PE_1

F_1

Output 1

Output 1=0 (no) iff$(I_1 W_1)+(I_2 W_2)+(I_3 W_3)+(I_4 W_4) < 5$

Output 1=1 (yes) iff$(I_1 W_1)+(I_2 W_2)+(I_3 W_3)+(I_4 W_4) \geq 5$

In the beginning there was the two-layer perceptron that provided the method of inputting data for a result.

frequently NOT used by firms who report neural net results in the financial market, resulting in an overstatement of the net's accuracy.

While these basic two layer nets had some success in forecasting weather, balancing brooms, and playing blackjack, they suffered from a serious flaw. They could not solve the exclusive OR (XOR) problem, as shown in Figure 2 (next page). This states that the output C will be 1, if and only if either A or B is 1, and shall be zero in all other cases. Since the two layer net can produce only a single line in the two dimensional case in Figure 2, it cannot possibly divide the space between the 1's and 0's. This is important because logicians have shown that any system that can't solve this problem cannot be very interesting in complex problem solving.

In the mid 1970's, Dr. Paul Werbos popularized the three and more layer net known as back-propagation (BP). It learns in a similar fashion to a two layer net, but has a third middle layer, or in rare cases even two or more middle layers. This is shown in Figure 3 (next page). While over 95% of the neural net systems in production today use this methodology, it too has some problems. BP does not

know when it doesn't know. This is illustrated in Figure 4 (two pages forward). Note that there are two solutions that BP could generate, the solid line solution and the dotted line solution. As a result, the classification of the question marks between the two solutions would depend upon which solution the net fell into. Always remember that nets are a non-deterministic system because the initial value of the weights are usually set randomly.

Recently, this problem has been addressed by a number of different learning algorithms which create closed surfaces like the circles shown around the outputs in Figure 4. In this case, any input that falls outside the circle is classified as unknown. The radius of these circles depend upon the data density around the correct solution and can be adjusted by the user. There are many neural net algorithms that can generate closed decision surfaces such as the Probabilistic Neural Net (PNN), Restricted Coulomb Energy (RCE) and Radial Basis Functions (RBF's). One should be aware that these classes of algorithms are much more memory intensive than BP, and require more compute cycles in the recall mode than BP. However, they can learn hundreds to even thousands of times faster than BP.

Figure 2. X-OR Problem

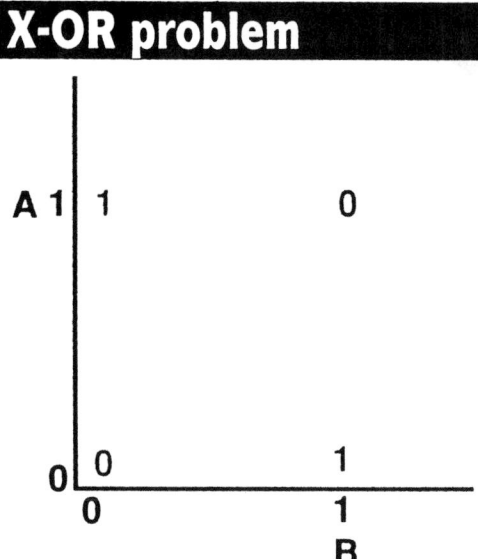

Truth table (Values of C in green)

A	B	C
0	0	0
1	0	1
0	1	1
1	1	0

A reasonable logical system must be able to learn this simple problem.

Today, there are at least 100 neural net learning algorithms with a new one surfacing each week. Which to use? In general, only about thirty of these are available in off-the-shelf software packages. The tried and true ones such as BP and its derivatives, along with the ones mentioned above, are the most popular. The result is that more is known about preprocessing and testing with these popular methods. Using these, you can build on the work of others rather than starting from scratch.

Preprocessing and Optimum Training Techniques

So far, not so hard? Yes, but there is no free lunch. Neural nets need help learning just as a child does. For instance, it would be very hard for a child to learn to read without a teacher to help present the material in a coherent fashion. Similarly, the net needs more than just data to learn. It needs someone who is familiar with the problem area, e.g. traders for trading, lending officers for loan approval and diagnostic engineers for diagnostics. These teachers, or domain experts, perform various

Figure 3. Back Propogation

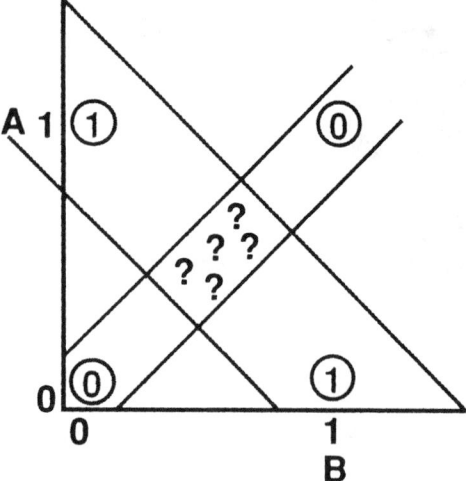

Today's methods can solve two-dimensionally, but need help to resolve the region of uncertainty.

forms of preprocessing when they solve a problem. By correctly preprocessing the data before it is presented to the net, the net can learn faster and more accurately.

For example, in the loan approval situation, a loan officer always does a "quick ratio" on the loan applicant. Knowing this, it would be foolish to put debt and assets as separate variables into a neural net, since you would be consuming valuable neural net learning resources (weights) while the net learned that the quick ratio was an important feature of the problem. Therefore, a good starting point for it would be to use the quick ratio as an input. Clearly, there are many preprocessing methods traders apply every day that can be used with neural nets. Since most aspects of trader preprocessing are instrument specific, and are well covered in the literature, we will focus on those methods that are useful for neural nets that are not covered in the literature.

Before we can go further, we need to have a little more insight into how a net learns, and the tradeoffs between generalization, net size, learning speed and accuracy.

Any mathematician will tell you that you can always derive an equation that can fit a time-series to any desired degree of accuracy. However, unless it is a periodic series like a sine wave, the ability for this equation to forecast the next data point in the

Figure 4. Closed Surfaces

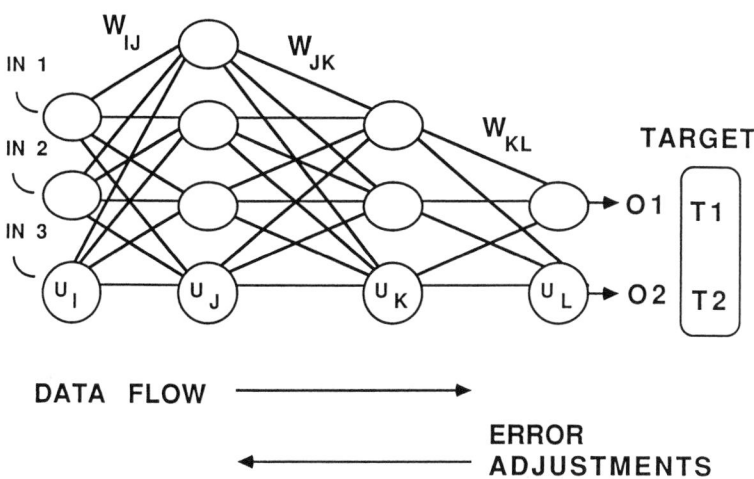

TYPICAL BACKPROP LAYOUT

time-series will suffer as a function of how closely one fits the series. This is known as overfitting and the same phenomenon appears in neural nets. One of the ways to minimize this is to use the smallest possible net (least PE's in the middle layer) that still meets your accuracy criteria.

There are many other reasons for seeking a minimum size net. First, the smaller the net, the less training data it will need. Surprisingly enough, in most forecasting problems you will NOT have enough data. Second, arriving at an optimum net is an iterative problem for the developer, although some of the newest software packages automate this function. As an iterative problem, you will try many neural net architectures to arrive at a satisfactory solution. The more experiments you can conduct in a finite period of time, the more accurate the resultant net will be. This repetitive experimental phase makes reducing training time a significant factor.

Since nets are susceptible to overfitting, one also needs to know when to stop training. Most packages will attempt to train to a given accuracy. A more sophisticated solution is to train until training accuracy and testing accuracy converge, a method that most software packages support. Additionally, it would be nice if more packages would flag those cases that have a very high error, e.g. ten times the average training error, since there is always a possibility of a data error.

How much data do I need? A general rule is that you need 2-10 examples for each weight in your net, with more examples needed for complex problems. For time-series problems, the minimum number of examples can be calculated with the following formula: the number of examples divided by three must be greater than the number of inputs

multiplied by the number of PE's in the middle layer.

Another issue in net resource allocation is input scaling. While it would be nice if a net input could be used for any number between +/- infinity, doing so would cause an over allocation of resources to very big numbers. If we were talking about the Standard & Poors 500 Stock Index (S&P 500) such an allocation would be ridiculous. One way to deal with this would be to say any number over 700 for the S&P 500 would be 700, and any number below 300 would be 300. This gives us a maximum and a minimum. Alternatively, one could use the logarithm of the S&P 500 index and have a range from 0 - 3. Today, most packages will find and set the maximum and minimum ranges for your data, and have logarithmic as well as other forms of scaling. Nevertheless, in some cases you may be interested in much more sophisticated forms of preprocessing. You can implement this on your own with Excel, or purchase one of the many preprocessing packages on the market. These tend to divide into two categories, those that are trading specific, and those that are neural net specific. At this time, many of the neural net specific products will snap into Excel, however, most of the trading specific packages won't, so make sure that these have ASCII interfaces for data import and export. Remember to check product reviews before purchasing since there seems to be little correlation between performance and price.

One form of preprocessing common to almost all forms of forecasting is computing a moving average. A moving average is used to smooth the data and remove the sharp changes common to most financial instruments. Today, many prefer an exponential moving average, while some of the more advanced technologists prefer an adaptive

Figure 5. Smoothing Data

Smoothing data

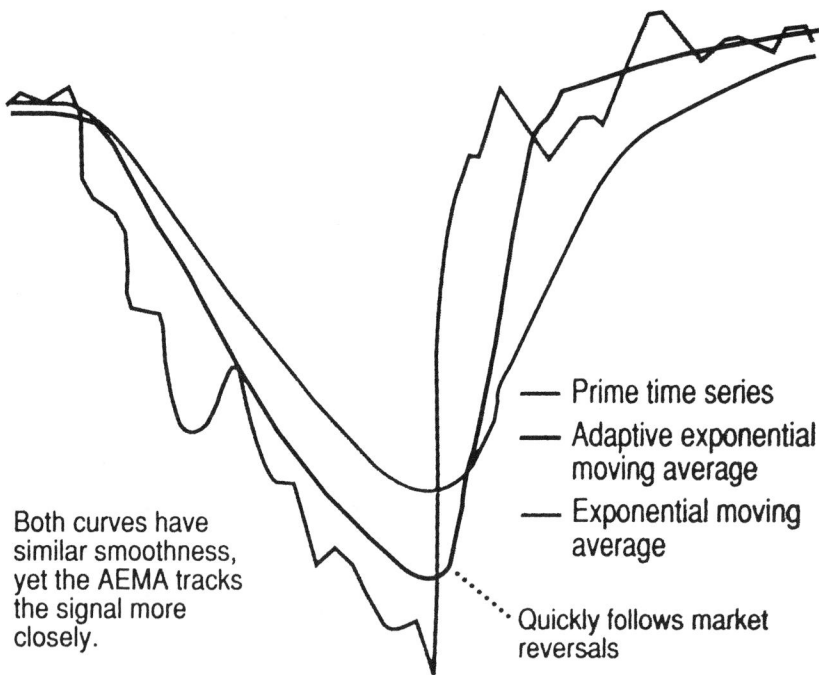

— Prime time series

— Adaptive exponential moving average

— Exponential moving average

Both curves have similar smoothness, yet the AEMA tracks the signal more closely.

Quickly follows market reversals

Better than raw data points, preprocessed inputs save time and are more accurate.

exponential moving average. A comparison of raw oil pricing data with both types of exponential averages is shown in Figure 5.

One final idea, currently used by John Deere in managing a portion of their retirement fund, is to normalize all stock prices relative to the S&P 500 and forecast percent change of value of the stock relative to the S&P 500. This method is one way in which they have improved system accuracy by decreasing the dynamic range of stock prices that the system had to deal with

Neural Net Specific Preprocessing

There are two issues near and dear to most time-series neural net architects--optimum time-series sampling and data decorrelation. Optimum sampling is another technique for reducing the size of the training set. For instance, suppose that you think there is a 5 week cycle in the S&P 500. How would you sample your data? The direct approach would be to take all five years of data and let the net learn on a daily basis. Wrong! This would lead to long training times, overfitting, loss of generalization and a much larger net than is really

needed. You could take every 25th trading day back for five years. A little better, but you still lose generalization since the cycle is probably not exactly every 25th day going back five years. The correct method is a mix of Nyquest and wavelet sampling theory. In this case, one would use the average of the 24th, 25th and-26th day back as the exact value for the 25th day. In this way, the noise around the 25th day back is averaged out making for a better performing net. This is similar to the fuzzifying of numbers in sampling offered by some packages, but with a few subtle differences.

Nets can be easily confused and waste resources when inputs are highly correlated. For instance, it is well known that the MACD and the ROC are highly correlated, as are the price of gold and the KR-CRB Index which both measure inflation. It would be redundant to use highly correlated inputs. Unfortunately, correlation between inputs is not always obvious. A data decorrelator analyzes all the inputs and remaps them in descending information content order. As an example, one chaotic time-series had 21 inputs and one output before decorrelation. After decorrelation, only 5 inputs accounted for over 98. 9% of the information, resulting in faster training and better generalization.

Excel, a Testbed for Forecasting

Anyone who forecasts is probably familiar with Lotus and Excel spread-sheets. Today, there are at least five forecasting tools for Excel and two for Lotus. They range in price from $99 to $4,000. The preference for Excel is that it is always available with the newest in DLL and OLE technology. This facility makes it easy to pass data and commands between other programs that support this technology, such as fuzzy logic, genetic algorithms (GA's), a variety of charting programs and a few data feed services. Fuzzy logic is good for creating dynamic stop-loss programs, where the stop-loss point can move as a function of market dynamics. GA's, on the other hand, find a place in portfolio optimization. Additionally, there are at least five vendors making products with DLL capability. These will take a little more work to hook into a spread sheet than the snap-ins, but may be worth considering. Again, look for product reviews in various publications for the latest information.

Each of these products offer some advantages and some disadvantages in their forecasting capability (frequently more a function of your preprocessing than the product), ease of use, level of automation and flexibility. An important caveat to remember is that you will usually build a better system by focusing on your preprocessing, than in spending time tweaking knobs in your neural net tool, because to do this with any facility you will have to become a neural net master.

It has recently come to light that some of the forecasting products do not do error checking on direct data feeds. Make sure the product you use does so. Neural nets are a GIGO (garbage in, garbage out) technology. This brings us to the question of historical data-scrubbing (getting rid of entry errors in the data you have purchased). It is the preferred method not to try to scrub, particularly for a weekly trading scenario. Since you are not getting live data there will always be entry problems, and your system should be able to deal with these errors as long as their percentage, relative to the total training set, is small. Additionally, really wild errors should be squashed to some degree by your input data scaling.

Where to Start

One of the easiest systems to build is a buy/sell oscillator forecaster. Many traders use a moving average, mixed with some small portion of the real price move, in combination with a lagged moving average to call market turns. By taking the difference between these two values one can get a curve which crosses a zero point. A buy signal is generated when the difference is greater than zero, and a sell signal when the difference is below zero.

Unfortunately, any prediction using this type of system will be late by the lag time of the moving average, and the fact that it is based upon historical data.

This can be easily improved upon in two ways. The first, is to use an adaptive exponential moving average to reduce the time lag. The second, is to teach a neural net to forecast the oscillator by one time period in your trading cycle, thereby predicting the position of the oscillator in future time. In actuality, you will probably use more than just the two moving averages. What inputs? That's where your market knowledge comes into play. In fact, input selection and preprocessing are much more important than what type of net you use.

Some Final Words

One of the big questions is *interday* trading or *intraday* trading. Interday trading data is cheaper, and you don't have to be at your machine each day. These systems are also easier to build. However, you do have a week-to-week anxiety problem. Intraday eliminates overnight anxiety, and in reality, you don't have to trade every day. But, you may want train your net on a frequent basis. Some neural net methods allow for data to be added incrementally without total retraining. Or, an accelerator board can be added ($2,000-$5,000) so that you can train fast enough to keep up with the market. The right compromise might be to start on interday and move up to intraday.

In some cases you may realize better performance by training one net to be a long identification net, and another to be a short identification net. Since long is not really the opposite of short, one can decide to stay out of the market. Also, once you have a system, you must have the confidence to NEVER second guess it or skip trades because the previous transaction was a loser. The neural net forecasting industry is ripe with stories of people who fell into these traps and lost in the long haul. While you may be right in second guessing a few times, the net should always be statistically better than you. If not, why are you even using this technology? Additionally, just because your system did well on a training set, don't start trading it immediately. You may have inadvertently done something that has biased (overtrained for instance) the net, so that results are good on your entire training set, but fall apart in the real world.

How often should you retrain? In general, if you have a daily system, most folks will tell you to retrain daily. With a weekly system, retrain weekly. Retraining with each tick will probably be hard to do because of speed, and may not be necessary. I know of one weekly system that does quite well with the S&P 500 that only retrains yearly.

What kind of results should you expect? With some work, you should be able to call direction on almost any instrument with 60-70% accuracy. With single stock systems, this usually translates to a 2-5% higher return than the index. Some futures traders report 40% annualized returns, with some index trading systems reporting higher. Index systems may be the best choice since they are usually closer to the efficient market hypothesis than most other choices. Finally, make sure that you don't overtrade, remember that commissions and slippage are a major expense. There is an old homily, "if the only tool you have is a hammer, all your problems look like nails." Once you achieve some proficiency in using neural nets, consider combining known trading technologies with other advanced technologies. For instance, one researcher is currently representing candlesticks as a fuzzy system, in tandem with his neural net system to realize even greater returns.

In 1984 Tom J. Schwartz founded The Schwartz Associates (TSA). The firm provides consulting to vendors and users of advanced computing technologies encompassing: expert systems, neural computing and fuzzy systems. Services include: on-site-training, video-courseware, (NeuroTapes, Genetic Algorithms Made Easy, Fuzzy Tapes & Expert Systems Made Easy) traveling seminars, custom and off-the shelf reports, problem and product selection, technology deployment strategies, turn-key systems for trading and fraud detection, technology licensing and strategic marketing. Currently, he is the Publicity Chair for the 1st IEEE Computational Intelligence in Financial Engineering Conference and a contributing editor to Wall Street and Technology, Futures Magazine and AI in Finance. Mr. Schwartz holds a BSEE, MSEE and MBA. He is a member of HKN, TBπ, IEEE, INNS, PATCA and co-founded: The IEEE Bay Area Special Interest Group for Computers in Finance, The Northern California Venture Capital Association and AI Forum Inc. (a non-profit corporation for the improvement of education in advanced computer technologies).

Mr. Schwartz has lectured and presented for IEEE, INNS, IJCNN, AAAI, IJCAI, ASME, Stanford University, the University of California, New York University, appeared on many national television broadcasts and been quoted in such publications as the Wall Street Journal, Time Magazine, Fortune and InfoWorld. He has written over 200 technology articles which have appeared in numerous national and international computer publications. He can be reached at 800-965-4561 or 415-965-4561.

*   *   *

Volume U.S.

U.S. FUTURES VOLUME HIGHLIGHTS

1994 in Comparison with 1993

1994 Rank	Contracts with Volume Over 100,000 during 1994	1994 CONTRACTS	%	1993 CONTRACTS	%	1993 Rank
1	Eurodollar, CME	104,823,245	24.59%	64,411,394	19.00%	2
2	T-Bonds, CBOT	99,959,881	23.45%	79,428,474	23.43%	1
3	Crude Oil, NYMEX	26,812,262	6.29%	24,868,602	7.33%	3
4	T-Notes (10 Year), CBOT	24,077,828	5.65%	16,601,258	4.90%	4
5	S&P 500 Index, CME	18,708,599	4.39%	13,204,413	3.89%	5
6	T-Notes (5 Year), CBOT	12,462,838	2.92%	8,123,939	2.40%	11
7	Corn, CBOT	11,529,884	2.70%	11,462,618	3.38%	8
8	Deutschemark, CME	10,956,479	2.57%	12,866,451	3.79%	6
9	Soybeans, CBOT	10,749,109	2.52%	11,649,333	3.44%	7
10	#2 Heating Oil, NYMEX	8,986,835	2.11%	8,625,061	2.54%	10
11	Gold (100 oz.), COMEX Div. of NYMEX	8,503,366	1.99%	8,916,195	2.63%	9
12	Unleaded Regular Gas, NYMEX	7,470,836	1.75%	7,407,809	2.18%	12
13	Japanese Yen, CME	6,612,993	1.55%	6,023,132	1.78%	13
14	Natural Gas, NYMEX	6,357,560	1.49%	4,671,533	1.38%	17
15	Silver (5,000 oz.), COMEX Div. of NYMEX	5,994,345	1.41%	4,855,924	1.43%	15
16	Swiss Franc, CME	5,217,236	1.22%	5,604,841	1.65%	14
17	Soybean Oil, CBOT	5,063,188	1.19%	4,612,229	1.36%	18
18	Sugar #11, CSC	4,719,218	1.11%	4,285,945	1.26%	19
19	Soybean Meal, CBOT	4,593,814	1.08%	4,718,095	1.39%	16
20	Wheat, CBOT	3,620,631	0.85%	3,019,629	0.89%	22
21	Live Cattle, CME	3,580,896	0.84%	3,306,952	0.98%	21
22	British Pound, CME	3,562,865	0.84%	3,701,427	1.09%	20
23	High Grade Copper, COMEX Div. of NYMEX	2,737,967	0.64%	2,064,629	0.61%	25
24	Coffee "C", CSC	2,658,073	0.62%	2,489,223	0.73%	23
25	Cocoa, CSC	2,417,006	0.57%	2,128,384	0.63%	24
26	Cotton, NYCE	2,289,998	0.54%	1,603,027	0.47%	26
27	One Month LIBOR, CME	1,911,184	0.45%	1,128,321	0.33%	30
28	Canadian Dollar, CME	1,740,205	0.41%	1,410,818	0.42%	27
29	Municipal Bond Index, CBOT	1,600,533	0.38%	1,120,510	0.33%	32
30	Live Hogs, CME	1,554,022	0.36%	1,401,754	0.41%	28
31	Wheat, KCBT	1,502,348	0.35%	1,348,500	0.40%	29
32	T-Bonds, MIDAM	1,385,904	0.33%	1,125,645	0.33%	31
33	T-Bills (90 Day), CME	1,020,491	0.24%	1,017,350	0.30%	33
34	T-Notes (2 Year), CBOT	939,043	0.22%	532,203	0.16%	41
35	Platinum, NYMEX	895,805	0.21%	651,222	0.19%	38
36	Soybeans, MIDAM	797,803	0.19%	966,244	0.28%	34
37	Wheat, MGE	737,089	0.17%	822,898	0.24%	36
38	NYSE Composite Index, NYFE	729,231	0.17%	848,522	0.25%	35
39	Orange Juice (Frozen Conc.), NYCE	653,824	0.15%	640,131	0.19%	39
40	Pork Bellies, CME	633,646	0.15%	698,799	0.21%	37
41	U.S. Dollar Index, NYCE	558,439	0.13%	599,112	0.18%	40
42	Nikkei 225, CME	548,233	0.13%	356,523	0.11%	44
43	Oats, CBOT	492,504	0.12%	455,335	0.13%	42
44	Feeder Cattle, CME	446,639	0.10%	419,888	0.12%	43
45	30 Day Federal Fund, CBOT	416,200	0.10%	182,319	0.05%	48
46	Australian Dollar, CME	355,183	0.08%	198,954	0.06%	47
47	S&P MidCap 400 Index, CME	285,962	0.07%	218,531	0.06%	46
48	Corn, MIDAM	232,855	0.05%	276,502	0.08%	45
49	Lumber, CME	172,963	0.04%	178,184	0.05%	49
50	Goldman Sachs Commodity Index, CME	154,511	0.04%	122,281	0.04%	53
51	Sugar #14, CSC	150,472	0.04%	133,898	0.04%	51
52	Major Market Index, CBOT	150,308	0.04%			
53	Palladium, NYMEX	143,773	0.03%	113,681	0.03%	54
54	Deutschemark Rolling Spot, CME	126,994	0.03%			
55	Deutschemark, MIDAM	113,166	0.03%	123,573	0.04%	52
56	CRB Index, NYFE	109,986	0.03%			
57	Wheat, MIDAM	102,145	0.02%	101,353	0.03%	55
	Contracts w/Volume Under 100,000	1,179,529	0.28%	1,076,720	0.32%	
	Other Contracts w/Volume Over 100,000**			155,338	0.04%	
	TOTAL	**426,307,942**	**100.00%**	**339,075,626**	**99.95%**	

** Contracts with volume over 100,000 in 1993, but less than 100,000 in 1994.

Volume U.S.

U.S. FUTURES VOLUME HIGHLIGHTS

1994 in Comparison with 1993

1994 RANK	EXCHANGE	1994 CONTRACTS	%	1993 CONTRACTS	%	1993 RANK
1	Chicago Board of Trade (CBOT)	175,697,680	41.21%	142,241,377	41.95%	1
2	Chicago Mercantile Exchange (CME)	162,696,029	38.16%	116,415,113	34.33%	2
3	New York Mercantile Exchange (NYMEX) **	68,010,380	15.95%	62,276,930	18.37%	3
4	Coffee, Sugar & Cocoa Exchange (CSCE)	9,947,040	2.33%	9,039,406	2.67%	5
5	MidAmerica Commodity Exchange (MidAm)	3,042,609	0.71%	2,966,474	0.87%	6
6	New York Cotton Exchange (NYCE)	3,662,614	0.86%	2,896,567	0.85%	7
7	Kansas City Board of Trade (KCBT)	1,604,508	0.38%	1,434,968	0.42%	8
8	New York Futures Exchange (NYFE)	839,228	0.20%	940,440	0.28%	9
9	Minneapolis Grain Exchange (MGE)	765,508	0.18%	839,255	0.25%	10
10	Philadelphia Board of Trade (PBOT)	42,346	0.01%	25,096	0.01%	11
	TOTAL	426,307,942	100.00%	339,075,626	100.00%	

** In 1993, the Commodity Exchange randed number 4 among U.S. futures exchanges. In August 1994, the Commodity Exchange and the New York Mercantile Exchange merged and is now listed as one exchange.

U.S. FUTURES VOLUME 1990 - 1994

FUTURE	CONTRACT UNIT	1994	1993	1992	1991	1990
Wheat	5,000 bu	3,620,631	3,019,629	3,498,814	3,146,844	2,876,270
Corn	5,000 bu	11,529,884	11,462,618	10,356,632	10,852,909	11,423,027
Oats	5,000 bu	492,504	455,335	459,578	354,953	433,567
Soybeans	5,000 bu	10,749,109	11,649,333	9,000,169	9,013,739	10,301,905
Soybean Oil	60,000 lbs	5,063,188	4,612,229	4,282,678	4,018,544	4,658,302
Soybean Meal	100 tons	4,593,814	4,718,095	4,145,397	4,498,287	4,904,471
Rice	200,000 lbs	16,693				
Diammonium Phosphate	100 tons	15,588	45,314	34,465	10,931	
Anhydrous Ammonia	100 tons	2,811	9,831	5,563		
Edible Oil Index	100 tons	298				
Barge Freight Index	%BF x $5/ton		6	20		
Structural Panel Index	100,000 sq. ft.	7,033				
Eastern Catastrophe Insurance	Loss/EP x $25,000		4,600	133		
Midwest Catastrophe Insurance	Loss/EP x $25,000		74			
National Catastrophe Insurance	Loss/EP x $25,000	4	4,782	79		
Silver	5,000 oz	10,278	1,022	472	640	2,256
Silver	1,000 oz	88,663	89,141	52,658	114,268	178,801
Gold	100 oz	984	778	56	825	7,814
Gold	Kilo	22,712	22,220	10,362	17,873	36,649
T-Bonds	$100,000	99,959,881	79,428,444	70,003,894	67,887,497	75,499,257
T-Notes (6 1/2-10 Year)	$100,000	24,077,828	16,601,258	11,217,938	6,341,432	6,054,222
T-Notes (5 Year)	$100,000	12,462,838	8,123,939	6,441,193	3,386,161	2,532,828
T-Notes (2 Year)	$200,000	939,043	532,203	445,394	285,567	110,789
Cash T-Note (2 Year)	$500,000				158	
Japanese Government Bonds	20 million Yen					3,062
30-Day Federal Funds	$5,000,000	416,200	182,319	233,727	115,958	81,300
Mortgage Backed 7.5%	$100,000			44		
Mortgage Backed 8.0%	$100,000			96	291	
Mortgage Backed 8.5%	$100,000				1,581	
Mortgage Backed 9.0%	$100,000				2,744	5,294
Mortgage Backed 9.5%	$100,000				1,163	11,554
Municipal Bond Index	$1,000 x Index	1,600,533	1,120,510	776,205	549,135	696,861
3 Year Swap	25 million	27,163			1,231	

Volume U.S.

FUTURE	CONTRACT UNIT	1994	1993	1992	1991	1990
5 Year Swap	25 million			2,389	5,675	
US Dollar Index	$1,250 x Index		733			
TOPIX	5,000 Yen x Index					230
MMI Maxi	$500 x Index		155,338	360,879	702,927	951,325
Wilshire Small Cap Index	$500 x Index		1,626			
CHICAGO BOARD OF TRADE (CBOT)		**175,697,680**	**157,697**	**363,268**	**708,602**	**951,555**
Live Hogs	40,000 lbs	1,554,022	1,401,754	1,556,092	1,582,234	2,241,272
Pork Bellies, Frozen	40,000 lbs	633,646	698,799	784,152	1,005,196	1,303,129
Broilers	40,000 lbs			1,312	5,956	
Live Cattle	40,000 lbs	3,580,896	3,306,952	3,319,618	3,792,824	3,797,376
Feeder Cattle	44,000 lbs	446,639	419,888	369,042	538,495	391,308
Lumber	160,000 bd ft	172,963	178,184	170,534	160,521	201,984
T-Bils (90-day)	$1,000,000	1,020,491	1,017,350	1,337,061	2,012,079	1,869,610
T-Bills (1 Year)	$500,000	586				
Eurodollar (3-month)	$1,000,000	104,823,245	64,411,394	60,531,066	37,244,223	34,695,625
Euromark (3-month)	$1,000,000	566	26,058			
Dollar/Pound Diff	$1,000,000				12	1,064
Dollar/Mark Diff	$1,000,000					1,478
Dollar/Yen Diff	$1,000,000					3,727
One Month LIBOR	$3,000,000	1,911,184	1,128,321	918,593	450,354	84,148
BP/DM Cross	50,000 x bp/dm X			15	3,605	
DM/JY Cross (Old)	125,000 x dm/jy X			718	8,561	
DM/JY Cross (New)	125,000 x dm/jy X		175	10,005		
DM/SF Cross	125,000 x dm/sf X			41	1,409	
British Pound	62,500	3,562,865	3,701,427	3,053,428	3,745,617	3,410,333
Canadian Dollar	100,000	1,740,205	1,410,818	1,171,640	1,139,397	1,408,799
Deutschemark	125,000	10,956,479	12,866,451	11,593,174	10,928,693	9,169,230
Japanese Yen	12,500,000	6,612,993	6,023,132	4,520,356	6,017,012	7,437,235
Swiss Franc	125,000	5,217,236	5,604,841	5,134,717	5,835,480	6,524,893
Australian Dollar	100,000	355,183	198,954	89,784	76,016	105,241
French Franc	250,000	49,005	19,343			50
Deutschemark Forward	$250,000	46,979				
British Pound Rolling Spot	250,000 sterling		1,729			
Deutschemark Rolling Spot	250,000 U.S.	126,994	28,936			
Nikkei 225	$5 x Index	548,233	356,523	383,755	246,948	52,046
S&P 500 Index	$500 x 500 Index	18,708,599	13,204,413	12,414,157	12,340,380	12,139,209
S&P MidCap 400 Index	$500 x 400 Index	285,962	218,531	102,708		
FT-SE 100	50 x FTSE Index		94	1,057		
Major Market	$500 x Index	150,308	49,286			
Russell 2000	$500 x Index	36,239	19,479			
Goldman Sachs Commodity Index	$250 x GSCI	154,511	122,281	36,320		
CHICAGO MERCANTILE EXCHANGE (CME)		**162,696,029**	**116,415,113**	**107,499,345**	**87,135,012**	**84,837,757**
Coffee "C"	37,500 lbs	2,658,073	2,489,223	2,152,383	1,772,648	1,774,050
Sugar #11	112,000 lbs	4,719,218	4,285,945	3,667,481	4,268,546	5,424,801
Sugar #14	112,000 lbs	150,472	133,898	138,609	131,791	139,143
White Sugar	50 metric tons			10	20	
Cocoa	10 metric tons	2,417,006	2,128,384	1,397,235	1,233,519	1,635,917
Euro-Diff Coffee	37,500 lbs				94	
Brazil-Diff Coffee	37,500 lbs		11	359		
Cheddar Cheese	40,000 lbs	1,366	669			
Non Fat Dry Milk	44,000 lbs	905	1,276			
COFFEE, SUGAR & COCOA EXCHANGE (CSCE)		**9,947,040**	**9,039,406**	**7,356,077**	**7,406,618**	**8,973,911**
Wheat	5,000 bu	1,502,348	1,348,500	1,339,842	1,412,510	1,136,234
Grain Sorghum	5,000 bu				1,064	1,210
Value Line Index	$500 x Index	50,259	45,806	46,195	57,705	35,558
Mini Value Line	$100 x Index	51,901	40,662	34,454	26,941	14,081
KANSAS CITY BOARD OF TRADE (KCBT)		**1,604,508**	**1,434,968**	**1,420,491**	**1,498,220**	**1,187,083**

Volume U.S.

FUTURE	CONTRACT UNIT	1994	1993	1992	1991	1990
Wheat	1,000 bu	102,145	101,353	239,180	153,949	147,033
Corn	1,000 bu	232,855	276,502	458,772	433,480	455,289
Oats	1,000 bu	5,208	4,555	8,008	4,681	13,502
Soybeans	1,000 bu	797,803	966,244	1,130,629	1,387,923	1,565,641
Soybean Meal New	20 tons	3,757	3,800	2,201	3,610	5,437
Live Cattle	20,000 lbs	15,895	16,314	15,366	16,937	19,284
Live Hogs	20,000 lbs	19,614	17,841	17,597	19,388	29,533
Rice, Rough New	200,000 lbs	68,379	65,970	25,291	39,310	55,385
New York Silver	1,000 oz	17,170	10,986	8,888	13,106	11,005
New York Gold	33.2 oz	24,926	19,803	6,813	6,785	15,084
Platinum	25 oz	2,841	1,750	861	562	1,012
T-Bonds	$50,000	1,385,904	1,125,645	1,342,251	1,397,225	1,461,046
T-Bills	$500,000	826	1,129	2,017	1,297	3,884
T-Notes (10 Year)	$50,000	35,303	11,615		4	9
T-Notes (5 Year)	$50,000	4	39			
Eurodollars	$500,000	8,987	7,229	2,885		
U.S. Dollar Index	$1,250 x USDI		7	1,755		
British Pound	12,500	66,162	67,208	44,120	30,019	25,846
Swiss Franc	62,500	64,501	73,532	62,788	74,349	75,819
Deutschemark	62,500	113,166	123,573	105,543	93,577	82,534
Japanese Yen	6,250,000	67,641	62,874	39,293	40,958	54,283
Canadian Dollar	50,000	9,522	8,505	4,802	4,030	9,287
MIDAMERICA COMMODITY EXCHANGE (MidAm)		**3,042,609**	**2,966,474**	**3,519,060**	**3,721,190**	**4,030,913**
Wheat	5,000 bu	737,089	822,898	742,703	624,826	477,043
White Wheat	5,000 bu	27,446	10,895	6,077	2,406	1,014
Oats	5,000 bu		4,025	118	116	20
White Shrimp	5,000 lbs	854	1,437			
Black Tiger Shrimp	5,000 lbs	119				
MINNEAPOLIS GRAIN EXCHANGE (MGE)		**765,508**	**839,255**	**748,898**	**627,348**	**478,077**
Cotton #2	50,000 lbs	2,289,998	1,603,027	1,701,258	1,614,244	1,534,611
Cotlook World Cotton	50,000 lbs X CWC	79	3,363	12,098		
Orange Juice Frozen Concentrate	15,000 lbs	653,824	640,131	339,230	287,538	342,574
European Currency Unit	$100,000			972	1,691	12,150
Mark Pound	$125,000 BP	12,351				
Mark Paris	$500,000 DM	10,295				
Dollar Mark	$125,000 DM	30,385				
Mark Yen	$125,000 DM	30,566				
Mark Lira	$250,000 DM	3,572				
U.S. Dollar/Swiss France	$125,000 SF	10				
U.S. Dollar/Japanese Yen	$12,500 Y	2				
U.S. Dollar/British Pound	$62,500 BP	2				
U.S. Dollar Index	$500 x Index	558,439	599,112	678,329	715,547	565,194
T-Note (5 Year)	$100,000	69,858	50,200	80,186	71,220	222,271
T-Note (2 Year)	$200,000	3,233	734	892	9,931	69,409
NEW YORK COTTON EXCHANGE (NYCE)		**3,662,614**	**2,896,567**	**2,812,965**	**2,700,171**	**2,746,209**
NYSE Composite Index	$500 x Index	729,231	848,522	1,315,438	1,486,166	1,574,641
NYSE Utility Index	$500 x Index	11	10			
T-Bond (30 Year)	$100,000				21	12,094
Commodity Research Bureau Index	$500 x Index	109,986	91,908	56,255	61,185	70,233
NEW YORK FUTURES EXCHANGE (NYFE)		**839,228**	**940,440**	**1,371,693**	**1,547,372**	**1,656,968**

Volume U.S.

FUTURE	CONTRACT UNIT	1994	1993	1992	1991	1990
High Grade Copper	25,000 lbs	2,737,967	2,064,629	1,674,163	1,640,065	1,853,185
Aluminum	40,000 lbs					96
Silver	5,000 oz	5,994,345	4,855,924	3,016,339	4,154,704	3,913,609
Gold	100 oz	8,503,366	8,916,195	6,002,009	6,799,917	9,730,041
Platinum	50 oz		342	9,963		
Paladium	100 oz		2	333		
Eurotop 100 Index	$100 x Price	62,231	56,497	26,453		
COMEX DIVISION		**17,297,909**	**15,893,589**	**10,729,260**	**12,594,686**	**15,496,931**
Palladium	100 oz	143,773	113,681	68,209	78,199	95,642
Platinum	50 oz	895,805	651,222	577,253	604,646	820,934
No. 2 Heating Oil, NY	1,000 bbl	8,986,835	8,625,061	8,005,462	6,680,171	6,376,871
Unleaded Gasoline, NY	1,000 bbl	7,470,836	7,407,809	6,674,757	5,509,926	5,205,995
Residual Fuel Oil	1,000 bbl					76
Natural Gas	10,000 MMBTU	6,357,560	4,671,533	1,920,986	418,410	132,820
Gulf Coast Unleaded Gas	42,000 gal	300	510	4,902		
Propane	42,000 gal	45,100	44,923	50,601	55,854	38,636
Crude Oil	1,000 bbl	26,812,262	24,868,602	21,109,562	21,005,867	23,686,897
Sour Crude Oil	1,000 bbl			10,331		
NYMEX DIVISION		**50,712,471**	**46,383,341**	**38,422,063**	**34,353,073**	**36,357,871**
NEW YORK MERCANTILE EXCHANGE (NYMEX)**		**68,010,380**	**46,383,341**	**38,422,063**	**34,353,073**	**36,357,871**
Australian Dollar	100,000	265	142	132		
British Pound	62,500	2,485	1,493	234	2	438
Canadian Dollar	100,000	639				96
ECU	125,000	1,768				
Deutschemark	125,000	21,661	11,469	60,647	350	12
Swiss Franc	125,000	3,038	614	130	66	
French Franc	500,000	7,167	8,814	16,432	110	38
Japanese Yen	12,500,000	5,323	2,564	5,780		192
PHILADELPHIA BOARD OF TRADE (PBOT)		**42,346**	**25,096**	**83,355**	**528**	**776**
TOTAL FUTURES		**426,307,942**	**339,075,626**	**295,292,042**	**262,895,551**	**276,536,280**
PERCENT CHANGE		**25.73%**	**14.83%**	**12.32%**	**-4.93%**	**3.42%**

** In August 1994, the Commodity Exchange and the New York Mercantile Exchange merged and is now listed as one exchange.

OPTIONS TRADED ON U.S. FUTURES EXCHANGES VOLUME HIGHLIGHTS

1994 in Comparison with 1993

1994 RANK	EXCHANGE	1994 CONTRACTS	%	1993 CONTRACTS	%	1993 RANK
1	Chicago Board of Trade (CBOT)	43,806,394	43.42%	36,531,698	44.63%	1
2	Chicago Mercantile Exchange (CME)	42,489,574	42.12%	30,331,877	37.05%	2
3	New York Mercantile Exchange (NYMEX) **	10,651,003	10.56%	11,989,619	14.65%	3
4	Coffee, Sugar & Cocoa Exchange (CSCE)	2,717,012	2.69%	2,265,417	2.77%	5
5	New York Cotton Exchange (NYCE)	1,017,664	1.01%	541,097	0.66%	6
6	Kansas City Board of Trade (KCBT)	93,358	0.09%	89,011	0.11%	7
7	Minneapolis Grain Exchange (MGE)	40,411	0.04%	37,521	0.05%	8
8	New York Futures Exchange (NYFE)	34,131	0.03%	36,389	0.04%	9
9	MidAmerica Commodity Exchange (MidAm)	31,953	0.03%	36,006	0.04%	10
	TOTAL	**100,881,500**	**100.00%**	**81,858,635**	**100.00%**	

** In 1993, the Commodity Exchange randed number 4 among U.S. futures exchanges. In August 1994, the Commodity Exchange and the New York Mercantile Exchange merged and is now listed as one exchange.

Volume U.S.

OPTIONS VOLUME ON U.S. FUTURES EXCHANGES 1990 - 1994

OPTION	CONTRACT UNIT	1994	1993	1992	1991	1990
Wheat	5000 bu	827,930	713,670	1,108,840	692,327	482,941
Corn	5000 bu	2,144,461	2,031,284	1,833,816	2,048,422	2,116,302
Oats	5000 bu	20,495	17,373	15,307	4,486	7,334
Soybeans	5000 bu	2,710,656	2,927,072	1,930,334	2,165,167	2,089,382
Soybean Oil	60,000 lbs	287,905	181,938	104,704	78,991	138,089
Soybean Meal	100 tons	263,734	306,523	152,394	116,433	181,429
Rice	200,000 lbs	1,750				
Eastern Catastrophe Insurance	Loss/EP x $25,000	7,742	2,482	28		
Midwest Catastrophe Insurance	Loss/EP x $25,000	44				
National Catastrophe Insurance	Loss/EP x $25,000	1,590	4,102	22		
Westerm Insurance-Annual	Loss/EP x $25,000	44				
Silver	1,000 oz	5,952	12,423	20,105	2,804	1,398
T-Bonds	$100,000	28,142,549	23,435,164	20,258,740	21,925,578	27,315,411
T-Notes (10 Year)	$100,000	6,437,215	4,844,272	2,564,191	890,293	936,754
T-Notes (5 Year)	$100,000	2,675,097	1,976,924	665,587	129,389	87,440
T-Notes (2 Year)	$200,000	12,862	8,235	6,677		
Japanese Government Bonds	20 million Yen					475
Mortgage Backed 7.5%	$100,000			20		
Mortgage Backed 8.0%	$100,000			45	831	
Mortgage Backed 8.5%	$100,000				5,079	
Mortgage Backed 9.0%	$100,000				3,847	3,394
Mortgage Backed 9.5%	$100,000				160	15,837
3 Year Swap	25 million				530	
5 Year Swap	25 million			400	5,877	
Muni Bonds	$1,000 x Index	24,772	68,816	38,200	52,692	85,613
Canadian Government Bonds	$100,000 C$	1,385				
Flexible U.S. T-Bonds		174,295				
Flexible T-Notes (10 Year)		46,606				
Flexible T-Notes (5 Year)		19,060				
Flexible T-Notes (2 Year)		250				
Major Market Index	$500 x Index		1,368	2,215	3,059	
Wilshire Small Cap Index	$500 x Index		52			
CHICAGO BOARD OF TRADE (CBOT)		**43,806,394**	**36,531,698**	**28,701,625**	**28,125,965**	**33,461,799**
Live Hogs	40,000 lbs	109,448	79,046	82,341	112,338	171,306
Pork Bellies, Frozen	40,000 lbs	24,173	32,698	32,507	32,780	46,286
Broilers	40,000 lbs			733	2,646	
Live Cattle	40,000 lbs	519,813	500,664	561,058	776,624	713,276
Feeder Cattle	44,000 lbs	95,845	79,264	85,807	168,966	168,310
Lumber	160,000 bd ft	17,603	25,934	5,278	8,117	29,717
T-Bill (90-day)	$1,000,000	5,269	14,485	29,670	49,261	32,283
Eurodollar (3-month)	$1,000,000	28,145,929	17,008,764	13,762,628	7,874,551	6,859,625
Euromark (3-month)	$1,000,000		8,923			
One Month LIBOR	$3,000,000	79,172	90,604	98,839	74,805	
BP/DM Cross	50,000 x bp/dm X			1	968	
DM/JY Cross (Old)	125,000 x dm/jy X				3,373	
DM/JY Cross (New)	125,000 x dm/jy X		82	29,106		
DM/SF Cross	125,000 x dm/sf X				756	
British Pound	62,500	920,109	528,239	597,352	650,472	501,187
Canadian Dollar	100,000	185,652	176,930	306,528	336,758	283,609
Deutschemark	125,000	4,793,639	5,916,463	6,354,248	5,643,031	3,430,374
Japanese Yen	12,500,000	2,946,432	2,261,977	1,518,409	2,397,141	3,116,130
Swiss Franc	125,000	767,583	627,923	1,026,974	998,002	1,130,447
Australian Dollar	100,000	7,800	3,482	13,132	37,519	27,381
French Franc	250,000	1,064	5,562			
British Pound Rolling Spot	250,000 sterling		286			
Deutschemark Rolling Spot	250,000 U.S.		420			

Volume U.S.

OPTION	CONTRACT UNIT	1994	1993	1992	1991	1990
Nikkei 225	$5 x Index	7,982	9,684	13,971	12,378	8,793
S&P 500 Index	$500 x 500 Index	3,820,893	2,916,047	2,209,529	1,813,118	1,638,131
S&P MidCap 400 Index	$500 x 400 Index	3,622	5,129	2,933		
FT-SE 100	50 x FTSE Index		2	73		
Major Market	$500 x Index	804	251			
Russell 2000	$500 x Index	2,793	1,428			
Goldman Sachs Commodity Index	$250 x GSCI	33,949	37,590	8,093		
CHICAGO MERCANTILE EXCHANGE (CME)		**42,489,574**	**30,331,877**	**26,739,210**	**20,993,604**	**18,156,855**
Coffee	37,500 lbs	1,208,925	1,022,017	860,943	411,550	282,566
Sugar	112,000 lbs	1,166,748	916,170	848,750	1,512,976	2,393,016
Cocoa	10 metric tons	341,131	326,760	209,938	163,610	344,944
Cheddar Cheese	40,000 lbs	150	174			
Non Fat Dry Milk	44,000 lbs	58	296			
COFFEE, SUGAR & COCOA EXCHANGE (CSCE)		**2,717,012**	**2,265,417**	**1,919,631**	**2,088,136**	**3,020,526**
5 Day Copper	25,000 lbs	41	534			
High Grade Copper	25,000 lbs	184,125	146,060	87,324	97,163	107,387
Silver	5,000 oz	1,316,650	1,094,702	676,543	1,019,093	747,499
5 Day Silver	5,000 oz	368	1,262	9,606	798	
Gold	100 oz	1,589,065	1,717,015	1,152,854	1,398,451	1,931,804
5 Day Gold	100 oz	911	418	17,233	13,464	
Platinum	50 oz			359		
Eurotop 100 Index	$100 x Price		533			
COMEX DIVISION		**3,091,160**	**2,960,524**	**1,943,919**	**2,528,969**	**2,786,690**
Platinum	50 oz	90,556	62,661	39,458	27,989	3,749
Heating Oil	42,000 gal	699,325	803,216	1,247,891	863,143	406,810
Crude Oil	1,000 bbl	5,675,072	7,156,518	6,562,163	4,968,742	5,254,612
Unleaded Gasoline	1,000 bbl	573,502	660,886	860,086	573,767	435,685
Natural Gas	10,000 MMBTU	493,491	345,814	80,756		
Gas-Crude Oil Spread	1,000 bbl	13,932				
Heating Oil-Crude Oil Spread	1,000 bbl	13,965				
NYMEX DIVISION		**7,559,843**	**9,029,095**	**8,790,354**	**6,433,641**	**6,100,856**
NEW YORK MERCANTILE EXCHANGE (NYMEX)**		**10,651,003**	**11,989,619**	**10,734,273**	**8,962,610**	**8,887,546**
Wheat	5,000 bu	89,954	87,214	85,565	91,060	65,794
Mini Value Line	$100 x Index	3,404	1,797	918		
KANSAS CITY BOARD OF TRADE (KCBT)		**93,358**	**89,011**	**86,483**	**91,060**	**65,794**
Corn	1,000 bu	5,765	6,274	8,333	4,581	
Soft Red Winter Wheat	5,000 bu	3,536	2,652	4,038	2,917	3,408
Soybeans	1,000 bu	13,498	19,062	15,786	19,797	23,578
Rough Rice	200,000 lbs	5,588	6,013	6,121		
T-Bonds	$50,000	3,149	1,966	3,657	2,113	
Gold	33.2 oz	417	39	289	255	2,324
MIDAMERICA COMMODITY EXCHANGE (MidAm)		**31,953**	**36,006**	**38,224**	**29,663**	**29,310**
American Spring Wheat	5,000 bu	26,441	27,822	13,556	5,132	4,509
European Spring Wheat	5,000 bu	284	48			22
White Wheat	5,000 bu	13,556	9,009	3,273	990	
Oats	5,000 bu		177			
White Shrimp	5,000 lbs	102	465			
Black Tiger Shrimp	5,000 lbs	28				
MINNEAPOLIS GRAIN EXCHANGE (MGE)		**40,411**	**37,521**	**16,829**	**6,122**	**4,531**

Volume U.S.

OPTION	CONTRACT UNIT	1994	1993	1992	1991	1990
Cotton	50,000 lbs	816,031	372,074	413,091	392,132	284,991
Cotlook World Cotton	50,000 lbs X CWC		206	1,188		
Orange Juice Frozen Concentrate	15,000 lbs	159,365	101,214	72,446	56,078	63,029
European Currency Unit	$100,000			4,570		
U.S. Dollar Index	$500 x Index	42,268	67,603	470,230	1,418,298	99,668
NEW YORK COTTON EXCHANGE (NYCE)		**1,017,664**	**541,097**	**961,525**	**1,866,508**	**447,688**
NYSE Composite Index	$500 x Index	26,636	29,571	43,386	34,570	25,501
Commodity Research Bureau Index	$500 x Index	7,495	6,818	3,589	3,667	3,544
NEW YORK FUTURES EXCHANGE (NYFE)		**34,131**	**36,389**	**46,975**	**38,237**	**29,045**
TOTAL OPTIONS		**100,881,500**	**81,858,635**	**69,244,775**	**62,201,905**	**64,103,094**
PERCENT CHANGE		**23.24%**	**18.22%**	**11.32%**	**-2.97%**	**15.61%**

** In August 1994, the Commodity Exchange and the New York Mercantile Exchange merged and is now listed as one exchange.

Volume Worldwide

	1994	1993	1992	1991
Live Hogs	41,382	46,117	0	0
Piglets	3,417	3,358	0	0
Potatoes	229,071	154,832	0	0
Agricultural Futures Markets, Amsterdam	**273,870**	**204,307**	**0**	**0**
Austrian Government Bond	124,070	43,410		
ATX Index	348,291	174,095	66,898	
ATX Index Options	1,252,782	672,985	176,219	
ATX LEOs (Long-term Equity Options)	9,077			
Australian Futures & Options Exchange	**1,734,220**	**890,490**	**243,117**	**0**
Belgian Government Bonds	687,987	584,970	263,832	
BIBOR 3 Months	150,238	190,936	51,547	
Bel 20 Index	154,574	12,281		
Belgian Government Bonds Options	51,989			
Bel 20 Index Options	561,012	345,510		
Stock Options			103,885	
USO (Dollar/Belgian Franc)	29,546			
BELFOX	**1,635,346**	**1,133,697**	**419,264**	**0**
Gold Options on Actuals	6,772,894	9,406,163	7,932,576	7,452,730
Gold Options Exercise	2,246,674	1,401,370	802,402	
U.S. $ Denominated Arabica Coffee Futures	79,220	87,753	50,873	12,931
U.S. $ Denominated Arabica Coffee Options	3,290,667	1,504,776	2,491	734
U.S. $ Denominated Arabica Coffee Options Exercise	1,359,128	268,159	476	
U.S. $ Denominated Robusta Coffee Futures		36	992	
U.S. $ Denominated Cotton			2	179
U.S. $ Denominated Live Cattle	5,687	7,438	7,046	1,561
Live Cattle Options	88,428			
U.S. $ Denominated Soybean Futures	11	375		
U.S. $ Denominated Calf Futures			916	
U.S. $ Denominated Gold Futures	132,240	11,720		
Bovespa Stock Index Futures	10,583,594	10,374,860	7,287,054	7,836,256
Bovespa Stock Options	11,875			
Interest Rate Futures	28,474,764	18,996,117	14,072,749	2,495,412
Interest Rate Options	320			
Interest Rate Options Exercise	120			
U.S. Dollar Futures	39,231,744	7,608,631	4,501,952	949,081
U.S. Dollar Options Exercise	80,703	50,190	38,176	19,680
U.S. Dollar Options on Actuals	588,911	359,411	374,441	71,092
Interest Rate Swap (Guaranteed) Futures	297,169	72,251		
Interest Rate Swap (Not Guaranteed) Futures	5,705,386	1,788,596		
Interest Rate x Exch. Rate Swap (Guaranteed) Futures	722,873	3,850		
Interest Rate x Exch. Rate Swap (Not Guaranteed) Futures	2,943,224	13,624		
Interest Rate x Reference Rate Swap (Guaranteed) Futures	740			
Interest Rate x Reference Rate Swap (Not Guaranteed) Futures	118,489			
Interest Rate x Gold Price Variation Swap (Not Guaranteed) Futures	737			
Central Bank Bills	10			
Exchange Rate Swap (Guaranteed) Futures	7,083			
Exchange Rate Swap (Not Guaranteed) Futures	163,579			
Inflation Rate Future	75,513	258,352		
BM&F, Brazil	**102,981,783**	**52,213,672**	**35,072,146**	**18,839,656**
DAX	5,140,803	3,976,882	3,271,055	1,251,453
BUND	14,160,460	7,624,604	5,327,846	2,282,896
Medium Term Notional Bond (BOBL)	5,647,859	4,533,543	1,667,799	235,729
BULX	89,150			
FIBOR	428,516			
DAX Options	23,499,552	21,419,890	13,944,986	2,045,707
Medium Term Notional Bond (BOBL) Options	46,145	54,373		
BUND Options	261,110	251,859	498,324	163,766
Options on DAX Futures	49,642	62,976	136,439	
Stock Options			9,996,329	9,390,179
DTB, Germany	**49,323,237**	**37,924,127**	**34,842,778**	**15,369,730**

Volume Worldwide

	1994	1993	1992	1991
Gold Options	133,412	284,040	72,815	132,956
Silver Options	5,100			
Dollar/Guilder Options	482,961	672,632	537,892	370,647
Pound/Sterling/Guilder Options				2,725
Dutch Government Bond Options	449,511	436,199	270,442	240,767
EOE Stock Index Options	2,851,170	2,694,680	2,452,238	2,355,299
Eurotop 100	853	2,647	10,424	9,632
Dutch Top 5 Index	393,584	411,757	493,466	329,509
Major Market Index Options	1,563	6,227	18,970	28,410
European - Options Exchange	**4,318,154**	**4,508,182**	**3,856,247**	**3,469,945**
EOE Stock Index (FTI)	1,031,333	811,882	510,517	484,937
Dutch Top 5 Index	61,957	58,483	51,896	46,740
Eurotop 100 Index	435	1,102	2,003	1,265
Deliverable Bond (FTO)	14,132	70,388	21,230	28,545
U.S. Dollar/Guilder (FUS)	13,395	22,000	11,101	1,901
Financial Futures Market, Amsterdam	**1,121,252**	**963,855**	**596,747**	**563,388**
Danish Government Bonds 9% 1995		480	117,684	
Danish Government Bonds 9% 1998	103,103	185,953	7,356	
Danish Government Bonds 9% 2000		1,250	396,181	282,575
Danish Government Bonds 8% 2003	343,101	391,969	27,235	
Danish Government Bonds 7% 2004	74,220			
6% 2026 Mortgage Bonds	172,239	28,618		
9% 2022 Mortgage Bonds		1,408	23,948	
9% 2006 Mortgage Bonds			9,889	99,863
9% 2006 Mortgage Bonds Options			120	35,492
Danish Government Bonds 9% 2000 Options		170	144,962	52,940
Danish Government Bonds 8% 2003 Options	76,548	85,580	8,100	
Danish Government Bonds 7% 2004 Options	24,045			
3 Month CIBOR	32,718	34,727		
KFX Stock Index	429,466	339,024	406,694	336,331
KFX Stock Index Options	79,952	87,246	193,598	134,581
Stock Options			186,992	142,765
Guarantee Fund Danish OPT&FUT	**1,335,392**	**1,156,425**	**1,522,759**	**1,084,547**
Crude Oil	10,082,761	8,852,549	6,172,156	5,230,892
Crude Oil Options	531,742	1,059,222	791,810	232,118
Dubai Crude				3,629
Gasoil	3,779,064	3,608,637	3,452,643	2,854,961
Gasoil Options	136,859	217,508	199,256	91,089
Unleaded Gasoline Options			58,938	
Unleaded Gasoline	3,977	32,062		
International Petroleum Exchange, UK	**14,534,403**	**13,769,978**	**10,674,803**	**8,412,689**
DIBOR	3,099	3,819	28,405	27,637
Long Gilt	12,123	9,888	3,900	9,714
Short Gilt	1,140	100	2,040	3,091
ISEQ Index				317
Irish Futures & Options Exchange	**16,362**	**13,807**	**34,345**	**40,759**
Crude Palm Oil	567,902	355,743	252,731	320,199
Crude Palm Kernel Oil (15 tonne)		4,474		
Crude Palm Kernel Oil (25 tonne)	230	2,741	2,721	
Tin			18	156
RDB Palm Olein				2,240
Cocoa			519	2,376
Kuala Lumpur Commodity Exchange	**568,132**	**362,958**	**255,989**	**324,971**
Financial Time Index (FT-SE 100)	4,227,490	3,119,971	2,618,629	1,727,382
Short Sterling (3 Month)	16,603,152	12,135,981	11,296,327	8,064,449
Long Gilt	19,048,097	11,808,998	8,804,639	5,639,081
3 Month ECU	622,457	720,788	316,781	114,810
Eurodollar	91,738	244,728	709,305	993,753
U.S. T-Bond		4,660	272,077	462,703
Eurotrack 100			81	2,721

Volume Worldwide

	1994	1993	1992	1991
Yen Bond	610,925	421,454	221,370	106,081
Spanish Government Bond		28,318		
Italian Government Bond	11,823,741	6,344,233	3,773,105	483,447
Euroswiss	1,698,736	1,846,376	1,970,438	547,883
Eurolira	3,456,437	1,479,012	375,514	
Euromark	29,312,222	21,318,942	12,173,431	4,783,649
ECU Bond			7,434	54,233
German BOBL	73,043	1,049,640		
German Government Bund	37,335,437	20,440,442	13,604,523	10,112,305
Financial Time Index (FT-SE Mid 250 Index)	40,674			
Eurodollar Options	12,400	20,015	72,906	30,628
Euromark Options	2,943,936	2,906,476	1,964,405	514,075
U.S. T-Bond Options		2,626	68,369	39,798
German Government Bond Options	8,574,137	4,416,480	2,749,670	2,452,554
Italian Government Bond Options	1,030,672	602,096	395,354	16,446
Euroswiss Options	19,245	32,163	17,412	
Long Gilt Options	2,357,348	2,059,142	1,812,576	843,561
Short Sterling Options	4,057,878	2,666,711	2,648,009	1,594,268
Equity (individual)			3,533,030	
Financial Times Index Option (FT-SE 100)	4,786,656	3,439,460	2,571,640	
LIFFE, UK	**148,726,421**	**97,108,712**	**71,977,025**	**38,583,827**
Arabica				3,469
Arabica Options				12
Barley	8,072	13,479	21,516	10,919
Barley Options	64	110	885	190
BIFFEX (Baltic Freight Index)	47,805	43,105	52,155	63,155
BIFFEX (Baltic Freight Index) Options	94	10	96	59
Cocoa	1,600,746	1,908,136	1,397,966	1,536,752
Cocoa Options	87,215	107,102	51,219	89,636
$ Coffee	1,269,477	908,963	876,687	125,606
$ Coffee Options	204,945	282,263	108,493	19,230
Hi Pro Soy		7,020	18,142	22,105
Hi Pro Soy Options		1	3,630	7,465
Lamb		110	650	259
Raw Sugar	30,959	14,898		
Pigs		2,291	8,749	14,102
Pigs Options		25		207
Potatoes in Bulk	36,672	23,073	25,384	29,300
Potato Options				20
Sugar (FOB)	1,104		75,052	252,457
Sugar Options				594
Wheat	84,212	62,546	63,202	33,733
Wheat Options	6,866	1,769	2,081	1,160
White Sugar	480,973	329,414	303,377	313,514
White Sugar Options	8,196			696
London Commodity Exchange, UK	**3,867,400**	**3,704,315**	**3,009,284**	**2,524,640**
High Grade Primary Aluminum	14,604,218	10,083,342	9,256,740	5,732,302
High Grade Primary Aluminum Options	1,231,794	900,266		
Aluminum Alloy	148,685	111,450	2,394	
Copper - Grade A	17,236,317	14,855,430	7,945,054	7,384,841
Copper - Grade A Options	2,155,587	1,156,352		
Standard Lead	1,942,234	1,020,579	986,000	706,795
Standard Lead Options	45,769	17,299		
Primary Nickel	3,404,942	2,118,710	1,485,064	731,625
Primary Nickel Options	142,107	70,607		
Special High Grade Zinc	5,303,060	4,167,832	4,527,594	2,022,384
Special High Grade Zinc Options	253,782	163,475		
Tin	1,192,735	613,952	534,074	359,962
Tin Options	26,487	10,638		
London Metal Exchange, UK	**47,687,717**	**35,289,932**	**24,736,920**	**16,937,909**

Volume Worldwide

	1994	1993	1992	1991
CAC 40 Index	7,464,449	5,908,739	3,601,476	2,311,196
ECU Bond	618,715	873,002	1,354,012	546,273
ECU Bond Options	790	7,797	82,820	21,179
Notional Bond	50,153,150	36,804,824	31,062,844	21,087,899
Notional Bond Options	18,024,502	11,572,671	10,047,391	8,411,903
3 Month Pibor	13,176,354	11,863,798	6,436,765	3,000,111
3 Month Pibor Options	3,361,277	4,830,198	2,659,534	1,373,717
French Treasury Bond		29,213		
French Medium Term	63	99,260		
Potatoes	33,302	11,029	10,437	26,787
Rapseed	7,026			
Sugar	297,940	262,940	218,250	199,413
Coffee	170	490	608	488
U.S. Dollar/French Franc Options	75,436			
U.S. Dollar/Deutschemark Options	225,497			
MATIF, Paris	**93,438,671**	**72,263,961**	**55,474,137**	**36,978,966**
MIBOR (90 Days)	3,730,008	2,319,132	747,191	455,778
360 Days MIBOR	446,160	44,130		
3 Year Notional Bond	12,112	15,585	235,804	482,698
5 Year Notional Bond			8,291	52,342
10 Year Notional Bond	13,191,835	4,537,765	770,480	
Spanish Peseta/U.S. Dollar		26	12,215	4,343
Spanish Peseta/Deutschemark		3,172	54,635	10,620
3 Year Notional Bond Options			41,900	
10 Year Notional Bond Options	2,047,754	1,087,972	339,877	
MIBOR Options (90 Days)	307,460	139,550	8,300	
MEFF RENTA FIJA, Spain	**19,735,329**	**8,147,332**	**2,218,693**	**1,005,781**
IBEX 35	27,020,886	10,856,012		
IBEX 35 Options	7,541,551	3,563,485		
MEFF RENTA VARIABLE, Spain	**34,562,437**	**14,419,497**	**0**	**0**
10 Year BTP	3,702,802	2,776,992		
5 Year BTP	667,115	1,637,256		
Mercato Italiano Dei Futures, Italy	**4,369,917**	**4,414,248**	**0**	**0**
Livestock (US $)	52	4,475	29,443	18,220
Livestock Options (US $)		7,924	22,513	5,803
Livestock ($)		155		
Livestock Options (Pesos)			25	
Livestock (Pesos)			398	
MERFOX, Argentina	**52**	**12,554**	**52,379**	**24,023**
CAC 40 Index (Short Term) Options	2,755,289	2,451,512	3,170,782	3,717,515
CAC 40 Index (Long Term) Options	2,996,181	1,760,763	547,495	86,881
MONEP, Paris	**5,751,470**	**4,212,275**	**3,718,277**	**3,804,396**
Canadian Government Bond Options	51,248	61,455	50,955	47,283
Bankers Acceptance Futures 3 Month	1,918,976	724,158	419,765	194,071
Bankers Acceptance Futures 1 Month	12,172	24,552	23,502	
Canadian Government Bond Futures	1,496,543	895,047	515,732	421,493
Options on Canadian Government Bond	6,363	9,489	5,195	15,439
Bankers Acceptance Futures 3 Month Options	29,464			
Equity Options			669,190	581,391
Montreal Exchange	**3,514,766**	**1,714,701**	**1,684,339**	**1,259,677**

Volume Worldwide

	1994	1993	1992	1991
U.S. Dollar	21	9	6	
3 Year Government Stock	101,229	74,128		
3 Year Government Stock Options	80	1,000		
5 Year Government Stock		50,836	209,232	267,152
5 Year Government Stock Options		1,652	28,048	21,654
10 Year Government Stock	42,541	20,996	5	296
10 Year Government Stock Options	4,200	120		
90 Day Bank Bill	608,460	463,141	393,172	408,357
90 Day Bank Bill Options	6,870	8,193	38,258	29,727
New Zealand Dollar				2
New Zealand Wool			56	1,478
Forty Index Futures	7,397	3,633	4,620	3,040
Forty Index Options	1,985	596	760	153
New Zealand Futures Exchange	**772,783**	**624,304**	**674,157**	**731,859**
OBr10	165,443	28,245		
OBr5	43,745			
OBX	4,151	16,650		
OBX Options	422,430	385,540		
OBX Long Options	1,370			
Oslo Stock Exchange	**637,139**	**430,435**	**0**	**0**
Gold	26	436	667	4,440
Eurodollar	8,687,969	5,535,806	5,617,972	3,432,820
Deutschemark	8,727	16,368	44,990	59,675
Japanese Yen	16,825	21,009	19,921	47,169
British Pound	1,741	3,912	4,111	3,604
Deferred Spot US$/JY	68,605	13,182		
Deferred Spot US$/DM	131,210	26,298		
Nikkei Stock Average	5,801,098	5,162,199	3,349,243	721,751
MSCI Hong Kong Index	317	80,245		
High Sulfur Fuel Oil	171,896	300,201	278,205	182,957
Dubai Crude Oil				286
Gasoil		23,288	25,806	4,212
Euroyen	6,820,673	3,532,998	2,472,931	1,491,742
Euromark	231,068	23,127	4,940	32,724
Japanese Government Bond	443,564	29,253		
Eurodollar Options	13,545	6,525	11,534	5,368
Euroyen Options	126,280	57,395	80,815	81,296
Nikkei Options	1,496,922	897,545	269,039	
Japanese Government Bond Options	39,808			
SIMEX, Singapore	**24,060,274**	**15,729,787**	**12,180,174**	**6,068,044**
Swiss Market Index	1,694,260	914,021	847,157	590,851
EUROTOP 100 Index			4	955
3 Month Euro Swiss Franc		353	184,084	121,854
5 Year Swiss Franc		28,548	199,829	58,708
Swiss Government Bond	949,657	270,653	233,761	
Swiss Market Index Options	6,678,779	5,595,388	7,793,949	6,175,416
Swiss Government Bond Options	49,749			
EUROTOP 100 Index Options			75	23,956
SOFFEX, Switzerland	**9,372,445**	**6,808,963**	**9,258,859**	**6,971,740**
All Share Index Futures	2,185,672	1,670,540		
All Share Index Options	2,804,855	1,236,263		
Industrial Index Futures	920,786	422,203		
Industrial Index Options	377,593	148,101		
Gold Index Futures	933,591	895,772		
Gold Index Options	132,230	102,136		
Krugerrand Futures	5,664			
Krugerrand Options	3,300			
3 Month Bank Bill	3,901	2,135		
R 150	1,750			
E168 (Long Bond) Futures	8,495	6,903		
E168 (Long Bond) Options	100	920		
South African Futures Exchange (SAFEX)	**7,377,937**	**4,484,973**	**0**	**0**

Volume Worldwide

	1994	1993	1992	1991
Stock Options			3,543,240	4,074,316
Stock Futures			21,180	5,192
Stocklending			74,888	
Interest Rate Options	86,410		19,584	94,367
Interest Rate Futures	14,123,881	11,272,285	7,420,164	4,134,275
OMX (Index) Options	5,812,435	4,073,852	5,605,059	4,826,172
OMX (Index) Futures	1,706,984	627,706	450,031	116,799
Financial Times Index (FT-SE Mid 250) Options	2,140			
Financial Times Index (FT-SE Mid 250) Futures	9,565			
GEMx Options			6,505	180,867
GEMx Futures			6,445	10,862
Stockholm Options Exchange	**21,741,415**	**15,973,843**	**17,147,096**	**13,442,850**
All Ordinaries Share Price Index	2,552,546	980,866	342,013	381,284
Fifty Leaders Share Price Index	1	1	203	
Bank Bills 90 Days	9,369,008	6,415,394	5,697,786	4,651,570
3 Year Treasury Bonds	9,709,791	6,939,811	5,434,795	2,119,469
10 Year Treasury Bonds	6,814,733	4,781,905	4,253,374	3,598,072
Live Cattle (Cash Set)		8	298	1,107
Wool (Cash Set)	4,833	3,271	1,259	632
3 Year Treasury Bond Options	507,252	514,539	317,356	106,797
90 Day Bank Bills Options	943,749	663,317	610,458	719,482
10 Year Treasury Bonds Options	800,263	712,686	745,994	669,623
Overnight 3 Year Treasury Bond Options	2,078	320		
Overnight 10 Year Treasury Bond Options	18,656	2,082		
Overnight Share Price Index Options	7			
All Ordinaries Share Price Options	833,667	466,896	154,149	247,982
Sydney Futures Exchange	**31,556,584**	**21,481,096**	**17,557,685**	**12,496,018**
TSE 35 Index	104,209	69,058	59,049	60,950
TSE 35 Options	247,482	221,232	302,444	465,124
TSE 100 Index	10,819			
TSE 100 Index Options	13,200			
TSE 300 Spot Index		4		
Silver Options	8,300	4,583	331	1,276
Toronto Futures Exchange	**384,010**	**294,877**	**361,824**	**527,350**
Wheat	191,696	210,074	199,060	131,946
Oats	52,550	59,244	45,913	24,627
Thunder Bay Barley	5,378	63,643	88,150	106,561
Cadadian Barley	31,600	4,150		
Rye	1,022	7,829	26,273	23,364
Flax Seed	105,338	104,110	144,581	122,240
Canola (Rapeseed)	1,167,447	972,354	839,715	815,373
Western Barley	115,376	40,248	22,655	14,868
Wheat Options	3,145	5,274	2,225	
Flax Options	1,692	4,907		
Cadadian Barley Options		80		
Western Barley Options	1,716	10		
Canola Options	82,565	44,121	50,262	4,950
Winnipeg Commodity Exchange	**1,759,525**	**1,516,044**	**1,418,834**	**1,243,929**
Hang Seng Index	4,192,574	2,415,739	1,089,037	499,246
Hang Seng Index Options	606,674	282,283		
3 Month HIBOR			205	1,261
Soybeans			4,688	31,200
Sugar			8,598	34,237
Gold	490	972	1,000	992
Hang Seng Comm. & Ind. Sub-Index			205	744
Hang Seng Properties Sub-Index			205	1,749
Hang Seng Finance Sub-Index			205	85
Hang Seng Utilities Sub-Index			205	43
Hong Kong Futures Exchange	**4,799,738**	**2,698,994**	**1,104,348**	**569,557**

Volume Worldwide

	1994	1993	1992	1991
Domestic Soybeans	18	24	24	24
Red Beans	241,555	182,611	220,096	233,862
White Beans	18	24	24	24
Potato Starch	18	24	24	24
Imyorted Soybeans	89,916	106,152	255,198	405,642
*Hokkaido Grain Exchange	**331,525**	**288,835**	**475,366**	**639,576**
Red Beans	492,294	579,751	488,167	320,390
Imported Soybeans	213,271	486,850	438,817	323,659
Refined Sugar	1,432	1,437	1,443	1,437
Corn	1,709,248	1,077,057	270,809	
*Kanmon Commodity Exchange	**2,416,245**	**2,145,095**	**1,199,236**	**645,486**
Red Beans	2,931,256	3,092,743	4,051,785	2,930,584
Imported Soybeans	1,298,180	2,113,812	2,340,144	1,927,076
Refined Sugar	2,864	2,874	2,880	2,874
Raw Sugar	664,683	1,063,480	648,833	1,426,146
Raw Sugar Options	63,789	26,793	95,802	
*Kansai Ag. Commodities Exchange	**4,960,772**	**6,299,702**	**7,139,444**	**6,286,680**
(Formerly the OGE, OSE, KGE)				
Raw Silk	695,172	687,723	195,037	207,012
*KOBE Raw Silk Exchange	**695,172**	**687,723**	**195,037**	**207,012**
Rubber (RSS3)	2,933,883	1,275,051	791,948	1,374,337
KOBE Rubber Exchange	**2,933,883**	**1,275,051**	**791,948**	**1,374,337**
Dried Cocoon	475,978	1,782,394	492,494	771,574
*Maebashi Dried Cocoon Exchange	**475,978**	**1,782,394**	**492,494**	**771,574**
Red Beans	919,371	1,217,337	1,376,017	726,200
Sweet Potato Starch	48	48	48	48
Imported Soybeans	177,513	287,612	348,733	314,200
Refined Sugar	1,789	2,874	2,886	2,874
*Nagoya Grain & Sugar Exchange	**1,098,721**	**1,507,871**	**1,727,684**	**1,043,322**
Cotton Yarn (40S)	1,100,388	822,683	1,145,017	1,082,950
Staple Fiber Yarn (Dull)	13,114	18,279	29,614	26,473
Wool Yarn	87,240	79,114	123,570	293,214
*Nagoya Textile Exchange	**1,200,742**	**920,076**	**1,298,201**	**1,402,637**
Nikkei 225 Index Futures	6,208 754	8,461,458	11,927,329	21,643,338
Nikkei 300 Index Futures	4,184,480			
Nikkei 225 Index Options	4,273,641	6,090,375	9,256,981	11,835,611
Nikkei 300 Index Options	269,067			
*Osaka Securities Exchange	**14,935,942**	**14,551,833**	**21,184,310**	**33,478,949**
Staple Fiber Yarn (Bright)	3,507	2,928	2,940	2,928
Staple Fiber Yarn (Dull)	2,910	2,928	4,715	2,928
Wool Yarn	266,974	524,699	258,487	563,941
Cotton Yarn (20S)	2,000,530	648,345	652,535	399,582
Cotton Yarn (40S)	833,307	574,724	644,897	444,400
*Osaka Textile Exchange	**3,107,228**	**1,753,624**	**1,563,574**	**1,413,779**
Gold	12,481,095	8,764,441	4,193,775	4,567,630
Silver	1,042,185	661,452	231,864	1,057,598
Palladium	774,284	2,275,843	404,091	
Platinum	4,551,406	4,984,480	4,631,724	5,403,596
Rubber	9,021,881	2,973,241	1,726,487	2,167,293
Cotton Yarn	2,573,963	1,865,469	2,330,029	1,607,228
Woolen Yarn	36,499	32,869	67,409	145,854
*Tokyo Commodity Exchange Industry	**30,481,313**	**21,557,795**	**13,585,379**	**14,949,199**

Volume Worldwide

	1994	1993	1992	1991
American Soybeans	2,559,288	3,750,291	4,000,410	3,427,300
Chinese Soybeans			208	3,175
Red Beans	5,122,015	6,353,667	7,804,868	6,253,789
Corn	3,053,244	1,263,357	556,501	
Refined Sugar	2,864	2,874	2,886	2,874
Raw Sugar	1,220,931	2,218,688	1,279,354	2,351,512
American Soybean Options	96,505	60,420	54,684	15,619
Raw Sugar Options	67,636	38,450	43,203	
*Tokyo Grain Exchange	**12,122,483**	**13,687,747**	**13,742,114**	**12,054,269**
(Formerly the TGE, TSE)				
3 Month Euroyen	37,425,846	23,386,958	14,959,373	14,665,521
3 Month Eurodollar				3,027
1 Year Euroyen	25,100	4,434	9,379	
U.S. Dollar - Japanese Yen	13,770	48,241	86,008	148,508
Euroyen Options	570,237	686,514	485,727	332,048
*Tokyo International Financial Futures Exchange	**38,034,953**	**24,126,147**	**15,540,487**	**15,149,104**
Yen Government Bond (10 Year)	12,999,698	15,162,159	11,868,414	12,822,430
Yen Government Bond (10 Year) Options	1,691,834	1,506,836	1,140,541	1,850,363
Yen Government Bond (20 Year)	3,194	3,106	3,972	6,575
TOPIX Stock Index Futures	2,623,067	2,156,960	1,358,723	1,676,798
TOPIX Options	20,078	37,831	48,576	120,280
U.S. T-Bond Futures	115,750	112,600	118,491	125,453
*Tokyo Stock Exchange	**17,453,621**	**18,979,492**	**14,538,717**	**16,601,899**
Dried Cocoon	488,558	1,066,374	519,045	836,629
*Toyahashi Dried Cocoon Exchange	**488,558**	**1,066,374**	**519,045**	**836,629**
Raw Silk	998,686	1,512,132	410,028	275,053
*Yokohama Raw Silk Exchange	**998,686**	**1,512,132**	**410,028**	**275,053**

*Exchange located in Japan

Conversion Factors

Commonly Used Agricultural Weights and Measurements

Bushel Weights:
wheat and soybeans = 60 lbs.
corn, sorghum and rye = 56 lbs.
barley grain = 48 lbs.
barley malt = 34 lbs.
oats = 32 lbs.

Bushels to tonnes:
wheat and soybeans = bushels X 0.027216
barley grain = bushels X 0.021772
corn, sorghum and rye = bushels X 0.0254
oats = bushels X 0.014515

1 tonne (metric ton) equals:
2204.622 lbs.
1,000 kilograms
22.046 hundredweight
10 quintals
(continued above)

1 tonne (metric ton) equals:
36.7437 bushels of wheat or soybeans
39.3679 bushels of corn, sorghum or rye
45.9296 bushels of barley grain
68.8944 bushels of oats
4.5929 cotton bales (the statistical bale used by the USDA and ICAC contains a net weight of 480 pounds of lint)

Area Measurements:
1 acre = 43,560 square feet = 0.040694 hectare
1 hectare = 2.4710 acres = 10,000 square meters
640 acres = 1 square mile = 259 hectares

Yields:
wheat: bushels per acre X 0.6725 = quintals per hectare
rye, corn: bushels per acre X 0.6277 = quintals per hectare
barley grain: bushels per acre X 0.538 = quintals per hectare
oats: bushels per acre X 0.3587 = quintals per hectare

Commonly Used Weights

The troy, avoirdupois and apothecaries' grains are identical in U.S. and British weight systems, equal to 0.0648 gram in the metric system. One avoirdupois ounce equals 437.5 grains. The troy and apothecaries' ounces equal 480 grains, and their pounds contain 12 ounces.

Troy weights and conversions:
24 grains = 1 pennyweight
20 pennyweights = 1 ounce
12 ounces = 1 pound
1 troy ounce = 31.103 grams
1 troy ounce = 0.0311033 kilogram
1 troy pound = 0.37224 kilogram
1 kilogram = 32.1507 troy ounces
1 tonne = 32,151 troy ounces

Avoirdupois weights and conversions:
27 11/32 grains = 1 dram
16 drams = 1 ounce
16 ounces = 1 lb.
1 lb. = 7,000 grains
14 lbs. = 1 stone (British)
100 lbs. = 1 hundredweight (U.S.)
112 lbs. = 8 stone = 1 hundredweight (British)
2,000 lbs. = 1 short ton (U.S. ton)
2,240 lbs. = 1 long ton (British ton)
160 stone = 1 long ton
20 hundredweight = 1 ton
1 lb. = 0.4536 kilogram
1 hundredweight (cwt.) = 45.359 kilograms
1 short ton = 907.18 kilograms
1 long ton = 1,016.05 kilograms

Metric weights and conversions:
1,000 grams = 1 kilogram
100 kilograms = 1 quintal
1 tonne = 1,000 kilograms = 10 quintals
1 kilogram = 2.204622 lbs.
1 quintal = 220.462 lbs.
1 tonne = 2204.6 lbs.
1 tonne = 1.102 short tons
1 tonne = 0.9842 long ton

U.S. dry volumes and conversions:
1 pint = 33.6 cubic inches = 0.5506 liter
2 pints = 1 quart = 1.1012 liters
8 quarts = 1 peck = 8.8098 liters
4 pecks = 1 bushel = 35.2391 liters
1 cubic foot = 28.3169 liters

U.S. liquid volumes and conversions:
1 ounce = 1.8047 cubic inches = 29.6 milliliters
1 cup = 8 ounces = 0.24 liter = 237 milliliters
1 pint = 16 ounces = 0.48 liter = 473 milliliters
1 quart = 2 pints = 0.946 liter = 946 milliliters
1 gallon = 4 quarts = 231 cubic inches = 3.785 liters
1 milliliter = 0.033815 fluid ounce
1 liter = 1.0567 quarts = 1,000 milliliters
1 liter = 33.815 fluid ounces
1 imperial gallon = 277.42 cubic inches = 1.2 U.S. gallons = 4.546 liters

ENERGY CONVERSION FACTORS

U.S. Crude Oil (average gravity)
1 U.S. barrel = 42 U.S. gallons
1 short ton = 6.65 barrels
1 tonne = 7.33 barrels

Barrels per tonne for various origins

Abu Dhabi	7.624
Algeria	7.661
Angola	7.206
Australia	7.775
Bahrain	7.335
Brunei	7.334
Canada	7.428
Dubai	7.295
Ecuador	7.580
Gabon	7.245
Indonesia	7.348
Iran	7.370
Iraq	7.453
Kuwait	7.261
Libya	7.615
Mexico	7.104
Neutral Zone	6.825
Nigeria	7.410
Norway	7.444
Oman	7.390
Qatar	7.573
Romania	7.453
Saudi Arabia	7.338
Trinidad	6.989
Tunisia	7.709
United Arab Emirates	7.522
United Kingdom	7.279
United States	7.418
Former Soviet Union	7.350
Venezuela	7.005
Zaire	7.206

Barrels per tonne of refined products:

aviation gasoline	8.90
motor gasoline	8.50
kerosene	7.75
jet fuel	8.00
distillate, including diesel	7.46
(continued above)	

residual feul oil	6.45
lubricating oil	7.00
grease	6.30
white spirits	8.50
paraffin oil	7.14
paraffin wax	7.87
petrolatum	7.87
asphalt and road oil	6.06
petroleum coke	5.50
bitumen	6.06
LPG	11.6

Approximate heat content of refined products:
(Million Btu per barrel, 1 British thermal unit is the amount of heat required to raise the temperature of 1 pound of water 1 degree F.)

Petroleum Product	Heat Content
asphalt	6.636
aviation gasoline	5.048
butane	4.326
distillate fuel oil	5.825
ethane	3.082
isobutane	3.974
jet fuel, kerosene	5.670
jet fuel, naptha	5.355
kerosene	5.670
lubricants	6.065
motor gasoline	5.253
natural gasoline	4.620
pentanes plus	4.620

Petrochemical feedstocks:

naptha less than 401°F	5.248
other oils equal to or greater than 401°F	5.825
still gas	6.000
petroleum coke	6.024
plant condensate	5.418
propane	3.836
residual fuel oil	6.287
special napthas	5.248
unfinished oils	5.825
unfractionated steam	5.418
waxes	5.537

Source: Department of Energy

Natural Gas Conversions

Although there are approximately 1,031 Btu in a cubic foot of gas, for most applications, the following conversions are sufficient:

Cubic Feet					MMBtu
1,000	(one thousand cubic feet)	=	1 Mcf	=	1
1,000,000	(one million cubic feet)	=	1 MMcf	=	1,000
10,000,000	(ten million cubic feet)	=	10 MMcf	=	10,000
1,000,000,000	(one billion cubic feet)	=	1 Bcf	=	1,000,000
1,000,000,000,000	(one trillion cubic feet)	=	1 Tcf	=	1,000,000,000

Cash Market Description for Monthly Charts

Aluminum
Pig Ingots - New York from 1910 thru 1986
Pig Ingots - Midwest from 11/14/86 to Date
Cast Scrap - New York 1929 thru 1984
Cast Scrap - Midwest (Chicago) 1985 to Date
Clippings - New York 1929 thru 1984 (1950-1951 N/A)
Clippings - Midwest (Chicago) 1985 to Date

Barley
No. 2 Minneapolis 08/09 thru 06/25
No. 3 Minneapolis (straight or better) 07/26 thru 06/76
No. 2 Feed Minneapolis 07/26 thru 12/86
No. 2 Feed Duluth 03/87 to Date

Beef Steers
Chicago All Grades 1909 thru 1934
Chicago Good 1935 thru 1939
Chicago All Grades 1940 thru 1962
Chicago Good - 1/2/48 to 12/31/64
Chicago Choice - 1/2/65 to 7/30/71
Omaha Choice Average - 8/2/71 to 8/25/87
Texas-Oklahoma Cattle Average - 8/26/87 to Date

Cocoa
Santos No. 4 NY - 1920 to 7/17/75
Brazilian NY - 1/6/76 to Date
Colombian Maniz NY - 1/2/48 to 7/6/53
Colombian Medellin NY - 1/4/54 to 6/8/76;
10/8/76 to 12/27/77
Colombian NY - 1/10/78 to 12/30/82;
1/2/83 to 7/1/83; 11/14/83 to 2/4/85; 8/29/85 to
10/15/87; 3/1/90 to Date

Copper
Electrolytic NY - 1910 thru 1983
Electrolytic US - 1984 to Date
Scrap No. 1 NY - 1927 thru 1955
Scrap No. 2 NY - 1956 thru 04/88
Scrap No. 2 Chicago - 5/88 to Date

Corn
No. 3 Yellow Chicago - 1901 to 04/47
No. 2 Yellow Chicago - 5/5/47 to 3/28/82
No. 2 Yellow Central Illinois - 3/29/82 to Date

Corn Oil
FOB Midwestern Mills (Decatur) - 07/24 thru 06/85
Wet Mill at Chicago - 10/85 to Date

Corporate AAA Bonds
Federal Reserve Bank of St. Louis - 1919 to Date

Cotton
7/8" at Designated Mkts Middling - 08/15 thru 07/30
15/16" at Designated Mkts Middling - 08/30 thru 07/73
11/16" at Designated Mkts Middling - 08/73 to Date

Cottonseed Meal
36% Protein Memphis - 08/10 thru 09/20
41% Protein Memphis - 10/21 thru 09/46
41% Protein (Expeller) Memphis - 10/46 thru 12/81
41% Protein (Solvent) Memphis - 01/82 to Date

Cottonseed Oil
FOB Southeastern Mills - 08/90 to Date

Discount Rate
Federal Reserve Bank of St. Louis - 1934 to Date

Eggs
NY Fresh Firsts - 1910 thru 1926
Chicago Fresh Firsts - 1927 thru 06/43
Chicago US Standards - 07/43 thru 1947
Chicago Large - 1948 to Date

Feeder Cattle
Oklahoma City - 1970 to Date

Five Year T-Bond Yield
Federal Reserve Bank of St. Louis - 1953 to Date

Flaxseed
No. 1 Minneapolis - 1901 thru 01/86
US Farm Price - 1980 to Date

Gold
NY Handy & Harman - 1968 to Date

Hides
Chicago (Paker's Heavy Native Steers) - 1920 to Date
Chicago (Light Native Steers) 1920 thru 1943

Hogs
Top Chicago - 1909 to 4/1/68
Live Hogs Farrowing Chicago - 4/2/68 to 5/15/70
Live Hogs Average Omaha - 5/18/70 to Date

Lard
Chicago - 1910 to Date

Lead
Raw - 1910 to Date
Scrap - 1985 to Date

Cash Market Description for Monthly Charts

Lumber
  White-Fir 2x4 - 1959 thru 1970
  Hem-Fir 2x4 - 1971 thru 03/80
  Spruce-Pine-Fir 2x4 - 03/80 to Date

Mercury
  N.Y. 75 pound Flask - 1920 thru 1931
  N.Y. 76 pound Flask - 1932 to Date

Molasses
  Blackstrap N.Y. - 1920 thru 1967
  Blackstrap (cane) New Orleans - 1968 to Date

Municipal Bonds
  Federal Reserve Bank of St. Louis - 1919 to Date

Oats
  No. 3 White Chicago - 1901 thru 1947
  Oats No. 2 White Chicago - 1/2/48 to 11/25/48
  Oats No. 1 White Hvy Chicago - 11/26/48 to 12/15/74
  Oats No. 2 White Hvy Chicago - 12/16/74 to Date

Pepper
  Black at N.Y. - 1920 to Date

Platinum
  N.Y. Producer Price - 1910 thru 1977
  N.Y. Merchants Price - 1978 to Date

Pork Bellies
  12-14 Lbs Chicago - 1/2/49 to 10/3/75
  Pork Bellies 12-14 Lbs Midwest - 10/6/75 to Date

Potatoes
  N.Y. - U.S. No. 1 White - 1913 thru 1960
  U.S. Farmers Price - 1961 to Date

Prime Rate
  Federal Reserve Bank of St. Louis - 1930 to Date

Rice
  New Orleans Fancy (Honduras Grade) - 8/9 thru 1924
  New Orleans Fancy (Blue Rose Grade) - 1925-1933
  New Orleans Medium to Good (Blue Rose Grade) -
  1934 thru 07/47
  New Orleans Fancy No. 2 Zenith Milled - 8/47-4/72
  Southwest Lousiana No. 2 Medium Grain - 5/72 to Date

Rubber
  N.Y. Plantation Smoked Sheets - 1908 to Date

Rye
  No. 2 Minneapolis - 07/09 to Date

  Winnipeg - 1950 thru 1982

Silver
  N.Y. Handy & Harman - 1910 to Date

Soybeans
  U.S. Farmers Price - 1913 thru 09/47
  No. 2 Yellow Chicago - 11/30/47 to 12/31/56
  No. 1 Yellow Chicago - 1/2/57 to 3/26/82
  No. 1 Yellow Central II - 3/29/82 to Date

Soybean Meal
  Chicago (Protein no specified) - 10/29 thru 10/36
  Chicago 41% Protein - 11/36 thru 06/50
  Chicago 44% Protein - 07/50 thru 09/65
  Decatur 44% Protein - 10/65 thru 11/16/92
  Decatur 48% Protein - 11/17/92 to Date

Soybean Oil
  N.Y. Crude (imported) - 1910 thru 09/29
  Decatur Crude - 10/29 to Date

Steel Scrap
  Chicago - 1929 to Date
  Pittsburg - 1910 to Date

Sugar
  N.Y. Raw-96 Centrifugal - 1980 to Date
  Raw (cif) NY Duty Pd #7 - 1/2/47 to 11/2/77
  #12 Raw New York - 8/20/79 to 12/30/82
  Spot Raw (cif) New York - 1/3/49 to 2/1/61
  No. 8 World Raw New York - 2/2/61 to 12/31/70
  No. 11 World Raw New York - 1/4/71 to 11/2/77
  No. 11 World Raw New York - 8/20/79 to Date
  Midwest Refined-Wholesale Beet - 1975 to Date

Tallow
  Chicago Inedible Prime - 1910 thru 1948
  Chicago Bleachable - 1949 to Date

Tin
  Staights - 1910 to Date

Wheat
  No. 2 Red Chicago - 1901 to 3/26/82
  No. 2 Red Spot St. Louis - 3/29/82 to Date

Wool
  Boston Territory Fine Scoured Staple - 1910 to 1971
  U.S. Mills Territory Fine Scoured Staple - 1972 to Date

Zinc
  East St. Louis Prime Western - 1910 to 1970
  U.S. Basis Prime Western - 1971 to Date

Aluminum

U.S. primary production of aluminum in July 1994 was 275,473 tonnes, 13 percent less than July 1993. For the January-July 1994 period, aluminum production was 1.93 million tonnes. During all of 1993, production totaled 3.7 million tonnes. Metallic recovery of new aluminum from purchased, tolled or imported scrap for the first seven-months of 1994 was 862,000 tonnes. For all of 1993, recovery of new aluminum was 1.31 million tonnes. Secondary recovery of old aluminum from purchased, tolled or imported scrap during the January-July 1994 period was 960,000 tonnes. During all of 1993, the total recovery of old aluminum was 1.63 million tonnes. In 1992, 13 companies operated 23 primary aluminum reduction plants. Washington, Oregon and Montana accounted for 40 percent of production while Kentucky, North Carolina, South Carolina and Tennessee accounted for 20 percent.

Estimated consumption of aluminum for the January-July 1994 period was 1.93 million tonnes. For all of 1993 consumption was 3.37 million tonnes. Consumption by secondary smelters for the first seven-months of 1994 was 633,000 tonnes. Integrated aluminum companies consumed 755,000 tonnes of aluminum over the same period. Independent mill fabricators used 467,000 tonnes while foundries consumed 70,000 tonnes. Aluminum consumption occurred at an estimated 25,000 firms centered in the east central U.S. Packaging accounts for about 35 percent of total domestic consumption; followed by transportation at 20 percent; building with 17 percent; electrical almost 9 percent; consumer durables 8 percent; and other uses approximately 11 percent.

U.S. imports for consumption of aluminum during the January-June 1994 period were 1.7 million tonnes. Imports of crude metal and alloys for the first half of 1994 were 1.28 million tonnes. The primary sources were Canada with 740,409 tonnes, Russia shipped 294,711 tonnes, while Venezuela provided 86,559 tonnes and Brazil 93,383 tonnes. Imports of aluminum plates, sheets and bars for January-June 1994 were 242,324 tonnes. Canada was by far the largest source providing 63 percent or 154,665 tonnes of U.S. needs. Other suppliers were Venezuela, Spain and Germany. Imports of aluminum scrap for the first half of 1994 were 180,360 tonnes. Canada again provided the majority of requirements with 94,103 tonnes, while Mexico shipped 28,414 tonnes and Venezuela 14,219 tonnes.

U.S. exports of aluminum during January-June 1994 were 632,743 tonnes. Exports of crude metals and alloys were 154,564 tonnes. The major destination was Japan which took 62,863 tonnes. Canada was the next largest market receiving 53,427 tonnes. Exports of aluminum plates, sheets and bars for the first half of 1994 were 341,695 tonnes. Canada imported over one-half the total with 177,265 tonnes. Mexico purchased 41,039 tonnes while Saudi Arabia took 20,780 tonnes. U.S. exports of aluminum scrap were 136,484 tonnes. The major destination was Japan with 42,190 tonnes, while Taiwan took 32,539 tonnes and Canada purchased 30,297 tonnes.

Aluminum prices surged higher in late-1994 in response to declines in stocks on the London Metal Exchange. Many in the trade did not believe the drawdown would continue, and that prices would begin to pull back during 1995.

Japan's Kirin Brewery Company announced that it would increase its imports of U.S.-made aluminum cans in 1995 by 20 percent. Anheuser-Busch Company, Inc. was expected to export 300 million empty aluminum beer cans to Kirin from the U.S. The cost of producing cans in the U.S. is one-half that of Japan. U.S. aluminum can stock makers announced earlier this year that due to rising aluminum prices worldwide, can stock prices would increase to more than $1.00 per pound for 1995 contracts, approximately 20¢ per pound higher than the previous year.

World Production of Primary Aluminum   In Thousands of Metric Tons

Year	Australia	Austria	Brazil	Canada	China	France	Germany	Italy	Japan	Norway	Russia[3]	Spain	Switzerland	United Kingdom	United States	Venezuela	World Total
1986	882	93	757	1,355	410	322	765	243	140	726	2,300	355	80	276	3,037	418	15,412
1987	1,004	93	843	1,540	615	323	793	233	41	853	2,400	341	73	294	3,343	428	16,514
1988	1,150	95	874	1,534	710	328	753	226	35	864	2,400	323	72	300	3,944	437	17,548
1989	1,244	93	890	1,555	750	335	796	219	35	863	3,300	352	71	297	4,030	540	19,010
1990	1,234	89	931	1,567	850	326	740	232	34	845	3,523	353	72	294	4,048	590	19,299
1991	1,228	80	1,140	1,822	963	286	690	206	32	833	3,251	355	66	294	4,121	601	19,575
1992	1,236	33	1,200	1,972	1,100	418	603	161	19	813	2,700	359	52	244	4,042	561	19,467
1993[1]	1,345	---	1,200	2,308	1,220	458	552	170	18	814	2,900	355	45	235	3,695	570	19,816
1994[2]	1,300		1,200	2,200		400					2,700				3,300	600	19,000

[1] Preliminary.   [2] Estimate.   [3] Formerly part of the U.S.S.R.; data not reported separately until 1992.   *Source: U.S. Bureau of Mines*

U.S. Production of Primary Aluminum (Domestic & Foreign Ores)   In Thousands of Metric Tons

Year	Jan.	Feb.	Mar.	Apr.	May	June	July	Aug.	Sept.	Oct.	Nov.	Dec.	Total
1985	329	289	312	295	304	288	292	289	280	285	265	271	3,858
1986	273	251	281	275	284	241	231	235	231	243	239	252	3,350
1987	262	238	266	263	275	272	282	286	286	301	301	316	3,349
1988	320	304	330	324	336	323	334	333	327	339	332	344	3,944
1989	346	312	347	334	347	335	346	341	323	328	328	343	4,030
1990	345	311	345	331	342	330	340	341	332	347	337	347	4,048
1991	349	317	352	340	353	343	354	350	336	347	337	343	4,121
1992	344	320	343	330	342	330	339	340	330	343	335	347	4,043
1993[1]	335	292	323	313	325	315	316	302	291	303	287	294	3,696
1994[1]	292	261	286	269	277	268	275	274	267	277	270	280	3,296

[1] Preliminary.   *Source: U.S. Bureau of Mines*

ALUMINUM

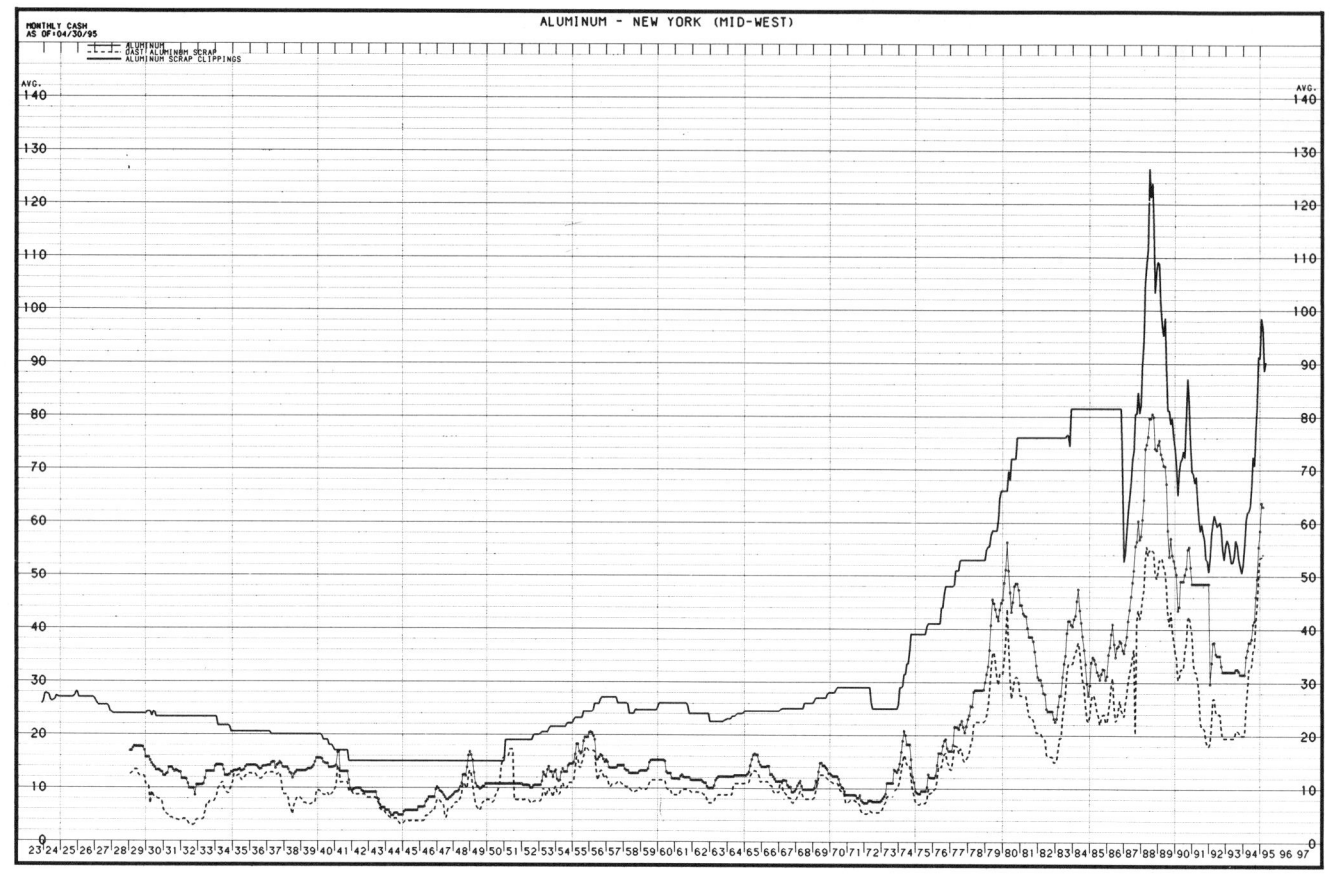

Salient Statistics of Aluminum in the U.S.   In Thousands of Metric Tons

	Net Import Reliance as a % of Apparent Con-sumption	-- Production -- Primary	-- Production -- Second-ary	Primary Ship-ments[2]	Recovery from ----- Scrap ----- Old	Recovery from ----- Scrap ----- New	Apparent Con-sumption	---- Wrought Products ---- Plate, Sheet, Foil	---- Wrought Products ---- Rolled Structural Shapes[3]	---- Wrought Products ---- Extruded Shapes[4]	All	Net Shipments[5] by Producers Castings Perma-nent Mold	Net Shipments[5] by Producers Castings Die	Net Shipments[5] by Producers Castings Sand	Net Shipments[5] by Producers Castings All	Total All Net Ship-ments
Year																
1986	26	3,037	1,773	6,545	784	989	5,143	3,397	337	1,335	5,179	155	749	77	1,032	6,211
1987	23	3,343	1,986	6,813	852	1,134	5,469	3,740	346	1,351	5,549	181	685	113	1,012	6,562
1988	7	3,944	2,122	6,851	1,045	1,077	5,373	3,787	343	1,341	5,589	201	700	115	1,055	6,621
1989	E	4,030	2,054	6,751	1,011	1,043	4,957	3,900	339	1,280	5,633	210	740	110	1,096	6,728
1990	E	4,048	2,393	6,592	1,359	1,034	5,264	3,799	301	1,211	5,425	208	620	103	968	6,393
1991	E	4,121	2,286	6,395	1,522	979	5,043	3,787	311	1,096	5,300	168	575	97	864	6,156
1992	1	4,042	2,756	6,809	1,612	1,145	5,725	4,097	303	1,186	5,691	198	595	99	804	6,609
1993[1]	19	3,695	2,944	7,231	1,648	1,217	6,540	4,030	297	1,294	5,807	NA	NA	NA	NA	NA

[1] Preliminary.   [2] To domestic industry.   [3] Also rod, bar & wire.   [4] Also rod, bar, tube blooms & tubing.   [5] Consists of total shipments less shipments to other mills for further fabrication.   NA = Not available.   E = Net exporter.   *Source: U.S. Bureau of Mines*

U.S. Supply and Distribution of Aluminum   In Thousands of Metric Tons

Year	Apparent Con-sumption	-- Production -- Primary	-- Production -- From Old Scrap	Imports	Exports	Inventories (Dec. 31) Private	Inventories (Dec. 31) Govern-ment	Year	Apparent Con-sumption	-- Production -- Primary	-- Production -- From Old Scrap	Imports	Exports	Inventories (Dec. 31) Private	Inventories (Dec. 31) Govern-ment
1985	5,174	3,500	850	1,420	908	2,343	2	1990	5,264	4,048	1,359	1,514	1,659	1,820	2
1986	5,143	3,037	784	1,967	753	2,235	2	1991	5,043	4,121	1,317	1,490	1,762	1,788	3
1987	5,469	3,343	852	1,850	917	2,000	2	1992	5,725	4,042	1,612	1,725	1,453	1,875	-----
1988	5,373	3,944	1,045	1,620	1,247	1,883	2	1993[1]	6,540	3,695	1,632	2,545	1,207	2,046	-----
1989	4,957	4,030	1,011	1,470	1,615	1,822	2	1994[2]	7,300	3,299	1,755	2,992	1,365	1,970	-----

[1] Preliminary.   [2] Estimate.   *Source: U.S. Burea of Mines*

2

U.S. Aluminum Products Distribution of End-Use Shipments   In Thousands of Metric Tons

Year	Building & Construction	Consumer Durables	Containers & Packaging	Electrical	Exports	Machinery & Equipment	Trans-portation	Other	Total
1986	1,432	540	1,926	626	413	383	1,372	252	6,958
1987	1,441	576	2,052	620	569	401	1,500	223	7,382
1988	1,316	588	2,036	671	787	435	1,536	269	7,638
1989	1,294	544	2,112	663	1,060	436	1,448	264	7,821
1990	1,208	509	2,157	594	1,131	452	1,388	261	7,700
1991	1,052	472	2,210	579	1,357	426	1,414	241	7,752
1992[1]	1,144	523	2,259	587	1,236	448	1,591	256	8,045
1993[1]	1,237	563	2,181	609	1,092	477	1,904	259	8,324

[1] Preliminary.   *Source: U.S. Bureau of Mines*

Average Annual Primary Aluminum Prices   In Dollars Per Pound

Year	Average Annual Price	Based on Constant 1987 Dollars	Year	Average Annual Price	Based on Constant 1987 Dollars
1909	.220	3.144	1952	.194	.894
1910	.223	3.140	1953	.209	.951
1911	.201	2.830	1954	.218	.977
1912	.220	2.972	1955	.237	1.026
1913	.236	3.233	1956	.240	1.003
1914	.186	2.479	1957 [5]	.254	1.029
1915	.340	4.359	1958	.248	.985
1916	.607	6.896	1959	.247	.958
1917	.516	4.825	1960	.260	.988
1918	.335	2.915	1961	.255	.961
1919	.321	2.359	1962	.239	.882
1920 [1]	.327	2.031	1963	.226	.823
1921	.221	1.673	1964	.237	.846
1922 [2]	.187	1.533	1965	.245	.853
1923	.254	1.999	1966	.245	.826
1924	.270	2.160	1967	.250	.820
1925	.272	2.141	1968	.256	.801
1926	.270	2.144	1969	.272	.805
1927	.254	2.065	1970	.287	.804
1928	.243	1.959	1971	.290	.769
1929 [3]	.243	1.959	1972	.250	.633
1930	.238	1.966	1973 [6]	.264	.628
1931	.233	2.118	1974	.431	.940
1932	.233	2.377	1975	.348	.689
1933	.233	2.453	1976	.412	.770
1934	.234	2.251	1977	.478	.837
1935	.200	1.886	1978	.510	.831
1936 [4]	.205	1.933	1979	.707	1.061
1937	.199	1.793	1980	.761	1.043
1938	.200	1.818	1981	.598	.748
1939	.200	1.852	1982	.468	.552
1940	.187	1.700	1983	.683	.772
1941	.165	1.411	1984	.611	.666
1942	.150	1.200	1985	.488	.517
1943	.150	1.172	1986	.559	.576
1944	.150	1.154	1987	.723	.723
1945	.150	1.128	1988	1.101	1.068
1946	.150	.909	1989	.878	.816
1947	.150	.798	1990	.740	.661
1948	.157	.782	1991	.595	NA
1949	.170	.850	1992	.575	NA
1950	.177	.873	1993	.533	NA
1951	.190	.891	1994	.650	NA

[1] 98% to 99% - pure aluminum.   [2] 98% - pure aluminum metal.   [3] 99% - pure aluminum metal.   [4] 99% plus - pure virgin ingot aluminum.   [5] 99.5% - pure unalloyed aluminum ingot.   [6] U.S. market spot price.   NA = Not available.   *Source: U.S. Bureau of Mines*

ALUMINUM

Average Price of Cast Aluminum Scrap (Crank Cases) in Chicago Area   In Cents Per Pound

Year	Jan.	Feb.	Mar.	Apr.	May	June	July	Aug.	Sept.	Oct.	Nov.	Dec.	Average
1987	25.75	27.56	30.00	31.64	33.10	34.82	36.20	40.24	41.55	43.68	41.87	42.82	29.50
1988	45.50	47.40	52.67	55.64	53.93	55.00	54.65	54.85	54.69	50.64	49.50	50.50	52.08
1989	53.02	52.97	53.41	51.90	51.14	47.59	42.97	40.63	43.30	40.14	37.75	35.65	45.87
1990	34.68	30.50	30.77	32.50	32.50	32.50	35.93	37.50	41.97	42.50	40.58	39.00	35.91
1991	33.50	32.00	32.00	30.64	28.45	22.40	21.50	21.50	21.13	19.00	18.11	18.00	24.85
1992	18.71	23.00	26.91	27.00	24.45	24.00	24.00	24.00	21.21	19.50	19.50	19.50	22.65
1993	19.50	19.50	19.50	19.50	19.50	19.50	20.79	21.00	20.62	20.00	20.00	20.00	19.95
1994	20.00	25.79	28.33	32.50	32.50	33.18	35.90	36.50	41.07	44.45	50.50	53.50	37.66

Source: American Metal Market

Aluminum Products (Ingot & Mill Products) Shipments[1] in the U.S.   In Million Pounds

Year	Jan.	Feb.	Mar.	Apr.	May	June	July	Aug.	Sept.	Oct.	Nov.	Dec.	Total
1987	1,170	1,241	1,329	1,284	1,306	1,433	1,346	1,261	1,334	1,307	1,219	1,353	15,584
1988	1,186	1,199	1,402	1,246	1,331	1,416	1,214	1,357	1,334	1,293	1,322	1,155	15,453
1989	1,266	1,232	1,419	1,246	1,306	1,365	1,205	1,369	1,299	1,278	1,169	1,071	15,468
1990	1,234	1,154	1,313	1,224	1,355	1,318	1,257	1,272	1,224	1,247	1,098	1,120	14,761
1991	1,177	1,087	1,261	1,244	1,313	1,287	1,387	1,389	1,276	1,371	1,265	1,241	15,298
1992	1,324	1,280	1,376	1,298	1,277	1,339	1,330	1,333	1,361	1,453	1,333	1,360	16,065
1993	1,251	1,291	1,486	1,408	1,377	1,440	1,296	1,410	1,382	1,306	1,364	1,284	16,294
1994[2]	1,496	1,518	1,906	1,572	1,767	1,621	1,539	1,740	1,593	1,622	1,721	1,635	19,729

[1] Mills products & pig & ingot (net shipments).   [2] Preliminary.   *Source: Bureau of Census, U.S. Department of Commerce*

U.S. Aluminum Inventories, Total (Ingot, Mill Products & Scrap)   In Million Pounds

Year	Jan. 1	Feb. 1	Mar. 1	Apr. 1	May 1	June 1	July 1	Aug. 1	Sept. 1	Oct. 1	Nov. 1	Dec. 1
1987	4,928	4,896	4,772	4,696	4,584	4,515	4,474	4,393	4,303	4,152	4,211	4,245
1988	4,175	4,272	4,363	4,343	4,941	4,344	4,215	4,235	4,175	4,175	4,134	4,119
1989	4,151	4,189	4,163	4,160	4,246	4,224	4,289	4,373	4,253	4,158	4,064	3,991
1990	4,016	4,019	4,035	3,914	3,974	3,808	3,916	4,070	3,980	4,040	4,119	4,013
1991	4,013	4,068	4,169	4,256	4,212	4,135	4,044	3,990	4,028	4,008	3,992	3,923
1992	3,913	4,321	4,346	4,375	4,411	4,486	4,482	4,333	4,376	4,418	4,336	4,263
1993[1]	4,131	4,059	4,091	4,146	4,216	4,241	4,294	4,357	4,374	4,345	4,318	4,251
1994[1]	4,330	4,324	4,435	4,455	4,470	4,403	4,435	4,482	4,484	4,437	4,351	4,345

[1] Preliminary.   *Source: Bureau of Census, U.S. Department of Commerce*

Aluminum Exports (Metal & Alloys, Crude) from the U.S.   In Cents Per Pound

Year	Jan.	Feb.	Mar.	Apr.	May	June	July	Aug.	Sept.	Oct.	Nov.	Dec.	Total
1987	15.4	23.9	21.3	23.6	15.2	14.6	26.3	27.8	27.9	20.6	29.1	35.5	281.1
1988	18.4	13.7	19.8	20.9	34.5	43.4	41.6	44.3	39.0	25.7	47.5	51.3	400.1
1989	34.8	41.8	40.2	33.3	34.1	44.6	46.2	52.0	46.1	68.8	72.7	80.0	593.0
1990	79.0	65.1	55.3	61.4	41.4	48.6	41.5	39.0	53.6	59.6	62.2	76.0	679.8
1991	61.1	54.8	46.7	82.8	56.4	71.3	69.0	80.1	54.6	68.0	80.7	67.3	792.8
1992	50.8	43.8	49.7	38.6	33.6	39.8	50.0	50.3	40.4	82.1	50.5	73.5	603.1
1993[1]	54.8	38.6	41.7	26.3	38.6	30.7	33.9	24.5	27.9	31.7	24.1	27.6	400.4
1994[1]	22.1	18.3	28.3	17.9	37.5	30.5	30.6	38.3	40.3	24.8	26.1	24.1	338.8

[1] Preliminary.   *Source: U.S. Bureau of Mines*

Aluminum General Imports (Metal & Alloys, Crude) from the U.S.   In Cents Per Pound

Year	Jan.	Feb.	Mar.	Apr.	May	June	July	Aug.	Sept.	Oct.	Nov.	Dec.	Total
1987	114.3	113.0	100.8	96.4	104.2	121.2	109.4	96.3	95.5	112.7	94.0	92.2	1,250.6
1988	101.2	92.0	104.9	89.0	92.1	80.6	79.6	80.0	92.4	81.9	82.0	55.0	1,030.6
1989	99.4	78.6	83.3	92.4	75.5	73.9	71.8	91.9	83.6	65.2	53.9	54.2	923.0
1990	84.4	73.4	85.4	85.1	90.4	94.0	102.6	82.1	76.4	66.8	58.7	60.6	959.6
1991	79.5	79.4	84.3	88.2	85.1	75.9	97.3	89.0	86.6	90.4	81.0	88.0	1,024.7
1992	100.7	93.1	97.1	94.6	96.3	87.8	82.4	103.4	94.3	108.4	100.5	96.8	1,155.4
1993[1]	120.8	123.9	165.8	172.0	152.1	152.6	125.1	162.7	173.5	149.4	182.9	155.6	1,836.4
1994[1]	200.2	157.8	282.0	206.9	251.9	179.3	202.8	198.3	160.0	183.4	240.1	222.2	2,484.8

[1] Preliminary.   *Source: U.S. Bureau of Mines*

Antimony

Antimony is primarily a by-product of mining, smelting and refining of other metals, usually lead and silver-copper ores. It is used in flame retardents, fabrics, plastics and ammunition. Reductions in the use of antimonial lead indicate that demand for this commodity is shifting away from metal products and into plastics and pigments. Most antimony is the U.S. is found in Idaho, Nevada, Alaska and Montana.

Domestic smelter production of antimony (primarily trioxide) in the first quarter of 1994 was 5,425 tonnes. According to the U.S. Bureau of Mines, smelter production for all of 1993 was 21,635 tonnes. In 1992, smelter production totaled close to 21,700 tonnes. Data on mine production of antimony was withheld to avoid disclosing company proprietary data. Secondary production of antimony for the first five months of 1994 totaled 4,825 tonnes. In 1993, secondary production of antimony totaled 10,699 tonnes.

U.S. imports of antimony ore and concentrate during the first five months of 1994 totaled 1,647 tonnes. This represented a significant increase from the 1993 calendar year total of 543 tonnes. In 1994, the major supplier was Bolivia which shipped 837, tonnes while Kyrgzstan sent 309 tonnes, and Canada 162. U.S. imports of antimony metal for the January-May 1994 period were 4,995 tonnes. For all of 1993 they were 14,364 tonnes. By far, the major supplier was China with 4,139 tonnes while Mexico shipped 520 tonnes. Antimony oxide imports for the first five months of 1994 were 6,765 tonnes. For 1993, imports were 16,037 tonnes. In 1994, the major suppliers were China with 2,162 tonnes, Bolivia 1,388 tonnes, Mexico 1,110 tonnes and South Africa with 1,012 tonnes.

Exports of antimony metal, alloys and scrap were 312 tonnes. For all of 1993, exports were only 318 tonnes. Exports of antimony oxide for January-May 1994 were 1,867 tonnes compared to 5,810 tonnes for calendar 1993.

Consumption of primary antimony for the first half of 1994 was 3,103 tonnes. Much of the data on uses, by class of material produced, has been withheld to avoid disclosing company proprietary data. Consumption in the first half of 1994 of antimonial lead was 559 tonnes. Use of antimony for ceramics and glass was 440 tonnes. Consumption of antimony in flame-retardant plastics was 1,140 tonnes.

Industry stocks of antimony on June 30, 1994 was 8,803 tonnes. Over the first half of 1994, the average New York dealer price for 99.5% to 99.6% metal antimony was 76 cents per pound. Sales of antimony from the National Defense Stockpile totaled 1,144 tonnes in the second quarter of 1994.

World Mine Production of Antimony (Content of Ore)   In Metric Tons

Year	Australia	Bolivia	Canada	China[2]	Czech Republic[3]	Guat-emala	Kyrgy-zstan[4]	Mexico[5]	Morocco	Peru[6]	Russia[4]	South Africa	Thailand	Turkey	United States	World Total[2]
1991	1,500	7,287	469	58,300	1,000	609	----	1,469	90	278	16,000	4,485	60	370	230	92,448
1992	1,701	6,022	948	45,000	1,000	582	2,000	1,200	90	339	10,000	3,779	269	309	232	75,011
1993[1]	1,700	4,500	741	50,000	250	600	1,600	1,469	90	340	6,000	3,500	270	310	W	73,288

[1] Preliminary. [2] Estimate. [3] Formerly part of Czechoslovakia, data not reported separately until 1993. [4] Formerly part of the USSR; data not reported separately until 1992. [5] Includes antimony content of miscellaneous smelter products. [6] Recoverable W = Withheld proprietary data. *Source: U.S. Bureau of Mines*

Salient Statistics of Antimony in the United States   In Metric Tons

Year	Avg. Price ¢ per pound CIF U.S. Ports	Production[3] — Primary[2] — Mine	Smelter	Secondary (Alloys)[2]	Imports[4] — Ore — Gross Weight	Sb Content	Oxide (Gross Weight)	Exports (Oxide)	Industry Stocks, December 31[3] — Metallic	Oxide	Sulfide	Residues and Slag	Total[5]
1991	82.0	W	16,032	19,294	4,395	3,381	14,397	3,752	3,598	3,338	W	W	10,170
1992	79.0	W	17,854	19,925	3,029	1,923	17,085	4,817	2,450	2,952	20	W	8,741
1993[1]	76.9	W	21,723	17,245	1,720	543	19,322	3,896	2,819	3,663	20	W	9,452

[1] Preliminary. [2] Estimate. [3] Antimony content. [4] Imports for consumption. [5] Including primary antimony residues & slag. W=Withheld proprietary data. *Source: U.S. Bureau of Mines*

Industrial Consumption of Primary Antimony in the United States   In Metric Tons (Antimony Content)

Year	Metal Products — Ammunition	Antimonial Lead	Sheet and Pipe	Bearing Metal and Pipe	Solder	Type Metal	Total All Metal Products	Flame Retardents — Plastics	Total	Non-Metal Products — Ceramics and Glass	Rubber Products	Pigments	Plastics	Total	Grand Total
1991	W	1,698	W	77	223	W	2,921	4,982	6,626	872	W	207	1,112	2,317	11,864
1992	W	1,642	W	36	248	W	3,297	5,113	6,826	928	W	314	717	2,102	12,225
1993[1]	W	2,659	W	45	242	W	4,485	8,050	9,801	1,191	W	W	1,035	2,761	17,047

[1] Preliminary. [2] Estimated coverage based on 77% of the industry. W=Withheld proprietary data. *Source: U.S. Bureau of Mines*

United States Prices of Antimony[1]   In Cents Per Pound

Year	January	February	March	April	May	June	July	August	September	October	November	December	Average
1992	133.00	133.00	133.00	133.00	133.00	133.00	133.00	133.00	133.00	133.00	133.00	133.00	133.00
1993	133.00	133.00	133.00	133.00	133.00	133.00	74.00	74.00	74.00	74.00	74.00	73.15	104.00
1994	73.00	73.00	78.04	87.50	111.07	153.75	182.50	235.00	250.00	260.00	288.00	293.00	173.74

[1] Prices thru June 1993 are for domestic refined antimony in alloy, content change only. From July 1993, prices are for antimony metal (99.65%) merchants, minimum 18-ton containers, c.i.f. U.S. Ports. *Source: American Metal Market Daily.*

Apples

World Production of Apples, Fresh (Dessert & Cooking)　　In Thousands of Metric Tons

Year	Argen-tina	Aus-tralia	Canada	France	Ger-many	Hun-gary	Italy	Japan	Mex-ico	Nether-lands	Slo-vakia[4]	South Africa	Spain	Tur-key	United States	World Total
1980	908	345	553	1,802	1,880	NA	1,966	960	282	450	483	450	859	NA	4,005	17,179
1981	804	294	422	1,502	884	1,156	1,774	846	280	325	508	486	1,008	1,450	3,517	17,006
1982	817	301	478	1,978	2,637	1,278	2,642	924	394	490	746	519	860	1,600	3,684	21,626
1983	872	267	485	1,575	1,313	1,141	2,057	1,048	302	403	557	513	1,012	1,750	3,800	19,205
1984	922	352	434	2,005	1,799	1,088	2,241	812	486	431	584	557	970	1,900	3,776	20,701
1985	594	288	479	1,793	1,410	954	2,012	910	443	300	368	517	988	1,900	3,590	18,775
1986	1,078	362	388	1,867	2,180	1,253	2,020	986	629	445	637	470	829	1,860	3,565	21,098
1987	925	309	506	1,985	1,077	1,064	2,273	998	615	340	423	526	971	1,680	4,873	20,922
1988-9	1,030	350	501	1,935	2,467	1,131	2,443	1,042	624	383	518	534	845	1,950	4,140	22,662
1989-90	1,050	333	538	1,818	1,727	959	2,162	1,045	545	417	546	557	747	1,850	4,519	21,654
1990-1	950	292	540	1,895	2,222	945	2,102	1,053	520	431	523	542	635	1,900	4,398	21,224
1991-2	1,043	289	513	1,236	1,165	859	1,869	760	550	223	480	605	517	1,900	4,413	18,250
1992-3	947	336	564	2,398	3,228	666	2,394	1,039	580	640	112	633	1,095	2,100	4,798	35,443
1993-4[1]	1,050	321	474	2,079	1,718	819	2,145	1,011	500	670	112	627	874	2,080	4,860	36,612
1994-5[2]	1,070	322	500	2,113	2,126	700	2,057	1,048	522	600	57	657	724	2,000	4,948	36,288

[1] Preliminary.　[2] Estimate.　[3] Commercial crop.　[4] Formerly part of Yugoslavia; data not reported separately until 1992.　NA = Not available.
Source: Foreign Agicultural Service, U.S. Department of Agriculture

Salient Statistics of Apples[2] in the United States

	Production		Growers Prices		Utilization of Quantities Sold						Avg. Farm Price ¢ Per Lb.	Farm Value Million $	Foreign Trade[4]			Fresh Per Capita Con-sump-tion Lbs.
							Processed[6]						Domestic		Imports	
Year	Total	Util-ized	Fresh ¢ Lb.	Pro-cessing $ Ton	Fresh	Canned	Dried	Frozen	Juice & Cider	Other[3]			Exports Fresh	Dried[5]	Fresh & Dried[5]	
				Millions of Pounds									Metric Tons			
1980	8,818	8,800	12.1	84.0	4,934	1,202	195	168	2,137	165	8.7	761.3	311.3	7.6	76.8	19.2
1981	7,740	7,693	15.4	102.0	4,442	1,002	190	173	1,798	87	11.1	851.1	269.2	8.3	128.3	16.9
1982	8,122	8,110	13.2	118.0	4,537	1,249	210	191	1,808	116	10.0	809.0	261.8	16.1	98.7	17.5
1983	8,379	8,358	14.8	104.0	4,621	1,204	283	170	1,985	95	10.5	879.0	228.7	12.0	126.0	18.3
1984	8,324	8,309	15.5	112.0	4,655	1,177	289	198	1,889	102	11.2	927.6	205.2	9.3	132.6	18.4
1985	7,915	7,827	17.3	103.0	4,222	1,255	242	194	1,839	74	11.7	914.3	147.1	5.5	152.6	17.3
1986	7,859	7,833	19.1	116.0	4,464	1,179	199	257	1,643	91	13.4	1,046.8	175.1	10.5	149.4	17.8
1987	10,742	10,451	12.7	79.3	5,610	1,306	284	249	2,929	74	8.6	903.1	296.2	7.7	132.7	20.8
1988	9,128	9,078	17.4	123.0	5,238	1,399	285	266	1,824	67	12.7	1,150.0	254.5	12.0	133.0	19.9
1989	9,963	9,917	13.9	107.0	5,865	1,320	282	322	2,071	57	10.4	1,034.4	357.4	23.7	119.7	21.4
1990	9,697	9,658	20.9	144.0	5,551	1,378	270	304	2,081	74	15.1	1,449.0	371.3	55.5	122.0	19.7
1991	9,729	9,659	25.1	171.0	5,469	1,311	299	286	2,194	100	17.9	1,733.1	530.1	44.2	143.9	18.3
1992[1]	10,579	10,474	19.5	130.0	5,781	1,497	324	247	2,471	155	13.4	1,421.8				19.3
1993[1]	10,723	10,611	18.2	107.0	6,161	1,344	366	281	2,371	88	12.8	1,557.4				19.5

[1] Preliminary.　[2] Commercial crop.　[3] Mostly crushed for vinegar, jam, etc.　[4] Year beginning July.　[5] Fresh weight basis.　*Source: Economic Research Service, U.S. Department of Agriculture*

U.S. Prices of Apples Received by Growers (for Fresh Use)　　In Cents Per Pound

Year	Jan.	Feb.	Mar.	Apr.	May	June	July	Aug.	Sept.	Oct.	Nov.	Dec.	Average
1980	14.1	14.9	16.6	17.0	17.9	21.0	24.6	17.5	15.7	12.5	11.5	10.7	16.2
1981	10.7	12.4	12.1	11.3	10.7	10.5	12.7	14.6	16.0	16.0	16.1	15.7	13.2
1982	14.1	15.7	16.0	14.5	16.2	17.7	15.3	12.8	16.3	14.5	13.9	13.0	15.0
1983	11.0	12.2	12.0	11.3	11.9	11.1	12.0	16.0	15.9	14.9	14.6	14.0	13.1
1984	14.3	15.1	15.2	14.8	15.0	14.6	14.9	16.5	18.5	17.4	16.4	15.6	15.7
1985	14.0	14.3	15.7	15.1	14.1	13.1	12.6	12.1	16.4	15.4	16.4	16.6	14.7
1986	16.6	17.2	17.2	17.2	20.7	21.0	28.5	27.6	20.9	18.0	17.3	16.5	19.9
1987	18.3	19.0	18.0	19.1	22.4	24.6	25.5	15.2	14.8	12.1	11.3	10.4	17.6
1988	11.1	12.9	12.5	11.0	10.9	10.4	22.8	27.7	23.7	18.5	17.5	17.4	16.4
1989	18.1	17.9	16.5	14.4	13.5	10.8	11.5	15.9	16.7	14.3	13.3	12.1	14.6
1990	12.2	12.4	12.3	12.0	12.6	13.7	20.3	22.3	22.2	19.3	19.6	20.9	16.7
1991	20.1	20.5	20.3	20.2	22.5	23.2	24.6	23.2	26.4	23.8	25.1	25.7	23.0
1992	24.6	24.8	24.3	24.1	25.0	25.2	28.6	33.3	27.1	21.2	19.4	19.9	24.8
1993[1]	18.3	16.7	14.5	14.3	14.9	16.1	17.8	24.4	24.5	21.1	19.4	18.6	18.4
1994[1]	18.7	17.8	16.6	15.6	14.4	13.7	13.1	20.3	21.7	20.0	16.7	17.9	17.2

[1] Preliminary.　*Source: Economic Research Service, U.S. Department of Agriculture*

Arsenic

Arsenic is a by-product of copper, lead, gold and zinc mining. With substantial quantities of these metals world-wide, availability of arsenic is ample. Arsenic is employed in a variety of products including laser materials, and as a doping agent in the manufacturing of various solid state devices. Arsenic trioxide is imported and converted to arsenic acid for use in producing wood preservative. In addition to chromated copper arsenate being the most common arsenic-based wood preservative, ammoniacal copper arsenate and fluor chrome arsenate phenol are also used.

According to the U.S. Bureau of Mines, agricultural uses for arsenic were as herbicides for weed control; arsenic acid is used in the mechanical harvesting of cotton and in glass-making. Arsenilic acid is an arsenical drug used for growth, pigmentation and disease control. Commercial grade arsenic metal, 99% pure, is used in lead and copper-based alloys to increase strength in the posts and grids of lead-acid storage batteries, and to increase corrosion resistance in copper alloys. Very high purity arsenic metal is utilized in the manufacturing of crystalline gallium arsenide. This semiconduction material, which is faster but more costly than silicon products, is used in optoelectronic circuitry and high-speed computers.

Current U.S. Bureau of Mines arsenic data is for the year ended 1993. The U.S. continued to import all of the arsenic it required in 1993. 97% of the arsenic was imported as trioxide and 3% as metal. U.S. imports of arsenic triozide in 1993 were 27,530 tonnes, down 10% from the 1992 total of 30,671 tonnes. The major suppliers of arsenic triox-

ide were China 11,710 tonnes, Chile 6,051 tonnes and Mexico 3,905 tonnes. In 1993, there were no imports of arsenic acid and no imports of arsenic sulfide. U.S. imports of arsenic metal in 1993 were 767 tonnes compared to 740 tonnes in 1992. China was by far the largest supplier with 691 tonnes.

Exports of arsenic in 1993 were 364 tonnes (arsenic content). This compares with 1992 exports of 94 tonnes.

Arsenic is used in many products. 1993 U.S. usage in agricultural chemicals was 3,000 tonnes, down 23% from 1992. Use in glass-making was estimated at 900 tonnes, the same as the prior year. Use of arsenic in wood preservatives, the major market for arsenic, was 16,200 tonnes, a decline of 9% from 1992. The future for arsenic consumption is related to new housing construction, particularly in the building of wood decks. Arsenic treated wood is also used in decks attached to existing homes. More importantly, no significant environmental problems are associated with the use of arsenicals in wood preservatives because of the low concentration of arsenic in the wood and because of the fact that arsenic does not readily leach from treated wood. Use of arsenic in nonferrous alloys and electronics in 1993 was estimated at 800 tonnes, the same as 1992.

World production of arsenic trioxide in 1993 was 47,740 tonnes, down 1% from 1992. The major producer was China with estimated production of 13,000 tonnes. The next largest producer was Ghana with 9,000 tonnes. This arsenic trioxide is a byproduct of gold processing and it is unclear how much is commercial grade.

World Production of White Arsenic (Arsenic Trioxide)   In Metric Tons

Year	Belgium	Bolivia	Canada[4]	Chile	China	France	Germany	Japan	Mexico	Namibia[3]	Peru	Phillipines	Russia[5]	Sweden	World Total
1984	3,000	144	3,000	3,500	-------	3,828	360	500	5,496	2,504	1,090	-------	8,000	10,000	48,402
1985	3,000	361	3,000	4,000	-------	8,000	360	500	4,782	2,471	1,257	5,000	8,100	10,000	53,235
1986	3,000	241	3,000	4,000	-------	10,000	360	500	5,315	2,208	1,273	5,000	8,100	10,000	53,173
1987	3,500	132	3,000	3,616	-------	10,000	360	500	5,304	1,864	1,757	5,000	8,100	10,000	52,351
1988	3,500	191	2,825	3,207	7,000	10,000	360	500	5,164	2,983	828	5,046	8,100	10,000	60,335
1989	3,500	338	1,825	5,000	7,000	10,000	360	500	5,551	2,399	563	4,652	8,100	10,000	61,026
1990	3,000	300	485	5,831	9,000	6,480	360	500	4,809	1,636	500	5,092	7,800	7,000	53,375
1991	2,500	463	236	6,822	10,000	2,000	300	500	4,922	1,804	661	5,000	7,000	2,500	45,960
1992	2,000	633	250	6,016	14,000	2,000	300	500	4,293	2,456	607	5,000	3,000	1,000	48,197
1993[1]	2,000	590	250	6,200	13,000	2,000	300	500	4,168	2,472	610	2,000	2,000	500	47,740
1994[2]	2,000			6,000	13,000				4,000	2,000		2,000	2,000		47,000

[1] Preliminary.   [2] Estimate.   [3] Output of Tsumeb Corp. Ltd. only.   [4] Includes low-grade dusts that were exported to the U.S. for further refining.
[5] Formerly part of the U.S.S.R.; reported seperately until 1992.   *Source: U.S. Bureau of Mines*

U.S. Arsenic Supply--Demand Relationships   In Metric Tons (Arsenic Content)

	------------------Supply--------------------				--Distribution--		------------------Estimated Demand Pattern-------------------						--Average Price--			
	------Imports------		Industry Stocks Jan. 1	Total	Apparent Demand	Industry Stocks Dec. 31	Agricultural Chemicals	Glass	Wood Preserv-atives	Non-Ferrous Alloys and Elec.	Other	Total	Trioxide Mexican	Metal Chinese	Imports Trioxide[3]	Exports
Year	Metal	Com-pounds											--¢ Per Pound--			
1989	928	21,498	100	22,526	22,300	100	4,900	900	15,600	700	200	22,300	27	47	28,348	126
1990	796	19,897	100	20,793	20,544	100	4,200	800	14,400	800	300	20,500	23	180	26,256	149
1991	1,008	20,741	100	21,849	21,615	-----	5,000	900	14,300	1,000	400	21,600	25	68	27,142	233
1992	740	23,256	-----	23,996	23,902	-----	3,900	900	17,900	800	400	23,900	29	56	30,671	94
1993[1]	767	20,850	-----	21,617	21,253	-----	3,000	900	16,200	800	400	21,300	33	44	27,530	364
1994[2]	1,400		-----	19,400	-----							19,400	34	50	23,900	100

[1] Preliminary.   [2] Estimate.   [3] For Consumption.   *Source: U.S. Bureau of Mines*

Barley

Barley is the third largest produced feed grain in the U.S., but annual production is a fraction of corn output. Barley production is much more important in other countries. The former Soviet Union was once the largest producer, but Canada is now the single largest producer with a 1994/95 crop of about 12.5 million tonnes. The U.S. crop totaled about 8.2 million tonnes. Most of the world's barley is produced in the European Community (EC-12) and Eastern Europe. World production and consumption in recent years has averaged near 160 million tonnes, with world stocks holding around 32 million tonnes.

In the U.S., the barley crop year begins June 1. Production has declined sharply since the mid-1980s when crops near 600 million bushels were realized. Production in 1994/95 of 375 million bushels was lower than initial forecasts that saw a crop about equal to the 400 million bushels produced in 1993/94. More significant is the decline in the acreage planted to barley, about 7.2 million acres in 1994/95, the lowest since 1934. The reason focuses mostly on barley's price as the average price of barley received by farmers in recent years, particularly in the Northern plains has been less favorable than wheat and sunflower. North Dakota generally accounts for more than a one-third of U.S. production followed by Montana and Idaho.

Lower barley supplies will restrict use in 1994/95 to about 450 million bushels compared with 484 million in 1993/94. Large corn supplies were expected to drop barley's feed and residual use to 215 million bushels, down 28 million bushels. Industrial use, mostly for beer and alcohol, should hold steady at 175 million bushels while exports increase to 70 million bushels. Imports of about 65 million bushels, mostly of malting quality barley from Canada, will offset some of the reduced U.S. supply. Imports have risen sharply since the late-1980s when they averaged about 12 million bushels per season. If the 1994/95 forecasts prove correct, carryover stocks on May 31, 1995 of 129 million bushels will compare with the year earlier lower total of 139 million.

Farmers' barley prices averaged about $1.99 per bushel in 1993/94, down 5¢ from 1992/93. Low quality of the 1993 crop contributed to the price drop, which trimmed the premium malting barley usually commands over feed barley. Little price recovery is expected for the 1994/95 crop year with initial United States Department of Agriculture estimates running from $1.90 per bushel to $2.10 per bushel.

U.S. Farm Program

For the 1994/95 marketing year, the national average loan rate was set at $1.54 per bushel and the target price was $2.36 per bushel, versus $1.40 per bushel and $2.36 in 1993/94, respectively.

Futures Market

A 20 tonne feed barley futures contract is traded on the Winnipeg Commodity Exchange (WCE). Futures are quoted in Canadian dollars per tonne.

World Barley Supply and Demand   In Thousands of Metric Tons

Crop Year	Australia	Canada	EC-12	Total Non-U.S.	U.S.	Total Exports	Saudi Arabia	Unaccounted	Total Imports	Production	Russia[3]	U.S.	Total Utilization	Canada	U.S.	Total Stocks
1985-6	3.7	4.8	7.3	17.6	0.8	18.4	6.6	NA	18.4	178.0	48.6	10.9	172.7	22.6	7.1	29.7
1986-7	2.2	6.0	6.2	15.6	3.0	18.6	9.0	NA	18.6	182.4	56.6	10.3	178.1	26.7	7.3	34.0
1987-8	1.6	3.5	7.0	13.1	2.9	16.0	4.8	NA	16.0	181.3	60.9	9.3	183.1	25.2	7.0	32.2
1988-9[4]	1,364	3,419	8,349	14,137	1,718	15,855	4,714	-12	15,855	162,722	44,245	7,540	162,536	2,800	4,276	30,674
1989-90	2,447	3,773	7,905	15,905	1,798	17,703	4,146	467	17,703	164,761	22,433	8,030	167,440	2,056	3,501	28,789
1990-1	2,683	4,460	7,053	17,016	1,507	18,523	4,342	742	18,523	178,056	29,156	8,283	174,898	2,646	2,948	32,317
1991-2	1,951	3,379	8,260	16,498	2,090	18,588	6,873	204	18,588	169,140	26,372	8,735	167,224	2,615	2,800	34,233
1992-3	2,600	2,859	5,544	13,695	1,611	15,306	3,917	761	15,306	165,656	24,565	7,916	162,489	3,271	3,292	37,400
1993-4[1]	4,305	3,789	6,500	16,978	1,553	18,531	4,550	1,105	18,531	170,008	27,028	9,053	169,856	3,388	3,023	37,552
1994-5[2]	500	4,000	6,000	14,150	1,300	15,450	4,500	305	15,450	160,830	26,800	8,709	167,845	3,090	2,476	30,537

[1] Preliminary. [2] Estimate. [3] Formerly part of the U.S.S.R.; data not reported separately until 1989-90. [4] Prior to 1988-89, reported in millions of metric tons. NA = Not available. *Source: Foreign Agricultural Service, U.S. Department of Agriculture*

World Production of Barley   In Thousands of Metric Tons

Year	Australia	Canada	China	Denmark	France	Germany	India	Japan	Kazakhstan[3]	Morocco	Saudi Arabia	Spain	Turkey	United Kingdom	United States	World Total
1985-6	4,868	12,387	6,200	5,251	11,470	9,690	1,556	378	46,500	2,225	12	9,980	5,800	9,740	12,876	178,000
1986-7	3,611	14,634	5,632	5,134	9,950	9,377	1,962	344	53,900	3,563	12	7,431	6,300	10,015	13,293	182,428
1987-8	3,477	13,957	6,041	4,292	10,528	8,571	1,669	353	58,409	1,543	80	9,282	6,000	9,225	11,354	181,511
1988-9	3,306	10,212	6,041	5,419	9,800	9,587	1,577	399	44,500	3,454	200	12,070	6,000	8,775	6,314	167,302
1989-90	4,044	11,666	6,180	4,982	9,840	9,716	1,721	371	48,500	2,999	331	9,100	4,900	8,025	8,784	169,680
1990-1	4,184	13,441	3,930	4,990	10,150	13,990	1,490	346	8,500	2,138	372	9,410	6,600	7,900	9,192	178,056
1991-2	4,606	11,617	3,928	5,040	10,800	14,490	1,630	268	3,085	3,253	394	9,140	6,800	7,700	10,110	169,140
1992-3	5,459	10,919	4,000	2,970	10,580	12,200	1,700	286	8,511	1,081	406	6,110	6,500	7,350	9,908	165,656
1993-4[1]	6,956	12,972	4,200	3,400	8,880	11,000	1,510	271	7,148	1,019	1,100	9,520	7,300	6,040	8,666	170,008
1994-5[2]	2,600	11,690	4,000	3,350	7,800	10,900	1,600	210	5,100	3,720	1,500	7,400	6,800	5,800	8,162	160,830

[1] Preliminary. [2] Estimate. [3] Formerly part of the U.S.S.R.; data not reported separately until 1990-91. *Source: Foreign Agricultural Service, U.S. Department of Agriculture*

U.S. Barley Acreage and Prices

Year Beginning June 1	Acreage ------ 1,000 Acres ------ Planted	Harvested for Grain	Yield Per Harvested Acre -- Bushels --	Received by Farmers[3]	Seasonal Prices Minneapolis[4] ------ or Better ------ Feed (No. 2)	Malting (No. 3)	Portland No. 2 Western	Government Price Support Operations National Average Loan Rate	Target Price	Put Under Support (Mil. Bu.)	% of Production
					Dollars per Bushel						
1985-6	13,139	11,591	50.9	1.98	1.53	2.24	2.23	2.08	2.60	159.1	27.0
1986-7	13,024	11,974	50.8	1.61	1.44	1.89	1.96	1.56	2.60	164.7	27.0
1987-8	10,929	9,957	52.4	1.81	1.78	2.04	2.09	1.49	2.60	122.7	23.6
1988-9	9,831	7,636	38.0	2.80	2.32	4.11	2.74	1.44	2.51	21.9	7.6
1989-90	3,125	8,313	48.6	2.42	2.20	3.28	2.61	1.34	2.43	24.0	5.9
1990-1	8,221	7,529	56.1	2.14	2.13	2.42	2.65	1.28	2.36	33.8	8.0
1991-2	8,941	8,413	55.2	2.10	2.17	2.38	2.66	1.32	2.36	38.0	8.2
1992-3	7,762	7,285	62.5	2.04	2.11	2.37	2.57	1.40	2.36	42.9	9.4
1993-4[1]	7,786	6,753	58.9	1.99	2.05	2.48	2.40	1.40	2.36	37.7	9.5
1994-5[2]	7,159	6,667	56.2	1.85-2.15				1.54	2.36	26.3	7.0

[1] Preliminary.　[2] Estimate.　[3] Excludes support payments.　[4] Duluth beginning March 1987.　[5] Available for total feed grains only.
Source: Economic Research Service, U.S. Department of Agriculture

Salient Statistics of Barley in the United States　In Millions of Bushels

Year Beginning June 1	Supply Beginning Stocks	Production	Imports	Total Supply	Disappearance Domestic Use Food & Alcohol Beverages	Seed	Feed & Residual	Total	Exports	Total Disappearance	Ending Stocks Gov't Owned	Privately Owned[3]	Total Stocks
1985-6	247.4	590.2	6.2	843.9	156.5	21.3	319.1	496.9	19.7	516.7	57.4	269.8	327.2
1986-7	327.2	608.5	6.7	942.4	156.9	17.9	297.7	472.5	133.6	606.1	75.5	260.8	336.3
1987-8	336.3	521.5	11.3	869.1	158.1	15.7	253.2	427.0	121.0	548.0	50.1	271.0	321.1
1988-9	321.1	290.0	10.5	621.6	160.4	15.0	170.9	346.3	78.9	425.2	30.4	166.0	196.4
1989-90	196.4	404.2	13.1	613.7	162.0	13.5	193.3	368.8	84.0	452.9	19.3	141.5	160.8
1990-1	160.8	422.2	13.5	596.5	161.1	14.6	204.8	380.5	80.6	461.1	8.4	127.0	135.4
1991-2	135.4	464.3	24.5	624.2	163.3	12.9	224.9	401.1	94.5	495.6	6.5	122.1	128.6
1992-3	128.6	455.1	11.4	597.9	158.4	13.2	194.9	366.5	80.3	444.0	5.0	146.2	151.2
1993-4[1]	151.2	398.0	71.5	621.0	175.0	12.1	243.0	430.1	66.1	482.0	5.2	133.7	138.9
1994-5[2]	138.9	374.9	60.0	574.0	175.0	------ 225.0 ------		400.0	70.0	470.0			129.2

[1] Preliminary.　[2] Estimate.　[3] Uncommitted inventory.　[4] Includes quantity under loan & farmer-owned reserves.　*Source: Economic Research Service, U.S. Department of Agriculture*

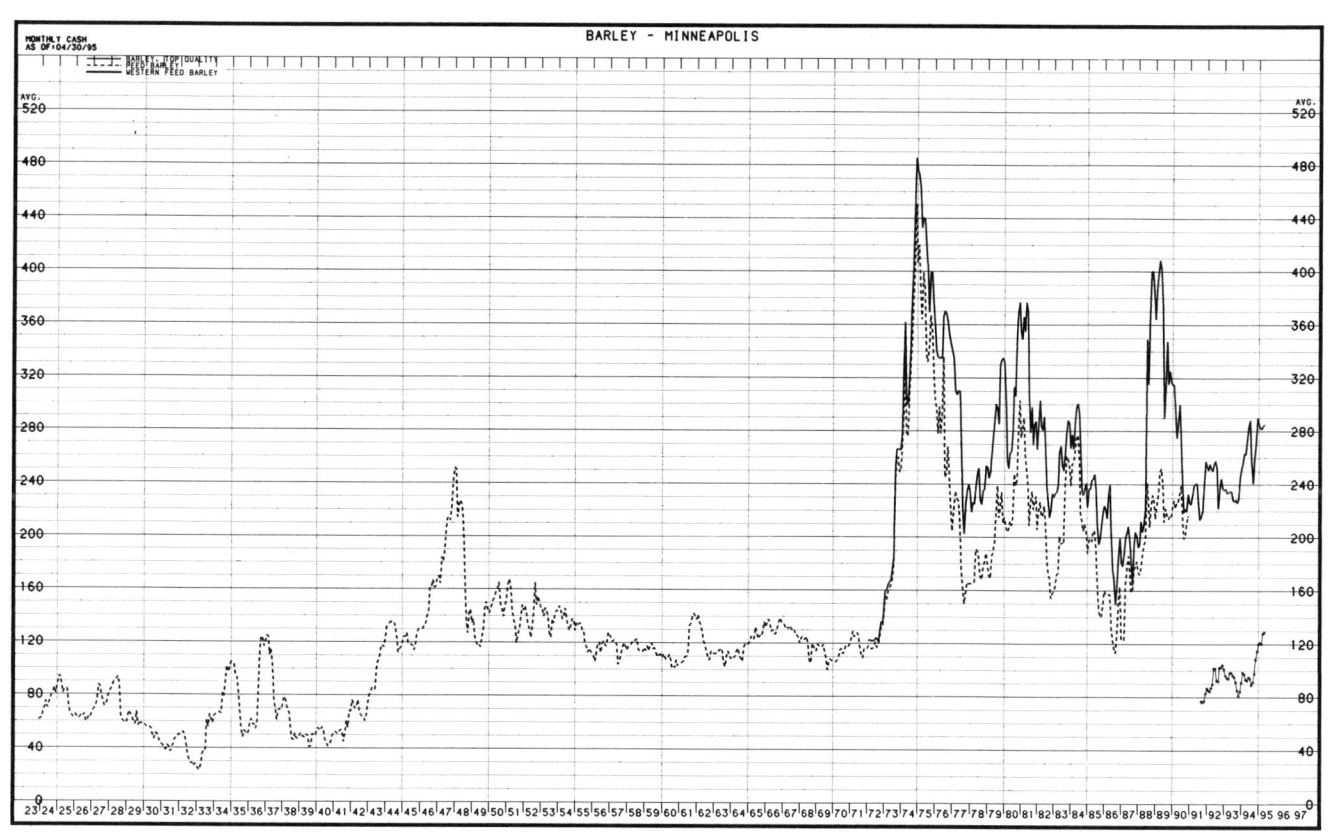

BARLEY

Average Cash Prices of No. 2 (or Better) Feed Barley, in Duluth   In Cents Per Pound

Year	June	July	Aug.	Sept.	Oct.	Nov.	Dec.	Jan.	Feb.	Mar.	Apr.	May	Average
1985-6	190	166	146	140	141	149	160	157	NQ	NQ	NQ	131	153
1986-7[2]	123	116	113	127	150	163	123	NQ	NQ	164	176	186	144
1987-8	173	159	160	176	178	182	174	172	177	188	194	198	178
1988-9	241	238	208	224	232	227	214	224	233	249	252	241	232
1989-90	212	211	217	213	216	215	223	228	220	227	227	233	220
1990-1	239	217	199	201	211	216	207	209	215	214	212	213	213
1991-2	202	189	192	208	218	223	218	220	228	230	235	238	217
1992-3	230	215	203	212	211	208	206	206	208	210	212	205	211
1993-4	199	196	189	189	201	216	214	215	216	207	208	211	205
1994-5[1]	205	202	199	204	195	204	200	202					

[1] Preliminary.   [2] Prior to March 1987, prices are at Minneapolis.   NQ = No quote.   *Source: Economic Research Service, U.S. Department of Agriculture*

Average Open Interest of Barley Futures at Winnipeg   In Contracts -- 20 Tonnes

Year	Jan.	Feb.	Mar.	Apr.	May	June	July	Aug.	Sept.	Oct.	Nov.	Dec.
1990	9,926	10,320	10,040	9,815	10,877	11,165	11,190	10,483	11,152	10,572	8,968	7,164
1991	7,005	6,808	5,952	6,410	5,520	6,169	6,287	6,198	6,240	5,558	6,746	5,977
1992	5,303	5,909	6,562	5,954	5,394	5,157	4,799	4,365	4,607	4,136	4,885	4,699
1993	5,715	7,017	6,074	5,568	5,070	4,869	3,573	2,675	2,373	2,779	2,675	2,213
1994[1]	1,862	1,686	700	351	86							

[1] Contract discontinued June 1994.   *Source: Winnipeg Commodity Exchange*

Average Open Interest of Western Feed Barley Futures at Winnipeg   In Contracts -- 20 Tonnes

Year	Jan.	Feb.	Mar.	Apr.	May	June	July	Aug.	Sept.	Oct.	Nov.	Dec.
1991		869	997	1,242	1,156	1,027	1,234	1,158	1,371	1,514	919	1,065
1992	940	662	1,060	1,572	2,025	2,692	3,168	2,605	2,994	2,746	1,519	1,685
1993	1,471	1,000	1,369	2,318	2,818	3,500	2,287	2,016	2,580	3,643	4,743	5,946
1994	7,600	8,164	7,650	8,212	8,153	9,019	8,511	8,558	9,633	12,340	10,802	9,457

Source: Winnipeg Commodity Exchange

Bauxite

Bauxite is the only raw material used in the production of alumina on a commercial scale in the U.S. However, production data for bauxite in the U.S. is withheld for proprietary reasons by the U.S. Bureau of Mines. Domestic production of bauxite in the second quarter of 1994 was approximately 60% higher than in the previous quarter and 1.5 times greater than the second quarter of 1993.

During the first five months on 1994, U.S. imports of crude and dried bauxite totaled 4.45 million tonnes. For all of 1993, imports were 11.6 million tonnes. The major sources were Jamaica, Guinea, Brazil and Guyana. Over the same period, U.S. exports of crude and dried bauxite were 54,185 tonnes, virtually all of it to Canada.

In the first five months of 1994, U.S. imports of calcined bauxite totaled 96,000 tonnes. Imports for all of 1993 were 237,000 tonnes. The major sources of calcined bauxite were China and Brazil. The U.S. exported 7,046 tonnes of calcined bauxite during the first five months of 1994. Most of the total was refractory bauxite. The major destinations were Mexico and Canada. For all of 1993, exports of calcined bauxite were 4,749 tonnes.

U.S. imports for consumption of alumina during the first five months of 1994 totaled 1.36 million tonnes compared to 3.94 million tonnes imported in all of 1993. Australia has supplied almost 66% of these imports with smaller shipments coming from Jamaica and Surinam. U.S. exports of alumina during January-May 1994 totaled 454 tonnes compared to 1993 exports of 1,237 tonnes. The export destinations were primarily Canada and Brazil.

In 1993, world production of bauxite totaled 105.6 million tonnes, an increase of 4% from 1992. Australia is by far the world's largest producer, accounting for 41.9 million tonnes in 1993. Guinea was the second largest producer with 14.1 million tonnes while Jamaica was third with 11.3 million tonnes. Other important producers include Brazil, Surinam, India, Russia and China.

World alumina production in 1993 was 43 million tonnes. This represented an increase of over 3% from the 1992 figure. Australia was again the largest producer, with output of 12.6 million tonnes, or close to 30% of the world total. The U.S. was the next largest producer with output of 5.3 million tonnes followed by Russia and Jamaica.

World Production of Bauxite   In Thousands of Metric Tons

Year	Australia	Brazil	China	France	Greece	Guinea	Guyana[2]	Hungary	Indo-nesia	Jamai-ca[3]	India	Suriname	Former USSR[3]	United States[3]	Yugo-slavia	World Total
1984	31,537	6,433	2,500	49	2,296	14,738	2,485	2,994	2,078	1,003	8,735	6,200	1,041	3,375	856	92,502
1985	31,839	5,846	2,800	170	2,435	13,956	2,206	2,815	2,341	830	6,239	6,400	1,185	3,738	674	89,747
1986	32,384	6,446	2,900	204	2,231	14,835	2,600	3,022	2,322	650	6,964	6,275	1,242	3,731	510	92,534
1987	34,102	6,567	3,200	196	2,467	16,282	2,785	3,101	2,816	635	7,660	5,700	1,391	2,581	576	96,517
1988	36,192	8,083	2,300	285	2,433	15,624	1,339	2,593	3,961	513	7,305	5,500	1,403	3,434	588	103,105
1989	38,584	8,665	2,388	347	2,550	15,792	1,321	2,644	4,471	862	9,601	5,500	1,548	3,530	670	103,722
1990	41,391	9,678	2,400	381	2,496	15,772	1,424	2,559	4,852	1,206	10,921	5,500	1,430	3,283	495	109,042
1991	40,503	10,414	2,600	353	2,133	15,466	2,204	2,037	4,735	1,406	11,552	5,000	1,288	3,198	50	107,916
1992	39,746	9,366	2,700	338	2,042	13,773	2,376	1,721	4,898	804	11,302	4,000	1,246	3,250	50	101,145
1993[1]	41,900	9,357	2,900	424	1,700	14,100	2,126	1,600	5,223	1,320	11,307	4,000	1,165	3,400	45	105,550
1994[2]	42,000	9,400			2,000	14,000	2,100	1,000	5,300	12,000				3,200		110,000

[1] Preliminary.   [2] Estimate.   [3] Dry Bauxite equivalent of ore processed.   [4] Formerly part of the U.S.S.R.; data not reported separetely until 1992.
Source: U.S. Bureau of Mines

U.S. Salient Statistics of Bauxite   In Thousands of Metric Tons

Year	Net Import Reliance as a % of Apparent Consumption	Average Price F.O.B. Mine $ per Ton	Mine Production Crude	Mine Production Dried Equivalent	Consumption by Industry Total	Consumption by Industry Alumina	Consumption by Industry Abrasive	Consumption by Industry Chemical	Consumption by Industry Refractory	Dry Equivalent Imports[3] (for Consumption)	Dry Equivalent Exports[4]	Dry Equivalent Consumption	Stocks, December 31 Producers and Consumers	Stocks, December 31 Govt.	Stocks, December 31 Total
1983	96	13-20	826	679	9,100	8,275	135	281	362	7,601	104	9,100	5,613	16,326	21,939
1984	96	13-20	1,054	856	10,519	9,465	328	251	420	9,435	110	10,519	4,881	17,338	22,219
1985	96	13-20	787	674	8,206	7,219	305	219	408	7,158	69	8,206	3,643	18,357	22,000
1986	96	13-17	617	510	6,901	5,980	259	231	372	6,456	85	6,901	3,319	18,472	21,791
1987	96	13-17	689	576	9,548	8,601	224	243	422	9,156	231	9,548	3,019	18,472	21,491
1988	97	13-17	714	588	10,074	8,970	274	236	524	9,944	71	10,074	3,021	18,474	21,495
1989	96	15-20	W	670	11,810	10,782	275	223	407	10,893	44	11,810	2,891	18,474	21,365
1990	98	15-20	W	495	12,042	11,064	276	212	387	12,144	74	12,042	2,318	18,477	20,795
1991	100	15-18	W	50	12,204	11,383	204	218	328	11,871	51	12,204	2,620	18,477	21,097
1992	100	15-18	W	50	11,873	11,066	223	190	334	10,939	63	11,873	2,319	17,805	20,124
1993[1]	100	15-24	W	45	11,917	11,002	203	225	429	11,621	90	11,917	1,045	16,938	17,983
1994[2]	99	15-18	W							11,200	150		2,200		

[1] Preliminary.   [2] Estomate.   [3] Including Concentrates.   W=Witheld to avoid disclosing company proprietary data.   *Source: Bureau of Mines*

11

Bismuth

Bismuth finds a wide variety of uses ranging from glass ceramics to pharmaceutical compounds to chemicals and pigments. Bismuth is used for treating stomach ulcers and is found in household pharmaceuticals like Pepto Bismol. In recent years, bismuth has been of interest as a non-toxic substitute for lead in many metallurgical and chemical applications. Bismuth is being tested as an additive to brass for plumbing fixtures, and there has been research into using it for shotgun pellets for hunting water fowl. Because of the limited supply of bismuth, neither of these applications is likely to find extensive usage. The U.S. Bureau of Mines has estimated that world production of bismuth would have to double just to meet the substitution for lead in plumbing fixtures.

Two companies have begun producing lead-free ceramic glazes containing bismuth for use on china and tableware. Glazes and enamels were also in use for decorative glass-coatings for automobiles and buildings. The bismuth glazes were shown to have the same durability as those with lead, while the manufacturing waste would not have to be treated as hazardous.

Domestic consumption of bismuth metal during the January-June 1994 period was 756,340 kilograms (bismuth content). Consumption in the second-quarter jumped 16 percent over the first-quarter. For all of 1993, consumption of bismuth was 1.46 million kilograms. Bismuth metals find use in chemicals which include cosmetic pigments, laboratory and industrial chemicals and pharmaceuticals. For the first half of 1994, bismuth metal used in chemicals was 383,804 kilograms or almost 51 percent of total consumption.

U.S. imports of bismuth metal for consumption over the first five-months of 1994 were 633,082 kilograms. During all of 1993, imports were 1.33 million kilograms. Mexico is by far the largest supplier of bismuth metal to the U.S. For January-May 1994, Mexico exported 241,132 kilograms of bismuth metal to the U.S.

Belgium exported 206,544 kilograms over the same period. Other suppliers included Peru, Canada and the United Kingdom. Imports of bismuth from China have posted a significant decline in 1994. Over the first five-months, China shipped only 16,916 kilograms of bismuth metal to the U.S. For all of 1993, China exported 264,369 kilograms. The U.S. Bureau of Mines reports that Chinese bismuth production in 1994 was likely to decline from 1993 because of several factors. The first is a reduction tungsten production, from which bismuth is recovered as a byproduct. China was also expected to have increased domestic consumption and sever flooding halted shipments. This resulted in a significant increase in bismuth prices in July 1994 on the order of 60 percent.

U.S. exports of bismuth, bismuth alloys and waste and scrap for the January-May 1994 period totaled 79,102 kilograms. This represents a substantial increase over 1993. For all of 1993, exports were only 70,070 kilograms. The difference is due to the situation in China. In 1993, the U.S. exported no bismuth or bismuth products to China. The other major export destination was Belgium. In the January-March 1994 period, the U.S. exported 35,084 kilograms of bismuth and bismuth products, while for all of 1993 the total was 38,478 kilograms.

In Japan, three major producers of lead announced that they would stop production by the end of 1994. All three companies recovered bismuth as a byproduct. This leaves only one significant producer of bismuth in Japan according to the Metal Bulletin (London).

World Production of Bismuth   In Metric Tons

| | ---- Mine Output, Metal Content ---- | | | | | | | | ---- Refined Metal ---- | | | | | | |
Year	Australia	Canada	China	Japan	Rep. of Korea	Mexico	Peru	Total	Belgium	China	Kazak-hastan[3]	Japan	Mexico	Peru	United Kingdom	Total
1988	400	181	750	160	132	958	363	3,220	795	750	85	524	622	341	300	3,669
1989	500	205	850	150	96	883	687	3,750	800	850	85	502	597	646	200	3,970
1990	400	87	1,000	133	79	733	555	3,375	750	1,000	80	442	549	521	125	3,882
1991	400	65	1,260	138	42	651	610	3,451	700	1,260	70	461	500	576	100	3,914
1992	300	224	1,200	159	9	807	550	3,164	700	1,200	35	530	550	418	100	3,767
1993[1]	-----	173	1,300	147	5	997	550	3,351	700	1,300	30	490	650	420	-----	3,762
1994[2]		150	1,100	140		1,000	500	3,100								

[1] Preliminary.   [2] Estimate.   [3] Formerly part of the U.S.S.R.; data not reported separately until 1992.   *Source: U.S. Bureau of Mines*

U.S. Salient Statistics of Bismuth   In Metric Tons

| | ---- Bismuth Consumed, By Uses ---- | | | | | | | Imports of Metallic Bismuth from | | | | Dealer Price $ Per Pound |
Year	Metallurgical Additives	Other Alloys & Uses	Fusible Alloys	Chemicals[3]	Total Consumption	Consumer Stocks Dec. 31	Exports of Metal & Alloys	Belgium	Mexico	Peru	Total	
1985	303	19	277	601	1,199	230	122	209.0	307.6	78.6	907	5.18
1986	350	21	290	663	1,324	346	42	384.4	362.9	107.0	1,129	3.25
1987	494	22	334	748	1,597	294	38	435.0	391.3	440.4	1,581	3.65
1988	493	27	332	679	1,531	433	147	340.2	448.5	188.9	1,641	5.78
1989	396	25	272	659	1,352	440	122	835.7	390.8	271.4	1,880	5.76
1990	424	24	249	577	1,274	344	122	668.1	404.8	262.7	1,612	3.56
1991	341	26	271	789	1,427	325	75	345.1	535.0	169.8	1,411	3.00
1992	381	33	278	758	1,450	253	90	467.4	550.5	75.7	1,621	2.66
1993[1]	392	59	255	749	1,455	330	70	275.1	479.1	117.2	1,335	2.50
1994[2]	402	39	253	796	1,490	425	127	453.7	610.2	114.9	1,505	4.10

[1] Preliminary.   [2] Estimate.   [3] Includes pharmaceuticals.   *Source: U.S. Bureau of Mines*

Broilers

U.S. broiler production appears to be expanding at a 5% annual rate. The steady growth reflects strong retail and food service demand, record exports, and positive net returns to producers owing to lower feed costs. 1994 production of 23.7 billion pounds compares with 22.2 billion in 1993 and 21 billion in 1992. Another 5% gain is forecast for 1995, which if realized would lift production to about 25 billion pounds. Still, producers cannot lapse into complacency. Competition from red meat pressured the domestic broiler market at times in 1994; in mid-October the boneless skinless breast price sagged about 20% from the year earlier level due to competitively priced beef and pork. Despite the late 1994 slippage, prices averaged approximately 56¢ per pound for the year, compared with the 1989 record level of 60¢ per pound. Price forecasts for 1995 average between 50¢ and 54¢ per pound.

1994 U.S. broiler exports of 2.6 million pounds set a new record, up more than 30% from 1993 and equivalent to almost 10% of production. Export growth continues to be stimulated by attractive prices of U.S. broilers, notably leg quarters. Development of foreign markets by individual companies and joint efforts by groups of companies is also promoting export growth. Exports go to a number of nations, but have generally been paced by Japan and Mexico. A major factor in the export surge of 1994 was the eightfold increase in Russian purchases during January-August. Hong Kong was a major importer in 1994, although they re-export approximately one-half the total to China, where the rapidly growing economy has increased the demand for poultry.

Broiler Supply and Prices in the United States

Year and Quarters	----------Federally Inspected Slaughter----------				Total Production RTC[3] (Mil. Lbs.)	Per Capita Consumption (Pounds)	-----Prices-----	
	Number (Millions)	Average Weight (Pounds)	Liveweight Pounds (Mil. Lbs.)	Certified RTC Weight (Mil. Lbs.)			Farm	Georgia Dock[4]
							-----Cents per Pound-----	
1989	5,499	4.34	23,882	17,334	17,227	66.2	36.00	55.79
1990	5,841	4.37	25,550	18,555	18,430	69.1	32.38	51.39
1991	6,140	4.43	27,171	19,728	19,591	72.3	30.91	49.15
1992	6,425	4.51	28,998	21,052	20,904	75.7	31.85	50.21
1993[1]	6,681	4.56	30,474	22,178	22,015	77.7	34.40	53.65
1994[2]	7,065	4.71	32,753	23,838	23,658	79.4	35.03	54.40
I	1,680	4.66	7826	5,674	5,631	19.4	34.30	53.03
II	1,784	4.60	8211	5,983	5,938	20.0	36.70	57.45
III	1,840	4.58	8450	6,160	6,114	20.7	35.83	55.67
IV	1,760	5.00	8266	6,020	5,975	19.3	33.30	51.46

[1] Preliminary. [2] Estimate. [3] Total production equals federal inspected slaughter plus other slaughter minus cut-up and further processing condemnation.
[4] Ready-to-cook basis. *Source: Economic Research Service*

Salient Broiler Statistics in the United States

Year	Commercial Production		------Average------		Value of Production Mil. $	----------Total Chickens[3] Supply and Distribution----------							
						-----Production-----			Storage Stocks January 1	Exports	Broiler Feed Ratio in Pounds	----Consumption----	
	Number Millions	Liveweight Mil. Lbs.	Liveweight Per Bird Pound	Average Price ¢ / Pound		Federally Inspected	Other Chickens	Total				Total Mil. Lbs.	Per Capita In Lbs.
						----------In Millions of Pounds----------							
1988	5,238	22,464	4.29	33.1	7,435	16,124	12	16,136	202	765	3.1	15,265	56.6
1989	5,517	23,979	4.35	36.6	8,778	17,334	31	17,365	179	814	3.0	16,371	58.5
1990	5,864	25,631	4.37	32.6	8,365	18,555	29	18,583	221	1,143	3.0	17,266	60.9
1991	6,137	27,203	4.43	30.8	8,383	19,728	32	19,760	242	1,261	3.0	18,271	63.6
1992	6,402	28,829	4.50	31.8	9,174	21,052	36	21,088	300	1,489	3.0	19,347	63.6
1993[1]	6,689	30,592	4.57	34.0	10,409	22,178	36	22,214	368	1,966	3.1	20,059	66.6
1994[2]	7,569					23,838	39	23,658	358	2,508	3.3	20,733	68.3
											3.3		69.9

[1] Preliminary. [2] Estimate. [3] Ready-to-cook. [4] Retail weight basis. *Source: Economic Research Service, U.S. Department of Agriculture*

Average Wholesale Broiler Prices RTC (Ready-to-Cook)

Year	January	February	March	April	May	June	July	August	September	October	November	December	Average
1988	43.86	44.89	48.37	48.66	56.55	61.46	66.54	68.86	62.77	57.69	57.14	58.81	56.30
1989	57.95	58.04	62.10	63.54	70.40	67.36	62.01	57.29	59.87	51.71	49.21	48.40	58.99
1990	51.70	57.37	60.39	55.28	57.93	56.44	59.47	54.89	57.35	48.79	48.02	49.63	54.77
1991	51.72	50.63	51.41	51.96	52.03	52.66	54.25	54.61	53.61	51.61	50.30	49.54	52.03
1992	50.14	50.28	50.24	49.45	55.06	52.38	56.04	56.13	51.29	53.67	54.98	51.17	52.57
1993	52.14	53.01	54.02	54.66	57.86	55.04	55.36	57.77	57.59	55.72	55.82	53.17	55.18
1994[1]	52.67	55.22	57.51	57.80	61.39	60.71	57.34	54.65	55.80	54.02	50.50	50.93	55.71

[1] Preliminary. *Source: Economic Research Service, U.S. Department of Agriculture*

Butter

U.S. butter production appears to have peaked in 1992 when 619,000 metric tons were produced. Production has since slipped, totaling 597,000 tons in 1993 and 585,000 tons in 1994, the lowest total since 1988. However, U.S. consumption of butter in the 1990's has maintained an upward trend; domestic use in 1994 was placed at 558,000 tons vs. 533,000 in 1993, and an average in 1990 and 1991 near 490,000 tons. Still, since the late 1980's, new supply has consistently outpaced domestic usage, although some of the slack has been absorbed by export demand. U.S. butter stocks, much of which is government owned, have recently-traversed a wide range; from a high at the end of 1991 of 206,000 tons to an estimated 50,000 at year-end 1994. U.S. per capita butter use, which slipped in the early 1990's to an estimated 4.3 pounds from 4.6 pounds in the 1980's, shows signs of picking up again, possibly to the 1980's level.

Butter production is derived directly from milk production. In 1994, U.S. milk output was estimated at 69.4 million metric tons, up 1% from 1993's total of 68.5 million. The increase does not reflect larger dairy herd numbers, which on balance had been declining, but more milk output per cow. By late 1994, however, cow numbers were estimated at less than 1% under a year earlier, a considerably slower decline than the near 2% drop in late 1993 and early 1994. If the trend continues, expect increased butter production in 1995. Butter manufacture is the third largest use of milk production, the first being milk as a fluid and secondly, its conversion into cheese.

Russia is the world's largest butter producer, accounting for about 15 percent of the 1994 global output of 5.4 million metric tons, followed by the U.S. with more than 10 percent. France and Germany are also large producers. Statistically, however, India shows the largest production, 1.1 million tons in 1994, but their product is mostly Ghee, a butter-like substance. World consumption almost mirrors production: India is first, Russia second, but Germany's use at times tops the U.S. for the third position. Global foreign trade in butter tends to be small. U.S. imports are insignificant, but exports totaled 161,000 tons in 1993 and 90,000 tons in 1994. Foreign demand for U.S. butter could quicken in 1995 as world stocks are relatively low. Import demand from the Middle East and North Africa may pick up after being weak for several years. However, the key to increased demand may rest with the former Soviet Union and how much they can afford to buy, as the world supply of sharply discounted butter has been greatly curtailed.

Wholesale butter prices in 1993 (Grade A, Chicago) averaged less than $.75 per pound in 1993, well under the 1980's which averaged more than $1.25 per pound. Prices trended even lower in 1994 with the year's average less than $.70. The downward pressure appears likely to persist into 1995; much will depend on how much butter the Government takes off and/or adds to the market. Early signs suggest that USDA purchases may be smaller than seen in recent years. In contrast, the industry was accustomed to drawing upon Government stocks to adjust supplies to market needs, a supply source that may now be tightening.

Supply and Distribution of Butter in the United States   In Millions of Pounds

	--------------------Supply--------------------				--Distribution--									------93 Score------	
		Cold Storage Stocks[3] Jan.1[6]			-Domestic Disappearance-					-Department of Agriculture-				AA Wholesale Price California Chicago	
Year	Production		Imports	Total Supply	Total	Donated	Pounds per capita	Exports	Ship-ments[4]	Jan. 1 Stocks[5]	Dec. 31 Stocks[5]	Removed by USDA	Total Use	Dollars per Pound	
1987	1,104	252	5	1,361	1,132	231	4.7	81	1	220	96	187.3	1,214	1.6748	1.4172
1988	1,208	147	5	1,359	1,102	195	4.5	41	1	96	173	312.6	1,144	1.6097	1.3412
1989	1,295	215	5	1,515	1,077	214	4.4	159	4	173	223	413.4	1,240	1.5660	1.2951
1990	1,302	256	5	1,582	1,095	182	4.4	68	2	223	373	400.3	1,165	1.3050	1.0346
1991	1,336	417	5	1,759	1,063	132	4.2	145	1	373	511	442.8	1,209	1.2856	1.0182
1992[1]	1,365	550	4	1,919	1,070	119	4.2	351	1	511	430	439.5	1,464	1.1386	.8427
1993[2]	1,315	455	4	1,774	1,175	149	4.5	354	1	430	432	288.8	1,530		

[1] Preliminary.   [2] Estimates.   [3] Includes butter equivalent.   [4] Includes USDA shipments to territories.   [5] Includes butteroil.   [6] Includes stocks held by USDA.   *Source: Economic Research Service, U.S. Department of Agriculture*

Commercial Disappearance of Creamery Butter in the U.S.   In Millions of Pounds

Year	First Quarter	Second Quarter	Third Quarter	Fourth Quarter	Total	Year	First Quarter	Second Quarter	Third Quarter	Fourth Quarter	Total
1983	209.5	198.6	217.0	256.6	881.7	1989	188.3	145.6	228.8	291.3	854.1
1984	194.0	241.3	215.6	251.9	902.7	1990	197.5	218.1	218.1	281.8	915.2
1985	200.0	203.9	241.5	272.9	918.2	1991	186.8	184.0	255.6	276.5	903.5
1986	198.6	220.1	234.4	269.8	922.9	1992	214.4	216.5	236.9	276.3	944.1
1987	222.7	222.1	218.4	239.3	902.5	1993	241.9	231.6	271.7	311.6	1,056.8
1988	194.5	221.6	219.7	274.0	909.8	1994[1]	261.7	254.9	287.5	292.4	1,096.5

[1] Preliminary.   *Source: Economic Research Service, U.S. Department of Agriculture*

World (Total) Butter[3] Production   In Thousands of Metric Tons

Year	Argen-tina	Australia	Brazil	Canada	Former Czecho-slovakia	Denmark	France	Ger-many[4]	India	Ireland	Japan	Nether-lands	New Zealand	Poland	Russia[5]	Sweden	Ukraine[5]	United Kingdom	United States
1984	29	111	70	119	152	104	621	572	690	171	78	241	287	322	------	77	1,588	205	500
1985	32	114	70	108	150	110	595	515	700	163	89	306	293	308	------	74	1,596	202	566
1986	32	105	65	109	156	112	633	567	720	160	88	377	299	289	------	66	1,700	222	545
1987	34	104	65	95	149	96	569	553	750	150	69	234	248	293	------	64	1,742	174	501
1988	35	98	65	105	148	94	521	585	850	139	68	214	276	293	------	61	1,724	140	547
1989	45	96	65	99	156	92	525	711	880	156	78	213	246	325	820	70	441	130	588
1990	40	111	75	100	159	93	514	640	970	159	76	209	276	300	833	76	444	138	591
1991	38	111	70	97	136	71	496	555	1,020	146	76	196	269	220	729	63	376	112	606
1992	37	116	65	86	118	62	453	474	1,060	142	95	191	268	180	762	65	345	99	619
1993[1]	48	131	68	87	115	59	445	480	1,110	135	108	193	267	165	716	69	325	108	597
1994[2]	53	146	70	90		58	450	460	1,110	134	85	190	289	160	670	72	310	98	585

[1] Preliminary.   [2] Forecast.   [3] Factory (including creameries and dairies) and farm.   [4] Includes the former East Germany after 1988.   [5] Formerly part of the U.S.S.R.; data not reported seperately until 1989.   *Source: Foreign Agricultural Service, U.S. Department of Agriculture*

Production of Creamery Butter in Factories in the United States   In Millions of Pounds

Year	January	February	March	April	May	June	July	August	September	October	November	December	Total
1984	127.3	108.9	107.6	103.0	105.1	81.8	72.7	70.2	67.5	84.4	79.8	95.1	1,103.4
1985	116.8	104.6	105.9	111.4	112.9	95.6	92.4	92.1	92.1	109.3	99.4	115.4	1,247.9
1986	136.7	119.3	119.2	122.7	114.7	93.0	79.7	69.9	80.2	85.3	80.3	101.3	1,202.3
1987	111.9	97.4	105.4	102.6	98.2	81.5	75.2	66.4	77.9	91.2	87.9	108.5	1,104.1
1988	126.1	119.7	115.5	113.8	108.0	90.8	76.3	74.1	83.3	92.3	95.6	112.0	1,207.5
1989	129.0	124.7	135.7	124.7	122.5	95.3	72.2	80.1	81.6	95.1	94.4	107.4	1,262.7
1990	134.0	127.3	136.2	125.6	118.6	96.7	84.6	84.2	83.4	106.7	110.1	112.2	1,319.6
1991	142.1	126.3	131.6	133.7	126.0	98.3	88.9	85.0	84.7	105.2	108.5	130.1	1,360.4
1992	156.0	132.0	129.9	119.7	118.2	103.0	97.8	86.7	96.6	101.6	98.3	119.8	1,365.2
1993[1]	144.4	138.9	139.1	121.8	116.4	102.3	86.2	80.7	86.3	97.8	97.3	120.3	1,315.2
1994[2]	131.8	119.6	117.8	119.3	118.8	102.4	86.2	88.7	90.6	101.5	101.8	118.7	1,297.2

[1] Preliminary.   [2] Estimate.   *Source: Economic Research Service, U.S. Department of Agriculture*

Cold Storage Holdings of Creamery Butter in the U.S. on First of Month   In Millions of Pounds

Year	January	February	March	April	May	June	July	August	September	October	November	December
1984	499.4	510.6	532.5	529.3	532.4	538.5	516.7	489.6	462.7	426.3	374.3	335.9
1985	296.6	277.3	289.4	291.7	272.7	283.2	286.8	280.7	264.6	247.0	231.6	206.9
1986	205.5	206.3	242.4	283.3	305.0	330.8	342.8	337.6	304.4	279.6	253.3	218.5
1987	193.0	206.6	231.6	254.0	247.9	251.1	237.9	211.2	187.3	176.2	165.6	158.5
1988	143.2	157.3	198.9	221.1	240.4	280.5	293.4	295.8	294.4	253.4	237.3	226.2
1989	214.7	246.6	314.4	341.9	377.2	438.3	464.1	461.3	439.7	407.9	370.6	294.1
1990	256.2	269.7	293.8	335.4	358.8	399.6	420.0	420.8	427.9	412.3	413.6	407.6
1991	416.1	470.8	524.8	555.9	620.5	646.7	662.7	659.8	629.4	597.2	567.1	539.4
1992	539.4	565.4	624.8	645.3	678.7	712.6	747.0	755.8	705.7	608.1	541.7	487.6
1993	447.7	489.1	492.5	515.6	552.7	559.0	569.0	516.4	473.3	395.4	341.1	276.3
1994[1]	234.7	251.0	243.2	253.5	265.7	281.4	275.1	245.9	206.6	163.4	124.6	84.5

[1] Preliminary.   *Source: Agricultural Statistics Board, U.S.Department of Agriculture*

Wholesale Price of 92 Score Creamery (Grade A) Butter at Chicago   In Cents Per Pound

Year	January	February	March	April	May	June	July	August	September	October	November	December	Average
1984	140.4	141.3	142.1	142.9	142.9	150.0	155.6	150.6	158.1	158.1	158.1	145.6	148.8
1985	141.5	141.3	141.3	141.9	141.9	141.9	141.5	140.7	141.2	141.6	139.5	139.1	141.1
1986	138.8	138.8	137.5	138.8	138.8	139.1	143.7	153.9	154.2	153.5	151.9	145.5	144.5
1987	137.3	136.8	137.8	138.8	138.4	144.6	149.0	148.1	145.3	136.8	135.6	134.0	140.2
1988	131.9	131.0	131.0	131.0	131.0	133.5	135.9	135.6	134.3	132.0	131.3	131.3	132.5
1989	131.0	131.0	131.0	131.0	131.0	131.0	130.3	132.8	125.1	120.5	120.5	120.0	127.9
1990	110.9	108.3	108.3	106.9	99.0	98.4	100.3	98.9	98.9	98.9	98.9	98.0	102.1
1991	97.3	97.3	97.3	97.3	97.3	98.6	98.9	98.9	100.7	106.3	104.6	98.4	99.3
1992	94.9	86.3	86.3	86.3	83.8	76.6	76.6	76.6	81.7	82.2	80.7	78.6	82.5
1993	75.3	75.3	75.3	75.3	75.3	76.2	73.5	74.6	74.3	74.2	73.6	69.7	74.4
1994	64.0	64.0	65.5	65.5	64.5	65.1	66.9	71.5	71.5	71.5	71.5	67.0	67.4

Source: Economic Research Service, U.S. Department of Agriculture

Cadmium

Cadmium is a rare chemical element that is the by-product of the smelting and refining of zinc ores. It is used primarily for plating of iron and steel to protect them from corrosion. Due to the cost of waste disposal and assorted problems because of its toxicity, the use of cadmium in electroplating has decreased. Because of environmental concerns, the outlook for cadmium usage is not bright. Cadmium is highly toxic and its disposal is problematic. Approximately 50% of cadmium usage is in battery production with 15% used for coatings and plating, 18% in pigments, 12% in alloys, and 12% in plastics and synthetic products. There were three companies in the U.S. which recovered cadmium as a by-product of smelting zinc concentrates, while a fourth company recovered cadmium from other sources.

Domestic production of primary and secondary cadmium metal in 1993 totaled 1,094 metric tonnes. This represented a significant decline from 1992 when production totaled 1,620 tonnes. Shipments of cadmium metal by producers in 1993 totaled 1,304 tonnes, down 37% from the 1992 total of 2,075 tonnes. U.S. production of cadmium sulfide in 1993 was 341 tonnes, a 26% increase from the 1992 total of 270 tonnes. Production of other cadmium compounds including oxide and plating salts was 731 tonnes, 32% less than in 1992.

Stocks of cadmium on January 1, 1993 were 868 tonnes.

With production of 1,094 tonnes and metal imports for consumption of 1,415 tonnes, the total supply was 3,377 tonnes. Exports were minimal at only 11 tonnes. Cadmium stocks on December 31, 1994 were 770 tonnes. Total apparent consumption of cadmium in 1993 was 2,596 tonnes, down 23% from 1992.

U.S. imports of cadmium metal in 1993 were 1,415 tonnes, valued at $1.69 million. Imports were 28% less than in 1992. The primary exporter was Canada with 614 tonnes. The second largest supplier was Mexico with 332 tonnes while Belgium exported 178 tonnes to the U.S.

World refinery production of cadmium in 1993 was 18,913 tonnes, down 6% from 1992. The major producer was Japan at 2,800 tonnes. Canada produced 1,944 tonnes while China produced 1,300 tonnes.

In 1993, the New York dealer average price per pound of cadmium was 45 cents, down sharply from 91 cents in 1992 and $6.28 in 1989.

According to the U.S. Bureau of Mines, while cadmium finds a wide range of uses, it is being used more and more in technologically sophisticated equipment such as helium-cadmium lasers and cadmium-telluride based solar cells. Advanced solar cells incorporating cadmium have tremendous potential as both terrestrial and extraterrestrial power sources.

World Refinery Production of Cadmium   In Metric Tons

Year	Australia	Belgium	Canada	China	Finland	France	Germany	Italy	Japan	Kazakhstan[4]	Mexico	Norway	Poland	United Kingdom	United States[3]	Zaire	World Total
1984	1,082	1,472	1,605	300	614	568	1,111	452	2,423	3,000	838	150	570	390	1,686	318	19,436
1985	910	1,252	1,717	540	565	337	1,095	526	2,535	3,000	734	159	600	370	1,603	296	18,924
1986	915	1,374	1,484	650	522	431	1,218	411	2,489	3,000	1,016	154	600	379	1,486	364	19,070
1987	944	1,308	1,481	680	690	457	1,125	320	2,450	3,000	935	147	600	498	1,515	299	19,066
1988	855	1,836	1,694	750	703	558	1,186	686	2,614	3,000	1,117	169	642	399	1,885	281	21,869
1989	696	1,764	1,620	800	612	170	1,234	776	2,694	3,000	976	207	555	395	1,550	224	20,873
1990	638	1,956	1,470	1,100	569	187	990	691	2,451	2,800	882	286	373	438	1,678	127	19,953
1991	1,076	1,807	1,829	1,200	593	271	1,060	658	2,889	2,500	688	227	364	449	1,676	65	20,463
1992	1,001	1,550	1,963	1,200	590	250	941	742	2,986	1,000	602	247	370	383	1,620	84	20,201
1993[1]	996	1,550	1,944	1,300	600	140	1,060	585	2,800	1,000	797	250	350	360	1,094	50	18,913
1994[2]	1,000	1,600	1,900						2,800		800				1,000		18,000

[1] Preliminary.   [2] Estimate.   [3] Primary and secondary metal.   [4] Formerly part of the U.S.S.R.; data not reported separately until 1992.
Source: U.S. Bureau of Mines

Salient Statistics of Cadmium in the United States   In Metric Tons of Contained Cadmium

Year	Net Import Reliance as a % of Apparent Consumption	Production (Metal)	Producer Shipments	Cadmium Sulfide Producton	Production Other Compounds	Imports of Cadmium Metal[3]	Exports[4]	Apparent Consumption	Industry Stocks December 31[5]	New York Dealer Price $ Per Pound[6]
1985	57	1,603	1,791	477	1,459	1,988	86	3,720	686	.92
1986	66	1,486	2,030	645	1,511	3,174	38	4,385	923	1.07
1987	64	1,515	1,916	540	1,497	2,701	241	4,178	720	1.60
1988	64	1,885	2,074	345	1,451	2,482	613	3,620	854	6.91
1989	48	1,550	2,015	267	1,451	2,787	369	4,096	726	6.28
1990	46	1,678	1,855	228	1,144	1,741	385	3,113	653	3.38
1991	50	1,676	1,736	263	1,089	2,040	158	3,369	835	2.01
1992	52	1,620	2,075	270	1,073	1,958	178	3,367	868	.91
1993[1]	61	1,094	1,304	341	731	1,415	11	2,596	770	.45
1994[2]	50	1,000				1,150	490	2,020	700	1.03

[1] Preliminary.   [2] Estimate.   [3] For Consumption.   [4] Cadmium Metal, alloys, dross, flue dust.   [5] Metallic, Compounds, Distributors (including in compounds from 1985).   [6] Sticks and Balls in 1 to 5 short ton lots.   Source: U.S. Bureau of Mines

Cassava

Cassava, or tapioca root, is used primarily as an animal feed and as a foodstuff in tropical countries. Cassava is looked upon as a possible solution to world hunger problems, and advances in technology hold the promise of increasing yields. Reports of new strains of cassava root being developed in Africa could in time prove to be important weapons in the fight against hunger. The possibility that cassava yields could be doubled would be an important improvement in productivity.

The Food and Agricultural Organization of the United Nations estimates that world production of cassava in 1993 was 153.6 million tonnes. This represents an increase of less than 1% from 1992. Harvested acreage was just over 16 million hectares while the yield was 9,601 kilograms per hectare. Both acreage and yields increased marginally. Most of the world's production of cassava occurs in Africa. For 1993, African production was estimated at 74.8 million tonnes, almost half of the world total. Over the 1979-81 period, cassava production in Africa averaged 49.1 million tonnes. The major producing country for cassava was Nigeria with 1993 output forecast at 21 million tonnes, down 2% from 1992. The other major producing country in Africa was Zaire with a crop of 20.8 million tonnes, up over 3% from 1992. Other important African producers of cassava were Tanzania, Uganda, Ghana and Mozambique.

Very little cassava is produced in North and Central America with the largest producers being Haiti and Cuba. South America, which contributes about 18% of the world total, is forecast to produce 27.5 million tonnes in 1993, nearly the same as the year before. By far the largest producing country is Brazil with 21.7 million tonnes in 1993, down 1% from 1992.

Asia, where cassava yields are the highest in the world, contributes about a third to the world production total with 1993 output of 50.2 million tonnes. The major producing country is Thailand which in 1993 had output of 19.6 million tonnes, down 1%. Indonesia, the other major producer, had a crop of 16.4 million tonnes, about the same as in 1992.

World trade in tapioca pellets and chips fell in 1993 to 8.3 million tonnes, down 14% from the 9.6 million tonnes exported in 1992, and 11% below the annual average of 9.3 million tonnes. The reason for the decline was a sharp drop in exports from Thailand. Thailand is a major producer and exporter of tapioca pellets and chips. Imports of tapioca pellets and chips also saw declines in South Korea to 658,000 tonnes, down 25% from 1992; Taiwan 58,000 tonnes, down 61%; Japan 151,000 tonnes, down 17%. Other Asian countries imports were 664,000 tonnes, down 25%. Imports of tapioca by the U.S. and Mexico also declined. Imports of tapioca by the European Union registered their third consecutive increase to 6.6 million tonnes, up 2% from the previous year.

World Cassava Production   In Thousands of Metric Tons

Year	Brazil	China	Columbia	Ghana	India	Indonesia	Mada-gascar	Mozam-bique	Nigeria	Paraguay	Phillipines	Tanzania	Thailand	Uganda	Viet Nam	Zaire	World Total
1989	23,668	3,320	1,509	3,327	4,833	17,117	2,277	4,000	15,425	3,978	1,873	7,792	15,128	3,568	2,585	17,400	151,773
1990	24,322	3,216	1,939	2,717	4,962	15,830	2,292	4,056	19,043	3,550	1,854	6,922	20,701	3,339	2,276	17,600	149,844
1991	24,538	3,310	1,645	3,600	5,416	15,954	2,307	3,690	20,000	2,585	1,816	7,460	20,356	3,229	2,455	19,500	153,562
1992	21,919	3,357	1,651	4,000	5,469	16,318	2,320	3,239	21,320	2,591	1,798	7,112	19,767	2,892	2,568	20,210	152,558
1993[1]	21,719	3,406	1,723	4,200	5,340	16,356	2,350	3,511	21,000	2,680	1,800	6,833	19,610	3,982	2,631	20,835	153,628

[1] Estimate.   Source: Food and Agricultural Organization of the United Nations

Prices of Tapioca, Hard Pellets, F.O.B. Rotterdam   U.S. Dollars Per Tonne

Year	January	February	March	April	May	June	July	August	September	October	November	December	Average
1991	187	186	163	160	168	158	158	177	187	187	202	197	178
1992	197	184	179	177	179	181	184	192	195	187	172	170	183
1993	160	150	140	149	145	133	130	131	136	127	120	125	137
1994	122	123	128	133	138	141	147	154	158	161	161	161	144

Source: Oil World

World Trade in Tapioca   In Thousands of Metric Tons

	Exports					Imports						
Year	China	Indonesia	Thailand	Viet Nam	Total World Exports	China	EC-12[2]	Japan	Republic of Korea	United States	Former U.S.S.R.	Total World Imports
1987	310	783	5,777	32	7,347	-----	7,141	34	138	-----	-----	7,484
1988	334	830	7,647	18	9,102	60	6,795	180	356	24	772	9,034
1989	251	1,146	9,231	42	10,910	529	6,777	279	685	185	797	10,478
1990	198	1,271	7,556	20	9,298	573	5,541	221	763	179	855	9,222
1991	410	859	6,187	3	7,674	175	6,150	162	444	127	-----	7,942
1992	316	873	8,045	32	9,572	230	6,506	181	876	217	22	9,454
1993[1]	266	936	6,707	38	8,310	150	6,636	151	658	60	8	8,722

[1] Estimate.   [2] Excluding trade between the EEC members.   Source: Oil World

Castor Beans

World production of castor beans in 1993 was estimated to be 1.25 million tonnes, over 10 percent more than the previous season, according to the Food and Agricultural Organization of the United Nations. In 1991, production was 1.2 million tonnes. By far the largest producer was India with output of 700,000 tonnes, some 13 percent more than in 1992. China is the next largest producer with a crop of 300,000 tonnes, up 11 percent from the prior season. China is becoming a larger producer in the castor bean market and is the largest exporter of castor beans. China is expanding acreage and has some of the highest yields in the world. Brazil is the third largest producer of castor beans. In 1993, production was put at 104,000 tonnes, up almost 2 percent from the previous season. Brazil's production has been in a general decline for several seasons.

Castor oil production for the October 1994-September 1995 season was forecast to be 465,000 tonnes. That represents an increase of almost 4 percent from the 1993/94 season. The major producing country was India with 281,000 tonnes. Chinese production was put at 97,000 tonnes while Brazilian output was 25,000 tonnes. World trade in castor oil was forecast at 191,000 tonnes. India is the largest exporter with 158,000 tonnes. Global use of castor oil was estimated at 453,000 tonnes. India was the largest consumer at 118,000 tonnes. Global ending stocks were placed at 72,000 tonnes.

World Production of Castorseed Beans — In Thousands of Metric Tons

Crop Year	Brazil	China	Ecuador	Ethiopia	India	Mexico	Paraguay	Pakistan	Phillipines	Romania	Sudan	Tanzania	Thailand	Former U.S.S.R.	World Total
1988-9	146	260	6	1	417	4	23	14	5	9	2	1	31	60	1,008
1989-90	128	270	7	1	517	4	41	10	7	7	2	2	29	43	1,099
1990-1	148	315	7	1	716	----	37	12	7	2	7	3	15	36	1,336
1991-2	133	310	5	1	575	1	33	13	7	1	6	3	13	32	1,163
1992-3[1]	135	270	12	1	700	1	20	14	7	1	6	3	10	20	1,230
1993-4[2]	60	300	13	1	670	1	10	14	7	1	6	3	9	4	1,130

[1] Preliminary.   [2] Estimate.   Sources: Foreign Agricultural Service, U.S. Department of Agriculture; Oil World

Castor Oil Consumption[2] in the United States — In Thousands of Pounds

Crop Year	October	November	December	January	February	March	April	May	June	July	August	September	Total
1988-9	5,720	6,565	5,018	5,539	4,665	5,424	5,062	4,827	4,914	3,155	5,680	2,644	59,213
1989-90	4,325	4,570	3,568	4,268	4,487	4,724	4,385	4,436	4,092	3,847	5,156	3,833	51,691
1990-1	3,334	2,815	3,507	----------11,787----------			----------10,958----------			----------11,096----------			44,030
1991-2	----------12,073----------			3,877	2,914	3,766	2,806	3,516	3,606	3,203	3,708	3,019	42,488
1992-3	4,712	3,250	3,100	3,287	4,271	3,924	4,098	3,965	4,496	4,902	5,073	4,400	49,478
1993-4[1]	5,046	5,649	5,092	5,510	4,982	5,766	4,548	6,335	5,258	4,603	4,929	4,543	62,261
1994-5[1]	5,032	4,204	6,578										

[1] Preliminary.   [2] In inedible products (Resins, Plastics, etc.).   Source: Bureau of the Census, U.S. Department of Commerce

Castor Oil Stocks in the United States — In Thousands of Pounds

Crop Year	Oct. 1	Nov. 1	Dec. 1	Jan. 1	Feb. 1	Mar. 1	Apr. 1	May 1	June 1	July 1	Aug. 1	Sept. 1
1988-9	9,614	13,826	15,402	14,448	6,738	9,620	13,256	10,794	13,257	13,934	12,898	10,201
1989-90	9,556	11,869	10,486	N.A.	N.A.	13,708	11,852	17,948	21,101	32,992	25,295	26,793
1990-1	18,819	18,118	25,245	-------------17,198-------------			-------------21,714-------------			-------------14,417-------------		
1991-2	-------------22,921-------------			20,382	23,499	17,293	21,511	19,429	13,036	20,383	16,066	11,346
1992-3	7,158	5,383	5,364	4,124	10,076	13,154	19,345	14,983	17,094	24,652	20,616	25,070
1993-4[1]	22,981	21,275	23,482	21,132	29,871	9,946	18,394	25,249	22,550	21,795	27,911	20,950
1994-5[1]	21,066	23,484	44,152	46,581								

[1] Preliminary.   Source: Bureau of the Census, U.S. Department of Commerce

Monthly Average Wholesale Prices of Castor Oil No. 1, Brazilian Tanks at New York — In Cents Per Pound

Year	January	February	March	April	May	June	July	August	September	October	November	December	Average
1988	46.50	46.50	52.50	51.38	49.88	49.50	48.75	48.00	48.00	48.00	48.50	49.00	48.88
1989	51.00	51.75	51.90	51.50	51.50	51.50	51.50	51.50	51.50	51.50	51.50	51.50	51.51
1990	54.50	53.50	52.60	52.00	51.20	51.00	51.00	51.00	51.50	51.50	51.50	51.50	48.70
1991	39.30	36.00	36.75	37.00	37.00	36.50	35.50	35.00	45.00	43.40	39.63	39.63	48.70
1992	37.50	37.50	37.50	36.00	34.50	34.50	34.50	34.50	34.50	34.00	34.00	34.00	35.21
1993	34.00	32.00	32.00	32.00	37.00	37.00	37.00	37.00	38.50	41.50	44.00	44.00	37.17
1994	44.00	42.50	41.00	41.00	46.50	45.00							43.33

Source: Foreign Agricultural Service, U.S.D.A.

Cattle and Calves

The expansion of the U.S. cattle herd carried into its sixth consecutive year during 1994 with the inventory placed at 103.5 million head on January 1, 1995, up 1.7% from a year earlier; the largest herd estimate since the beginning of the 1986 inventory of 105.4 million head. The July 1, 1994, beef cow inventory was estimated at 36.3 million head, up 2.5% from mid-1993, indicating a moderate expansion of the beef herd through 1994, abetted by favorable forage supplies. This was the largest beef cow inventory since 1984. However, a decline in dairy cows which has occurred since 1984 has caused the total cow inventory to fall more than 5% during the ten year period.

In recent years, the dairy sector has been an increasingly important contributor to feeder cattle supplies and nearly every available young animal not retained for the breeding herd is now being placed on feed. Calf slaughter, meanwhile, has declined from near 3.5 million head in the mid-1980's to near 1.2 million. The 1994 calf crop was expected to rise 2% to 40.6 million head, the largest calf crop since 1986, but only 4% over the cyclical peak of 39 million head in 1991.

Following a large slaughter pace in mid-1994 the stage was thought to be set for a seasonal decline in slaughter and rising fed cattle prices. However, the expectations exceeded reality as prices declined into early fall and then recovered only moderately owing to large supplies of beef and record large supplies of competing meats, notably pork at sharply lower prices. Third quarter steer and heifer slaughter was up more than 3% from the large year earlier level, but cow slaughter fell about 7%; average slaughter weights in the quarter were at a record high and about 23 pounds per head above a year earlier. The rise in fourth quarter steer and heifer slaughter relative to 1993 was moderate, but cow slaughter rose about 5%, and average slaughter weight hit a record high for the October-December period. The upward trend in slaughter and average weight is expected to carry into 1995; average dressed weights are estimated at 710 pounds, a shade higher than the record 1994 average.

Beef production in 1994 reached a record 24.1 billion pounds compared with 22.9 billion in 1993. The outlook for 1995 was placed at nearly 24.5 billion pounds, the increase reflecting the large 1994 calf crop and continued large placement of cattle onto feedlots. Despite the U.S. consumer's apparent concern about beef's high cholesterol content, the impact was muted during the past few years by relatively low retail beef prices, aggressive advertising by the beef industry promoting the product, and the stronger U.S. economy. Per capita beef consumption in 1993 of 65.1 pounds was eclipsed by 1994's total of 67.4; a rise to 67.8 pounds is forecast for 1995. Choice steer prices (basis, Nebraska) averaged about $68-$70/cwt. in 1994, vs. $76.36 in 1993; for 1995, the average is forecast at $64-70/cwt. Retail choice beef prices around $2.80 a pound during 1994's third quarter were at a three year low and expected to slide towards $2.70 in 1995.

The U.S. is a net beef and live cattle importer. Beef imports in 1994 of 1.09 million tons approximately equaled 1993's. The 1994 U.S. Voluntary Restraint Agreements (VRA's) with Australia and New Zealand limited 1994 U.S. meat imports from the two countries to 302,000 tons, and 184,000 tons, respectively; the two countries normally supply more than 50% of U.S. beef imports. U.S. beef imports in 1995 are forecast at 1.13 million tons, up 3.5% from 1994. Greater production in Australia, Canada and New Zealand will ensure larger supplies of manufacturing grade beef marketed to the U.S. Beef exports in 1995 are estimated at 721,000 tons, up about 5% from 1994. Larger exports are forecast to Japan, Mexico and Korea. The U.S. imports live cattle from Canada and Mexico and exports much smaller numbers to the same two countries. Most of the Mexican imports are feeder cattle while slaughter ready cattle comes from Canada.

Futures Markets

Live cattle futures and options on futures are traded on the Chicago Mercantile Exchange (CME) with a smaller futures contract on the Midamerica Exchange (MCE). Feeder cattle futures and options are also traded on the CME.

World Cattle and Buffalo Numbers as of January 1   In Thousands of Head

Year	Argentina	Australia	Brazil	Canada	China	Columbia	France	Germany[3]	India	Mexico	Russia[4]	South Africa	Turkey	Ukraine[4]	United Kingdom	United States	World Total (Mil. Head)
1984	54,375	22,161	93,300	11,629	78,084	21,694	23,519	15,552	267,510	33,917	--------	12,125	16,000	119,558	13,131	113,700	1,033
1985	54,684	22,784	94,700	11,330	82,593	21,188	23,102	15,688	271,390	33,853	--------	12,000	15,500	121,055	12,985	109,582	1,041
1986	53,484	23,436	122,463	10,956	86,820	19,904	22,803	15,627	275,340	32,167	--------	11,750	15,000	120,888	12,695	105,378	1,067
1987	51,683	23,540	128,000	10,802	91,670	18,819	22,171	21,109	274,822	33,603	--------	12,002	14,450	122,103	12,476	102,118	1,073
1988	56,482	23,469	130,000	10,756	94,650	18,400	21,053	20,608	268,720	35,378	--------	12,187	14,000	115,824	11,849	99,622	1,070
1989	56,482	23,938	130,500	10,984	97,948	17,627	21,340	20,369	268,470	34,999	59,300	12,675	13,400	25,621	11,902	98,065	1,037
1990	56,482	24,673	140,400	11,220	100,752	16,835	21,394	20,287	270,070	31,747	58,800	13,398	12,700	25,195	11,922	98,162	1,038
1991	56,982	25,026	142,900	11,289	102,884	16,225	21,446	19,488	272,300	29,847	57,000	13,512	12,200	24,623	11,843	98,896	1,038
1992	57,282	25,857	143,600	11,713	104,590	16,008	20,970	17,134	271,200	30,232	54,700	13,311	12,000	23,728	11,623	99,559	1,033
1993	55,577	26,154	145,200	11,786	107,840	16,391	20,383	16,207	271,255	30,649	52,200	13,239	11,900	22,457	11,620	100,611	1,032
1994[1]	54,875	26,775	144,300	12,028	113,160	16,614	20,112	15,897	272,655	30,702	48,900	12,506	11,800	21,607	11,709	101,749	1,034
1995[2]	54,725	26,620	143,710	12,485	119,000	16,886	20,047	15,750	274,155	30,162	45,800	12,630	11,700	20,855	11,735	103,400	1,039

[1] Preliminary.   [2] Forecast.   [3] Prior to 1987, data only reported for the Federal Republic of Germany.   [4] Formerly part of the U.S.S.R.; country data not shown seperately prior to 1989.   *Source: Foreign Agricultural Service, U.S.D.A.*

CATTLE AND CALVES

Cattle Supply and Distribution in the United States   In Thousands of Head

Year	Cattle and Calves on Farms January 1	Imports	Calves Born	Total Supply	Livestock Slaughter - Cattle and Calves / Commercial / Federally Inspected	Other[3]	All Commercial	Farm	Total Slaughter	Deaths on Farms	Exports	Total Disappear-ance
1984	113,360	753	42,470	156,583	38,910	1,969	40,879	388	41,269	5,464	71	46,794
1985	109,582	836	41,050	151,468	37,933	1,745	39,678	370	40,048	5,046	125	45,219
1986	105,378	1,407	41,182	147,967	39,108	1,588	40,696	349	41,046	4,992	108	46,146
1987	102,118	1,200	40,152	143,470	37,148	1,314	38,462	330	38,792	4,800	131	43,723
1988	99,622	1,332	40,293	141,247	36,459	1,126	37,585	280	37,889	4,657	321	42,858
1989	96,740	1,459	40,102	139,626	35,110	980	36,089	240	36,329	4,452	169	40,950
1990	95,816	2,135	39,249	139,546	34,133	800	35,032	245	35,277	4,432	120	39,829
1991	96,393	1,939	39,026	139,861	33,285	841	34,126	242	34,368	4,347	311	39,027
1992	97,556	2,255	38,933	141,104	33,428	817	34,245	243	34,489	4,486	322	39,297
1993[1]	99,176	2,499	39,448	142,750	33,753	767	34,519			4,755	153	39,654
1994[2]	100,988	2,083	40,729	143,900	34,719	750	35,469			4,370	231	40,300

[1] Preliminary.   [2] Estimate.   [3] Wholesale and retail.   Source: Economic Research Service, U.S.D.A.

United States Beef Supply and Utilization

Year	Qtr.	Beginning Stocks	Production / Commercial	Total	Imports	Total Supply	Exports	Ending Stocks	Total Disappear-ance	Per Capita Disappearance / Carcass Weight	Retail Weight
					Million Pounds					Pounds	
1992		419	22,968	23,086	2,440	25,944	1,324	360	24,261	95.0	66.5
	I	419	5,597	5,638	632	6,689	317	415	5,957	23.4	16.4
	II	415	5,726	5,744	737	6,896	323	396	6,177	24.2	17.0
	III	396	5,991	6,009	599	7,005	346	363	6,296	24.6	17.2
	IV	363	5,654	5,695	471	6,529	338	360	5,831	22.7	15.9
1993		360	22,942	23,049	2,401	25,810	1,275	529	24,006	93.0	65.1
	I	360	5,357	5,394	741	6,495	267	390	5,838	22.7	15.9
	II	390	5,690	5,706	580	6,676	346	362	5,968	23.1	16.2
	III	362	6,076	6,092	607	7,061	334	433	6,294	24.3	17.0
	IV	433	5,819	5,857	473	6,763	328	529	5,906	22.8	15.9
1994		529	24,282	24,389	2,392	27,310	1,581	557	25,172	96.5	67.5
	I[1]	529	5,744	5,781	682	6,992	359	560	6,073	23.4	16.4
	II[1]	560	6,044	6,060	603	7,223	391	506	6,326	24.3	17.0
	III[2]	506	6,378	6,394	587	7,487	416	536	6,535	25.0	17.5
	IV[2]	529	6,116	6,154	520	7,210	415	557	6,238	23.8	16.7
1995[3]		557	24,625	24,732	2,635	27,924	1,735	450	25,739	97.7	68.4
	I[3]	557	5,975	6,012	705	7,274	405	500	6,369	24.3	17.0
	II[3]	500	6,100	6,116	695	7,311	435	450	6,426	24.4	17.1
	III[3]	450	6,400	6,416	640	7,506	450	425	6,631	25.1	17.6
	IV[3]	425	6,150	6,188	595	7,208	445	450	6,313	23.9	16.7

[1] Preliminary.   [2] Estimate.   [3] Forecast.   Source: Economic Research Service, U.S.D.A.

U.S. Cattle on Feed in 13 States, Quarterly   In Thousands of Head

Year	Qtr.	Number on Feed[3]	Placed on Feed	Marketings	Other Disappearance	Year	Qtr.	Number on Feed[3]	Placed on Feed	Marketings	Other Disappearance
1991		10,827	23,208	22,383	1,517	1992		10,135	24,251	21,981	1,431
	I	10,827	5,702	5,328	462		I	10,135	5,423	5,411	404
	II	10,739	5,006	5,820	464		II	9,743	5,253	5,665	444
	III	9,461	5,414	5,973	282		III	8,887	6,117	5,751	263
	IV	8,620	7,086	5,262	309		IV	8,990	7,458	5,154	320
1993		10,974	24,102	22,376	1,504	1994		1,196	23,441	22,979	1,060
	I	10,974	5,351	5,354	439		I[1]	11,196	5,372	5,559	275
	II	10,532	5,334	5,858	465		II[1]	10,734	4,675	5,951	334
	III	9,543	6,341	5,918	275		III[2]	9,124	6,305	5,986	191
	IV	9,691	7,076	5,246	325		IV[2]	9,252	7,089	5,483	260

[1] Preliminary.   [2] Estimate.   [3] Beginning of Period.   Source: Economic Research Service, U.S.D.A.

U.S. Cattle on Feed in 7 States   In Thousands of Head

Year	January 1	February 1	March 1	April 1	May 1	June 1	July 1	August 1	Sept. 1	October 1	Nov.1	Dec.1
1984	8,006	7,917	7,515	7,568	7,391	7,333	7,155	6,851	6,787	7,482	8,251	8,554
1985	8,635	8,184	7,891	7,826	7,526	7,490	7,127	6,509	6,270	6,591	7,732	8,062
1986	8,150	7,894	7,552	7,523	7,337	7,326	6,773	6,561	6,619	7,031	7,796	8,101
1987	7,953	7,614	7,473	7,527	7,548	7,875	7,488	6,983	7,098	7,830	8,659	8,752
1988	8,411	8,204	7,912	8,056	7,829	8,134	7,736	7,140	6,944	7,404	8,194	8,255
1989	8,045	7,970	7,931	8,252	8,087	7,795	7,235	6,763	6,631	6,958	7,911	8,331
1990	8,378	8,526	8,319	8,483	8,181	7,867	7,310	6,998	6,975	7,635	8,669	9,039
1991	8,992	8,963	8,874	8,941	8,590	8,570	7,877	7,388	7,064	7,216	8,013	8,477
1992	8,397	8,223	8,195	8,058	7,868	7,876	7,377	7,050	7,018	7,565	8,704	8,984
1993	9,163	9,140	8,851	8,781	8,409	8,393	7,973	7,703	7,794	8,224	9,096	9,397
1994[1]	9,370	9,232	9,011	8,977	8,701	8,325	7,654	7,463	7,486	7,840	8,629	8,914

[1] Preliminary.   *Source: Economic Research Service, U.S.D.A.*

U.S. Cattle Placed on Feedlots in 7 States   In Thousands of Head

Year	January	February	March	April	May	June	July	August	September	October	November	December	Total
1984	1,566	1,301	1,764	1,525	1,798	1,455	1,333	1,680	2,265	2,536	1,925	1,647	20,795
1985	1,449	1,341	1,592	1,436	1,691	1,296	1,098	1,520	2,000	2,829	1,801	1,590	19,643
1986	1,581	1,220	1,650	1,565	1,756	1,162	1,544	1,822	2,123	2,433	1,854	1,515	20,225
1987	1,581	1,442	1,719	1,701	1,984	1,432	1,289	1,915	2,474	2,614	1,676	1,390	21,217
1988	1,663	1,379	1,848	1,521	2,175	1,387	1,251	1,660	2,209	2,450	1,690	1,421	20,654
1989	1,706	1,610	1,975	1,539	1,624	1,293	1,291	1,638	1,953	2,652	2,001	1,537	20,819
1990	1,881	1,383	1,862	1,362	1,597	1,325	1,530	1,745	2,199	2,726	1,987	1,433	21,030
1991	1,721	1,455	1,703	1,427	1,772	1,102	1,327	1,459	1,826	2,539	1,917	1,456	19,704
1992	1,565	1,502	1,516	1,425	1,724	1,319	1,432	1,641	2,189	2,688	1,813	1,694	20,508
1993	1,641	1,262	1,626	1,326	1,801	1,430	1,513	1,865	2,148	2,494	1,878	1,490	20,474
1994[1]	1,543	1,356	1,640	1,416	1,415	1,205	1,594	1,846	2,060	2,478	1,854	1,585	19,992

[1] Preliminary.   *Source: Economic Research Service, U.S.D.A.*

CATTLE AND CALVES

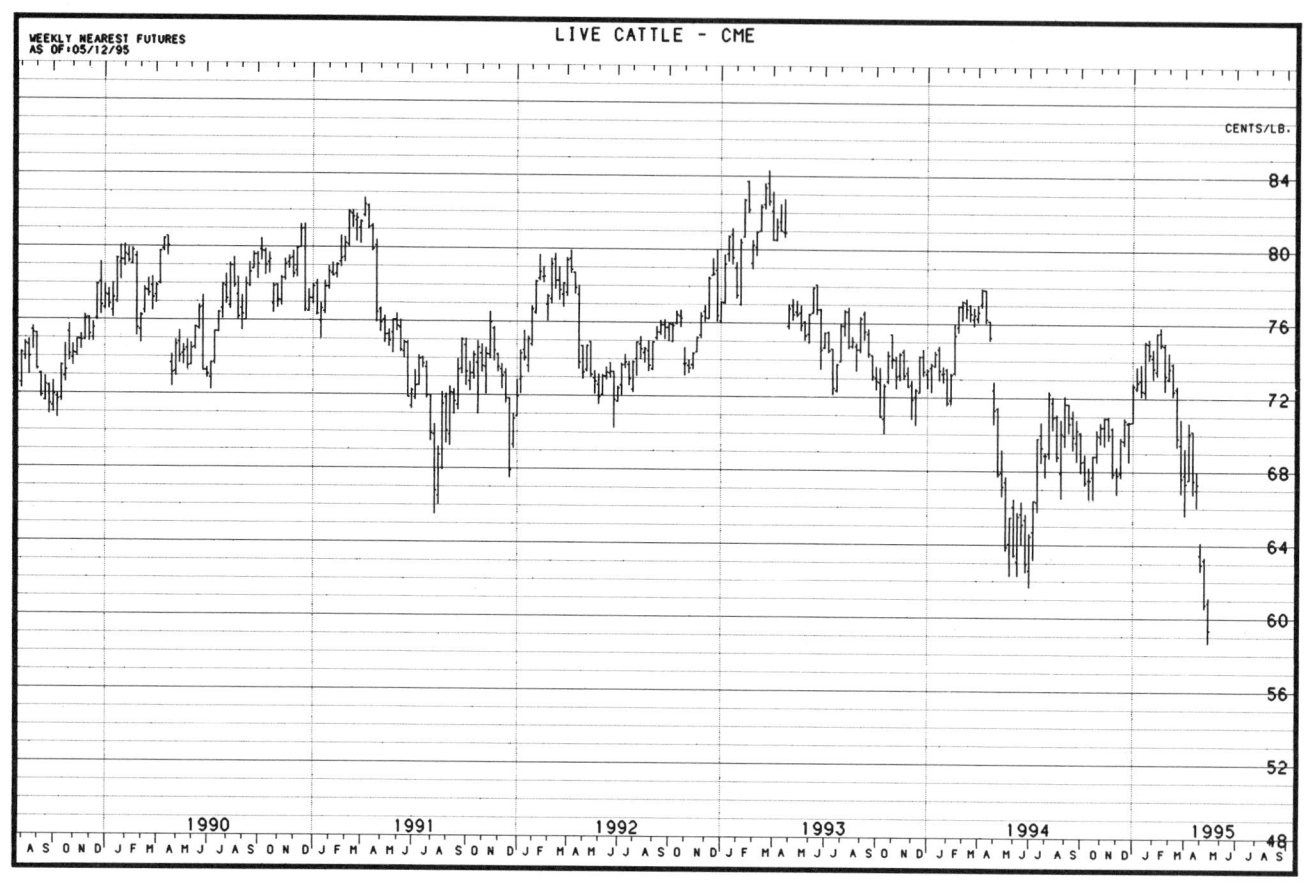

U.S. Cattle Marketings in 7 States   In Thousands of Head

Year	January	February	March	April	May	June	July	August	September	October	November	December	Total
1984	1,569	1,621	1,594	1,523	1,637	1,544	1,553	1,683	1,489	1,657	1,501	1,429	18,800
1985	1,782	1,540	1,559	1,603	1,604	1,577	1,655	1,697	1,598	1,603	1,395	1,401	19,014
1986	1,750	1,470	1,593	1,631	1,635	1,648	1,692	1,694	1,652	1,587	1,462	1,559	19,373
1987	1,793	1,478	1,571	1,541	1,514	1,732	1,723	1,732	1,671	1,700	1,478	1,612	19,545
1988	1,764	1,545	1,593	1,609	1,724	1,717	1,785	1,790	1,682	1,576	1,517	1,516	19,818
1989	1,677	1,534	1,579	1,580	1,752	1,791	1,700	1,694	1,579	1,628	1,490	1,403	19,407
1990	1,619	1,495	1,578	1,539	1,761	1,809	1,765	1,686	1,460	1,605	1,522	1,359	19,198
1991	1,632	1,431	1,499	1,650	1,651	1,681	1,724	1,716	1,598	1,665	1,376	1,443	19,066
1992	1,640	1,410	1,536	1,490	1,594	1,702	1,674	1,592	1,581	1,473	1,442	1,414	18,548
1993	1,534	1,441	1,585	1,572	1,681	1,743	1,702	1,692	1,652	1,546	1,469	1,431	19,048
1994[1]	1,610	1,501	1,588	1,610	1,699	1,770	1,730	1,767	1,656	1,633	1,498	1,540	19,602

[1] Preliminary.   *Source: Economic Research Service, U.S.D.A.*

Condition[1] of Pasture and Range Feed in the United States, on First of Month   In Percent of Normal

Year	May 1	June 1	July 1	August 1	Sept. 1	Oct. 1	Nov. 1	Year	May 1	June 1	July 1	August 1	Sept. 1	Oct. 1	Nov. 1
1983	80	85	88	76	63	66	73	1989	68	74	77	73	72	74	69
1984	75	79	80	75	70	66	74	1990	75	79	76	73	71	70	71
1985	83	81	77	70	75	76	79	1991	79	87	84	76	72	77	72
1986	76	80	83	76	79	83	85	1992	84	80	80	86	83	82	78
1987	81	84	82	78	76	79	71	1993[2]	84	88	88	83	81	83	82
1988	73	68	46	51	54	60	59	1994[2]	83	85	81	80	77	77	78

[1] Indicates current supply of feed grazing on non-irrigated pastures and ranges relative to that expected from existing stands under very favorable weather conditions. (80 and over, good to excellent; 65-79, poor to fair; 50-64, very poor; 35-49, severe drought; under 35, extreme drought.)   [2] Preliminary.   *Source: Statistical Reporting Service, U.S.D.A.*

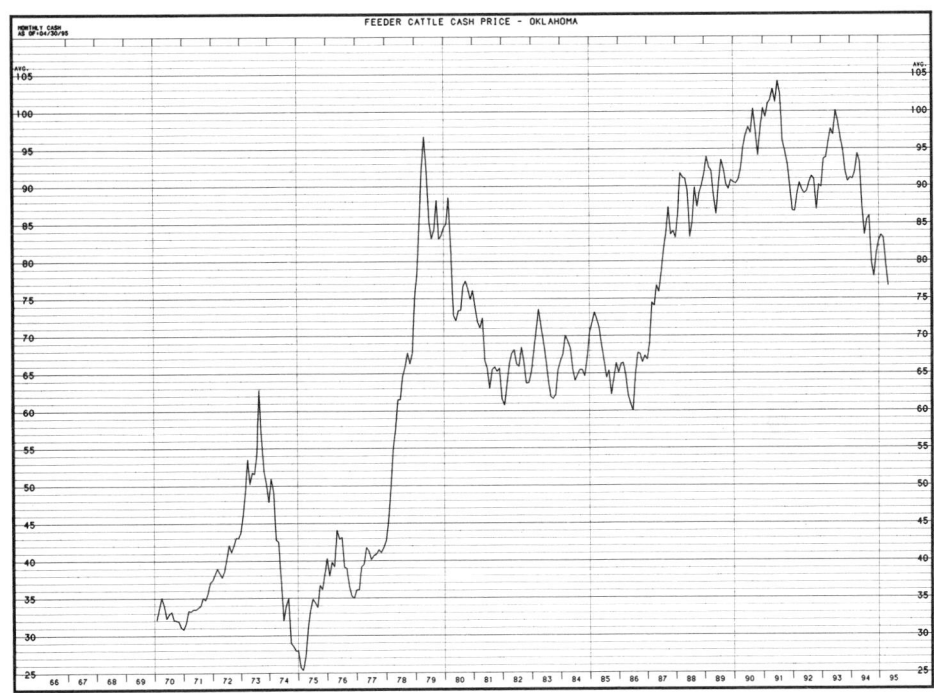

Average Wholesale Prices of Beef Steers at Omaha, Choice (1000-1100 Lbs.[1])   In Dollars Per 100 Pounds

Year	January	February	March	April	May	June	July	August	September	October	November	December	Average
1985	64.35	62.80	59.58	58.72	57.58	56.69	53.26	51.94	51.29	58.02	63.30	62.94	58.37
1986	59.69	56.42	55.55	53.68	55.79	54.08	58.27	59.04	59.43	59.58	61.54	59.82	57.74
1987	58.79	61.02	61.58	66.30	70.66	68.83	65.80	64.50	64.81	64.81	64.20	63.93	64.60
1988	65.00	68.31	71.53	73.21	75.15	70.58	65.96	67.08	67.71	69.13	70.07	71.21	69.58
1989	72.35	72.92	75.75	75.31	74.52	71.71	70.74	71.09	68.44	69.69	72.48	75.21	72.52
1990	76.73	76.61	78.15	79.36	77.57	75.63	74.46	76.22	75.75	77.50	79.93	80.88	77.40
1991	78.95	78.63	80.75	80.77	78.28	74.63	72.08	67.25	67.20	68.91	69.90	68.64	73.83
1992	71.20	75.71	76.58	76.93	76.31	74.15	73.05	73.08	73.68	74.13	74.41	76.58	74.65
1993	79.15	80.38	82.45	81.47	80.97	76.13	72.22	73.28	71.46	69.78	69.93	69.98	75.60

[1] Prior to 1986, 900-1100 lb.   *Source: Economic Research Service, U.S.D.A.*

Average Prices of Steers (Feeder) Oklahoma City   In Dollars Per 100 Pounds

Year	January	February	March	April	May	June	July	August	September	October	November	December	Average
1988	86.23	91.73	91.14	90.97	89.29	83.20	85.23	89.82	87.19	89.14	90.14	91.67	88.81
1989	93.94	92.49	92.02	88.67	86.26	90.16	93.52	92.18	90.19	89.58	90.78	90.52	90.86
1990	90.32	90.81	92.32	95.21	96.90	97.90	97.12	100.35	97.54	94.13	97.82	100.42	95.90
1991	99.22	101.01	101.50	103.00	101.22	104.05	102.32	96.09	94.62	92.90	89.93	86.69	97.71
1992	86.63	88.90	90.43	89.48	88.96	89.27	90.43	91.30	90.87	86.65	90.12	89.83	89.41
1993	93.59	93.80	95.82	97.65	96.85	100.09	98.58	96.48	94.78	91.82	90.57	91.04	95.09
1994	90.90	91.88	94.34	93.18	87.21	83.45	85.48	85.97	79.77	77.88	80.99	82.58	86.14

Source: Chicago Mercantile Exchange

Federally Inspected Slaughter of Cattle in the United States   In Thousands of Head

Year	January	February	March	April	May	June	July	August	September	October	November	December	Total
1987	3,084	2,564	2,805	2,875	2,780	2,945	3,009	2,972	2,977	3,024	2,640	2,793	34,468
1988	2,836	2,679	2,812	2,707	2,830	2,983	2,898	3,120	2,927	2,871	2,698	2,685	34,048
1989	2,711	2,500	2,744	2,576	2,947	2,951	2,730	2,975	2,706	2,876	2,694	2,600	33,010
1990	2,775	2,437	2,690	2,550	2,920	2,873	2,796	2,918	2,553	2,877	2,622	2,380	32,391
1991	2,809	2,408	2,444	2,674	2,786	2,650	2,784	2,843	2,634	2,855	2,508	2,491	31,887
1992	2,856	2,377	2,599	2,525	2,688	2,863	2,802	2,721	2,748	2,793	2,490	2,632	32,094
1993[1]	2,601	2,411	2,712	2,623	2,720	2,957	2,811	2,883	2,810	2,729	2,632	2,706	32,593
1994[1]	----------------------13,415----------------------					2,984	2,770	3,001	2,885	2,878	2,744	2,806	33,483

[1] Preliminary.   *Source: Agricultural Statistics Board, U.S.D.A.*

CATTLE AND CALVES

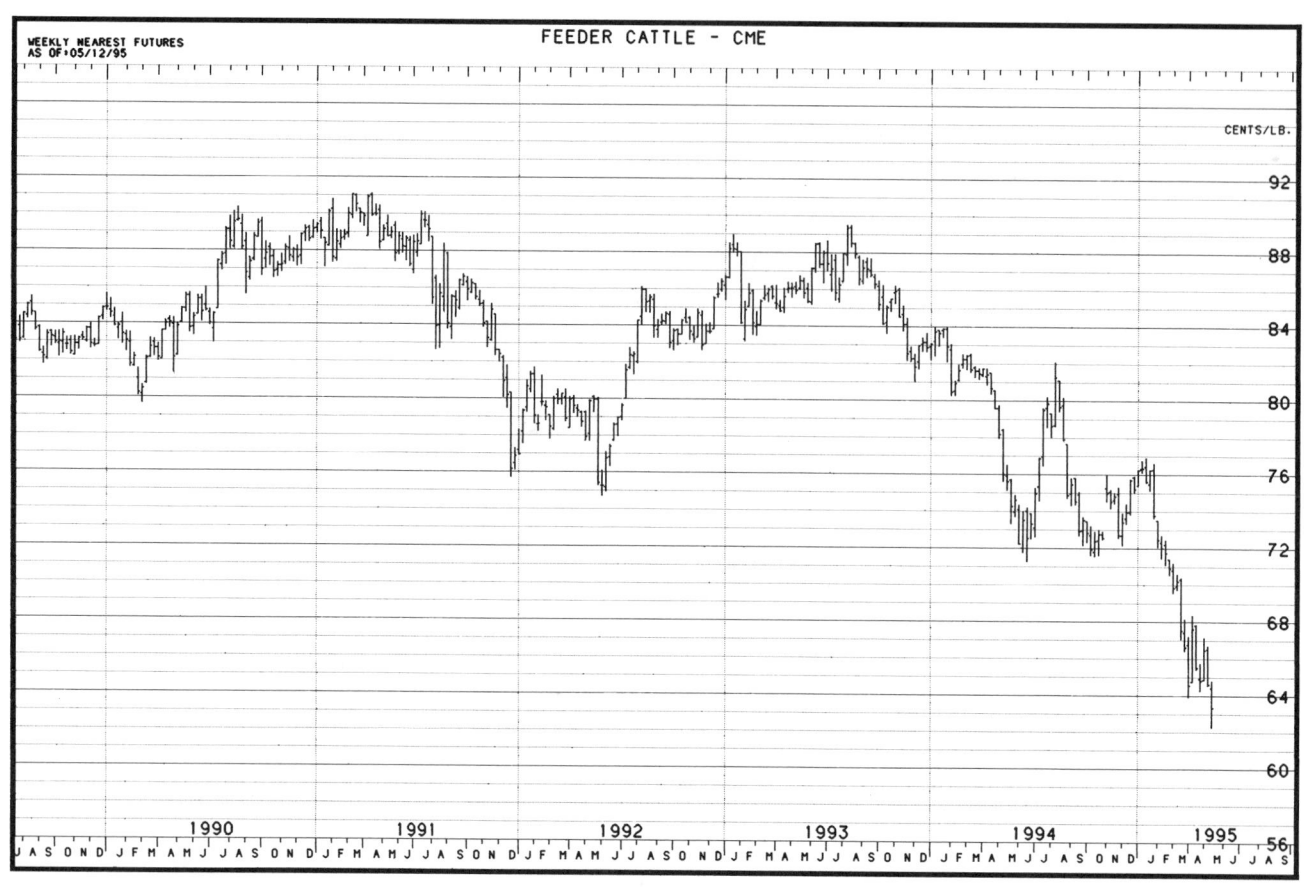

Average Open Interest of Live Cattle Futures at Chicago   In Contracts

Year	January	February	March	April	May	June	July	August	September	October	November	December
1984	55,430	53,303	59,509	55,090	48,169	41,389	40,280	36,359	38,724	39,975	56,086	58,501
1985	58,544	57,763	60,999	59,309	53,332	48,603	49,092	43,730	49,443	55,616	67,849	63,076
1986	57,943	54,947	55,427	49,185	56,179	55,018	64,385	63,170	64,401	56,402	62,751	58,561
1987	62,770	83,958	91,018	89,818	98,350	86,144	81,399	81,315	90,915	80,156	75,379	74,839
1988	77,436	92,363	105,307	97,582	91,480	85,257	82,080	81,025	80,935	80,356	82,790	76,683
1989	80,464	84,909	93,240	82,267	81,588	69,981	78,045	76,582	73,530	65,807	73,962	71,508
1990	95,515	108,149	104,647	95,709	86,875	76,130	70,462	68,375	69,611	67,122	70,576	69,647
1991	74,392	79,695	84,574	83,322	78,284	70,107	67,868	68,359	74,483	70,395	75,788	74,687
1992	79,638	97,500	97,222	90,823	83,112	68,135	67,828	62,656	61,783	60,761	63,945	67,125
1993	78,481	79,256	88,113	78,144	72,183	68,287	66,617	66,560	70,275	70,559	73,571	76,042
1994	87,923	87,578	83,949	70,287	72,851	75,470	76,663	72,988	73,391	67,924	74,152	68,600

Source: Chicago Mercantile Exchange

Volume of Trading of Live Cattle Futures at Chicago   In Thousands of Contracts

Year	January	February	March	April	May	June	July	August	September	October	November	December	Total
1984	457.4	397.6	404.2	323.2	256.4	215.5	265.3	202.6	181.0	245.9	345.7	258.5	3,553.3
1985	340.7	290.3	327.9	304.3	412.0	317.2	440.5	370.2	400.2	445.3	405.0	383.8	4,437.3
1986	492.6	381.0	408.2	462.1	424.2	374.5	448.7	373.0	387.1	376.9	289.4	273.0	4,690.5
1987	376.6	426.7	474.2	456.6	523.7	357.8	394.8	412.7	485.8	580.4	363.1	377.0	5,229.3
1988	425.1	455.6	543.9	468.0	467.8	571.3	463.4	511.8	415.0	417.5	383.9	353.9	5,477.2
1989	452.9	357.7	409.0	404.2	382.9	370.3	327.9	331.9	376.9	345.4	266.2	240.2	4,265.7
1990	400.5	350.0	354.1	327.6	372.2	263.9	298.5	327.7	273.3	320.3	268.4	240.8	3,797.4
1991	344.2	252.1	288.9	300.4	247.2	254.8	311.2	406.1	321.2	386.3	327.7	352.8	3,792.9
1992	375.6	322.5	353.8	319.1	275.9	263.9	268.9	231.0	196.0	227.9	203.8	246.7	3,319.6
1993	328.8	294.2	363.4	263.5	199.7	255.4	269.3	226.0	269.5	297.6	248.4	291.1	3,307.0
1994	280.9	295.6	262.4	264.2	372.9	363.9	318.2	317.1	270.0	308.9	275.9		

Source: Chicago Mercantile Exchange

Beef Steer-Corn Price Ratio at Omaha[1]

Year	January	February	March	April	May	June	July	August	September	October	November	December	Average
1988	36.4	37.4	38.2	39.4	38.6	29.5	24.4	26.1	26.4	26.4	28.4	27.9	31.59
1989	28.1	28.7	29.4	30.2	29.3	29.1	29.6	32.0	30.8	31.1	32.2	32.8	30.28
1990	34.2	34.0	32.6	31.1	29.3	27.9	28.5	30.9	34.5	36.5	37.3	36.5	32.78
1991	35.3	34.3	34.0	32.8	32.7	32.0	31.3	28.5	28.8	29.9	30.5	29.7	31.65
1992	29.9	31.0	30.4	31.6	30.6	29.4	32.2	34.7	35.1	37.4	38.0	38.8	33.26
1993[2]	39.6	40.0	38.7	37.6	37.5	36.8	31.4	32.8	32.0	29.6	26.4	25.0	33.95
1994[2]	24.8	25.1	26.9	28.4	26.0	23.9	28.8	29.5	30.9				27.14

[1] Based on price of choice beef-steers, 900-1100 pounds.   [2] Preliminary.   *Source: Agricultural Statistics Board, U.S.D.A.*

U.S. Farm Value, Income and Wholesale Prices of Cattle and Calves

Year	January 1 Per Head Dollars	January 1 Total Million $	Gross Income From C. & C.[2] Million $	At Omaha[3] Steers[3] Choice	At Omaha[3] Steers[3] Select	At Omaha[3] Heifers[4] Select	At Omaha[3] Heifers[4] Choice	Feeder Heifers at Oklahoma City[5]	Cows, Boning Utility Sioux Falls[6]	Vealer, Choice Albany, New York	Cows, Commercial Sioux Falls	Wholesale Prices, Central U.S. Choice, 700-850 lb.	Wholesale Prices, Central U.S. Select, 700-850 lb.	Cow[6] Canners[7]
1988	523	52,148	36,810	69.58	67.06	65.35	68.16	77.11	47.21	95.82	49.46	NA	NA	88.61
1989	580	56,908	36,894	72.52	70.28	69.52	71.93	80.00	48.98	97.57	52.14	NA	NA	94.43
1990	614	60,285	39,945	77.40	75.24	73.94	76.82	85.31	53.60	97.61	57.13	123.11	116.49	99.96
1991	654	64,662	39,644	73.83	72.46	71.44	73.86	86.04	50.66	94.66	56.08	117.24	112.73	99.42
1992[1]	629	62,656	37,958	74.65	73.65	72.88	74.91	78.41	44.84	87.01	51.22	116.02	111.66	93.85
1993[1]	649	65,287	39,986	75.60	74.80	74.76	75.90	82.79	47.52	89.11	56.47	117.71	113.53	95.43
1994[1]	659	66,968						74.55	42.51	88.01	48.28	106.73	102.08	84.39

[1] Preliminary.   [2] Excludes interfarm sales and Government payments. Cash receipts from farm marketings and value of farm consumption.   [3] 1,000 to 1,100 pound weight range.   [4] 1,000 to 1,200 pound weight range.   [5] 700 to 750 pound weight range. Prior to 1992, 600 to 700 pound weight range.   [6] All weights.   [7] & cutter.   NA=Not available.   *Source: Economic Research Service, U.S.D.A.*

Average Price Received by Farmers for Beef Cattle   In Dollars Per 100 Pounds

Year	January	February	March	April	May	June	July	August	September	October	November	December	Average
1987	56.40	58.80	59.30	62.60	63.00	62.50	61.10	61.90	63.70	62.90	62.00	62.20	61.37
1988	65.40	67.40	68.30	69.00	69.30	65.00	63.20	65.90	67.20	67.00	66.70	67.20	66.80
1989	70.60	71.60	72.00	70.10	68.80	67.60	68.00	69.70	68.20	68.70	69.80	71.00	69.68
1990	73.70	74.60	74.20	74.60	74.60	74.20	73.60	76.00	75.00	75.50	75.30	77.10	74.87
1991	76.60	77.00	78.50	78.20	75.90	73.60	71.60	68.80	68.70	70.40	67.90	67.40	72.88
1992	68.90	72.50	72.90	72.60	71.90	70.20	70.60	71.80	71.70	71.80	70.90	70.80	71.38
1993	73.20	75.80	77.30	77.30	77.10	74.50	72.50	72.70	71.40	69.10	69.30	68.50	73.23
1994[1]	70.00	70.20	72.20	72.00	67.20	62.70	62.90	65.90	63.50	63.10	64.40	64.40	66.54

[1] Preliminary.   *Source: Crop Reporting Board, U.S.D.A.*

Average Price Received by Farmers for Calves   In Dollars Per 100 Pounds

Year	January	February	March	April	May	June	July	August	September	October	November	December	Average
1987	66.40	70.60	72.50	75.10	77.40	78.80	80.30	82.30	85.90	81.40	82.90	83.00	78.05
1988	88.20	92.60	93.50	93.20	93.40	84.90	87.70	91.00	89.50	87.80	87.80	88.60	89.85
1989	92.80	95.90	94.00	90.40	91.10	94.10	94.60	94.20	91.10	88.10	86.70	89.10	91.84
1990	90.10	96.00	99.10	100.40	101.00	98.10	95.90	98.90	95.40	92.80	93.80	97.80	96.61
1991	98.00	104.00	107.00	104.00	107.00	106.00	103.00	98.30	96.20	93.90	90.20	87.60	99.60
1992	88.30	92.80	94.10	92.00	89.60	88.40	90.10	90.60	87.40	88.30	87.20	87.00	89.65
1993	91.40	95.90	98.20	99.60	99.20	99.10	96.90	95.10	93.50	93.90	91.60	92.80	95.60
1994[1]	94.00	95.00	97.90	95.70	89.60	84.90	83.90	84.50	80.10	78.40	80.90	81.90	87.23

[1] Preliminary.   *Source: Crop Reporting Board, U.S.D.A.*

Federally Inspected Slaughter of Calves and Vealers in the U.S.   In Thousands of Head

Year	January	February	March	April	May	June	July	August	September	October	November	December	Total
1987	248	225	251	215	189	214	220	202	229	233	211	242	2,679
1988	205	203	216	169	171	204	207	227	207	197	202	203	2,410
1989	196	175	194	152	157	161	169	189	173	191	175	167	2,137
1990	175	145	165	128	137	131	139	147	132	158	149	136	1,743
1991	150	120	119	105	102	90	108	108	115	127	125	131	1,408
1992	128	111	120	108	103	105	106	107	107	111	109	121	1,328
1993	101	97	116	96	82	91	90	95	94	94	101	103	1,159
1994[1]	99	94	112	92	90	98	93	106	106	112	114	103	1,237

[1] Preliminary.   *Source: Crop Reporting Board, U.S.D.A.*

Cement

Portland cement shipments in the U.S. and Puerto Rico in June 1994 were 8.6 million tonnes, according to the U.S. Bureau of Mines. This represented an 8 percent increase from June 1993. Cumulative shipments for the first six-months of 1994 were 37.7 million tonnes, 11 percent above cumulative shipments through the first half of 1993. The leading portland cement producing states were California, Texas, Michigan, Pennsylvania and Missouri. They shipped 41 percent of the June total. The leading consuming states were California, Texas, Florida, Illinois and Ohio. They took 32 percent of the total shipments.

Masonry cement shipments in June 1994 were 327,676 tonnes, a 10 percent increase from June 1993. For the first half of 1994, cumulative masonry shipments were 1,578,224 tonnes. This represented a 12 percent increase on the first six-months of 1993. The leading producers of masonry cement were Indiana, Pennsylvania, Florida, Alabama and Michigan, which together shipped 50 percent of the total.

The leading consuming states were Florida, North Carolina, Texas, Ohio and Georgia, which took 39 percent of the shipments.

The increase in consumption of cement appears due to the continued improvement in the U.S. economy. The residential housing sector continues to show expansion despite sharp increases in interest rates. Because of overbuilding in the commercial sector in the 1980s, that sector is likely to remain subdued. It appears that the U.S. economy will continue to expand, though probably at a slower rate as interest rates have increased. That should mean further increases in cement consumption.

Imports of hydraulic cement and clinker in May 1994 were 1,019,977 tonnes. This represented an increase of 63 percent from May 1993. Cumulative imports over January-May 1994 were 3,011,007 tonnes, some 63 percent higher than in the same period of 1993. The major suppliers were Canada, Spain, Colombia, Mexico and Greece.

World Production of Hydraulic Cement by Selected Countries   In Thousands of Short Tons

Year	Brazil	Canada	China	France	Germany	India	Italy	Japan	Poland	Rep. of Korea	Russia[3]	Spain	Turkey	United Kingdom	United States	World Total
1988	27,922	13,267	231,000	27,888	42,694	44,864	41,760	85,489	18,722	31,961	153,771	28,000	24,995	18,195	78,252	1,232,686
1989	28,578	13,879	228,000	29,580	44,934	50,706	43,414	87,873	18,877	33,592	154,804	30,175	26,231	18,573	78,559	1,266,064
1990	28,496	12,947	224,000	29,088	41,539	54,013	44,692	93,085	13,889	37,038	151,371	30,966	26,914	18,432	78,713	1,265,514
1991	30,303	10,357	273,000	29,219	37,915	56,218	44,883	98,723	13,260	42,257	140,000	30,403	28,689	12,855	73,583	1,311,590
1992	30,975	9,352	335,000	23,810	41,340	55,115	45,577	99,980	13,200	47,000	75,000	29,000	31,534	11,820	78,734	1,382,107
1993[1]	28,000		356,000	22,000	37,000	52,000	42,000	87,000		47,000	60,000	26,000	30,000	32,000	76,000	1,300,000
1994[2]	29,000		360,000	24,000	40,000	55,000	45,000	90,000		50,000	62,000	30,000	32,000		81,000	1,300,000

[1] Preliminary.   [2] Estimate.   [3] Formerly part of the U.S.S.R.; data not reported separately until 1992.   *Source: U.S. Bureau of Mines*

Salient Statistics of Cement in the United States

Year	Net Import Reliance as a % of Apparent Consumption	Production — Portland Thousand Tons	Production — Others[3] Thousand Tons	Production — Total Thousand Tons	Capacity Used at (Portland Mills) %	Shipments From Mills — Total Mil. Tons	Shipments From Mills — Value[4] Mil. $	Average Value (F.O.B. Mill) $ per ton	Stocks at Mills Dec. 31 Million Tons	Exports[5] Million Tons	Apparent Consumption Million Tons	Imports for Consumption[6] by Country — Canada Thousand Short Tons	Japan	Mexico	Spain	Total
1988	19	73,272	3,595	76,867	74.3	89,460	4,370	48.85	5,997	101	93,256	3,628	1,758	4,992	1,857	17,488
1989	16	73,895	3,294	77,189	75.3	86,238	4,243	49.20	6,300	512	90,676	3,420	2,415	4,411	1,562	15,741
1990	14	73,902	3,209	77,111	76.3	86,200	4,280	54.73	5,637	554	89,623	3,216	2,101	2,307	1,309	13,273
1991	10	70,729	2,856	73,585	72.2	74,481	3,705	54.84	5,700	698	79,484	3,127	331	1,044	699	8,701
1992	7	74,261	3,093	77,354	78.4	77,073	3,824	54.69	5,492	823	82,075	3,304	306	909	492	6,797
1993[1]	8	NA	NA	74,532		81,404		55.61	5,352	710	81,106	3,682	47	812	598	7,060
1994[2]	12	NA	NA	80,007		86,540		56.22	5,262	599	90,492	4,704	15	705	1,479	12,459

[1] Preliminary.   [2] Estimate.   3 Masonry, natural & pozzolan (slag-line).   [4] Value received F.O.B. mill, excluding cost of containers.   [5] Hydraulic & clinker cement.   NA = Not available.   *Source: U.S. Bureau of Mines*

Average Price of Bulk Cement in 20 Cities   In Dollars Per Metric Ton

Year	Jan.	Feb.	Mar.	Apr.	May	June	July	Aug.	Sept.	Oct.	Nov.	Dec.	Average
1990	62.56	62.20	62.31	62.72	63.06	62.95	63.47	63.22	62.62	62.44	62.20	62.10	62.65
1991[1]	68.45	69.88	70.37	69.54	70.03	70.32	70.53	70.67	70.42	70.33	70.14	68.82	69.96
1992	69.94	69.52	68.53	68.53	68.67	68.92	68.99	68.13	69.00	68.13	68.13	68.13	68.72
1993	68.13	68.31	68.31	68.31	70.31	70.87	71.17	71.18	69.91	69.69	69.88	70.05	69.68
1994	70.05	70.07	70.07	72.60	72.33	73.65	74.27	74.90	73.99	73.88	74.31	74.54	72.89

[1] Reported in dollars per short ton prior to 1991.   *Source: U.S. Bureau of Mines*

Shipments of Finished Portland Cement from Mills in the U.S.   In Thousands of Short Tons

Year	Jan.	Feb.	Mar.	Apr.	May	June	July	Aug.	Sept.	Oct.	Nov.	Dec.	Total
1991				---------- 38,750.1 ----------				7,382.0	6,780.3	7,586.8	5,310.9	4,434.4	70,245
1992	4,121.8	4,204.5	5,258.7	6,577.3	7,061.2	7,675.4	7,668.1	7,652.7	7,732.9	8,285.3	5,531.8	4,817.7	76,829
1993	3,715.7	4,039.0	5,381.5	6,375.9	7,294.4	8,079.0	7,936.4	8,330.6	8,747.2	8,920.2	7,463.4	5,968.1	86,386
1994[1]	4,112.0	4,551.6	7,033.3	7,566.9	8,859.2	9,465.7	8,567.7	9,896.8	9,338.7	9,255.6	7,703.6	6,347.0	92,698

[1] Preliminary.   *Source: U.S. Bureau of Mines*

Cheese

World production and consumption of cheese reached a record high in 1994 with the U.S., the largest participant, accounting for almost a third of the totals. Production neared 11 million metric tons vs 10.7 million in 1993. U.S. production totaled 3.1 million and 3 million, respectively, the increase reflecting higher milk production. France, the second largest producer, turns out about half the U.S. total. Most of the world's cheese is consumed where produced, with total exports less than 10% of production. World stocks at the end of 1994 of about 1.7 million tons were fractionally lower than a year earlier. Demand is sensitive to economic conditions: the improvement in the U.S. economy in 1994 boosted U.S. usage to more than 3.2 million tons, up from less than 3.1 million in 1993; consumption averaged 3 million tons during the 1990-94 period. France and Italy together consumed about 2.3 million tons in 1994, marginally higher than in 1993.

American cheese accounts for the largest individual variety of U.S. production. Since the late 1980's, however, other varieties--mostly Italian--have had a combined production that exceeds American cheese. U.S. per capita cheese consumption has shown irregular patterns in recent years. American cheese, of which cheddar is the largest variety, apparently peaked in the mid 1980's at around 12 1/4 pounds and has since slipped about one pound. Italian cheese varieties, however, have increased sharply rising from about 6 pounds in the mid 1980's to near 10 pounds recently. Mozzarella makes up the bulk of Italian cheese use. For most dairy products, statistical data is a product of the fat or skim solids content. Cheese, however, is handled somewhat differently. Making cheese exhausts virtually all the value of the skim component of raw milk, even though most of the solids-not-fat are left in the liquid whey. To account for this, the factors used for cheese reflect the total skim solids needed to produce a pound, not just the casein and minerals actually in the cheese.

The U.S. does import some cheese, a few varieties of which are under a quota. Imports in 1994 of 150,000 tons compares with 145,000 in 1993. The U.S. is the world's largest importer of cheese, but a very minor exporter relative to Europe.

U.S. cheese prices have a seasonal pattern, generally strengthening in autumn. When counterseasonal price strength develops, as it did in the spring of 1994, it usually reflects regional conditions more than national supply/demand factors. U.S. wholesale cheese prices (40-lb. blocks, Wisconsin) averaged $1.315 per pound in 1993; the average for 1994 was expected to be moderately higher.

World Cheese (Total[1]) Production — In Millions of Metric Tons

Year	Argentina	Australia	Brazil	Canada	Denmark	France	Germany	Italy	Mexico	Netherlands	New Zealand	Russia[3]	Sweden	Switzerland	Ukraine	United Kingdom	United States
1984	239	161	200	192	293	1,287	465	661	188	515	110	-----	116	130	780	245	2,120
1985	210	160	205	213	253	1,300	495	684	187	522	118	-----	109	126	809	260	2,305
1986	256	170	185	226	252	1,320	530	694	262	534	127	-----	106	131	844	256	2,363
1987	277	177	195	246	271	1,342	817	704	298	552	113	-----	107	128	861	263	2,424
1988	265	176	200	252	258	1,378	849	737	370	559	128	-----	115	134	895	299	2,527
1989	260	190	220	247	275	1,485	885	760	373	568	128	460	109	137	184	280	2,546
1990	270	175	200	255	293	1,471	749	811	384	593	122	458	108	138	184	316	2,749
1991	290	178	210	262	285	1,500	777	885	395	610	125	394	107	142	162	303	2,730
1992	310	197	215	262	290	1,489	783	890	390	634	142	299	110	141	160	324	2,943
1993[1]	315	211	200	267	321	1,509	830	885	395	635	145	304	115	141	140	330	2,961
1994[2]	330	218	200	271	315	1,540	830	880	410	633	190	305	120	141	130	314	3,070

[1] Preliminary. [2] Estimate. [3] Formerly part of the U.S.S.R.; data not reported seperately prior to 1989. *Source: Foreign Agricultural Service, U.S. Department of Agriculture*

Supply and Distribution of All Cheese in the United States — In Millions of Pounds

	Supply					Distribution						
	Production					Cheese 40-Lb. Blocks Wisconsin Assembly		Government		American Cheese Removed by USDA Programs	Total Disappearance	Domestic Disappearance		
Year	Whole Milk[2]	All Cheese[3]	January 1 Commercial Stocks	Imports[4]	Total Supply	Points Cents per Pound	Exports and Shipments	January 1 Stocks	December 31 Stocks			American Cheese Donated	Total	Per Capita
1984	2,648	4,674	1,266	306	6,246	137.96	108	793.0	621.0	447.3	5,184	560	5,077	21.48
1985	2,855	5,081	1,062	303	6,446	127.72	125	621.0	543.7	629.0	5,501	636	5,376	22.54
1986	2,798	5,209	945	295	6,449	127.30	97	543.7	420.1	468.4	5,660	560	5,563	23.12
1987	2,717	5,344	789	265	6,399	123.19	88	420.1	81.2	282.0	5,939	607	5,851	24.10
1988	2,757	5,572	460	252	6,284	123.80	76	81.2	36.7	238.1	5,886	257	5,810	23.71
1989	2,674	5,615	398	276	6,289	138.79	74	36.7	6.6	37.4	5,959	67	5,885	23.79
1990	2,894	6,059	330	298	6,689	136.69	75	6.6	8.2	21.5	6,231	21	6,156	24.63
1991	2,769	6,055	458	297	6,810	124.41	72	8.2	23.1	76.9	6,393	60	6,321	25.02
1992[1]	2,937	6,488	417	285	7,191	131.91	78	23.1	16.5	14.4	6,720	0	6,641	26.00
1993[1]	2,925	6,528	471	320	6,719	131.52	87	16.5	2.2	8.3	6,853	0	6,772	26.22

[1] Preliminary. [2] Whole milk American cheddar. [3] All types of cheese except cottage, pot and baker's cheese. [4] Imports for consumption.
[5] Commercial. *Source: Economic Research Service, U.S. Department of Agriculture.*

CHEESE

Cheese Production in the United States   In Millions of Pounds

Year	American Whole Milk	American Part Skim	American Total	Swiss, Including Block	Muenster	Brick	Limburger	Cream and Neufchatel Cheese	Italian Varieties	Blue Mond	All Other Varieties	Total of All Cheese[2]	Cottage Cheese Lowfat	Cottage Cheese Curd[3]	Cottage Cheese Creamed[4]
1984	2,649	2.7	2,652	208.0	76.0	16.0	1.2	276.5	1,318.8	34.1	92.2	4,674	229.3	606.2	736.1
1985	2,855	2.4	2,858	222.9	82.1	20.1	1.0	293.8	1,491.3	33.4	77.7	5,081	244.4	598.8	715.6
1986	2,798	2.1	2,800	227.3	88.5	20.4	1.1	321.5	1,632.9	34.2	82.1	5,209	265.5	600.1	704.8
1987	2,717	0.9	2,718	227.2	92.6	28.9	1.1	342.2	1,799.8	35.9	99.1	5,344	270.5	573.8	674.8
1988	2,757	1.1	2,758	250.1	83.3	24.8	1.0	375.9	1,937.1	37.8	104.3	5,572	290.9	556.7	647.1
1989	2,674	0.8	2,675	231.2	91.1	17.5	0.9	401.0	2,042.9	34.6	121.2	5,615	300.9	526.9	572.3
1990	2,894	0.8	2,895	261.1	100.2	17.3	0.8	430.8	2,207.0	36.4	110.7	6,059	301.8	493.5	530.6
1991	2,769	0.8	2,770	234.5	106.4	15.3	0.7	446.7	2,328.6	34.3	118.5	6,055	321.1	490.9	497.9
1992[1]	2,937	1.2	2,938	237.3	116.4	15.5	1.0	516.7	2,508.6	33.2	121.9	6,488	329.5	502.4	457.3
1993[1]			2,957						2,494.5			6,528	317.8		431.6
1994[1]			2,983						2,610.2			6,713	311.0		411.8

[1] Preliminary.   [2] Excludes full-skim cheddar and cottage cheese.   [3] Includes cottage, pot, and baker's cheese with a butterfat content of less than 4%.
[4] Includes cheese with a butterfat content of 4 to 19%.   *Source: Economic Research Service, U.S. Department of Agriculture*

Wholesale Price of Cheese, 40-lb. Blocks, Wisconsin Assembly Points   In Cents Per Pound

Year	January	February	March	April	May	June	July	August	September	October	November	December	Average
1984	135.8	135.5	135.9	135.9	135.9	136.0	136.7	138.6	144.3	143.8	139.7	137.5	138.0
1985	136.5	134.3	132.1	129.9	128.0	126.8	124.7	124.3	124.3	124.3	123.8	123.9	127.7
1986	123.8	124.5	123.2	125.0	126.0	125.4	126.7	129.5	129.7	130.2	133.4	130.4	127.3
1987	127.8	122.5	122.3	122.4	122.0	122.0	123.2	125.5	126.6	121.9	121.3	120.8	123.2
1988	118.4	116.1	115.6	115.1	115.0	116.2	118.3	127.6	134.6	136.4	136.3	136.0	123.8
1989	129.1	117.6	117.9	120.4	123.9	130.8	140.6	143.3	155.8	160.3	163.6	162.2	138.8
1990	152.3	131.6	130.7	140.5	145.8	149.5	151.0	150.3	142.6	114.9	112.0	112.7	136.2
1991	111.4	111.5	111.5	111.7	115.0	121.4	128.4	136.1	139.7	140.2	135.8	130.2	124.4
1992	125.4	119.0	119.8	131.9	140.0	141.3	141.8	142.0	136.9	132.4	129.4	123.2	131.9
1993	119.3	118.6	124.3	140.8	141.8	133.7	126.3	124.8	137.4	138.9	138.7	133.7	131.5
1994[1]	132.2	134.2	140.0	143.3	125.7	120.2	129.1	132.2	135.6	135.4	127.9	121.3	131.5

[1] Preliminary.   *Source: Economic Research Service, U.S. Department of Agriculture*

United States Total Cheese Production[1]   In Millions of Pounds

Year	January	February	March	April	May	June	July	August	September	October	November	December	Total
1984	382.1	366.0	412.3	409.9	432.9	415.4	379.9	371.3	357.9	381.2	368.9	396.3	4,674
1985	395.0	361.5	416.0	435.3	461.1	447.2	443.8	427.3	403.6	432.9	415.4	441.8	5,081
1986	433.9	400.0	457.1	459.5	482.5	457.4	436.6	421.8	410.1	410.2	401.0	439.4	5,209
1987	422.0	398.6	457.4	462.1	477.8	465.6	453.8	426.0	430.7	448.6	431.8	469.7	5,344
1988	439.5	436.2	491.6	475.3	488.2	476.7	454.9	442.0	451.9	470.0	458.9	486.5	5,572
1989	456.6	419.5	488.4	472.6	494.9	485.5	464.6	460.4	448.5	464.0	453.0	489.5	5,614
1990	483.7	471.9	531.7	521.1	542.8	522.8	502.2	495.0	472.6	505.9	495.5	522.1	6,061
1991	501.7	458.0	530.1	515.4	532.3	509.0	499.5	498.2	485.0	521.0	502.3	533.7	6,061
1992	514.1	497.1	542.7	534.7	550.9	549.8	541.8	534.6	528.3	558.2	547.5	571.6	6,488
1993	517.3	492.5	563.2	561.4	576.9	563.2	537.9	525.8	531.1	560.0	540.1	558.9	6,528
1994[2]	538.4	507.5	584.8	553.3	587.5	563.5	549.8	552.8	563.9	573.9	561.0	577.1	6,713

[1] Excludes cottage and full skim American.   [2] Preliminary.   *Source: National Agricultural Statistics Service, U.S. Department of Agriculture*

Cold Storage Holdings of All Varieties of Cheese in the U.S., on First of Month   In Millions of Pounds

Year	January	February	March	April	May	June	July	August	September	October	November	December
1984	1,205	1,201	1,220	1,217	1,182	1,208	1,193	1,186	1,148	1,115	1,078	1,044
1985	986.2	968.9	944.4	907.7	898.6	911.0	954.2	963.5	962.9	941.0	891.8	877.5
1986	852.9	835.8	813.2	815.7	838.4	873.3	892.8	915.6	916.2	859.0	805.0	757.0
1987	693.6	683.9	652.4	646.5	645.1	666.8	659.0	642.5	606.6	580.8	538.0	495.9
1988	457.1	455.1	448.3	443.8	451.9	460.1	480.9	496.1	460.8	421.3	400.7	366.7
1989	388.1	395.3	404.4	396.6	412.1	431.9	429.6	430.4	419.8	370.2	331.4	330.6
1990	328.0	358.4	374.9	395.8	413.4	441.6	465.0	484.6	475.7	459.9	445.4	437.3
1991	457.8	483.9	475.1	492.4	510.3	512.1	521.5	511.5	494.1	477.9	429.3	409.0
1992	415.4	440.9	445.9	449.0	449.7	455.9	465.2	496.2	487.3	449.7	441.1	462.0
1993	462.0	476.1	454.4	460.0	453.6	480.5	541.2	533.3	517.7	500.1	471.9	462.4
1994[1]	465.2	495.2	473.6	473.3	487.9	513.4	521.4	506.3	474.7	453.0	448.3	434.2

[1] Preliminary.   [2] Quantities are given in "net weight."   *Source: National Agricultural Statistics Service, U.S. Department of Agriculture*

Chromite

Chromite is the ore mineral of chromium. It is used in making stainless steel and other alloys, for which resistance to oxidation and corrosion is important. Chromium is used for plating and as a tanning agent. The mineral chromite is made into refractory linings for steel-making furnaces. Since the U.S. mines no chromite ore, imports are essential. South Africa is the leading producer of ferrochromium, and its exports to the U.S. are for use in the defense industry. Outside of South Africa, the next largest chromite producers are Kazakhstan and Albania, and in the Western Hemisphere, Brazil and Cuba produce small amounts.

U.S. consumption of chromite over the first seven months of 1994 was 170,118 tonnes. For the first half of 1994 consumption was running slightly below the first half of 1993. For all of 1993, chromite consumption was 336,582 tonnes. Consumption by the chemical and metallurgical industry over the first seven months of 1994 was 158,170 tonnes, while refractory use was 11,948 tonnes. In terms of consumption by end use, stainless and heat resisting steel consumed 81%; carbon steel 2.4%; high strength, low-alloy and electric steel were nearly 4%; and superalloys 2%.

Stocks of chromite at the end of July 1994 were 274,292 tonnes. At the end of 1993, stocks were 274,756 tonnes. Chromite stocks of the chemical and metallurgical industry on July 31, 1994 were 259,771 tonnes, while stocks of the refractory industry were 14,521 tonnes.

Since the U.S. mines no chromite ore, and there are no substitutes for chromite ore in the production of ferrochromium, chromium chemical or chromite refractories, imports are important. Over the first six months of 1994 the U.S. Bureau of Mines reported that imports of chromite ore totaled 89,442 tonnes. This compares with imports over the same period in 1993 of 150,972 tonnes. For all of 1993 chromite ore imports reached 254,802 tonnes. In 1994 the Republic of South Africa supplied 91% of the U.S. import needs, while the rest was supplied by the Philippines. U.S. imports of ferrochromium during the first half of 1994 were 184,971 tonnes. During the same period of 1993 imports were 192,486 tonnes, and for all of 1993 imports totaled 387,015 tonnes. The major suppliers of ferrochromium were Turkey, South Africa, Russia, Croatia and Finland. U.S. imports of chromium metal during January-June 1994 were 3,345 tonnes. For all of 1993 chromium metal imports were 6,185 tonnes.

U.S. exports of chromite ore during the first half of 1994 were 41,210 tonnes. Chromium ferroalloy exports were 5,728 tonnes, while chromium metal exports were 244 tonnes. U.S. government stockpiles of chromite ore on July 31, 1994 stood at 1.57 million tonnes, chromium ferroalloys 1.09 mil. tonnes, and chromium metal 7.610 mil. tonnes.

World Mine Production of Chromite — In Thousands of Metric Tons (Gross Weight)

Year	Albania	Brazil	China	Cuba	Finland	Greece	India	Iran	Kazak-hstan[3]	Mada-gascar	Phillip-ines	South Africa	Sudan	Turkey	Zim-babwe	World Total[1]
1984	720	260	------	38	446	61	423	59	2,940	59	261	3,407	22	487	477	9,776
1985	825	190	------	38	506	59	565	56	3,360	127	272	3,699	10	589	536	10,945
1986	850	223	50	50	678	62	638	56	3,640	83	174	3,907	9	543	533	11,555
1987	1,075	338	32	52	543	64	624	92	3,570	107	188	3,789	13	762	570	11,919
1988	1,109	410	26	52	700	50	821	60	3,700	64	129	4,245	8	851	561	12,896
1989	900	476	25	51	513	62	1,003	73	3,800	63	217	4,951	25	1,077	627	14,006
1990	910	267	25	50	504	35	939	77	3,800	73	186	4,618	13	836	573	12,959
1991	500	340	25	50	473	37	1,087	90	3,800	63	191	5,100	10	940	564	13,320
1992	150	460	25	50	499	------	1,312	130	3,600	69	102	3,363	10	531	522	10,993
1993[1]	90	430	25	50	500	------	1,070	150	2,900	69	105	2,840	10	490	400	9,301
1994[2]	90	400			500		1,100		2,900		100	2,900		500	400	9,400

[1] Estimate. [2] Preliminary. [3] Formerly part of the U.S.S.R.; data not reported seperately until 1992. *Source: U.S. Bureau of Mines*

U.S. Salient Statistics of Chromite — In Thousands of Metric Tons (Gross Weight)

Year	% Net Import Reliance of Apparent Consumption	Production of Ferro-chromium	Exports	Imports for Consumption	Reexports	Consumption by Primary Consumer Groups — Total	Metallurgical & Chemical	Refractory	Consumer Stocks, December 31 — Metallurgical & Chemical	Refractory	Total Stocks	Dollars Per Metric Ton — South Africa	Turkish
1985	75	100	91	376	3	508	449	59	228	44	272	42	125
1986	79	95	84	443	1	388	342	45	249	35	285	42	125
1987	75	107	1	490	5	506	459	48	309	23	332	46	115
1988	78	120	4	615	1	551	495	56	366	23	390	56	180
1989	78	147	40	525	2	561	517	44	368	24	392	65	185
1990	71	109	6	306	4	405	361	44	333	21	355	55	135
1991	72	68	9	212	-----	375	339	36	310	11	321	50	130
1992	76	61	7	219	-----	362	335	27	308	13	321	60	110
1993[1]	74	63	10	255	2	337	314	23	259	15	275	60	110
1994[2]	75		28	281								60	110

[1] Preliminary. [2] Estimate. [3] Cr_2O_3, 44% (Transvaal). *Source: U.S. Bureau of Mines*

29

Coal

During the first-quarter of 1994, the Department of Energy reported that domestic coal production totaled over 254 million short tons. This compares with the first-quarter of 1993 when the total output was over 243 million tons. For all of 1993, coal production was over 945 million tons. The record high output was established in 1990 with just over a billion tons. Imports of coal over the January-March 1994 period was 1.85 million tons.

Producer and distributor stocks as of March 31, 1994 were 34.1 million tons. Consumption of coal over the first-quarter of 1994 was over 237 million tons. In the prior quarter, it was just over 229 million tons. For all of 1993, U.S. coal consumption was nearly 926 million tons. Exports of coal in the first-quarter were 14.9 million tons. This was down 21 percent from the like quarter of 1993. Exports were off to their slowest start in several years. Consumer stocks have been drawndown significantly. As of March 31, 1994, consumer coal stocks were only 112 million tons. This represented a decline of 27 percent from March 31, 1993.

U.S. coke production, used in the manufacture of pig iron, by the iron and steel industry, during the first-quarter of 1994 was 5.3 million tons. Imports were 292,000 tons while producer and distributor stocks were just over a one million tons. Coke consumption in the first-quarter was 5.9 million tons with exports of 99,000 tons.

The major coal producing states in 1994 were Wyoming, Kentucky, West Virginia and Pennsylvania.

World Coal Production (Monthly Average)[3]   In Thousands of Metric Tons

Year	Australia	Canada	China	Czech Rep.[4]	France	Germany	India	Indonesia	Kazakhstan[5]	Rep. of Korea	Poland	Romania	Russia[5]	Ukraine[5]	United Kingdom	United States
1986	11,115	2,545	74,500	2,138	1,360	7,260	13,839	144	------	1,934	16,007	725	42,741	------	9,008	61,577
1987	12,309	2,721	74,910	2,145	1,124	6,865	14,748	157	------	1,920	16,084	733	43,257	------	8,703	63,528
1988	11,234	3,215	78,872	2,159	1,012	6,610	15,692	238	------	1,889	16,085	742	43,587	------	8,649	65,405
1989	12,317	3,233	87,833	2,089	1,025	6,454	16,569	380	------	1,583	14,830	691	48,083	------	8,190	67,608
1990	13,236	3,139	90,000	1,842	879	6,363	16,819	611	------	1,328	12,306	319	39,300	------	7,442	71,137
1991	13,720	3,326	88,212	1,623	842	6,063	18,905	1,143	------	1,148	11,698	270	33,769	------	8,028	68,755
1992	14,594	2,693	91,278	NA	790	6,013	19,490	1,760	10,546	928	10,960	292	16,123	NA	7,273	75,618
1993[1]	18,949	2,943	96,177	1,345	654	5,347	20,503	2,299	9,323	373	10,937	331	16,200	9,545	5,282	71,352
1994[2]	17,894	2,877	97,701	1,216	829	4,670	22,988	2,319	8,733	553	10,746	345	14,500	9,222	3,976	79,130

[1] Preliminary.   [2] Estimate.   [3] All grades of anthracite and bituminous coal, but excludes recovered slurries, lignite and brown coal.   [4] Formerly part of Czechoslovakia; data not reported separately until 1993.   [5] Formerly part of the U.S.S.R.; data not reported separately until 1992.   NA = Not available.
Source: United Nations

United States Production of Coal by Principal States   In Thousands of Short Tons

----- Bituminous & Lignite -----

Year	Alabama	Colorado	Illinois	Indiana	Kentucky	Montana	Ohio	Pennsylvania	Texas	West Virginia	Virginia	Wyoming	Total	Total U.S.
1986	25,826	15,237	61,866	32,852	153,933	33,978	36,441	67,356	48,590	41,178	129,907	136,826	886,023	890,315
1987	25,540	14,420	59,155	34,208	165,192	34,399	35,788	66,863	50,529	44,543	136,676	146,850	915,202	918,762
1988	26,518	15,913	58,594	31,271	157,852	38,881	34,043	67,091	52,281	45,886	145,005	164,014	946,711	950,265
1989	27,992	17,123	59,267	33,641	167,389	37,742	33,689	67,248	53,854	43,006	153,580	171,558	980,729	980,729
1990	29,030	18,910	60,393	35,907	128,396	37,616	35,252	67,008	55,755	46,917	169,205	184,249	1,025,569	1,029,076
1991	27,269	17,834	60,258	31,468	158,980	38,237	30,569	61,936	53,825	41,954	167,352	193,854	992,539	995,984
1992	25,796	19,226	59,857	30,466	161,068	38,889	30,403	65,498	55,071	43,024	162,164	190,172	994,062	997,545
1993[1]	24,768	21,886	41,098	29,295	156,299	35,917	28,816	55,394	21,847	39,317	130,525	210,129	941,119	945,424
1994[2]	23,143	24,681	52,780	32,540	158,870	41,631	29,778	63,980	23,417	39,784	156,850	231,398	1,026,818	1,030,501

[1] Preliminary.   [2] Estimate.   *Source: Energy Information Administration, U.S. Department of Energy*

Bituminous Coal Production[1] in the United States   In Thousands of Short Tons

Year	Jan.	Feb.	Mar.	Apr.	May.	June	July	Aug.	Sept.	Oct.	Nov.	Dec.	Total
1986	78,282	72,686	77,569	74,894	73,137	72,671	67,818	76,549	75,022	76,832	68,671	70,264	886,023
1987	74,256	71,253	75,396	70,524	70,256	76,555	69,207	80,087	81,854	85,335	78,677	79,275	915,202
1988	75,325	76,757	83,943	75,324	73,981	76,443	69,176	88,175	83,196	80,799	82,925	80,260	946,711
1989	81,969	75,040	88,981	77,233	82,486	78,544	66,269	90,824	84,618	87,657	82,925	80,260	980,729
1990	90,304	81,796	91,357	83,350	86,615	84,720	79,585	91,558	83,107	93,418	86,772	75,676	1,025,569
1991	85,810	82,592	85,012	79,324	79,917	76,896	79,745	88,851	81,533	90,307	81,730	79,383	992,539
1992	87,979	82,102	85,835	82,364	80,197	79,968	80,768	84,401	83,555	86,265	80,240	83,021	994,062
1993	80,508	76,341	84,782	79,329	73,759	80,949	70,771	76,209	79,705	80,628	79,404	79,905	941,119
1994[2]	76,376	81,370	95,727	87,386	81,960	86,065	76,856	93,204	87,702	85,713	86,659	87,801	1,026,818

[1] Includes small amounts of lignite.   [2] Preliminary.   *Source: Energy Information Administration, U.S. Department of Energy*

Pennsylvania Anthracite Coal Production[1]   In Thousands of Short Tons

Year	Jan.	Feb.	Mar.	Apr.	May	June	July	Aug.	Sept.	Oct.	Nov.	Dec.	Total
1986	261	243	260	300	294	297	298	330	333	431	373	340	4,292
1987	256	264	305	339	333	359	426	441	441	371	331	310	3,560
1988	215	268	279	265	296	282	246	360	315	377	302	253	3,555
1989	281	282	337	273	280	256	197	311	299	373	339	291	3,519
1990	237	221	259	297	329	327	225	280	323	354	310	183	3,506
1991	248	243	259	230	224	235	253	313	285	346	299	238	3,445
1992	247	257	279	296	274	287	305	337	311	322	321	306	3,483
1993	272	266	290	175	305	358	222	277	351	603	315	271	4,306
1994[2]	241	254	315	294	290	293	261	355	319	377	365	319	3,683

[1] Represents production in Pennsylvania only..   [2] Preliminary.   *Source: Energy Information Administration, U.S. Department of Energy*

Salient Statistics of Coal in the United States   In Thousands of Short Tons

Year	Production	Imports	Consumption	Exports Brazil	Exports Canada	Exports Europe	Exports Asia	Exports Total	Total Ending Stocks[2]	Losses & Unaccounted For[3]
1986	890,315	2,212	804,231	5,720	14,774	42,552	19,639	85,518	207,319	-1,175
1987	918,762	1,747	836,941	5,830	16,464	34,159	20,206	79,607	213,780	-2,499
1988	950,265	2,134	883,642	5,252	19,232	45,137	23,075	95,023	188,831	-1,316
1989	980,729	2,851	889,699	5,681	16,777	51,604	22,734	100,815	178,087	6,811
1990	1,029,076	2,699	895,480	5,847	15,511	58,382	22,725	105,804	201,629	3,949
1991	995,984	3,390	887,621	7,052	11,178	65,520	21,788	108,969	200,682	3,731
1992	997,545	3,803	892,421	6,370	15,140	57,255	20,540	102,516	197,685	9,407
1993[1]	945,424	7,309	925,944	5,197	8,889	37,575	19,500	74,519	145,742	4,213

[1] Preliminary.   [2] Producer & distributor and consumer stocks, excludes stocks held by retail dealers for consumption by the residential and commercial sector.   [3] Equals production plus imports minus the change in producer & distributor and consumer stocks minus consumption minus exports.
Source: Energy Information Administration, U.S. Department of Energy

U.S. Consumption and Stocks of Total Coal   In Thousands of Short Tons

Year	Electric Utilities Anthracite	Electric Utilities Bituminous	Electric Utilities Lignite	Electric Utilities Total	Industrial Coke Plants	Industrial Other Industrial[2]	Residential and Commercial	Total	Consumer Electric Utilities	Consumer Coke Plants	Consumer Other Industrials	Producers and Distributors
1986	829	616,134	69,093	685,056	35,924	75,583	7,667	804,231	161,806	2,992	10,429	32,093
1987	972	647,824	69,098	717,894	36,957	75,175	6,914	836,941	170,797	3,884	10,777	28,321
1988	1,063	681,048	76,260	758,372	41,888	76,252	7,130	883,642	146,507	3,137	8,768	30,418
1989	1,049	688,504	77,335	766,888	40,508	76,134	6,167	889,699	135,860	2,864	7,363	29,000
1990	1,031	694,317	78,201	773,549	38,877	76,330	6,724	895,480	156,166	3,329	8,716	33,418
1991	994	691,275	79,999	772,268	33,854	75,405	6,094	887,621	157,876	2,773	7,061	32,971
1992	986	698,626	80,248	779,860	32,366	74,042	6,153	892,421	154,130	2,597	6,965	33,993
1993[1]	951	732,736	79,821	813,508	31,323	74,892	6,221	925,944	111,341	2,401	6,716	25,284

[1] Preliminary.   [2] Including transportation.   [3] Excludes stocks held at retail dealers for consumption by the residential and commercial sector.
Source: *Energy Information Administration, U.S. Department of Energy*

Average U.S. Price of Coal   In Dollars Per Short Ton

Year	End-Use Sector Electric Utilities	End-Use Sector Coke Plants	End-Use Sector Other Industrial[3]	Imports[4]	Exports Steam	Exports Metallurgical	Exports Total Average[4]	Year	End-Use Sector Electric Utilities	End-Use Sector Coke Plants	End-Use Sector Other Industrial[3]	Imports[4]	Exports Steam	Exports Metallurgical	Exports Total Average[4]
1985	34.53	54.30	37.21	36.04	NA	NA	48.18	1990	30.45	47.73	33.59	34.45	36.81	46.51	42.63
1986	33.30	50.83	35.84	36.02	43.37	47.14	45.95	1991	30.02	48.88	33.54	33.12	36.91	46.15	42.39
1987	31.83	46.55	33.71	32.04	39.22	44.49	42.77	1992	29.36	47.92	32.78	33.46	35.73	45.41	41.34
1988	30.64	47.70	33.43	29.96	38.59	44.17	42.23	1993[1]	28.58	47.44	32.23	29.89	36.03	44.11	41.41
1989	30.15	47.50	33.03	34.14	37.64	45.19	42.52	1994[2]	28.25	46.59	32.47	29.50	34.23	42.97	40.25

[1] Preliminary.   [2] Estimate.   [3] Manufacturing plants only.   [4] Based on the free alongside ship (F.A.S) value.   NA = Not available.
Source: Energy Information Administration, U.S. Department of Energy

Cobalt

Cobalt is found widely in the ores of iron and copper. Most cobalt is utilized in the production of superalloys which are used in jet engines. Because of its properties, cobalt is used in heavy-wear, high-temperature and magnetic applications. In addition, radioactive isotope of cobalt has medical and industrial uses, and cobalt can be found as a coloring agent in ceramic materials, printing ink and pigments. Cobalt salt is used for electroplating baths.

According to U.S. Bureau of Mines data, cobalt was consumed in the following products: just over 40% went toward aircraft gas turbine engines; over 10% was used in paint driers; magnetic alloys used 10%; and cemented carbides took 7%.

The cobalt resources of the U.S. are estimated to be 1.3 million tonnes. Most deposits are located in Minnesota, but not in large enough concentrations to be mined. There are plans to open a mine in Maine. Most cobalt is produced through recycling superalloy or cemented carbine scrap.

Cobalt consumption during the first six months of 1994 was 3,370 tonnes compared to 3,036 tonnes consumed in the same period of 1993. U.S. consumption of cobalt metal totaled 1,456 tonnes compared to 1,218 tonnes for the same period of 1993. Consumption of oxide and other chemicals was 1,110 tonnes against 999 tonnes in 1993. Scrap consumption was 804 tonnes compared with 999 tonnes in 1993. Total U.S. consumption of cobalt materials in 1993 was 6,473 tonnes. Consumption of cobalt materials by end use over the January-June 1994 period showed stainless and heat resisting steel used 17 tonnes; superalloys consumed 1,316 tonnes; cutting and wear-resistant materials used 350 tonnes; magnetic alloys 356 tonnes; chemical catalysts 489 tonnes while paint driers consumed 451 tonnes.

Most data on cobalt use is withheld to avoid disclosing company proprietary data.

U.S. reported stocks of cobalt materials on June 30, 1994 were as follows: cobalt metal 377 tonnes; cobalt oxide and other chemical compounds 346 tonnes; scrap 155 tonnes. Total stocks were 877 tonnes. This compares with stocks on December 31, 1993 of 875 tonnes.

Since the U.S. does not mine cobalt, it must rely on imports to meet its needs. For the first five months of 1994 U.S. imports of cobalt content material were 706,463 kilograms. Imports of cobalt metal were 605,231 kilograms; cobalt oxides and hydroxides 100,322 kilograms; and cobalt salts and compounds 97,468 kilograms. The major suppliers of cobalt metal were Canada, Norway and Zambia. Oxides and hydroxides were supplied mainly by Zaire and Finland. Cobalt salts and compounds came primarily from Finland. The U.S. also imports smaller amounts of cobalt material like unwrought cobalt alloys, cobalt matte, waste and scrap and wrought cobalt.

For the first five months of 1994 U.S. exports of unwrought cobalt, powders, matte, waste and scrap were 260,347 kilograms (gross weight). Exports of cobalt oxides and hydroxides for January-May 1994 were 471,630 kilograms, while exports of salt and compounds were 108,741 kilograms. Exports of wrought cobalt and cobalt articles were 263,555 kilograms. Exports of cobalt ores and concentrates were 84,643 kilograms.

Platt's Metals Week indicated that the price of electrolytic cobalt in June 1994 averaged $24.34 per pound, while in July 1994 prices averaged $23.24 per pound. At the end of 1993, cobalt prices were averaging $11.00 per pound to $14.75 per pound.

World Mine Production of Cobalt — In Metric Tons (Cobalt Content)

Year	Albania	Australia	Botswana	Brazil	Canada	Cuba	Finland (Refinery)	France (Refinery)	Japan (Refinery)	Morocco	New Caledonia	Norway (Refinery)	Russia[3]	South Africa	Zaire	Zambia	World Total
1986	600	1,237	163	150	2,297	1,553	1,348	158	1,338	-----	700	1,574	2,800	690	33,373	5,869	50,199
1987	600	1,261	181	150	2,490	1,566	1,234	136	124	224	750	1,576	2,800	380	23,200	7,365	41,245
1988	600	1,200	291	150	2,398	1,783	1,132	176	109	253	800	1,951	2,850	300	26,000	7,090	43,819
1989	600	1,100	215	300	6,167	1,825	1,295	165	99	121	800	1,946	5,700	300	18,400	7,255	42,873
1990	600	1,200	205	400	5,470	1,600	1,300	150	199	194	800	1,830	5,500	350	19,000	6,999	42,420
1991	600	1,400	208	400	5,274	1,600	1,503	123	185	325	800	1,983	5,000	300	9,900	6,994	32,906
1992	20	1,600	208	400	5,102	1,500	2,100	150	105	461	800	2,293	4,000	350	5,700	6,910	27,131
1993[1]	10	1,700	200	400	5,738	1,500	2,200	150	190	397	800	2,414	3,300	350	2,459	5,300	22,224
1994[2]		1,900			5,700	1,500					800		3,300		2,500	5,300	22,000

[1] Preliminary. [2] Estimate. [3] Formerly part of the U.S.S.R.; data not reported seperately until 1992. *Source: U.S. Bureau of Mines*

U.S. Salient Statistics of Cobalt — In Metric Tons (Cobalt Content)

Year	% Net Import Reliance of Apparent Consumption	Cobalt Secondary Production	Processors and Consumer Stocks December 31	Imports for Consumption	Ground Coat Frit	Stainless and Heat Resisting	Catalysts	Super-Alloys	Tool Steel	Magnetic Alloys	Pigments	Drier in Paints, etc.[3]	Cutting and Wear-Resistant Material	Welding Materials	Total (Apparent)	Price Dollars Per Pound[4]
1987	87	1,025	2,043	8,832	360	26	497	2,873	174	666	258	799	654	W	7,986	6.56
1988	87	1,018	1,766	7,051	332	26	617	2,865	180	878	378	892	522	206	7,824	7.09
1989	83	1,184	1,456	5,793	366	74	819	2,860	219	870	319	718	538	136	7,172	7.64
1990	84	1,225	1,853	6,529	357	41	W	3,345	123	710	W	751	541	180	7,512	10.09
1991	80	1,578	1,622	6,924	W	51	W	3,066	W	713	W	781	525	135	7,240	16.92
1992	75	1,613	896	5,757	257	26	949	2,697	47	670	197	745	522	128	6,471	22.93
1993[1]	79	1,566	875	5,945	W	41	935	2,614	59	629	193	732	569	171	6,473	13.79
1994[2]	79	1,600		7,300											7,800	25.00

[1] Preliminary. [2] Estimate. [3] Or related usage. [4] Annual spot for cathodes. W = Witheld proprietary data. *Source: U.S. Bureau of Mines*

Cocoa

World cocoa prices neared a five-year high in mid-1994, which for a time overshadowed prospects of a record large 1994/95 production. The strength reflected fears that the world crop would trail initial expectations, but the bullish enthusiasm proved short lived and by yearend 1994 prices (based on New York futures values) were about midway between the year's high and low. Historically, cocoa's initial statistical data tends to have a wide margin of error and price swings, in either direction, are inclined to carry further than later data can support.

World cocoa bean production for 1994/95 (October-September) was forecast at a record 2.55 million tonnes, 2.3 percent over the year earlier 2.49 million tonnes, and slightly over the previous record of 2.52 million tonnes of 1990/91. The record production largely reflected increased production in Brazil, Cote d'Ivoire and Ghana. Production in the early-1980s averaged about 1.6 million tonnes, by the turn of the 1990s the average was close to 2.4 million tonnes.

The Cote d' Ivoire, the world's largest grower, produced about 860,000 tonnes in 1994/95, marginally above 1993/94. Cocoa's higher price trend since mid-1992 has encouraged producers to implement better farm management, such as increased tree spraying and more complete harvesting of trees. Cote d'Ivoire cocoa bean exports in 1993 totaled 790,721 tonnes, one-half of which went to the Netherlands. Another 80,000 plus tonnes of cocoa butter and paste were exported. Ghana's estimated 1994/95 production of 315,000 tonnes, of which 285,000 tonnes was from the main crop and the balance mid-crop, compares with a 1993/94 total of 260,000 tonnes. In mid-1994 the Ghana government more than doubled prices paid to producers which is expected to see growers better maintain their farms. Ghana's 1993 cocoa bean exports of 255,967 tonnes compares with 223,774 tonnes in 1992. Brazil's crop of 306,000 tonnes compares with the poor 1993/94 harvest of only 276,000 tonnes. The Bahia main and temporao crops were both higher than in 1993/94. The U.S. is the major market for Brazil's cocoa bean and product exports with over 100,000 tonnes in 1993.

Indonesia's production has surged since the early-1980s, although a drought held 1994/95 production to about 260,000 tonnes from the year earlier record of 280,000 tonnes. Uncertainty persists as to how much acreage Indonesia is actually placing into cocoa production, and the same might be said of Malaysia as much of their crops are produced on small farms. However, the Indonesian government appears committed to stimulating cocoa production with various incentives to growers, which if successful could see crops of about 450,000 tonnes by the year 2000.

Indonesia's cocoa bean exports in 1993 totaled a record 200,112 tonnes. Malaysia's production appears to have stagnated and has drifted steadily lower in the 1990s, from 235,000 tonnes in 1990/91 to 200,000 tonnes in 1994/95. Acreage under cultivation for cocoa since 1990 has dropped from 420,000 hectares to 320,000 hectares.

World cocoa bean grindings for 1994/95 are estimated at 2.52 million tonnes, which if realized would place world supply/demand in a virtual balance with no change in world stocks as of September 30, 1995. From 1984/85 through 1990/91, world production exceeded consumption, resulting in large global stocks and depressed market prices. During the next three years world stocks dropped modestly, but still totaled about 1.3 million tonnes at the end of the 1993/94 season, the equivalent of about a six-month supply at current annual grinding rates. The International Cocoa Organization (ICCO) continues its controlled liquidation of an initial 230,000 tonnes buffer stock inventory, which are being sold in monthly installments over a four and one-half year period in order to check bearish pressure on prices. The new International Cocoa Agreement (ICCA) is based on production management and consumption promotion, rather than on a buffer stock mechanism to stabilize prices. The agreement's success remains uncertain as some producing nations are reluctant to voluntarily limit their production.

Raw cocoa consumption is reflected by grindings, most of which occurs in Europe and the U.S. The U.S. grind in 1993 of almost 320,000 tonnes compares with 314,000 tonnes in 1992, but the total for 1994 is expected to lag 1993. The German 1993 grind of 299,000 tonnes and the total for 1994 should about equal 1993. Grinding totals can be restrained (or increased) by slack economies, as in Germany in 1993, or by reporting discrepancies.

The U.S. imported 411,937 tonnes of cocoa beans and about 380,000 tonnes of cocoa products in 1993. Norfolk, Virginia is the major port of entry for beans, while processed cocoa products went mostly through Philadelphia. Cocoa products come mostly from Canada. U.S. per capita consumption of cocoa (bean equivalent) in 1992/93 of 2.3 kilograms was fractionally under 1991/92. Per capita consumption is higher in a number of European nations.

Futures Markets

Cocoa futures are traded on the Coffee, Sugar, and Cocoa Exchange (CSCE) in New York and on the London Terminal Market. Options are traded on the CSCE and the London Futures and Options Exchange.

World Cocoa Supply and Demand   In Thousands of Metric Tons

Crop Year Beginning October	Stock Oct. 1	Net World Pro- duction[4]	Total Avail- ability	Seasonal Grindings	Closing Stocks	Stock Change	Crop Year Beginning October	Stock Oct. 1	Net World Crop[4]	Total Avail- ability	Seasonal Grindings	Closing Stocks	Stock Change
1981-2	642	1,720	2,362	1,606	747	+114	1988-9	822	2,445	3,267	2,124	1,133	+321
1982-3	747	1,530	2,277	1,635	645	-105	1989-90	1,133	2,395	3,528	2,216	1,307	+179
1983-4	645	1,531	2,176	1,719	450	-188	1990-1	1,307	2,501	3,808	2,339	1,431	+162
1984-5	450	1,947	2,397	1,857	513	+90	1991-2	1,431	2,278	3,709	2,304	1,362	-26
1985-6	513	1,927	2,440	1,875	580	+52	1992-3[1]	1,362	2,387	3,749	2,417	1,362	-30
1986-7	580	1,993	2,573	1,896	652	+97	1993-4[2]	1,362	2,371	3,733	2,462	1,271	-91
1987-8	652	2,192	2,844	1,997	822	+195	1994-5[3]	1,271	2,427	3,698	2,516	1,182	-89

[1] Preliminary. [2] Estimate. [3] Forecast. [4] Obtained by adjusting the Gross World Crop for one percent loss in weight. *Source: E D & F Man Cocoa, Ltd.*

COCOA

World Production of Cocoa Beans in Principal Producing Countries   In Thousands of Metric Tons

Crop Year Beginning October	Brazil	Came-roon	Colom-bia	Domin-ican Republic	Ecuador	Ghana	Indo-nesia	Ivory Coast	Mal-aysia	Mexico	Nigeria	Papua New Guinea	Peru	Philip-pines	Togo	Vene-zuela	World Total
1984-5	415	120	42.0	39.2	128.0	175	32.4	565	100	42.1	170	30.8	10	6.0	7.0	10.5	1,966.6
1985-6	380	119	45.6	39.0	112.0	219	34.3	555	130	39.2	130	32.7	10	6.5	12.8	11.2	1,946.1
1986-7	365	123	52.0	45.2	77.0	228	167.0	620	167	37.9	100	34.0	10	6.6	15.7	13.9	2,013.5
1987-8	400	133	53.8	50.0	76.0	188	70.0	674	227	47.5	145	35.0	10	7.2	12.0	12.5	2,214.2
1988-9	334	124	56.3	44.3	82.0	300	98.0	849	225	41.0	160	48.0	10	7.8	10.0	11.5	2,471.3
1989-90	356	122	58.0	57.0	102.0	295	135.0	710	240	38.5	155	41.0	10	9.0	7.6	14.4	2,419.1
1990-1	375	100	60.0	42.3	104.0	293	165.0	804	235	38.9	160	34.0	10	9.0	6.8	16.5	2,525.5
1991-2	301	107	60.5	48.8	82.4	243	200.0	747	217	41.5	110	41.0	10	9.0	8.0	16.0	2,301.4
1992-3[1]	330	100	60.0	50.8	76.0	312	240.0	700	225	43.5	140	39.0	10	9.0	6.0	16.5	2,417.4
1993-4[2]	276	105	60.0	55.0	78.0	260	280.0	850	210	38.0	140	35.0	10	9.0	6.0	16.0	2,487.5
1994-5[3]	306	100	60.0	51.0	79.0	315	260.0	860	200	44.0	130	40.0	10	9.0	6.0	16.0	2,545.2

[1] Preliminary.   [2] Estimate.   [3] Forecast.   Source: Foreign Agricultural Service, U.S. Department of Agriculture

World Absorption (Consumption) of Cocoa[1]   In Thousands of Metric Tons

Crop Year Beginning October	Belgium	Brazil	Canada	Colom-bia	Cote d'Ivoire	France	Ger-many	Italy	Japan	Mal-aysia	Nether-lands	Singa-pore	Spain	United Kingdom	United States	Former USSR	World Total
1984-5	36	249	22	39	97	42	205	47	34	25	165	23	33	95	202	165	1,857
1985-6	34	240	20	51	117	41	218	45	35	27	176	30	31	83	193	144	1,875
1986-7	34	233	19	48	89	35	225	43	36	36	190	33	33	94	228	164	1,896
1987-8	35	241	21	46	102	40	245	46	40	40	215	40	43	100	241	132	1,998
1988-9	41	210	22	41	110	44	265	46	40	47	234	46	40	112	237	201	2,124
1989-90	47	243	24	45	111	59	287	51	47	72	241	52	42	120	265	106	2,220
1990-1	49	283	25	47	115	70	295	56	52	77	268	51	45	145	265	83	2,347
1991-2	45	225	31	44	108	67	306	62	49	87	294	50	46	153	307	25	2,304
1992-3[2]	45	222	41	45	100	76	305	57	37	99	309	46	44	169	326	95	2,417
1993-4[3]	46	226	42	46	108	78	297	59	39	104	329	48	46	170	315	90	2,462
1994-5[4]		220			111		300			108	341			167	328	80	2,516

[1] Figures represent the "grindings" of cocoa beans in each country.   [2] Preliminary.   [3] Estimate.   [4] Forecast.   Source: Foreign Agricultural Service, U.S. Department of Agriculture

Raw Cocoa Grindings in Selected Countries   In Metric Tons

Year	Total	First Quarter	Second Quarter	Third Quarter	Fourth Quarter	Total	First Quarter	Second Quarter	Third Quarter	Fourth Quarter
			Germany[2]					Netherlands		
1984	193,468	49,900	48,570	42,381	52,617	161,420	44,350	39,970	34,960	42,140
1985	206,806	57,042	51,722	44,047	53,995	167,353	44,633	41,690	36,970	44,060
1986	201,037	53,643	50,641	42,589	54,164	182,570	46,200	45,050	40,290	51,030
1987	208,684	55,190	49,224	46,424	57,846	195,627	49,141	47,399	42,772	56,315
1988	232,794	60,039	53,990	53,008	65,757	216,499	56,074	51,712	50,539	58,174
1989	245,997	61,960	59,211	56,994	67,832	233,529	61,071	56,392	55,129	60,937
1990	281,855	69,125	64,613	70,994	77,123	247,590	62,243	58,817	58,702	67,828
1991	290,703	73,172	72,396	70,934	73,661	274,741	64,299	71,643	63,973	74,826
1992	319,251	78,661	73,797	80,111	86,682	293,157	77,954	71,537	69,871	73,795
1993	298,681	74,119	69,805	74,010	80,747	320,060	78,338	75,548	81,183	84,991
1994[1]		80,242	68,033	67,706			83,963	78,055	81,750	
			United Kingdom					United States[3]		
1984	89,552	22,338	21,864	21,120	24,230	164,442	42,416	41,590	40,904	39,532
1985	91,295	26,547	24,435	19,981	20,332	153,911	38,970	37,519	40,549	36,873
1986	87,243	21,109	21,998	20,088	24,048	153,621	33,761	37,014	42,264	40,582
1987	95,396	24,469	22,941	22,405	25,581	180,811	39,665	45,930	49,864	45,352
1988	100,507	26,309	24,997	22,407	26,794	186,885	45,197	47,327	48,376	45,985
1989	114,669	28,506	30,113	26,873	29,177	192,837	43,802	49,185	47,071	52,779
1990	124,791	32,116	29,322	29,419	33,934	216,740	51,559	51,683	58,278	55,220
1991	148,191	32,902	36,016	41,863	37,410	255,781	51,191	64,365	66,544	73,681
1992	159,284	39,831	37,903	37,120	44,430	313,921	70,335	74,515	84,109	84,962
1993	170,208	44,575	41,975	37,496	46,162	321,905	78,968	77,720	84,593	80,624
1994[1]		44,131	39,063	39,591			71,397	76,282	86,247	

[1] Preliminary.   [2] Beginning October 1990, includes former East Germany.   [3] Data incomplete January 1984-March 1991, excludes one major processor.
Source: Foreign Agricultural Service, U.S. Department of Agriculture

Imports of Cocoa Butter--Selected Countries   In Metric Tons

Year	Australia	Austria	Belgium	Canada	Finland	France	Germany	Greece	Italy	Japan	Netherlands	Norway	Russia[2]	Sweden	Switzerland	United Kingdom	United States
1982	5,419	3,382	12,281	4,860	2,333	14,008	30,564	1,859	1,631	10,615	16,225	2,083	NA	4,451	9,982	25,820	37,325
1983	6,067	3,535	12,128	5,313	2,428	16,690	30,581	1,788	2,151	9,947	20,224	1,892	NA	7,404	10,224	31,581	47,981
1984	6,445	3,763	13,451	5,437	2,156	17,325	35,241	1,561	2,337	8,346	25,072	2,139	4,200	5,103	9,798	30,203	51,711
1985	8,538	3,682	15,416	5,535	2,039	19,908	33,378	1,225	3,056	8,632	24,595	1,957	7,150	4,920	11,175	31,372	70,146
1986	8,204	4,387	13,795	5,377	1,966	19,397	25,513	1,557	3,246	8,474	14,925	2,295	3,450	4,866	11,369	32,669	70,264
1987	8,370	3,879	14,312	5,833	1,971	23,704	27,436	1,860	3,509	9,330	16,152	2,734	1,000	5,272	11,932	29,689	79,773
1988	9,405	4,315	12,869	7,371	2,246	24,562	33,590	2,812	4,731	12,497	20,431	2,523	1,008	5,596	12,821	34,329	78,285
1989	10,291	4,599	17,748	8,224	2,469	26,597	41,765	2,806	5,932	15,280	22,924	2,706	2,500	5,735	16,276	35,045	64,353
1990	10,331	6,047	22,123	8,830	2,536	28,541	50,402	2,892	6,183	15,686	34,647	2,897	4,750	5,854	16,306	34,397	92,165
1991	10,466	5,170	24,794	8,682	2,745	28,630	54,450	2,162	7,807	15,745	29,730	3,024	610	6,314	16,545	26,886	93,239
1992	10,418	5,250	31,904	11,358	3,452	25,211	44,906	2,562	8,419	15,835	31,702	2,962	870	5,885	17,415	25,917	99,512
1993[1]	11,644	5,416	26,642	10,222	4,530	30,517	35,876	2,503	9,846	16,423	51,428	3,567	1,308	6,390	16,732	28,297	83,399

[1] Preliminary.   [2] Formerly part of the U.S.S.R.; data not reported separately until 1992.   NA = Not available.   Source: Food and Agricultural Organization of the United Nations

Imports of Cocoa Liquor and Cocoa Powder (Selected Countries)   In Metric Tons

	Cocoa Liquor							Cocoa Powder							
Year	France	Germany	Netherlands	Japan	United Kingdom	United States	Former U.S.S.R.	Belgium	France	Germany	Italy	Japan	Netherlands	Sweden	United Kingdom	United States
1982	13,871	2,196	13,519	3,684	2,283	31,419	8,700	3,770	7,609	13,524	6,673	2,832	2,974	3,872	3,284	60,563
1983	15,164	2,288	14,216	4,303	3,829	45,477	15,425	3,895	8,527	13,886	7,964	3,157	3,009	3,806	3,014	78,968
1984	20,268	3,075	13,622	2,928	2,184	45,457	32,000	4,204	9,652	13,554	7,462	3,260	3,574	3,996	3,654	89,978
1985	24,031	3,570	14,822	2,792	3,400	53,042	37,510	4,586	8,269	16,624	8,313	3,841	4,669	3,928	2,591	81,775
1986	28,426	2,006	10,915	3,346	4,091	50,705	30,110	4,844	8,984	15,654	9,059	4,844	4,669	3,980	3,258	89,454
1987	31,171	391	8,805	3,402	1,870	38,105	21,680	5,229	8,967	16,989	9,330	5,517	3,624	3,982	3,897	103,455
1988	31,157	793	9,014	3,445	3,022	34,454	21,000	5,572	9,750	16,455	9,498	6,470	3,432	4,330	3,576	91,337
1989	29,257	1,040	9,315	3,451	2,524	27,556	31,504	6,138	10,920	18,470	10,233	6,033	5,862	4,125	3,255	53,736
1990	35,146	1,860	9,875	3,123	1,713	25,047	18,580	6,235	12,244	21,294	11,418	6,284	6,446	4,357	3,619	58,280
1991	40,251	3,242	7,443	2,057	1,918	25,320	NA	6,665	12,215	25,315	12,189	6,557	6,239	4,314	4,315	55,636
1992	45,056	2,540	6,391	2,246	3,145	24,255	NA	6,665	14,896	27,745	14,469	6,067	9,412	3,533	3,109	56,089

[1] Preliminary.   NA = Not available.   Source: E D & F Man Cococa, Ltd.

United States Imports of Cocoa and Products   In Thousands of Metric Tons

Year	Jan.	Feb.	Mar.	Apr.	May	June	July	Aug.	Sept.	Oct.	Nov.	Dec.	Total
1982	10	29	18	15	17	12	13	20	14	14	14	17	194
1983	46	43	19	36	14	11	10	7	6	5	8	8	214
1984[3]	16	21	29	17	25	15	13	11	10	5	11	18	191
1985	43	44	40	10	31	16	14	13	11	10	13	25	270
1986	30	17	15	9	19	16	22	23	12	8	15	18	209
1987	27	28	23	31	21	10	11	14	6	23	24	45	263
1988	27	31	27	19	15	21	15	20	9	9	14	31	237
1989	44	24	30	29	25	18	18	23	14	20	10	10	266
1990[2]	72	53	70	110	83	60	NA	61	41	NA	72	49	716
1991	70	53	51	74	62	66	65	59	53	NA	NA	73	761
1992	83	66	62	55	50	60	52	60	67	67	64	69	755
1993	67	57	56	61	58	61	77	58	59	71	71	88	801
1994[1]	89	68	56	56	49	51	49	58	58	61	45	48	672

[1] Preliminary.   [2] Prior to 1990, data for cocoa bean imports only.   [3] Prior to 1984, data are in thousands of long tons.   NA = Not available.
Source: Foreign Agricultural Service, U.S. Department of Agriculture

Visible Stocks of Cocoa at Port of Hampton Road Warehouses[1], End of Month   In Thousands of Bags

Year	Jan.	Feb.	Mar.	Apr.	May	June	July	Aug.	Sept.	Oct.	Nov.	Dec.
1988	140.8	274.8	347.3	434.9	480.8	474.3	511.2	464.1	486.4	465.8	442.1	419.6
1989	528.4	653.3	777.7	775.0	875.0	741.6	655.8	583.2	509.1	594.2	567.0	552.3
1990	403.6	445.9	583.2	674.3	807.4	1,064.7	917.2	67.2	1,046.5	19.0	996.5	958.2
1991	946.5	953.3	910.1	946.0	906.1	1,036.6	1,174.5	1,291.2	1,386.2	1,429.0	1,426.0	1,502.9
1992	1,588.3	1,892.1	2,233.1	2,236.2	2,236.9	2,204.8	2,150.8	2,087.4	1,982.4	2,018.6	2,043.9	2,188.5
1993	2,209.9	2,497.3	2,443.9	2,676.8	2,771.8	2,689.7	2,920.0	2,708.6	2,740.1	2,418.7	2,328.3	2,356.9
1994	2,329.6	2,441.1	2,684.1	2,522.9	2,543.0	2,457.6	2,445.4	2,335.0	2,308.4	2,360.2	2,306.9	2,253.7

[1] Licensed and unlicensed warehouses approved by the CSCE.   Source: Coffee, Sugar & Cocoa Exchange, Inc. (CSCE)

COCOA

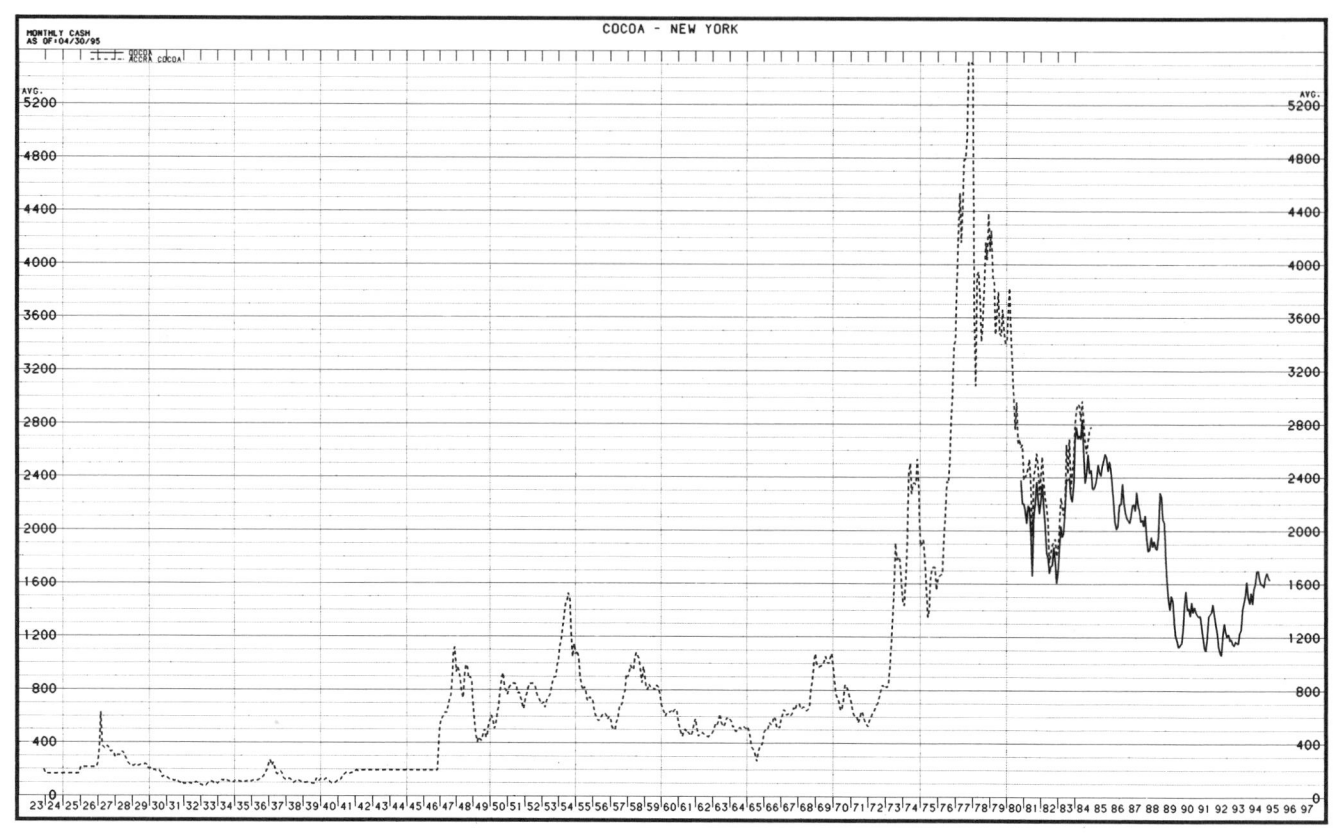

Visible Stocks of Cocoa in Philadelphia (Delaware River) Warehouses[1], End of Month   In Thousands of Bags

Year	Jan.	Feb.	Mar.	Apr.	May	June	July	Aug.	Sept.	Oct.	Nov.	Dec.
1985	221.3	282.0	333.6	420.9	416.4	389.1	315.9	323.9	320.7	316.3	289.1	280.6
1986	281.3	276.4	258.8	255.8	237.9	201.3	208.7	182.0	209.5	137.1	136.7	188.5
1987	209.8	210.8	228.9	224.1	243.6	276.2	291.4	259.7	236.6	177.9	189.6	206.3
1988	164.6	149.2	154.9	211.1	227.3	232.0	238.1	193.3	185.5	157.6	123.4	112.0
1989	86.0	67.5	88.7	96.2	114.0	112.5	100.3	100.0	54.6	46.1	51.9	53.5
1990	35.1	61.1	87.5	107.9	120.5	204.4	297.1	231.2	185.9	193.0	195.3	215.1
1991	216.2	226.9	249.3	254.9	309.2	376.8	382.8	376.8	375.5	355.1	280.5	282.7
1992	344.6	345.5	412.1	547.6	576.7	632.0	637.7	654.0	616.4	606.0	565.8	612.4
1993	562.2	589.8	603.9	606.0	653.1	678.0	665.7	648.9	600.6	611.5	685.2	781.8
1994	271.0	275.0	280.8	296.6	358.6	394.1	447.5	447.5	467.3	427.3	407.2	818.9

[1] Licensed and unlicensed warehouses approved by the CSCE.   *Source: Coffee, Sugar & Cocoa Exchange, Inc. (CSCE)*

Visible Stocks of Cocoa in New York Warehouses[1], End of Month   In Thousands of Bags

Year	Jan.	Feb.	Mar.	Apr.	May	June	July	Aug.	Sept.	Oct.	Nov.	Dec.
1985	34.7	22.0	13.2	36.4	167.8	170.9	161.3	155.7	164.6	150.6	131.8	107.1
1986	99.2	96.9	95.6	89.7	87.4	90.3	88.9	103.6	102.1	87.5	70.6	59.9
1987	51.9	43.5	40.0	39.4	55.2	46.1	58.7	43.5	49.4	44.8	107.7	149.1
1988	138.7	115.4	100.1	96.8	102.8	135.4	140.8	146.8	114.3	105.8	73.7	59.8
1989	65.0	81.9	47.3	82.2	214.8	245.3	274.2	215.6	181.3	247.7	313.6	293.5
1990	288.4	267.5	311.9	335.3	294.8	359.2	431.3	409.0	442.2	406.3	413.4	397.2
1991	355.6	219.6	295.9	294.1	250.4	292.6	313.3	317.1	271.5	253.9	292.9	282.4
1992	321.2	303.7	278.7	302.6	273.4	287.8	329.7	301.5	280.5	252.3	212.7	183.3
1993	150.9	144.1	122.0	125.0	119.8	119.8	119.8	119.8	119.8	118.6	132.4	187.7
1994	271.0	275.0	280.8	296.6	358.6	394.1	447.5	447.5	467.3	427.3	407.2	556.1

[1] Licensed and unlicensed warehouses approved by the CSCE.   *Source: Coffee, Sugar & Cocoa Exchange, Inc. (CSCE)*

U.S. Spot Cocoa Prices[1] for Selected Origins of Cocoa Beans and Products   Dollars Per Metric Ton

Crop Year Beginning October	Cocoa Beans					Chocolate Liquor		Cocoa Butter		Cocoa Cake 10-12% Fat
	Brazil	Cote d'Ivoire	Dominican Republic	Ecuador	Malaysia	Brazil	Ecuador	African	Other	
1984-5	2,407	2,433	2,197	2,239	NA	2,919	2,784	5,331	5,276	951
1985-6	2,207	2,281	2,020	2,048	NA	2,720	2,552	4,940	4,897	825
1986-7	2,087	2,155	1,942	1,975	NA	2,634	2,554	4,643	4,608	965
1987-8	1,807	1,952	1,664	1,700	NA	2,280	2,216	4,001	3,919	916
1988-9	1,669	1,773	1,442	1,466	1,364	2,136	1,912	3,543	3,515	945
1989-90	1,259	1,307	1,142	1,250	1,162	1,775	1,640	3,176	3,151	666
1990-1	1,222	1,289	1,091	1,168	1,131	1,704	1,646	3,232	3,199	394
1991-2	1,234	1,262	1,051	1,136	1,111	1,656	1,540	2,763	2,815	393
1992-3	1,109	1,199	969	1,123	1,020	1,571	1,513	2,517	2,572	539
1993-4	1,378	1,560	1,277	1,393	1,326	2,076	2,028	3,348	3,393	649

[1] All prices are nominal and are net ex-dock or ex-warehouse, U.S. eastern seaboard north of Hatteras, for merchandise physically available in interstate commerce, in truckload and regular commercial quantities.   NA = Not available.   *Source: Foreign Agricultural Service, U.S. Department of Agriculture*

Average Open Interest of Cocoa Futures at New York   In Contracts

Year	Jan.	Feb.	Mar.	Apr.	May	June	July	Aug.	Sept.	Oct.	Nov.	Dec.
1985	23,224	24,349	26,565	26,226	21,935	21,122	21,242	19,817	19,891	20,736	19,636	17,778
1986	18,507	19,543	20,841	21,267	22,520	23,172	24,287	24,376	25,795	24,769	23,678	24,576
1987	25,412	23,578	24,541	23,372	24,869	26,115	32,859	32,063	30,946	32,643	29,666	27,674
1988	27,704	28,713	32,178	33,589	35,239	36,444	37,772	38,841	38,762	38,222	37,834	36,697
1989	36,747	35,492	32,917	36,597	41,341	45,016	47,222	45,700	42,731	46,366	48,062	49,553
1990	52,094	52,599	55,796	51,299	51,076	50,385	49,603	49,083	47,332	50,084	44,944	41,955
1991	42,446	38,205	40,198	45,250	47,764	49,111	53,153	53,886	53,974	54,854	53,390	53,412
1992	54,464	54,797	52,110	49,904	48,076	47,690	49,924	50,532	51,706	56,101	57,426	60,521
1993	64,886	68,307	69,464	68,533	71,802	71,792	87,011	83,057	88,000	94,844	96,507	91,573
1994	89,174	87,349	91,715	82,500	82,970	72,288	72,249	69,614	73,436	74,163	72,232	75,995

Source: Coffee, Sugar & Cocoa Exchange, Inc.

Volume of Trading of Cocoa Futures at New York   In Contracts

Year	Jan.	Feb.	Mar.	Apr.	May	June	July	Aug.	Sept.	Oct.	Nov.	Dec.	Total
1985	86,748	83,988	94,863	72,564	64,716	62,989	74,583	57,842	52,912	58,358	53,056	37,954	800,573
1986	52,774	61,836	70,859	74,249	57,525	77,335	79,029	65,963	75,673	64,729	54,090	43,703	777,765
1987	67,268	61,641	73,341	67,954	68,521	93,849	111,728	66,990	71,591	70,164	81,605	60,813	895,465
1988	84,590	83,826	92,644	85,144	111,277	121,184	128,859	106,031	87,684	137,635	142,016	87,160	1,268,050
1989	138,883	122,374	116,082	132,208	135,783	129,943	98,922	137,879	73,741	95,531	101,152	59,352	1,341,850
1990	121,610	128,357	166,277	191,007	194,759	181,377	126,596	143,323	75,757	120,689	116,175	69,990	1,635,917
1991	94,609	92,450	104,973	99,176	76,435	104,327	96,840	146,379	104,136	135,677	106,888	72,629	1,234,519
1992	122,576	119,375	94,131	116,804	66,185	135,373	104,660	145,815	113,589	109,888	137,815	95,024	1,397,235
1993	145,378	139,932	111,751	149,771	82,961	189,474	225,901	215,044	240,371	217,697	229,752	183,352	2,128,384
1994	178,303	190,804	205,623	188,004	267,188	251,300	193,883	241,340	142,589	183,975	210,635	164,917	2,417,006

Source: Coffee, Sugar & Cocoa Exchange, Inc.

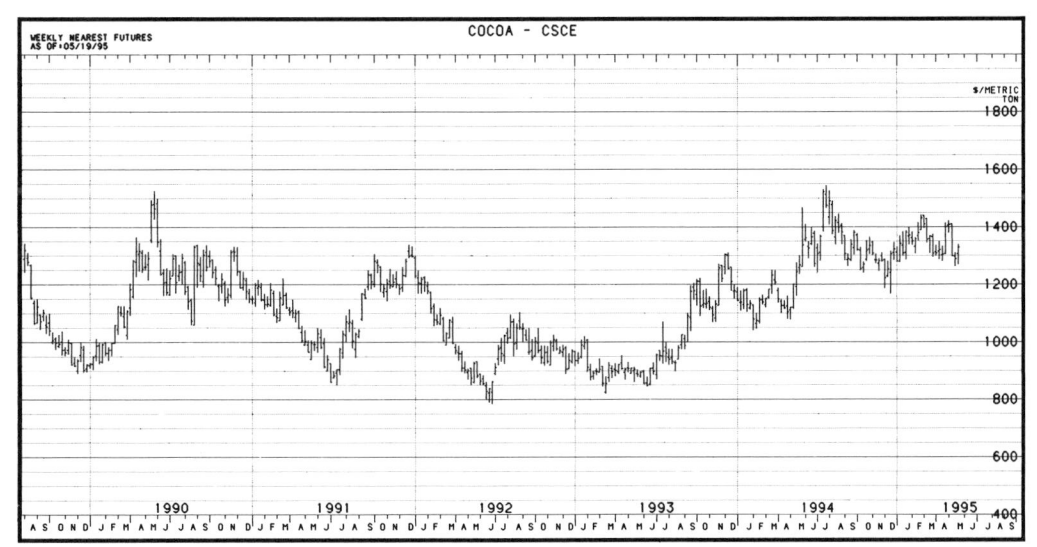

Coconut Oil and Copra

Copra, dried coconut meat, is crushed or processed to yield coconut oil and copra meal. Coconut oil is an important ingredient in cosmetics and soap, and is also used as a food ingredient. However, as an edible oil used in a variety of foods, its continued use, at least in the developed nations, is questionable, as the oil has a high level of saturated fats. The U.S. has imported in recent years an average of about 450,000 tons of coconut oil, most of which is processed into inedible products. Coconut oil for food use has dropped sharply from the mid 1980's when over 300,000 tons were used; recent figures place yearly use under 200,000 tons.

World production is small relative to the major oilseed, usually less than 5 percent that of soybeans. Total production in 1994/95 of 5 million metric tons compares with 4.8 million in 1993/94, and the highest outturn so far in the 1990's. Most of the crop is processed into oil which in 1994/95 totaled 3.1 million tons vs. copra meal production of less than 2 million tons, about the same for both as in 1993/94. The Philippines account for almost 40 percent of world copra output, Indonesia about 25 percent followed by India with 10 percent. Production in the three major producing nations has basically held steady in recent years, but percentage-wise, Vietnam's production has tripled since the mid-1980's, from about 70,000 tons to over 200,000. However, relative to the mid-1980's, Philippine production has dropped from a record high 2.5 million tons, then almost half the world total. Foreign trade in copra is small, but yearly coconut oil trade runs about 1.5 million tons. World copra stocks at the end of 1994/95 of about 130,000 tons are nearly twice the year earlier level; coconut oil stocks of 210,000 tons compare with 250,000, respectively.

U.S. 1994/95 imports of lauric oils (coconut and palm kernel) at 1.4 billion pounds are expected to be nearly unchanged from 1993/94, with coconut oil imports totally flat at slightly more than one billion pounds. U.S. coconut oil usage, however, was expected to edge higher in 1994/95 to 1.364 billion pounds (up 13 million from 1993/94), necessitating a draw on stocks from the expected 207 million pound carryover as of October 1, 1994.

Crude coconut oil prices, basis New York, recovered in 1994 from a year earlier. During the first half of the year prices averaged about 6 cents a pound over 1993, pointing to an average for the year above 30 cents a pound vs 25.25 cents in 1993.

World Copra Production by Principal Countries   In Thousands of Metric Tons

Year	India	Indonesia	Ivory Coast	Malaysia	Mexico	Mozambique	Papua New Guinea	Philipines	Solomon Islands	Sri Lanka	Thailand	Vanuatu	Vietnam	World Total
1982	268	1,091	27	208	110	50	120	2,015	31	131	30	45	40	4,600
1983	300	1,225	36	214	100	55	158	1,237	43	62	35	47	60	3,781
1984	360	1,260	60	166	100	55	176	1,813	45	240	93	39	65	4,681
1985	380	1,250	53	162	100	55	160	2,500	31	242	65	41	70	5,306
1986	320	1,270	48	97	115	65	149	2,100	28	125	74	36	70	4,709
1987	434	1,195	64	81	201	68	136	1,700	29	62	49	30	118	4,450
1988	487	1,021	52	97	203	70	134	1,710	35	130	62	24	139	4,444
1989	470	1,381	70	96	202	70	117	2,345	30	128	59	45	188	5,488
1990	450	1,392	75	76	175	72	91	1,950	24	61	62	28	192	4,933
1991	440	1,110	79	82	175	72	110	1,845	29	70	65	27	220	4,612
1992	440	1,110	65	82	200	72	117	1,845	23	70	65	24	220	4,624
1993[1]	445	1,100	60	65	173	73	120	1,950	23	60	68	26	200	2,648
1994[2]	455	1,260	65	55	170	74	115	1,880	25	62	69		200	2,742
1995[3]	470	1,270	68	52	169	74	100	2,000	27	62	69		215	2,896

[1] Preliminary.   [2] Estimate.   [3] Forecast.   *Source: The Oil World*

World Coconut Oil Supply and Distribution   In Thousands of Metric Tons

	Production							Consumption						Ending Stocks		
Year	India	Indonesia	Malaysia	Philippines	Total	Exports	Imports	EC-12	India	Indonesia	Philippines	United States	Total	Philippines	United States	Total
1983-4	189	672	125	786	2,273	1,053	908	374	199	577	223	415	2,424	104	50	253
1984-5	226	708	104	919	2,607	1,186	1,102	410	226	574	253	386	2,553	115	59	223
1985-6	236	720	86	1,587	3,296	1,613	1,523	575	236	710	286	461	3,040	178	140	389
1986-7	198	731	56	1,320	2,934	1,487	1,340	553	198	610	257	488	2,800	187	123	375
1987-8	253	721	38	1,141	2,851	1,451	1,490	535	246	479	304	416	2,891	122	151	589
1988-9	285	669	40	957	2,685	1,219	1,287	473	282	517	297	396	2,911	100	68	432
1989-90	284	782	34	1,314	3,212	1,587	1,554	521	284	576	278	386	3,039	115	128	571
1990-1	273	843	31	1,283	3,175	1,525	1,563	639	278	682	278	402	3,317	52	127	467
1991-2	267	701	29	1,092	2,807	1,406	1,360	497	280	380	253	409	2,817	102	85	412
1992-3[1]	267	681	30	1,294	2,987	1,653	1,602	491	280	430	249	491	2,980	38	114	372
1993-4[2]	271	746	23	1,051	2,791	1,354	1,410	502	279	389	269	483	2,926	47	74	293
1994-5[3]	280	757	22	1,270	3,036	1,524	1,520	483	287	436	274	475	2,990	63	80	335

[1] Preliminary.   [2] Estimate.   [3] Forecast.   *Source: The Oil World*

Supply and Distribution of Coconut Oil in the United States   In Millions of Pounds

Year	Rotterdam Copra Ton	Coconut Oil, CIF	Imports for Con-sumption	Stocks October 1	Total Supply	Exports	Total Domestic	Edible Products	Inedible Products	Total	Oct.-Dec.	Jan.-Mar.	Apr.-June	July-Sept.
1983-4	707	1,123	917	145	1,061	37	915	299	602	688.7	172.5	163.1	186.0	167.1
1984-5	476	746	891	112	1,001	20	851	275	376	658.5	176.4	161.3	175.7	145.1
1985-6	200	304	1,217	132	1,347	22	1,019	333	683	546.3	134.1	130.7	133.9	147.6
1986-7	285	413	1,087	308	1,395	49	1,076	319	720	685.5	151.8	197.9	180.4	155.4
1987-8	385	547	1,074	271	1,344	77	935	233	700	786.1	181.7	194.2	214.9	195.3
1988-9	371	545	778	332	1,111	55	904	211	713	712.7	199.3	165.1	182.0	166.3
1989-90	251	371	1,038	152	1,190	44	866	161	705	703.1	195.4	163.8	187.3	156.6
1990-1	247	364	946	279	1,216	51	897	169	742	754.6	196.8	150.8	141.8	265.2
1991-2	397	605	838	277	1,000	22	906	164	699	733.9	145.3	158.8	159.3	270.5
1992-3	292	446	1,190	187		22	1,080	202	692	650.5	156.0	158.8	166.6	169.1
1993-4[1]	388	564	1,047	275		22	1,047	234	716	536.2	155.6	129.0	131.8	119.8

[1] Preliminary.   *Source: Bureau of Census, U.S. Department of Commerce*

U.S. Consumption of Coconut Oil in End Products (Edible and Inedible)   In Millions of Pounds

Year	January	February	March	April	May	June	July	August	September	October	November	December	Total
1984	71.5	68.5	66.0	67.0	72.6	70.9	61.8	70.7	48.1	63.4	56.6	45.3	762.4
1985	53.4	57.1	46.1	52.5	51.7	52.8	53.2	57.2	61.2	53.0	57.7	50.0	645.9
1986	67.7	43.8	44.7	52.5	45.7	50.0	49.5	67.2	52.8	78.7	65.9	52.2	670.7
1987	63.7	58.0	76.2	74.1	72.8	81.4	73.8	79.1	82.5	89.6	70.0	72.8	894.0
1988	76.1	71.2	59.1	59.6	66.8	65.8	55.1	53.8	48.7	65.2	57.8	57.9	737.1
1989	52.6	51.6	64.3	55.0	65.9	58.0	60.5	51.3	48.7	55.1	49.7	39.6	652.3
1990	45.4	44.9	44.3	44.6	43.2	39.4	39.8	39.5	39.2	49.7	41.0	43.9	514.9
1991	------------137.6------------			------------150.6------------			------------134.4------------			------------122.1------------			544.7
1992	72.5	70.6	76.5	70.7	78.7	74.8	65.2	70.6	77.4	75.8	76.2	66.4	875.4
1993	74.4	75.9	81.3	77.6	72.1	71.0	73.6	78.2	72.6	85.9	90.9	84.6	938.1
1994[1]	71.1	74.6	74.8	75.9	85.5	85.2	73.3	86.0	61.8	71.1	82.2	90.1	931.6

[1] Preliminary.   *Source: Bureau of Census, U.S. Department of Commerce*

Stocks of Coconut Oil (Crude and Refined) in the United States   In Millions of Pounds

Year	Jan. 1	Feb. 1	Mar. 1	Apr. 1	May 1	June 1	July 1	Aug.1	Sept.1	Oct. 1	Nov. 1	Dec. 1
1984	175.2	215.5	193.8	165.0	150.2	121.8	78.7	90.9	100.2	111.0	119.8	107.3
1985	121.4	128.0	91.9	81.3	75.9	86.0	116.0	121.7	140.5	130.0	177.4	162.8
1986	206.5	259.0	262.1	285.1	247.4	289.3	275.0	273.4	273.8	308.0	295.5	320.5
1987	323.3	323.6	355.7	318.1	336.9	271.2	203.6	243.9	240.8	270.2	288.5	370.9
1988	367.7	358.8	370.7	371.1	356.0	353.6	336.6	290.2	287.5	335.0	332.7	307.0
1989	275.7	278.9	247.4	205.3	167.7	134.7	189.9	177.5	149.8	150.8	218.6	238.5
1990	297.3	304.4	307.0	348.0	305.6	306.6	292.2	264.3	315.4	281.1	309.3	304.6
1991	-------	--------	359.0	--------	--------	364.3	--------	--------	279.3	--------	--------	298.0
1992	-------	266.3	274.2	239.7	211.2	173.7	178.3	141.1	187.1	187.7	225.1	278.8
1993	355.7	406.7	418.9	348.7	338.3	305.2	257.2	233.8	321.4	250.8	335.0	299.1
1994[1]	291.7	316.5	284.4	251.5	237.6	199.8	151.3	164.1	156.0	164.1	166.2	152.8

[1] Preliminary.   *Source: U.S. Department of Commerce*

Average Price of Coconut Oil (Crude) Tank Cars at New York   In Cents Per Pound

Year	January	February	March	April	May	June	July	August	September	October	November	December	Average
1984	49.20	54.30	53.00	50.80	63.00	69.90	73.30	70.00	64.60	65.60	56.20	52.60	60.20
1985	42.20	40.20	41.00	41.00	N A	N A	31.70	27.50	25.00	24.00	22.80	17.40	31.30
1986	20.60	18.00	15.60	15.50	13.80	13.90	13.80	13.00	13.30	16.80	19.80	20.70	16.20
1987	21.40	20.88	19.30	20.38	21.44	24.25	25.75	25.13	24.40	24.69	24.50	27.15	23.27
1988	28.81	26.06	25.45	25.25	26.50	30.45	31.88	28.30	27.38	27.44	28.06	27.81	27.80
1989	26.75	27.63	27.90	28.94	29.90	29.56	28.94	27.75	28.63	27.25	26.35	24.75	27.86
1990	24.31	23.69	22.10	21.63	21.15	20.31	19.16	18.58	18.26	18.18	20.45	20.13	22.69
1991	20.22	20.31	20.50	19.38	19.69	21.69	26.19	25.63	25.63	28.50	31.50	32.38	24.72
1992	39.33	36.00	34.57	34.75	33.56	32.13	29.63	27.31	27.88	26.94	27.00	25.50	31.33
1993	24.94	24.33	23.65	23.25	24.13	24.95	25.50	25.75	24.25	23.75	26.50	32.00	25.25
1994[1]	28.00	30.00	30.00	30.25	31.75	32.75							

[1] Preliminary.   N A = Not available.   *Source: Economic Research Service, U.S. Department of Agriculture*

Coffee

Coffee prices surged in mid-1994 in the wake of a severe freeze in Brazil, and the market fevered perception of it having a potentially devastating effect on the crop of the world's largest producer. From late June to late July, prices (basis December 1994 futures, N.Y.) spiked from about $1.30 per pound to nearly $2.50 per pound, and then lost almost one-half the gain by mid-August. As calendar 1994 moved into its closing months, prices drifted back towards $1.50 per pound as the early crop fears dissipated, and expectation that the mid-year price rise would choke off consumer demand. Still, coffee prices closed the year at nearly double late-1993 values.

Dramatic price swings, in either direction, are not unusual for the coffee market. In 1976, prices surged from about 75¢ per pound to a record high $3.25 per pound in 1977, and then collapsed to under $1.50 per pound. In the mid-1980s, prices about doubled from a base of $1.25 per pound, and by the close of the 1980s prices were under $1 per pound. Based on coffee's price history during the past 20 years, some dramatic action has occurred at least once each decade.

World coffee production in 1994/95 was initially forecast at about 90.6 million bags, the smallest crop since 1986/87 (79.5 million bags) and compares with 1993/94 production of 94.2 million bags. Early crop forecasts are often suspect, as some crop damage news is likely and the odds are that it will prove less damaging than expected. A record high 103.4 million bags were produced in 1991/92. Global exportable production in 1994/95 (total harvested production less domestic consumption in producing countries) was forecast at 66 million bags compared with 69.9 million bags in 1993/94. World coffee consumption has been basically flat in recent years at about 73 million bags in importing nations, owing largely to strong competition from other beverages. Usage in producing nations in 1994/95 was estimated at almost 25 million bags, up about one million bags from 1993/94.

Producer stocks at the beginning of the 1994/95 marketing year of about 30 million bags, were expected to slide to a record low 22 million bags by the end of the season. Stocks in importing nations in early-1994 totaled only about 16 million bags to 17 million bags, versus about 20 million bags a year earlier. More than one-third of the stocks were in the U.S. and much of the balance in Western Europe. U.S. stocks towards mid-1994 of about 6 million bags were under a year earlier, but about one million bags over normal carryover levels. The adequate stocks in importing nations helped arrest the sharp price surge in mid-1994. Moreover, 1994's high prices likely encouraged producers to plant more trees and implement better cultural practices, that with normal crop weather should lead to record large coffee production a few years.

Brazil is the world's leading producer of green coffee and Columbia a distant second. In the 1980s, Brazil's production varied from 38 million bags in 1987/88 to 13.9 million bags in 1986/87. In the first-half of the 1990s, the highest production was 31 million bags in 1990/91. During the following four crop years, Brazil's production averaged about 26 million bags with 28.5 million bags produced in 1993/94 and an initial forecast of only 23.5 million for 1994/95. The decline cannot just be attributed to adverse crop weather, be it freeze or drought. It is estimated that farmers uprooted over one billion coffee trees between 1991-1993, the equivalent of one-quarter of Brazil's coffee tree population. This factor alone is believed to have reduced Brazil's annual production to a maximum of 27 million bags to 30 million bags under optimum crop conditions. The reason is attributed to farmer dissatisfaction with low world prices in the early-1990s and rising production costs. How the price recovery of 1994 will effect future plantings remains to be seen, but production is likely to rebound in 1995/96 given normal crop weather. Brazil's 1993 exports of green and roasted coffee totaled 15.1 million bags of which 22 percent went to the U.S. In the first half of 1994, Brazil's exports were nearly 10 percent over the like 1993 period.

Indonesia is the world's largest producer of Robust coffee and third largest producer of all coffees. Java is the Indonesian synonym for coffee. Japan and Germany are the largest importer of Indonesian coffee. Indonesia produces about one-half of total Asian coffee production, estimated at 16.5 million bags in 1994/95 about the same as in 1993/94. Africa's total coffee production in 1994/95 also totaled about 16.5 million bags versus 15.8 million bags in 1993/94. The U.S. is not a major importer of African coffee because of higher ocean freight rates and the preference for Latin American coffees. Western Europe takes most of Africa's exports.

The U.S. is the world's largest consumer of coffee, importing the equivalent of 19.3 million bags 1993 (18 million green coffee and the balance processed) with a value of about $1.5 billion, versus nearly 23 million bags in 1992 with a value of $1.7 billion. The largest exporters to the U.S. are Brazil, Columbia and Mexico. New Orleans is the major port of entry for green coffee followed by New York. U.S. per capita coffee consumption has been dropping while use of soft drinks has been expanding. In 1970, U.S. per capita coffee use totaled 35.7 gallons, by 1990 per capita use had dropped to 26.4 gallons and was estimated at 25.9 gallons in 1993. Bottled water use is also expanding rapidly and may be having some marginal adverse effect on coffee use. The U.S. retail price for roasted coffee in the first half of 1994 averaged about $2.52 per pound, and the wholesale soluble price $8.30 per pound. In 1993, the retail roasted price averaged $2.47 per pound and soluble $8.32 per pound.

A new five-year International Coffee Agreement (ICA) became effective October 1, 1994 and is to run until September 30, 1999. The new pact will not have economic provisions such as export quotas but will attempt to take measures, when needed, designed to balance world supply and demand for coffee. The U.S. is not a member of the new ICA as funding for U.S. membership in the International Coffee Organization (ICO) was withdrawn.

Futures Markets

Arabica (Coffee "C") futures are traded on the New York Coffee, Sugar and Cocoa Exchange (CSCE). Robust coffee futures are traded on the London Commodity Exchange and the Marche a Terme International de France (MATIF). Options are traded in New York and London.

World Coffee Supply and Distribution — In Thousands of 60 Kilogram Bags (132.276 Lbs. Per Bag)

Crop Year	Beginning Stocks	Production	Imports	Supply	Total Exports	Bean Exports	Rst/Grn Exports	Soluble Exports	Domestic Use	Ending Stocks
1980-1	25,523	86,174	675	112,372	59,787	56,692	179	2,916	20,463	32,122
1981-2	32,122	98,152	755	131,029	65,340	61,037	235	4,068	21,056	44,633
1982-3	44,633	82,074	733	127,440	65,454	62,739	220	2,495	20,620	41,366
1983-4	41,366	88,975	606	130,947	68,202	65,080	351	2,771	21,080	41,665
1984-5	41,665	90,508	456	132,629	72,140	68,493	306	3,341	22,968	37,521
1985-6	37,521	95,837	397	133,755	70,121	67,367	248	2,506	21,386	42,248
1986-7	42,248	79,549	262	122,059	66,408	63,777	298	2,333	22,201	33,450
1987-8	33,450	103,285	296	137,031	67,150	64,484	337	2,329	23,074	46,807
1988-9	46,807	94,363	415	141,585	70,892	67,874	162	2,856	22,165	48,528
1989-90	48,528	97,286	258	146,072	83,321	79,953	129	3,239	21,536	41,215
1990-1	41,215	100,417	352	141,984	76,957	73,898	83	2,976	21,806	43,221
1991-2	43,221	104,245	349	147,815	80,727	77,642	53	3,032	19,697	47,391
1992-3[1]	47,391	93,405	770	141,566	77,668	73,571	113	3,984	21,328	42,570
1993-4[2]	42,570	93,538	1,032	137,140	77,609	73,011	136	4,462	23,997	35,534
1994-5[3]	35,534	94,306	1,060	130,900	77,297	73,095	145	4,057	22,655	30,948

[1] Preliminary. [2] Estimate. [3] Forecast. *Source: Foreign Agricultural Service, U.S. Department of Agriculture*

World Green Coffee (Total) Production — In Thousands of 60 Kilogram Bags (132.276 Lbs. Per Bag)

Crop Year	Brazil	Cameroon	Colombia	Costa Rica	El Salvador	Ethiopia	Guatemala	India	Indonesia	Ivory Coast	Mexico	Papua New Guinea	Uganda	Zaire	World Total
1980-1	21,500	1,959	13,500	2,140	2,940	3,264	2,702	1,977	5,365	6,090	3,862	870	2,133	1,526	86,344
1981-2	33,000	1,850	14,342	1,782	2,886	3,212	2,653	2,540	5,785	4,160	3,900	910	2,885	1,425	98,189
1982-3	17,750	1,830	13,300	2,300	3,100	3,670	2,530	2,170	4,750	4,510	3,900	910	3,000	1,425	82,778
1983-4	30,000	1,000	13,000	2,070	2,400	3,300	2,340	1,667	5,515	4,120	4,530	640	3,000	1,354	88,595
1984-5	27,000	2,316	11,000	2,516	2,680	2,587	2,703	3,250	5,600	4,609	4,530	925	2,700	1,350	90,266
1985-6	33,000	2,067	12,000	1,514	2,300	2,833	2,650	2,033	5,800	4,420	4,250	775	2,800	1,540	95,934
1986-7	13,900	2,191	11,000	2,566	2,275	2,700	2,843	3,350	5,900	4,405	4,826	860	2,700	1,610	79,549
1987-8	38,000	1,251	13,000	2,375	2,538	3,200	3,020	2,050	5,965	3,103	5,297	756	2,700	1,875	103,231
1988-9	25,000	1,760	10,700	2,758	1,492	3,400	3,022	3,590	6,750	3,989	4,717	1,100	2,600	2,000	94,363
1989-90	26,000	1,440	13,300	2,453	2,787	3,400	3,472	2,150	7,100	4,734	5,500	1,175	3,300	1,750	97,286
1990-1	31,000	1,450	14,500	2,565	2,603	3,500	3,282	2,970	7,480	3,300	5,100	1,092	2,500	2,000	100,417
1991-2	28,500	1,920	17,980	2,530	2,357	3,000	3,549	3,200	7,100	3,967	4,550	964	2,700	1,695	104,245
1992-3[1]	24,000	837	14,950	2,620	2,894	2,800	3,584	2,700	7,350	2,500	4,620	841	2,900	1,500	93,405
1993-4[2]	28,500	1,250	11,400	2,475	2,115	3,000	3,078	3,450	7,400	2,700	4,180	1,060	2,800	1,790	93,538
1994-5[3]	26,000	1,300	12,500	2,300	2,520	3,500	3,027	3,000	7,000	3,400	4,300	1,100	3,000	1,300	94,306

[1] Preliminary. [2] Estimate. [3] Forecast. *Source: Foreign Agricultural Service, U.S. Department of Agriculture*

World Green Coffee (Exportable)[4] Production — In Thousands of 60 Kilogram Bags (132.276 Lbs. Per Bag)

Crop Year	Brazil	Cameroon	Colombia	Costa Rica	El Salvador	Ethiopia	Guatemala	Indonesia	Ivory Coast	Kenya	Mexico	Papua New Guinea	Uganda	Zaire	World Total
1980-1	13,500	1,926	11,675	1,932	2,740	1,664	2,381	4,137	6,026	1,648	2,362	837	2,090	1,346	66,064
1981-2	24,500	1,815	12,492	1,539	2,686	1,596	2,328	4,630	4,095	1,434	2,450	901	2,840	1,240	77,311
1982-3	9,750	1,785	11,445	2,077	2,900	2,108	2,195	3,636	4,445	1,501	2,830	631	2,954	1,159	62,366
1983-4	21,500	945	11,140	1,837	2,200	1,728	2,000	4,375	1,395	1,938	3,030	923	2,653	1,150	67,676
1984-5	16,500	2,261	9,135	2,281	2,480	1,087	2,373	4,590	4,582	1,488	2,635	762	2,752	1,340	67,449
1985-6	24,000	1,987	10,130	1,276	2,120	1,293	2,350	4,800	4,391	1,951	3,326	842	2,650	1,410	74,841
1986-7	4,900	2,058	9,000	2,324	2,095	1,034	2,543	4,950	4,375	1,591	3,797	738	2,649	1,670	57,786
1987-8	28,000	1,206	10,980	2,140	2,369	1,756	2,720	4,915	3,071	1,985	3,137	1,087	2,547	1,791	80,390
1988-9	15,500	1,725	8,891	2,508	1,332	1,767	2,717	5,478	3,957	1,787	3,880	1,160	3,250	1,530	71,891
1989-90	17,000	1,405	11,538	2,198	2,607	2,239	3,162	5,820	4,700	1,665	3,650	1,081	2,450	1,780	75,944
1990-1	22,000	1,420	12,885	2,305	2,423	1,800	2,972	6,185	3,264	1,433	3,150	954	2,650	1,480	78,814
1991-2	21,900	1,895	16,580	2,270	2,173	1,300	3,239	5,550	3,929	1,483	3,170	832	2,845	1,300	84,744
1992-3[1]	15,920	812	13,647	2,365	2,677	1,100	3,274	5,570	2,461	1,195	2,880	1,051	2,745	1,615	72,471
1993-4[2]	18,066	1,225	10,000	2,225	1,885	1,200	2,777	5,635	2,661	1,208	2,950	1,021	2,640	950	70,019
1994-5[3]	17,000	1,275	11,100	2,055	2,283	1,700	2,747	5,040	3,361	1,308	3,100	1,091	2,940	1,150	72,061

[1] Preliminary. [2] Estimate. [3] Forecast. [4] Marketing year begins in October in some countries and April or July in others. Exportable production represents total harvested production minus estimated domestic consumption. *Source: Foreign Agricultural Service, U.S. Department of Agriculture*

COFFEE

Origin of Green Coffee Imports (for Consumption) into the U.S.   In Thousands of 60 Kilogram Bags[2]

Year	Brazil	Colombia	Costa Rica	Domin. Republic	Ecuador	El Salvador	Ethiopia	Guate- mata	Indonesia	Ivory Coast	Mexico	Peru	Philip- pines	Uganda	Vene- zuela	Grand Total
1981	3,243	1,727	226	359	701	779	547	645	1,516	602	1,393	439	270	863	27	16,555
1982	3,372	1,710	248	500	773	919	578	844	1,118	998	1,377	513	308	1,229	16	17,416
1983	3,417	1,755	226	430	857	1,214	519	887	1,079	674	1,495	439	276	729	26	16,449
1984	3,866	2,170	258	447	961	1,052	423	1,118	1,030	1,144	1,553	557	296	570	88	17,734
1985	4,148	2,554	360	438	974	1,366	195	1,054	1,041	951	1,812	543	407	739	107	18,698
1986	2,200	2,629	413	488	1,371	1,108	243	1,658	1,346	694	2,125	675	440	739	224	19,483
1987	3,928	2,549	551	446	1,285	1,117	421	1,439	911	476	2,764	573	105	587	163	19,906
1988	4,213	2,235	233	366	811	829	218	609	731	654	1,719	436	298	481	72	15,348
1989	4,155	2,413	393	402	1,137	790	432	1,404	635	335	3,937	673	362	458	87	19,377
1990	3,633	2,771	403	445	876	843	234	1,871	830	54	3,305	473	107	246	222	19,566
1991	5,335	3,048	603	343	785	868	31	1,489	536	54	2,993	610	61	287	108	18,849
1992	4,253	4,852	662	254	753	1,344	23	1,812	581	407	3,042	526	13	223	104	21,673
1993	3,376	2,957	437	213	671	1,274	192	1,815	542	273	2,947	158	6	163	444	18,023
1994[1]	2,850	2,372	325	207	969	376	215	1,403	558	114	2,516	249	78	191	295	14,872

[1] Preliminary.   [2] 132.276 pounds per bag.   *Source: Bureau of Census, U.S. Department of Commerce*

Total Coffee (Green) Imports (for Consumption) into the U.S.   In Thousands of 60 Kilogram Bags[2]

Year	Jan.	Feb.	Mar.	Apr.	May	June	July	Aug.	Sept.	Oct.	Nov.	Dec.	Total
1981	1,858	1,738	1,395	1,299	1,356	1,026	922	1,213	1,150	1,487	1,565	1,547	16,555
1982	1,287	1,195	1,490	1,147	1,476	1,335	1,282	1,602	1,640	2,005	1,356	1,253	17,416
1983	1,556	1,332	1,373	1,253	1,502	1,034	1,319	1,230	1,532	1,685	1,380	1,187	16,449
1984	1,598	1,299	1,440	1,905	1,615	1,059	1,722	1,735	1,432	1,614	1,127	1,785	17,734
1985	1,622	1,681	1,702	1,430	1,324	1,751	1,217	1,757	1,773	1,385	1,272	1,785	18,698
1986	2,360	1,836	1,645	1,667	1,810	1,286	1,549	1,513	1,641	1,535	1,449	1,192	19,483
1987	1,092	1,218	1,841	1,789	1,883	2,181	1,717	1,481	1,770	2,631	1,246	1,056	19,906
1988	1,175	1,683	1,427	1,179	1,141	832	1,543	1,621	1,238	1,272	1,195	1,040	15,348
1989	1,646	1,323	1,368	1,398	1,296	1,199	1,634	1,974	1,951	2,180	1,748	1,660	19,337
1990	1,950	1,989	2,358	1,783	1,658	1,548	1,451	1,261	1,229	1,611	1,140	1,591	19,566
1991	2,106	1,946	1,590	1,748	1,556	984	1,056	1,335	1,424	1,368	1,616	2,122	18,849
1992	2,262	1,944	2,125	1,698	1,534	1,795	1,806	1,692	1,644	1,615	1,508	2,050	21,673
1993	1,782	1,663	2,012	1,481	1,631	1,253	1,442	1,344	1,374	1,464	1,018	1,561	18,023
1994[1]	1,538	1,152	1,409	1,077	1,082	1,151	1,195	1,560	1,266	1,127	1,103	1,213	14,872

[1] Preliminary.   [2] 132.276 pounds per bag.   *Source: Bureau of Census, U.S. Department of Commerce*

Average Spot Price of Coffee (Brazilian[1]) at New York   In Cents Per Pound

Year	Jan.	Feb.	Mar.	Apr.	May	June	July	Aug.	Sept.	Oct.	Nov.	Dec.	Average
1981	221.72	NA	218.58	218.50	NA	224.76	169.43	143.05	137.50	149.18	158.56	154.21	181.54
1982	148.95	153.11	143.70	143.86	141.33	144.42	138.17	142.05	142.92	141.31	141.63	142.69	143.68
1983	140.73	142.29	142.02	140.86	141.51	142.81	142.51	138.70	136.65	145.31	146.88	152.76	142.75
1984	155.15	155.38	152.82	149.80	145.91	149.45	146.99	150.62	151.55	147.63	144.93	145.59	149.65
1985	152.10	157.25	155.56	146.33	143.84	136.71	130.81	133.25	139.03	150.27	174.28	201.70	151.76
1986	303.42	276.26	286.68	288.55	280.24	229.10	183.40	190.43	210.36	187.89	175.58	162.40	231.19
1987	119.75	114.42	97.41	101.68	111.96	98.34	89.95	91.40	100.67	111.68	122.05	117.09	106.37
1988	117.35	130.40	126.21	123.30	121.02	122.81	120.01	111.89	118.79	115.65	118.53	136.10	121.84
1989	145.29	128.72	128.06	131.45	128.94	115.02	78.75	67.32	67.75	60.32	65.53	67.93	98.76
1990	70.36	77.59	86.17	87.45	86.31	82.94	78.94	90.25	92.20	85.78	77.46	80.17	82.97
1991	75.59	79.39	83.83	81.58	75.56	72.44	69.24	68.15	75.08	65.91	66.03	62.14	72.91
1992	62.03	58.05	59.60	54.94	51.11	49.08	48.53	46.40	49.43	59.64	64.64	74.39	56.49
1993	67.13	66.34	62.60	54.92	57.26	55.70	65.76	73.25	75.58	71.65	74.20	74.51	66.58
1994	71.42	80.14	84.72	87.14	118.37	136.43	211.81	192.38	212.73	191.21	172.83	159.73	143.24

[1] And other Arabicas.   NA = Not available.   *Source: Foreign Agricultural Service, U.S. Department of Agriculture*

WEEKLY NEAREST FUTURES
AS OF 05/12/95

COFFEE 'C' - CSCE

CENTS/LB.

U.S. Average Monthly Wholesale Prices of Coffee   In Cents Per Pound

Year	Jan.	Feb.	Mar.	Apr.	May	June	July	Aug.	Sept.	Oct.	Nov.	Dec.	Average
Ground Roast -- All Packs													
1986	334.5	357.5	361.7	367.6	368.9	373.9	366.5	358.0	352.6	350.9	347.7	247.6	357.3
1987	329.6	329.4	319.4	310.1	302.5	300.2	296.4	296.0	279.0	281.4	284.3	283.4	301.0
1988	286.1	287.2	292.8	295.6	295.2	295.7	287.4	288.5	289.4	292.4	288.1	288.8	290.6
1989	294.1	305.3	306.2	305.5	304.8	304.8	303.8	297.8	289.3	285.3	280.6	280.6	296.5
1990	279.8	276.7	275.9	277.6	277.1	278.2	278.2	279.0	278.7	275.6	282.8	282.8	278.5
1991	281.3	275.0	283.0	283.5	284.2	283.6	281.6	273.3	274.6	276.1	276.1	275.7	279.0
1992	275.2	275.7	275.1	274.9	273.8	273.2	268.1	266.4	264.2	261.9	262.0	262.6	269.4
1993	263.3	268.9	266.0	267.6	266.4	265.6	266.4	265.9	266.6	266.2	265.9	267.1	266.3
1994[1]	270.8	270.9	264.0	265.5	266.7	283.3	371.0						
Ground Roast in One Pound Cans													
1986	334.2	345.4	346.7	345.7	350.7	349.4	348.4	350.3	341.7	343.8	334.5	334.5	343.8
1987	311.4	314.3	298.1	296.6	297.3	296.9	291.7	292.5	281.0	282.0	285.6	284.6	294.3
1988	284.0	283.2	294.9	294.2	294.2	298.0	279.5	284.1	283.4	286.7	285.0	285.1	287.7
1989	288.8	301.3	311.1	314.0	314.0	315.2	315.0	308.0	298.5	300.4	301.0	303.0	305.9
1990[2]	303.7	303.0	302.8	308.6	309.8	309.2	309.2	309.2	309.1	304.2	331.3	333.8	311.2
1991	333.4	333.8	335.0	334.4	334.5	332.9	319.9	306.0	306.0	304.8	304.8	302.6	320.7
1992	301.0	300.7	299.1	299.2	299.2	299.2	296.6	294.0	291.4	291.9	291.9	291.9	296.3
1993	291.9	304.4	300.7	306.6	306.2	304.1	310.9	310.8	311.0	310.5	304.7	305.2	305.6
1994[1]	304.8	309.7	290.7	290.7	291.0	313.3	458.2						
Soluble Per 16 Ounces													
1986	932.4	995.4	1,012.8	1,020.3	1,016.1	1,014.0	1,003.4	956.4	970.8	952.2	977.7	977.7	985.8
1987	943.2	885.2	861.9	861.9	866.5	866.5	846.3	846.3	825.6	830.6	830.6	830.6	857.9
1988	805.8	805.8	815.3	812.6	812.6	812.6	922.0	922.0	922.0	922.0	922.0	922.0	866.4
1989	915.4	948.4	941.9	941.9	941.9	952.3	952.3	921.0	921.0	915.6	915.6	915.6	931.9
1990	915.6	915.6	902.5	918.2	918.2	918.2	918.2	918.2	918.1	912.9	912.9	912.9	915.1
1991	912.9	967.2	967.2	967.2	944.1	940.8	929.6	915.2	915.2	868.1	868.1	868.1	922.0
1992	861.6	861.6	850.7	850.7	850.7	850.7	833.3	833.3	833.3	837.9	837.9	837.9	845.0
1993	837.9	830.3	826.2	829.2	829.2	829.2	829.2	829.2	829.2	838.8	838.8	838.8	832.2
1994[1]	838.8	826.0	826.0	826.0	826.0	867.0	1,014.3						

[1] Price survey discontinued as of August 1994.   [2] Includes gourmet coffee beginning November 1990.   *Source: Foreign Agricultural Service, U.S. Department of Agriculture*

COFFEE

Average Open Interest of Coffee Futures at New York   In Contracts

Year	Jan.	Feb.	Mar.	Apr.	May	June	July	Aug.	Sept.	Oct.	Nov.	Dec.
1983	9,718	10,346	10,498	11,692	11,552	9,930	8,154	8,957	8,950	9,260	9,103	8,787
1984	7,928	9,664	11,925	12,058	11,343	9,844	9,969	9,776	9,347	10,696	10,192	11,320
1985	13,493	13,291	12,952	12,885	12,811	12,393	11,722	11,015	10,198	10,504	11,652	13,287
1986	13,104	14,391	15,714	15,972	16,684	15,712	15,917	16,374	16,798	18,079	16,995	14,905
1987	15,317	16,034	17,415	20,445	22,455	21,160	22,536	23,943	25,857	26,418	22,757	21,064
1988	22,581	26,100	24,591	21,413	22,228	23,346	21,570	24,525	22,460	21,961	19,424	20,356
1989	24,544	23,684	23,246	25,870	23,663	24,716	27,184	31,410	32,404	35,019	32,687	32,096
1990	37,352	43,516	46,187	43,978	41,756	40,464	39,856	41,428	39,278	39,523	43,750	41,365
1991	42,320	41,326	39,948	39,410	41,726	43,717	42,037	40,661	42,126	43,940	41,819	40,628
1992	47,042	51,183	48,961	51,979	59,275	58,304	59,096	58,401	56,446	59,808	57,527	58,257
1993	59,193	54,249	53,618	55,578	51,797	50,918	53,871	48,541	47,649	49,809	46,901	48,812
1994	54,796	50,230	53,713	57,226	58,574	54,589	43,056	35,052	35,800	34,258	31,046	31,134

Source: Coffee, Sugar & Cocoa Exchange, Inc.

Volume of Trading of Coffee "C" Futures at New York   In Contracts

Year	Jan.	Feb.	Mar.	Apr.	May	June	July	Aug.	Sept.	Oct.	Nov.	Dec.	Total
1983	30,567	32,884	44,211	37,399	44,917	45,575	26,065	32,818	22,579	38,999	34,428	36,999	427,441
1984	33,327	44,890	46,793	46,833	51,174	42,891	34,956	48,979	43,159	29,703	37,457	36,094	499,133
1985	48,733	54,809	52,365	58,531	38,755	54,725	42,222	39,425	23,615	58,870	83,845	94,671	650,768
1986	113,305	95,509	76,787	82,308	75,176	87,323	78,670	106,366	93,465	112,685	89,713	61,835	1,073,142
1987	69,564	81,427	78,671	104,350	71,189	86,564	77,621	106,182	77,207	85,315	72,846	53,650	964,586
1988	67,955	119,075	85,154	80,772	73,379	125,684	91,569	118,956	88,460	83,713	85,366	129,627	1,149,710
1989	141,903	106,019	102,594	129,018	95,902	134,848	100,700	122,207	97,744	104,100	111,434	82,484	1,328,953
1990	130,223	174,115	211,105	144,641	128,121	147,605	127,767	172,947	119,088	113,569	175,067	119,802	1,774,050
1991	138,642	174,688	188,842	153,436	103,344	135,887	107,058	170,113	180,017	148,640	159,099	112,882	1,772,648
1992	153,332	199,420	174,662	188,232	156,944	164,586	177,493	182,741	163,214	108,707	211,678	199,374	2,152,383
1993	290,120	214,771	183,354	209,607	176,559	197,761	193,002	233,479	202,363	187,763	217,947	182,486	2,489,223
1994	188,508	219,455	208,113	284,734	380,119	304,542	210,479	196,685	159,574	177,424	184,172	142,713	2,658,073

Source: Coffee, Sugar & Cocoa Exchange, Inc.

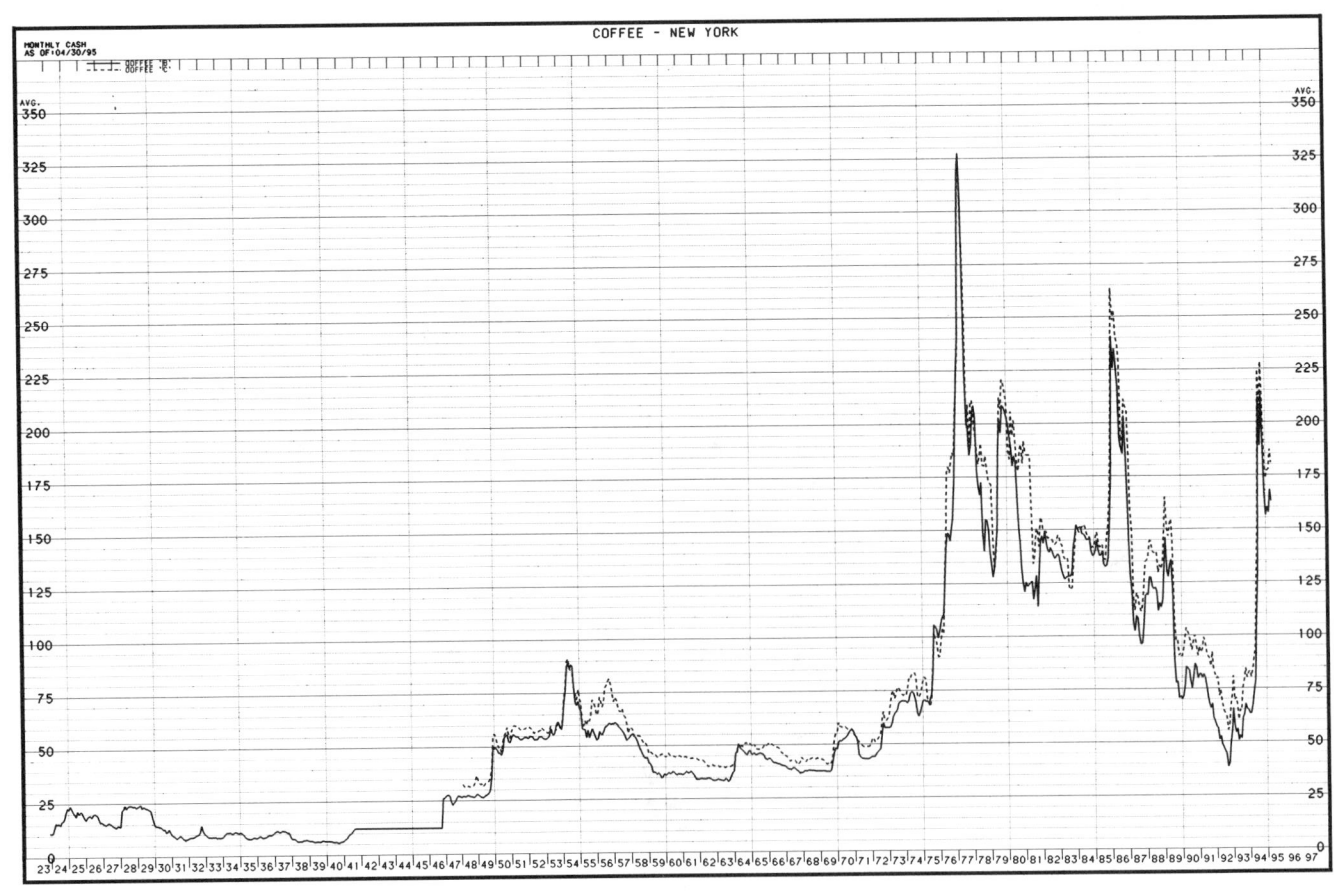

Coke

U.S. Salient Statistics of Coke   In Thousands of Short Tons

| | Production at Coke Plants | | | | | | Exports | | | Producer & Distributor | Avg. Price of Coal |
Year	Merchant Coke Plants	Furance Coke Plants	Total Coke	Breeze	Imports	Consump-tion[2]	Total	Canada	Mexico	Ending Stocks	Receipts at Coke Plants
1986	3,289	22,251	24,917	2,065	329	24,729	1,004	477	78	2,066	50.83
1987	3,551	24,486	26,304	2,252	922	27,654	574	248	106	1,064	46.55
1988	3,868	28,536	28,945	2,478	2,688	30,021	1,093	348	101	1,583	47.70
1989	-----------	28,045	-----------	2,342	2,311	28,935	1,085	644	157	1,919	47.50
1990	3,724	23,892	27,617	1,736	765	27,811	572	376	94	1,918	47.73
1991	3,251	20,795	24,046	1,734	1,099	24,216	740	239	98	2,107	48.95
1992	3,248	20,162	23,410	1,721	1,739	24,731	642	310	76	1,883	47.92
1993[1]	3,209	19,973	23,182	3,424	1,534	24,303	835	417	92	1,461	47.44

[1] Preliminary.   [2] Equal to production plus imports minus the change in producer and distributor stocks minus exports.   *Source: Energy Information Administration, U.S. Department of Energy*

Petroleum Coke Production in the United States   In Thousands of Barrels[2]

Year	Jan.	Feb.	Mar.	Apr.	May	June	July	Aug.	Sept.	Oct.	Nov.	Dec.	Total
1985	2,469	2,215	2,502	2,608	2,748	2,892	2,962	2,978	2,684	2,942	2,899	3,305	33,204
1986	3,161	2,825	3,027	2,865	3,191	3,176	3,059	3,230	3,171	3,066	2,925	3,206	36,903
1987	3,228	2,960	3,034	2,794	3,087	3,121	3,190	3,138	3,047	3,060	3,158	3,384	37,380
1988	3,436	3,171	3,415	3,164	3,367	3,282	3,333	3,347	3,205	3,281	3,347	3,462	39,811
1989	3,505	2,931	3,201	3,200	3,337	3,406	3,509	3,447	3,255	3,252	3,104	3,227	39,533
1990	3,336	3,142	3,329	3,278	3,357	3,291	3,437	3,617	3,304	3,366	3,351	3,502	40,332
1991	3,518	3,056	3,276	3,303	3,527	3,404	3,537	3,575	3,410	3,501	3,505	3,808	41,493
1992	3,710	3,266	3,565	3,523	3,692	3,737	3,866	3,656	3,569	3,533	3,540	3,877	43,599
1993	18,551	17,289	19,226	18,200	18,587	18,715	20,196	19,319	18,547	18,695	18,954	19,737	226,016
1994[1]	19,122	16,823	18,522	18,406	19,697	19,258	19,940	19,405	17,800	18,685	18,927	19,632	226,217

[1] Preliminary.   [2] Prior to 1993, data shown in thousands of short tons (5 barrels = 1 short ton).   *Source: Energy Information Administration, U.S. Department of Energy*

Coal Receipts and Carbonization at Coke Plants in the U.S.   In Thousands of Short Tons

| | Coal Receipts at Coke Plants | | | | | By Plant Type | | Coal Carbonized at Coke Plants | | | | | By Plant Type | |
| | By State | | | | | Merchant Coke Plants | Furance Coke Plants | By State | | | | | Merchant Coke Plants | Furance Coke Plants |
Year	Alabama	Indiana	Ohio	Pennsyl-vania	Total			Alabama	Indiana	Ohio	Pennsyl-vania	Total		
1986	2,720	8,671	5,024	6,790	35,837	4,246	31,592	2,674	8,518	5,184	7,007	36,006	4,325	31,680
1987	3,250	9,774	5,770	8,504	37,744	4,660	33,084	3,150	9,791	5,361	8,395	36,957	4,536	32,422
1988	3,313	11,251	5,041	10,179	41,115	5,008	36,107	3,383	11,287	5,448	10,146	41,910	5,034	36,876
1989	3,330	10,558	5,143	9,822	41,019	4,959	36,060	3,314	10,568	5,265	9,877	41,369	5,010	36,876
1990	3,304	10,497	5,021	10,604	40,736	4,988	35,749	3,288	8,867	4,949	10,456	38,877	4,950	33,927
1991	3,114	8,141	3,595	8,912	33,090	4,399	28,692	3,166	8,234	3,698	8,812	33,854	4,482	29,371
1992	3,334	6,894	3,717	9,761	32,027	4,295	27,732	3,297	7,153	3,755	9,868	32,366	4,316	28,050
1993[1]	3,184	6,515	2,853	10,424	31,104	4,184	26,921	3,206	6,591	2,892	10,333	31,323	4,267	27,056

[1] Preliminary.   *Source: Energy Information Administration, U.S. Department of Energy*

United States Coke Distribution and Stocks   In Thousands of Short Tons

| | Distribution | | | | | | | Coke Plant Stocks, Dec. 31 | | | |
| | By Plant Type | | By Consumer Category | | | | | | By Plant Type | | |
Year	Merchant Coke Plants	Furance Coke Plants	Blast Furance	Foundries	Other Industrial Plants	Total Coke	Breeze	Total Coke	Merchant Coke Plants	Furance Coke Plants	Breeze
1986	3,382	22,583	23,654	1,494	817	25,966	2,454	2,066	288	1,778	260
1987	3,639	26,163	27,236	1,552	1,014	29,802	2,151	1,064	218	846	332
1988	3,953	29,758	30,499	1,630	1,581	33,710	2,448	1,583	163	1,420	189
1989	3,755	30,286	30,676	1,535	1,830	34,041	2,251	1,919	216	1,703	179
1990	3,724	29,564	30,877	1,437	974	33,289	1,882	1,918	244	1,674	228
1991	3,246	24,267	25,669	1,213	630	27,513	2,057	2,107	252	1,856	259
1992	3,253	26,718	28,075	1,290	606	29,971	2,255	1,883	267	1,616	215
1993[1]	3,226	27,009	28,295	1,373	567	30,235	3,563	1,461	272	1,189	486

[1] Preliminary.   *Source: Energy Information Administration, U.S. Department of Energy*

Copper

Copper metal and copper alloy have considerable commercial importance due to their electrical, mechanical and physical properties. Copper for commercial purposes is obtained by the reduction of the copper compounds in ores, followed by electrolytic refining. Copper is used largely in alloys such as brass, which is composed of copper and zinc.

Fourteen mines accounted for more than 95 percent of production in the U.S., with principal mining states including Arizona, New Mexico, Utah, Michigan and Montana. The U.S. Bureau of Mines indicated that U.S. production of recoverable mine copper during January-July 1994 was just over one million tonnes. In 1993, mine production was 1.78 million tonnes. Smelter production of copper over the first seven-months of 1994 totaled 736,392 tonnes, while for all of 1993 smelter production was 1.27 million tonnes. Refinery production of copper so far in 1994 totaled 1.06 million tonnes. Electrolytic processes produced 779,798 tonnes, while the electrown process produced 284,486 tonnes. For all of 1993, refinery production of copper was 1.79 million tonnes. Copper is also recovered from scrap, which provides a sizable source of copper supply. January-July production was 1.15 million tonnes.

Total apparent consumption of copper during the January-July 1994 period was 1.59 million tonnes, while for all of 1993 it was 2.51 million tonnes. Refined copper consumption in the first seven-months of 1994 was 1.58 million tonnes, while purchased copper-base scrap consumed was 992,278 tonnes.

The U.S. exports various forms of copper. For the first six-months of 1994, exports of refined copper were 64,560 tonnes. The major market was Taiwan which received 20,542 tonnes. U.S. exports of unalloyed copper scrap for the first six-months of 1994 were 58,823 tonnes. Canada was by far the largest market taking 31,131 tonnes, much above their pace of 1993. Exports of copper-base scrap in the data period for 1994 were 90,158 tonnes. The largest market was India with 34,525 tonnes. This pace was far above 1993, when for the entire year they imported 39,423 tonnes. China was another important market for copper-base scrap, taking 21,375 tonnes in the first half of 1994.

U.S. imports for consumption of copper alloy scrap for the January-June 1994 period were 64,664 tonnes (gross weight), with a copper content of 46,558 tonnes. Imports of copper sulfate for the first half of 1994 were 7,314 tonnes, a much higher pace than in 1993 when imports for the entire year were 9,431 tonnes.

Total stocks of refined copper on July 31, 1994 were 112,654 tonnes. This represented a significant decline from July 31, 1993 when stocks were 199,118 tonnes. Stocks of crude copper on July 31 were 116,863 tonnes, 29 percent less than stocks on July 31 of the prior year.

As a result of the significant drawdown in stocks and a strong recovery in the U.S. economy, the price of copper has undergone a substantial increase. In July 1994, the average price of U.S. producer copper cathode averaged 115.692¢ per pound. During 1993, the average price was 91.555¢ per pound.

FUTURES MARKETS

High-grade copper futures and options are traded on the Commodity Exchange (COMEX), now a division of the New York Mercantile Exchagne. Cash copper futures and options are listed on the London Metals Exchange (LME).

World Mine Production of Copper (Content of Ore) In Thousands of Metric Tons

Year	Aus- tralia	Canada³	Chile	China	Indo- nesia	Mexico	Mon- golia	Peru	Philip- pines	Poland	Russia⁴	South Africa	United States³	Zaire	Zambia	World Total²
1985	259.8	738.6	1,359.8	200	88.7	171.3	128.0	400.8	222.2	432.0	600	203.2	1,102.6	525.2	519.6	7,988
1986	248.4	698.6	1,398.8	185	95.8	189.1	136.0	399.9	222.6	434.0	620	184.2	1,144.2	527.8	462.4	7,939
1987	232.7	802.2	1,418.1	250	102.1	252.7	120.8	417.6	216.1	438.0	630	188.1	1,243.6	515.6	463.2	8,243
1988	238.3	776.5	1,451.0	282	121.5	284.9	121.7	337.5	218.1	437.0	1,000	168.5	1,419.7	495.8	456.6	8,727
1989	296.0	723.1	1,609.3	276	144.0	264.2	123.6	387.9	193.0	384.0	1,000	181.9	1,507.3	466.2	466.3	9,058
1990	330.0	793.7	1,588.4	300	164.1	320.5	123.9	334.0	182.1	329.3	950	178.7	1,587.8	372.8	436.3	9,017
1991	311.0	808.1	1,814.3	300	211.7	324.6	90.1	399.9	148.3	320.3	900	184.6	1,631.0	250.5	410.2	9,187
1992	378.0	764.2	1,932.7	309	282.0	277.1	105.1	367.7	123.5	332.0	375	197.8	1,765.1	144.0	432.6	9,240
1993¹	334.9	711.2	2,035.7	309	277.6	296.8	105.1	374.9	136.5	332.0	NA	204.1	1,786.6	80.0	418.3	9,161
1994²	340.0	620.0	2,150.0	340	320.0			360.0	110.0	350.0	500		1,840.0	50.0	420.0	9,300

¹ Preliminary. ² Estimate. ³ Recoverable. ⁴ Formerly part of the U.S.S.R.; data not reported separately until 1992. NA = Not available.
Source: U.S. Bureau of Mines

Commodity Exchange, Inc. (COMEX) Warehouse Stocks of Copper In Thousands of Short Tons

Year	Jan. 1	Feb. 1	Mar. 1	Apr. 1	May 1	June 1	July 1	Aug. 1	Sept. 1	Oct. 1	Nov. 1	Dec. 1
1985	276.3	258.2	238.8	224.8	214.3	201.0	186.4	167.7	155.0	149.0	136.4	124.6
1986	120.3	120.1	118.5	116.4	114.5	108.5	103.4	95.7	90.6	86.6	81.0	84.0
1987	93.3	102.8	108.9	97.5	88.4	71.4	65.3	69.0	73.5	89.2	66.2	33.7
1988	18.5	16.9	16.8	11.8	10.2	19.0	16.9	24.6	22.3	13.6	9.5	5.9
1989	13.4	14.9	17.3	29.7	21.2	25.2	23.0	20.4	15.2	11.4	10.4	9.1
1990	16.3	7.2	4.1	4.5	6.0	14.7	18.1	11.5	8.9	6.7	8.3	9.3
1991	20.2	14.7	16.4	30.2	30.9	25.0	25.1	35.9	33.6	24.4	26.8	29.3
1992	33.7	34.8	29.5	28.2	30.3	32.4	31.8	36.0	40.4	51.7	70.1	73.8
1993	105.9	124.0	114.8	107.6	110.8	108.3	105.5	113.8	100.1	94.1	96.6	80.5
1994	74.0	56.2	50.9	37.2	32.7	31.0	36.5	39.5	28.5	17.4	19.7	21.8

Source: Commodity Exchange, Inc. of New York (COMEX)

U.S. Salient Statistics of Copper — In Thousands of Metric Tons

	New Copper Produced						Imports[3]		Exports			Stocks, Dec. 31			Apparent Consumption[6]	
	From Domestic Ores															
Year	Mines	Smelters	Refineries	From Foreign Ores[3]	Total New	Secondary Recovered[4]	Unmanufactured	Refined	Ore Concentrate[6]	Refined[7]	COMEX	Primary Producers (Refined)	Blister & Material in Solution	Refined Copper (Reported)	Primary & Old Copper[8]
1984	1,103	990	1,090	75	1,165	461	552	445	69	91	251	125	245	2,123	2,107
1985	1,105	939	1,004	54	1,057	503	444	378	116	38	109	320	146	1,976	2,144
1986	1,144	908	1,033	41	1,074	479	597	502	174	12	84	225	136	2,097	2,138
1987	1,244	972	1,127	W	1,127	498	568	469	125	9	17	113	150	2,127	2,197
1988	1,417	1,043	1,282	124	1,406	518	513	332	211	58	12	97	121	2,210	2,214
1989	1,498	1,120	1,352	125	1,477	548	515	300	267	130	15	107	132	2,203	2,185
1990	1,588	1,158	1,502	75	1,577	537	512	262	258	211	18	101	119	2,150	2,168
1991	1,631	1,123	1,501	77	1,577	518	512	289	253	263	31	132	135	2,048	2,105
1992	1,765	1,180	1,615	96	1,711	554	593	289	266	177	96	205	166	2,178	2,311
1993[1]	1,801	1,265	1,214	89	1,793	460	526	344	227	217	67	153	146	2,364	2,525
1994[2]	1,795	1,311	1,282	55	1,826	392		750	140	680	24	117	171	2,674	

[1] Preliminary. [2] Estimate. [3] Also from matte, etc., refinery reports. [4] From scrap only. [5] For consumption. [6] Blister (copper content). [7] Ingots, bars, etc. [8] Old scrap only. *Source: U.S. Bureau of Mines*

Consumption of Refined Copper[3] in the United States — In Thousands of Metric Tons

	By-Products						By Class of Consumer						Total Consumption
Year	Cathodes	Wire Bars	Ingot & Ingot Bars	Cakes & Slabs	Billets	Other	Wire Rod Mills	Brass Mills	Chemical Plants	Ingot Makers	Foundries	Miscellaneous	
1984	1,635.1	72.1	74.4	127.7	118.5	8.2	1,401.7	514.0	.7	5.3	19.8	34.6	1,976.0
1985	1,563.4	70.3	64.2	115.8	139.6	22.8	1,401.7	564.9	.9	1.4	20.6	22.9	2,101.5
1986	1,717.7	52.5	105.9	81.6	127.9	16.9	1,491.9	564.9	.9	1.4	20.6	22.9	2,102.6
1987	1,852.9	13.8	74.0	71.9	92.7	20.3	1,593.9	488.6	1.1	1.4	14.2	26.4	2,125.7
1988	1,967.4	14.0	54.2	63.0	99.0	12.7	1,667.2	493.2	1.0	2.6	14.5	31.9	2,210.4
1989	1,981.6	6.1	34.4	64.9	104.9	11.2	1,698.4	461.0	.9	1.3	14.9	26.5	2,203.1
1990	1,922.4	6.6	50.5	57.9	---- 113.0 ----		1,653.5	445.2	1.1	4.5	14.6	31.6	2,150.4
1991	1,854.9	W	24.7	33.3	---- 135.4 ----		1,591.8	458.5	.9	3.4	12.7	25.3	2,048.3
1992	1,974.9	W	20.0	43.7	---- 139.6 ----		1,675.0	458.5	.9	3.0	15.0	25.8	2,178.2
1993[1]	2,174.3	W	41.2	55.3	---- 83.2 ----		1,819.1	504.1	------------------ 44.7 ------------------				2,364.0
1994[2]	2,473.9	2.6	50.1	72.5	---- 85.3 ----		2,064.7	568.7	------------------ 40.8 ------------------				2,674.3

[1] Preliminary. [2] Estimate. [3] Primary & secondary. *Source: U.S. Bureau of Mines*

London Metals Exchange (LME) Warehouse Stocks of Copper (End of Period) — In Thousands of Metric Tons

Year	Jan.	Feb.	Mar.	Apr.	May	June	July	Aug.	Sept.	Oct.	Nov.	Dec.
1986	218.9	198.5	186.3	161.2	162.8	173.9	188.7	191.1	196.4	210.5	214.3	212.9
1987	213.2	170.6	159.9	176.0	133.5	126.4	118.3	139.6	128.0	82.9	69.1	64.3
1988	59.6	74.4	69.4	54.8	86.8	109.1	145.8	148.4	122.4	86.2	78.3	79.9
1989	96.6	104.2	117.4	138.7	125.2	99.2	96.1	100.8	126.7	117.8	142.2	131.2
1990	121.5	106.8	71.9	67.0	92.8	67.7	126.8	161.1	227.1	221.1	199.9	220.6
1991	189.0	202.8	213.9	237.9	275.0	264.9	266.5	307.1	308.4	291.7	308.3	332.3
1992	308.6	302.7	296.4	279.7	265.4	259.1	246.8	275.2	299.7	317.8	327.0	315.8
1993	313.5	333.1	365.8	403.5	429.1	446.9	464.3	521.7	600.7	612.3	590.9	599.5
1994[1]	597.6	554.5	504.4	446.4	379.0	350.9	338.9	367.8	359.3	333.1	318.4	301.8

[1] Preliminary. *Source: American Bureau of Metal Statistics*

U.S. Copper Refined from Scrap — In Thousands of Metric Tons

Year	Jan.	Feb.	Mar.	Apr.	May	June	July	Aug.	Sept.	Oct.	Nov.	Dec.	Total
1984	26.8	21.0	24.3	26.4	27.3	25.3	22.9	31.0	29.0	24.4	19.9	20.6	298.8
1985	29.5	29.5	32.0	31.6	31.2	34.7	32.0	30.0	29.6	25.9	28.7	28.5	377.5
1986	42.5	44.9	45.2	42.6	42.4	40.8	39.1	37.4	43.9	43.5	36.0	36.7	405.9
1987	28.7	31.6	40.1	44.3	34.0	35.1	39.5	33.2	34.5	35.8	30.8	37.1	414.7
1988	34.2	35.2	42.9	38.1	38.0	38.4	30.4	37.9	42.3	37.0	37.5	40.2	453.3
1989	37.4	40.8	47.0	40.1	40.8	41.1	36.6	41.4	40.6	41.3	35.9	37.1	479.9
1990	37.3	35.2	37.1	38.5	39.3	38.1	34.6	39.2	29.9	34.3	31.9	32.0	440.8
1991	35.4	32.8	40.5	39.6	38.2	35.7	32.6	33.0	28.5	37.3	32.1	32.6	417.7
1992	27.8	34.1	39.8	34.8	36.7	39.4	27.8	35.4	39.8	40.0	34.3	35.8	433.2
1993	38.1	45.9	38.9	37.8	36.4	41.1	35.0	37.6	37.4	43.0	35.4	32.2	459.8
1994[1]	33.3	28.3	37.9	30.7	37.1	28.7	26.9	33.0	38.7	27.0	34.3	37.3	391.7

[1] Preliminary. *Source: U.S. Bureau of Mines*

COPPER

Average Open Interest of Copper Futures[1] at COMEX   In Contracts

Year	Jan.	Feb.	Mar.	Apr.	May	June	July	Aug.	Sept.	Oct.	Nov.	Dec.
1986	87,280	83,713	86,713	79,370	71,169	68,505	63,529	61,827	62,779	65,073	73,414	78,164
1987	77,851	77,433	76,967	70,108	74,628	84,725	85,391	75,725	65,678	59,073	47,279	41,781
1988	43,177	41,220	35,505	34,787	31,410	35,949	31,750	29,520	34,946	35,724	36,607	33,094
1989	33,397	33,756	34,664	35,694	30,459	27,606	24,462	25,128	23,742	19,439	14,955	2,898
1990	31,401	33,908	34,654	34,405	31,552	30,113	32,780	31,515	32,578	36,145	35,088	30,128
1991	34,927	35,978	35,026	34,096	44,153	39,879	33,100	33,333	40,347	42,028	41,618	44,283
1992	47,109	47,929	48,700	45,114	39,986	48,129	47,065	38,397	37,041	41,658	44,927	45,541
1993	47,433	48,707	48,220	51,217	52,762	56,856	54,861	54,571	54,929	57,406	63,632	69,311
1994[2]	65,518	65,446	66,177	59,346	63,825	60,383	51,616	46,855	56,344	59,060	59,158	51,078

[1] High grade copper contracts from 1990.   *Source: Commodity Exchange, Inc. of New York (COMEX)*

Volume of Trading of Copper Futures[1] at COMEX   In Contracts

Year	Jan.	Feb.	Mar.	Apr.	May	June	July	Aug.	Sept.	Oct.	Nov.	Dec.	Total
1983	306,001	381,645	230,574	278,655	226,482	309,540	213,832	295,470	188,201	230,063	289,111	147,340	3,186,914
1984	199,461	259,881	217,635	269,765	196,382	223,551	152,424	215,226	149,465	170,568	279,151	172,856	2,514,311
1985	254,052	261,784	167,686	310,487	215,079	209,506	146,396	195,882	138,803	178,728	200,142	166,007	2,444,552
1986	190,983	206,513	197,818	240,770	106,750	200,547	89,818	145,468	123,779	121,361	162,963	85,439	1,872,209
1987	124,845	178,598	165,216	170,827	208,696	306,029	272,794	214,181	193,035	276,491	278,985	179,481	2,569,178
1988	210,209	222,625	194,722	151,177	130,289	179,991	120,088	142,945	141,899	186,220	258,725	173,569	2,112,459
1989	216,828	200,945	226,425	201,677	193,956	174,055	132,793	173,273	151,097	176,822	154,241	93,243	2,096,547
1990	152,156	148,766	179,445	181,726	164,489	163,372	141,602	154,383	156,924	161,814	133,718	114,790	1,853,185
1991	159,621	131,044	108,191	150,390	148,777	139,207	110,025	149,702	132,354	125,757	153,910	135,132	1,643,310
1992	145,245	168,015	105,003	157,473	77,722	182,091	138,225	177,581	137,423	121,392	146,062	117,931	1,674,163
1993	152,387	148,388	132,705	212,086	160,751	181,427	165,727	169,428	222,099	133,364	203,729	182,538	2,064,629
1994	197,959	233,016	231,239	207,963	247,143	297,393	188,644	242,393	219,788	208,957	290,585	178,887	2,737,967

[1] Beginning May 1989 thru December 1989, high grade contracts are included (May total was 353 contracts)   *Source: Commodity Exchange, Inc. of New New York (COMEX)*

Producers' Prices of Electrolytic (Wirebar) Copper, Delivered U.S. Destinations   In Cents Per Pound

Year	Jan.	Feb.	Mar.	Apr.	May	June	July	Aug.	Sept.	Oct.	Nov.	Dec.	Average
1985	66.23	68.32	67.19	72.17	71.89	68.86	68.53	68.32	67.66	68.60	68.37	70.10	68.85
1986	71.57	70.21	71.78	70.55	68.69	69.15	65.47	64.12	66.82	65.61	65.06	65.91	67.91
1987	67.29	67.87	70.50	69.83	73.54	76.71	83.10	84.94	88.04	91.52	109.59	134.71	84.80
1988	135.63	110.58	111.99	107.51	106.91	116.46	107.90	103.62	118.04	126.38	159.08	167.80	122.66
1989	164.21	146.17	154.89	150.26	132.72	121.45	119.27	133.75	143.60	137.61	123.59	115.64	136.93
1990	116.36	119.35	136.22	134.38	132.32	124.93	133.91	142.53	142.45	138.41	127.76	124.39	131.08
1991	122.59	122.73	121.24	120.35	133.11	111.72	111.90	113.48	118.92	118.90	117.26	110.33	118.54
1992	108.16	112.52	113.56	112.35	112.56	116.74	125.66	124.30	119.39	112.09	108.23	111.13	114.72
1993	112.57	110.26	107.80	99.03	92.35	94.98	93.41	97.06	92.36	81.69	86.07	91.08	96.56
1994	95.65	99.13	101.76	99.87	112.30	120.58	123.68	121.38	132.53	130.91	141.92	148.86	119.05

Source: American Metal Market

Dealers' Buying Price of No. 2 Heavy Copper Scrap In the Chicago Area[1]   In Cents Per Pound

Year	Jan.	Feb.	Mar.	Apr.	May	June	July	Aug.	Sept.	Oct.	Nov.	Dec.	Average
1983	42.55	46.71	51.50	51.50	53.74	54.50	54.50	53.54	51.74	48.12	43.30	42.50	49.52
1984	41.17	40.60	43.59	44.50	43.30	42.21	39.36	38.50	38.08	36.20	34.50	35.67	39.81
1985	37.50	37.50	37.50	37.50	37.50	37.50	37.50	37.50	37.50	37.50	37.50	37.50	37.50
1986	38.23	39.50	39.50	39.50	39.50	39.50	39.50	37.79	37.50	37.50	37.50	37.50	38.59
1987	37.50	37.50	37.86	39.50	41.15	42.50	44.68	49.07	49.50	53.32	55.39	64.73	46.06
1988[1]	77.10	68.00	63.50	63.12	70.07	70.59	69.80	69.54	72.36	78.93	83.66	85.50	72.68
1989	89.83	87.13	95.33	95.95	91.14	80.27	74.45	75.54	86.50	90.32	86.00	80.25	86.06
1990	78.27	71.00	78.73	88.00	88.00	84.38	84.00	85.50	91.84	89.50	86.48	83.00	84.06
1991	83.00	79.50	82.21	82.50	78.66	72.40	71.00	71.00	72.05	75.39	75.08	74.50	76.44
1992	73.21	73.37	75.23	75.16	74.00	74.27	77.18	78.38	75.38	70.27	69.00	67.18	73.55
1993	67.95	67.00	67.00	62.95	55.12	53.59	56.33	54.18	52.67	49.10	47.00	48.00	56.74
1994	50.80	56.11	59.61	62.00	64.86	72.32	76.40	74.30	75.69	76.45	78.10	82.95	69.13

[1] Prior to May 1988, prices are for the New York area.   *Source: American Metal Market*

COPPER

U.S. Foreign Trade of Refined Copper   In Thousands of Metric Tons

Year		Jan.	Feb.	Mar.	Apr.	May	June	July	Aug.	Sept.	Oct.	Nov.	Dec.	Total
1986	Imports	51.9	43.9	49.5	38.2	54.9	36.8	36.0	36.0	37.3	31.7	55.6	31.2	503.1
	Exports	1.3	1.5	1.2	1.0	2.4	.9	.8	1.8	1.7	.6	.9	.8	14.9
1987	Imports	34.4	38.7	55.8	38.9	60.2	69.3	37.0	45.0	28.6	35.9	40.8	31.1	515.6
	Exports	.8	1.9	2.4	2.8	.8	1.1	.6	.5	.8	.7	2.3	3.2	17.9
1988	Imports	49.4	38.0	39.0	33.7	25.9	25.1	22.3	27.7	25.7	44.2	39.2	20.2	390.4
	Exports	4.9	2.0	3.8	5.7	7.7	9.5	3.5	4.4	14.3	2.3	4.0	4.5	66.5
1989	Imports	32.7	24.8	18.7	20.9	24.1	25.9	20.9	24.4	28.1	30.5	32.3	16.9	300.1
	Exports	6.2	4.8	5.9	13.5	4.3	6.6	21.4	15.8	23.4	13.7	6.3	12.1	130.2
1990	Imports	24.7	15.8	26.5	25.3	31.3	24.0	20.6	18.0	21.4	18.4	20.8	16.7	263.6
	Exports	18.1	20.8	12.2	7.6	15.6	12.2	23.9	20.1	22.4	21.5	17.2	19.8	211.3
1991	Imports	22.7	27.1	21.7	30.9	17.5	23.6	23.7	17.4	22.9	36.3	26.8	18.0	288.6
	Exports	33.6	21.4	37.4	16.8	31.5	23.9	20.6	20.9	17.9	13.4	15.4	17.9	270.7
1992	Imports	22.6	24.5	31.9	25.2	25.3	26.1	24.7	25.3	24.0	19.6	20.3	20.8	289.1
	Exports	21.7	18.4	10.8	12.3	11.7	12.0	9.3	13.0	13.6	24.1	14.1	16.1	176.9
1993	Imports	21.8	25.6	28.2	35.9	29.5	26.9	30.6	28.3	22.5	31.6	32.2	30.5	343.4
	Exports	14.0	24.9	23.6	16.3	15.4	13.1	10.7	10.1	19.5	19.5	14.9	14.5	216.7
1994[1]	Imports	28.7	33.6	49.8	36.8	36.1	46.8	35.6	34.4	34.7	62.4	35.9		
	Exports	13.0	10.2	10.7	6.8	14.8	9.1	15.6	10.9	15.4	15.9	13.1		

[1] Preliminary.   Source: U.S. Bureau of Mines

Refined Copper Stocks in the U.S.A.   In Thousands of Short Tons (Recoverable Copper Content)

Year	Jan. 1	Feb. 1	Mar. 1	Apr. 1	May 1	June 1	July 1	Aug. 1	Sept. 1	Oct. 1	Nov. 1	Dec. 1
1979	367.0	318.4	287.5	262.1	237.4	197.8	176.0	174.6	158.0	154.6	148.6	167.3
1980	186.3	203.5	228.2	237.1	269.1	277.3	295.7	310.6	301.0	274.6	265.0	246.0
1981	253.0	261.6	249.4	236.8	245.5	243.4	264.7	276.9	276.0	275.5	281.6	301.2
1982	338.6	351.9	375.9	387.3	409.8	422.5	448.1	463.7	449.9	436.2	438.2	470.8
1983	484.5	489.6	501.6	508.9	524.1	519.4	498.7	509.0	522.7	509.1	514.2	505.2
1984	475.3	497.8	499.6	483.3	478.3	463.4	483.2	493.4	490.7	467.1	475.2	457.3
1985	469.7	452.9	380.9	368.2	358.4	363.2	344.1	331.4	310.9	275.7	257.3	264.1
1986	270.7	271.0	261.6	242.0	231.1	201.4	188.0	209.6	214.4	188.1	189.0	211.3
1987	238.4	211.5	206.8	170.1	175.7	161.6	136.4	141.0	140.4	151.3	121.1	86.7
1988	81.4	79.8	81.6	89.0	83.1	75.7	42.0	48.8	52.5	42.9	40.6	39.8
1989	56.3	67.5	56.3	60.6	54.3	54.4	49.1	61.8	66.1	42.3	48.1	48.2
1990	72.7	42.4	38.6	45.2	55.9	60.2	67.5	67.2	67.6	27.4	27.9	45.4
1991	72.3	72.8	53.2	68.6	63.2	52.8	52.4	71.4	64.4	48.5	48.3	63.1
1992	75.3	76.3	67.2	69.7	75.9	65.0	62.2	71.2	87.1	99.5	110.3	107.1
1993	135.4	152.7	144.3	132.3	146.0	153.6	137.1	151.0	128.4	117.2	124.6	107.1
1994[1]	103.0	87.7	83.6	72.8	70.7	70.4	73.3	81.1	74.6	66.5	52.7	53.6

[1] Preliminary.   Source: American Bureau of Metal Statistics

Refined Copper Stocks Outside the U.S.A.   In Thousands of Short Tons (Recoverable Copper Content)

Year	Jan. 1	Feb. 1	Mar. 1	Apr. 1	May 1	June 1	July 1	Aug. 1	Sept. 1	Oct. 1	Nov. 1	Dec. 1
1979	942.2	878.2	862.4	765.1	758.8	756.7	727.2	687.1	696.6	648.2	635.4	641.3
1980	619.5	598.3	560.9	534.6	516.5	525.9	531.2	530.9	553.2	527.9	489.1	472.6
1981	476.2	485.2	471.0	463.0	458.8	449.8	446.0	454.9	454.7	433.4	419.4	403.0
1982	432.5	466.3	448.4	459.6	452.0	458.7	479.3	492.0	503.6	522.7	575.1	642.9
1983	699.9	760.8	766.4	759.1	795.5	780.0	722.2	683.0	757.4	767.2	765.2	810.4
1984	832.8	817.5	730.0	653.0	618.5	519.3	551.9	526.5	516.0	493.9	483.9	430.0
1985	425.0	420.7	385.7	361.9	364.6	380.4	368.8	464.0	546.7	558.4	533.6	486.6
1986	502.8	501.5	451.8	435.7	422.6	418.7	396.8	430.4	455.1	455.4	458.5	464.8
1987	473.7	467.5	410.5	397.5	387.4	348.5	337.8	336.8	341.1	314.7	254.9	269.6
1988	260.9	292.1	301.1	290.2	277.4	317.9	329.9	374.7	348.7	310.9	282.8	272.2
1989	337.5	325.7	341.0	350.3	406.5	385.7	374.2	389.8	335.8	368.7	348.1	358.3
1990	362.3	382.0	335.6	320.0	332.6	356.3	291.8	370.9	417.9	484.6	483.0	447.6
1991	439.5	464.2	447.1	501.1	559.5	595.4	593.1	605.4	664.7	653.5	644.9	676.9
1992	640.4	718.1	704.2	715.7	714.9	723.2	726.4	737.9	816.5	822.5	873.8	896.1
1993	757.1	765.9	789.6	817.2	885.1	912.2	910.4	943.8	1,040.3	1,124.3	1,133.9	1,106.1
1994[1]	1,075.0	1,095.5	1,046.8	984.9	913.7	859.5	843.7	839.7	874.6	870.7	835.1	824.1

[1] Preliminary.   Source: American Bureau of Metal Statistics

Refined Copper Production in the U.S.A.   In Thousands of Short Tons (Recoverable Copper Content)

Year	Jan.	Feb.	Mar.	Apr.	May	June	July	Aug.	Sept.	Oct.	Nov.	Dec.	Total	Crude
1984	98.8	100.7	117.1	120.5	127.9	125.6	123.0	126.1	101.8	119.5	95.4	101.4	1,358	1,270
1985	113.5	101.2	118.8	122.4	124.1	100.8	99.9	96.8	93.0	112.9	119.7	106.7	1,310	1,387
1986	109.5	98.3	103.5	115.0	122.4	112.1	109.3	108.9	106.7	114.4	116.6	138.1	1,355	1,323
1987	118.0	110.5	105.4	127.7	118.5	95.5	107.7	106.4	121.8	131.3	123.3	127.7	1,394	1,308
1988	124.5	127.2	145.6	122.5	133.7	116.7	112.7	146.0	133.8	121.1	137.7	131.8	1,553	1,527
1989	129.5	128.1	137.2	118.3	132.2	142.6	121.3	150.8	116.5	137.0	127.4	130.7	1,572	1,555
1990	136.0	122.0	150.4	140.1	147.5	136.1	125.5	132.5	130.1	141.6	141.0	125.5	1,628	1,630
1991	129.0	127.7	134.9	119.7	137.1	124.8	136.8	142.7	135.6	153.1	141.0	149.7	1,632	1,393
1992	139.9	135.6	150.6	142.8	123.0	138.5	140.3	150.1	146.9	155.3	156.8	153.7	1,734	1,503
1993	153.9	153.8	173.2	166.0	160.3	177.0	151.4	153.7	160.2	157.3	157.2	166.2	1,930	1,269
1994[1]	160.9	150.0	167.8	157.2	165.5	160.4	148.9	165.5	162.1	157.3	153.3	165.4	1,915	1,743

[1] Preliminary.   Source: American Bureau of Metal Statistics

Refined Copper Production Outside the U.S.A.   In Thousands of Short Tons (Recoverable Copper Content)

Year	Jan.	Feb.	Mar.	Apr.	May	June	July	Aug.	Sept.	Oct.	Nov.	Dec.	Total	Crude
1984	380.3	376.9	412.4	375.1	374.1	382.5	357.4	381.5	373.8	405.2	380.8	358.7	4,559	5,114
1985	371.6	338.8	388.5	376.1	377.4	351.4	384.2	385.6	380.4	387.6	385.5	394.9	4,522	5,217
1986	366.5	351.5	401.7	409.7	373.1	361.2	361.7	374.8	400.3	407.4	396.4	403.6	4,608	5,132
1987	385.8	375.4	410.6	412.2	399.9	403.6	393.3	370.6	391.2	402.7	402.5	407.5	4,755	5,233
1988	397.7	387.8	434.2	370.6	389.4	391.5	366.6	386.9	365.9	412.8	417.0	414.9	4,735	5,210
1989	387.8	372.7	411.9	404.3	430.1	388.7	409.5	413.5	421.7	436.1	434.0	402.7	4,913	5,439
1990	423.7	396.7	424.6	412.8	414.1	395.6	372.6	407.1	404.6	422.6	417.4	411.0	4,902	5,278
1991	416.5	381.1	427.7	405.5	425.3	404.5	375.1	378.7	411.4	411.8	409.2	424.5	4,871	5,533
1992	441.2	412.6	447.0	418.0	438.7	449.5	418.5	425.8	418.7	438.9	431.3	426.1	5,166	5,730
1993	429.2	405.6	475.1	426.2	440.9	447.5	421.6	449.4	448.0	425.9	447.2	436.5	5,253	5,378
1994[1]	447.5	405.8	447.7	415.6	447.9	436.1	402.8	428.8	436.5	431.3	458.0	444.0	5,202	6,558

[1] Preliminary.   Source: American Bureau of Metal Statistics

Refined Copper Deliveries to Fabricators Outside the U.S.A.   In Thousands of Short Tons[2]

Year	Jan.	Feb.	Mar.	Apr.	May	June	July	Aug.	Sept.	Oct.	Nov.	Dec.	Total
1984	118.3	146.1	185.7	184.4	190.7	163.8	150.7	159.3	101.8	167.1	149.5	124.2	1,906
1985	170.2	188.7	159.8	153.0	144.3	135.2	122.3	130.0	93.0	151.5	137.9	120.7	1,767
1986	123.8	120.1	150.5	155.3	164.5	131.5	113.1	127.1	106.7	141.1	114.7	128.4	1,631
1987	160.2	138.7	166.9	152.3	165.6	152.3	131.6	127.2	121.8	188.3	192.7	168.2	1,885
1988	152.0	151.5	162.5	149.6	150.1	161.2	116.5	164.7	133.8	148.2	159.1	139.0	1,824
1989	127.8	147.7	148.4	141.1	153.2	168.4	131.4	173.2	116.5	156.8	149.2	121.9	1,781
1990	167.4	132.8	163.3	156.6	153.3	144.5	129.5	132.5	130.1	140.9	130.7	108.6	1,733
1991	128.4	153.3	125.3	126.7	152.7	115.0	125.4	152.8	135.6	167.7	130.4	132.9	1,684
1992	144.9	159.0	165.9	155.5	149.4	161.4	145.8	144.1	146.9	150.4	166.2	130.0	1,813
1993	142.9	165.3	201.6	170.4	162.5	209.6	144.8	191.4	178.9	164.3	194.8	182.7	2,109
1994[1]	193.3	168.5	204.6	178.3	187.8	171.9	154.3	194.6	188.2	188.7	171.9	173.9	2,176

[1] Preliminary.   [2] Recoverable copper content.   Source: American Bureau of Metal Statistics

Refined Copper Deliveries to Fabricators Outside the U.S.A.   In Thousands of Short Tons[2]

Year	Jan.	Feb.	Mar.	Apr.	May	June	July	Aug.	Sept.	Oct.	Nov.	Dec.	Total
1984	375.0	448.8	477.8	377.1	453.1	358.8	372.5	371.5	382.7	394.6	420.7	360.6	4,793
1985	356.6	372.1	408.2	369.8	379.8	395.9	300.4	319.9	384.6	422.0	419.6	375.9	4,505
1986	364.5	396.9	403.4	403.2	375.6	387.9	331.0	334.1	376.2	384.9	380.9	380.8	4,519
1987	386.0	413.0	413.9	406.8	426.7	401.8	384.1	359.4	416.4	468.8	377.1	396.8	4,851
1988	359.6	375.2	448.7	385.1	366.8	403.2	340.9	405.9	401.8	437.4	455.6	356.6	4,737
1989	426.0	369.9	411.8	360.9	459.0	398.0	386.8	464.2	393.2	456.9	423.0	399.1	4,949
1990	419.9	466.3	436.7	392.9	408.3	466.7	303.7	373.5	370.8	448.9	469.1	420.7	4,972
1991	405.0	404.4	391.5	361.2	406.3	433.5	368.5	323.4	420.7	499.1	391.4	483.4	4,807
1992	453.7	408.9	441.8	416.4	413.4	432.4	410.4	364.7	432.6	403.5	406.1	461.3	5,045
1993	427.9	392.9	452.3	361.7	422.2	442.6	384.4	347.9	387.5	414.8	463.4	458.5	4,956
1994[1]	414.8	444.5	496.2	481.5	483.9	443.1	402.9	384.2	438.5	463.9	467.6	439.8	5,361

[1] Preliminary.   [2] Recoverable copper content.   Source: American Bureau of Metal Statistics

Corn

The U.S. produced a record high 10 billion bushels of corn in 1994, up dramatically from the previous year's midwestern flood and southeastern drought, which damaged 6.3 billion bushels. This is approximately 160 million bushels over the previous record set in 1992/93. The huge crop will result in a doubling of stocks to 2.1 billion bushels, from a near 20-year low of 850 million bushels at the end of the 1993/94 season (August 31). The stock-to-use ratio is forecast at 22 percent, up sharply from 11 percent in the previous year.

A record yield of 138.4 bushels per acre was realized in 1994, versus the weather damaged 100.7 bushels per acre in 1993. In addition, the quality of the 1994 crop was markedly better than in the previous two years, owing to the generally excellent crop weather. Acreage was up, but not to the record levels of the early-1980s. The impact of the large crop was quickly manifested in futures values in mid-1994, as prices plunged approximately 40¢ per bushel before stabilizing near $2.20 per bushel, basis nearby futures. The 1994 price action was something of a mirror image of 1993, when futures soared about 60¢ per bushel during the second half of the year. In 1993/94, the average price received by farmers for corn was $2.50 per bushel and for 1994/95, a price range of $1.85 per bushel to $2.25 per bushel was forecast, which if realized would be the lowest average of the early-1990s.

Corn is the leading U.S. feed grain with a record large 5.5 billion bushels allocated to this usage in 1994/95, about 61 percent of total disappearance. The latter is in-line with normal feed use patterns, but it could prove higher if livestock producers opt to increase their livestock numbers more than expected, owing to lower feeding costs. The U.S. exports about 1.5 billion bushels of corn on average, but a larger total is forecast for 1994/95, owing to reduced competition from other corn exporting nations. China, for example, the leading competitor of the U.S. for corn exports, will ship less in 1994/95. U.S. corn imports are minor. Food, seed and industrial (FSI) use accounts for almost 20 percent of total U.S. corn usage, 7.2 billion bushels in 1994/95. Within FSI, the biggest gains of late have been for fuel alcohol and corn sweetners. In 1994/95, High fructose corn syrup (HFCS) production is forecast at a record large 455 million bushels. In the early-1980s, HFCS was absorbing less than 200 million bushels of corn. Fuel alcohol use has expanded even more since 1980, from the equivalent of less than 100 million bushels to a projected record high 510 million bushels in 1994/95. Alcohol producers are planning on an increase in alcohol demand when the reformulated gasoline requirements take effect on January 1, 1995, at which time a portion of a new oxygenated cleaner-burning fuel known as reformulated gasoline must be used, beginning

with a 15 percent requirement. Ethanol, which is derived from corn, is expected to be used. Nine major U.S. cities with heavy smog would be required to use the new gasoline as of early-1995.

Total world corn production in 1994/95 of 556 million tonnes compares with 467 million tonnes in 1993/94. The increase largely reflected the large U.S. crop. China, since 1987/88, is the second largest producer with 104 million tonnes in 1994/95, about 20 percent of total production. Rapid increases in per capita income and meat consumption in recent years has led to a large increase in China's corn demand for feed. Whether these gains can be sustained is questionable, but if so, it may cloud China's ability to remain a major corn exporter, which in-turn is apt to benefit U.S. corn producers. Global, consumption in 1994/95 of about 531 million tonnes compares with 503 million tonnes in 1993/94. The U.S. is the largest consumer. World stocks are forecast to increase in 1994/95 by 25 million tonnes, ending the season around 94 million tonnes and in sharp contrast to the draw on world stocks during 1993/94 of nearly 37 million tonnes. The larger global corn supplies were expected to dampen world prices during 1994/95. However, what happens to world corn prices is dependent on the quality and availability of other coarse grains from local harvests, of which wheat can play an important role and world wheat production in 1994/95 is down from 1993/94.

U.S. #2 yellow corn prices vary with the location. Typically, Gulf port prices are about 30¢ per bushel higher than prices in Central Illinois, while quotes at St. Louis run about 10¢ per bushel to 12¢ per bushel higher than Illinois prices.

U.S. Farm Program

The target price for 1994/95 corn is $2.75 per bushel, the same as the previous four crop years. However, the price support loan rate was raised to $1.89 per bushel from $1.72 per bushel in 1993/94. Government controlled corn stocks have been minuscule in recent years, at less than 100 million bushels. On August 31, 1987, the government's inventory exceeded 1.4 billion bushels.

Futures Markets

Corn futures and options are traded on the Chicago Board of Trade (CBOT). A smaller contract is also traded on the Mid-America Commodity Exchange (MidAm). Internationally, the Tokyo Grain Exchange lists corn and futures and continues to experience significant increases in trading volume.

World Production of Corn or Maize   In Thousands of Metric Tons

Crop Year	Argentina	Brazil	Canada	China	France	Hungry	India	Indo-nesia	Italy	Mexico	Romania	South Africa	Ukraine[3]	United States	Yugo-slavia	World Total
1980-1	12,900	22,555	5,434	62,600	9,219	6,535	6,957	3,991	6,377	10,400	10,300	14,645		9,454	168,787	9,317	406,691
1981-2	9,600	22,932	6,673	59,205	8,956	6,998	6,897	4,509	8,197	12,500	11,892	8,355		8,000	208,330	9,807	441,237
1982-3	9,000	19,500	6,513	60,295	10,400	7,800	6,594	3,235	6,847	7,000	12,620	4,083		13,500	209,181	11,126	438,354
1983-4	9,200	21,000	5,933	68,210	10,400	6,426	7,922	5,087	6,669	9,300	11,982	4,405		12,000	106,042	10,719	345,817
1984-5	11,500	22,000	7,024	73,410	10,384	6,686	8,356	5,288	6,776	9,900	13,274	7,755		12,500	194,929	11,293	456,959
1985-6	12,400	21,000	6,970	63,830	12,567	8,818	6,643	4,330	6,357	10,500	11,000	8,078		14,400	225,479	9,896	479,797
1986-7	9,250	26,500	5,912	70,856	11,470	7,261	7,457	5,000	6,401	10,000	15,000	7,150		12,479	209,556	12,526	477,912
1987-8	9,000	24,790	7,015	79,150	12,454	7,234	5,721	4,800	5,762	9,900	10,500	7,075		14,808	181,143	8,863	448,762
1988-9	5,000	26,050	5,369	77,350	14,578	6,028	8,229	5,200	6,318	10,100	10,000	12,384		16,030	125,194	7,697	401,962
1989-90	5,200	22,300	6,571	78,928	13,400	6,747	9,409	5,000	6,359	9,750	6,760	8,900	7,026	191,156	9,415	460,484
1990-1	7,600	24,330	7,067	96,820	9,500	4,317	8,962	5,000	5,864	14,100	6,800	8,300	4,737	201,534	6,724	477,855
1991-2	10,600	30,800	7,413	98,770	12,930	7,745	7,980	5,400	6,240	14,500	10,500	3,125	4,747	189,868	11,500	486,885
1992-3[1]	10,200	29,200	4,883	95,380	14,870	4,301	10,200	5,650	7,410	17,000	6,829	9,985	2,851	240,719	6,650	533,194
1993-4[1]	10,000	32,000	6,501	102,700	15,100	4,000	9,700	5,400	8,030	17,000	8,000	12,875	3,780	160,954	5,900	467,519
1994-5[2]	10,500	30,000	7,050	104,000	12,750	4,500	10,500	5,200	7,500	16,000	8,500	8,000	2,700	256,629	6,500	555,894

[1] Preliminary.   [2] Estimate.   [3] Formerly part of the U.S.S.R.; data not reported separately until 1989.   *Source: U.S. Foreign Agricultural Service, U.S. Department of Agriculture*

World Course Grains Supply & Demand   In Millions of Metric Tons/Hectares

Crop Year Beginning Oct. 1	Area Harvested	Yield	Pro-duction	World Trade	Total Con-sumption	Ending Stocks	Stocks as % of Consump-tion[3]
1980-1	340.5	2.1	723.1	107.9	739.2	126.4	17.1
1981-2	348.5	2.2	758.8	97.4	734.1	151.1	20.6
1982-3	337.8	2.3	775.2	89.8	744.0	182.3	24.5
1983-4	332.7	2.0	677.5	93.1	748.8	111.1	14.8
1984-5	334.3	2.4	805.8	100.0	772.2	144.7	18.7
1985-6	339.9	2.5	832.3	82.7	767.8	209.3	27.3
1986-7	336.0	2.5	822.4	82.9	796.5	235.2	29.5
1987-8	323.3	2.4	784.2	88.3	807.2	215.1	26.7
1988-9	323.4	2.2	721.0	95.5	784.6	151.5	19.3
1989-90	321.1	2.5	791.2	103.9	814.2	128.5	15.8
1990-1	314.5	2.6	821.8	88.3	809.7	140.6	17.4
1991-2	318.2	2.5	803.2	94.4	805.7	138.1	17.1
1992-3[1]	318.9	2.7	863.0	90.0	833.7	167.4	20.1
1993-4[1]	310.5	2.5	785.9	84.6	828.7	124.7	15.1
1994-5[2]	310.9	2.8	866.4	89.4	856.8	134.2	15.7

[1] Preliminary.   [2] Estimate.   [3] Represents the ratio of marketing year ending stocks to total consumption.   *Source: Foreign Agricultural Service, U.S. Department of Agriculture*

Acreage and Supply of Corn in the United States   In Millions of Bushels

Crop Year Beginning Sept. 1[3]	Planted	Harvested For Grain	Harvested For Silage	Yield Per Harvested Acre Bushels	Carry-over, Sept. 1 On Farms[3]	Carry-over, Sept. 1 Off Farms[3]	Supply Beginning Stocks	Supply Pro-duction	Supply Imports	Total Supply
		In Thousands of Acres								
1983-4	60,207	51,479	7,808	81.1	1,510.4	1,609.5	3,523	4,174	2	7,699
1984-5	80,517	71,897	7,535	106.7	347.9	375.4	1,006	7,672	2	8,680
1985-6	83,398	75,209	7,155	118.0	678.9	701.8	1,648	8,875	10	10,534
1986-7	76,580	68,907	6,418	119.4	NA	NA	4,040	8,226	2	12,267
1987-8	66,200	59,505	5,994	119.8	2,284.5	2,597.2	4,882	7,131	3	12,016
1988-9	67,717	58,250	8,294	84.6	2,002.8	2,256.3	4,259	4,929	3	9,191
1989-90	72,221	64,703	6,606	116.3	967.5	962.9	1,930	7,525	2	9,458
1990-1	74,171	66,952	6,124	118.5	754.8	589.7	1,344	7,934	3	9,282
1991-2	75,951	68,847	6,101	108.6	691.2	830.0	1,521	7,475	20	9,016
1992-3[1]	79,340	72,162	6,069	131.4	605.0	494.8	1,100	9,482	7	10,589
1993-4[1]	73,323	62,991	6,831	100.7	1,070.7	1,042.0	2,113	6,344	21	8,478
1994-5[2]	78,767	71,757	5,563	133.8	395.4	454.8	850	9,602	5	10,457

[1] Preliminary.   [2] Estimate.   [3] Data prior to 1986-87 are as of October 1.   NA = Not available.   *Source: Economic Research Service, U.S. Department of Agriculture*

CORN

U.S. Corn Supply and Disappearance   In Millions of Bushels

Crop Year Beginning Sept. 1	Supply Beginning Stocks	Supply Pro-duction	Supply Imports	Total Supply	Disappearance Domestic Use Food, Alcohol & Industrial	Seed	Feed & Residual	Total	Exports	Total Disap-pearance	Ending Stocks Gov't Owned[3]	Ending Stocks Privately Owned[4]	Total
1991-2	1,521	7,476	19.6	9,016	1,434	20.2	4,878	6,332	1,584	7,916	113	987	1,100
Sept.-Nov.	1,521	7,476	6.5	9,003	349	0	1,692	2,041	421	2,462	250	6,291	6,541
Dec.-Feb.	6,541	--------	4.4	6,546	344	0	1,279	1,623	362	1,985	199	4,362	4,561
Mar.-May	4,561	--------	5.4	4,566	369	19.9	1,068	1,456	372	1,828	147	2,591	2,739
June-Aug.	2,739	--------	3.3	2,742	372	.3	839	1,212	430	1,642	113	987	1,100
1992-3[1]	1,100	9,477	7.1	10,584	1,511	18.7	5,296	6,826	1,663	8,471	56	2,058	2,113
Sept.-Nov.	1,100	9,477	1.3	10,578	360	0	1,825	2,185	488	2,672	87	7,819	7,906
Dec.-Feb.	7,906	--------	1.0	7,907	350	0	1,416	1,766	463	2,229	87	5,591	5,678
Mar.-May	5,678	--------	2.0	5,680	403	16.4	1,157	1,576	411	1,971	64	3,645	3,709
June-Aug.	3,709	--------	2.8	3,712	399	2.3	899	1,300	301	1,599	56	2,058	2,113
1993-4[1]	2,113	6,336	20.8	8,470	1,588	20.1	4,704	6,312	1,328	7,620	45	805	850
Sept.-Nov.	2,113	6,336	5.2	8,455	378	0	1,705	2,083	435	2,518	53	5,884	5,937
Dec.-Feb.	5,937	--------	8.0	5,945	371	0	1,248	1,619	330	1,949	50	3,946	3,996
Mar.-May	3,996	--------	6.3	4,002	419	19.5	954	1,393	270	1,642	48	2,312	2,360
June-Aug.	2,360	--------	1.4	2,361	420	.6	798	1,219	293	1,511	45	805	850
1994-5[2]	850	10,103	5.0	10,958	---- 1,700 ----		5,650	7,350	1.950	9,300			1,658
Sept.-Nov.	850	10,103	1.0	10,954	410	0	2,004	2,414	460	2,874			8,081

[1] Preliminary.   [2] Estimate.   [3] Uncommitted inventory.   [4] Includes quantity under loan and farmer-owned reserves.   *Source: Economic Research Service, U.S. Department of Agriculture*

Corn Production Estimates and Cash Prices in the U.S.

Crop Year	Corn for Grain Production Estimates In Thousands of Bushels Aug. 1	Sept. 1	Oct. 1	Nov. 1	Final	St. Louis No. 2 Yellow	Omaha No. 2 Yellow	Los Angeles No. 2 Yellow	Kansas City No. 2 White	Chicago No. 2 Yellow	Average Farm Price[2]	Value of Pro-duction (Million Dollars)
						Dollar Per Bushel						
1989-90	7,348,155	7,321,005	7,448,875	7,589,715	7,525,493	2.58	2.41	3.38	3.10	2.54	2.36	17,897
1990-1	7,850,164	8,118,117	8,021,697	7,934,892	7,934,028	2.49	2.28	3.33	2.98	2.41	2.28	18,192
1991-2	7,474,480	7,295,071	7,479,421	7,485,901	7,475,480	2.53	2.36	3.39	3.06	2.52	2.37	17,864
1992-3	8,762,060	7,873,436	8,592,821	9,328,850	9,476,698	2.25	2.10			2.22	2.07	19,378
1993-4[1]	7,423,142	7,229,427	6,961,902	6,503,237	6,336,470	2.67	2.57			2.68	2.50	
1994-5[1]	9,214,420	9,257,170	9,602,340	10,010,310	10,103,030						2.00-2.40	

[1] Preliminary.   [2] Season-average price based on monthly weighted by monthly marketings.   *Source: Economic Research Service, U.S. Department of Agriculture*

Production of Corn (for Grain) in the United States   In Millions of Bushels

Year	Colo-rado	Illinois	Indiana	Iowa	Kansas	Mich-igan	Minn-esota	Missouri	Nebraska	Ohio	Penn-slvania	South Dakota	Texas	Wis-consin
1988	128.0	700.8	415.0	898.8	143.8	112.0	347.8	153.5	818.4	255.0	59.2	132.0	129.6	130.7
1989	134.9	1,322.3	691.6	1,445.5	155.0	222.6	700.0	219.8	847.0	342.2	98.9	190.8	148.4	310.8
1990	128.7	1,320.8	703.1	1,562.4	188.5	238.1	762.6	205.8	934.4	417.5	109.6	234.0	130.5	354.0
1991	128.5	1,177.0	510.6	1,427.4	206.3	253.0	720.0	213.4	999.6	326.4	68.4	240.5	165.0	380.8
1992	130.2	1,646.5	877.6	1,903.7	259.5	241.5	741.0	324.0	1,066.5	507.7	118.8	277.2	202.5	306.8
1993	106.8	1,300.0	712.8	880.0	216.0	225.5	322.0	166.5	785.2	360.8	93.1	160.7	212.8	216.2
1994[1]	133.5	1,786.2	858.2	1,930.4	304.6	260.9	915.9	273.7	1,153.7	486.5	123.6	367.2	238.7	437.1

[1] Preliminary.   *Source: National Agricultural Statistics Service, U.S. Department of Agriculture*

Distribution of Corn in the United States   In Millions of Bushels

Year Crop Beginning Sept. 1	Food, Seed and Industrial Use HFCS	Glucose & Dextrose	Starch	Alcohol Fuel	Beve-rage[3]	Seed	Cereal & Other Products	Total	Livestock Feed[4]	Exports (Including Grain Equiv. of Products)	Domestic Disap-pearance	Total Utilization
1988-9	361	182	223	287	107	19	114	1,293	3,941	2,026	5,234	7,260
1989-90	368	193	230	321	109	19	115	1,355	4,389	2,368	5,745	8,113
1990-1	379	200	232	349	80	19	114	1,373	4,663	1,725	6,036	7,761
1991-2	392	210	237	398	81	20	116	1,454	4,878	1,584	6,332	7,916
1992-3	414	215	238	426	83	19	117	1,493	5,296	1,663	6,826	8,471
1993-4[1]	442	223	244	458	83	20	118	1,568	4,704	1,328	6,312	7,620
1994-5[2]	465	230	250	535	83	20	117	1,680	5,650	1,950	7,350	9,300

[1] Preliminary.   [2] Estimate.   [3] Also includes nonfuel industrial alcohol.   [4] Feed and waste (residual, mostly feed).   *Source: Economic Research Service, U.S. Department of Agriculture*

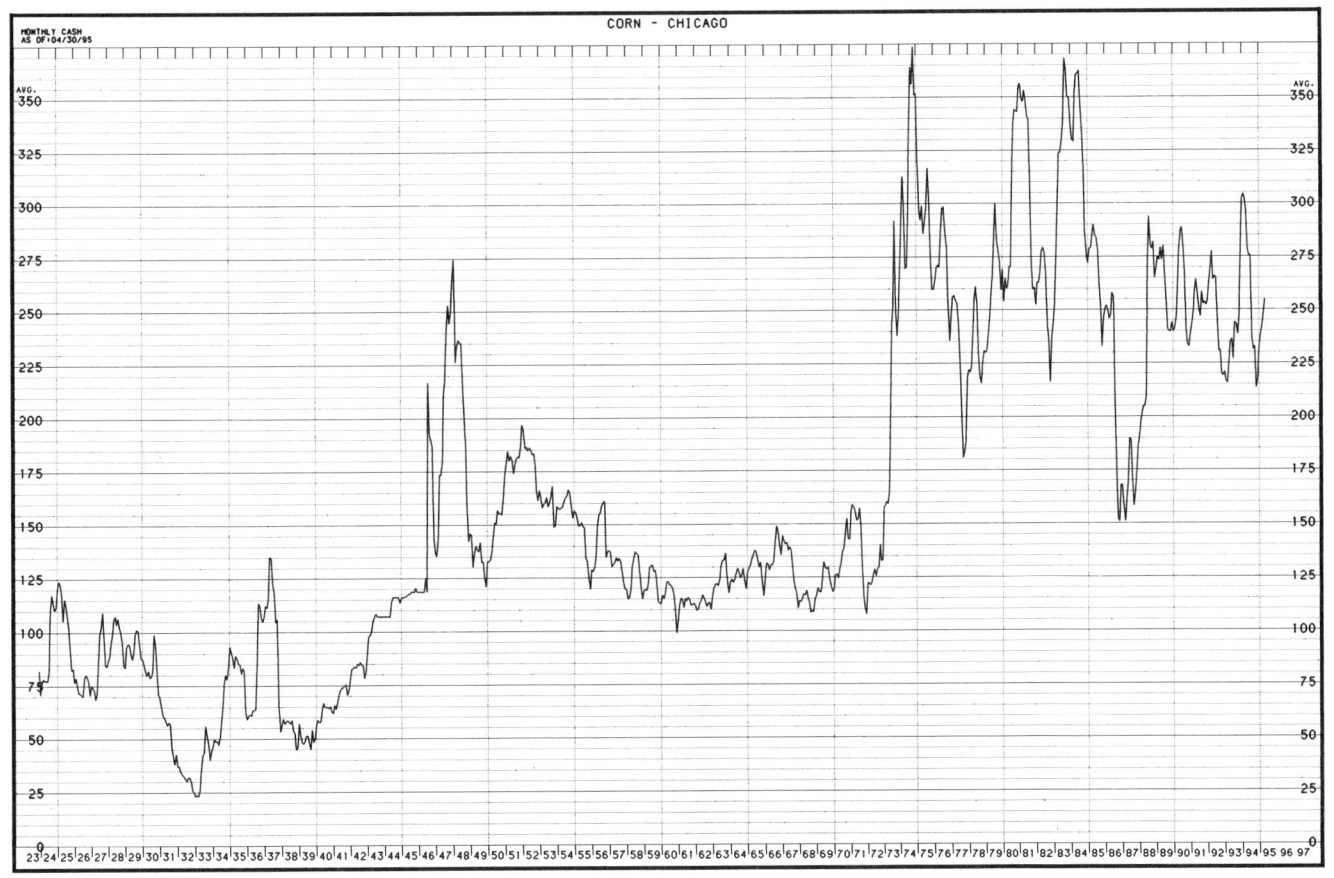

CORN - CHICAGO

MONTHLY CASH
AS OF 04/30/95

Average Cash Price of Corn, No. 2 Yellow in Central Illinois[2]   In Dollars Per Bushel

Crop Year	Sept.	Oct.	Nov.	Dec.	Jan.	Feb.	Mar.	Apr.	May	June	July	Aug.	Average
1983-4	3 52	3.47	3.51	3.38	3.30	3.29	3.52	3.61	3.61	3.62	3.45	3.23	3.46
1984-5	2.95	2.81	2.79	2.72	2.79	2.79	2.84	2.90	2.95	2.83	2.76	2.50	2.80
1985-6	2.28	2.10	2.32	2.38	2.36	2.33	2.29	2.31	2.42	2.41	1.93	1.52	2.22
1986-7	1.34	1.34	1.55	1.52	1.44	1.38	1.46	1.56	1.75	1.74	1.60	1.46	1.51
1987-8	1.50	1.64	1.74	1.78	1.84	1.90	1.92	1.92	1.97	2.66	2.85	2.70	2.04
1988-9	2.68	2.70	2.54	2.56	2.62	2.60	2.64	2.58	2.64	2.53	2.44	2.30	2.57
1989-90	2.35	2.25	2.29	2.29	2.29	2.34	2.44	2.64	2.73	2.70	2.68	2.54	2.46
1990-1	2.25	2.18	2.20	2.27	2.31	2.36	2.45	2.50	2.41	2.34	2.34	2.45	2.34
1991-2	2.39	2.41	2.41	2.42	2.49	2.58	2.64	2.50	2.51	2.51	2.31	2.17	2.45
1992-3	2.13	1.97	1.99	2.05	2.07	2.05	2.16	2.23	2.20	2.09	2.25	2.27	2.12
1993-4	2.22	2.27	2.63	2.81	2.89	2.82	2.75	2.60	2.57	2.61	2.19	2.13	2.54
1994-5[1]	2.08	1.92	2.04	2.17	2.22								

[1] Preliminary.   [2] Data prior to 1985-86 are for Omaha.   *Source: Economic Research Service, U.S. Department of Agriculture*

Average Cash Price of Corn, No. 2 Yellow at Gulf Ports[2]   In Dollars Per Bushel

Crop Year	Sept.	Oct.	Nov.	Dec.	Jan.	Feb.	Mar.	Apr.	May	June	July	Aug.	Average
1983-4	3.75	3.76	3.74	3.64	3.60	3.48	3.74	3.76	3.71	3.73	3.62	3.52	3.67
1984-5	3.31	3.08	2.98	2.90	3.03	3.04	3.05	3.05	2.96	2.95	2.92	2.67	2.99
1985-6	2.59	2.50	2.69	2.75	2.72	2.63	2.56	2.57	2.68	2.63	2.12	1.85	2.52
1986-7	1.68	1.66	1.83	1.81	1.73	1.70	1.83	1.89	2.06	2.06	1.95	1.81	1.83
1987-8	1.86	1.99	2.08	2.11	2.20	2.23	2.29	2.28	2.29	3.05	3.22	3.02	2.39
1988-9	3.08	3.07	2.89	2.99	3.01	2.99	3.02	2.93	2.99	2.87	2.73	2.57	2.93
1989-90	2.60	2.40	2.75	2.75	2.69	2.70	2.72	3.01	3.08	3.05	2.92	2.79	2.79
1990-1	2.59	2.55	2.54	2.60	2.68	2.70	2.77	2.80	2.69	2.65	2.67	2.79	2.67
1991-2	2.76	2.76	2.72	2.71	2.70	2.8	2.96	2.77	2.77	2.80	2.61	2.48	2.74
1992-3	2.50	2.40	2.42	2.39	2.39	2.40	2.48	2.55	2.50	2.36	2.59	2.55	2.46
1993-4	2.57	2.68	2.94	3.08	3.22	3.14	3.05	2.88	2.81	2.85	2.51	2.44	2.85
1994-5[1]	2.48	2.44	2.43	2.61	2.72								

[1] Preliminary.   [2] Barge delivered to Louisiana Gulf.   *Source: Economic Research Service, U.S. Department of Agriculture*

CORN

Weekly Outstanding Export Sales & Cumulative Exports -- U.S. Corn   In Thousands of Metric Tons

1992/93			1993/94			1994/95		
Marketing Year 1992/93 Week Ending	Out-standing Sales	Cumu-lative Exports	Marketing Year 1993/94 Week Ending	Out-standing Sales	Cumu-lative Exports	Marketing Year 1993/94 Week Ending	Out-standing Sales	Cumu-lative Exports
Sept. 3, 1992	9,224	271	Sept. 2, 1993	6,624	176	Sept. 1, 1994	5,728	53
10	9,076	1,214	9	6,623	708	8	6,210	510
17	9,463	1,975	16	7,332	1,456	15	6,370	1,162
24	9,377	2,755	23	7,610	2,246	22	6,681	1,805
Oct. 1	9,540	3,626	30	7,881	3,122	29	6,923	2,622
8	9,854	4,339	Oct. 7	7,873	4,029	Oct. 6	7,460	3,151
15	10,299	5,342	14	7,601	4,882	13	7,974	3,840
22	11,180	6,136	21	7,385	5,744	20	8,053	4,522
29	11,599	6,883	28	7,395	6,518	27	8,350	5,308
Nov. 5	4,344	7,805	Nov. 4	7,230	7,315	Nov. 3	8,164	6,332
12	11,242	8,627	11	7,031	8,204	10	7,955	7,453
19	10,960	9,714	18	6,918	9,072	17	8,745	8,317
26	10,178	10,879	25	6,567	9,784	24	9,147	9,478
Dec. 3	9,408	12,315	Dec. 2	6,392	10,609	Dec. 1	10,437	10,991
10	9,122	13,492	9	6,059	11,689	8	10,953	12,089
17	9,315	14,489	16	5,647	12,544	15	10,669	13,218
24	9,455	15,226	23	5,122	13,362	22	13,065	14,097
31	9,424	15,904	30	4,921	13,950	29	13,403	15,185
Jan. 6, 1993	9,342	16,691	Jan. 6, 1994	4,975	14,348	Jan. 5, 1995	13,278	16,408
13	9,594	17,251	13	5,278	15,153	12	13,973	17,460
20	9,584	18,217	20	5,490	15,771	19	13,531	18,815
27	9,126	19,248	27	5,521	16,399	26	13,347	19,938
Feb. 4	8,937	20,060	Feb. 3	5,306	17,036	Feb. 2	12,613	21,330
11	8,873	21,037	10	5,289	17,361	9	11,853	22,750
18	8,615	21,993	17	5,044	17,940	16	11,409	23,896
25	8,696	22,782	24	4,724	18,564	23	11,190	24,789
Mar. 3	8,745	23,282	Mar. 3	4,664	19,005	Mar. 2	10,699	26,039
11	8,276	24,357	10	4,271	19,633	9	10,305	27,263
18	8,366	25,058	17	3,719	20,411	16		
25	7,782	25,971	24	3,637	20,814	23		
Apr. 1	7,718	26,528	31	3,312	21,440	30		
8	7,462	27,045	Apr. 7	3,103	21,891	Apr. 6		
15	7,150	27,967	14	3,339	22,277	13		
22	6,972	28,889	21	3,097	22,817	20		
29	6,884	29,548	28	2,796	23,292	27		
May 6	6,507	30,235	May 5	2,690	23,668	May 4		
13	6,050	31,032	12	2,863	24,124	11		
20	6,309	31,651	19	2,944	24,701	18		
27	6,491	32,021	26	3,161	25,053	25		
June 3	5,970	32,863	June 2	3,230	25,334	June 1		
10	5,649	33,495	9	3,452	25,716	8		
17	5,349	34,106	16	3,510	26,096	15		
24	5,114	34,834	23	3,770	26,604	22		
July 1	4,958	35,229	30	3,727	27,179	29		
8	4,717	35,741	July 7	3,995	27,489	July 6		
15	4,280	36,334	14	4,089	27,854	13		
22	3,786	36,831	21	3,721	28,409	20		
29	3,709	37,306	28	3,434	28,895	27		
Aug. 5	3,306	37,754	Aug. 4	3,228	29,375	Aug. 3		
12	3,185	38,081	11	2,848	30,146	10		
19	2,233	39,068	18	2,598	30,723	17		
26	1,603	39,840	25	3,802	0	24		

Source: Foreign Agricultural Service, U.S. Department of Agriculture

U.S. Exports[1] of Corn (Including Seed), by Country of Destination   In Thousands of Metric Tons

Year Beginning Oct.	Algeria	Brazil	Canada	Dominican Republic	Egypt	Israel	Japan	Mexico	Rep. of Korea	Russia[3]	Saudi Arabia	Spain	Taiwan	Vene-zuela	Total
1986-7	974	1,162	428	341	2,055	401	12,459	3,256	4,080	3,907	301	468	3,184	0	39,297
1987-8	1,113	0	158	394	1,078	415	14,816	2,900	4,411	5,585	545	1,836	4,169	0	43,955
1988-9	973	20	896	392	1,014	304	13,016	3,113	4,591	15,573	616	1,280	3,625	0	50,676
1989-90	1,146	12	637	421	1,135	250	13,885	4,585	5,680	16,371	707	1,712	5,009	593	59,854
1990-1	1,328	393	302	442	1,756	299	13,639	1,901	1,982	9,077	725	1,434	5,086	321	44,497
1991-2	827	148	314	531	1,058	369	13,481	1,041	1,508	6,533	602	1,273	4,998	552	40,693
1992-3	1,224	71	1,189	614	1,543	539	14,235	396	1,021	3,380	787	1,075	5,450	777	41,766
1993-4[2]	1,182		640	604	1,437	268	12,032	1,678	631	2,337	851	1,116	4,955	751	33,057

[1] Excludes exports of corn by-products.   [2] Preliminary.   [3] Formerly part of the U.S.S.R.; data not reported separately until 1992.
Source: Economic Research Service, U.S. Department of Agriculture

Corn (Shelled & Ear) Stocks in the United States   In Millions of Bushels

Year	On Farms Mar. 1	On Farms June 1	On Farms Sept. 1	On Farms Dec. 1	Off Farms Mar. 1	Off Farms June 1	Off Farms Sept. 1	Off Farms Dec. 1	Total Stocks Mar. 1	Total Stocks June 1	Total Stocks Sept. 1	Total Stocks Dec. 1
1985[2]	2,833.8	2,007.8	NA	NA	1,131.7	827.7	NA	NA	3,965.5	2,835.5	1,648.2	8,614.7
1986	NA	3,143.1	2,049.4	6,795.5	NA	1,847.0	1,990.1	3,510.0	6,587.1	4,990.0	4,039.5	10,305.5
1987	5,024.0	3,491.8	2,284.5	6,100.0	3,224.2	2,840.4	2,597.2	3,668.5	8,248.2	6,332.2	4,881.7	9,768.5
1988	4,421.0	3,241.0	2,002.8	4,280.2	3,214.6	2,594.5	2,256.3	2,791.4	7,635.6	5,835.5	4,259.1	7,071.6
1989	3,021.0	2,022.0	967.5	4,698.8	2,182.9	1,397.3	962.9	2,383.3	5,203.9	3,419.3	1,930.4	7,082.1
1990	2,910.5	1,623.5	754.8	4,874.0	1,901.9	1,219.7	589.7	2,066.3	4,812.4	2,843.2	1,344.5	6,940.3
1991	3,064.5	1,755.0	691.2	4,294.5	1,724.5	1,237.0	830.0	2,246.6	4,789.0	2,992.0	1,521.2	6,541.1
1992	2,610.2	1,517.5	605.5	5,736.9	1,950.8	1,221.1	494.8	2,169.5	4,561.0	2,738.6	1,100.3	7,906.4
1993	3,630.0	2,216.5	1,070.7	3,803.0	2,048.2	1,492.9	1,042.3	2,133.5	5,678.2	3,709.4	2,113.0	5,936.5
1994[1]	2,210.0	1,203.0	395.4	5,417.5	1,785.5	1,156.9	454.7	2,663.2	3,995.7	2,359.9	850.1	8,080.7

[1] Preliminary.   [2] April 1 stocks.   NA = Not available.   *Source: National Agricultural Statistics Service, U.S. Department of Agriculture*

CORN

Volume of Trading of Corn Futures at Chicago   In Millions of Bushels

Year	Jan.	Feb.	Mar.	Apr	May	June	July	Aug.	Sept.	Oct.	Nov.	Dec.	Total
1984	3,518	3,866	4,248	4,407	4,259	4,111	4,868	3,975	3,289	2,883	3,619	2,439	45,543
1985	2,406	2,369	2,746	2,608	2,346	2,494	3,231	2,743	2,629	2,597	3,545	2,248	31,964
1986	2,629	2,153	2,203	2,840	3,029	2,390	2,605	2,217	2,486	3,103	2,591	2,555	30,801
1987	2,343	2,901	3,088	3,646	3,579	3,984	2,978	2,498	2,620	3,380	2,923	2,327	36,266
1988	3,040	3,333	3,212	3,478	4,235	7,898	6,818	5,352	4,353	4,661	5,597	3,549	55,528
1989	4,170	3,384	3,818	4,138	3,930	4,485	4,323	3,433	2,827	4,702	4,352	2,793	46,354
1990	3,248	3,991	4,623	5,742	7,146	6,767	5,509	4,541	3,028	3,939	5,682	2,899	57,114
1991	4,284	3,484	4,663	5,205	4,227	5,064	6,268	5,486	3,462	4,420	4,539	3,161	54,264
1992	4,506	5,013	4,761	4,343	4,691	5,076	4,328	3,975	3,443	3,442	4,981	3,222	51,783
1993	2,588	3,182	3,870	4,474	3,440	5,237	6,978	5,071	4,480	5,180	7,872	4,941	57,313
1994	6,257	5,178	5,228	5,544	5,396	7,275	3,738	3,009	3,075	3,515	5,127	4,307	57,649

Source: Chicago Board of Trade

Average Open Interest of Corn Futures at Chicago   In Thousands of Barrels

Year	Jan.	Feb.	Mar.	Apr.	May	June	July	Aug.	Sept.	Oct.	Nov.	Dec.
1984	1,037,167	995,724	997,533	1,003,501	807,738	759,022	681,895	723,519	698,227	737,381	715,814	629,253
1985	667,033	655,735	592,298	630,084	525,072	513,082	549,368	627,919	639,756	637,095	716,065	656,807
1986	603,350	562,749	545,073	572,669	548,970	586,031	574,077	607,718	621,703	712,114	773,156	590,845
1987	651,105	708,597	692,102	706,486	650,705	632,792	568,933	591,430	593,557	689,305	690,809	631,781
1988	728,517	759,008	787,238	813,253	826,970	1,072,313	1,229,357	1,174,962	1,164,763	1,236,846	1,211,708	1,112,098
1989	1,081,102	994,058	963,200	917,720	819,439	783,908	719,030	727,027	706,896	857,567	971,254	839,719
1990	890,470	1,014,224	1,149,729	1,260,776	1,250,101	1,212,310	1,063,743	1,039,755	1,033,015	1,056,112	1,151,665	1,019,404
1991	1,050,031	1,096,179	1,145,049	1,147,020	1,024,140	1,010,500	992,637	1,098,500	1,077,634	1,212,331	1,285,325	1,141,737
1992	1,270,977	1,474,784	1,427,144	1,302,633	1,151,794	1,160,944	1,056,106	1,098,981	1,043,064	1,199,439	1,311,724	1,224,013
1993	1,280,564	1,304,929	1,243,192	1,249,999	1,145,079	1,162,948	1,328,361	1,324,688	1,219,460	1,378,962	1,662,225	1,636,129
1994	1,730,383	1,681,711	1,637,696	1,528,608	1,313,103	1,231,541	1,075,406	1,044,950	1,064,915	1,218,389	1,314,246	1,253,229

Source: Chicago Board of Trade

Corn Price Support Data in the United States

Crop Year Beginning Sept. 1	National Average Loan Rate[3] ----- $ Per Bushel -----	Target Price	Placed Under Loan	% of Production	Acquired by CCC	Owned by CCC Aug. 31	CCC Owned	Under CCC Loan	Quantity Pledged -- Ths. Bu --	Face Amount Ths. $
1983-4	2.65	2.86	162	3.9	9	202	1,230	1,450	369	1,058
1984-5	2.55	3.03	1,100	14.3	65	225	296	1,056	2,290	627
1985-6	2.55	3.03	3,163	35.6	580	546	477	2,811	56,868	156,478
1986-7	1.92	3.03	4,894	59.5	1,332	1,443	1,265	4,905	59,188	114,611
1987-8	1.82	3.03	4,186	58.7	787	835	1,843	4,436	290,323	53,745
1988-9	1.77	2.93	756	15.3	151	363	679	982	18,757	35,688
1989-90	1.65	2.84	920	12.2	361	233	679	1,110	11,335	20,889
1990-1	1.57	2.75	1,071	13.5	285	371	214	1,071	6,945	11,895
1991-2	1.62	2.75	1,006	13.5	291	113	265	678	26,636	45,609
1992-3[1]	1.72	2.75	1,645	17.4	0	56	87			
1993-4[1]	1.72	2.75	618	9.7	0	45	50			
1994-5[2]	1.89	2.75	1,311	13.7	0					

[1] Preliminary.   [2] Estimate.   [3] Finley or announced loan rate.   *Source: National Agricultural Statistics Service, U.S. Department of Agriculture*

Corn Under Price Support Through the End of the Month
(Cumulative Total from Current Season's Crop)   In Millions of Bushels

Crop Year	Aug.	Sept.	Oct.	Nov.	Dec.	Jan.	Feb.	Mar.	Apr	....May	....June	July
1984-5	-----	2.3	47.2	278.5	631.5	969.6	1,028.0	1,055.0	1,063.0	1,068.0	1,070.0	-----
1985-6	11.1	56.9	369.8	1,069.0	2,016.0	2,055.0	2,828.0	2,916.0	2,996.0	3,278.0	3,040.0	-----
1986-7	8.1	59.2	535.6	1,583.0	2,810.0	3,922.0	4,455.0	4,612.0	4,765.0	4,814.0	4,839.0	4,850.0
1987-8	3.8	290.3	967.9	2,385.0	3,051.0	3,899.0	4,092.0	4,140.0	4,168.0	4,181.0	4,187.0	4,187.0
1988-9	1.3	16.0	95.3	266.2	505.7	704.7	733.4	749.3	752.9	754.0	756.0	755.9
1989-90	2.3	11.3	75.9	434.0	668.0	870.9	896.4	916.4	918.6	919.5	919.9	919.9
1990-1	1.4	6.9	56.7	431.0	700.3	-----	1,041.3	1,063.5	1,067.1	1,069.4	1,070.9	1,071.0
1991-2	2.4	26.6	165.4	526.2	693.8	966.4	991.2	1,000.9	1,004.2	1,005.4	1,006.0	1,645.2
1992-3	2.9	16.7	91.9	418.6	1,032.3	1,492.5	1,578.7	1,620.4	1,638.0	1,642.3	1,645.1	1,006.0
1993-4	3.2	13.5	45.0	225.0	459.0	584.5	601.5	612.9	616.1	617.9	618.2	

Source: Agricultural Stabilization and Conservation Service, U.S. Department of Agriculture

Corn Oil

Supply & Distribution of Corn Oil   In Millions of Pounds

| Crop Year Beginning Oct. 1 | Supply | | | | Disappearance | | | | | | |
	Stocks Oct. 1	Pro-duction	Imports	Total Supply	Baking and Frying Fats	Salad and Cooking Oil	Marg-arine	Total Edible Products	Domestic Disap-pearance	Exports	Total Disap-pearance
1984-5	70	1,194	-----	1,265	W	511	206	774	930	260	1,190
1985-6	74	1,253	-----	1,327	W	524	200	837	863	344	1,207
1986-7	120	1,400	-----	1,520	W	491	248	934	1,143	268	1,411
1987-8	109	1,435	-----	1,546	W	555	212	946	1,065	370	1,435
1988-9	111	1,415	2.0	1,528	227	615	218	1,060	1,073	356	1,429
1989-90	99	1,470	-----	1,569	W	659	218	1,129	1,028	414	1,442
1990-1	127	1,656	1.8	1,785	304	589	195	1,143	1,149	498	1,647
1991-2	138	1,821	5.1	1,965	411	565	185	1,085	1,202	566	1,768
1992-3[1]	196	1,878	7.2	2,081	241	547	W	945	1,219	712	1,931
1993-4[1]	150	1,906	6.6	2,062	86	412	W	648	1,239	705	1,944
1994-5[2]	118	2,040	2.0	2,160					1,275	740	2,051

[1] Preliminary.   [2] Estimate.   W = Withheld proprietary data.   *Source: Economic Research Service, U.S. Department of Agiculture*

Crude Corn Oil Production in the United States[2]   In Millions of Pounds

Year	Oct.	Nov.	Dec.	Jan.	Feb.	Mar.	Apr.	May	June	July	Aug.	Sept.	Total
1984-5	88.8	75.5	89.6	87.7	84.2	107.3	107.0	110.1	107.7	130.1	101.9	104.0	1,194
1985-6	114.2	101.5	97.1	72.8	97.9	102.2	109.8	118.4	106.3	108.6	119.9	104.1	1,253
1986-7	134.6	120.2	114.0	100.1	102.2	119.3	111.2	123.8	117.5	123.0	114.7	119.5	1,400
1987-8	121.5	115.9	110.6	107.1	110.2	113.4	117.3	125.6	125.4	131.7	132.1	124.5	1,435
1988-9	123.8	107.5	127.8	125.5	108.6	128.9	122.0	125.1	119.9	118.6	98.7	108.5	1,415
1989-90	130.2	106.1	128.6	127.7	122.0	131.4	135.6	115.5	140.7	150.4	145.2	132.2	1,566
1990-1	142.0	129.4	129.3	----------- 405.0 -----------			----------- 422.3 -----------			----------- 427.6 -----------			1,656
1991-2	----------- 436.7 -----------			138.1	137.5	164.5	153.3	150.2	160.0	165.0	162.4	153.6	1,821
1992-3	168.1	151.8	151.6	135.5	139.0	165.6	153.5	161.6	164.5	163.0	158.5	165.1	1,878
1993-4[1]	160.8	153.4	162.5	140.6	138.6	166.9	155.3	164.2	171.8	164.8	162.3	165.1	1,906
1994-5[1]	175.5	165.3	180.9	163.2									685

[1] Preliminary.   [2] Not seasonally adjusted.   *Source: Bureau of Census, U.S. Department of Commerce*

U.S. Corn Oil Consumption in Refining   In Millions of Pounds

Year	Oct.	Nov.	Dec.	Jan.	Feb.	Mar.	Apr.	May	June	July	Aug.	Sept.	Total
1984-5	82.1	86.7	91.0	84.0	71.3	89.4	75.5	106.0	97.4	109.1	96.2	90.8	1,080
1985-6	106.0	95.8	87.1	94.1	87.8	100.9	95.1	103.4	91.2	105.2	97.4	98.1	1,162
1986-7	101.2	98.9	98.3	95.7	98.4	104.0	88.7	83.1	90.9	82.6	77.1	92.3	1,111
1987-8	99.2	90.5	78.3	77.7	93.4	90.0	91.7	103.6	104.1	100.6	119.0	110.6	1,159
1988-9	100.8	101.2	107.9	116.5	98.6	118.0	89.5	110.1	106.2	100.1	107.5	98.0	1,254
1989-90	119.8	99.2	105.2	109.1	94.3	96.9	99.8	102.2	105.6	118.3	107.6	102.2	1,260
1990-1	115.4	100.0	108.2	----------- 330.2 -----------			----------- 287.2 -----------			----------- 293.5 -----------			1,235
1991-2	----------- 287.2 -----------			138.1	137.5	164.5	153.3	150.2	160.0	165.0	162.4	153.6	1,672
1992-3	168.1	151.8	151.6	81.2	93.6	110.5	102.4	85.8	99.9	88.0	90.9	96.4	1,320
1993-4[1]	106.7	101.7	114.3	71.8	76.5	92.6	79.4	91.5	91.7	90.6	106.4	109.1	1,132
1994-5[1]	103.5	107.2	116.9										328

[1] Preliminary.   *Source: Bureau of Census, U.S. Department of Commerce*

Corn Oil Spot Price, Wet Mill at Chicago   In Cents Per Pound

Year	Oct.	Nov.	Dec.	Jan.	Feb.	Mar.	Apr.	May	June	July	Aug.	Sept.	Average
1984-5	30.50	34.20	30.70	28.70	30.00	31.00	32.50	31.50	30.80	NA	NA	NA	31.10
1985-6[2]	20.90	20.20	20.10	20.80	18.70	17.10	17.90	18.00	17.30	17.00	16.70	16.70	18.45
1986-7	19.60	20.47	21.48	22.45	24.61	22.65	20.94	21.43	22.90	21.48	20.00	19.14	21.43
1987-8	20.68	20.69	21.49	23.09	22.46	21.26	20.44	21.61	26.43	29.56	26.58	24.94	23.27
1988-9	23.35	21.78	21.22	20.65	20.30	21.61	21.40	21.75	21.44	20.05	19.21	19.39	21.01
1989-90	20.84	22.67	23.25	22.61	23.57	24.96	26.05	24.99	26.56	25.09	28.49	28.00	24.76
1990-1	26.61	24.24	22.15	25.89	27.29	28.50	29.98	28.87	29.61	29.76	29.55	28.50	27.58
1991-2	27.75	27.25	28.75	29.00	28.45	27.19	26.75	26.04	24.75	22.48	20.40	21.00	25.82
1992-3	20.43	20.60	20.75	20.75	20.87	20.79	20.80	20.75	20.60	20.67	21.50	22.23	20.90
1993-4[1]	22.25	23.06	26.93	28.00	29.89	30.30	29.50	29.50	29.50				27.66

[1] Preliminary.   [2] Prior to October 1985, prices are for F.O.B. Decatur (Tank Cars).   NA = Not available.   *Source: Economic Research Service, U.S. Department of Agriculture*

Cotton

World cotton production in 1994/95 totaled nearly 87 million bales (480 pounds per bale), more than initially forecast and up more than 10 million bales from the yield averaged 1993/94 crop. A record high 96 million bales was produced in 1991/92. China, the world's largest producer, with about 19.5 million bales in 1994/95 versus 17 million bales in 1993/94, encouraged producers to increase output. The results so far appear mixed as cotton growers failed to meet the government target of 6 million hectares for the 1994/95 crop. Cotton is China's only major crop with a prohibition on any private sales, but a parallel private market exists, nonetheless, with prices above those paid by the Chinese government. China produced a record large 28.7 million bales in 1984/85. The U.S. record high 1994/95 crop of 19.3 million bales compares with 15.8 million in 1993/94.

Owing to the hefty increase in the 1994/95 crop, production will top world consumption by one million bales and increase world stocks by at least that amount. Usage is estimated at a record large 86 million bales, up 1.5 million bales from 1993/94. World consumption in the early-1990s has trended irregularly higher, but carryover supplies have dropped from 40 million bales at the end of 1991/92 to about 31 million bales as of July 31, 1995. The most broadly favorable factor for increased cotton usage is improved economic growth overseas. If, as expected, Japan and Europe emerge from their worst recession since the 1970s, demand for textile goods will abet mill use and imports. Meanwhile, developing nations are expected to maintain GDP growth rates well in excess of 5 percent on average through 1995. China accounts for almost one-fourth of world consumption, and at times has been forced to import large quantities of cotton to help augment disappointing production.

World trade during 1994/95 may about equal 1993/94, with about 27 million bales shipped. The U.S. share of world exports is expected to remain at about 26 percent of the total, with 7.2 million bales versus 6.9 million bales in 1993/94. The U.S. is the world's largest cotton exporter followed by Uzbekistan. However, the latter along with Australia were expected to have less exportable supplies in 1994/95.

The record U.S. 1994/95 crop reflected a larger than expected harvested acreage of 13.4 million acres, and hefty jump in yield to about 695 pounds per acre versus 606 pounds per acre in 1993/94. The increase will help to replenish stocks from a 1994/95 carryin of 3.5 million bales to a 4.9 million bales carryover. In August 1994, the first month of the 1994/95 year, mills used 44,000 bales per day, the largest average daily use since 1950/51, and for the month about 100,000 bales over a year earlier. Moreover, cotton's share of total fiber use was a hefty 77 percent, suggesting that cotton's high use was at the expense of man-made fibers. For the year, a near record large 11 million bales was forecast for domestic mills (the record 11.6 million bales was set in 1941), nearly 6 percent over 1993/94. If realized, this would place mill operations at near capacity levels. Domestic cotton use has steadily increased since the early-1980s. Between 1985 and 1993, the average annual gain was 490,000 bales while cotton's share of total fiber use during the period increased nearly 12 percent. Larger textile export demand has supported the domestic mill usage. For 1994, cotton textile exports were estimated at a record 2.2 million bale-equivalents. Countries in the Caribbean basis and Mexico have been growing markets for U.S. textiles and expected to remain so.

The U.S. spot price averaged 66¢ per pound in 1993//94, while the adjusted world price (AWP) averaged 56¢ per pound, but the averages are somewhat misleading as both prices strengthened sharply late in the season. U.S. prices at the start of the 1994/95 season declined slightly from late 1993/94 levels, but were well above a year earlier. For the year, the U.S. and world price are likely to average 5¢ per pound to 10¢ per pound higher than in 1993/94.

U.S. Government Program

The 1994/95 price support loan rate for Upland (1-1/16") cotton was 50¢ per pound, dropping from 52.35¢ per pound in 1993/94, and the target price remained unchanged at 72.9¢ per pound. The United State Department of Agriculture cotton programs cover a wide spectrum of requirements and grades. Shorter staple grades have lower loan rates, and longer lengths have higher loans rates.

Futures Markets

Cotton futures and options are traded on the New York Cotton Exchange (CTN). A world cotton futures contract is also traded on the CTN.

Supply and Distribution of All Cotton in the United States — In Thousands of 480-Pound Bales

Crop Year Beginning Aug. 1	Area — 1,000 acres — Planted	Harvested	Yield Lbs./acre	Supply Beginning Stocks[3]	Pro-duction[4]	Imports	Total	Disappearance Mill Use	Exports	Total	Unac-counted	Ending Stocks	Farm Price[5]	"A" Index Price[6] -- Cents Per Lb. --	of Pro-duction Million $
1984	11,145	10,379	600	2,775	12,982	24	15,781	5,540	6,215	11,755	76	4,102	57.8	69.18	3,671
1985	10,685	10,229	630	4,102	13,432	33	17,567	6,399	1,960	8,359	140	9,348	56.3	48.90	3,628
1986	10,045	8,468	552	9,348	9,731	3	19,082	7,452	6,684	14,136	80	5,026	52.4	61.98	2,449
1987	10,397	10,030	706	5,026	14,760	2	19,788	7,617	6,582	14,199	182	5,771	64.3	72.26	4,555
1988	12,515	11,948	619	5,771	15,411	5	21,187	7,785	6,148	13,930	-165	7,092	56.6	66.42	4,190
1989	10,587	9,538	614	7,092	12,196	2	19,290	8,759	7,694	16,453	163	3,000	66.2	82.34	3,878
1990	12,348	11,732	634	3,000	15,505	4	18,509	8,657	7,793	16,450	285	2,344	67.1	82.87	5,076
1991	14,052	12,960	652	2,344	17,614	13	19,971	9,613	6,646	16,259	-8	3,704	58.1	62.90	4,913
1992[1]	13,240	11,143	699	3,704	16,218	1	19,923	10,250	5,201	15,451	190	4,662	54.9	56.87	4,184
1993[1]	13,488	12,783	606	4,662	16,134	6	20,802	10,418	6,862	17,280	8	3,530	59.0	70.75	

[1] Preliminary. [2] Estimate. [3] Excludes preseason ginnings (adjusted to 480-lb. bale net weight basis). [4] Includes preseason ginnings. [5] Marketing year average price. [6] Average of 5 cheapest types of SLM 1 3/32" staple length cotton offered on the European market. *Source: Economic Research Service, U.S. Department of Agriculture*

World Production of Cotton (All Types) In Thousands of 480-Lb. Bales

Crop Year Beginning Aug. 1	Argen- tina	Brazil	China	Colom- bia	Egypt	India	Iran	Israel	Mexico	Pakistan	Sudan	Turkey	United States	Uzbek- istan[3]	World Total
1980-1	384	2,862	12,429	527	2,428	6,256	262	359	1,620	3,281	446	2,297	11,122	12,224	63,741
1981-2	696	2,941	13,632	404	2,293	6,559	356	423	1,440	3,435	712	2,242	15,641	11,267	68,892
1982-3	515	2,976	16,526	151	2,115	6,755	431	400	840	3,783	944	2,246	11,963	10,380	66,472
1983-4	826	3,423	21,298	352	1,838	6,122	420	427	1,038	2,271	1,021	2,398	7,771	9,976	66,460
1984-5	786	4,423	28,700	575	1,840	7,925	512	402	1,240	4,628	945	2,664	12,982	11,876	88,146
1985-6	547	3,812	19,000	531	1,999	8,355	482	455	970	5,669	652	2,379	13,432	12,777	79,613
1986-7	482	3,008	16,300	493	1,822	7,418	510	308	630	6,060	757	2,376	9,731	12,157	70,447
1987-8	1,295	3,514	19,500	614	1,614	7,388	487	271	1,010	6,741	612	2,465	15,411	11,491	81,349
1988-9	896	3,376	19,100	554	1,405	8,276	551	285	1,416	6,547	700	2,985	12,196	12,621	84,774
1989-90	1,272	3,030	17,400	481	1,324	10,599	524	212	769	6,687	584	2,835	12,196	7,605	79,780
1990-1	1,355	3,215	20,700	581	1,378	9,135	553	236	813	7,522	380	3,007	15,505	7,317	86,980
1991-2	1,148	3,445	26,100	725	1,338	9,430	525	90	831	10,000	420	2,578	17,614	6,790	95,965
1992-3[1]	643	2,113	20,700	292	1,620	10,931	465	133	138	7,073	276	2,635	16,218	6,000	82,783
1993-4[2]	1,079	1,860	17,200	244	1,882	9,600	418	124	109	6,282	243	2,766	16,134	6,240	76,922
1994-5[2]	1,425	2,300	20,700	250	1,400	10,000	520	230	480	6,300	380	2,900	19,573	6,000	85,819

[1] Preliminary. [2] Estimate. [3] Formerly part of the U.S.S.R.; data not reported separately until 1989. *Source: Foreign Agricultural Service, U.S. Department of Agriculture*

Cotton World Supply and Demand In Thousands of 480-Lb. Bales

Crop Year Beginning Aug. 1	Beginning Stocks — United States	Uzbek- istan[3]	China	World Total	Production — United States	Uzbek- istan[3]	China	World Total	Consumption — United States	Russia[3]	China	World Total	Exports — United States	Uzbek- istan[3]	China	World Total
1980-1	3,000	2,154	1,548	21,177	11,122	12,224	12,429	63,741	5,891	8,250	15,024	65,281	5,926	4,070	6	19,713
1981-2	2,668	2,585	2,392	20,455	15,641	11,267	13,632	68,892	5,264	7,855	16,285	64,666	6,567	4,295	0	20,239
1982-3	6,632	2,527	1,892	25,181	11,963	10,380	16,526	66,472	5,513	7,600	16,822	66,412	5,207	3,890	75	19,452
1983-4	7,937	1,900	3,101	25,198	7,771	9,976	21,298	66,460	5,926	7,900	15,714	67,353	6,786	3,202	760	19,166
1984-5	2,775	707	8,305	23,952	12,982	11,928	28,720	88,364	5,540	8,630	16,002	69,392	6,215	2,994	944	20,206
1985-6	4,102	1,460	20,146	43,246	13,432	12,778	19,046	79,863	6,399	9,200	18,909	76,070	1,960	3,170	2,799	20,299
1986-7	9,348	2,260	16,848	47,026	9,731	12,217	16,261	70,107	7,452	9,400	20,976	83,793	6,684	3,462	3,169	26,014
1987-8	5,026	2,031	10,795	35,926	14,760	11,345	19,500	81,109	7,617	9,000	20,065	83,500	6,582	3,457	2,322	23,227
1988-9	5,771	1,302	7,559	32,850	15,412	12,704	19,056	84,423	7,782	9,200	20,533	85,352	6,148	3,656	1,636	25,869
1989-90	7,092	473	5,971	31,423	12,196	7,605	17,400	79,741	8,759	5,831	20,000	86,579	7,694	6,810	865	31,275
1990-1	3,000	460	4,379	25,771	15,505	7,317	20,700	86,964	8,657	5,469	20,000	85,492	7,793	5,393	928	29,678
1991-2	2,344	1,555	6,356	28,102	17,614	6,790	26,100	95,991	9,613	4,539	19,000	84,507	6,646	5,200	602	28,120
1992-3[1]	3,704	2,295	14,184	40,114	16,218	6,000	20,700	82,747	10,250	2,200	21,500	85,585	5,201	5,500	684	25,379
1993-4[2]	4,662	1,845	12,342	37,539	16,134	6,240	17,200	76,922	10,418	2,000	20,900	84,516	6,862	6,200	749	26,810
1994-5[2]	3,530	960	8,467	30,384	19,573	6,000	20,700	85,819	11,000	1,800	21,200	85,801	5,450		650	27,244

[1] Preliminary. [2] Estimate. [3] Formerly part of the U.S.S.R.; data not reported separately until 1989. *Source: Foreign Agricultural Service, U.S. Department of Agriculture*

World Consumption of All Cottons in Specific Countries In Thousands of 480-Lb. Bales

Crop Year Beginning Aug. 1	Agren- tina	Brazil	China	Egypt	France	Ger- many	India	Italy	Japan	Mexico	Pakistan	Poland	United Kingdom	United States	Uzbek- istan[3]	World Total
1980-1	413	2,700	15,500	1,340	785	740	6,100	950	3,150	760	1,990	735	215	5,891	9,300	66,271
1981-2	360	2,600	15,700	1,341	743	745	5,843	1,024	3,426	620	2,238	711	207	5,264	9,400	65,647
1982-3	460	2,600	16,400	1,370	765	928	6,250	1,030	3,290	625	2,450	650	230	5,513	9,200	67,862
1983-4	514	2,435	16,000	1,310	745	976	6,531	1,170	3,300	528	2,030	650	234	5,921	9,300	68,612
1984-5	464	2,665	15,500	1,367	724	1,000	7,117	1,200	3,187	550	2,264	712	248	5,538	9,500	69,401
1985-6	551	3,100	19,500	1,550	672	1,000	7,191	1,170	3,146	670	2,342	750	248	6,413	9,600	76,888
1986-7	575	3,285	20,200	1,290	710	1,100	7,847	1,419	3,445	580	2,990	600	225	7,452	9,350	82,239
1987-8	575	3,399	20,000	1,334	690	1,110	7,612	1,381	3,477	600	3,600	715	216	7,617	9,300	83,499
1988-9	551	3,766	20,500	1,300	640	910	8,139	1,424	3,408	650	3,904	725	193	7,782	9,100	85,565
1989-90	533	3,445	20,000	1,352	600	1,435	8,667	1,450	3,229	725	4,801	650	170	8,759	9,200	86,579
1990-1	597	3,215	20,000	1,457	530	955	9,018	1,470	3,027	712	5,648	410	140	8,657	8,700	85,492
1991-2	606	3,215	19,000	1,465	484	830	8,674	1,447	2,783	772	6,482	275	100	9,613	860	84,507
1992-3[1]	588	3,445	21,500	1,640	470	680	9,761	1,400	2,301	740	6,634	390	85	10,250	950	85,585
1993-4[2]	550	3,675	20,900	1,530	500	750	9,950	1,375	2,060	825	6,500	400	85	10,418	925	84,516
1994-5[2]	565	3,800	21,200	1,375	520	780	10,200	1,375	1,900	865	6,300	425	90	11,000	900	85,801

[1] Preliminary. [2] Estimate. [3] Formerly part of the U.S.S.R.; data not reported separately until 1991. *Source: Foreign Agricultural Service, U.S. Department of Agriculture*

COTTON

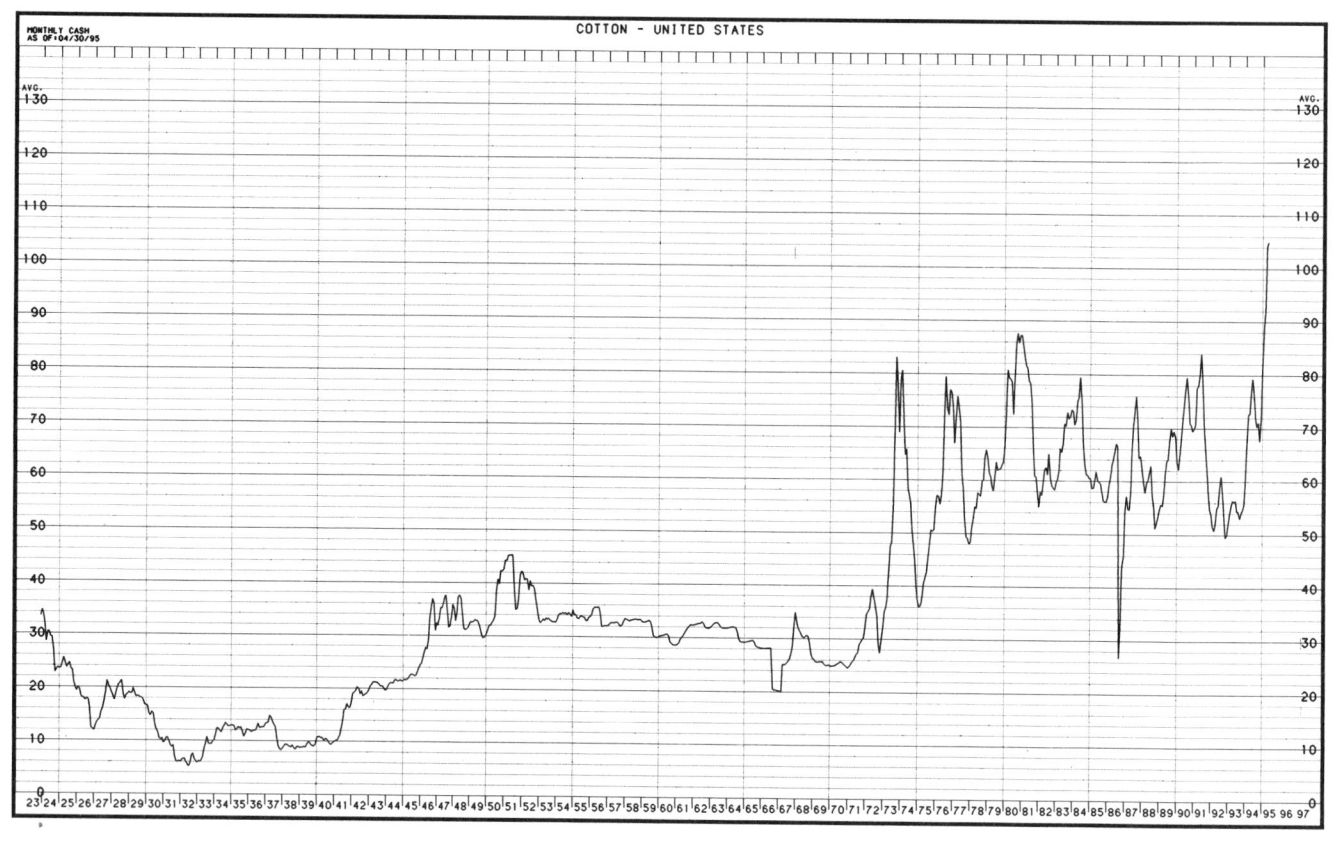

Average Spot Cotton Prices[2], C.I.F. Northern Europe   In U.S. Cents Per Pound

Crop Year Beginning Aug. 1	Argentina "C"[3] 1 1/16"	Australia M 13/32"	Central America[4] M 13/32"	China Type 329	Cotlook Index A	Cotlook Index B	Egypt Giza[5] 81	Greece M 13/32"	Mexico M 13/32"	Pakistan Sind/ Punjab[6]	Tanzania AR[7] Type 3	Turkey Izmir[8] 13/32"	U.S. Calif. ACALA SJV[9]	U.S. Memphis Terr.[10] M 13/32"	U.S. Orleans/ Texas[11] M 1 1/32"
1978-9	71.60	------	74.42	------	76.05	67.95	------	82.44	76.02	66.99	90.13	77.38	82.96	76.27	67.22
1979-80	75.04	------	83.46	------	85.40	74.55	136.37	84.00	77.87	75.45	84.01	------	90.69	78.47	75.36
1980-1	82.06	------	98.25	------	94.20	84.20	137.66	100.41	95.48	85.11	103.78	97.43	101.85	99.99	89.14
1981-2	63.55	------	72.99	------	73.80	64.40	115.73	81.06	75.36	65.56	87.92	77.65	79.79	75.87	66.76
1982-3	62.63	------	76.13	------	76.65	66.60	110.07	85.25	76.37	65.58	87.19	83.28	84.94	77.95	68.11
1983-4	83.32	90.83	86.86	------	87.65	80.40	134.07	94.42	87.54	75.51	95.23	92.64	94.90	87.23	78.41
1984-5	60.95	60.33	67.22	62.50	69.15	59.55	134.01	76.14	70.10	56.20	77.29	75.92	76.20	73.88	65.95
1985-6	49.42	50.05	42.39	42.39	49.00	40.95	111.40	50.98	53.16	37.92	55.81	57.06	59.43	65.01	52.26
1986-7	68.97	66.59	62.76	62.11	62.05	55.05	112.59	63.53	64.64	55.11	67.41	64.63	74.27	61.96	56.38
1987-8	64.13	76.14	71.94	71.94	72.30	67.50	145.11	83.85	73.75	65.88	87.96	86.43	81.17	74.24	72.07
1988-9	64.11	72.14	60.69	60.69	66.35	61.30	176.85	63.07	61.54	56.98	69.09	68.98	77.13	69.00	63.92
1989-90	77.05	84.16	80.63	85.92	82.40	77.40	189.54	83.76	82.50	76.75	86.68	90.49	88.59	83.90	78.93
1990-1	77.06	85.58	83.28	87.45	82.90	77.80	177.43	84.24	84.46	77.19	89.62	81.32	92.84	88.13	80.35
1991-2	55.08	65.97	68.40	71.72	63.05	58.50	128.10	65.90	68.19	58.14	68.90	74.66	74.47	66.35	63.41
1992-3	64.31	64.01	NA	61.59	57.70	53.70	99.24	56.92	NA	52.66	62.24	------	68.37	63.08	58.89
1993-4[1]	55.08	72.81	NA	73.49	70.60	67.30	88.35	58.81	NA	54.42	69.83	59.80	77.55	72.80	69.78

[1] Preliminary.   [2] Generally for prompt shipment.   [3] 1 1/32 inches prior to January 20, 1984; 1 1/16 inches since.   [4] Guatemala SM 1 1/16 inches 1971/72 through 1985/86; Central American Middling 13/32 inches since.   [5] Giza 67 1969/70 until December 1983; Giza 69/75/81 until November 1990; Giza 81 since.   [6] Punjab until 1979/80; Sind SG until June 1984; Sind/Punjab SG until January 1985; Afzal 1 inch until January 1986; Afzal 1 1/32 inches since.   [7] No. 1 until 1978/79; No. 1/2 until January 1987; Izmir/Antalya ST 1 White 13/32 inches RG since.   [9] SM 1 1/8 inches.   [10] SM 1 1/16 inches prior to 1981-82; Middling 13/32 inches since.   [11] Middling 1 inch prior to 1988/89; Middling 1 1/32 inches since.   *Source: International Cotton Advisory Committee*

Average Price of Strict Low Middling 1¹/₁₆", Cotton at Designated U.S. Markets   ¢ Per Pound (Net Weight)

Year	Aug.	Sept.	Oct.	Nov.	Dec.	Jan.	Feb.	Mar.	Apr.	May	June	July	Average
1984-5	63.01	61.16	61.15	60.43	60.45	59.96	58.65	60.18	61.71	60.11	59.76	59.55	60.51
1985-6	57.87	56.38	56.14	56.03	56.25	58.39	59.81	61.75	62.62	63.95	65.24	65.73	60.01
1986-7	26.81	33.56	43.95	45.74	54.19	57.17	54.75	54.60	57.72	65.94	70.42	73.07	53.16
1987-8	75.89	71.41	64.30	64.66	62.26	59.69	57.83	59.64	60.07	61.55	62.86	57.40	63.13
1988-9	55.20	51.25	52.20	53.40	54.80	55.67	55.37	57.59	61.43	63.70	64.06	67.39	57.67
1989-90	69.88	68.46	69.40	68.33	63.56	62.21	64.95	68.06	71.31	74.61	77.06	79.53	69.78
1990-1	76.27	71.01	70.54	69.48	69.92	70.50	77.69	77.92	79.94	83.94	79.05	71.33	74.80
1991-2	66.44	62.39	58.28	54.70	53.89	51.54	50.76	52.01	54.97	55.45	58.82	60.93	56.68
1992-3	57.56	53.49	49.47	49.98	51.85	53.72	55.38	56.45	56.17	56.37	54.38	54.35	54.10
1993-4	53.04	54.01	54.58	55.61	60.29	66.53	72.69	72.74	76.12	79.30	76.85	71.71	66.12
1994-5[1]	70.32	71.10	67.58	72.00	81.92	88.11	91.89						

[1] Preliminary.   Note: Grade 41, staple 34 cotton.   *Source: Agricultural Marketing Service, U.S Department of Agriculture*

Average Spot Cotton, 1³/₃₂", Price (SLM) at Designated U.S. Markets   In Cents Per Pound (Net Weight)

Year	Aug.	Sept.	Oct.	Nov.	Dec.	Jan.	Feb.	Mar.	Apr.	May	June	July	Average	1 ¹/₃₂"	1"
1984-5	63.45	61.60	60.71	59.99	60.01	59.52	58.21	59.74	61.27	59.67	59.32	59.99	60.29	58.30	55.98
1985-6	57.40	55.89	55.66	55.55	55.77	57.92	59.34	61.28	62.15	63.48	64.77	66.20	59.62	57.87	55.81
1986-7	27.39	35.56	44.53	46.27	54.71	57.70	55.26	55.12	58.24	66.46	70.94	73.59	53.81	50.78	47.77
1987-8	76.42	71.99	64.84	65.17	62.76	60.14	58.28	60.12	60.55	62.03	63.34	57.88	63.63	60.81	59.33
1988-9	55.69	51.80	52.66	53.80	55.20	56.07	55.77	58.04	61.94	64.21	64.57	67.92	58.14	53.99	52.32
1989-90	70.42	69.00	69.89	68.75	63.99	62.63	65.37	68.48	71.73	75.03	77.48	79.95	70.23	66.02	64.89
1990-1	76.69	71.43	70.97	69.97	70.43	71.09	78.45	78.63	80.65	84.60	79.69	71.99	75.38	71.52	69.15
1991-2	66.88	62.75	58.63	55.04	54.23	51.92	51.16	52.41	55.37	55.85	59.22	61.33	57.07	54.15	53.23
1992-3	57.96	53.88	49.99	50.65	52.49	54.43	56.09	57.23	56.95	57.15	55.16	55.13	54.76	52.42	52.46
1993-4	53.81	54.78	55.36	55.65	61.02	67.22	73.38	73.43	76.81	79.71	77.25	72.11	66.71	64.28	63.91
1994-5[1]	70.72	71.50	67.92												

[1] Preliminary.   *Source: Economic Research Service, U.S. Department of Agriculture*

Average Spot Prices of U.S. Cotton,[1] Base Quality--(SLM) at Designated Markets   In Cents Per Pound

Crop Year Beginning Aug. 1	Dallas (East Tex.-Okl.)	Fresno (San Joaquin Valley)	Greenville (South-east)	Green-wood (South Delta)	Lubbock (West Texas)	Memphis (North Delta)	Phoenix Desert (South-west)	Average
1984-5	58.94	61.29	61.08	60.98	58.93	60.73	61.57	60.51
1985-6	58.96	60.35	60.52	60.69	59.17	60.40	59.84	60.01
1986-7	51.03	60.97	51.66	51.99	51.20	51.70	55.38	53.16
1987-8	61.14	66.02	63.37	62.41	61.09	62.54	65.69	63.13
1988-9	55.88	63.30	57.26	56.67	55.77	56.71	59.67	57.90
1989-90	67.11	73.47	70.64	69.50	67.06	69.51	71.19	69.78
1990-1	71.40	78.30	75.90	75.53	71.09	75.49	75.90	74.80
1991-2	55.63	57.50	57.70	56.21	55.79	56.18	57.77	56.68
1992-3	53.78	52.84	56.73	55.03	53.53	55.03	51.61	54.10
1993-4[2]	66.22	65.04	67.46	67.04	65.92	67.04	64.16	66.12

[1] Prices are for mixed lots, net weight, uncompressed in warehouse.   [2] 1993 prices are for mixed lots, net weight, compressed, F.O.B. car/truck.
Source: Agricultural Marketing Service, U.S. Department of Agriculture

Average Price[1] Received by Farmers for Upland Cotton in the U.S.   In Cents Per Pound

Year	Aug.	Sept.	Oct.	Nov.	Dec.	Jan.	Feb.	Mar	Apr.	May	June	July	Average
1984-5	67.3	65.6	64.4	62.0	56.1	52.2	49.5	56.1	57.0	57.5	60.3	60.5	58.7
1985-6	56.6	55.9	57.3	56.5	53.7	54.0	56.9	58.1	59.2	58.5	58.5	61.5	56.8
1986-7	46.8	48.6	50.0	52.6	52.7	52.1	46.4	47.5	50.4	60.0	66.2	68.3	51.5
1987-8	63.8	65.4	65.1	65.6	64.6	61.7	57.0	57.9	59.9	58.3	62.0	59.5	63.7
1988-9	53.9	51.9	55.1	57.5	55.3	54.7	52.8	55.6	58.7	58.3	57.2	59.5	55.6
1989-90	60.4	63.8	65.8	65.6	61.9	60.2	61.0	63.9	65.8	66.2	64.0	63.9	63.6
1990-1	64.6	65.1	67.7	68.4	67.1	64.9	67.9	68.9	69.5	70.1	67.5	66.3	67.1
1991-2	66.3	64.9	62.9	61.2	55.7	51.7	49.8	50.3	53.1	53.2	58.0	56.3	56.8
1992-3	52.7	52.8	53.9	52.7	54.3	53.0	53.8	56.3	55.1	54.4	53.6	53.7	53.7
1993-4	53.1	51.9	52.4	53.3	56.5	63.7	66.0	66.1	67.7	69.3	63.5	58.4	58.1
1994-5[2]	65.5	65.1	65.7	69.3	73.2	79.7	81.0						

[1] Weighted average by sales.   [2] Preliminary.   *Source: Agricultural Marketing Service, U.S. Department of Agriculture*

COTTON

Purchases Reported by Exchanges in Designated U.S. Spot Markets[1]   In Running Bales

Year Beginning Aug. 1	Aug.	Sept.	Oct.	Nov.	Dec.	Jan.	Feb.	Mar.	Apr.	May	June	July	Market Total
1984	258,511	154,557	271,195	558,999	1,153,086	1,015,087	570,259	287,483	303,501	159,540	123,089	131,035	4,986,342
1985	166,725	152,795	258,891	395,097	570,460	671,758	389,436	416,654	487,813	626,319	968,185	690,947	7,250,658
1986	585,628	638,356	392,451	422,542	1,353,241	1,055,081	633,852	354,643	501,265	354,008	163,307	160,474	6,614,848
1987	152,935	252,669	650,349	718,829	1,065,457	622,727	571,851	463,739	266,545	572,702	336,191	117,645	5,791,639
1988	288,187	166,692	230,724	163,642	323,025	383,699	811,630	388,169	307,937	282,564	261,958	282,288	3,890,515
1989	119,516	49,237	89,853	214,910	258,849	388,519	333,417	206,528	157,187	86,966	42,299	46,312	1,993,593
1990	36,735	53,948	154,499	376,790	600,752	516,421	180,949	66,869	138,503	101,180	45,731	40,551	2,312,928
1991	50,469	55,637	179,671	347,393	776,233	1,043,190	1,063,959	699,026	302,102	110,764	134,500	105,795	4,868,739
1992	81,778	233,424	325,600	853,846	1,049,780	1,321,861	317,451	330,381	224,874	208,962	189,401	231,390	5,368,748
1993	143,237	173,896	321,119	1,071,518	1,213,655	500,246	602,766	318,008	234,331	318,244	83,083	40,699	5,020,802
1994	92,401	98,251	426,371	1,075,829	1,491,429	608,701	233,159						4,026,141

[1] Commencing March 28, 1983, spot transactions are for eight markets; and commencing September 1, 1988, spot transactions are for seven months.
Source: Agricultural Marketing Service, U.S. Department of Agriculture

Average Open Interest of Cotton Futures at New York   In Contracts

Year	Jan.	Feb.	Mar.	Apr.	May	June	July	Aug.	Sept.	Oct.	Nov.	Dec.
1985	18,347	18,741	18,216	15,915	15,048	15,986	17,439	20,003	21,220	22,049	23,489	22,354
1986	23,451	21,654	20,686	20,088	22,473	23,566	22,399	26,058	26,379	24,227	22,056	22,320
1987	25,196	25,048	22,482	23,760	26,074	27,996	32,012	37,426	39,204	39,912	38,017	33,888
1988	35,240	35,974	30,507	29,933	29,753	31,804	28,307	34,637	38,453	37,162	33,210	30,682
1989	31,415	30,978	36,725	36,657	40,761	38,693	40,059	45,894	49,629	49,072	48,136	42,349
1990	40,237	36,291	36,073	37,829	37,908	38,556	36,083	34,042	35,250	40,431	43,997	40,241
1991	43,003	46,793	44,001	43,957	50,086	46,637	40,924	39,616	38,252	39,772	39,295	36,066
1992	38,097	40,095	38,592	36,228	37,839	36,861	35,891	42,241	46,168	46,577	40,425	38,487
1993	41,946	38,657	38,576	33,641	33,012	34,057	32,118	33,872	37,393	36,479	38,567	45,975
1994	54,424	55,558	53,724	54,670	52,830	51,001	52,357	50,597	50,955	51,561	53,563	59,065

Source: New York Cotton Exchange

Volume of Trading of Cotton Futures at New York   In Contracts

Year	Jan.	Feb.	Mar.	Apr.	May	June	July	Aug.	Sept.	Oct.	Nov.	Dec.	Total
1985	61,860	57,034	61,921	65,709	47,606	47,604	41,069	40,524	42,747	55,046	63,829	51,543	636,492
1986	73,576	77,152	57,433	74,520	57,479	64,742	75,545	94,025	130,898	111,359	113,812	84,618	1,015,392
1987	110,165	106,520	88,621	106,620	110,303	132,180	98,339	127,048	131,214	124,319	126,582	107,124	1,395,980
1988	114,672	119,832	97,533	118,614	127,880	149,303	89,907	100,447	108,285	135,221	124,221	84,334	1,370,249
1989	124,764	135,963	113,028	118,573	135,044	167,442	91,381	151,034	165,255	143,713	178,889	124,034	1,649,120
1990	135,260	116,806	126,820	121,203	139,489	135,040	132,329	129,081	103,936	142,670	150,958	98,895	1,534,611
1991	133,415	179,656	148,918	156,978	174,690	122,242	116,458	115,175	107,742	125,558	150,545	82,867	1,614,244
1992	134,531	134,184	149,711	167,778	173,128	153,194	105,534	142,323	144,844	129,680	161,194	105,157	1,701,258
1993	171,180	135,400	136,965	135,300	105,920	128,985	130,886	122,280	110,989	107,571	178,350	139,344	1,603,027
1994	210,011	207,421	210,363	252,614	178,942	208,945	161,688	128,879	140,574	179,604	205,936	203,021	2,289,998

Source: New York Cotton Exchange

United States Government Crop Forecasts and Actual Cotton Crops

Year	Forecast of Production (1,000 Bales of 480 Lbs.[1])						Actual Crop	Forecasts of Yields (Lbs. Per Harvested Acre)						Actual Yield
	Aug. 1	Sept. 1	Oct. 1	Nov. 1	Dec. 1	Jan. 1		Aug. 1	Sept. 1	Oct. 1	Nov. 1	Dec. 1	Jan. 1	
1980	12,812	11,689	11,589	11,224	11,125	------	11,122	461	421	419	408	411	------	404
1981	14,789	15,507	15,476	15,560	15,733	------	15,646	515	540	540	543	546	------	542
1982	11,143	11,029	11,365	11,947	12,102	------	11,963	563	569	587	605	613	------	590
1983	7,810	7,776	7,550	7,497	7,725	------	7,771	503	501	487	504	506	------	508
1984	12,569	13,276	13,272	13,271	13,292	------	12,982	583	615	620	613	610	------	600
1985	13,780	13,655	13,638	13,875	13,810	13,534	13,432	638	632	633	644	644	630	630
1986	10,676	10,506	10,006	9,875	9,792	9,785	9,731	573	565	539	546	539	553	552
1987	12,907	12,846	13,336	13,936	14,281	14,724	14,760	615	616	640	671	695	703	706
1988	14,934	14,709	14,714	14,837	15,197	15,446	15,411	616	605	605	612	627	623	619
1989	11,834	12,279	11,991	12,102	12,083	1,233	12,196	618	603	607	608	619	619	614
1990	14,864	14,722	14,540	14,905	15,399	15,617	15,499	622	616	609	622	640	640	634
1991	17,648	17,868	17,614	13,429	14,052	17,542	17,614	630	638	620	635	630	656	652
1992	16,533	17,943	15,885	16,204	16,259	16,260	16,219	696	685	694	698	696	700	699
1993	18,545	17,867	17,014	16,297	16,284	16,176	16,134	668	645	614	594	597	607	606
1994	19,195	19,025	19,303	19,453	19,573	19,728	19,728	690	690	690	695	699	710	710

[1] Net weight bales.   Source: Agricultural Statistics Board, U.S. Department of Agriculture

COTTON #2 - NYCE

WEEKLY SELECTED FUTURES
AS OF 05/12/95

CENTS/LB.

U.S. Production of Cotton (Upland) & American-Pima In Thousands of 480-Pound Bales

						Upland									Total
Year	Ala-bama	Arizona	Arkan-sas	California	Georgia	Louis-iana	Missis-sippi	Missouri	New Mexico	North Carolina	Okla-homa	South Carolina	Ten-nessee	Texas	American-Pima
1978	291	1,068	660	1,940	111	478	1,378	188	101	45	355	115	235	3,792	93.4
1979	324	1,280	606	3,408	152	690	1,437	157	104	43	522	116	171	5,515	98.6
1980	275	1,354	444	3,109	86	460	1,143	177	107	52	205	77	200	3,320	104.2
1981	422	1,556	604	3,535	159	742	1,565	168	141	95	440	164	315	5,663	79.6
1982	460	1,095	534	3,073	235	870	1,760	204	78	102	238	155	339	2,700	98.7
1983	183	725	323	1,971	112	532	900	73	70	43	145	53	151	2,380	94.7
1984	447	1,097	612	2,913	281	1,056	1,650	187	87	120	183	170	337	3,680	130.4
1985	545	928	703	3,114	370	742	1,655	204	71	117	285	180	419	3,910	155.1
1986	330	675	602	2,245	185	673	1,190	196	62	109	210	87	396	2,535	205.9
1987	397	849	901	2,989	338	977	1,745	330	89	98	346	106	634	4,635	284.6
1988	380	865	1,044	2,824	370	948	1,825	306	102	133	303	140	584	5,215	334.2
1989	383	649	851	2,661	342	868	1,555	269	80	141	173	154	476	2,870	691.7
1990	375	811	1,081	2,734	405	1,177	1,850	314	95	263	382	145	495	4,965	358.5
1991	553	898	1,576	2,548	722	1,414	2,275	429	63	640	240	344	701	4,710	398.4
1992	621	725	1,681	2,817	744	1,299	2,131	541	48	468	210	226	834	3,265	508.3
1993	469	790	1,094	2,918	733	1,105	1,550	376	78	429	270	204	545	5,095	369.3
1994[1]	740	790	1,760	2,720	1,550	1,500	2,150	595	70	820	240	380	890	5,000	342.0

[1] Preliminary. Source: Agricultural Statistics Board, U.S. Department of Agriculture

COTTON

Gross Entries of Cotton into U.S. Government Loan Program   In Thousands of Bales

Crop Year	Aug.	Sept.	Oct.	Nov.	Dec.	Jan.	Feb.	Mar.	Apr.	May[1]	June[1]	July[1]	Total
1978-9	0	5	26	89	215	584	352	189	68	16	14	[2]	1,560
1979-80	0	[2]	23	294	319	600	316	110	51	35	8	[2]	1,759
1980-1	0	[2]	8	253	528	912	343	204	36	28	16	[2]	2,328
1981-2	0	9	132	293	1,081	2,796	1,120	473	117	39	21	2	6,083
1982-3	0	46	143	674	1,857	1,590	4,503	4,160	43	23	13	3	5,062
1983-4	0	0	165	227	253	513	188	264	127	9	32	5	1,765
1984-5	0	1	11	98	563	776	1,057	324	62	44	32	5	2,977
1985-6	31	202	771	1,497	1,406	2,375	781	159	61	12	40	60	7,365
1986-7	22	136	775	1,146	1,124	1,664	662	504	97	40	30	6	6,204
1987-8	[2]	25	400	839	745	1,503	1,305	321	170	44	18	9	5,381
1988-9	10	192	1,131	2,015	2,649	2,400	2,441	354	19	7	8	----	11,238
1989-90	----	21	119	997	765	1,718	130	22	8	1	1	0	3,743
1990-1	0	1	363	575	762	1,302	153	310	281	743	764	0	5,254
1991-2	384	423	465	1,315	2,586	1,307	420	196	2,015	2,833	604	326	12,874
1992-3	-358	6,514	476	2,867	2,463	2,019	350	78	11	19	6	0	14,445
1993-4	26	130	823	2,707	2,060	1,314							

[1] Entries after April 30 represent late reporting.   [2] Less than one thousand bales.   Note: Seasonal totals are net, due to allowances for rejections.
Sources: New York Cotton Exchange; Commodity Credit Corporation

U.S. Daily Rate of Upland Cotton Mill Consumption[2] on Cotton-System Spinning Spindles
In Thousands of Running Bales

Crop Year Beginning Aug. 1	Aug.	Sept.	Oct.	Nov.	Dec.	Jan.	Feb.	Mar.	Apr.	May.	June	July	Average
1980-1	22.1	22.8	23.9	22.9	19.0	21.8	22.3	21.5	21.7	22.1	21.3	19.3	21.7
1981-2	21.4	20.7	22.4	20.1	16.0	18.9	19.9	19.7	20.5	19.6	18.4	16.0	19.5
1982-3	19.3	19.0	20.8	19.5	17.0	20.2	21.5	22.0	21.5	22.0	21.7	18.4	20.2
1983-4	22.6	22.4	22.9	22.3	18.7	23.5	22.4	21.9	21.5	22.1	20.1	17.7	21.6
1984-5	21.4	20.4	21.4	19.5	16.9	20.0	20.9	20.8	21.0	21.9	21.0	18.5	20.3
1985-6	22.9	22.5	24.6	23.9	19.5	23.8	24.9	24.6	24.8	25.2	24.4	20.9	23.4
1986-7	26.7	26.2	27.3	26.5	23.1	27.3	28.1	29.4	28.7	29.3	28.3	27.0	27.3
1987-8	30.3	30.1	31.0	30.3	24.4	28.4	29.5	29.5	27.8	27.6	26.5	21.7	28.1
1988-9	28.8	27.7	27.6	26.1	22.9	28.3	29.2	30.0	31.2	32.2	31.9	27.9	28.6
1989-90	32.9	32.8	33.0	30.6	25.9	29.9	31.4	31.5	30.9	31.8	32.8	27.8	30.9
1990-1	33.8	41.4	33.2	30.2	29.7	------------ 32.3 ------------			------------ 34.0 ------------			------------	33.5
1991-2	33.6 ------------		------------ 33.1 ------------			34.6	36.3	35.7	35.6	37.3	35.2	33.9	35.0
1992-3	38.5	37.8	39.7	37.6	31.5	39.1	39.5	38.8	38.7	39.4	37.8	34.5	37.8
1993-4[1]	39.8	38.4	39.4	36.4	31.4	36.9	39.0	39.7	40.0	41.1	41.0	36.9	38.3
1994-5[1]	42.4	41.8	42.6	40.8	34.9								40.5

[1] Preliminary.   [2] Not seasonally adjusted.   *Source: Bureau of Census, U.S. Department of Commerce*

Consumption of American and Foreign Cotton in the United States   In Thousands of Running Bales

Year	Aug.	Sept.	Oct.	Nov.	Dec.	Jan.	Feb.	Mar.	Apr.	May	June	July	Total
1980-1	443	456	597	458	475	435	446	539	435	441	531	385	5,641
1981-2	429	517	448	403	400	378	398	493	410	392	460	317	5,038
1982-3	386	474	416	391	425	404	430	549	431	441	543	369	5,259
1983-4	453	560	459	446	468	469	448	548	430	442	503	354	5,628
1984-5	428	509	428	390	423	399	418	519	419	439	525	369	5,268
1985-6	458	562	493	477	486	595	499	492	620	503	489	522	6,198
1986-7	534	523	683	529	576	546	562	734	573	586	708	540	7,096
1987-8	606	753	621	606	610	568	590	738	556	551	662	433	7,294
1988-9	577	693	552	523	572	568	584	751	623	645	798	559	7,444
1989-90	689	860	690	642	685	630	658	826	650	667	826	559	8,383
1990-1	680	835	671	610	601	---------- 2,068 ------------			--------- 2,212 ------------			---------	8,367
1991-2	2,215 ------------		--------- 2,199 ------------			870	730	898	718	752	885	682	9,949
1992-3	776	950	799	756	792	788	796	976	778	792	951	694	9,846
1993-4	801	965	792	731	790	743	785	999	806	830	1,032	744	10,019
1994-5[1]	855	1,052	858	823	882	843	861						

[1] Preliminary.   *Source: Bureau of Census, U.S. Department of Commerce*

Exports of All Cotton from the United States — In Thousands of Running Bales

Year	Aug.	Sept.	Oct.	Nov.	Dec.	Jan.	Feb.	Mar.	Apr.	May	June	July	Total
1980-1	403	461	195	422	674	660	608	792	438	404	402	222	5,639
1981-2	233	198	211	545	698	669	756	793	765	450	560	386	6,263
1982-3	348	304	248	442	357	472	355	435	557	511	381	467	4,961
1983-4	369	329	308	438	566	821	737	783	839	494	429	370	6,419
1984-5	454	249	340	472	712	755	705	692	556	435	359	299	5,943
1985-6	166	218	180	198	236	189	202	206	125	69	68	19	1,875
1986-7	374	496	489	525	664	591	518	750	500	465	554	439	6,366
1987-8	355	304	316	612	536	698	879	649	565	537	486	359	6,297
1988-9	248	173	292	352	524	756	514	597	575	795	515	649	5,987
1989-90	431	384	507	469	516	909	840	882	818	495	510	550	7,310
1990-1	480	355	433	591	639	1,112	950	804	960	488	404	273	7,488
1991-2	219	126	239	396	674	961	725	791	787	535	430	466	6,386
1992-3	252	263	277	342	528	501	502	533	639	401	317	395	4,950
1993-4[1]	246	299	317	385	557	522	598	841	623	727	855	614	6,584
1994-5[1]	430	523	238	503	952	991	1,307						

[1] Preliminary.   Source: Foreign Agricultural Service, U.S. Department of Agriculture

U.S. Exports of American Cotton to Countries of Destination — In Thousands of 480-Pound Bales

Crop Year Beginning Aug. 1	Canada	China	Egypt	Germany	Hong Kong	Indonesia	Italy	Japan	Rep. of Korea	Mexico	Philippines	Sweden	Taiwan	Thailand	United Kingdom	Former USSR	Total
1980-1	238	1,309	0	112	205	227	54	1,139	1,303	-----	81	10	351	196	38	0	5,926
1981-2	167	847	0	119	243	243	106	1,626	1,412	-----	58	17	777	167	43	0	6,567
1982-3	238	20	0	163	158	268	105	1,286	1,322	-----	72	23	378	197	50	192	5,207
1983-4	227	12	0	195	283	320	252	1,709	1,269	-----	59	28	495	244	67	351	6,785
1984-5	195	6	126	195	125	258	301	1,464	1,257	-----	58	22	513	139	72	329	6,211
1985-6	98	0	120	85	1	105	91	520	513	-----	8	15	46	17	35	0	1,958
1986-7	70	0	68	263	52	324	263	1,723	1,330	-----	153	15	907	239	56	0	6,685
1987-8	153	0	93	376	88	287	406	1,569	1,450	-----	135	19	424	248	69	98	6,582
1988-9	148	793	102	255	108	307	239	1,381	1,302	-----	50	16	254	172	37	2	6,147
1989-90	197	670	242	368	244	499	431	1,594	1,365	117	134	22	320	375	74	5	7,694
1990-1	191	1,233	243	214	306	561	425	1,437	1,168	202	132	22	358	317	36	5	7,793
1991-2	181	792	339	101	335	739	240	1,107	1,024	213	181	18	380	368	60	0	6,646
1992-3[1]	154	1	170	74	100	429	144	839	1,031	557	117	20	279	150	65	0	5,201
1993-4[2]	165	1,183	0	50	314	653	96	790	976	653	168	12	356	277	65	0	6,862

[1] Preliminary.   [2] Estimate.   Source: Foreign Agricultural Service, U.S. Department of Agriculture

Cotton[1] Government Loan Program in the United States

Crop Year Beginning Aug. 1	Support Price ¢ per Pound	Target Price ¢ per Pound	Put Under Support Ths Bales	% of Production	Acquired Ths Bales	Owned July 31 Ths Bales	Crop Year Beginning Aug. 1	Support Price ¢ per Pound	Target Price ¢ per Pound	Put Under Support Ths Bales	% of Production	Acquired Ths Bales	Owned July 31 Ths Bales
1983-4	55.00	76.00	1,743	22.7	0	158	1989-90	50.00	73.40	3,732	32.4	1	NA
1984-5	55.00	81.00	2,957	23.0	649	123	1990-1	50.27	72.90	3,205	21.2	644	NA
1985-6	57.30	81.00	7,287	54.9	161	767	1991-2	50.77	72.90	6,311	36.7	8	NA
1986-7	55.00	81.00	6,169	64.8	12	73	1992-3[2]	52.35	72.90	8,302	55.5	10	NA
1987-8	52.25	79.40	5,362	37.1	105	3	1993-4[2]	52.35	72.90	7,721	51.4	3	NA
1988-9	51.80	75.90	11,231	74.4	66	50	1994-5[2]	50.00	72.90	3,300	17.9	0	NA

[1] Upland.   [2] Preliminary.   NA = Not available.   Source: Economic Research Service, U.S. Department of Agriculture

Cotton Cloth[1] Production in the United States — In Millions of Square Yards

Year	First Quarter	Second Quarter	Third Quarter	Fourth Quarter	Total Year	Year	First Quarter	Second Quarter	Third Quarter	Fourth Quarter	Total Year
1983	1,068	1,052	1,032	1,040	4,192	1989	1,157	1,192	1,134	1,106	4,589
1984	1,069	1,031	947	955	4,002	1990	1,202	1,127	1,087	1,048	4,463
1985	1,030	1,002	933	955	3,921	1991	1,081	1,148	1,082	1,093	4,404
1986	1,037	1,103	1,095	1,129	4,364	1992	1,154	1,172	1,130	1,144	4,600
1987	1,158	1,217	1,219	1,178	4,772	1993	1,150	1,144	1,071	1,039	4,403
1988	1,252	1,255	1,072	1,052	4,632	1994[2]	1,076	1,111	1,102		

[1] Cotton broadwoven goods over 12 inches in width.   [2] Preliminary.   Source: Bureau of Census, U.S. Department of Commerce

COTTON

United States Cotton Ginnings[1] To: In Thousands of Running Bales

Crop Year	Aug. 1	Aug. 15	Sept. 1	Sept. 15	Oct. 1	Oct. 15	Nov. 1	Nov. 15	Dec. 1	Dec. 15	Jan. 1	Jan. 15	Feb. 1	Total Crop
1982-3	40	NA	453	578	1,529	2,660	5,288	7,202	8,823	9,627	10,574	10,974	11,300	11,488
1983-4	2	NA	315	397	763	1,748	3,348	4,638	6,003	6,880	7,209	7,389	7,476	7,665
1984-5	163	NA	634	780	1,175	2,277	4,321	7,025	8,972	10,478	11,079	11,682	12,319	12,452
1985-6	70	NA	681	1,073	2,431	4,342	6,246	8,216	10,052	11,372	12,365	12,776	12,948	13,063
1986-7	145	NA	624	1,022	2,407	3,618	5,292	6,369	7,491	8,263	8,588	9,093	9,270	9,294
1987-8	1	NA	429	1,242	3,196	5,359	7,531	9,135	11,082	12,588	13,276	13,733	14,177	14,493
1988-9	136	NA	804	1,147	2,279	4,116	6,922	9,535	11,845	13,257	14,248	14,686	14,904	14,939
1989-90	90	NA	382	523	981	2,772	5,948	8,388	10,353	11,246	11,548	11,681	11,771	11,884
1990-1	120	NA	583	1,090	2,616	4,739	7,955	10,207	12,428	13,863	14,516	14,809	14,963	15,064
1991-2	---------- 699 ----------			983	2,467	4,955	8,351	10,752	13,260	15,067	15,888	16,402	16,765	17,146
1992-3	---------- 446 ----------			740	1,664	4,046	7,584	10,296	12,597	14,083	14,944	15,311	15,527	15,786
1993-4[2]	---------- 435 ----------			748	1,846	4,471	7,975	10,952	13,244	14,695	15,321	15,517	15,590	15,686
1994-5[2]	---------- 680 ----------			943	2,333	4,996	8,970	12,627	15,610	17,491	18,440	18,846	19,006	

[1] Excluding linters.   [2] Preliminary.   NA = Not available.   *Source: National Agricultural Statistics Service, U.S. Department of Agriculture*

U.S. Fiber Prices   In Cents Per Pound

Year	Cotton[1] Actual	Cotton[1] Raw[5] Equivalent	Rayon[2] Actual	Rayon[2] Raw[5] Equivalent	Polyester[3] Actual	Polyester[3] Raw[5] Equivalent	Price Ratios[4] in Percent Cotton/ Rayon	Price Ratios[4] in Percent Cotton/ Polyester
1983	78	86	80	84	73	76	1.02	1.13
1984	76	84	84	88	79	82	.95	1.02
1985	66	73	79	82	66	69	.89	1.06
1986	61	68	76	79	62	65	.86	1.04
1987	73	81	81	84	66	69	.96	1.18
1988	65	72	91	94	74	77	.77	.94
1989	72	80	110	114	86	89	.70	.90
1990	79	88	120	125	83	86	.71	1.03
1991	79	88	122	127	74	77	.69	1.15
1992	62	69	114	119	74	77	.58	.90
1993	62	69	111	116	73	76	.59	.91
1994 Jan.	72	79	104	108	72	75	.73	1.06
Feb.	80	88	104	108	71	74	.82	1.20
Mar.	79	88	103	107	71	74	.82	1.19
Apr.	81	90	103	107	72	75	.84	1.21
May	85	95	102	106	75	78	.89	1.22
June	83	92	102	106	76	79	.86	1.16
July	76	84	102	106	76	79	.79	1.07
Aug.	75	84	102	106	76	79	.79	1.06
Sept.	76	84	102	106	76	79	.79	1.06
Oct.	73	81	104	108	78	81	.75	1.00
Nov.	77	85	104	108	78	81	.79	1.05
Dec.	87	97	104	108	78	81	.90	1.20

[1] SLM-1¹/₁₆" at group B Mill points, net weight.   [2] 1.5 and 3.0 denier, regular rayon staples.   [3] Reported average market price for 1.5 denier polyester staple for cotton blending.   [4] Raw fiber equivalent.   [5] Actual prices converted to estimated raw fiber equivalent as follows: cotton, divided by 0.90, rayon and polyester, divided by 0.96.   *Source: Economic Research Service, U.S. Department of Agriculture*

Average Producer Price Index of Gray Cotton Boardwovens   Index 1982=100

Year	Jan.	Feb.	Mar.	Apr.	May	June	July	Aug.	Sept.	Oct.	Nov.	Dec.	Average
1985	103.7	102.7	102.6	102.4	102.0	102.1	101.8	100.6	100.4	101.5	102.0	102.0	102.0
1986	101.6	101.2	100.8	100.7	101.0	101.0	101.2	101.0	101.3	101.2	101.5	101.2	101.1
1987	101.8	101.8	101.9	102.5	103.0	103.3	106.0	103.9	107.1	109.5	110.6	111.5	105.2
1988	112.7	114.3	114.5	115.9	116.2	116.1	115.9	115.6	114.8	111.9	112.5	112.3	114.4
1989	112.4	111.3	110.9	110.9	110.5	110.1	109.4	109.8	109.8	110.8	110.9	113.5	110.9
1990	113.7	113.8	113.8	114.0	114.1	109.9	115.1	115.1	112.3	112.5	116.1	116.4	113.8
1991	113.3	113.6	114.1	114.5	114.9	115.2	115.3	115.3	115.3	115.4	115.7	115.6	114.9
1992	116.9	116.8	116.7	116.7	116.8	117.5	117.3	117.3	117.2	116.9	117.1	117.2	117.0
1993	117.0	116.8	115.9	116.3	115.7	115.7	115.2	115.2	112.5	114.1	114.1	114.9	115.3
1994[1]	109.9	110.8	115.4	115.7	114.9	114.9	115.0	117.5	117.6	118.9	117.2	118.0	115.5

[1] Preliminary.   *Source: Bureau of Labor Statistics (0337-01), U.S. Department of Commerce*

Cottonseed and Products

Cottonseed production in the U.S. has benefitted from strong demand for cotton fiber. U.S. acreage planted to cotton in 1994 was just over 14 million acres, an increase of almost 5 percent from 1993. Production was forecast at just over 7 million tons, up 11 percent. Beginning stocks were 375,000 tons, up slightly from 1993, and total supply of cotton in 1994 was forecast at 7.43 million tons.

The U.S. cottonseed crush was forecast at 3.9 million tons, up almost 11 percent from 1993. The use of cottonseed, primarily for whole-seed feeding was projected to reach almost 2.8 million tonnes, an increase of over 4 percent from 1993. Exports were forecast at 200,000 tons, a sharp increase of over 30 percent from 1993. Total use of cottonseed was forecast at 6.88 million tonnes, up 8 percent. Projected ending stocks were expected to increase close to 50 percent to 550,000 tons. Large crops of soybeans and corn were expected to pressure cottonseed prices, with the average price received by farmers forecast at between $80 per ton to $95 per ton. In 1993, the average price was $113 per ton.

U.S. production of cottonseed meal in 1994 was forecast at 1.78 million tons, up 14 percent. With beginning stocks of 30,000 tons, total supply will be 1.8 million tonnes. Domestic use of this feed was forecast to be 1.65 million tons, up 14 percent. With exports of 110,000 tons, total use was forecast at 1.76 million tons. Prices for cottonseed meal are expected to be under pressure from a large soybean crop.

Cottonseed oil production in 1994 was forecast at 1.25 million tons, and total use was put at 1.24 million tons. Ending stocks were projected to increase to 115,000 tons, up 35 percent. World production of cottonseed in 1994/95 was forecast at 33 million tonnes, up 1 percent. Global production of cottonseed meal was estimated at 11.8 million tonnes, and use was forecast at 11.9 million tonnes. Global production of cottonseed oil was forecast at 3.69 million tonnes, just under 1993/94. World consumption of cottonseed oil was predicted to be 3.75 million tonnes.

World Production of Cottonseed   In Thousands of Metric Tons

Crop Year	Agrentina	Australia	Brazil	China	Colombia	Egypt	Greece	India	Mexico	Pakistan	South Africa	Spain	Turkey	United States	Former U.S.S.R.	World Total
1986-7	174	330	1,070	6,550	184	673	330	3,170	226	2,639	70	138	829	3,448	4,529	27,365
1987-8	467	445	1,620	7,853	235	584	255	3,110	414	2,936	97	138	859	5,234	4,446	31,759
1988-9	367	449	1,338	7,676	229	532	390	3,600	491	2,852	119	195	920	5,499	4,779	32,699
1989-90	495	493	1,255	7,008	201	498	440	4,610	255	2,911	99	100	987	4,243	4,600	31,242
1990-1	538	686	1,352	8,340	265	504	365	3,980	294	3,275	108	139	977	5,415	4,550	33,919
1991-2	435	724	1,313	10,499	298	491	355	4,090	307	4,352	87	137	878	6,283	4,283	37,691
1992-3[1]	275	528	800	8,340	123	571	410	4,740	52	3,080	36	104	905	5,652	3,557	32,232
1993-4[1]	390	466	920	6,956	125	655	460	4,120	36	2,720	26	46	940	5,754	3,671	30,025
1994-5[2]	580	376	1,070	7,863	120	420	560	4,250	77	2,500	47	62	1,000	6,957	3,450	32,317

[1] Preliminary.   [2] Estimate.   Source: The Oil World

Salient Statistics of Cottonseed in the United States

Crop Year Beginning Aug. 1	Supply — Stocks	Supply — Production	Supply — Total Supply	Disappearance — Crush	Disappearance — Exports	Disappearance — Other	Total Disappearance	Farm Price $/Ton	Value of Production Mil. $	Products Produced — Oil Millions Lbs.	Products Produced — Meal Thousand Sh. Tons
	In Thousands of Short Tons										
1986-7	347	3,801	4,148	2,520	17	1,422	3,959	80.0	304.0	781	1,112
1987-8	189	5,769	5,958	3,396	50	2,153	5,599	83.0	474.7	1,204	1,647
1988-9	359	6,062	6,421	3,730	39	1,987	5,756	118.0	718.3	1,243	1,689
1989-90	665	4,677	5,342	2,974	46	1,957	4,977	105.0	492.7	1,039	1,327
1990-1	366	5,969	6,337	3,369	53	2,264	5,686	121.0	722.3	1,154	1,691
1991-2	651	6,926	7,579	3,981	161	2,977	7,119	71.0	492.3	1,279	1,765
1992-3	460	6,230	6,690	3,629	192	2,504	6,325	98.0	608.4	1,137	1,533
1993-4[1]	365	6,347	6,714	3,525	150	2,664	6,339	113.0	705.2	1,125	1,555
1994-5[2]	375	7,050	7,427	3,900	200	2,777	6,877	80-95		1,250	1,775

[1] Preliminary.   [2] Estimate.   Source: Economic Research Service, U.S. Department of Agriculture

Average Wholesale Price of Cottonseed Meal (41% Solvent) at Memphis   In Dollars Per Short Ton

Year	Jan.	Feb.	Mar.	Apr.	May	June	July	Aug.	Sept.	Oct.	Nov.	Dec.	Average
1986	146.25	128.75	115.60	129.25	133.75	132.50	137.00	150.60	152.50	141.90	157.50	160.50	140.51
1987	146.25	138.10	128.00	133.75	149.60	154.50	166.90	163.80	141.50	150.60	177.50	195.00	153.79
1988	187.50	160.00	141.00	143.10	147.50	230.00	223.75	181.00	205.00	212.50	293.00	199.40	193.65
1989	200.50	191.25	196.25	184.40	161.50	163.30	157.50	172.00	190.00	181.25	180.00	180.00	179.83
1990	160.00	150.00	146.25	150.00	155.00	147.50	161.50	169.50	178.75	163.00	147.50	141.25	155.85
1991	125.00	118.10	125.00	122.50	118.10	117.20	127.50	130.90	133.10	131.00	144.40	162.00	129.57
1992	156.25	140.10	124.25	121.25	127.50	132.50	133.75	146.90	163.00	154.40	157.50	174.50	144.33
1993	164.40	149.40	153.50	149.00	143.10	153.00	170.30	178.50	193.75	173.10	181.00	180.00	165.75
1994[1]	170.30	173.10	174.00	166.25	157.75	154.10	152.50	144.50	145.00	134.40	120.50	114.20	150.55

[1] Preliminary.   Source: Economic Research Service, U.S. Department of Agriculture

COTTONSEED AND PRODUCTS

COTTONSEED MEAL - MEMPHIS

Supply & Distribution of Cottonseed Oil in the United States   In Millions of Pounds

Crop Year Beginning Oct. 1	Supply				Disappearance			Per Capita Consump. of Salad & Ck. Oils – In Lbs.–	Utilization Food Uses			Prices	
	Stocks	Pro-duction	Imports	Total Supply	Domestic	Exports	Total		Short-ening	Salad & Cooking Oils	Total	U.S.[3] (Crude) ----- $/Tonne -----	Rott[4] (Cif)
1986-7	85	781	11	877	573	214	787	24.2	135	408	494	390	491
1987-8	90	1,204	25	1,319	750	409	1,159	25.4	164	579	743	481	585
1988-9	160	1,243	0	1,403	850	406	1,256	25.8	191	680	917	439	567
1989-90	147	1,039	13	1,199	765	354	1,119	24.0	235	507	801	514	650
1990-1	80	1,154	3	1,237	851	249	1,100	24.2	272	438	777	492	614
1991-2	137	1,279	18	1,434	1,075	281	1,356	25.2	247	375	685	443	545
1992-3	78	1,137	38	1,253	995	177	1,172	25.6	238	353	640	550	688
1993-4[1]	81	1,125	4	1,225	940	200	1,140	24.3	245	284	560	613	749
1994-5[2]	85	1,250		1,355	1,040	200	1,240					544	683

[1] Preliminary.   [2] Estimate.   [3] Valley Points F.O.B.; Tank Cars.   [4] Rotterdam;US PBY   *Source: Economic Research Service, U.S. Department of Agriculture.*

U.S. Consumption of Crude Cottonseed Oil in Refining   In Millions of Pounds

Year	Oct.	Nov.	Dec.	Jan.	Feb	Mar.	Apr.	May	June	July	Aug.	Sept.	Total
1986-7	75.6	91.1	99.8	106.1	100.0	92.6	77.6	62.1	52.4	46.6	47.2	58.5	909.6
1987-8	74.4	113.4	124.4	122.1	121.8	136.7	120.2	122.8	106.5	112.5	86.9	63.0	1,304.7
1988-9	97.1	127.5	131.9	144.1	125.8	141.9	117.5	121.4	106.2	74.3	91.1	73.3	1,352.1
1989-90	87.5	121.1	121.6	133.7	103.4	114.2	83.8	79.1	68.0	53.3	62.2	56.5	1,084.4
1990-1	79.4	99.7	92.8	---------- 264.7 ----------			---------- 265.9 ----------			---------- 227.7 ----------			1,030.2
1991-2	---------- 265.0 ----------			104.6	108.9	101.3	88.7	76.0	84.2	84.6	72.7	48.6	1,034.6
1992-3	75.7	93.3	95.5	107.3	85.1	77.5	92.8	79.3	74.7	65.1	68.6	57.6	972.5
1993-4	82.7	113.0	103.8	110.8	96.7	111.5	69.6	74.8	73.2	74.2	88.4	64.2	1,062.9
1994-5[1]	81.9	97.2	110.7										289.8

[1] Preliminary.   *Source: Bureau of Census, U.S. Department of Commerce*

U.S. Exports of Cottonseed Oil (Crude & Refined)   In Thousands of Pounds

Year	Jan.	Feb.	Mar.	Apr.	May	June	July	Aug.	Sept.	Oct.	Nov.	Dec	Total
1986	21,901	39,640	32,613	52,638	59,589	27,297	25,087	46,678	13,167	..9,348	20,904	25,243	374,105
1987	7,070	14,081	27,544	10,455	25,024	27,000	..9,562	12,172	25,823	17,112	32,870	32,797	241,510
1988	24,381	36,614	37,088	50,426	29,851	88,494	18,531	18,626	21,800	..6,743	29,110	15,417	377,081
1989	47,178	41,019	49,938	11,840	16,583	14,094	38,654	63,633	72,349	49,077	17,030	40,066	461,461
1990	34,922	37,220	39,152	14,018	39,665	35,560	16,860	21,412	..8,721	18,285	..9,452	46,463	321,730
1991	---------- 55,378 ----------			---------- 67,155 ----------			---------- 52,469 ----------			---------- 38,291 ----------			213,293
1992	68,977	69,631	19,704	19,753	13,071	13,443	16,027	..7,947	13,090	..8,101	..4,625	17,308	271,677
1993	23,904	14,238	..6,294	27,370	25,849	17,685	..5,066	..7,065	19,246	..7,079	15,103	14,075	182,974
1994[1]	32,011	11,093	21,156	26,595	34,775	11,023	24,000	24,000	24,250	17,487	33,385	36,613	296,388

[1] Preliminary.   *Source: Economic Research Service, U.S. Department of Agriculture*

COTTONSEED AND PRODUCTS

Cottonseed Crushed (Consumption) in the United States   In Thousands of Short Tons

Year	Aug.	Sept.	Oct.	Nov.	Dec.	Jan.	Feb.	Mar.	Apr.	May	June	July	Total
1986-7	141.4	167.7	208.5	262.2	283.2	323.5	278.4	255.8	214.7	171.3	134.2	78.8	2,520
1987-8	71.4	137.7	251.8	344.2	363.2	373.4	352.4	340.1	310.7	312.5	275.5	263.6	3,397
1988-9	216.8	179.5	299.3	375.3	376.7	399.7	325.4	383.3	336.6	321.7	287.0	228.9	3,730
1989-90	218.8	150.6	273.4	338.3	335.1	346.6	285.1	254.8	245.5	201.5	194.9	129.3	2,974
1990-1	157.3	176.1	274.9	339.4	320.8	------------ 973.0 ------------			------------ 864.5 ------------			--------	3,106
1991-2	813.6 -----------		--------- 1,145.2 ------------			420.6	378.3	381.3	297.8	245.4	292.1	270.2	4,245
1992-3	245.7	162.9	323.2	353.3	372.1	413.3	334.6	324.1	323.8	296.4	242.7	237.2	3,629
1993-4[1]	182.9	162.6	300.4	391.4	375.0	391.0	335.2	358.6	265.7	257.7	239.4	210.2	3,470
1994-5[1]	192.1	195.5	343.9	386.2	397.5	394.6							

[1] Preliminary.   *Source: Economic Research Service, U.S. Department of Agriculture*

Production of Cottonseed Cake and Meal in the United States   In Thousands of Short Tons

Year	Aug.	Sept.	Oct.	Nov.	Dec.	Jan.	Feb.	Mar.	Apr.	May	June	July	Total
1986-7	64.4	77.7	95.0	121.2	130.3	151.1	128.7	116.1	100.0	80.0	61.3	37.3	1,163
1987-8	32.2	58.3	121.7	156.9	169.3	169.4	160.2	155.7	144.0	144.0	124.7	120.6	1,557
1988-9	100.7	80.1	135.4	170.0	172.5	183.2	151.6	175.3	152.7	157.6	126.7	106.1	1,712
1989-90	98.5	69.3	126.1	154.9	152.6	157.1	130.6	116.6	111.9	90.7	86.6	56.6	1,352
1990-1	68.7	77.4	128.2	160.1	148.8	------------ 456.2 ------------			------------ 409.1 ------------			-------	1,449
1991-2	388.6 -----------		------------ 533.9 ------------			192.6	170.5	173.5	138.2	111.7	129.9	127.8	1,967
1992-3	111.2	76.0	143.7	150.2	160.5	176.2	146.6	136.4	140.9	126.1	103.0	101.0	1,572
1993-4[1]	76.7	71.5	130.1	172.2	166.6	161.8	151.8	164.0	119.6	116.1	106.9	93.4	1,531
1994-5[1]	90.6	89.4	154.3	171.5	176.9	180.2							

[1] Preliminary.   *Source: Bureau of Census, U.S. Department of Commerce*

U.S. Production of Crude Cottonseed Oil[2]   In Millions of Pounds

Year	Aug.	Sept.	Oct.	Nov.	Dec.	Jan.	Feb.	Mar.	Apr.	May	June	July	Total
1986-7	48.0	54.5	64.5	83.5	91.4	103.7	90.3	83.3	70.6	55.6	43.5	25.4	814
1987-8	22.6	46.9	84.0	118.2	124.8	125.7	115.8	113.2	104.4	105.8	91.2	91.0	1,144
1988-9	72.7	56.9	98.6	125.3	125.0	129.3	106.0	127.1	111.7	109.7	94.5	76.6	1,233
1989-90	81.9	56.8	97.6	115.3	117.4	118.4	98.2	89.4	88.8	74.7	75.4	48.0	1,062
1990-1	58.7	57.6	86.2	104.0	102.3	------------ 309.9 ------------			------------ 283.0 ------------			------	1,002
1991-2	263.7 -----------		------------ 398.9 ------------			137.4	127.2	121.5	97.5	79.3	91.8	91.3	1,409
1992-3	77.8	56.8	99.5	110.2	117.6	134.7	107.2	104.9	101.7	96.1	77.7	76.5	1,161
1993-4[1]	59.1	51.7	93.5	122.2	117.5	124.7	99.9	119.6	85.3	85.2	78.4	69.8	1,107
1994-5[1]	61.7	61.0	109.8	122.6	125.6								

[1] Preliminary.   [2] Not seasonally adjusted.   *Source: Bureau of Census, U.S. Department of Commerce*

United States Production of Refined Cottonseed Oil   In Millions of Pounds

Year	Aug.	Sept.	Oct.	Nov.	Dec.	Jan.	Feb.	Mar.	Apr.	May	June	July	Total
1986-7	60.3	51.2	73.5	90.9	97.6	103.7	96.8	90.3	74.9	59.8	51.0	45.5	896
1987-8	45.8	56.9	71.5	110.3	120.9	119.9	117.8	132.6	116.5	119.2	103.3	109.6	1,224
1988-9	83.2	61.7	94.1	124.8	127.8	139.7	121.9	137.0	116.3	119.1	102.8	71.6	1,300
1989-90	86.6	69.1	79.8	111.8	111.6	122.3	94.4	109.7	80.4	74.8	65.0	50.8	1,056
1990-1	57.8	53.7	75.4	96.0	90.0	------------ 253.9 ------------			------------ 256.3 ------------			-------	883
1991-2	209.3 -----------		------------ 205.0 ------------			103.2	105.6	97.9	85.6	73.4	82.1	81.1	1,043
1992-3	69.3	46.3	72.6	90.2	91.9	103.1	82.0	74.5	88.8	75.6	70.8	62.4	928
1993-4[1]	65.1	54.6	79.4	109.1	100.6	107.2	93.4	107.8	66.9	71.6	70.0	72.1	998
1994-5[1]	86.3	62.9	80.0	94.4	107.1								

[1] Preliminary.   *Source: Bureau of Census, U.S. Department of Commerce*

U.S. Stocks of Cottonseed Oil (Crude & Refined) at End of Month   In Millions of Pounds

Year	Aug.	Sept.	Oct.	Nov.	Dec.	Jan.	Feb.	Mar.	Apr.	May	June	July
1986-7	90.4	84.9	77.0	101.1	130.6	165.4	188.1	207.5	204.2	263.2	190.8	165.9
1987-8	127.3	90.2	107.2	136.1	169.8	210.0	197.6	184.7	177.2	197.8	175.6	176.0
1988-9	172.9	160.4	163.9	188.6	206.1	266.3	274.0	276.6	263.7	249.2	266.7	247.6
1989-90	191.4	147.3	138.3	163.2	189.6	186.8	180.9	174.8	168.8	156.1	135.6	111.8
1990-1	75.9	80.4	83.0	93.5	102.7	------------ 145.8 ------------			------------ 124.3 ------------			-------
1991-2	136.3 -----------		------------ 163.3 ------------			193.1	183.6	180.3	171.5	154.0	139.9	119.8
1992-3	94.3	81.0	98.4	101.7	123.2	148.4	152.6	167.1	157.0	159.2	144.8	143.8
1993-4[1]	85.8	54.6	79.4	109.1	100.6	107.2	93.4	107.8	66.9	71.6	70.0	72.1
1994-5[1]	112.4	105.6	103.5	117.0	114.7	119.1						

[1] Preliminary.   *Source: Bureau of Census, U.S. Department of Commerce*

71

COTTONSEED AND PRODUCTS

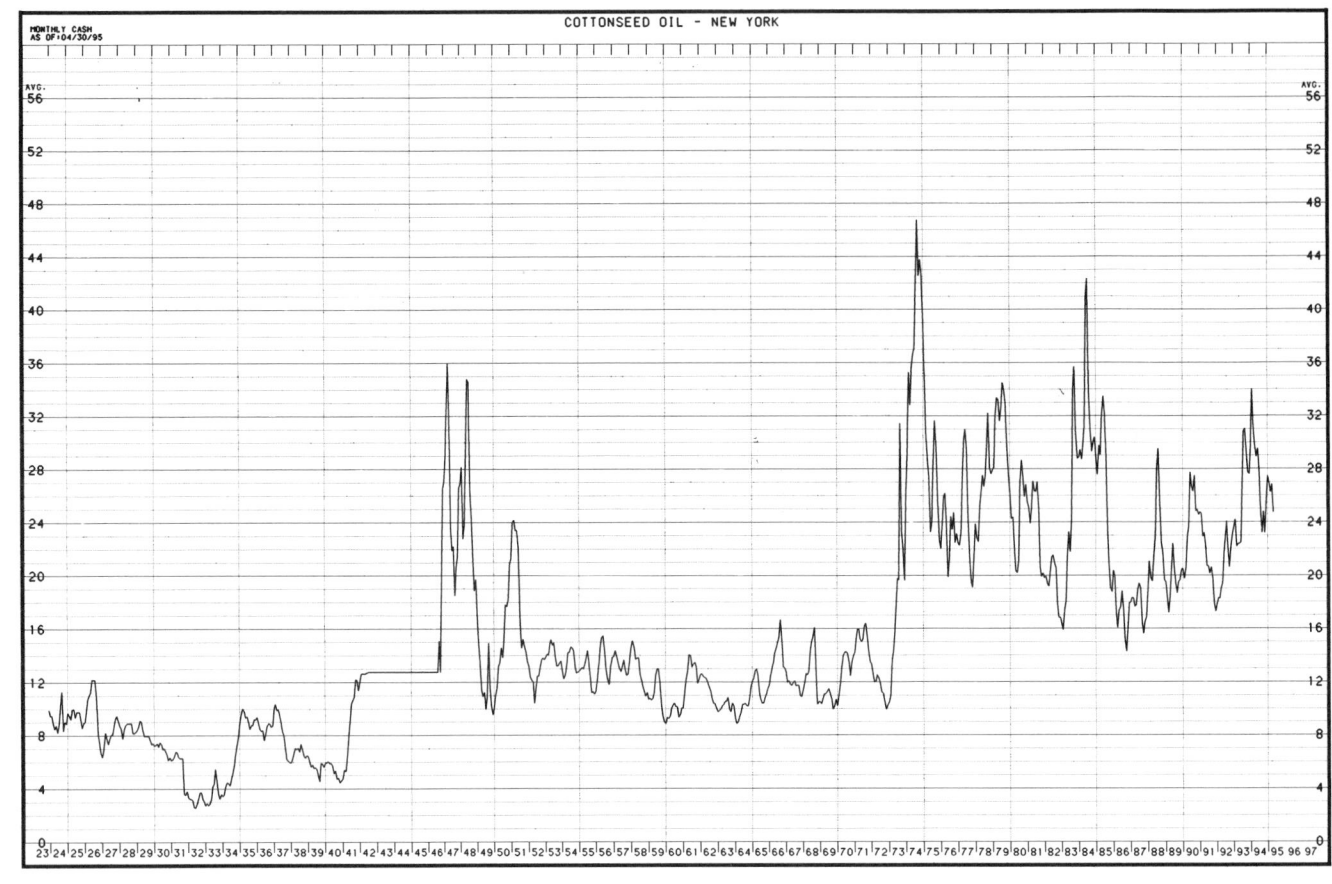

Average Price of Crude Cottonseed Oil, F.O.B. Valley Points[1] (Tank Cars)   In Cents Per Pound

Year	Jan.	Feb.	Mar.	Apr.	May	June	July	Aug.	Sept.	Oct.	Nov.	Dec.	Average
1985	27.30	30.10	30.10	32.30	33.30	32.50	29.10	23.70	20.60	18.25	18.88	20.60	26.39
1986	19.88	17.63	15.75	17.50	17.69	17.90	15.38	17.44	14.25	15.38	17.44	17.75	17.00
1987	18.38	18.56	17.85	17.88	18.94	19.25	19.00	16.70	15.44	16.75	17.00	18.35	17.84
1988	21.31	20.19	19.60	21.00	22.88	26.65	30.25	15.00	23.00	21.44	19.70	19.94	21.75
1989	19.19	17.56	20.25	21.06	21.80	20.25	19.63	18.60	19.75	19.95	20.81	20.50	19.95
1990	19.95	20.19	22.88	22.83	26.90	26.94	26.00	24.60	24.88	24.80	24.19	24.75	24.08
1991	23.75	22.88	23.00	22.13	20.67	20.31	20.50	21.00	19.88	17.98	17.41	18.07	20.63
1992	18.50	18.13	19.25	19.38	21.38	22.58	24.45	21.86	21.04	22.17	22.96	23.91	21.30
1993	24.09	22.03	22.24	22.55	22.70	26.76	30.74	30.45	28.98	24.79	26.69	30.39	26.03
1994	33.16	29.96	29.60	29.06	29.66	27.55	24.29	23.71	24.51	23.64	24.85	25.50	27.12

[1] Southeastern mills.   *Source: Economic Research Service, U.S Department of Agriculture*

U.S. Exports of Cottonseed Oil to Important Countries   In Thousands of Metric Tons

Year	Canada	Dominican Republic	Egypt	Guat- emala	Japan	Mexico	Nether- lands	Salvador	South Korea	Turkey	Venez- uela	Total
1984	3.8	4.5	50.3	-----	11.7	.2	3.1	5.2	2.3	-----	79.0	171.3
1985	2.5	7.6	57.1	9.8	24.9	.3	5.8	19.4	2.3	-----	51.9	191.4
1986	2.9	2.2	16.5	11.6	27.3	9.3	8.0	25.9	5.7	-----	50.9	173.7
1987	3.2	5.0	1.9	2.4	15.7	3.1	2.9	15.6	7.8	-----	47.3	109.9
1988	4.8	3.1	29.6	.5	21.5	8.2	2.7	26.3	7.7	13.5	46.2	167.8
1989	6.6	5.1	39.4	6.0	34.3	3.2	3.4	30.5	21.0	2.0	53.7	209.4
1990	6.8	6.0	14.7	.4	36.7	1.4	2.9	21.0	36.0	-----	9.2	136.3
1991	7.8	2.1	14.7	-----	24.1	4.8	3.4	13.0	13.0	5.5	4.2	97.0
1992	11.3	1.0	8.2	3.2	15.3	8.5	17.4	26.5	10.9	7.0	3.7	123.3
1993[1]	10.9	-----	-----	.5	17.6	5.8	.2	30.8	6.6	.5	1.5	83.1

[1] Prelminary.   *Source: The Oil World*

Currencies

The world's major currencies slowly strengthened against the U.S. dollar during 1994; on a trade-weighted basis the dollar declined 8%. In retrospect the action proved the forerunner for a major slide of the dollar's value in early 1995.

The dollar's weakness seemed to defy rationality: the U.S. economy's real growth in 1994 was second to none relative to the world's major industrialized nations, and the Federal Reserve lifted short term interest rates almost 3% during the year; both variables that should have buoyed the dollar. However, there was a flip side to the U.S. economy's strength in that strong consumer demand for foreign goods pushed the merchandise trade deficit to $166 billion in 1994, although it should also be noted that imports account for only about 12% of U.S. demand for goods and services. Mexico's economic crisis likely distorted the U.S. trade deficit in late 1994 and early 1995 as U.S. exports to Mexico plunged.

The continued failure of the U.S. congress to come to grips with the nation's budget deficit is an underlying longer term variable that continues to erode confidence in the dollar's value. An estimated $2.1 trillion of U.S. government debt was pumped into the world economy during the past decade with little sign that the massive borrowing will diminish, bringing the dollar's fundamental problem into high profile--a strong reliance on foreign capital to finance the U.S. economy's growth. Moreover, the FOREX market was unsettled during 1994 by U.S. government flipflops as to whether a strong or weaker dollar is preferred, uncertainties of which enhanced the value of the D-Mark and J-Yen.

The D-Mark closed 1994 on a strong note. In early 1994 the D-Mark traded near $.56 against the U.S. dollar, at yearend it was $.64, and in early 1995 above $.70. The D-Mark's value was buoyed by an improving German economy and by safe-haven buying against the tangential European currencies such as the Greek drachma and Italian lira. The strength may have carried too far: In late 1994, short term U.S. interest rates were more than 100 basis points over like German rates and apt to widen further in 1995. From a traditional economic stance the D-Mark value should slip against the dollar in 1995. However, the current FOREX psychology has the D-Mark as the world's pivotal currency, a factor likely to hold any slippage in check.

The B-Pound was the least volatile hard currency in 1994, at least against the U.S. Dollar and D-Mark. In early 1994 the Pound pivoted about $1.50 to the Dollar, by mid-year the Pound pushed to $1.57, spurted towards $1.65 in October, and finished the year back near $1.55. A restrictive monetary policy helped to support the currency, but the higher interest rates may choke off consumer demand in 1995 and possibly force the central bank to ease its policy.

In early 1995 the J-Yen reached a historic low against the Dollar, however, the underlying impetus had been building throughout 1994. During the second half of 1994 the Yen/Dollar parity held near y100 to $1, partially reflecting Japan's persistent one-sided trade surplus with the U.S. Moreover, Japan's foreign investment has tapered off despite extremely low domestic interest rates, suggesting that until capital outflows improve any weakness in the Yen's value should be minimal.

The one bright spot for the U.S. Dollar in 1994 was its strength against the C-Dollar, the latter declining from about $.76 to nearly $.70 by yearend. Ironically, Canada's economic outlook seems to be improving, but Canada's debt relative to its GDP is one of the highest among the industrialized nations. Moreover, political uncertainties abound, especially in Quebec. In 1995 Canada's central bank may tighten interest rates in an effort to bolster the C-Dollar, but positive results may prove elusive.

Futures Markets

The Chicago Mercantile Exchange's International Monetary Market (IMM) trades futures and options on the British Pound, Swiss Franc, Deutsche Mark, Japanese Yen, and the Canadian and Australian Dollars. The exchange also trades a D-Mark rolling spot contract and a D-Mark forward contract. Typically, the D-Mark and J-Yen have the largest market following if total open interest is used as a benchmark. Chicago's MidAmerica Exchange (MidAm) trades smaller futures contracts on some of the IMM's currencies. The FINEX division of the New York Cotton Exchange (NYCE) trades futures and options on a composite Dollar index and also offers crossrate contracts: D-Mark/J-Yen, D-Mark/French Franc and D-Mark/B-Pound. Currency futures and options are also traded on the Philadelphia Board of Trade (PBOT).

Monthly Close of the Knight-Ridder CRB Currency Futures Index   1977 = 100

Year	January	February	March	April	May	June	July	August	September	October	November	December
1984	93.9	97.1	97.7	95.1	94.1	92.2	88.8	89.8	86.2	86.5	84.3	83.1
1985	81.6	78.0	84.2	83.4	84.8	85.5	91.4	90.3	93.9	95.9	98.7	98.8
1986	99.5	103.9	103.3	108.5	104.3	109.6	112.4	113.2	112.3	109.2	112.0	114.4
1987	118.5	119.5	123.3	125.7	123.4	122.9	120.6	123.8	122.6	128.7	134.8	141.3
1988	134.0	133.6	138.3	137.0	134.5	129.2	127.1	125.1	126.7	131.3	136.3	133.7
1989	128.2	130.0	126.0	125.5	119.3	120.2	125.2	119.7	123.6	122.6	123.9	126.1
1990	127.3	126.3	124.9	125.8	127.5	129.1	134.8	136.6	137.4	141.5	141.8	140.8
1991	142.8	139.8	129.3	130.6	129.0	125.5	128.0	128.3	132.4	132.5	134.5	138.8
1992	134.4	132.0	129.8	130.2	134.0	137.9	140.6	145.6	141.1	132.7	128.9	127.6
1993	127.4	127.2	130.2	133.5	134.7	129.4	129.6	130.7	131.8	129.3	128.6	127.7
1994	129.6	131.0	131.8	133.2	132.3	137.1	136.3	136.9	140.2	143.2	138.2	138.7

Source: Knight-Ridder Financial

CURRENCIES

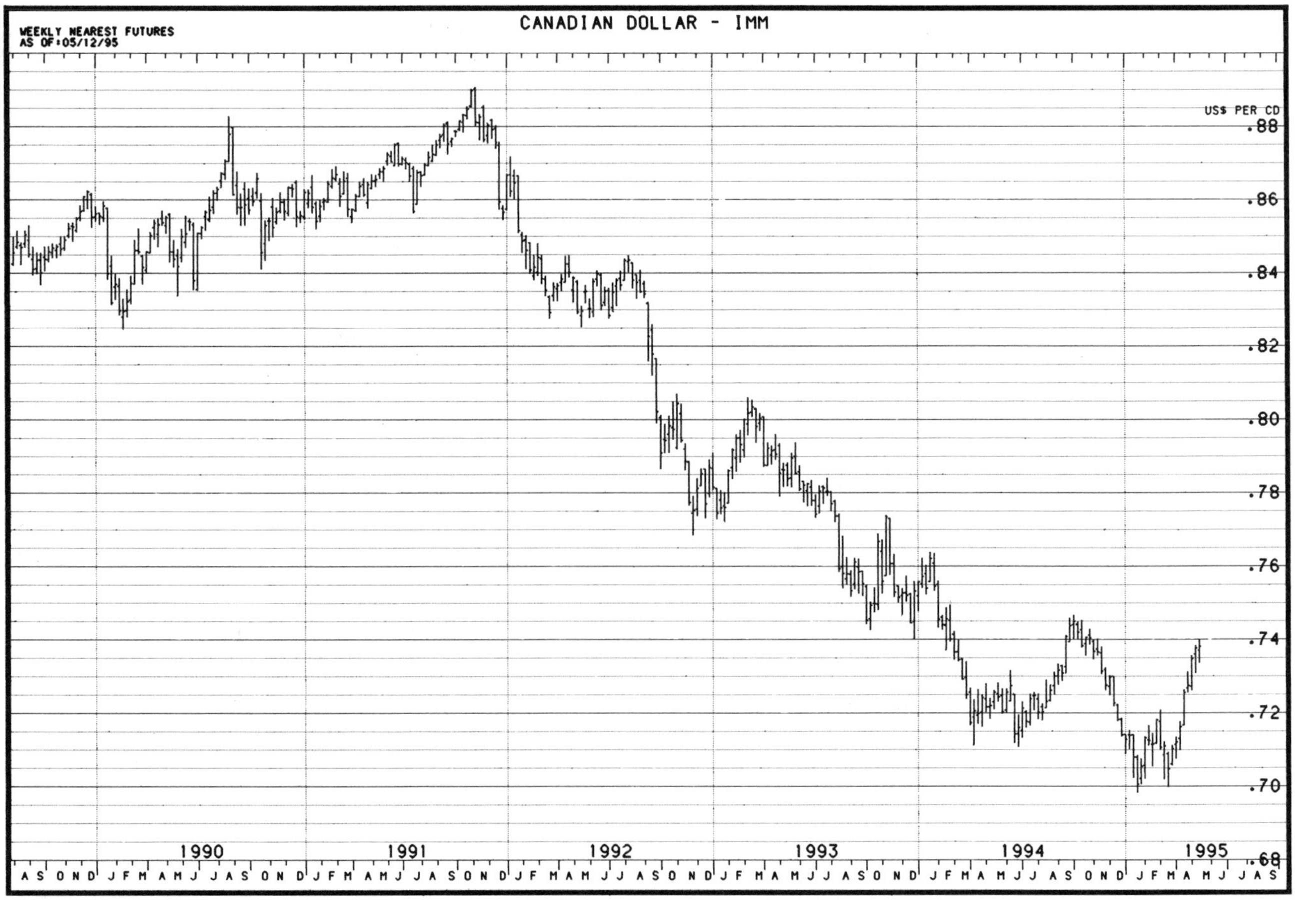

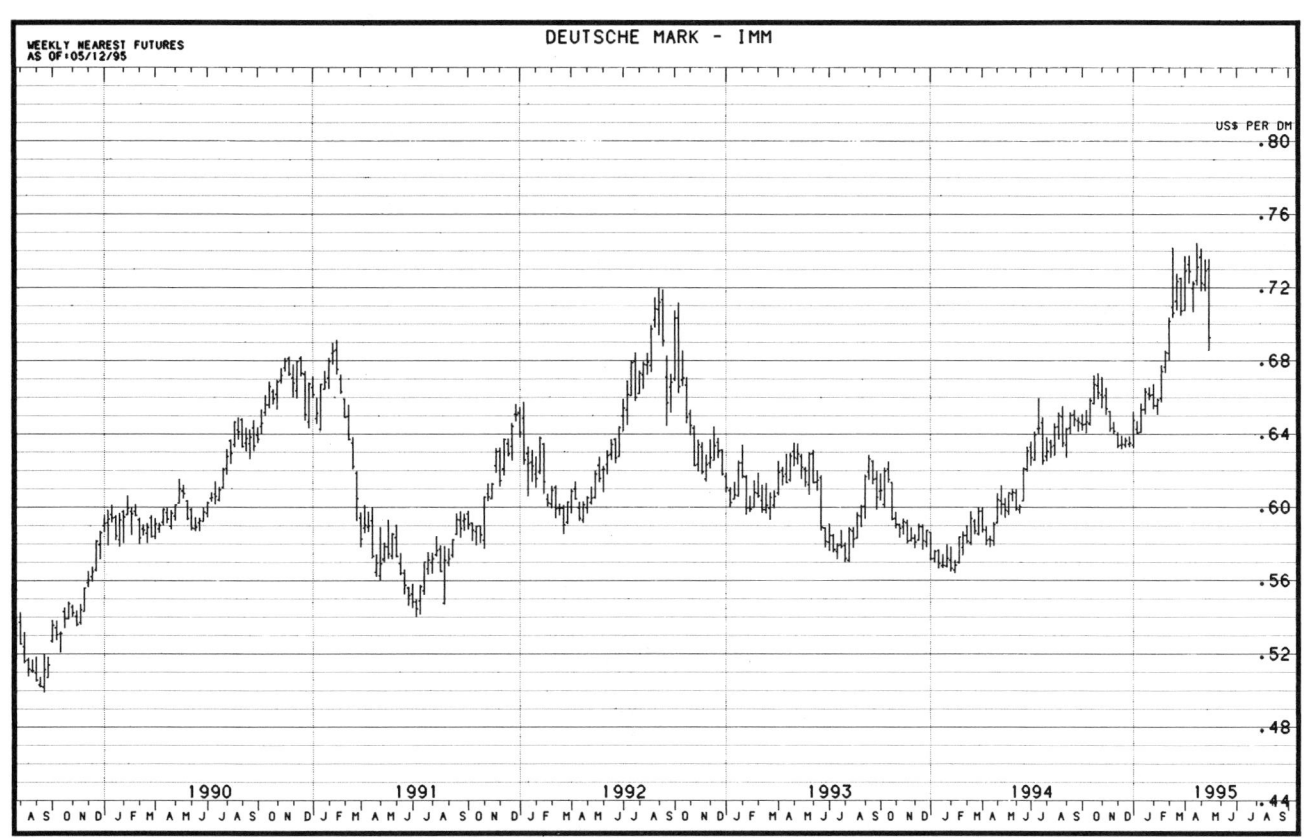

DEUTSCHE MARK - IMM

WEEKLY NEAREST FUTURES
AS OF:05/12/95

US$ PER DM

1990 1991 1992 1993 1994 1995

JAPANESE YEN - IMM

WEEKLY NEAREST FUTURES
AS OF:05/12/95

US$ PER
100 JY

1990 1991 1992 1993 1994 1995

CURRENCIES

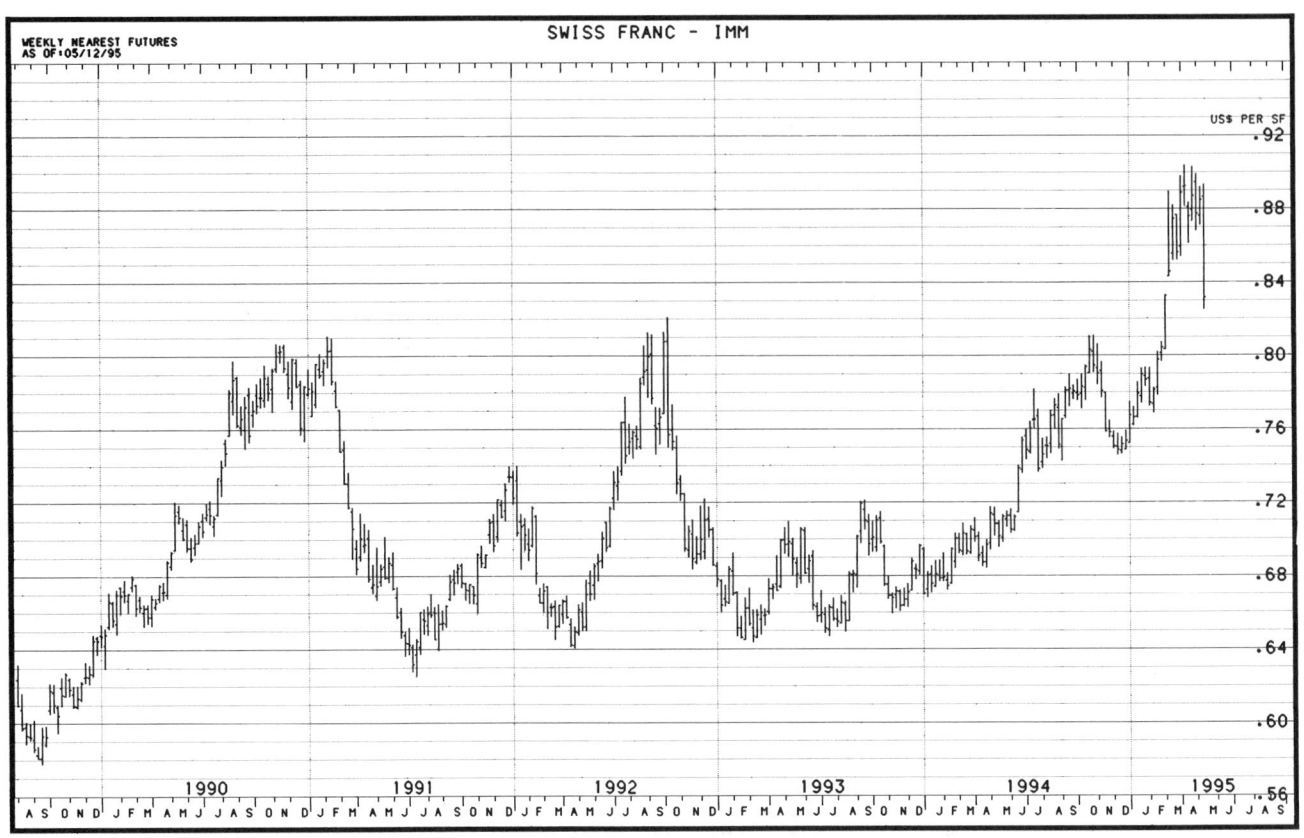

Canadian Dollars per U.S. Dollar

Year	January	February	March	April	May	June	July	August	September	October	November	December	Average
1987	1.360	1.334	1.319	1.319	1.341	1.338	1.326	1.325	1.315	1.309	1.316	1.307	1.326
1988	1.284	1.268	1.249	1.235	1.237	1.217	1.208	1.224	1.227	1.206	1.218	1.196	1.231
1989	1.191	1.189	1.195	1.189	1.193	1.199	1.189	1.176	1.192	1.202	1.169	1.161	1.187
1990	1.172	1.197	1.180	1.168	1.170	1.170	1.160	1.150	1.160	1.160	1.164	1.160	1.168
1991	1.156	1.155	1.157	1.154	1.150	1.144	1.124	1.145	1.139	1.121	1.131	1.145	1.143
1992	1.157	1.218	1.192	1.187	1.199	1.196	1.192	1.191	1.221	1.244	1.268	1.271	1.211
1993	1.277	1.260	1.247	1.262	1.269	1.279	1.282	1.308	1.321	1.325	1.316	1.331	1.290
1994	1.318	1.342	1.365	1.382	1.381	1.383	1.382	1.378	1.354	1.350	1.365	1.390	1.366

Source: Knight-Ridder Financial

German (Deutsche) Marks per U.S. Dollar

Year	January	February	March	April	May	June	July	August	September	October	November	December	Average
1987	1.858	1.823	1.834	1.810	1.787	1.819	1.848	1.855	1.812	1.798	1.682	1.634	1.797
1988	1.654	1.697	1.676	1.671	1.693	1.757	1.846	1.888	1.867	1.817	1.748	1.756	1.756
1989	1.836	1.851	1.869	1.869	1.946	1.979	1.889	1.927	1.949	1.866	1.766	1.736	1.874
1990	1.692	1.677	1.704	1.688	1.660	1.680	1.640	1.570	1.570	1.540	1.486	1.498	1.617
1991	1.509	1.481	1.612	1.703	1.718	1.782	1.783	1.743	2.122	1.686	1.620	1.561	1.693
1992	1.580	1.619	1.659	1.649	1.621	1.572	1.489	1.446	1.449	1.486	1.587	1.583	1.562
1993	1.614	1.643	1.646	1.594	1.605	1.654	1.714	1.693	1.620	1.640	1.700	1.711	1.653
1994	1.742	1.734	1.691	1.697	1.656	1.627	1.571	1.564	1.549	1.519	1.541	1.571	1.622

Source: Knight-Ridder Financial

Japanese Yen per U.S. Dollar

Year	January	February	March	April	May	June	July	August	September	October	November	December	Average
1987	154.7	153.3	151.3	142.8	140.4	144.5	150.3	147.3	143.2	143.1	135.4	128.3	144.6
1988	127.6	129.1	127.0	124.9	124.7	127.4	133.0	133.8	134.3	128.7	123.2	123.6	128.1
1989	127.4	127.7	130.6	132.0	137.9	144.0	140.4	141.4	144.9	141.4	143.4	143.7	137.9
1990	145.0	145.7	153.2	158.4	156.2	153.8	149.0	147.4	138.5	129.6	128.2	133.9	144.9
1991	133.7	130.5	137.4	137.1	138.0	139.6	137.6	136.9	134.8	130.5	129.7	128.0	134.5
1992	125.3	127.7	132.8	133.5	130.7	126.7	125.7	126.1	122.6	121.2	123.8	123.9	126.7
1993	124.9	120.8	117.0	112.2	110.1	107.3	107.6	103.7	105.4	107.0	107.8	109.9	111.1
1994	111.3	106.2	105.0	103.4	103.8	102.4	98.7	99.9	98.8	98.4	98.1	100.1	102.2

Source: Knight-Ridder Financial

Swiss Francs per U.S. Dollar

Year	January	February	March	April	May	June	July	August	September	October	November	December	Average
1987	1.561	1.541	1.539	1.494	1.470	1.509	1.537	1.538	1.503	1.494	1.381	1.329	1.491
1988	1.349	1.393	1.387	1.383	1.413	1.463	1.534	1.584	1.575	1.539	1.463	1.480	1.464
1989	1.562	1.574	1.611	1.647	1.729	1.706	1.629	1.663	1.687	1.632	1.618	1.567	1.635
1990	1.518	1.489	1.513	1.485	1.420	1.425	1.391	1.309	1.306	1.281	1.256	1.280	1.389
1991	1.271	1.269	1.389	1.438	1.456	1.530	1.551	1.520	1.482	1.480	1.436	1.383	1.434
1992	1.403	1.457	1.507	1.518	1.490	1.423	1.332	1.295	1.276	1.319	1.428	1.423	1.406
1993	1.478	1.520	1.520	1.457	1.447	1.477	1.514	1.495	1.416	1.442	1.497	1.463	1.477
1994	1.471	1.456	1.430	1.436	1.412	1.372	1.326	1.318	1.290	1.264	1.297	1.328	1.366

Source: Knight-Ridder Financial

British Pounds per U.S. Dollar

Year	January	February	March	April	May	June	July	August	September	October	November	December	Average
1987	1.507	1.528	1.925	1.632	1.667	1.628	1.609	1.600	1.645	1.663	1.777	1.829	1.668
1988	1.799	1.757	1.834	1.877	1.868	1.777	1.704	1.696	1.684	1.738	1.812	1.824	1.781
1989	1.774	1.753	1.713	1.701	1.628	1.554	1.626	1.593	1.572	1.586	1.573	1.597	1.639
1990	1.651	1.696	1.625	1.638	1.678	1.711	1.810	1.901	1.880	1.948	1.964	1.921	1.785
1991	1.935	1.964	1.821	1.751	1.726	1.649	1.648	1.684	1.725	1.721	1.778	1.831	1.769
1992	1.811	1.778	1.725	1.756	1.810	1.856	1.919	1.945	1.851	1.655	1.527	1.550	1.765
1993	1.533	1.438	1.462	1.547	1.549	1.509	1.497	1.493	1.525	1.503	1.481	1.490	1.502
1994	1.493	1.479	1.492	1.483	1.504	1.526	1.545	1.542	1.565	1.607	1.586	1.558	1.532

Source: International Monetary Market (Chicago)

CURRENCIES

Average Open Interest of Canadian Dollar Futures in Chicago   In Contracts

Year	January	February	March	April	May	June	July	August	September	October	November	December
1987	16,546	24,662	28,830	26,584	25,050	22,193	22,005	19,876	22,244	21,292	18,744	16,504
1988	22,411	24,244	22,965	24,095	27,747	35,787	33,207	28,513	22,645	23,138	19,548	24,844
1989	24,221	27,726	23,102	21,146	24,900	24,807	20,007	31,041	27,206	25,903	29,645	29,116
1990	26,426	29,204	23,848	24,048	33,823	30,809	39,843	42,092	34,998	29,434	31,250	25,272
1991	29,072	28,214	25,550	24,894	29,310	33,136	25,113	25,310	30,909	28,805	27,453	22,311
1992	19,724	24,020	24,118	21,354	24,020	22,860	24,773	27,665	28,221	27,827	28,025	24,923
1993	20,410	24,376	25,877	23,639	27,438	29,784	29,385	45,397	40,639	43,476	32,469	28,879
1994	28,277	38,157	48,411	42,730	44,363	42,845	35,370	39,582	49,312	40,706	42,353	59,763

Source: International Monetary Market (Chicago)

Average Open Interest of Deutsche Mark Futures in Chicago   In Contracts

Year	January	February	March	April	May	June	July	August	September	October	November	December
1987	55,518	57,619	47,105	44,425	54,018	42,127	37,790	47,875	39,754	36,319	52,866	48,644
1988	32,849	45,974	42,134	37,759	53,511	60,575	48,574	60,803	48,777	46,456	53,695	46,461
1989	51,439	65,251	52,869	52,693	70,062	72,766	62,365	66,520	65,666	70,976	91,393	93,491
1990	63,745	73,216	72,357	63,058	70,475	65,113	64,765	72,684	58,241	61,839	76,650	67,322
1991	51,211	73,463	72,824	71,737	79,162	80,318	68,046	73,860	70,525	59,236	85,248	77,632
1992	60,390	69,246	76,614	74,945	85,123	74,761	79,297	93,027	82,287	87,679	126,380	132,676
1993	134,432	140,184	126,046	118,747	131,816	159,334	165,356	147,140	108,958	103,720	135,960	145,414
1994	146,742	144,594	118,301	99,177	125,321	108,586	94,767	106,647	108,742	88,784	101,376	101,548

Source: International Monetary Market (Chicago)

Average Open Interest of Japanese Yen Futures in Chicago   In Contracts

Year	January	February	March	April	May	June	July	August	September	October	November	December
1987	31,056	31,040	35,526	47,220	47,151	36,330	35,526	41,918	49,034	42,477	54,093	51,804
1988	48,680	54,426	54,728	45,399	49,150	45,113	49,300	51,337	49,228	45,162	54,522	47,509
1989	39,467	48,400	53,654	52,013	67,213	73,355	48,261	30,235	71,230	50,594	60,283	57,748
1990	60,012	67,723	82,783	71,709	79,850	62,252	62,760	65,050	77,686	74,890	77,115	65,365
1991	43,552	64,694	57,115	49,060	52,964	55,727	53,045	56,496	66,174	74,353	74,585	64,219
1992	63,856	67,714	71,702	63,938	63,079	64,596	56,465	58,353	53,462	44,488	45,941	46,887
1993	50,066	70,195	81,979	76,696	82,028	81,103	72,186	80,780	73,002	83,097	84,812	95,817
1994	101,792	94,470	73,286	57,281	65,835	70,759	73,734	72,798	63,419	63,091	80,053	92,834

Source: International Monetary Market (Chicago)

Average Open Interest of Swiss Franc Futures in Chicago   In Contracts

Year	January	February	March	April	May	June	July	August	September	October	November	December
1987	30,600	35,576	30,208	31,226	34,140	28,592	27,380	30,406	28,379	25,998	36,015	31,866
1988	25,852	32,781	26,245	25,640	36,244	33,748	28,750	33,839	29,886	25,733	37,820	29,276
1989	27,442	31,287	34,749	34,074	42,256	36,445	35,625	41,613	38,429	31,432	39,757	47,927
1990	36,339	42,435	34,953	32,853	45,464	42,862	39,769	48,544	40,269	37,216	44,166	37,220
1991	31,489	36,483	49,061	40,026	38,601	43,476	36,031	35,881	29,833	24,949	32,342	32,439
1992	24,653	33,640	42,825	36,230	38,269	36,668	30,159	33,707	33,167	34,767	45,428	44,901
1993	52,713	49,472	48,002	43,514	47,832	42,343	40,703	44,329	60,446	49,320	58,406	49,670
1994	41,914	46,280	44,134	37,450	42,071	49,162	45,223	43,746	44,495	39,587	51,539	55,424

Source: International Monetary Market (Chicago)

Average Open Interest of British Pound Futures in Chicago   In Contracts

Year	January	February	March	April	May	June	July	August	September	October	November	December
1987	27,535	30,539	44,786	39,453	44,235	39,266	36,803	42,365	36,672	37,032	43,073	36,700
1988	29,433	40,278	41,665	43,291	45,745	29,892	18,052	18,917	18,149	17,930	21,850	23,829
1989	22,870	24,705	27,436	21,170	25,871	26,512	22,899	22,559	27,661	21,971	24,850	26,124
1990	23,272	30,729	26,219	23,909	33,355	35,528	37,898	41,820	33,458	32,213	39,623	32,790
1991	23,686	34,680	33,558	29,900	30,697	33,792	26,443	21,578	28,215	22,882	31,792	26,443
1992	21,578	28,215	22,882	31,595	36,426	35,529	27,160	28,041	30,137	30,330	33,121	27,935
1993	26,614	41,752	40,238	38,544	39,654	34,953	26,056	32,446	33,560	29,733	37,246	33,606
1994	39,223	43,878	35,554	44,725	46,577	41,801	37,633	34,988	40,751	42,648	49,684	65,834

Source: International Monetary Market (Chicago)

United States Merchandise Trade Balance   In Millions of Dollars

Year	January	February	March	April	May	June	July	August	September	October	November	December	Total
1985	-11,408	-8,095	-8,960	-10,588	-10,387	-12,068	-10,447	-9,846	-14,559	-10,561	-12,267	-13,311	-122,173
1986	-12,166	-9,027	-9,961	-11,618	-10,706	-10,212	-13,056	-12,157	-13,144	-12,470	-13,140	-10,623	-145,081
1987	-13,453	-10,956	-10,628	-11,613	-12,410	-13,721	-14,431	-13,747	-12,484	-15,298	-11,932	-11,445	-159,557
1988	-9,874	-11,179	-7,656	-8,233	-7,915	-11,738	-10,211	-11,006	-9,237	-10,251	-10,824	-10,402	-126,959
1989	-8,639	-8,622	-6,954	-7,191	-9,463	-8,724	-10,582	-11,034	-8,971	-11,780	-10,754	-6,687	-115,249
1990	-9,640	-6,150	-6,369	-6,527	-7,308	-6,476	-10,759	-10,509	-9,157	-12,805	-10,529	-6,211	-109,033
1991	-7,079	-4,201	-1,889	-3,411	-4,158	-3,948	-7,894	-7,450	-7,111	-8,735	-4,942	-5,908	-74,068
1992	-5,470	-2,178	-3,527	-5,772	-5,409	-6,718	-9,893	-10,218	-9,693	-9,706	-8,644	-7,276	-96,097
1993	-6,113	-5,905	-8,886	-8,428	-6,542	-11,749	-12,609	-11,949	-12,516	-12,638	-11,120	-7,322	-132,575
1994	------------	-31,766	----------	------------	-38,278	-----------	-----------	-50,116	-----------				

Not seasonally adjusted.   *Source: Bureau of Economic Analysis, U.S. Department of Commerce*

Index of Real Trade-Weighted Dollar Exchange Rates for Total Agricultural[2]   1985 = 100

Year	January	February	March	April	May	June	July	August	Sept.	October	Nov.	Dec.
1988 U.S. Markets	76.4	76.8	75.8	74.8	74.9	76.0	77.8	78.3	79.3	77.8	75.7	75.6
U.S. Competitors	83.1	83.4	82.6	81.9	81.8	82.2	83.2	84.2	84.4	83.5	82.1	81.9
1989 U.S. Markets	77.2	77.5	79.4	79.1	81.0	82.1	79.5	80.6	81.4	79.5	79.5	78.5
U.S. Competitors	82.1	81.4	81.9	85.0	88.7	88.7	86.8	85.7	85.2	83.7	82.4	83.9
1990 U.S. Markets	78.3	78.1	79.3	79.4	78.5	78.9	79.2	79.1	78.5	76.6	74.7	75.3
U.S. Competitors	80.1	81.2	79.6	79.2	77.8	77.5	76.4	76.1	76.3	75.0	75.3	73.5
1991 U.S. Markets	75.8	75.0	78.4	79.4	79.7	80.8	80.5	79.8	78.4	78.3	77.1	76.3
U.S. Competitors	75.3	75.1	76.4	77.0	77.3	77.8	77.8	76.9	75.8	77.0	76.4	76.2
1992 U.S. Markets	75.5	76.4	80.9	78.2	76.5	76.0	74.7	74.2	74.2	75.2	77.6	77.3
U.S. Competitors	76.2	76.8	81.1	76.6	77.4	76.6	75.6	75.1	77.2	75.7	77.7	77.4
1993 U.S. Markets	78.2	78.4	78.3	77.0	77.3	76.0	77.1	76.8	76.0	76.6	77.4	77.9
U.S. Competitors	78.3	78.6	79.1	78.4	78.9	77.7	78.5	78.7	78.0	78.3	78.6	78.1
1994[1] U.S. Markets	77.0	77.0	76.7	76.6	76.2	76.2	74.6	74.7	72.8	72.5	71.8	71.1
U.S. Competitors	78.3	78.3	78.0	78.5	77.4	76.5	74.1	70.7	67.1	63.8	61.7	59.5

[1] Preliminary.   [2] Real indexes adjust nominal exchange rates for differences in rates of inflation to avoid the distortion caused by high-inflation countries. A higher value means the dollar has appreciated. Federal Reserve Board Index of trade-weighted value of the U.S. Dollar against ten major currencies. Weights are based on relative importance in world financial markets.   *Source: Economic Research Service, U.S.D.A.*

United States Balance on Current Account   In Millions of Dollars

Year	1st Quarter	2nd Quarter	3rd Quarter	4th Quarter	Annual
1985	-21,499	-31,427	-37,171	-35,276	-125,372
1986	-31,159	-37,629	-42,687	-39,726	-151,201
1987	-35,631	-42,034	-46,171	-43,261	-167,097
1988	-28,905	-31,188	-34,381	-33,721	-128,194
1989	-21,184	-25,207	-30,244	-26,186	-102,820
1990	-16,468	-19,511	-30,311	-25,458	-91,748
1991	16,214	2,953	-16,703	-9,416	-6,952
1992	-2,133	-14,757	-24,159	-26,837	-67,886
1993	-12,587	-24,364	-33,850	-33,095	-103,896
1994	-24,938	-36,023	-47,667		

Not seasonally adjusted.   *Source: Bureau of Economic Analysis, U.S. Department of Commerce*

Merchandise Trade and Account Balances   In Billions of Dollars

Year	-----Merchandise Trade Balance-----					-----Current Account Balance-----				
	Canada	Germany	Japan	Switzerland	U.K.	Canada	Germany	Japan	Switzerland	U.K.
1986	7.7	56.1	92.8	-2.0	-14.0	-10.1	39.5	85.8	6.9	-1.3
1987	9.0	70.5	96.4	-3.1	-18.9	-11.8	45.9	87.0	7.6	-8.1
1988	8.1	79.9	95.0	-3.2	-38.2	-17.1	50.6	79.6	9.0	-29.6
1989	6.0	77.9	76.9	-4.1	-40.4	-22.8	57.5	57.2	7.0	-36.8
1990	8.3	72.4	63.5	-3.2	-33.4	-21.6	46.9	35.8	8.6	-32.4
1991	3.7	23.8	103.0	-2.1	-18.1	-24.1	-19.4	72.9	10.6	-13.5
1992	6.1	32.0	132.3	2.7	-23.5	-21.9	-22.0	117.5	15.0	-18.5
1993	7.6	43.4	141.4	5.0	-20.5	-23.8	-20.1	131.4	18.6	-16.3
1994[1]	7.7	53.1	152.1	6.2	-16.1	-21.4	-25.2	139.8	16.3	-8.8
1995[2]	12.9	68.9	154.1	7.1	-17.6	-19.0	-13.0	145.0	20.0	-13.0

[1] Estimate.   [2] Projections.   *Source: Organization for Economic Cooperation and Development*

CURRENCIES

80

Diamonds

World Production of Natural Gem Diamonds   In Thousands of Carats

Year	Angola	Aus-tralia	Bots-wana	Brazil	Central African Republic	China	Ghana	Guinea	Namibia	Russia[3]	Sierra Leone	South Africa	Tan-zania	Zaire	World Total
1984	652	3,415	5,810	200	236	200	35	44	884	4,300	240	4,516	193	5,169	26,093
1985	464	4,242	6,318	233	190	200	60	123	865	4,400	243	4,550	165	4,032	26,233
1986	240	13,145	9,590	310	259	200	88	190	970	7,400	215	4,473	133	4,661	42,038
1987	180	13,650	9,368	300	304	200	65	163	971	7,400	150	4,063	87	3,885	41,024
1988	950	17,413	10,660	350	284	200	55	136	925	11,000	12	3,800	105	2,724	49,206
1989	1,165	17,540	10,680	350	334	200	395	137	910	11,500	90	4,000	105	2,663	50,665
1990	1,060	17,331	12,150	600	303	200	520	119	750	12,000	66	3,800	60	2,914	52,459
1991	899	17,978	11,550	600	296	200	560	91	1,170	10,000	160	3,900	70	3,000	51,090
1992[1]	1,100	17,750	11,160	653	307	200	570	90	1,500	9,000	200	4,400	48	8,934	56,757
1993[2]	470	19,000	12,000	600	307	230	600	90	1,100	8,000	90	4,300	48	9,500	57,205

[1] Preliminary.   [2] Estimate.   [3] Formerly part of the U.S.S.R.; data not reported separately until 1992.   *Source: U.S. Bureau of Mines*

World Production of Natural Industrial Diamonds   In Thousands of Carats

Year	Angola	Aus-tralia	Bots-wana	Brazil	Central African Republic	China	Ghana	Liberia	Russia[3]	Sierra Leone	South Africa	Tan-zania	Vene-zuela	Zaire	World Total
1984	250	2,277	7,104	550	101	800	311	132	6,400	105	5,627	84	232	13,290	37,359
1985	250	2,828	6,317	217	87	800	576	72	6,400	106	5,652	71	180	16,127	39,785
1986	10	16,066	3,500	315	99	800	498	189	7,400	100	5,755	57	165	18,643	53,702
1987	10	16,683	3,840	200	108	800	400	183	7,400	75	4,990	37	68	15,540	50,464
1988	50	17,413	4,570	180	59	800	465	100	11,000	6	4,700	45	75	15,439	55,122
1989	80	17,540	4,570	150	81	800	99	93	11,500	39	5,100	45	185	15,092	55,562
1990	73	17,331	5,200	900	78	800	130	60	12,000	12	4,900	25	248	16,513	58,452
1991	62	17,978	4,950	900	82	800	140	60	10,000	83	4,530	30	112	14,814	54,737
1992	80	22,250	4,790	665	107	800	140	93	9,000	96	5,750	20	176	4,567	48,773
1993[1]	30	23,200	5,000	900	106	850	150	90	8,000	68	6,050	20	200	5,500	50,390
1994[2]		23,000	5,000	900		800			8,000		6,000			5,000	50,000

[1] Preliminary.   [2] Estimate.   [3] Formerly part of the U.S.S.R.; data not reported separately until 1992.   *Source: U.S. Bureau of Mines*

World Production of Synthetic Diamonds   In Thousands of Carats

Year	Belarus[3]	China	Czech Republic[4]	France	Greece	Ireland	Japan	Russia[3]	South Africa	Sweden	Ukraine[3]	States	Total
1988	------	15,000	5,000	4,000	1,000	60,000	25,000	41,500	55,000	25,000	------	W	241,500
1989	------	15,000	10,000	4,000	1,000	60,000	25,000	120,000	60,000	25,000	------	W	325,000
1990	------	15,000	10,000	5,000	1,000	60,000	25,000	120,000	60,000	25,000	------	W	269,000
1991	------	15,000	10,000	4,000	1,000	60,000	30,000	120,000	60,000	25,000	------	90,000	423,000
1992[1]	30,000	15,000	10,000	3,500	750	60,000	30,000	80,000	60,000	25,000	10,000	90,000	419,250
1993[2]	30,000	15,500	5,000	3,500	1,000	66,000	32,000	80,000	75,000	25,000	10,000	103,000	456,000

[1] Preliminary.   [2] Estimate.   [3] Formerly part of the U.S.S.R.; data not reported separately until 1992.   [4] Formerly part of Czechoslovakia; data not reported separately until 1993.   W = Withheld proprietary data.   *Source: U.S. Bureau of Mines*

U.S. Salient Statistics of Industrial Diamonds   In Millions of Carats

	Bort, Grit & Powder & Dust Natural and Synthetic								Stones (Natural)					
	Production													
Year	Manu-factured Diamond	Secon-dary	Imports for Con-sumption	Exports & Re-exports	In Manu-factured Products	Gov't Sales	Apparent Con-sumption	Price Value of Imports $ Per Carat	Secon-dary Pro-duction	Imports for Con-sumption	Exports & Re-exports	Gov't Sales	Apparent Con-sumption	Price Value of Imports $ Per Carat	Net Import Reliance % of Con-sumption
---	---	---	---	---	---	---	---	---	---	---	---	---	---	---	---
1987	W	3.0	45.0	56.8	.6	-----	W	1.28	.3	3.9	3.0	2.0	1.2	10.86	75
1988	W	6.6	64.3	74.5	.6	-----	W	1.03	.6	6.9	3.0	1.8	4.5	9.31	87
1989	W	3.0	61.6	78.2	.6	-----	75.8	.72	.6	8.8	2.8	-----	6.6	6.94	91
1990	90.0	5.9	85.4	71.0	.6	3.0	112.7	.76	.5	11.0	1.7	-----	9.8	6.57	95
1991	90.0	3.5	70.0	78.8	.6	5.0	89.1	.83	.3	7.6	2.9	-----	5.0	6.68	94
1992	95.0	3.4	97.3	83.6	.6	10.4	121.9	.70	.1	9.8	5.6	-----	4.3	4.56	98
1993[1]	100.3	15.8	15.0	96.1	.6	-----	134.4	.61	.1	5.5	3.7	1.3	1.8	6.85	95
1994[2]	108.0	41.1	140.0	110.0		2.0	181.0	.62	.1	3.0	1.0	3.1	2.0	6.90	95

[1] Preliminary.   [2] Estimate.   W = Withheld proprietary data.   *Source: U.S. Bureau of Mines*

Eggs

U.S. annual egg production has slowly increased since the mid-1980s, but the U.S. remains the world's second largest producer with about 12 percent of total production. China is the largest producer and consumer of eggs, accounting for more than one-third of world totals. However, a major difference persists between the two nations in respect to utilization. Much of China's large production is directly consumed as fresh brown eggs, whereas, in the U.S. about one-third of production is processed and white eggs are favored for table use.

However, a change in attitude towards eggs may be taking hold in the U.S. that only a few years ago was not anticipated. Per capita egg consumption in 1995 is forecast at 233 eggs to 234 eggs, one egg lower than in 1994 and about the same as in 1991. During the 1980s, per capita consumption declined about 4 eggs per year. However, a shift in usage will persist that favors egg products relative to table use. U.S. consumers now appear less concern about the connection of the overall cholesterol content of eggs and heart disease than noted in previous years, perhaps because the cause and effect is now seen as questionable. In either case, per capita egg usage remains much higher, and/or gaining much more rapidly abroad than in the U.S. Japan's per capita egg use, as it nears 300, is probably the world's highest.

Foreign trade in eggs is widespread, but relatively small. The net totals gives a slight edge to exports. Trade within the European Community accounts for about one-half of the world's egg trade. The U.S. is a consistent net exporter while Japan is a net importer, with a breakdown that includes hatched, table, dried and preserved eggs and egg albumen. Japan is generally the largest buyer of U.S. egg yolks. U.S. egg and egg product exports in 1994 were up about 11 percent from 1993. The Export Enhancement Program (EEP) was an important factor in increasing U.S. table egg exports 20 percent in the first half of 1994. Hong Kong was a strong buyer of table eggs, with other strong buyers of egg products including Japan, Canada and Mexico.

There are definitive seasonal swings in U.S. egg production and table consumption. The table egg flocks typically reach a low in mid-summer and then increase throughout the year, with monthly production peaking during the winter. Table egg consumption tends to be highest when consumers have more time for leisurely meals, in the U.S. generally the summer. Wholesale prices (at Chicago) lack a clear seasonality, but on balance appear highest during the winter months. U.S. egg production in 1994 of 6.1 billion dozen compares with almost 6 billion dozen in 1993. Forecasts for 1995, pointed to another fractional gain as the positive return to producers in the second half of 1994 ended flock liquidation and encouraged increased pullet hatch. The larger production could depress prices in 1995 to about a 67¢ per dozen average, basis New York from a 1994 average of 68¢ per dozen to 69¢ per dozen and 72.53¢ per dozen in 1993.

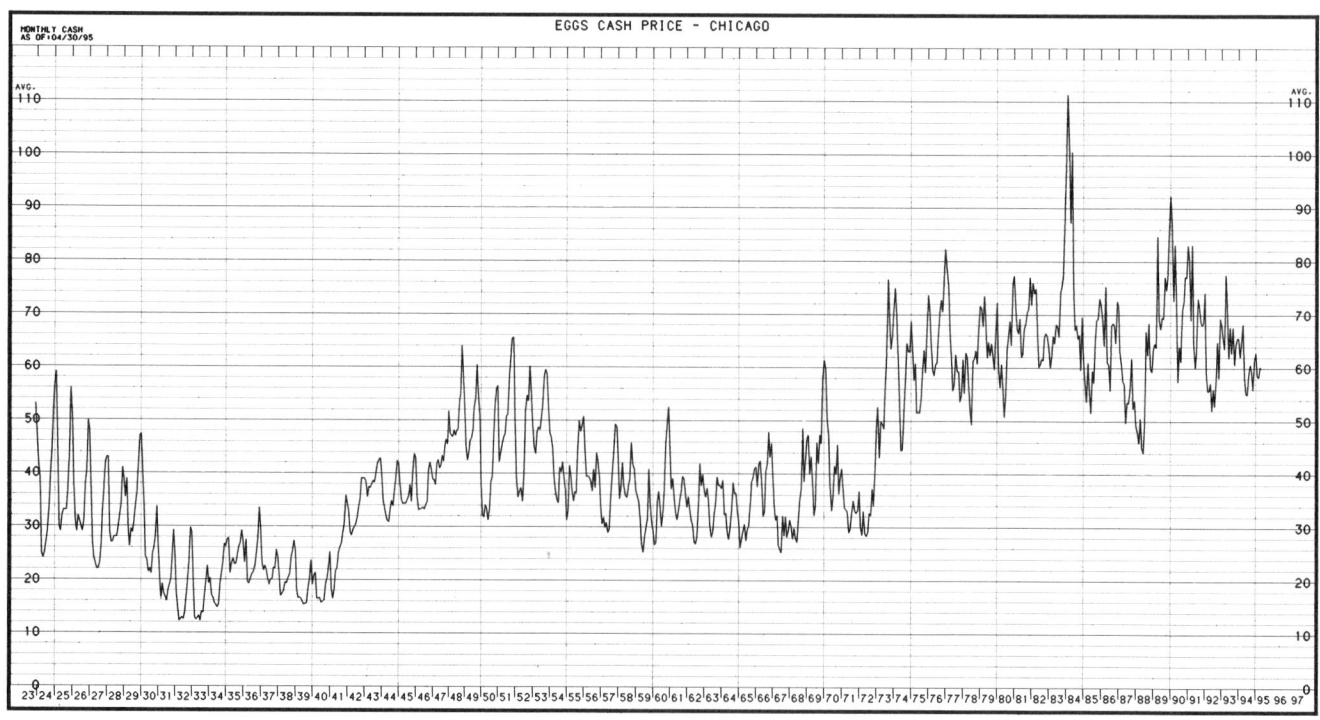

World Production of Eggs   In Millions of Eggs

Year	Brazil	Canada	China	France	Germany	Italy	Japan	Rep. of Korea	Mexico	Netherlands	Poland	Russia[4]	Spain	Ukraine[4]	United Kingdom	United States
1985	11,800	5,855	------	14,910	13,150	10,900	35,700	5,250	18,092	11,051	8,636	------	10,164	77,255	13,117	68,256
1986	13,000	5,898	111,000	14,970	12,765	10,300	37,080	6,011	18,563	10,930	8,303	------	10,877	79,892	13,150	69,196
1987	15,400	5,706	118,000	14,540	17,995	10,743	39,567	6,574	18,039	10,930	7,966	47,447	10,500	17,425	13,300	70,418
1988	12,174	5,719	139,100	15,050	17,960	11,234	40,383	7,204	17,950	10,660	8,220	49,144	10,856	17,672	13,500	67,174
1989	12,174	5,719	140,900	15,050	17,794	11,223	40,356	6,919	17,950	10,660	8,200	49,042	10,140	17,393	10,547	67,178
1990	13,454	5,661	158,920	14,629	16,800	11,454	40,318	7,145	18,040	10,801	7,649	47,470	10,659	16,287	10,658	67,987
1991	13,655	5,666	184,400	15,300	15,525	11,568	41,638	7,770	19,840	10,762	6,500	46,900	10,184	15,188	11,006	69,352
1992	14,190	5,670	230,980	15,375	15,165	11,454	42,911	7,750	19,650	10,458	6,300	42,900	8,675	13,445	10,699	70,618
1993[1]	12,700	5,689	235,960	15,355	13,678	11,502	43,252	8,200	20,140	10,019	5,450	40,300	8,454	11,800	10,645	71,522
1994[2]	13,600	5,640	260,000	15,600	14,000	11,600	42,800	8,400	22,150	9,800	5,600	38,700	8,700	11,000	10,640	73,834
1995[3]	14,800	5,675	290,000	15,400	14,000	11,550	42,400	8,600	21,700	9,700	5,800	37,900	8,800	11,000	10,615	74,880

[1] Preliminary.   [2] Estimate.   [3] Forecast.   [4] Formerly part of the U.S.S.R.; data not reported separately until 1987.   *Source: Foreign Agricultural Service, U.S. Department of Agriculture*

Salient Egg Statistics in the United States

Year	Hens & Pullets On Farm Dec. 1[3] (Thousands)	Hens & Pullets Average Number During Year (Thousands)	Rate of Lay Per Layer During Year[4] (Number)	Eggs Total Produced (Millions)	Eggs Price in ¢ Per Dozen	Value of Production[5] Million $	Total Egg Production (Million Dozen)	Imports[6] (Million Dozen)	Exports[6] (Million Dozen)	Used for Hatching (Million Dozen)	Consumption Total	Consumption Per Capita Eggs[6] (Number)
1985	281,519	277,592	247	68,521	57.2	3,262	5,710	12.7	70.6	548.1	5,104	256.0
1986	283,193	279,046	248	69,196	61.5	3,543	5,766	13.7	101.6	566.8	5,112	254.9
1987	288,320	283,872	248	70,418	54.7	3,209	5,868	5.6	111.2	599.1	5,159	255.0
1988	275,447	277,781	251	69,410	52.8	3,067	5,784	5.3	141.8	606.0	5,041	246.8
1989	271,064	269,347	250	67,178	68.9	3,861	5,598	25.2	91.6	641.8	4,894	237.4
1990	271,963	269,862	251	67,987	70.9	4,010	5,666	9.1	100.8	678.5	4,894	235.0
1991	279,325	274,287	252	69,352	67.8	3,909	5,779	2.3	154.5	708.6	4,917	233.5
1992	282,034	278,830	253	70,618	57.6	3,387	5,885	4.3	157.0	732.0	5,000	233.5
1993[1]	290,626	284,776	252	70,715	63.4	3,771	5,960	4.7	158.9	769.3	5,039	234.9
1994[2]	298,509	290,823	251	72,892			6,128	4.2	185.0	802.3	5,142	236.6

[1] Preliminary.   [2] Estimate.   [3] All layers of laying age.   [4] Number of eggs produced during the year divided by the average number of all layers of laying age on hand during the year.   [5] Value of sales plus value of eggs consumed in households of producers.   [6] Shell-egg equivalent of eggs and egg products.
Source: National Agricultural Statistics Service, U.S. Department of Agriculture

Average Wholesale Prices of Shell Eggs (Large) Delivered, Chicago   In Cents Per Dozen

Year	Jan.	Feb.	Mar.	Apr.	May	June	July	Aug.	Sept.	Oct.	Nov.	Dec.	Average
1985	58.4	55.1	62.3	57.3	52.9	60.8	58.6	66.4	70.5	70.7	74.6	73.2	63.4
1986	70.6	65.7	76.9	62.6	62.0	57.3	69.4	70.0	69.4	66.3	74.1	72.8	68.1
1987	64.4	62.0	59.2	59.0	51.8	55.6	55.4	58.7	64.8	55.5	56.3	52.1	57.9
1988	51.2	48.9	53.6	47.9	47.1	52.8	69.8	65.4	71.4	63.1	62.2	66.1	58.3
1989	67.8	66.6	91.0	71.6	69.8	72.0	71.8	79.6	77.2	79.4	89.1	94.3	77.5
1990	88.6	75.1	86.1	78.6	60.3	66.9	64.2	73.9	75.4	80.0	80.0	83.1	76.0
1991	86.0	72.0	85.8	67.6	60.9	63.4	73.1	71.3	68.8	67.9	68.7	73.9	71.6
1992	59.1	55.7	55.7	57.4	52.0	56.0	53.0	57.9	64.9	58.2	69.4	68.0	58.9
1993	65.7	63.6	77.5	70.9	61.9	67.6	62.8	67.6	60.6	64.2	65.6	65.5	66.1
1994[1]	62.1	64.9	68.3	58.3	55.1	55.1	58.8	60.6	59.2	55.9	61.5	62.9	60.2

[1] Preliminary.   *Source: National Agricultural Statistics Service, U.S. Department of Agriculture*

Total Egg Production in the United States   In Cents Per Dozen

Year	Jan.	Feb.	Mar.	Apr.	May	June	July	Aug.	Sept.	Oct.	Nov.	Dec.	Total
1985	5,970	5,310	5,938	5,688	5,743	5,521	5,680	5,704	5,564	5,783	5,688	5,932	68,521
1986	5,904	5,340	5,943	5,698	5,844	5,655	5,763	5,766	5,613	5,865	5,783	6,022	69,196
1987	5,989	5,417	6,093	5,864	5,925	5,685	5,863	5,861	5,756	6,008	5,873	6,084	70,418
1988	6,047	5,667	6,050	5,767	5,839	5,575	5,740	5,762	5,589	5,838	5,697	5,839	69,410
1989	5,758	5,182	5,782	5,569	5,696	5,498	5,648	5,613	5,450	5,658	5,543	5,781	67,178
1990	5,708	5,172	5,838	5,655	5,769	5,533	5,703	5,718	5,533	5,783	5,696	5,879	67,987
1991	5,865	5,316	5,935	5,666	5,796	5,643	5,840	5,855	5,675	5,915	5,811	6,035	69,352
1992	5,951	5,558	6,042	5,832	5,918	5,693	5,908	5,919	5,753	6,019	5,913	6,112	70,618
1993[1]	6,030	5,432	6,067	5,861	6,009	5,816	5,992	6,015	5,876	6,144	6,085	5,388	70,715
1994[2]	6,137	5,559	6,279	6,035	6,158	5,962	6,188	6,262	6,114	6,367	6,265	5,566	72,892

[1] Preliminary.   [2] Estimate.   *Source: National Agricultural Statistics Service, U.S. Department of Agriculture*

EGGS

Shell Eggs: Per Capita Disappearance in the United States   In Number of Eggs

Year	Jan.	Feb.	Mar.	Apr.	May	June	July	Aug.	Sept.	Oct.	Nov.	Dec.	Total	Total Consumption (Million Dozen)
1983	20.2	17.7	20.0	18.9	19.0	17.7	18.8	18.4	18.0	19.0	18.8	19.9	226.4	4,421
1984	19.4	17.2	19.2	18.8	18.5	17.7	18.7	18.4	18.3	18.8	18.8	20.2	224.0	4,412
1985	19.5	17.0	19.5	17.9	17.7	17.4	17.6	18.0	17.6	18.1	18.3	19.2	217.9	4,331
1986	18.9	17.0	19.3	17.5	18.0	17.2	17.5	17.8	17.3	17.9	18.5	18.8	215.8	4,327
1987	18.6	16.5	18.5	17.8	17.8	16.6	17.3	17.6	17.3	18.1	17.5	18.1	211.6	4,282
1988	18.4	16.8	18.0	17.0	16.7	15.6	16.9	16.4	16.1	16.8	16.6	17.3	202.6	4,138
1989	16.8	15.1	17.3	16.1	15.9	15.2	16.2	15.8	15.5	16.0	15.9	17.1	192.2	3,978
1990	16.2	14.5	16.3	15.9	15.5	14.9	15.4	15.3	15.3	15.6	15.5	16.6	186.8	3,891
1991	15.9	14.4	16.4	14.6	14.8	14.4	15.0	15.2	14.9	15.1	15.7	16.2	182.6	3,844
1992	15.4	14.3	15.4	15.1	15.0	14.0	14.7	15.2	14.5	15.3	15.5	15.9	180.3	3,838
1993[1]	15.9	14.0	15.6	14.8	14.7	13.9	14.6	14.6	14.1	15.0	15.0	15.6	177.8	3,825
1994[2]	----------- 44.5 -----------			----------- 42.6 -----------			----------- 43.7 ----------						175.8	3,820

[1] Preliminary.   [2] Estimate.   Source: Economic Research Service, U.S. Department of Agriculture

Egg-Feed Ratio[1] in the United States

Year	Jan.	Feb.	Mar.	Apr.	May	June	July	Aug.	Sept.	Oct.	Nov.	Dec.	Average
1983	5.7	5.8	6.1	5.8	6.0	5.8	5.7	6.1	6.0	6.2	6.9	7.7	6.2
1984	8.8	8.5	7.4	8.5	6.5	5.8	5.8	5.8	5.9	5.7	6.5	6.3	6.8
1985	5.5	5.6	6.3	5.7	5.5	5.9	5.9	6.5	7.1	7.3	7.5	7.4	6.4
1986	7.2	6.9	7.6	6.4	6.4	5.7	6.9	7.3	7.3	7.0	8.0	7.8	7.0
1987	7.3	7.1	6.6	6.6	5.9	6.0	5.7	5.6	6.5	6.0	6.4	5.7	6.3
1988	5.5	5.3	5.6	5.2	5.0	5.3	4.9	4.9	5.4	5.3	5.4	5.4	5.3
1989	5.9	5.8	7.5	6.2	5.9	6.0	6.1	6.8	6.8	7.1	7.9	8.3	6.7
1990	8.4	7.1	8.0	7.3	6.2	6.4	5.4	6.4	6.7	7.3	7.3	7.7	7.0
1991	7.9	6.9	7.8	6.8	6.1	6.1	6.8	6.7	6.5	6.2	6.3	7.0	6.8
1992	5.7	5.5	5.4	5.5	5.1	5.3	5.2	5.3	5.9	5.8	6.6	6.5	5.7
1993	6.4	6.3	7.0	6.9	6.3	6.6	5.7	6.1	5.5	5.8	6.1	6.1	6.2
1994[2]	5.7	5.8	6.0	5.7	5.4	5.4	5.6	5.8	5.9	5.7	6.2	6.2	5.8

[1] Pounds of laying feed equivalent in value to one dozen eggs.   [2] Preliminary.   Source: Economic Research Service, U.S. Department of Agriculture

Total Eggs -- U.S. Supply and Distribution   In Millions of Dozen

Year & Quarters	Beginning Stocks	Production	Imports[4]	Total Supply	Exports[4]	Eggs Used for Hatching	Ending Stocks	Total	Per Capita (Number)
1990 I	10.7	1,391	1.9	1,404	18.4	167.3	13.4	1,205	58.1
II	13.4	1,411	4.1	1,428	18.8	173.1	14.4	1,222	58.8
III	14.4	1,413	2.7	1,430	25.9	168.9	13.1	1,222	58.6
IV	13.1	1,445	.4	1,458	37.5	166.6	11.6	1,243	59.4
1991 I	11.6	1,422	.2	1,434	34.9	174.9	11.1	1,213	57.9
II	11.1	1,420	.3	1,432	38.0	182.2	11.2	1,200	57.1
III	11.2	1,441	.7	1,453	38.8	176.6	12.9	1,224	58.1
IV	12.9	1,475	.5	1,488	42.7	174.3	13.0	1,258	59.6
1992 I	13.0	1,464	.8	1,477	40.5	180.0	15.8	1,241	58.5
II	15.8	1,454	1.0	1,471	36.1	186.9	17.0	1,231	57.9
III	17.0	1,464	1.3	1,482	34.5	180.6	15.8	1,251	58.7
IV	15.8	1,501	1.2	1,518	45.9	178.9	13.5	1,280	59.8
1993[1] I	13.5	1,461	.9	1,475	37.1	187.3	11.9	1,237	57.7
II	11.9	1,474	1.5	1,487	34.5	196.6	11.7	1,244	57.9
III	11.7	1,490	1.4	1,503	42.0	192.4	11.4	1,258	58.4
IV	11.4	1,535	.9	1,548	45.3	191.4	10.7	1,300	60.2
1994[2] I	10.7	1,498	1.0	1,510	40.2	195.0	12.1	1,262	58.3
II	12.1	1,513	1.1	1,526	45.5	204.7	11.9	1,264	58.2
III	11.9	1,547	1.0	1,560	49.3	202.6	13.6	1,294	59.5
IV	13.6	1,570	1.1	1,585	50.0	200.0	13.0	1,322	60.6
1995[3] I	13.0	1,530	1.0	1,544	40.0	205.0	12.0	1,287	58.8
II	12.0	1,535	1.1	1,548	43.0	215.0	12.0	1,278	58.3
III	12.0	1,550	1.1	1,563	43.0	210.0	12.0	1,298	59.1
Year	13.0	6,200	4.3	6,217	170.0	835.0	12.0	5,200	236.9

[1] Preliminary.   [2] Estimate.   [3] Forecast.   [4] Shell-egg equivalent of eggs and egg products.   Source: Economic Research Service, U.S. Department of Agriculture

Hens and Pullets of Laying Age (Layers) in the U.S., First of Month   In Thousands

Year	Jan. 1	Feb. 1	Mar. 1	Apr. 1	May 1	June 1	July 1	Aug. 1	Sept. 1	Oct. 1	Nov. 1	Dec. 1
1986	281,997	281,882	281,622	279,730	277,532	275,728	274,059	276,072	275,840	279,157	282,233	283,193
1987	285,939	287,082	285,877	285,536	282,109	280,642	278,452	280,232	282,032	285,954	286,409	288,320
1988	286,470	285,670	283,225	279,221	277,449	272,482	270,282	271,220	273,136	275,191	276,415	275,447
1989	272,243	272,780	271,590	269,278	267,269	267,239	267,088	266,253	267,656	267,919	270,006	271,064
1990	271,164	272,826	271,921	272,813	270,664	269,040	265,647	266,767	267,004	268,835	270,274	271,963
1991	273,917	275,533	274,446	272,541	272,150	272,944	272,779	272,998	274,277	276,187	278,433	279,325
1992	280,697	279,274	279,117	279,009	276,757	275,645	275,179	275,091	274,010	279,233	280,183	282,034
1993	281,639	282,933	282,005	282,480	281,468	280,795	280,517	282,201	282,341	284,771	285,298	290,626
1994[1]	288,048	287,767	288,866	289,510	287,905	287,225	286,458	288,359	292,002	294,536	295,798	298,509

[1] Preliminary.   *Source: National Agricultural Statistics Service, U.S. Department of Agriculture*

Eggs Laid Per Hundred Layers in the United States   In Number of Eggs

Year	Jan.	Feb.	Mar.	Apr.	May	June	July	Aug.	Sept.	Oct.	Nov.	Dec.	Average
1986	2,128	1,922	2,146	2,068	2,134	2,079	2,120	2,117	2,053	2,118	2,078	2,155	2,093
1987	2,126	1,919	2,166	2,103	2,137	2,060	2,123	2,114	2,053	2,129	2,078	2,157	2,097
1988	2,154	2,027	2,189	2,103	2,150	2,081	2,150	2,150	2,073	2,152	2,105	2,179	2,126
1989	2,154	1,937	2,178	2,111	2,165	2,089	2,148	2,135	2,071	2,142	2,099	2,182	2,118
1990	2,150	1,940	2,185	2,120	2,173	2,105	2,179	2,181	2,104	2,189	2,149	2,208	2,140
1991	2,186	1,978	2,218	2,124	2,168	2,108	2,186	2,189	2,106	2,175	2,134	2,206	2,148
1992	2,174	2,036	2,216	2,148	2,186	2,110	2,196	2,204	2,125	2,201	2,156	2,227	2,165
1993	2,138	1,923	2,149	2,078	2,137	2,072	2,130	2,131	2,073	2,155	6,085	2,169	2,437
1994[1]	2,131	1,928	2,171	2,090	2,141	2,078	2,153	2,158	2,085	2,157	6,265	2,182	2,462

[1] Preliminary.   *Source: National Agricultural Statistics Service, U.S. Department of Agriculture*

Egg-Type Chicks Hatched by Commercial Hatcheries in the United States   In Thousands

Year	Jan.	Feb.	Mar.	Apr.	May	June	July	Aug.	Sept.	Oct.	Nov.	Dec.	Total
1986	34,538	34,826	39,523	42,359	42,465	37,253	33,575	33,382	32,638	32,444	27,456	33,262	423,721
1987	34,156	35,815	41,708	42,356	40,858	37,256	33,375	34,667	31,800	33,959	30,593	31,242	427,785
1988	29,274	28,433	35,615	34,749	35,984	33,049	24,876	27,838	30,918	31,007	27,181	27,311	366,235
1989	26,602	27,271	32,597	36,135	38,376	34,708	29,828	32,217	32,862	33,456	29,666	29,284	383,002
1990	32,004	32,107	36,509	36,915	37,895	34,471	31,582	32,949	31,219	32,926	29,809	31,046	398,432
1991	34,487	34,837	37,041	39,775	38,404	36,227	33,696	33,656	34,007	34,307	30,400	32,717	419,554
1992	32,496	31,950	36,490	35,755	38,513	34,568	32,265	28,349	28,760	32,843	27,718	31,612	391,319
1993	34,852	33,984	38,232	37,143	36,741	35,587	33,980	31,455	31,775	31,634	30,073	30,446	405,902
1994[1]	32,816	31,056	33,335	35,718	35,179	31,916	30,260	31,518	30,855	31,764	25,432	28,575	378,424

[1] Preliminary.   *Source: National Agricultural Statistics Service, U.S. Department of Agriculture*

U.S. Cold Storage Holdings of Shell Eggs, First of Month   In Thousands Cases (One Case = 30 Dozen)

Year	Jan.	Feb.	Mar.	Apr.	May	June	July	Aug.	Sept.	Oct.	Nov.	Dec.
1986	24	28	21	20	32	44	38	25	33	29	20	29
1987	22	20	25	22	28	38	32	34	32	33	51	40
1988	43	67	53	32	14	21	30	28	25	23	24	26
1989	9	12	7	33	18	26	27	12	17	23	6	11
1990	12	22	16	16	12	21	22	29	19	18	11	16
1991	15	17	9	23	12	15	13	13	10	13	12	13
1992	21	20	25	14	27	34	30	29	23	22	17	15
1993	15	12	12	15	6	6	7	6	6	15	13	6
1994[1]	10	7	8	9	8	8	8	14	14	9	7	3

[1] Preliminary.   *Source: National Agricultural Statistics Service, U.S. Department of Agriculture*

U.S. Cold Storage Holdings of Frozen Eggs, First of Month   In Millions of Pounds[1]

Year	Jan.	Feb.	Mar.	Apr.	May	June	July	Aug.	Sept.	Oct.	Nov.	Dec.
1986	13.2	12.7	12.8	10.7	12.5	11.6	14.2	15.1	15.0	14.0	14.0	13.0
1987	12.8	14.3	13.5	14.5	14.9	17.4	16.9	17.3	17.5	16.5	17.9	17.4
1988	17.3	18.3	18.3	14.1	17.3	20.3	25.3	22.9	24.5	22.2	20.0	17.9
1989	19.6	19.7	19.0	14.8	15.3	16.2	15.1	16.5	15.0	14.4	14.9	13.4
1990	13.6	14.2	15.2	16.8	19.7	16.8	18.1	17.1	17.1	16.6	16.8	17.2
1991	14.7	14.8	14.0	14.1	13.0	13.5	14.2	18.1	16.3	16.5	17.0	15.1
1992	16.0	20.0	19.2	19.7	18.8	18.9	21.1	19.5	20.2	20.0	21.7	18.7
1993	17.2	16.7	16.9	15.1	14.3	15.5	15.1	17.6	18.1	14.4	14.0	13.5
1994[2]	13.7	14.8	15.8	15.6	16.3	15.2	15.4	19.0	19.7	17.8	20.0	19.1

[1] Converted on basis 39.5 pounds frozen eggs equal 1 case   [2] Preliminary.   *Source: National Agricultural Statistics Service, U.S. Department of Agriculture*

Electric Power

According to the Energy Information Administration, total U.S. net generation of electricity in June 1994 was 264 billion kilowatthours, 6 percent more than the amount reported for June 1993. Temperatures (measured by cooling-degree days) were 20 percent warmer than those of June 1993, and 29 percent warmer than normal across the nation. This contributed to the higher generation levels seen during the month. For the January-June 1994 period, electric utility net generation was 1.424 trillion kilowatthours. Of the electricity provided during the first half of 1994, energy sources were varied. Coal accounted for 57 percent, petroleum 4 percent, gas 8.5 percent, hydroelectric 9.3 percent, nuclear 20.9 percent and other .3 percent. Other included geothermal, wood, wind, waste and solar. Net generation from coal-fired plants for the first half of 1994 was 811 billion kilowatthours, up almost 4 percent from the like period of 1993. Electricity generated from petroleum sources was almost 57 billion kilowatthours, up over 38 percent from 1993. Net generation from gas sources was 121 billion kilowatthours, up 13 percent. Electricity generated from nuclear sources in the January-June 1994 period was 298 billion kilowatthours, decreasing 2 percent from the previous year. Hydroelectric sources generated almost 134 billion kilowatthours during the first half of 1994, an 11 percent decline form 1993.

For the first six-months of 1994, electricity generation consumed 404 million short tons of coal, over 4 percent more than in 1993. Petroleum consumed in electricity generation reached over 94 million barrels, a substantial 40 percent increase from the like period of 1993. Gas consumed in electricity generation over the first half of 1994 was to 1.25 trillion cubic feet, 12 percent more than 1993.

Sales of electricity to residential customers during the very warm month of June 1994 were nearly 84 billion kilowatthours. This was a substantial increase over the June 1993 total of almost 77 billion kilowatthours. For the first half of 1994, residential customers consumed 494 billion kilowatthours, over 5 percent more than the like period of 1993. Commercial customers in June 1994 purchased 73 billion kilowatthours, or almost 8 percent more than in June 1993. Cumulative purchases for the first half of 1994 were 394 billion kilowatthours, or 5 percent more than 1993. In June 1994, industrial customers purchased over 86 billion kilowatthours of electricity, almost 2 percent more than in June 1993. Cumulative first half 1994 purchases were 490 billion kilowatthours, or nearly 2 percent more than in the like period of 1993.

The average cost of electricity for residential users in the January-June 1994 period was 8.2¢ per kilowatthour. For commercial customers, the average was 7.61¢ per kilowatthour, while industrial customers paid 4.7¢ per kilowatthour.

World Electricity Production (Monthly Average)   In Millions of Kilowatt Hours

Year	Australia	Canada	China	France	Germany	India	Italy	Japan	Poland	Rep. of Korea	Russia[3]	South Africa	Sweden	Ukraine[3]	United Kingdom	United States
1983	3,242	34,037	29,283	23,441	39,741	11,658	15,009	51,510	10,490	4,071	116,333	10,240	9,072	------	22,965	197,303
1984	9,412	36,499	31,417	25,596	41,908	13,053	14,962	54,048	11,275	4,484	124,340	10,133	10,273	------	23,368	206,609
1985	10,083	38,254	34,225	27,144	43,379	14,186	15,190	55,996	11,476	4,834	128,676	10,125	11,378	------	24,477	214,027
1986	10,518	39,049	37,458	28,586	43,474	15,626	15,749	55,981	11,691	4,167	133,244	12,210	11,502	------	24,846	216,610
1987	11,027	41,361	41,442	29,383	34,873	16,824	16,748	58,248	12,153	6,166	138,744	12,550	10,802	------	25,161	226,561
1988	11,592	42,164	49,460	30,456	35,228	18,427	16,931	62,811	12,028	7,122	142,090	13,062	12,451	------	25,761	239,875
1989	12,316	41,628	49,549	33,908	36,716	20,428	17,570	66,563	12,124	7,873	143,500	13,527	11,992	------	25,153	246,659
1990	12,923	40,169	51,500	35,011	37,433	22,025	18,074	71,439	11,361	8,972	139,455	12,270	12,204	------	26,581	250,979
1991	13,071	42,326	55,918	37,846	44,949	23,893	18,503	74,007	11,225	9,885	136,156	12,411	12,282	------	26,900	254,818
1992	13,260	41,803	61,562	38,522	44,761	25,081	18,854	74,611	11,070	10,914	------	12,385	12,187	------	27,240	256,209
1993[1]	13,595	42,591	67,723	35,728	37,722	26,317	18,182	65,959	11,256	12,036	79,382	13,075	11,883	19,083	26,834	240,184

[1] Preliminary.   [2] Estimate.   [3] Formerly part of the U.S.S.R.; data not reported separately until 1992.   *Source: United Nations*

Installed Capacity, Capability & Peak Load of the U.S. Electric Utility Industry   In Millions of Kilowatt Hours

	Total Electric Utility Industry	Hydro	Gas Turbine & Steam	Nuclear Power	Internal Combustion	Investor Owned	Cooperative	Sub-total Gov't.	Municipal Utilities	Federal	Power Districts, State Projects	Capability at Winter Peak Load	Non-Coincident Winter Peak Load	Capacity Margin Based on Non-Coincident Peak Load (%)	Total Electric Utility Industry Generation	Annual Peak Load Factor (%)
1984	672.5	80.6	516.5	70.5	4.8	514.9	24.7	132.9	36.7	63.3	32.8	622.1	436.4	25.3	2,416	61.7
1985	688.7	83.0	520.3	80.4	5.0	530.4	24.6	133.8	37.0	63.7	33.0	636.5	423.7	25.9	2,470	62.0
1986	707.7	85.2	524.1	92.4	5.9	544.2	26.4	137.1	38.6	63.9	34.6	646.7	422.9	24.8	2,487	60.7
1987	718.1	85.9	524.3	101.6	6.2	552.8	26.4	138.9	39.4	64.7	34.9	663.0	448.3	23.4	2,572	60.8
1988	723.9	86.9	526.6	103.4	7.0	557.8	26.4	139.7	40.4	64.8	34.5	676.9	466.5	20.0	2,704	59.5
1989	730.9	87.5	529.1	106.7	7.5	562.1	26.4	142.4	40.7	67.2	34.5	685.2	496.4	22.3	2,784	62.2
1990	735.1	87.2	531.1	108.0	8.7	568.8	26.3	139.9	40.1	65.4	34.4	696.8	484.0	20.4	2,808	60.4
1991	740.0	88.7	534.1	108.4	8.8	573.0	26.5	140.5	40.4	65.6	34.5	703.2	485.4	20.2	2,825	60.9
1992[1]	741.7	89.7	534.5	107.9	9.6	572.9	26.0	142.7	41.6	66.1	35.0	707.8	493.0	21.1	2,797	61.1
1993[1]	745.0	89.8	537.7	107.8	9.6	576.0	26.1	143.0	41.7	66.1	35.1	712.0	521.7	17.1	2,883	61.0

[1] Preliminary.   *Source: Edison Electric Institute*

Available Electricity & Energy Sales in the United States   In Billions of Kilowatt Hours

	Net Generation — Electric Utility Industry								Sales to Ultimate Customers						
Year	Total[2]	Hydro	Natural Gas	Coal	Fuel Oil	Nuclear	Other Sources[3]	Total	Total Million $	Total	Resi-dential	Inter-Depart-mental	Com-mercial	Indust-rial	Street & Highway Lighting	Other Public Author-ities	Rail-ways & Rail-roads
1980	2,286	276	346	1,162	246	251	5.5	2,354	95,462	2,126	734.4	6.4	524.1	793.8	14.8	48.3	4.3
1981	2,295	261	346	1,204	206	273	6.1	2,359	111,001	2,151	730.5	6.2	521.7	819.6	14.7	53.7	4.2
1982	2,241	309	305	1,192	146	283	5.2	2,302	121,584	2,100	732.7	5.4	517.0	770.4	14.2	55.7	4.3
1983	2,310	332	274	1,259	144	294	6.5	2,368	129,589	2,160	750.3	5.4	545.6	783.0	13.9	57.3	4.3
1984	2,416	321	297	1,342	120	328	8.6	2,488	143,093	2,281	782.6	5.8	578.1	835.5	14.2	59.9	4.5
1985	2,470	281	292	1,402	100	384	10.7	2,568	149,162	2,306	792.9	5.3	605.9	820.3	14.6	62.2	4.7
1986	2,487	291	249	1,386	137	414	11.5	2,599	152,467	2,355	820.0	5.2	629.0	819.0	15.0	61.9	4.7
1987	2,572	250	273	1,464	118	455	12.3	2,719	155,700	2,435	846.5	4.5	658.4	843.7	14.4	63.0	4.9
1988	2,704	223	253	1,541	149	527	12.0	2,879	162,388	2,554	886.1	4.2	697.8	881.8	14.6	64.6	5.1
1989	2,784	265	267	1,554	158	529	11.3	2,985	169,627	2,621	898.8	4.3	715.9	912.8	14.6	69.3	5.3
1990	2,808	280	264	1,560	117	577	10.7	3,041	176,468	2,684	915.8	4.2	738.9	931.9	15.2	72.8	5.3
1991	1,825	276	264	1,551	111	613	10.1	3,100	185,118	2,764	948.8	2.6	753.3	934.9	15.6	76.1	5.3
1992	2,797	240	264	1,576	89	619	10.2	3,107	187,283	2,735	929.3	2.6	755.7	949.3	15.8	77.2	5.2
1993[1]	2,883	265	259	1,639	100	610	9.6	3,210	196,432	2,836	990.1	2.4	781.8	963.7	16.2	76.6	5.1

[1] Preliminary.   [2] Includes internal combustion.   [3] Includes electricity produced from geothermal, wood, waste, wind, solar, etc.
Source: Edison Electric Insititute

Electric Power Production by Electric Utilities in the U.S.   In Millions of Kilowatt Hours

Year	Jan.	Feb.	Mar.	Apr.	May	June	July	Aug.	Sept.	Oct.	Nov.	Dec.	Total
1980	200,005	188,715	187,464	168,720	175,734	189,430	216,776	215,393	191,485	178,555	178,550	195,613	2,286,439
1981	206,467	179,613	185,553	172,545	177,806	202,702	220,373	210,403	186,838	181,352	175,570	195,590	2,294,812
1982	209,403	180,299	187,687	172,580	177,147	186,128	210,584	205,656	180,662	172,966	173,377	184,722	2,241,211
1983	195,579	172,479	182,488	170,372	174,392	191,048	220,165	229,957	195,604	182,931	183,949	212,319	2,310,285
1984	216,632	189,564	200,107	181,084	192,217	209,648	221,245	229,296	195,198	190,936	190,380	199,996	2,416,304
1985	227,856	198,242	194,970	184,877	196,790	205,363	226,722	226,050	202,499	194,789	192,427	219,255	2,469,841
1986	217,470	192,336	196,834	186,074	197,315	215,015	242,672	225,166	206,692	197,754	196,432	213,551	2,487,310
1987	222,749	194,034	201,849	189,496	206,074	225,589	247,915	247,645	213,008	203,009	200,258	220,500	2,572,127
1988	237,897	216,937	214,013	196,000	208,371	232,747	257,461	267,693	220,179	210,608	209,593	232,752	2,704,250
1989	232,747	219,826	226,742	208,042	220,124	235,689	257,050	258,687	227,150	219,910	219,300	259,038	2,784,304
1990	237,289	212,880	226,034	211,070	222,908	249,175	266,375	268,527	237,017	224,694	213,748	237,434	2,808,151
1991	248,455	210,821	221,400	209,004	234,373	248,427	271,976	268,115	233,885	223,430	221,377	233,760	2,825,023
1992	243,970	217,761	224,665	210,837	220,355	236,842	266,148	255,203	234,760	221,289	221,263	244,126	2,797,219
1993	245,782	224,617	234,801	211,374	222,396	249,633	282,292	279,132	236,603	223,629	225,855	246,412	2,882,525
1994[1]	261,035	225,051	231,144	214,813	227,681	263,843	278,137	274,392	237,953	227,975	224,569	242,760	2,909,352

[1] Preliminary.   *Source: Energy Information Administration, U.S. Department of Energy*

Use of Fuels for Electric Generation in the United States

Year	Consumption of Fuel			Total Fuel in Coal Equivalent[3] (Thousand Short Tons)	Net Generation by Fuels[4] (Million Kw. Hr.)	Pounds of Coal Per Kw. Hr. (Pounds)	Cost of Fossil-Fuel at Electric Utilities ¢ Mil. BTU	Average Cost of Fuel Per Kw. Hr. (¢)	Heat Rate BTU Per Kw. Hr.	Cost Per Million BTU Consumed (¢)
	Coal (Thousand Short Tons)	Fuel Oil (Thousand Barrels)[2]	Gas (Million Cubic Feet)							
1980	569,453	420,214	3,681,595	916,952	1,753,749	.980	192.8	2.07	10,489	197.0
1981	596,936	351,111	3,640,154	922,133	1,755,401	.992	225.6	2.42	10,506	230.2
1982	593,666	249,771	3,225,518	858,869	1,644,062	.996	224.9	2.46	10,517	234.0
1983	625,211	245,497	2,910,767	867,621	1,678,021	.993	220.6	2.40	10,547	227.1
1984	664,399	204,479	3,111,342	909,156	1,758,882	.990	219.1	2.41	10,385	232.0
1985	693,841	173,414	3,044,083	926,793	1,794,276	.990	209.4	2.27	10,429	217.7
1986	685,056	230,482	2,602,370	907,720	1,770,925	.989	175.0	1.92	10,423	184.5
1987	717,894	199,378	2,844,051	944,420	1,854,895	.981	170.6	1.84	10,354	177.7
1988	758,372	248,096	2,635,613	984,969	1,942,353	.984	164.3	1.76	10,328	170.7
1989	766,888	267,451	2,787,012	1,004,964	1,978,577	.987	167.5	1.79	10,312	174.0
1990	773,549	196,054	2,787,332	988,300	1,940,712	.997	168.9	1.80	10,366	174.1
1991	772,268	184,886	2,789,014	987,469	1,926,801	.996	160.3	1.75	10,322	169.6
1992	779,860	147,335	2,765,608	983,484	1,928,683	.990	159.0	1.72	10,340	166.6
1993[1]	813,508	162,454	2,682,440	1,017,086	1,997,605	.993	159.5	1.72	10,351	166.6

[1] Preliminary.   [2] 42-gallon barrels.   [3] Beginning in 1980, coal equivalents are calculated on the basis of Btu instead of generation data.   [4] Excludes wood & waste fuels.   *Source: Edison Electric Institute*

Fertilizer

The three primary fertilizer chemicals in the U.S. are nitrogen, phosphorus and potassium. These chemicals provide the basic nutrients to plants. The basic nitrogen fertilizer is ammonia, which is comprised of natural gas and nitrogen. Ammonia can be applied in liquid form below the surface of the soil or converted into solid nitrogenous fertilizers. Made from phosphate rock and sulfuric acid, phosphoric acid is the source of most phosphatic acid fertilizer. Diammonium phosphate is the only major fertilizer containing the two basic nutrients, nitrogen and phosphatic fertilizer. Potassium chloride, or potash is the major potassium fertilizer. Nitrogen-based fertilizers account for more than one-half of total fertilizer consumption.

According to the U.S. Bureau of Mines, U.S. apparent domestic consumption of ammonia in 1993 was just over 15 million tonnes. Fertilizer materials account for about 80 percent of domestic ammonia demand. Urea and ammonium nitrate find extensive use in the fertilizer sector. Anhydrous ammonia continued to be the leading direct application fertilizer material in the U.S. Urea-ammonium nitrate fertilizers that contain 28 percent to 32 percent nitrogen have increased in popularity due to their safe handling and storage characteristics. In 1993, ammonia and ammonia derivatives accounted for 10.3 million tonnes, or over one-half of the primary fertilizer nutrient market in the U.S.

During 1993, a 13 percent decline in direct application ammonia consumption, due to wet weather in the Midwest, was almost offset by increases in direct application solid urea, urea-ammonium nitrate fertilizer solutions and granular bulk-blend fertilizers.

In 1993, global ammonia production fell sharply for the fourth year in a row to 91.5 million tonnes. Production fell in almost every part of the world except for the Middle East. Ammonia production has been declining most in the countries of Eastern Europe and the former Soviet Union. Anhydrous ammonia is produced in about 79 countries.

U.S. production of phosphate rock declined substantially in 1993 as sales of phosphate fertilizer products declined. Domestic production of phosphate rock declined by 24 percent in 1993, while world production fell 10 percent. World trade in phosphate rock declined by 7 percent in 1993, while U.S. phosphate rock exports fell 14 percent. The reason for the decline was reduced demand for raw material, due primarily to the closure of a number of phosphoric acid plants in Western Europe. Exports of diammonium phosphate, phosphoric acid, triple superphosphate and elemental phosphorus also declined.

The decline in world production of phosphate rock was a result of lower phosphate fertilizer consumption, notably in China and the former Soviet Union. However, U.S. farmers were expected to use more fertilizer after the huge floods of 1993.

Domestic potash production, in terms of potassium oxide content, declined about 12 percent to 1.5 million tonnes. Sales of agricultural potash, in terms of potassium oxide, were 4.33 million tonnes. World potash production was estimated by the U.S. Bureau of Mines to have declined about 13 percent from 1992.

FUTURES MARKET

Diammonium phosphate futures are traded on the Chicago Board of Trade (CBOT).

World Production of Ammonia   In Thousands of Metric Tons of Contained Nitrogen

Year	Bulgaria	Canada	China	France	Germany	India	Indonesia	Italy	Japan	Mexico	Netherlands	Poland	Romania	Russia[3]	United Kingdom	United States	Total
1988	1,342	3,289	16,500	1,832	2,980	6,205	2,67	1,561	1,524	2,067	2,695	2,338	2,795	20,200	1,105	12,544	99,265
1989	1,326	3,339	17,000	1,476	2,932	6,661	2,526	1,446	1,539	2,100	2,901	2,360	2,736	19,400	1,037	12,280	99,331
1990	1,309	3,054	17,500	1,586	2,371	7,010	2,789	1,197	1,531	2,164	3,188	1,962	1,785	18,200	1,148	12,680	97,160
1991	1,093	3,016	18,000	1,604	2,123	7,132	2,706	1,147	1,553	2,221	3,033	1,531	1,800	17,100	1,011	12,803	94,472
1992	910	3,104	18,000	1,848	2,113	7,038	2,688	1,098	1,60	2,203	2,588	1,490	1,100	8,786	869	13,643	93,253
1993[1]	750	3,410	19,000	1,800	2,000	7,124	2,888	729	1,447	1,758	2,500	1,500	1,100	8,138	873	12,865	91,497
1994[2]		3,550		1,500	2,000	7,300		850	1,500	2,100	2,500				870	13,050	92,000

[1] Preliminary.   [2] Estimate.   [3] Formerly part of the U.S.S.R.; data not reported separately until 1992.   *Source: U.S. Bureau of Mines*

U.S. Salient Statistics of Nitrogen[3] (Ammonia)   In Thousands of Metric Tons

Year	Net Import Reliance as a % of Apparent Consumption	Production[3] (Fixed) Fertilizer	Non-fertilizer	Total	Imports[4] (Fixed)	Exports	Nitrogen[5] Compounds Produced	Consumption	Ammonia	Stocks, Dec. 31 Fixed Nitrogen Compounds	Ammonia Consumption (Apparent)	Average Price ($ Per Tonne) Urea F.O.B. Gulf[6] Coast	F.O.B. Corn Belt	Ammonium Nitrate: F.O.B. Corn Belt	Ammonia F.O.B. Gulf Coast
1986[7]	13	10,852	1,057	11,909	2,048	531	8,100	8,147	1,507	NA	13,714	75-78	90-110	100-120	75
1987	13	10,903	1,101	12,004	2,38	769	8,468	8,514	955	NA	13,783	114-117	125-135	100-120	95
1988	14	11,400	1,144	12,544	2,751	582	9,279	9,333	925	705	14,742	139-145	150-155	128-135	109
1989	17	11,131	1,148	12,2 0	2,861	346	9,634	9,687	849	787	14,871	139-145	110-120	105-115	104
1990	15	11,573	1,107	12,680	2,673	482	9,851	9,902	797	1,451	14,923	155-156	155-165	120-125	106
1991	14	11,559	1,244	12,803	2,742	580	9,770	9,815	936	1,607	14,826	142-143	146-160	108-130	117
1992	14	12,294	1,349	13,643	2,690	354	10,404	10,448	1,059	1,789	15,856	142-146	149-160	138-149	106
1993[1]	17	11,226	1,639	12,865	2,657	378	9,618	9,662	855	1,625	15,348	139-141	141-165	138-149	121
1994[2]	18			13,050	3,100	200			800		16,000				215

[1] Preliminary.   [2] Estimate.   [3] Anhydrous ammonia, synthetic.   [4] For consumption.   [5] Major downstream nitrogen compounds.   [6] Granular.   [7] Reported in short tons before 1987.   NA = Not available.   *Source: U.S. Bureau of Mines*

World Production of Phosphate Rock, Basic Slag & Guano   In Thousands of Metric Tons (Gross Weight)

Year	Algeria	Brazil	China	Egypt	Israel	Jordan	Morocco	Nauru Island	Russia[3]	Senegal	Syria	Togo	Tunisia	United States	World Total
1985	1,207	4,214	6,970	1,074	4,076	6,067	20,737	1,508	33,750	1,814	1,270	2,452	4,530	50,835	148,849
1986	1,203	4,509	6,700	1,271	3,673	6,249	21,178	1,494	33,900	1,850	1,606	2,314	5,951	38,710	138,869
1987	1,073	4,777	15,000	1,175	3,798	6,800	21,300	1,376	34,100	1,874	1,986	2,644	6,390	40,954	151,962
1988	1,332	4,672	17,000	1,154	3,479	6,611	25,015	1,541	37,000	2,326	2,186	3,464	6,103	45,389	166,436
1989	1,124	3,655	20,000	1,355	3,922	6,900	18,067	1,181	37,500	2,273	2,256	3,355	6,610	49,817	167,342
1990	1,128	2,968	21,550	1,151	3,516	6,082	21,396	926	36,800	2,147	1,633	2,314	6,258	46,343	162,783
1991	1,090	3,280	22,000	1,660	3,370	4,433	17,900	530	28,400	1,741	1,359	2,965	6,352	48,096	150,731
1992	1,136	2,825	23,000	2,008	3,595	4,296	19,146	747	11,500	2,284	1,266	2,100	6,400	46,965	147,017
1993[1]	1,136	3,000	24,000	2,008	3,590	4,200	18,305	600	10,400	2,200	1,275	2,100	6,400	35,494	132,629
1994[2]			24,000		3,600	4,500	19,500		8,500	2,000		2,000	6,200	41,000	130,000

[1] Preliminary.   [2] Estimate.   [3] Formerly part of the U.S.S.R.; data not reported separately until 1992.   *Source: U.S. Bureau of Mines*

U.S. Salient Statistics of Phosphate Rock   In Thousands of Metric Tons

Year	Mine Production	Marketable Production	Value Million $	Imports for Consumption	Exports	Apparent Consumption	Stocks, Dec. 31 (Producer)	Price - $ Avg. Per Metric Ton (F.O.B. Mine)	Avg. Price of Florida & North Carolina --$ Tonne - F.O.B. Mine (-60% to +74%)-- Domestic	Export	Average
1985	175,227	50,835	1,236	34	9,136	37,532	15,534	24.31	23.08	26.72	23.81
1986	135,683	40,320	897	528	7,848	34,456	13,277	22.25	21.64	25.02	22.31
1987	148,426	40,954	793	464	8,454	35,683	10,884	19.37	18.93	22.87	19.77
1988	162,299	45,389	888	676	8,092	41,025	9,323	19.56	18.29	25.24	19.56
1989	170,268	49,817	1,084	705	7,842	42,143	11,027	21.76	20.65	28.67	21.76
1990	151,277	46,343	1,075	451	6,238	43,967	8,912	23.20	22.44	30.43	23.55
1991	154,485	48,096	1,109	552	5,082	40,177	10,168	23.06	22.67	31.69	23.69
1992	154,936	46,965	1,058	1,530	3,723	42,920	12,612	22.53	22.47	31.69	23.32
1993[1]	106,790	35,494	759	1,434	3,198	38,287	9,215	21.38	21.26	28.11	21.89
1994[2]		41,000		1,500	3,400	42,000	6,300	22.00			

[1] Preliminary.   [2] Estimate.   *Source: U.S. Bureau of Mines*

World Production of Marketable Potash   In Thousands of Metric Tons (K₂O Equivalent)

Year	Belarus[3]	Brazil	Canada	Chile	China	France	Germany	Israel	Italy	Jordan	Russia[3]	Spain	United Kingdom	United States	World Total
1985	------	------	6,661	21	40	1,750	6,048	1,200	205	561	10,367	659	343	1,296	29,151
1986	------	18	6,753	20	40	1,617	5,646	1,255	158	660	10,228	795	396	1,202	28,788
1987	------	62	7,668	23	40	1,539	5,709	1,253	178	734	10,888	741	429	1,262	30,526
1988	------	54	8,154	25	22	1,502	5,800	1,244	95	785	11,301	855	460	1,521	31,820
1989	------	97	7,333	45	42	1,195	5,388	1,273	112	792	10,200	741	462	1,595	29,276
1990	------	66	6,989	50	29	1,292	4,960	1,311	68	841	9,000	686	488	1,713	27,493
1991	------	101	7,406	55	32	1,129	3,855	1,320	31	818	8,560	585	495	1,749	26,136
1992	3,311	85	7,270	55	21	1,141	3,473	1,320	86	808	3,454	594	524	1,705	24,044
1993[1]	1,947	173	6,841	55	25	1,000	3,250	1,300	80	800	2,597	600	530	1,506	20,864

[1] Preliminary.   [2] Estimate.   [3] Formerly part of the U.S.S.R.; data not reported separately until 1992.   *Source: U.S. Bureau of Mines*

U.S. Salient Statistics of Potash   In Thousands of Metric Tons (K₂O Equivalent)

Year	Net Import as a % of Consumption	Production	Sale by Producers	Value Million $	Imports for Consumption	Exports	Apparent Consumption	Producer Stocks, Dec. 31	------- $ Per Ton ------- Avg. Value Per ton of Product - $	Average Value of K₂O Equiv.	Average Price[3] $ Per Tonne
1985	76	1,296	1,266	178.4	4,593	513	5,346	336	71.22	140.89	96
1986	75	1,202	1,147	144.9	4,212	547	4,843	378	63.24	126.28	82
1987	75	1,262	1,485	197.7	4,073	470	5,088	155	67.98	131.73	93
1988	71	1,521	1,427	240.3	4,217	380	5,264	248	85.75	168.37	132
1989	65	1,595	1,536	271.5	3,410	446	7,680	307	90.28	176.74	137
1990	68	1,713	1,716	303.3	4,164	470	9,327	303	89.46	176.80	130
1991	69	1,749	1,709	304.5	4,158	624	8,933	343	91.52	178.20	131
1992	68	1,705	1,766	334.4	4,248	663	9,150	283	96.45	189.36	134
1993[1]	72	1,506	1,484	286.0	4,363	415	9,300	305	94.36	192.72	124
1994[2]	74	1,425			4,400	400	5,390	340			128

[1] Preliminary.   [2] Estimate.   [3] Unit of K₂O, standard 60% muriate F.O.B. mine.   *Source: U.S. Bureau of Mines*

Fish

Domestic fish supplies come mainly from landings by the wild catch industry and imports. Aquaculture or domestically raised fish, have become an increasingly important industry in the U.S. According to the United States Department of Agriculture (USDA), U.S. fishery landings in 1993 totaled just under nine billion pounds. Of the total, pollack made up 36 percent, menhaden 22 percent, Pacific salmon 10 percent, flounder 7 percent and tuna less than 1 percent. Shellfish landings were 1.5 billion pounds with crabs making up 41 percent, shrimp 20 percent, squid 11 percent and clams 10 percent.

The aquaculture industry has been growing because of declining supplies of wild stocks of many seafood species. Other factors in its growth have been the demand for year round supplies and specific qualities and appearance. Cited examples are the trout and catfish industries. Wild harvest of these species could not possibly have supplied enough fish to meet demand. The depletion of wild seafood stocks is expected to continue, which should support the development of the aquaculture industry.

According to the USDA, one area of growth in aquaculture is to aid in the expansion of the harvest of wild stocks of fish. Using aquaculture methods, hatcheries can raise large numbers of young fish, which can then be released to form larger wild stocks. This is currently taking place in Alaska, where the massive release of hatchery raised smolts has enabled the salmon industry to expand its harvests. Aquaculture researchers are looking at the possibility of using a similar approach, massive releases of hatchery raised fish, to increase the stock of other marine species.

Catfish production was expected to remain below year-ago levels over the remainder of 1994 and into 1995. The forecast is based on July 1, 1994 grower inventory estimates. At the beginning of the third-quarter of 1994, grower-held inventories were down in a number of categories. Low inventories, as well as, low stocks of finished products held by processors means that market-size catfish will be relatively tight in the last half of 1994 and the first half of 1995. For the first eight-months of 1994, roundweight processed catfish were 291 million pounds. For the same period of 1993, the total was 311 million pounds. Total processor sales of catfish during the January-August 1994 period was 147 million pounds, compared to nearly 160 million pounds in the same period of 1993. In 1994, there were 1,351 catfish operations in the U.S., 100 less than the year before. Total water surface was 153,640 acres, up almost 3 percent from 1993. The average water surface size per catfish operation in 1994 was 114 acres.

U.S. Fishery Products -- Supply   In Millions of Pounds[2]

Year	Grand Total	-For Human Food- Finfish	Shellfish[3]	For Industrial Use[4]	Total	% of Grand Total	-For Human Food- Finfish	Shellfish[3]	For Industrial Use[4]	Total	% of Grand Total	For Finfish	Shellfish[3]	For Industrial Use[4]
					Domestic Catch					Imports				
1983	12,252	6,358	2,055	3,939	6,439	52.1	2,351	887	3,201	5,913	47.9	4,007	1,168	738
1984	12,552	6,303	2,195	4,054	6,438	51.3	2,348	972	3,118	6,114	48.7	3,955	1,223	936
1985	15,150	6,991	2,346	5,813	6,258	41.3	2,273	1,021	2,964	8,892	58.7	4,718	1,325	2,849
1986	14,368	7,087	2,533	4,748	6,031	42.0	2,240	1,153	2,638	8,337	58.0	4,847	1,380	2,110
1987	15,744	7,919	2,642	5,183	6,896	43.8	2,769	1,177	2,950	8,848	56.2	5,150	1,465	2,233
1988	14,628	7,786	2,719	4,123	7,192	49.2	3,306	1,282	2,604	7,436	50.8	4,480	1,437	1,519
1989	15,485	9,735	2,533	3,217	8,463	54.7	4,897	1,307	2,259	7,022	45.3	4,838	1,226	958
1990	16,349	10,120	2,542	3,687	9,404	57.5	5,747	1,294	2,363	6,945	42.5	4,373	1,248	1,324
1991	16,364	10,186	2,834	3,344	9,484	58.0	5,564	1,467	2,453	6,879	42.0	4,622	1,367	890
1992[1]	16,106	10,297	2,945	2,864	9,637	59.8	6,182	1,436	2,019	6,469	40.2	4,115	1,509	845

[1] Preliminary.   [2] Live weight, except percent.   [3] For univalue and bivalues mollusks (conchs, clams, oysters, scallops, etc.) the weight of meats, excluding the shell is reported.   [4] Fish meal and sea herring.   Source: Fisheries Statistics Division, U.S. Department of Commerce

U.S. Fisheries -- Landings of Principal Species   In Millions of Pounds

Year	Cod, Atlantic	Flounder	Halibut	Herring, Sea	Menhaden	Pollock	Salmon, Pacific	Tuna	Whiting	Clams (Meats)	Crabs	Lobsters (American)	Oysters (Meats)	Scallops (Meats)	Shrimp
1986	61	169	78	210	2,391	185	659	88	40	145	356	46	41	22	400
1987	59	200	76	207	2,712	598	562	100	35	134	386	46	40	41	363
1988	76	229	82	222	2,086	1,290	606	111	36	132	456	49	32	43	331
1989	78	202	75	209	1,989	2,385	786	89	39	138	458	53	30	41	352
1990	96	255	70	221	1,962	3,129	733	62	44	139	499	61	29	42	346
1991	93	405	66	230	1,977	2,873	783	36	37	134	650	63	32	40	320
1992[1]	62	646	67	282	1,644	2,968	716	57	36	142	624	56	36	34	338
1993[1]		599		216	1,983	3,270	888	55		148	604		34	19	293

[1] Preliminary.   Source: Fisheries Statistics Division, U.S. Department of Commerce

U.S. Fisheries: Quantity & Value of Domestic Catch & Consumption & World Fish Oil Production

Year	Fresh & Frozen	Canned	Cured	For Meal, Oil, Etc.	Total	For Human Food	For Industrial Products	Ex-vessel Value[3] Million $	Average Price ¢ Lb.	Fish Per Capita Consumption Lbs.	World[2] Fish Oil Production 1,000 Tonnes
	--- Disposition ---			Millions Pounds							
1983	2,304	1,087	80	2,968	6,439	3,238	3,201	2,355	36.6	13.3	1,482
1984	2,336	1,128	82	2,892	6,438	3,320	3,118	2,350	36.5	14.1	1,369
1985	2,725	749	70	2,714	6,258	3,294	2,964	2,326	37.2	15.0	1,517
1986	2,487	1,134	60	2,350	6,031	3,393	2,638	2,763	45.8	15.4	1,384
1987	3,157	1,009	89	2,641	6,896	3,946	2,950	3,115	45.2	16.1	1,544
1988	3,813	1,017	86	2,276	7,192	4,588	2,604	3,520	48.9	15.1	1,613
1989	5,585	798	128	1,952	8,463	6,204	2,259	3,238	38.3	15.6	1,393
1990	6,501	751	126	2,026	9,404	7,041	2,363	3,522	37.4	15.0	1,406
1991	6,541	674	119	2,150	9,484	7,031	2,453	3,308	34.9	14.8	1,128
1992[1]	7,288	543	110	1,696	9,637	7,618	2,019	3,678	38.2	14.7	1,119

[1] Preliminary. [2] Crop year on a marketing year basis. [3] At the Dock Prices. *Source: Fisheries Statistics Division, U.S. Department of Commerce*

Imports of Seafood Products into the U.S.   In Thousands of Pounds

Year	Atlantic Salmon	Pacific Salmon	Shrimp	Trout	Atlantic Salmon	Pacific Salmon	Shrimp	Oysters[1]	Mussels[2]	Clams[3]	Canned Salmon	Prepared Shrimp[4]
	Fresh				Frozen							
1990	35,948	43,296	11,193	4,866	6,362	10,293	464,529	18,971	5,853	10,267	1,371	25,622
1991	39,709	47,487	12,206	3,331	3,687	8,245	499,859	17,914	6,595	6,975	990	27,531
1992	48,843	33,734	8,348	5,820	5,302	8,627	558,580	16,800	7,657	6,192	964	28,434
1993	62,860	32,091	11,649	4,229	7,714	11,151	556,213	17,293	9,658	5,818	419	33,116

[1] Oysters fresh or prepared. [2] Mussels fresh or prepared. [3] Clams, fresh or prepared. [4] Shrimp, canned, breaded or prepare.
Source: Bureau of Census, U.S. Department of Commerce

Exports of Seafood Products into the U.S.   In Thousands of Pounds

Year	Atlantic Salmon	Pacific Salmon	Shrimp	Trout	Atlantic Salmon	Pacific Salmon	Shrimp	Oysters[1]	Mussels[2]	Clams[3]	Canned Salmon	Prepared Shrimp[4]
	Fresh				Frozen							
1990	0	22,372	1,971	1,336	112	281,289	18,071	1,010	1,508	3,893	49,401	11,601
1991	473	14,389	2,927	1,040	123	195,821	14,980	929	1,665	4,405	66,025	9,937
1992	1,396	20,446	3,558	1,201	406	239,114	18,082	1,105	2,317	4,999	85,369	11,134
1993	4,018	23,115	2,776	955	373	256,790	16,524	1,454	2,291	4,217	84,520	11,539

[1] Oysters fresh or prepared. [2] Mussels fresh or prepared. [3] Clams, fresh or prepared. [4] Shrimp, canned, breaded or prepare.
Source: Bureau of Census, U.S. Department of Commerce

World Production of Fish Meal   In Thousands of Metric Tons

Year	Chile	Spain	Denmark	EC-12	FSU-12	Iceland	Japan	Mexico	Norway	Peru	South Africa	Thailand	United States	World Total
1983-4	943.8	84.8	322.9	542.9	659.0	132.3	1,174.3	58.2	307.5	423.8	130.4	220.1	417.8	5,630.2
1984-5	1,056.2	87.5	290.7	508.9	658.6	166.9	1,181.6	73.0	263.0	567.7	120.0	221.6	410.9	6,064.8
1985-6	1,169.0	88.7	316.7	523.1	725.3	181.3	1,132.9	84.2	200.2	965.0	122.2	215.9	366.3	6,526.5
1986-7	1,073.2	88.7	268.0	469.1	761.1	202.0	1,073.0	100.3	164.0	1,008.4	260.7	219.9	389.4	6,554.4
1987-8	1,066.0	83.4	306.0	538.9	768.8	184.3	1,042.5	84.1	193.2	892.6	215.7	237.2	346.1	6,436.7
1988-9	1,305.2	128.0	340.6	579.5	754.1	181.4	977.4	86.4	196.3	1,405.9	151.7	260.8	338.8	7,002.9
1989-90	1,124.6	129.6	256.4	499.0	705.0	140.9	1,000.8	85.0	166.8	1,180.4	103.8	284.9	299.5	6,341.2
1990-1	1,144.2	130.6	302.6	544.7	643.9	87.1	841.8	80.1	221.2	1,308.5	87.9	292.9	310.4	6,280.2
1991-2[1]	1,322.1	122.8	351.7	585.4	547.1	163.9	534.6	84.9	240.4	1,095.6	150.3	255.3	312.2	6,016.2
1992-3[2]	1,091.2	112.0	299.1	522.1	490.0	204.6	405.0	88.0	250.8	1,767.3	128.3	245.0	327.6	6,249.3
1993-4[3]	1,250.0	110.0	345.0	565.2	418.0	178.0	440.0	90.0	215.0	1,550.0	115.0	255.0	315.0	6,130.0

[1] Preliminary. [2] Estimate. [3] Forecast. *Source: The Oil World*

Flaxseed and Linseed Oil

The United States Department of Agriculture (UDSA) lists flaxseed as a minor oilseed, with recent crop year production totals of about 3 million bushels. Linseed oil is derived from the flaxseed, and annual production has average only about 165,000 short tons since 1990.

The area planted to U.S. flaxseed production has been falling for several years with little sign of any trend reversal. Planted acreage for the 1994/95 crop of 189,000 acres was down 8 percent from 1993/94. Acreage in the mid-1980s averaged more than 600,000 acres, less than one-half the acreage of the 1970s. Production in 1994/95 of 3.3 million bushels compares with 3.5 million bushels in 1993/94. Annual production in the mid-1980s averaged about 8 million bushels and over 15 million bushels in the early 1970s. The U.S crop is produced mostly in the Northern Plains states with North Dakota the largest producer. The crop year begins on June 1.

A stronger demand for linseed oil in 1994/95 was expected to marginally lift the flaxseed crush to 9 million bushels, more than twice U.S. production. Imported seed, mostly from Canada, covered the shortfall. A dramatic shift in U.S. foreign trade of flaxseed developed since the mid-1970s when the U.S. was net exporter of flaxseed, at times by a substantial margin. The U.S. is now a net importer with a near record large 6.4 million bushels in 1994/95, while exports hover at a paltry 150,000 bushels. The large imports will help to supplement the 1994/95 carryin of approximately 1.2 million bushels, down from 1.5 million bushels in the previous year.

U.S. demand for linseed oil in 1994/95 of 180 million pounds compares with 173 million pounds in 1993/94, and 158 million pounds in 1992/93. Linseed oil is used as a drying agent in paint. Although its use has fallen in-line with the acceptance of water based latex paints, overall demand for paint tends to reflect the strength in housing starts, which in 1994 was increasing with the economy's recovery. Still, U.S. demand for linseed oil for domestic and export apparently peaked approximately 20 years, when domestic usage totaled 541 million pounds and exports totaled 256 million pounds. Since then, exports have fallen drastically, averaging only 10 million pounds to 12 million pounds since the mid-1980s, with 8 million pounds forecast for 1994/95.

Canada is the world's largest flaxseed producer, accounting for almost one-third of total production of approximately two million tonnes. China is the second largest producer followed by India and Argentina.

The average price received by U.S. farmer for flaxseed in 1994/95 was expected to average between $3.60 per bushel to $4.20 per bushel, versus the year earlier average of $4.20 per bushel. Linseed oil prices in 1994/95 were forecast between 27¢ per pound to 36¢ per pound, and compare with 32.5¢ per pound in 1993/94, basis Minneapolis.

Futures Markets

Flaxseed futures are traded on the Winnipeg Commodity Exchange (WCE). Prices are quoted in Canadian dollars per metric ton.

World Production of Flaxseed   In Thousands of Metric Tons

Crop Year	Argentina	Australia	Bangladesh	Canada	China	Czechoslovakia	Egypt	France	Hungary	India	Poland	Romania	Turkey	United States	Uruguay	Former USSR	World Total
1984-5	626	6	8	694	427	15	20	29	9	389	18	35	2	178	7	248	2,316
1985-6	460	12	8	902	535	15	22	34	7	380	18	36	5	211	6	201	2,350
1986-7	622	9	8	1,026	485	15	19	24	6	317	15	32	4	293	3	233	2,658
1987-8	535	8	43	701	400	10	29	21	20	393	11	38	4	189	5	228	2,755
1988-9	446	3	43	328	490	12	28	32	11	361	12	38	3	41	5	220	2,215
1989-90	526	2	47	498	400	16	21	31	11	326	12	49	3	31	4	227	2,352
1990-1	458	4	48	889	535	16	28	34	10	339	11	53	2	97	6	197	2,923
1991-2	341	5	55	635	410	14	24	26	13	292	5	23	1	158	8	140	2,458
1992-3[1]	177	5	49	334	430	14	21	29	10	268	2	18	1	84	4	130	1,969
1993-4[2]	112	8	49	627	430	12	22	27	11	330	2	28	1	88	2	120	2,197
1994-5[3]	129	6	50	960	420	12	23	35	11	345	2	27	1	74	3	115	2,435

[1] Preliminary.   [2] Estimate.   [3] Forecast.   *Source: The Oil World*

U.S. Supply and Distribution of Flaxseed   In Thousands of Bushels

Crop Year Beginning June	Planted	Harvested	Yield Per Acre Bushels	Beginning Stocks	Production	Imports	Total Supply	Seed	Crush	Exports	Residual	Total Distribution
	---- 1,000 Acres ----											
1984-5	555	538	13	1,716	7,022	3,796	12,534	511	9,935	238	201	10,885
1985-6	620	584	14	1,649	8,293	2,927	12,869	517	10,313	250	160	11,240
1986-7	720	683	17	1,629	11,538	2,224	15,391	362	10,000	1,448	280	12,090
1987-8	470	463	16	3,301	7,444	2,925	13,671	223	10,800	156	167	11,346
1988-9	275	226	7	2,325	1,615	6,730	10,670	158	8,500	764	-59	9,363
1989-90	195	163	8	1,307	1,215	7,260	9,782	211	8,250	1,054	23	9,538
1990-1	260	253	15	244	3,812	6,715	10,771	288	8,800	549	163	9,800
1991-2	356	342	18	971	6,200	4,371	11,542	139	9,050	541	256	9,986
1992-3[1]	171	165	20	1,556	3,288	6,035	10,879	167	8,600	230	337	9,334
1993-4[2]	206	191	18	1,545	3,480	5,110	10,135	144	8,650	126	60	8,980
1994-5[3]	178	171	17	1,155	2,922	6,345	10,422	156	8,750	150	117	9,173

[1] Preliminary.   [2] Estimate.   [3] Forecast.   *Source: Economic Research Service, U.S. Department of Agriculture*

FLAXSEED AND LINSEED OIL

U.S. Production of Flaxseed, by States   In Thousands of Bushels

Crop Year	Minnesota	North Dakota	South Dakota	Other States	Total	Crop Year	Minnesota	North Dakota	South Dakota	Other States	Total
1985	950	6,008	1,335	------	8,293	1990	238	3,118	456	------	3,812
1986	544	9,538	1,456	------	11,538	1991	640	4,860	578	122	6,200
1987	224	6,518	702	------	7,444	1992	220	2,730	322	16	3,288
1988	110	1,295	210	------	1,615	1993	170	2,886	323	101	3,480
1989	95	980	140	------	1,215	1994[1]	126	2,450	304	42	2,922

[1] Preliminary.   *Source: National Agricultural Statistics Service, U.S. Department of Agriculture*

Average Price Received by Farmers for Flaxseed in the U.S.   In Dollars Per Bushel

Year	July	Aug.	Sept.	Oct.	Nov.	Dec.	Jan.	Feb.	Mar.	Apr.	May	June	Average
1984-5	6.25	6.07	5.72	5.67	5.95	6.05	6.59	6.64	6.18	6.67	6.94	6.54	6.09
1985-6	6.10	5.72	5.39	5.01	4.80	4.79	4.77	4.94	4.95	4.88	4.87	4.95	5.05
1986-7	4.39	3.80	3.69	3.46	3.39	3.41	3.18	3.13	3.04	3.15	3.35	3.44	3.47
1987-8	3.47	3.33	3.15	3.07	3.03	3.20	3.45	3.80	3.95	4.11	4.19	5.28	3.39
1988-9	6.29	7.19	7.67	7.85	8.09	8.34	8.34	8.70	8.09	7.78	7.54	6.79	7.56
1989-90	5.90	6.49	7.07	7.09	7.15	7.14	7.24	7.69	8.03	8.60	8.23	8.31	7.20
1990-1	7.56	5.86	5.36	5.15	5.16	5.15	5.12	4.80	4.90	4.66	4.33	3.98	5.32
1991-2	3.91	3.68	3.55	3.40	3.31	3.46	3.39	3.43	3.52	3.53	3.61	3.67	3.50
1992-3	3.70	3.71	4.12	4.09	4.10	4.21	4.12	4.47	4.54	4.41	4.37	4.44	4.19
1993-4	4.29	3.80	4.25	4.09	4.05	4.18	4.38	4.58	4.65	4.61	4.34	4.30	4.29
1994-5[1]	4.28	4.48	4.55	4.49	4.51	4.71	4.75	4.90					

[1] Preliminary.   *Source: National Agricultural Statistics Service, U.S. Department of Agriculture*

United States Linseed Oil Consumption in Inedible Products   In Millions of Pounds

Crop Year	July	Aug.	Sept.	Oct.	Nov.	Dec.	Jan.	Feb.	Mar.	Apr.	May	June	Total
1989-90	12.2	13.6	14.5	8.7	8.7	7.5	10.3	8.6	12.8	9.7	9.6	10.0	126.2
1990-1	9.5	10.2	6.8	8.3	6.3	4.7	----------- 19.4 -----------			----------- 24.2 -----------			89.4
1991-2	----------- 29.0 -----------			----------- 23.2 -----------			15.5	15.5	13.0	15.0	15.3	11.4	137.9
1992-3	16.3	14.8	11.5	11.2	6.9	8.0	8.3	8.5	11.8	10.5	12.6	13.0	133.4
1993-4	14.9	8.1	11.2	9.0	7.2	10.7	12.7	8.6	11.0	10.2	14.0	14.5	132.1
1994-5[1]	12.7	12.7	14.2	14.2	10.6	12.2							76.6

[1] Preliminary.   *Source: Bureau of Census, U.S. Department of Commerce*

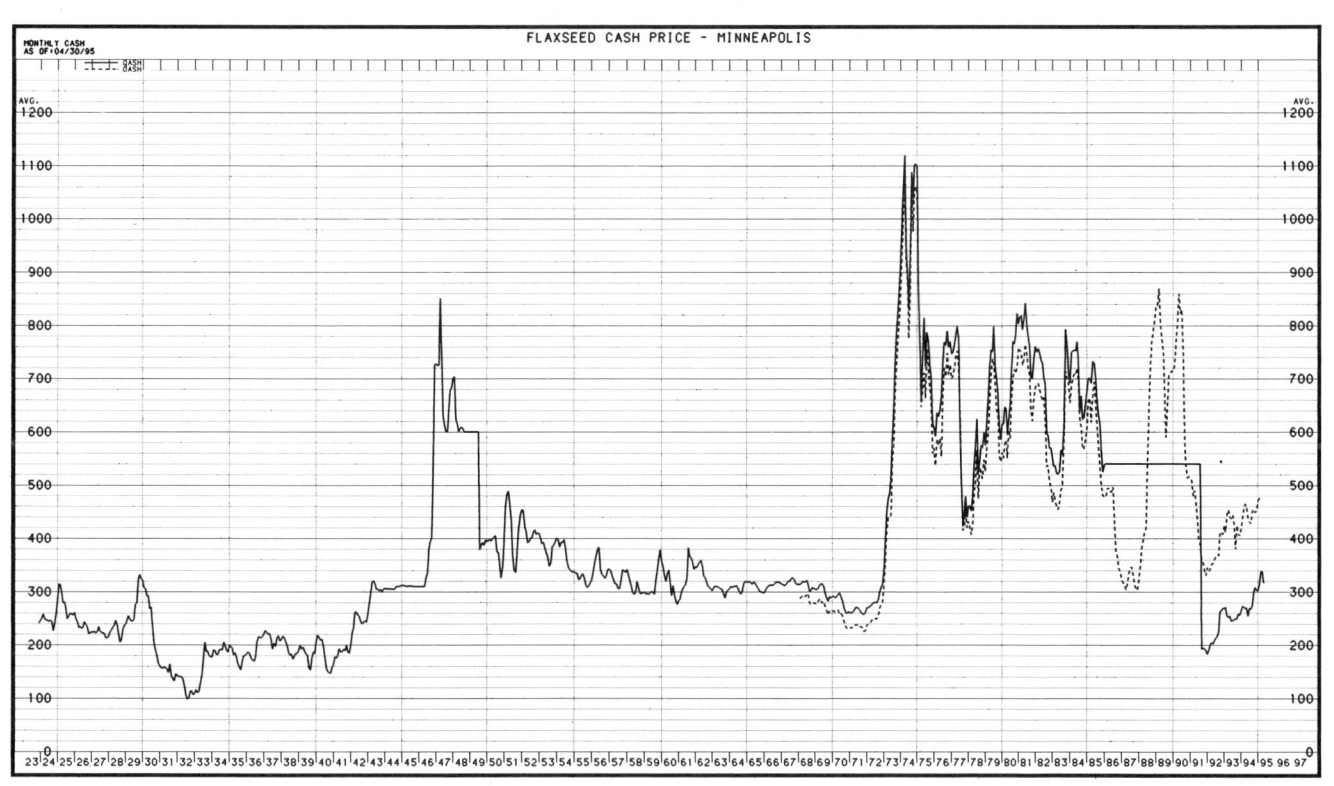

FLAXSEED CASH PRICE - MINNEAPOLIS

93

FLAXSEED AND LINSEED OIL

Supply and Distribution of Linseed Oil in the U.S. In Millions of Pounds

Crop Year Beginning June	Supply: Stocks June 1	Supply: Production	Total	Disappearance: Exports	Disappearance: Domestic	Total Disappearance	Average Price at Minneapolis Cents/Lb.
1984-5	48	194	242	15	194	209	32.00
1985-6	33	205	238	15	184	199	30.80
1986-7	39	201	240	6	183	189	26.40
1987-8	51	217	268	8	219	227	24.70
1988-9	41	170	211	12	151	163	39.50
1989-90	48	165	213	12	164	176	40.20
1990-1	37	176	213	6	167	173	38.00
1991-2	40	182	222	12	170	182	32.10
1992-3	40	172	212	8	150	158	31.00
1993-4[1]	54	174	228	7	158	165	32.50
1994-5[2]	63	175	238	8	170	178	31-36

[1] Preliminary. [2] Forecast. Source: Economic Research Service, U.S. Department of Agriculture

World Production and Price of Linseed Oil In Thousands of Metric Tons

Year	Argentina	Bangladesh	Belgium	China	Egypt	Ethiopia	Germany	India	Japan	United Kingdom	United States	Former U.S.S.R.	World Total	Price Rotterdam Ex-Tank $ Tonne
1984-5	183.7	------	2.4	117.5	13.0	11.7	78.9	109.7	34.9	16.9	94.3	8.0	761.7	639
1985-6	143.7	------	7.1	139.7	13.0	13.3	113.1	104.7	36.5	14.0	90.8	7.3	784.2	475
1986-7	198.5	9.2	6.2	125.2	12.3	12.7	135.3	90.8	31.6	17.1	97.3	11.8	837.0	319
1987-8	175.5	10.3	8.3	111.3	11.1	10.5	81.1	105.7	33.6	13.5	82.4	12.6	734.9	441
1988-9	137.7	10.8	9.6	127.5	11.8	8.2	41.6	103.4	33.2	12.2	76.0	10.5	658.3	716
1989-90	158.8	11.6	12.9	104.1	11.7	6.6	44.9	92.9	31.4	11.4	76.1	11.5	646.6	756
1990-1	141.5	12.0	12.2	126.9	12.3	12.1	57.5	93.9	34.7	16.8	84.0	10.1	685.5	502
1991-2	114.0	13.5	14.7	115.5	11.7	11.7	56.1	83.6	31.9	27.0	87.9	9.1	642.4	377
1992-3[1]	62.3	12.6	19.6	109.5	9.6	10.5	56.8	78.2	28.6	27.2	80.0	9.6	563.5	450
1993-4[2]	36.0	12.7	18.0	109.5	9.8	10.1	64.7	78.9	30.0	25.8	77.7	9.9	550.3	459

[1] Preliminary. [2] Forecast. Source: The Oil World

Factory Shipments of Paints, Varnish and Lacquer in the U.S. In Millions of Dollars

Year	Jan.	Feb.	Mar.	Apr.	May	June	July	Aug.	Sept.	Oct.	Nov.	Dec.	Total
1984	624.5	672.4	760.7	754.3	839.2	839.9	785.1	833.0	744.4	765.3	633.0	566.5	8,818
1985	630.5	621.2	754.3	865.3	930.1	880.5	862.2	864.3	805.9	820.4	673.6	571.0	9,279
1986	698.6	681.1	760.0	903.9	913.8	891.0	862.7	856.3	841.5	863.4	660.1	614.3	9,547
1987	696.7	754.6	849.5	903.2	916.0	933.0	906.6	890.8	879.6	895.4	751.7	681.3	10,168
1988	751.5	822.3	958.0	970.1	1,034.0	1,067.0	937.5	1,000.0	932.6	908.1	819.7	751.5	10,783
1989	820.5	841.3	952.6	985.7	1,072.7	1,091.5	965.9	1,114.4	1,019.7	995.9	914.3	755.5	11,239
1990	853.2	881.1	1,020.4	1,035.1	1,076.3	1,077.2	1,032.7	1,084.3	963.1	1,046.8	854.9	730.9	11,762
1991	---------- 2,498.4 ------------			---------- 3,158.7 ----------			---------- 3,123.0 ----------			---------- 2,611.2 ------------			11,707
1992	---------- 2,852.3 ------------			---------- 3,464.1 ----------			---------- 3,308.7 ----------			---------- 2,816.4 ------------			12,441
1993	---------- 2,894.1 ------------			---------- 3,600.5 ----------			---------- 3,448.9 ----------			---------- 2,993.7 ------------			12,937
1994[1]	---------- 3,147.7 ------------			---------- 3,874.1 ----------			---------- 3,791.9 ----------						

[1] Preliminary. Source: Bureau of Census, U.S. Department of Agriculture

U.S. Stocks of Linseed Oil (Crude & Refined) at Factories & Warehouses In Millions of Pounds

Year	July 1	Aug. 1	Sept. 1	Oct. 1	Nov. 1	Dec. 1	Jan. 1	Feb. 1	Mar. 1	Apr. 1	May 1	June 1
1984-5	50.7	40.8	24.9	48.3	41.3	36.1	39.3	38.3	34.1	30.1	35.1	33.4
1985-6	32.7	36.9	25.4	47.0	62.3	55.2	60.6	62.7	64.6	66.0	56.1	40.1
1986-7	46.0	45.3	40.4	40.0	50.3	68.0	60.0	68.0	60.0	64.6	55.0	51.1
1987-8	52.2	45.9	40.2	52.1	54.3	50.4	50.8	56.0	39.0	35.5	35.6	40.8
1988-9	35.6	36.0	44.8	24.4	33.5	36.6	46.8	54.6	47.6	49.1	54.6	47.5
1989-90	48.4	43.8	23.2	21.5	23.9	30.3	29.9	39.5	36.7	39.1	38.3	36.8
1990-1	28.2	21.9	17.2	41.8	41.4	47.5	------------ 61.7 ------------			------------ 75.4 --------------		
1991-2	------------ 60.6 ------------			------------ 64.2 ------------			73.1	51.2	62.3	45.6	45.7	41.4
1992-3	34.6	35.5	29.7	41.3	49.1	47.7	39.9	44.2	45.1	49.1	42.8	43.1
1993-4	45.2	39.0	42.1	47.0	27.9	19.3	22.5	38.1	41.9	49.4	52.0	62.7
1994-5[1]	60.2	56.5	49.3	60.6	48.1	39.3	37.3					

[1] Preliminary. Source: Bureau of Census, U.S. Department of Commerce

FLAXSEED - WPG

CAN.$/ METRIC TON

Wholesale Price of Raw Linseed Oil at Minneapolis in Tank Cars   In Cents Per Pound

Year	July	Aug.	Sept.	Oct.	Nov.	Dec.	Jan.	Feb.	Mar.	Apr.	May	June	Average
1984-5	33.40	38.00	31.00	28.80	28.50	30.00	31.20	32.00	NA	NA	NA	NA	31.60
1985-6	34.60	33.30	33.00	30.00	30.00	27.60	30.00	30.00	30.00	30.00	30.00	29.40	30.70
1986-7	29.00	29.00	29.00	25.00	25.00	25.00	25.00	25.00	25.00	25.00	25.00	25.00	26.00
1987-8	25.00	25.00	25.00	22.75	24.25	25.00	25.00	25.00	25.00	24.75	24.75	28.20	24.98
1988-9	35.00	37.00	41.50	42.00	42.00	41.50	41.00	41.00	41.40	42.00	42.00	39.75	40.51
1989-90	39.00	39.00	39.50	40.00	40.00	40.00	40.00	40.00	41.60	42.00	42.00	43.00	40.51
1990-1	44.00	40.40	39.75	36.80	36.00	36.00	36.00	36.00	36.00	36.00	36.50	36.00	37.45
1991-2	36.00	36.00	36.00	30.00	30.00	30.00	30.00	30.00	30.00	30.00	30.00	30.00	31.50
1992-3	30.00	30.00	32.00	32.00	32.00	32.00	32.00	32.00	32.00	32.00	32.00	28.50	31.38
1993-4[1]	32.00	32.00	32.00	32.00	32.00	32.00	32.00	32.00	32.00	32.00	32.00	32.00	32.00

[1] Preliminary.   Source: Economic Research Service, U.S. Department of Agriculture

Average Open Interest of Flaxseed Futures in Winnipeg   In Contracts

Year	Jan.	Feb.	Mar.	Apr.	May	June	July	Aug.	Sept.	Oct.	Nov.	Dec.
1986	4,960	5,417	4,631	6,212	6,244	6,440	5,403	6,150	6,910	4,986	4,860	4,662
1987	4,356	4,284	4,034	5,665	6,938	6,932	6,348	6,953	7,901	5,880	5,705	5,210
1988	5,838	6,341	5,583	6,189	6,089	7,219	5,964	7,018	7,791	8,777	10,662	7,621
1989	7,864	7,875	5,422	6,038	6,479	8,297	8,609	9,234	8,191	5,120	4,613	3,349
1990	3,812	5,165	5,701	5,790	4,839	4,985	4,950	4,908	4,651	4,477	5,079	4,502
1991	4,033	4,140	4,175	4,861	4,137	4,642	5,317	6,106	6,173	5,733	5,669	5,333
1992	5,620	6,772	7,864	7,984	7,786	7,321	6,299	6,553	5,623	4,860	6,734	5,979
1993	7,810	8,052	6,203	5,672	5,505	5,321	4,246	5,777	5,923	3,568	3,763	3,922
1994	6,118	6,201	5,946	5,519	4,683	3,945	4,301	4,654	4,997	3,077	4,888	5,251

Source: Winnipeg Commodity Exchange

Fruits

The United States Department of Agriculture (USDA) indicated that utilized production of fresh apples in the 1993/94 season was 6.2 billion pounds, an increase of nearly 7 percent from 1992/93. Imports were estimated at 234 million pounds, down 10 percent. Exports of fresh apples were estimated at 1.35 billion pounds, up 24 percent from the previous season. Consumption of fresh apples was put at 5.05 billion pounds, up nearly 2 percent. Per capita consumption was estimated at 19.45 pounds, the highest level since 1990/91. In 1993, the largest producing states in terms of utilized production were Washington, Michigan, California, New York and Pennsylvania.

Production of canned apples in 1993/94 was 1.08 billion pounds, down 10 percent from the previous year. Imports were minimal at almost 4 million pounds. Consumption of canned apples in 1993/94 were 1.08 billion pounds, producing per capita consumption of 4.15 pounds.

Fresh grape utilized production in 1993/94 was 1.6 billion pounds, or 4 percent more than the previous season. Imports fell 5 percent to 681 million pounds, and exports were 454 million pounds, up 11 percent. Consumption of fresh grapes was 1.8 billion pounds, while per capita consumption was just over seven pounds.

Utilized production of fresh pears in 1993/94 was 1.02 billion pounds, some 14 percent more than the previous season. Imports of fresh pears were marginally higher at 144 million pounds. Exports rose 28 percent to 282 million pounds. Consumption of fresh pears was 879 million pounds, some 8 percent more than the previous season. Per capita consumption was 3.38 pounds, the highest level since 1987/88.

Fresh grapefruit utilized production in 1993/94 was 2.6 billion pounds, up very slightly from 1992/93. Imports were minimal at 32 million pounds. Exports of fresh grapefruit reached just over one billion pounds, up 3 percent from the previous year. Consumption of grapefruit was 1.6 billion pounds, down 1 percent. Per capita consumption fell to 6.08 pounds from 6.23 pounds in 1992/93.

Utilized production of fresh lemons in 1993/94 was 946 million pounds, down marginally from the previous season. Imports were nearly 17 million pounds, and exports of fresh lemons were 268 million pounds, down 6 percent from 1992/93. Consumption of fresh lemons in 1993/94 reached 695 million pounds, an increase of approximatley 2 percent. Per capita consumption was 2.68 pounds. Fresh lime utilized production was 13 million pounds, while imports were 247 million pounds. Exports were minimal at less than 6 million pounds. Consumption of fresh limes was 254 million pounds, and per capita consumption was .98 pounds.

Fresh orange utilized production was 4.68 billion pounds. Imports were small at 29 million pounds. Exports in 1993/94 were estimated by the USDA at 1.18 billion pounds. Total consumption was 3.53 billion pounds, down 4 percent from 1992/93. Per capita consumption of fresh oranges was 13.54 pounds, down from 14.24 during the 1992/93 season.

U.S. Commercial Production for Selected Fruits   In Thousands of Short Tons

Year	Apples	Cherries[2]	Cran-berries	Grapes	Grape-fruit	Lemons	Nect-arines	Oranges	Peaches	Pears	Pine-apples	Prunes & Plums	Straw-berries	Tangelos	Tang-erines	Total All Fruits
1989	4,981	325	187	5,931	2,844	759	220	8,949	1,178	917	580	1,018	571	171	239	29,551
1990	4,848	261	170	5,660	1,978	706	232	7,745	1,117	964	575	729	627	132	164	26,517
1991	4,864	244	211	5,556	2,224	766	215	8,909	1,343	904	555	831	685	117	166	27,033
1992	5,237	349	208	6,032	2,791	942	236	10,992	1,240	924	550	828	657	137	247	29,568
1993	5,303	289	196	6,018	2,655	984	205	10,281	1,244	948	370	586	724	150	318	31,830
1994[1]	5,367	333	227	5,923	2,881	958	242	11,364	1,176	1,036	365	865	813	144	303	32,639

[1] Preliminary.   [2] Sweet and tart.   *Source: Economic Research Service, U.S. Department of Agriculture*

U.S. Commercial Production of Selected Fruits   In Thousands of Short Tons

Year	Utilizated Production			Value of Production		
	Citrus[1]	Noncitrus[2]	Total	Citrus[1]	Noncitrus[2]	Total
	In Thousands of Short Tons			In Thousands of Dollars		
1989	13,186	16,365	29,551	2,663,248	5,288,195	7,951,443
1990	10,860	15,657	26,517	2,242,862	5,533,543	7,776,405
1991	11,285	15,748	27,033	2,414,933	6,028,490	8,443,423
1992	12,452	17,116	29,568	2,401,351	6,025,322	8,428,874
1993	15,274	16,566	31,840	2,160,513	6,143,220	8,330,463
1994[3]	15,778	16,861	32,639		6,022,373	

[1] Year harvest was completed.   [2] Includes bushberries (beginning 1992), cranberries and strawberries.   [3] Preliminary.   *Source: Economic Research Service, U.S. Department of Agriculture*

U.S. Annual-Average Retail Prices for Selected Fruits   In Dollars Per Pound

Year	Red Delicious Apples	Bananas	Anjou Pears	Thompson Seedless Grapes	Lemons	Grapefruit	Oranges	
							Navel	Valen-cias
1989	.688	.449	.733	1.205	.995	.525	.516	.599
1990	.719	.463	.763	1.256	1.074	.657	.570	.558
1991	.885	.481	.840	1.400	1.227	.618	.784	.925
1992	.890	.458	.830	1.288	1.007	.607	.586	.559
1993	.834	.439	.858	1.465	1.084	.607	.586	.559
1994[1]	.826	.467	.797	1.428	1.089	.512	.538	.591

[1] Estimate.   *Source: Economic Research Service, U.S. Department of Agriculture*

U.S. Utilization of Fruit Production, and Value   In Thousands of Short Tons (Fresh Equivalent)

Year	Utilized Pro-duction	Fresh	Canned	Dried	Juice	Frozen	Wine	Other	Value of Utilized Production $1,000
					Processed				
1985	10,525	4,749	2,119	2,192	1,226	263	2,921	212	3,380,152
1986	11,058	4,896	2,211	1,668	1,135	286	2,909	259	3,699,956
1987	11,993	5,553	2,369	2,367	1,893	306	2,647	317	3,868,619
1988	12,761	5,465	2,374	2,546	1,372	296	2,983	267	4,552,348
1989	13,186	5,692	2,266	2,857	1,547	341	2,869	222	4,750,439
1990	10,860	5,676	2,244	2,440	1,450	314	2,717	189	4,943,385
1991	11,285	6,517	2,119	2,417	1,557	504	2,765	164	6,028,490
1992	17,116	6,517	2,382	2,369	1,742	592	3,256	257	6,025,321
1993[1]	16,566	6,599	2,040	2,339	1,742	629	3,033	184	6,143,220

[1] Preliminary.   Source: Economic Research Service, U.S. Department of Agriculture

U.S. Average Price Indexes for Fruits

Year	Index of all Fruit Prices Received by Growers (1982 = 100)	Fresh Fruit	Dried Fruit	Canned Fruits and Juices	Frozen Fruits and Juices	Fresh Fruit	Processed Fruit
		Producer Price Index				Consumer Price Index	
				1982 = 100		1982-84 = 100	
1985	103	108.1	88.7	113.8	118.5	116.3	109.5
1986	97	112.9	91.9	111.0	103.0	118.7	106.3
1987	104	112.0	95.0	115.4	113.3	132.0	110.6
1988	106	112.8	98.9	120.3	130.0	143.0	121.9
1989	111	110.4	103.1	122.6	124.5	152.4	125.9
1990	106	116.1	107.0	126.9	138.9	170.9	136.6
1991	151	129.4	111.5	128.6	115.1	193.9	131.8
1992	100	83.2	114.3	134.6	125.7	181.6	137.7
1993	100	84.3	117.6	126.1	110.9	188.8	132.3
1994[1]	84	84.2	121.7	126.3	112.7	200.2	133.2

[1] Estimate.   Source: Economic Research Service, U.S. Department of Agriculture

U.S. Fresh Fruit: Per Capita Consumption[1]   In Pounds

Year	Oranges	Tangerines & Tangelos	Lemons	Grapefruit	Total	Apples	Apricots	Avocados	Bananas	Cherries	Cran-berries
		Citrus Fruit				Noncitrus Fruit					
1985	13.43	1.51	2.47	6.13	21.47	17.26	.16	2.21	23.48	.42	.13
1986	12.81	1.59	2.48	6.32	24.21	17.84	.10	1.88	25.82	.49	.14
1987	13.90	1.78	2.47	6.66	23.90	20.83	.08	1.37	25.01	.72	.13
1988	12.17	1.77	2.39	6.58	25.36	19.87	.15	2.36	24.28	.53	.11
1989	12.38	1.71	2.60	4.43	23.54	21.39	.10	1.63	24.71	.53	.20
1990	8.46	1.31	2.60	5.87	21.37	19.74	.16	1.52	24.37	.39	.24
1991	12.91	1.38	2.54	5.95	19.06	18.26	.13	1.25	25.12	.40	.26
1992	14.24	1.94	2.65	6.23	24.36	19.30	.15	1.50	27.26	.53	.24
1993[2]	13.54	1.87	2.68	6.08	25.96	19.45	.13	2.05	26.79	.43	.19

[1] All data on calendar-year basis except for citrus fruits; apples, August; grapes and pears, July; grapefruit, September; lemons, August of prior year; all other citrus, November.   [2] Preliminary.   Source: Economic Research Service, U.S. Department of Agriculture

U.S. Fresh Fruit: Per Capita Consumption[1]   In Pounds

Year	Grapes	Kiwifruit	Mangos	Nectarines & Peaches	Pears	Pine-apples	Papaya	Plums & Prunes	Straw-berries	Total Noncitrus	Total Fruit
				Noncitrus - Continued							
1985	6.84	.14	.43	5.50	2.79	1.49	.18	1.43	2.99	65.44	86.91
1986	7.10	.15	.49	5.84	2.97	1.75	.18	1.29	2.89	68.94	93.15
1987	7.05	.25	.56	6.05	3.51	1.70	.19	1.91	3.12	72.48	96.38
1988	7.70	.25	.38	6.58	3.22	1.81	.16	1.72	3.33	72.44	97.81
1989	7.94	.33	.51	5.74	3.21	2.04	.14	1.41	3.25	73.13	96.67
1990	7.92	.49	.54	5.52	3.23	2.05	.18	1.55	3.24	71.14	92.52
1991	7.26	.44	.85	6.38	3.16	1.92	.17	1.42	3.59	70.61	89.68
1992	7.18	.33	.68	5.99	3.16	2.00	.24	1.78	3.53	73.87	98.23
1993[2]	7.04	.53	.90	5.93	3.38	2.05	.28	1.28	3.55	73.98	99.94

[1] All data on calendar-year basis except for citrus fruits; apples, August; grapes and pears, July; grapefruit, September; lemons, August of prior year; all other citrus, November.   [2] Preliminary.   Source: Economic Research Service, U.S. Department of Agriculture

Gas

Total dry natural gas production over the first seven-months of 1994 in the U.S. was 10.9 trillion cubic feet. This compared with production of 10.6 trillion in the same period of 1993, and 10.3 trillion cubic feet in the like period of 1992. For all of 1993, dry natural gas production in the U.S. was 18.4 trillion cubic feet. During the January-July 1994 period there were 1.7 trillion cubic feet of dry natural gas withdrawn from storage. Imports of natural gas have been increasing as U.S. energy use continues to grow. During the January-July 1994 period, imports of dry natural gas were 1.5 trillion cubic feet. This represented an 11 percent increase from the same period of 1993, and a 23 percent increase from the first seven-months of 1992. For all of 1993, natural gas imports into the U.S. were 2.35 trillion cubic feet, an increase of close to 10 percent from 1992. It is of interest to note that 1993 imports were over 80 percent more than were imported in 1988.

The major suppliers of natural gas to the U.S. are Canada, Mexico and Algeria. For the first seven-months of 1994, Canada supplied the U.S. with 1.42 trillion cubic feet. That represented over a 10 percent increase from the same period of 1993. Imports from Canada have been on a steady increase for the past several years. Mexico has just started exporting natural gas to the U.S. Over the January-July 1994 period, Mexican exports were 9.8 billion cubic feet. Algeria exports liquefied natural gas to the U.S. For the first seven-months of 1994, exports were 48.3 billion cubic feet, an increase of almost 5 percent from the same period of 1993. In the like period of 1992, Algeria's exports were only 20.2 billion cubic feet.

The major natural gas producing states are Texas, Louisiana and Oklahoma. For the first five-months of 1994, Texas marketed production of 2.62 trillion cubic feet while Louisiana produced 2.18 trillion and Oklahoma 841 billion cubic feet. Smaller producers include New Mexico, Wyoming and Kansas.

During the January-July 1994 period, consumption of dry natural gas in the U.S. totaled 12.85 trillion cubic feet. This represents an increase of almost 5 percent from the like period of 1993. For all of 1993, natural gas consumption was 20.3 trillion cubic feet, up 4 percent from 1992.

FUTURES MARKET

Natural gas futures and options are traded on the New York Mercantile Exchange (NYMEX).

World Natural Gas Production (Average Monthly Marketed Production[3])   In Terajoule[4]

Year	Australia	Canada	China	France	Germany	Indonesia	India	Italy	Mexico	Netherlands	Romania	Russia[5]	United Kingdom	United States	Venezuela
1981	33,850	229,032	41,300	23,080	56,088	4,887	54,435	44,436	86,085	247,910	127,656	1,351,213	114,517	1,588,064	53,902
1982	36,000	235,377	38,696	21,417	48,360	7,386	53,862	48,621	136,482	211,053	129,070	1,451,200	123,574	1,471,285	56,870
1983	36,939	228,371	39,597	24,725	52,899	8,881	64,428	41,240	121,028	224,209	128,083	1,553,149	127,258	1,332,128	55,640
1984	39,195	247,646	39,824	20,562	51,422	10,450	78,373	43,706	92,630	226,410	127,167	1,705,724	124,522	1,445,086	61,718
1985	51,070	265,709	41,834	18,067	48,670	12,196	78,115	44,956	89,002	236,580	126,833	1,845,787	138,724	1,491,513	60,574
1986	47,591	248,984	45,600	13,713	38,755	17,467	93,305	45,105	82,043	212,582	112,177	1,974,833	145,609	1,454,350	67,116
1987	49,077	271,207	45,063	17,172	48,527	89,971	24,374	46,133	82,603	195,827	106,431	2,107,896	140,085	1,506,613	66,607
1988	50,286	313,592	46,331	10,104	45,312	101,638	28,441	47,009	79,163	173,213	102,977	2,184,357	134,778	1,550,343	68,799
1989	51,406	331,923	48,816	6,774	44,734	121,871	33,715	49,618	75,131	210,184	92,312	2,245,667	143,708	1,569,198	69,877
1990	66,445	342,826	49,380	6,450	44,162	131,545	36,795	54,389	79,594	211,717	79,931	2,311,092	158,628	1,614,310	79,683
1991	70,068	362,029	49,955	7,739	52,460	151,618	43,284	53,037	79,009	239,349	68,977	2,286,626	176,344	1,609,083	83,097
1992[1]	76,096	397,229	50,052	7,470	51,911	168,471	43,297	57,117	80,500	240,043	67,900	------	176,661	1,614,941	79,784
1993[2]	75,917	437,922	52,297	10,828	47,904	247,656	44,409	61,757	136,703	225,259	68,891	2,068,113	196,792	1,670,207	111,415
1994[2]	82,318	499,337	54,222	10,500	47,364	------	45,191	61,125	135,783	------	63,615	2,081,380	195,824	1,671,268	------

[1] Preliminary.   [2] Estimate.   [3] Compares all gas collected & utilized as fuel or as a chemical industry raw material, including gas used in oilfields as a fuel by producers.   [4] Terajoule = 10 to the 12th power Joule = approximately 10 to the 9th power BTU.   [5] Formerly part of the U.S.S.R., data not reported separately until 1992.   *Source: United Nations*

Marketed Production of Natural Gas by Important States in the U.S.   In Million of Cubic Feet

Year	Alaska	California	Colorado	Kansas	Louisiana	Michigan	Mississippi	New Mexico	Oklahoma	Texas	Wyoming	Total
1988	378,638	399,663	191,544	592,845	5,180,267	146,145	124,053	791,819	2,167,050	6,286,029	509,058	17,918,465
1989	393,729	362,860	216,737	601,196	5,078,125	155,988	102,645	854,615	2,237,037	6,241,425	665,699	18,095,147
1990	402,907	362,748	242,997	573,603	5,241,989	172,151	94,616	965,104	2,258,471	6,343,146	735,728	18,593,792
1991	437,822	378,384	285,961	628,459	5,034,361	195,749	108,031	1,038,284	2,153,852	6,280,654	776,528	18,532,439
1992	443,597	365,632	323,041	658,007	4,914,300	194,815	91,697	1,268,863	2,017,356	6,145,862	842,576	18,711,808
1993[1]	430,350	315,851	400,985	686,347	5,165,992	204,635	80,695	1,409,429	2,049,942	6,249,624	778,956	19,305,087

[1] Preliminary.   *Source: Energy Information Administration, U.S. Department of Energy*

World Natural Gas Plant Liquids Production   Thousand Barrels Per Day

Year		Algeria	Canada	Mexico	Saudi Arabia	Former USSR	United States	Persian Gulf[2]	OAPEC[3]	OPEC[4]	World
1978	Average	25	281	115	250	255	1,567	410	447	566	3,078
1979	Average	30	331	150	303	270	1,584	458	535	637	3,285
1980	Average	36	331	193	369	285	1,573	534	618	732	3,444
1981	Average	49	330	241	433	300	1,609	599	691	825	3,625
1982	Average	58	318	255	430	315	1,550	612	721	842	3,626
1983	Average	56	309	265	330	330	1,559	552	655	780	3,635
1984	Average	105	336	257	355	340	1,630	604	761	869	3,869
1985	Average	120	337	271	375	350	1,609	645	808	892	3,938
1986	Average	120	328	352	385	440	1,551	700	860	969	4,150
1987	Average	140	367	338	418	495	1,595	721	900	1,006	4,344
1988	Average	120	381	370	499	525	1,625	808	979	1,077	4,556
1989	Average	130	410	384	503	515	1,546	851	1,041	1,188	4,593
1990	Average	130	426	428	620	520	1,559	930	1,107	1,281	4,735
1991	Average	140	431	457	680	525	1,659	950	1,132	1,312	4,955
1992	Average	145	459	446	720	525	1,697	1,013	1,190	1,380	5,118
1993[1]	Average	145	476	457	704	525	1,736	1,034	1,211	1,403	5,221

[1] Preliminary.   [2] Bahrain, Iran, Iraq, Kuwait, Qatar, Saudi Arabia and the United Arab Emirates.   [3] Organization of Arab Petroleum Exporting Countries.
[4] Organization of Petroleum Exporting Countries.   *Source: Energy Information Administration, U.S. Department of Energy*

United States Recoverable Reserves and Deliveries of Natural Gas   In Billions of Cubic Feet

Year	Gross Withdrawals of Natural Gas	Recoverable Reserves of Natural Gas Dec. 31[2]	Residential	Commercial	Lease & Plant Fuel	Used as Pipeline Fuel	Industrial	Total Deliveries	Electric Utility Plants[2]	Heating Value BTU per Cubic Foot
1981	21,587	201,730	4,546	2,520	928	642	7,128	17,834	3,640	1,027
1982	20,272	201,512	4,633	2,606	1,109	596	5,831	16,295	3,226	1,028
1983	18,659	200,247	4,381	2,433	978	490	5,643	15,367	2,911	1,031
1984	20,267	197,463	4,555	2,524	1,077	529	6,154	16,345	3,111	1,031
1985	19,607	193,369	4,433	2,432	966	504	5,901	15,811	3,044	1,032
1986	19,131	191,586	4,314	2,318	923	485	5,579	14,814	2,602	1,030
1987	20,140	187,211	4,315	2,430	1,149	519	5,953	15,542	2,844	1,031
1988	20,999	168,024	4,630	2,670	1,096	614	6,383	16,320	2,636	1,029
1989	21,074	167,116	4,781	2,718	1,070	629	6,816	17,102	2,787	1,031
1990	21,523	169,346	4,391	2,623	1,236	660	7,018	16,820	2,786	1,031
1991	21,750	167,062	4,556	2,729	1,129	601	7,231	17,305	2,789	1,030
1992	22,132	165,015	4,690	2,803	1,171	588	7,527	17,896	2,766	1,027
1993[1]	22,912	162,415	4,957	2,912	1,180	624	7,942	18,494	2,682	1,027

[1] Preliminary.   [2] Estimated proved recoverable reserves of dry natural gas.   [3] Figures include gas other than natural (impossible to segregate); therefore,
shown separately from other consumption.   *Source: Energy Information Administration, U.S. Department of Agriculture*

Gas Utility Sales in the United States by Types & Class of Service   In Trillions of BTU's

Year	Total Utility Sales	Number of Customers (Millions)	Class of Service — Residential	Commercial	Industrial	Electric Generation	Other	Revenue -- Million $ From Sales to Customers — Total	Residential	Commercial	Industrial	Electric Generation	Other
1980	15,413	48.5	4,826	2,453	5,856	2,110	168	48,303	17,432	8,183	16,648	5,592	473
1981	15,375	46.5	4,610	2,375	5,977	2,262	150	56,110	19,180	9,286	19,796	7,328	520
1982	14,183	45.4	4,770	2,471	4,861	1,933	147	63,200	23,700	11,666	19,292	7,908	634
1983	12,858	46.8	4,450	2,298	4,364	1,606	140	65,837	26,173	12,659	19,576	6,739	690
1984	13,162	47.2	4,628	2,396	4,241	1,750	146	67,496	27,485	13,205	18,705	7,389	713
1985	12,615	47.3	4,513	2,338	3,686	1,949	130	63,293	26,864	12,723	15,658	7,428	620
1986	11,125	52.0	4,381	2,239	2,891	1,447	167	51,201	24,759	11,274	10,546	3,949	673
1987	10,543	53.6	4,385	2,156	2,339	1,509	155	45,492	23,622	10,271	7,279	3,789	530
1988	10,705	52.1	4,695	2,306	2,208	1,336	160	46,162	24,828	10,681	6,713	3,400	538
1989	10,551	47.2	4,798	2,322	1,963	1,280	188	47,493	26,172	11,074	9,217	3,449	582
1990	9,842	47.8	4,468	2,192	1,890	1,120	171	45,153	25,000	10,604	6,034	2,962	553
1991	9,601	50.3	4,546	2,198	1,743	888	226	44,647	25,729	10,669	5,326	2,250	674
1992	9,907	45.5	4,694	2,209	1,959	813	231	46,178	26,702	10,865	5,837	2,077	698
1993[1]	10,224	57.2	4,923	2,291	1,957	842	211	50,024	29,113	11,754	6,237	2,214	701
1994[2]	10,153	NA	4,859	2,270	1,983	861	180	50,913	29,558	11,957	6,349	2,213	664

[1] Preliminary.   [2] Estimate.   NA = Not available.   *Source: American Gas Association*

GAS

Salient Statistics of Gas in the United States

Year	Marketed Production	Extraction Loss	Dry Production	Storage Withdrawals	Imports (Consumed)	Total Supply	Consumption	Exports	Added to Storage	Total Disposition	Wellhead Price	Imports	Exports	Residential	Commercial	Industrial	Electric Utilities
					In Billions of Cubic Feet									$ Per Thousand Cubic Feet			
1980	20,180	777	19,403	1,972	985	21,875	19,877	49	1,949	21,875	1.59	4.28	4.70	3.68	3.39	2.56	2.27
1981	19,956	775	19,181	1,930	904	21,691	19,404	59	2,228	21,691	1.98	4.88	5.90	4.29	4.00	3.14	2.89
1982	18,520	762	17,820	2,164	933	20,525	18,001	52	2,472	20,525	2.46	5.03	5.81	5.17	4.82	3.87	3.48
1983	16,822	790	16,094	2,270	920	18,712	16,835	55	1,822	18,712	2.59	4.78	5.10	6.06	5.59	4.18	3.58
1984	18,230	838	17,466	2,908	843	20,300	17,953	55	2,295	20,300	2.66	4.08	4.92	6.12	5.55	4.22	3.70
1985	17,198	816	16,454	2,397	950	19,499	17,281	55	2,163	19,499	2.51	3.19	4.77	6.12	5.50	3.95	3.55
1986	16,791	800	16,059	1,837	750	18,266	16,221	61	1,984	18,266	1.94	2.53	2.81	5.83	5.08	3.23	2.43
1987	17,349	812	16,621	1,905	993	19,176	17,211	54	1,911	19,176	1.67	2.17	3.07	5.54	4.77	2.94	2.32
1988	17,918	816	17,103	2,270	1,294	20,315	18,030	74	2,211	20,315	1.69	1.84	2.74	5.47	4.63	2.95	2.33
1989	18,095	785	17,311	2,854	1,382	21,435	18,801	107	2,528	21,435	1.69	1.82	2.51	5.64	4.74	2.96	2.43
1990	18,594	784	17,810	1,986	1,532	21,302	18,716	86	2,499	21,300	1.71	1.94	3.10	5.80	4.83	2.93	2.38
1991	18,532	835	17,698	2,752	1,773	21,836	19,035	129	2,672	21,836	1.64	1.82	2.59	5.82	4.81	2.69	2.18
1992	18,712	872	17,840	2,772	2,138	22,360	19,544	216	2,599	22,360	1.74	1.85	2.25	5.89	4.88	2.84	2.36
1993[1]	19,305	886	18,419	2,799	2,350	23,273	20,298	140	2,835	23,273	2.03	1.99	2.59	6.16	5.16	3.09	2.61
1994[2]	19,698	918	18,780	2,405	2,539	23,461	20,598	144	2,718	23,461	1.86	1.73	2.55	6.47	5.38	3.07	2.34

[1] Preliminary. 2 Estimate. *Source: Energy Information Administration, U.S. Department of Energy*

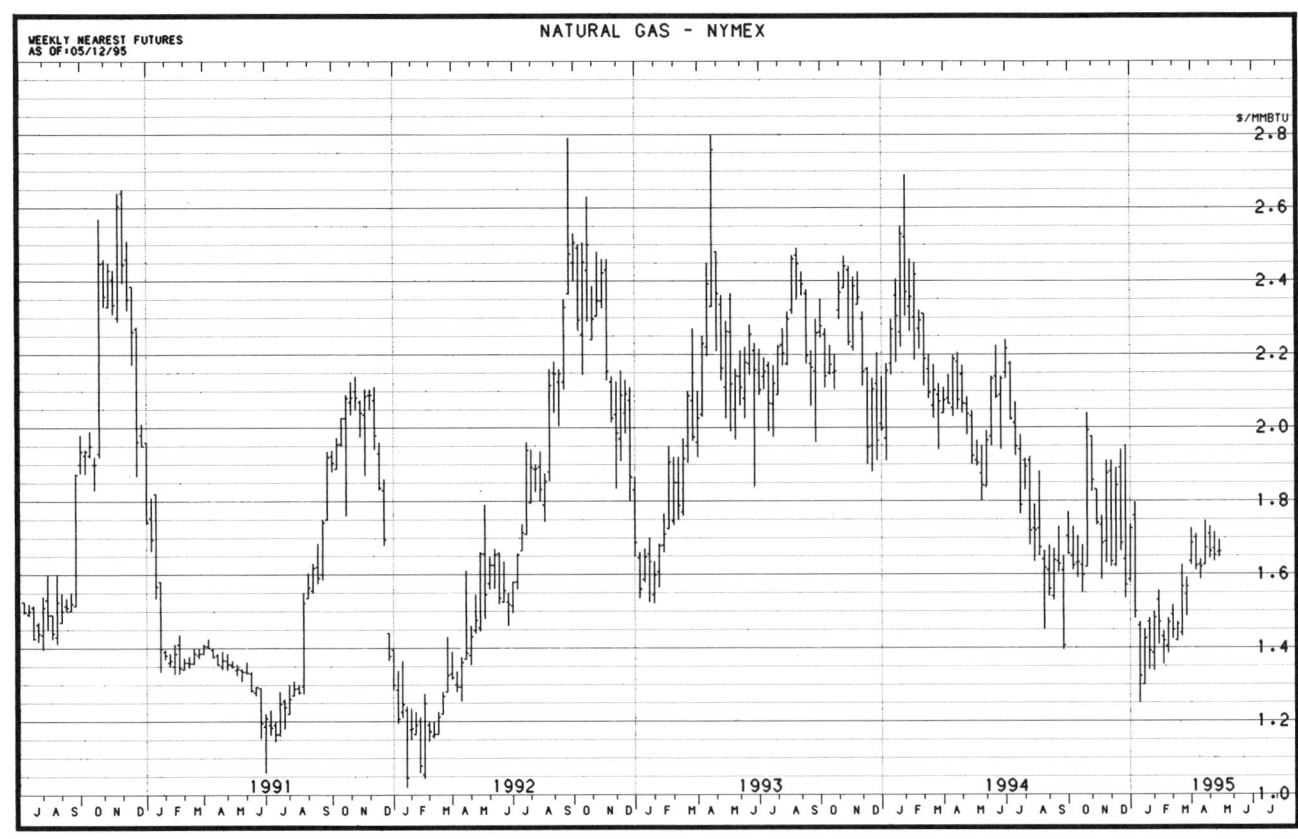

Gasoline

Unleaded gasoline prices fell sharply in late-summer 1994, as the summer driving season came to an end and there were large imports. Between August-September 1994, futures prices for unleaded gasoline on the New York Mercantile Exchange (NYMEX) fell over 8¢ per gallon. An important factor in the price slide included the fact that oil refiners had begun preparing for the winter season and new gasoline specifications, by unloading summer grade material onto the market. After bottoming in late-September to early-October, futures prices staged an impressive rebound on concerns about the availability of gasoline which will be produced under standards defined in the 1990 Clean Air Act. On January 1, 1995, reformulated gasoline (RFG) standards will go into effect and there are concerns about the availability of supplies. In addition, questions have been risen concerning the ability of the current energy products distribution infrastructure to handle the new grades of gasoline that will be offered.

It has been estimated that RFG account for around 40 percent of U.S. gasoline use after the January 1, 1995 starting date. Because it is meant to improve air quality, the use will be concentrated in areas which have the lowest air quality. These include Southern California, parts of the east coast between Washington and Boston,as well as, cities like Chicago and Houston. The implementation of the guidelines is not expected to go smoothly. The NYMEX has adapted the standards starting with its December 1994 contract. One problem with the specifications concerns foreign production. The northeast U.S. is very reliant on gasoline imports to meet demand. It is possible that many foreign gasoline suppliers will not be able to meet the specifications. There are fines involved for those who do not comply

with the specifications. Another concern is about the processing ability of the existing infrastructure. There will be a larger number of gasoline product grades, which will increase the number of batches that must be separated. This will work to reduce the capacity of pipeline. There also will be problems with existing storage capacity since the different product grades will have to be separated.

Another problem concerns the use of corn-based ethanol. Legislation, passed this summer, will require that at least 15 percent of the new gasoline's oxygenate content use corn-based ethanol rather than methanol-based oxygenate. Since ethanol production is largely based in the Midwest, there are expected to be difficulties shipping it to the Northeast for blending to produce .

U.S. production of finished motor gasoline over the first eight-months of 1994 averaged 7.156 million barrels per day, down 1 percent from the same period of 1993. For all of 1993, daily average gasoline production was 7.36 million barrels. Imports of motor gasoline averaged 402,000 barrels per day during January-August 1994, some 60 percent more than in the like period of 1993. Between April and August of 1994, imports of gasoline increased significantly. U.S. exports of gasoline averaged 80,000 barrels per day in the first eight-months of 1994, down from 100,000 barrels per day in 1993. At the end of August 1994, total gasoline stocks were 204 million barrels, up slightly from 202 barrels million in August 1993.

FUTURES MARKETS

Unleaded gasoline futures and options are traded on the New York Mercantile Exchange (NYMEX).

Average Spot Prices of Unleaded Gasoline   In Cents Per Gallon

Year	Jan.	Feb.	Mar.	Apr.	May	June	July	Aug.	Sept.	Oct.	Nov.	Dec.	Average
1986	67.71	46.38	40.65	47.18	55.10	42.01	33.84	42.51	42.02	41.04	41.08	43.12	45.22
1987	49.23	47.64	51.13	50.54	54.18	55.75	55.78	52.43	51.71	54.03	51.68	45.58	51.64
1988	45.14	45.79	45.25	50.89	52.20	51.70	55.12	48.18	46.40	51.15	52.39	47.22	49.29
1989	50.24	48.47	54.91	69.98	67.97	63.75	56.34	52.81	59.29	55.76	50.80	53.94	57.02
1990	64.20	59.59	56.15	61.86	64.24	64.55	65.25	89.61	99.85	95.68	88.10	68.07	73.10
1991	68.88	65.82	74.25	72.07	70.28	63.59	65.23	69.90	62.17	64.41	65.10	55.55	66.44
1992	53.04	55.14	54.10	59.75	63.48	64.51	59.94	62.06	61.63	60.81	58.22	53.24	58.83
1993	52.96	52.54	54.33	59.35	59.37	54.78	51.80	53.13	48.61	50.22	44.30	37.68	51.59
1994	42.40	43.75	44.04	48.98	50.62	52.84	54.52	55.61	46.53	51.14	52.32	46.87	49.14

Source: New York Mercantile Exchange

Average Open Interest of Unleaded Regular Gasoline Futures in New York   In Contracts

Year	Jan.	Feb.	Mar.	Apr.	May	June	July	Aug.	Sept.	Oct.	Nov.	Dec.
1987	28,026	32,240	41,440	40,630	37,152	32,453	28,977	27,463	27,522	29,271	31,998	38,327
1988	39,887	43,055	44,006	46,094	46,517	50,754	57,897	51,064	49,636	49,649	49,877	50,893
1989	55,838	57,011	59,012	69,547	68,478	61,519	56,913	52,158	51,910	55,312	65,392	71,464
1990	77,580	80,425	75,368	71,132	62,121	72,105	68,826	59,528	60,558	61,253	56,332	56,569
1991	54,807	75,337	81,393	74,801	71,900	73,633	74,503	87,073	90,680	100,606	111,745	125,578
1992	124,896	117,155	108,388	89,775	79,680	80,394	81,110	76,741	71,264	68,059	71,110	77,508
1993	80,610	93,630	100,657	96,607	88,311	94,926	104,260	103,371	100,921	107,339	126,649	150,359
1994	135,366	120,204	118,977	122,092	96,525	89,854	86,401	76,213	67,881	70,258	71,245	63,679

Source: New York Mercantile Exchange

GASOLINE

Volume of Trading of Unleaded Regular Gasoline Futures in New York   In Contracts

Year	Jan.	Feb.	Mar.	Apr.	May	June	July	Aug.	Sept.	Oct.	Nov.	Dec.	Total
1987	135,208	139,885	211,590	214,982	178,735	175,585	182,661	154,685	155,352	166,365	152,176	190,014	2,056,238
1988	196,616	191,231	245,019	217,139	257,507	330,009	401,196	254,010	294,512	355,982	308,438	240,366	3,292,055
1989	354,167	258,669	373,936	510,964	407,445	443,205	356,939	310,546	412,753	375,489	328,277	352,168	4,484,558
1990	540,633	349,439	461,438	481,665	527,637	472,377	456,342	549,702	373,102	386,472	314,051	248,137	5,205,995
1991	366,772	351,188	525,432	541,073	482,943	446,350	396,429	562,085	386,421	477,111	537,834	529,940	5,594,915
1992	565,922	558,476	604,678	668,490	580,088	620,114	600,897	545,520	469,844	563,856	435,847	461,025	6,674,757
1993	531,780	558,770	584,899	539,785	571,860	611,951	594,740	721,852	642,959	629,733	674,814	729,717	7,407,809
1994	634,027	526,505	615,594	677,891	636,990	673,034	601,980	783,181	569,384	684,670	582,359	519,987	7,470,836

Source: New York Mercantile Exchange

United States Production of Finished Motor Gasoline   Thousand Barrels Per Day

Year	Jan.	Feb.	Mar.	Apr.	May	June	July	Aug.	Sept.	Oct.	Nov.	Dec.	Average
1983	6,065	5,848	5,906	6,201	6,397	6,655	6,707	6,537	6,611	6,188	6,634	6,308	6,340
1984	6,036	6,317	6,359	6,525	6,650	6,619	6,450	6,405	6,516	6,388	6,709	6,478	6,453
1985	5,926	5,914	6,072	6,344	6,564	6,780	6,788	6,814	6,299	6,356	6,480	6,651	6,419
1986	6,522	6,302	6,061	6,498	7,095	7,101	6,956	7,092	6,891	6,616	6,895	6,970	6,752
1987	6,714	6,365	6,569	6,850	6,991	7,089	7,043	6,933	6,921	6,668	6,907	7,015	6,841
1988	6,730	6,736	6,715	6,907	6,851	6,983	7,159	7,209	6,948	6,858	7,060	7,303	6,956
1989	6,937	6,650	6,612	6,811	6,894	7,275	7,360	7,155	7,069	6,845	7,046	6,884	6,963
1990	6,879	6,989	6,613	6,775	6,610	7,101	7,238	7,326	7,274	6,880	6,940	6,887	6,959
1991	6,629	6,573	6,643	6,742	7,063	7,351	7,274	7,247	7,030	6,749	7,018	7,354	6,975
1992	7,013	6,726	6,683	6,954	7,092	7,198	7,195	6,817	7,071	7,198	7,323	7,411	7,058
1993	7,228	7,144	6,904	7,126	7,446	7,442	7,337	7,335	7,573	7,394	7,652	7,725	7,360
1994[1]	7,098	6,780	6,740	7,171	7,282	7,448	7,372	7,432	7,387	7,149	7,849	7,860	7,300

[1] Preliminary.   *Source: Energy Information Adminstration, U.S. Department of Energy*

United States Disposition of Finished Motor Gasoline, Total Product Supplied   Thousand Barrels Per Day

Year	Jan.	Feb.	Mar.	Apr.	May	June	July	Aug.	Sept.	Oct.	Nov.	Dec.	Average
1985	6,348	6,587	6,664	6,956	7,060	6,997	7,008	7,242	6,629	6,897	6,770	6,792	6,831
1986	6,502	6,469	6,955	7,105	7,106	7,209	7,436	7,435	6,864	7,250	6,879	7,143	7,034
1987	6,535	6,796	6,964	7,314	7,460	7,539	7,581	7,338	7,205	7,305	7,151	7,251	7,206
1988	6,693	7,039	7,323	7,430	7,303	7,817	7,482	7,556	7,404	7,271	7,379	7,344	7,336
1989	6,745	7,119	7,421	7,157	7,381	7,780	7,296	7,717	7,240	7,302	7,353	7,410	7,328
1990	6,643	7,179	7,338	7,121	7,358	7,519	7,496	7,796	6,914	7,226	7,241	6,978	7,235
1991	6,645	6,838	7,017	7,137	7,437	7,456	7,561	7,528	7,083	7,281	7,008	7,224	7,188
1992	6,869	6,963	7,137	7,238	7,328	7,460	7,639	7,380	7,344	7,338	7,102	7,396	7,268
1993	6,639	7,112	7,389	7,435	7,585	7,700	7,785	7,864	7,607	7,382	7,533	7,661	7,476
1994[1]	6,916	7,272	7,379	7,530	7,592	7,926	7,846	8,007	7,619	7,547	7,479	7,902	7,587

[1] Preliminary.   *Source: Energy Information Adminstration, U.S. Department of Energy*

Stocks of Finished Gasoline[2] on Hand in the United States   In Millions of Barrrels

Year	Jan.	Feb.	Mar.	Apr.	May	June	July	Aug.	Sept.	Oct.	Nov.	Dec.
1985	200.9	191.8	188.2	184.2	183.4	188.5	194.4	190.4	189.7	182.3	185.6	192.4
1986	203.2	207.8	186.2	176.0	189.8	197.8	192.0	189.7	198.5	187.0	193.0	196.4
1987	213.0	209.0	207.2	202.9	197.7	194.5	190.8	190.0	193.4	184.1	190.2	191.1
1988	203.1	205.1	196.4	192.1	190.8	176.7	181.2	185.4	184.6	182.3	185.8	192.0
1989	207.8	205.7	191.1	190.6	185.8	180.1	192.1	183.8	187.5	184.8	187.1	179.1
1990	197.6	203.3	187.9	186.3	180.3	177.7	182.0	175.4	190.5	181.9	178.7	182.4
1991	189.1	182.7	174.4	171.9	173.7	178.5	173.5	172.8	179.1	168.3	173.3	183.3
1992	192.8	191.4	182.9	185.0	187.4	189.5	182.0	168.2	170.0	168.7	178.2	179.1
1993	197.8	201.9	189.0	184.0	186.8	184.2	176.8	166.7	171.2	175.6	182.6	187.1
1994[1]	194.7	186.6	176.0	176.9	179.7	176.9	174.1	167.6	168.9	154.8	135.5	175.0

[1] Preliminary. [2] Includes oxygenated and other finished.   *Source: Energy Information Administration, U.S. Department of Energy*

Refiner Sales Prices of Finished Motor Gasoline to End Users (Excluding Taxes)[1]   In Cents Per Gallon

Year	Jan.	Feb.	Mar.	Apr.	May	June	July	Aug.	Sept.	Oct.	Nov.	Dec.	Average
1985	84.6	83.6	87.1	92.4	94.4	95.2	95.4	94.0	91.9	90.8	91.7	91.9	91.2
1986	89.3	80.5	65.4	59.1	63.8	64.9	58.0	55.5	56.2	53.2	53.2	54.2	62.4
1987	59.7	62.1	62.7	64.9	66.3	67.7	69.6	71.6	70.5	69.7	69.4	67.4	66.9
1988	64.9	63.3	62.5	66.0	68.4	68.1	69.9	71.8	70.0	68.0	67.6	66.1	67.3
1989	65.6	66.1	68.4	81.7	85.5	84.5	82.0	76.6	74.9	74.7	72.7	72.1	75.6
1990	78.8	76.5	75.1	77.9	80.2	81.5	80.8	92.4	101.2	108.7	107.2	98.4	88.3
1991	88.8	79.5	74.0	77.0	82.0	81.9	78.9	81.1	80.2	77.9	79.1	76.0	79.7
1992	71.2	70.2	71.0	74.6	80.3	84.0	83.5	82.3	82.3	81.3	81.4	78.5	78.4
1993	76.9	76.1	75.7	77.8	80.1	79.8	77.6	76.2	74.9	75.3	72.5	68.0	75.9
1994[2]	66.7	67.6	67.3	69.5	71.1	74.1	77.0	81.5	79.6	76.9	77.4		73.5

[1] Excludes aviation. [2] Preliminary.   *Source: Energy Information Administration, U.S. Department of Energy*

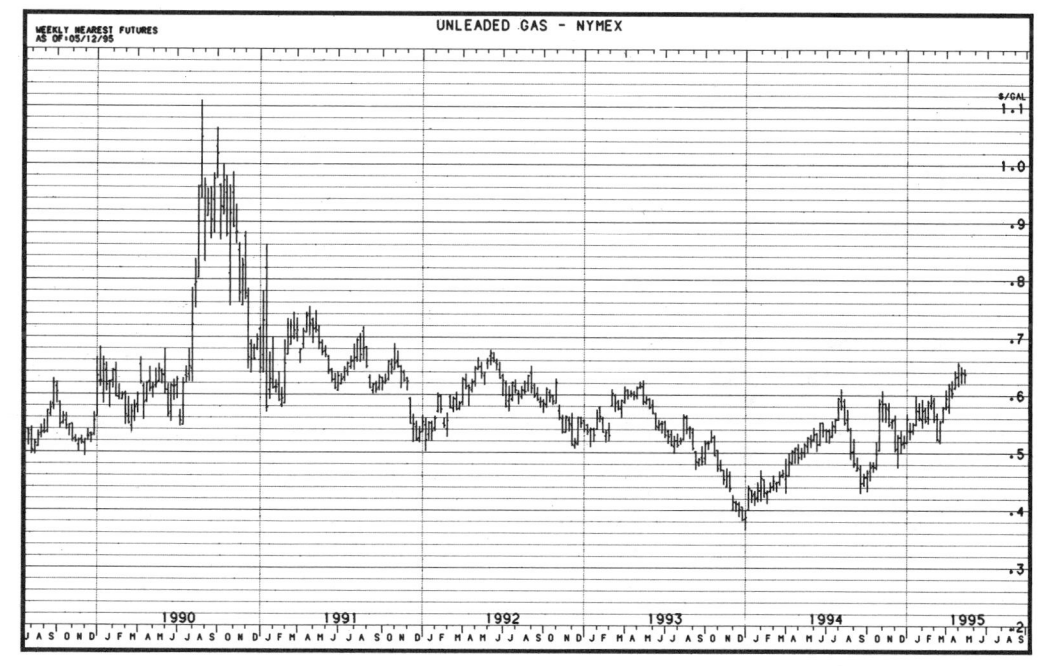

GASOLINE

U.S. Average Retail Selling Prices of Motor Gasoline (Including Taxes)   In Cents Per Gallon

Year	Jan.	Feb.	Mar.	Apr.	May	June	July	Aug.	Sept.	Oct.	Nov.	Dec.	Average
						Unleaded Premium							
1982	146.6	144.8	140.8	135.1	135.5	141.8	144.3	143.9	142.9	142.1	141.2	139.4	141.5
1983	137.6	133.8	130.8	136.0	139.7	141.1	142.1	141.9	141.0	139.5	138.4	137.6	138.3
1984	136.9	136.1	136.2	137.5	138.0	137.7	137.0	135.5	136.0	136.5	136.4	135.4	136.6
1985	130.4	129.0	131.0	134.0	136.0	137.1	136.7	135.9	134.9	134.2	133.9	134.4	134.0
1986	133.6	128.2	116.0	106.1	107.5	110.0	104.5	99.9	101.0	98.7	98.0	98.4	108.5
1987	100.7	104.7	105.2	107.3	107.9	109.8	111.5	113.9	113.6	112.8	112.5	111.9	109.3
1988	109.5	108.2	107.4	108.8	110.5	111.1	112.3	113.8	113.0	111.9	111.6	110.1	110.7
1989	109.1	110.0	111.5	122.1	127.8	127.8	126.4	123.3	121.3	120.9	118.7	117.0	119.7
1990	123.0	122.7	121.8	123.3	124.8	127.1	127.2	136.9	146.7	155.4	155.9	153.7	134.9
1991	143.1	132.1	126.4	128.1	133.1	133.8	131.3	131.8	132.4	130.7	131.8	130.9	132.1
1992	126.7	124.8	125.0	126.8	131.7	135.9	136.3	134.8	134.6	134.5	135.1	133.0	131.6
1993	131.3	130.1	129.4	130.4	131.9	132.1	130.5	129.4	128.2	132.3	130.5	126.8	130.2
1994[1]	124.0	124.5	124.3	126.0	127.4	130.0	132.7	136.7	136.4	134.5	135.4	133.7	130.5
						Unleaded Regular							
1982	135.8	133.4	128.4	122.5	123.7	130.9	133.1	132.3	130.7	129.5	128.3	126.0	129.6
1983	123.0	118.7	115.2	121.5	125.9	127.7	128.8	128.5	127.4	125.5	124.1	123.1	124.1
1984	121.6	120.9	121.0	122.7	123.6	122.9	121.2	119.6	120.3	120.9	120.7	119.3	121.2
1985	114.8	113.1	115.9	120.5	123.1	124.1	124.2	122.9	121.6	120.4	120.7	120.8	120.2
1986	119.4	112.0	98.1	88.8	92.3	95.5	89.0	84.3	86.0	83.1	82.1	82.3	92.7
1987	86.2	90.5	91.2	93.4	94.1	95.8	97.1	99.5	99.0	97.6	97.6	96.1	94.8
1988	93.3	91.3	90.4	93.0	95.5	95.5	96.7	98.7	97.4	95.7	94.9	93.0	94.6
1989	91.8	92.6	94.0	106.5	111.9	111.4	109.2	105.7	102.9	102.7	99.9	98.0	102.1
1990	104.2	103.7	102.3	104.4	106.1	108.8	108.4	119.0	129.4	137.8	137.7	135.4	116.4
1991	124.7	114.3	108.2	110.4	115.6	116.0	112.7	114.0	114.3	112.2	113.4	112.3	114.0
1992	107.3	105.4	105.8	107.9	113.6	117.9	117.5	115.8	115.8	115.4	115.9	113.6	112.7
1993	111.7	110.8	109.8	111.2	112.9	113.0	110.9	109.7	108.5	112.7	111.3	107.0	110.8
1994[1]	104.3	105.1	104.5	106.4	108.0	110.6	113.6	118.2	117.7	115.2	116.3	114.3	111.2
						All-Types[2]							
1982	134.1	131.8	126.8	121.0	122.4	129.6	131.8	131.0	129.2	128.0	126.8	124.4	128.1
1983	121.4	117.0	113.5	119.8	124.3	126.1	127.2	126.9	125.7	123.9	122.4	121.5	122.5
1984	120.0	119.3	119.4	121.1	122.1	121.4	119.7	118.4	118.9	119.5	119.3	117.9	119.8
1985	114.5	112.8	115.5	119.9	122.3	123.3	123.3	122.2	120.9	119.8	120.1	120.3	119.6
1986	119.0	111.9	98.3	89.5	92.7	95.8	89.5	84.8	86.4	83.7	82.7	83.0	93.1
1987	86.8	91.1	91.8	94.0	94.8	96.6	98.0	100.4	100.0	98.8	98.7	97.5	95.7
1988	94.7	92.8	92.0	94.6	97.0	97.1	98.4	100.4	99.2	97.6	97.2	95.3	96.3
1989	94.4	95.5	97.4	109.8	115.2	115.0	113.2	109.6	107.3	107.1	104.6	103.0	106.0
1990	109.0	108.6	107.6	109.6	111.4	114.0	113.9	124.6	134.7	143.1	143.2	141.0	121.7
1991	130.4	119.8	113.8	115.9	120.9	121.4	118.5	119.6	119.9	118.0	119.3	118.2	119.6
1992	113.5	111.7	112.2	114.3	119.7	123.9	123.8	122.1	122.2	121.9	122.3	120.1	119.0
1993	118.2	117.2	116.3	117.5	119.3	119.4	117.4	116.3	115.1	119.3	117.8	113.6	117.3
1994[1]	110.9	111.4	110.9	112.8	114.3	116.9	119.9	124.3	123.7	121.2	122.2	120.3	117.4

[1] Preliminary.   [2] Also includes types of motor oil not shown separately.   *Source: Energy Information Administration, U.S. Department of Energy*

U.S. Refiner Sales Prices of Finished Aviation Gasoline to End Users[2]   In Cents Per Gallon

Year	Jan.	Feb.	Mar.	Apr.	May	June	July	Aug.	Sept.	Oct.	Nov.	Dec.	Average
1982	132.0	132.8	133.6	131.5	131.5	131.3	133.2	131.4	128.8	130.3	129.5	129.1	131.2
1983	129.2	127.2	126.6	125.2	125.4	125.6	125.1	125.9	124.2	124.7	124.5	124.4	125.5
1984	123.9	123.7	123.8	124.4	123.9	124.6	124.3	123.2	123.7	123.3	119.3	121.9	123.4
1985	121.7	121.1	121.4	121.2	121.9	121.7	120.2	118.9	119.5	118.9	118.3	117.0	120.1
1986	116.2	117.2	111.5	104.3	102.2	101.0	98.2	94.9	93.2	91.2	87.2	88.8	101.1
1987	87.9	89.7	90.3	89.8	90.6	91.3	91.5	92.4	91.9	91.4	91.0	90.0	90.7
1988	88.4	88.2	87.7	87.6	89.2	87.2	89.7	92.2	90.8	88.7	89.2	89.2	89.1
1989	89.2	89.7	90.6	99.1	107.0	107.1	105.5	101.9	100.7	100.4	98.6	97.3	99.5
1990	102.0	102.4	100.9	101.4	103.6	104.2	103.9	112.8	125.6	134.4	131.7	122.5	112.0
1991	112.1	106.4	101.3	101.2	105.3	105.2	103.6	105.8	105.7	104.6	104.3	102.0	104.7
1992	98.5	98.5	98.0	99.1	102.4	106.4	106.8	105.7	104.9	104.3	103.4	101.3	102.7
1993	100.3	99.9	99.4	100.7	102.2	102.5	99.7	98.8	98.2	98.0	95.7	91.2	99.0
1994[1]	88.6	88.4	89.0	91.3	92.3	95.6	95.9	101.7	101.1	100.0	100.0	99.2	95.6

[1] Preliminary.   [2] Excluding taxes.   *Source: Energy Information Administration, U.S. Department of Energy*

Gold

Gold's price was largely uneventful during 1994, encompassing a trading range of about $35 per troy ounce. The year started on a firm note as gold neared $410 per troy ounce. By yearend, prices were hovering near $375 per troy, basis December N.Y. futures. As usual, a tug of war persisted between the confirmed gold bull who believed that gold would see $500 per troy ounce during 1994, and the less dogmatic bear who, while generally reluctant to pinpoint a downside price objective, saw little reason for gold to strengthen. At yearend the bears had the edge. The psychology towards gold has changed, which became quite evident during 1994. The world financial markets now offer so many accessible alternatives, the currency and fixed instrument markets being the most prominent, as hedges against economic and/or political uncertainties which have cut deeply into gold's long standing appeal as the one true hedge.

Gold, however, will always retain a speculative following and certainly the metal's industrial use is not apt to diminish, but barring no world shaking events during 1995, the odds are that gold's following will slip further and so will prices. Gold's production costs are generally thought to average in the low $200 per troy ounce range, suggesting that much of the metal's market price above costs and profit margins is a speculative based premium that is rooted in psychology and almost impossible to quantify. During 1994, the U.S. financial markets were under the threat of budding inflationary pressures, but the gold market seemed to pay little attention. Moreover, the many military and/or political flareups in the world, while attracting a lot of media attention, were also seen as happening in countries that really had little adverse effect on the major industrialized nations. In the past, such fears would have at least for a brief time kicked gold's price higher. It would be premature to suggest that such response no longer holds, but it may not be necessarily inaccurate to state that gold's pivotal role in the world's financial structure is dissipating.

World mine production of gold in the early-1990s has averaged about 66 million troy ounces, nearly twice the annual average of the early-1980s. Production in 1993 totaled about 66 million troy ounces. South Africa produces almost one-third of total output followed by the U.S. The former Soviet Union generally accounted for about 12 percent of world production. China's demand for gold has increased as the country moves towards a market economy. In mid-1994, China's government stated its intention to reassert control over its gold industry. All unauthorized gold markets were to be closed, and China's central bank was given control of all mining, processing and trading of gold. China also said it would selectively introduce overseas investment and technologies to mine its gold resources that are of low grade. Brazil, whose gold production has doubled from the early-1980s, also indicated in mid-1994 plans to better control production in parts of the Amazon basin.

The U.S. supply of primary gold in 1993 totaled about 1.1 million kilograms, which included production from domestic and foreign ores of 249,792 kilograms, recovery of 54,815 kilograms obtained from old scrap, imports and deliveries from foreign accounts (held at the New York Federal Reserve Bank). Refinery production from ores in the first half of 1994 suggested a total for the year close to 1993. Secondary production from old scrap, however, was running at a faster pace with nearly 36,000 kilograms obtained. Nevada accounts for nearly two-thirds of U.S. mine production and California a distant second. The U.S. imports refined gold, mostly from Canada, but the year-to-year totals vary sharply. In 1993, about 130,045 kilograms were imported, whereas, in the first half of 1994 less than 40,000 kilograms were apparently imported.

U.S. consumption of gold for industry and arts totaled 89,409 kilograms in 1993, with karat gold for jewelry using two-thirds. In the first half of 1994, about 44,000 kg were consumed. U.S. exports of refined and unrefined gold in 1993 totaled 792,680 kilograms. In the first half of 1994, about 230,000 kg were exported, with most of the consisting of refined bullion. U.S. known gold stocks at yearend 1993 totaled 9,081,303 kilograms, with over 8 million kilograms held by the U.S. Treasury. In mid-1994, the total inventory is believed to have slipped to under 9 million kilograms.

Futures Markets

Gold futures and options on those futures are traded on the COMEX, a division of the New York Mercantile Exchange. Gold futures are also traded on exchanges in Chicago, Tokyo, Sydney and Hong Kong.

World Mine Production of Gold   In Kilograms (1 Kilogram = 32.1507 Troy Ounces)

Year	Australia	Brazil	Canada	Chile	China	Colombia	Ghana	Indonesia	Papua N.Guinea	Philippines	Russia[3]	South Africa	United States	Uzbekistan[3]	Zimbabwe	Total World
1981	18,374	37,324	52,033	12,456	52,876	16,460	10,606	1,687	16,806	23,586	262,000	656,942	42,897	------	11,539	1,283,037
1982	26,961	46,655	64,734	16,907	55,986	14,702	10,295	2,236	18,328	25,954	266,000	664,219	45,588	------	13,250	1,340,730
1983	30,591	57,542	73,510	17,759	57,542	13,266	8,585	2,391	18,022	25,397	267,000	679,528	62,286	------	14,101	1,404,737
1984	40,309	61,585	83,444	16,829	59,097	22,726	8,927	2,447	25,971	25,727	269,000	679,952	64,839	------	14,877	1,459,671
1985	58,521	72,160	87,561	17,240	61,000	35,532	9,322	2,619	36,908	33,063	270,000	670,754	75,495	------	14,691	1,531,858
1986	75,079	67,500	102,899	17,947	66,000	39,995	8,931	3,304	35,075	40,322	275,000	638,047	116,297	------	14,853	1,606,570
1987	110,696	83,700	115,818	17,035	72,000	26,546	10,201	3,643	33,250	32,599	260,000	607,000	153,870	------	14,710	1,660,535
1988	156,950	112,159	134,813	20,614	78,000	29,014	11,601	4,738	38,129	30,482	277,600	621,000	200,914	------	14,191	1,873,803
1989	203,563	52,527	159,527	22,559	90,000	29,506	13,358	6,155	27,538	30,040	304,000	607,460	265,731	------	16,003	2,013,913
1990	244,137	101,913	169,412	27,503	100,000	29,352	16,840	11,158	31,938	24,591	302,000	605,100	294,189	------	16,900	2,182,307
1991	234,218	89,369	176,552	28,879	120,000	34,844	26,311	16,879	60,780	25,916	260,000	601,110	294,062	------	17,820	2,187,462
1992	243,400	85,862	161,402	33,774	140,000	32,118	31,032	37,983	71,190	22,702	146,000	614,071	330,212	80,000	18,278	2,298,809
1993[1]	247,196	85,000	152,929	30,300	160,000	27,845	39,235	42,097	60,587	15,826	149,500	619,201	331,013	80,000	18,916	2,330,321
1994[2]	250,000	80,000	150,000		160,000						150,000	600,000	330,000	80,000		2,300,000

[1] Preliminary.   [2] Estimate.   [3] Formerly part of the U.S.S.R.; data not reported separately until 1992.   *Source: U.S. Bureau of Mines*

GOLD

Salient U.S. Gold Statistics   In Kilograms (1 Kilogram = 32.1507 Troy Ounces)

			Refinery Production				-------- Stocks, Dec. 31 ---------			Official	---------- Consumption ----------			
Year	Mine Production	Value Million $	Domestic & Foreign Ores	Secondary (Old Scrap)	Exports (Excluding Coinage)	Imports for Con-sumption	Treasury Department[3]	Futures Exch.	Industry	World Reserves[4]	Dental	Industrial[5]	Jewelry & Arts	Total
1985	75,495	771.0	64,583	49,824	123,378	255,857	8,170,019	65,628	18,538	35,616	9,309	35,828	50,951	96,318
1986	155,365	1,819.0	75,618	47,266	155,365	489,863	8,149,938	87,370	28,771	35,743	7,921	36,858	65,827	110,795
1987	153,870	2,216.0	112,368	63,843	119,630	119,539	8,160,251	81,647	23,390	35,655	6,944	35,245	71,024	113,319
1988	200,914	2,831.3	137,829	61,391	328,237	92,457	8,145,696	44,634	38,360	35,829	7,576	37,226	67,027	111,836
1989	265,731	3,268.6	183,685	51,943	211,091	152,504	8,147,169	69,727	30,462	35,603	7,927	37,621	69,524	115,078
1990	294,189	3,640.8	225,183	43,980	296,397	97,519	8,146,432	50,881	37,065	35,572	8,700	30,996	78,514	118,216
1991	294,062	3,434.7	224,675	48,088	284,127	178,749	8,145,696	49,893	39,411	35,501	8,485	21,793	84,096	114,375
1992	330,212	3,662.4	283,951	53,396	368,851	174,341	8,145,000	46,453	36,713	35,199	6,543	20,360	83,508	110,410
1993[1]	331,013	3,840.9	243,135	65,964	792,680	169,305	8,143,000	78,514	32,728	34,632	6,173	19,663	64,575	90,411
1994[2]	330,000		250,000			140,000	8,142,000							90,000

[1] Preliminary.   [2] Estimate.   [3] Includes gold in Exchange Stabilization Fund.   [4] Held by market economy country central banks and governments and inter-national monetary organizations.   [5] Including space and defense.   *Source: U.S. Bureau of Mines*

Monthly Average Gold Price (Handy & Harman at New York)   Dollars Per Troy Ounce

Year	Jan.	Feb.	Mar.	Apr.	May	June	July	Aug.	Sept.	Oct.	Nov.	Dec.	Average
1981	557.4	500.3	498.8	494.9	479.8	460.8	408.8	411.0	444.1	437.2	413.7	408.7	549.61
1982	384.1	374.1	330.3	350.0	334.4	315.0	340.1	366.0	435.6	421.8	414.1	445.4	375.94
1983	479.9	490.4	419.7	432.2	437.6	412.8	423.1	416.3	411.5	393.2	382.3	387.1	423.83
1984	370.9	386.0	394.4	381.7	377.3	377.7	346.4	347.7	340.9	340.1	340.9	319.0	360.23
1985	302.8	298.8	303.9	324.9	316.1	316.5	317.8	330.2	322.6	326.2	325.5	322.4	317.31
1986	345.5	339.3	345.4	304.6	340.5	342.8	348.9	376.9	419.0	423.6	398.8	391.2	367.70
1987	408.3	401.3	408.9	438.7	460.1	449.6	450.8	460.9	460.2	465.5	466.5	486.0	446.40
1988	476.6	441.9	443.6	451.8	450.8	451.3	437.6	431.3	412.8	406.8	420.1	418.5	436.93
1989	404.0	387.8	390.1	384.4	371.3	367.6	394.7	364.9	361.9	366.9	392.3	408.1	382.92
1990	410.1	416.8	393.1	374.3	369.2	352.3	362.5	395.0	389.5	380.7	381.7	378.2	383.61
1991	383.6	363.8	363.4	358.4	356.8	366.7	367.5	356.2	348.8	358.7	359.5	361.1	362.18
1992	354.5	353.9	344.3	338.5	337.2	340.8	353.0	343.0	345.4	344.4	335.1	334.7	343.74
1993[1]	329.0	329.4	330.1	341.9	366.7	371.9	392.4	378.5	354.9	364.2	373.5	383.7	359.67
1994[1]	387.0	382.0	384.1	378.2	381.2	385.6	385.4	380.4	391.8	389.8	384.4	379.6	384.14

[1] Preliminary.   *Sources: U.S. Bureau of Mines; American Metal Market*

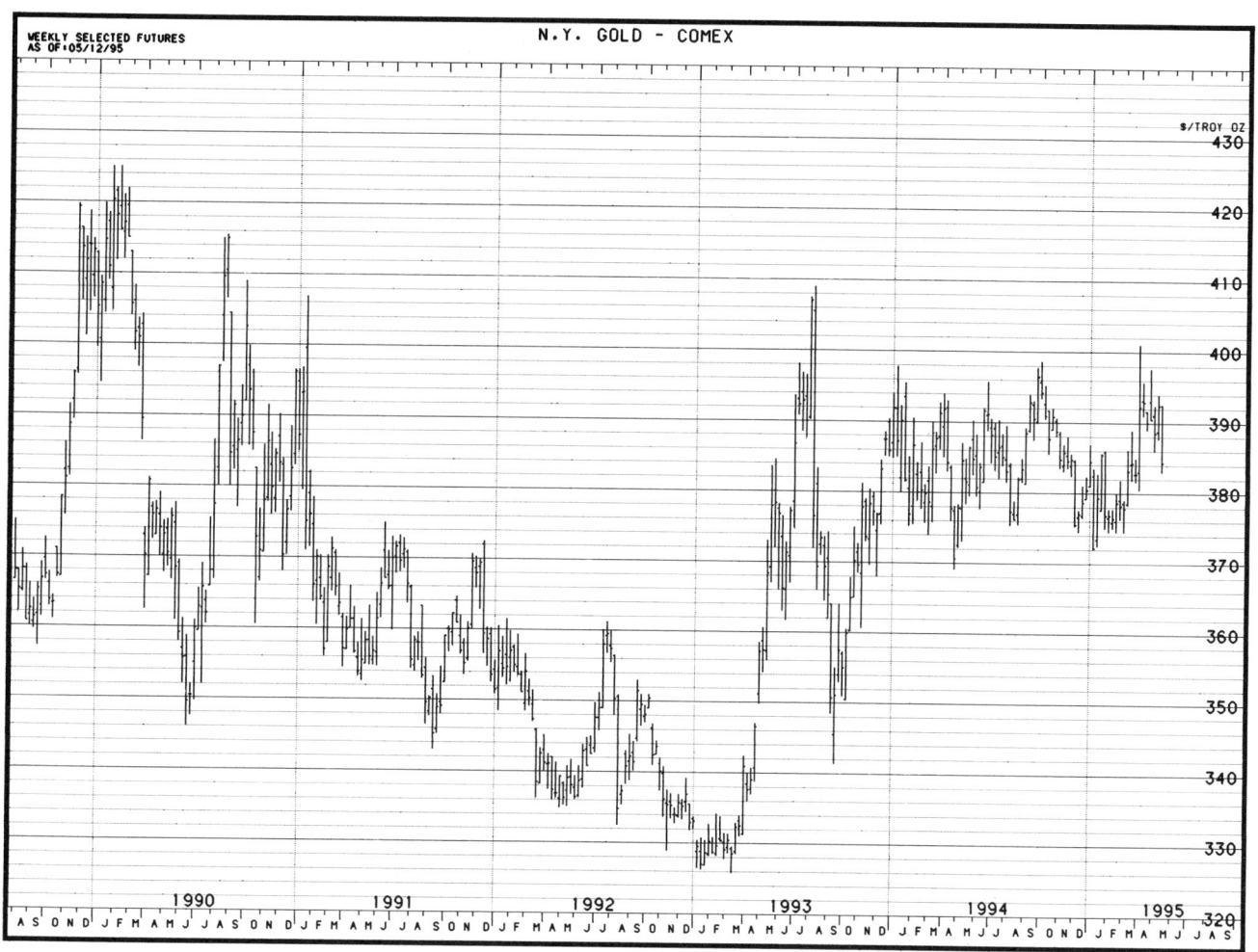

WEEKLY SELECTED FUTURES
AS OF·05/12/95

N.Y. GOLD - COMEX

$/TROY OZ

Gold Average Open Interest at New York (COMEX)   In Thousands of Contracts

Year	Jan.	Feb.	Mar.	Apr.	May	June	July	Aug.	Sept.	Oct.	Nov.	Dec.
1986	147,771	139,118	141,941	137,748	130,605	116,896	121,769	133,225	149,013	140,621	145,940	135,533
1987	137,650	134,151	146,896	172,605	169,606	147,703	147,005	149,345	147,346	139,482	137,383	154,110
1988	147,067	152,789	158,224	154,788	153,465	145,951	147,822	140,311	153,556	160,591	153,497	154,110
1989	162,226	166,455	167,419	160,215	180,709	164,196	154,517	150,414	151,836	146,262	153,497	144,839
1990	147,884	132,400	126,890	118,750	117,707	113,958	105,496	120,579	116,331	113,873	154,927	151,788
1991	104,666	98,000	98,429	101,266	100,341	88,961	94,467	99,790	105,053	96,302	111,638	110,343
1992	106,110	103,319	109,796	106,485	109,947	98,127	111,039	102,239	102,376	102,232	109,030	109,004
1993	112,420	10 ,093	115,505	142,208	172,491	170,829	200,168	180,509	166,201	152,531	109,965	100,328
1994	156,045	139,354	146,269	144,386	147,738	146,255	148,915	155,641	167,981	166,041	166,536	178,998

Source: Commodity Exchange, Inc. of New York (COMEX)

Total Volume of Trading of Gold Futures at New York (COMEX)   In Thousands of Contracts

Year	Jan.	Feb.	Mar.	Apr.	May	June	July	Aug.	Sept.	Oct.	Nov.	Dec.	Total
1986	1,126.2	574.2	703.9	617.9	482.2	451.6	527.6	711.1	1,054.7	846.9	724.3	579.6	8,400
1987	936.4	706.9	794.9	1,135.2	1,021.2	793.4	796.9	760.3	747.9	951.3	847.1	748.2	10,240
1988	815.0	778.7	965.0	637.7	866.2	946.3	884.2	587.5	790.9	694.5	895.5	634.9	9,496
1989	900.4	800.0	993.8	682.4	932.0	936.6	756.1	591.1	630.0	681.2	1,228.4	876.4	9,989
1990	1,327.1	885.1	975.6	472.4	745.2	541.0	747.4	1,191.5	729.4	879.9	705.3	530.1	9,730
1991	957.3	497.8	617.7	446.1	584.4	520.0	551.4	457.2	429.1	551.0	677.3	510.6	6,771
1992	729.8	388.4	607.3	425.4	485.4	427.2	734.6	500.2	465.3	414.1	504.1	320.1	6,002
1993	506.0	446.2	661.4	640.4	1,140.7	809.6	1,171.7	808.8	728.9	565.2	892.3	533.2	8,916
1994	981.8	584.0	88 .5	589.2	922.6	749.2	723.8	626.0	645.6	651.2	687.8	461.5	8,503

Source: Commodity Exchange, Inc. of New York (COMEX)

GOLD

Commodity Exchange, Inc. (COMEX) Depository Warehouse Stocks of Gold   In Thousands of Troy Ounces

Year	Jan. 1	Feb. 1	Mar. 1	Apr. 1	May 1	June 1	July 1	Aug. 1	Sept. 1	Oct. 1	Nov. 1	Dec. 1
1983	2,247	2,621	2,754	2,645	2,636	2,723	2,630	2,648	2,570	2,538	2,500	2,485
1984	2,481	2,472	2,408	2,452	2,412	2,426	2,376	2,395	2,387	2,391	2,349	2,366
1985	2,308	2,308	2,273	2,109	2,136	2,142	2,133	2,107	2,119	2,083	2,099	2,105
1986	2,109	2,352	2,580	2,593	2,567	1,986	1,992	1,621	1,664	1,726	1,787	2,193
1987	2,890	2,798	2,817	2,903	2,628	2,665	2,614	2,624	2,670	2,636	2,644	2,645
1988	2,624	2,605	2,586	1,596	1,566	1,675	1,834	2,099	2,189	1,949	1,629	1,267
1989	1,434	1,408	1,454	1,532	1,606	1,634	1,602	1,602	1,433	1,483	1,731	2,263
1990	2,241	2,225	2,245	2,220	2,048	1,809	1,582	1,530	1,539	1,564	1,585	1,347
1991	1,636	1,686	1,540	1,298	1,458	1,711	1,772	1,875	1,220	1,342	1,302	1,479
1992	1,605	1,362	1,435	1,411	1,591	1,618	1,605	1,733	1,688	1,947	1,766	1,524
1993	1,507	1,340	1,365	1,426	1,383	2,231	2,247	2,448	2,437	2,425	2,349	2,552
1994	2,524	2,928	2,958	2,862	2,802	2,567	2,665	2,574	1,988	1,904	1,843	1,867

Source: Commodity Exchange, Inc. of New York (COMEX)

Central Gold Bank Reserves   In Millions of Troy Ounces

Year	Belgium	Canada	France	Germany	Italy	Japan	Netherlands	Switzerland	United Kingdom	United States	Industrial Total	Developing Oil	Developing Non-Oil	IMF[2]	Bank for Int'l Settlements	World Total
1985	34.2	20.1	81.9	95.2	66.7	24.2	43.9	83.3	19.0	262.7	896.5	43.8	94.7	103.4	6.7	1,145.2
1986	34.2	19.7	81.9	95.2	66.7	24.2	43.9	83.3	19.0	262.0	895.6	43.7	100.3	103.4	6.4	1,149.5
1987	33.6	18.5	81.9	95.2	66.7	24.2	43.9	83.3	19.0	262.4	894.3	43.6	99.1	103.4	6.1	1,146.5
1988	33.7	17.1	81.9	95.2	66.7	24.2	43.9	83.3	19.0	261.9	895.1	42.0	99.1	103.4	6.4	1,146.1
1989	30.2	16.1	81.9	95.2	66.7	24.2	43.9	83.3	19.0	261.9	891.5	42.1	103.3	103.4	6.1	1,146.4
1990	30.2	14.8	81.9	95.2	66.7	24.2	43.9	83.3	18.9	261.9	889.4	41.5	101.3	103.4	6.6	1,142.2
1991	30.2	13.0	81.9	95.2	66.7	24.2	43.9	83.3	18.9	261.9	887.3	42.0	101.6	103.4	6.6	1,141.0
1992	25.0	9.9	81.9	95.2	66.7	24.2	43.9	83.3	18.6	261.8	877.4	42.0	102.2	103.4	7.8	1,132.8
1993[1]	25.0	6.8	81.9	95.2	66.7	24.2	33.7	83.3	18.5	261.8	860.7	42.0	101.7	103.4	6.6	1,114.4

[1] Thru October only.   [2] International Monetary Fund.   *Source: American Metal Market*

U.S. Mine Production of Recoverable Gold   In Kilograms

Year	Arizona	California	Idaho	Montana	Nevada	Alaska	Colorado	South Dakota	New Mexico	Utah	Other States	Total
1987	1,791	18,277	3,041	7,143	83,342	3,812	5,561	-------------------- 30,903 --------------------				153,870
1988	4,549	22,442	3,218	9,175	114,322	4,210	5,126	13,981	------------ 23,891 ------------			200,914
1989	2,768	29,804	3,057	12,434	153,995	5,756	3,448	16,123	1,076	----- 37,270 -----		265,731
1990	5,000	29,607	W	13,012	179,078	3,232	2,357	17,870	888	----- 43,145 -----		294,189
1991	6,195	30,404	3,348	13,715	180,382	3,200	3,181	16,371	------------ 39,161 ------------			295,957
1992	6,656	33,335	3,177	13,994	203,165	5,003	3,763	18,681	------------ 41,350 ------------			329,124
1993[1]	3,042	35,356	4,324	20,265	206,304	------------------------------ 62,803 ------------------------------						332,091

[1] Preliminary.   W = Withheld proprietary data, included in "Other States."   *Source: U.S. Bureau of Mines*

U.S. Consumption of Gold, by End-Use   In Kilograms

Year	Jewelry and the Arts — Gold-filled & Other	Electro-plating	Karat Gold	Total	Dental	Industrial — Gold-filled & Other	Electro-plating	Karat Gold	Total	Grand Total
1987	9,256	3,133	58,635	71,024	6,944	21,010	12,343	1,892	35,245	113,319
1988	7,598	1,469	57,959	67,027	7,576	21,034	15,088	1,104	37,226	111,836
1989	7,364	1,283	60,877	69,524	7,927	15,723	20,684	1,215	37,621	115,078
1990	8,132	429	69,952	78,514	8,700	12,725	17,251	1,020	30,996	118,216
1991	3,848	373	79,875	84,096	8,485	8,102	12,624	1,068	21,793	114,375
1992	3,546	581	79,381	83,508	6,543	8,802	10,476	1,082	20,360	110,410
1993[1]	3,532	528	60,514	64,575	6,173	9,474	9,094	1,095	19,663	90,411

[1] Preliminary.   *Source: U.S. Bureau of Mines*

GOLD IN BRITISH POUNDS

WEEKLY CASH
AS OF:05/19/95

GOLD IN DEUTSCHE MARKS

WEEKLY CASH
AS OF:05/12/95

GOLD IN JAPANESE YEN

WEEKLY CASH
AS OF:05/19/95

GOLD IN SWISS FRANCS

WEEKLY CASH
AS OF:05/12/95

Grain Sorghum

World sorghum production was 57 million tonnes in 1994/95, up from 53 million in 1993/94. U.S. production was 16.1 million tonnes, up from 14.4 million in 1993/94. India produces about 20 percent of world output, but their domestic usage about equals if not trails production. India is now the world's largest consumer of sorghum. World trade is small, averaging under 9 million tonnes per crop year. The U.S. supplies about 75 percent of exports and Argentina supplies most of the balance. Mexico and Japan vie for the top import position for U.S. sorghum.

In the U.S. the sorghum crop year begins September 1. Kansas and Texas are the largest producing states. During 1991-93, about 1.1 million acres of sorghum were harvested for silage, abandoned or used as fodder for livestock, resulting in less than 9.4 million acres of sorghum harvested for the 1994/95 crop. Applying a trend yield of 65.7 bushels per acre, the initial 1994/95 crop forecast was placed at 585 million bushels, up slightly from the weather reduced 1993/94 crop of 568 million. The forecast proved low as production reached 640 million bushels.

Total supplies in 1994/95 of about 670 million bushels, including a low 48 million carry-in (the U.S. imports no sorghum), would be the lowest total since the 1970s. However, prices are not likely to benefit very much, partially owing to large competing supplies of corn. Moreover, the lower sorghum supply is expected to force a reduction in use of perhaps 90 million bushels, placing disappear-ance around 603 million bushels—the lowest use in more than twenty years—and replenish carryover stocks to about 66 million as of September 1, 1995.

Export demand for U.S. sorghum still accounts for nearly a third of total disappearance, even though it has been falling in recent years. Exports declined in 1993/94 to 202 million bushels from 277 million in 1992/93 owing largely to reduced demand from Mexico. Export prospects do not look much better than 220 million in 1994/95, as Mexico opts for corn rather than sorghum, which effectively offsets any increase in demand from Japan.

Through the first half of 1993/94, sorghum prices received by farmers remained relatively strong, averaging nearly 95 percent of corn prices. With continued weak export demand and lower domestic use during the second half of 1993/94, the sorghum farm price fared poorly relative to corn. However, prices were still up about 25 percent compared to 1992/93. Prices received by farmers for sorghum were forecast to decline in 1994/95 and average between $1.65-$2.05 per bushel vs. $2.31 in 1993/94.

Government Program

The target price for 1994/95 sorghum was $2.61 per bushel and the national average loan rate was $1.80. The levels in 1993/94 were $2.61 per bushel and $1.63, respectively.

World Sorghum Supply and Demand   In Thousands of Metric Tons

Crop Year	Exports Argentina	Non-U.S.	U.S.	Total	Imports Japan	Mexico	Unac-counted	Total	Total Pro-duction	China	Japan	Mexico	U.S.	Total	Ending Stocks Non-U.S.	U.S.	Total
1990-1	1,330	1,966	5,788	7,754	3,587	3,026	57	7,754	52,859	5,049	3,587	6,826	10,627	55,511	3,982	3,622	7,604
1991-2	1,300	1,907	7,457	9,364	3,247	4,996	22	9,364	51,394	4,851	3,217	7,596	9,717	53,052	4,592	1,351	5,943
1992-3[1]	1,023	2,018	6,634	8,652	3,221	3,951	25	8,652	64,317	4,597	3,210	6,631	12,091	60,755	5,059	4,446	9,505
1993-4[2]	425	1,315	5,318	6,633	2,841	3,089	108	6,633	52,244	4,900	2,991	5,329	11,687	57,986	2,555	1,208	3,763
1994-5[3]	500	800	5,600	6,400	2,800	2,100	205	6,400	56,651	5,900	2,900	4,200	10,351	56,784	1,723	1,907	3,630

[1]Preliminary. [2]Estimate. [3]Forecast. *Source: Foreign Agricultural Service, U.S. Department of Agriculture*

Salient Statistics of Grain Sorghum in the United States

Year	Acreage Planted[4] for All Purposes 1,000 Acres	For Grain Acreage Harvested 1,000 Acres	Pro-duction 1,000	Yield Per Harvested Acre Bushels	Price in Cents Per Bushels	Value of Pro-duction Million $	For Silage Acreage Harvested 1,000 Acres	Pro-duction 1,000 Acres	Yield Per Harvested Acre Tons	Sorghum Grain Stocks Dec. 1 On Farms Tons	Off Farms 1,000 Bushels	June 1 On Farms	Off Farms
1989-90	12,642	11,103	615,420	55.4	210	1,287.7	541	5,647	10.4	NA	NA	44,500	290,484
1990-1	10,535	9,089	573,303	63.1	212	1,220.5	527	5,377	10.2	NA	NA	43,750	178,250
1991-2	11,064	9,870	584,860	59.3	225	1,331.3	483	4,846	10.0	140,000	372,340	34,140	76,247
1992-3[1]	13,177	12,050	875,022	72.6	189	1,693.1	453	5,468	12.1	110,200	340,262	58,465	206,348
1993-4[2]	9,882	8,916	534,172	59.9	231		351	3,914	11.2	105,950	340,198	32,075	96,035
1994-5[3]	9,772	8,967	655,021	73.0	170-210		329	3,932	12.0	126,650	295,497		

[1]Preliminary. [2]Estimate. [3]Forecast. *Source: Foreign Agricultural Service, U.S. Department of Agriculture*

Production of All Sorghum for Grain in the United States, by State   In Thousands of Bushels

Year	Alabama	Arkansas	Colorado	Illinois	Kansas	Louisiana	Miss-issippi	Missouri	Nebraska	New Mexico	North Carolina	Oklahoma	South Dakota	Texas
1989	1,500	21,080	11,375	11,620	198,750	6,175	4,505	45,030	102,300	12,500	3,240	17,640	11,600	164,300
1990	990	18,150	10,340	14,625	184,800	8,320	5,525	42,640	108,750	3,250	1,840	16,450	14,300	135,200
1991	1,265	15,390	10,800	13,840	176,400	10,120	4,760	37,440	90,450	10,200	1,250	13,800	13,020	176,900
1992	1,250	31,160	6,660	26,780	244,000	15,232	10,500	62,080	143,820	12,300	1,000	17,490	14,060	279,000
1993	817	12,470	7,140	17,430	176,400	7,200	4,225	39,420	73,750	7,425	675	14,500	10,500	156,750
1994[1]	900	18,375	7,650	17,820	231,000	8,364	5,250	49,500	122,500	6,840	1,100	14,000	12,350	153,400

[1]Preliminary.   *Source: National Agricultural Statistics Service, U.S. Department of Agriculture*

U.S. Grain Sorghum Quarterly Supply and Disappearance   In Millions of Bushels

Sept. 1	Supply Beginning Stocks	Supply Pro-duction	Supply Imports	Total Supply	Food, Alcohol & Industrial	Seed	Feed & Residual	Total	Export	Total	Ending Stocks Gov't. Owned[3]	Ending Stocks Privately Owned[4]	Total Stocks
1991-2	142.6	584.9	0	727.5	6.8	1.7	374.0	382.5	291.7	674.3	8.0	45.0	53.2
Sept.-	142.6	584.9	0	727.4	2.1	0	228.3	230.4	46.5	277.0	34.3	416.2	450.5
Dec.-Feb.	450.5	------	0	450.5	1.8	0	89.2	91.0	108.2	199.2	19.6	231.6	251.2
Mar.-May	251.2	------	0	251.2	1.9	1.1	32.9	35.9	105.0	140.9	14.3	96.1	110.4
June-Aug.	110.4	------	0	110.4	1.0	.6	23.6	25.2	32.0	57.2	8.0	45.0	53.2
1992-3	53.2	884.0	0	937.2	6.1	1.4	477.5	485.0	277.2	762.2	4.0	171.0	175.0
Sept.-	53.2	884.0	0	937.2	1.5	0	273.9	275.4	56.4	331.9	2.5	602.8	605.3
Dec.-Feb.	605.3	------	0	605.3	1.2	0	68.2	69.4	101.5	170.9	4.0	430.4	434.4
Mar.-May	434.4	------	0	434.4	1.8	.7	79.7	82.2	87.4	169.6	3.9	260.9	264.8
June-Aug.	264.8	------	0	264.8	1.6	.7	55.6	57.9	31.9	89.8	4.0	171.0	175.0
1993-4[1]	175.0	534.2	0	709.2	6.2	1.3	453.0	461.0	201.6	662.0	.7	46.9	47.6
Sept.-	175.0	534.2	0	709.2	1.7	0	222.0	223.7	39.2	263.0	1.9	446.9	446.0
Dec.-Feb.	448.8	------	0	446.0	1.5	0	108.0	109.5	60.4	170.0	2.0	274.2	276.2
Mar.-May	276.2	------	0	276.2	1.6	.9	81.9	84.4	63.7	148.1	2.0	126.1	128.1
June-Aug.	128.1	------	0	128.1	1.4	.4	40.5	42.3	38.2	80.5	.7	46.9	47.6
1994-5[2]	47.6	655.0	0	702.6	------ 8.0 ------			400.0	408.0	220.0	628.0		

[1] Preliminary. [2] Forecast. [3] Uncommitted inventory. [4] Includes quantity under loan & farmer-owned reserves.
Source: Economic Research Service, U.S. Department of Agriculture

Average Price of Sorghum Grain, No. 2, Yellow at Kansas City   In Dollars Per Hundred Pounds (Cwt.)

Year	Sept	Oct	Nov	Dec	Jan	Feb	Mar	Apr	May	June	July	Aug	Average
1986-7	2.47	2.6	2.7	2.62	2.5	2.57	2.8	2.85	3.1	3.2	2.8	2.55	2.73
1987-8	2.64	2.75	2.9	2.95	3.05	3.24	3.27	3.16	3.21	4.58	4.79	4.28	3.4
1988-9	4.27	4.17	4	4.23	4.24	4.26	4.32	4.17	4.29	4.15	3.96	3.92	4.17
1989-90	4.73	3.91	4	3.98	3.91	3.84	4.01	4.32	4.47	4.54	4.48	4.27	4.21
1990-1	3.89	3.79	3.85	3.97	4.12	4.21	4.35	4.34	4.13	4.02	4.05	4.22	4.08
1991-2	4.24	4.3	4.27	4.35	4.44	4.62	4.78	4.41	4.54	4.51	4.05	3.77	4.36
1992-3	3.76	3.6	3.61	3.7	3.7	3.66	3.7	3.72	3.82	3.58	3.99	4.01	3.74
1993-4[1]	3.89	4.03	4.6	4.91	4.93	4.81	4.64	4.33	4.38	4.43	3.79	3.73	4.37
1994-5[1]	3.72	3.55											

[1] Preliminary.   *Source: Economic Research Service, U.S. Department of Agriculture*

U.S. Exports of Grain Sorghum, by Country of Destination   In Metric Tons

Year Beginning October	Canada	Ecuador	Ethiopia	Israel	Japan	Jordan	Mexico	South Africa	Spain	Sudan	Turkey	World Total
1988-9	1,130	31,370	0	414,630	2,633,562	135,995	2,193,506	0	226,489	9,999	550,717	8,036,892
1989-90	1,167	29,999	8,497	347,639	3,028,529	254,907	3,022,079	0	233,080	0	52,150	7,240,836
1990-1	1,325	33,060	0	165,906	1,853,079	20,500	3,015,944	0	181,501	91,400	114,636	5,778,792
1991-2	1,613	36,000	42,150	104,952	1,738,075	120,001	4,956,607	19,031	174,758	122,183	99,394	7,454,616
1992-3[1]	1,795	9,501	0	217,110	1,933,012	0	3,970,069	56,186	188,893	4,287	132,182	6,651,528
1993-4[2]			86,697	66,264	1,681,976		3,089,255		169,454	48,042	0	5,216,640

[1] Preliminary. [2] Estimate.   *Source: Economic Research Service, U.S. Department of Agriculture*

Grain Sorghum Price Support Program & Market Prices

Year	Put Under Price Support Quantity	Price Support % of Pro-duction	Acquired by CCC	Owned by CCC at Year End	Basic Loan Rate	Target Price	Findley Loan Rate	Effective Base[3] Mil. Acres	Partici-pation Rate[4] % of Base	No. 2 Yellow Kansas City	No. 2 Yellow Texas High Plains	No. 2 Yellow Los Angeles	No. 2 Yellow Gulf Ports
	Million Cwt.				$ Per Bushel								
1986-7	222.1	42.2	127.9	229.0	2.28	2.88	------	19.0	75	2.73	3.24	4.50	3.22
1987-8	201.3	49.2	119.7	259.6	2.17	2.88	1.82	17.4	84	3.40	3.81	5.18	3.96
1988-9	22.7	7.0	17.0	190.9	2.10	2.78	1.74	16.8	82	4.17	4.66	6.08	4.81
1989-90	11.7	3.4	10.1	91.0	1.96	2.70	1.57	16.2	71	4.21	4.38	5.53	4.76
1990-1	12.1	3.8	5.0	36.2	1.86	2.61	1.49	15.4	70	4.08	4.48	5.52	4.65
1991-2	9.5	2.9	5.4	5.0	1.80	2.61	1.54	13.5	77	4.36	4.78	5.69	4.86
1992-3	27.2	5.5	0	1.1	1.91	2.61	1.63	13.6	79	3.74	4.06		4.27
1993-4[1]	8.2	2.8	0		1.89	2.61	1.63	13.5	82	4.37	4.95		4.90
1994-5[2]	23.1	6.3	0		1.89	2.61	1.80	13.5	81				

[1] Preliminary. [2] Estimate. [3] National effective crop acreage base as determined by ASCS

Hay

U.S. producers harvested nearly 60.3 million acres for hay in 1994, vs. 60.4 million in 1993. Production totaled about 154 million tons, placing total 1994/95 supplies near 177 millions tons, including carry-in stocks of 22.7 million. That total was up from 170 million tons in 1993/94. The number of roughage consuming animal units (RCAU) was placed at 78.7 million, the highest so far in the 1990s and suggesting a supply of 2.18 tons per RCAU, about the same as in 1993/94. Disappearance of hay per RCAU during 1994/95, however, may rebound slightly from the previous season's 1.91, which was the lowest since the 1989/90 sea-son that followed the 1988 drought.

The key to hay prices rests largely on the number of dairy cows and producer intentions to plant acreage to hay for forage. In 1994, California and Arizona planted more acreage to hay to help feed increased dairy cow numbers, but in Wisconsin where dairy cow numbers were lower, farmers still opted for more hay acreage owing to the crop's low quality in 1993. The higher hay supply in 1994/95 was expected to see the average farm price of hay slip from the $81.60/ton of 1993/94 despite the anticipated higher RCAU's.

Salient Statistics of All Hay in the United States

Year Crop Beginning May	Acres Harvested 1,000 Acres	Yield Per Acre Tons	Pro- duction	Carryover May 1	Disap- pearance	Supply Per Animal Unit	Disap- pearance Per Animal Unit	Animal Units Fed[3] Millions	Farm Price $ Per Ton	Farm Pro- duction Value Million $	Alfalfa (Certified)	Timothy	Red Clover	Sudan- Grass
			---- Millions Tons ----			---- In Tons ----					---- Dollars Per Cwt. ----			
1988-9	65,055	1.94	126.0	27.1	135.6	2.03	1.80	75.5	85.20	10,457	245.00	132.00	143.00	42.00
1989-90	63,300	2.30	145.5	17.5	135.9	2.16	1.80	75.5	85.40	11,197	249.00	132.00	143.00	45.30
1990-1	61,407	2.39	146.8	27.1	146.9	2.30	1.94	75.5	80.60	10,462	253.00	82.10	145.00	47.70
1991-2	62,475	2.45	153.3	27.0	152.0	2.36	1.98	76.4	71.20	10,006	266.00	66.40	134.00	48.10
1992-3	58,903	2.49	146.9	28.6	156.4	2.32	2.04	76.6	72.10	10,506	252.00	66.30	122.00	47.10
1993-4[1]	59,679	2.46	146.8	21.1	147.3	2.21	1.91	77.1	74.30		269.00	80.60	148.00	45.20
1994-5[2]	58,744	2.56	150.1	22.7		2.18		80.7	81.60		266.00	76.00	148.00	47.90

Header note: Retail Price Paid by Farmers for Seed, April 15

[1]Preliminary. [2]Estimate. [3]Roughage-consuming animal units fed annually. *Source: Economic Research Service, U.S. Department of Agriculture*

Production of All Hay in the United States by Important States   In Thousands of Tons

Year	California	Idaho	Illinois	Iowa	Michigan	Minna-sota	Missouri	Nebraska	New York	North Dakota	Ohio	Oklahoma	Pennsyl-vania	South Dakota	Texas	Wis-consin
1989	8,524	4,043	2,365	6,650	5,205	6,400	6,764	5,705	4,538	3,020	4,553	5,115	4,709	4,290	9,582	8,080
1990	8,307	4,084	2,220	7,095	5,335	6,560	6,865	7,205	4,377	3,745	4,620	3,926	4,719	6,300	8,000	9,120
1991	8,610	4,294	3,162	6,285	5,255	8,090	7,110	7,473	4,102	4,780	3,150	4,360	4,026	8,045	9,700	9,060
1992	7,755	3,655	3,316	6,615	4,280	6,550	6,780	7,793	3,590	3,515	4,240	4,750	4,740	6,780	9,800	6,090
1993	7,590	4,844	4,106	4,803	5,370	5,970	7,335	7,323	3,605	5,043	3,475	4,248	4,352	8,190	7,506	6,260
1994[1]	8,210	4,438	3,175	5,775	4,865	7,530	6,770	7,415	3,961	4,510	4,384	4,128	4,528	7,330	8,455	6,550

[1]Preliminary. *Source: Agricultural Statistics Board, U.S. Department of Agriculture*

U.S. Types of Hay Production & Farm Stocks   In Thousands of Short Tons

Year	Alfalfa & Mixtures	All Others	All Hay	Corn for Silage[1]	Sorghum Silage[1]	Farm Stocks May 1	Farm Stocks Dec. 1
	---- Production ----					---- Farm Stocks ----	
1989	77,370	68,142	145,512	86,109	5,647	17,507	101,194
1990	83,555	63,265	146,820	86,844	5,377	27,089	104,873
1991	83,795	69,530	153,325	80,543	4,846	27,023	111,404
1992	79,140	67,763	146,903	87,663	5,468	28,599	105,601
1993	80,305	66,494	146,799	81,829	3,914	21,102	101,888
1994[2]	81,398	68,726	150,124	87,949	3,932	22,714	

[1]Not included in all tame hay. [2]Preliminary. *Source: Agricultural Statistics Board, U.S. Department of Agriculture*

Mid-Month Price Received by Farmers for All Hay (Baled)   In Dollars Per Ton

Year	May	June	July	Aug	Sept	Oct	Nov	Dec	Jan	Feb	Mar	Apr	Average[2]
1988-9	79.70	77.00	81.60	81.40	82.90	85.10	86.40	87.60	89.50	91.80	96.90	101.00	85.20
1989-90	100.00	90.20	83.40	81.60	85.70	83.20	83.20	83.50	84.90	85.70	87.50	95.00	85.40
1990-1	96.00	85.00	81.60	81.00	83.20	84.00	81.40	78.70	77.90	77.80	80.50	85.50	80.60
1991-2	81.10	75.20	71.80	70.80	69.80	68.50	68.20	68.90	68.70	71.10	69.90	70.90	71.20
1992-3	79.50	75.80	69.70	71.90	70.10	70.30	71.00	73.50	76.10	78.00	80.50	83.60	74.30
1993-4	86.60	79.60	76.90	77.50	78.80	82.30	84.20	83.50	85.70	86.90	90.80	98.20	81.60
1994-5[1]	100.00	88.70	82.50	83.10	82.40	86.80	86.60	85.50	84.80				

[1]Preliminary. [2]Weighted average by sales. *Source: Economic Research Service, U.S. Department of Agriculture*

Heating Oil

Heating oil consumption in the U.S. is concentrated in the Northeastern states and is used mainly for residential purposes. There is vigorous competition between heating oil distributors and regulated natural gas distributors, which are mostly utilities. The trend over the past several years has been for consumers to either choose natural gas, or switch to natural gas heating from heating oil. Natural gas pipelines have now been installed in many older neighborhoods, and consumers have responded by replacing aging heating oil units with natural gas. At the same time, heating oil distributors have met the competition by hedging in the futures market to lock in "guaranteed" low prices. While natural gas is often considered the cleaner and more environmentally safe fuel, heating oil burners have been designed to be more efficient and require less fuel to operate.

The trend in use appears to be working against heating oil. In many areas, restrictions have been put on heating oil. New oil tanks are now required to be located above ground, which many home owners are not likely to find acceptable. Natural gas travels through underground pipelines. While heating oil distributors often call into question the safety of natural gas use, there have been few incidents of residential natural gas accidents. The future trend appears to be toward residential heating with natural gas and not heating oil.

In late-summer, it was expected that heating oil prices would follow their normal seasonal path upward, in response to increased use in the northeast U.S. It is the distillate pool (heating oil, diesel, kerosene, jet fuel) that benefits the most from the seasonal increase in heating demand. Already, distillate demand, specifically in the form of diesel fuel, has increased due to the strong increase in U.S. economic activity. A wild card is the implementation of the new reformulated gasoline (RFG) standards which will go into effect on January 1, 1995. These standards will require an increased number of new gasoline specifications to be available in the Northeast to fight pollution. It is still not known how refineries will respond to the challenge of producing this gasoline. It is possible that refineries will have to curtail production of heating oil to meet potential demand for the new gasolines.

Heating oil traders will remember the situation in the Northeast last winter when a very severe winter held its grip for several weeks. Use of residual fuel oil soared to some of the highest levels seen since the cold wave of 1989. So far in late-1994, the fall and winter in the Northeast has been much milder than normal.

Over the first eight-months of 1994, average daily U.S. production of distillate fuel oil was 3.2 million barrels per day. That represented an increase of over 6 percent from the like period of 1993, and an 11 percent increase from 1992. Imports of distillate fuel oil during the January-August 1994 period were 211,000 barrels per day. That is much above the same period of 1993. Exports over the eight-month period were 240,000 barrels per day. Distillate product supplied averaged 3.18 million barrels per day, up 6 percent from the same period of 1993. Ending stocks at the end of August 1994 were 138,000 barrels.

During the January-August 1994 period, U.S. production of residual fuel oil averaged 812,000 barrels per day. This represented a decline of 1 percent from the like period of 1993, and 11 percent below 1992. The decline in residential heating oil consumption is evident since 1979, when the average daily production of residual fuel oil was 1.7 million barrels per day. Imports for the first eight-months of 1994 averaged 352,000 barrels per day. Imports have also significantly declined, as compared to 1979 daily imports of 1.2 million barrels. During last February's extreme cold wave in the Northeast, fuel oil stocks decreased by 152,000 barrels per day, the largest stock drawdown in many years. Exports of residual fuel oil averaged 119,000 barrels per day in 1994. Product supplied, a measure of consumption, averaged 1.06 million barrels per day in the January-August 1994 period. In February 1994, the daily average was 1.5 million barrels, the highest level since 1982. In August 1994, stocks of residual fuel oil were at 39 million barrels.

Futures Markets

Heating oil futures and options are traded on the New York Mercantile Exchange (NYMEX). In London, gas oil futures and options are listed on the International Petroleum Exchange (IPE).

Average Spot Prices of Heating Oil #2   In Cents Per Gallon

Year	Jan.	Feb.	Mar.	Apr.	May	June	July	Aug.	Sept.	Oct.	Nov.	Dec.	Average
1984	93.24	86.26	79.31	85.35	84.23	77.89	75.43	76.50	79.83	78.10	76.35	74.28	80.56
1985	74.28	75.88	80.57	79.24	72.63	70.31	68.80	72.90	78.97	83.72	86.94	81.45	77.14
1986	66.81	53.31	59.69	43.70	46.90	37.84	33.33	40.93	40.31	39.47	42.17	44.52	45.49
1987	52.34	47.36	49.18	48.58	51.75	52.30	54.62	52.46	52.33	56.14	55.84	53.75	52.22
1988	51.73	48.10	47.43	51.46	50.82	44.76	42.79	43.41	40.71	40.52	44.84	50.91	46.46
1989	54.35	51.47	56.86	53.98	50.76	48.51	49.35	49.75	55.78	58.80	59.20	80.91	55.81
1990	73.26	57.48	57.93	58.51	53.99	48.22	53.14	75.23	88.82	93.95	87.51	79.73	68.98
1991	74.96	70.80	61.92	56.36	55.04	53.67	57.74	60.48	61.54	66.58	64.33	53.35	61.31
1992	51.72	53.39	52.49	56.22	57.38	61.26	60.24	58.29	61.90	62.72	56.52	54.98	57.25
1993	53.14	56.02	58.13	55.49	54.53	52.62	49.74	50.70	51.96	54.00	50.30	43.47	52.51
1994	49.93	55.81	49.18	48.01	47.98	49.37	49.93	49.51	47.90	48.23	49.62	48.41	49.49

Source: New York Mercantile Exchange

HEATING OIL

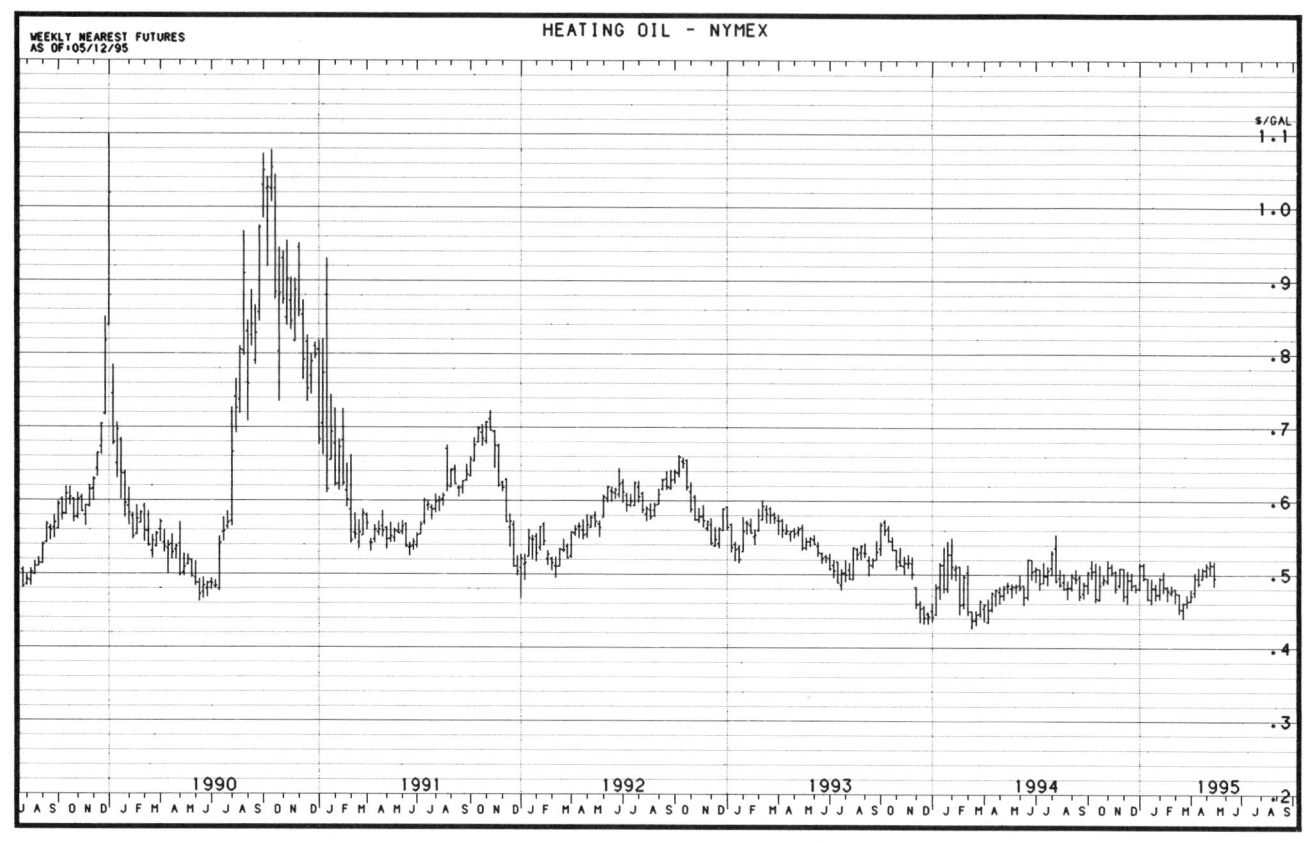

Average Open Interest of Heating Oil Futures (No. 2) in New York   In Contracts

Year	Jan.	Feb.	Mar.	Apr.	May	June	July	Aug.	Sept.	Oct.	Nov.	Dec.
1984	31,359	24,817	17,751	17,421	17,818	17,491	18,646	20,928	23,968	28,550	26,520	25,306
1985	23,197	16,243	16,881	17,196	16,970	20,150	21,419	25,061	29,626	31,726	35,062	33,275
1986	28,866	29,476	32,783	33,841	37,897	50,299	63,935	65,337	70,994	79,030	75,477	70,723
1987	66,228	60,479	47,798	45,494	40,865	44,530	52,480	54,696	65,781	70,167	74,093	74,945
1988	59,605	51,640	49,705	44,674	49,155	58,960	77,018	77,777	87,942	93,762	85,350	80,093
1989	75,038	63,791	60,455	57,533	49,174	49,527	59,799	69,578	88,642	97,064	99,293	105,240
1990	83,020	68,065	67,389	76,954	85,349	112,506	116,108	103,280	97,589	93,631	92,399	81,864
1991	74,216	81,742	81,103	82,419	89,482	102,887	115,896	125,463	135,804	144,026	128,330	117,182
1992	108,337	96,543	91,508	90,816	87,459	101,185	98,623	109,787	119,595	129,951	140,952	135,380
1993	130,536	125,603	130,438	107,363	102,708	113,898	131,816	142,054	166,253	172,940	175,781	199,299
1994	196,390	185,607	186,539	164,417	140,658	129,005	124,764	149,571	172,071	165,475	152,570	148,298

Source: New York Mercantile Exchange

Volume of Trading of Heating Oil Futures[1] In New York   In Contracts

Year	Jan.	Feb.	Mar.	Apr.	May	June	July	Aug.	Sept.	Oct.	Nov.	Dec.	Total
1984	254,788	209,802	144,326	144,041	161,689	144,182	120,668	153,913	137,011	281,183	182,005	163,938	2,091,546
1985	286,264	149,403	162,503	137,064	122,699	133,339	148,117	157,552	202,785	246,558	219,126	242,323	2,207,733
1986	274,057	221,156	214,501	207,748	223,943	247,552	309,662	282,636	285,246	387,054	271,497	349,992	3,275,044
1987	399,813	328,327	348,204	282,109	238,048	273,708	329,078	343,355	347,152	437,157	422,982	543,462	4,293,395
1988	506,182	377,379	403,181	267,233	286,365	380,550	431,231	363,276	441,939	578,648	475,675	423,356	4,935,015
1989	534,041	422,660	430,447	372,640	334,973	445,822	372,388	402,420	475,402	554,733	574,693	820,748	5,740,967
1990	754,945	415,420	462,479	451,708	516,989	463,263	518,993	723,152	505,810	612,310	521,969	429,833	6,376,871
1991	603,683	523,870	392,484	387,232	399,919	425,082	507,755	595,913	538,240	689,143	781,291	835,559	6,680,165
1992	815,199	574,007	550,113	592,056	586,707	601,067	645,020	663,743	625,675	709,532	808,201	807,142	8,005,462
1993	829,340	660,546	747,299	537,543	481,957	543,356	632,168	721,852	833,800	761,764	886,565	988,871	8,625,061
1994	1,085,683	875,714	766,788	631,664	629,295	723,677	612,316	783,181	706,822	721,375	652,257	798,063	8,986,835

[1] No. 2 heating oil.   *Source: New York Mercantile Exchange*

Stocks of Distillate Fuel in the U.S., First of the Month   In Millions of Barrels

Year	Jan.	Feb.	Mar.	Apr.	May	June	July	Aug.	Sept.	Oct.	Nov.	Dec.	Residual Fuel Oil Stocks Jan. 1	July 1
1984	140.3	119.3	132.2	109.6	97.7	98.1	112.8	124.4	133.3	142.9	152.2	161.0	48.5	46.9
1985	161.1	142.4	121.4	99.3	96.8	104.4	109.7	115.7	113.8	117.4	123.4	139.7	53.0	39.6
1986	143.7	136.5	112.4	98.8	95.9	98.9	107.9	118.9	137.7	152.4	151.6	158.3	50.4	42.8
1987	155.1	141.3	123.7	109.3	100.3	101.3	104.4	114.6	124.7	126.8	121.0	128.0	47.4	41.4
1988	134.5	128.1	110.3	89.8	95.0	104.9	110.4	120.0	125.7	131.5	128.2	128.8	47.4	42.2
1989	123.5	120.3	107.5	96.6	98.4	99.3	99.6	115.0	116.3	123.2	121.7	119.8	44.6	44.1
1990	105.7	118.0	112.2	99.7	99.5	102.8	109.4	125.2	136.0	136.3	132.4	132.2	43.8	46.8
1991	112.1	111.7	101.6	98.2	102.9	106.9	113.7	124.7	131.4	140.1	138.3	144.5	47.6	43.7
1992	143.5	126.7	108.8	97.7	92.1	96.4	104.5	114.6	122.8	127.8	136.8	146.3	49.9	40.9
1993	140.6	130.7	110.4	97.3	99.5	102.8	110.0	120.7	128.2	131.3	145.3	149.2	42.6	45.7
1994[1]	140.9	118.1	104.0	99.6	102.6	112.4	119.6	133.8	138.4	144.6	146.0	147.3	44.2	39.3

[1] Preliminary.   Source: *Energy Information Administration, U.S. Department of Energy*

U.S. Production of Distillate Fuel Oil   Thousand Barrels Per Day

Year	Jan.	Feb.	Mar.	Apr.	May	June	July	Aug.	Sept.	Oct.	Nov.	Dec.	Average
1984	2,591	2,867	2,479	2,342	2,624	2,880	2,719	2,661	2,707	2,691	2,826	2,798	2,681
1985	2,631	2,504	2,267	2,490	2,686	2,647	2,646	2,592	2,594	2,902	3,102	3,176	2,687
1986	2,899	2,563	2,643	2,788	2,858	2,729	2,710	2,922	2,865	2,717	2,917	2,943	2,798
1987	2,759	2,556	2,421	2,553	2,563	2,689	2,700	2,706	2,748	2,780	3,035	3,242	2,731
1988	3,010	2,667	2,706	2,867	2,936	2,893	2,784	2,848	2,778	2,827	2,909	3,068	2,859
1989	2,974	2,797	2,713	2,789	2,750	2,809	2,848	2,907	2,952	2,906	3,063	3,266	2,899
1990	3,130	2,753	2,657	2,803	2,874	2,996	3,008	3,131	2,968	2,928	2,915	2,917	2,925
1991	2,845	2,870	2,865	2,819	2,929	2,941	2,998	2,961	3,055	3,040	3,103	3,107	2,962
1992	2,818	2,661	2,749	2,930	2,933	2,995	3,067	2,865	2,983	3,251	3,240	3,179	2,974
1993	2,914	2,815	2,919	3,047	2,994	3,093	3,186	3,100	3,205	3,432	3,474	3,382	3,132
1994[1]	3,117	3,019	3,095	3,250	3,319	3,287	3,211	3,189	3,286	3,206	3,274	3,236	3,208

[1] Preliminary.   Source: *Energy Information Administration, U.S. Department of Energy*

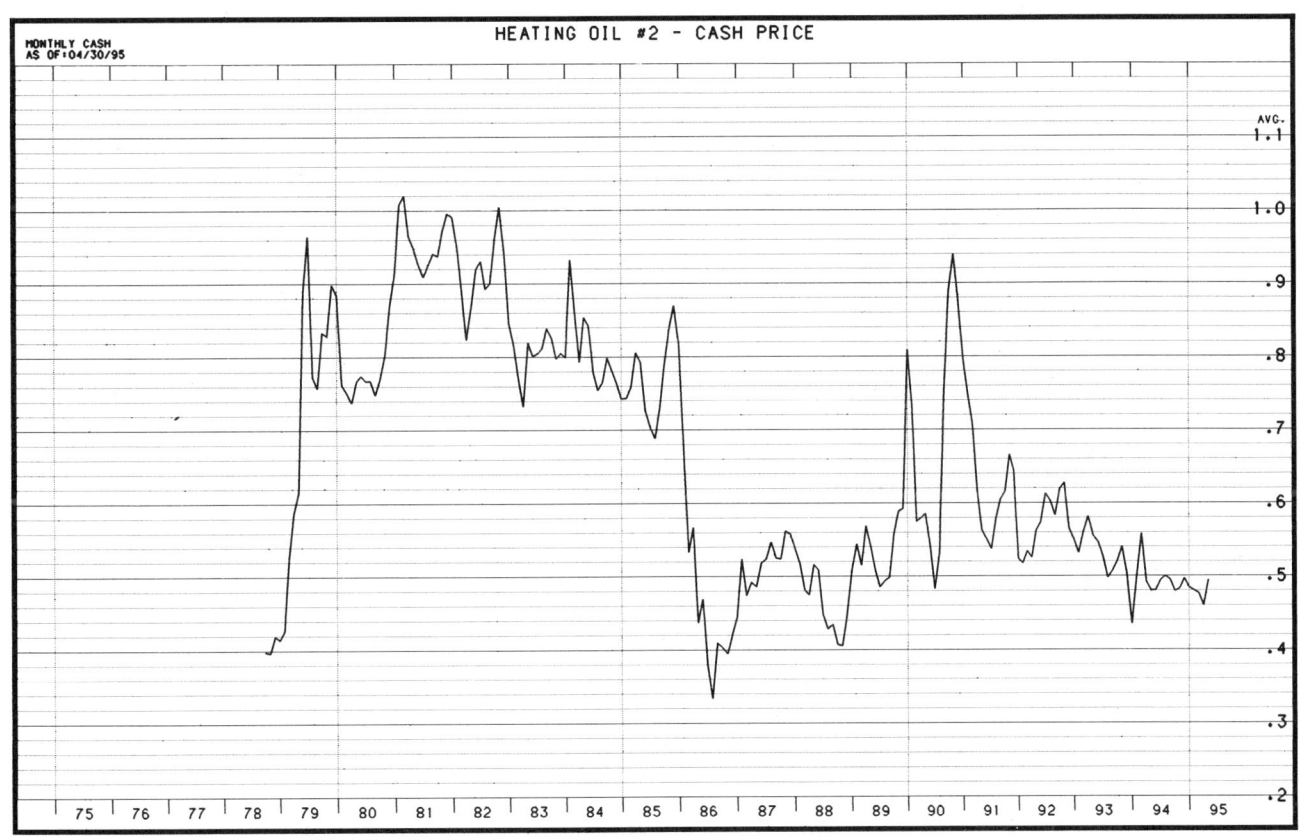

HEATING OIL #2 - CASH PRICE

MONTHLY CASH AS OF:04/30/95

HEATING OIL

U.S. Imports of Distillate Fuel Oil   Thousand Barrels Per Day

Year	Jan.	Feb.	Mar.	Apr.	May	June	July	Aug.	Sept.	Oct.	Nov.	Dec.	Average
1984	299	454	115	220	253	256	199	259	291	421	316	190	272
1985	272	143	156	253	197	152	95	81	222	262	280	287	200
1986	325	169	217	147	149	169	313	370	262	243	254	339	247
1987	222	253	297	192	203	265	381	222	222	237	187	378	255
1988	424	383	247	210	253	222	222	279	307	336	327	409	302
1989	346	331	439	301	290	233	334	254	249	261	307	324	306
1990	505	357	281	308	209	257	236	293	226	190	238	239	278
1991	192	139	206	258	186	209	155	168	237	207	249	252	205
1992	232	217	238	202	179	157	172	229	237	263	236	229	216
1993	182	224	235	209	153	168	130	159	137	242	214	160	184
1994[1]	160	276	313	226	202	181	164	211	193	159	166	185	202

[1] Preliminary.   Source: Energy Information Administration, U.S. Department of Energy

U.S. Disposition of Distillate Fuel Oil, Total Product Supplied   Thousand Barrels Per Day

Year	Jan.	Feb.	Mar.	Apr.	May	June	July	Aug.	Sept.	Oct.	Nov.	Dec.	Average
1984	3,525	2,834	3,259	2,926	2,814	2,593	2,504	2,559	2,654	2,765	2,827	2,865	2,845
1985	2,465	3,330	3,093	2,398	2,607	2,594	2,436	2,636	2,575	2,901	2,747	3,254	2,868
1986	3,330	3,416	3,168	2,904	2,762	2,544	2,592	2,621	2,540	2,912	2,877	3,329	2,914
1987	3,310	3,345	3,116	2,991	2,684	2,790	2,713	2,553	2,838	3,151	2,932	3,318	2,976
1988	3,558	3,557	3,539	2,864	2,765	2,854	2,640	2,873	2,821	3,218	3,183	3,560	3,122
1989	3,303	3,427	3,428	2,975	2,954	3,002	2,596	2,966	2,889	3,127	3,311	3,914	3,157
1990	3,185	3,260	3,277	3,043	2,900	2,923	2,726	3,218	2,864	2,960	3,094	2,816	3,021
1991	3,367	2,976	2,984	2,839	2,765	2,775	2,648	2,770	2,865	3,047	2,921	3,087	2,921
1992	3,231	3,219	3,207	3,039	2,753	2,679	2,710	2,705	2,908	3,056	2,929	3,316	2,979
1993	3,128	3,465	3,420	2,943	2,685	2,863	2,674	2,820	2,973	2,983	3,218	3,357	3,041
1994[1]	3,692	3,565	3,330	3,124	2,915	3,061	2,694	3,060	3,135	3,063	3,185	3,207	3,166

[1] Preliminary.   Source: Energy Information Administration, U.S. Department of Energy

U.S. Production of Residual Fuel Oil   Thousand Barrels Per Day

Year	Jan.	Feb.	Mar.	Apr.	May	June	July	Aug.	Sept.	Oct.	Nov.	Dec.	Average
1984	961	1,003	889	847	840	849	770	800	850	907	928	1,053	891
1985	1,004	1,040	963	912	793	702	732	742	808	912	932	1,055	882
1986	940	856	813	933	913	818	850	896	854	827	975	987	889
1987	920	825	863	831	813	864	901	882	904	887	928	1,001	885
1988	1,002	994	948	960	862	880	906	866	852	852	916	1,069	926
1989	949	930	937	904	934	953	862	903	856	1,001	1,075	1,140	954
1990	1,163	1,060	976	882	884	926	987	944	909	799	846	1,021	950
1991	1,001	1,050	995	916	929	933	871	925	838	814	896	1,051	934
1992	965	957	990	900	964	894	838	815	810	818	895	862	892
1993	820	840	818	896	908	795	762	752	822	841	899	869	835
1994[1]	813	859	841	825	830	770	791	828	809	756	836	873	819

[1] Preliminary.   Source: Energy Information Adminstration, U.S. Department of Energy

United States Residual Fuel Oil Supply and Disposition

Year	Supply — Total Production	Supply — Imports	Disposition — Stock Change	Disposition — Exports	Disposition — Product Supplied	Ending Stocks Million Barrels	Average Sales to End Users[3] ¢ per Gallon
	← Thousand Barrels Per Day →						
1984	1,070	776	-32	209	1,716	66	68.7
1985	852	699	-55	185	1,421	49	61.0
1986	891	681	12	190	1,369	53	34.3
1987	882	510	-7	197	1,202	50	42.3
1988	889	669	-8	147	1,418	47	33.4
1989	885	565	[2]	186	1,264	47	38.5
1990	950	504	13	211	1,229	49	44.4
1991	934	453	4	226	1,158	50	34.0
1992	892	375	-20	193	1,094	43	33.6
1993	835	373	4	123	1,080	44	33.7
1994[1]	819	302	-6	125	1,002	42	35.0

[1] Preliminary.   [2] Less than +500 barrels per day and greater than -500 barrels per day.   [3] Refiner price excluding taxes.
Source: Energy Information Administration, U.S. Department of Energy

Hides and Leather

According to the United States Department of Agriculture (USDA), world production of hides and skins in 1994 is forecast to increase to 3.47 million tonnes from 3.42 million in 1993. The increase is attributed to higher livestock slaughter in the Western Hemisphere. U.S. production of bovine hides and skins in 1994 was forecast at 1.11 million tonnes, an increase of almost 3 percent from 1993. The next largest producer of hides and skins is Brazil with 1994 production forecast at 430,000 tonnes, up nearly 5 percent from 1993. Argentine production was forecast at 305,000 tonnes, slightly more than the previous year's 300,000 tonnes. In Europe, the largest producer is France with 1994 production of 190,000 tonnes, up marginally from 1993. German production was forecast at 178,000 tonnes. German production has fallen considerably from 1991 when it reached 251,000 tonnes. Total European Union production was forecast at 790,000 tonnes. Australia is also an important producer of hides and skins with 1994 production forecast at 153,000 tonnes.

World exports of bovine hides and skins in 1994 was forecast by the USDA at 1.16 million tonnes, excluding European Union intra-trade. The U.S. is by far the largest exporter of hides and skins. U.S. exports for 1994 were forecast at 592,000 tonnes, up almost 2 percent from 1993. The U.S. exports a variety of hides and skins, with the major destinations being Taiwan, South Korea and Mexico for cattle hides. The major market for whole calf skins has been Italy. Exports of whole kip skins have gone mostly to Japan and South Korea. Brazilian exports of hides and skins in 1994 were predicted to be 75,000 tonnes. Exports by the European Union were put at 141,000 tonnes. Australian exports were forecast at 134,000 tonnes.

The U.S. also imports lesser amounts of hides and skins. For 1994, imports were forecast at 59,000 tonnes, up 4 percent. Mexican imports were placed at 62,000 tonnes. European Union imports, excluding intra-trade, were 344,000 tonnes. The major importers of hides and skins are the Pacific Rim countries. South Korea was forecast to import 350,000 tonnes, down 6 percent. Japan is also an importer with 1994 purchases put at 170,000 tonnes, down 6 percent. Taiwan was forecast to import 90,000 tonnes while Hong Kong took 81,000 tonnes.

Utilization of hides and skins for 1994 was forecast at 3.49 million tonnes, virtually unchanged from 1993. U.S. utilization was forecast at 576,000 tonnes, up 4 percent. The next largest user was Italy with 435,000 tonnes. Brazil was forecast to utilize 365,000 tonnes, up 3 percent. South Korea production was also forecast at 365,000 tonnes, down 5 percent. Argentine use was put at 305,000 tonnes while Japan was 200,000 tonnes.

Cattle hide prices were increasing over the first four months of 1994. Average prices for light native cow hides, Chicago Packer hides, were 68.1 cents per pound. Heavy native steer prices averaged 78.5 cents during the January-April 1994 period.

World Production of Bovine Hides and Skins — In Thousands of Metric Tons

Year	Argentina	Australia	Brazil	Canada	Colombia	France	Germany	Italy	Mexico	New Zealand	Russia[3]	South Africa	Turkey	United Kingdom	United States
1985	319	124	340	94	92	190	207	101	139	41	942	-----	61	110	1,028
1986	332	131	324	92	92	186	209	95	120	36	1,022	59	62	104	1,115
1987	314	144	350	85	86	193	203	91	122	54	1,060	59	62	101	1,128
1988	303	139	390	82	93	185	191	89	176	41	1,089	51	63	90	1,022
1989	304	137	429	84	97	170	228	88	222	35	1,090	55	65	91	1,086
1990	307	149	447	78	105	175	247	92	181	40	1,050	55	67	92	1,057
1991	308	153	436	75	104	182	251	95	155	44	1,029	54	64	93	1,061
1992	298	162	472	77	88	180	205	98	160	44	110	57	66	88	1,073
1993[1]	303	154	461	75	79	160	175	95	161	46	145	54	65	77	1,078
1994[1]	290	153	443	79	77	158	172	94	163	48	140	47	64	81	1,109
1995[2]	295	156	465	81	78	164	168	94	164	49	135	45	63	83	1,128

[1]Preliminary. [2]Forecast. [3]Formerly part of U.S.S.R.; data not reported separately until 1992. *Source: Foreign Agricultural Service, U.S.D.A.*

Salient Statistics of Hides & Leather in the United States

Year	Federally Inspected	Uninspected[4]	Total Production	Net Exports	Heavy Native Cows[2]	Heavy Native[3] Steers	All U.S. Tanning	Cattle Hide Equiv. Hides	Value of Leather Exports $1,000	Men	Women	Production[5]	Export
1985	34,765	1,528	36,293	24,398	57.55	54.0	15,230	12,616	283,704	104.2	103.6	265,098	11,320
1986	35,913	1,375	37,288	26,522	68.06	63.7	14,460	12,598	313,408	107.2	104.3	241,273	12,452
1987	34,468	1,179	35,647	24,007	83.43	79.9	14,800	12,754	395,536	111.4	107.2	225,888	14,575
1988	34,048	1,031	35,079	24,527	86.50	87.3	13,375	11,475	506,483	121.3	112.5	234,852	18,394
1989	33,010	907	33,917	22,500	83.16	89.4	13,029	11,242	624,925	127.5	116.2	221,790	14,358
1990	32,391	851	33,242	20,920	92.58	92.0	14,995	13,018	750,836	135.8	120.9	184,568	15,174
1991	31,887	803	32,690	18,636	76.92	78.9	14,850	13,021	680,348	141.0	124.0	167,386	18,109
1992[1]	32,094	780	32,874	17,810	81.71	75.9	16,000	14,474	705,038	145.0	126.4	168,451	21,401
1993[1]	32,593	731	33,324	17,117		78.9	18,100	16,931	764,120	145.3	129.3	163,757	20,700

Column groups: New Supply of Cattle Hides — Domestic Slaughter (Thousands of Equivalent Hides): Federally Inspected, Uninspected[4], Total Production, Net Exports. Wholesale Prices - ¢ Lb.: Heavy Native Cows[2], Heavy Native[3] Steers. Production (In Thous. Equiv. Hides): All U.S. Tanning, Cattle Hide. Value of Leather Exports $1,000. Wholesale Leather Indexes — Upper (1982 = 100): Men, Women. Footwear (Mil. Pairs): Production[5], Export.

[1]Preliminary. [2]Central U.S., heifers. [3]F.O.B. Chicago. [4]Includes farm slaughter; diseased & condemned animals & hides taken off fallen animals. [5]Other than rubber. *Sources: Leather Industries of America; Bureau of Labor Statistics, U.S. Department of Commerce*

HIDES AND LEATHER

U.S. Production of All Footwear (Shoes, Sandals, Slippers, Athletic, Etc.)   In Millions of Pairs

Year	Jan.	Feb.	Mar.	Apr.	May	June	July	Aug.	Sept.	Oct.	Nov.	Dec.	Total
1983	27.7	31.6	31.3	26.9	29.8	28.4	22.4	30.2	29.3	28.9	27.6	24.8	339.2
1984	27.3	29.1	30.2	27.7	28.6	24.6	20.7	26.0	21.9	25.2	22.3	19.6	303.2
1985	22.5	21.0	22.2	22.2	24.9	21.1	19.7	24.5	22.4	24.8	21.1	18.7	265.1
1986	22.5	21.6	21.3	21.2	20.8	18.4	18.4	20.8	19.7	21.4	18.4	16.6	240.9
1987	18.2	19.2	20.7	20.0	19.7	20.7	16.1	20.6	20.9	20.6	18.2	15.2	230.0
1988	16.7	20.8	21.6	19.3	20.2	19.7	14.0	21.4	21.3	21.2	21.3	17.6	234.8
1989	18.1	18.5	19.6	16.6	18.7	17.5	13.7	19.7	17.4	19.0	17.5	14.3	221.9
1990	17.8	17.2	18.5	16.7	18.9	16.7	14.3	18.8	16.5	18.2	15.4	12.6	184.6
1991	----------	48.1	----------	----------	37.8	----------	----------	41.8	----------	----------	41.2	----------	169.0
1992	----------	41.1	----------	----------	40.8	----------	----------	43.6	----------	----------	39.3	----------	164.8
1993	----------	43.3	----------	----------	44.6	----------	----------	42.8	----------	----------	41.0	----------	171.7
1994[1]	----------	40.0	----------	----------	39.2	----------	----------	38.2	----------	----------	39.3	----------	156.7

[1]Preliminary. *Source: U.S. Department of Commerce*

U.S. Imports and Exports of All Cattle Hides   In Thousands of Hides

	Imports		U.S. Exports – By Country of Destination													
Year	Total	From Canada	Total	Canada	France	Germany	Italy	Japan	Repub. of Korea	Mexico	Nether-lands	Portugal	Romania	Spain	Taiwan	Thailand
1983	664	570	21,861	1,235	332	343	823	6,413	4,635	1,296	174	133	1,318	246	2,433	10
1984	711	669	25,889	1,145	316	256	1,243	7,394	5,447	1,888	257	202	1,088	540	2,765	2
1985	1,044	883	25,428	796	220	125	1,169	6,835	6,453	2,309	82	180	1,168	340	2,831	17
1986	761	594	26,963	714	275	85	1,553	6,626	9,324	1,042	156	247	688	255	3,579	20
1987	490	338	24,235	924	158	56	394	5,998	10,077	1,437	85	82	308	200	3,184	37
1988	642	481	24,687	759	93	97	319	7,140	9,986	1,865	100	44	624	142	2,493	35
1989	901	1,043	23,401	614	17	68	343	6,268	10,322	1,284	132	46	1,154	64	1,886	70
1990	661	678	21,582	674	28	78	136	6,802	9,839	1,438	99	29	253	175	1,476	91
1991	1,549	1,258	20,185	561	4	52	138	4,662	9,300	2,702	65	7	-----	39	2,058	123
1992	1,536	1,302	19,347	684	2	-----	107	4,647	8,589	2,729	56	100	4	30	1,823	160
1993	1,660		18,777	965	8	1	354	4,167	7,919	2,217	9	79	1	60	1,950	386

[1]Preliminary. *Source: Leather Industries of America*

Average Factory Price[2] of Footwear in the United States   In Dollars Per Pair

Year	Jan.	Feb.	Mar.	Apr.	May	June	July	Aug.	Sept.	Oct.	Nov.	Dec.	Average
1983	12.88	13.72	13.18	13.54	14.20	13.57	12.91	14.14	14.06	15.02	14.69	15.55	13.96
1984	14.95	14.19	14.00	14.99	15.20	14.43	14.88	14.59	15.11	14.56	15.00	15.62	14.79
1985	15.24	14.97	14.10	14.87	14.86	15.35	14.24	14.55	14.12	13.71	13.56	15.13	14.56
1986	14.60	13.86	13.82	14.22	15.00	14.98	15.53	14.38	14.64	14.38	14.40	16.50	14.69
1987	15.09	14.58	14.05	15.15	15.89	15.63	16.47	15.60	15.63	15.23	15.89	17.96	15.60
1988	16.57	14.80	13.88	15.97	13.77	14.46	17.27	14.92	15.32	15.18	14.98	16.73	15.32
1989	15.94	15.35	15.00	16.90	15.77	16.45	16.36	17.17	17.38	17.20	17.73	18.68	16.98
1990	----------	18.04	----------	----------	18.65	----------	----------	19.91	----------	----------	20.72	----------	19.37
1991	----------	22.14	----------	----------	20.40	----------	----------	19.74	----------	----------	18.52	----------	20.14
1992	----------	20.19	----------	----------	22.21	----------	----------	21.15	----------	----------	20.46	----------	20.96
1993	----------	21.62	----------	----------	21.67	----------	----------	21.37	----------	----------	21.79	----------	21.61
1994[1]	----------	24.58	----------	----------	24.35	----------	----------	20.92	----------	----------	20.41	----------	22.31

[1]Preliminary. [2]Average value of factory shipments per pair. *Source: U.S. Department of Commerce*

HIDES AND LEATHER

Wholesale Price of Hides (Packer Heavy Native Steers) F.O.B. Chicago   In Cents Per Pound

Year	Jan.	Feb.	Mar.	Apr.	May	June	July	Aug.	Sept.	Oct.	Nov.	Dec.	Average
1983	37.1	37.7	40.4	46.0	50.8	51.8	59.2	57.3	53.3	53.8	56.7	54.8	49.9
1984	54.8	56.0	62.0	61.7	64.5	64.7	66.5	69.2	68.9	61.7	52.5	47.9	60.9
1985	46.0	41.7	45.5	54.7	57.0	53.1	54.0	55.7	57.1	57.6	63.5	60.8	53.9
1986	57.7	58.4	57.7	63.1	68.6	68.7	68.3	69.9	64.5	65.9	65.2	61.8	64.2
1987	61.8	64.2	69.7	82.4	83.5	81.7	82.5	83.8	89.0	89.9	85.4	83.7	79.8
1988	82.9	86.3	97.4	100.0	99.2	87.6	84.2	93.7	87.3	80.5	77.1	76.7	87.7
1989	84.0	87.4	94.6	87.5	85.2	85.0	90.3	91.7	95.9	94.7	92.9	90.9	90.0
1990	92.7	92.8	95.5	100.0	99.6	97.9	96.7	91.7	87.5	84.6	83.0	84.4	92.2
1991	81.6	76.4	75.7	86.3	88.8	86.7	84.1	77.2	74.1	75.4	75.4	71.3	79.4
1992	70.6	67.8	69.9	76.0	80.0	76.8	76.5	72.8	77.6	81.2	80.1	81.0	75.9
1993	79.8	81.8	81.5	81.4	80.4	76.9	76.6	79.3	80.5	81.8	80.8	79.8	80.1
1994	75.1	75.1	79.0	84.8	87.3	88.8	90.4	89.8	93.9	93.7	93.2	91.1	86.9

Source: Wall Street Journal; Knight-Ridder CRB

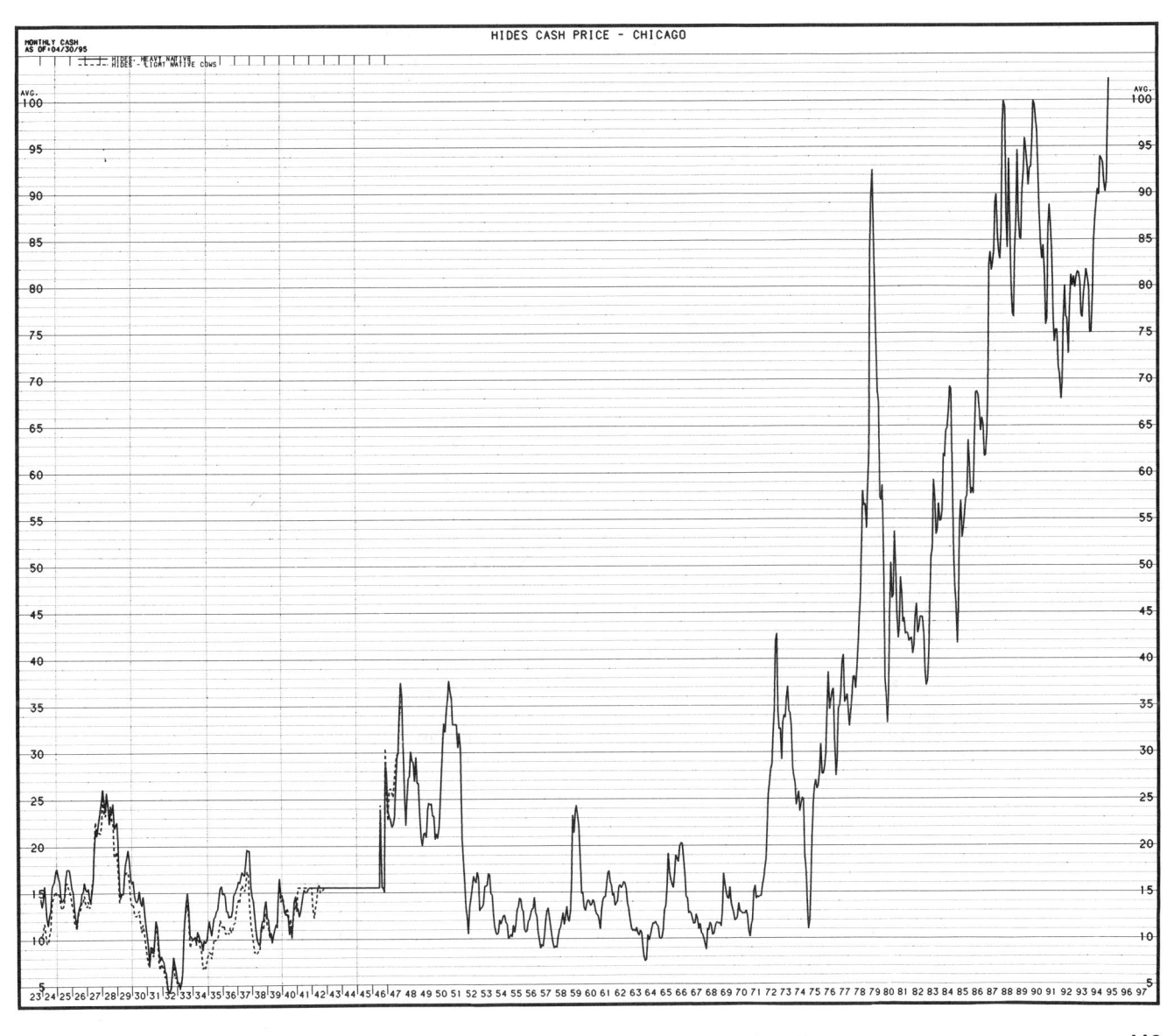

Hogs

The hog producing industry has witnessed major changes since the early-1980s, and the change is apt to persist into the late-1990s. The number of small hog farms (less than 500 head) has dropped nearly one-half, while the number of larger operations (over 500 head) has almost doubled. Percentagewise, of the nearly 230,000 U.S. hog producing farms in 1994, about 60 percent had less than 100 head. Twelve years ago, there were nearly 500,000 farms, with 75 percent having under 100 head. Despite the contraction, the U.S. hog population has steadily pushed to new highs. Iowa is the leading producing state. The U.S. follows China as world's largest hog producers, accounting for 8 percent and 50 percent, respectively, of total output.

On September 1, 1994, the market hog inventory of 54.2 million head was the largest since quarterly U.S. numbers were first reported in 1988. Producers at the time also indicated intentions to farrow approximately 3.1 million head during September-November, and another 3 million in December-February, up 5 percent and 4 percent, respectively, from a year earlier. If realized, record large pork production is likely for each quarter of 1995. The estimated large hog slaughter is expected to dampen prices and pressure the survival of the smaller hog producing farms. As it is, the expansion of breeding herds in late-1994 was occurring in large commercial operations in states where contracting is more prevalent. However, even the greater efficiency of larger operations will not offset market losses from weak prices, which cash hogs trading in the low $30 per hundred pounds are considered. Still, any slowing in hog production is not expected to at least mid-1995, and even then pork supplies are likely to range 3 percent to 4 percent higher than a year earlier. Moreover, the United States Department of Agriculture (USDA) expects pork supplies to stay at near record levels into the late-1990s. For 1995, hog slaughter is forecast at 99.7 million head, pork production at 18.4 billion pounds and per capita pork consumption at 55.2 pounds, all record highs. Total 1995 pork supplies of 19.6 billion pounds compare with 18.6 billion in 1994, while total use is estimated at 18.7 billion pounds. Dress weight averaged was about 184 pounds in 1994, and is estimated to reach 185 pounds in 1995.

The U.S. is a net importer of pork products and hogs. Canada is the largest supplier followed by Denmark. U.S. pork exports go largely to Japan, but Mexico returned as a strong market in 1994, partially owing to the North American Free Trade Act (NAFTA) pact. Total pork exports for 1994 of 450 million pounds were up about 3.5 percent from 1993. With stronger world demand expected in 1995 and if U.S. prices remain low, pork exports in 1995 are forecast to reach 480 million pounds. Canada is the sole exporter of live hogs to the U.S. and Mexico is the largest importer of U.S. hogs. Feeder pigs account for about 40 percent of all hogs imported from Canada.

Hog prices during 1994 traversed an unusual pattern in that they failed to rally in late-April and peak in June-July, when pork production reaches a seasonal low. The lack of seasonal price strength and larger production pressured prices during the fourth-quarter to the low $30 per hundred pounds area. Barrow and gilt prices averaged about $40 per hundred pound in 1994, down from $46.10 per hundred pounds in 1993 and expected to slip to $37.50 per hundred pounds in 1995. Composite retail pork prices held better during 1994, owing partially to aggressive industry advertising pushing pork as a white meat and alternative to high cholesterol red meats.

Futures Markets

Live hog futures and options are traded on the Chicago Mercantile Exchange (CME). A smaller contract is also traded on the Mid-America Commodity Exchange in Chicago (MCE).

World Hog Numbers in Specified Countries as of January 1   In Thousands of Head

Year	Brazil	Canada	China	Denmark	France	Germany	Italy	Japan	Meixco	Philip-pine	Poland	Russia	Spain	Ukraine	United Kingdom	United States
1990	32,120	10,650	352,810	9,120	12,275	34,178	9,261	11,816	8,563	8,124	18,685	40,000	16,910	19,947	7,383	53,821
1991	32,550	10,468	362,408	9,282	12,013	30,818	8,837	11,355	8,593	8,007	19,739	38,500	16,001	19,427	7,380	54,477
1992	33,050	10,498	369,650	9,767	12,067	26,063	8,549	10,966	9,928	8,022	20,725	35,400	17,209	17,839	7,519	57,684
1993[1]	31,050	10,577	384,210	10,345	12,564	26,514	8,307	10,783	11,298	7,954	21,059	31,500	18,260	16,175	7,705	58,116
1994[2]	31,200	11,209	393,000	10,870	12,868	26,075	8,000	10,622	12,083	8,227	17,422	28,600	18,100	15,298	7,869	57,938
1995[3]	32,100	11,650	401,000	11,085	13,000	25,400	7,900	10,450	12,373	8,235	19,000	26,000	18,200	14,400	7,910	60,500

[1] Preliminary.   [2] Estimate.   [3] Forecast.   Source: Foreign Agricultural Service, U.S. Department of Agricultures

Salient Statistics of Pigs and Hogs in the U.S.

	Pig Crop						Value of Hogs on Farms, Dec. 1		Hog Marketings	Quantity Produced (Live Wt.)	Value of Pro-duction	Hogs Slaughtered in Thousand Heads -- Commercial				
	Spring[3]			Fall[4]								Federally				
	Sows Farrowed	Pig Crop	Pigs Per Liter	Sows Farrowed	Pig Crop	Pigs Per Liter	$ Per Head	Total Million $	Thousand Head	Mil. Lbs.	Mil. $	Inspected	Other	Total	Farm	Total
Year	- 1,000s of Head -			- 1,000s of Head -												
1987	6,030	46,883	7.77	5,810	44,927	7.73	76.00	4,133	84,249	20,446	10,444	78,913	2,168	81,081	341	81,422
1988	6,041	47,238	7.82	6,036	46,000	7.62	66.30	3,678	90,334	21,670	9,145	85,517	2,278	87,795	341	88,136
1989	5,745	45,321	7.89	5,775	44,836	7.76	79.10	4,256	92,550	21,942	9,294	86,328	2,364	88,692	315	89,007
1990	6,001	47,507	7.92	5,717	44,939	7.86	85.40	4,655	89,373	21,347	11,376	82,901	2,235	85,136	296	85,431
1991	6,275	50,577	8.06	6,074	47,926	7.89	68.90	3,972	92,351	22,809	11,104	85,952	2,217	88,169	276	88,445
1992	6,004	48,806	8.13	6,006	48,626	8.10	71.60	4,281	99,115	24,279	9,991	92,611	2,278	94,888	268	95,157
1993[1]	6,028	49,006	8.13	5,954	48,044	8.07	74.90	4,338				90,933	2,135	93,068		
1994[2]	6,274	51,344	8.18	6,067	49,773	8.20	53.20	3,172				93,434	2,283	95,717		

[1] Preliminary.   [2] Estimate.   [3] December-May.   [4] June-November.   Source: Economic Research Service, U.S. Department of Agriculture

Hogs and Pigs on U.S. Farms on December 1   In Thousands of Head

Year	Georgia	Illinois	Indiana	Iowa	Kansas	Kentucky	Minne-sota	Missouri	Nebraska	North Carolina	Ohio	Penn-slvanyia	South Dakota	Wis-consin	Total
1988	1,210	5,600	4,300	14,000	1,500	1,090	4,690	2,850	4,150	2,700	2,210	970	1,810	1,275	55,469
1989	1,200	5,700	4,350	13,500	1,450	975	4,450	2,700	4,200	2,570	2,080	975	1,720	1,150	53,821
1990	1,100	5,700	4,400	13,800	1,500	920	4,500	2,800	4,300	2,800	2,000	920	1,770	1,200	54,477
1991	1,130	5,900	4,600	15,000	1,430	950	4,900	2,700	4,500	3,650	1,925	920	1,950	1,180	57,684
1992	1,100	5,900	4,600	16,400	1,440	870	4,700	2,850	4,650	4,500	1,800	950	1,830	1,210	59,815
1993	1,000	5,450	4,300	15,000	1,350	850	4,750	3,000	4,300	5,400	1,630	1,060	1,750	1,170	57,904
1994[1]	1,020	5,350	4,500	14,200	1,310	780	4,850	3,450	4,350	7,000	1,800	1,090	1,740	1,040	59,612

[1] Preliminary.   Source: National Agricultural Statistics Service, U.S. Department of Agriculture

Quarterly 10 -- U.S. State Hogs & Pigs Report   In Thousands of Head

Year[2]	Inventory[3]	Breeding[3]	Market[3]	Farrowings	Pig Crop	Year[2]	Inventory[3]	Breeding[3]	Market[3]	Farrowings	Pig Crop
1989	43,210	5,335	37,875	9,203	71,807	1992	45,735	5,610	40,125	10,202	82,497
I	43,210	5,335	37,875	2,109	16,439	I	45,735	5,610	40,125	2,296	18,532
II	41,655	5,440	36,215	2,580	20,309	II	44,800	5,555	39,245	2,663	21,570
III	44,020	5,565	38,455	2,324	18,167	III	47,255	5,845	41,410	2,501	20,395
IV	45,200	5,335	39,865	2,190	16,890	IV	49,175	5,840	43,335	2,398	19,351
1990	42,200	5,275	36,925	8,960	70,589	1993[1]	46,240	5,515	40,725	9,449	76,560
I	42,200	5,275	36,925	2,013	15,748	I	46,240	5,515	40,725	2,220	18,117
II	40,190	5,245	34,945	2,458	19,576	II	45,080	5,480	39,650	2,531	20,546
III	42,630	5,405	37,225	2,236	17,684	III	46,420	5,630	40,790	2,332	18,849
IV	44,120	5,300	38,820	2,238	17,459	IV	46,920	5,610	41,310	2,366	19,048
1991	42,900	5,257	37,643	9,516	75,330	1994[1]	46,180	5,595	40,585	9,742	80,020
I	42,900	5,257	37,643	2,129	16,700	I	46,180	5,595	40,585	2,296	18,607
II	41,990	5,450	36,540	2,577	20,555	II	45,830	5,595	40,235	2,673	22,173
III	44,520	5,700	38,820	2,413	19,260	III	47,965	5,845	42,670	2,443	20,116
IV	46,950	5,685	41,265	2,433	18,551	IV	49,150	5,850	43,950	2,330	19,124

[1] Preliminary.   [2] Quarters are December preceding year-February (I), March-May (II), June-August (III) and September-November (IV).   [3] Beginning of period.   Source: National Agricultural Statistics Service, U.S.Department of Agriculture

Hog-Corn Price Ratio[1] in the U.S.

Year	Jan.	Feb.	Mar.	Apr.	May	June	July	Aug.	Sept.	Oct.	Nov.	Dec.	Average
1984	18.2	18.4	16.3	15.3	15.4	16.9	17.6	17.4	16.0	16.5	18.4	19.0	16.9
1985	19.0	18.4	17.6	17.3	19.2	22.7	29.5	35.9	17.3	20.4	19.5	19.8	22.5
1986	31.9	33.9	32.2	33.4	32.8	35.0	37.3	39.9	40.2	37.9	35.9	33.7	34.6
1987	24.3	25.0	22.7	22.3	23.9	19.5	16.2	16.9	36.4	31.5	25.2	23.4	21.4
1988	15.7	15.6	15.1	14.4	16.1	17.9	18.6	20.1	15.7	15.0	14.4	15.7	16.7
1989	20.5	20.8	21.6	21.4	23.4	22.9	23.2	23.3	19.0	21.0	20.1	21.2	22.1
1990	22.0	22.5	21.5	21.0	22.7	23.7	23.9	22.0	22.3	23.3	25.9	21.5	22.4
1991	22.0	22.5	21.5	21.0	22.7	23.7	23.9	22.0	19.9	18.9	16.6	16.6	20.9
1992	15.3	16.3	15.7	16.5	18.1	18.9	19.1	20.5	19.5	20.5	20.8	21.2	18.5
1993	20.3	22.0	22.1	21.0	21.9	23.0	20.6	21.0	21.6	20.6	17.3	15.2	20.6
1994[2]	16.1	17.5	16.2	16.1	16.1	16.3	18.6	19.4	16.1	15.5	14.1	14.5	16.4

[1] Bushels of corn equal in value to 100 pounds of hog, live weight   [2] Preliminary.   Source: Economic Research Service, U.S. Department of Agriculture

Cold Storage Holdings of Frozen Pork[1] in the U.S., on First of Month   In Millions of Pounds

Year	Jan.	Feb.	Mar.	Apr.	May	June	July	Aug.	Sept.	Oct.	Nov.	Dec.
1984	300.6	295.1	311.7	350.7	390.4	437.7	405.2	345.0	269.5	256.6	275.6	269.4
1985	274.3	291.9	286.3	314.1	368.2	410.3	385.0	343.1	294.7	277.0	277.5	265.0
1986	229.4	235.4	239.1	253.5	282.0	275.6	247.7	214.9	184.7	185.9	215.8	206.2
1987	197.1	217.7	228.5	221.8	217.8	218.8	189.2	181.1	175.1	186.2	212.2	251.7
1988	285.4	291.5	308.2	345.8	397.3	388.6	362.8	337.2	287.0	288.0	320.8	361.3
1989	357.9	377.6	393.5	392.8	432.6	428.1	380.1	342.6	277.9	278.0	275.8	279.2
1990	255.8	272.5	303.9	294.6	320.3	320.3	292.6	256.4	224.7	225.8	231.9	221.5
1991	233.6	247.0	281.2	289.0	340.0	333.3	312.3	277.9	282.4	280.5	299.7	308.0
1992	311.1	341.2	364.0	372.2	362.6	344.9	319.0	307.0	266.7	297.3	306.8	316.7
1993	314.5	329.5	344.4	330.4	378.5	371.6	351.3	342.5	308.9	311.2	324.8	313.0
1994[2]	299.2	348.8	356.9	393.1	429.7	437.6	410.8	396.2	364.0	352.7	385.4	383.2

[1] Excludes lard.   [2] Preliminary.   Source: Economic Research Service, U.S. Department of Agriculture

HOGS

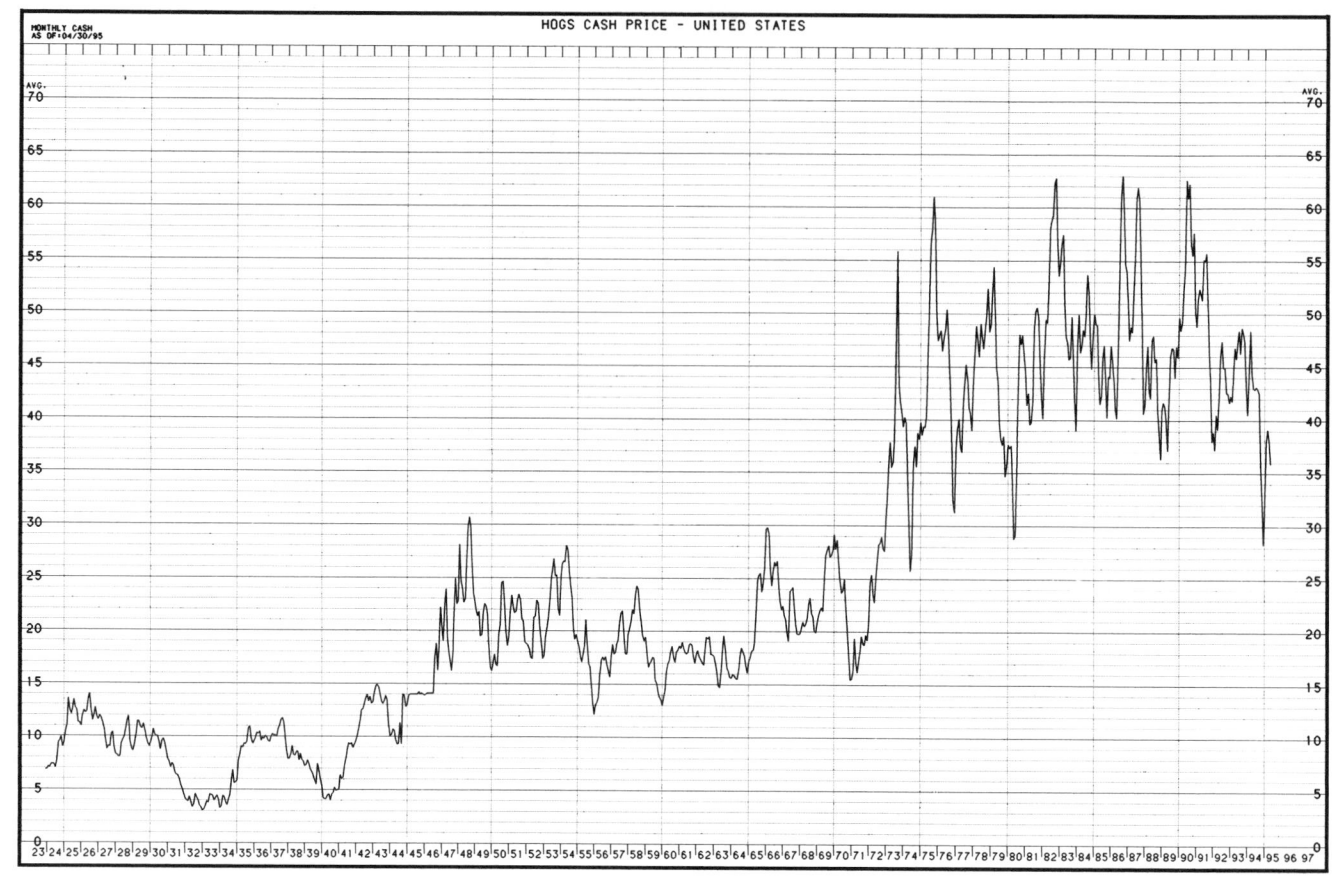

Average Wholesale Price of Hogs, Average (All Weights) at Sioux City   In Dollars Per Hundred Pounds (Hwt.)

Year	Jan.	Feb.	Mar.	Apr.	May	June	July	Aug.	Sept.	Oct.	Nov.	Dec.	Average
1987	47.56	49.08	48.67	52.10	55.79	61.37	62.69	50.56	55.19	49.28	40.74	41.56	51.22
1988	44.59	47.45	43.19	42.28	47.75	48.26	45.60	45.98	41.28	38.92	36.52	40.58	43.53
1989	41.64	41.11	39.88	37.22	42.40	46.24	47.26	47.04	44.58	47.49	47.21	49.65	44.31
1990	48.41	49.48	52.56	54.63	62.80	61.34	62.54	56.37	55.64	58.02	50.17	48.96	55.08
1991	51.32	52.31	51.92	51.42	54.83	54.79	55.74	51.11	46.76	43.51	38.29	38.93	49.24
1992	37.15	40.45	39.09	42.01	45.90	47.59	44.98	44.88	42.50	42.57	41.98	42.12	42.60
1993	41.66	44.57	46.76	45.46	47.10	48.52	46.38	48.67	48.40	47.27	42.76	40.38	45.66
1994[1]	43.99	48.12	44.30	42.72	42.27	42.76	42.62	42.37	35.49	32.56	28.25	32.39	39.82

[1] Preliminary.   *Source: Economic Research Service, U.S. Department of Agriculture*

Average Price Received by Farmers for Hogs in the U.S.   In Cents Per Pound

Year	Jan.	Feb.	Mar.	Apr.	May	June	July	Aug.	Sept.	Oct.	Nov.	Dec.	Average
1987	47.20	48.20	47.40	50.80	54.40	59.20	59.60	58.60	54.30	48.90	40.60	40.30	50.79
1988	43.00	45.80	42.20	41.90	46.30	47.10	44.10	44.70	40.70	38.70	36.20	39.70	42.53
1989	40.90	40.40	39.30	36.90	41.60	45.10	45.90	45.60	43.40	46.60	45.00	48.20	43.24
1990	47.30	48.20	51.30	53.80	61.20	60.30	60.80	55.90	54.30	56.80	50.20	47.80	53.99
1991	50.00	52.20	51.50	50.90	54.10	54.70	54.20	51.20	46.40	43.60	38.00	38.60	48.78
1992	36.40	40.20	39.10	41.00	45.10	46.40	44.40	43.90	41.90	42.60	40.90	41.80	41.98
1993	41.40	44.20	46.80	45.50	47.00	48.20	45.70	47.30	47.80	46.90	42.50	40.60	45.33
1994[1]	43.50	47.90	45.00	42.70	42.60	42.60	42.30	41.80	35.30	32.90	28.00	30.70	39.61

[1] Preliminary.   *Source: Economic Research Service, U.S. Department of Agriculture*

U.S. Federally Inspected Hog Slaughter   In Thousands of Head

Week Ended	1992	1993	1994	Week Ended	1992	1993	1994
January[1]				July			
1	1,471	1,515	1,596	2	1,437	1,544	1,644
8	1,870	1,948	1,777	9	1,620	1,422	1,444
15	1,914	1,944	1,857	16	1,708	1,621	1,751
22	1,812	1,812	1,601	23	1,722	1,654	1,652
29	1,818	1,824	1,732	30	1,683	1,642	1,713
Februray				August			
5	1,783	1,784	1,730	6	1,722	1,679	1,680
12	1,779	1,771	1,643	13	1,791	1,698	1,773
19	1,727	1,652	1,698	20	1,792	1,747	1,757
26	1,773	1,715	1,714	27	1,799	1,712	1,780
March				September			
5	1,797	1,750	1,756	3	1,840	1,743	1,819
12	1,841	1,780	1,826	10	1,679	1,577	1,638
19	1,687	1,725	1,769	17	1,981	1,846	1,973
28	1,799	1,735	1,751	24	1,949	1,834	1,999
April				October			
2	1,773	1,697	1,799	1	1,932	1,853	1,970
9	1,777	1,745	1,729	8	1,907	1,861	1,961
16	1,757	1,773	1,817	15	1,963	1,877	1,984
23	1,647	1,857	1,810	22	1,867	1,843	2,037
30	1,699	1,823	1,802	29	1,994	1,822	2,027
May				November			
7	1,631	1,803	1,796	5	1,947	1,874	2,053
14	1,704	1,719	1,767	12	1,917	1,825	1,985
21	1,698	1,701	1,749	19	1,909	1,936	2,059
28	1,480	1,670	1,729	26	1,677	1,606	1,697
June				December			
4	1,615	1,488	1,488	3	1,921	1,960	2,097
11	1,651	1,701	1,729	10	1,938	1,947	2,087
18	1,640	1,618	1,675	17	1,882	1,847	2,002
25	1,644	1,666	1,638	24	1,358	1,545	1,795

[1] Corresponding dates to 1994: 1992, January 4; 1993, January 2.   *Source: Economic Research Service, U.S. Department of Agriculture*

Federally Inspected Hog Slaughter in the United States   In Thousands of Head

Year	Jan.	Feb.	Mar.	Apr.	May	June	July	Aug.	Sept.	Oct.	Nov.	Dec.	Total
1987	6,723	5,886	6,787	6,492	5,922	5,987	6,019	6,019	6,855	7,519	7,121	7,583	78,913
1988	6,803	6,518	7,505	6,929	6,713	6,715	6,199	7,101	7,534	7,887	7,908	7,703	85,516
1989	7,116	6,619	7,569	7,199	7,277	6,881	6,131	7,392	7,493	7,823	7,815	7,012	86,328
1990	7,407	6,643	7,279	6,785	6,799	6,152	5,938	7,110	6,716	7,546	7,334	7,140	82,901
1991	7,461	6,469	7,044	7,320	6,948	6,296	6,557	7,098	7,177	8,292	7,744	7,708	85,951
1992	8,144	7,153	7,934	7,610	6,897	7,166	7,461	7,494	8,217	8,599	7,796	8,142	92,613
1993	7,649	6,921	7,958	7,840	6,988	7,338	7,010	7,473	7,763	7,857	7,952	8,184	90,993
1994[1]	7,285	6,783	8,148	7,609	7,382	7,452	6,941	7,997	8,192	8,585	8,516	8,547	93,464

[1] Preliminary.   *Source: National Agricultural Statistics Service, U.S. Department of Agriculture*

Average Live Weight of all Hogs Slaughtered Under Federal Inspection   In Pounds Per Head

Year	Jan.	Feb.	Mar.	Apr.	May	June	July	Aug.	Sept.	Oct.	Nov.	Dec.	Average
1984	242	241	240	243	245	248	245	243	242	245	246	246	244
1985	245	242	242	245	247	248	245	243	242	246	248	247	245
1986	246	244	244	246	246	246	245	244	245	248	250	252	246
1987	251	248	246	247	247	248	246	244	246	249	252	250	248
1988	248	247	247	249	250	250	249	247	248	251	253	251	249
1989	249	247	247	251	251	251	247	247	246	248	251	250	249
1990	249	248	248	250	251	252	249	249	248	250	253	252	250
1991	251	250	250	252	254	253	251	250	251	253	256	255	252
1992	255	253	252	253	254	254	251	250	252	252	255	255	253
1993	254	253	253	254	254	256	254	252	252	254	257	258	254
1994[1]	254	254	254	256	255	256	252	252	255	259	261	260	256

[1] Preliminary.   *Source: Economic Research Service, U.S. Department of Agriculture*

HOGS

Average Open Interest of Live Hogs Futures at Chicago   In Contracts

Year	Jan.	Feb.	Mar.	Apr.	May	June	July	Aug.	Sept.	Oct.	Nov.	Dec.
1983	47,316	44,412	41,019	36,564	33,103	31,593	27,269	30,683	34,621	31,472	30,666	30,323
1984	33,760	32,849	34,212	33,930	35,009	33,006	27,643	23,016	22,755	20,871	24,145	23,141
1985	26,589	29,408	27,125	24,248	24,019	23,545	20,878	18,894	19,799	21,567	27,843	24,852
1986	22,480	21,273	19,769	17,522	23,209	25,855	30,480	31,697	34,611	28,256	30,491	27,062
1987	26,275	28,125	30,794	30,195	32,431	32,889	30,752	31,553	34,197	28,562	25,138	24,440
1988	26,681	30,532	31,329	28,156	31,801	31,221	27,466	26,476	31,507	30,092	34,251	31,458
1989	31,923	30,853	29,014	30,414	29,646	27,353	25,375	25,345	28,308	33,936	35,913	29,693
1990	30,335	31,018	37,789	39,257	47,291	43,631	32,942	29,964	26,982	25,691	27,648	25,757
1991	22,742	24,798	24,449	22,400	25,871	21,275	18,154	16,771	17,281	18,462	21,572	19,167
1992	23,854	31,545	32,441	32,430	30,947	26,362	24,935	24,535	27,535	32,555	32,738	30,468
1993	27,210	25,620	28,264	24,139	22,581	19,840	19,026	20,761	20,544	20,051	21,167	24,096
1994	31,899	32,123	31,012	31,713	30,889	27,327	26,414	25,335	28,957	32,077	36,304	33,516

Source: Chicago Mercantile Exchange

Volume of Trading of Live Hogs Futures at Chicago   In Thousands of Contracts

Year	Jan.	Feb.	Mar.	Apr.	May	June	July	Aug.	Sept.	Oct.	Nov.	Dec.	Total
1983	291.6	254.7	213.8	230.6	254.1	262.1	217.4	279.9	220.8	174.2	197.5	194.2	2,790.7
1984	232.2	212.7	243.8	172.3	211.0	192.6	189.2	143.9	109.1	140.7	181.0	140.5	2,169.0
1985	155.0	128.3	160.2	141.7	156.2	141.9	134.7	120.2	136.1	156.8	145.2	143.5	2,719.9
1986	156.3	108.5	113.7	153.6	157.4	160.8	224.3	168.8	196.5	183.4	171.0	142.5	1,936.7
1987	159.2	138.5	172.7	190.3	189.7	212.1	219.5	169.8	174.0	175.5	121.1	118.0	2,040.5
1988	172.9	143.0	172.4	137.6	169.6	267.0	171.4	140.3	160.7	150.3	166.8	156.7	2,008.8
1989	188.2	135.0	152.8	130.7	175.2	147.5	141.9	131.8	149.6	181.5	205.9	151.6	1,891.9
1990	181.0	119.9	189.7	188.8	278.3	277.0	212.5	170.4	147.0	160.3	186.1	130.4	2,241.3
1991	177.9	150.3	148.0	157.0	155.7	120.8	131.1	120.9	102.9	118.4	104.5	94.8	1,695.8
1992	135.2	137.0	140.4	138.2	116.7	131.2	148.8	102.2	116.6	149.5	117.0	123.3	1,556.1
1993	131.5	101.9	160.0	131.0	120.2	121.1	112.5	91.5	109.4	102.7	116.1	103.0	1,401.8
1994	144.8	97.6	146.9	93.1	127.4	144.4	116.2	122.1	110.7	129.0	150.7	172.1	1,554.0

Source: Chicago Mercantile Exchange

Honey

Annual honey production in the world's key producing countries averaged about 445,000 tonnes during the first half of the 1990s, of which the U.S. produced about 20 percent. Total production in 1994 at 417,500 tonnes, was the lowest in a number of years and compares with 444,751 tonnes in 1993, and annual average during the 1980s of about 700,000 tonnes. Historically, the former Soviet Union was the world's largest producer, but China now leads with an estimated production in 1994 of 170,000 tonnes, and the U.S. a distant second. Several factors influence a country's annual honey production, not the least of which is dry weather and disease. However, another factor is the displacement of honey producing bees by more aggressive and less productive bees, notably Africanized bees. The latter have virtually wiped out honey production in some countries.

China's honey production has declined from the early-1990s when production averaged 200,000 tonnes. The reason seems to have its roots in the nation's sociological changes as farmers no longer are welcomed beekeepers. The Chinese government, however, appears to be trying to change that attitude and the downsizing of bee colonies was expected to end by late-1994. If the latter is realized, China's honey output should improve in 1995, abetted by higher prices. About 50 percent of China's production is exported, suggesting that total supply may lag well under demand.

Mexico and Canada together produced about 48,000 tonnes and 31,000 tonnes, respectively in 1994. Mexico's recent output has been contained by Africanized bees, but the Government has implemented procedures to help minimize the damage, including the changing of the queen bee in the hive at least once a year. If successful, Mexico's production could again near the 59,000 tonnes realized in 1991. U.S. production for 1994 is expected to total about 100,000 tonnes versus 104,493 tonnes in 1993.

World Production of Honey   In Metric Tons

Year	Argentina	Australia	Brazil	Canada	China	Germany[2]	Japan	Mexico	Russia[3]	United States	Total[4]
1982	33,000	22,400	25,000	30,500	136,000	18,000	7,400	45,000	186,000	104,300	-----
1983	30,000	24,963	22,000	38,771	138,000	19,000	6,869	68,000	210,000	93,000	650,603
1984	35,000	27,997	25,000	43,298	140,000	16,000	6,798	60,000	193,000	75,000	622,093
1985	45,000	26,871	28,000	36,120	150,000	11,000	7,225	56,000	204,000	68,000	632,216
1986	36,000	25,077	27,000	34,041	160,000	16,000	5,553	54,000	210,000	90,900	658,571
1987	44,000	28,000	30,500	39,776	204,000	16,000	6,023	47,850	219,245	102,875	738,269
1988	46,000	27,622	30,000	37,105	156,000	18,000	4,870	46,140	243,000	97,114	705,851
1989	40,000	26,198	32,000	27,815	189,000	29,000	5,343	48,530	225,000	80,266	703,152
1990	47,000	27,561	30,000	32,115	193,000	23,000	4,854	51,000	236,219	89,717	732,466
1991	54,000	20,604	32,300	31,606	206,000	25,000	4,202	58,770	240,000	99,414	714,790
1992	61,000	18,948	19,000	30,339	178,000	24,677	3,800	48,852	47,000	100,055	489,923
1993	59,000	22,556	20,100	30,901	176,000	26,357	3,500	48,000	49,600	104,493	494,351
1994[1]	45,000			33,000	170,000	23,000		46,500	54,000	100,000	471,500

[1] Preliminary.   [2] Data prior to 1989 are for West Germany.   [3] Formerly part of the U.S.S.R.; data not reported separately until 1992.   [4] Only for countries listed.   *Source: Foreign Agricultural Service, U.S. Department of Agriculture*

Salient Statistics of Honey in the United States   In Millions of Pounds

Year	Number of Colonies (1,000)	Yield Per Colony Pounds	Stocks Jan. 1	Total U.S. Production	Imports for Consumption	Domestic Disappearance	Exports	Total Supply	Placed Under Loan	CCC Take Over	Net Gov't. Expenditure[3] Mil. $	Domestic Avg. Price All Honey ¢ Lb.	National Avg. Price Support ¢ Lb.	Per Capita Consumption Lbs.
1980	4,141	48.2	37.7	199.8	49.0	226.2	8.5	234.7	41.1	6.0	8.7	61.5	50.3	.8
1981	4,213	44.1	51.8	185.9	77.3	232.0	9.2	241.2	55.2	35.2	8.4	63.2	57.4	.8
1982	4,250	54.1	73.8	230.0	92.0	250.8	8.5	259.3	88.4	74.5	27.4	56.8	60.4	.9
1983	4,275	48.0	136.5	205.0	109.8	269.0	7.5	276.5	113.6	106.4	48.0	54.4	62.2	1.0
1984	4,300	38.4	174.8	165.1	128.7	251.7	7.5	259.2	107.5	105.8	90.2	49.5	65.8	.9
1985	4,325	34.7	209.4	150.1	138.2	256.9	6.5	263.4	102.0	98.0	80.8	45.5	65.3	.9
1986	3,205	62.5	234.3	200.4	120.0	282.9	9.2	292.1	180.4	41.0	89.4	51.3	64.0	1.0
1987	3,190	71.1	262.6	226.8	58.3	320.9	12.4	333.3	218.0	52.7	72.6	50.3	61.0	1.1
1988	3,219	66.3	214.4	214.1	55.9	278.0	14.0	292.0	209.5	32.0	100.1	50.0	59.1	.9
1989	3,443	51.4	192.4	177.0	77.3	292.0	10.0	302.0	161.7	2.8	41.7	49.8	56.4	1.0
1990	3,210	61.6	144.7	197.8	77.0	303.4	12.4	315.8	183.5	1.1	46.7	53.7	53.8	1.0
1991	3,181	68.9	103.7	219.2	92.2	303.4	9.6	313.0	112.9	3.2	18.6	55.6	53.8	1.0
1992	3,030	72.8	102.1	220.6	114.6	298.2	10.4	308.6	122.4	2.9	16.6	55.0	53.8	1.0
1993[1]	2,876	80.1	128.7	230.4	133.6	304.2	8.5	312.7	130.7	.1	22.1	54.4	53.8	1.0
1994[2]	2,700	80.4	117.0	220.4	132.3	355.4	5.6	469.7	65.3		10.0			1.0

[1] Preliminary.   [2] Forecast.   [3] Fiscal year.   *Source: Economic Research Service, U.S. Department of Agriculture*

Interest Rates, U.S.

Monetary policy tightened steadily during 1994, perhaps more so than appeared warranted on the basis of prevailing inflationary pressure on the U.S. economy. The Federal Reserve (Fed), however, perceived the U.S. economy's cyclical expansion as having more staying power than seen in most post World War II cycles. By late-1994, the expansion was nearing four years in duration, and showing only little sign of slippage despite six increases in short-term rates by the Fed. Indeed, 1994 witnessed the strongest economic growth since 1988, with a near 4 percent gain in the Gross Domestic Product (GDP) during the fourth-quarter. Strong consumer spending and business investment, coupled with a buildup in inventories, all contributed to the GDP's buoyancy. Ironically, inflation proved less of a problem than expected with the Consumer Price Index (CPI) rising only 2.7 percent in 1994. Moreover, the Fed publicly stated that the CPI was probably overstating inflation by .5 percent to 1 percent, which if true, might suggest the Fed's tightening in 1994 was an over reaction to perception than fact. It could be argued that the Fed's policy, especially during the second half of 1994, was aimed more at strengthening the dollar than offsetting inflation . Fed funds rose from 3 percent to 5.5 percent during 1994. The yield curve flattened somewhat, but long-term rates still pushed towards 8 percent as the persistent publicity about inflation spooked bond traders. Bond holders took a beating, especially mutual funds that focused mostly on fixed assets. The Dow-Jones 20 Bond Index fell, losing about 10 percent of its value in 1994. The early-1994 jump in commodity prices, may have been the catalyst that prompted the Fed to lift the funds rate 25 basis points to 3.25 percent on February 4. Another .25 percent followed in late-March, a .25 percent in mid-April, and within a month later, a hefty .5 percent jump. During the second half of 1994, the Fed tightened twice.

Significantly, commodity prices flattened as 1994 progressed. By early-1995, Knight-Ridder Commodity Research Bureau (KR-CRB) Futures Index was approximately 3 percent over the previous year, hardly a basis for a cost-induced inflation spiral.

In either case, the Fed's 1994 monetary policy is not likely to be repeated in 1995. The initial market consensus focused on perhaps another 1 percent increase in short-term rates, but any further tightening was seen as counterproductive. Inflation for the year was forecast between 3 percent to 3.5 percent, which suggests a funds rate of about 6 percent if the normal relationship of about 300 basis points over inflation still holds. However, the odds favored a slackening in the GDP and official unemployment near 6 percent as the year progressed. If realized, these conditions could keep inflationary pressures subdued and set the stage for a moderate reversal in Fed policy, notwithstanding the dollar's value. Indeed, the Fed chairman indicated a willingness to accommodate the U.S. economy during 1995 if recession fears took root.

Futures Markets

A futures and options contract exists for almost every maturity on the yield curve, as well as for municipal and commercial credit risks. Major U.S. contracts include T-bills and Eurodollars CDs on Chicago's International Monetary Market (IMM), and T-bonds and municipal bonds on the Chicago Board of Trade (CBOT). Futures are also traded in Chicago on two, five, and ten year T-notes, 30 day fed funds and one month LIBOR. Smaller size contracts on interest rate instruments are listed at the MidAmerica Commodity Exchange (MidAm).

It should be noted that the IMM's Eurodollar futures contract permits trading in deliveries up to ten years ahead.

U.S. Producer Commodity Price Index (Wholesale, All Commodities)   1982 = 100

Year	Jan.	Feb.	Mar.	Apr.	May	June	July	Aug.	Sept.	Oct.	Nov.	Dec.	Average
1986	103.2	101.7	100.3	99.6	100.0	99.9	99.4	99.3	99.4	99.7	99.8	99.7	100.2
1987	100.5	101.0	101.2	101.9	102.6	103.0	103.5	103.8	103.7	104.1	104.2	104.2	102.8
1988	104.6	104.8	104.9	105.8	106.5	107.2	107.9	108.0	108.1	108.2	108.3	109.0	106.9
1989	110.5	110.8	111.5	112.3	113.2	112.9	112.8	112.0	112.3	112.7	112.7	113.0	112.2
1990	114.9	114.4	114.2	114.1	114.6	114.3	114.5	116.5	118.3	120.8	120.1	118.7	116.3
1991	119.0	117.2	116.2	116.0	116.5	116.4	116.1	116.2	116.1	116.4	116.4	115.9	116.5
1992	115.6	116.0	116.1	116.3	117.2	118.0	117.9	117.7	118.0	118.1	117.8	117.6	117.2
1993[1]	118.0	118.4	118.7	119.3	119.7	119.5	119.2	118.7	118.7	119.1	119.0	118.6	118.9
1994[1]	119.1	119.3	119.7	119.7	119.9	120.5	120.7	121.2	120.9	120.9	121.5	121.8	120.4

[1] Preliminary.   Source: Bureau of Labor Statistics, U.S. Department of Commerce

U.S. Consumer Price Index[2] (Retail Price Index for All Items: Urban Consumers)   1982-1984 = 100

Year	Jan.	Feb.	Mar.	Apr.	May	June	July	Aug.	Sept.	Oct.	Nov.	Dec.	Average
1986	109.6	109.3	108.8	108.6	108.9	109.5	109.5	109.7	110.2	110.3	110.4	110.5	109.6
1987	111.2	111.6	112.1	112.7	113.1	113.5	113.8	114.4	115.0	115.3	115.4	115.4	113.6
1988	115.7	116.0	116.5	117.1	117.5	118.0	118.5	119.0	119.8	120.2	120.3	120.5	118.3
1989	121.1	121.6	122.3	123.1	123.8	124.1	124.4	124.6	125.0	125.6	125.9	126.1	124.0
1990	127.4	128.0	128.7	128.9	129.2	129.9	130.4	131.6	132.7	133.5	133.8	133.8	130.7
1991	134.6	134.8	135.0	135.2	135.6	136.0	136.2	136.6	137.2	137.4	137.8	137.9	136.2
1992	138.1	138.6	139.3	139.5	139.7	140.2	140.5	140.9	141.3	141.8	142.0	141.9	140.3
1993[1]	142.6	143.1	143.6	144.0	144.2	144.4	144.4	144.8	145.1	145.7	145.8	145.8	144.5
1994[1]	146.2	146.7	147.2	147.4	147.5	148.0	148.4	149.0	149.4	149.5	149.7	149.7	148.2

[1] Preliminary.   [2] Not seasonally adjusted.   Source: Bureau of Labor Statistics, U.S. Department of Commerce

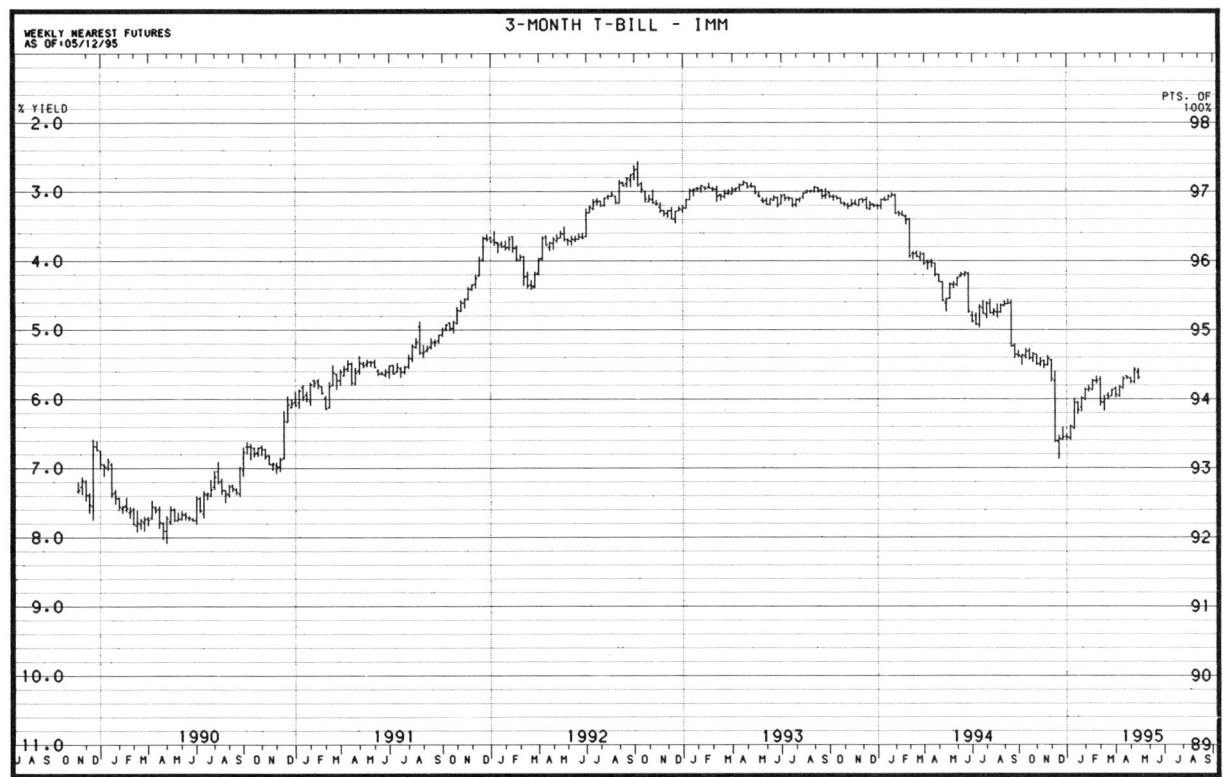

WEEKLY NEAREST FUTURES AS OF 05/12/95

3-MONTH T-BILL - IMM

Average Open Interest of 13 Week[1] Treasury Bill Futures in Chicago   In Thousands of Contracts

Year	Jan.	Feb.	Mar.	Apr.	May	June	July	Aug.	Sept.	Oct.	Nov.	Dec.
1981	44,158	42,982	35,939	29,695	31,495	36,427	42,853	46,297	38,106	34,350	37,361	34,174
1982	33,765	33,854	37,029	41,262	49,754	43,235	48,025	60,055	55,414	48,690	48,006	49,035
1983	48,730	47,608	39,257	42,777	44,259	42,574	43,574	44,782	42,656	49,731	51,947	45,577
1984	44,814	50,417	47,490	51,299	58,668	47,626	45,713	43,931	42,313	42,337	48,923	42,866
1985	47,022	47,171	40,954	40,069	39,624	33,712	35,817	37,911	35,473	36,887	40,830	35,963
1986	37,365	43,008	48,572	51,145	43,394	36,479	40,676	40,819	37,532	36,107	37,940	36,271
1987	40,710	48,375	39,691	35,671	32,202	23,431	24,077	25,454	20,539	26,014	24,222	20,989
1988	19,571	22,956	21,460	26,134	28,166	19,081	21,812	21,626	21,374	21,930	24,711	26,923
1989	29,023	26,612	25,672	20,433	21,864	19,934	20,950	22,687	25,216	29,118	34,224	33,469
1990	39,168	38,358	27,668	31,274	25,128	21,171	26,524	37,903	35,723	46,974	53,284	50,146
1991	55,371	53,484	38,259	43,538	53,941	51,178	55,514	55,999	47,509	50,865	57,680	51,750
1992	51,312	45,902	35,539	44,757	47,734	41,091	38,399	35,638	29,781	32,556	35,379	29,566
1993	32,544	35,756	32,556	39,115	40,724	34,614	30,895	34,177	28,983	30,121	33,800	30,996
1994	36,456	41,150	43,243	51,485	41,164	34,580	32,572	29,559	24,522	32,325	30,077	22,322

[1] 90-day U.S. Treasury Bill.   *Source: International Monetary Market (Chicago Mercantile Exchange)*

Volume of Trading of 13 Week[1] Treasury Bill Futures in Chicago   In Thousands of Contracts

Year	Jan.	Feb.	Mar.	Apr.	May	June	July	Aug.	Sept.	Oct.	Nov.	Dec.	Total
1981	446.6	414.4	408.5	407.6	426.1	511.0	487.8	482.0	525.8	516.0	509.5	496.5	5,631.3
1982	503.5	465.5	638.7	529.1	595.1	546.0	615.2	738.4	628.6	521.4	442.4	374.7	6,598.8
1983	302.2	337.9	361.4	308.5	331.4	366.2	283.9	371.1	273.5	309.8	275.7	268.5	3,790.0
1984	200.0	213.4	304.9	300.2	489.1	342.8	315.1	242.5	201.6	203.6	264.0	215.5	3,293.0
1985	231.3	245.4	314.5	217.9	206.2	205.6	180.6	165.8	206.8	159.9	142.1	138.1	2,413.0
1986	175.0	215.4	149.5	212.8	169.7	152.9	117.8	135.7	160.8	114.2	106.3	105.1	1,815.2
1987	137.9	218.8	151.8	197.6	207.8	125.5	97.5	125.4	110.1	262.2	161.0	131.6	1,927.0
1988	103.2	111.6	129.2	125.6	163.4	105.3	84.3	117.9	97.9	101.6	129.1	104.5	1,373.6
1989	109.6	146.5	143.2	119.2	126.3	101.4	89.3	126.9	135.9	149.1	130.1	124.9	1,502.4
1990	169.3	153.6	118.5	120.3	102.4	96.7	138.1	206.6	168.9	178.5	223.7	193.1	1,869.6
1991	252.9	197.9	166.8	164.0	188.2	173.3	141.7	223.2	111.0	110.8	140.8	141.6	1,912.2
1992	143.8	137.9	145.0	115.9	106.5	106.1	85.8	76.2	103.0	127.0	106.5	83.4	1,337.1
1993	86.1	100.4	97.0	65.6	103.2	106.0	71.7	75.7	89.3	69.1	87.4	66.0	1,071.3
1994	59.8	137.5	115.9	104.4	99.4	89.4	53.7	60.9	77.6	57.4	81.2	83.8	1,020.5

[1] 90-day U.S. Treasury Bill.   *Source: International Monetary Market (Chicago Mercantile Exchange)*

INTEREST RATES

Average Open Interest of U.S. Treasury Bond Futures in Chicago   In Thousands of Contracts

Year	Jan.	Feb.	Mar.	Apr.	May	June	July	Aug.	Sept.	Oct.	Nov.	Dec.
1982	210,528	207,766	185,227	190,176	195,945	166,256	157,216	167,606	164,364	164,761	170,415	178,211
1983	172,930	165,131	148,170	148,017	141,917	140,684	157,193	155,511	148,115	166,725	186,617	186,063
1984	174,827	163,119	168,705	168,980	193,248	198,144	193,662	205,630	209,920	223,808	244,596	217,550
1985	196,826	223,282	224,553	215,742	224,351	209,985	209,823	229,284	229,382	279,083	315,082	307,137
1986	320,040	317,197	266,005	253,991	237,236	212,415	203,921	207,524	196,672	223,588	241,717	239,695
1987	256,822	286,198	237,005	285,491	297,998	250,315	272,633	303,192	336,976	383,640	337,855	293,160
1988	296,133	328,081	307,004	317,891	366,723	406,493	441,064	489,339	475,841	478,585	472,628	411,888
1989	395,874	366,704	303,891	308,850	330,016	312,318	325,851	321,493	283,133	301,719	355,555	314,252
1990	315,671	324,954	294,968	280,745	303,544	278,889	285,934	317,197	297,075	286,291	288,581	254,775
1991	257,229	279,378	250,028	283,473	279,443	254,983	273,774	325,303	310,110	304,198	317,445	301,604
1992	343,156	353,782	318,737	313,742	346,542	347,293	370,850	427,723	385,645	364,250	362,231	321,706
1993	336,327	375,435	361,675	362,404	370,485	349,285	361,393	396,411	388,188	360,859	359,739	337,575
1994	380,057	422,902	454,539	500,790	497,296	421,286	441,884	451,462	447,924	436,684	449,642	397,554

Source: Chicago Board of Trade

Volume of Trading of Treasury Bond Futures in Chicago   In Thousands of Contracts

Year	Jan.	Feb.	Mar.	Apr.	May	June	July	Aug.	Sept.	Oct.	Nov.	Dec.	Total
1982	1,266	1,306	1,414	1,259	1,408	1,255	1,146	1,670	1,474	1,644	1,545	1,352	16,740
1983	1,334	1,448	1,600	1,263	1,679	1,705	1,579	2,313	1,606	1,839	1,687	1,498	19,551
1984	1,476	1,891	2,629	2,069	3,374	2,594	2,692	2,792	2,557	2,924	2,781	2,185	29,963
1985	2,974	3,250	2,906	2,272	3,339	3,755	3,308	3,409	3,149	3,558	4,118	3,965	40,448
1986	4,640	5,220	4,445	5,115	4,783	4,486	4,114	4,175	4,638	3,853	3,595	3,534	52,599
1987	4,188	4,308	4,128	7,110	6,120	5,518	4,839	6,185	7,769	7,388	4,861	4,428	66,841
1988	5,550	5,765	6,088	4,984	5,570	7,495	5,133	6,346	5,641	6,136	6,431	5,171	70,307
1989	5,806	6,300	5,605	4,858	6,673	7,995	5,231	7,640	4,792	6,329	5,828	3,244	70,303
1990	7,215	7,438	7,175	5,653	6,189	5,279	4,895	8,855	4,939	6,659	6,570	4,691	75,559
1991	5,804	5,717	5,658	5,957	6,186	5,582	4,293	6,592	4,765	6,450	6,239	4,643	67,886
1992	7,523	6,270	6,793	4,810	5,418	4,829	6,081	6,085	5,953	6,871	5,288	4,083	70,005
1993	5,577	6,483	7,903	6,156	6,800	5,817	6,218	6,914	7,444	6,537	8,193	5,385	79,428
1994	7,288	8,430	10,837	9,557	9,999	9,804	6,987	7,910	7,913	7,004	8,533	5,699	99,960

Source: Chicago Board of Trade

Average Open Interest of Eurodollar Futures in Chicago   In Contracts

Year	Jan.	Feb.	Mar.	Apr.	May	June	July	Aug.	Sept.	Oct.	Nov.	Dec.
1984	47,635	56,464	61,886	70,114	83,396	87,492	94,201	92,177	85,973	84,727	93,860	89,077
1985	93,554	105,150	107,654	105,703	122,952	120,183	118,905	129,144	125,433	127,799	154,873	144,419
1986	135,703	151,853	148,114	157,288	171,319	164,950	163,345	186,915	213,502	219,995	228,157	219,868
1987	232,311	267,832	229,482	263,086	291,824	269,490	279,309	316,878	361,431	379,188	354,892	323,502
1988	317,384	358,496	340,855	375,951	422,663	421,907	440,567	510,188	509,180	477,860	519,843	566,951
1989	574,799	672,315	731,344	749,690	756,850	720,434	690,204	713,979	637,947	591,502	663,588	661,925
1990	638,515	662,860	653,188	616,948	662,787	676,324	690,639	740,018	697,837	678,167	728,362	664,136
1991	630,859	722,741	741,075	767,644	857,350	835,233	797,940	883,085	916,708	949,479	1,054,742	1,067,187
1992	1,129,756	1,213,739	1,244,564	1,269,120	1,377,229	1,382,685	1,434,127	1,549,891	1,537,036	1,537,640	1,546,965	1,418,669
1993	1,429,428	1,586,690	1,643,285	1,653,433	1,782,750	1,739,140	1,777,713	1,918,439	1,940,677	2,026,541	2,148,959	2,150,194
1994	2,300,466	2,529,469	2,568,095	2,627,293	2,734,294	2,565,180	2,599,129	2,703,830	2,699,588	2,561,170	2,660,339	2,606,336

Source: International Monetary Market (Chicago Mercantile Exchange)

Volume of Trading of Eurodollar Futures in Chicago   In Thousands of Contracts

Year	Jan.	Feb.	Mar.	Apr.	May	June	July	Aug.	Sept.	Oct.	Nov.	Dec.	Total
1984	105	127	235	202	435	448	439	355	435	491	532	388	4,193
1985	525	724	877	765	754	892	798	698	769	694	695	711	8,901
1986	889	825	628	934	983	1,018	755	847	1,289	1,047	836	775	10,825
1987	1,072	1,472	1,197	2,562	1,825	1,760	1,292	1,514	2,495	2,849	1,202	1,177	20,416
1988	1,466	1,681	1,635	1,575	1,830	2,288	1,604	1,893	1,957	1,586	2,236	1,952	21,705
1989	2,257	3,107	3,848	4,471	3,941	4,116	3,193	3,980	2,977	3,971	2,914	2,043	40,818
1990	3,244	2,459	2,727	2,566	3,132	2,473	2,947	3,857	2,730	2,898	2,982	2,680	34,696
1991	2,859	2,635	3,445	3,208	2,458	2,972	2,629	4,035	3,000	3,505	3,301	3,196	37,243
1992	5,366	4,419	5,583	4,942	4,819	4,603	5,358	4,016	4,705	6,692	5,461	4,568	60,531
1993	5,557	5,004	6,014	4,059	5,978	5,673	5,657	4,494	6,341	4,888	6,270	4,477	64,411
1994	6,538	9,394	9,469	9,639	11,494	9,348	7,810	7,128	7,641	7,992	9,715	9,766	104,823

Source: International Monetary Market (Chicago Mercantile Exchange)

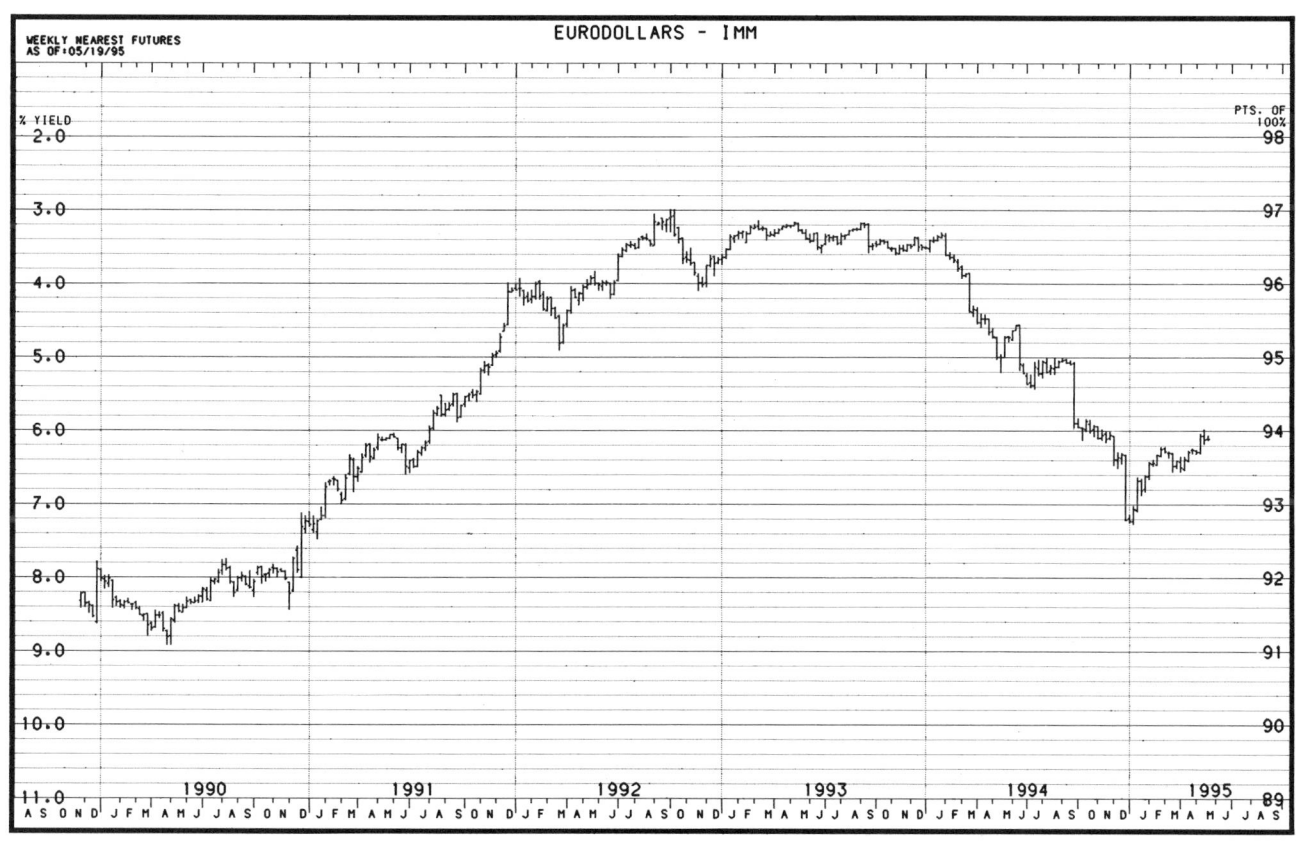

INTEREST RATES

Average Open Interest of U.S. Treasury Note (10-year) Futures in Chicago   In Contracts

Year	Jan.	Feb.	Mar.	Apr.	May	June	July	Aug.	Sept.	Oct.	Nov.	Dec.
1984	16,395	24,443	23,245	26,115	28,797	32,818	35,645	35,824	33,998	33,006	35,352	37,430
1985	38,462	44,251	49,909	42,744	48,416	52,963	55,676	62,118	59,587	66,796	70,300	69,603
1986	76,661	78,528	75,024	63,804	70,568	72,565	67,048	62,122	60,839	56,955	64,397	58,763
1987	58,926	56,177	55,093	64,924	68,797	71,033	72,033	78,281	88,939	82,672	75,139	77,631
1988	76,066	75,884	73,083	75,836	78,038	84,349	84,612	101,470	96,821	91,811	89,307	74,602
1989	76,964	84,605	78,966	86,661	88,511	76,364	77,211	76,538	71,138	82,844	82,149	72,238
1990	73,155	82,211	76,939	76,030	82,174	78,498	71,413	75,644	72,900	67,309	73,744	76,697
1991	72,621	79,355	79,413	71,451	84,203	81,884	85,527	94,379	96,836	93,187	95,450	87,063
1992	119,739	114,521	106,497	102,862	112,666	126,228	143,924	158,831	179,045	191,725	199,990	195,705
1993	190,018	206,852	198,653	209,221	229,378	217,521	233,458	238,189	237,243	237,877	273,336	262,831
1994	264,848	258,643	300,080	328,821	294,091	254,612	232,373	253,233	273,564	277,313	301,000	271,992

Source: Chicago Board of Trade

Volume of Trading of U.S. Treasury Note (10-year) Futures in Chicago   In Thousands of Contracts

Year	Jan.	Feb.	Mar.	Apr.	May	June	July	Aug.	Sept.	Oct.	Nov.	Dec.	Total
1984	59.7	110.5	126.8	105.3	199.1	145.1	147.2	162.8	139.5	149.2	166.0	150.7	1,662
1985	171.8	216.0	215.9	175.8	274.9	266.9	219.4	282.9	212.7	234.3	297.5	292.5	2,860
1986	269.7	401.4	383.1	381.7	434.8	470.3	309.7	363.1	459.5	319.9	328.1	305.2	4,426
1987	304.9	358.3	347.6	643.8	541.3	405.1	269.6	446.0	512.9	662.0	369.4	392.8	5,254
1988	335.3	462.8	420.6	298.8	467.8	469.6	327.4	566.0	455.4	383.2	537.4	476.7	5,201
1989	450.5	547.9	468.3	431.6	625.6	637.3	453.0	629.6	465.8	555.8	516.7	327.4	6,110
1990	491.3	650.5	480.9	381.1	638.7	427.4	415.0	703.0	399.3	449.6	574.3	442.6	6,054
1991	507.7	519.6	508.3	466.5	566.9	456.6	318.9	705.9	467.2	573.2	661.3	591.4	6,342
1992	929.6	866.4	824.9	531.2	758.9	683.3	859.4	1,047.7	1,138.5	1,300.2	1,225.8	1,052.1	11,218
1993	1,134.6	1,286.3	1,763.1	1,089.5	1,341.4	1,390.6	1,147.0	1,390.7	1,523.7	1,279.5	1,926.6	1,328.2	16,601
1994	1,484.3	1,935.7	2,572.4	2,213.5	2,399.4	2,250.2	1,621.8	2,028.7	1,932.9	1,635.1	2,253.6	1,750.2	24,078

Source: Chicago Board of Trade

WEEKLY NEAREST FUTURES
AS OF:05/12/95

CBT 5-YR T-NOTE - CBOT

PTS-64THS
OF 100%

Average Open Interest of 5-Year Treasury Notes Futures in Chicago   In Contracts

Year	Jan.	Feb.	Mar.	Apr.	May	June	July	Aug.	Sept.	Oct.	Nov.	Dec.
1988					2,545	5,292	10,584	11,424	12,677	18,403	24,569	34,267
1989	34,728	40,203	45,320	46,371	48,195	42,496	44,985	34,675	37,474	42,669	57,901	73,798
1990	81,705	74,568	74,999	60,841	59,417	56,485	54,004	64,100	75,955	78,370	82,981	93,549
1991	80,059	82,666	83,109	74,612	75,799	65,543	72,197	86,981	85,794	91,096	102,890	99,291
1992	116,322	121,667	125,155	130,826	135,111	144,386	143,928	143,203	127,418	122,113	129,548	127,690
1993	139,207	150,443	152,711	158,607	169,234	152,262	152,403	160,258	159,754	154,501	181,492	206,914
1994	200,812	213,037	200,626	185,083	192,659	186,026	189,828	182,027	181,518	181,578	176,322	205,150

Source: Chicago Board of Trade

Volume of Trading of 5-Year Treasury Notes Futures in Chicago   In Thousands of Contracts

Year	Jan.	Feb.	Mar.	Apr.	May	June	July	Aug.	Sept.	Oct.	Nov.	Dec.	Total
1988					20.6	56.5	45.6	66.4	73.8	54.8	97.1	91.8	244
1989	91.1	156.8	128.1	89.2	167.3	162.0	142.3	205.2	121.2	148.3	253.4	116.9	519
1990	184.5	277.5	164.9	107.6	266.6	140.8	131.6	320.4	189.0	197.9	305.7	40.8	544
1991	220.5	318.5	252.3	181.4	307.6	232.4	179.7	385.4	243.9	291.5	419.9	353.1	1,065
1992	498.6	543.8	560.0	322.2	590.1	551.5	484.2	565.7	582.1	539.0	640.8	563.2	1,743
1993	539.5	673.1	886.0	447.6	755.9	753.8	506.4	711.3	753.8	472.6	908.0	715.8	2,096
1994	695.9	1,235.1	1,295.4	917.1	1,202.0	1,154.9	834.8	944.9	1,107.3	840.6	1,156.7	1,078.0	12,463

Source: Chicago Board of Trade

INTEREST RATES

U.S. Federal Funds Rate   In Percent

Year	Jan.	Feb.	Mar.	Apr.	May	June	July	Aug.	Sept.	Oct.	Nov.	Dec.	Annual
1976	4.87	4.77	4.84	4.82	5.29	5.48	5.31	5.29	5.25	5.03	4.95	4.65	5.05
1977	4.61	4.68	4.69	4.73	5.35	5.39	5.42	5.90	6.14	6.47	6.51	6.56	5.54
1978	6.70	6.78	6.79	6.89	7.36	7.60	7.81	8.04	8.45	8.96	9.76	10.03	7.93
1979	10.07	10.06	10.09	10.01	10.24	10.29	10.47	10.94	11.43	13.77	13.18	13.78	11.19
1980	13.82	14.13	17.19	17.61	10.98	9.47	9.03	9.61	10.87	12.81	15.85	18.90	13.36
1981	19.08	15.93	14.70	15.72	18.52	19.10	19.04	17.82	15.87	15.08	13.31	12.37	16.38
1982	13.22	14.78	14.68	14.94	14.45	14.15	12.59	10.12	10.31	9.71	9.20	8.95	12.26
1983	8.68	8.51	8.77	8.80	8.63	8.98	9.37	9.56	9.45	9.48	9.34	9.47	9.09
1984	9.56	9.59	9.91	10.29	10.32	11.06	11.23	11.64	11.30	9.99	9.43	8.38	10.23
1985	8.35	8.50	8.58	8.27	7.97	7.53	7.88	7.90	7.92	7.99	8.05	8.27	7.41
1986	8.14	7.86	7.48	6.99	6.85	6.92	6.56	6.17	5.89	5.85	6.04	6.91	6.81
1987	6.43	6.10	6.13	6.37	6.85	6.73	6.58	6.73	7.22	7.29	6.69	6.77	6.66
1988	6.83	6.58	6.58	6.87	7.09	7.51	7.76	8.01	8.19	8.30	8.35	8.76	7.57
1989	9.12	9.36	9.85	9.84	9.81	9.53	9.24	8.99	9.02	8.84	8.55	8.45	9.22
1990	8.23	8.24	8.28	8.26	8.18	8.29	8.15	8.13	8.20	8.11	7.81	7.31	8.10
1991	6.91	6.25	6.12	5.91	5.78	5.90	5.82	5.66	5.45	5.21	4.81	4.43	5.69
1992	4.03	4.06	3.98	3.73	3.82	3.76	3.25	3.30	3.22	3.10	3.09	2.92	3.52
1993	3.02	3.03	3.07	2.96	3.00	3.04	3.06	3.03	3.09	2.99	3.02	2.96	3.02

Source: Bureau of Economic Analysis, U.S. Department of Commerce

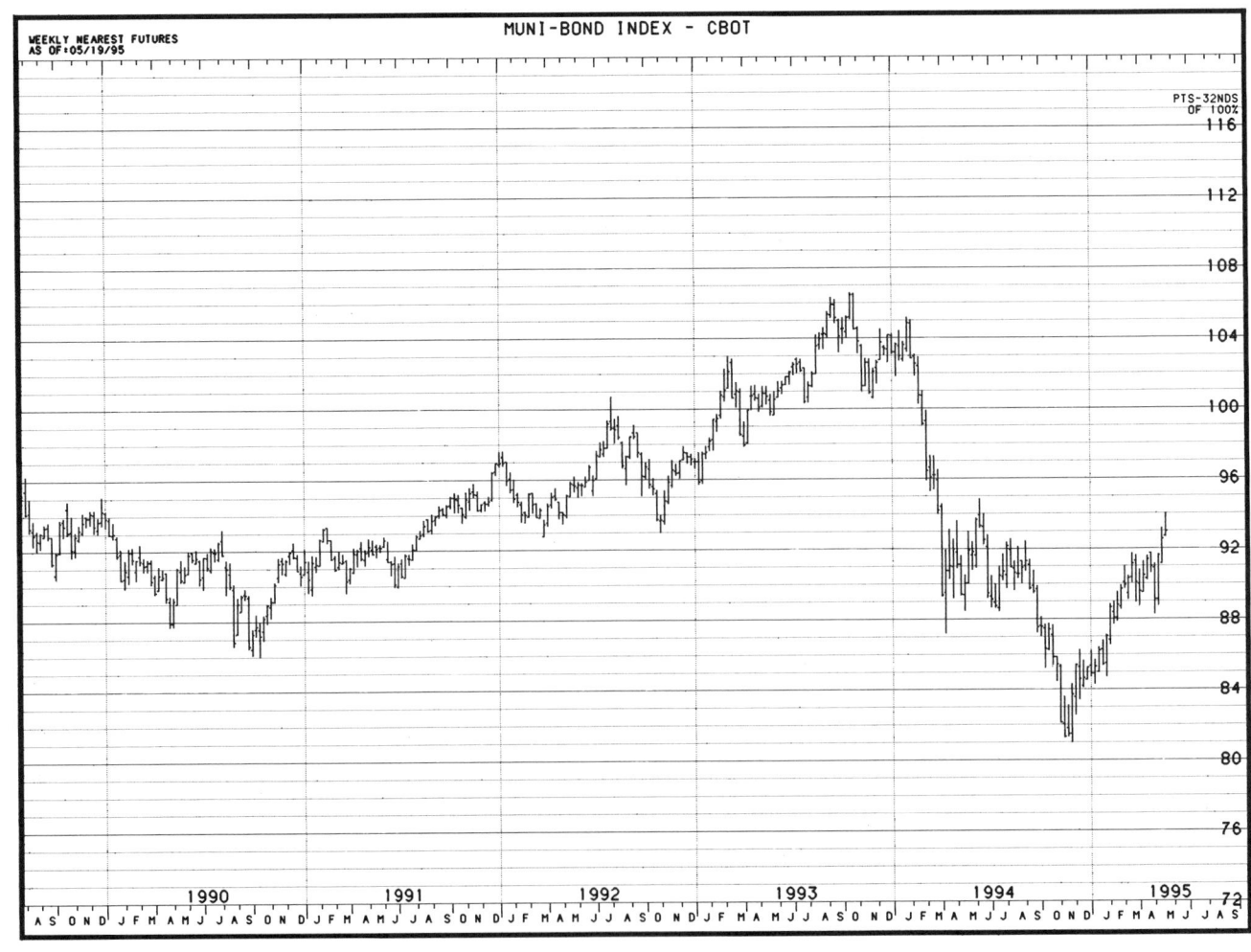

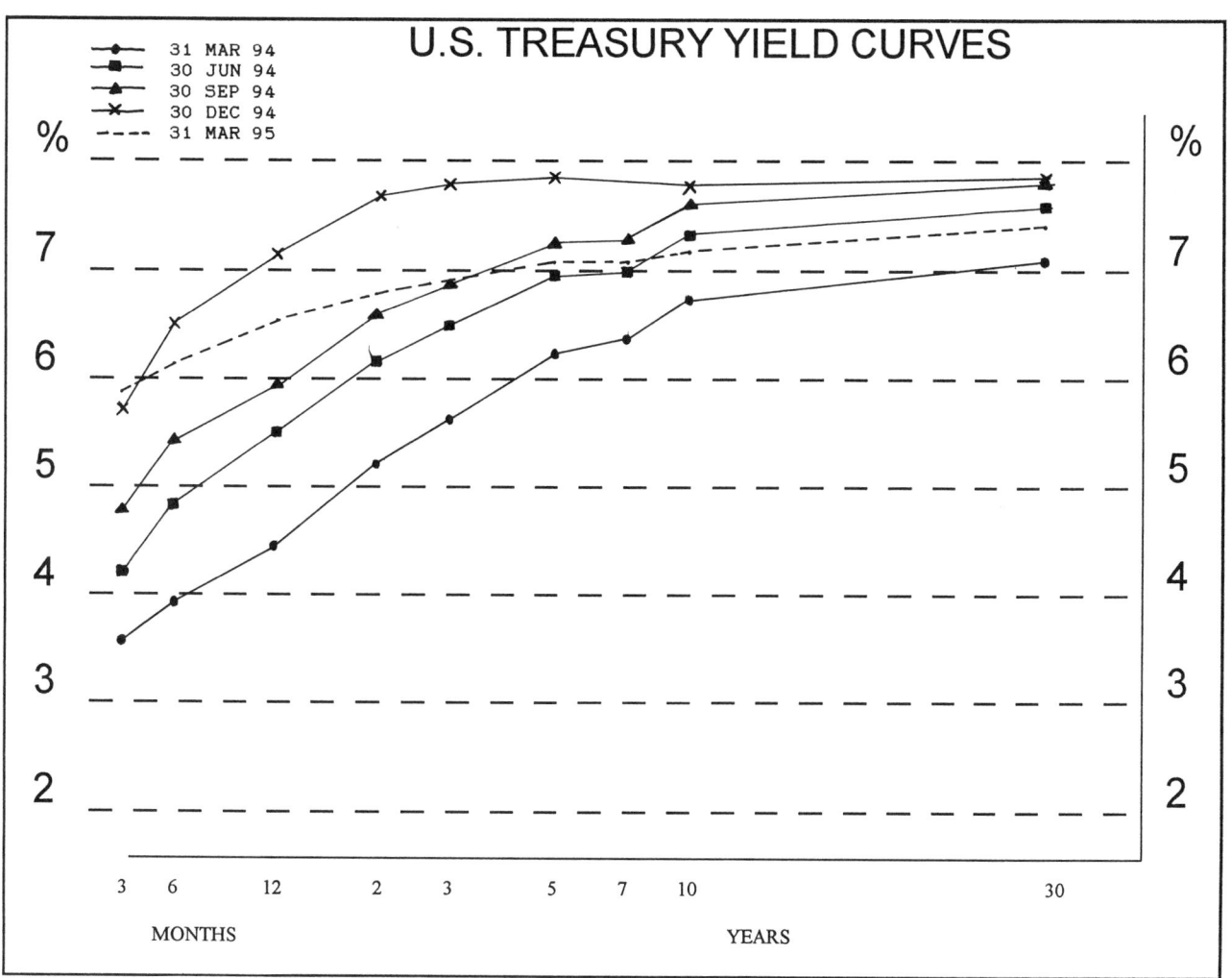

U.S. TREASURY YIELD CURVES

Legend:
- 31 MAR 94
- 30 JUN 94
- 30 SEP 94
- 30 DEC 94
- 31 MAR 95

MONTHS: 3 6 12
YEARS: 2 3 5 7 10 30

U.S. Industrial Production Index[1] (Seasonally Adjusted)   1987 = 100

Year	Jan.	Feb.	Mar.	Apr.	May	June	July	Aug.	Sept.	Oct.	Nov.	Dec.	Average
1979	85.1	85.8	86.1	85.2	86.2	86.1	85.6	85.3	85.5	86.0	85.7	85.6	85.7
1980	85.9	86.2	86.2	84.5	82.5	81.5	81.2	82.4	83.5	84.0	85.5	85.9	84.1
1981	85.2	85.4	85.7	85.0	85.6	86.1	87.1	86.9	86.5	85.8	84.8	84.1	85.7
1982	82.4	84.2	83.7	83.2	82.7	82.4	82.0	81.6	81.0	80.3	80.0	79.3	81.9
1983	80.8	80.7	81.3	82.3	83.2	83.7	85.3	86.5	87.9	88.6	88.8	89.2	84.9
1984	91.0	90.9	91.9	92.4	93.0	93.5	93.9	94.0	93.9	93.2	93.3	92.8	92.8
1985	93.1	93.8	94.1	94.5	94.7	94.4	94.1	94.5	95.0	94.2	94.6	95.6	94.4
1986	96.1	95.5	94.6	94.8	94.8	94.4	94.8	95.0	95.1	95.6	96.2	96.7	95.3
1987	96.5	97.6	98.2	98.3	99.2	100.1	100.8	101.0	100.9	102.3	102.2	102.6	100.0
1988	103.5	103.5	103.9	104.3	104.8	105.0	106.1	106.4	106.2	106.5	106.9	107.4	105.4
1989	107.7	107.6	107.7	108.6	108.3	108.4	107.8	108.2	108.2	107.7	108.1	108.6	108.1
1990	107.5	108.5	108.9	108.8	109.4	110.1	110.4	110.5	110.4	109.9	108.3	107.2	109.2
1991	106.6	105.7	105.0	105.5	106.4	107.3	108.1	108.0	108.4	108.4	108.1	107.4	107.1
1992	106.6	107.2	105.6	106.3	106.7	106.0	106.8	106.6	106.2	107.5	108.4	108.9	106.9
1993	109.2	109.9	110.0	110.5	110.0	110.4	110.9	111.1	112.5	112.7	113.7	114.7	112.0
1994[2]	114.7	115.6	116.6	116.7	117.4	118.0	118.2	119.1	119.0	119.4	120.3	121.4	118.1

[1] Total Index of the Federal Reserve Index of Quantity Output.   [2] Preliminary.   *Source: Bureau of Economic Analysis, U.S. Department of Commerce*

INTEREST RATES

U.S. Money Supply M1 in 1987 Dollars[3] In Billions of Dollars

Year	Jan.	Feb.	Mar.	Apr.	May	June	July	Aug.	Sept.	Oct.	Nov.	Dec.	Average
1984	496.1	496.0	497.7	498.2	499.3	502.3	501.3	500.5	502.4	499.3	501.6	504.9	500.0
1985	507.8	511.4	512.0	513.3	517.1	523.0	527.3	534.1	539.6	540.4	541.7	546.7	526.2
1986	545.5	551.3	562.1	569.4	577.7	583.2	591.5	599.0	603.5	609.0	618.0	633.0	585.4
1987	632.7	631.0	630.7	636.8	635.9	629.8	629.5	629.2	629.5	635.3	630.9	628.0	632.7
1988	630.4	630.8	631.8	634.7	632.0	634.4	636.7	634.5	633.0	631.4	630.8	631.7	632.7
1989	625.0	622.9	619.0	612.0	605.0	601.6	604.0	603.0	605.5	606.7	605.4	607.2	609.9
1990	600.8	602.6	602.4	603.4	601.0	600.9	598.4	598.6	598.8	594.2	593.6	593.4	599.6
1991	591.8	598.7	601.6	600.6	605.2	608.0	609.5	611.9	613.7	618.6	623.8	627.2	609.2
1992[2]	635.2	644.1	647.6	650.0	656.7	655.6	661.2	668.2	677.2	685.2	692.3	696.5	664.2
1993[1]	823.1	822.4	824.2	827.1	841.4	847.7	854.4	859.1	866.1	869.8	874.1	876.8	848.9
1994[1]	880.7	882.6	882.8	880.5	879.8	880.4	882.4	878.0	876.6	873.4	870.7	868.7	878.0

[1] Preliminary.   [2] Prior to 1993, shown in 1982 dollars.   [3] M1--This measure is currency, travelers checks, plus demand deposits at commercial banks and interest-earning checkable deposits at all depository institutions.   *Source: Bureau of Economic Analysis, U.S. Department of Commerce*

U.S. Money Supply M2 in 1987 Dollars[2] In Billions of Dollars

Year	Jan.	Feb.	Mar.	Apr.	May	June	July	Aug.	Sept.	Oct.	Nov.	Dec.	Average
1984	2,451.3	2,462.1	2,470.3	2,478.7	2,489.7	2,498.4	2,501.1	2,503.4	2,512.3	2,518.1	2,538.8	2,560.3	2,498.7
1985	2,582.3	2,594.7	2,594.7	3,591.5	2,600.6	2,624.2	2,636.3	2,648.9	2,662.4	2,661.8	2,664.3	2,671.2	2,627.7
1986	2,668.3	2,682.2	2,719.3	2,753.8	2,772.9	2,787.0	2,812.1	2,832.7	2,844.2	2,863.0	2,873.4	2,891.2	2,791.7
1987	2,889.9	2,881.9	2,874.2	2,875.2	2,871.2	2,862.9	2,860.4	2,862.8	2,866.7	2,876.7	2,867.7	2,868.4	2,871.5
1988	2,881.2	2,896.8	2,905.6	2,910.0	2,918.3	2,917.4	2,913.9	2,909.3	2,895.7	2,895.9	2,899.5	2,898.6	2,903.5
1989	2,886.2	2,877.2	2,870.4	2,852.7	2,838.8	2,852.2	2,864.1	2,880.0	2,893.2	2,892.5	2,902.0	2,910.3	2,876.6
1990	2,893.6	2,893.0	2,888.0	2,892.3	2,889.5	2,887.1	2,880.6	2,871.7	2,865.1	2,848.0	2,837.0	2,837.6	2,873.6
1991	2,827.7	2,835.9	2,852.7	2,851.4	2,853.6	2,856.4	2,849.0	2,845.1	2,836.6	2,835.5	2,834.8	2,838.4	2,843.1
1992	2,833.3	2,840.0	2,830.9	2,821.5	2,819.1	2,807.8	2,801.9	2,801.8	2,803.4	2,801.0	2,799.2	2,795.8	2,813.0
1993[1]	2,791.1	2,775.4	2,769.3	2,763.0	2,775.3	2,778.5	2,778.1	2,773.4	2,777.7	2,772.0	2,772.8	2,772.3	2,774.9
1994[1]	2,777.7	2,769.1	2,769.9	2,771.2	2,767.7	2,756.5	2,757.9	2,745.2	2,737.9	2,732.0	2,727.0	2,725.5	2,753.1

[1] Preliminary.   [2] M2--This measure adds to M1 ovenight repurchase agreements (RPs) issued by commercial banks and certain overnight Eurodollars (those issued by Caribbean branches of member banks) held by U.S. nonbank residents, general purpose and broker/dealer money market mutual shares (MMMF), and savings and small-denomination time deposits.   *Source: Bureau of Economic Analysis, U.S. Department of Commerce*

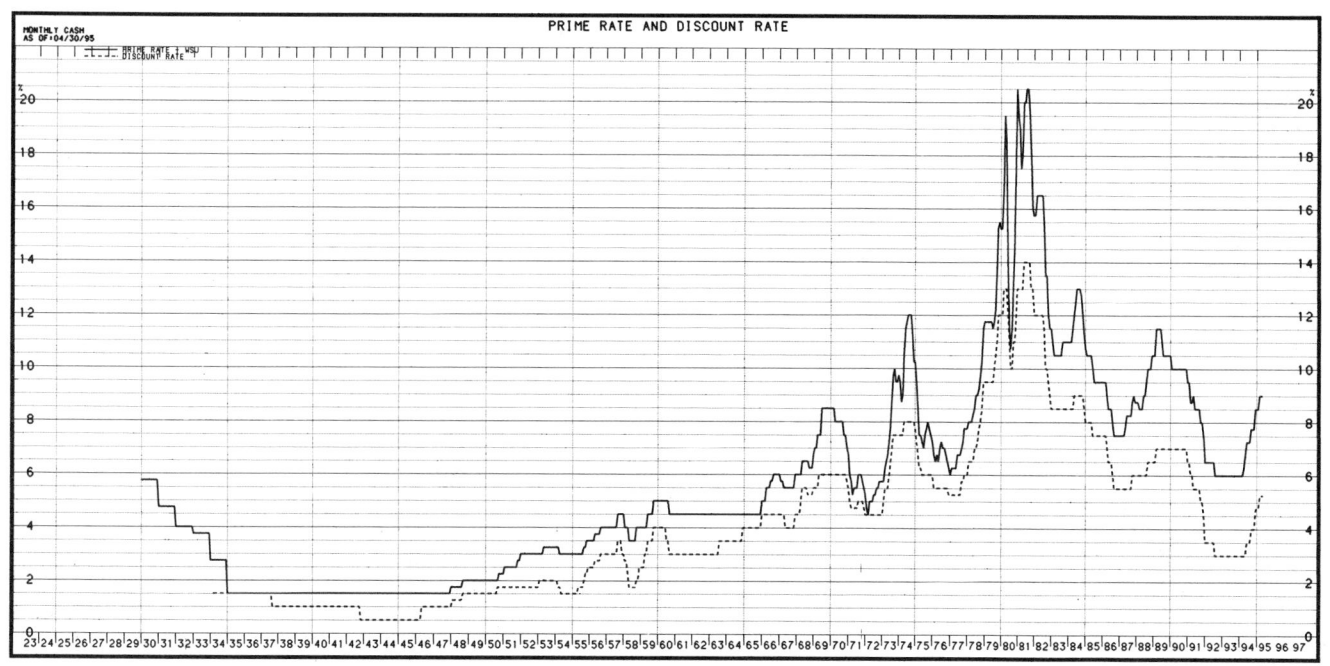

PRIME RATE AND DISCOUNT RATE
MONTHLY CASH
AS OF:04/30/95
PRIME RATE + WSD
DISCOUNT RATE
%
20
18
16
14
12
10
8
6
4
2
0
23 24 25 26 27 28 29 30 31 32 33 34 35 36 37 38 39 40 41 42 43 44 45 46 47 48 49 50 51 52 53 54 55 56 57 58 59 60 61 62 63 64 65 66 67 68 69 70 71 72 73 74 75 76 77 78 79 80 81 82 83 84 85 86 87 88 89 90 91 92 93 94 95 96 97

MUNICIPAL AND CORPORATE AAA BOND YIELDS
MONTHLY CASH
AS OF:04/30/95
MUNICIPAL BOND YIELD
CORPORATE AAA BOND YIELD
AVG.
15
14
13
12
11
10
9
8
7
6
5
4
3
2
1
23 24 25 26 27 28 29 30 31 32 33 34 35 36 37 38 39 40 41 42 43 44 45 46 47 48 49 50 51 52 53 54 55 56 57 58 59 60 61 62 63 64 65 66 67 68 69 70 71 72 73 74 75 76 77 78 79 80 81 82 83 84 85 86 87 88 89 90 91 92 93 94 95 96 97

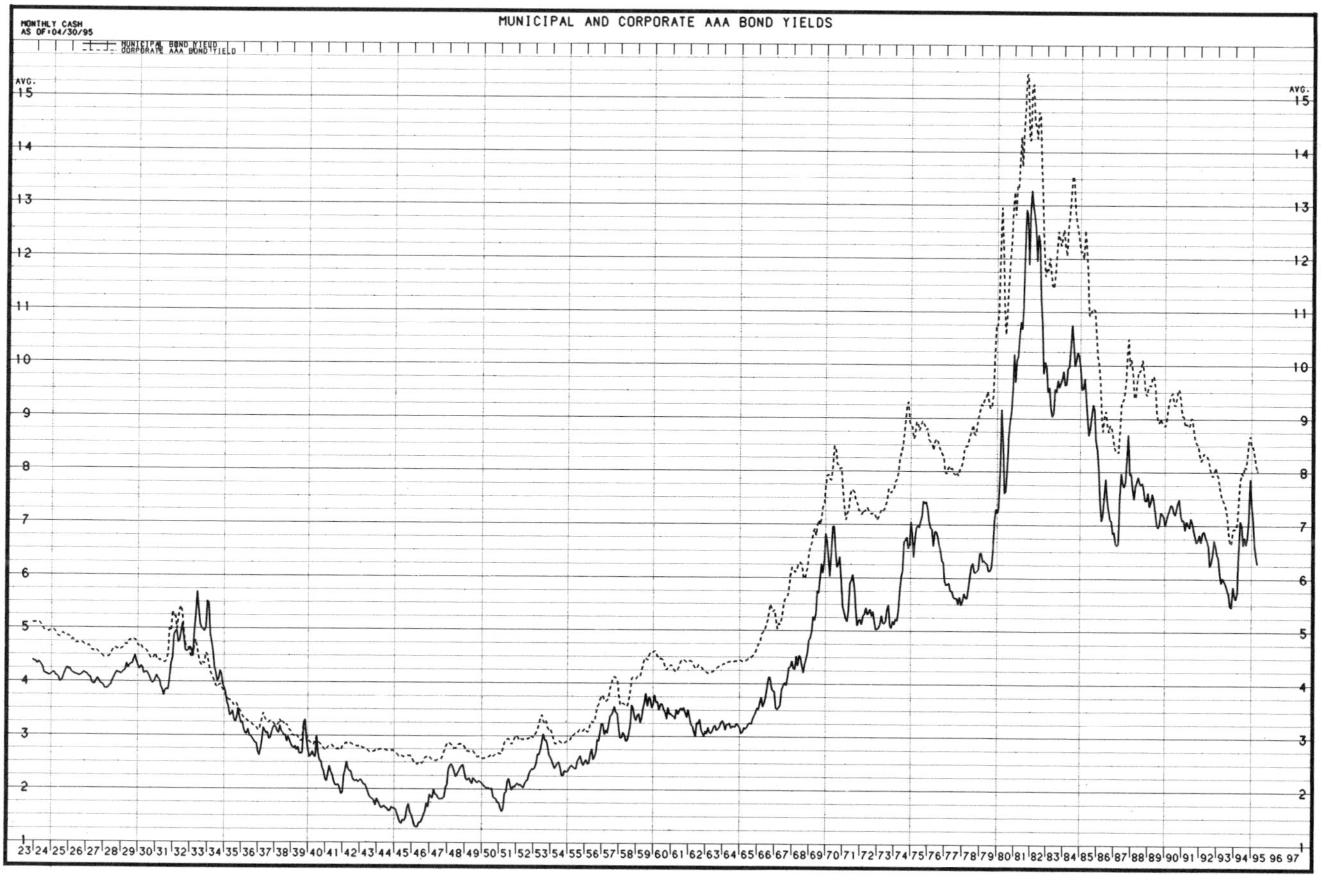

INTEREST RATES

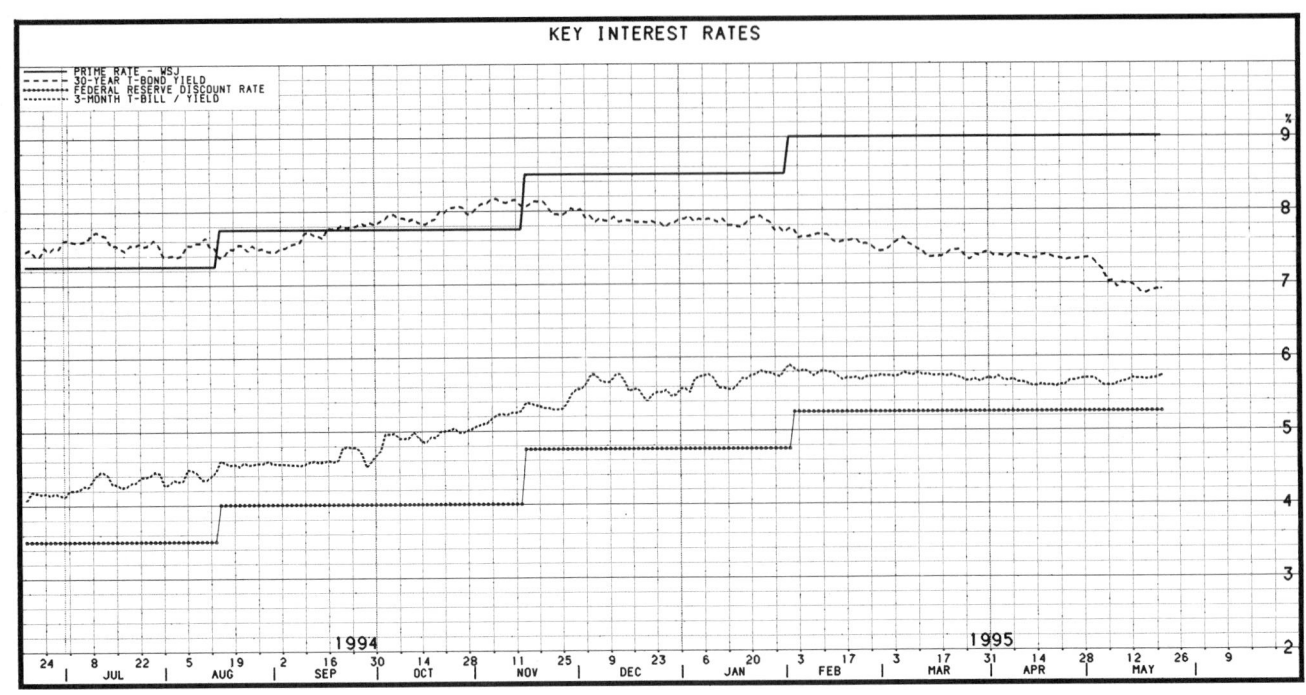

KEY INTEREST RATES

PRIME RATE - WSJ
30-YEAR T-BOND YIELD
FEDERAL RESERVE DISCOUNT RATE
3-MONTH T-BILL / YIELD

U.S. Gross National Product, National Income, and Personal Income   In Billions of Current Dollars[1]

Year	Gross Domestic Product					National Income					Personal Income				
	I	II	III	IV	Annual Average	I	II	III	IV	Annual Average	I	II	III	IV	Annual Average
1981	2,979	3,018	3,100	3,114	3,053	2,388	2,415	2,483	2,487	2,444	2,441	2,485	2,568	2,591	2,521
1982	3,113	3,160	3,179	3,213	3,166	2,483	2,514	2,528	2,548	2,518	2,614	2,656	2,684	2,729	2,671
1983	3,266	3,367	3,444	3,546	3,406	2,599	2,686	2,742	2,852	2,720	2,753	2,813	2,847	2,942	2,839
1984	3,675	3,754	3,808	3,852	3,772	2,962	3,009	3,047	3,096	3,029	3,034	3,075	3,138	3,188	3,109
1985	3,926	3,979	4,047	4,108	4,015	3,162	3,209	3,252	3,313	3,234	3,263	3,308	3,332	3,399	3,325
1986	4,181	4,195	4,253	4,297	4,232	3,363	3,395	3,419	3,473	3,413	3,457	3,510	3,540	3,598	3,526
1987	4,412	4,498	4,578	4,691	4,545	3,572	3,646	3,722	3,829	3,692	3,716	3,760	3,814	3,919	3,802
1988	4,764	4,863	4,952	5,054	4,908	3,889	3,966	4,028	4,128	4,003	3,968	4,038	4,103	4,195	4,076
1989	5,144	5,218	5,280	5,351	5,248	4,203	4,231	4,245	4,301	4,245	4,304	4,352	4,391	4,474	4,380
1990	5,433	5,506	5,577	5,583	5,525	4,396	4,461	4,475	4,507	4,460	4,581	4,655	4,719	4,765	4,680
1991	5,615	5,674	5,726	5,764	5,695	4,493	4,529	4,555	4,599	4,544	4,753	4,807	4,846	4,907	4,828
1992	5,897	5,971	6,044	6,169	6,020	4,752	4,807	4,794	4,965	4,830	5,032	5,102	5,148	5,335	5,154
1993[2]	6,240	6,300	6,359	6,478	6,343	5,031	5,094	5,139	5,262	5,131	5,256	5,365	5,396	5,485	5,375
1994[2]	6,575	6,690	6,792	6,891	6,737	5,309	5,431	5,495		5,41	5,556	5,660	5,728	5,857	5,702

[1] Seasonally adjusted at annual rates.   [2] Preliminary.   *Source: Bureau of Economic Analysis, U.S. Department of Commerce*

Interest Rates, Worldwide

Most of the world's equity markets during 1994 proved unexciting in dollar terms. The big loser was Mexico, down nearly 45 percent following the peso's surprise devaluation in late-1994. The major European markets posted lackluster results, reflecting relatively tight credit conditions. In the Pacific rim, the Hong Kong market was the major loser as values fell approximately 30 percent, reflecting uncertainties as to the nation's future if China opts to take control from the British in 1997.

However, when viewed in a longer term perspective, world equity markets have performed well since the late 1980s . Using 1988 as a base year (100), prices by yearend 1994 had almost doubled during the six-years in the U.S. and Germany, and more than doubled in France. United Kingdom values lagged but were still up about 75 percent, while Italy's and Canada's gain neared 50 percent. Significantly, Japan's equity values fell sharply in 1990 to 1992 and the recovery since could be viewed as anemic.

In the U.S., stock prices proved mixed in 1994 in that prices of the more seasoned blue chip companies did reasonably well. The well publicized Dow Jones 30 Industrial Index closed the year up 2.3 percent from 1993. However, the Standard's & Poor's (S & P) 500 lost about 1.2 percent, while the National Association of Security Dealers Automated Quotation System (NASDAQ) fell almost 4.5 percent. Trading volume was a record high despite steadily rising interest rates during the year, which in the past would have typically siphoned traders enthusiasm away from equities and into higher yielding capital assets.

However, the rout in U.S. bond prices apparently proved to volatile for many market participants and they opted to remain in equities, especially those of seasoned corporations. Moreover, a sense of optimism prevailed towards the U.S. economy's growth despite the tightening monetary policy. Corporate downsizing was perceived as still in effect, which could only enhanced earnings and ultimately dividend payout. Patience was apparently seen as necessary during 1994 and it proved rewarding as 1995 unfolded. Equities soared to record-highs, paced by the blue chips, and fostering expectations that the strength could easily be maintained across the equity market spectrum through the year. The Federal Reserve (Fed) sees the U.S. economy slowly losing its momentum in 1995, but experiencing little more than a "soft landing" and minimal inflationary pressures, a positive setting for equity markets.

In the United Kingdom, the Financial Time's Stock Equity (FT-SE) 100 Index market lost nearly 4 percent in 1994, while French values fell nearly 6 percent. Germany's DAX Index, however, rose nearly 5 percent, and Swiss prices gained nearly 3 percent. Percentagewise, the Netherlands market featured nearly a 13 percent gain. Despite Europe's mixed results in 1994, forecasts were generally positive for 1995. Most economies seemed to be on the right monetary and fiscal policy paths, and inflation fears were generally subdued. Germany holds the key to Europe's recovery, perhaps to the chagrin of bordering nations, but if Germany's economic growth persists its apt to have a beneficial impact on most of Europe's equity markets in 1995.

Japan's Nikkei 225 Index collapsed in early-1995, nearing its mid-1992 record low. The U.S. dollar's weakness against the Japanese yen is seen as cutting strongly into Japanese exports to the U.S., which may or may not happen. Contributing to the Nikkei weakness was the devastating earthquake in Kobe, Japan's sixth largest city. Recovery costs could run into the billions of dollars. Moreover, it could redirect Japan's economic powers to domestic needs at the expense of exports. It will take time for the equity markets to assess the longer term effect on the Nikkei.

Futures Markets

A number of stock index futures and options markets are traded in the world's major financial centers. The Chicago Mercantile Exchange (CME) offers a S & P 500 Index, a S & P Midcap 400 Index, and a Major Market Index. A Nikkei 225 Index average is traded in Chicago, Tokyo, Osaka and Singapore. In New York, a New York Stock Exchange (NYSE) Composite Index is offered. The Kansas City Board of Trade (KCBT) trades the Value-Line Index. A Canadian 25 Stock Index is traded on the Toronto Futures Exchange (TFE). The Sydney Futures Exchange (SFE) trades an Australian All Ordinaries Share Price Index. In Europe, an FT-SE 100 Index is traded on the London International Financial Futures Exchange (LIFFE), and in Paris, a CAC-40 Stock Index is traded on the Marche a Terme International de France (MATIF).

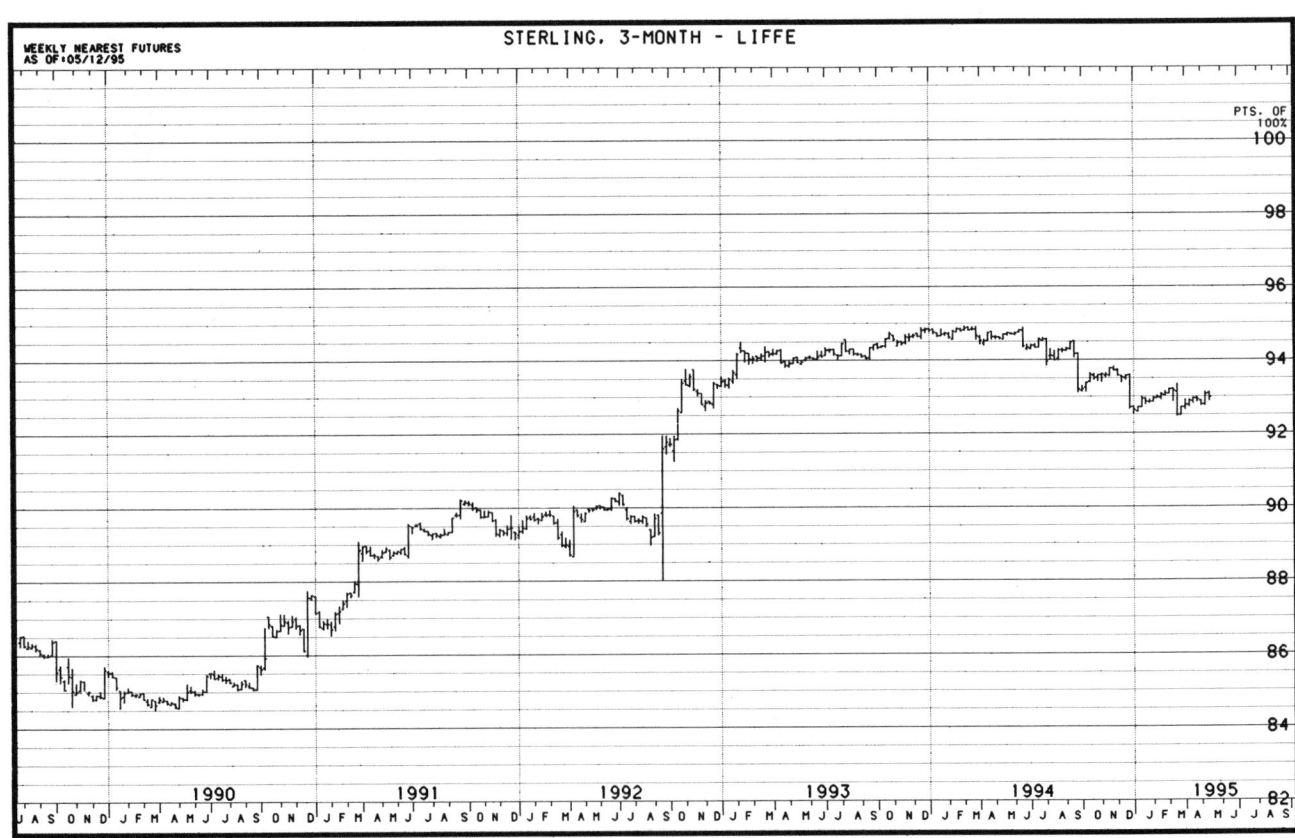

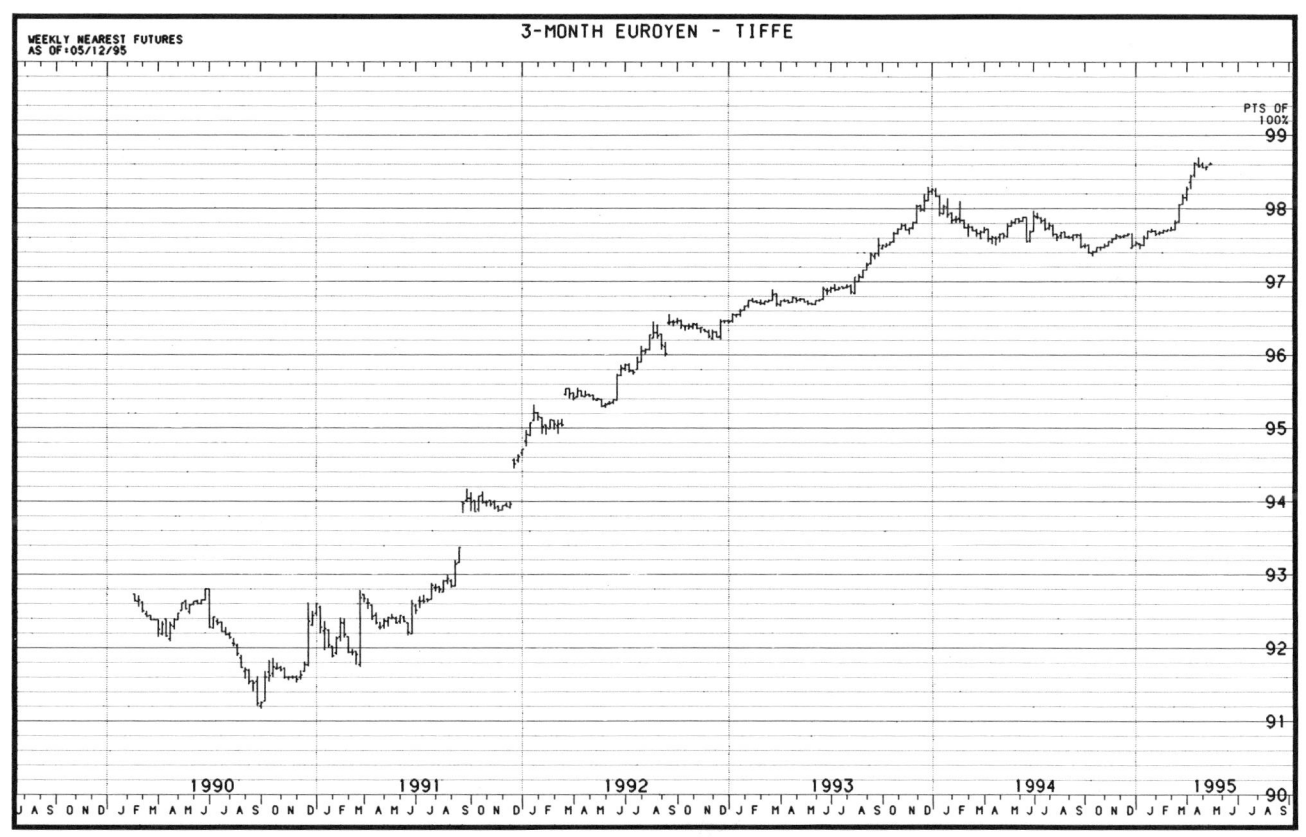

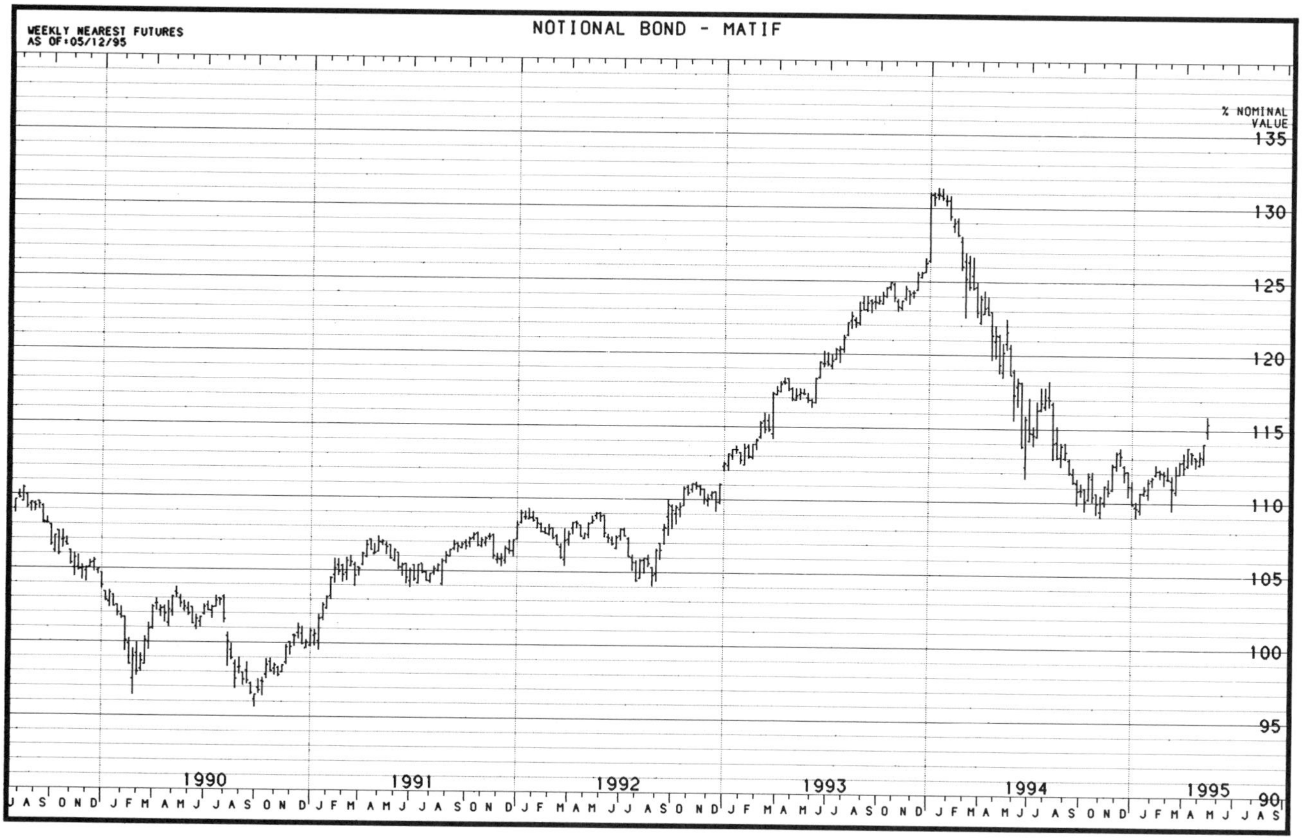
WEEKLY NEAREST FUTURES
AS OF:05/12/95
NOTIONAL BOND - MATIF
% NOMINAL VALUE
135
130
125
120
115
110
105
100
95
90
1990
1991
1992
1993
1994
1995
J A S O N D J F M A M J J A S O N D J F M A M J J A S O N D J F M A M J J A S O N D J F M A M J J A S O N D J F M A M J J A S O N D J F M A M J J A S

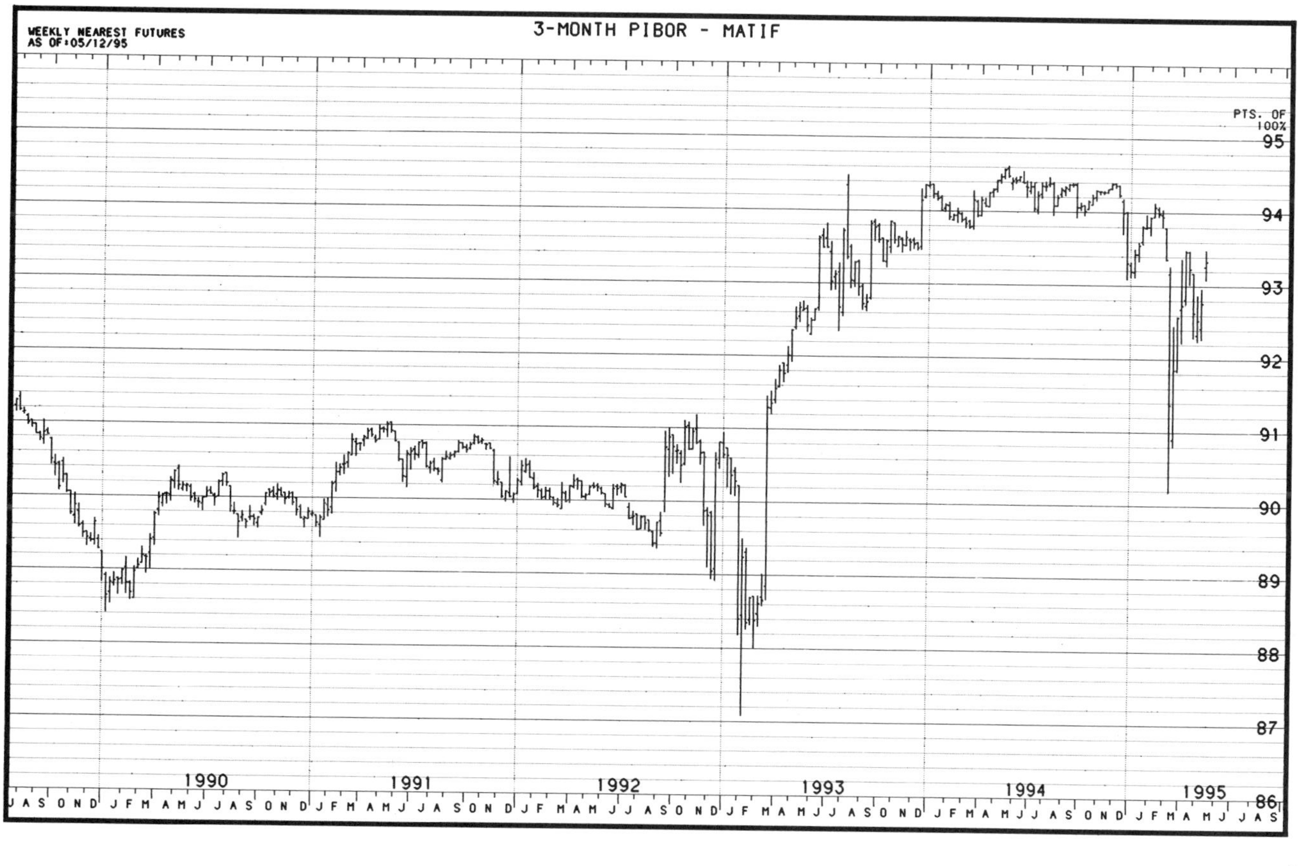
WEEKLY NEAREST FUTURES
AS OF:05/12/95
3-MONTH PIBOR - MATIF
PTS. OF 100%
95
94
93
92
91
90
89
88
87
86
1990
1991
1992
1993
1994
1995
J A S O N D J F M A M J J A S O N D J F M A M J J A S O N D J F M A M J J A S O N D J F M A M J J A S O N D J F M A M J J A S O N D J F M A M J J A S

INTEREST RATES, WORLDWIDE

Japan--Economic Statistics — Percentage Change from Previous Period

Year	Real GDP	Nominal GDP	Real Private Consumption	Real Public Consumption	Grossed Fixed Investment	Real Total Domestic Demand	Real Exports of Goods & Services	Real Imports of Goods & Services	Consumer Prices[1]	Unemployment Rate
1986	2.6	4.4	3.4	4.5	4.8	3.7	-4.9	2.4	.4	2.8
1987	4.1	4.1	4.2	.4	9.6	5.1	.1	7.8	.2	2.8
1988	6.2	6.6	5.2	2.2	11.9	7.6	7.0	18.7	-.1	2.5
1989	4.7	6.7	4.3	2.0	9.3	5.8	9.0	17.6	1.8	2.3
1990	4.8	7.2	3.9	1.9	8.8	5.0	7.3	8.6	2.6	2.1
1991	4.0	6.2	2.2	1.7	3.0	2.7	4.9	-4.5	2.5	2.1
1992	1.3	3.2	1.7	2.4	-1.0	.6	4.9	0	2.0	2.2
1993	.1	1.1	1.1	3.2	-1.3	.4	1.0	3.2	1.3	2.5
1994	.8	1.5	2.1	2.6	.6	1.5	1.1	6.6	.9	2.9
1995[2]	2.7	3.6	3.6	2.2	3.0	3.4	2.7	7.5	.9	2.8

[1] National accounts implicit private consumption deflator.   [2] Forecast.   *Source: Organization for Economic Co-operation and Development (OECD)*

United Kingdom--Economic Statistics — Percentage Change from Previous Period

Year	Real GDP	Nominal GDP	Real Private Consumption	Real Public Consumption	Grossed Fixed Investment	Real Total Domestic Demand	Real Exports of Goods & Services	Real Imports of Goods & Services	Consumer Prices[1]	Unemployment Rate
1986	3.9	7.7	6.4	1.8	2.4	4.7	4.7	6.9	4.3	11.2
1987	4.8	10.0	5.5	1.2	9.6	5.4	5.6	7.8	4.3	10.3
1988	4.3	11.3	7.4	.6	14.2	8.0	-.1	12.2	5.1	8.6
1989	2.3	9.3	3.3	.9	7.2	3.3	3.8	7.4	5.9	7.2
1990	.5	6.8	.7	3.2	-3.1	-.5	4.9	1.0	5.3	5.9
1991	-2.2	4.2	-2.0	3.2	-9.9	-3.1	.1	-3.1	7.1	8.3
1992	-.6	3.8	0	0	-.5	.4	2.7	5.6	5.0	10.0
1993	1.9	5.4	2.5	-.5	.8	2.0	3.1	3.5	1.6	10.3
1994	2.8	6.1	2.8	1.4	4.0	3.3	5.7	7.0	3.2	9.6
1995[2]	3.2	5.7	3.0	1.7	5.3	3.4	6.9	7.3	3.0	8.9

[1] National accounts implicit private consumption deflator.   [2] Forecast.   *Source: Organization for Economic Co-operation and Development (OECD)*

France--Economic Statistics — Percentage Change from Previous Period

Year	Real GDP	Nominal GDP	Real Private Consumption	Real Public Consumption	Grossed Fixed Investment	Real Total Domestic Demand	Real Exports of Goods & Services	Real Imports of Goods & Services	Consumer Prices[1]	Unemployment Rate
1986	2.5	7.9	3.9	1.7	4.5	4.5	-1.4	7.1	2.7	10.4
1987	2.3	5.3	2.9	2.8	4.8	3.3	3.1	7.7	3.2	10.5
1988	4.5	7.5	3.3	3.4	9.6	4.7	8.1	8.6	2.7	10.0
1989	4.3	7.4	3.1	.5	7.9	3.9	10.2	8.1	3.4	9.4
1990	2.5	5.6	2.9	2.0	2.9	2.8	5.3	6.3	2.9	8.9
1991	.7	3.7	1.4	2.5	-1.5	.5	3.9	2.9	3.0	9.5
1992	1.4	3.7	1.7	2.7	-2.0	.4	7.0	3.1	2.4	10.4
1993	-.9	1.4	.7	.5	-5.1	-1.9	0	-3.4	2.1	11.7
1994	1.8	3.6	1.5	1.0	1.1	1.2	5.2	2.8	1.9	12.3
1995[2]	2.9	4.5	2.3	.5	4.2	2.8	6.6	6.0	2.1	12.2

[1] National accounts implicit private consumption deflator.   [2] Forecast.   *Source: Organization for Economic Co-operation and Development (OECD)*

Germany[2]--Economic Statistics — Percentage Change from Previous Period

Year	Real GDP	Nominal GDP	Real Private Consumption	Real Public Consumption	Grossed Fixed Investment	Real Total Domestic Demand	Real Exports of Goods & Services	Real Imports of Goods & Services	Consumer Prices[1]	Unemployment Rate
1986	2.2	5.6	3.4	2.5	3.6	3.3	-.6	2.8	-.5	6.4
1987	1.4	3.4	3.3	1.5	2.1	2.6	.4	4.2	.6	6.2
1988	3.7	5.3	2.7	2.2	4.6	3.6	5.5	5.1	1.4	6.2
1989	3.4	6.1	2.7	-1.7	6.5	2.8	10.1	8.5	3.1	5.6
1990	5.1	8.1	5.4	2.4	8.7	4.9	10.4	10.2	2.6	6.2
1991	4.5	8.7	4.5	.3	6.1	3.6	13.7	12.1	3.7	4.6
1992	2.1	7.5	2.3	3.8	4.2	2.7	.1	2.6	4.7	7.7
1993	-1.3	2.6	.1	-.7	-3.3	-1.4	-9.5	-10.1	4.1	8.9
1994	1.8	4.6	-.2	-.1	4.1	1.0	4.4	1.1	3.0	10.0
1995[3]	2.6	4.6	.9	.1	6.0	2.2	7.4	5.8	2.2	10.0

[1] National accounts implicit private consumption deflator.   [2] Data are for Western Germany only, except for foreign trade statistics.   [3] Forecast.   *Source: Organization for Economic Co-operation and Development (OECD)*

Iron and Steel

U.S. raw steel production during the first seven months of 1994 totaled 51.2 million tonnes. For the same period of 1993, production was 50.7 million tonnes while for 1992 the total was 49.2 million, according to the American Iron and Steel Institute. For all of 1993, raw steel production was 88.8 million tonnes. The American Iron and Steel Institute reported that for the January-July 1994 period, raw steel capability utilization was 89.8 percent. This compares with 87.4 percent for the like period of 1993 and 82.3 percent for 1992. Continuous cast steel production over the first seven months of 1994 accounted for 88.3 percent of total steel production. For the same period of 1993 the figure was 85 percent while for 1992 it was 77.2 percent.

The monthly composite price for No. 1 heavy melting steel scrap in August 1994, as reported by the American Metal Market, was $127.86 per tonne while for the first eight months of 1994 the average price was $127.49 per tonne. For all of 1993, the average monthly composite price was $112.44 per tonne, compared to $84.67 per tonne in 1992.

Total consumption of iron and steel scrap for steel producers during the first seven months of 1994 was 30.7 million tonnes. Integrated steel producers consumed 9.6 million tonnes while electric furnace steel producers used 21.1 million tonnes. Iron and steel scrap shipments for the January-July 1994 period were 1.5 million tonnes with integrated steel producers shipping 95 percent of the total. Stocks of iron and steel scrap on July 31, 1994 were 3.3 million tonnes with integrated steel producers holding 29 percent and electric furnace steel producers 71 percent.

Production of pig iron for the first seven months of 1994 was 28.7 million tonnes. All was produced by integrated steel producers. Consumption of pig iron over the same period was 29 million tonnes. Consumption data by type of producer was withheld to avoid disclosing company proprietary data. Shipments of pig iron for the same period were 1.5 million tonnes. Virtually all was shipped by integrated steel producers. Pig iron stocks on July 31, 1994 were 254,423 tonnes with integrated steel producers holding 54 percent and electric furnace steel producers 46 percent.

Direct-reduced or pre-reduced iron consumption during the January-July 1994 period was 785,490 tonnes. Integrated steel producers used 309,731 tonnes while electric furnace steel producers consumed 475,759 tonnes. Shipments were minor at 3,299 tonnes. On July 31, 1994, stocks of direct-reduced or pre reduced iron were 178,084 tonnes.

U.S. exports of iron and steel scrap for the January-June 1994 period were 4.1 million tonnes. The major destinations were South Korea, Canada, Turkey, Mexico and China. U.S. imports of iron and steel scrap for the first half of 1994 were 823,408 tonnes. The largest source was Canada with shipments of 637,178 tonnes. Other important sources were Mexico and Japan.

U.S. production of iron ore during the first seven months of 1994 were 27.8 million tonnes. Consumption of iron ore and agglomerates for the first half of 1994 were 35.4 million tonnes compared to 34.7 million in the same period of 1993. Stocks of iron ore and agglomerates on June 30, 1994 were 10.2 million tonnes. This was down 28 percent from stocks held on June 30, 1993.

World Production of Raw Steel (Ingots & Castings) In Thousands of Metric Tons

Year	Belgium	Brazil	Canada	China	Czech-oslovakia	France	Germany	Italy	Japan	Rep. of Korea	Russia³	Spain	Ukraine³	United Kingdom	United States	World Total
1985	10,683	20,456	14,600	46,720	15,036	18,833	48,350	23,898	105,281	13,539	154,670	14,235	-----	15,723	80,069	718,131
1986	9,771	21,234	14,101	52,070	15,112	17,624	45,101	22,883	98,277	14,554	160,553	11,976	-----	14,811	74,033	712,704
1987	9,787	22,231	14,737	56,280	15,356	17,693	44,491	22,859	98,513	16,782	161,887	11,691	-----	17,425	80,877	734,319
1988	11,222	24,657	14,866	59,430	15,319	19,122	49,154	23,760	105,681	19,117	163,037	11,685	-----	19,013	90,650	780,318
1989	10,952	25,055	15,458	61,200	15,465	19,335	48,902	25,213	107,908	21,873	160,096	12,684	-----	18,813	88,852	786,712
1990	11,419	20,567	12,281	66,100	14,877	19,032	43,981	25,439	110,339	23,125	154,414	12,705	-----	17,908	89,726	771,169
1991	11,334	22,617	12,987	70,570	12,133	18,437	42,169	25,046	109,649	26,001	77,093	12,933	45,002	16,511	79,738	736,007
1992	10,332	23,939	13,840	80,953	10,846	17,965	39,720	24,843	98,154	28,061	67,018	12,111	41,768	16,215	84,323	735,040
1993¹	10,173	25,160	14,297	88,696	10,741	17,110	37,633	25,695	99,645	33,023	58,249	12,977	30,544	16,629	88,794	739,021
1994²		25,000		92,000					96,000	34,000	46,000		23,000		90,000	720,000

¹Preliminary. ²Estimate. ³Formerly part of the U.S.S.R.; data not reported separately until 1991. *Source: U.S. Bureau of Mines*

Average Wholesale Prices of Iron and Steel in the U.S.

Year	No. 1 Heavy Melting Steel Scrap Pittsburgh	Chicago	Hot Rolled Sheet²	Sheet Bars Hot Rolled	Sheet Bars Cold Finished	Hot Rolled Strip	Carbon Steel Plates	Cold Rolled Strip	Galvanized Sheets	Rail Road Steel Scrap³	Used Steel Cans⁴
	---$ Per Gross Ton---		Cents Per Pound (Pittsburgh Prices)							---$ Per Gross Ton---	
1985	77.43	72.89	23.60	24.10	32.00	23.49	24.50	37.24	30.15	98.03	NA
1986	74.87	73.49	21.15	24.10	32.00	23.30	18.27	37.24	27.89	94.07	NA
1987	90.58	87.22	21.92	17.12	21.23	22.50	19.29	37.24	29.97	117.65	NA
1988	113.78	113.47	21.50	17.25	21.23	22.10	21.64	37.24	31.05	150.25	NA
1989	106.80	108.33	22.21	19.60	25.21	22.10	23.50	37.24	32.48	145.23	60.18
1990	106.61	108.62	22.25	20.43	25.37	22.10	23.75	37.24	33.55	131.59	77.16
1991	95.18	95.19	22.88	20.60	25.75	23.15	24.50	38.86	35.35	129.69	89.00
1992	88.72	88.52	19.13	17.48	24.03	23.50	24.50	39.40	30.88	117.40	88.73
1993¹	116.30	115.26	17.25	18.44	23.83	23.50	25.12	39.40	30.90	142.18	91.79

¹Preliminary. ²10 Gauge. ³Specialties scrap. ⁴Consumer buying prices. NA = Not available. *Source: American Metal Market*

IRON AND STEEL

Salient Statistics of Steel in the United States   In Thousands of Net Tons

Year	Pig Iron Production	Producer Price Index for Steel Mill Products (1982=100)	Raw Steel Production By Type of Furnace Basic Oxygen	Open Hearth	Electric/2	Stainless	Carbon	Alloy	Total	Net Shipments Steel Mill Products	Total — Steel Products — Exports	Imports
1985	50,446	104.9	51,885	6,428	29,946	1,683	76,699	9,877	88,259	73,043	1,293	25,857
1986	43,952	99.7	47,885	3,330	30,390	1,689	71,413	8,505	81,606	70,263	1,215	22,355
1987	48,410	102.3	52,496	2,666	33,989	2,028	77,976	9,147	89,151	76,654	1,647	22,005
1988	55,745	110.7	57,960	5,118	36,846	2,199	86,823	10,902	9,924	83,840	2,469	22,989
1989	55,873	114.5	58,348	4,442	35,154	1,926	86,230	9,786	97,943	84,100	5,098	19,699
1990	54,750	112.1	58,471	3,496	36,939	2,037	86,590	10,279	98,606	84,981	5,001	19,401
1991	48,637	109.5	52,714	1,408	33,774	1,878	77,879	8,139	87,896	78,846	7,112	17,743
1992	52,224	106.4	57,642	NA	35,308	1,993	82,458	8,498	92,949	82,241	5,016	19,033
1993[1]	53,082	108.2	59,353	NA	38,524	1,956	86,865	9,056	97,877	89,022	4,727	21,796

[1]Preliminary. [2]Includes crucible steels. NA = Not available. *Sources: American Iron & Steel Institute; U.S. Bureau of Mines*

U.S. Production of Steel Ingots, Rate of Capability Utilization[1]   In Percents

Year	Jan	Feb	Mar	Apr	May	Jun	Jul	Aug	Sep	Oct	Nov	Dec	Average
1985	60.9	66.1	72.1	71.6	68.9	66.3	62.1	63.2	63.4	65.2	64.7	59.7	66.1
1986	69.4	71.8	71.9	73.5	69.5	63.5	59.2	52.8	54.3	56.8	56.5	54.9	63.8
1987	65.5	69.5	77.3	80.3	80.2	79.7	77.3	79.1	83.9	84.4	85.2	82.8	79.5
1988	88.1	89.7	92.2	91.4	93.1	87.4	88.0	86.6	90.1	87.7	85.8	83.8	89.2
1989	88.2	89.8	90.9	92.2	88.1	86.2	80.8	79.2	80.0	83.0	77.4	73.3	84.5
1990	83.1	85.1	85.7	85.2	85.7	84.5	82.0	85.5	84.6	85.1	83.8	75.0	84.0
1991	74.6	73.1	71.7	72.5	70.0	71.7	74.8	75.2	78.5	78.0	78.0	74.4	74.2
1992	80.5	82.4	83.5	85.3	83.5	82.1	78.9	78.7	78.3	80.9	80.4	77.7	82.2
1993	84.8	89.0	87.0	87.4	88.3	87.5	86.9	86.2	87.7	90.2	86.3	85.9	89.1
1994[2]	87.7	92.2	91.3	91.4	91.2	88.7	87.1	87.7	90.0	92.0	92.6	94.3	93.8

[1]Based on tonnage capability to produce raw steel for a full order book. [2]Preliminary. *Sources: American Iron and Steel Institute; U.S. Bureau of Mines*

United States Production of Steel Ingots   In Thousands of Short Tons

Year	Jan	Feb	Mar	Apr	May	Jun	Jul	Aug	Sep	Oct	Nov	Dec	Total
1985	6,984	6,851	8,269	7,872	7,830	7,292	7,010	7,130	6,924	7,351	7,051	6,728	88,259
1986	7,666	7,171	7,947	7,787	7,616	6,730	6,352	5,668	5,644	6,087	5,860	5,877	81,606
1987	6,248	5,992	7,375	7,402	7,641	7,349	7,324	7,494	7,694	8,073	7,882	7,916	89,151
1988	8,380	7,984	8,763	8,398	8,832	8,031	8,313	8,181	8,237	8,332	7,883	7,954	99,924
1989	8,729	8,022	8,997	8,738	8,633	8,171	7,955	7,790	7,617	8,175	7,386	7,222	97,943
1990	8,241	7,624	8,505	8,209	8,529	8,142	8,101	8,452	8,094	8,424	8,021	7,422	98,906
1991	7,577	6,608	7,283	7,089	7,076	7,017	7,338	7,386	7,457	7,711	7,461	7,348	87,896
1992	7,754	7,432	8,043	7,875	7,968	7,584	7,542	7,526	7,249	7,742	7,449	7,438	92,949
1993[1]	7,942	7,528	8,148	7,926	8,278	7,937	8,066	8,001	7,878	8,409	7,786	8,008	97,877
1994[1]	8,003	7,598	8,323	8,180	8,437	7,941	7,996	8,053	7,993	8,477	8,256	8,686	97,884

[1]Preliminary. *Source: American Iron and Steel Institute*

Shipments of Steel Products[1] by Market Classifications in the United States   In Thousands of Net Tons

Year	Appliances Utensils & Cutlery	Auto-motive	Containers, Packaging & Shipping Materials	Construction Including Maint.	Con-tactors Products	Electrical Equip-ment	Export	Machinery, Industrial Equip. & Tools	Oil and Gas	Rail Trans-portation	Steel for Converting & Pro-cessing[2]	Steel Service Center & Dis-tributors	All Other[3]	Total Ship-ments
1985	1,466	12,950	4,089	7,900	3,330	1,869	494	2,271	2,044	1,061	5,484	18,439	11,646	73,043
1986	1,648	11,889	4,113	7,336	3,278	2,113	495	2,076	1,023	798	5,635	17,478	12,381	70,263
1987	1,633	11,343	4,372	7,681	3,337	2,373	515	2,277	1,489	758	7,195	19,840	13,841	76,654
1988	1,638	12,555	4,421	8,607	3,495	2,459	1,233	2,798	1,477	1,146	8,792	21,037	14,182	83,840
1989	1,721	11,763	4,459	8,318	3,182	2,449	3,183	2,409	1,203	1,229	8,235	20,769	15,180	84,100
1990	1,540	11,100	4,474	9,245	2,870	2,453	2,487	2,388	1,892	1,080	9,441	21,111	14,900	84,981
1991	1,388	10,015	4,278	9,161	2,306	2,102	4,476	1,982	1,425	999	8,265	19,464	12,985	78,846
1992	1,503	11,092	3,974	9,536	2,694	2,136	2,650	1,951	1,454	1,052	9,226	21,328	13,645	82,241
1993	1,592	12,719	4,355	10,516	2,913	2,213	2,110	2,191	1,526	1,223	9,451	23,714	14,499	89,022

[1]All grades including carbon, alloy and stainless steel. [2]Net total after deducting shipments to reporting companies for conversion or resale. [3]Includes agricultural; bolts, nuts, rivets & screws; forgings (other than automotive); shipbuilding & marine equipment; aircraft; mining, quarrying & lumbering; other domestic & commercial equipment machinery; ordnance & other direct military; 7 shipments of non-reporting companies.
Source: American Iron and Steel Institute

Net Shipments of Steel Products in the United States[1]   In Thousands of Net Tons

Year	Cold Finished Bars	Rails & Accessories	Wire Drawn	Tin Mill Products	Plates (Cut & Coils)	Sheet & Strip Galv. (Hot Dipped)	Hot Rolled Bars	Pipe & Tubing	Structural Shapes & Steel Piling	Reinforcing Bars	Hot Rolled Sheets	Cold Rolled Sheets	Carbon	Alloy	Stainless
1985	1,255	121	874	3,773	4,327	6,850	5,698	4,096	4,373	4,326	12,952	13,574	64,360	7,432	1,251
1986	1,257	101	802	3,801	3,565	7,224	5,648	2,836	4,233	4,299	12,167	13,250	62,520	6,556	1,187
1987	1,361	62	800	3,988	4,048	7,660	6,048	3,569	4,839	4,918	13,048	13,859	68,116	7,120	1,418
1988	1,499	118	1,073	4,069	7,328	8,115	6,460	4,443	4,860	5,091	12,969	13,871	77,702	4,552	1,586
1989	1,472	95	1,002	4,126	7,384	8,543	6,301	4,011	4,987	5,015	13,281	13,854	78,485	4,143	1,472
1990	1,486	99	918	4,031	7,945	7,878	6,655	4,652	5,670	5,305	13,388	13,199	78,818	4,647	1,516
1991	1,341	89	865	4,041	6,942	6,910	5,431	4,488	5,245	4,859	13,161	11,532	73,480	3,917	1,449
1992	1,458	122	900	3,927	7,102	8,199	5,806	4,198	5,081	4,781	13,361	12,692	76,625	4,101	1,514
1993	1,580	129	802	4,123	7,538	9,712	6,339	4,445	4,973	5,033	14,873	12,758	83,106	4,381	1,534

[1]All grades, including carbon, alloy and stainless steel. *Source: American Iron and Steel Institute*

World Production of Pig Iron (Excludes Ferro-Alloys)   In Thousands of Metric Tons

Year	Australia	Belgium	Brazil	Canada	China	Czech Republic[3]	France	Germany	India	Italy	Japan	Poland	Russia[4]	Ukraine[4]	United Kingdom	United States	World Total
1987	5,569	8,244	21,509	10,446	55,030	9,788	13,449	31,272	11,083	11,335	73,418	10,476	115,038	-----	12,017	44,034	522,720
1988	5,730	9,147	23,649	10,245	57,040	9,706	14,786	34,676	11,925	11,349	79,295	10,264	116,158	-----	13,056	50,861	553,395
1989	6,094	8,868	24,621	10,849	58,200	9,911	15,071	35,197	12,420	11,795	80,197	9,488	116,628	-----	12,638	50,977	561,762
1990	6,125	9,416	21,401	8,076	62,380	9,667	14,415	32,058	13,395	11,883	80,229	8,658	111,763	-----	12,277	50,058	550,077
1991	5,647	9,354	23,921	8,821	67,200	8,479	13,646	30,868	15,356	10,856	79,985	6,355	90,900	-----	11,883	44,533	525,741
1992	6,000	8,524	23,382	9,260	72,000	8,039	13,051	28,788	16,440	10,462	73,144	6,351	45,834	35,300	11,351	47,767	517,278
1993[1]	6,500	8,000	24,140	9,391	87,300	5,000	13,000	27,250	17,600	12,000	73,738	6,400	45,580	27,005	11,000	48,595	527,907
1994[2]		25,000		96,000							73,000		42,500	22,000		49,000	510,000

[1]Preliminary. [2]Estimate. [3]Formerly part of Czechoslovakia; data not reported separately until 1993. [4]Formerly part of the U.S.S.R.; data not reported separately until 1992. *Source: U.S. Bureau of Mines*

U.S. Pig Iron Production (Excluding Production of Ferro-Alloys)   In Thousands of Short Tons

Year	Jan	Feb	Mar	Apr	May	Jun	Jul	Aug	Sep	Oct	Nov	Dec	Total
1987	3,214	3,069	3,891	4,048	4,256	4,079	4,235	4,165	4,208	4,407	4,351	4,447	48,137
1988	4,683	4,443	4,842	4,699	4,932	4,497	4,762	4,584	4,612	4,646	4,455	4,712	55,745
1989	4,964	4,654	5,112	4,990	4,917	4,707	4,604	4,172	4,403	4,692	4,322	4,202	55,873
1990	4,638	4,221	4,681	4,549	4,746	4,530	4,656	4,788	4,629	4,673	4,523	4,264	54,925
1991	4,077	3,470	4,047	3,830	3,885	3,830	4,179	4,121	4,175	4,251	4,300	4,338	48,503
1992	4,390	4,175	4,524	4,400	4,444	4,232	4,347	4,299	4,065	5,329	4,268	4,306	52,224
1993[1]	4,503	4,503	4,454	4,328	4,555	4,351	4,522	4,504	4,367	4,652	4,218	4,514	53,103
1994[1]	3,970	3,858	3,957	4,099	4,394	4,519	4,518	4,446	4,320	4,564	4,618	4,928	54,431

[1]Preliminary. *Source: American Iron and Steel Institute*

Salient Statistics of Ferrous Scrap & Pig in the U.S.   In Thousands of Metric Tons

	Consumption: Ferrous Scrap & Pig Iron Charged To						Mfg. of Steel Castings (Scrap)	All Uses			Imports of Scrap[2]	Exports of Scrap[3]	Stocks--Dec. 31 Ferrous Scrap & Pig Iron at Consumers		
	Mfg. of Pig Iron & Steel Ingots & Castings			Iron Foundries & Misc. Users											
Year	Scrap	Pig Iron	Total	Scrap	Pig Iron	Total		Ferrous Scrap	Pig Iron	Grand Total			Scrap	Pig Iron	Total Stocks
------	------	------	------	------	------	------	------	------	------	------	------	------	------	------	------
1985	48,264	45,208	93,472	13,805	1,370	15,175	1,882	63,951	46,640	110,591	554	9,027	4,630	241	4,871
1986	45,053	40,211	85,264	13,034	1,113	14,147	1,657	59,745	41,372	101,117	657	10,618	3,941	171	4,112
1987	46,870	44,421	91,291	13,371	955	14,326	1,723	61,964	45,387	107,351	765	9,405	4,394	255	4,649
1988	51,054	52,163	103,217	16,513	1,393	17,906	2,126	69,692	53,567	123,259	942	9,161	4,131	188	4,319
1989	52,733	50,210	102,943	13,270	892	14,162	1,894	67,897	51,122	119,019	1,016	11,149	4,293	246	4,539
1990	54,361	49,337	103,698	13,085	835	13,920	1,850	69,296	50,193	119,489	1,324	11,580	4,292	147	4,439
1991	48,778	44,095	92,873	11,126	656	11,782	1,609	61,513	44,765	106,278	1,073	9,502	4,072	190	4,262
1992	50,144	47,263	97,407	11,444	619	12,063	1,640	63,228	47,894	111,122	1,316	9,262	3,752	181	3,933
1993[1]	53,084	48,092	101,176	12,658	676	13,334	1,729	67,472	48,777	116,249	1,545	9,805	3,725	220	3,945

[1]Preliminary. [2]Includes tinplate and terneplate. [3]Excludes used rails for rerolling and other uses and ships, boats, and other vessels for scrapping.
Source: U.S. Bureau of Mines

IRON AND STEEL

Consumption of Pig Iron in the U.S., by Type of Furnace or Equipment   In Thousands of Metric Tons

Year	Open Hearth	Electric	Cupola	Basic Oxygen Process	Air & Other Furnace	Direct Casting	Total	Year	Open Hearth	Electric	Cupola	Basic Oxygen Process	Air & Other Furnace	Direct Casting	Total
1982	3,298	450	436	34,975	128	1,000	40,288	1988	3,500	1,269	679	47,199	40	879	53,567
1983	3,554	309	386	40,216	83	875	45,424	1989	1,582	1,051	389	49,380	30	536	52,969
1984	5,187	334	425	41,324	83	909	48,265	1990	2,072	982	332	47,307	19	387	51,100
1985	4,297	456	455	40,384	51	998	46,640	1991	997	574	265	42,955	13	106	44,911
1986	2,109	284	388	37,723	53	816	41,372	1992	------	429	215	47,194	7	49	47,894
1987	1,866	1,322	336	38,468	51	891	39,790	1993[1]	------	519	292	47,848	34	84	48,777

[1]Preliminary. [2]Estimate. *Source: U.S. Bureau of Mines*

Wholesale Price of No. 1 Heavy Melting Steel Scrap at Chicago   In Dollars Per Gross Ton

Year	Jan	Feb	Mar	Apr	May	Jun	Jul	Aug	Sep	Oct	Nov	Dec	Average
1984	88.29	89.00	87.09	85.14	85.00	84.71	79.00	78.00	81.00	81.09	83.00	76.00	83.12
1985	78.86	82.16	84.76	79.59	68.00	62.00	64.24	73.00	72.00	71.87	69.00	69.19	72.89
1986	74.23	76.89	74.05	74.00	74.00	71.00	71.00	76.71	73.14	70.87	73.00	73.00	73.49
1987	78.00	78.00	73.00	72.00	74.15	77.00	78.73	84.00	96.52	116.00	115.47	103.73	87.22
1988	100.80	119.43	119.02	117.24	111.38	108.55	120.00	119.78	115.00	115.00	109.16	106.33	113.47
1989	114.10	118.32	113.00	113.00	113.00	113.00	108.00	108.00	108.00	101.09	96.00	94.50	108.33
1990	104.00	102.29	98.00	109.43	114.55	111.67	108.50	116.00	113.76	112.50	107.73	105.00	108.62
1991	104.76	100.74	98.00	97.80	93.18	87.50	87.74	94.14	98.50	97.50	91.97	90.50	95.19
1992	90.50	90.50	90.50	90.50	89.70	87.68	87.50	87.55	88.50	85.50	85.50	88.36	88.52
1993	98.34	109.50	109.50	106.50	106.50	111.27	118.50	114.18	113.50	125.88	131.50	138.00	115.26
1994	138.00	138.00	138.00	138.00	123.64	110.50	117.20	133.63	134.50	132.50	137.50	141.50	131.91

Source: American Metal Market

World Production of Iron Ore[3], by Specified Countries   In Thousands of Metric Tons (Gross Weight)

Year	Australia	Brazil	Canada	Chile	China	France	India	Mauritania	Mexico	North Korea	Russia[4]	South Africa	Sweden	Ukraine[4]	United States	Venezuela	World Total
1985	97,447	128,251	39,502	6,534	80,000	14,447	42,545	9,333	7,820	8,000	247,639	24,414	20,454	——	49,533	14,710	860,556
1986	94,015	129,405	36,167	6,981	90,000	12,437	47,800	9,170	7,298	8,500	249,959	24,483	20,475	——	39,486	16,753	863,650
1987	101,748	134,497	37,702	6,637	113,000	11,267	51,018	9,002	7,523	8,500	250,874	22,008	19,636	——	47,648	17,782	902,737
1988	99,450	146,008	39,934	7,710	154,380	9,872	49,961	10,004	8,431	9,000	249,754	25,248	20,440	——	57,515	18,932	967,218
1989	105,810	157,900	40,509	9,030	171,850	9,368	53,418	12,110	15,000	9,500	241,348	29,958	21,763	——	59,032	18,053	1,013,383
1990	110,508	152,300	34,855	7,903	168,300	8,729	54,579	11,590	15,000	10,000	236,000	30,291	19,877	——	56,408	20,119	984,048
1991	117,134	150,500	36,383	8,692	176,070	7,472	57,638	10,246	13,000	10,000	199,000	28,958	19,328	——	56,596	21,296	955,552
1992	117,170	151,000	32,697	8,270	197,600	5,707	54,000	8,202	15,000	10,500	82,500	28,226	19,277	75,700	55,593	18,070	963,159
1993[1]	120,534	151,000	30,568	8,500	234,600	3,520	61,000	9,300	15,000	10,500	75,000	29,385	18,728	70,000	55,651	16,851	988,797
1994[2]	120,000	150,000	35,000		240,000	3,500	62,000	10,000				29,000	20,000		57,000		1,000,000

[1]Preliminary. [2]Estimate. [3]Iron ore, iron ore concentrates and iron ore agglomerates. [4]Formerly part of the U.S.S.R.;data not reported separately until 1992. *Source: U.S. Bureau of Mines*

Salient Statistics of Iron Ore[3] in the U.S.   In Thousands of Metric Tons

Year	Net Import Reliance % of Apparent Consumption	Production Total	Production Lake Superior	Production Other Regions	Shipments	Value Million $ (at Mine)	Average Value $ at Mine Per Ton	Stocks–Dec. 31 Mines	Stocks–Dec. 31 Consuming Plants	Stocks–Dec. 31 Lake Erie Docks	Imports	Exports	Consumption	Value Million $ Imports
1985	21	49,533	48,148	1,385	50,204	2,076.7	41.37	6,046	21,631	2,442	16,024	5,114	71,708	452.3
1986	33	39,486	38,203	1,283	41,991	1,472.5	35.07	3,307	17,439	2,019	17,011	4,553	62,097	460.6
1987	22	47,648	46,756	892	47,983	1,503.1	31.33	2,402	16,565	2,056	16,849	5,093	67,768	408.8
1988	18	57,515	56,038	1,477	57,113	1,716.7	30.06	2,957	18,005	2,537	20,183	5,285	83,694	484.5
1989	22	59,032	56,981	2,052	58,299	1,939.9	33.27	4,575	15,730	2,171	19,596	5,365	80,447	522.3
1990	21	56,408	54,628	1,780	57,010	1,740.9	30.54	4,795	15,911	2,273	18,054	3,199	76,855	559.5
1991	11	56,761	55,636	1,124	56,775	1,674.1	29.49	4,853	17,612	2,981	13,335	4,045	66,366	436.8
1992	12	55,593	55,018	575	55,569	1,732.4	31.18	3,783	16,093	2,981	12,504	5,055	75,067	395.8
1993[1]	14	55,661	54,814	848	56,251	1,642.8	29.21	2,504	16,548	2,288	14,097	5,061	76,793	420.8
1994[2]	18	57,000			57,000			20,000			15,000	4,000	78,000	

[1]Preliminary. [2]Estimate. [3]Usable iron ore exclusive of ore containing 5% or more manganese and includes byproduct ore. *Source: U.S. Bureau of Mines*

U.S. Imports (for Consumption) of Iron Ore[2] from Principal Countries   In Thousands of Metric Tons

Year	Australia	Brazil	Canada	Chile	Mauritania	Peru	Sweden	Venezuela	Total
1985	—	2,304	7,763	149	—	110	59	1,876	14,307
1986	10	3,752	8,836	94	66	92	106	2,346	17,011
1987	194	3,698	7,981	636	412	84	139	2,622	16,849
1988	1,076	4,935	9,157	139	522	181	88	3,568	20,183
1989	394	5,169	8,538	61	594	186	57	4,232	19,596
1990	14	4,276	9,344	138	666	59	54	3,503	18,054
1991	—	2,481	7,299	103	459	157	51	2,763	13,335
1992	163	2,442	6,834	107	280	70	64	2,540	12,504
1993[1]	254	2,872	7,442	68	206	1	60	3,189	14,097

[1]Preliminary. [2]Including agglomerates. *Source: U.S. Bureau of Mines*

Total[1] Iron Ore Stocks at End of Month in the U.S.   In Thousands of Metric Tons

Year	Jan	Feb	Mar	Apr	May	Jun	Jul	Aug	Sep	Oct	Nov	Dec
1986	26,829	25,770	24,743	23,618	24,652	24,677	24,546	23,047	23,331	23,251	22,336	21,783
1987	21,472	21,406	20,580	19,571	18,875	19,008	19,235	19,085	19,343	19,994	20,264	20,613
1988	20,997	20,925	20,041	20,119	19,789	19,341	19,835	20,801	22,210	22,140	22,485	22,755
1989	23,189	23,252	22,685	21,145	21,670	21,544	22,286	22,275	22,588	21,429	21,448	22,476
1990	22,088	21,986	20,958	20,609	20,501	21,019	21,863	22,110	22,268	22,027	22,042	22,978
1991	22,572	22,218	21,316	20,757	21,756	23,174	23,319	24,329	25,148	25,117	25,358	25,445
1992	24,527	23,162	20,922	20,550	21,501	22,492	23,046	21,721	22,735	23,190	23,433	22,856
1993[2]	21,296	20,806	19,235	18,996	19,180	22,036	22,905	21,575	22,629	21,355	21,615	21,341
1994[2]	18,765	17,826	15,953	14,883	15,249	16,592	17,863	18,931	20,554	20,760	21,552	21,339

[1]All stocks at mines, furnace yards and at U.S. docks. [2]Preliminary. *Source: U.S. Bureau of Mines*

KR-CRB Futures Index

Developed in 1957, the Knight-Ridder Commodity Research Bureau's Futures Price Index was designed to monitor broad changes in the commodity markets. Because it averages the prices of 21 important futures markets, it measures anticipated inflation and is followed widely by traders, analysts and economists. U.S. bond traders are particularly interested in the movement of this Index because of the well documented inverse correlation with bond prices over the past decade.

In 1993, the KR-CRB Index rose for the second consecutive year. The December 30, 1994 closing value of 236.64 was 10.33 higher, or 4.56 percent above the December 31, 1993 level. Unlike 1993, when all seven sub-index groups advanced, 1994's gain was almost exclusively a result of the 51.3 percent rise in the imported group. Also contributing to the year-on-year gain was a 9.9 percent rise in the industrial components.

Futures Market

Futures and options on the KR-CRB Index are traded on the New York Futures Exchange (NYFE).

KR-CRB Component Commodities by Group

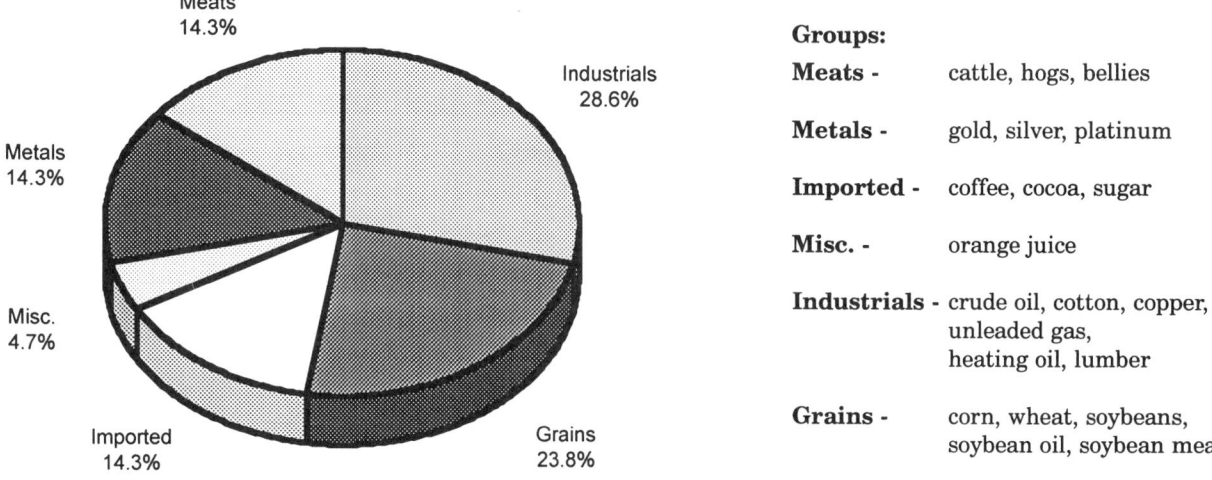

Groups:	
Meats -	cattle, hogs, bellies
Metals -	gold, silver, platinum
Imported -	coffee, cocoa, sugar
Misc. -	orange juice
Industrials -	crude oil, cotton, copper, unleaded gas, heating oil, lumber
Grains -	corn, wheat, soybeans, soybean oil, soybean meal

The Index is calculated in a three-step fashion:

1) Each of the Index's 21 component commodities is averaged arithmetically using the prices for all of the futures months which expire on or before the end of the ninth calendar month from the current date, excluding non-cycle months. This means that the Index extends between nine and 10 months into the future depending on where one is in the current month. For example, live cattle's average price on July 29, 1994 would be computed as follows:

$$\frac{\text{Aug 94} + \text{Oct 94} + \text{Dec 94} + \text{Feb 95} + \text{Apr 95}}{5}$$

2) These 21 component averages are then geometrically averaged by multiplying all of the numbers together and taking the 21st root.

$$\sqrt[21]{\text{LC Avg x CC Avg x ....W Avg}}$$

3) The resulting value is divided by 50.7161, the 1967 base-year average for these commodities, and then multiplied by an adjustment factor of .94128. The adjustment factor is necessitated by several changes made to the Index since 1987. The first was the July 20, 1987 changeover from 26 commodities averaged over 12 months, to 21 commodities averaged over nine months. The second change was the July 24, 1989 elimination of non-cycle component months, and the third was the July 6, 1992 substitution of oat futures (traded on the Chicago Board of Trade) with unleaded gasoline (NYMEX).

Finally that result is multiplied by 100 in order to convert the Index into percentage terms:

$$\frac{\text{Current Geometric Average}}{\text{1967 Geometric Average (50.7161)}} \times .94128 \times 100$$

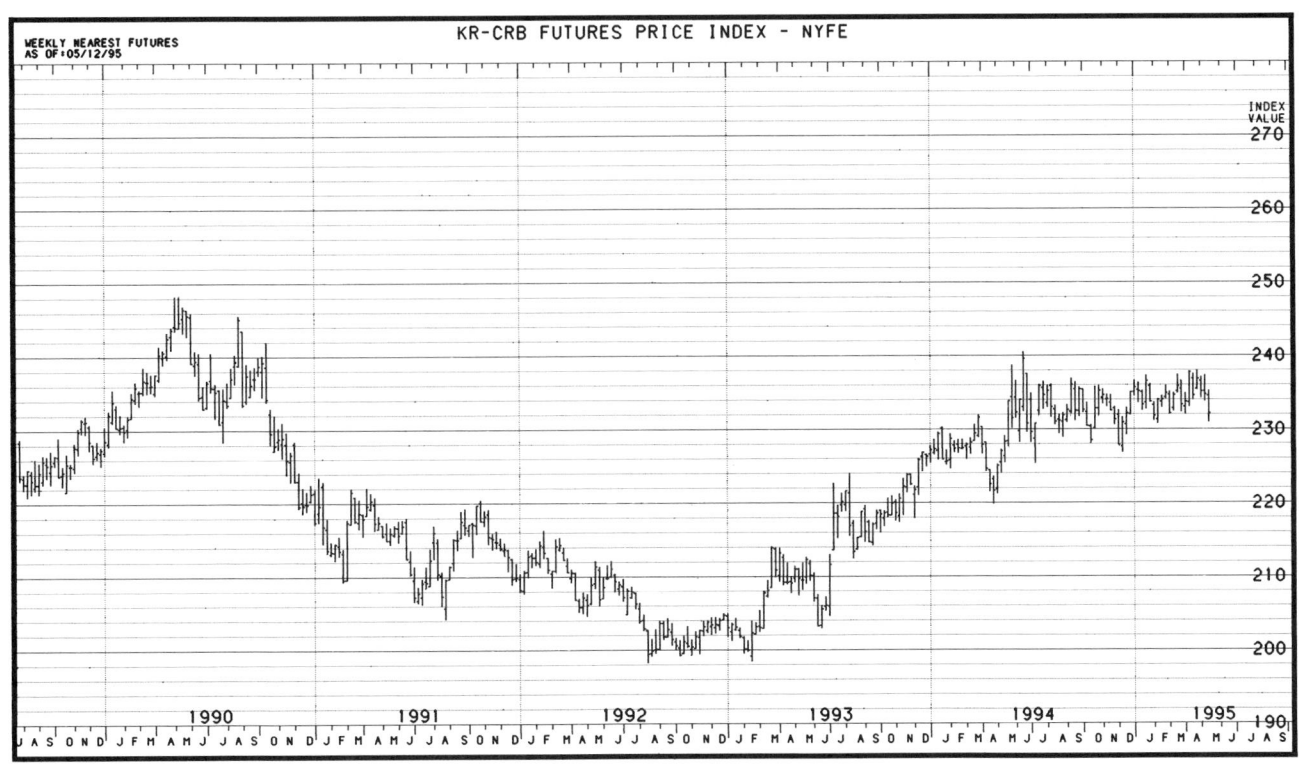

Average Open Interest of Knight-Ridder CRB Futures at New York   In Contracts

Year	Jan.	Feb.	Mar.	Apr.	May	June	July	Aug.	Sept.	Oct.	Nov.	Dec.
1988	2,597	2,607	2,682	2,819	3,592	3,934	2,846	2,795	2,659	2,419	2,529	2,556
1989	2,679	3,008	2,491	2,274	2,117	2,104	1,891	1,992	1,861	1,907	2,215	2,209
1990	1,889	1,229	1,476	1,858	1,499	1,459	1,289	1,286	1,181	1,247	1,505	1,530
1991	1,443	1,593	1,524	1,620	1,511	1,524	1,168	1,071	1,045	1,172	1,357	1,383
1992	1,435	1,472	1,185	1,347	1,311	1,087	951	1,179	1,075	1,226	1,283	1,406
1993	1,969	1,984	1,842	2,201	2,564	2,947	2,616	2,409	2,128	2,383	2,432	2,351
1994	2,607	3,146	2,680	2,691	2,339	2,698	3,838	5,146	4,562	4,942	4,535	2,800

Source: New York Futures Exchange

Volume of Trading of Knight-Ridder CRB Futures at New York   In Contracts

Year	Jan.	Feb.	Mar.	Apr.	May	June	July	Aug.	Sept.	Oct.	Nov.	Dec.	Total
1988	9,557	10,726	13,841	9,480	20,299	43,591	31,043	22,020	15,615	9,044	9,691	11,044	205,951
1989	8,805	10,045	12,035	11,437	13,145	13,824	11,917	9,846	7,918	7,412	9,613	8,551	124,548
1990	6,505	5,829	7,042	6,670	7,191	6,687	6,477	6,415	4,096	4,744	4,409	3,842	69,907
1991	5,835	5,391	6,715	6,432	3,671	5,557	4,853	5,876	4,414	3,766	4,132	4,543	61,185
1992	4,895	6,031	4,136	5,697	5,496	4,487	4,162	4,617	3,874	3,183	5,277	4,400	56,255
1993	3,620	5,720	8,050	7,340	8,680	10,722	12,418	8,590	6,192	4,350	8,535	6,954	91,908
1994	6,956	7,473	10,085	10,274	11,298	14,652	10,560	8,967	7,445	6,575	10,186	5,515	109,986

Source: New York Futures Exchange

Lard

Production of lard is directly related to commercial pork production. U.S. lard production in 1994/95 (October-September) is forecast by the U.S. Department of Agriculture to be 985 million pounds. This represents an increase of 1 percent from 1993/94. Over the last five years, lard production averaged 970 million pounds. Initial stocks on October 1, 1994 were 30 million pounds, an increase of 15 percent from October 1, 1993.

While most lard is used domestically in food products, a certain percentage is exported. For the 1994/95 marketing year, lard exports were forecast by the USDA to increase over 15 percent to 105 million pounds. While this represents a significant increase from the past season, in recent years lard exports have been much higher. As recently as the 1992/93 season, lard exports were 135 million pounds while the year prior to that they were 131 million.

Despite consumer preferences toward healthier food products, lard finds widespread use in edible foods. The major uses of lard for edible purposes are in baking and frying fats and margarine. For October 1993-May 1994, use of lard for baking and frying fats was nearly 166 million pounds. For October 1992-September 1993, use of lard in baking or frying fats was 272 million pounds. For the October 1993-May 1994 period, lard usage for margarine (which includes edible tallow) was nearly 26 million pounds. Total usage for margarine was 30 million pounds for the 1992/93 marketing year. Use of lard for edible purposes over the first 8 months of the marketing year was just over 190 million pounds. Of all fats and oils used in edible products, lard comprises about 2 percent of the total. The major oil used is soybean oil followed by corn oil and cottonseed oil.

The average wholesale price of loose lard in Chicago tanks was 15.4 cents per pound in 1993. That was up from 14.2 cents in 1992. Per capita consumption of lard in 1993 was 3.8 pounds.

World Production of Lard   In Thousands of Metric Tons

Crop Year Beginning Oct. 1	Brazil	Canada	China	Czecho-slovak	France	Germany	Italy	Japan	Poland	Romania	Spain	Taiwan	United States	Former U.S.S.R.	World Total
1988-9	147.5	79.0	1,438.3	124.6	126.5	518.7	181.0	91.0	137.7	130.4	154.8	54.9	426.2	852.1	5,382.8
1989-90	151.0	75.6	1,519.5	123.9	129.2	534.4	178.5	91.0	136.8	130.1	156.1	59.1	412.3	844.4	5,441.8
1990-1	158.6	75.6	1,605.6	112.4	137.3	476.3	187.6	87.0	150.1	129.0	169.7	65.5	415.0	762.8	5,444.0
1991-2[1]	165.7	76.9	1,714.8	111.0	140.4	411.3	188.0	85.0	156.9	117.7	170.6	66.7	447.7	653.6	5,365.6
1992-3[2]	175.5	77.0	1,856.3	98.4	150.4	417.6	192.0	85.8	148.9	114.4	185.8	69.4	445.0	582.9	5,481.1
1993-4[3]	189.0	76.0	1,956.5	94.4	153.8	409.4	195.4	83.7	137.7	117.3	180.6	71.4	439.0	583.4	5,590.0

[1] Preliminary. [2] Estimate. [3] Forecast. *Source: The Oil World*

Supply and Distribution of Lard in the United States   In Millions of Pounds

Year	Supply Pro-duction	Supply Stocks Jan. 1	Supply Total Supply	Disappearance Domestic	Disappearance Baking or Frying Fats	Disappearance Mar-garine[2]	Disappearance Exports	Disappearance Total Disap-pearance	Direct Use	Per Capita (Lbs.)
1985	927	39	966	826	289	65	105	931	426	3.5
1986	876	35	911	785	274	48	104	889	417	3.2
1987	863	22	885	745	224	22	107	852	441	3.1
1988	932	33	965	801	265	35	127	928	433	3.2
1989	935	37	972	830	295	32	110	940	442	3.3
1990	919	32	954	832	264	35	97	929	468	3.3
1991	952	25	980	822	274	43	121	943	429	3.3
1992	1,025	37	1,064	906	310	37	136	1,042	426	3.5
1993[1]	1,005	23	1,031	878	296	31	114	992	448	3.8

[1] Preliminary. [2] Includes edible tallow. *Source: Economic Research Service, U.S. Department of Agriculture*

Consumption (Edible & Inedible) of Lard in the United States   In Millions of Pounds

Year	Jan	Feb	Mar	Apr	May	June	July	Aug	Sept	Oct	Nov	Dec	Total
1986	33.3	31.4	35.6	38.1	35.6	33.8	26.3	23.3	27.5	28.4	28.9	25.6	367.8
1987	20.2	22.1	25.9	21.3	18.5	28.0	26.8	22.3	33.0	27.4	26.3	32.4	304.2
1988	25.6	27.7	31.1	29.3	28.5	27.4	25.9	28.0	37.9	34.6	36.3	35.3	367.6
1989	28.9	27.5	34.0	31.1	33.5	32.2	28.9	33.5	34.1	39.0	42.5	32.7	397.9
1990	27.0	27.3	30.9	26.3	32.1	29.2	22.8	32.0	31.3	34.6	33.8	30.6	384.9
1991	---------	97.3	----------	----------	94.7	----------	----------	95.2	----------	----------	105.9	------------	393.1
1992	33.9	31.6	39.9	40.0	38.7	39.6	42.9	41.1	47.6	46.4	41.0	37.2	479.7
1993	40.1	34.4	45.9	36.8	38.2	38.8	32.6	38.4	41.8	44.0	43.0	40.3	474.3
1994[1]	31.5	31.7	33.9	32.4	33.8	32.0	30.2	34.8	40.4	40.6	41.6	39.0	421.9

[1] Preliminary. *Source: Bureau of Census, U.S. Department of Commerce*

Average Wholesale Price of Lard -- Loose, Tank Cars, Chicago   In Cents Per Pound

Year	Jan	Feb	Mar	Apr	May	June	July	Aug	Sept	Oct	Nov	Dec	Average
1987	15.50	14.40	14.60	13.70	14.70	14.90	15.70	14.50	15.50	14.70	14.70	14.40	14.78
1988	17.00	16.70	16.60	16.40	16.30	17.60	17.70	16.50	16.40	16.30	13.20	14.60	16.28
1989	14.50	14.40	14.10	13.80	13.70	14.10	14.40	13.50	14.20	14.60	14.80	13.20	14.11
1990	13.50	13.80	13.20	12.50	12.30	13.20	13.40	12.10	12.70	14.00	14.50	14.10	13.28
1991	13.50	13.50	13.50	13.70	12.50	12.50	12.40	13.40	14.00	14.40	13.60	12.20	13.27
1992	12.50	12.50	12.60	12.60	13.90	15.00	15.00	15.30	15.50	15.40	16.10	16.30	14.39
1993	15.80	15.00	14.70	16.20	16.70	15.50	14.60	15.40	15.50	15.90	15.30	14.30	15.41
1994	14.50	14.60	15.40	15.70	15.80	16.30	17.20	18.90	20.10	20.40	20.40	20.90	17.52

Source: The Wall Street Journal

United States Cold Storage Holdings of all Lard[1], on First of Month   In Millions of Pounds

Year	Jan	Feb	Mar	Apr	May	June	July	Aug	Sept	Oct	Nov	Dec
1987	21.90	31.50	30.90	27.20	28.90	29.90	27.40	27.80	28.90	28.80	38.20	36.20
1988	33.00	37.20	33.80	37.10	31.20	31.90	37.80	41.10	30.10	39.00	41.70	36.70
1989	37.40	38.20	37.10	27.30	34.20	37.60	41.30	32.40	28.90	41.60	29.00	36.60
1990	32.00	33.70	37.60	28.50	31.60	27.40	25.20	25.90	22.80	22.90	22.20	30.30
1991	------------	24.40	------------	------------	28.30	------------	------------	24.00	------------	------------	24.10	------------
1992	37.40	27.20	28.90	28.30	26.70	23.20	24.80	29.20	26.90	27.20	22.20	24.80
1993	22.70	25.90	27.20	24.60	22.80	25.80	31.10	27.40	23.60	26.20	24.60	30.10
1994[2]	37.70	38.00	31.80	28.80	27.40	27.00	27.00	25.50	29.70	34.40	33.97	35.78

[1] Stocks in factories and warehouses (except that in hands of retailers).   [2] Preliminary.   *Source: Bureau of Census, U.S. Department of Commerce*

Lead

Lead finds widespread use in batteries, fuel tanks, ammunition, building construction, electrical equipment, cans and containers, and as solder for pipes and plumbings. Lead and compounds that contain lead are very toxic. As a result, there has been a concerted effort to reduce the use of lead, especially in areas where humans are exposed to it. Substitutes for lead include plastic, aluminum, tin and iron. There has been research into the use of bismuth as a non-toxic substitute for lead in a variety of uses from ceramic glazes to solder. Currently there is a great deal of research occurring in developing a new type of battery using lithium-polymer materials. Lithium polymer batteries have some obvious advantages over lead-acid batteries. Lithium is the lightest metal on the atomic chart while lead is one of the heaviest. The other components of lithium-polymer batteries, including plastics and hydrocarbons, are also light materials.

U.S. lead is mined primarily in Missouri, Alaska, Colorado, Idaho and Montana. Missouri accounts for most of U.S. production. Primary refinery lead production during January-July 1994 was 215,023 tonnes, compared with 335,014 tonnes for all of 1993. Lead production by secondary refineries for the first seven months of 1994 totaled 553,100 tonnes, compared with 908,200 tonnes for all of 1993.

Consumption of lead during the first seven months of 1994 was 800,600 tonnes. For 1993, total lead usage was 1,318,800 tonnes. Usage of lead by product is dominated by storage batteries. Usage for that category totaled 404,880 tonnes in the January-July 1994 period. Ammunition, including shot and bullets, used 32,093 tonnes. Other uses include brass and bronze ingots, cable covering, casting metals, sheet lead, solder and pipes.

Exports of lead ore and concentrates over the first six months of 1994 totaled 13,305 tonnes. For all of 1993, exports of ore and concentrates totaled 41,766 tonnes. Lead material exports for January-June 1994 totaled 27,855 tonnes, compared with 58,584 for all of 1993. Ash and residue exports were 11,915 tonnes, compared to only 1,728 tonnes in 1993. Total exports of lead scrap were 35,962 tonnes in first half 1994. U.S. imports of refined metal lead during the first seven months of 1994 were 104,991 tonnes. For all of 1993, refined metal lead imports totaled 195,572 tonnes with Canada and Mexico supplying most of the requirements.

It was reported that lead mine output in the former Soviet Union continued to decline in 1994 due to a lack of funding. Toll-smelting arrangements helped smelters in 1993, but due to the worldwide shortage of concentrates, further tolling appears limited. Domestic and foreign transportation and freight costs have also been factors limiting the industry's ability to recover. In another development, Japan's Matsushita Battery Industrial Company announced it would build a new lead-acid battery plant in China. The plant will use an estimated 4,000 tonnes of lead per year. The facility will build small sealed lead-acid storage batteries for use in small-sized uninterruptable power systems, communication base stations and switching systems.

Futures Market

Lead futures and options are traded on the London Metals Exchange (LME).

World Smelter (Primary & Secondary) Production of Lead — In Thousands of Metric Tons

Year	Australia[3]	Belgium[4]	Bulgaria	Canada[3]	China[2]	France	Germany	Italy	Japan	Kazakhstan[5]	Mexico[3]	Peru[3]	Spain	United Kingdom[3]	United States	World Total
1986	175.0	90.5	96.0	264.9	239.6	230.4	366.6	132.4	361.5	755.0	248.6	67.4	124.9	328.6	931.8	5,210
1987	220.7	89.6	100.6	230.7	246.4	245.5	340.4	168.3	338.5	750.0	253.6	71.4	122.7	347.0	1,042.0	5,411
1988	185.0	105.2	101.0	268.1	241.4	255.7	345.1	177.7	340.0	727.0	250.0	53.6	110.8	373.8	1,090.5	5,518
1989	205.0	109.4	101.5	242.8	260.0	427.6	184.2	186.2	332.4	745.0	235.0	78.4	114.5	350.5	1,287.8	6,077
1990	229.0	105.8	66.6	183.6	296.0	432.7	177.9	166.8	327.4	700.0	232.2	74.3	110.0	329.4	1,325.9	5,907
1991	239.0	110.7	56.2	212.4	330.0	438.0	171.2	208.2	332.4	630.0	161.8	79.5	169.0	311.0	1,230.3	5,780
1992[1]	232.0	116.3	550.0	359.1	365.0	444.6	175.3	186.3	330.2	210.0	172.6	87.5	120.0	346.8	1,221.1	5,517
1993[2]	234.0	122.0	550.0	336.0	387.4	438.0	129.8	197.0	258.0	195.0	188.4	87.5	110.0	345.0	1,238.6	5,420

[1]Preliminary. [2]Estimate. [3]Refined & bullion. [4]Includes scrap. [5]Formerly part of the U.S.S.R.; data not reported separately until 1992.
Source: U.S. Bureau of Mines

Consumption of Lead in the United States by Product — In Metric Tons

Year	Ammunition	Bearing Metals	Pipes, Traps & Bends[2]	Cable Covering	Calking Lead	Casting Metals	Other Metal Products[3]	Total Other Oxides[4]	Sheet Lead	Solder	Storage Battery — Grids, Post, etc.	Storage Battery — Oxides	Brass and Bronze	Total Consumption
1986	44,382	5,525	12,542	17,061	1,833	10,268	7,481	69,527	17,275	21,302	488,932	364,878	9,057	1,125,521
1987	46,835	5,260	11,532	20,140	1,893	19,909	7,119	68,094	17,400	19,758	529,362	424,236	9,868	1,230,373
1988	52,708	6,034	11,193	16,170	1,618	15,872	7,614	62,524	17,458	19,064	514,694	454,964	9,994	1,245,170
1989	57,310	2,586	9,818	22,605	1,831	16,175	6,850	57,984	20,987	17,009	552,308	459,847	9,610	1,283,234
1990	58,210	5,212	9,281	18,253	1,688	14,843	3,812	56,484	21,013	16,490	571,187	448,450	9,943	1,275,226
1991	58,458	3,669	8,975	17,472	1,074	14,141	3,254	59,617	22,334	14,750	591,884	415,233	8,997	1,246,337
1992	64,845	4,785	11,652	15,992	1,045	17,111	3,024	63,225	21,006	13,518	629,147	373,185	9,175	1,236,571
1993	51,151	2,639	1,361	17,165	961	18,458	3,896	45,295	11,230	6,509	697,222	422,636	6,069	1,318,800
1994[1]	52,317	W	1,121	---- 15,594 ------			3,999	45,153	10,155	7,639	---- 705,219 ----		6,540	1,384,300

[1]Preliminary. [2]Including building. [3]Includes terne metal, type metal, and lead consumed in foil, collapsible tubes, annealing, plating, galvanizing and fishing weights. [4]Includes paints, glass and ceramic products, and other pigments and chemicals. W = Withheld proprietary data.
Source: U.S. Bureau of Mines

Salient Statistics of Lead in the United States   In Thousands of Metric Tons

Year	Net Import Reliance as a % of Apparent Consumption	Production of Refined Lead from — Domestic Ores[3]	Foreign Ores[3]	Total Primary	Total Value of Refined Million $	Secondary Lead Recovered — As Soft Lead	In Antimonial Lead	In Other Alloys	Total	Total Value of Secondary Million $	Stocks, Dec. 31 — Primary	Consumer[4]	Average Price ¢ Per Pound — New York	London[5]
1979	5	530.0	45.6	575.6	668.0	352.2	378.8	70.3	801.4	930.0	89.3	153.2	52.64	54.52
1980	E	508.2	39.4	547.6	512.6	315.2	306.7	53.7	675.6	632.4	126.0	126.2	42.46	41.21
1981	1	440.2	55.1	495.3	398.9	282.2	304.4	54.6	641.1	516.3	140.2	123.2	36.53	33.30
1982	11	459.9	52.3	512.2	288.4	240.5	284.4	46.4	615.7	321.7	125.5	97.2	25.54	24.66
1983	20	463.9	55.2	519.2	248.1	189.6	271.6	42.3	503.5	240.7	53.4	100.8	21.68	19.27
1984	20	324.0	65.4	389.4	219.3	263.4	327.8	42.1	633.4	266.3	45.1	97.1	25.55	20.12
1985	12	422.7	71.4	494.0	207.7	273.7	299.3	42.7	615.7	258.9	84.5	93.1	19.07	17.84
1986	20	348.2	22.1	370.3	180.0	289.5	291.9	43.3	624.8	303.7	20.4	83.8	22.05	18.43
1987	17	336.5	37.1	373.6	296.0	345.1	323.3	41.7	710.1	562.6	21.6	88.6	35.94	26.99
1988	13	371.3	20.7	392.1	321.0	367.1	331.3	38.0	736.4	603.0	15.4	89.9	37.14	29.73
1989	8	379.0	17.4	396.5	343.9	438.0	418.6	34.7	891.3	773.3	15.6	82.4	39.35	30.63
1990	3	385.6	18.0	403.7	409.5	461.4	425.4	35.6	922.2	935.6	25.5	86.3	46.02	37.05
1991	6	323.9	21.9	345.7	255.2	421.9	426.9	35.8	884.6	652.9	9.1	71.7	33.48	25.30
1992	10	284.0	20.8	304.8	235.9	452.9	424.5	23.1	916.3	709.1	20.5	82.3	35.10	24.50
1993[1]	15	310.7	24.9	335.7	234.4	425.6	445.0	17.0	903.6	632.3	14.3	80.8	31.74	18.40
1994[2]	17	330.0	39.4	369.4					949.0		9.3	52.0	37.17	24.00

[1] Preliminary. [2] Estimator. [3] And base bullion. [4] Also at secondary smelters. [5] LME data in dollars per metric ton beginning July 1993.
E = Net Exporter. *Source: U.S. Bureau of Mines*

U.S. Mine Production of Recoverable Lead   In Metric Tons

Year	Total	Missouri	Missouri's % of Total	Year	Total	Missouri	Missouri's % of Total
1983	449,295	409,280	91%	1989	410,915	366,931	89%
1984	322,677	278,329	86%	1990	483,704	380,781	79%
1985	413,955	371,008	90%	1991	465,931	351,995	76%
1986	339,793	319,900	94%	1992	397,923	300,589	76%
1987	311,381	W	NA	1993[1]	353,607	276,569	78%
1988	384,983	353,194	92%	1994[2]	363,443	290,738	80%

[1] Preliminary. [2] Estimate. W = Withheld. NA = Not available. *Source: U.S. Bureau of Mines*

U.S. Foreign Trade of Lead   In Thousands of Metric Tons

Year	Exports — Ore Concentrate	Unwrought Lead[3]	Wrought Lead[4]	Scrap	Ash & Residues[5]	Imports for Consumption — Ores, Flue Dust or Re-Fume & Mattes	Base Bullion	Pigs & Bars	Reclaimed Scrap, Etc.	Value Million $	General Imports From: Ore, Flue Dust & Matte — Australia	Canada	Peru	Pigs & Bars — Australia	Canada	Mexico	Peru
1979	32.9	7.4	3.3	119.7	-----	44.4	1.7	182.6	4.0	248.3	1.9	12.8	12.4	17.3	-----	73.6	17.9
1980	27.6	156.5	8.0	119.7	-----	29.6	.3	81.3	2.9	116.5	3.0	8.5	18.0	11.3	34.9	28.6	3.3
1981	33.0	16.8	6.5	59.4	-----	27.2	.4	100.1	2.7	110.5	2.2	23.5	14.1	10.9	50.8	33.7	2.9
1982	29.1	51.0	4.6	51.8	-----	18.9	-----	94.9	4.8	69.9	7.7	4.8	14.5	7.3	49.8	23.5	8.3
1983	20.1	17.7	2.8	50.9	-----	19.8	.1	134.4	4.2	89.9	10.0	6.1	22.7	10.9	72.7	34.9	10.1
1984	11.9	5.0	2.5	45.1	9.1	29.9	-----	161.5	5.0	104.2	17.0	14.1	22.7	10.9	94.9	39.5	9.2
1985	10.0	25.4	2.0	59.9	10.0	2.6	.8	131.4	3.2	56.5	12.3	5.2	15.2	3.6	90.1	33.8	5.2
1986	4.4	11.2	1.4	59.0	7.2	4.6	.1	140.2	3.3	62.1	11.5	62.9	8.4	-----	105.3	29.5	1.1
1987	8.8	4.4	5.8	52.8	3.5	.9	10.8	185.7	6.6	133.8	1.7	201.2	19.1	.1	92.6	42.6	.4
1988	20.9	7.5	6.0	81.9	15.5	20.6	4.0	148.6	7.3	124.8	1.4	221.8	11.4	6.7	104.8	30.9	-----
1989	57.0	28.5	5.4	59.9	10.0	5.1	5.8	115.7	.7	95.7	1.9	189.9	12.9	-----	90.5	19.2	2.3
1990	56.6	57.2	6.8	75.0	13.0	10.7	2.7	90.6	.3	91.2	1.2	124.3	7.1	6.9	70.7	25.0	1.0
1991	88.0	94.4	7.6	72.0	11.0	12.4	.4	116.5	.1	82.6	1.0	226.7	3.9	8.0	83.6	11.9	.5
1992	72.3	64.3	5.3	63.2	2.1	5.3	.2	190.7	.2	120.6	-----	239.9	21.2	-----	124.7	56.1	9.8
1993[1]	41.8	51.4	7.1	54.1	1.7	.5	.0	195.6	.1	95.8	-----	55.7	13.6	1.0	130.8	40.3	18.3
1994[2]	38.7	←— 70.0 —→				88.1	20.6	.5	.6	230.8	.1	-----		.3	11.7	.5	159.1

[1] Preliminary. [2] Estimate. [3] And lead alloys. [4] Blocks, pigs, etc. [5] Formerly drosses & flue dust. *Source: U.S. Bureau of Mines*

LEAD

Average Price of Pig Lead, U.S. Primary Producers (Common Corroding)[1] In Cents Per Pound

Year	Jan	Feb	Mar	Apr	May	Jun	Jul	Aug	Sep	Oct	Nov	Dec	Total
1983	51,737	46,215	47,923	44,397	42,847	38,143	35,857	41,081	37,400	45,335	46,164	42,077	519,167
1984	46,721	46,630	39,010	36,288	35,562	23,769	25,764	26,400	22,952	37,014	25,402	24,041	389,398
1985	39,100	45,632	51,075	47,809	48,444	46,176	29,484	42,276	40,733	35,653	27,307	40,370	494,003
1986	43,001	37,740	44,816	36,469	36,469	24,041	15,332	28,395	24,948	25,946	25,855	27,307	370,288
1987	35,199	30,482	32,659	30,119	31,026	26,762	26,127	28,032	30,300	34,111	35,834	33,113	373,610
1988	31,117	32,115	35,472	31,117	32,841	31,571	28,849	22,952	29,121	44,997	36,288	35,653	392,087
1989	37,195	32,659	35,381	30,845	32,841	32,206	32,387	34,474	35,653	31,480	32,024	29,303	396,455
1990	34,927	34,383	33,476	35,018	33,022	30,210	30,845	34,474	33,929	38,375	33,476	31,571	403,657
1991	30,763	30,863	33,771	30,248	27,031	22,371	27,973	28,204	29,411	29,846	26,428	28,813	345,714
1992	29,121	27,691	33,366	27,456	26,742	22,441	24,993	21,587	19,365	22,945	23,674	25,414	304,791
1993	29,627	26,693	30,197	27,578	29,814	28,253	16,734	22,817	32,725	31,220	27,953	31,312	335,014
1994[2]	29,907	30,685	31,419	29,059	31,587	31,706	30,660	27,334	34,375	32,874	29,300	30,447	369,353

[1]New York Delivery. *Source: American Metal Market*

Refiners Production[1] of Lead in the United States In Metric Tons

Year	Jan	Feb	Mar	Apr	May	Jun	Jul	Aug	Sep	Oct	Nov	Dec	Total
1983	51,737	46,215	47,923	44,397	42,847	38,143	35,857	41,081	37,400	45,335	46,164	42,077	519,167
1984	46,721	46,630	39,010	36,288	35,562	23,769	25,764	26,400	22,952	37,014	25,402	24,041	389,398
1985	39,100	45,632	51,075	47,809	48,444	46,176	29,484	42,276	40,733	35,653	27,307	40,370	494,003
1986	43,001	37,740	44,816	36,469	36,469	24,041	15,332	28,395	24,948	25,946	25,855	27,307	370,288
1987	35,199	30,482	32,659	30,119	31,026	26,762	26,127	28,032	30,300	34,111	35,834	33,113	373,610
1988	31,117	32,115	35,472	31,117	32,841	31,571	28,849	22,952	29,121	44,997	36,288	35,653	392,087
1989	37,195	32,659	35,381	30,845	32,841	32,206	32,387	34,474	35,653	31,480	32,024	29,303	396,455
1990	34,927	34,383	33,476	35,018	33,022	30,210	30,845	34,474	33,929	38,375	33,476	31,571	403,657
1991	30,763	30,863	33,771	30,248	27,031	22,371	27,973	28,204	29,411	29,846	26,428	28,813	345,714
1992	29,121	27,691	33,366	27,456	26,742	22,441	24,993	21,587	19,365	22,945	23,674	25,414	304,791
1993	29,627	26,693	30,197	27,578	29,814	28,253	16,734	22,817	32,725	31,220	27,953	31,312	335,014
1994[2]	29,907	30,685	31,419	29,059	31,587	31,706	30,660	27,334	34,375	32,874	29,300	30,447	369,353

[1]Represents Production1 of lead produced from domestic ores by primary smelters plus small amounts of secondary material passing through these smelters. Includes GSA metal purchased for remelt. [2]Preliminary. *Source: U.S. Bureau of Mines*

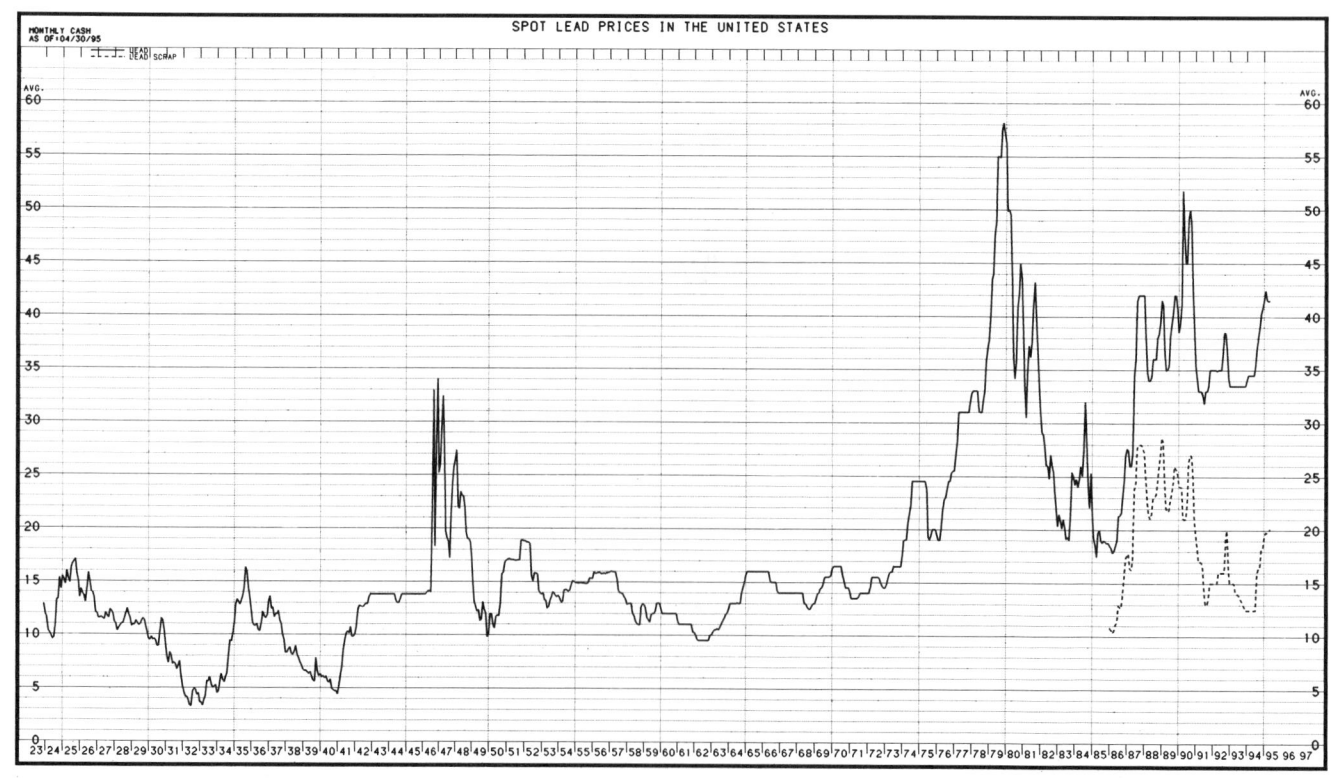

U.S. Mine Production of Recoverable Lead   In Thousands of Metric Tons

Year	Jan	Feb	Mar	Apr	May	Jun	Jul	Aug	Sep	Oct	Nov	Dec	Total
1987	24.2	23.9	27.9	23.6	27.0	26.3	29.0	24.1	28.2	28.4	23.2	25.5	311.4
1988	27.9	28.2	36.0	32.7	30.3	32.5	30.4	36.3	33.1	34.4	31.1	31.8	385.0
1989	33.3	31.0	34.4	33.2	33.8	36.1	33.2	38.6	34.3	35.1	32.9	30.1	410.9
1990	42.4	39.0	39.9	37.4	40.8	38.8	42.3	47.2	37.9	43.0	38.5	36.6	483.7
1991	41.5	41.1	41.6	37.8	43.5	36.4	47.5	41.1	36.1	38.9	28.0	26.1	465.9
1992	36.0	34.0	34.0	31.2	31.5	32.4	33.8	32.5	32.5	33.3	30.8	31.7	392.7
1993	33.3	30.5	34.2	30.6	28.5	29.5	25.8	27.5	28.4	27.3	29.5	28.5	355.2
1994[1]	27.6	28.8	33.0	31.3	32.4	29.1	29.4	30.4	31.2	28.0	31.7	29.9	363.4

[1]Preliminary. *Source: U.S. Bureau of Mines*

Total Stocks of Lead[1] in the United States at Refiners, at End of Month   In Metric Tons

Year	Jan	Feb	Mar	Apr	May	Jun	Jul	Aug	Sep	Oct	Nov	Dec
1987	31,026	33,839	35,653	28,577	29,575	18,598	10,614	10,977	11,521	14,878	18,053	21,591
1988	22,408	27,670	27,397	28,849	24,041	15,060	14,697	5,988	4,627	10,524	11,884	15,422
1989	26,037	32,931	39,191	37,558	29,665	28,940	31,389	27,942	27,488	18,779	14,606	15,604
1990	14,697	18,325	16,420	21,138	19,323	195,696	20,775	19,958	20,593	23,769	22,771	25,492
1991	24,177	24,333	26,990	21,261	17,474	16,195	15,362	9,072	6,608	4,091	4,491	9,089
1992	9,774	15,785	21,682	25,220	28,940	26,490	26,634	22,347	17,736	14,971	14,796	20,543
1993	28,069	33,338	34,058	34,306	35,775	32,162	22,753	14,797	15,086	14,408	13,456	14,289
1994[2]	11,964	12,633	12,048	11,445	11,598	10,251	12,368	9,256	9,807	10,659	9,060	9,271

[1]Stocks at own plant & elsewhere. [2]Preliminary. *Source: U.S. Bureau of Mines*

Total[1] Lead Consumption in the United States   In Thousands of Metric Tons

Year	Jan	Feb	Mar	Apr	May	Jun	Jul	Aug	Sep	Oct	Nov	Dec	Total
1987	96.5	91.1	103.0	101.0	101.4	103.5	97.4	103.2	108.5	119.1	105.8	100.1	1,230
1988	99.8	101.4	116.0	99.3	104.0	103.6	92.1	102.5	103.0	110.6	103.4	95.1	1,231
1989	104.7	98.3	101.2	99.2	101.3	101.6	95.2	102.7	105.9	114.0	106.2	97.3	1,283
1990	104.1	106.7	111.9	101.1	106.2	103.2	97.7	112.4	104.6	109.0	104.3	97.3	1,275
1991	101.3	105.3	101.2	101.3	98.4	92.4	90.8	101.9	102.7	106.9	102.4	92.7	1,246
1992	102.5	99.3	108.3	98.5	96.0	103.5	94.8	104.8	106.6	105.4	98.2	92.9	1,215
1993	108.9	107.5	112.3	104.6	109.2	113.8	106.8	112.6	117.1	113.2	109.3	102.2	1,357
1994[1]	107.0	115.2	112.8	111.6	113.5	115.2	114.3	115.5	115.9	121.2	118.7	113.0	1,384

[1]Represents total consumption of primary & secondary lead as metal, in chemicals, or in alloys. [2]Preliminary. *Source: U.S. Bureau of Mines*

U.S. Lead Recovered from Scrap   In Thousands of Metric Tons (Lead Content)

Year	Jan	Feb	Mar	Apr	May	Jun	Jul	Aug	Sep	Oct	Nov	Dec	Total
1987	50.0	49.9	54.4	55.6	59.3	53.9	59.9	63.4	53.3	67.3	55.9	55.1	710.2
1988	52.2	57.5	60.1	55.9	52.2	59.4	55.3	56.3	60.7	61.8	61.6	59.7	737.0
1989	62.1	58.6	67.5	64.1	65.3	66.3	61.6	65.9	64.4	73.5	67.1	66.9	808.6
1990	68.7	69.6	73.0	69.4	66.9	67.9	67.0	71.8	71.0	77.5	72.3	77.3	923.0
1991	79.0	74.4	71.0	72.0	72.0	70.7	69.8	70.0	72.3	74.6	70.7	75.9	883.7
1992	76.1	71.5	66.5	71.0	73.3	72.3	71.1	77.7	77.5	79.6	76.9	74.3	888.5
1993	71.1	76.8	71.7	80.2	78.9	72.5	70.3	76.6	76.3	77.0	77.9	79.3	903.6
1994[1]	74.0	76.0	84.2	81.7	81.1	79.0	78.9	79.8	78.4	76.4	81.0	80.4	949.0

[1]Preliminary. *Source: U.S. Bureau of Mines*

Domestic Shipments[1] of Lead in the United States by Refiners   In Thousands of Short Tons

Year	Jan	Feb	Mar	Apr	May	Jun	Jul	Aug	Sep	Oct	Nov	Dec	Total
1987	27.0	30.5	34.1	41.1	34.8	40.0	37.8	30.1	33.1	33.8	35.7	32.7	410.7
1988	33.5	29.5	39.2	33.0	41.4	44.7	32.0	34.7	33.7	43.0	38.5	35.5	438.7
1989	29.3	28.5	32.2	35.7	45.1	36.4	32.8	41.5	40.0	44.2	40.2	31.1	437.1
1990	39.3	33.9	39.1	33.5	38.4	32.9	32.6	38.9	36.6	38.9	37.9	26.7	433.7
1991	35.4	33.8	34.3	39.8	33.9	26.0	31.8	37.9	35.1	35.7	28.7	26.7	399.2
1992	31.3	23.9	30.4	26.3	25.6	27.2	27.3	28.7	26.3	28.5	26.3	21.7	323.5
1993	24.6	23.6	32.5	30.0	31.3	35.1	28.9	34.0	35.5	35.5	31.7	33.5	376.2

[1]Includes GSA metal. *Source: American Metal Market*

Lumber & Plywood

The forest products industry in 1994 was affected by a host of factors including a strong economic recovery in the U.S. and overseas, the continued problem of logging restrictions in the Northwest and a series of increases in interest rates. The strong level of economic activity in the U.S. going into 1995 was expected to increase demand for wood products in the housing and furniture industries and for home improvements. Logging restrictions in the Northwest U.S. also insure that there will be tightness in supplies of lumber. Overall, the lumber industry has very little capacity to increase production in the near term. Therefore, large excess supplies of lumber appear unlikely. Higher interest rates at some point will take their effect on housing starts and consumer demand at the retail level, an may pressure prices.

A court ruling has allowed timber sales in the Northwest and it has met the Clinton Administration's timber plan criterion. The administration had hoped to get timber sales to the 1.2 billion board foot level within two years. To get to this level, lumber market analysts calculate that it will take federally sponsored timber sales to about 25 percent of pre-1990 levels. A more important market factor is likely to be Canada's decision to reduce its timber harvest. This, when coupled with reduced harvests in the Pacific Northwest is expected to keep the supply of lumber tight in coming years.

The American Forest and Paper Association reported that U.S. softwood lumber production in September 1994 in the Southern Pine region was 1.229 billion board feet. Softwood lumber production in the West Coast region was 735 million board feet while the Inland region produced 696 million board feet. The California Redwood region had production of 151 million board feet. Total softwood lumber production in September 1994 was 2.952 billion board feet, a slight increase from August 1994 and a 9.1 percent increase from September 1993.

Total hardwood lumber production in September 1994 was 1.142 billion board feet, down 2.1 percent from August 1994, but 2.1 percent higher than September 1993 production. Total lumber production in September 1994 was 4.094 billion board feet, unchanged from August 1994 but 7.1 percent greater than in the same period of 1993. Structural panel production in September 1994 was 2.311 billion board feet, down 3.1 percent from the prior month but 3.2 percent more than in September 1993.

For the first nine months of 1994, total softwood lumber production was 25.72 billion board feet, up 4.4 percent from 1993. Total hardwood production was 9.65 billion board feet, up 6.5 percent from the first nine months of 1993. Total lumber production over the January-September 1994 period was 35.36 billion board feet, a five percent increase from the same period of 1993. Total structural panel production over the period was 20.19 billion board feet, up 4.2 percent.

Softwood lumber use for the first nine months of 1994 was 36.22 billion board feet. This represented an increase of almost eight percent from the same period of 1993. Hardwood lumber consumption was 9.2 billion board feet, a 10 percent increase over the first nine months of 1993. Total lumber consumption was 45.42 billion board feet, up eight percent.

U.S. exports of softwood lumber over the January-September 1994 period were 1.646 billion board feet which represented a decline of 10.3 percent from the nine months of 1993. Exports of softwood logs were 1.773 billion board feet, a decline of 13.8 percent from the prior year. Exports of hardwood veneer were 1.822 billion square feet, up almost 27 percent from the 1993 period.

U.S. imports of softwood lumber for the first nine months of 1994 were 12.346 billion board feet, up 10.8 percent from 1993. Imports of softwood logs were 82.5 million board feet, an increase of 62.8 percent from a year earlier. Imports of hardwood logs were 10.4 million board feet, up 73.9 percent from 1993.

In Canada, timber production in the first nine months of 1994 was up 4.6 percent from the 1993 level. British Columbia's lumber production in the first nine months of 1994 rose only 0.6 percent while Eastern Canada's production was up 10.2 percent. Operable timber inventories are reportedly being stretched to the limits. Securing an adequate timber supply in British Colombia is reportedly becoming as difficult as in the Pacific Northwest.

Futures Markets

Lumber futures and options are traded on the Chicago Mercantile Exchange (CME). The Chicago Board of Trade (CBOT) began listing a Structural Panel Index Futures contract in 1994.

U.S. Housing Starts: Seasonally Adjusted Annual Rate   In Thousands (Total is Actual Starts)

Year	Jan	Feb	Mar	Apr	May	June	July	Aug	Sept	Oct	Nov	Dec	Average
1986	1,972	1,848	1,876	1,933	1,854	1,847	1,782	1,807	1,687	1,681	1,623	1,833	1,805
1987	1,840	1,787	1,715	1,622	1,607	1,583	1,592	1,587	1,685	1,535	1,659	1,391	1,621
1988	1,391	1,511	1,528	1,576	1,392	1,463	1,478	1,459	1,463	1,532	1,567	1,577	1,488
1989	1,678	1,465	1,409	1,343	1,308	1,414	1,424	1,325	1,263	1,423	1,347	1,273	1,376
1990	1,568	1,488	1,307	1,216	1,206	1,189	1,153	1,131	1,107	1,026	1,130	971	1,207
1991	844	1,008	918	978	983	1,036	1,053	1,053	1,022	1,085	1,085	1,118	1,113
1992	1,180	1,285	1,318	1,095	1,197	1,141	1,106	1,229	1,218	1,226	1,226	1,286	1,200
1993[1]	1,170	1,194	1,092	1,232	1,241	1,238	1,245	1,319	1,359	1,409	1,406	1,612	1,293
1994[1]	1,266	1,328	1,519	1,471	1,491	1,358	1,439	1,461	1,497	1,419	1,545	1,527	1,443

[1] Preliminary.   Total Privately Owned.   *Source: American Forest & Paper Association.*

World Production of Industrial Roundwood by Selected Countries   In Thousands of Cubic Meters

Year	Austria	Canada	Czech[3] Republic	Finland	France	Germany	Japan	Norway	Poland	Russia[4]	Spain	Sweden	Switzer- land	Turkey	United Kingdom	United States
1989	13,575	170,625	16,856	42,670	34,276	41,806	31,202	10,590	18,980	305,300	15,691	51,430	3,729	5,728	6,207	416,900
1990	14,160	174,415	16,398	40,196	34,913	40,934	29,300	10,900	15,549	305,300	16,227	49,071	5,383	5,960	6,125	430,200
1991	13,135	171,215	13,770	31,616	33,754	29,823	27,938	10,325	14,334	275,300	16,510	47,300	3,751	5,502	6,122	391,770
1992[1]	9,255	179,215	8,820	35,279	32,131	29,159	27,729	9,180	15,720	164,000	15,112	49,700	3,638	5,600	5,740	401,285
1993[2]	9,108	NA	8,800	35,158	29,720	29,357	NA	NA	15,943	117,900	NA	47,000	NA	NA	5,940	NA

[1] Preliminary. [2] Estimate. [3] Formerly part of Czechoslovakia; data not reported separately until 1992. [4] Formerly part of the U.S.S.R.; data not reported-separately until 1992. NA = Not available. *Source: Food and Agriculture Organization of the United States.*

United States Lumber Production and Consumption   In Millions of Board Feet

| | Production | | | | | | Domestic Consumption | | | | | | | |
| | Softwood | | | | | | Softwood | | | | | | | |
Year	California Redwood	Inland Region	Southern Pine	West Coast	Total	Total Hardwood	Inland Region	Southern Pine	West Coast	Softwood Imports	Total	U.S. Hardwood	Hardwood Imports	Total Lumber
1984	1,664	8,992	10,674	8,329	31,174	9,865	8,764	10,401	7,551	13,270	42,832	9,501	328	52,661
1985	1,730	9,276	10,730	8,062	31,321	8,866	8,977	10,480	7,250	14,608	44,240	8,864	364	53,468
1986	2,021	10,482	11,678	9,412	35,273	10,024	10,273	11,383	8,377	14,238	47,492	9,609	347	57,448
1987	2,181	11,407	12,473	10,354	38,235	11,160	11,008	12,240	9,117	14,680	50,558	10,685	511	61,754
1988	2,214	11,395	12,676	10,029	38,130	11,446	11,180	12,108	8,096	13,806	48,513	9,931	390	58,834
1989	2,053	11,348	12,544	9,811	37,545	10,988	11,134	12,125	7,950	13,638	47,975	10,497	375	58,847
1990	1,972	10,452	12,911	8,751	35,791	10,704	10,390	12,388	7,184	12,148	45,003	9,224	255	54,482
1991	1,657	9,510	12,507	7,908	33,161	10,213	9,302	12,147	6,454	11,742	41,998	8,909	226	51,134
1992	1,571	9,263	14,106	7,948	34,526	12,109	9,107	13,893	6,709	13,381	45,737	11,330	276	57,343
1993	1,354	8,312	14,392	7,319	32,947	12,300	8,129	14,020	6,043	15,260	45,810	10,932	335	57,078
1994[1]	1,592	7,983	14,930	7,874	33,999	13,012	7,852	14,558	6,859	16,380	48,196	11,825	394	60,415
I	352	2,148	3,532	1,963	8,394	3,204	1,925	3,242	1,573	3,735	10,995	3,066	89	14,150
II	403	1,960	3,940	1,953	8,670	3,147	1,987	3,888	1,735	4,442	12,702	2,980	106	15,789
III	438	1,997	2,877	2,019	8,748	3,296	2,076	3,876	1,793	4,169	12,622	2,861	98	15,580
IV	399	1,878	2,581	1,939	8,187	3,365	1,863	3,552	1,759	4,034	11,877	2,919	101	14,897

[1] Preliminary. *Source: American Forest & Paper Association*

Stocks (Gross) of Softwood Lumber in the United States, Beginning of Month   In Millions of Board Feet

Year	Jan	Feb	Mar	Apr	May	June	July	Aug	Sept	Oct	Nov	Dec
1984	4,606	4,424	4,494	4,602	4,717	4,715	4,658	4,560	4,509	4,573	4,515	4,590
1985	4,594	4,533	4,637	4,733	4,508	4,415	4,633	4,680	4,687	4,699	4,850	4,870
1986	4,765	4,842	4,959	4,846	4,886	4,748	4,605	4,615	4,722	4,840	4,929	5,038
1987	5,040	5,039	5,112	5,203	5,181	5,097	4,927	4,928	4,755	4,855	4,787	4,823
1988	4,771	4,867	4,950	4,994	4,939	4,894	4,685	4,677	4,765	4,823	4,951	4,979
1989	4,999	4,896	4,818	4,837	4,810	4,740	4,746	4,748	4,797	4,762	4,908	4,934
1990	4,898	5,022	5,022	5,020	4,961	5,043	4,831	4,783	4,752	4,810	4,834	4,809
1991	4,734	4,925	4,949	4,946	4,849	4,600	4,699	4,684	4,793	4,786	4,741	4,710
1992	4,616	4,603	4,567	4,608	4,730	4,731	4,678	4,606	4,418	4,419	4,365	4,263
1993	4,206	4,211	4,187	4,239	4,407	4,593	4,599	4,599	4,488	4,445	4,364	4,303
1994[1]	4,207	----------		4,772	----------		4,649	----------		4,400	----------	4,271

[1] Preliminary. *Source: American Forest & Paper Association*

Lumber Production in the United States   In Millions of Board Feet

Year	Jan	Feb	Mar	Apr	May	June	July	Aug	Sept	Oct	Nov	Dec	Total
1984	2,740	2,678	3,104	2,983	2,828	2,968	2,685	2,933	2,776	3,154	2,814	2,295	41,039
1985	2,727	2,718	3,085	3,296	3,256	3,101	3,034	3,299	3,196	3,387	2,851	2,649	40,187
1986	3,092	3,046	3,347	3,362	3,405	3,355	2,961	3,441	3,397	3,820	3,496	3,623	45,297
1987	3,293	3,307	3,742	3,616	3,518	3,905	3,662	3,737	3,617	3,942	3,458	3,829	49,395
1988	3,814	4,042	4,389	4,247	4,245	4,137	3,671	4,056	4,180	4,040	3,715	3,641	49,576
1989	3,849	3,311	3,758	3,773	4,025	4,273	3,683	4,023	3,787	4,172	3,811	3,615	48,533
1990	4,160	3,862	4,300	4,121	4,084	3,944	3,976	4,060	3,602	4,015	3,412	2,914	46,495
1991	3,534	3,410	3,661	3,958	3,837	3,762	3,664	3,808	3,682	3,933	3,473	3,254	43,374
1992	3,836	3,628	4,121	3,862	3,632	3,911	3,882	3,746	3,736	4,048	3,617	3,425	46,635
1993	----------	11,095	----------		----------	11,151	----------		----------	11,439	----------		----------	11,562	----------		45,247
1994[1]	----------	11,598	----------		----------	11,817	----------		3,770	4,093	4,094	4,142	3,634	3,774	47,011

[1] Preliminary. *Source: American Forest & Paper Association*

LUMBER

United States Lumber Shipments   In Millions of Board Feet

Year	Jan	Feb	Mar	Apr	May	June	July	Aug	Sept	Oct	Nov	Dec	Total
1984	2,589	2,603	3,002	2,875	2,852	2,993	2,756	2,950	2,688	3,154	2,922	2,397	40,693
1985	2,666	2,602	3,013	3,496	3,349	3,031	2,944	3,294	3,162	3,221	2,828	2,809	39,784
1986	2,955	2,899	3,478	3,321	3,538	3,498	2,979	3,344	3,291	3,689	3,480	3,791	45,239
1987	3,350	3,302	3,735	3,686	3,656	4,039	3,671	3,812	3,540	4,034	3,470	3,865	49,761
1988	3,790	4,092	4,320	4,257	4,261	4,309	3,688	3,929	4,038	3,871	3,656	3,649	49,134
1989	3,914	3,417	3,877	3,846	4,163	4,420	3,760	3,977	3,823	4,081	3,854	3,626	49,003
1990	4,035	3,870	4,317	4,173	3,952	4,176	3,912	3,987	3,453	3,890	3,357	2,873	45,927
1991	3,240	3,301	3,617	4,037	4,028	3,764	3,412	3,926	3,676	4,012	3,477	3,370	43,190
1992	3,912	3,693	4,078	3,682	3,565	3,936	3,884	3,878	3,692	4,147	3,745	3,491	47,314
1993	-------	11,076	---------	---------	10,724	---------	---------	11,442	---------	---------	11,626	---------	44,868
1994[1]	-------	11,151	---------	---------	12,041	---------	4,022	4,133	3,874	4,339	3,601	3,617	46,868

[1]Preliminary.   *Source: American Forest & Paper Association*

United States Trade of Lumber by Type   In Millions of Board Feet

Year	Cedar	Douglas Fir	Hemlock	Pine	Spruce	Total	Total Hardwood	Total Lumber	Douglas Fir	Hemlock	Ponderosa/ White Pine	Southern Pine	Total	Total Hardwood	Total Lumber
		Imports[2] — Softwood							Exports[2] — Softwood						
1984	704.1	603.0	514.9	901.6	9471.4	13,270.2	327.7	13,622.2	532.1	337.4	174.1	172.4	1,599.3	466.5	2,150.4
1985	807.9	765.1	643.9	817.2	10,393.4	14,607.8	363.6	14,999.1	475.6	364.4	167.7	164.4	1,515.4	397.1	1,945.3
1986	800.6	686.2	488.4	668.7	10,389.1	14,238.2	346.9	14,608.2	512.4	532.0	209.4	178.6	1,877.0	498.3	2,398.6
1987	792.2	631.4	553.6	499.6	10,964.1	14,680.4	511.0	15,219.3	660.8	663.9	269.1	247.5	2,423.3	775.1	3,216.9
1988	786.8	721.4	539.7	332.3	10,284.5	13,806.0	390.1	14,225.3	888.6	714.9	233.4	492.3	3,263.9	1,232.0	4,528.0
1989	786.0	603.4	469.5	335.8	7,387.4	13,638.4	375.1	14,032.5	1,018.2	670.9	197.0	442.3	3,319.1	856.0	4,213.1
1990	652.8	375.4	362.4	87.6	3,535.7	12,148.2	255.4	12,429.4	818.5	549.4	215.2	374.7	2,970.4	877.7	3,900.0
1991	700.6	354.1	287.8	55.7	2,248.3	11,741.5	226.2	11,998.2	798.1	497.7	222.9	396.0	3,089.6	934.3	4,085.3
1992	666.4	3,555.3	300.0	91.4	2,410.5	13,380.5	276.4	13,681.9	735.0	396.7	308.7	440.5	2,650.7	977.2	3,687.1
1993	615.3	327.6	354.9	84.6	3,104.1	15,259.9	335.0	15,625.4	664.9	340.4	273.3	339.6	2,376.4	1,008.9	3,468.9
1994[1]	702.6	336.2	399.2	97.2	2,948.5	16,380.3	394.4	16,787.1	591.9	283.2	157.2	356.7	2,186.6	1,040.9	3,333.4
I	183.1	57.0	91.2	27.0	672.9	3,734.6	89.5	3,827.0	149.6	70.1	45.2	83.8	569.0	256.4	844.4
II	192.4	121.6	95.1	24.2	815.3	4,442.2	106.3	4,552.0	138.4	59.2	42.8	98.8	533.0	268.0	827.1
III	176.5	83.4	104.4	22.1	784.6	4,169.4	97.6	4,270.1	153.7	73.2	32.5	85.0	544.1	259.5	837.6
IV	150.7	74.3	108.5	23.9	675.7	4,034.0	101.0	4,138.0	150.2	80.7	36.7	89.1	540.5	257.0	824.4

[1]Preliminary.   [2]Includes sawed timber, board planks & scantlings, flooring, box shook and railroad ties.   *Source: American Forest & Paper Association.*

LUMBER CASH PRICE - SPF 2X4

Average Open Interest of Lumber Futures at Chicago   In Contracts

Year	Jan	Feb	Mar	Apr	May	June	July	Aug	Sept	Oct	Nov	Dec
1985	9,953	9,704	8,102	9,115	9,115	10,038	8,823	8,672	7,672	7,247	6,819	6,567
1986	5,486	6,121	8,866	9,287	8,171	6,112	5,441	5,197	5,701	5,262	5,275	5,732
1987	6,077	7,330	6,406	6,950	6,019	6,770	6,563	7,439	6,961	7,247	6,579	6,572
1988	6,212	6,701	5,791	6,395	5,548	5,644	5,586	6,272	5,527	5,697	5,368	5,919
1989	7,982	7,484	7,436	8,244	7,363	7,921	8,248	8,055	7,065	7,192	6,600	6,167
1990	6,078	6,061	4,991	4,957	4,538	4,359	3,570	3,028	2,881	3,105	2,632	2,001
1991	1,922	2,003	2,023	2,354	2,076	2,601	2,571	2,181	2,276	2,480	2,206	1,606
1992	1,969	2,651	2,743	2,467	1,900	1,774	1,338	1,369	1,507	1,441	1,745	2,155
1993	2,194	2,432	2,163	2,055	2,302	2,658	2,254	2,141	2,011	2,080	2,140	2,721
1994	2,571	2,814	2,638	2,563	1,936	1,838	1,705	1,854	2,102	2,169	1,702	1,967

Source: Chicago Mercantile Exchange

Volume of Trading of Lumber Futures at Chicago   In Contracts

Year	Jan	Feb	Mar	Apr	May	June	July	Aug	Sept	Oct	Nov	Dec	Total
1984	51,170	70,031	57,075	68,314	88,009	59,592	60,156	65,739	60,035	61,012	52,496	59,939	753,568
1985	71,719	55,737	56,718	65,762	62,766	57,422	43,525	39,151	36,517	34,703	29,556	27,972	581,548
1986	29,570	34,647	61,718	64,176	44,778	49,929	35,203	42,212	44,961	35,847	28,912	30,577	502,530
1987	40,351	49,167	40,504	39,211	27,954	33,505	31,345	38,876	34,039	39,437	32,052	30,648	437,089
1988	35,451	32,410	32,886	30,386	28,100	37,508	27,550	33,454	29,743	24,632	26,131	23,238	371,489
1989	29,963	25,857	23,947	31,427	26,789	26,712	20,258	19,514	18,790	18,965	17,286	14,395	273,903
1990	27,416	21,914	20,948	18,362	19,053	16,084	16,465	13,446	8,914	11,839	15,794	11,749	201,984
1991	10,535	13,460	10,326	11,309	15,135	19,029	19,350	14,912	12,214	14,054	10,295	9,902	160,521
1992	17,073	16,778	17,557	13,713	14,059	13,807	12,177	13,043	12,127	11,261	11,514	17,425	170,534
1993	14,915	15,080	14,808	14,661	14,241	15,308	13,287	13,358	12,400	13,248	18,150	18,728	178,184
1994	16,865	15,442	17,323	17,380	14,996	14,348	11,542	13,327	14,856	13,032	10,997	13,121	172,963

Source: Chicago Mercantile Exchange

Magnesium

With a density only two-thirds that of aluminum, magnesium is used in many applications where weight is a consideration. Magnesium alloys find extensive use in aircraft parts, photo optical instruments, engines, automobiles, luggage, pipelines, water heaters and dry-cell batteries. Among the magnesium compounds, magnesium sulfate is consumed in explosives, fertilizer and paper production. Magnesium oxide is used in water treatment, household cleaners and pharmaceuticals. The U.S. is the world's largest producer of magnesium followed by the former Soviet Union, Norway and Canada.

The U.S. Bureau of Mines reported that domestic magnesium production in the second quarter of 1994 reached 35,779 tonnes, an increase of more than 36 percent from the previous quarter. Producer shipments during the April-June 1994 period increased slightly to 35,357 tonnes. End-of-quarter inventories had increased 6 percent to total 11,664 tonnes.

U.S. exports of magnesium over the first five-months of 1994 were 19,857 tonnes. For all of 1993, exports were 38,815 tonnes. Most exports are of magnesium metal. For the first five-months of 1994, metal exports were 12,051 tonnes. Other export forms were waste and scrap totaling 883 tonnes; alloys by gross weight were 1,649 tonnes; and other materials including sheet, tubing, ribbons, wire and powder by gross weight were 5,274 tonnes.

The U.S. Bureau of Mines reported that imports of magnesium over the first five-months of 1994 totaled 15,883 tonnes. For all of 1993, imports were 37,249 tonnes. For the January-May 1994 period, imports of magnesium metal totaled 10,621 tonnes; waste and scrap at 1,213 tonnes; alloys by magnesium content were 3,735 tonnes; and sheet, tubing, ribbons, wire, powder and other by magnesium content ran 313 tonnes.

During the year, the Magnesium Corporation of America and Dow Chemical filed an antidumping suit against magnesium imports from China and the former Soviet States of Russia and Ukraine, citing that the flow of magnesium from those countries has resulted in idle capacity, lost jobs and economic hardship.

In the automotive market, Chrysler finalized plans to install magnesium steering column brackets on 1997 models of the Dodge Dakota pickup truck. General Motors Corporation approved the use of magnesium alloy steering column supports in three redesigned car lines that are due out in 1996 and 1997.

World Production of Magnesium (Primary and Secondary)   In Metric Tons

	Primary Production											Secondary Production		
Year	Brazil	Canada	China	France	Italy	Japan	Kazak-hstan[3]	Norway	Russia[4]	United States	World Total[2]	Japan	United Kingdom	United States	Former USSR
1982	331	8,700	7,700	10,593	10,960	6,123	-----	39,598	89,000	102,197	279,899	23,887	1,940	43,232	9,000
1983	551	6,600	7,700	12,208	8,473	6,643	-----	32,897	91,000	115,431	286,755	14,343	1,900	46,329	9,000
1984[3]	1,323	8,800	7,700	14,299	8,257	7,830	-----	54,343	94,000	159,207	360,459	17,258	1,102	48,357	9,000
1985	2,615	7,200	3,000	13,639	7,863	8,456	-----	54,704	87,000	135,728	325,183	20,894	900	41,298	8,000
1986	4,356	5,100	3,000	13,361	12,417	8,116	-----	56,522	89,000	125,639	322,408	13,400	1,000	41,807	8,000
1987	5,488	8,800	3,000	13,601	7,626	8,180	-----	56,907	90,000	124,396	323,930	10,124	1,000	45,165	8,000
1988	5,865	7,600	3,200	13,776	5,436	9,012	-----	50,317	91,000	141,983	334,348	15,099	1,000	50,207	8,000
1989	6,200	7,000	3,500	14,600	5,768	8,381	-----	49,827	91,000	152,066	344,447	20,270	1,000	51,200	8,000
1990	8,700	26,726	5,900	14,000	5,725	12,843	-----	48,222	88,000	139,333	355,237	23,308	900	54,808	7,500
1991	7,800	35,512	8,600	14,000	3,919	11,559	-----	44,322	80,000	131,288	341,000	17,158	800	50,543	7,000
1992	7,300	25,700	10,000	13,700	1,211	7,119	20,000	30,404	40,000	136,947	306,381	12,978	800	57,045	6,500
1993[1]	9,700	23,300	12,000	13,000	-----	7,500	20,000	27,300	30,000	132,144	283,944	13,215	500	58,890	6,000

[1] Preliminary.   [2] Estimate.   [3] Data prior to 1985 reported in short tons.   [4] Formerly part of the U.S.S.R.; data not reported separately until 1992.
Source: U.S. Bureau of Mines

Salient Statistics of Magnesium in the United States   In Metric Tons

	Production								Domestic Consumption of Primary Magnesium					
	Primary	Secondary				Imports for Con-sumption	Stocks, Dec. 31[4]	$ Price Per Pound[5]	Castings	Wrought	Total	Aluminum Alloys	Other Uses[6]	Total
Year	(Ingot)	New Scrap	Old Scrap	Total	Exports[3]				Structural Products					
1982	102,197	19,801	23,431	43,232	39,613	4,784	46,000	1.34	3,600	10,128	13,728	39,878	20,993	74,599
1983	115,431	21,591	24,738	46,329	46,690	6,350	28,000	1.38	3,341	11,435	14,776	46,026	21,174	81,976
1984[7]	159,207	21,594	26,763	48,357	48,337	9,381	35,000	1.43-1.48	4,193	10,246	14,439	48,673	26,775	89,887
1985	135,728	19,579	25,944	41,298	36,680	8,411	39,000	1.48-1.53	4,536	10,840	15,376	31,059	31,317	83,752
1986	125,639	18,813	22,994	41,807	39,909	8,355	39,000	1.53	5,767	7,737	13,504	39,290	26,167	78,961
1987	134,396	21,712	23,452	45,164	44,182	10,851	28,000	1.53	6,285	8,300	14,585	52,172	27,863	94,620
1988	141,983	22,567	27,640	50,207	49,802	14,407	25,000	1.58-1.63	7,069	10,138	17,207	53,671	29,915	100,793
1989	152,066	23,229	27,971	51,200	56,631	12,289	26,000	1.63	7,455	9,653	17,108	53,821	34,297	88,118
1990	139,333	23,424	31,384	54,808	51,834	26,755	26,000	1.43-1.63	9,078	10,944	20,022	45,060	31,026	76,086
1991	131,288	23,059	27,484	50,543	55,160	31,863	27,000	1.43	8,857	8,802	17,659	45,809	28,404	74,213
1992	136,947	26,191	30,854	57,045	51,951	11,844	13,000	1.46-1.53	10,223	8,843	19,066	41,003	33,758	74,761
1993[1]	132,144	28,313	30,577	58,890	38,815	37,248	26,000	1.43-1.46	12,094	9,871	21,963	46,498	32,110	78,608
1994[2]	135,000			59,000	48,000	28,000		1.48-1.53						

[1] Preliminary.   [2] Estimate.   [3] Metal & alloys in crude form & scrap.   [4] Estimate of Industry Stocks, metal.   [5] Magnesium (99.8%), F.O.B. Valasco, Texas.
[6] Distributive or sacrificial purposes.   [7] Data prior to 1985 reported in short tons.   *Source: U.S. Bureau of Mines*

Manganese

Manganese finds its primary use in the steel industry, where it is used as an alloy. Virtually all steel contains some amount of manganese, which increases hardness. Manganese ore, when converted to a metallic alloy with iron, forms the compound known as ferromanganese. Some nonmetallurgical uses for manganese include plant fertilizers and animal feed. It also finds use in dry cell batteries. Manganese dioxide is used in the brick industry to provide a red-brown tint, in glassmaking, photographic developing, and in paint and dye production.

The world's largest producers of manganese include various countries that made up the former Soviet Union, China, South Africa and Brazil. In the U.S., manganese ore was consumed by approximately 20 firms located principally in the Eastern and Midwestern states. Most ore consumption is directly related to steel production. The U.S. Bureau of Mines reported that consumption of manganese ore containing 35 percent or more manganese, exclusive of that at iron and steel plants, was 30,400 tonnes in July 1994. This brought the year-to-date total to 215,000 tonnes. Industry stocks of manganese ore from the end of July 1994 increased 6 percent from June 1994 to 249,000 tonnes.

For the first six-months of 1994, U.S. imports of manganese ore and dioxide had a manganese content of 78,850 tonnes. This compares with 54,747 tonnes in the same period of 1993.

Low-carbon ferromanganese imports over the first half of 1994 had a gross weight of 4,707 tonnes, with manganese content of 4,158 tonnes. Italy and South Africa were the major suppliers. Medium-carbon imports for the same period of 1994 were 50,358 tonnes, with manganese content of 40,649 tonnes. The major sources included Mexico and Norway. Imports of high-carbon ferromanganese were 135,297 tonnes, with manganese content of 104,758 tonnes. The main suppliers were South Africa and France. U.S. imports of silicomanganese for the first half of 1994 were 171,546 tonnes, with manganese content of 112,292 tonnes. South Africa, Brazil and Australia were the major suppliers.

The U.S. exports small amounts of manganese material. For the first six-months of 1994, exports of manganese ore were 6,007 tonnes; ferromanganese 3,190 tonnes; silicomanganese 4,119 tonnes; and manganese metal 2,160 tonnes. The principal destinations were Canada, the Netherlands, Chile and Belgium.

World Production of Manganese Ore   In Thousands of Metric Tons (Gross Weight)

Year	Australia 37-53[4]	Brazil 30-50	Bulgaria 29	China 30	Gabon 50-53	Georgia 29-30	Ghana 30-50	Hungary[3] 30-33	India 10-54	Iran 25-35	Mexico 27-50	Morocco 50-53	South Africa 30-48 +	Ukraine[5] 29-30	World Total
1984	2,038	2,969	50	1,760	2,336	-----	296	74	1,246	73	525	65	3,361	11,100	26,100
1985	2,208	2,781	42	2,900	2,579	-----	351	69	1,367	61	437	48	3,969	10,900	27,948
1986	1,818	2,973	41	3,000	2,767	-----	335	69	1,337	37	506	44	4,100	10,300	27,523
1987	2,043	2,279	42	2,900	2,649	-----	303	86	1,435	69	425	47	3,631	10,313	26,404
1988[6]	1,985	1,991	34	3,212	2,254	-----	260	81	1,333	75	444	30	4,023	9,108	25,013
1989	2,124	1,904	32	3,200	2,592	-----	297	84	1,334	81	394	32	4,884	9,141	26,260
1990	1,920	2,300	39	4,080	2,423	-----	247	60	1,385	54	451	49	4,402	8,500	26,108
1991	1,482	2,000	34	5,150	1,620	-----	320	30	1,401	48	254	59	3,146	7,240	22,937
1992	1,200	1,703	17	5,300	1,556	1,200	276	18	1,400	40	407	44	2,464	5,819	21,608
1993[1]	1,789	1,900	-----	5,400	1,460	1,000	295	18	1,750	40	363	43	2,507	5,000	21,757

[1] Preliminary.   [2] Metallurgical Ore.   [3] Concentrate.   [4] Range of percentage of manganese.   [5] Formerly part of the U.S.S.R.; data not reported separately until 1992.   [6] Data reported in short tons prior to 1988.   *Source: U.S. Bureau of Mines*

Salient Statistics of Manganese in the United States   In Thousands of Metric Tons (Gross Weight)

Year	Net Import Reliance as a % of Consumption	Manganese Ore (35% of More Manganese) — Imports for Consumption	Exports	Consumption	Stocks, Dec. 31[3]	Ferromanganese — Imports for Consumption	Exports	Consumption	Price Avg. Value Mn. Metallurgical Ore $ Large Ton Unit[4]	Silicomanganese — Exports	Imports
1984	98	338	238	615	582	409	7	492	1.42	5.3	138.5
1985	100	387	56	545	589	367	7	466	1.43	3.1	165.5
1986	100	463	42	500	455	396	4	376	1.34	2.0	198.6
1987	100	341	63	533	456	368	3	409	1.27	.7	191.4
1988[5]	100	464	62	503	415	482	3	425	1.75	8.3	256.0
1989	100	580	52	559	470	432	8	399	2.76	6.5	281.5
1990	100	307	70	497	379	380	7	413	3.78	1.8	224.5
1991	100	234	66	473	275	320	15	346	3.72	2.9	258.3
1992	100	247	13	438	276	304	13	339	3.25	9.2	257.2
1993[1]	100	232	16	389	302	347	18	341	2.60	9.4	316.1

[1] Preliminary.   [2] Estimate.   [3] Including bonded warehouses; excludes Government stocks; also excludes small tonnages of dealers' stocks.   [4] 46-48% Mn, C.I.F., U.S. Ports.   [5] Data reported in short tons prior to 1988.   *Source: U.S. Bureau of Mines*

MANGANESE

U.S. Consumption of Manganese by End Uses   In Thousands of Metric Tons

Year	Appliances & Equipment	Batteries	Cans & Containers	Chemicals	Con-struction	Machinery	Oil & Gas Industry	Trans-portation	Other	Total
1979	59	17	61	59	291	217	70	296	180	1,250
1980	49	17	49	50	243	167	79	214	161	1,029
1981[3]	46	15	42	45	229	155	81	194	125	932
1982	27	19	28	26	138	83	36	104	147	610
1983	30	23	25	20	137	82	25	117	147	606
1984	33	31	34	31	154	88	33	126	39	569
1985	29	35	32	20	149	71	31	112	154	633
1986	24	39	28	21	134	59	23	86	248	662
1987	28	39	32	40	150	70	27	95	153	634
1988	17	44	28	42	221	100	19	93	119	682
1989	11	41	21	39	138	75	9	49	340	723
1990	9	42	22	36	138	74	14	45	250	630
1991[1]	8	52	20	33	122	45	10	47	260	598
1992[2]	8	50	20	34	101	63	10	60	250	596

[1] Preliminary.   [2] Estimate.   [3] Data reported in short tons prior to 1981.   Source: U.S. Bureau of Mines

Manganese Ore (20% or More Mn) Imported[3] into the U.S.   In Metric Tons (Mn Content)

Year	Australia	Brazil	Gabon	Mexico	Morocco	South Africa	Total	Customs Value Thous. $
1978	32,598	52,095	126,962	18,355	14,522	10,976	278,212	33,581
1979	55,316	51,660	49,222	2,059	10,719	52,117	243,553	27,485
1980	106,043	33,648	79,858	18,568	5,260	86,373	329,750	46,413
1981	34,259	38,909	90,629	25,813	13,594	97,536	300,740	42,643
1982	18,842	2,962	23,156	1,492	4,996	57,873	111,054	16,160
1983	15,118	39,112	85,509	25,598	20	12,703	178,060	19,867
1984	21,005	44,259	66,135	16,298	39	17,286	165,023	16,024
1985	43,104	59,816	64,093	21,761	65	-----	188,840	22,561
1986	35,539	38,728	119,068	14,771	186	13,988	225,608	23,122
1987	48,747	29,673	88,413	3,712	30	-----	170,576	15,079
1988[4]	39,324	27,004	146,654	35,490	94	-----	248,566	29,074
1989	60,436	93,283	109,637	9,828	20	21,618	298,485	43,794
1990[5]	35,873	22,776	74,766	3,012	20	10,977	164,180	40,054
1991	16,485	2,583	79,997	4,673	44	-----	117,255	40,332
1992[1]	25,519	15,541	75,354	3,930	56	-----	120,400	29,967
1993[2]	30,171	5,573	66,659	7,317	43	6,006	115,770	24,927

[1] Preliminary.   [2] Estimate.   [3] Imports for consumption.   [4] Manganese content of 35% or more prior to 1989.   [5] Data reported in short tons prior to 1991.
Source: U.S. Bureau of Mines

Average Price of Ferromanganese[1] (High Carbon[2] - F.O.B. Plant)   In Dollars Per Gross Ton -- Carloads

Year	Jan.	Feb.	Mar.	Apr.	May	June	July	Aug.	Sept.	Oct.	Nov.	Dec.	Average
1976	432.50	432.50	432.50	432.50	432.50	432.50	432.50	432.50	432.50	432.50	425.00	417.50	430.63
1977	417.50	417.50	417.50	399.50	399.50	399.50	399.50	399.50	399.50	399.50	399.50	399.50	404.00
1978	399.50	399.50	399.50	399.50	422.17	425.00	425.00	425.00	425.00	425.00	425.00	425.00	416.26
1979	440.00	440.00	440.00	465.00	490.00	490.00	490.00	490.00	490.00	493.00	510.00	510.00	479.04
1980	510.00	510.00	510.00	510.00	510.00	510.00	510.00	510.00	510.00	510.00	510.00	510.00	510.00
1981	510.00	510.00	510.00	510.00	510.00	510.00	510.00	510.00	510.00	510.00	510.00	510.00	510.00
1982	510.00	510.00	510.00	510.00	510.00	510.00	510.00	510.00	510.00	510.00	510.00	510.00	510.00
1983	510.00	510.00	510.00	510.00	510.00	510.00	510.00	510.00	510.00	510.00	510.00	510.00	510.00
1984	510.00	510.00	510.00	510.00	510.00	510.00	510.00	510.00	510.00	NQ	NQ	NQ	510.00
1985	NQ	NQ	NQ	NQ	NQ	NQ	NQ	NQ	NQ	NQ	NQ	NQ	NQ
1986	NQ	NQ	NQ	NQ	NQ	NQ	NQ	NQ	NQ	NQ	NQ	NQ	NQ
1987	NQ	NQ	NQ	NQ	326.25	331.88	339.50	345.00	355.00	358.00	363.00	373.00	348.95
1988	382.50	382.50	414.50	422.50	435.63	440.00	457.50	475.00	530.00	550.00	550.00	550.00	465.84
1989	550.00	550.50	573.75	597.50	640.00	640.00	640.00	634.00	610.00	610.00	610.00	610.00	605.48
1990	610.00	610.00	610.00	610.00	610.00	610.00	610.00	610.00	610.00	610.00	610.00	610.00	610.00
1991	610.00	610.00	610.00	610.00	610.00	610.00	610.00	610.00	610.00	610.00	610.00	610.00	610.00
1992	610.00	610.00	610.00	610.00	610.00	610.00	610.00	610.00	610.00	610.00	610.00	610.00	610.00
1993	610.00	610.00	610.00	610.00	610.00	610.00	610.00	610.00	610.00	610.00	610.00	610.00	610.00

[1] Domestic standard.   [2] Prior to May 1987, prices are for 78% Mn-F.O.B. plant.   NQ = No quote.   Source: American Metal Market

Meats

U.S. red meat and poultry production continue to set new year-to-year production records. Total meat production in 1994 was 71.5 billion pounds, compared with the previous records of 68.1 billion and 67.2 billion in 1993 and 1992, respectively. Red meat accounted for almost 60 percent of total production, about the same as in 1993. A further breakdown shows beef accounting for 58 percent of red meat output in 1994 and pork the balance, vs. 57 percent for beef in 1993. Within the poultry sector, chicken production accounts for more than 80 percent of output and turkeys the balance. Further gains in production are expected in 1995 in the usual proportional pattern, with a forecast of 74.3 billion pounds.

U.S. per capita meat usage (retail weight) reached a record high 212.1 pounds in 1994, vs. the 1993 total 207.6 pounds and the previous high of 208.4 pounds set in 1992. Within the per capita usage complex, broilers are the largest with 70 pounds in 1994 followed by beef at 67.4 pounds, both up about 2 pounds from 1993. Initial forecasts for 1995 place total per capita use at a new record high 217.6 pounds with broiler use at a record high 72.7 pounds. U.S. consumer meat demand is sensitive to the nation's economic strength and level of disposable income. If the economy's strength in 1994 that saw a near 3 percent gain in personal income carries into 1995, the indicated per capita meat use forecasts are apt to be realized.

Large supplies pressured most prices across the meat complex in 1994. Live hog prices were the lowest since the early 1980s and fed cattle for a time were at an 8-year low.

Lower prices are expected in 1995. Choice steers (basis Nebraska) are forecast at $65-71/cwt., vs. $68-70 in 1994; midwest barrow prices are forecast at $37-40/cwt., vs. $40-41 in 1993; and broiler prices are expected to average between $.52-.56/lb., down from $.56-.57/lb. in 1994.

The U.S. is a net meat exporter, owing largely to poultry. Total 1994 meat exports were almost 5.0 billion pounds, compared to imports of 3.2 billion. Exports were up significantly from 1993 while imports were about unchanged. Forecasts for 1995 place exports at a record high 5.1 billion pounds and imports once again near 3.2 billion. The U.S. is consistently a net importer of beef and veal and net exporter of poultry. Trade in live cattle decidedly favors imports, exclusively from Canada and Mexico. Foreign trade in pork is relatively small with imports usually higher. Beef and veal are mostly imported from Australia and New Zealand. Japan is the largest importer of U.S. beef. U.S. broiler exports are widespread, but the Far East is generally the major buyer.

World Total Meat Production[4]   In Thousands of Metric Tons

Year	Argentina	Australia	Brazil	Canada	China[5]	Denmark	France	Germany	Italy	Japan	Mexico	New Zealand	Poland	Russia[6]	Ukraine[6]	United Kingdom	United States
1986	2,936	2,332	2,800	2,020	19,183	1,387	1,552	4,554	2,417	2,111	2,185	1,077	2,631	------	14,635	2,334	17,822
1987	2,782	2,423	3,450	2,108	19,859	1,385	3,605	4,565	2,428	2,146	2,228	1,190	2,609	------	15,517	2,410	17,547
1988	2,697	2,377	3,600	2,161	21,870	1,386	3,532	4,477	2,378	2,147	2,791	1,811	2,635	------	15,893	2,314	18,146
1989	2,696	2,452	4,750	2,164	23,262	1,372	3,670	6,006	2,515	2,142	3,125	1,168	2,621	------	16,501	2,326	17,963
1990	2,738	2,683	4,650	2,022	25,132	1,100	3,816	6,111	2,583	2,104	2,658	1,014	2,736	8,204	3,608	2,331	17,597
1991	2,735	2,704	5,513	2,022	27,238	1,485	3,963	5,552	2,608	2,057	2,535	1,053	2,768	7,526	3,339	2,389	17,956
1992	2,602	2,810	5,923	2,119	29,406	1,600	3,997	4,994	2,648	2,024	2,626	1,036	2,708	6,748	2,874	2,297	18,589
1993[1]	2,630	2,810	5,864	2,075	32,255	1,731	4,018	4,817	2,642	2,026	2,718	1,095	2,028	6,150	2,466	2,238	18,487
1994[2]	2,555	2,823	5,830	2,195	34,200	1,757	4,100	4,655	2,602	2,002	2,792	1,065	1,714	5,810	2,280	2,295	19,196
1995[3]	2,580	2,852	6,060	2,260	36,700	1,805	4,209	4,600	2,582	1,990	2,830	1,057	1,825	5,480	2,186	2,313	19,772

[1]Preliminary. [2]Estimate. [3]Forecast. [4]Includes beef, veal, pork, sheep and goat meat. [5]Predominately pork production. [6]Formerly part of the U.S.S.R.; data not reported separately until 1990.   Source: Foreign Agricultural Service, U.S. Department of Agriculture

Production and Consumption of Red Meats in The United States (Carcass Weight)

Year	Beef Commercial Production - Million Pounds -	Beef Consumption Total	Beef Consumption Per Capita Lb.[4]	Veal Commercial Production - Million Pounds -	Veal Consumption Total	Veal Consumption Per Capita Lb.[4]	Lamb & Mutton Commercial Production - Million Pounds -	Lamb & Mutton Consumption Total	Lamb & Mutton Consumption Per Capita Lb.[4]	Pork (Excluding Lard) Commercial Production - Million Pounds -	Pork Consumption Total	Pork Consumption Per Capita Lb.[4]	All Meats Commercial Production - Million Pounds -	All Meats Consumption Total	All Meats Consumption Per Capita Lb.[4]
1984	23,418	25,048	106.0	495	479	2.2	371	401	1.7	14,720	15,630	66.1	38,988	41,587	176.0
1985	23,557	25,523	107.0	515	499	2.2	352	389	1.6	14,728	15,865	66.5	39,136	42,311	177.4
1986	24,213	25,257	108.0	524	509	2.3	331	378	1.6	13,998	15,135	62.9	39,051	42,051	174.7
1987	23,405	25,252	104.0	430	417	1.9	309	362	1.5	14,311	15,352	63.2	38,442	41,422	170.6
1988	23,424	24,330	103.1	396	387	1.7	329	387	1.6	15,623	16,549	67.5	39,763	42,599	173.9
1989	22,974	24,030	98.4	355	344	1.4	341	386	1.6	15,759	16,571	67.0	39,418	41,644	168.4
1990	22,634	24,114	96.2	327	316	1.3	358	397	1.6	15,300	16,030	64.1	38,608	40,782	163.2
1991	22,800	24,261	95.4	306	296	1.2	358	397	1.6	15,948	16,399	64.9	39,402	41,214	163.1
1992	22,968	24,261	95.0	310	299	1.2	343	388	1.5	17,185	17,475	68.4	40,795	42,437	166.1
1993[1]	22,942	24,006	93.0	267	286	1.1	329	381	1.5	17,030	17,419	67.5	40,588	42,092	163.0
1994[2]	24,262	25,148	98.6	277	298	1.1	304	353	1.3	17,651	17,899	68.4	42,530	43,698	167.4
1995[3]	24,625	25,452	97.7	264	296	1.2	285	359	1.3	17,925	18,728	69.4	43,119	44,835	169.5

[1]Preliminary. [2]Estimate. [3]Forecast. [4]Carcass Weight   Source: Economic Research Service, U.S. Department of Agriculture

MEATS

Total Red Meat Imports (Carcass Weight Equivalent) of Principal Countries — In Thousands of Metric Tons

Year	Belgium & Lux.	Canada	Czecho-slovakia	France	Germany	Greece	Hong Kong	Italy	Japan	Rep. of Korea	Nether-lands	Russia[4]	Singa-pore	Spain	Switzer-land	United Kingdom	United States
1981	88	110	21	579	687	80	------	690	612	45	146	786	------	16	31	1,072	1,058
1982	79	112	29	618	692	157	68	824	546	82	119	679	3	28	25	1,137	1,175
1983	107	121	25	676	728	216	82	832	599	78	108	779	24	26	27	1,072	1,212
1984	79	130	15	711	796	194	238	823	636	39	105	691	22	36	21	1,015	1,280
1985	79	132	15	760	843	208	296	948	647	19	116	587	0	36	15	955	1,476
1986	77	130	15	841	837	221	300	961	712	14	104	537	38	92	16	1,007	1,506
1987	78	157	15	829	880	246	281	952	869	16	109	495	42	90	20	1,036	1,602
1988	76	170	15	869	940	232	313	906	994	45	132	353	40	93	18	1,081	1,630
1989	81	175	25	908	952	239	292	974	1,150	111	119	355	47	127	14	1,033	1,421
1990	110	198	15	967	1,033	209	311	1,025	1,153	145	143	545	43	971	17	76	1,503
1991	88	232	0	1,035	1,240	179	306	1,106	1,206	221	181	740	41	140	13	896	1,463
1992	81	237	108	1,027	1,338	248	265	1,231	1,388	26	202	292	54	147	14	885	1,423
1993[1]	71	292	44	989	1,480	236	265	1,235	1,480	31	201	87	54	164	18	889	1,449
1994[2]	74	325	61	946	1,547	230	270	1,294	1,576	50	205	340	56	170	18	891	1,474
1995[3]	74	325	42	965	1,626	238	275	1,350	1,644	67	180	480	58	170	20	884	1,506

[1]Preliminary. [2]Estimate. [3]Forecast. [4]Formerly part of the U.S.S.R.; data not reported separately until 1992. *Source: Foreign Agricultural Service, U.S. Department of Agriculture*

Total Red Meat Exports (Carcass Weight Equivalent) of Principal Countries — In Thousands of Metric Tons

Year	Argen-tina	Aus-tralia	Brazil	Canada	China	Den-mark	France	India	Ireland	Nether-lands	New Zealand	Poland	Ro-mania	Ukraine[4]	United Kingdom	United States	Uruguay
1981	508	966	281	207	------	905	415	59	324	932	817	60	245	53	243	240	185
1982	546	1,184	361	247	230	909	401	62	311	879	846	52	160	32	194	213	182
1983	438	947	404	242	264	945	387	83	341	957	938	93	185	25	296	225	236
1984	266	747	483	280	273	952	489	88	301	1,066	815	68	177	27	344	227	142
1985	272	860	540	313	278	958	503	65	370	1,158	876	13	265	30	284	210	131
1986	261	1,031	355	376	222	1,007	649	64	473	1,216	863	122	280	353	306	279	198
1987	294	1,122	304	394	238	986	604	79	496	1,265	922	128	310	1,157	313	327	104
1988	464	1,102	567	405	227	1,005	630	69	431	1,309	901	131	305	747	270	402	142
1989	369	1,069	304	407	261	990	586	70	478	1,357	908	140	320	704	301	606	177
1990	461	1,312	243	424	395	995	644	133	469	1,395	794	107	25	545	188	565	192
1991	402	1,391	290	375	494	1,097	757	151	529	1,438	845	31	31	740	299	669	117
1992	301	1,510	422	453	195	1,173	864	110	643	1,485	884	34	40	291	348	787	123
1993[1]	283	1,501	426	494	315	1,311	987	120	677	1,513	858	33	64	256	421	779	62
1994[2]	294	1,470	488	565	365	1,408	940	130	734	1,530	934	26	60	181	470	893	70
1995[3]	303	1,503	540	630	420	1,414	991	140	548	1,510	926	35	60	167	458	943	90

[1]Preliminary. [2]Estimate. [3]Forecast. [4]Formerly part of the U.S.S.R.; data not reported separately until 1992. *Source: Foreign Agricultural Service, U.S. Department of Agriculture*

U.S. Exports and Imports of Meats into the United States (Carcass Weight Equivalent)[3]

Year	Exports — Beef and Veal	Exports — Lamb and Mutton	Exports — Pork[4]	Exports — All Meat	Imports — Beef and Veal	Imports — Lamb and Mutton	Imports — Pork[4]	Imports — All Meat
				In Millions of Pounds				
1980	177	2	252	430	2,085	33	550	2,668
1981	221	2	307	531	1,761	31	541	2,333
1982	254	2	214	470	1,958	21	612	2,591
1983	276	1	219	497	1,974	18	707	2,717
1984	335	2	164	500	1,847	20	954	2,821
1985	332	1	128	461	2,091	36	1,128	3,255
1986	526	1	86	613	2,156	41	1,122	3,319
1987	611	1	109	722	2,293	44	1,195	3,533
1988	690	1	195	887	2,406	51	1,137	3,594
1989	1,023	5	262	1,290	2,178	46	896	3,120
1990	1,006	6	238	1,250	2,356	41	898	3,295
1991	1,188	10	283	1,481	1,406	41	775	3,223
1992	1,324	8	407	1,739	2,440	50	645	3,135
1993[1]	1,275	7	435	1,717	2,401	53	740	3,194
1994[2]	1,611	9	532	2,152	2,371	49	744	3,164

[1]Preliminary. [2]Estimate. [3]Includes meat content of minor meats and of mixed products. *Source: Economic Research Service, U.S. Department of Ag.*

United States Meat Imports by Type of Product   In Metric Tons

Year	Beef and Veal Fresh, Chilled & Frozen	Beef and Veal Canned, including Sausage	Beef and Veal Other Prepared or Preserved	Lamb Mutton and Goat, Except Canned	Pork Fresh and Frozen	Pork Canned[2]	Pork Other Prepared or Preserved	Pork Sausage, all Types	Mixed Sausage	Other Meats[3]	Variety Meats, Fresh or Frozen	Total
1983	565,997	59,073	16,766	8,752	121,707	125,593	2,300	2,176	1,911	3,606	3,935	911,814
1984	516,960	57,863	19,864	8,693	207,703	142,423	3,372	2,243	2,121	5,088	5,707	972,037
1985	594,476	64,277	19,314	15,565	254,538	160,802	6,312	2,192	2,672	5,305	5,622	1,130,075
1986	637,718	45,779	20,778	16,596	263,488	151,730	8,221	2,640	2,849	4,621	6,475	1,160,895
1987	671,152	56,653	17,450	17,204	302,392	145,464	9,387	2,688	4,222	4,126	9,590	1,240,328
1988	703,415	66,919	10,367	19,239	282,728	139,847	10,214	2,906	2,732	3,977	8,905	1,251,249
1989	638,999	68,710	1,434	20,917	225,304	107,267	8,651	2,656	2,620	3,509	11,102	1,091,169
1990	694,163	67,054	1,520	19,056	232,253	98,479	10,055	3,421	1,874	1,239	11,423	1,140,537
1991	709,997	71,570	1,870	19,100	215,933	72,666	11,760	2,144	1,533	3,904	18,266	1,128,744
1992[1]	728,922	72,631	2,112	23,853	185,672	54,114	13,104	2,453	1,674	1,514	20,059	1,118,900
1993[1]	720,075	------ 74,342 -----		24,463	207,651	----- 87,559 ------		2,695	1,368	1,839	25,673	1,152,861

[1]Preliminary. [2]Includes canned hams, shoulders and bacon. [3]Mostly mixed luncheon meats. *Source: Foreign Agricultural Service, U.S.Dept. of Agriculture*

United States Meat Exports by Type of Product   In Metric Tons

Year	Beef and Veal Fresh, Chilled & Frozen	Beef and Veal Prepared and Preserved	Lamb and Mutton, Fresh or Frozen	Pork Fresh, Chilled & Frozen	Pork Hams & Shoulders, Cured	Pork Bacon	Pork Other Preserved or Not Canned	Pork Other Preserved Canned	Sausage, Bologna & Frankfurters	Variety Meats, Fresh, Chilled & Frozen	Other Meats[2]	Total
1978	40,390	14,878	1,375	84,120	3,934	1,655	7,524	2,932	3,653	181,164	67,549	387,109
1979	45,908	11,495	562	83,058	3,380	912	8,912	1,123	3,003	164,125	64,631	412,326
1980	48,255	11,248	595	69,966	3,327	820	8,438	1,667	3,296	195,182	69,532	443,338
1981	62,371	12,297	972	86,652	2,363	1,079	9,130	1,662	3,819	206,891	56,102	530,835
1982	71,621	14,046	676	58,541	1,358	774	7,514	1,289	3,404	222,688	48,924	416,095
1983	80,976	12,070	632	62,141	1,794	601	5,581	695	3,139	213,155	36,176	416,960
1984	99,208	12,322	878	46,098	1,474	621	3,837	513	2,603	213,180	35,457	416,191
1985	99,923	9,605	460	34,394	1,175	450	4,066	638	2,908	239,451	38,395	431,465
1986	173,884	10,519	558	20,969	650	474	4,796	349	3,214	241,051	46,760	503,224
1987	200,180	10,789	668	29,145	1,227	617	3,597	376	4,582	222,342	61,812	535,335
1988	214,530	14,083	619	54,598	2,138	1,045	4,924	268	8,439	302,087	75,084	677,815
1989	373,110	8,810	2,076	79,318	6,101	3,788	2,204	1,395	11,968	245,235	78,550	812,555
1990	339,925	7,783	2,490	66,756	5,567	4,518	4,310	1,036	14,208	226,623	70,558	731,566
1991	395,697	10,248	3,790	76,193	4,702	5,443	6,133	1,278	24,025	280,721	61,440	869,670
1992[1]	436,455	12,064	3,278	116,496	8,181	7,396	5,812	2,352	22,796	303,295	57,154	975,279
1993[1]	410,997	14,467	3,606	129,240	5,209	7,094	4,578	2,351	34,195	329,603	47,917	1,169,145

[1]Preliminary. [2]Includes sausage ingredients, cured (excluding canned); meat and meat products canned; and baby food, canned. *Source: Foreign Agricultural Service, U.S. Department of Agriculture*

Average Wholesale Prices of Meats   In Cents Per Pound

Year	Composite Retail Price of Beef, Choice, Grade[3]	Composite Retail Price of Pork[3]	Wholesale Value[4] Beef	Wholesale Value[4] Pork	Net Farm Value of Pork[5]	Cow Beef Canner & Cutter, Central US	Boxed Beef Cut-out, Choice 1-3, Central US 550-700 lbs.	Pork Carcass Cut-out, U.S., No. 2	Lamb Carcass, Choice-Prime, East Coast, 55-65 lbs.	Pork[6] Loins, Central US, 14-18 lbs.	Skinned Ham, Central US, 17-20 lbs.	Pork Bellies, Central US, 12-14 lbs.
1984	235.50	162.00	162.50	110.10	77.40	74.70	103.80	61.35	130.99	96.36	75.41	60.31
1985	228.60	162.00	148.80	101.10	71.50	74.13	97.95	50.38	140.23	91.51	67.27	59.51
1986	226.80	178.40	146.50	110.90	80.60	71.31	94.61	69.05	140.32	104.78	77.96	65.82
1987	238.40	188.40	160.00	113.00	82.70	85.26	103.85	69.40	150.41	106.23	79.29	63.11
1988	250.30	183.40	169.40	101.00	69.40	87.77	110.35	59.57	137.81	97.49	69.05	41.25
1989	265.70	182.90	176.80	99.20	70.40	94.43	114.78	60.62	131.35	101.11	69.25	34.14
1990	281.00	212.60	189.60	118.30	87.20	102.41	123.21	74.00	121.47	117.52	84.87	53.80
1991	288.30	211.90	182.50	108.90	78.40	99.42	118.31	67.02	117.33	108.39	75.68	47.79
1992	284.60	198.00	179.60	98.90	67.80	93.85	116.73	58.37	131.66	101.41	67.42	30.39
1993[1]	293.40	197.60	182.50	102.90	72.50	95.31	118.74	62.19	143.97	107.47	67.85	41.62
1994[2]	282.90	198.00	166.70	96.90	62.80	84.39	108.47	57.28	147.62	104.54	58.29	39.98

[1]Preliminary. [2]Estimate. [3]Sold as retail cuts (ham, bacon, loin, etc.). [4]Quantity equivalent to 1 pound of retail cuts. [5]Portion of gross farm value minus farm by-product allowance. [6]Prior to 1983, 8-14 pounds. *Source: Economic Research Bureau, U.S. Department of Agriculture*

MEATS

Average Wholesale Price of Boxed Beef Cut-Out[1], Choice, at Central Markets   In Cents Per Pound

Year	Jan	Feb	Mar	Apr	May	June	July	Aug	Sept	Oct	Nov	Dec	Average
1985	105.48	102.77	98.73	96.40	97.31	94.89	91.02	91.48	91.83	97.37	105.12	103.03	97.95
1986	96.70	91.22	89.02	88.17	90.56	90.37	96.05	98.40	98.48	98.00	101.41	96.95	94.61
1987	96.71	98.56	98.40	106.45	114.03	113.18	104.55	101.52	104.33	103.97	102.62	101.82	103.85
1988	102.55	105.94	108.50	110.79	116.73	111.96	107.09	110.37	112.72	112.74	112.37	112.45	110.35
1989	113.62	114.30	117.09	118.58	118.53	114.53	113.17	112.83	110.08	110.04	115.06	119.52	114.78
1990	121.75	120.97	122.10	123.62	124.56	121.53	118.54	121.52	121.18	124.96	128.32	129.48	123.21
1991	125.04	123.24	125.45	125.96	123.76	120.61	115.82	111.54	110.61	113.04	113.43	111.18	118.31
1992	114.38	119.65	119.14	118.66	119.18	117.53	112.79	114.36	114.40	115.51	115.26	119.95	116.73
1993	122.69	122.13	124.80	126.12	127.19	120.52	114.48	116.73	114.65	111.52	113.26	110.83	118.74
1994[2]	112.11	112.23	115.03	114.98	108.85	102.92	104.19	108.38	105.49	103.63	106.66	107.22	108.47

[1]Choice 1-3, 550-700 pounds.   [2]Preliminary.   *Source: Economic Research Service, U.S. Department of Agriculture*

Production (Commercial) of all Red Meats in the U.S.   In Millions of Pounds (Carcass Weight)

Year	Jan	Feb	Mar	Apr	May	June	July	Aug	Sept	Oct	Nov	Dec	Total
1985	3,421	2,938	3,163	3,296	3,489	3,084	3,277	3,403	3,251	3,545	3,123	3,146	39,136
1986	3,483	2,942	3,133	3,476	3,388	3,157	3,281	3,179	3,260	3,505	2,986	3,261	39,051
1987	3,410	2,875	3,198	3,161	2,976	3,103	3,158	3,135	3,330	3,521	3,197	3,378	38,442
1988	3,246	3,071	3,355	3,158	3,206	3,319	3,170	3,507	3,462	3,512	3,399	3,358	39,763
1989	3,265	3,004	3,325	3,131	3,397	3,343	3,048	3,483	3,317	3,523	3,411	3,171	39,418
1990	3,354	2,972	3,259	3,049	3,320	3,175	3,100	3,431	3,096	3,499	3,273	3,080	38,608
1991	3,430	2,954	3,081	3,285	3,291	3,059	3,253	3,425	3,308	3,708	3,324	3,284	39,402
1992	3,623	3,090	3,376	3,259	3,237	3,423	3,441	3,406	3,560	3,656	3,289	3,434	40,794
1993	3,304	3,012	3,396	3,299	3,212	3,481	3,342	3,504	3,516	3,499	3,449	3,554	40,568
1994[1]	3,367	3,125	3,591	3,383	3,429	3,616	3,361	3,683	3,721	3,799	3,666	3,715	42,531

[1]Preliminary.   *Source: Economic Research Service, U.S. Department of Agriculture*

Cold Storage Holdings of All[1] Meats in the United States, at End of Month   In Millions of Pounds

Year	Jan	Feb	Mar	Apr	May	June	July	Aug	Sept	Oct	Nov	Dec
1985	735.0	702.9	721.2	772.7	784.9	758.6	738.2	677.1	654.2	645.2	633.0	607.4
1986	616.8	615.3	622.5	658.2	667.2	638.8	618.6	572.0	541.1	572.4	564.3	566.2
1987	597.6	599.0	598.2	590.8	560.2	498.7	515.6	495.9	523.0	575.6	613.8	622.9
1988	664.6	689.5	716.6	759.4	721.2	670.7	670.7	633.9	644.3	644.0	701.5	716.4
1989	745.0	758.7	474.5	747.5	763.7	683.5	652.0	576.3	557.0	538.2	554.2	536.0
1990	564.7	609.6	637.5	653.0	632.8	591.6	565.9	507.4	507.5	536.7	536.7	536.4
1991	566.2	588.6	606.2	597.7	640.1	614.1	589.7	593.2	592.8	594.7	650.2	644.9
1992	707.9	690.5	725.4	706.8	692.2	665.3	646.0	595.6	613.4	637.8	626.6	615.1
1993	649.4	654.6	652.9	692.0	671.0	660.8	664.2	650.7	671.7	702.4	720.3	726.7
1994[2]	809.5	802.4	843.9	859.6	839.2	822.5	822.5	818.8	771.9	783.5	827.5	801.0

[1]Includes beef and veal, mutton and lamb, pork and products, rendered pork fat, and miscellaneous meats. Excludes lard.   [2]Preliminary.
Source: Economic Research Service, U.S. Department of Agriculture

Cold Storage Holdings of Frozen Beef in the United States   In Millions of Pounds

Year	Jan. 1	Feb. 1	Mar. 1	Apr. 1	May 1	June 1	July 1	Aug. 1	Sept. 1	Oct. 1	Nov. 1	Dec. 1
1985	357.7	375.1	347.0	334.0	328.0	300.9	295.5	319.7	310.6	308.4	294.9	302.3
1986	317.4	318.4	302.3	297.1	301.2	318.5	321.6	337.0	319.4	291.6	292.3	297.5
1987	310.6	320.6	306.0	311.1	312.3	280.1	252.7	278.7	269.3	286.5	307.6	304.3
1988	288.7	316.7	325.4	313.2	305.0	275.1	248.4	269.6	294.9	307.6	296.5	300.4
1989	317.5	315.1	313.4	298.9	275.4	244.1	241.8	249.2	242.4	231.8	220.7	237.6
1990	251.7	259.8	267.6	304.3	293.3	270.4	256.5	265.4	240.5	243.0	267.4	277.2
1991	300.4	298.9	271.3	276.9	265.6	234.7	247.1	273.2	259.4	276.7	298.2	306.3
1992	315.9	329.1	298.9	313.7	302.1	303.5	299.4	294.1	288.9	275.2	291.2	275.9
1993	272.8	286.4	279.9	293.9	276.7	262.1	271.7	285.3	307.5	326.8	344.4	376.3
1994[1]	401.0	430.2	414.4	423.2	399.5	367.9	379.4	388.9	377.2	401.8	410.6	419.5

[1]Preliminary.   *Source: Economic Research Service, U.S. Department of Agriculture*

Mercury

Mercury's use continues to fall, owing to its toxicity. Worldwide, several major uses already have been virtually eliminated. In the U.S., environmental legislation has limited the use and disposal of mercury and the restrictions may further tighten. The trend for several years has been to substitute other materials for mercury rather than develop large-scale recycling programs. However, secondary mercury will be a large part of the world mercury supply as more chlor-alkali plants are dismantled, and recycling of other products increases. In short, mercury is likely to be used only where it is absolutely necessary.

At ordinary temperatures mercury is a liquid, has a high specific value and good electrical conductivity. However, there are substitutes as the metal is seen as an environmental hazard. In the U.S., the last producing primary mercury mine (in Nevada) was closed in 1990; it produced 448 tonnes that year. Since 1990, U.S. primary mercury has been recovered only as a byproduct of gold mining operations in California, Nevada and Utah; the recovery is required to prevent contamination of the environment.

World production of mercury is limited to a few countries. China produced about 800 tonnes in 1993, almost one-third of the world total 2,563 tonnes. Spain, once the world's largest producer with output in 1986 greater than current total world output, opted to replenish stocks during 1993 and produced about 643 tonnes versus no reported production in 1990-1992. World resources are estimated at nearly 600,000 tonnes, mostly in Spain and the former Soviet Union; at current production rates it could easily last more than 100 years. Mercury occurs with gold ores and must be recovered to avoid contamination, but recovery restrictions are lax in some countries, notably along the Amazon River basin in South America where exploration of gold is intense.

Mercury is a recoverable metal. In the U.S., secondary production nearly doubled in 1993, to 350 tonnes, owing largely to new Enviromental Protection Agency's restrictions banning landfill disposal and/or transport of mercury-containing wastes, which in turn encouraged more efficient methods. Mercury's recovery from fluorescent lamps has become a growing industry with 11 plants operating in the U.S. Stockpiled mercury is another source of world supply and the total is expected to increase as more mercury using plants are closed. Industry stocks at U.S. sites in late-1993 totaled 384 tonnes versus 436 tonnes reported the previous year. The U.S. government has a mercury stockpile with tight restrictions are in place as to how much can be sold each year, but the stated goal is to reduce the inventory to zero.

U.S. mercury consumption fell 10 percent in 1993 and by yearend had dropped 63 percent since 1988. All domestic battery manufacturers now produce alkaline and zinc-carbon batteries without any added mercury. Chlorine and caustic soda manufacture remains the largest domestic use for mercury, taking about 180 tonnes in 1993, one-third of its total use. Substitutes for mercury include lithium and composite ceramic materials.

U.S. foreign trade in mercury is small, but exports are well in excess of imports; totaling 389 tonnes and 40 tonnes, respectively, in 1993. The Netherlands were the largest importer, while Canada and Germany were the sole exporters to the U.S.

Mercury is usually sold in 34.5 kilogram flasks. The U.S. average price in 1993 was $187.00 per flask (at New York) versus $201.39 in 1992. Prices during the 1980's averaged near $300 per flask. European prices are generally lower than in the U.S. and considered more reflective of true market values.

World Mine Production of Mercury   In Metric Tons (1 tonne = 29.008216 flasks)

Year	Algeria	China	Finland	Kyrgz-stan[3]	Mexico	Spain	Tajik-istan[3]	Turkey	Ukraine[3]	United States	Total
1986	759	700	146	------	104	2,757	------	291	2,250	NA	7,247
1987	705	700	144	------	124	1,395	------	211	2,300	100	5,810
1988	662	940	130	------	345	1,716	------	97	850	378	5,357
1989	587	1,200	159	------	651	1,224	------	197	850	414	5,464
1990	637	1,000	141	------	735	425	------	60	800	562	4,098
1991	431	760	74	------	340	100	------	25	750	58	2,542
1992	476	800	85	300	21	56	100	5	100	64	2,108
1993[1]	475	800	85	250	20	643	80	5	80	70	2,563
1994[2]	400	700			20	345			80		2,200

[1] Preliminary.   [2] Estimate.   [3] Formerly part of the U.S.S.R.; data not reported separately until 1992.   NA = Not available.   *Source: U.S. Bureau of Mines*

Salient Statistics of Mercury in the U.S.   In Metric Tons

Year	Producing Mines	Secondary Production — Industrial	Government[3]	N.D.S.[4] Shipments	Consumer & Dealer Stocks Dec. 31	Industrial Demand	Exports	Imports
1988	10	278	214	52	338	1503	NA	329
1989	10	137	180	170	217	121	221	131
1990	9	108	193	52	197	720	311	15
1991	8	165	215	103	313	554	786	56
1992	9	176	103	267	436	621	977	92
1993[1]	9	350		543	384	558	389	40
1994[2]		400		86	320	550	400	20

[1] Preliminary.   [2] Estimate.   [3] Secondary mercury shipped from the Department of Energy.   [4] National Defense Stockpile.   NA = Not available.
Source: U.S. Bureau of Mines

MERCURY

Average Price of Mercury in New York   In Dollars Per Flask of 76 Pounds (34.5 Kilograms)

Year	Jan.	Feb.	Mar.	Apr.	May	June	July	Aug.	Sept.	Oct.	Nov.	Dec.	Average
1984	318.67	295.68	300.45	324.26	328.27	325.48	314.64	302.09	317.18	329.07	327.13	320.08	316.92
1985	317.30	315.00	314.38	309.34	297.27	309.05	316.74	324.61	325.00	325.00	325.00	325.00	316.97
1986	285.68	261.97	252.44	272.05	277.50	276.07	260.00	218.10	181.91	193.80	215.19	219.43	242.85
1987	216.70	211.03	223.73	260.00	297.63	297.73	286.82	306.55	337.86	345.91	348.95	342.27	289.60
1988	354.00	357.00	350.00	337.14	326.90	352.28	367.13	360.43	349.29	322.74	299.34	293.45	339.14
1989	292.50	318.42	330.00	327.50	315.68	308.86	293.03	273.80	265.13	267.61	282.50	292.50	297.29
1990	292.50	292.50	287.84	285.00	285.00	285.00	281.45	262.50	259.34	235.54	198.75	182.50	262.33
1991	181.55	169.08	150.36	140.68	129.77	119.75	110.36	102.50	98.00	94.02	127.50	150.12	131.14
1992	162.86	177.24	180.00	180.00	190.63	202.50	202.50	203.45	207.50	207.50	207.50	207.50	194.10
1993	207.50	207.50	207.50	207.50	207.50	201.30	191.00	191.00	185.00	185.00	181.00	175.00	195.57
1994	175.00	175.00	179.78	180.00	180.95	186.64	196.50	200.00	203.10	205.00	217.50	230.71	194.18

Source: American Metal Market

Mercury Consumed in the United States   In Metric Tons

Year	Batteries	Chlorine & Caustic Soda	Catalysts, Misc.	Dental Equipment	Electrical Lighting	General Lab Use	Measuring Control Instrument	Paints	Wiring Devices & Switches	Other Uses	Total
1983	23,350	8,054	484	1,597	1,273	280	2,465	6,047	2,316	1,356	49,138
1984[3]	29,700	7,347	359	1,432	1,487	269	2,856	4,651	2,730	1,404	54,669
1985	952	235	61	50	40	14	79	169	95	20	1,718
1986	750	259	90	52	41	20	63	179	103	31	1,588
1987	533	311	59	56	45	20	59	198	131	34	1,446
1988	448	354	86	53	31	26	77	197	176	55	1,503
1989	250	379	40	39	31	18	87	192	141	32	1,212
1990	106	247	29	44	33	32	108	14	70	38	720
1991	18	184	26	41	39	30	90	6	71	49	554
1992[1]	13	209	20	42	55	28	80		82	92	621
1993[2]	10	180	18	35	38	26	65		83	103	558

[1] Preliminary.   [2] Estimate.   [3] Data reported in flasks prior to 1985.   *Source: U.S. Buraeu of Mines*

Milk

U.S. milk production in 1994 of 69.4 million tonnes was up 1 percent from 1993's total of 68.5 million. The increase reflected gains in milk production per cow which more than offset a small year-to-year decline in milk cow numbers. This pattern was expected to carry into 1995 with production forecast to be up about 2 percent from 1994 as producers respond to 1) the carryover effect of moderately strong 1992-94 milk prices, 2) ample supplies of feed and 3) continued adoption of bovine somatotropin (bST). The latter, a genetically engineered hormone approved for use by the FDA in late 1993, increases the amount of milk produced by dairy cows. The early adverse response to bST by producers and consumer groups slowly dissipated during 1994. Farmers increased the number of cows injected with bST during the year while at the same time voicing doubts as to its use. The drug's producer estimated that some 800,000 cows had been injected by late summer, higher than the FDA's estimate, but close to the USDA's assumed adoption rate. Milk per cow is expected to grow 3 percent in 1995, following an increase of more than 2 percent in 1994.

Seasonally, milk production is highest during the April-June quarter and this pattern basically held in 1994 as nearly 40 billion pounds were produced, vs. 37.7 billion in the first quarter. However, the third-quarter growth in milk per cow of almost 3 percent was the strongest since 1992; data from the 21 key reporting states indicated output per cow more robust during August-September than during June-July. The use of bST likely contributed to the boost in monthly production and output in the third quarter of 38.4 billion pounds, compared to 37.4 billion a year earlier.

Since 1992, returns to milk production are thought to have neither encouraged rapid expansion by producers nor brought large additional numbers of farm under financial stress. What appears to have occurred in the industry are structural changes that in turn released long standing pent-up pressures as reflected by the stability in cow numbers during 1994.

Following the breakup of the USSR, the U.S. became the world's largest milk producer, accounting for nearly 20 percent of the 1994 world total of 381 million tonnes. Russia's production runs a distant second; their annual output dropping to under 50 million tonnes since 1992, vs. an annual outturn of more than 55 million in the late 1980s. The Ukraine's production also collapsed— to 17.5 million tonnes in 1994 from nearly 25 million five years earlier. Other large producing nations include: France, Germany and India. U.S. milk prices are generally lower than in most nations. The U.S. producer price for fluid grade milk in 1993 of $12.86 per cwt. and about $13.00 in 1994 compares with about $20/cwt. in Europe and even higher prices in Japan. Despite seemingly favorable U.S. milk prices, U.S. per capita consumption continues to slide; 226 pounds in 1993 vs. an average near 240 pounds in the 1980s.

U.S. milk prices in 1995 will reflect the more ample supplies and could slip 5-7 percent, possibly to the 1986-88 average of $12.54/cwt. One key uncertainty for 1995 prices pivots on the number of additional cows injected with bST. During the 1993/94 marketing year, manufacturing grade milk prices averaged $.91/cwt. above the $10.10 support price. The last marketing year in which prices averaged within 5 percent of the support price was 1987/88. Milk prices continue relatively independent of the support price owing to small surpluses, the effect of the Dairy Export Incentive Program (DEIP) and the lack of flexibility of converting milk into cheese.

World Fluid Milk Production (Cow's Milk)   In Thousands of Metric Tons

Year	Australia	Brazil	Canada	France	Germany	India	Italy	Japan	Mexico	Nether-lands	New Zealand	Poland	Russia[3]	Ukraine[3]	United Kingdom	United States
1988	6,297	13,200	8,229	26,000	32,000	22,000	10,671	7,607	8,830	11,406	7,936	15,450	------	106,622	14,880	65,840
1989	6,465	13,400	7,980	26,150	32,400	24,000	10,828	8,059	8,970	11,321	7,406	16,371	55,742	24,237	14,647	65,424
1990	6,435	14,500	7,975	26,400	31,200	27,500	11,491	8,190	9,330	11,285	7,746	15,801	55,715	24,360	14,952	67,276
1991	6,578	14,200	7,790	25,700	28,916	28,200	11,400	8,260	10,200	11,047	8,122	14,504	51,971	22,409	14,503	67,348
1992	6,918	15,000	7,633	25,315	28,106	29,400	11,300	8,581	10,700	10,901	8,603	13,060	47,237	19,078	14,428	68,786
1993[1]	7,530	15,200	7,500	24,992	28,200	30,500	10,800	8,625	10,720	10,925	8,735	12,650	46,900	18,100	14,529	68,472
1994[2]	8,119	15,300	7,700	24,900	27,800	30,500	10,300	8,500	11,010	10,750	9,763	12,500	46,800	17,500	14,440	69,400

[1]Preliminary.   [2]Estimate.   [3]Formerly part of the U.S.S.R.; data not reported separately until 1989.
Source: Foreign Agricultural Service, U.S. Department of Agriculture

U.S. Milk-Feed Price Ratio[1]   In Pounds

Year	Jan	Feb	Mar	Apr	May	June	July	Aug	Sept	Oct	Nov	Dec	Average
1988	1.51	1.47	1.43	1.40	1.37	1.36	1.15	1.19	1.26	1.32	1.36	1.38	1.35
1989	1.38	1.35	1.30	1.29	1.28	1.29	1.37	1.43	1.52	1.63	1.71	1.76	1.44
1990	1.67	1.56	1.49	1.48	1.49	1.52	1.55	1.58	1.54	1.45	1.40	1.29	1.50
1991	1.31	1.30	1.27	1.27	1.27	1.28	1.37	1.44	1.49	1.53	1.58	1.57	1.39
1992	1.50	1.44	1.40	1.41	1.43	1.47	1.51	1.52	1.52	1.51	1.48	1.45	1.47
1993	1.38	1.35	1.35	1.41	1.44	1.45	1.43	1.39	1.43	1.45	1.50	1.49	1.42
1994[2]	1.43	1.41	1.41	1.44	1.41	1.36	1.35	1.37	1.41	1.48	1.48	1.46	1.42

[1]Pounds of 16% protein mixed dairy feed equal in value to one pound of whole milk.   [2]Preliminary.
Source: Economic Research Service, U.S. Department of Agriculture

MILK

Salient Statistics of Milk in the United States   In Millions of Pounds

Year	Number of Milk Cows on Farms[3] (Thousands)	Production Per Cow[4] (Pounds)	Production Total[4]	Beginning Stocks[5]	Imports	Total Supply	Exports[5]	Fed to Calves	Humans	Total Use	All Milk, Whole-sale	Milk Eligible for Fluid Market	Milk, Manu-facturing Grade	Per Capita Consump-tion[6] (Fluid Milk in Lbs.)
1988	10,262	14,145	145,152	7,473	2,394	155,019	1,582	1,620	142,824	146,641	12.26	12.36	11.15	235
1989	10,126	14,245	144,239	8,378	2,498	155,115	3,995	1,503	139,802	146,079	13.56	13.66	12.38	236
1990	10,127	14,645	148,313	9,036	2,690	160,039	1,886	1,517	142,626	146,680	13.74	13.89	12.34	233
1991	9,992	14,860	148,477	13,359	2,625	164,461	3,673	1,511	142,818	148,621	12.27	12.30	11.05	233
1992	9,835	15,419	151,647	15,840	2,521	170,008	8,532	1,454	145,230	155,794	13.15	13.19	11.91	231
1993[1]	9,705	15,554	150,954	14,214	2,806	167,974	8,643	1,450	147,733	158,404	12.86	12.88	11.80	227
1994[2]	9,624	16,010	154,093	9,570	3,000						13.04	13.09	11.88	

[1]Preliminary. [2]Estimate. [3]Average number on farms during year including dry cows, excluding heifers not yet fresh. [4]Excludes milk sucked by calves. [5]Government and commercial. [6]Product pounds of commercial sales and on farm consumption.
Source: Economic Research Service, U.S.Department of Agriculture

Utilization of Milk in the United States   In Millions of Pounds (Milk Equivalent)

Year	Butter from Whey Cream	Creamery Butter[2]	Cheese[3]	Cottage Cheese (Creamed)	Canned Milk[4]	Bulk Condensed Whole Milk Unsweet-ened	Bulk Condensed Whole Milk Sweet-ened	Dry Whole Milk Products	Ice Cream[5]	Other Frozen Dairy Products	Other Manu-factured Pro-ducts[6]	Used on Farms Farm-Churned Butter	Total
1988	4,017	27,116	44,111	857	1,285	640	172	1,263	2,155	12,960	388	623	2,242
1989	3,961	28,486	43,548	704	1,144	428	215	1,286	2,069	12,531	357	579	2,082
1990	4,348	29,391	47,368	672	1,332	351	243	1,292	2,014	12,307	332	522	2,039
1991	4,296	30,039	46,769	644	1,194	364	236	785	2,092	12,726	356	508	2,019
1992[1]	4,150	30,478	49,458	592	1,872	417	301	1,227	2,367	11,825	188	470	1,919

[1]Preliminary. [2]Excludes whey butter. [3]American and other. [4]Includes evaporated and sweetened condensed. [5]Milk equivalent of butter and condensed milk used in ice cream. [6]Whole milk equivalent of dry cream, malted milk powder, part-skim milk, dry or concentrated ice cream mix, dehydrated butterfat and other miscellaneous products using milk-fat.   *Source: National Agricultural Statistics Service, U.S. Department of Agriculture*

Milk Production[1] in the United States   In Millions of Pounds

Year	Jan	Feb	Mar	Apr	May	June	July	Aug	Sept	Oct	Nov	Dec	Total
1988	11,998	11,550	12,582	12,426	12,974	12,440	12,321	11,985	11,614	11,811	11,436	12,015	145,152
1989	12,296	11,412	12,733	12,582	12,973	12,147	11,981	11,838	11,338	11,657	11,380	11,902	144,239
1990	12,283	11,491	12,988	12,749	13,256	12,635	12,562	12,312	11,737	12,098	11,831	12,372	148,314
1991	12,587	11,732	13,106	12,888	13,268	12,477	12,348	12,202	11,705	12,102	11,763	12,347	148,477
1992	12,671	12,132	13,155	12,838	13,346	12,893	12,844	12,577	12,094	12,476	12,064	12,626	151,747
1993	10,728	9,908	11,060	10,927	11,410	10,940	10,913	10,573	10,138	10,331	9,994	10,461	127,383
1994[2]	10,637	9,802	11,079	11,038	11,452	10,998	10,996	10,830	10,471	10,707	10,383	10,826	129,219

[1]Excludes milk sucked by calves. [2]Preliminary.   *Source: Economic Research Service, U.S. Department of Agriculture*

Average Price Received by U.S. Farmers for All Milk (Sold to Plants)   In Dollars Per Hundred Pounds (Cwt.)

Year	Jan	Feb	Mar	Apr	May	June	July	Aug	Sept	Oct	Nov	Dec	Average
1988	12.50	12.20	11.90	11.60	11.40	11.30	11.40	11.80	12.50	13.00	13.40	13.60	12.26
1989	13.50	13.20	12.70	12.40	12.30	12.40	12.60	13.20	14.00	14.80	15.60	16.00	13.56
1990	15.50	14.50	13.90	13.40	13.50	13.80	14.00	14.20	13.90	13.10	12.70	11.70	13.74
1991	11.70	11.60	11.40	11.30	11.30	11.40	11.80	12.40	12.80	13.50	13.90	13.80	12.27
1992	13.40	12.90	12.50	12.60	12.80	13.20	13.40	13.50	13.50	13.40	13.10	12.80	13.15
1993	12.50	12.20	12.20	12.60	12.90	13.00	12.80	12.40	12.80	13.10	13.60	13.50	12.86
1994[1]	13.70	13.50	13.50	13.50	12.90	12.70	12.30	12.50	12.80	13.10	13.10	12.90	13.04

[1]Preliminary.   *Source: Economic Research Service, U.S. Department of Agriculture*

Farm Price of Milk Eligible for Fluid Market   In Dollars Per Hundred Pounds (Cwt.)

Year	Jan	Feb	Mar	Apr	May	June	July	Aug	Sept	Oct	Nov	Dec	Average
1988	12.70	12.40	12.10	11.70	11.50	11.40	11.50	12.00	12.60	13.10	13.50	13.70	12.36
1989	13.60	13.40	12.90	12.50	12.40	12.50	12.70	13.30	14.10	14.90	15.60	16.10	13.66
1990	15.60	14.70	14.00	13.40	13.60	13.90	14.10	14.30	14.00	13.30	12.90	11.80	13.89
1991	11.80	11.70	11.50	11.40	11.40	11.50	11.90	12.40	12.90	13.60	13.90	13.90	12.30
1992	13.50	13.00	12.50	12.60	12.90	13.30	13.40	13.50	13.60	13.50	13.20	12.90	13.19
1993	12.60	12.30	12.20	12.70	13.00	13.10	12.80	12.50	12.80	13.10	13.60	13.60	12.88
1994[1]	13.70	13.50	13.60	13.60	13.00	12.80	12.30	12.50	12.90	13.10	13.10	13.00	13.09

[1]Preliminary.   *Source: Economic Research Service, U.S. Department of Agriculture*

Molasses

U.S. supplies of molasses (including production and imports) amount to about three million tonnes a year. Of this total, about a third comes from mainland cane sugar mills, a quarter from beet sugar refiners, smaller amounts from Hawaiian cane and cane refiners' blackstrap, and the remainder from imports. Beet molasses is used primarily as a livestock feed and as a yeast by the pharmaceutical industry. In 1993, blackstrap molasses averaged $55.48 per short ton, down about 10 percent from 1992. The average price in Baltimore was $76.03 per ton. The average price of beet molasses in the Red River Valley of the northern Plains states in 1993 was $64.44 per ton, compared to $57.50 in 1992.

According to the U.S. Department of Agriculture, production of cane molasses from mainland mills in 1993 was 1.03 million metric tons, up seven percent from 1992. Cane refiners' blackstrap molasses production in 1993 was 120,000 tonnes, down five percent. Shipments of cane molasses from Hawaii to the U.S. mainland were nearly 177,000 tonnes, down 12 percent. Production of molasses from beets in 1993 was 692,000 tonnes, down 27 percent.

U.S. imports of molasses in 1993 were 1.04 million tonnes, down 7 percent from 1992. The major supplier of molasses was Australia with 275,663 tonnes, up 37 percent from the previous year. The next largest supplier was the Dominican Republic with 163,180 tonnes, up 28 percent. Guatemala was the third largest supplier with 109,220 tonnes, down 54 percent.

Hawaiian production of molasses in 1993 was 187,915 tonnes, down seven percent. Puerto Rican production was 25,097 tonnes, unchanged from 1992. Edible molasses production in Louisiana was 1.48 million gallons, up one percent from 1992.

World Production of Sugarcane and Sugarbeets by Selected Countries — In Thousands of Metric Tons

Crop Year	Australia	Brazil	China	Cuba	India	Indonesia	Pakistan	Thailand	China	France	Germany	Poland	Russia[3]	Turkey	Ukraine[3]	United States
	Sugarcane								**Sugarbeets**							
1980-1	23,976	90,000	22,330	72,000	150,500	13,288	9,140	18,652	6,305	25,248	19,083	10,139	-----	6,766	79,559	21,321
1981-2	25,136	88,170	29,690	77,000	110,200	17,642	14,552	30,264	6,360	33,332	24,353	15,867	-----	11,165	60,843	24,982
1982-3	24,908	98,900	35,882	75,000	189,000	17,846	12,511	24,407	6,712	29,680	22,692	16,364	-----	12,732	71,648	18,955
1983-4	24,190	100,000	31,141	75,000	177,020	21,092	13,486	23,087	9,182	22,643	16,255	16,364	-----	12,770	81,800	19,044
1984-5	25,513	98,000	39,519	75,000	173,569	21,141	14,692	25,053	8,284	26,803	20,024	16,048	-----	11,108	85,251	20,080
1985-6	24,402	247,199	58,711	67,400	170,319	22,621	27,856	25,055	8,919	29,977	28,210	14,664	-----	9,830	82,392	20,438
1986-7	25,413	238,493	56,483	68,500	170,648	26,208	29,926	24,093	8,306	25,830	28,007	14,217	-----	10,662	79,299	22,827
1987-8													-----			
1988-9													-----			
1989-90	26,940	252,643	55,423	81,003	203,040	29,421	36,976	36,668	9,243	27,694	20,767	14,374	-----	10,929	97,414	22,798
1990-1	24,370	262,674	63,451	76,230	225,569	27,980	35,494	33,561	14,525	31,735	23,310	16,721	32,327	13,986	44,265	24,959
1991-2	20,640	260,888	72,695	71,000	241,046	28,133	35,989	47,480	16,289	29,520	25,926	11,412	24,280	15,474	36,168	25,585
1992-3[1]	27,958	271,475	78,869	58,000	253,995	32,000	38,865	34,860	15,069	31,675	27,150	11,052	25,548	15,126	28,783	26,438
1993-4[2]	31,700	251,408	68,419	44,000	230,832	32,400	38,743	34,710	12,100	31,748	28,610	15,621	25,500	15,563	33,717	23,946

[1]Preliminary. [2]Estimate. [3]Formerly part of the U.S.S.R.; data not reported separately until 1990.
Source: Food and Agriculture Organization of the United Nations

U.S. Annual Average Prices of Molasses, by Types (F.O.B. Tank Car or Truck) — In Dollars Per Short Tons[2]

Year	New Orleans	South Florida	Baltimore	Upper Mississippi[3]	Savannah[4]	California Ports	Colorado	Montana/Wyoming & Neb.	Red River Valley[5]
	Blackstrap							**Beet Molasses**	
1978	51.50	52.40	59.25	67.30	72.55	54.00	60.40	58.35	60.95
1979	82.95	85.50	91.20	107.90	107.75	84.05	85.30	82.65	NA
1980	96.50	96.80	106.75	124.45	128.85	101.70	95.60	96.55	NA
1981	84.90	90.00	99.30	111.20	119.40	89.20	85.30	95.20	NA
1982	48.00	56.55	64.15	70.85	81.90	60.50	69.40	63.70	44.50
1983	56.50	63.10	73.05	76.90	91.90	70.40	79.45	65.95	60.55
1984	61.50	71.00	77.65	81.00	94.45	71.95	82.50	79.15	70.65
1985	50.28	59.79	64.66	72.83	85.00	61.89	NA	67.50	57.33
1986	69.61	78.10	83.05	92.03	NA	73.26	80.33	73.75	68.44
1987	53.23	61.96	72.83	80.05	NA	67.17	60.31	54.69	62.22
1988	64.89	74.54	82.93	90.07	NA	74.61	72.95	69.94	55.71
1989	55.63	65.31	75.15	81.12	NA	70.36	79.94	74.50	55.00
1990	61.70	68.37	80.59	88.48	76.13	74.50	82.83	75.00	58.33
1991	67.02	74.58	89.15	94.78	82.52	80.00	85.00	71.92	66.16
1992	61.27	68.36	80.41	92.95	76.70	78.43	DISC	67.81	57.50
1993[1]	55.48	62.36	76.03	89.26	70.00	74.24	DISC	72.63	64.44

[1]Preliminary. [2]To convert dollars per short ton to cents per gallon divide by 171. [3]Prior to 1989, prices are for Minneapolis. [4]Prior to 1989, prices are for Omaha. DISC = Discontinued. NA = Not available. *Source: Agricultural Marketing Service, U.S. Department of Agriculture*

MOLASSES

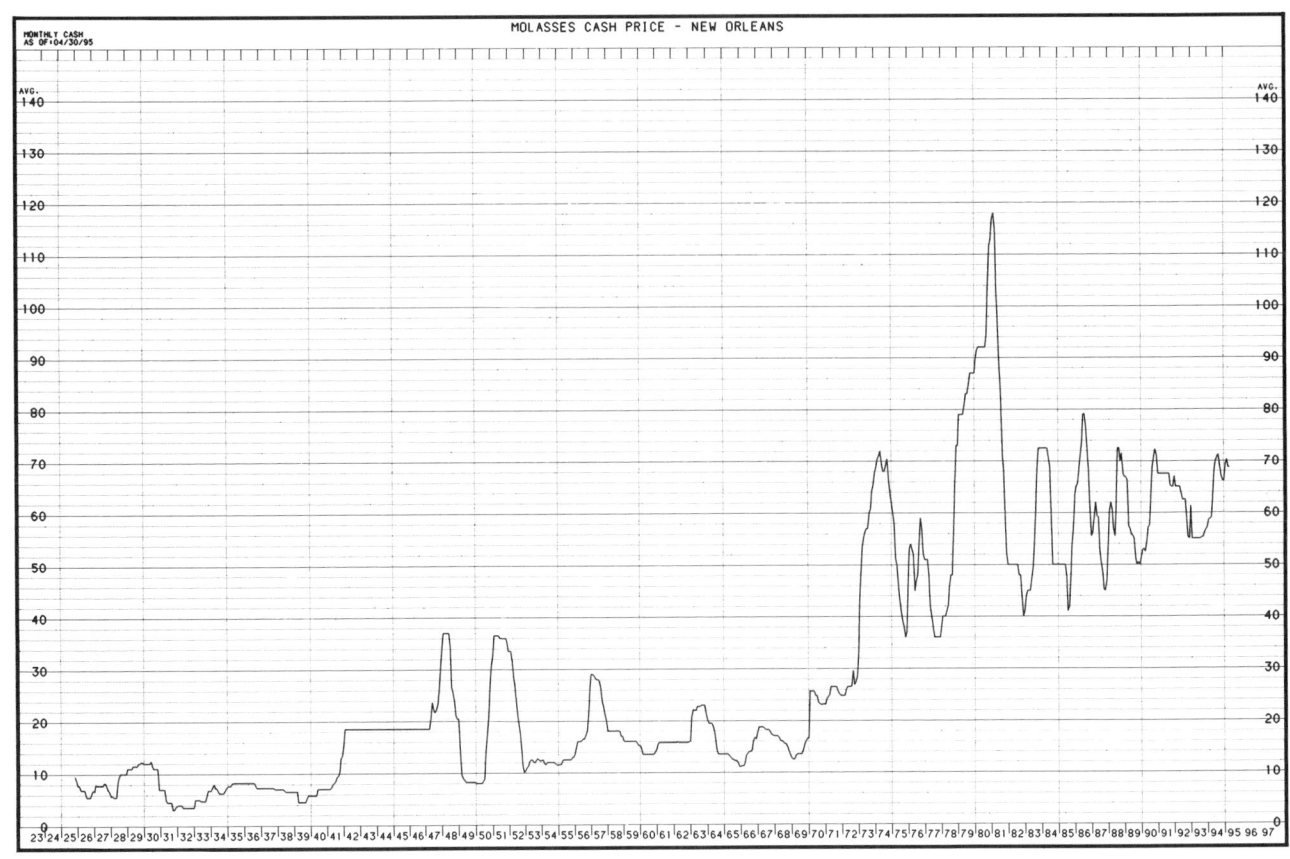

MOLASSES CASH PRICE - NEW ORLEANS

Salient Statistics of Molasses³ in the United States   In Metric Tons

| | | Production | | | | Inedible Imports From | | | | | Pro-duction of Edible |
| | | Mainland | | | In Ship-ments | | | | | | Molasses |
Year	Hawaii	Mainland Mills⁴	Refiners Black-strap	Beet	Puerto Rico	From Hawaii	Total Imports	Brazil	Dominican Republic	Mexico	Mainland Exports⁵	Total U.S. Supply	(1,000 Gallons)
1985	NA	697,007	184,237	907,535	NA	235,987	1,643,535	203,080	99,113	161,142	196,134	3,395,601	1,650
1986	268,305	731,056	136,184	879,019	31,354	273,683	123,055	309,340	136,687	97,436	329,936	3,058,167	1,700
1987	260,930	726,854	110,784	1,137,014	35,385	152,087	962,151	95,004	123,619	183,525	366,957	2,721,954	1,630
1988	252,516	775,936	101,257	1,006,353	40,694	178,476	969,870	142,897	102,792	93,605	299,217	2,749,692	1,925
1989	218,009	808,355	122,786	974,179	34,864	169,270	926,870	107,109	147,235	75,634	293,535	2,707,925	1,990
1990	228,968	741,749	105,124	948,820	24,959	214,045	1,078,924	70,986	145,543	88,401	212,263	2,876,399	1,405
1991	188,252	807,652	126,000	1,165,962	27,882	184,337	1,258,637	10,342	137,271	235,244	242,635	3,299,953	1,825
1992¹	201,553	967,400	126,000	950,312	25,097	201,690	1,115,863	0	127,500	117,722	282,098	3,079,167	1,460
1993²	187,915	1,034,384	120,000	692,465	25,097	176,603	1,040,876	0	163,180	47,596	255,907	2,808,424	

¹Preliminary.   ²Estimate.   ³Feed and industrial molasses.   ⁴Includes high-test molasses from frozen cane.   ⁵Excluding exports from Hawaii and Puerto Rico.   NA = Not available.   *Source: Agricultural Marketing Service, U.S. Department of Agriculture*

Wholesale Price of Blackstrap Molasses (Cane) at New Orleans   In Dollars Per Short Ton

Year	Jan	Feb	Mar	Apr	May	June	July	Aug	Sept	Oct	Nov	Dec	Average
1985	50.00	50.00	50.00	50.00	50.00	47.75	41.00	41.90	48.00	53.75	57.50	63.50	50.28
1986	65.00	65.60	68.50	71.00	73.75	79.00	79.13	76.60	72.30	68.10	60.25	55.50	69.56
1987	56.25	59.40	62.00	59.40	59.10	53.00	50.60	48.60	45.30	45.00	47.00	53.10	53.23
1988	60.30	62.00	60.60	56.90	55.50	62.50	72.50	72.50	70.00	71.50	67.50	66.90	64.89
1989	66.90	66.25	57.50	56.90	55.75	55.60	55.00	51.25	50.00	50.50	50.00	51.25	55.58
1990	52.75	53.13	52.50	54.25	57.19	57.50	62.75	68.75	70.63	72.25	71.25	67.50	61.70
1991	67.50	67.50	67.50	67.50	67.50	67.50	67.50	67.50	65.25	65.00	65.00	65.00	67.02
1992	65.00	65.00	65.00	65.00	63.75	62.50	62.50	62.50	58.75	55.31	55.00	55.00	61.27
1993	55.00	55.00	55.00	55.00	55.00	55.00	55.00	55.25	55.31	56.25	56.75	57.19	55.48
1994¹	57.75	57.50	59.40	62.50	68.00	70.00	70.40	71.30	69.50	67.50	66.25	66.25	65.53

¹Preliminary.   *Source: Agricultural Marketing Service, U.S. Department of Agriculture*

Molybdenum

Molybdenum is a high-melting, silver-gray metal which is strong at high temperatures, hard and resistant to corrosion. It finds use in alloy steels, stainless steel and armor plating. It is added to iron-, cobalt- and nickel-based alloys for heat and corrosion-resistant applications finding use in electronic circuitry and filaments for light bulbs.

U.S. production of molybdenum concentrate for the first six months of 1994 was 21,438 tonnes (molybdenum content). For all of 1993, production was 36,803 tonnes. Domestic shipments during the first half of 1994 totaled 10,204 tonnes, compared with 22,361 tonnes for 1993 as a whole. Exports for January-June were 6,211 tonnes. For all of 1993, they were 16,304 tonnes.

Gross production of molybdenum products for the first six months of 1994 totaled 13,013 tonnes, compared with 22,703 tonnes for all of 1993. Shipments of molybdenum products for January-June 1994 were 11,882 tonnes. For all of 1993, shipments were 15,981 tonnes.

By end use, U.S. reported consumption of molybdenum materials in June 1994 included full alloy steel at 3,068 tonnes, stainless and heat-resisting steel at 2,108 tonnes, mill products made from metal powder at 1,642 tonnes,

tool steel at 977 tonnes, and superalloys at 443 tonnes. Stocks of molybdenum materials on June 30, 1994 were 19,609 tonnes.

The U.S. engages in active and widespread trade in molybdenum ore and concentrate. For 1994, the leading export destinations were Belgium, the Netherlands, Japan, the United Kingdom and Chile. U.S. exports of ferromolybdenum during the January-May 1994 period totaled 1,070 tonnes. For all of 1993, exports totaled 2,236 tonnes. The major destinations were Mexico, Canada and Taiwan.

On a gross weight basis, U.S. imports of roasted ore and concentrates during the January-May 1994 period totaled 17.4 million kilograms, while imports of ferromolybdenum reached 19.3 million kilograms. Total imports of molybdenum products were 55.7 million kilograms. For 1993 as a whole, imports were almost 118.6 million kilograms.

World mine production of molybdenum in 1993 was estimated by the U.S. Bureau of Mines at 95,286 tonnes. The U.S. was the leading producer with 36,803 tonnes, followed by China at 16,000 tonnes, Chile with 15,400 tonnes and Canada with 10,098 tonnes.

World Mine Production of Molybdenum   In Metric Tons (Contained Molybdenum)

Year	Bulgaria	Canada[3]	Chile	China	Iran	Kazak hstan[4]	Mexico	Mongolia	Peru	Russia[4]	United States	Uzbek isten[4]	World Total
1983	420	22,474	33,651	4,400	------	------	13,932	2,120	5,825	24,500	33,593	------	140,616
1984	420	25,479	37,172	4,400	1,100	------	8,938	2,200	6,557	24,700	103,664	------	214,275
1985[5]	420	17,311	40,541	4,400	1,100	------	8,292	2,200	8,393	24,900	108,409	------	216,959
1986	190	11,251	16,581	2,000	900	------	3,350	1,100	3,484	11,400	42,627	------	93,218
1987	200	14,771	16,941	12,000	500	------	4,400	1,400	3,353	11,500	34,063	------	89,871
1988	200	13,535	15,515	14,400	700	------	4,456	1,400	2,444	17,000	43,051	------	112,860
1989	190	14,073	16,550	15,700	785	------	4,189	1,580	3,177	17,000	63,105	------	136,494
1990	150	11,994	13,830	15,700	542	------	2,000	1,578	2,510	17,000	61,611	------	127,028
1991	120	11,329	14,434	13,200	395	------	1,716	1,716	3,031	16,000	53,364	------	115,459
1992	120	9,405	14,840	16,000	1,320	3,000	1,458	1,522	3,220	5,000	49,725	1,000	107,610
1993[1]	120	10,098	15,400	16,000	1,500	3,000	1,705	1,500	2,860	4,800	36,803	1,000	95,286
1994[2]	500	11,000	15,000	16,000	1,500	3,000	1,700	1,500	140	4,800	40,000	1,000	110,000

[1]Preliminary. [2]Estimate. [3]Shipments. [4]Formerly part of the U.S.S.R.; data not reported separately until 1992. [5]Data reported in thousands of pounds prior to 1986. *Source: U.S. Bureau of Mines*

U.S. Salient Statistics of Molybdenum   In Metric Tons (Contained Molybdenum)

Year	Concentrate — Pro- duction	Total (Includes Exports)	Value Mil. $	For Exports	Con- sumption	Imports for Con- sumption	Stocks, Dec. 31[3]	Primary Products[4] — Net Production — Grand Total	Molybdic Oxide[5]	Molyb- denum Metal Powder	Price Avg. Value $ Kl.[6]	Shipments — To Domestic Dest- inations	Oxide for Exports (Gross Weight)	Con- sumption	Producer Stocks, Dec. 31
1983	33,593	48,805	166.6	18,979	27,014	1,673	11,637	18,288	11,148	3,667	3.64	50,562	19,877	27,225	28,352
1984	103,664	102,405	326.8	41,687	54,843	28	12,450	53,353	40,186	4,302	3.56	65,527	24,553	34,792	22,155
1985	108,409	111,936	347.8	38,646	W	112	9,322	61,901	48,750	3,734	3.33	73,861	36,268	33,451	21,014
1986[7]	93,976	95,006	240.5	18,267	53,061	1,120	8,715	17,953	6,147	4,256	2.92	57,855	21,325	31,898	20,699
1987	34,073	31,692	179.3	18,377	16,983	2,954	6,841	11,257	7,076	4,181	7.28	18,447	5,567	14,800	10,055
1988	43,051	45,240	266.9	23,500	35,690	514	4,777	29,782	25,404	4,378	7.61	20,535	W	17,422	7,116
1989	63,105	61,733	421.4	51,232	41,877	238	6,969	16,545	16,545	W	8.05	18,277	1,391	17,204	6,675
1990	61,611	61,580	346.3	41,380	35,455	478	7,672	15,727	15,727	W	7.39	17,983	787	18,060	5,919
1991	53,364	53,607	249.9	22,424	32,998	161	5,291	20,782	18,739	2,043	5.27	19,105	1,571	16,901	9,422
1992	49,725	45,098	189.9	33,439	15,243	831	11,905	13,880	11,916	1,964	4.85	17,305	557	17,168	7,480
1993[1]	36,803	39,209	165.1	28,280	13,794	3,398	10,762	11,989	10,697	1,292	5.13	15,981	1,042	17,715	6,149
1994[2]	40,000										7.70			18,000	

[1]Preliminary. [2]Estimate. [3]At mines & at plants making molybdenum products. [4]Comprises ferromolybdenum, molybdic oxide, & molybdenum salts & metal. [5]Includes molybdic oxide briquests, molydic acid, molybdenum trioxide, all other. [6]U.S. producer price per kilogram of molybdenum contained in technical-grade molybdic acid, molybdenum trioxide, all other. [6]U.S. producer price per kilogram of molybdenum contained in technical-grade molybdic oxide. [7]Data reported in thousands of pounds and dollars per pound prior to 1987. W = Withheld proprietary data. *Source: U.S. Bureau of Mines*

Nickel

Most commercial nickel is used in stainless steel and other corrosion-resistant alloys. Approximately one-fifth of the nickel produced in the U.S. is used in plating to give hard, tarnish-resistant, polishable surfaces. Plating techniques, like electroless coating or single-slurry coating, are employed for such applications as helicopter rotors, turbine blades, extrusion dies and rolled steel strip. Nickel finds use in coins to replace silver and has been utilized in ceramics, rechargeable batteries and electronic circuitry. Nickel-base alloys are consumed in wire, bars, sheets and tubular forms fabricated into finished products.

According to the U.S. Bureau of Mines, U.S. consumption of nickel over the first six-months of 1994 totaled 45,463 tonnes (nickel content). For the same period of 1993, nickel consumption was 45,798 tonnes. By form and use, stainless and heat-resistant steel accounted for 27 percent of use, electroplating took 15 percent while other nickel and nickel alloys used 23 percent. Consumption of secondary nickel, which is composed of ferrous and nonferrous scrap totaled 18,534 tonnes over the first half of 1994.

Ending stocks of nickel for June 1994 were 6,029 tonnes. Almost 40 percent of the stocks were held as steel (stainless, heat resisting and alloy), while the remainder were held as nonferrous alloys and chemicals. Ending stocks of secondary nickel for June 1994 were 442 tonnes.

U.S. imports of nickel for consumption over the first five-months of 1994 were 59,738 tonnes, compared to 53,222 tonnes over the same period of 1993. U.S. imports of cathodes, pellets and briquets over January-May 1994 were 43,601 tonnes, while ferronickel was 5,668 tonnes and powder and flakes 4,363 tonnes. Among the major suppliers were Canada which shipped nearly one-half of the U.S. import requirement. Other major suppliers included Norway, Australia, the Dominican Republic and Russia. U.S. imports of nickel alloys for the first five-months of 1994 were 2,998 tonnes. Most of the imports were in the form of unwrought alloyed ingot. The major suppliers of nickel alloy included Germany, Canada, Sweden and France.

U.S. exports of nickel for the first five-months of 1994 were 15,626 tonnes, up 19 percent from the comparable period of 1993. Over one-half of the exports were in the form of stainless steel scrap. Other significant forms of exports were waste and scrap and nickel oxide. Exports of nickel alloys during January-May 1994 were 6,995 tonnes, 12 percent higher than the same period in 1993.

Russia's nickel exports over the first seven-months of 1994 was reported to be up sharply. Russia's demand for nickel has been dropping since 1993 with reduced output of stainless steel. A similar situation is occurring in China where domestic nickel consumption is declining which should in turn increase exports in 1994.

World Mine Production of Nickel In Metric Tons (Contained Nickel)

Year	Aus-tralia[3]	Bots-wana	Brazil	Canada	China	Dominican Republic	Finland[3]	Greece	Indo-nesia	New Caledonia	Philip-pines	Russia[4]	South Africa	United States	Zim-babwe	World Total
1985	85,759	26,301	16,473	169,974	25,000	25,394	8,547	22,045	40,337	72,395	28,159	185,000	25,039	5,558	11,116	812,622
1986	76,740	25,583	21,103	163,642	25,000	21,878	11,886	14,424	53,680	61,780	12,791	259,000	31,026	1,066	3,720	852,151
1987	74,554	25,900	22,092	189,086	25,000	32,521	10,557	9,202	57,764	56,850	7,819	270,000	34,300	------	6,300	890,539
1988	62,358	26,000	18,677	216,589	32,700	29,345	11,699	13,131	57,982	71,200	10,349	280,000	30,000	------	12,600	952,215
1989	67,041	23,700	18,826	200,899	34,250	31,264	10,480	16,097	62,987	96,200	15,380	280,000	28,900	------	12,721	984,078
1990	67,000	23,200	18,788	196,225	33,000	28,700	11,524	15,727	68,308	85,100	15,818	280,000	29,000	330	12,654	965,326
1991	69,000	23,500	20,456	192,259	31,000	29,062	9,900	16,005	71,681	114,492	13,658	245,000	27,700	5,523	12,371	948,796
1992	64,000	23,500	21,000	192,086	37,000	25,000	9,171	15,400	78,100	113,100	15,400	215,000	28,400	6,671	12,200	921,929
1993[1]	64,717	23,000	22,700	188,378	29,100	23,863	8,287	12,940	65,757	98,100	10,200	243,000	28,900	2,464	12,769	900,000
1994[2]	75,000	24,000	21,000	150,000	30,000	24,000	8,100	12,800	78,000	100,000	12,000	215,000	32,000	------	13,000	850,000

[1] Preliminary. [2] Estimate. [3] Content of nickel and sulfate and concentrates. *Source: U.S. Bureau of Mines*

Salient Statistics of Nickel in the United States In Metric Tons (Contained Nickel)

Year	Net Import Reliance as a % of Apparent Con-sumption	Production Plant[4]	Secon-dary[5]	Alloy Steels	Cast Irons	Copper Base Alloys	Electro-plating Anodes	Nickel Alloys	Stainless & Heat Re-sisting Steels	Super Alloys	Chem-icals	Apparent Con-sumption	At Con-sumers' Plants	At Pro-ducer Plants	Primary & Secondary Nickel Exports	Imports	Avg. Price LME[6] $ Lb.
1985	71	33,006	32,332	8,712	2,820	13,488	22,560	22,927	61,668	12,351	1,863	198,818	23,050	15,785	31,974	143,056	2.26
1986	73	1,498	41,039	7,458	2,370	9,609	19,050	18,086	54,580	11,563	1,692	164,483	19,256	9,344	19,586	117,114	1.76
1987	79	------	32,331	8,139	1,591	10,169	20,548	17,377	71,797	16,605	1,765	183,397	13,474	6,191	20,951	134,511	2.19
1988	74	------	49,371	7,330	2,359	6,890	19,520	19,046	80,107	13,537	1,816	159,156	15,081	6,967	27,916	127,680	6.25
1989	71	347	42,565	6,094	2,318	9,928	21,604	18,757	68,866	10,956	1,164	147,059	15,403	6,326	31,460	137,017	6.04
1990	64	3,701	46,079	7,007	2,646	7,594	15,550	16,315	96,120	15,713	1,500	170,042	12,576	8,065	37,057	145,179	4.02
1991	61	7,065	40,304	5,536	1,185	6,938	15,474	16,882	84,292	13,787	1,363	156,663	14,291	11,794	36,902	138,659	3.70
1992	59	8,962	51,139	4,988	1,202	6,313	16,538	15,946	83,460	10,872	51	159,373	15,913	10,140	33,867	128,266	3.18
1993[2]	63	4,878		3,450	W	84	14,693	15,409	30,155	10,559	W	130,233	15,534	15,534	33,199	133,065	2.40
1994[3]	66		5,048	W	W	13,567	19,013	32,408	11,476			126,171	13,000	13,000	37,070	135,960	2.88

[1] Exclusive of scrap. [2] Preliminary. [3] Estimate. [4] Smelter & refinery. [5] From purchased scrap (ferrous & nonferrous). [6] London Metal Exchange
W = Withheld proprietary data. *Source: U.S. Bureau of Mines*

Oats

Within the U.S. feed grain complex, oats production is the smallest. The 1994/95 crop (June to May) totaled 230 million bushels obtained from a harvested acreage of 4.0 million acres and average yield of about 57.2 bushels per acre. The totals were somewhat lower than the USDA's initial forecasts for the 1994/95 crop and compare with a record low crop of 206 million bushels in 1993/94. Despite the rebound, the production trend is distinctly lower. Harvested acreage averaged over six million acres as recently as the late 1980s and crops in excess of 350 million bushels were typical. For the 1994/95 crop almost all of the increase in harvested acreage was in Iowa and North Dakota. The larger crop is expected to cut import demand by at least 25 million bushels from the record large 107 million imported during 1993/94.

Oats 1994/95 carry-in stocks of 106 million bushels were down seven million from a year earlier and the lowest since 1989/90 when carry-in was 98 million bushels. Despite low total supply during 1993/94, average farm prices did not increase to the same extent as corn and sorghum prices owing to large imports and extremely low quality of the 1993 oats crop. The total supply for the 1994/95 season of 415 million bushels will trail 1993/94 by about 11 million bushels, but feed and residual usage is expected to fall to a record low 175 million bushels, vs. 193 million in 1993/94 and 234 million in 1992/93. Estimated total disappearance of only 301 million bushels will allow carry-in stocks to increase to 114 million bushels as of June 1, 1995, up 8 million from a year earlier.

Government-owned oats stocks are an insignificant part of total carryover. U.S. oats exports are minimal, averaging less than 4 million bushels per year since 1992/93, but that represented a hefty percentage gain from less than one million per season in the 1980s.

Lower corn prices in 1994/95 are expected to generally dampen support for oats farm prices. Prices received by farmers were forecast to average between $1.20 and $1.30 per bushel, vs. $1.36 during 1993/94. Initial forecasts of average farm prices during 1993/94 ranged from $1.25 to as high as $1.65 per bushel, but large imports subsequently depressed prices.

World trade in oats in 1994/95 was forecast at 1.5 million tonnes, compared with 2.4 million in 1993/94. Canada is the single largest exporter with almost half the world total, most of which goes to the U.S., the world's largest importer.

U.S. Farm Program

The national average loan rate for 1994/95 oats was 97¢ per bushel and the target price was $1.45 per bushel vs. $.88 and $1.45, respectively, in 1993/94.

Futures Markets

Oat futures and options are traded on the Chicago Board of Trade. A smaller futures contract is traded on the Mid-America Commodity Exchange.

World Production of Oats In Thousands of Metric Tons

Crop Year	Argentina	Australia	Canada	China	Denmark	France	Germany	Italy	Poland	Spain	Sweden	Turkey	United Kingdom	United States	Former U.S.S.R.	World Total
1979-0	522	1,411	2,978	1,600	163	1,845	3,697	432	2,186	456	1,524	370	542	7,643	15,200	45,165
1980-1	433	1,128	3,028	1,800	160	1,927	3,249	450	2,245	680	1,567	355	601	6,652	15,544	44,543
1981-2	339	1,617	3,188	1,700	176	1,774	3,200	422	2,731	445	1,816	325	620	7,391	15,000	45,343
1982-3	637	848	3,637	1,660	178	1,802	3,777	359	2,608	443	1,663	330	575	8,602	15,500	47,866
1983-4	593	2,296	2,773	1,650	86	1,374	2,489	307	2,377	464	1,268	310	465	6,923	17,000	45,115
1984-5	610	1,367	2,670	780	150	1,892	2,973	433	2,604	780	1,904	300	516	6,875	19,200	48,391
1985-6	400	1,339	2,997	664	152	1,803	3,278	363	2,682	719	1,668	314	615	7,559	20,500	50,062
1986-7	400	1,584	3,251	599	111	1,007	2,687	397	2,486	433	1,486	300	505	5,608	21,929	47,471
1987-8	650	1,738	2,995	642	94	1,045	2,406	361	2,428	502	1,440	310	450	5,424	18,495	43,270
1988-9	451	1,867	2,993	670	202	984	2,941	383	2,222	537	1,330	300	545	3,158	15,287	37,506
1989-0	620	1,640	3,546	622	125	970	2,010	296	2,186	494	1,455	270	530	5,423	14,972	39,554
1990-1	434	1,530	2,692	685	121	830	2,104	298	2,119	512	1,584	270	550	5,189	15,081	39,042
1991-2	400	1,669	1,794	650	125	740	1,867	359	1,873	410	1,426	280	545	3,534	12,342	32,763
92-3[1]	450	1,500	2,400	640	125	700	1,750	325	1,800	400	1,405	280	545	3,992	14,309	33,879
93-4[2]	440	1,650	3,550	640		700	1,700	360	1,500		1,300	280	500	3,000	14,620	35,320
94-5[3]	450	670	3,700	600		670	1,650	360	1,200		1,060	300	490	3,340	13,780	33,250

[1] Preliminary. [2] Estimate. [3] Forecast. *Source: Foreign Agricultural Service, U.S. Department of Agriculture*

United States Official Oat Crop Production Reports In Thousands of Bushels

Year	July 1	Aug. 1	Sept. 1	Oct. 1	Dec.	Final	Year	July 1	Aug. 1	Sept. 1	Oct. 1	Dec.	Final
1983	519,002	504,201	472,541	------	477,303	476,961	1989	387,593	380,690	380,690	370,693	------	373,587
1984	454,747	455,190	472,460	------	471,921	473,661	1990	374,457	365,337	365,337	358,288	------	357,524
1985	498,953	519,028	537,443	------	518,626	520,800	1991	280,016	259,666	259,666	242,526	------	243,451
1986	------	443,183	413,025	------	383,553	386,356	1992	256,381	276,381	------	------	------	294,229
1987	------	392,843	------	------	------	373,713	1993	262,860	249,830	249,830	208,138	------	206,770
1988	------	206,330	206,330	210,766	------	217,600	1994	248,151	247,753	247,753	229,717	------	229,857

Source: National Agricultural Statistics Service, U.S. Department of Agriculture

OATS

Oats Stocks in the United States as of June 1   In Thousands of Bushels

	On Farms				Off Farms				Total Stocks			
Year	Mar. 1	June 1	Sept. 1	Dec. 1	Mar. 1	June 1	Sept. 1	Dec. 1	Mar. 1	June 1	Sept. 1	Dec. 1
1990	140,000	82,850	234,700	194,700	74,749	74,062	117,009	99,398	214,749	156,912	351,709	294,098
1991	138,600	92,400	173,600	148,100	90,659	78,831	110,487	96,508	229,259	171,231	284,087	244,608
1992	98,150	61,000	199,900	161,200	76,735	66,721	94,717	81,292	174,885	127,721	294,617	242,492
1993	110,250	66,130	161,000	124,200	64,875	47,063	58,004	69,517	175,125	113,193	219,004	193,717
1994[1]	85,050	53,940	144,300	113,400	61,502	51,583	75,551	78,551	146,552	105,523	219,851	191,951

[1] Preliminary   Source: National Agricultural Statistics Service, U.S. Department of Agriculture

Oats Supply and Utilization in the United States

Crop Year Beginning June 1	Acreage Planted	Harvested	Yield Per Acre	Pro-duction	Imports	Total Supply	Feed & Residual	Food, Alcohol & Industrial	Seed	Exports	Total Use	Ending Stocks	Farm Price	Findley Loan Rate	Target Price
	— 1,000 Acres —		(Bushels)	In Millions of Bushels									In Dollars Per Bushel		
1980-1	13,381	8,657	53.0	458.8	1.1	696.3	436.5	41.0	33.0	8.8	519.3	177.0	1.72	1.16	0
1981-2	13,632	9,407	54.2	509.5	1.5	688.0	458.0	41.2	34.2	2.7	536.1	151.9	1.88	1.24	0
1982-3	13,951	10,258	57.8	592.6	3.5	748.0	442.4	41.7	43.3	.8	528.2	219.8	1.49	1.31	1.50
1983-4	20,289	9,062	52.6	476.5	29.9	726.2	474.0	40.9	29.5	.9	545.3	180.9	1.62	1.36	1.60
1984-5	12,414	8,163	58.0	473.7	33.6	688.2	435.6	41.0	31.2	.5	508.3	179.9	1.67	1.31	1.60
1985-6	13,235	8,147	63.6	518.5	27.2	725.6	464.2	44.0	32.5	1.2	541.9	183.7	1.23	1.31	1.60
1986-7	14,671	6,840	56.3	385.0	32.4	601.0	384.4	45.0	38.0	.9	468.3	132.7	1.21	.99	1.60
1987-8	17,907	6,888	54.3	373.7	45.7	552.1	358.2	49.8	31.6	.5	440.1	112.0	1.56	.94	1.60
1988-9	13,910	5,533	39.3	217.6	62.9	392.5	193.8	72.7	27.1	.6	294.2	98.3	2.61	.90	1.55
1989-0	12,085	6,882	54.3	373.6	66.4	539.3	265.6	91.6	23.4	.8	381.4	156.9	1.49	.85	1.50
1990-1	10,423	5,945	60.1	357.5	63.4	577.8	286.0	100.9	19.1	.6	406.6	171.2	1.14	.81	1.45
1991-2	8,654	4,806	50.7	243.5	74.8	489.4	234.8	107.2	17.8	1.9	361.7	127.7	1.21	.83	1.45
1992-3	7,961	4,492	65.6	294.8	55.0	477.5	233.6	107.2	17.8	5.7	364.3	113.2	1.32	.88	1.45
1993-4[1]	7,944	3,798	54.4	206.4	106.8	426.4	192.9	109.8	15.2	3.0	320.9	105.5	1.36	.88	1.45

[1] Preliminary.   [2] Forecasted.   Source: Economic Research Service, U.S. Department of Agriculture

Production of Oats in the United States by State   In Thousands of Bushels

Year	California	Illinois	Indiana	Iowa	Michigan	Minne-sota	Missouri	Nebraska	New York	North Dakota	Ohio	Oregon	Penn-sylvania	South Dakota	Texas	Wis-consin
1981	3,600	13,530	5,525	59,520	21,080	90,090	4,590	15,800	17,920	44,160	17,010	4,550	20,010	70,520	18,860	52,606
1982	3,350	11,800	6,720	54,150	28,350	97,920	3,276	26,680	18,200	55,650	23,460	6,375	19,765	123,540	10,730	49,290
1983	2,925	12,600	4,560	38,250	15,600	76,950	2,538	13,640	11,400	63,630	15,360	6,000	16,200	79,200	24,000	45,050
1984	3,450	11,385	4,960	47,360	21,700	78,000	1,584	15,680	10,620	49,980	13,860	6,600	15,960	86,800	8,750	53,320
1985	3,015	12,480	7,590	57,760	26,130	77,000	5,775	25,620	17,710	44,520	26,350	9,200	21,000	79,520	15,000	51,480
1986	3,150	14,400	6,390	39,060	17,010	43,350	5,000	21,240	12,920	38,500	12,160	7,600	16,120	46,200	8,400	52,700
1987	2,800	13,110	6,365	35,750	17,100	45,600	3,420	17,640	12,000	36,400	17,500	5,200	14,820	52,900	9,900	43,200
1988	2,730	9,180	3,000	25,000	6,000	24,750	1,520	12,160	7,540	7,200	9,000	6,500	13,000	20,000	9,000	46,860
1989	3,375	16,000	6,840	54,000	20,100	46,750	3,600	8,640	9,145	20,150	15,750	6,860	13,770	44,000	6,600	46,860
1990	3,375	11,560	4,830	40,800	13,050	48,180	2,226	13,440	8,235	16,100	2,280	4,590	15,840	53,200	9,225	47,570
1991	3,375	6,600	2,565	21,250	5,400	22,800	1,632	11,880	5,000	10,200	1,292	4,725	8,400	38,500	7,200	26,500
1992	2,800	7,930	2,800	25,125	8,400	35,000	2,430	15,400	7,700	37,400	12,070	4,230	13,735	42,900	5,720	34,410
1993	2,400	4,590	2,240	9,000	7,150	23,750	686	6,880	6,510	37,100	9,000	3,000	10,000	26,520	7,420	24,150
1994[1]	2,800	5,490	1,855	26,660	6,270	24,750	1,768	7,500	7,040	33,550	6,720	4,500	8,480	31,360	5,200	25,380

[1] Preliminary.   [2] Forecasted.   Source: Economic Research Service, U.S. Department of Agriculture

Volume of Trading in Oats Futures at the Chicago Board of Trade   In Millions of Bushels

Year	July	Aug	Sept	Oct	Nov	Dec	Jan	Feb	Mar	Apr	May	June	Total
1987-8	103.7	153.6	109.4	135.4	139.4	116.6	92.1	121.2	146.6	162.1	162.6	267.1	1,709.8
1988-9	160.3	121.1	107.6	108.1	183.0	141.1	168.5	136.6	150.7	188.7	138.7	195.2	1,799.6
1989-90	148.7	174.9	104.2	86.7	191.9	64.5	123.3	158.7	169.4	225.7	270.0	231.8	1,949.8
1990-1	160.2	248.0	126.0	139.0	236.9	77.8	100.2	151.4	151.6	213.6	102.9	224.7	1,932.3
1991-2	185.5	205.3	89.3	101.5	172.8	76.0	155.1	420.1	211.3	235.3	210.1	272.7	2,335.0
1992-3	111.0	200.8	125.5	82.9	176.1	97.0	102.4	132.5	130.3	315.7	167.1	215.6	1,856.9
1993-4	166.5	160.4	134.4	203.9	361.6	186.3	239.9	285.3	199.0	269.1	171.5	348.8	2,726.7
1994-5	103.8	196.7	144.2	124.5	284.7	98.4	67.6						

Source: Chicago Board of Trade

Average Open Interest of Oats at the Chicago Board of Trade   In Thousands of Bushels

Year	Jan	Feb	Mar	Apr	May	Jun	July	Aug	Sept	Oct	Nov	Dec
1987	31,648	36,004	33,508	30,655	26,271	24,536	28,090	36,166	35,212	35,173	28,988	29,724
1988	35,008	42,084	39,209	43,132	43,594	48,130	40,230	35,936	34,095	35,978	45,844	46,842
1989	50,341	51,226	50,761	50,283	47,606	48,831	48,967	47,272	48,824	55,834	59,311	56,240
1990	56,134	59,043	56,777	61,213	62,563	54,455	53,714	60,559	64,824	74,022	75,574	58,791
1991	59,450	64,161	69,476	78,100	71,117	65,457	55,584	54,469	51,842	57,798	56,284	46,776
1992	47,776	77,496	76,797	75,261	76,646	73,863	63,793	55,501	49,345	45,889	43,906	36,433
1993	36,990	38,696	38,274	57,897	66,783	60,098	54,472	56,906	55,855	70,578	100,285	102,734
1994	105,964	100,687	100,971	99,412	91,561	72,873	58,550	69,616	73,715	81,330	76,768	66,882

Source: Chicago Board of Trade

OATS

Average Cash Price of No. 2 Heavy White Oats at Minneapolis   In Dollars Per Bushel

Year	June	July	Aug	Sept	Oct	Nov	Dec	Jan	Feb	Mar	Apr	May	Average	No. 2 — Heavy, White — Portland	Toledo
1978-9	1.36	1.24	1.28	1.36	1.39	1.47	1.40	1.47	1.54	1.60	1.48	1.55	1.43	1.79	1.37
1979-0	1.68	1.60	1.47	1.55	1.65	1.67	1.59	1.52	1.50	1.48	1.52	1.62	1.57	1.87	1.60
1980-1	1.67	1.80	1.70	1.86	1.96	2.15	2.16	2.20	2.25	2.23	2.21	2.23	2.04	2.42	2.17
1981-2	2.18	2.02	1.99	2.02	2.09	2.28	2.10	2.23	2.26	2.16	2.21	2.16	2.14	2.36	2.23
1982-3	2.12	1.87	1.53	1.51	1.51	1.67	1.67	1.67	1.63	1.63	1.73	1.71	1.69	2.18	1.55
1983-4	1.67	1.60	1.79	1.94	2.00	1.97	1.94	1.98	1.82	1.88	1.89	1.96	1.87	1.95	2.01
1984-5	1.92	1.84	1.77	1.79	1.84	1.92	1.87	1.81	1.82	1.79	1.73	1.65	1.81	2.12	1.92
1985-6	1.59	1.44	1.23	1.24	1.19	1.32	1.39	1.37	1.30	1.27	1.16	1.22	1.31	1.60	1.08
1986-7	1.18	1.05	1.12	1.29	1.39	1.72	1.66	1.64	1.56	1.46	1.59	1.83	1.46	1.53	1.20
1987-8	1.64	1.61	1.77	1.85	1.97	2.05	2.02	2.10	2.06	1.93	1.94	2.12	1.92	1.76	1.68
1988-9	3.26	3.25	3.09	3.07	2.99	2.71	2.74	2.87	2.59	2.49	2.30	2.22	2.80	2.24	2.26
1989-0	1.97	1.72	1.59	1.58	1.61	1.68	1.70	1.56	1.48	1.57	1.63	1.68	1.65	1.63	1.40
1990-1	1.52	1.37	1.25	1.23	1.29	1.30	1.24	1.22	1.18	1.27	1.32	1.36	1.30	1.58	1.17
1991-2	1.25	1.33	1.38	1.35	1.41	1.42	1.49	1.50	1.68	1.66	1.57	1.59	1.47	1.60	1.37
1992-3	1.55	1.49	1.45	1.58	1.52	1.59	1.63	1.66	1.63	1.63	1.66	1.57	1.58	1.73	1.51
1993-4	1.54	1.63	1.63	1.66	1.56	1.51	1.56	1.57	1.52	1.55	1.46	1.37	1.55		1.40
1994-5[1]	1.47	1.36	1.44	1.44	1.44	1.41									

[1]Preliminary.   Source: Economic Research Service, U.S. Department of Agriculture

Average Price Received by U.S. Farmers for Oats   In Dollars Per Bushel

Year	Jan	Feb	Mar	Apr	May	June	July	Aug	Sept	Oct	Nov	Dec	Marketing Year Average
1980	1.48	1.50	1.53	1.63	1.65	1.84	1.92	1.98	2.01	2.08	2.05	2.05	1.72
1981	1.99	1.84	1.72	1.74	1.78	1.88	1.94	1.97	1.99	2.02	1.99	1.99	1.88
1982	1.88	1.57	1.39	1.35	1.32	1.40	1.44	1.46	1.48	1.49	1.54	1.54	1.49
1983	1.51	1.46	1.45	1.55	1.62	1.67	1.73	1.81	1.88	1.81	1.82	1.84	1.62
1984	1.80	1.68	1.62	1.60	1.69	1.64	1.72	1.74	1.69	1.68	1.68	1.60	1.67
1985	1.59	1.31	1.16	1.10	1.08	1.17	1.20	1.18	1.16	1.14	1.13	1.21	1.23
1986	1.10	.90	.86	.99	1.10	1.32	1.44	1.46	1.47	1.45	1.50	1.57	1.21
1987	1.52	1.29	1.40	1.49	1.60	1.62	1.76	1.79	1.84	1.78	1.82	1.84	1.56
1988	2.63	2.86	2.54	2.57	2.56	2.41	2.47	2.52	2.46	2.41	2.24	2.13	2.61
1989	2.52	2.46	2.41	2.24	2.13	1.82	1.53	1.47	1.38	1.47	1.48	1.53	1.49
1990	1.47	1.43	1.39	1.44	1.45	1.33	1.15	1.06	1.09	1.14	1.16	1.17	1.14
1991	1.13	1.13	1.16	1.16	1.16	1.08	1.08	1.09	1.12	1.21	1.25	1.25	1.21
1992	1.31	1.44	1.44	1.46	1.43	1.38	1.32	1.23	1.28	1.31	1.35	1.36	1.32
1993	1.42	1.42	1.43	1.45	1.51	1.43	1.36	1.32	1.31	1.33	1.39	1.42	1.36
1994[1]	1.42	1.42	1.39	1.32	1.49	1.31	1.20	1.16	1.18	1.22	1.19	1.18	1.20

[1]Preliminary.   Source: National Agricultural Statistics Service, U.S. Department of Agriculture

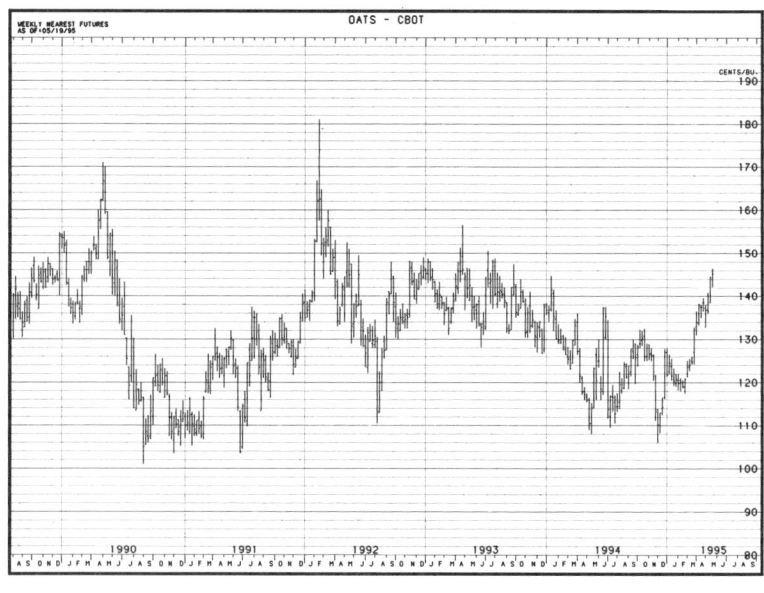

Olive Oil

World olive oil production in 1994/95 was forecast by the United States Department of Agriculture (USDA) to increase 7 percent to 1.72 million tonnes. Olive production is very cyclical, with large crops followed by small ones. The 1990/91 crop was small at only 1.5 million tonnes. That was followed by the 1991/92 crop which increased almost 43 percent to 2.14 million tonnes. By 1992/93, the crop declined 17 percent to 1.78 million tonnes. The 1993/94 crop was countercyclical in that it was 10 percent smaller.

The olive harvest begins in the northern Mediterranean region in mid-November and moves south ending in March. The main producers are Italy, Spain and Greece, with Tunisia, Turkey and Morocco accounting for smaller amounts. Tunisia has emerged in recent seasons as a more important supplier. Among the various countries, the production cycle also deviates, with some producers harvesting small crops while others harvest large ones.

While a larger crop is expected in 1994/95, global exports of olive oil were expected to decline 30,000 tonnes to 600,000 tonnes. The European Union has in the past subsidized olive production with the payments acting as income support in the poorer regions where olives are grown. While much of the olive oil is consumed in the countries where it is produced, the U.S. remains the major importer. U.S. imports of olive oil during the June-October 1994 period were 94,072 tonnes, an increase of less than 1 percent from the same period of 1992/93. The value of these imports was just over $174 million.

Despite its steep price premium to other cooking oils, olive oil remains the oil of choice for many, due to its taste and health benefits. Perhaps due to its higher price, olive oil consumption has shown virtually no growth in recent years. World olive oil consumption in 1994/95 was estimated at 1.86 million tonnes, down 5 percent from the previous year. Olive oil consumption by the European Union was forecast at 1.34 million tonnes. Global ending stocks of olive oil were projected at 630,000 tonnes, compared with 670,000 tonnes in the 1993/94 season.

World Production of Olive Oil (Pressed Oil)   In Thousands of Metric Tons

Crop Year	Algeria	Argentina	Greece	Israel	Italy	Jordan	Lebanon	Libya	Morocco	Portugal	Spain	Syria	Tunisia	Turkey	World Total
1983-4	10.0	10.8	258.6	4.0	705.0	8.4	15.0	15.0	23.5	21.0	294.2	32.2	162.0	46.0	1,607.0
1984-5	15.0	9.7	266.0	4.0	371.8	7.1	7.0	12.0	28.5	48.0	724.2	66.6	99.8	91.0	1,769.8
1985-6	18.0	9.5	386.4	2.0	656.0	9.1	5.0	9.0	43.4	36.0	432.2	52.0	114.7	81.0	1,870.3
1986-7	15.0	7.5	257.0	3.0	383.1	15.4	6.0	7.4	38.0	44.0	529.8	81.0	127.5	138.0	1,670.2
1987-8	10.0	9.5	322.0	3.0	742.5	3.1	5.0	6.5	41.5	38.0	792.0	36.0	101.5	63.0	2,198.0
1988-9	10.0	11.0	319.2	4.0	390.0	13.0	5.0	6.0	31.5	24.6	431.4	100.0	61.0	102.0	1,552.0
1989-0	16.0	10.5	316.3	2.5	624.2	7.5	5.5	8.0	70.0	44.3	594.9	33.0	137.0	39.0	1,938.6
1990-1	6.0	10.5	170.0	7.5	163.3	8.0	6.5	7.0	36.0	20.0	639.4	92.0	175.0	80.0	1,453.0
1991-2	37.0	90.0	385.0	2.5	674.5	5.0	5.0	10.0	50.0	62.0	593.0	51.0	250.0	60.0	2,207.2
1992-3[1]	26.5	10.0	310.0	7.5	435.0	14.0	8.0	6.0	38.0	22.0	623.0	86.0	120.0	56.0	1,813.0
1993-4[2]	21.0	8.0	254.0	1.5	418.0	8.5	2.0	8.0	40.0	23.0	545.0	95.0	230.0	50.0	1,715.0
1994-5[3]	14.0	9.5	345.0	8.0	400.0	15.0	8.5	6.5	50.0	22.0	490.0	90.0	130.0	120.0	1,757.5

[1] Preliminary.   [2] Estimate.   *Source: Oil World*

Average Unit Value of U.S. Olive Oil Imports   In Dollars Per Metric Ton

Year	Jan	Feb	Mar	Apr	May	June	July	Aug	Sept	Oct	Nov	Dec	Average
1985	1,256	1,169	1,215	1,235	1,256	1,249	1,251	1,257	1,308	1,333	1,292	1,338	1,263
1986	1,402	1,400	1,402	1,469	1,492	1,495	1,587	1,554	1,751	1,572	1,732	1,589	1,537
1987	1,690	1,763	1,652	1,726	1,635	1,577	1,588	1,608	1,563	1,646	1,609	1,696	1,646
1988	1,682	1,694	1,736	1,699	1,701	1,669	1,465	1,562	1,691	1,582	1,493	1,606	1,632
1989	1,642	1,642	1,890	1,930	2,005	1,981	1,919	1,919	1,862	1,917	1,910	2,017	1,886
1990	1,892	1,940	1,931	2,034	2,047	2,047	2,044	2,169	2,142	2,029	2,245	2,170	2,058
1991	2,195	2,213	2,355	2,188	2,283	2,274	2,281	2,282	2,401	2,250	2,417	2,523	2,305
1992	2,448	2,365	2,317	2,271	2,270	2,267	2,299	2,302	2,206	2,204	2,189	2,295	2,286
1993[1]	2,132	2,071	1,853	1,823	1,779	1,820	1,805	1,815	1,836	1,788	1,885	1,852	1,872
1994[1]	1,838	1,752	1,891	1,850	1,872	1,889	1,943	2,001	2,032	2,141			1,921

[1] Preliminary.   *Source: Foreign Agricultural Service, U.S. Department of Agriculture*

World Olive Oil Supply and Distribution   In Thousands of Metric Tons

Crop Year	Production	Exports	Imports	Consumption	Ending Stocks	Crop Year	Production	Exports	Imports	Consumption	Ending Stocks
1982-3	1,908	360	401	1,627	1,022	1989-0	1,939	579	573	1,861	706
1983-4	1,644	296	338	1,810	908	1990-1	1,579	821	801	1,868	394
1984-5	1,600	484	503	1,729	799	1991-2	2,400	352	347	1,930	860
1985-6	1,626	367	500	1,718	839	1992-3[1]	1,973	382	372	2,072	750
1986-7	1,670	746	730	1,849	764	1993-4[2]	1,855	385	392	2,029	583
1987-8	2,095	509	519	1,929	1,936	1994-5[3]	1,918	376	386	1,946	564

[1] Preliminary.   [2] Estimate.   [3] Forecast.   *Source: Oil World*

Onions

Salient Statistics of Onions in the United States

Crop Year	Harvested Acres	Yield Per Acre	Pro-duction 1,000 Cwt.	Price Per Cwt.	Farm Value $1,000	Jan. 1 Stocks Frozen	Annual Pack Frozen	Imports Canned	Exports (Fresh)	Imports (Fresh)	Per Capita[2] Utilization --Lbs., Farm Weight-- All	Fresh
						------------------------- Millions of Pounds -----------------------						
1985	122,760	367	45,059	9.08	347,328	23.4	142.0	14.0	195.1	263.7	15.2	13.6
1986	115,540	375	43,615	11.10	439,239	27.4	185.5	12.3	261.1	247.7	15.6	13.7
1987	123,720	364	45,113	12.50	505,163	35.7	185.2	13.0	282.0	371.2	14.9	13.4
1988	128,950	362	46,733	9.75	413,996	29.6	198.9	14.1	322.9	407.0	16.2	14.5
1989	132,660	361	47,902	11.40	496,971	33.4	208.8	3.3	250.0	359.7	16.4	14.8
1990	138,340	382	52,781	10.50	488,786	39.6	243.1	3.7	370.8	377.0	17.1	15.1
1991	133,970	378	50,702	12.50	582,556	34.4	226.5	3.4	339.0	491.7	17.3	15.7
1992	141,730	386	54,731	13.00	629,019	32.1	202.3	3.4	355.9	417.3	17.5	16.1
1993	150,680	379	57,062	16.70	813,259	34.2	213.7	4.7	341.8	507.1	17.8	15.7
1994[1]	160,050	394	63,033	10.50	602,003	36.1			301.5		18.0	16.2

[1] Preliminary.   [2] Includes fresh and processing.   *Source: Economic Research Service, U.S. Department of Agriculture*

Production of Onions in the United States   In Thousands of Hundredweight (Cwt.)

	Spring				Summer										
Year	Arizona	California	Texas	Total (All)	California	Colorado	Idaho	Michigan	Minne-sota	New Mexico	New York	Oregon (Malheur)	Texas	Total (All)	Grand Total
1985	564	3,510	3,230	7,304	9,250	5,355	3,740	2,535	194	1,463	3,960	6,785	943	37,755	45,059
1986	660	2,886	3,600	7,146	9,953	4,590	3,710	1,653	208	1,810	3,456	5,945	1,537	36,155	43,301
1987	585	3,198	2,750	6,533	10,730	4,688	4,620	1,900	195	2,106	3,132	7,032	799	39,334	45,867
1988	450	3,315	3,220	6,985	10,512	5,535	4,028	2,000	126	2,752	2,925	6,649	861	39,748	46,733
1989	440	3,080	3,225	7,380	10,125	5,520	3,996	2,212	161	3,000	2,912	6,710	1,040	40,516	47,902
1990	473	3,570	2,520	7,655	12,675	5,130	4,180	2,442	208	2,870	5,120	6,865	1,377	45,853	53,508
1991	441	3,160	3,264	7,093	11,250	4,953	4,543	2,044	294	2,960	3,510	7,588	960	42,017	49,110
1992	450	3,600	2,793	8,229	10,313	5,460	5,063	2,448	285	3,200	4,392	6,649	740	46,502	54,213
1993	631	3,300	2,768	8,193	13,035	5,735	4,698	2,201	22	3,740	3,720	5,940	936	48,869	57,062
1994[1]	688	2,948	4,704	10,297	12,400	6,125	5,547	2,308	312	3,570	3,844	7,378	837	52,736	63,033

[1] Preliminary.   *Source: Agricultural Statistics Board, U.S. Department of Agriculture.*

Cold Storage of Fresh Onions in the United States   In Thousands of Pounds

Year	Jan. 1	Feb. 1	Mar. 1	Apr. 1	May 1	June 1	July 1	Aug. 1	Sept. 1	Oct. 1	Nov. 1	Dec. 1
1985	7,465	5,518	4,454	2,248	810	4,806	2,804	1,280	6,205	6,526	5,890	6,128
1986	5,171	5,325	2,572	1,573	545	1,769	1,627	1,001	346	2,116	4,693	7,784
1987	6,773	5,330	2,710	1,883	1,560	2,403	1,181	137	1,276	2,500	3,823	6,641
1988	4,406	1,982	192	35	575	2,551	1,587	268	3,508	7,453	10,499	9,018
1989	7,608	4,914	2,348	70	462	670	184	140	2,133	13,283	16,492	16,000
1990	11,858	12,787	7,282	5,226	2,633	3,346	2,394	984	2,296	13,927	23,224	21,731
1991	17,030	14,387	5,918	2,885	995	1,957	2,225	1,695	2,164	26,746	35,362	29,414
1992	9,894	7,717	5,799	595	357	2,072	1,882	951	6,476	22,115	28,573	16,839
1993	12,032	5,196	3,536	1,642	733	600	747	1,270	16,948	11,735	19,967	16,875
1994[1]	6,353	2,668	1,678	1,390	838	2,973	2,106	2,060	1,631	3,858	6,300	4,058

[1] Preliminary.   *Source: National Agricultural Statistics Service, U.S. Department of Agriculture.*

FOB Price Received by Growers for Onions in the United States   In Dollars Per Hundred Pounds (Cwt.)

Year	Jan	Feb	Mar	Apr	May	June	July	Aug	Sept	Oct	Nov	Dec	Season Average
1985	10.20	8.82	7.93	9.09	12.90	10.90	18.80	11.20	7.61	6.41	6.97	8.19	9.08
1986	7.84	6.89	7.26	9.71	9.45	10.80	11.20	9.72	10.30	11.10	11.50	12.40	11.10
1987	16.50	18.30	20.60	26.30	22.30	16.80	14.90	10.60	9.71	8.77	9.38	10.60	12.50
1988	15.70	15.70	15.00	16.80	8.90	8.52	10.40	8.97	12.50	12.10	12.20	12.00	9.75
1989	11.50	10.90	9.70	10.90	9.47	12.90	16.90	16.00	11.20	10.10	9.62	9.70	11.40
1990	10.90	15.70	18.40	19.40	13.40	10.50	9.49	10.80	9.01	8.29	9.54	10.90	10.50
1991	13.80	10.20	11.90	18.40	21.50	14.10	17.70	12.90	11.20	10.00	10.60	10.40	12.50
1992	10.70	12.80	20.80	23.60	12.40	10.00	12.20	13.80	12.40	11.60	12.00	14.80	13.00
1993	16.60	14.00	17.30	31.00	23.60	10.40	12.60	14.70	13.20	12.10	19.00	24.10	16.70
1994[1]	31.70	34.50	18.00	10.20	8.34	8.25	12.80	9.13	9.55	9.72			10.50

[1] Preliminary.   *Source: Economic Research Service, U.S. Department of Agriculture.*

Oranges and Orange Juice

The United States Department of Agriculture (USDA) forecast the 1994/95 Florida orange crop at 196 million boxes, the second largest crop on record. This represented an increase of over 12 percent from the 1993/94 crop of 174 million boxes. The crop developed under near ideal conditions. The biggest orange crop ever harvested in Florida was 206.7 million boxes in 1979/80. Florida dominates U.S. citrus production, accounting for three-fourths of the country's annual citrus crop and over 90 percent of the orange juice supply. Early, midseason and navel oranges accounted for 118 million boxes, an increase of close to 10 percent from the previous season. Valencia oranges accounted for 78 million boxes, representing an increase of almost 17 percent from 1993/94.

Texas was forecast to produce one million boxes. Early midseason and navel oranges accounted for 900,000 boxes while valencias were 100,000 boxes. The Texas crop was over 80 percent larger than in 1993/94. Arizona orange production was put at 1.7 million boxes, down 11 percent from the previous season. Early, midseason and navel oranges accounted for 800,000 boxes of the total while valencias were 900,000 boxes.

California is the other major orange producing state with 1994/95 production of 65 million boxes, up almost four percent. Early, midseason and navel orange production was 37 million boxes while valencia production was 28 million boxes. The total U.S. orange crop was forecast to be 263.7 million boxes, up 10 percent from 1993/94. Early, midseason and navel oranges were expected to total 156.7 million boxes while valencias accounted for 107 million.

Based on USDA forecasts, the Florida Department of Citrus indicated that Florida orange juice production would reach 1.175 billion gallons, single strength equivalent, up over 12 percent from 1993/94. This would represent the second highest level on record. USDA forecast Florida frozen concentrated orange juice yields would decline to 1.54 gallons per box, 42 degrees Brix in 1994/95. The previous season's yield was 1.57 gallons. Single strength equivalent (SSE) is the form in which people normally drink orange juice, while 42 degree Brix is the form in which FCOJ is packed.

About 185 million gallons of Florida oranges were expected to be processed during the 1994/95 season. Almost 126 million boxes would be processed for frozen concentrated orange juice, up 13 percent while 57 million boxes would be used for chilled juice, up 12 percent. The number of boxes utilized for chilled juice has been increasing due to growth in pasteurized orange juice consumption. Some 833 million gallons (SSE) would be in frozen concentrated orange juice while Florida chilled orange juice production would use 341 million gallons (SSE).

Non-Florida orange juice production is expected to total over 85 million SSE gallons in 1994/95, or 6 percent of the U.S. total. Florida FCOJ ending inventories were forecast at almost 54 million gallons, 42 degree Brix, in 1994/95, down slightly from 1993/94. This is equivalent to about a 12-week supply. Orange juice imports, the majority of which come from Brazil, were forecast to be 40 million gallons.

Futures Market

Frozen concentrated orange juice futures and options are traded on the Citrus Associates of the New York Cotton Exchange (NYCE).

WEEKLY NEAREST FUTURES AS OF 05/12/95 — ORANGE JUICE - NYCE — CENTS/LB.

ORANGES AND ORANGE JUICE

World Production of Oranges   In Thousands of Metric Tons

Season	Argentina	Australia	Brazil	Cuba	Cyprus	Egypt	Greece	Israel	Italy	Mexico	Morocco	South Africa	Spain	Turkey	United States	Grand Total
1985-6	623	523	11,015	447	157	1,168	554	685	2,257	1,410	841	497	1,942	505	6,913	29,905
1986-7	621	475	10,650	496	204	1,235	881	815	2,424	1,683	650	577	2,059	750	7,122	31,196
1987-8	650	394	10,400	508	138	1,387	462	627	1,343	1,942	891	681	2,442	700	7,903	30,990
1988-9	620	544	14,150	474	170	1,199	770	546	2,170	2,000	994	629	2,216	740	8,272	35,835
1989-0	750	458	12,036	604	223	1,397	932	877	2,067	1,900	775	697	2,400	740	7,083	33,361
1990-1	600	485	12,362	600	169	1,574	819	567	1,760	2,300	1,103	648	2,590	735	7,222	33,938
1991-2	640	595	14,974	428	168	1,694	820	513	1,842	2,100	780	680	2,651	830	8,175	38,193
1992-3[1]	660	572	14,484	379	160	1,771	1,042	377	2,111	2,700	874	664	2,926	820	10,074	41,315
1993-4[2]	630	622	13,260	350	160	1,489	890	476	1,891	2,530	916	650	2,320	840	9,419	38,173
1994-5[3]	NA	NA	NA	350	166	1,350	900	500	1,655	2,570	700	NA	2,561	850	10,415	NA

[1] Preliminary.   [2] Estimate.   [3] Forecast.   NA = Not available.   Source: Foreign Agricultural Service, U.S. Department of Agriculture.

U.S. Salient Statistics of Oranges & Orange Juice

Season	Production[4] California	Florida	Total U.S.	Farm Price $ Per Box	Farm Value Million $	Florida Crop Processed — Frozen Concentrates	Chilled Products	Total Processed	Yield Per Box Gallons[5]	Frozen Concentrated Orange Juice-Florida — Carry-in	Pack	Total Supply	Total Season Movement	Pack	Brazilian U.S. Imports of Frozen Concentrated OJ — Exports — Total	To U.S.
	Million Boxes					Million Boxes				In Million Gallons (42° Brix)						
1985-6	53.9	119.2	175.7	6.18	1,090.4	96.1	17.3	114.7	1.4	48.3	215.1	263.4	226.4	285.9	190.7	112.2
1986-7	57.9	119.7	181.2	7.29	1,322.5	96.2	19.7	116.8	1.5	37.0	227.9	264.9	225.1	210.4	277.8	139.8
1987-8	59.0	138.0	200.3	8.52	1,773.7	103.9	23.6	138.0	1.6	39.8	240.9	280.7	238.5	244.8	254.5	120.5
1988-9	58.9	146.6	207.2	8.90	1,848.5	107.4	29.5	146.6	1.5	42.1	239.1	281.2	235.0	245.8	243.8	123.1
1989-0	71.4	110.2	184.5	7.96	1,465.1	70.1	33.5	110.2	1.2	46.3	184.7	231.0	191.1	362.0	330.7	132.4
1990-1	25.6	151.6	179.0	8.69	1,582.4	100.4	38.2	151.6	1.5	40.0	221.2	261.2	229.2	294.8	284.5	87.7
1991-2	67.4	139.8	209.6	7.72	1,599.1	90.6	37.0	139.8	1.6	31.8	211.7	243.5	212.6	274.1	279.3	107.8
92-93[1]	66.8	186.6	255.8			128.3	47.2	186.5	1.6	31.0	292.0	322.9	269.4	394.8	418.2	103.1
93-94[2]	62.6	174.2	239.3			111.7	51.0	174.2	1.6	53.5	182.2	303.2	244.5	388.2	387.5	102.0
94-95[3]	64.0	203.0	269.5			136.2	55.0	203.0		58.6	211.7	308.3	252.0	356.9	370.7	

[1] Preliminary.   [2] Estimate.   [3] Forecast.   [4] Fruit ripened on trees , but destroyed prior to picking is not included.   [5] 42° Brix equivalent.

Sources: Economic Research Service, U.S. Department of Agriculture, Florida Department of Citrus,

U.S. Cold Storage Stocks of Orange Juice Concentrate [2]   In Millions of Pounds

Year	Jan. 1	Feb. 1	Mar. 1	Apr. 1	May 1	June 1	July 1	Aug. 1	Sept. 1	Oct. 1	Nov. 1	Dec. 1
1985	651.6	883.4	1,050.6	1,102.7	1,188.6	1,229.5	1,063.7	1,036.1	912.4	882.2	778.8	656.0
1986	679.2	888.4	966.8	911.5	1,031.6	1,047.5	1,056.9	920.3	855.3	715.4	577.8	524.8
1987	621.2	874.8	1,012.7	933.8	999.0	1,109.1	1,105.1	942.1	792.6	840.0	652.8	569.0
1988	662.4	903.8	1,072.9	1,004.1	1,019.0	1,122.1	1,171.8	998.5	827.0	693.3	638.7	589.5
1989	721.6	980.9	1,155.9	1,087.0	1,144.8	1,296.1	1,324.8	1,167.5	932.6	808.4	725.7	669.7
1990	749.6	926.6	1,046.5	1,119.2	980.9	1,148.2	1,074.8	1,008.1	901.4	797.1	802.0	871.3
1991	1,031.6	1,195.8	1,199.5	1,236.9	1,363.2	1,304.7	1,110.6	1,007.5	876.9	765.2	617.3	655.4
1992	828.4	1,130.7	1,150.0	1,102.9	1,269.3	1,294.8	1,143.8	978.0	874.9	741.9	665.5	638.0
1993	892.9	1,135.9	1,282.8	1,297.5	1,440.9	1,462.3	1,351.8	1,147.0	1,029.6	875.7	813.3	890.9
1994[1]	955.5	1,248.9	1,429.0	1,273.8	1,499.6	1,615.2	1,521.8	1,449.1	1,257.5	1,119.6	1,026.1	1,055.9

[1] Preliminary.   Source: Agricultural Statistics Board, U.S. Department of Agriculture.

Average Open Interest of Frozen Concentrated Orange Juice Futures   In Contracts

Year	Jan	Feb	Mar	Apr	May	June	July	Aug	Sept	Oct	Nov	Dec
1985	8,023	7,094	6,378	6,588	6,027	5,854	5,214	4,826	4,367	5,092	6,352	11,571
1986	10,440	8,532	7,986	7,010	6,909	6,860	7,198	6,669	6,924	8,287	9,270	10,849
1987	11,222	10,283	10,031	9,206	8,658	8,104	6,994	6,665	7,229	8,810	9,000	10,212
1988	11,683	14,089	16,708	14,576	11,861	11,427	11,235	11,192	9,708	6,564	9,170	8,697
1989	7,169	6,959	7,009	7,821	8,374	9,767	8,340	7,531	6,857	7,218	7,029	9,887
1990	9,667	11,067	11,877	11,952	10,528	10,229	9,413	7,485	6,867	5,939	5,802	6,983
1991	6,773	6,457	5,739	6,255	5,762	6,338	5,653	6,556	9,854	11,924	9,877	9,101
1992	9,095	10,033	9,872	11,309	10,791	9,776	10,109	12,132	11,910	14,224	16,669	17,455
1993	17,733	18,199	19,030	20,210	18,525	19,267	20,000	18,899	18,287	18,825	18,422	20,367
1994	17,544	18,137	19,073	21,607	21,450	23,530	24,829	21,874	22,739	23,385	26,859	26,413

Source: Citrus Associates of the N.Y. Cotton Exchange.

Volume of Trading of Frozen Concentrated Orange Juice Futures   In Contracts

Year	Jan	Feb	Mar	Apr	May	June	July	Aug	Sept	Oct	Nov	Dec	Total
1985	28,768	20,572	8,135	11,529	9,514	10,011	8,238	7,893	9,395	16,320	11,115	49,268	190,758
1986	39,756	24,971	21,413	13,209	13,909	14,979	10,469	9,887	10,940	17,513	9,551	24,946	211,543
1987	28,566	24,342	27,999	19,569	10,651	15,470	8,805	10,710	12,330	20,321	20,724	26,758	266,641
1988	40,976	42,153	37,295	28,937	22,931	36,877	23,752	27,118	26,228	26,922	19,399	25,451	358,039
1989	26,156	26,419	28,501	26,855	30,272	32,051	23,403	19,698	17,119	18,069	15,893	39,668	304,104
1990	53,133	32,035	31,676	28,025	23,656	45,028	21,302	24,029	13,131	21,793	16,473	30,739	342,574
1991	35,037	28,221	17,298	17,116	17,991	20,956	14,905	20,187	26,412	42,016	23,228	24,171	287,076
1992	30,508	28,177	21,371	31,725	21,253	22,473	21,877	27,208	26,912	29,604	33,133	44,979	339,230
1993	43,634	46,067	58,298	52,554	53,566	60,330	49,415	52,381	56,838	63,808	44,167	58,073	640,131
1994	46,166	51,123	43,075	55,955	48,236	60,110	37,069	55,711	52,209	73,155	54,978	76,037	653,824

Source: Citrus Associates of the N.Y. Cotton Exchange.

U.S. Retail and Nonretail Sales of Orange Juice   In Millions of SSE Gallons

Crop Year	Retail Sales	% Change[2]	Nonretail Sales	% Change[2]	Apparent Consumption	% Change[2]	Per Capita Consumption	% Change[2]
1980-1	808	0	259	-38.8%	1,067	-13.3%	4.6	-14.8%
1981-2	804	-.5%	256	-1.2%	1,060	-.7%	4.6	0
1982-3	863	7.3%	441	72.3%	1,304	23.0%	5.6	21.7%
1983-4	856	-.8%	218	-50.6%	1,074	-17.6%	4.5	-19.6%
1984-5	817	-4.6%	376	72.5%	1,193	11.1%	5.0	11.1%
1985-6	884	8.2%	321	-14.6%	1,205	1.0%	5.0	0
1986-7	701	-20.7%	385	19.9%	1,243	3.2%	5.1	2.0%
1987-8	667	-4.9%	432	12.2%	1,229	-1.1%	5.0	-2.0%
1988-9	690	3.4%	401	-7.2%	1,238	.7%	5.0	0
1989-90	628	-9.0%	317	-20.9%	1,079	-12.8%	4.3	-14.0%
1990-1	701	11.6%	296	-6.6%	1,146	6.2%	4.5	4.7%
1991-2	689	-1.7%	268	-9.5%	1,112	-3.0%	4.4	-2.2%
1992-3	743	7.8%	371	38.4%	1,328	19.4%	5.1	15.9%
1993-4[1]	738	-.7%			1,436	8.1%	5.5	7.8%
1994-5[1]	735	-.4%			1,392	-3.1%	5.3	-3.6%

[1] *Estimate.*   *Source: Florida Department of Citrus.*

Producer Price Index of Frozen Orange Concentrate   1982 = 100

Year	Jan	Feb	Mar	Apr	May	June	July	Aug	Sept	Oct	Nov	Dec	Average
1986	328.5	321.7	307.2	297.0	296.3	296.7	296.5	296.7	295.0	302.1	310.4	319.2	305.6
1987[1]	106.9	106.9	107.4	109.5	109.7	110.0	110.1	111.0	110.6	110.6	117.2	129.9	111.7
1988	132.1	140.1	142.4	140.5	142.0	141.1	141.6	142.0	141.7	140.7	140.8	139.1	140.3
1989	136.4	127.7	126.5	126.5	131.7	139.2	140.6	140.3	134.0	131.6	123.1	121.7	131.6
1990	137.6	162.4	162.8	159.9	159.7	160.0	160.4	160.8	150.9	147.2	120.9	117.8	150.0
1991	114.4	114.4	111.7	111.7	111.0	111.0	111.0	107.2	107.4	116.0	127.3	131.5	114.5
1992	135.1	134.7	134.7	134.3	126.2	118.5	115.5	114.5	112.5	106.5	104.2	98.8	119.6
1993	91.6	88.8	88.2	89.0	89.3	97.5	104.5	104.5	104.7	104.7	107.9	107.9	98.2
1994[1]	107.9	104.8	104.2	104.2	102.7	101.2	100.2	100.1	99.8	99.8	100.8	100.5	102.2

[1] *Preliminary.*   [2] *Prior to 1987, price index shown as 1967 = 100.*   *Source: Bureau of Labor Statistics, U.S. Department of Labor.*

Average Price of Oranges (Equivalent On-Tree) Received by Growers   In Dollars Per Box

Year	Jan	Feb	Mar	Apr	May	June	July	Aug	Sept	Oct	Nov	Dec	Average
1986	4.20	4.01	4.07	3.76	4.24	4.18	3.58	3.91	4.59	6.50	6.46	4.79	4.52
1987	4.64	4.80	4.96	5.40	5.99	6.40	6.02	5.41	7.43	10.43	9.10	6.35	6.41
1988	6.43	6.59	6.87	7.76	8.79	8.78	6.47	5.44	5.56	3.39	6.15	6.76	6.58
1989	6.51	6.45	6.26	7.28	8.39	8.51	7.27	6.52	6.54	6.29	7.34	6.34	6.98
1990	5.92	5.82	6.00	6.47	6.97	6.61	5.74	4.38	4.48	5.04	5.78	5.76	5.75
1991	5.64	6.28	6.94	7.09	7.95	19.43	17.40	18.45	21.39	9.87	6.27	5.79	11.04
1992	5.90	6.02	5.81	6.14	6.16	4.26	1.85	1.02	1.05	2.43	4.10	3.67	4.03
1993	3.37	3.21	3.41	4.00	4.03	4.09	5.02	7.25	11.85	11.44	5.95	3.81	5.62
1994[1]	3.94	4.20	4.76	5.20	5.53	5.15	4.44	4.56	2.53	2.62	2.60	2.91	4.04

[1] *Preliminary.*   *Source: Economic Research Service, U.S. Department of Agriculture.*

Palm Oil

World palm oil production and consumption is second only to soybean oil, but it is the leading vegetable oil in foreign trade. Palm oil is a tropical oil, but competes directly with other cooking oils such as soybean and sunflower oils that are grown in more temperate climates. Almost all the world's production comes from Malaysia and Indonesia and the balance from equatorial nations in Africa, South America and Pacific islands.

Production in 1994/95 trailed initial forecasts, but still reached a record high 13.9 million tonnes, vs. 13.4 million in 1993/94. Much of the production is exported to meet world consumption, estimated at 13.8 million tonnes in 1994/95, vs. 13.7 million in 1993/94 and an early 1990's average of about 11.5 million tonnes. However, there are signs that consumption may have reached at least a temporary plateau. World palm oil stocks declined from the 1.72 million tonnes at the end of 1992/93 to 1.42 million a year later, but it no further draw upon stocks is likely during 1994/95.

Malaysian production during the year ending July 1994, totaled 7.2 million tonnes, a gain of only 4.8 percent above a year earlier and under the percentage gains of earlier years. The lagged effect of improved rainfall with expanded bearing tree numbers is expected to increase Malaysia's oil output through the 1994/95 crop year, but the percentage year to year gain could prove minimal. Higher palm oil prices have cut into world demand, even in producing countries. Total domestic consumption of palm oil in Malaysia in 1994/95 is expected to fall to 1.2 million tonnes, 116,000 tonnes below 1993/94. Malaysian exports for 1994/95 were forecast at 6.3 millions tonnes, well above the 1980s, but down from 6.35 million in 1993/94. In August, 1994 Malaysia hiked FOB palm oil prices 18 percent to a level that was 65 percent above a year earlier. From the late 1980s to mid-1994 Malaysian palm oil prices were under U.S. soybean oil prices, but then went to a premium the effect of which, if maintained, could further dampen world palm oil demand.

World palm oil foreign trade in 1994/95 approximated nine million tonnes in 1994/95, about the same as in 1993/94. The major importers include Pakistan, China and Japan. U.S. imports are relatively small, less than 200,000 tonnes in 1993/94.

World Palm Oil Statistics   In Thousands of Metric Tons

Crop Year	Colombia	Ecuador	Indonesia	Ivory Coast	Malaysia	Nigeria	Papua/ N. Guinea	Thailand	World Total	China	Pakistan	Singapore	World Total	Indonesia	Malaysia	Singapore	World Total
				— Production —						— Imports —					— Exports —		
1989-0	230	119	2,272	264	6,418	592	135	221	11,129	988	721	790	8,270	1,033	5,817	673	8,325
1990-1	251	127	2,574	277	6,036	631	184	231	11,233	1,291	818	848	8,763	1,626	5,717	644	8,827
1991-2	281	148	2,803	278	6,224	633	195	252	11,794	877	1,002	696	8,341	1,267	5,783	572	8,291
1992-3[1]	303	162	3,355	300	7,122	640	232	297	13,423	1,161	1,102	744	9,319	1,733	6,212	501	9,300
1993-4[2]	339	163	3,521	317	7,103	642	249	318	13,697	1,668	1,080	469	10,143	1,897	6,742	346	10,109
1994-5[3]	340	179	4,000	336	7,500	647	257	335	14,686	1,300	1,260	540	10,066	2,170	6,500	380	10,142

[1] Preliminary.   [2] Estimate.   [3] Forecast.   *Source: Oil World*

Palm Oil – U.S. Supply & Distribution   In Thousands of Metric Tons

Year Beginning Oct.	Stocks Oct. 1	Imports	Total Supply	Edible Products	Inedible Products	Total End Products	Total Disappearance	Exports	Import Value/4	U.S. F.O.B., RBD	Palm Kernel Oil, Malaysia, C.I.F. Rotterdam
				— Consumption —						— Prices —	
				— In Millions of Pounds —					— U.S. $ Per Metric Ton —		
1989-90	16.9	112.7	129.6	124.0	53.6	177.6	115.0	1.8	267	272	359
1990-1	12.8	129.0	141.8	97.8	71.1	168.9	115.0	3.1	323	317	362
1991-2	23.7	100.1	123.8	98.6	101.5	200.1	100.4	3.3	347	365	586
1992-3[1]	20.1	120.6	140.7	83.5	113.5	197.0	122.5	3.3	377	379	439
1993-4/[2]	14.9	167.0	181.9	86.2	118.2	204.4	162.0	3.5	370	451	566
1994-5[3]	16.0	141.0	157.0				138.0	4.0		668	788

[1] Preliminary.   [2] Estimate.   [3] Forecast.   [4] Market value in the foreign country, excluding import duties, ocean freight and marine insurance.

Sources: Oil World, Economic Research Service, U.S. Department of Agriculture.

Average Wholesale Palm Oil Prices, CIF, Bulk, U.S. Ports   In Cents Per Pound

Year	Jan	Feb	Mar	Apr	May	June	July	Aug	Sept	Oct	Nov	Dec	Average
1988	24.71	22.56	19.36	19.93	20.67	22.83	24.21	20.95	20.34	20.13	20.90	20.11	21.39
1989	19.27	19.45	19.20	18.79	20.37	20.26	18.88	15.31	15.82	16.10	16.05	15.16	17.89
1990	15.14	13.94	14.53	14.68	13.91	14.98	14.16	15.04	14.63	15.21	16.24	15.73	14.85
1991	19.49	19.50	19.25	19.18	19.05	19.40	20.32	19.14	18.86	20.63	21.63	18.99	19.62
1992	21.91	21.05	21.92	22.05	21.51	21.77	21.19	21.00	21.50	21.86	22.18	22.24	21.68
1993	23.18	23.09	22.99	22.26	21.95	21.01	20.31	19.84	19.43	18.83	19.74	21.90	21.21
1994[1]	20.83	20.88	20.81	22.30	24.25	26.19							22.54

[1] Preliminary.   *Source: Economic Research Service, U.S. Department of Agriculture*

Paper

According to the American Forest and Paper Association, North American Production of newsprint in 1994 was 15.7 million tonnes, a marginal increase over 1993 production. North American shipments of newsprint for calendar year 1994 were 15.8 million tonnes, an increase of nearly 2 percent from 1993. Stocks of newsprint on December 31, 1994 were nearly 302,000 tonnes, almost 33 percent lass than a year earlier.

Production of newsprint in the U.S. in 1994 was 6.34 million tonnes, down just over one percent from 1993. U.S. newsprint shipments were 6.36 million tonnes, virtually unchanged from the previous year. U.S. stocks of newsprint on December 31, 1994 were 59,600 tonnes, over 26 percent less than on the same date in 1993. Canadian production of newsprint in calendar year 1994 was 9.31 million tonnes, up nearly 2 percent from 1993. Newsprint shipments were 9.44 million tonnes or almost 4 percent more than in 1993. December 31, 1994 newsprint stocks were 242,100 tonnes, down sharply from the year-earlier level of 367,300 tonnes.

Most U.S. consumption of newsprint is by daily newspapers. For 1994, daily newspapers consumed just over 80 percent of all newsprint. For 1994, the daily newspaper consumption was 9.42 million tonnes, an increase of close to five percent from the prior year. Total U.S. demand for newsprint in 1994 was 11.69 million tonnes, up just over one percent from 1993. Seasonally adjusted stocks of newsprint by daily newspaper publishers on December 31, 1994 were 926,000 tonnes, down nearly seven percent from a year earlier.

Production of Paper and Paperboard by Selected Countries — In Thousands of Metric Tons

Year	Austria	Canada	Czech[2] Republic	Finland	France	Germany	Italy	Japan	Nether-lands	Norway	Russia[3]	Spain	Sweden	Switzer-land	United Kingdom	United States
1989	2,754	16,555	1,305	8,754	6,754	12,610	5,640	26,809	2,572	1,790	10,735	3,446	8,362	1,259	4,475	69,514
1990	2,932	16,466	1,300	8,967	7,049	12,759	5,587	28,088	2,770	1,820	10,718	3,446	8,419	1,295	4,824	71,965
1991	3,090	16,559	1,087	8,776	7,190	13,018	5,795	29,056	2,862	1,784	9,590	3,579	8,349	1,259	4,951	72,868
1992	3,252	16,597	688	9,147	7,690	13,200	6,040	28,324	2,835	1,684	5,765	3,449	8,372	1,305	5,151	75,244
1993[1]	3,301	17,519	624	9,990	7,824	13,109	6,019	-----	2,855	1,968	4,464	3,348	8,781	1,332	5,243	76,551

[1] Preliminary. [2] Formerly part of Czechoslovakia; data not reported separately until 1992. [3] Formerly part of the U.S.S.R.; data not reported separately until 1992. *Source: Food and Agriculture Organization of the United Nations.*

Production of Newsprint by Selected Countries (Monthly Average) — In Thousands of Metric Tons

Year	Australia	Brazil	Canada	China	Finland	France	Germany	India	Japan	Rep. of Korea	Norway	Russia[3]	Sweden	United Kingdom	United States
1989	33.4	19.1	803.3	32.3	98.6	31.5	79.4	22.8	268.1	36.9	87.4	143.3	213.3	47.4	460.3
1990	32.6	20.5	755.7	33.3	119.1	35.2	92.7	23.3	289.9	44.3	82.4	143.5	212.3	58.0	500.0
1991	33.2	21.3	748.1	36.5	108.8	34.8	94.1	24.3	292.9	47.4	79.6	128.6	192.3	56.0	517.2
1992	33.6	18.9	729.0	40.8	104.8	55.8	94.2	24.7	271.1	50.2	77.9	78.6	147.5	58.3	535.3
1993[1]	33.1	22.2	761.0	51.9	118.7	66.8	105.4	23.5	243.1	61.9	83.9	62.9	193.8	61.8	534.3
1994[2]	34.6	21.7	766.8	53.1	120.3	-----	117.5	24.0	244.4	71.4	-----	-----	199.6	-----	528.4

[1] Preliminary. [2] Estimate. [3] Formerly part of the U.S.S.R.; data not reported separately until 1992. *Source: Statistical Division, United Nations.*

Paper and Board Production in the United States — In Thousands of Short Tons

Year	-- Paper --							All Paperboard Total
	Newsprint (Metric Tons)	Coated (Shipments)	Tissue Paper	Uncoated Free Sheet (Shipments)	Groundwood Paper Uncoated (Shipments)	Packaging & Industrial Converting (Shipments)	All Paper Total	
1989	5,523	7,171	5,636	11,097	1,741	2,681	38,266	38,519
1990	5,997	7,430	5,802	11,479	1,868	2,377	39,359	39,423
1991	6,206	7,358	5,669	11,504	1,716	2,280	39,082	40,416
1992	6,424	8,119	5,784	12,170	1,609	2,380	40,973	40,973
1993[1]	6,412	8,183	6,008	12,336	1,742	2,254	41,546	41,546

[1] Preliminary. *Source: Bureau of Census, U.S. Department of Commerce.*

Salient Statistics of Newsprint in the United States and Canada — In Thousands of Metric Tons

Year	Production	Exports	---------------- United States ---------------- Imports by Countries of Origin									Consumption	Stocks, Dec. 31		--------- Canada ---------		
			Canada	Finland	Italy	Norway	South Africa	Sweden	United Kingdom	Total			At Mills	At Publishers	Production	Exports	Stocks at Mills
1989	5,523	485	7,558	23	0	37	0	130	0	7,760	12,241	56	749	9,640	8,465	321
1990	5,997	427	7,365	30	0	33	0	96	0	7,528	12,127	46	801	9,068	7,999	315
1991	6,206	570	6,695	22	0	29	0	46	0	6,795	11,268	98	932	8,855	7,602	565
1992	6,424	753	6,577	14	0	25	0	38	0	6,658	11,482	59	938	8,753	7,924	351
1993[1]	6,412	768	6,922	14	0	37	0	54	6	7,061	11,563	81	956	9,136	8,003	367
1994[1]	6,339	672	7,047	12	0	28	.9	30	.7	7,150	11,689	60	881	9,312	8,326	242

[1] Preliminary. Not seasonally adjusted. *Source: Newsprint Division, American Forest and Paper Association.*

PAPER

Index Price of Paperboard   1982 = 100

Year	Jan	Feb	Mar	Apr	May	June	July	Aug	Sept	Oct	Nov	Dec	Average
1988	126.6	127.1	130.5	132.6	133.4	134.0	134.3	134.5	136.3	136.4	136.5	136.5	133.2
1989	137.7	138.7	140.4	142.3	142.5	141.0	139.5	140.0	139.7	139.8	139.7	140.0	140.1
1990	139.2	138.9	138.9	137.6	136.0	135.5	135.0	133.4	133.1	134.3	134.2	132.8	135.9
1991	132.6	132.0	129.6	128.4	127.0	127.2	127.1	127.8	131.8	132.7	132.8	132.9	130.2
1992	133.4	133.6	133.4	134.3	134.3	134.3	134.2	134.6	135.9	135.7	133.9	133.6	134.3
1993	133.0	131.6	131.3	130.6	129.9	128.9	128.6	128.0	128.0	129.7	130.2	130.5	130.0
1994/1	130.2	130.1	131.4	133.4	133.1	133.5	137.8	143.5	145.3	151.4	156.5	156.6	140.2

[1] Preliminary.   Source: Bureau of Labor Statistics, U.S. Department of Commerce

Index Price of Wood Pulp, Bleached Sulphate Softwood   1982 = 100

Year	Jan	Feb	Mar	Apr	May	June	July	Aug	Sept	Oct	Nov	Dec	Average
1988	138.6	143.7	144.4	149.3	151.0	154.8	159.9	161.3	161.5	163.0	165.7	167.5	155.1
1989	176.2	176.9	178.1	180.7	184.8	184.8	184.4	184.4	184.4	185.8	185.8	184.0	182.5
1990	183.2	183.0	180.9	179.3	177.1	174.9	174.5	173.5	173.5	170.2	170.9	170.4	176.0
1991	152.2	150.0	143.6	142.1	136.8	132.4	126.2	124.2	123.2	120.0	120.7	114.8	132.2
1992	121.6	123.7	125.2	131.8	132.1	131.4	134.2	136.1	135.1	133.7	132.0	132.8	130.8
1993	121.6	118.1	112.7	112.3	112.7	112.7	110.7	108.9	108.6	107.1	105.5	104.0	111.2
1994/1	106.7	106.9	108.0	113.5	112.9	118.0	119.4	124.3	132.7	144.0	140.8	145.7	122.7

[1] Preliminary.   Source: Bureau of Labor Statistics, U.S. Department of Commerce.

Index Price of Shipping Sack Paper[2]   1982 = 100

Year	Jan	Feb	Mar	Apr	May	June	July	Aug	Sept	Oct	Nov	Dec	Average
1988	125.4	125.4	129.2	130.4	133.2	133.2	133.2	133.2	133.2	133.2	133.2	133.2	131.3
1989	133.2	144.4	144.4	144.4	144.4	144.4	144.4	144.4	144.4	144.4	144.4	144.4	143.5
1990	144.4	144.4	144.4	144.4	144.4	144.4	144.4	144.4	NA	NA	NA	NA	144.4
1991	148.9	148.9	148.9	148.9	148.9	148.9	148.9	148.9	148.9	148.9	148.9	148.9	148.9
1992	148.9	148.9	154.0	154.0	154.0	148.9	148.9	148.9	155.7	155.7	155.7	155.7	152.4
1993	155.7	155.7	155.7	155.7	151.8	151.8	151.8	151.8	151.8	151.8	152.5	152.5	153.3
1994[1]	151.3	150.9	154.5	154.5	159.3	163.9	169.9	170.3	176.1	180.5	184.9	185.6	166.8

[1] Preliminary.   [2] Unbleached kraft.   NA = Not available.   Source: Bureau of Labor Statistics, U.S. Department of Commerce.

Producer Price Index of Standard Newsprint   1982 = 100

Year	Jan	Feb	Mar	Apr	May	June	July	Aug	Sept	Oct	Nov	Dec	Average
1988	127.1	127.9	127.9	127.7	127.9	127.9	127.8	127.7	127.8	127.7	127.5	126.6	127.6
1989	126.5	126.0	126.6	126.5	123.2	122.0	121.3	120.7	120.4	119.3	119.0	118.3	122.5
1990	116.8	115.4	115.6	115.5	116.6	121.6	122.2	122.2	121.8	122.5	122.3	122.7	119.5
1991	126.8	127.2	127.1	121.7	121.4	120.1	119.5	118.8	118.1	117.3	116.4	115.8	120.9
1992	115.3	114.8	112.3	108.8	108.3	106.6	106.6	106.7	109.5	109.2	110.6	109.6	109.9
1993	110.4	111.2	114.1	113.9	113.0	113.1	112.7	112.6	111.3	111.2	111.0	111.0	112.1
1994/1	109.9	109.5	110.4	110.6	112.2	113.4	116.9	116.9	121.8	122.2	124.4	125.8	116.2

[1] Preliminary.   Source: Bureau of Labor Statistics, U.S. Department of Commerce.

Index Price of Coated Printing Paper, No. 3   1982 = 100

Year	Jan	Feb	Mar	Apr	May	June	July	Aug	Sept	Oct	Nov	Dec	Average
1988	120.9	121.2	122.2	121.8	122.0	122.0	124.0	126.3	127.5	127.5	127.7	127.8	124.2
1989	127.8	127.8	129.3	130.3	130.5	130.7	130.5	130.5	130.3	130.2	130.3	130.1	129.9
1990	130.3	130.2	130.2	130.3	130.3	130.3	130.2	130.2	130.2	130.2	130.2	127.8	128.6
1991	129.3	129.4	129.4	129.1	128.7	128.1	128.1	128.1	128.1	128.7	128.7	127.8	128.6
1992	126.8	123.6	123.7	123.7	122.3	121.7	122.1	121.7	121.7	124.2	123.4	123.3	123.2
1993	123.4	123.3	123.3	123.4	123.4	123.3	123.0	123.0	123.2	122.9	122.9	122.9	123.2
1994/1	122.0	122.1	122.2	122.2	121.6	121.6	121.6	125.2	127.8	129.0	130.7	135.7	125.1

[1] Preliminary.   Source: Bureau of Labor Statistics, U.S. Department of Commerce.

Peanuts and Peanut Oil

World peanut production averaged about 23 million tonnes during the 1990-94 period. Total production for the 1994 crop year was 23.4 million tonnes, compared with 23.8 million in 1993/94. India and China produce more than half the world's crop; the U.S. is a distant third with less than 10 percent. The world crop was larger than expected owing to heavy monsoon rains in India that boosted 1994 production to 8.2 million tonnes. U.S. production of 1.9 million tonnes compared with 1.54 million in 1993/94, but was in line with average production during the 1988-92 period.

Foreign trade in raw peanuts is small as most of the crop is consumed locally. Among the world's major oilseed only peanuts has shown virtually no increase in allotted acreage in recent years. In the U.S., acreage has dropped slightly. World stocks at the end of the 1994/95 season was forecast at 670,000 tonnes, about the same as a year earlier and a fraction of the estimated 21-million-tonne soybean carryover. More of the world's crop is allocated to meal production than oil. Some 5.2 million tonnes of peanut meal was produced in 1994/95, while oil production totaled 3.7 million tonnes, both slightly higher than in 1993/94 and continuing the upward trend of the early 1990s.

U.S. peanut production is largely concentrated in the Southeast. Peanuts are also grown in the Southern Plains States. Due to drought, the U.S. peanut crops in 1990 and 1993 fell dramatically from initial forecasts and prices skyrocketed. In mid-1994, a hurricane inundated fields in parts of Georgia, Alabama and Florida, but the damage proved less than initially feared. A crop of about 4.1 billion pounds was likely, up from 3.4 billion in 1993, but well under the near five billion produced in 1991. Total supplies in 94/95 of about five billion pounds, including a near one billion carry-in as of August 1, 1994 could exceed total usage of about four billion, pointing to a near doubling of carryover stocks during the crop year.

The U.S. peanut crush in 1994/95 is forecast at 930 million pounds, up from 700 million in 1993/94. Food use may dip to about 2.1 billion pounds while exports rise to 650 million pounds from 550 million in 1993/94. U.S. peanut exports at times have exceeded one billion pounds, but that quantity was last seen in 1985/86. The U.S. does import peanut butter, the quantity of which is dependent on U.S./world price differentials. Peanut butter imports in 1993/94 totaled more than 15,000 tonnes (product basis), but well under initial forecasts. The lower total was attributed to the erratic price swings during the year: the short 1993/94 crop caused world prices to initially jump, increasing the costs to domestic peanut butter manufacturers that buy peanuts on the world market and ship the product to the U.S. However, as U.S. prices eased, so did demand for foreign peanuts. World prices then retreated even faster, which triggered a late 1993/94 surge in U.S. imports.

The average peanut price received by farmers in 1993/94 of 29.6 cents per pound was a shade under 1992/93. For the 1994/95 season the average price was initially forecast near 31 cents. Peanut oil prices, however, showed more buoyancy during 1993/94 and the trend was expected to carry into 1994/95.

U.S. Government Program

For quota peanuts, the 1994 price support is 33.92 cents per pound, vs. 33.75 cents in 1993/94. There is also an additional 6.6 cents allotted, the same as in the previous two crop years.

World Production of Peanuts (in the Shell) In Thousands of Metric Tons

Crop Year	Argentina	Brazil	Burma	China	India	Indonesia	Mali	Nigeria	Senegal	South Africa	Sudan	Taiwan	Thailand	United States	Zaire	World Total
1981-2	270	305	564	3,826	7,223	728	92	428	116	878	740	83	147	1,806	347	19,832
1982-3	250	250	541	3,916	5,282	795	80	396	89	1,109	497	63	145	1,560	357	17,435
1983-4	329	220	532	3,951	7,086	747	50	591	72	568	413	87	147	1,495	367	18,738
1984-5	270	337	667	4,815	6,436	755	45	500	196	560	390	89	172	1,998	375	19,683
1985-6	439	216	560	6,664	5,120	780	90	400	111	587	275	77	172	1,870	375	1,990
1986-7	518	195	544	5,882	5,875	750	90	400	235	817	350	83	169	1,677	380	20,383
1987-8	450	170	519	6,170	5,854	786	100	475	204	932	435	100	162	1,640	380	20,863
1988-9	243	156	438	5,693	9,000	843	115	350	163	350	450	74	164	1,806	380	23,279
1989-0	336	137	459	5,365	8,088	875	90	350	113	350	400	58	161	1,810	380	22,059
1990-1	574	157	440	6,368	7,514	860	100	250	703	112	325	73	162	1,634	380	22,206
1991-2	400	160	440	6,300	7,065	890	95	220	724	114	400	83	160	2,235	380	22,138
1992-3[1]	225	150	425	5,953	8,850	890	95	250	580	172	390	65	162	1,943	380	23,050
1993-4[1]	230	150	370	8,420	7,630	980	-----	250	630	180	390	-----	170	1,540	380	23,970
1994-5[2]	230	150	420	7,300	8,400	1,000	-----	250	640	140	390	-----	170	1,930	380	24,120

[1] Preliminary.   [2] Estimated.   [3] Forecast.   *Source: Foreign Agricultural Service, U.S.D.A.*

PEANUTS AND PEANUT OIL

Salient Statistics of Peanuts in the United States

Crop Year	Acreage Planted ----(1,000 Acres)-----	Acreage Harvested for Nuts	Average Yield Per Acre In Lbs.	Pro- duction 1,000 Lbs.	Season Farm Price ¢ Lb.	Farm Value Million Dollars	Exports Unshelled	Exports Shelled	Imports Unshelled	Imports Shelled
1982-3	1,311.4	1,277.4	2,693	3,440,255	25.1	862.7	51,321	473,416	844	1,323
1983-4	1,411.0	1,373.5	2,399	3,295,530	24.7	814.6	39,509	529,949	298	1,715
1984-5	1,558.6	1,528.0	2,883	4,405,745	27.9	1,230.8	72,907	592,333	79	2,167
1985-6	1,490.4	1,467.4	2,810	4,122,787	24.3	1,003.4	83,747	721,690	1,493	1,942
1986-7	1,564.7	1,535.2	2,408	3,700,745	29.2	1,073.3	75,687	441,954	328	1,598
1987-8	1,567.4	1,547.4	2,337	3,619,440	28.0	1,021.9	76,345	407,557	880	1,949
1988-9	1,657.4	1,628.4	2,445	3,980,917	27.9	1,115.2	105,746	437,867	650	2,094
1989-0	1,665.2	1,644.7	2,426	3,989,995	28.0	1,116.5	126,682	577,807	55	1,477
1990-1	1,840.0	1,809.5	1,991	3,602,770	34.9	1,257.2	250,851	401,149	6,429	20,571
1991-2	2,039.2	2,015.7	2,444	4,926,570	28.3	1,392.0	------- 997,000 -------		-------- 5,000 --------	
1992-3	1,686.6	1,669.1	2,567	4,284,416	30.0	1,285.3	------- 951,000 -------		-------- 2,000 --------	
1993-4/1	1,733.5	1,689.8	2,008	3,392,415	29.6	1,002.6	------- 550,000 -------		-------- 9,000 --------	
1994-5/2	1,645.0	1,613.5	2,643	4,264,550	29-33		------ 650,000 -------		--------10,000 --------	

[1] Preliminary.   [2] Estimate.   Source: Economic Research Service, U.S. Department of Agriculture.

Peanuts Supply & Disposition (Farmers' Stock Basis) & Support Program in the United States

Crop Year Beginning Aug. 1	Supply Pro- duction	Supply Imports	Supply Stocks Aug. 1	Supply Total	Disposition Exports	Disposition Crushed for Oil	Disposition Seed, Loss & Residual	Disposition Food	Total Disap- pearance	Support Price ¢ per Lb.	Addi- tional ¢ per Lb.	Amount Put Under Support Quantity Mil. Lbs.	Amount Put Under Support % of Prod.
1981-2	3,982	2	413	4,397	576	573	795	1,696	3,640	22.75	12.5	835	20.9
1982-3	3,440	2	757	4,199	681	342	463	1,849	3,335	27.50	10.0	539	15.7
1983-4	3,296	2	864	4,162	744	387	564	1,856	3,551	27.50	9.3	367	11.1
1984-5	4,406	2	611	5,019	860	625	199	1,911	3,595	27.50	9.3	1,370	30.9
1985-6	4,123	2	1,424	5,549	1,043	812	826	2,023	4,704	27.95	7.4	1,359	33.0
1986-7	3,697	2	845	4,544	663	514	291	2,073	3,541	30.37	7.5	290	7.8
1987-8	3,616	2	1,003	4,621	618	560	539	2,071	3,788	30.37	7.5	700	19.3
1988-9	3,981	2	833	4,816	688	814	217	2,254	3,973	30.76	7.5	540	13.6
1989-0	3,990	2	843	4,835	989	624	209	2,312	4,134	30.79	7.5	401	10.0
1990-1	3,603	27	701	4,331	652	689	287	2,020	3,647	31.57	7.5	576	16.0
1991-2	4,927	5	683	5,615	997	1,103	253	2,207	4,560	32.14	7.5	1,070	21.7
1992-3	4,284	2	1,055	5,341	951	891	227	2,122	3,991	33.75	6.6	436	10.2
1993-4[1]	3,392	9	1,350	4,752	550	700	426	2,075	3,752	33.75	6.6		
1994-5[2]	4,265	10	1,000	4,875	650	930	245	2,050	3,875	33.92	6.6		

[1] Preliminary.   [2] Estimate.   Source: Economic Research Service, U.S. Department of Agriculture

U.S. Production of Peanuts (Harvested for Nuts) by States   In Thousands of Pounds

Crop Year	Alabama	Florida	Georgia	New Mexico	North Carolina	Okla- homa	South Carolina	Texas	Virginia	Total
1981	602,730	178,200	1,655,450	24,900	555,560	189,280	39,000	393,250	330,750	3,981,850
1982	522,150	153,000	1,517,480	25,220	417,200	174,580	30,000	325,125	275,500	3,440,255
1983	454,500	166,800	1,567,980	25,630	318,255	176,540	25,000	362,275	198,550	3,295,530
1984	648,550	246,400	2,160,000	32,190	449,500	189,000	39,150	371,295	269,660	4,405,745
1985	590,000	216,000	1,921,320	31,992	451,990	170,980	34,200	422,625	283,680	4,122,787
1986	494,940	233,160	1,632,575	28,700	440,440	184,500	25,530	385,000	275,900	3,700,745
1987	465,300	215,800	1,575,000	29,760	392,200	222,750	31,200	441,000	243,000	3,616,010
1988	561,680	228,600	1,801,550	30,552	419,985	225,040	32,110	417,500	263,900	3,980,917
1989	537,750	214,890	1,849,500	43,680	370,120	210,700	32,500	484,700	246,155	3,989,995
1990	386,560	233,120	1,347,500	50,000	475,600	235,320	30,105	534,650	309,915	3,602,770
1991	638,485	279,660	2,228,550	51,075	461,700	243,800	33,600	682,500	307,200	4,926,570
1992	591,180	202,510	1,820,465	58,236	406,980	236,180	32,500	680,150	256,215	4,284,416
1993	473,220	194,880	1,383,545	56,680	299,585	233,580	24,500	550,175	176,250	3,392,415
1994[1]	446,000	214,200	1,864,050	58,750	483,200	258,000	39,150	616,000	285,200	4,264,550

[1] Preliminary.   Source: Agricultural Statistics Board, U.S. Department of Agriculture

188

Supply and Reported Uses of Shelled Peanuts and Products in the U.S.   In Millions of Pounds

Crop Year Beginning Aug. 1	Shelled Peanuts — Stocks Aug.1 — Edible	Oil Stock[2]	Shelled Peanuts — Production — Edible	Oil Stock[2]	Candy[3]	Snacks[4]	Sandwich Spread	Butter[5]	Other Products	Total	Shelled Peanuts Crushed[6]	Crude Oil Production	Meal Production
1983-4	537,855	19,208	1,776,069	342,477	298,065	301,971	24,279	671,430	15,469	1,311,214	291,084	119,008	159,340
1984-5	402,449	33,063	2,414,852	422,026	290,318	309,050	26,240	697,137	19,201	1,341,945	470,264	187,283	264,658
1985-6	860,508	30,407	2,238,427	496,928	313,836	358,542	24,623	701,289	23,515	1,421,805	610,897	256,545	336,232
1986-7	559,256	4,734	2,123,054	299,651	321,191	384,286	33,858	679,373	41,065	1,459,773	386,388	152,423	214,526
1987-8	683,622	21,300	2,015,144	301,379	325,583	373,773	45,808	701,436	37,791	1,484,391	421,214	168,263	247,851
1988-9	565,779	22,647	2,095,351	406,626	326,907	381,481	28,373	831,928	35,978	1,604,667	612,200	250,498	348,662
1989-0	513,679	44,397	2,319,780	374,859	330,158	392,811	—— 897,318 ——		36,682	1,656,969	469,351	193,000	261,465
1990-1	455,586	15,194	1,836,052	330,102	305,324	355,258	—— 742,384 ——		37,888	1,440,854	517,712	213,112	299,820
1991-2	386,155	65,950	2,538,398	616,170	327,617	346,255	—— 886,367 ——		34,173	1,594,412	828,986	356,276	459,457
1992-3	871,207	57,829	2,376,782	533,641	328,324	352,775	—— 797,910 ——		24,981	1,503,990	669,942	285,904	377,301
1993-4[1]	681,470	41,430	1,749,139	425,327	362,418	348,896	—— 727,006 ——		36,301	1,474,621	503,674	212,216	292,093

[1] Preliminary. [2] Includes straight run oil stock peanuts. [3] Includes peanut butter made by manufacturers for own use in candy. [4] Formerly titled "Salted Peanuts." [5] Includes peanut butter made by manufacturers for own use in cookies and sandwiches, but excludes peanut butter used in candy. [6] All crushings regardless of grade.   *Source: National Agricultural Statistics Service, U.S. Department of Agriculture.*

Shelled Peanuts (Raw Basis) Used in Primary Products by Type   In Thousands of Pounds

Crop Year Beginning Aug. 1	Virginia Candy[2]	Snack Peanuts	Peanut Butter[3]	Total	Runner Candy[2]	Snack Peanuts	Peanut Butter[3]	Total	Spanish Candy[2]	Snack Peanuts	Peanut Butter[3]	Total
1983-4	15,402	101,980	44,091	163,268	237,075	164,389	600,226	1,032,248	45,588	35,602	33,263	115,698
1984-5	31,276	96,181	46,735	176,237	209,765	175,404	620,057	1,050,877	49,276	37,466	26,896	114,831
1985-6	32,900	113,577	54,794	206,557	240,198	207,503	648,566	1,091,850	40,739	37,463	43,159	123,400
1986-7	27,591	171,679	61,405	280,765	261,630	169,715	633,307	1,053,159	31,970	42,892	48,706	125,849
1987-8	40,251	120,084	42,841	216,987	249,673	220,511	613,231	1,152,848	35,659	33,178	43,224	114,556
1988-9	37,145	112,101	75,436	241,130	259,680	237,008	644,555	1,256,252	30,082	32,372	43,668	107,285
1989-0	28,701	130,000	90,622	263,014	278,062	234,661	773,985	1,306,810	23,395	28,150	32,711	87,145
1990-1	26,043	142,113	101,069	286,242	259,995	189,254	580,691	1,049,423	19,286	23,841	60,624	105,189
1991-2	51,312	142,514	89,045	297,570	244,815	180,609	759,747	1,203,233	31,490	23,132	37,575	93,609
1992-3	49,223	124,875	92,355	275,895	259,498	203,732	674,962	1,152,775	19,603	24,168	30,593	75,320
1993-4[1]	44,889	99,381	63,270	222,641	298,325	227,315	365,047	1,179,425	19,204	22,200	28,689	72,555

[1] Preliminary. [2] Includes peanut butter made by manufacturers for own use in candy. [3] Includes peanut butter made by manufacturers for own use in cookies and sandwiches, but excludes peanut butter used in candy.   *Source: National Agricultural Statistics Service, U.S. Department of Agriculture.*

Production, Consumption, Stocks and Foreign Trade of Peanut Oil in the U.S.   In Millions of Pounds

Crop Year Beginning Aug. 1	Production Crude	Refined	Consumption In Refining	In End Products	Stocks Dec. 31 Crude	Refined	Imports for Consumption	Exports
1982-3	106.9	168.8	133.5	174.0	NA	3.9	3.7	5
1983-4	119.0	139.6	183.9	132.9	17.9	4.0	0.6	7
1984-5	187.3	119.9	148.4	NA	9.6	4.8	2.2	29
1985-6	256.5	139.7	124.6	NA	64.9	4.0	0.5	93
1986-7	152.4	160.0	145.7	153.2	17.0	3.6	2.4	6
1987-8	168.3	199.6	169.0	179.3	10.9	3.8	33.1	7
1988-9	250.5	185.5	207.5	NA	18.6	4.4	1.9	11
1989-0	193.0	212.5	192.4	NA	17.6	4.1	5.0	19
1990-1	213.1	131.7	229.1	169.0	19.3	5.8	10.0	25
1991-2	261.5	125.6	132.3	141.0	27.5	3.1	1.0	151
1992-3	285.9	181.1	188.4	182.1	46.2	5.3	0.0	59
1993-4[1]	212.2	155.2	163.7	149.1	6.5	3.9	15.0	50

[1] Preliminary.   NA = Not available.   *Source: Bureau of Census, U.S. Department of Commerce.*

PEANUTS AND PEANUT OIL

Average price Received by Producers in U.S. for Peanuts in the Shell   In Cents Per Pound

Crop Year	Aug	Sept	Oct	Nov	Dec	Jan	Feb	Mar	Apr	May	June	July	Average/[1]
1979-80	NQ	21.4	20.3	20.4	20.4	20.4	NQ	NQ	NQ	NQ	NQ	NQ	20.6
1980-1	NQ	22.5	23.2	27.9	37.3	47.7	NQ	NQ	NQ	NQ	NQ	NQ	31.7
1981-2	25.7	28.9	26.7	25.1	25.8	24.9	NQ	NQ	NQ	NQ	NQ	NQ	26.2
1982-3	27.1	25.1	24.9	25.3	26.1	22.9	NQ	NQ	NQ	NQ	NQ	NQ	25.2
1983-4	NQ	25.2	24.3	24.5	26.0	27.8	NQ	NQ	NQ	NQ	NQ	NQ	25.6
1984-5	NQ	29.9	27.1	25.6	26.3	NQ	NQ	NQ	NQ	NQ	NQ	NQ	27.2
1985-6	24.7	24.4	24.3	24.6	23.3	20.6	NQ	NQ	NQ	NQ	NQ	NQ	23.7
1986-7	29.6	27.0	28.8	29.8	32.5	24.5	NQ	NQ	NQ	NQ	NQ	NQ	28.7
1987-8	29.7	29.2	27.9	27.4	27.6	28.5	NQ	NQ	NQ	NQ	NQ	NQ	28.4
1988-9	20.0	29.9	28.0	26.4	25.8	27.8	NQ	NQ	NQ	NQ	NQ	NQ	26.3
1989-0	28.4	28.2	27.7	26.9	28.2	24.6	NQ	NQ	NQ	NQ	NQ	NQ	27.3
1990-1	26.5	32.2	34.0	40.1	43.6	44.8	NQ	NQ	NQ	NQ	NQ	NQ	36.9
1991-2	30.4	29.3	28.1	24.4	25.1	NQ	NQ	NQ	NQ	NQ	NQ	NQ	27.5
1992-3	NQ	31.3	29.9	28.2	25.7	29.5	NQ	NQ	NQ	NQ	NQ	NQ	28.9
1993-4[2]	NQ	31.9	29.8	28.2	27.2	36.0	NQ	NQ	NQ	NQ	NQ	NQ	30.6
1994-5[2]	NQ	30.3	28.8	25.6	25.4	25.7							27.2

[1] Weighted average by sales.   [2] preliminary.   NQ = No quote.   *Source: National Agricultural Statistics Service, U.S. Department of Agriculture.*

Crude Peanut oil Produced in the United States   In Millions of Pounds

Year	Jan	Feb	Mar	Apr	May	June	July	Aug	Sept	Oct	Nov	Dec	Total
1980	6.2	15.1	16.7	25.9	30.7	22.9	23.5	21.2	5.9	2.1	6.3	5.9	182.4
1981	6.1	6.0	10.5	17.3	19.1	19.5	13.6	9.8	5.3	9.7	12.0	12.7	141.6
1982	11.3	11.1	19.4	26.3	22.3	19.0	15.0	11.8	NA	NA	NA	NA	NA
1983	NA	NA	NA	NA	NA	NA	NA	NA	NA	NA	NA	NA	NA
1984	12.1	13.3	10.8	12.5	10.1	8.9	5.1	5.3	4.3	9.9	8.6	7.3	108.2
1985	9.8	13.9	15.8	15.5	14.5	12.4	10.4	10.0	10.1	9.2	10.2	14.9	146.7
1986	19.2	21.1	19.9	20.8	24.0	26.4	14.2	9.6	NA	4.1	11.9	10.7	181.9
1987	9.8	13.6	20.5	11.6	17.8	15.8	14.5	9.7	4.2	7.5	13.7	13.1	151.8
1988	13.8	14.9	10.1	8.3	19.5	12.5	17.0	11.4	2.8	9.7	17.0	18.4	155.4
1989	10.5	20.8	27.8	24.3	19.0	33.4	26.6	22.4	NA	7.4	11.6	9.8	213.6
1990	11.1	15.8	14.2	22.2	24.9	24.1	14.0	8.5	2.1	14.4	12.5	15.9	179.7
1991	----------- 70.8	-----------	----------	71.1	---------	------------	59.5	-----------	------------	60.1	-----------		261.5
1992	28.0	26.8	42.5	40.9	39.8	40.6	37.3	31.3	35.1	24.2	19.2	15.6	381.5
1993	16.9	17.0	24.1	28.8	23.3	29.0	25.6	22.5	3.6	8.6	16.4	14.6	233.8
1994[1]	18.1	18.0	20.6	23.1	25.3	20.2	21.2	15.9	16.5	11.4	18.4	24.3	232.9

[1]Preliminary.   NA = Not available.   *Source: Bureau of Census, U.S. Department of Commerce.*

Average Price of Domestic Crude Peanut Oil (in Tanks) F.O.B. Southeast Mills   In Cents Per Pound

Year	Oct	Nov	Dec	Jan	Feb	Mar	Apr	May	June	July	Aug	Sept	Average
1980-1	35.8	48.7	49.1	47.7	39.3	34.1	34.0	37.1	38.0	38.1	43.2	40.3	40.5
1981-2	34.5	34.5	30.9	27.3	31.4	23.3	29.1	29.9	26.2	24.7	22.7	22.5	28.1
1982-3	22.9	25.2	26.1	25.6	25.7	24.1	25.1	26.4	26.4	26.7	30.7	50.5	28.0
1983-4	50.7	48.8	48.1	47.3	46.5	48.4	52.6	58.2	59.1	57.7	54.8	39.2	47.3
1984-5	36.7	41.2	41.4	39.2	38.8	40.3	49.6	46.2	40.7	39.7	37.6	33.9	40.4
1985-6	38.3	42.2	36.1	29.5	22.6	21.5	24.4	27.6	28.0	27.5	30.5	28.3	29.7
1986-7	27.80	29.80	26.50	25.10	25.00	23.75	24.00	26.15	25.68	25.27	24.61	26.74	25.87
1987-8	33.48	31.50	32.10	35.73	32.40	29.61	29.50	30.02	34.00	39.80	37.86	36.0	33.50
1988-9	42.50	36.75	34.25	26.50	25.09	29.98	32.39	36.25	39.80	NA	35.75	34.4	33.97
1989-90	39.06	41.50	41.60	43.25	46.00	43.40	41.25	45.25	46.90	46.88	49.05	51.13	44.61
1990-1	48.13	44.20	43.00	41.00	42.83	47.60	46.75	43.33	42.25	41.50	35.33	30.66	42.38
1991-2	34.33	27.67	23.50	23.50	23.63	23.17	25.00	27.88	25.60	26.19	23.88	22.0	25.52
1992-3	23.63	25.58	30.30	30.88	27.17	26.00	27.50	30.00	30.20	33.00	39.50	35.93	29.97
1993-4[1]	40.20	43.33	43.17	46.38	46.13	44.50	43.40	44.25	43.75				

[1] Preliminary.   *Source: Agricultural Marketing Service, U.S. Department of Agriculture*

Pepper

After a three and a half year stretch of depressed prices, the price of Indonesian Muntok white pepper began to increase in August 1993. This was the result of a significant decline in Indonesian production due to unfavorable growing conditions. Over the first seven months of 1993, the price of pepper averaged just over 86 cents per pound. For the January-May 1994 period, Muntok while pepper averaged nearly $1.41 per pound. The higher prices met resistance from consumers who looked to utilize stocks from previous years, according to the USDA. Indonesia accounts for most global production of white pepper.

Much of the statistical data on pepper is laggard. Production estimates are further complicated by the tendency of third-world producing countries to hold stocks in lieu of local currency, in hopes of avoiding inflation and currency risk. Additionally, pepper can be stored for long periods, so actual world stocks are likely to be underestimated. Countries experiencing high inflation are likely to build stocks as a hedge against inflation.

One trend in the world market, as evidenced by prices, is that production is expanding. The major producers of pepper are Indonesia, Brazil, India and Malaysia. These countries account for about 90 percent of production.

According to USDA data, world exports of black and white pepper by the principle producing countries in 1992 were approximately 165,000 tonnes, a slight decline from 167,000 a year earlier. Exports of black and white pepper in 1992 by India, Indonesia, Brazil and Malaysia totaled 128,471 tonnes. India's exports were 19,399 tonnes. The principal destination was the U.S., which took 9,500 tonnes while Canada received 1,519 tonnes. The former Soviet Union took 1,460 tonnes, a decline of close to 90 percent from 1991. Indonesia's exports were 61,438 tonnes, an increase of 24 percent from 1991. The principle market was the U.S., which took 26,071 tonnes or nearly 90 percent more than in 1991. Exports to Germany were 4,643 tonnes, down 24 percent. Shipments to the Netherlands were 2,993 tonnes, a decline of 37 percent from 1991. Brazil exported 25,702 tonnes of pepper in 1992, a 46 percent decline from 1991. The major market was the U.S. which took 6,041 tonnes, a decrease of over 40 percent from 1991. Other major destinations were Morocco with 4,705 tonnes and Germany with 3,591 tonnes. Malaysian exports in 1992 were 21,932 tonnes, down 14 percent. Exports to the U.S. declined over 80 percent to only 1,315 tonnes. Japan took 3,868 tonnes while Germany imported 2,815 tonnes.

World exports of pepper in 1993 were estimated at 130,000 tonnes, according to the USDA. Smaller shipments were made from Indonesia, Malaysia, Brazil and Vietnam. The U.S. is the largest importer of pepper and accounts for about a quarter of world trade. U.S. imports in 1993 totaled 42,110 tonnes with a value of $54.4 million. Imports in 1992 were 46,642 tonnes with a value of $50.1 million.

World Exports of Pepper (Black & White) and U.S. Prices

Year	Brazil	India	Indonesia	Mada-gascar	Malaysia	Mexico	Sri Lanka	Thailand	Vietnam	Indonesian Lampong Black	Indonesian Muntok White	Brazilian Black	Indian Malabar Black	Indian Telli-cherry[2]
1983	30,363	27,982	45,061	2,802	23,481	(2)	1,120	1,014	(2)	72.1	96.7	65.5	76.0	86.5
1984	36,499	28,381	33,817	2,097	16,502	1,562	2,202	2,325	(2)	98.6	153.9	96.5	98.9	115.2
1985	24,676	19,538	26,202	2,002	19,070	2,283	1,260	1,785	1,335	169.6	190.6	167.4	169.6	185.3
1986	22,069	49,808	29,566	972	15,380	1,794	1,286	1,816	3,133	215.0	275.3	212.5	214.6	235.1
1987	26,260	32,971	29,995	1,851	14,185	2,125	2,014	1,477	4,275	237.1	267.7	235.9	236.0	262.8
1988	24,393	47,258	41,568	2,497	19,190	2,602	2,714	910	2,612	173.9	243.4	170.3	170.3	220.6
1989	27,717	25,120	42,138	1,417	26,260	2,388	1,576	2,077	7,551	138.2	146.2	136.2	135.9	174.8
1990	28,014	34,429	47,675	1,222	27,706	2,663	2,609	4,042	1,288	99.1	90.3	97.1	97.1	139.1
1991	47,553	18,735	49,667	1,844	25,458	1,861	2,058	3,838	16,252	71.1	70.1	67.1	67.1	117.8
1992	25,702	19,399	61,438	1,948	21,932	3,441	2,127	6,158	22,358	56.1	70.8	54.7	54.7	86.1
1993[1]	29,202	56,000	46,010	2,383	23,733	3,645	5,279	5,292	14,000	62.5	114.6	62.3	62.3	84.0

[1]Preliminary. [2]Data not available. *Source: Foreign Agricultural Service, U.S. Department of Agriculture.*

United States Imports of Unground Pepper from Specified Countries   In Metric Tons

Year	Black: Brazil	China	India	Indonesia	Malaysia	Mexico	Singapore	Spain	Sri Lanka	Total	White: Brazil	China	Germany	Indonesia	Malaysia	Singapore	Total
1985	12,227	378	4,024	9,814	131	3	322	34	158	27,421	246	260	10	3,805	100	100	4,762
1986	9,416	243	20,976	5,980	634	7	120	1	255	38,063	134	171	7	2,846	65	140	3,578
1987	11,981	107	9,341	6,958	1,667	23	379	-----	388	31,372	65	6	1	4,238	22	110	4,533
1988	6,033	14	7,481	11,131	1,400	119	104	-----	344	26,939	20	2	25	4,169	12	26	4,326
1989	11,038	109	1,272	11,016	6,732	20	324	-----	375	31,819	37	38	1	5,272	63	90	5,549
1990	8,778	70	6,679	8,444	6,768	20	457	20	644	32,980	17	15	1	5,506	24	86	5,721
1991	15,069	4	2,308	11,330	8,154	20	391	-----	396	38,860	2	7	1	4,938	37	96	5,174
1992	6,601	1	9,892	20,768	2,073	160	52	1	310	40,590	51	2	-----	5,089	29	261	5,544
1993[1]	4,580	6	21,985	7,666	209	-----	-----	-----	539	35,969	322	114	3	4,304	137	363	5,481

[1]Preliminary.   *Source: Foreign Agricultural Service, U.S. Department of Agriculture.*

PEPPER

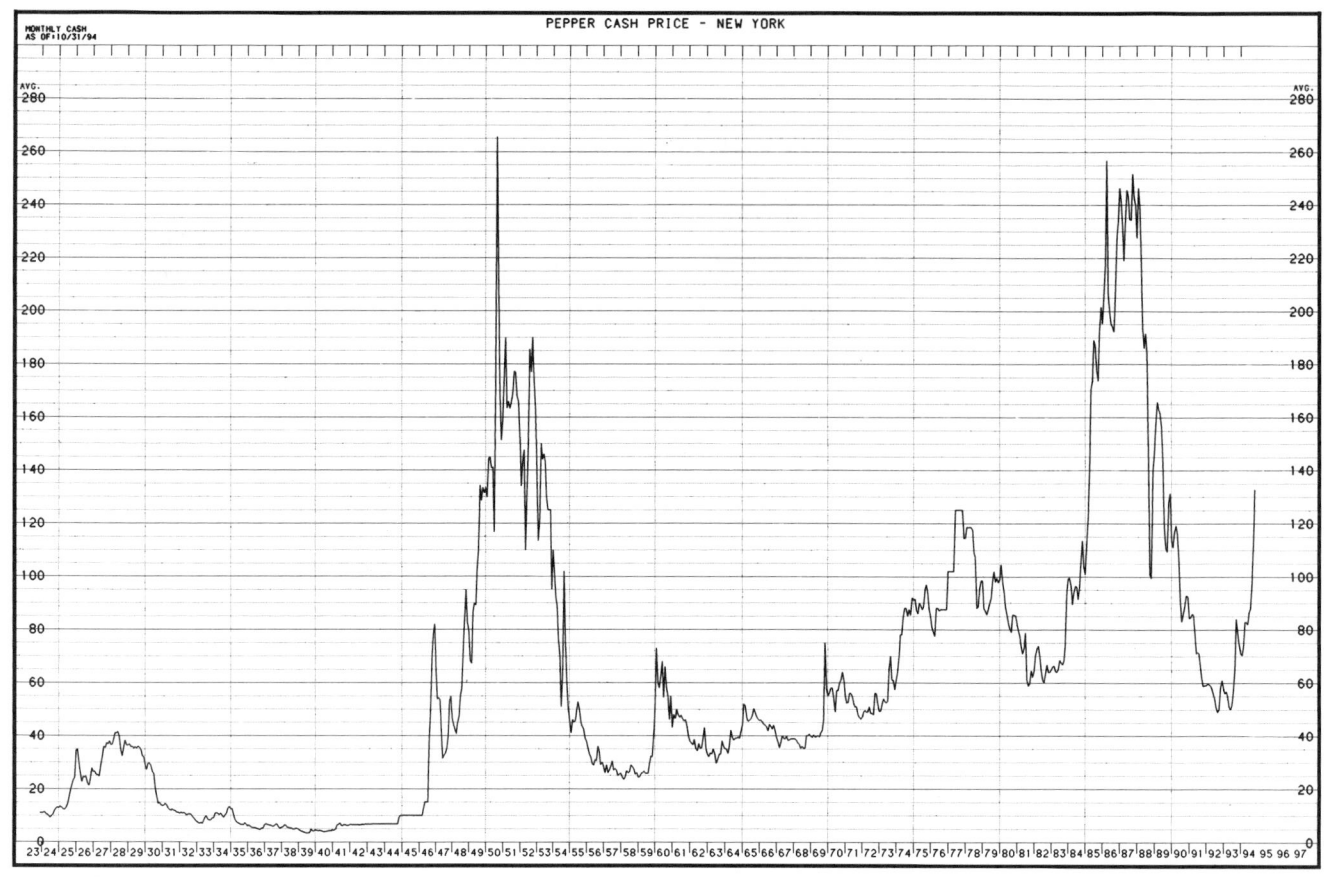

PEPPER CASH PRICE - NEW YORK

MONTHLY CASH AS OF 10/31/94

Average Black Pepper Prices in New York   In Cents Per Pound

Year	Jan	Feb	Mar	Apr	May	June	July	Aug	Sept	Oct	Nov	Dec	Average
1975	91.5	87.0	86.0	90.0	89.0	87.5	88.5	95.0	97.0	94.0	87.5	85.0	89.8
1976	81.0	79.0	77.5	88.0	88.0	87.0	87.5	87.5	NA	NA	NA	102.0	86.4
1977	102.0	102.0	102.0	102.0	125.0	125.0	125.0	125.0	125.0	125.0	114.5	NA	115.7
1978	118.5	118.5	118.5	118.5	117.5	109.0	107.5	88.0	88.5	95.5	98.5	98.5	106.4
1979	105.0	NA	130.0	NA	NA	95.0	97.0	110.0	108.0	108.0	102.0	101.3	106.3
1980	108.0	101.0	96.3	93.0	87.0	84.3	82.8	79.0	79.0	88.0	86.5	89.3	89.5
1981	88.5	93.3	92.0	81.0	83.0	82.3	84.0	82.5	82.3	82.3	82.5	82.5	84.7
1982	82.5	82.5	75.0	75.0	70.0	69.0	67.0	63.0	69.0	70.5	68.5	68.3	71.7
1983	68.3	66.5	66.3	65.5	65.5	65.5	75.0	69.3	76.3	77.3	83.5	83.5	71.9
1984[1]	99.5	96.5	89.4	93.9	96.4	96.2	89.3	94.8	104.0	110.5	100.0	97.5	97.3
1985	108.0	119.3	137.6	167.5	170.4	188.0	186.0	175.8	172.5	190.8	199.8	192.5	167.4
1986	197.6	210.5	250.0	206.0	198.2	193.8	193.8	190.8	204.8	226.0	232.0	246.2	212.5
1987	241.4	231.0	218.8	232.5	245.2	241.8	232.6	232.5	251.5	241.4	238.5	233.8	236.8
1988	233.3	228.8	210.5	190.3	184.3	190.5	182.8	141.5	100.2	99.5	138.3	143.0	170.3
1989	156.8	161.8	159.0	160.0	154.5	141.8	115.5	108.0	108.2	124.7	131.3	112.4	136.2
1990	107.0	110.8	115.4	115.0	106.0	91.0	82.3	85.8	88.5	92.3	89.6	81.8	97.1
1991	79.0	78.5	78.6	74.5	66.8	70.0	68.8	61.6	59.5	56.8	55.8	55.0	67.1
1992	55.6	54.5	56.0	55.3	54.0	54.0	50.8	49.0	50.0	57.8	61.0	58.0	54.7
1993	56.0	56.5	54.3	51.2	50.0	51.5	55.8	64.8	84.0	79.0	74.2	70.8	62.3
1994	69.3	74.3	82.0	82.8	82.0	86.5	87.8	97.8	112.2	131.5	123.5		93.6

[1]Brazilian black since 1984.   NA = Not available.   *Source: Foreign Agricultural Service, U.S. Department of Agriculture.*

Petroleum

Global oil stocks, including crude oil and petroleum products, were at historically low levels as the second quarter of 1994 began. This was due to a very cold winter in North America, higher than expected demand and steady foreign production. Worldwide demand for petroleum was expected to increase in 1994. Most of the demand growth was expected to occur in North America due to higher levels of economic activity.

U.S. field production of crude oil during the first eight months of 1994 averaged 6.65 million barrels per day. This compared with the average over the first eight months of 1993 of 6.68 million barrels, and 7.22 million in the like period of 1992. For all of 1993, field production of crude oil averaged 6.85 million barrels per day.

U.S. crude oil production has been in a downtrend for several years. In 1973, daily average crude oil production was 9.21 million barrels while by 1983 the average had fallen to 8.69 million barrels. Alaskan crude oil field production during January-August 1994 averaged 1.55 million barrels per day. Production has been falling since 1988 when it was 2.02 million barrels per day.

Ending stocks of crude oil and petroleum products in August 1994 were 1.65 billion barrels. This represented a slight decline from stocks in August 1993 of 1.68 billion barrels. Stocks in the Strategic Petroleum Reserve in August 1994 were 592 million barrels.

U.S. imports of crude oil continue to rise. During the January-August 1994 period, crude oil imports averaged 6.56 million barrels per day according to the Energy Information Administration. For the same period of 1993, crude oil imports averaged 6.73 million barrels per day. In 1973, U.S. imports of crude oil averaged 3.24 million barrels per day while by 1983 that figure had increased to 3.33 million.

Many countries export crude oil to the U.S. Imports of crude oil from Saudi Arabia during the January-July 1994 period averaged 1.24 million barrels per day, down 12 percent from the same period of 1993. Import levels from Saudi Arabia have fluctuated widely over the last twenty years. In 1991 they averaged 1.7 million barrels per day while in 1985 they had fallen to 132,000 barrels per day. Imports from Kuwait have recovered since the Gulf War. During the first seven months of 1994 they averaged 344,000 barrels per day, up substantially from the average over the like period of 1993 of 251,000 barrels. Another important supplier of U.S. crude oil needs is Venezuela. During the January-July 1994 period, Venezuela's daily exports to the U.S. averaged 986,000 barrels, about the same as in 1993. Nigeria's daily average exports were 587,000 barrels, down 30 percent from the like period of 1993.

The Organization of Petroleum Exporting Countries (OPEC) produced 25.86 million barrels of crude oil per day during the January-June 1994 period, virtually unchanged from 1993 and 1992.

U.S. consumption of petroleum during the January-April 1994 period averaged 17.72 million barrels per day. This represented an increase of over 4 percent from 1993. the increased use was attributable to the extremely cold winter in the Northeast. During February 1994, average daily use was 18.3 million barrels.

In late 1994, OPEC met to discuss goals for 1995. There was a general consensus that the current production ceiling of 24.52 million barrels a day would be extended for six more months. The ceiling was currently in place for the first quarter of 1995. There were conflicting opinions as to whether such an extension would actually increase prices or weaken them. It was felt that a six-month rollover could improve prices by between $1.50 and $2.00 a barrel in the first quarter of 1995. The price improvement would be due to colder weather in Europe and the U.S. OPEC was also due to appoint a new secretary-general.

Futures Markets

Futures and options contracts on light sweet crude oil, heating oil and unleaded gasoline are traded on the New York Mercantile Exchange (NYMEX). Propane and natural gas futures also are traded there.

London's International Petroleum Exchange (IPE) trades Brent crude oil futures and options on those futures. The IPE also trades heating oil futures and options (termed gas oil) and unleaded gasoline futures. High-sulfur fuel oil futures are traded on the SIMEX in Singapore.

World Production of Crude Petroleum, by Specified Countries   In Thousands of Barrels Per Day

Year	Algeria	Canada	China	Libya	Indo-nesia	Iran	Iraq	Kuwait	Mexico	Nigeria	Russia[3]	Saudi Arabia	United Kingdom	United States	Vene-zuela	World Total
1982	987	1,271	2,045	1,150	1,339	2,214	1,012	823	2,748	1,295	11,912	6,483	2,065	8,649	1,895	53,481
1983	968	1,356	2,120	1,105	1,343	2,440	1,005	1,064	2,689	1,241	11,972	5,086	2,291	8,688	1,801	53,255
1984	1,014	1,438	2,296	1,087	1,412	2,174	1,209	1,157	2,780	1,388	11,861	4,663	2,480	8,879	1,798	54,488
1985	1,037	1,471	2,505	1,059	1,325	2,250	1,433	1,023	2,745	1,495	11,585	3,388	2,530	8,971	1,677	53,981
1986	945	1,474	2,620	1,034	1,390	2,035	1,690	1,419	2,435	1,467	11,895	4,870	2,539	8,680	1,787	56,227
1987	1,048	1,535	2,690	972	1,343	2,298	2,079	1,585	2,548	1,341	11,985	4,265	2,406	8,349	1,752	56,601
1988	1,040	1,616	2,730	1,175	1,342	2,240	2,685	1,492	2,512	1,450	11,978	5,086	2,232	8,140	1,903	58,662
1989	1,095	1,560	2,757	1,150	1,409	2,810	2,897	1,783	2,520	1,716	11,625	5,064	1,802	7,613	1,907	59,773
1990	1,175	1,553	2,774	1,375	1,462	3,088	2,040	1,175	2,553	1,810	10,880	6,410	1,820	7,355	2,137	60,471
1991	1,230	1,548	2,805	1,483	1,613	3,334	298	187	2,676	1,892	9,887	8,181	1,797	7,417	2,375	60,221
1992	1,217	1,598	2,838	1,483	1,566	3,429	450	1,029	2,668	1,982	7,386	8,438	1,825	7,171	2,334	60,255
1993[1]	1,190	1,678	2,911	1,377	1,507	3,650	512	1,872	2,671	2,050	6,425	8,198	1,909	6,847	2,377	60,070
1994[2]	1,170	1,735	2,945	1,376	1,514	3,600	547	2,033	2,691	2,017	5,820	8,133	2,353	6,626	2,512	60,610

[1] Estimate.   [2] Preliminary.   [3] Formerly part of the U.S.S.R.; data not reported separately until 1992.   Source: Energy Information Administration.

U.S. Department of Energy

PETROLEUM
Refiner Sales Prices of Petroleum Products for Resale (Excluding Taxes) (In Cents Per Gallon)

Year	Jan.	Feb.	Mar.	Apr.	May	June	July	Aug.	Sept.	Oct.	Nov.	Dec.	Average
				Residual Fuel Oil (Sulfur 1% or less) to End Users									
1988	36.5	35.2	32.4	33.5	34.0	32.9	31.8	32.7	31.4	29.2	31.9	35.6	33.3
1989	38.8	37.0	38.8	44.1	43.6	39.3	39.0	37.3	38.2	40.2	40.5	47.7	40.7
1990	56.0	44.4	39.7	36.1	34.5	31.1	33.2	49.1	56.4	64.1	63.3	57.6	47.2
1991	52.1	36.5	36.0	33.6	36.6	32.1	32.6	33.4	33.7	34.1	36.6	34.8	36.4
1992	30.3	32.7	30.8	31.6	33.1	35.9	38.0	37.7	37.9	41.4	39.2	35.9	35.1
1993	36.8	35.5	39.1	38.4	34.8	33.7	32.7	31.6	31.9	32.1	30.7	27.5	33.7
1994/1	33.8	39.3	30.0	29.4	31.7	35.8	37.8	37.1	32.6	32.6	35.7		34.2
				No. 2 Fuel Oil									
1988	52.0	48.9	47.6	50.7	50.1	46.6	43.3	44.3	43.3	41.9	45.1	49.9	47.3
1989	53.2	51.1	54.4	56.5	52.6	49.6	50.4	51.2	56.4	60.1	60.4	72.8	56.5
1990	73.8	57.8	57.9	57.4	54.5	49.4	51.9	72.1	85.3	95.0	90.6	80.9	69.7
1991	76.6	67.9	59.6	57.2	56.0	54.0	56.7	60.6	62.1	66.3	66.6	55.9	62.2
1992	51.9	54.0	53.7	56.5	58.8	61.7	61.3	60.1	62.7	64.6	58.8	55.7	57.9
1993	54.4	56.9	59.0	57.5	56.9	55.0	51.0	51.0	54.8	58.1	53.1	45.1	54.4
1994/1	50.8	54.1	49.7	48.9	48.9	49.8	50.9	51.4	50.1	50.8	51.0		50.6
				No. 2 Diesel Fuel									
1988	51.0	49.0	49.2	51.9	51.3	47.9	44.0	45.0	44.7	42.0	44.6	48.0	47.3
1989	51.1	52.8	56.0	59.5	54.0	50.8	50.5	52.4	58.5	62.2	62.0	68.4	56.7
1990	69.3	57.1	57.6	57.6	55.4	50.5	52.0	73.7	87.2	99.4	93.6	79.8	69.4
1991	75.5	67.4	57.7	57.4	57.2	54.5	57.1	61.9	62.9	65.6	66.5	55.6	61.5
1992	51.4	54.1	54.0	57.0	60.1	62.7	61.8	60.4	63.3	65.5	60.4	56.4	59.1
1993	54.9	57.4	60.0	59.8	59.6	57.2	53.2	53.2	58.9	65.8	58.9	46.8	57.0
1994/1	49.1	52.8	52.9	52.3	51.7	52.2	53.7	54.1	54.2	55.2	55.1		53.0
				Kerosene-Type Jet Fuel									
1988	53.2	52.4	50.4	50.4	51.4	51.0	47.5	47.9	46.9	45.2	46.4	50.1	49.5
1989	56.2	55.4	56.5	59.5	56.6	54.4	53.5	54.5	58.6	63.2	63.4	67.3	58.3
1990	76.6	66.7	61.6	59.5	57.1	54.6	55.5	71.4	92.9	114.7	107.0	90.1	77.3
1991	82.0	74.0	62.4	58.9	60.8	58.8	59.4	63.3	65.9	67.1	68.2	60.1	65.0
1992	53.9	55.2	54.6	56.9	60.8	63.3	64.8	63.9	64.3	66.0	61.5	58.9	60.5
1993	57.7	60.4	60.3	59.8	60.1	58.5	55.1	55.1	56.6	60.5	58.7	51.0	57.7
1994/1	52.6	56	52.4	50.8	50.6	51.5	53.8	54.4	54	54.4	56.3		53.3
				Propane (Consumer Grade)									
1988	26.8	26.6	25.6	25.2	24.9	24.3	21.8	22.1	22.5	22.1	22.1	22.9	24.0
1989	24.0	22.7	22.5	22.7	22.1	21.4	20.7	21.7	23.1	24.4	24.3	36.4	24.7
1990	54.4	34.1	27.1	25.2	24.0	24.9	27.3	36.3	43.5	53.5	50.5	44.6	38.6
1991	42.2	31.6	31.3	31.8	31.9	29.3	27.6	29.6	34.9	40.2	43.0	37.7	34.9
1992	30.9	30.2	29.5	29.0	29.4	31.6	31.5	32.9	35.4	36.6	36.2	36.3	32.8
1993	40.2	36.7	38.2	36.2	34.0	33.8	33.3	33.3	34.1	34.7	33.6	30.9	35.1
1994/1	32.3	34.0	31.8	30.5	30.4	29.9	29.8	31.0	31.7	33.5	35.0		31.8

[1] Preliminary.   Source: Energy Information Administration

United States Crude Oil Supply & Distribution

Yearly Average	Field Production – Total Domestic	Alaskan	Imports Total	SPR[2]	Other	Unaccounted for Crude Oil	Stock Withdrawal/[3] SPR/[2]	Other	Disposition Refinery Inputs	Exports	Ending Stocks Total	SPR[2]	Other Primary
					Thousands of Barrels Per Day							Million of Barrels	
1985	8,971	1,825	3,201	118	3,083	145	117	67	12,002	204	814	493	321
1986	8,680	1,867	4,178	48	4,130	139	50	28	12,716	154	843	512	331
1987	8,349	1,962	4,674	73	4,601	145	80	49	12,854	151	890	541	349
1988	8,140	2,017	5,107	51	5,055	196	52	-51	13,246	155	890	560	330
1989	7,613	1,874	5,843	56	5,787	200	56	30	13,401	142	921	580	341
1990	7,355	1,773	5,894	27	5,867	258	16	-51	13,409	109	908	586	323
1991	7,417	1,798	5,782	0	5,782	195	-47	5	13,301	116	893	569	325
1992	7,171	1,714	6,083	10	6,073	258	17	-18	13,411	89	893	575	318
1993	6,847	1,582	6,787	15	6,772	168	34	47	13,613	98	922	587	335
1994/1	6,627	1,557	7,027	12	7,014	342	13	5	13,872	99	929	592	337

[1] Preliminary.   [2] Strategic Petroleum Reserve.   [3] A negative number indicates a decrease in stocks and a positive number indicates an increase.
Note: Crude oil includes lease condensate. Stocks of Alaskan crude oil in transit were included beginning in January 1981.
Source: Energy Information Administration; U.S. Department of Energy

Crude Petroleum Refinery Operations Ratio[1]   (In Percent of Capacity)

Year	Jan.	Feb.	Mar.	Apr.	May	June	July	Aug.	Sept.	Oct.	Nov.	Dec.	Average
1985	74	74	74	76	78	79	81	78	77	79	80	81	78
1986	81	78	76	82	86	86	84	87	86	83	84	84	83
1987	82	80	79	81	82	85	87	87	86	83	82	84	83
1988	83	81	83	84	86	86	86	87	84	83	84	85	84
1989	86	83	84	84	86	90	89	89	88	86	86	84	86
1990	88	88	84	85	87	89	93	91	91	84	84	83	87
1991	83	84	83	85	87	90	89	89	88	83	84	87	86
1992	83	81	85	86	89	92	92	89	91	89	90	88	88
1993	87	87	89	91	93	95	95	93	93	92	92	91	92
1994[2]	90	89	87	92	95	96	96	97	95	90	93		93

[1] Based on the ration of the daily average crude runs to stills to the rated capacity of refineries per day.   [2] Preliminary
Source: Bureau of Mines

United States Crude Oil Refinery Inputs   In Thousands of Barrels Per Day

Year	Jan	Feb	Mar	Apr	May	June	July	Aug	Sept	Oct	Nov	Dec	Average
1985	11,445	11,367	11,372	11,805	12,094	12,292	12,445	12,045	11,925	12,209	12,410	12,570	12,002
1986	12,374	11,918	11,652	12,512	13,279	13,261	12,917	13,287	13,097	12,636	12,831	12,777	12,716
1987	12,570	12,290	12,081	12,512	12,653	13,202	13,430	13,380	13,168	12,733	12,981	13,212	12,854
1988	12,920	12,644	13,016	13,135	13,425	13,487	13,617	13,752	13,261	13,126	13,156	13,381	13,246
1989	13,330	12,765	12,963	12,956	13,405	13,905	13,848	13,861	13,791	13,360	13,420	13,165	13,401
1990	13,491	13,487	12,876	13,051	13,386	13,689	14,212	14,142	14,104	12,825	12,953	12,708	13,409
1991	12,735	13,046	12,839	13,042	13,539	13,918	13,703	13,800	13,694	12,896	12,929	13,465	13,301
1992	12,923	12,486	13,083	13,260	13,679	14,059	13,953	13,426	13,714	13,584	13,547	13,194	13,411
1993	12,938	12,865	13,200	13,538	13,829	14,129	14,136	13,844	13,841	13,729	13,686	13,571	13,613
1994[1]	13,285	13,132	12,978	13,817	14,269	14,364	14,356	14,505	14,240	13,537	13,978	13,958	13,872

[1] Preliminary.   *Source: Energy Information Administration, U.S. Department of Energy*

Production of Major Refined Petroleum Products in Continental U.S.   In Millions of Barrels

Year	Asphalt	Aviation Gasoline	Fuel Oil Distillate	Fuel Oil Residual	Gasoline	Jet Fuel	Kerosene	Natural Gas Plant Liquids	Lubri-cants	Liquefied Gases Total	Liquefied Gases at L.P.G./2	Liquefied Gases at L.P.G./3
1985	146.3	9.3	980.9	322.0	2,352	433.9	34.5	607.5	53.1	622.0	479.3	142.6
1986	149.7	11.7	1,021.2	324.3	2,476	472.0	32.6	587.1	58.2	618.5	466.2	152.3
1987	158.4	9.1	996.6	323.2	2,506	490.1	28.7	605.6	60.9	638.2	474.5	163.7
1988	162.1	9.3	1,046.3	338.7	2,555	501.3	28.8	614.2	62.3	665.2	482.6	182.6
1989	154.9	9.2	1,152.2	500.1	2,684	543.6	30.8	586.1	58.1	653.5	451.3	202.2
1990	164.0	8.5	1,067.5	346.6	2,650	555.6	15.5	598.3	59.7	638.4	456.2	182.2
1991	156.8	8.0	1,081.0	341.1	2,554	525.0	14.0	639.2	57.0	683.1	487.5	195.6
1992	153.0	7.9	1,088.4	326.1	2,591	512.0	14.8	668.0	57.5	738.7	499.7	222.2
1993[1]	165.6	7.9	1,139.7	303.9	2,644	518.8	17.5	631.2	58.4	509.9	297.3	212.6

[1] Preliminary.   [2] Gas processing plants.   [3] Refineries.   *Source: Energy Information Administration, U.S. Department of Energy*

Stocks of Petroleum & Products in the United States on January 1   (In Millions of Barrels)

Year	Crude Petroleum	Strategic Reserve	Refined Products Total	Asphalt	Aviation Gasoline	Fuel Oil Distillate	Fuel Oil Residual	Finished Gasoline	Jet Fuel	Kero-sene	Liquefied Gases[2]	Lubri-cants	Motor Gasoline Total	Motor Gasoline Finished[3]
1985	795.9	450.5	620.6	17.2	2.7	161.1	53.0	207.9	42.0	11.9	100.8	12.7	223	190
1986	814.2	493.3	556.6	21.2	2.1	143.7	50.4	192.4	40.5	7.5	73.5	11.8	233	194
1987	842.8	511.6	609.4	17.7	2.2	155.1	47.4	196.4	49.7	8.4	102.7	14.2	226	189
1988	889.6	540.6	579.5	18.8	2.3	134.5	47.4	191.1	49.9	8.4	97.1	13.3	228	190
1989	889.9	559.5	561.6	20.8	2.1	123.5	44.6	192.0	43.8	7.3	97.3	13.3	213	177
1990	921.1	579.9	508.3	20.6	2.1	105.7	43.8	179.1	40.9	5.1	80.2	13.8	220	181
1991	908.4	585.7	566.8	18.7	1.7	132.2	48.6	182.4	52.1	5.6	97.9	12.4	219	182
1992	893.1	568.5	576.7	22.3	1.6	143.5	49.9	183.3	48.8	5.8	92.3	12.3	216	178
1993	892.9	574.7	549.1	17.7	1.6	140.6	42.6	179.1	43.1	5.7	88.7	13.3	221	182
1994[1]	922.5	587.1	465.8	19.1	1.8	140.9	44.2	185.7	40.4	4.1	106.6	11.8	227	187

[1] Preliminary.   [2] Includes ethane & ethylene at plants and refineries.   [3] Includes oxygenated.   *Source: Energy Info. Administration; U.S. Dept. of Energy*

PETROLEUM

Stocks of Crude Petroleum in the United States at Beginning of Month — In Millions of Barrels

Year	Jan.	Feb.	Mar.	Apr.	May	June	July	Aug.	Sept.	Oct.	Nov.	Dec.
1985	795.9	793.5	781.6	791.2	806.8	828.6	820.6	810.5	805.6	806.6	803.6	812.4
1986	814.2	826.1	827.1	837.8	836.6	828.5	828.4	845.2	837.7	844.2	851.4	848.6
1987	842.8	847.9	848.6	852.4	850.9	849.8	854.8	853.8	864.4	871.1	891.5	902.2
1988	889.6	888.3	892.2	898.9	904.6	907.6	908.9	900.8	885.7	883.2	895.6	895.7
1989	889.9	894.8	896.6	892.5	907.4	915.7	903.0	907.6	916.3	912.0	914.3	930.5
1990	921.1	932.9	924.0	955.9	953.1	968.7	970.9	966.2	959.2	932.7	935.7	924.7
1991	908.4	905.3	912.8	905.3	907.2	924.3	915.3	910.6	913.8	909.1	910.7	912.0
1992	893.1	909.7	914.8	907.1	916.5	912.0	894.6	902.2	898.3	893.5	906.2	899.4
1993	892.9	902.0	908.1	914.7	930.4	935.0	935.1	935.2	919.6	906.4	916.5	924.1
1994/1	922.5	922.0	917.4	927.9	926.2	919.5	913.4	919.2	917.9	921.3	930.4	933.5

[1] Preliminary.   *Source: Energy Information Administration; U.S. Department of Energy*

Production of Crude Petroleum in the Unites States — In Thousands of Barrels Per Day

Year	Jan.	Feb.	Mar.	Apr.	May	June	July	Aug.	Sept.	Oct.	Nov.	Dec.	Average
1984	8,868	8,874	8,672	8,862	8,955	8,852	8,885	8,809	8,993	8,906	8,979	8,897	8,879
1985	8,740	9,025	9,095	9,043	9,132	9,022	8,949	8,803	8,954	8,970	8,902	9,030	8,971
1986	9,137	9,173	9,013	8,864	8,838	8,623	8,660	8,374	8,328	8,419	8,412	8,352	8,680
1987	8,480	8,389	8,464	8,498	8,336	8,279	8,251	8,210	8,205	8,364	8,397	8,318	8,349
1988	8,250	8,374	8,374	8,288	8,229	8,170	8,040	8,079	7,895	8,023	8,023	7,942	8,140
1989	7,937	7,788	7,575	7,772	7,816	7,624	7,444	7,544	7,548	7,453	7,536	7,337	7,613
1990	7,546	7,497	7,433	7,407	7,328	7,106	7,173	7,287	7,224	7,542	7,387	7,338	7,355
1991	7,500	7,637	7,546	7,509	7,409	7,320	7,347	7,316	7,368	7,437	7,328	7,299	7,417
1992	7,361	7,389	7,348	7,293	7,169	7,167	7,131	6,922	7,030	7,126	7,024	7,103	7,171
1993/1	6,961	6,943	6,974	6,881	6,847	6,795	6,688	6,758	6,712	6,839	6,912	6,858	6,847
1994/2	6,777	6,745	6,719	6,634	6,658	6,567	6,528	6,547	6,551	6,578	6,542	6,686	6,627

[1] Preliminary.   [2] Estimate.   *Source: Energy Information Administration; U.S. Department of Energy*

U.S. Foreign Trade of Petroleum and Products — In Thousands of Barrels Per Day

	Exports		Imports						Exports		Imports			
Year	Total[2]	Petroleum Products	Crude	Petroleum Products	Distillate Fuel Oil	Residual Fuel Oil	Net Imports[3]	Year	Total[2]	Petroleum Products	Crude	Petroleum Products	Distillate Fuel Oil	Residual Fuel Oil	Net Imports[3]
1975	209	204	4,105	1,951	1	15	5,846	1985	781	577	3,201	1,866	67	197	4,286
1976	223	215	5,287	2,026	1	12	7,090	1986	785	631	4,178	2,045	100	147	5,439
1977	243	193	6,615	2,193	1	6	8,565	1987	764	613	4,674	2,004	66	186	5,914
1978	362	204	6,356	2,008	3	13	8,002	1988	815	661	5,107	2,295	69	200	6,587
1979	471	236	6,519	1,937	3	9	7,985	1989	859	717	5,843	2,217	97	215	7,202
1980	544	258	5,263	1,646	3	33	6,365	1990	857	748	5,894	2,123	109	211	7,161
1981	595	367	4,396	1,599	5	118	5,401	1991	1,001	885	5,782	1,844	215	226	6,626
1982	815	579	3,488	1,325	74	209	4,298	1992	950	861	6,083	1,805	219	193	6,938
1983	739	575	3,329	1,722	64	185	4,312	1993	1,003	904	6,787	1,833	274	123	7,618
1984	722	541	3,426	2,011	51	190	4,715	1994/1	942	843	7,027	1,902	234	125	7,986

[1] Preliminary.   [2] Includes crude oil.   [3] Equals imports minus exports.   *Source: Energy Information Administration; U.S. Department of Energy*

Domestic First Purchase Price of Crude Petroleum at Wells[1] — In Dollars Per Barrel

Year	Jan.	Feb.	Mar.	Apr.	May	June	July	Aug.	Sept.	Oct.	Nov.	Dec.	Average
1985	24.26	23.64	23.89	24.19	24.18	24.07	24.04	23.99	23.96	24.10	24.27	24.51	24.09
1986	23.12	17.65	12.62	10.68	10.75	10.68	9.25	9.77	11.09	11.00	11.05	11.73	12.51
1987	13.79	14.51	14.54	14.95	15.29	15.95	16.88	17.06	16.25	15.95	15.46	14.27	15.40
1988	13.64	13.43	12.96	13.92	14.12	13.59	12.38	12.22	11.63	10.62	10.31	11.99	12.58
1989	13.80	14.24	15.65	17.04	16.76	16.42	16.32	15.01	15.58	16.25	16.30	17.01	15.86
1990	18.49	18.16	16.57	14.52	13.82	12.79	14.03	21.87	28.46	30.86	27.53	22.63	20.03
1991	19.60	16.28	15.13	16.16	16.44	15.58	16.36	16.60	16.71	17.72	17.12	14.68	16.54
1992	13.99	14.04	14.12	15.36	16.38	17.96	17.80	17.07	17.20	17.16	16.00	14.94	15.99
1993	14.70	15.53	15.94	16.15	16.03	15.06	13.83	13.75	13.39	13.72	12.45	10.38	14.25
1994/2	10.51	10.73	10.81	12.33	14.03	14.95	15.31	14.50	13.62	13.84	14.14		13.16

[1] Buyers posted prices.   [2] Preliminary.   *Source: Energy Information Administration; U.S. Department of Energy*

Volume of Trading of Crude Oil Futures in New York   In Thousands of Contracts

Year	Jan.	Feb.	Mar.	Apr.	May	June	July	Aug.	Sept.	Oct.	Nov.	Dec.	Total
1985	385	263	299	273	290	342	330	270	340	366	338	387	3,981
1986	520	491	560	691	677	613	861	702	667	986	604	942	8,314
1987	873	968	1,199	1,059	937	1,196	1,412	1,505	1,126	1,205	1,287	1,813	14,582
1988	1,626	1,336	1,809	1,352	1,205	1,507	1,754	1,219	1,956	2,040	1,609	1,450	18,859
1989	1,919	1,524	2,053	2,070	1,911	2,082	1,663	1,343	1,541	1,521	1,425	1,483	20,535
1990	2,164	1,790	1,794	1,813	1,945	1,839	2,046	2,716	2,073	2,437	1,769	1,302	23,687
1991	1,997	1,478	1,605	1,885	1,741	1,411	1,675	1,598	1,543	2,064	2,051	1,960	21,008
1992	2,097	1,630	1,620	1,889	1,885	2,006	1,796	1,531	1,541	1,797	1,542	1,778	21,110
1993	2,139	1,886	1,895	1,459	1,641	2,018	2,616	2,200	2,679	1,945	2,378	2,122	24,869
1994	2,296	1,933	2,228	2,382	2,602	2,576	2,186	2,544	1,897	2,195	2,196	1,778	16,812

Source: New York Mercantile Exchange

Average Open Interest of Crude Oil Futures in New York   In Contracts

Year	Jan.	Feb.	Mar.	Apr.	May	June	July	Aug.	Sept.	Oct.	Nov.	Dec.
1987	127,129	144,569	160,668	155,686	143,305	147,501	177,760	195,468	197,623	183,276	165,489	199,806
1988	202,830	200,813	210,878	192,074	177,155	180,019	177,978	177,879	220,973	221,628	196,454	196,109
1989	204,066	210,299	224,322	248,032	231,390	222,748	221,389	209,702	230,990	235,716	242,677	257,974
1990	273,193	300,069	287,013	287,538	278,600	285,384	275,771	262,746	266,313	269,167	242,500	232,405
1991	249,759	272,396	285,417	303,942	286,159	277,587	278,704	267,186	264,223	298,434	292,889	284,453
1992	310,763	331,050	316,544	340,315	335,545	364,155	331,972	316,066	314,446	301,381	308,467	330,134
1993	352,316	369,180	385,768	381,954	384,309	396,832	423,041	428,418	404,172	397,121	404,046	427,756
1994	427,705	438,929	424,462	410,974	427,071	414,257	409,251	396,657	395,194	413,206	388,932	391,151

Source: New York Mercantile Exchange

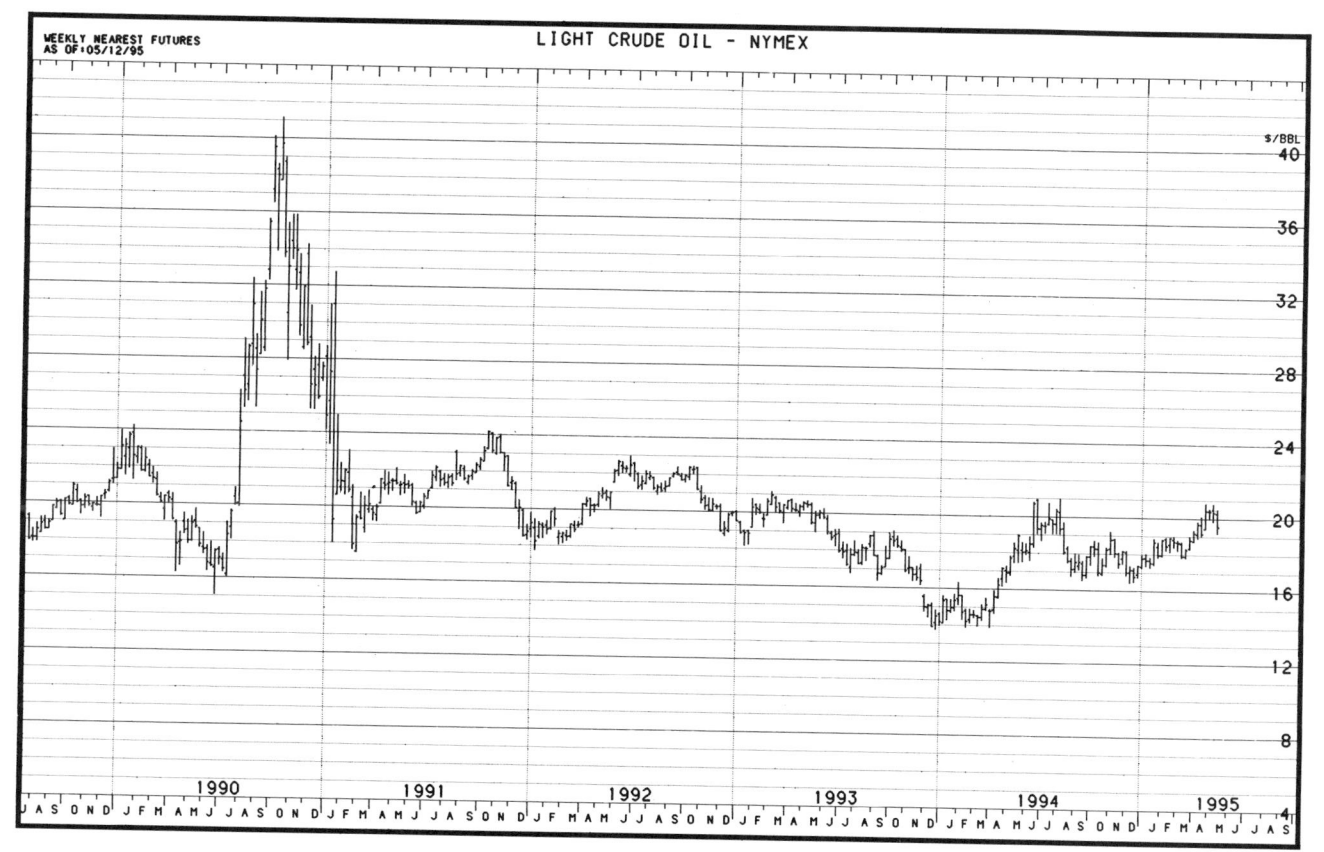

Plastics

Plastics find wide use in a variety of products ranging from packaging materials to replacement material for wood, metals, glass and paper. A major concern of the industry has been the environmental impact of the disposal of items containing plastic material. The recycling of plastic material has taken on increasing importance in many communities.

One area where plastic is making a significant contribution is in the automobile industry. This has been attributed to the need by automakers to keep the prices of cars down and partly to increase gasoline efficiency by making vehicles lighter. New high-temperature plastics continue to find increasing use in a variety of products and have many applications in the aviation and aerospace industries. In automobile production, these new products find use in bumpers, gas tanks, hoods and fenders. In 1993, the fastest growing segments of the plastics industry were engineering resin, high-density polyethylene polyvinyl chloride, and polyolefins.

According to the Society of the Plastics Industry, Inc., plastic production using thermoset resins in the U.S. in 1993 was 6.87 billion pounds, up eight percent from 1992. Production using polyester unsaturated thermosets in 1993 was 1.19 billion pounds, about one percent more than in 1992. Production using phenolic thermosets was 2.08 billion pounds in 1993, up 5 percent.

Plastic production using thermoplastic resin in 1993 was 51.2 billion pounds, up almost three percent from

1992. Plastic production using low density polyethylene resin in 1993 was 12.1 billion pounds while plastic output using high density polyethylene resin in 1993 was 9.94 billion pounds. Total plastic production in the U.S. in 1993 was 68.9 billion pounds, up close to four percent from the 1992 total of 66.4 billion pounds.

In terms of use by market, plastic resins are used in a number of important industries. By far the dominant use is in packaging, which in 1993 used 19.6 billion pounds (dry weight) of plastic resins, an increase of seven percent from 1992. Packing takes about 30 percent of the total use of plastic resins. The next largest use is building and construction, which took 12.9 billion pounds of plastic resins in 1993, a yearly increase of eight percent. Consumption of plastic resin for consumer and industrial purposes was just over 6 billion pounds, down one percent. Transportation absorbed 3.2 billion pounds while furniture and furnishings took 2.8 billion pounds. Between 1991 and 1992, plastic resin use by transportation rose 21 percent, while between 1992 and 1993 it increased 14 percent. Between 1991 and 1992, the furniture and furnishings industry increased use by 13 percent while between 1992 and 1993 it rose almost eight percent.

Exports of plastic resin have been declining. In 1993, they were 6.6 billion pounds, down five percent from 1992 while in 1992 the export total of seven billion pounds was down six percent from 1991.

Plastic Production by Resin in the United States   In Millions of Pounds

Year	Thermosets Polyester Unsaturated	Phenolic	Epoxy	Total Thermosets	Thermoplastics Thermoplastic Polyester	Polyvinyl Chloride	Poly-styrene	Poly-propylene	Nylon	Density Polyethylene[1]	Density Polyethylene	Total Thermoplastics	Total Selected Plastics	Other Plastics	Total Plastics
1985	1,223	2,640	385	5,631	965	6,772	4,054	5,139	399	8,889	6,671	34,004	39,635	8,311	47,946
1986	1,271	2,735	398	5,848	1,175	7,256	4,470	5,812	465	8,903	7,182	36,447	42,295	8,554	50,849
1987	1,367	2,869	433	6,263	1,394	7,971	4,780	6,647	507	9,599	7,995	40,194	46,457	9,294	55,751
1988	1,404	3,066	486	6,588	1,652	8,350	5,187	7,274	566	10,397	8,400	43,251	49,839	9,923	59,762
1989	1,319	2,879	510	6,407	1,630	8,478	5,104	7,238	569	9,695	8,102	42,189	48,596	9,933	58,529
1990	1,221	2,946	499	6,364	1,879	9,096	5,021	8,310	558	11,148	8,337	45,646	52,010	9,950	61,960
1991	1,075	2,658	497	5,909	2,115	9,164	4,954	8,330	576	11,582	9,213	47,146	53,055	9,731	62,786
1992	1,175	2,923	457	6,335	2,413	9,989	5,096	8,421	668	11,917	9,808	49,751	56,086	10,285	66,371
1993	1,185	3,078	512	6,868	2,549	10,257	5,382	8,628	768	12,067	9,941	51,159	58,027	10,777	68,854

[1] Includes LDPE and LLDPE.   *Source: The Society of the Plastics Industry, Inc.*

Total Resin Sales and Captive Use by Important Markets   In Millions of Pounds (Dry Weight Basis)

Year	Adhesive, Inks & Coatings	Building & Construction	Consumer & Industrial	Electrical & Electronics	Exports	Furniture & Furnishings	Industrial & Machinary	Packaging	Transportation	Other	Total
1989	1,211	11,096	6,217	3,145	[1]	2,285	475	14,711	2,547	10,911	52,598
1990	1,373	11,803	5,861	3,165	[1]	2,190	636	16,568	2,504	11,811	55,910
1991	1,391	10,650	5,689	2,896	7,418	2,255	587	16,723	2,328	6,616	56,553
1992	1,723	11,876	6,093	2,766	6,950	2,559	617	18,284	2,817	6,877	60,562
1993	1,572	12,885	6,015	2,981	6,632	2,759	768	19,569	3,221	7,234	63,636

[1] Included in other.   *Source: The Society of the Plastics Industry, Inc.*

Average Producer Price Index of Plastic Materials in the United States (1982 = 100)

Year	Jan	Feb	Mar	Apr	May	June	July	Aug	Sept	Oct	Nov	Dec	Average
					Plastic Resins and Materials (066)								
1986	300.9	302.4	301.8	296.6	295.6	295.2	296.7	294.4	290.1	292.9	295.0	290.3	296.0
1987[1]	102.6	102.4	103.2	106.3	107.0	109.7	112.8	113.1	114.2	116.8	117.4	117.7	110.3
1988	121.5	123.5	124.4	127.6	130.1	131.2	134.8	136.9	138.9	139.8	140.2	140.1	132.4
1989	140.3	141.1	140.6	140.7	139.8	138.0	135.3	127.7	126.1	124.7	123.7	123.3	133.4
1990	122.2	121.6	122.2	123.0	123.5	123.0	122.1	122.3	123.6	125.1	128.6	131.2	124.0
1991	131.1	128.7	125.4	122.9	120.6	117.0	115.0	114.9	114.9	116.4	116.7	116.0	120.0
1992	115.4	115.6	114.2	114.2	114.7	115.2	115.9	117.7	117.5	118.2	118.1	118.1	116.2
1993	118.3	118.0	117.6	117.1	116.3	116.9	116.9	117.6	117.4	116.9	116.2	116.2	117.1
1994[3]	1,153.0	114.7	114.7	116.5	117.7	119.1	119.6	121.5	126.2	130.4	133.0	136.0	208.5
					Thermoplastic Resins (0662)								
1986	108.7	109.4	109.0	106.9	106.3	105.9	106.7	105.7	103.6	105.2	106.2	103.9	106.5
1987[2]	102.3	102.1	103.1	107.3	107.9	111.1	113.9	114.1	115.3	118.5	119.3	119.7	111.2
1988	124.4	126.7	127.8	131.1	133.7	134.9	139.0	141.2	143.5	144.3	144.4	142.2	136.3
1989	114.5	145.2	144.4	143.9	143.2	141.1	137.7	128.5	126.7	125.1	124.0	124.0	133.2
1990	122.9	121.9	122.5	123.5	124.1	123.4	122.4	122.5	124.1	125.8	130.5	134.0	124.8
1991	132.1	129.4	125.5	122.9	120.2	116.2	113.8	113.7	114.6	115.5	116.0	115.3	119.6
1992	114.7	114.7	113.0	112.9	113.4	114.1	114.8	117.1	116.8	117.6	117.6	117.5	115.4
1993	117.5	117.1	116.3	115.8	114.8	115.4	115.5	116.4	116.4	116.4	115.5	114.6	116.0
1994[3]	113.0	112.7	112.7	115.0	116.2	117.9	118.4	120.1	125.2	129.9	132.2	135.8	120.8
					PE Resin, Low, Film & Sheeting (0662-0301)								
1986	224.7	224.7	224.7	224.7	224.7	224.7	224.7	224.7	NA	224.0	222.5	224.5	224.4
1987[2]	112.3	113.1	110.5	113.9	114.6	121.5	123.9	127.8	127.9	131.9	138.8	140.7	123.1
1988	145.9	150.3	153.8	157.9	171.4	172.0	178.3	192.3	201.3	203.5	202.7	201.6	177.6
1989	202.0	206.6	206.0	204.0	200.8	195.3	191.9	151.5	150.3	150.9	152.3	153.0	180.4
1990	151.9	145.3	146.1	145.9	152.5	151.7	144.9	141.9	152.3	145.6	149.8	157.4	148.8
1991	158.1	150.7	142.6	135.8	130.1	121.9	117.8	114.8	113.9	123.2	131.3	124.6	130.4
1992	126.5	130.9	126.7	121.3	123.5	122.4	132.9	138.9	145.2	149.3	148.6	150.6	134.7
1993	NA	151.4	145.6	141.8	135.5	137.1	132.2	136.6	129.2	128.4	127.6	127.4	135.7
1994[3]	121.6	119.4	119.3	120.8	127.6	134.5	136.3	140.8	146.7	153.9	166.3	183.1	139.2
					Styrene Plastics Materials (0662-06)								
1987[2]	96.0	96.1	101.3	108.3	110	116.8	119.6	115.4	117.6	116.6	119.5	119.7	111.4
1988	122.2	125.2	127.0	128.9	129.0	131.7	133.6	134.1	134.1	135.4	134.7	134.8	130.9
1989	135.3	136.3	134.4	135.8	135.1	133.1	124.6	119.5	119.0	116.8	114.2	114.4	126.5
1990	113.1	114.7	117.2	116.8	116.8	115.2	113.7	113.7	116.8	123.4	127.8	124.2	117.8
1991	123.3	122.7	115.4	115.5	112.4	121.9	109.2	107.7	108.3	113.0	113.0	111.5	114.5
1992	109.5	109.6	109.1	109.1	110.3	109.4	110.4	112.6	111.2	112.5	111.7	111.5	110.6
1993	110.7	110.5	110.0	110.4	111.0	111.3	111.2	111.1	110.6	109.1	106.5	106.4	109.9
1994[3]	105.8	104.1	104.1	108.1	108.3	109.2	110.4	110.6	115.5	122.7	125.0	120.6	112.0
					Thermosetting Resins (0663)								
1986	114.9	115.0	115.1	113.7	113.5	114.0	114.0	113.4	113.3	112.7	112.8	112.7	113.8
1987[2]	101.5	101.4	101.9	102.2	103.6	105.5	110.6	111.1	111.8	111.8	111.3	111.0	107.0
1988	110.2	110.4	110.7	113.5	115.4	115.7	116.8	118.4	119.2	120.0	122.4	122.7	116.3
1989	122.4	124.0	124.9	127.9	126.6	126.5	126.8	127.5	126.9	126.6	125.9	123.8	125.8
1990	122.8	124.0	124.1	124.4	124.3	124.7	124.7	124.8	125.0	125.6	124.0	126.6	124.6
1991	130.1	129.1	128.9	127.1	126.3	125.2	124.9	124.9	123.9	124.5	123.8	123.1	126.0
1992	123.1	124.1	123.9	124.3	124.4	124.4	124.7	125.0	125.0	125.3	125.1	125.2	124.5
1993	126.1	126.5	127.4	127.5	127.8	128.0	127.7	127.7	127.9	127.8	127.8	128.3	127.5
1994[3]	128.2	128.1	128.2	127.8	128.7	129.1	129.7	132.1	135.1	137.7	141.4	141.5	132.3
					Phenolic & Tar Acid Resins (0663-02)								
1986	113.4	113.4	113.3	111.5	110.6	110.0	109.9	110.0	110.0	110.0	110.0	110.2	111.0
1987	103.7	103.0	105.1	104.8	111.8	117.9	127.1	129.7	132.8	132.1	130.6	129.8	119.0
1988	126.8	126.2	126.4	128.8	135.4	136.2	141.6	143.6	147.1	150.9	154.8	157.1	139.6
1989	156.7	158.9	162.6	166.8	164.2	164.4	166.2	159.5	158.6	158.0	156.9	152.3	160.4
1990	148.2	149.4	149.1	148.7	148.5	147.3	143.9	142.5	141.5	139.0	138.2	143.7	145.0
1991	146.4	147.3	142.4	140.7	138.3	132.8	131.6	131.5	128.3	129.7	126.5	125.5	135.1
1992	125.4	126.4	125.1	124.7	125.6	125.6	127.7	127.6	127.9	129.7	128.8	128.5	126.9
1993	128.5	130.3	130.5	131.4	133.7	134.1	133.9	132.8	133.1	132.1	132.0	132.9	132.1
1994[2]	133.0	130.9	129.7	131.3	134.1	135.9	139.2	143.7	147.6	155.1	160.2	160.9	141.8

[1] Indexes prior to 1987=100. [2] Indexes prior to 1987 are Dec. 1980=100. [3] Preliminary. NA = Not available.

Source: Bureau of Labor Statistics, U.S. Dept. of Commerce

Platinum-Group Metals

Platinum prices trended higher during much of 1994, extending the advance that took root around $350 per ounce in September 1993 and carrying to $435 nine months later, basis nearby futures values in New York. The price strength largely reflected the stronger U.S. economy and the likelihood that it would enhance the demand for platinum. Towards the close of 1994, however, prices retreated to under $400/oz. in sympathy with the slippage in gold and silver prices and the fear that higher U.S. interest rates would slow the economy's growth.

Palladium price trends generally take their cue from platinum, but in 1994 a lag developed in that nearby palladium futures did not peak until early November at $164 per ounce and the slippage into year-end was contained towards $150. The short-term variables effecting the price of both metals is generally more supply sensitive, especially to developments in South Africa. Significantly, the marketplace took in stride the profound changes in South Africa's political structure during 1994. The historic all-race elections in April brought about only a holiday-based moderate loss in production.

Both metals had a protracted basing action during 1991 and 1992; for platinum near $350/oz and palladium around $80 that likely helped support the firmness in 1994 and carried platinum to its highest level since 1990 and palladium to a five-year high. Palladium's price action since 1992 has been the more dramatic, on a percentage basis, but that partially reflects the relatively low liquidity of the palladium market. Indeed, both metals have low market liquidity (relative to gold and silver) if the open interest in the futures markets serves as a clue: for platinum in 1994 it averaged about 25,000 contracts, while palladium averaged around 7,500, well under the 150,000 or so for gold and 100,000 contracts for silver.

Six metals make up the platinum group, but reasonably up to date statistical data is limited to platinum and palladium; for iridium, osmium, rhodium and ruthenium the data is spotty at best. The world's annual platinum group metal production averages about 280,000 kilograms with more than half produced by South Africa. In the late 1980s Russia produced about a third of world output. Production has since declined, but by how much is not readily known. Canada's recent annual production has averaged about 11,500 kilograms and U.S. production, most of which is palladium, has averaged less less than 8,000 kilograms. The U.S. is almost totally dependent on foreign supplies. Reportedly, the U.S. has large deposits of platinum metals in the Montana region, but the extracting costs for full scale operations exceed the metals' value.

The platinum group's inherent properties make it a needed industrial metal(s). The U.S. imports half the world's production, but re-exports a portion as refined platinum. In 1993, U.S. apparent platinum metal consumption totaled 121,564 kilograms, vs. 109,469 kg in 1992. Apparent is defined by the U.S. Bureau of Mines as: mine production + non-toll production refined imports − refined exports + beginning stocks − ending stocks.

The automotive industry is the largest consumer of platinum due to the metal's use as an emissions control catalyst. The electrical industry takes less than half the automotive needs and the jewelry industry less than 10 percent. Apparent consumption in the first half of 1994 suggests that the year's consumption will lag 1993. In either case, more than half of 1993's consumption was palladium (63,597 kg) with platinum taking 46,602 kg.

U.S. imports of platinum group metals in 1993 totaled about 153,000 kilograms, of which palladium accounted for almost 79,000 kg and platinum much of the balance (and included platinum coins). The market value of 1993 imports totaled about $1.3 billion. South Africa is the largest supplier to the U.S. followed by Russia. However, The U.K. and Belgium also export relatively large quantities of refined platinum–group metals to the U.S. In the first quarter of 1994 the U.S. imported almost 36,000 kg., vs. 34,000 in the same period of 1993 with a market value of $303 million vs. $297 million, respectively. The U.S. exported 35,380 kg. in the first quarter of 1994, compared to 24,319 a year earlier. Almost all U.S. exports are relegated to the category known as waste and scrap, of which Belgium took almost half with Japan and the U.K. accounting for most of the balance.

Producers maintain an artificial price for the platinum group metals: Through the first half of 1994 and for all of 1993 it was $600 per ounce for platinum, $150 for palladium, $1275 for rhodium and osmium at $400. Dealer or market prices are generally much lower: platinum averaged $370 in 1993 and near $400 in 1994; palladium averaged $120 in 1993 and in the $140 during 1994 while rhodium in the first half of 1994 averaged about $730 per kg. Through 1994 platinum maintained a premium to gold, as it usually does, with the differential averaging about $25 per ounce in the second half of 1994, wider than seen during the first.

Futures Markets

Platinum and palladium futures and options are traded on the New York Mercantile Exchange (NYMEX). In Japan, platinum and palladium futures are listed on the Tokyo Commodity Exchange (TOCOM).

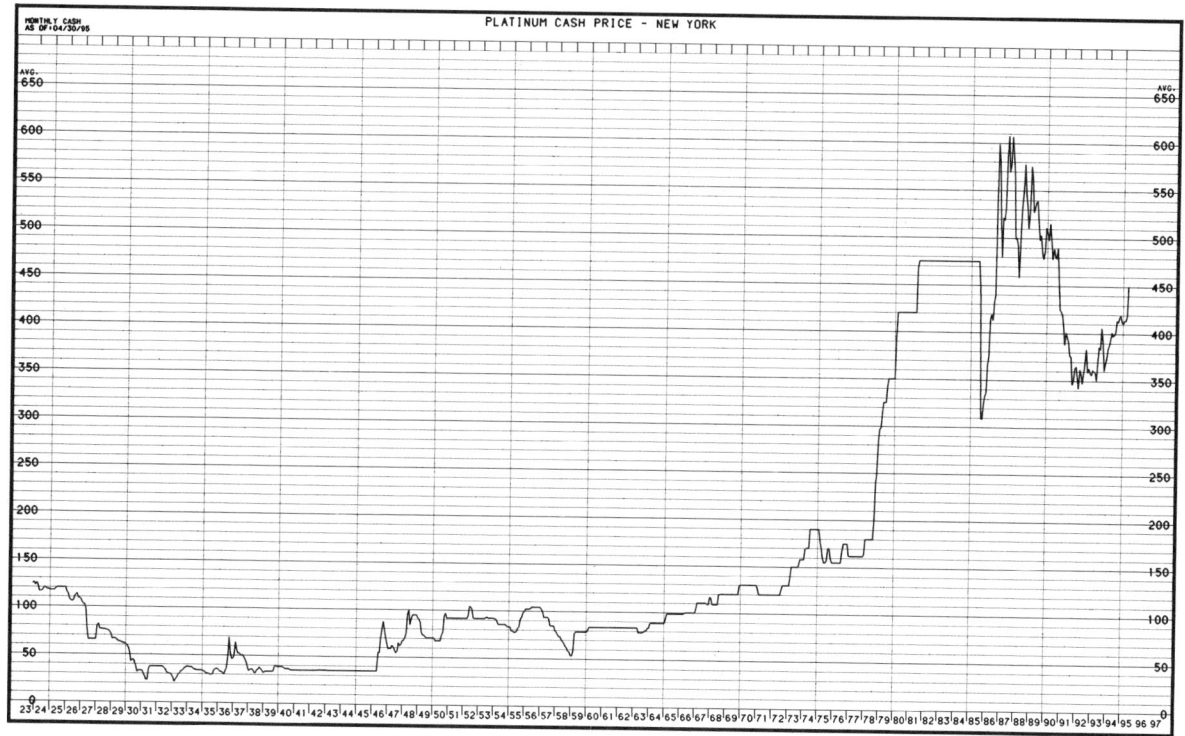

PLATINUM CASH PRICE - NEW YORK

World Mine Production of Platinum–Group Metals   In Kilograms

Year	Australia	Canada Platinum	Canada Palladium	Canada Total	Colombia[3]	Japan Platinum	Japan Palladium	Russia[4] Platinum	Russia[4] Palladium	Russia[4] Total	South Africa Platinum	South Africa Palladium	South Africa Total	United States Platinum	United States Palladium	World Total
1985	571	-----	-----	10,485	362	691	1,359	-----	-----	118,200	-----	-----	115,100	W	W	246,988
1986	543	5,242	5,486	12,190	447	663	1,453	30,000	81,000	121,300	73,100	32,300	123,200	W	W	260,193
1987	620	4,354	5,910	10,930	638	753	1,417	31,000	83,000	124,400	78,400	33,900	128,000	780	2,330	270,281
1988	517	5,393	5,643	12,541	815	647	1,170	32,000	85,000	127,500	80,322	34,400	131,722	1,240	3,730	280,282
1989	500	4,467	4,676	10,389	973	1,031	821	32,000	85,000	127,500	82,884	35,800	133,684	1,430	4,850	280,282
1990	500	5,044	5,269	11,709	1,316	1,425	1,047	32,000	85,000	127,500	82,884	35,800	133,684	1,430	4,850	281,629
1991	500	4,683	6,439	11,708	1,603	988	1,053	31,000	84,000	125,000	87,813	38,300	141,913	1,810	5,930	291,015
1992	500	4,800	5,800	11,907	1,956	629	986	30,000	82,000	121,500	88,861	38,000	142,861	1,730	6,050	288,343
1993[1]	500	5,500	6,900	13,807	2,000	660	1,200	28,000	70,000	104,000	94,891	41,000	152,891	1,840	6,470	281,438
1994[2]				13,000				20,000	50,000	74,000	82,000	41,000	150,000	1,800	6,500	250,718
										74,000			150,000	--------- 8,300 ---------		

[1] Preliminary. [2] Estimate. [3] Placer platinum. [4] Formerly part of the U.S.S.R.; data not reported separately until 1992.
W = Withheld proprietary data. *Source: U.S. Bureau of Mines.*

Salient Statistics of Platinum and Allied Metals[3] in the U.S.   In Kilograms

Year	Net Import Reliance as a % of Apparent Con-sumption	Mine Production Platinum	Mine Production Palladium	Refinery Produc-tion (Secon-dary)	Total Refined	Refiner, Importer & Dealer Stocks as of Dec. 31 Platinum	Palladium	Other[4]	Total	Imports for Consumption Refined	Total	Exports Refined	Total	Apparent Con-sumption
1985	92	W	W	40,336	40,563	17,783	14,152	3,171	35,106	106,928	124,090	16,369	27,640	104,511
1986	90	W	W	46,939	47,074	20,426	16,958	2,803	40,187	115,925	139,256	11,880	23,349	104,511
1987	91	780	2,330	50,053	50,243	19,004	17,356	2,052	38,412	98,878	118,397	13,423	22,031	109,904
1988	91	1,240	3,730	51,190	51,488	18,438	14,837	2,239	35,514	110,947	124,324	20,301	28,787	95,458
1989	90	1,430	4,850	50,186	50,525	14,791	15,182	2,570	32,543	111,107	113,278	23,082	38,301	103,302
1990	88	1,810	5,930	71,248	71,312	13,421	14,425	2,478	30,324	120,631	125,354	20,148	55,044	101,209
1991	90	1,730	6,050	72,349	72,564	10,349	12,263	1,701	24,313	121,741	125,661	27,401	39,624	117,043
1992	87	1,840	6,470	64,309	64,309	14,187	10,641	2,118	26,946	129,419	132,006	31,060	57,830	111,798
1993[1]	89	1,800	6,500	65,792	65,792	10,263	8,324	1,612	20,199	148,790	153,165	43,798	78,521	109,469
1994[2]	91	1,800	6,500	63,000	63,000				20,000	160,000	160,000	45,000	90,000	123,273
														127,000

[1] Preliminary. [2] Estimate. [3] Includes platinum, palladium, iridium, osmium, rhodium, and ruthenium. [4] Includes iridium, osmium, rhodium, and ruthenium.
W = Withheld proprietary data. *Source: U.S. Bureau of Mines.*

PLATINUM-GROUP METALS

Average Merchant's Price of Platinum in the U.S.   In Dollars Per Troy Ounce

Year	Jan	Feb	Mar	Apr	May	Jun	Jul	Aug	Sep	Oct	Nov	Dec	Average
1975	195.00	180.53	175.00	163.06	160.00	160.00	162.73	175.00	175.00	172.17	160.00	160.00	169.87
1976	160.00	160.00	160.00	160.00	160.00	163.54	175.60	182.50	182.50	182.50	167.00	167.00	168.39
1977	167.00	167.00	167.00	167.00	167.00	167.00	167.00	167.00	167.00	167.00	167.65	174.81	167.71
1978[1]	186.55	206.58	217.07	220.00	220.00	227.73	237.89	241.74	250.23	253.18	284.00	300.00	237.08
1979	303.41	325.00	325.00	327.38	350.00	350.00	350.00	357.83	380.00	380.00	380.00	393.33	351.83
1980	420.00	420.00	420.00	420.00	420.00	420.00	420.00	425.24	475.00	475.00	475.00	475.00	436.77
1981	475.00	475.00	475.00	475.00	475.00	475.00	475.00	475.00	475.00	475.00	475.00	475.00	475.00
1982	369.26	361.95	322.46	338.95	314.43	278.26	286.90	290.41	334.98	324.58	346.65	370.95	328.32
1983	441.07	468.34	400.17	410.38	446.69	420.23	431.63	438.30	431.93	399.87	389.33	399.70	423.14
1984	375.11	391.38	398.47	395.17	388.95	386.31	345.55	336.03	327.36	324.65	328.45	309.11	358.83
1985	275.76	274.37	255.36	287.23	273.24	267.94	269.52	303.91	304.59	321.73	334.53	327.75	291.33
1986	362.77	377.74	412.48	422.93	415.52	431.23	436.50	526.52	597.92	578.50	524.65	480.14	463.91
1987	520.08	518.30	533.27	587.38	607.08	569.14	573.57	610.12	590.55	568.65	500.02	479.29	554.79
1988	494.14	458.64	496.49	527.73	548.91	581.32	548.51	532.80	513.16	527.35	577.74	567.36	531.18
1989	528.69	532.66	538.26	539.96	517.20	498.81	503.16	485.20	479.29	485.48	508.73	507.24	510.39
1990	949.93	517.34	500.32	478.33	485.89	486.60	476.93	492.02	463.87	423.78	424.12	446.94	474.26
1991	408.92	385.53	403.12	398.16	373.06	374.25	375.38	351.68	348.01	362.52	364.01	356.65	375.11
1992	341.88	362.97	356.84	347.73	354.75	368.17	378.89	360.20	361.60	359.75	355.81	361.98	359.21
1993	359.99	361.53	349.31	365.98	385.50	384.54	401.10	394.69	365.29	369.19	376.98	383.85	374.75

[1] Prior to 1978 prices are for producer prices.   *Source: American Metal Market*

Platinum–Group Metals Sold to Consuming Industries in the United States   In Kilograms

Year	Automotive Platinum	Automotive Other[3]	Chemical Platinum	Chemical Other[3]	Electrical Platinum	Electrical Other[3]	Dental & Medical Platinum	Dental & Medical Other[3]	Jewelry & Decorative Platinum	Jewelry & Decorative Other[3]	Petroleum Platinum	Petroleum Other[3]	All Platinum–Group Metals Platinum	Palladium	Other[3]	Total
1985	19,251	7,785	2,651	2,718	3,603	11,169	762	10,576	499	397	895	2,518	31,901	32,976	5,765	70,642
1986	19,438	7,234	2,416	2,346	3,219	11,082	645	8,363	352	304	951	1,896	30,509	27,677	6,511	64,698
1987	18,816	6,935	1,919	1,283	1,821	10,879	479	10,526	177	478	543	1,286	25,469	30,953	3,851	60,273
1988	19,346	7,186	3,184	4,499	3,494	14,429	581	6,650	385	407	1,027	1,560	31,125	34,241	5,632	70,998
1989	18,774	6,869	2,424	2,233	3,894	19,514	632	8,601	418	396	2,859	2,570	33,698	39,273	5,512	78,483
1990	20,967	5,990	2,080	2,574	3,907	19,791	687	6,287	431	387	3,274	1,488	36,055	35,116	6,316	77,487
1991	18,643	5,338	861	1,749	3,910	14,428	598	4,918	626	500	3,163	181	31,112	25,747	5,738	62,597
1992	20,503	5,860	1,716	2,299	2,865	15,993	635	5,208	905	1,086	1,036	792	31,245	28,523	7,033	66,801
1993[1]	19,446	10,124	2,364	3,121	2,125	9,837	687	5,291	1,179	1,159	1,204	709	29,801	23,837	6,634	60,272

[1] Preliminary.   [2] Estimate.   [3] Includes palladium, iridium, osmium, rhodium, and ruthenium.   Source: U.S. Bureau of Mines

Average Open Interest of Platinum Futures in New York   In Contracts

Year	Jan	Feb	Mar	Apr	May	Jun	Jul	Aug	Sep	Oct	Nov	Dec
1984	12,460	12,838	14,246	14,544	15,827	15,911	15,768	15,743	16,556	15,305	14,885	15,651
1985	15,107	14,770	14,307	12,934	11,787	11,844	11,585	14,225	15,229	12,615	14,618	16,534
1986	17,496	18,587	20,993	17,591	16,007	18,867	17,473	20,989	27,426	19,825	20,256	17,485
1987	16,641	16,544	18,629	20,777	19,675	17,977	17,290	22,890	24,421	22,631	20,458	19,756
1988	17,133	18,080	16,737	16,718	18,643	22,735	19,668	17,671	19,936	19,097	22,022	24,384
1989	19,334	18,648	19,736	19,895	19,661	20,597	17,310	19,121	19,165	16,981	19,934	20,392
1990	19,510	17,970	15,888	15,915	16,688	15,652	15,496	17,254	18,494	17,472	16,313	16,994
1991	15,497	16,043	16,083	14,334	15,779	18,273	17,503	19,214	18,611	15,933	13,579	14,533
1992	15,464	14,231	14,272	14,130	15,353	19,070	20,402	18,444	17,574	14,079	13,532	14,282
1993	11,889	14,315	12,990	15,490	19,641	17,919	20,931	18,892	16,883	15,690	16,658	19,633
1994	18,779	19,655	21,673	22,834	21,880	22,835	24,804	25,049	24,245	24,159	26,287	26,661

Source: New York Mercantile Exchange

Volume of Trading of Platinum Futures in New York   In Thousands of Contracts

Year	Jan	Feb	Mar	Apr	May	Jun	Jul	Aug	Sep	Oct	Nov	Dec	Total
1984	44.7	43.7	68.9	54.5	44.9	53.8	55.2	38.4	52.2	35.9	38.3	40.7	571.1
1985	41.0	26.2	53.5	48.8	43.1	42.2	40.3	98.1	82.7	68.6	64.8	84.0	693.3
1986	101.3	114.7	139.8	100.3	77.0	122.2	75.4	189.8	289.4	164.8	136.6	113.3	1,624.6
1987	117.2	85.7	134.1	149.3	110.8	116.5	87.1	133.2	122.7	127.2	88.6	89.2	1,361.5
1988	82.8	77.6	119.2	74.3	123.3	182.2	111.5	105.8	125.1	114.6	164.8	179.2	1,460.5
1989	113.6	96.6	148.5	107.3	111.6	126.9	69.8	86.8	85.1	56.4	99.8	88.1	1,190.5
1990	85.6	80.9	81.3	55.3	65.2	70.1	52.7	73.8	77.2	68.0	50.1	56.8	817.1
1991	50.8	42.3	72.7	43.0	51.1	55.7	40.6	45.7	55.8	42.9	41.9	60.3	598.6
1992	47.9	38.3	54.1	29.3	37.7	82.0	61.0	50.6	51.8	28.5	42.3	53.8	577.3
1993	29.4	55.6	61.4	50.6	65.8	72.5	59.8	56.4	58.6	37.0	44.0	60.3	651.2
1994	18.8	19.7	21.7	22.8	21.9	22.8	24.8	25.0	24.2	24.2	26.3	81.6	895.8

Source: New York Mercantile Exchange

Average Open Interest of Palladium Futures in New York   In Contracts

Year	Jan	Feb	Mar	Apr	May	Jun	Jul	Aug	Sep	Oct	Nov	Dec
1988	6,094	6,434	6,194	6,269	6,419	7,038	7,330	7,160	6,360	6,263	6,188	6,289
1989	6,460	6,758	6,636	9,082	9,173	9,116	8,307	7,616	7,105	6,847	7,123	6,660
1990	6,296	6,350	5,276	5,359	5,476	5,361	5,493	5,717	5,165	5,100	5,316	4,565
1991	4,658	4,559	4,319	4,686	4,559	4,302	4,454	4,429	4,429	4,384	4,337	4,042
1992	3,984	4,071	4,101	4,206	4,137	3,852	3,762	3,362	3,041	2,982	2,901	3,246
1993	3,718	4,213	4,365	4,897	5,312	4,513	4,655	5,080	4,360	4,495	4,472	4,484
1994	4,626	4,995	4,672	4,303	5,116	4,530	5,807	6,851	6,625	6,511	7,726	6,917

Source: New York Mercantile Exchange

PLATINUM-GROUP METALS

Volume of Trading of Palladium Futures in New York   In Contracts

Year	Jan	Feb	Mar	Apr	May	Jun	Jul	Aug	Sep	Oct	Nov	Dec	Total
1987	9,870	14,469	9,849	19,005	22,323	7,728	9,660	18,270	6,741	17,514	17,724	9,303	162,456
1988	12,348	16,065	8,673	11,970	15,435	15,456	15,393	11,781	6,363	7,077	14,973	11,739	147,273
1989	12,852	16,296	12,978	48,699	28,266	13,062	15,477	15,351	11,235	8,862	17,745	10,836	211,659
1990	4,893	19,026	6,930	5,355	13,104	5,670	4,452	11,130	5,407	7,150	9,592	3,178	95,887
1991	5,017	10,542	5,380	7,245	10,521	4,447	5,230	10,114	2,914	5,668	8,150	2,971	78,199
1992	7,217	7,323	3,429	2,833	8,011	2,881	4,965	6,752	5,066	5,359	6,461	7,912	68,209
1993	7,708	14,461	8,057	10,034	12,190	7,368	7,043	13,356	6,977	9,220	12,477	4,790	113,681
1994	8,250	14,953	6,067	6,676	15,481	6,514	9,024	21,741	15,690	9,603	21,384	8,390	143,773

Source: New York Mercantile Exchange

Average Dealer[1] Price of Palladium in the United States   In Dollars Per Troy Ounce

Year	Jan	Feb	Mar	Apr	May	Jun	Jul	Aug	Sep	Oct	Nov	Dec	Average
1986	101.83	103.18	110.62	110.64	109.23	110.40	112.00	127.05	142.30	136.68	125.36	118.15	117.29
1987	124.13	121.32	122.74	136.58	146.55	140.00	141.34	143.32	137.93	132.72	113.42	121.99	131.84
1988	125.26	120.40	122.67	123.62	124.06	128.77	126.25	123.84	121.04	122.59	126.80	133.30	124.89
1989	135.74	141.79	152.84	165.46	155.17	152.92	151.36	135.97	137.85	137.84	139.35	139.75	145.50
1990	135.80	136.63	131.25	128.18	120.08	117.40	116.60	116.17	106.62	96.12	94.84	90.93	115.89
1991	86.61	85.11	86.44	95.25	96.61	97.39	95.57	84.55	82.49	81.87	85.96	82.72	88.38
1992	82.96	86.04	84.50	83.71	82.90	80.98	86.49	86.04	90.67	95.07	95.01	104.88	88.27
1993	110.39	112.57	106.22	113.79	119.94	125.36	139.74	137.37	121.95	130.04	123.62	125.60	122.22
1994[2]	124.00	130.00	132.00	132.00	135.00	137.00	145.00	151.00	151.00	153.00	156.00	153.00	142.00

[1]Based on wholesale quantities, prompt delivery.   [2]Estimate.   *Sources: American Metal Market; U.S. Bureau of Mines*

Pork Bellies

Pork bellies, the source of bacon, are obtained from the underside of a hog. A hog has two bellies, generally weighing about 8-18 pounds, depending on the hog's commercial slaughter weight. Slaughter weights now generally average 250 pounds per head. Bellies account for about 12 percent of a hog's live weight, but represent a somewhat larger percentage of the total cutout value of the realized pork products. Bellies deliverable against futures generally weigh around 12-14 pounds.

There are definitive seasonal trends for pork bellies. Bellies are storable and the movement into cold storage builds early in the calendar year and peaks about mid-year. Net withdrawals from storage then carry stocks to a low around October. The cycle then begins anew. Retail bacon demand also follows a well-established pattern. Demand is strongest in the summer when consumer preference shifts to lighter foods and then tapers off to a low during the winter months.

A weak price seasonality is evident if the swings in futures values serve as a clue. Demand patterns would suggest the highest prices in the summer and the lowest in the winter. Just the opposite is not unusual, however. Such contra-seasonal price moves can be partially attributed to supply logistics; notably, the availability of storage stocks deliverable against futures at exchange-approved warehouses. When it happens, underlying demand factors for bacon are on the back burner as a market making variable. The fact that there are no futures contracts between August and the following February adds to the price distortion and one should be aware of the gap when looking at a belly futures continuation chart.

Belly prices (cash and futures) are sensitive to the inventory in cold storage during the year and to the weekly net movement in and out of storage. Storage movements give a clue to demand, although a better measure is the weekly quantity of bellies being sliced into bacon. In mid-1994, the monthly domestic belly stocks averaged higher than in the same period of 1993 period, but no where near some of the mid-year monthly highs seen in the late 1980s.

Cash belly prices averaged higher in the first half of 1994 relative to 1993, but the picture reversed during the second half, basis midwest 12-14 pound bellies. Retail bacon prices, however, held firm most of the year, at times averaging more than 10 cents a pound higher than in the like 1993 period. Mid-1994 prices averaged about $2.00/lb., vs. $1.95 a year earlier. Still, retail prices are not likely to see, at least in the foreseeable future, the levels of the early 1990s when prices averaged near $2.20/lb. Bacon is not a food necessity and consumer demand for the product is sensitive to trends in disposable income and the state of the economy. The stronger economy in 1994 helped support retail bacon prices as the economy's weakness in 1992/93 had a dampening effect. More importantly is the change in consumer food preferences with increased emphasis away from fatty foods and/or those requiring chemicals in their processing, as bacon does. The latter factors could easily contain retail bacon demand during 1994, despite the likelihood of lower prices and/or more aggressive retail promotional activity. Initial prospects for retail bacon in 1995 are for prices to average below 1994 levels, perhaps even more than expected if the economy and consumer disposable income slips.

Futures Markets

Pork belly futures and options are traded on the Chicago Mercantile Exchange (CME).

Average Bureau of Labor Statistics Retail Price of Bacon, Sliced   In Dollars Per Pound

Year	Jan	Feb	Mar	Apr	May	June	July	Aug	Sept	Oct	Nov	Dec	Average
1987	2.12	2.09	2.10	2.08	2.11	2.13	2.23	2.28	2.28	2.19	2.07	2.02	2.14
1988	1.95	1.94	1.92	1.91	1.90	1.90	1.91	1.88	1.84	1.86	1.80	1.79	1.88
1989	1.80	1.80	1.79	1.75	1.68	1.69	1.71	1.72	1.72	1.77	1.82	1.96	1.77
1990	1.97	2.01	1.99	1.98	2.04	2.15	2.21	2.24	2.18	2.21	2.24	2.28	2.13
1991	2.26	2.30	2.32	2.27	2.31	2.31	2.31	2.22	2.16	2.12	2.07	1.99	2.22
1992	1.96	1.95	1.92	1.92	1.90	1.93	1.95	1.94	1.93	1.89	1.85	1.86	1.92
1993	1.87	1.84	1.80	1.89	1.91	1.95	2.00	1.95	1.98	1.99	2.01	2.02	1.93
1994[1]	2.04	2.02	2.02	2.06	1.99	1.99	2.00	1.99	1.97	1.97	1.92	1.89	1.99

[1] Preliminary.   Source: Economic Research Service, U.S. Department of Agriculture

U.S. Frozen Pork Belly Storage Stocks   In Thousands of Pounds, First of the Month

Year	Jan	Feb	Mar	Apr	May	June	July	Aug	Sept	Oct	Nov	Dec
1985	57,361	53,623	51,633	68,315	83,836	96,040	88,367	61,397	35,764	20,158	29,787	47,427
1986	51,314	47,633	51,218	62,508	68,325	65,895	61,547	40,333	20,797	12,941	17,022	24,528
1987	37,771	34,900	34,717	41,821	50,482	58,245	47,367	28,649	18,938	12,620	14,850	35,487
1988	62,089	62,996	67,035	90,347	102,543	111,484	103,401	73,747	42,623	31,054	49,550	93,254
1989	113,137	116,191	121,556	127,617	143,751	142,340	126,676	94,107	49,083	32,031	39,358	67,489
1990	85,026	77,255	85,789	96,945	102,899	105,482	87,983	55,859	23,352	4,785	5,506	24,044
1991	46,998	48,750	54,529	68,094	80,382	79,936	72,032	45,915	29,832	15,944	25,558	48,311
1992	71,318	76,894	75,925	85,095	96,653	92,677	78,646	54,544	26,854	21,973	26,044	49,970
1993	70,576	65,280	65,919	66,064	79,430	77,903	70,251	46,630	20,811	10,964	14,345	33,563
1994[1]	53,168	55,999	54,921	63,099	72,230	79,018	73,583	57,747	30,636	18,260	22,656	40,725

[1] Preliminary.   Source: National Agricultural Statistics Service, U.S. Department of Agriculture

PORK BELLIES

Weekly Pork Belly Storage Movement

1993 Week Ending		In	Out	On Hand	Net Move-ment	1994 Week Ending		In	Out	On Hand	Net Move-ment	Certified Delivery
Jan.	2	2,043	280	60,793	+1,763	Jan.	1	3,017	78	43,348	+2,939	9,720
	9	1,687	892	61,588	+795		8	1,522	153	44,717	+1,369	10,760
	16	872	1,613	60,422	-741		15	1,250	142	45,825	+1,108	12,440
	23	314	2,725	58,011	-2,411		22	670	124	46,370	+546	14,800
	30	203	1,138	55,283	-935		29	274	369	46,276	-95	17,600
Feb.	6	146	1,769	56,218	-1,793	Feb.	5	103	859	45,520	-756	19,680
	13	203	1,138	55,283	-935		12	626	576	45,570	+50	20,840
	20	378	581	55,079	-203		19	394	135	45,829	+259	22,960
	27	321	366	55,035	-45		26	1,077	39	46,867	+1,038	23,320
Mar.	6	648	388	55,295	+260	Mar.	5	833	615	47,085	+218	24,160
	13	1,572	566	56,301	+1,006		12	2,004	577	48,512	+1,427	24,320
	20	1,450	277	57,474	+1,173		19	2,369	495	50,386	+1,874	25,120
	27	1,208	715	57,967	+493		26	1,519	276	51,629	+1,243	26,200
Apr.	3	1,316	312	58,970	+1,004	Apr.	2	1,794	198	53,225	+1,596	27,520
	10	1,578	276	60,273	+1,302		9	2,410	140	55,495	+2,270	27,680
	17	2,768	245	62,796	+2,523		16	1,467	227	56,735	+1,240	28,720
	24	2,766	347	62,215	+2,419		23	2,256	553	58,438	+1,703	29,280
May	1	2,400	808	66,807	+1,592		30	2,322	456	60,304	+1,866	30,040
	8	1,633	249	68,191	+940	May	7	1,055	735	60,624	+320	30,240
	15	1,008	176	68,856	+832		14	1,138	1,364	60,398	-221	30,080
	22	351	1,317	67,890	-966		21	1,104	1,063	60,439	+41	29,920
	29	276	1,587	66,579	-1,311		28	798	366	60,891	+432	30,080
June	5	569	1,133	66,015	-564	June	4	473	741	60,603	-268	29,960
	12	269	1,704	64,580	-1,435		11	66	1,020	59,649	-954	29,840
	19	875	1,853	63,602	-978		18	369	1,742	58,276	-1,373	29,520
	26	239	4,168	59,673	-3,929		25	24	1,457	56,843	-1,433	29,200
July	3	201	3,903	55,971	-3,702	July	2	71	1,516	55,398	-1,445	28,680
	10	182	4,419	51,734	-4,237		9	231	2,834	52,795	-2,603	27,960
	17	54	5,551	46,237	-5,497		16	0	3,878	48,917	-3,878	27,080
	24	3	6,108	40,132	-6,105		23	77	3,554	45,440	-3,477	26,040
	31	43	5,085	35,090	-5,042		30	67	3,529	41,978	-3,462	25,640
Aug.	7	41	5,625	29,866	-5,224	Aug.	6	10	4,178	37,810	-4,168	24,280
	14	33	4,766	25,133	-4,733		13	41	4,915	32,936	-4,874	21,176
	21	-----	4,824	20,309	-4,824		20	2	4,188	28,750	-4,186	17,760
	28	8	4,195	16,122	-4,187		27	8	4,875	23,883	-4,867	0
Sept.	4	96	3,405	12,813	-3,309	Sept.	3	161	4,391	19,653	-4,230	0
	11	464	2,364	10,913	-1,900		10	699	2,920	17,432	-2,221	0
	18	133	2,020	9,026	-1,887		17	1,621	2,972	16,081	-1,351	0
	25	55	1,676	7,405	-1,621		24	276	2,075	14,282	-1,799	0
Oct.	2	1,173	968	7,610	+205	Oct.	1	121	2,517	11,886	-2,396	0
	9	445	574	7,481	-129		8	255	1,956	10,185	-1,701	0
	16	625	311	7,795	+314		15	897	1,023	10,059	-126	0
	23	909	605	8,099	+304		22	2,119	266	11,912	+1,853	0
	30	1,301	202	9,198	+1,099		29	1,669	110	13,471	+1,559	0
Nov.	6	3,562	322	12,057	+3,240	Nov.	5	2,310	659	15,122	+1,651	0
	13	3,453	142	15,749	+3,311		12	3,455	529	18,048	+2,926	0
	20	3,458	367	18,840	+3,091		19	4,633	698	21,983	+3,935	0
	27	4,299	122	23,017	+3,710		26	5,028	122	26,889	+4,906	0
Dec.	4	3,477	271	26,223	+3,206	Dec.	3	4,043	287	30,645	+3,756	2,760
	11	5,427	42	31,608	+5,835		10	4,516	447	34,714	+4,069	3,880
	18	4,772	160	36,220	+4,612		17	4,059	488	38,285	+3,571	5,400
	25	4,229	40	40,409	+4,189		24	3,333	162	41,456	+3,171	7,000
							31	2,605	365	43,696	+2,240	8,840

Stocks¹ in Thousands of Pounds

[1] 57 Chicago and Outside Combined Chicago Mercantile Exchange approved warehouses.   *Source: Chicago Mercantile Exchange*

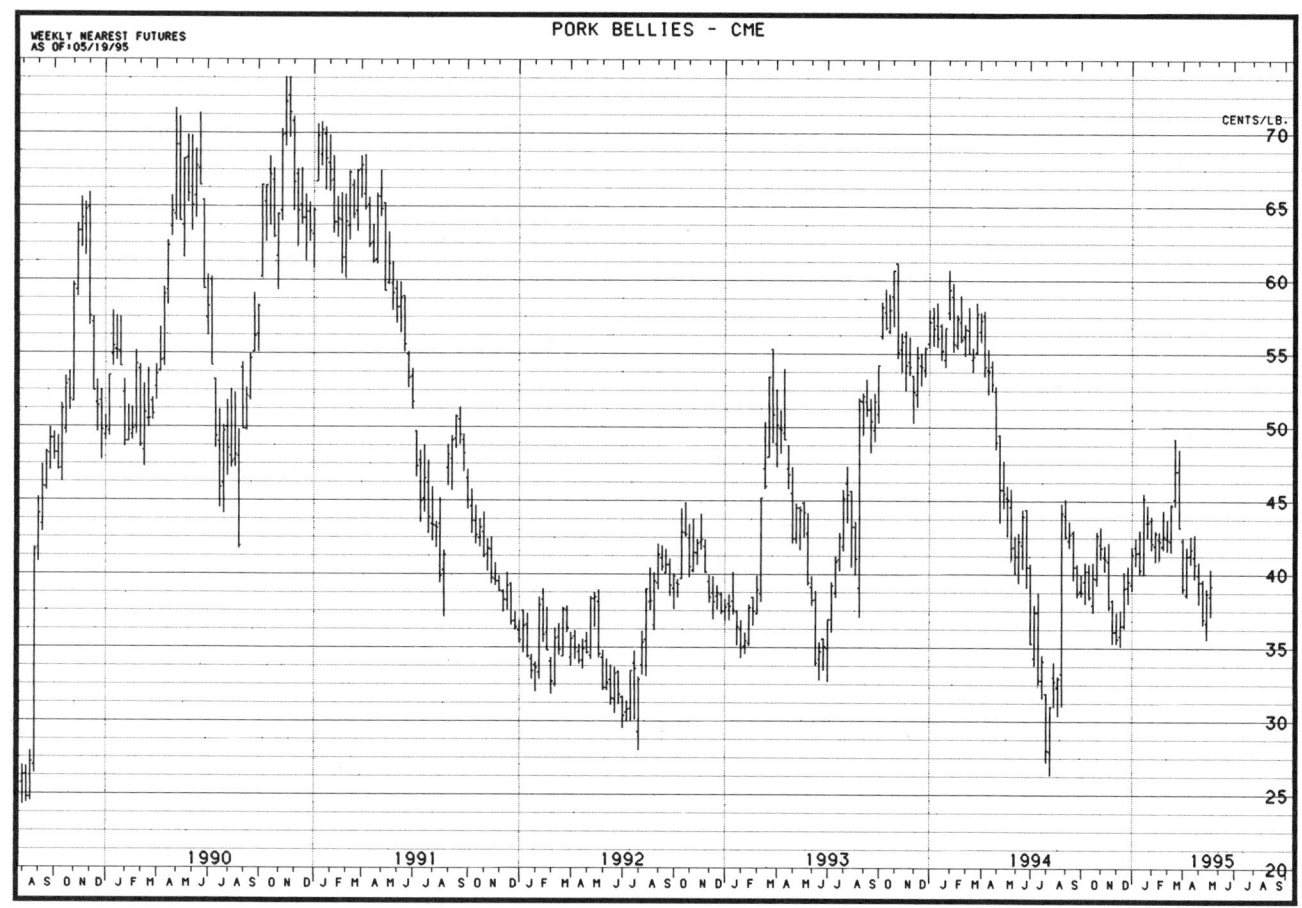

WEEKLY NEAREST FUTURES
AS OF : 05/19/95

PORK BELLIES - CME

CENTS/LB.

Average Open Interest of Pork Bellies Futures at Chicago   In Contracts

Year	Jan	Feb	Mar	Apr	May	June	July	Aug	Sept	Oct	Nov	Dec
1985	13,804	14,545	13,138	12,356	11,526	11,315	9,770	6,878	6,710	7,507	8,481	9,018
1986	8,313	7,969	7,357	8,635	9,509	10,781	9,135	7,462	8,515	8,287	10,412	11,440
1987	11,617	10,159	10,936	13,586	14,277	12,863	11,291	8,940	8,301	9,550	9,924	11,846
1988	11,250	10,942	13,421	16,229	17,887	18,428	15,782	11,874	14,678	15,860	19,292	19,723
1989	20,453	20,444	21,897	22,117	24,931	25,898	20,053	12,724	11,916	12,501	14,802	13,844
1990	12,885	12,114	13,017	15,338	14,513	13,038	11,146	6,104	6,059	7,851	11,419	12,589
1991	11,777	10,187	9,776	11,509	10,436	10,111	7,356	6,176	7,532	10,813	13,173	12,844
1992	12,521	12,195	11,901	12,345	12,497	13,598	12,623	7,149	6,540	7,033	9,251	10,953
1993	10,623	9,244	8,283	8,626	10,096	11,092	9,031	5,427	4,644	7,241	8,701	9,121
1994	11,053	10,426	9,375	9,894	8,092	8,248	7,836	7,841	8,398	10,072	10,141	10,216

Source: Chicago Mercantile Exchange

Volume of Trading of Pork Bellies Futures at Chicago   In Contracts

Year	Jan	Feb	Mar	Apr	May	June	July	Aug	Sept	Oct	Nov	Dec	Total
1985	173,488	137,334	133,509	148,489	149,809	135,139	136,026	89,784	77,326	99,291	85,377	91,634	1,457,386
1986	92,033	81,768	75,830	96,642	106,958	100,331	109,981	78,967	91,470	87,712	91,779	86,868	1,100,339
1987	104,134	95,108	92,707	118,107	112,112	120,598	118,996	89,564	60,670	66,423	53,903	64,688	1,097,010
1988	70,150	76,741	85,947	99,754	116,780	179,505	112,356	90,371	79,667	94,646	84,236	96,446	1,186,599
1989	107,577	89,922	84,768	90,353	145,975	152,207	119,733	91,200	75,155	106,389	141,983	105,714	1,310,976
1990	109,036	100,813	129,476	133,946	165,880	143,663	122,187	74,653	53,428	76,549	112,752	80,746	1,303,129
1991	106,078	89,975	88,056	111,195	119,773	96,273	74,255	59,176	65,604	80,707	63,331	50,773	1,005,196
1992	80,697	79,700	67,470	57,565	73,137	73,081	78,588	54,663	39,839	64,248	60,724	54,440	784,152
1993	77,380	62,871	63,988	62,403	62,400	70,124	65,496	42,613	37,992	47,780	60,163	49,099	698,799
1994	61,013	67,770	58,183	53,839	56,575	58,424	50,450	47,626	38,375	45,525	49,280	47,803	633,646

Source: Chicago Mercantile Exchange

PORK BELLIES

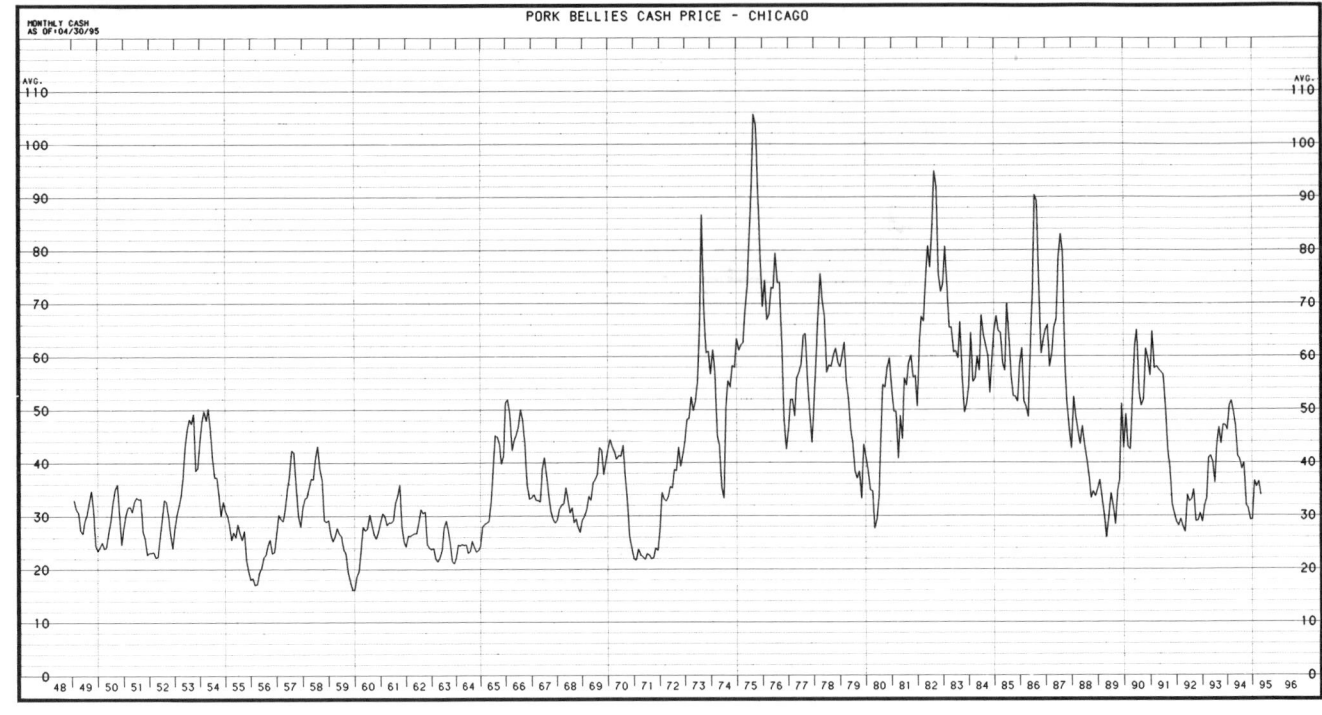

PORK BELLIES CASH PRICE - CHICAGO

MONTHLY CASH AS OF 04/30/95

Average Price of Pork Bellies (12-14 Pounds) Midwest   In Cents Per Pound

Year	Jan	Feb	Mar	Apr	May	June	July	Aug	Sept	Oct	Nov	Dec	Average
1983	80.91	73.88	65.11	64.71	60.81	60.19	59.06	65.72	55.25	49.10	50.96	54.59	61.69
1984	65.03	54.68	56.04	59.53	57.38	67.12	64.75	62.17	58.00	52.80	61.88	64.31	60.31
1985	67.50	64.14	64.25	58.83	58.64	70.15	62.53	54.17	51.40	52.09	51.73	58.63	59.51
1986	61.27	51.50	50.80	49.45	61.82	71.83	90.08	89.10	75.64	60.32	63.29	64.72	65.82
1987	66.32	57.81	60.02	65.79	67.21	78.44	83.62	80.46	59.74	49.39	45.87	42.60	63.11
1988	51.82	48.40	45.32	43.13	46.09	45.51	40.84	37.46	33.05	34.97	33.64	34.82	41.25
1989	36.91	31.41	30.19	25.49	29.11	32.90	31.52	28.82	34.23	36.88	49.96	42.23	34.14
1990	48.65	42.53	42.60	52.60	61.48	65.15	53.18	51.08	51.31	59.83	60.57	56.58	53.80
1991	64.11	57.20	58.52	57.25	57.50	56.48	50.40	42.01	38.97	32.26	30.04	28.79	47.79
1992	28.05	29.44	28.01	26.93	34.09	32.78	32.77	35.13	29.09	29.13	30.48	28.80	30.39
1993	31.97	33.22	41.28	41.19	39.86	36.24	44.51	46.68	43.82	47.25	47.21	46.21	41.62
1994[1]	50.63	51.66	49.68	46.84	41.40	40.39	38.64	39.60	31.50	31.33	29.09	29.29	40.00

[1] Preliminary.   Source: Economic Research Service, U.S. Department of Agriculture

Potatoes

U.S. annual potato production trended irregularly higher during the first half of the 1990s as generally higher average yield tended to offset a slippage in planted acreage. On the consumption side an uptrend that remained solidly in place and apt to carry to new record levels is the allocation of the crop into processed potatoes. The latter topped 240 million cwt. in 1993, up 20 million cwt. in just three years while annual tablestock (fresh potatoes) use stagnated near 125 million cwt.

Potatoes are grown in all fifty states. However, the crop is divided into four seasonal groups based on harvest time. The fall crop accounts for 85-90 percent of total production and is harvested September through November in about two dozen states. The winter crop is the smallest and harvested only in Florida and California from January into March. Spring and summer crop production tends to be fairly close in size. The pronounced seasonal disparities reflect major differences in planted acreage and realized yield which is consistently higher in the fall producing states. The marketing season follows the harvest, but the movement of the fall crop can extend into the following July with supplies drawn from storage. The inventoried fall crop, however, can serve as a supply buffer in the event the spring and summer crops are short, but large Fall stocks can also be a depressant on prices should earlier crops prove large. Generally about 30 percent of farm marketings occur in September/October and 15 percent in March and April.

A record large 429 million cwt. crop was harvested in 1993, up one percent from 1992. Harvested acreage of 1.32 million acres was four percent under 1991, but a record high average yield of 326 cwt./acre was 22 cwt. above 1991. The fall crop at 386 million cwt. was up 6 million from 1992

as yield averaged 341 cwt./acre vs. 335 cwt., respectively. Idaho was the largest producer at 125 million cwt. with Washington a distant second at 88 million cwt., but Washington's average yield of 590 cwt./acre was the nation's highest; Idaho's yield averaged under 400 cwt./acre.

About 60 percent of U.S. production is processed, either into frozen products or as a direct consumer food, as chips. Frozen french fries account for most of all frozen use. Chips and shoestrings account for more than 20 percent of total processing use. Per capita use of potatoes, the largest U.S. vegetable crop, totaled a record high 133.5 pounds in 1992, but slipped in 1993 to 132.7 pounds as tablestock use dipped to 46.7 pounds while processed potatoes reached a record high 86 pounds. Per capita use was expected to hold steady in 1994, but the continued expansion in fast food eateries is likely to see processed use twice that of tablestock in the late 1990s.

Foreign trade in U.S. potatoes is relatively small. The U.S. is a net exporter. Japan is the largest importer of U.S. processed potatoes, mostly french fries. Canada exports fresh potatoes to the U.S. which are used mostly for seed.

Retail fresh potato prices have averaged over $.30 a pound since 1990, vs. an average in the mid-$.20's in the 1980s. Processed potato prices have also trended higher with frozen potato prices averaging near a record high $.85-.90 per pound since 1992. The value of the 1993 crop was estimated at a near record $2.64 billion, up 13 percent from 1992 and 29 percent above 1991. The average price received by farmers in 1993 of $6.18 per cwt. compared with $5.52 in 1992. The 1994 average price will top 1993, but prove less than the record high $7.36 realized in 1989.

Salient Statistics of Potatoes in the United States

Crop Year	Acreage Planted – 1,000 Acres –	Acreage Harvested – 1,000 Acres –	Yield Per Harvested Acre Cwt.	Total Production	Seed & Feed In Thousands of Cwt.	Shrinkage & Loss In Thousands of Cwt.	Sold[2] In Thousands of Cwt.	Farm Price $ Cwt.	Value of Production[3] Million $	Value of Sales Million $	Stocks on Jan. 1 1,000 Cwt	Foreign Trade (Fresh) Domestic Exports Millions of Lbs.	Foreign Trade (Fresh) Imports Millions of Lbs.	Consumption Per Capita Fresh In Pounds	Consumption Per Capita Total In Pounds
1987	1,317	1,293	301	389,320	5,654	31,901	351,765	4.38	1,683	1,539	180,915	363.2	402.8	47.9	126.0
1988	1,285	1,259	283	356,438	5,810	25,067	325,561	6.02	2,144	1,958	196,760	422.0	388.4	49.6	122.4
1989	1,305	1,282	289	370,444	5,722	24,974	339,748	7.36	2,717	2,501	177,750	467.8	509.3	50.0	127.1
1990	1,400	1,371	293	402,110	5,949	28,329	367,832	6.08	2,409	2,240	173,550	327.3	482.9	45.8	127.7
1991	1,408	1,375	304	417,622	5,995	32,429	379,198	4.96	2,043	1,880	194,460	341.7	437.3	46.4	130.4
1992	1,339	1,315	323	425,367	5,925	33,807	385,637	5.52	2,336	2,129	211,005	537.9	273.5	48.9	132.4
1993[1]	1,385	1,317	326	428,693	5,931	30,152	392,610	6.18	2,641	2,427	215,990	539.3	541.4	51.9	135.7
1994[1]	1,414	1,377	334	459,342							217,800			49.1	133.9

[1]Preliminary. [2]For all purposes, including food, seed processing & livestock feed. [3]Farm weight basis, excluding canned and frozen potatoes.
Source: Economic Research Service, U.S. Department of Agriculture

U.S. Cold Storage Stocks of All Frozen Potatoes (First of Month)   In Millions of Pounds

Year	Jan	Feb	Mar	Apr	May	June	July	Aug	Sept	Oct	Nov	Dec
1987	894.1	786.7	795.9	856.6	886.7	962.9	1,003.3	816.4	675.5	774.2	947.5	966.1
1988	882.6	899.0	977.7	965.1	950.7	963.9	1,000.8	882.5	835.0	917.9	1,047.5	1,044.4
1989	988.7	927.4	944.3	947.3	968.7	986.7	961.5	739.9	611.3	734.2	878.7	938.0
1990	917.3	932.7	995.6	1,041.2	1,059.0	1,061.3	977.6	769.3	688.1	852.5	995.6	999.5
1991	975.8	993.3	988.9	1,041.5	1,052.3	1,167.2	1,216.5	935.5	880.1	985.5	1,148.0	1,037.2
1992	980.8	996.5	1,036.3	1,082.7	1,077.6	1,137.3	1,131.4	966.4	948.7	949.1	1,067.1	1,038.7
1993	963.2	971.2	1,028.2	1,046.6	912.7	979.5	989.8	932.8	902.8	1,019.5	1,184.7	1,130.7
1994[1]	1,006.4	1,019.9	1,057.1	1,054.4	1,050.5	1,118.9	1,099.9	979.8	1,028.2	1,108.7	1,189.0	1,163.5

[1]Preliminary.   *Source: Agricultural Statistics Board, U.S. Department of Agriculture*

POTATOES

Potato Crop Production Estimates, Stocks & Disappearance in the U.S.   In Millions of Cwt.

| | Crop Production Estimates | | | | | Total Storage Stocks[2] | | | | | | Fall Crop — 1,000 Cwt. | | | | |
| | Total Crop | | | Fall Crop | | | Following Year | | | | | Pro-duction | Disap-pearance (Sold) | Dec. 1 Stocks | Average Price $/Cwt. | Value of Sales $1,000 |
Year	Oct. 1	Nov. 1	Dec. 1	Oct. 1	Nov. 1	Dec. 1	Jan. 1	Feb. 1	Mar. 1	Apr. 1	May 1					
1981	329.9	329.9	333.7	287.1	287.1	193.6	164.4	137.8	111.8	82.3	50.8	297,080	265,085	193,610	4.74	1,261,531
1982	350.0	350.0	349.3	306.9	308.9	206.5	179.0	150.2	122.5	90.1	57.3	309,134	272,611	206,525	3.92	1,067,863
1983	329.8	329.8	325.7	292.7	292.7	192.5	165.3	138.9	112.7	81.7	50.4	294,679	265,598	192,150	5.46	1,449,394
1984	358.8	358.8	361.6	310.0	346.1	201.4	173.4	144.8	118.4	86.4	52.5	312,662	279,270	201,410	5.03	1,402,425
1985	——	400.4	404.1	——	307.5	235.5	202.8	171.5	138.7	104.5	65.4	343,984	295,032	235,475	3.42	1,007,953
1986	——	352.3	352.3	——	342.7	209.4	180.9	154.5	128.7	95.1	59.8	307,928	284,721	209,435	4.68	1,335,419
1987	——	361.5	——	——	309.9	225.9	196.8	167.3	138.8	105.9	70.0	335,607	309,279	225,890	3.69	1,142,731
1988	——	352.1	——	——	322.7	206.4	177.8	151.1	124.5	92.6	59.4	305,623	284,205	206,420	5.82	1,652,864
1989	——	367.3	——	——	342.5	202.1	173.6	144.3	116.6	84.3	50.7	316,097	295,605	202,050	6.76	1,999,104
1990	——	393.2	——	——	371.7	225.5	194.5	162.9	134.5	101.2	63.0	344,200	320,033	225,500	5.42	1,734,476
1991	——	417.6	——	——	379.5	242.1	211.0	178.5	145.8	108.9	69.1	363,541	334,893	242,070	4.16	1,393,749
1992	——	425.4	——	——	372.4	246.8	216.0	184.6	152.8	115.8	75.0	368,516	341,209	246,820	5.17	1,762,984
1993	——	414.8	——	——	372.4	249.7	217.8	186.1	154.1	116.0	73.9	375,004	351,161	249,710	5.65	1,984,205
1994[1]	——	458.5	——	——	412.4	263.6	229.4	196.0				400,385		263,630		

[1] Preliminary. [2] Held by growers and local dealers in the fall producing areas. *Source: Agricultural Statistics Board, U.S. Department of Agriculture*

Potato Crop Production Estimates, Stocks & Disappearance in The U.S.   In Millions of Cwt.

| | Crop Production Estimates | | | | | Total Storage Stocks[2] | | | | | | Fall Crop — 1,000 Cwt. | | | | |
| | Total Crop | | | Fall Crop | | | Following Year | | | | | Pro-duction | Disap-pearance (Sold) | Dec. 1 Stocks | Average Price $/Cwt. | Value of Sales $1,000 |
Year	Oct. 1	Nov. 1	Dec. 1	Oct. 1	Nov. 1	Dec. 1	Jan. 1	Feb. 1	Mar. 1	Apr. 1	May 1					
1981	329.9	329.9	333.7	287.1	287.1	193.6	164.4	137.8	111.8	82.3	50.8	297,080	265,085	193,610	4.74	1,261,531
1982	350.0	350.0	349.3	306.9	308.9	206.5	179.0	150.2	122.5	90.1	57.3	309,134	272,611	206,525	3.92	1,067,863
1983	329.8	329.8	325.7	292.7	292.7	192.5	165.3	138.9	112.7	81.7	50.4	294,679	265,598	192,150	5.46	1,449,394
1984	358.8	358.8	361.6	310.0	346.1	201.4	173.4	144.8	118.4	86.4	52.5	312,662	279,270	201,410	5.03	1,402,425
1985	——	400.4	404.1	——	307.5	235.5	202.8	171.5	138.7	104.5	65.4	343,984	295,032	235,475	3.42	1,007,953
1986	——	352.3	352.3	——	342.7	209.4	180.9	154.5	128.7	95.1	59.8	307,928	284,721	209,435	4.68	1,335,419
1987	——	361.5	——	——	309.9	225.9	196.8	167.3	138.8	105.9	70.0	335,607	309,279	225,890	3.69	1,142,731
1988	——	352.1	——	——	322.7	206.4	177.8	151.1	124.5	92.6	59.4	305,623	284,205	206,420	5.82	1,652,864
1989	——	367.3	——	——	342.5	202.1	173.6	144.3	116.6	84.3	50.7	316,097	295,605	202,050	6.76	1,999,104
1990	——	393.2	——	——	371.7	225.5	194.5	162.9	134.5	101.2	63.0	344,200	320,033	225,500	5.42	1,734,476
1991	——	417.6	——	——	379.5	242.1	211.0	178.5	145.8	108.9	69.1	363,541	334,893	242,070	4.16	1,393,749
1992	——	425.4	——	——	372.4	246.8	216.0	184.6	152.8	115.8	75.0	368,516	341,209	246,820	5.17	1,762,984
1993	——	414.8	——	——	372.4	249.7	217.8	186.1	154.1	116.0	73.9	375,004	351,161	249,710	5.65	1,984,205
1994[1]	——	458.5	——	——	412.4	263.6	229.4	196.0				400,385		263,630		

[1] Preliminary. [2] Held by growers and local dealers in the fall producing areas. *Source: Agricultural Statistics Board, U.S. Department of Agriculture*

United States Potato Production by Seasonal Groups   In Millions of Cwt.

| | Spring | | | | Summer | | | Fall | | | | | | | | |
Year	Winter	California	Florida	Total	New Mexico	Virginia	Total	Colorado	Idaho	Maine	Minnesota	North Dakota	Oregon	Washington	Wisconsin	Total
1981	2.2	10.3	5.3	20.8	1.3	2.3	20.5	11.6	84.5	26.5	13.3	20.1	21.7	52.9	18.2	297.1
1982	2.3	9.6	5.7	21.0	2.2	2.5	22.8	12.8	91.8	27.0	11.5	17.3	21.1	52.8	22.6	309.1
1983	2.2	8.3	5.1	18.3	1.6	1.0	18.5	14.0	86.0	22.6	10.3	20.5	20.7	54.1	18.9	294.7
1984	2.6	11.1	6.7	24.0	2.6	1.5	22.7	17.2	86.6	21.4	13.8	20.6	23.5	56.9	21.4	312.7
1985	2.7	10.6	6.6	23.0	2.9	3.3	27.3	17.9	102.5	28.2	14.1	23.6	26.9	63.6	24.1	353.6
1986	3.0	7.6	7.0	19.9	2.8	1.1	20.7	18.8	90.2	21.9	13.7	21.6	23.2	62.0	20.1	318.2
1987	2.5	7.9	5.6	19.0	3.5	2.0	22.8	19.5	99.7	23.2	16.3	24.1	25.9	67.0	22.1	345.0
1988	2.6	7.5	6.8	20.1	3.1	2.0	20.2	19.0	102.6	22.0	12.1	15.5	20.7	63.3	20.0	313.6
1989	2.8	7.9	6.9	20.9	4.0	1.4	22.2	20.6	102.5	22.0	13.9	15.1	23.3	64.3	23.1	324.7
1990	2.3	8.4	8.7	24.2	3.4	2.0	23.1	22.7	119.1	20.5	14.3	16.7	23.5	68.0	23.1	352.5
1991	2.6	8.3	6.6	20.6	3.5	1.5	22.6	23.8	122.2	18.2	17.2	30.0	22.2	75.4	23.3	371.7
1992	3.0	7.2	7.8	21.5	1.0	2.0	21.3	22.1	127.1	24.3	16.1	27.7	21.1	69.3	25.2	379.5
1993	2.6	7.5	6.1	19.7	1.3	1.8	20.6	25.3	126.2	19.9	12.7	21.1	23.1	88.5	22.6	385.9
1994[1]	2.4	7.8	8.6	22.6	1.1	1.4	22.2	25.8	134.3	17.3	17.8	28.2	25.8	88.9	25.7	412.1

[1] Preliminary. *Source: Agricultural Statistics Board, U.S. Department of Agriculture*

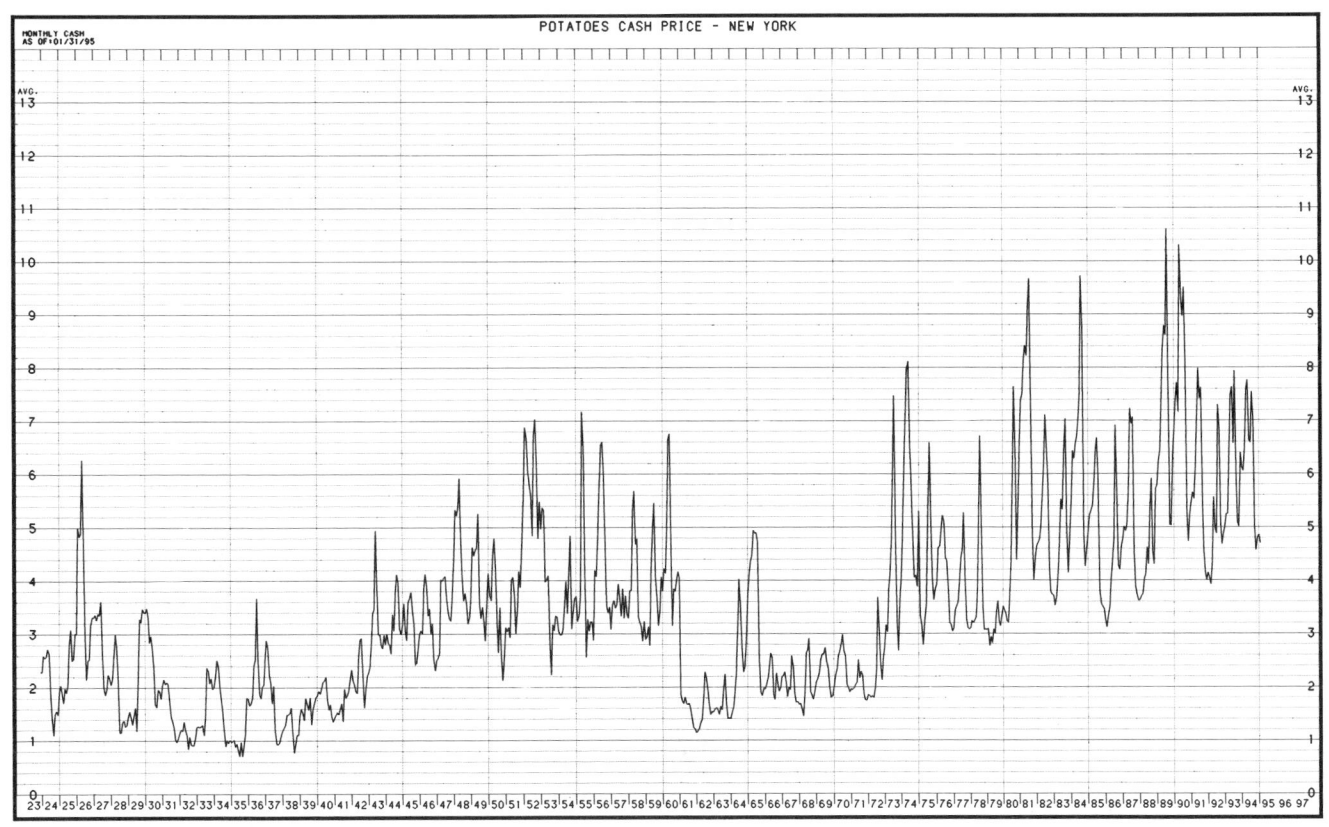

POTATOES CASH PRICE - NEW YORK

MONTHLY CASH
AS OF:01/31/95

U.S. Average Price Received by Farmers for Potatoes   In Dollars Per Cwt.

Year	Jan	Feb	Mar	Apr	May	June	July	Aug	Sept	Oct	Nov	Dec	Season Average
1982	4.71	4.78	5.03	5.59	6.21	7.11	6.52	5.80	4.25	3.78	3.73	3.71	4.45
1983	3.53	3.69	4.07	4.65	5.52	5.33	6.36	7.03	4.94	4.14	4.87	5.46	5.82
1984	6.43	6.29	6.55	6.69	7.04	7.52	9.72	8.75	4.87	4.26	4.60	4.90	5.69
1985	5.22	5.31	5.40	5.80	6.44	6.67	5.84	3.83	3.56	3.51	3.46	3.26	3.92
1986	3.12	3.35	3.50	3.99	4.39	4.79	6.91	5.68	4.28	4.20	4.63	4.78	5.03
1987	5.01	4.93	5.05	5.66	7.23	6.94	7.06	4.52	3.89	3.74	3.62	3.63	4.38
1988	3.70	3.74	4.02	4.11	4.62	4.30	5.28	5.91	4.55	4.30	5.72	5.79	6.02
1989	6.24	6.43	7.34	8.33	8.78	8.61	10.60	7.58	5.06	5.03	6.32	6.81	7.36
1990	7.36	7.71	9.17	10.30	9.32	8.96	9.50	8.09	5.36	4.73	5.24	5.46	6.08
1991	5.66	5.53	6.15	7.03	7.98	7.51	7.95	5.39	4.51	4.06	3.99	4.29	4.96
1992	4.07	4.08	4.64	5.16	4.43	4.71	7.00	6.64	4.89	4.55	4.90	5.06	5.52
1993	5.15	5.29	6.06	7.19	7.18	6.45	7.61	6.05	5.12	4.96	6.40	6.12	6.22

[1]Preliminary.   Source: Agricultural Statistics Board, U.S. Department of Agriculture

POTATOES

United States Potatoes Processed[1], Eight States   In Thousands of Cwt.

States	Storage Season	to Dec. 1	to Jan. 1	to Feb. 1	to Mar. 1	to Apr. 1	to May 1	Entire Season
Oregon-	1987-8	18,260	23,320	28,680	34,340	40,380	46,440	64,495
Malheur Co	1988-9	18,740	24,270	29,420	34,720	41,360	48,080	64,425
Idaho and	1989-0	22,200	28,140	34,240	40,270	46,330	51,810	66,010
	1990-1	24,780	31,100	37,550	44,220	51,030	58,660	78,500
	1991-2	22,980	28,910	35,700	42,840	50,260	57,290	78,690
	1992-3	22,180	29,080	35,710	42,800	50,090	57,090	80,570
	1993-4	24,090	30,540	37,150	44,720	53,070	61,440	85,780
	1994-5	26,620	34,230	42,330				
Maine[2]	1987-8	1,770	2,440	3,145	3,745	4,410	4,865	6,745
	1988-9	1,685	2,190	2,830	3,455	4,230	4,915	6,915
	1989-0	2,055	2,660	3,510	4,000	4,620	5,210	6,900
	1990-1	2,105	2,690	3,420	3,900	4,460	5,120	6,750
	1991-2	2,015	2,450	3,050	3,350	3,900	4,445	5,210
	1992-3	1,195	1,630	2,205	2,720	3,390	4,020	5,055
	1993-4	1,350	1,720	2,210	2,505	2,890	3,275	4,555
	1994-5	1,510	1,840	2,275				
Washington	1987-8	22,265	25,950	30,790	35,800	40,900	44,925	58,085
Oregon-Other	1988-9	19,200	23,455	27,280	31,960	37,575	41,795	51,555
	1989-0	23,635	28,015	33,170	38,610	44,510	49,595	57,695
	1990-1	24,780	29,830	35,170	39,950	45,600	50,780	61,450
	1991-2	26,345	30,570	35,320	41,320	47,120	52,605	65,210
	1992-3	26,840	31,550	35,950	41,670	46,530	51,630	63,510
	1993-4	28,260	33,350	39,010	45,020	51,290	57,180	70,690
	1994-5	28,690	33,500	39,120				
Other States[3]	1987-8	5,750	7,370	9,200	11,250	13,305	15,270	20,155
	1988-9	5,805	7,450	9,040	10,645	12,340	14,075	18,385
	1989-0	6,340	8,010	9,860	11,535	13,240	15,100	20,610
	1990-1	6,585	8,605	10,405	12,425	14,635	17,010	24,005
	1991-2	7,515	9,350	11,580	13,585	15,685	17,935	24,990
	1992-3	7,140	9,220	11,265	13,305	15,550	17,555	25,070
	1993-4	7,605	9,515	11,605	13,720	16,080	18,705	25,690
	1994-5	8,790	12,045	14,605				
Total	1987-8	48,045	59,080	71,815	85,135	98,995	111,500	149,480
	1988-9	45,430	57,365	68,570	80,780	95,505	108,865	144,280
	1989-0	54,230	66,825	80,780	94,415	108,700	121,715	151,215
	1990-1	58,250	72,225	86,545	100,495	115,725	131,570	170,705
	1991-2	58,855	71,280	85,650	101,095	116,965	132,275	174,100
	1992-3	57,355	71,480	85,130	100,495	115,560	130,295	174,205
	1993-4	61,305	75,125	89,975	105,965	123,330	140,600	186,715
	1994-5	65,610	81,615	98,330				

[1] Total quanitity received and used for processing regardless of the state in which the potatoes were produced. Excludes quantities used for potato chips in Maine, Michigan, Minnesota, North Dakota or Wisconsin. [2] Includes Maine grown potatoes only. [3] Michigan, Minnesota, North Dakota and Wisconsin.
Source: National Agricultural Statistics Service, U.S. Department of Agriculture

Potatoes U.S. Total Per Capita Utilization in Pounds (Farm Weight)

Year	Total	Fresh	Freezing	Processing — Chips & Shoe-string	Processing — Dehy-drating	Canning	Total
1984	122.1	48.3	43.7	18.0	10.3	1.8	73.8
1985	122.4	46.3	45.4	17.6	11.2	1.9	76.1
1986	126.0	48.8	46.3	18.2	10.9	1.8	77.2
1987	126.0	47.9	47.9	17.6	10.8	1.8	78.1
1988	122.4	49.6	43.3	17.2	10.4	1.9	72.8
1989	127.1	50.0	46.8	17.5	10.8	2.0	77.1
1990	127.7	45.8	50.2	17.0	12.8	1.9	81.9
1991	130.4	46.4	51.3	17.3	13.7	1.7	84.0
1992	132.4	48.9	51.0	17.5	13.2	1.8	83.5
1993	135.7	51.9	51.3	17.5	13.1	1.9	83.8
1994[1]	133.9	49.1	52.1	17.4	13.4	1.9	84.8

[1] Preliminary.   *Source: Agricultural Statistics Board, U.S. Department of Agriculture*

Rapeseed (Canola)

Rapeseed (or Canola) is the world's third largest oilseed crop behind soybeans and cottonseed, but slowly closing the gap for second place. World production in 1994/95 of a record high 30 million tonnes was slightly more than 12 percent of total world oilseed production of 246 million tonnes. In the early 1980s the crop averaged about 13 million tonnes, but by the end of the decade production was over 20 million. Significantly, 1994/95 rapeseed production was only 3 million tonnes under cottonseed. In the early 1990s the difference exceeded 8 million tonnes; if the trend persists rapeseed is apt to be the world's second largest oilseed crop in the late 1990s.

World rapeseed production is widespread. China retains the top spot with almost a fourth of total production—about 7.2 million tonnes in 1994/95, but Canada is rapidly closing the gap with a record large 1994/95 crop of 7.0 million tonnes. In the early 1980s Canada produced on average less than 3 million tonnes. In India, the second largest producer until 1994/95, production totaled 5.5 million tonnes. Rapeseed is also produced in Europe. Germany's production during the past decade soared to a record large 2.85 million tonnes in 1993/94, but slipped to 2.75 million in 1994/95. France and the U.K. now also produce more than 1.2 million tonnes. World acreage has increased substantially since the mid-1980s, and in 1994/95 at 22.5 million hectare was about one-third that of soybeans. Yield, however, is lower than beans. The world average of 1.33 tonnes per hectare in 1994/95 compares with 2.06 for soybeans. China's 1994/95 rapeseed yield of 1.30 tonnes/hectare compares with Western Europe's 2.62 tonnes.

In foreign trade, rapeseed is second only to soybeans. World exports in 1994/95 of 5.8 million tonnes compares with 5 million in 1993/94. The 1994/95 world rapeseed carryover of 1.8 million tonnes is more than twice the ending 1993/94 carryover and the highest so far of the 1990s.

U.S. production of Canola seed is small, but growing as more acreage is planted to the crop as producers see a strong demand for canola oil. A record large 321,000 acres was planted for the 1994/95 crop compared to the previous record of 199,000 acres in 1993/94. A record 419 million pounds were produced in 1994/95 up from 252 million in 1993/94. Production is well below demand, estimated at 1.4 billion pounds in 1994/95, up from less than a billion pounds in 1993/94, necessitating record large imports of nearly one billion pounds in 1994/95 up from 772 million in 1993/94; Canada is the major supplier. The large imports will help to replenish stocks to about 132 million pounds as of May 31, 1995 from the 95 million pound carry-in a year earlier. In the mid-1980s, canola seed carryover stocks were virtually insignificant. Production of canola oil in 1994/95 of 440 million pounds compares with 336 million the previous year. Canola oil imports, mostly from Canada, were 993 million pounds in 1994/95, compared to 904 million in 1993/94.

The primary reason for the increase in U.S. canola seed output reflects 1) the development of low-erucic canola varieties that can be grown in the U.S., 2) the wider acceptance of canola oil in cooking due to its lower content of saturated fats, and 3) it's competitively priced against sunflowerseed oil. Canola oil is now readily accepted as a salad and cooking oil; it is reported to be about 94 percent saturated fat free, the lowest of any leading oil. The U.S. remains almost entirely dependent on imported canola oil to satisfy domestic usage. This dependency is apt to persist into the foreseeable future. Demand for canola meal has also grown impressively as a livestock feed owing to very aggressive pricing by producers.

Despite the increase in world production, rapeseed prices are still highly sensitive to changes in either supply or demand. The N.Y. monthly wholesale denatured rapeseed oil price in 1993 trended steadily lower during the year, from 62.25 cents per pound to 50 cents at year end, and the downward pressure continued to 43.75 cents through the first half of 1994. Futures values broke sharply in mid-1994 from $400/ton to $340 in mid-summer before staging a rally in late 1994 that carried to new contract highs.

Futures Markets

Canola futures are traded on the Winnipeg Commodity Exchange (WPG) and quoted in Canadian dollars per ton. The market generally has the largest open interest among the futures traded on the WPG.

World Production of Rapeseed   In Thousands of Metric Tons

Year	Australia	Bangladesh	Canada	China	Czecho-slovakia	Denmark	France	Germany	India	Pakistan	Poland	Sweden	United Kingdom	Former U.S.S.R.	World Total
1981-2	------	123	1,849	4,065	200	290	990	284	2,382	238	496	282	325	------	12,345
1982-3	7	120	2,225	5,656	178	334	1,147	878	2,207	246	533	320	580	47	14,804
1983-4	17	131	2,609	4,287	314	309	906	859	2,608	217	554	318	565	69	14,259
1984-5	32	140	3,412	4,205	300	474	1,305	1,017	3,073	234	911	327	925	55	16,935
1985-6	87	261	3,498	5,607	285	544	1,340	1,184	2,681	250	1,073	320	895	74	18,699
1986-7	77	229	3,787	5,881	306	618	1,071	1,472	2,605	217	1,298	321	940	144	19,550
1987-8	66	222	3,847	6,605	337	556	2,645	1,723	3,455	204	1,192	250	1,353	296	23,435
1988-9	58	207	4,218	5,044	380	504	2,303	1,642	4,377	249	1,199	250	1,040	420	22,646
1989-0	78	217	3,209	5,436	387	655	1,748	1,908	4,125	233	1,586	370	976	424	22,096
1990-1	99	228	3,266	6,958	380	793	1,926	2,155	5,152	228	1,206	367	1,258	506	25,301
1991-2	170	248	4,224	7,436	490	734	2,270	3,030	5,863	219	1,043	252	1,308	410	28,534
1992-3[1]	179	250	3,872	7,653	430	405	1,810	2,617	4,872	235	758	247	1,159	388	25,601
1993-4[2]	327	252	5,480	6,939	475	417	1,550	2,848	5,300	230	594	313	1,228	335	26,965
1994-5[3]	228		7,388	6,500	559	370	1,800	2,788	5,500		680	250	1,370	350	29,200

[1] Preliminary. [2] Estimate. [3] Forecast. *Source: Oil World*

RAPESEED

WEEKLY NEAREST FUTURES
AS OF •05/12/95

CANOLA - WPG

CAN.$/METRIC TON

World Supply & Distribution of Rapeseed & Products   In Thousands of Metric Tons

Crop Year	Rapeseed Pro-duction	Exports	Imports	Crush	Ending Stocks	Rapeseed Meal Pro-duction	Exports	Imports	Con-sumption	Ending Stocks	Rapeseed Oil Pro-duction	Exports	Imports	Con-sumption	Ending Stocks
1980-1	11,104	2,305	2,366	10,477	1,489	6,297	808	636	6,075	199	3,933	814	756	3,914	210
1981-2	12,345	2,142	2,216	11,959	911	7,331	845	683	7,182	186	4,383	824	775	4,404	140
1982-3	14,804	2,469	2,540	13,826	740	8,449	768	871	8,500	238	4,991	841	790	4,925	155
1983-4	14,263	2,537	2,704	13,312	647	8,130	1,198	1,303	8,206	267	4,856	984	980	4,827	180
1984-5	16,935	3,153	3,291	15,369	1,033	9,419	1,463	1,451	9,454	220	5,602	1,298	1,199	5,497	186
1985-6	18,699	3,632	3,648	16,986	1,267	10,260	1,823	1,734	10,109	282	6,233	1,313	1,203	5,978	331
1986-7	19,550	4,577	4,923	18,439	1,037	11,112	1,692	2,225	11,568	359	6,849	1,662	1,409	6,540	387
1987-8	23,383	4,456	4,296	20,370	1,250	12,264	2,113	2,088	12,139	169	7,701	1,852	1,806	7,461	922
1988-9	22,646	4,417	4,610	20,252	3,760	12,160	2,709	2,675	12,213	81	7,671	1,939	1,807	7,775	687
1989-0	22,096	4,471	4,486	21,075	3,240	12,706	2,595	2,646	12,678	160	7,943	1,963	2,026	7,959	733
1990-1	25,301	4,416	4,359	23,231	3,130	14,028	2,994	2,920	14,001	114	8,756	2,021	2,047	8,733	782
1991-2	28,534	4,768	4,841	25,332	3,700	15,338	3,707	3,735	15,382	98	9,547	2,093	2,209	9,620	825
1992-3[1]	25,601	3,132	3,000	23,920	780	14,482	2,726	2,657	14,414	97	9,093	1,205	1,185	9,155	760
1993-4[2]	26,965	4,114	3,983	25,158	780	15,093	2,590	2,683	15,168	116	9,686	1,618	1,550	9,613	765
1994-5[3]	29,200	4,580	4,660	26,569	1,280	15,923	2,725	2,691	15,882	123	10,237	1,865	1,895	10,193	840

[1] Preliminary. [2] Estimate. [3] Forecast.   *Source: Oil World*

Salient Statistics of Rapeseed and Canola Oil in the United States   In Millions of Pounds

Crop Year Beginning June 1	Rapeseed (Canola Seed) Supply				Rapeseed Disappearance			Canola Oil Supply				Canola Oil Disappearance		
	Stocks June 1	Pro-duction	Imports	Total	Crush	Exports	Total[3]	Stocks June 1	Pro-duction	Imports	Total	Domestic	Exports	Total
1988	2	39	37	78	71	4	75	29	54	430	513	486	8	494
1989	3	95	231	329	298	10	308	20	130	391	541	510	6	516
1990	21	97	141	259	195	32	227	24	18	583	625	577	7	584
1991	32	191	2	225	109	97	212	41	32	815	888	801	15	816
1992	13	144	27	184	59	104	174	71	49	861	981	898	16	914
1993[1]	10	252	773	1,035	850	78	940	67	406	902	1,375	1,228	76	1,304
1994[2]	95	447	992	1,534	1,290	110	1,417	71	481	963	1,515	1,355	85	1,440

[1] Preliminary.   [2] Forecast.   [3] Includes planting seed and residual.   *Source: Economic Research Service, U.S. Department of Agriculture*

Wholesale Price of Rapeseed Oil, Refined (Denatured), in Tanks at N.Y.   In Cents Per Pound

Year	Jan	Feb	Mar	Apr	May	June	July	Aug	Sept	Oct	Nov	Dec	Average
1985	55.20	55.20	55.20	NA	NA	68.30	67.90	64.00	62.50	62.50	62.50	60.50	61.40
1986	60.00	60.00	60.00	60.00	60.00	60.00	60.00	60.00	60.50	60.50	60.50	60.50	60.10
1987	60.50	62.00	62.50	62.50	64.25	69.50	69.50	65.00	63.50	63.50	63.50	63.50	64.15
1988	63.56	63.50	63.50	63.50	63.50	63.50	63.50	63.50	63.50	64.63	66.25	70.00	64.37
1989	70.00	70.00	80.25	80.25	80.25	80.75	80.25	80.25	80.25	80.25	80.25	80.25	78.58
1990	81.75	82.25	82.23	82.25	82.25	82.25	82.25	82.25	79.25	77.25	77.25	81.00	81.02
1991	82.25	82.25	82.25	82.25	82.25	82.25	82.25	82.25	82.25	82.25	82.25	82.25	82.25
1992	82.25	82.25	82.25	82.25	82.25	82.25	82.25	82.25	67.25	62.25	62.25	62.25	76.00
1993	62.25	62.25	62.25	62.25	55.88	53.75	53.25	53.00	53.00	52.00	52.50	50.00	56.03
1994[1]	43.75	43.75	43.75	43.75	43.75	43.75							43.75

[1] Preliminary.   NA = Not available.   *Source: Economic Research Service, U.S. Department of Agriculture.*

Average Open Interest of Rapeseed Futures in Winnipeg   In 20 Metric Ton Units

Year	Jan	Feb	Mar	Apr	May	June	July	Aug	Sept	Oct	Nov	Dec
1985	19,122	22,206	21,260	22,202	19,611	17,591	17,675	19,058	16,757	14,511	14,717	17,232
1986	15,553	18,146	19,741	20,435	22,262	19,193	17,192	20,594	22,570	26,838	28,391	28,972
1987	25,143	32,141	34,152	31,564	30,761	28,903	26,599	24,083	25,075	25,893	23,049	26,576
1988	28,875	33,387	31,798	34,056	34,587	31,318	30,224	29,509	26,289	29,510	28,974	29,221
1989	22,435	20,889	18,591	22,690	24,587	21,025	22,280	22,027	16,153	21,556	20,981	21,749
1990	18,431	20,340	17,599	19,825	24,718	22,546	23,073	24,353	24,872	25,688	18,706	22,057
1991	22,000	22,829	24,815	26,637	30,072	28,240	28,288	27,547	27,558	29,079	23,880	20,117
1992	15,943	17,556	20,559	21,410	23,727	28,885	26,013	25,674	28,049	32,724	35,693	37,375
1993	34,098	37,658	36,715	38,210	38,231	29,743	39,763	43,844	50,616	55,107	54,998	54,475
1994	50,335	55,280	54,899	58,012	60,567	55,434	54,733	57,044	57,049	54,375	55,045	49,475

Source: Winnipeg Commodity Exchange

Average Price of Cash Canola at Vancouver   In Canadian Dollars Per Tonne

Year	Jan	Feb	Mar	Apr	May	June	July	Aug	Sept	Oct	Nov	Dec
1985	381.52	387.69	385.37	398.63	393.49	375.08	354.84	330.12	334.24	313.57	314.21	321.75
1986	321.49	304.19	294.97	283.29	282.19	267.79	252.73	234.95	239.20	246.00	252.73	244.59
1987	242.61	227.73	219.03	221.67	243.97	256.27	247.85	235.66	243.24	257.22	267.19	281.15
1988	302.56	303.16	294.22	305.27	336.31	413.98	395.28	381.19	379.83	349.68	333.96	344.35
1989	329.54	321.64	333.29	331.44	335.18	306.10	300.49	289.44	297.10	293.79	303.10	302.54
1990	300.01	301.45	311.00	318.78	322.24	303.89	300.83	299.43	292.74	295.23	290.08	290.01
1991	285.01	280.36	291.50	298.57	293.83	277.25	258.12	269.40	275.00	270.30	262.90	261.60
1992	264.15	273.35	282.70	276.85	288.08	292.35	272.20	282.26	320.62	302.10	327.22	331.57
1993	344.22	329.26	328.67	325.06	318.85	319.23	331.29	322.85	311.29	311.66	331.44	366.37
1994	408.60	413.10	422.23	454.90	481.44	484.95	388.63	382.54	381.70	379.99	401.38	432.35

Source: Winnipeg Commodity Exchange

Rayon and Other Synthetic Fibers

Worldwide Cellulosic Fiber Production   In Thousands of Metric Tons

Year	Austria	Brazil	China	Czech Republic	Finland	Germany	India	Japan	Poland	Romania	Taiwan	United Kingdom	United States	Former U.S.S.R.	Yugo-slavia	Total
1986	123.9	50.4	183.0	55.2	55.0	276.7	140.0	320.0	72.0	64.0	119.9	58.0	280.7	589.0	71.1	2,860
1987	120.0	48.9	187.0	55.2	54.0	274.6	167.5	300.5	73.3	66.0	119.6	55.0	274.6	591.5	63.3	2,826
1988	132.0	51.5	184.4	58.3	60.4	277.1	174.1	290.6	74.2	75.6	125.8	64.0	278.3	601.0	68.0	2,896
1989	136.0	55.0	204.0	56.9	64.8	278.4	198.7	272.9	65.6	95.9	147.6	55.0	263.3	584.0	71.1	2,943
1990	135.0	54.5	214.3	55.0	63.8	199.1	216.7	275.8	36.2	59.9	147.9	71.0	229.2	544.0	72.7	2,757
1991	120.0	53.0	212.0	40.9	47.4	118.0	215.4	266.4	25.6	38.0	149.1	63.0	220.7	401.7	49.3	2,411
1992	128.3	54.2	217.0	39.3	56.0	139.9	219.9	254.4	22.1	28.5	139.3	65.0	224.5	295.5	18.2	2,288
1993[1]	131.2	56.0	255.0	41.0	56.5	127.1	238.9	244.4	23.0	13.3	130.8	67.2	228.9	241.3	15.0	2,246
1994[2]	134.1	74.0	262.0	51.2	62.0	157.4	282.0	332.3	56.0	55.0	153.0	72.0	279.0	463.0	51.0	3,114
1995[2]	134.1	74.0	280.0	51.2	62.0	162.4	297.0	332.3	51.0	55.0	153.0	72.0	305.3	463.0	77.0	3,244

[1] Preliminary. [2] Producing Capacity.   Source: Fiber Economics Bureau, Inc.

Worldwide Noncellulosic Fiber Production (Except Olefin)   In Thousands of Metric Tons

Year	Brazil	China	France	Germany	India	Italy/Malta	Japan	Rep. of Korea	Mexico	Romania	Spain	Taiwan	United Kingdom	United States	Former U.S.S.R.	Total
1986	237.0	747.4	167.2	745.0	220.7	576.9	1,355.6	862.4	296.3	199.7	276.2	1,232.1	208.2	2,918.8	589.0	12,927
1987	248.1	846.0	161.0	759.3	266.0	564.6	1,340.6	970.1	333.2	201.9	268.5	1,391.3	203.0	3,094.3	591.5	13,741
1988	239.7	1,074.5	159.1	926.3	321.6	568.2	1,351.9	1,115.0	340.3	192.3	302.3	1,430.2	193.0	3,146.9	601.0	14,418
1989	245.8	1,223.2	152.1	952.3	366.7	547.7	1,380.9	1,189.9	352.8	159.3	252.3	1,523.1	178.5	3,119.4	874.0	14,747
1990	207.8	1,342.8	137.2	908.4	436.6	578.3	1,425.0	1,269.7	366.8	139.9	255.0	1,621.5	179.8	2,886.0	893.5	14,913
1991	219.1	1,488.9	107.0	797.0	439.6	564.6	1,429.8	1,364.1	395.3	138.8	241.1	1,841.4	179.3	2,902.9	804.8	15,282
1992	229.0	1,586.7	105.2	817.3	538.0	589.9	1,448.8	1,455.5	426.6	110.1	257.0	2,043.4	187.4	2,980.6	656.8	15,963
1993[1]	233.2	1,652.9	103.7	758.8	603.7	551.6	1,365.1	1,583.0	420.2	103.5	240.3	2,122.8	174.3	3,016.1	598.8	16,182
1994[2]	352.6	2,351.0	159.0	1,015.9	782.0	681.1	1,820.5	1,823.4	537.3	203.0	320.0	2,407.3	227.4	3,622.4	1,194.0	21,854
1995[2]	379.9	2,634.0	159.0	1,017.5	1,061.3	679.9	1,820.5	1,991.7	557.3	203.0	321.5	2,489.4	235.0	3,794.8	1,209.0	23,454

[1] Preliminary. [2] Producing capacity.   Source: Fiber Economics Bureau, Inc.

World Production of Synthetic Fibers   In Thousands of Metric Tons

Year	Noncellulosic Fiber Production (Except Olefin) — By Fibers — Acrylic & Modacrylic	Nylon & Aramid	Polyester	Other Fibers[3]	World Total — Yarn & Monofilaments	Staple & Tow & Fiberfill	Total	Glass Fiber Production — Europe	Japan	Other Americas	United States	Total	China	Former U.S.S.R.	Cigarette Tow Production
1986	2,445	3,500	6,842	140	5,683	7,244	12,927	364	240	35	630	1,299	50	100	362
1987	2,521	3,638	7,438	144	6,040	7,701	13,741	407	300	50	725	1,517	55	110	400
1988	2,452	3,725	8,102	138	6,572	7,845	14,417	465	340	65	730	1,655	65	125	412
1989	2,341	3,795	8,459	152	6,847	7,900	14,747	470	345	65	735	1,680	70	133	443
1990	2,320	3,738	8,697	158	7,054	7,859	14,913	445	371	60	675	1,631	75	120	464
1991	2,385	3,605	9,125	167	7,264	8,018	15,282	441	293	75	650	1,561	65	133	480
1992	2,363	3,674	9,769	157	7,723	8,240	15,963	442	307	83	700	1,652	75	130	475
1993[1]	2,294	3,621	10,125	142	7,989	8,193	16,182	508	312	86	794	1,865	77	133	482
1994[2]	2,999	5,184	13,389	282	11,221	10,633	21,854	653	346	105	989	2,289	130	190	

[1] Preliminary. [2] Producing capacity. [3] Alginate, azlon, spandex, saran, etc.   Source: Fiber Economics Bureau, Inc.

Man-Made Fiber Production in the United States   In Millions of Pounds

Year	Artificial (Cellulosic) Fibers Rayon & Acetate - Filament Yarn & Monofilament	Staple & Tow	Total Cellulosic	Synthetic (Noncellulosic) Fibers — Yarn & Monofilament — Nylon	Polyester	Olefin	Total Yarn	Staple & Tow — Nylon	Polyester	Acrylic & Modacrylic	Olefin	Total Staple	Total Noncellulosic	Total Manufactured Fibers	Total Glass Fiber
1987	191	414	605	1,697	1,179	1,134	4,010	992	2,362	592	360	4,306	8,316	8,921	1,598
1988	214	400	614	1,728	1,228	1,224	4,180	942	2,452	588	364	4,346	8,526	9,140	1,609
1989	217	363	580	1,759	1,209	1,257	4,225	981	2,385	543	382	4,291	8,516	9,096	1,620
1990	206	299	505	1,672	1,105	1,417	4,194	990	2,090	506	405	3,991	8,185	8,690	1,488
1991	213	273	486	1,666	1,208	1,408	4,282	869	2,203	454	458	3,984	8,266	8,752	1,433
1992	220	275	495	1,652	1,269	1,528	4,449	904	2,307	439	474	4,124	8,573	9,068	1,543
1993[1]	227	278	505	1,700	1,284	1,659	4,643	959	2,273	433	483	4,148	8,791	9,296	1,750
1994[2]	225	273	498	1,812	1,492	1,860	5,164	935	2,366	442	545	4,288	9,452	9,950	2,180

[1] Preliminary. [2] Estimate.   Source: Fiber Economics Bureau, Inc.

U.S. Artificial (Cellulosic) Distribution   In Millions of Pounds

Year	Yarn & Monofilament					Staple & Tow					Fiber Ship-ments
	Producers' Shipments				Domestic Con-sumption	Producers' Shipments				Domestic Con-sumption	
	Domestic	Exports	Total	Imports		Domestic	Exports	Total	Imports		
1985	187.1	23.0	210.1	13.9	201.0	324.2	35.0	359.2	12.3	336.5	1,259.6
1986	192.1	20.2	212.3	17.0	209.1	373.5	30.8	404.3	17.4	390.9	1,339.3
1987	166.8	24.9	191.7	12.8	179.6	383.6	32.4	416.0	13.8	397.4	1,513.1
1988	182.6	34.1	216.7	17.6	200.2	386.0	20.5	406.5	20.4	406.4	1,587.6
1989	187.3	31.7	219.0	26.3	213.6	338.2	16.2	354.4	54.0	392.2	1,530.1
1990	172.7	34.0	206.7	24.2	196.9	291.7	12.5	304.2	111.6	403.3	1,519.1
1991	179.9	32.3	212.2	30.8	210.7	255.5	8.1	263.6	92.0	347.5	1,488.5
1992	182.9	35.1	218.0	32.1	215.0	260.7	6.9	267.6	85.6	346.3	1,629.7
1993[1]	196.5	31.5	228.0	40.4	236.9	273.6	10.3	283.9	89.5	363.1	1,780.6

[1] Preliminary.   *Source: Fiber Economics Bureau, Inc.*

U.S. Domestic Distribution of Synthetic (Noncellulosic) Fibers   In Millions of Pounds

Year	Yarn & Monofilament								Staple & Tow							
	Producers' Shipments						Domestic Con-sumption		Producers' Shipments							Domestic Con-sumption
	Domestic				Exports	Total	Import		Domestic		Acrylic & Mod-acrylic						
	Nylon	Polyester	Olefin	Total					Nylon	Polyester		Olefin	Total	Exports	Total	Imports	
1985	1,417.4	1,204.2	937.6	3,559.2	240.2	3,799.4	104.6	3,663.8	830.3	1,872.7	458.7	279.7	3,441.4	372.8	3,814.2	159.4	3,600.8
1986	1,479.6	1,092.4	1,049.2	3,621.2	200.6	3,821.8	126.1	3,747.3	894.9	1,998.6	531.2	312.7	3,737.4	239.8	3,977.2	182.8	3,920.2
1987	1,554.3	1,113.4	1,135.5	3,803.2	214.7	4,017.9	123.9	3,927.1	966.0	2,201.0	479.3	341.1	3,987.4	325.6	4,313.0	189.0	4,176.4
1988	1,572.4	1,157.4	1,199.8	3,929.6	260.5	4,190.1	116.3	4,045.9	944.9	2,311.8	421.1	344.2	4,022.0	344.8	4,366.8	196.2	4,218.2
1989	1,575.3	1,110.7	1,226.0	3,912.0	237.9	4,149.9	182.2	4,094.2	955.3	2,261.3	414.8	363.4	3,994.8	253.3	4,248.1	192.4	4,187.2
1990	1,537.5	1,046.2	1,404.9	3,988.6	265.1	4,253.7	154.7	4,143.3	950.2	2,015.4	352.2	387.9	3,705.7	278.9	3,984.6	209.8	3,915.5
1991	1,493.9	1,114.0	1,380.6	3,988.5	246.9	4,235.4	174.8	4,163.3	835.0	2,127.9	319.2	437.5	3,719.6	277.8	3,997.4	263.1	3,982.7
1992	1,570.1	1,229.6	1,496.1	4,295.8	194.8	4,490.6	209.3	4,505.1	891.7	2,202.1	322.3	441.0	3,857.1	267.2	4,124.3	397.7	4,255.0
1993[1]	1,612.7	1,228.4	1,631.5	4,472.6	174.6	4,647.2	295.8	4,768.4	907.9	2,157.8	333.0	468.2	3,866.9	297.1	4,164.0	509.0	4,375.9

[1] Preliminary.   *Source: Fiber Economics Bureau, Inc.*

U.S. Mill Consumption of Fiber & Products & Per Capita Consumption   In Millions of Pounds

Year	Cellulosic Fibers				Noncellulosic Fibers			Total Manu-factured Fibers[2]	Cotton	Wool	Other Fibers[3]	Grand Total	Per Capita[4] Mill Consumption (Pounds)				
	Yarn & Monofil-ament	Staple & Tow	Net Waste	Total Cellu-lostic	Noncellu-lostic	Net Waste	Total Noncellu-lostic						Man-made Fibers[2]	Cotton	Wool	Other Fibers[3]	Total AllFibers
1985	201.0	336.5	8.1	545.6	7,264.6	225.3	7,489.9	8,035.5	2,796.0	134.7	103.6	11,069.8	37.7	17.6	1.5	2.7	59.5
1986	209.1	390.9	8.3	608.3	7,667.5	178.1	7,845.6	8,453.9	3,301.7	164.5	103.3	12,023.4	39.9	20.4	1.7	2.4	64.4
1987	179.6	397.4	8.6	585.6	8,103.5	172.6	8,276.1	8,861.7	3,736.5	167.6	104.8	12,870.6	41.3	23.7	1.7	2.5	69.2
1988	200.2	406.4	5.8	612.4	8,264.1	140.9	8,405.0	9,017.4	3,470.1	156.1	83.8	12,727.4	40.9	21.4	1.5	2.1	65.9
1989	213.6	392.2	-5.0	600.8	8,281.4	127.4	8,408.8	9,009.6	3,985.9	139.6	77.9	13,213.0	40.6	23.4	1.1	2.0	67.1
1990	196.9	403.3	-1.3	598.9	8,058.8	179.3	8,238.1	8,837.0	4,036.5	135.4	75.7	13,084.6	39.3	23.2	1.1	2.2	65.8
1991	210.7	347.5	-1.7	556.5	8,146.0	168.8	8,314.8	8,871.3	4,347.5	159.0	78.6	13,456.4	39.1	24.6	1.2	2.0	66.9
1992	215.0	346.3	-3.6	557.7	8,760.1	192.9	8,953.0	9,510.7	4,714.7	159.1	76.3	14,460.8	41.5	27.6	1.2	1.9	72.2
1993[1]	236.9	363.1	-5.6	594.4	9,144.3	198.6	9,342.9	9,937.3	4,847.5	164.6	73.8	15,023.2	43.2	28.9	1.3	1.8	75.2

[1] Preliminary.   [2] Excludes Glass Fiber.   [3] Includes silk, linen, jute and sisal & others.   [4] Mill consumption plus imports less exports of semimanufactured and unmanufactured products.   *Source: Fiber Economic Bureau, Inc.*

Producer Price Index of Grey Synthetic Broadwovens   (1982 = 100)

Year	Jan	Feb	Mar	Apr	May	June	July	Aug	Sept	Oct	Nov	Dec	Average
1985	104.0	103.1	102.5	102.3	103.0	102.4	101.9	101.7	101.8	102.0	102.3	102.4	102.5
1986	102.4	102.5	102.5	103.0	102.4	102.6	102.7	101.5	100.3	101.0	100.9	101.0	101.9
1987	101.9	101.9	102.2	103.4	103.9	105.3	106.4	106.9	107.9	108.6	109.0	109.2	105.6
1988	110.0	111.1	111.6	111.8	112.2	113.0	113.4	113.8	113.0	113.5	113.9	114.6	112.7
1989	114.3	112.0	112.2	112.2	112.1	113.1	114.7	115.0	115.0	115.8	115.9	115.3	114.0
1990	115.6	115.7	115.6	115.7	115.5	115.6	115.7	115.2	115.3	115.6	115.8	116.1	115.7
1991	115.7	114.7	114.4	114.1	114.3	113.9	114.8	116.4	116.5	116.5	116.8	118.2	115.5
1992	119.0	119.9	120.3	120.9	121.8	122.0	122.6	122.0	121.7	120.8	119.4	119.9	120.9
1993	119.6	119.1	119.1	119.2	117.1	118.4	118.0	118.0	116.9	117.3	115.2	114.5	117.7
1994[1]	113.5	112.8	110.3	113.2	113.2	113.3	113.1	113.3	114.2	111.8	112.8	113.8	112.9

[1] Preliminary.   *Source: Bureau of Labor Statistics, U.S. Department of Commerce.*

Rice

Rice is the world's second most popular foodstock after wheat. International trading in rice is relatively small, however, as much of the crop is consumed in the producing country. Still a record foreign trade was realized in rice during calendar 1994. Despite the increase in trade, however, prices were relatively subdued and lower relative to 1993 when a shortfall in Japanese production triggered a sharp increase in 1994 imports. Japan's need has since dissipated with imports of only 400,000 tonnes forecast for 1995. World rough rice production in the past few years has averaged near 520 million tonnes (equal to about 365 million tonnes, milled basis), but only 12-15 million milled tonnes moved in world trade. Prices can be very sensitive to any significant changes, real or perceived, in supply and demand, as occurred in the wake of Japan's recent import needs.

World rough rice production in 1994/95 was 522.9 million tonnes (352.9 million milled), compared to 519.2 million in 1993/94. The world's largest producer and consumer is China, with nearly a third of each. India is a distant second.

Thailand, whose rice production is about 12 percent that of China's, is the largest exporter, followed by the U.S. Importing nations are far more numerous, but on a consistent basis the larger importers include Brazil, Mexico, Saudi Arabia, Iran and Iraq. The Mideast typically is the largest importing region of U.S. rice, but Brazil has emerged as a major buyer. U.S. export prices are traditionally higher than its competitors, notably Thailand, but U.S. producers have shown increasing adaptability to changes in world trade and the trend is expected to persist.

U.S. rough rice production in 1994/95 was a record large 8.7 million tonnes, compared to 7.1 million in 1993/94. Export totals were expected to be 2.7 million tonnes in 1994/95, compared to 2.5 million a year earlier. The large U.S. crop was due to increased acreage and higher yields. U.S. rice acreage peaked in 1981 at over 3.8 million acres and has never returned to that level, but yields have escalated owing to higher-yielding varieties introduced in the 1980s. The 1994 yield of 5,954 pounds per acre surpassed the previous record of 5,749 pounds in 1989 and was more than 20 percent higher than the 1981 yield.

World milled rice consumption in 1994/95 was 358 million tonnes, compared to 355 million in 1993/94. This was the seventh consecutive year of growth, necessitating another draw upon carryover stocks during the year. For the start of the 1995/96 season, world stocks may total only 45 million tonnes (milled), vs. 50 million a year earlier, the lowest in nearly twenty years.

U.S. rice prices, farm level, in 1994/95 were forecast to range between $5.25 and $6.75 per cwt., substantially lower than the $8.08/cwt. of 1993/94. World prices are also expected to average much lower.

Futures Markets

Rough rice futures and options are traded on the Chicago Board to Trade (CBOT).

World Rice Supply and Distribution   In Thousands of Metric Tons

Year	Pro-duction	Exports U.S.	Exports Non-U.S.	Exports Total	Imports Brazil	Imports Iran	Imports Saudi Arabia	Imports Unac-counted	Imports Total	Utilization China	Utilization India	Utilization Total	Ending Stocks China	Ending Stocks India	Ending Stocks Total
1990-1	517,966	2,197	9,862	12,059	776	565	533	1,483	12,059	126,725	73,291	345,922	28,220	14,500	58,650
1991-2	516,872	2,106	11,975	14,081	450	926	625	1,445	14,081	128,537	74,975	351,545	27,510	13,500	56,651
1992-3[1]	521,472	2,641	12,097	14,738	716	1,050	869	1,795	14,738	127,000	75,110	355,059	29,602	10,600	54,174
1993-4[2]	520,203	2,650	13,272	15,922	850	475	750	1,635	15,922	128,000	75,975	356,731	25,192	12,000	48,370
1994-5[3]	523,263	2,800	12,597	15,397	800	800	750	1,084	15,397	127,000	76,800	355,962	20,192	12,600	45,717

[1] Preliminary. [2] Estimate. [3] Forecast. [4] Production is on a rough basis; all other data are reported on a milled basis.
Source: Foreign Agricultural Service, U.S. Department of Agriculture.

World Production of Rough Rice   In Thousands of Metric Tons

Year	Bang-ladesh	Brazil	Burma	China	Egypt	India	Indonesia	Japan	Kazak-hstan	Rep. of Korea	Pakistan	Philip-pines	Russia	Thailand	Vietnam
1990-1	26,781	10,000	13,695	189,331	3,167	111,448	45,178	13,124	578	7,732	4,898	9,885	895	17,192	18,776
1991-2	27,378	10,100	12,800	183,810	3,447	112,031	44,680	12,005	522	77,428	4,865	9,132	772	20,400	22,179
1992-3[1]	27,513	9,901	13,400	186,220	3,908	108,926	48,231	13,216	468	7,257	4,674	9,523	755	19,917	21,703
1993-4[2]	26,800	10,515	15,086	177,700	4,198	117,012	48,185	9,793	403	6,511	5,993	9,923	769	19,200	22,197
1994-5[3]	27,003	10,515	15,517	173,751	4,516	117,012	46,000	14,973	277	6,882	5,269	10,000	538	21,000	22,348

[1] Preliminary. [2] Estimate. [3] Forecast. *Source: Foreign Agricultural Service, U.S. Department of Agriculture.*

World Exports of Rice (Milled Basis), by Country of Origin   In Thousands of Metric Tons

Year	Argentina	Australia	Burma	China	Egypt	European Union	Guyana	India	Indonesia	Pakistan	Taiwan	Thailand	Uruguay	Vietnam	United States
1988	21	417	368	698	108	228	56	350	0	923	104	4,791	273	97	2,241
1989	36	450	456	315	32	239	26	400	104	789	68	6,036	260	1,383	2,967
1990	53	470	186	326	85	271	51	505	50	904	79	3,938	288	1,670	2,420
1991	75	450	176	689	159	391	54	711	0	1,297	229	3,988	260	1,048	2,197
1992	204	500	185	933	209	376	114	563	60	1,358	188	4,776	327	1,914	2,106
1993[1]	276	500	223	1,374	133	153	122	625	450	937	101	4,798	350	1,765	2,641
1994[2]	225	600	650	1,500	250	150	150	600	225	1,375	175	4,750	350	2,000	2,650
1995[3]	300	500	1,000	500	200	200	150	800	0	1,300	150	4,900	350	2,000	2,800

[1] Preliminary. [2] Estimate. [3] Forecast. *Source: Foreign Agricultural Service, U.S. Department of Agriculture.*

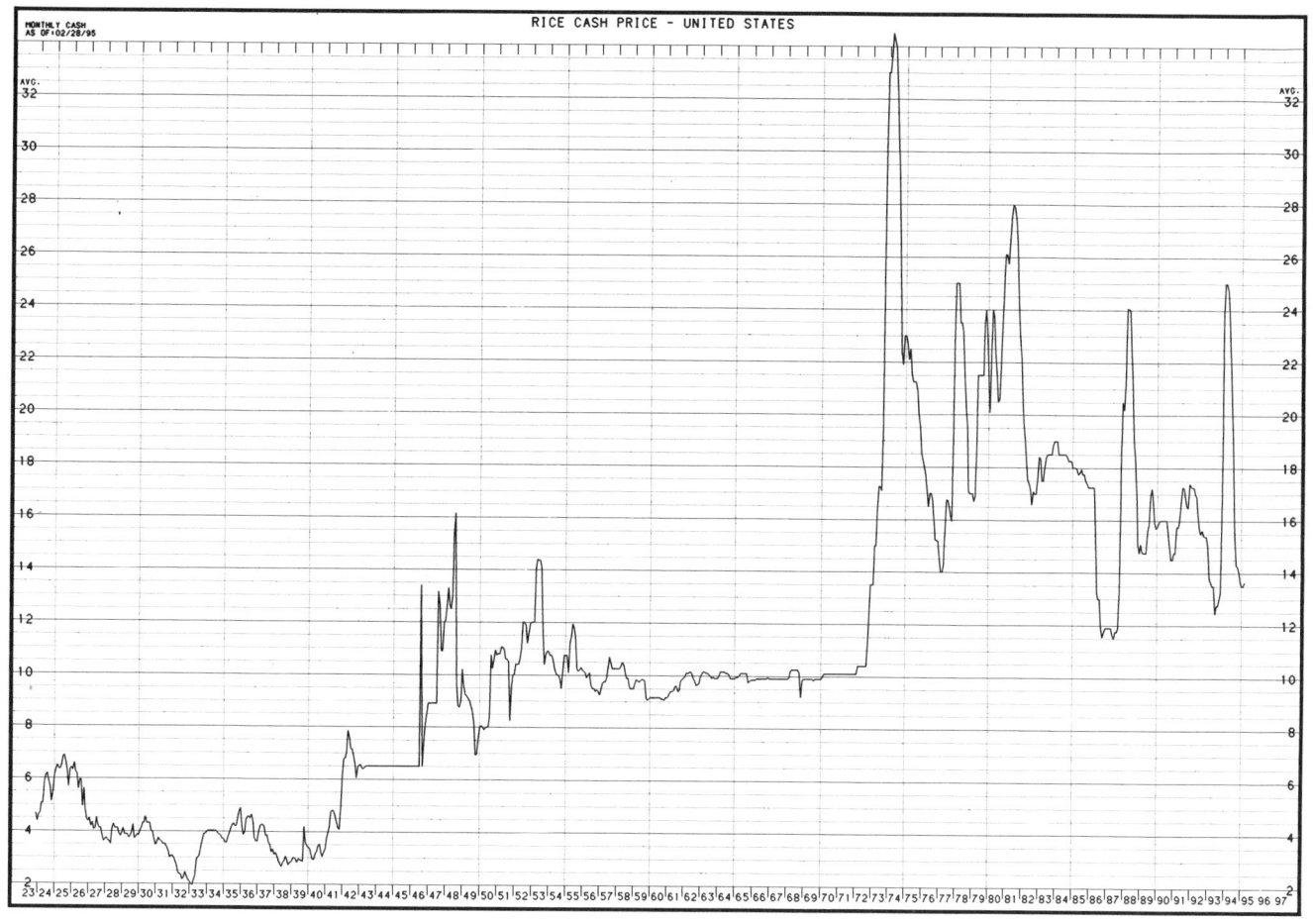

RICE CASH PRICE - UNITED STATES

Average Wholesale Price of Rice No. 2 (Medium)[1] Southwest Louisiana   In Dollars Per Cwt. Bagged

Year	Aug	Sept	Oct	Nov	Dec	Jan	Feb	Mar	Apr	May	June	July	Average
1981-2	26.40	24.20	22.90	21.20	20.00	18.80	17.80	16.10	16.00	16.40	16.20	16.00	19.30
1982-3	16.50	16.50	16.50	16.70	17.80	17.30	16.50	16.50	16.50	17.10	17.50	17.50	16.90
1983-4	17.50	17.50	17.50	17.50	17.50	17.50	17.50	17.50	17.50	17.50	17.50	17.50	17.50
1984-5	16.00	16.00	15.50	15.50	15.50	15.50	15.50	16.00	16.20	16.30	18.00	16.20	16.00
1985-6	16.00	16.00	16.00	16.00	16.00	16.00	15.67	15.50	14.60	11.90	12.00	11.35	14.75
1986-7	10.00	10.00	10.00	10.00	10.00	10.00	10.00	10.50	11.25	11.15	11.20	11.20	10.45
1987-8	11.10	11.95	16.60	17.25	16.75	18.50	19.80	20.15	20.00	18.00	17.40	16.70	17.00
1988-9	16.40	16.20	14.50	14.50	14.00	13.90	13.75	13.50	13.50	14.60	14.65	15.75	14.60
1989-0	15.55	15.30	14.80	14.30	14.04	14.80	15.13	15.13	15.50	15.75	15.65	15.30	15.10
1990-1	14.75	13.90	13.50	13.50	13.50	14.90	14.90	15.05	16.05	16.15	16.50	16.35	14.90
1991-2	15.85	16.00	16.00	16.00	16.00	16.00	15.90	15.50	15.50	15.15	14.50	14.50	15.60
1992-3	14.50	14.00	14.50	14.15	13.40	13.40	13.00	12.80	12.40	11.94	12.00	12.00	13.15
1993-4	12.25	12.45	15.65	21.95	24.00	24.00	23.88	23.80	24.00	23.70	22.00	20.00	20.65
1994-5[2]	18.30	15.90											

[1] U.S. No. 2 – broken not to exceed 4%.   [2] Preliminary.   Source: Economic Research Service, U.S. Department of Agriculture.

U.S. Rice (Rough) Production by Type and Variety   In Thousands of Cwt.

Year	Long Grain	Medium Grain	Short Grain	Total	Year	Long Grain	Medium Grain	Short Grain	Total
1987	88,995	37,651	2,957	129,603	1991	109,137	47,567	753	157,457
1988	119,364	36,891	3,642	159,897	1992	128,015	50,633	1,010	179,658
1989	109,161	41,441	3,885	154,487	1993	103,064	51,873	1,173	156,110
1990	107,806	47,328	954	156,088	1994[1]	133,445	63,390	944	197,779

[1] Preliminary.   Source: National Agricultural Statistics Service, U.S. Department of Agriculture.

RICE

Salient Statistics of Rice, Rough & Milled (Rough Equivalent) in the United States In Million of Cwt.

Crop Year Beginning August	Stocks August 1	Pro-duction	Imports	Total Supply	Food	Brewers	Seed	Total	Exports	Resid-ual	Total Disap-pearance	CCC Stocks July 31	Put Under Price Support	Long	Medium	All Classes	Milled Long
1989-90	26.7	154.5	4.4	185.6	60.0	15.4	3.6	79.0	77.2	3.0	159.2	0	121.9	6.68	6.13	6.50	10.81
1990-1	26.4	156.1	4.8	187.2	63.8	15.3	3.6	82.7	70.9	9.0	162.7	.1	143.7	6.68	6.21	6.50	10.84
1991-2	24.6	157.5	5.3	187.3	65.2	15.4	3.9	84.5	66.4	9.0	159.9	.4	108.3	6.65	6.11	6.50	10.74
1992-3	27.4	179.7	6.1	213.2	69.0	15.1	3.6	87.7	77.0	9.0	173.7	.1	125.8	6.66	6.13	6.50	10.74
1993-4[1]	39.4	156.1	7.0	202.5	71.3	15.0	4.2	90.5	79.4	6.5	176.4	.1	30.9	6.66	6.13	6.50	10.75
1994-5[2]	26.0	192.3	8.0	226.3	74.0	15.0	4.0	93.0	81.0	9.0	183.0	.1	125.3	6.65	6.12	6.50	10.72

[1] Preliminary. [2] Forecast. [3] Loan rate for each class of rice is the sum of the whole kernels' loan rate weighted by its milling yield (average 56%) and the broken kernels' loan rate weighted by its milling yield (average 12%).   *Source: Economic Research Service, U.S. Department of Agriculture.*

Acreage, Yield, Production and Prices of Rice in the United States

Crop Year	Southern States	California	United States	California	United States	Southern States	California	United States	Value of Pro-duction $1,000	Arkan-sas[2]	Hous-ton[3]	U.S. No. 2[4]	Thai "A"[5]	Thai "B"[5]
1989-90	2,277	410	2,690	7,900	5,749	122,097	32,390	154,487	1,055,889	15.75	16.20	338	397	336
1990-1	2,428	395	2,823	7,700	5,529	125,659	30,429	156,088	1,047,242	15.55	15.55	340	405	339
1991-2	2,425	350	2,775	8,100	5,674	129,107	28,350	157,457	1,200,629	16.20	17.15	359	396	328
1992-3	2,738	394	3,132	8,500	5,736	146,168	33,490	179,658	1,098,874	14.30	15.15	287	385	290
1993-4	2,396	437	2,833	8,300	5,510	119,839	36,271	156,110		21.20	20.75	413	413	335
1994-5[1]	2,831	485	3,316	8,500	5,964	156,555	41,224	197,779		15.68	15.65	312	412	302

[1] Preliminary. [2] F.O.B. mills, Arkansas, medium. [3] Houston, Texas (long grain). [4] Milled, 4%, container, FAS. [5] SWR, 100%, bulk.   *Source: Economic Research Service, U.S. Department of Agriculture.*

U.S. Exports of Milled Rice, by Country of Destination In Thousands of Metric Tons

Trade Year Beginning October	Canada	Germany	Haiti	Iran	Ivory Coast	Jamaica	Mexico	Nether-lands	Peru	Russia[2]	Saudi Arabia	Senegal	South Africa	Switzer-land	United Kingdom	Total
1990-1	127.4	49.9	124.8	0.0	69.4	75.5	96.5	91.6	61.5	0.0	189.1	63.2	115.9	108.6	38.8	2,395.1
1991-2	143.7	44.9	116.9	11.6	73.4	46.3	157.0	67.7	43.6	55.6	179.6	61.7	136.6	94.2	59.8	2,279.0
1992-3	146.0	67.6	152.9	184.3	107.3	39.4	241.5	120.9	61.6	74.8	223.5	91.5	122.1	71.2	72.2	2,709.9
1993-4[1]	141.3	41.7	57.2	60.4	34.2	53.8	234.0	92.9	47.0	6.4	180.5	90.1	110.9	64.8	82.4	2,432.7

[1] Preliminary. [2] Formerly part of the U.S.S.R.; data not reported separately until 1992.
Source: Economic Research Service, U.S. Department of Agriculture.

U.S. Rice Exports by Export Program In Thousands of Metric Tons

Fiscal Year	PL 480	Section 416	CCC Credit Pro-grams[2]	CCC African Relief Exports	EEP[3]	Export Pro-grams[4]	Exports Outside Specified Export Programs	Total U.S. Rice Exports	% Export Pro-grams as a Share of Total Exports
1989	408	0	826	0	20	1,254	1,862	3,116	40
1990	375	0	663	0	0	1,038	1,459	2,497	42
1991	411	0	183	0	76	669	1,726	2,395	28
1992	404	0	220	0	358	982	1,297	2,279	43
1993	594	0	235	0	278	1,108	1,499	2,607	43
1994[1]	375	0	167	0	46	588	2,012	2,600	23

[1] Preliminary. [2] May not completely reflect exports made under these programs. [3] Sales not shipments. [4] Adjusted for estimated overlap between CCC export credit and EEP shipments.   *Source: Economic Research Service, U.S. Department of Agriculture.*

Average Price Received by Farmers for Rice (Rough) in the U.S. In Dollars Per Hundred Pounds (Cwt.)

Year	Aug	Sept	Oct	Nov	Dec	Jan	Feb	Mar	Apr	May	June	July	Average[2]
1989-90	7.41	7.59	7.41	7.03	7.05	7.44	7.57	7.55	7.41	7.28	7.18	7.05	7.35
1990-1	6.66	6.21	6.02	6.29	6.13	6.39	6.75	7.07	7.43	7.44	7.43	7.21	6.68
1991-2	7.16	7.67	7.65	7.84	7.98	7.84	7.97	7.78	7.46	7.18	6.97	6.99	7.58
1992-3	6.60	6.41	6.40	6.40	6.38	6.35	6.06	5.63	5.50	5.23	5.02	4.90	5.89
1993-4[1]	5.19	5.21	6.10	8.06	8.91	8.98	10.10	10.20	9.93	10.00	8.88	7.80	8.09
1994-5[1]	6.75	6.82	6.47	6.39									

[1] Preliminary. [2] Weighted average by sales.   *Source: Economic Research Service, U.S. Department of Agriculture.*

Rubber

World rubber demand is largely dependent on new and replacement tire needs. Over the first five months of 1994, estate production of natural rubber was 430,000 tonnes, down from 485,000 tonnes in the same months of 1993. For all of 1993, estate production of natural rubber was 1.22 million tonnes. Production by small holdings for the January-May 1994 period was 1.72 million tonnes. This represented an almost 2 percent increase from the same period of 1993. For all of 1993, small holding production of natural rubber was 4.26 million tonnes.

Total consumption of natural rubber during the first five months of 1994 was 2.15 million tonnes, down slightly from 2.17 million tonnes over the like period of 1993. Producer stocks of natural rubber in May 1994 were 420,000 tonnes, down 11 percent from the May 1993 stock total. Consumer's total stocks in May 1994 were 540,000 tonnes, down 5 percent from June 1993. Stocks afloat in May 1994 were 590,000 tonnes, up 10,000 tonnes from the year-earlier stock level. Total stocks of natural rubber in May 1994 were 1.55 million tonnes, down 4 percent from May 1993.

Production of synthetic rubber during January-May 1994 was 3.71 million tonnes, marginally higher than output for the same period of 1993. For all of 1993, synthetic rubber production was 8.54 million tonnes. Total stocks of synthetic rubber in May 1994 were 1.64 million tonnes, down 12 percent from the May 1993 stocks of 1.86 million tonnes.

Consumption of synthetic rubber over the first five months of 1994 was 3.76 million tonnes. For the same period of 1993, consumption was 3.71 million tonnes. The U.S., with its huge automobile manufacturing capacity, is the world's largest user of natural and synthetic rubber. Over the first six months of 1994, the U.S. consumed 1.59 million tonnes, compared to 1.52 million tonnes in the same period of 1993. For all of 1993, the U.S. consumed 2.97 million tonnes of both natural and synthetic rubber. In 1992, U.S. consumption was 2.87 million tonnes. During the recession year of 1991, U.S. consumption was 2.52 million tonnes. The CIS use of rubber continues to decline. Over the January-May 1994 period, the CIS consumed 310,000 tonnes of rubber compared with 476,000 tonnes in the same period of 1993. Another large user of both natural and synthetic rubber is Japan, which also has a huge automobile industry. In 1993, Japan consumed 1.65 million tonnes, down 6 percent from 1992. China consumed 1.15 million tonnes of rubber in 1993, up almost 6 percent from 1992. Other large consumers in 1993 were Germany (668,000 tonnes), Brazil (436,000 tonnes), India (555,000 tonnes) and South Korea (578,000 tonnes).

The largest producer of natural rubber is Thailand, which in 1993 produced 1.57 million tonnes, up slightly from 1992. Indonesia produced 1.3 million tonnes of natural rubber in 1993, down 6 percent from 1992. Malaysian production has been in a state of serious decline. For 1993, production was 1.07 million tonnes, down 8 percent from 1992. In 1988, Malaysia produced 1.66 million tonnes of natural rubber. Other important producers in 1993 were India (428,100 tonnes), China (325,000 tonnes) and the Philippines (172,000 tonnes).

The major exporters of natural rubber are Thailand and Indonesia. Thailand exported 1.39 million tonnes of natural rubber in 1993, down 1 percent. Indonesia exported 1.21 million tonnes, down 4 percent. Other exporters include Nigeria, Malaysia, Vietnam and Cambodia.

The U.S. is the largest importer of natural rubber. In 1993, the U.S. imported almost 988,000 tonnes, up 8 percent from 1992. Japan imported almost 634,000 tonnes in 1993, down 6 percent. Other large importers in 1993 were Korea 275,000 tonnes, China at 270,000 tonnes, Germany took 170,000 tonnes and the United Kingdom 120,000.

The U.S. is the largest producer of synthetic rubber. For the January-June 1994 period, the U.S. produced 1.18 million tonnes. For all of 1993, U.S. production was 2.17 million tonnes. This was 6 percent lower than in 1992. The CIS produced 1.02 million tonnes in 1993, down sharply from 1.6 million in 1992. Japan's output of synthetic rubber in 1993 was 1.31 million tonnes, down 6 percent. German production was 572,000 tonnes, up 16 percent. France was also an important producer with 486,000 tonnes while China's output was 385,000 tonnes. It was reported that rubber producers and consumers could not agree on a new pact to stabilize prices. Producers wanted a 5 percent increase in the reference price which controls the price at which buffer stocks can be bought and sold. Consuming countries did not agree on the increase. Rubber prices have staged a rally which has allowed the sale of almost all of the 200,000 tonnes of rubber in the buffer stockpile.

U.S. Imports of Natural Rubber (Includes Latex & Guayule)   In Thousands of Metric Tons

Year	Jan	Feb	Mar	Apr	May	Jun	Jul	Aug	Sep	Oct	Nov	Dec	Total
1984	87.8	57.8	75.5	69.2	70.3	41.5	73.8	56.2	67.5	62.0	62.4	62.2	786.0
1985[2]	72.8	72.8	89.5	65.0	86.0	48.9	60.9	46.0	41.4	70.6	73.0	65.5	792.3
1986	66.7	71.5	77.9	84.5	48.4	54.9	70.1	45.2	63.9	73.5	54.0	56.7	721.0
1987	55.9	91.3	82.0	33.3	64.6	58.9	64.2	47.6	59.4	57.7	63.9	78.9	769.1
1988	83.2	69.6	87.0	68.6	67.2	64.9	49.5	83.3	59.1	69.3	77.4	74.7	791.8
1989	99.3	52.2	99.1	74.6	87.5	63.8	77.9	65.6	69.1	69.5	78.9	69.1	880.9
1990	72.3	58.6	81.9	63.1	89.5	77.7	60.4	61.0	83.0	55.7	81.7	75.7	820.1
1991	59.9	54.1	69.5	90.9	59.6	56.7	53.4	52.4	65.5	74.4	71.3	68.9	776.2
1992	77.5	75.2	84.7	64.7	79.0	73.8	80.5	77.2	73.9	81.3	68.1	77.5	913.4
1993[1]	95.3	79.9	93.9	86.3	74.1	81.2	83.6	77.8	69.2	73.4	86.0	86.9	987.6
1994[1]	87.5	74.7	102.6	78.9	88.3	77.8	66.7	85.0	78.8	89.3			

[1] Preliminary. [2] Data prior to 1985 are in thousands of long tons.   *Source: International Rubber Study Group*

RUBBER

World Rubber Production [1] In Thousands of Metric Tons

				Natural										Synthetic			
Year	China	India	Indo-nesia	Malaysia	Nigeria	Philip-pines	Sri Lanka	Thailand	Vietnam	World Total	Canada	Germany	Japan	United Kingdom	United States	Former U.S.S.R.	World Total
1985	187.9	198.3	1,130.2	1,469.5	51.6	150.1	137.5	723.8	52.5	4,400	209.2	447.6	1,158.0	232.6	2,026.0	2,125.0	8,960
1986	209.7	219.0	1,049.2	1,538.6	36.8	146.0	137.8	786.0	54.0	4,490	187.1	452.5	1,150.1	249.2	2,119.1	2,320.0	9,260
1987	237.6	227.4	1,203.3	1,578.7	55.3	147.2	121.8	925.6	55.0	4,840	179.8	468.4	1,191.9	257.0	2,182.1	2,366.0	9,450
1988	239.8	254.8	1,235.0	1,661.6	80.5	51.6	122.4	978.9	60.0	5,020	197.0	499.6	1,298.8	312.8	2,334.7	2,435.0	10,160
1989	242.8	288.6	1,256.0	1,415.6	118.4	56.7	110.7	1,178.9	84.0	5,130	188.0	507.6	1,352.7	311.4	2,261.4	2,358.0	10,110
1990	264.2	323.5	1,262.0	1,291.0	152.0	61.2	113.1	1,271.1	102.0	5,140	213.0	524.5	1,425.8	274.3	2,114.5	2,277.0	9,880
1991	296.4	360.2	1,284.0	1,255.7	155.7	59.6	103.9	1,340.8	88.0	5,230	190.0	504.4	1,377.3	251.3	2,050.0	2,105.0	9,250
1992[2]	309.0	383.0	1,387.0	1,173.2	126.0	56.9	106.1	1,531.0	113.0	5,480	211.0	494.3	1,388.0	280.1	2,300.0	1,600.0	9,180
1993[2]	325.0	428.1	1,301.3	1,074.3	105.0	56.0	104.2	1,569.8	111.0	5,350	198.0	572.0	1,309.8	289.8	2,170.0	1,020.0	8,520

[1] Including rubber in the form of latex. [2] Preliminary. *Source: International Rubber Study Group*

World Consumption of Natural and Synthetic Rubber In Thousands of Metric Tons

				Natural									Synthetic				
Year	Australia	Brazil	Canada	France	Germany	Japan	United Kingdom	United States	World Total	Canada	France	Germany	Japan	United Kingdom	United States	World Total
1984	35.9	88.7	102.0	162.0	190.0	525.0	118.0	750.7	4,230	208.0	287.0	403.0	915.0	195.0	2,062.3	8,955
1985	35.8	97.6	95.0	156.0	202.2	539.9	126.0	764.0	4,350	173.0	311.8	411.3	947.5	201.0	1,962.0	9,000
1986	30.6	105.6	86.0	158.7	198.7	535.0	130.0	743.0	4,460	190.2	315.0	426.0	910.0	195.0	2,019.6	9,280
1987	35.5	115.4	98.0	170.0	198.5	568.0	134.0	789.0	4,800	210.0	316.4	453.4	946.0	216.0	2,017.3	9,650
1988	40.5	125.3	82.5	181.0	203.6	623.0	140.0	858.3	5,100	202.0	315.0	471.0	1,042.0	226.5	2,016.8	9,940
1989	43.5	124.3	84.9	184.0	221.1	657.0	132.5	866.9	5,220	191.1	358.0	476.0	1,103.0	240.0	2,051.0	10,050
1990	34.0	121.3	84.0	179.0	208.7	677.0	136.0	807.5	5,210	185.4	351.0	511.0	1,133.0	223.0	1,820.8	9,710
1991	34.0	125.0	76.3	183.0	210.7	689.5	119.0	755.8	5,120	183.9	342.0	502.0	1,118.5	201.0	1,768.1	9,300
1992[1]	36.5	119.4	86.5	179.0	212.8	685.4	124.5	910.2	5,310	198.0	365.4	507.0	1,080.6	229.0	1,959.6	9,300
1993[1]	45.0	125.0	91.5	170.0	175.0	631.0	119.0	966.7	5,350	210.0	320.0	490.0	1,022.0	222.0	2,001.0	8,690

[1] Preliminary. *Source: International Rubber Study Group*

World Stocks[1] of Natural & Synthetic Rubber (by Countries) on Jan. 1 In Thousands of Metric Tons

				In Producing Countries								In Consuming Countries (Reported Stocks)				
Year	Total Synthetic	Africa	Cam-bodia	Indo-nesia	Malaysia	Singa-pore	Sri Lanka	Thailand	Vietnam	Other Asia	Total Natural	Brazil	India	Japan	United States	Total
1985	1,790	------	1.0	95.0	228.8	36.8	10.2	41.3	5.0	30.0	545	15.9	58.0	70.7	96.4	925
1986[2]	1,750	17.8	1.0	90.0	191.8	22.0	12.2	47.1	6.0	16.0	520	13.5	58.2	70.7	95.2	238
1987	1,710	16.2	1.0	90.0	207.3	21.6	23.6	32.5	6.0	15.1	530	13.3	85.5	61.9	73.0	234
1988	1,520	19.1	1.0	100.0	208.5	21.6	20.0	37.8	6.0	13.8	510	13.5	58.2	70.7	95.2	224
1989	1,800	23.2	1.0	100.0	286.5	32.2	23.2	53.0	6.0	6.7	540	20.5	80.9	97.2	61.7	260
1990	1,860	26.9	1.0	110.0	248.3	24.0	27.0	53.7	8.0	7.0	510	15.6	78.4	105.6	92.0	292
1991	2,030	23.4	1.0	114.0	190.3	20.2	29.8	74.9	10.0	7.3	490	11.4	92.9	91.6	94.3	290
1992	1,980	23.3	1.0	68.0	196.1	25.9	17.3	80.1	9.0	7.2	450	8.8	106.0	92.7	109.4	317
1993[1]	1,860	22.2	1.0	70.0	187.2	15.3	16.0	79.8	11.0	6.9	500	5.7	90.9	82.9	108.0	288
1994[1]	1,690	18.6	1.0	40.0	159.2	10.6	17.2	121.0	11.0	7.2	480	10.0	96.4	85.4	71.3	263

[1] Preliminary. [2] Prior to 1986 data shown for all consuming countries. *Source: International Rubber Study Group*

Net Exports of Natural Rubber from Producing Areas In Thousands of Metric Tons

Year	Cambodia	Guat-emala	Indonesia	Liberia	Malaysia	Nigeria	Sri Lanka	Thailand	Vietnam	Other Africa[2]	Other Asia[3]	World Total
1985	14.0	10.6	1,000.9	87.2	1,465.8	29.1	120.4	685.3	35.5	69.0	29.8	3,640
1986	20.0	6.2	958.7	90.4	1,485.2	26.0	110.0	755.2	35.0	78.0	35.2	3,630
1987[4]	20.0	10.4	1,092.8	91.1	1,578.5	43.7	106.0	873.2	35.0	94.0	28.1	3,950
1988	21.0	9.8	1,132.0	105.6	1,563.6	65.8	99.3	906.4	37.9	107.0	36.8	4,070
1989	21.0	11.0	1,151.8	106.0	1,364.8	101.3	86.0	1,100.6	57.7	115.0	38.2	4,150
1990	23.0	13.4	1,077.3	40.0	1,185.6	121.0	86.7	1,150.8	75.9	120.0	37.6	4,010
1991	23.5	14.3	1,220.0	19.0	1,041.2	139.0	76.4	1,231.9	62.9	122.0	43.7	4,010
1992[1]	29.0	15.7	1,268.1	28.0	939.1	107.0	78.6	1,412.9	80.9	131.0	43.5	4,080
1993[1]	30.0	16.9	1,214.3	3.0	769.8	87.0	69.6	1,393.6	75.0	133.6	50.6	3,910

[1] Preliminary. [2] Includes Cameroon, Cote d'Ivoire, Gabon, Ghana and Zaire. [3] Includes Myanmar, Papua New Guinea and the Philippines. [4] Prior to 1987 data shown for Central American Common Market (C.A.C.M.) *Source: International Rubber Study Group*

Average Spot Crude Rubber Prices (Smoked Sheets¹) in New York   In Cents Per Pound

Year	Jan	Feb	Mar	Apr	May	Jun	Jul	Aug	Sep	Oct	Nov	Dec	Average
1983	44.0	48.5	57.8	57.8	56.8	54.5	58.3	59.3	60.5	60.5	58.3	-----	56.0
1984	57.3	58.3	58.0	56.8	51.8	47.0	46.0	46.0	46.0	43.0	42.8	42.0	49.6
1985	42.3	42.3	41.8	42.3	40.8	42.0	40.3	41.8	41.8	43.8	42.5	39.8	41.8
1986	40.7	42.8	42.0	39.2	40.1	41.0	43.5	43.5	45.3	46.9	44.7	44.7	42.9
1987	45.9	46.5	43.8	47.4	49.1	50.6	53.5	53.7	54.2	53.8	53.1	54.0	50.5
1988	54.6	53.8	54.9	55.7	58.6	67.6	66.1	63.8	60.1	55.2	53.0	54.1	58.1
1989	56.0	59.3	54.1	55.2	52.1	49.5	49.2	47.2	46.1	46.1	45.6	44.8	50.4
1990	44.7	45.8	45.9	45.6	45.8	46.0	45.8	47.5	48.4	46.5	46.3	47.1	46.3
1991	47.5	48.8	49.1	46.0	45.2	45.3	44.6	44.4	44.3	44.5	44.8	44.2	45.7
1992	43.1	44.0	44.5	45.9	46.4	46.6	46.8	47.1	46.9	47.8	48.0	48.0	46.3
1993	48.5	48.3	46.4	44.2	43.8	43.8	43.3	43.9	44.5	44.2	44.9	44.7	45.0
1994	44.9	46.1	49.6	50.8	51.4	55.1	62.5	66.4	67.2	73.5	71.8	77.4	59.7

¹No. 1, ribbed, plantation rubber.   *Source: Wall Street Journal; KR-CRB*

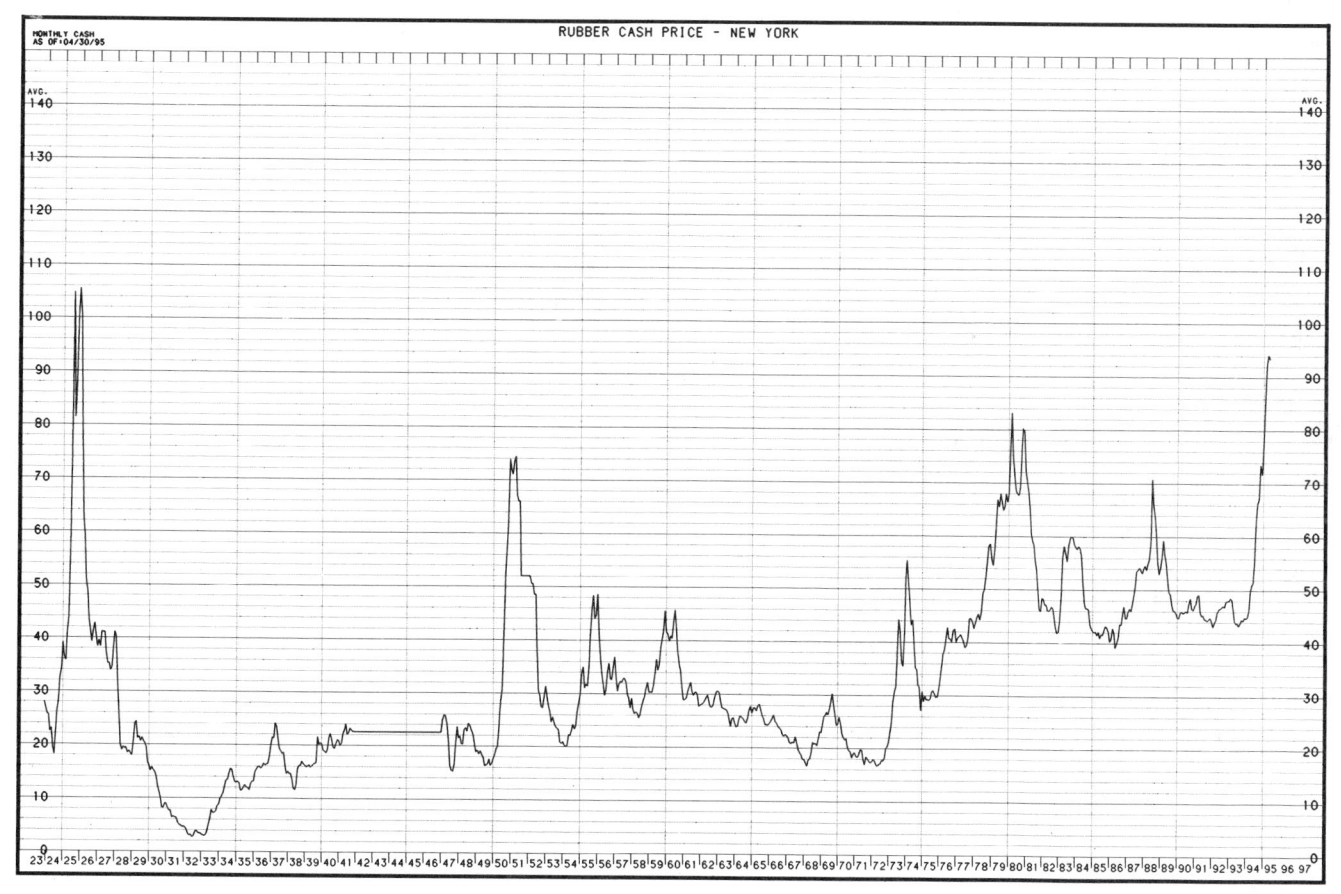

RUBBER

Consumption of Natural Rubber in the United States   In Thousands of Metric Tons

Year	Jan	Feb	Mar	Apr	May	Jun	Jul	Aug	Sep	Oct	Nov	Dec	Total
1983	64.5	44.5	55.3	55.3	56.9	67.0	48.8	39.2	50.2	75.3	69.7	49.6	676.3
1984	73.8	56.8	83.1	68.2	65.1	42.4	73.9	56.1	63.7	58.3	55.4	54.1	750.7
1985	71.8	65.7	91.5	51.7	89.0	45.2	55.4	47.3	68.1	47.2	65.7	52.4	774.7
1986	59.4	71.8	71.3	81.9	45.5	54.6	69.9	49.9	57.0	80.3	50.8	51.2	743.0
1987	49.9	85.4	81.3	62.3	62.6	56.3	67.4	61.4	61.9	57.4	60.6	69.4	789.0
1988	80.9	66.3	91.6	60.8	68.7	66.2	53.5	80.6	64.6	74.5	75.4	75.2	858.3
1989	89.9	51.1	96.6	68.4	87.9	65.1	82.7	70.8	72.0	62.1	84.6	50.9	866.9
1990	62.6	57.3	79.0	65.2	87.4	73.9	57.4	74.1	78.8	59.8	75.6	69.8	807.5
1991	60.0	60.0	65.0	65.0	65.0	60.0	55.0	55.0	65.0	70.0	65.0	66.0	755.8
1992	83.4	63.3	85.9	66.9	80.6	78.6	82.6	79.5	70.2	84.6	64.4	70.2	910.2
1993[1]	96.3	76.0	93.4	93.4	67.9	76.8	77.3	84.9	72.0	73.6	82.9	72.2	966.7
1994[1]	92.8	85.0	93.1	82.7	89.6	84.6	76.2	87.8	74.8	91.5			

[1] Preliminary.   Source: International Rubber Study Group

Stocks of Natural Rubber in the United States, Beginning of Month   In Thousands of Metric Tons

Year	Jan	Feb	Mar	Apr	May	Jun	Jul	Aug	Sep	Oct	Nov	Dec
1985	96.4	94.3	97.3	91.4	101.9	95.9	95.6	97.9	93.9	84.9	81.1	85.1
1986	95.2	97.0	96.9	100.4	98.6	98.6	96.7	93.8	86.4	91.6	75.3	78.2
1987	38.5	76.7	78.8	70.2	80.2	79.5	79.0	82.5	77.0	70.6	65.9	65.5
1988	72.5	74.9	75.3	70.7	74.6	72.9	71.6	68.7	71.2	63.9	57.9	58.4
1989	61.7	71.1	67.5	77.4	82.2	86.7	86.2	86.2	88.1	83.3	87.7	83.9
1990	92.0	100.2	100.2	101.6	97.1	97.3	99.8	101.6	87.2	90.3	84.7	89.6
1991	94.3	94.0	88.0	93.0	119.0	113.0	110.0	108.0	106.0	106.0	110.0	117.0
1992	109.4	103.6	112.7	110.4	107.5	105.9	101.1	99.0	96.7	100.3	97.0	100.7
1993[1]	108.0	49.4	53.3	53.7	46.7	52.9	57.3	63.6	56.5	53.7	53.4	56.5
1994[1]	71.3	65.9	55.7	65.2	61.4	60.0	53.2	43.8	41.0	45.0	42.8	

[1] Preliminary.   Source: International Rubber Study Group

Stocks of Synthetic Rubber in the United States, Beginning of Month   In Thousands of Metric Tons

Year	Jan	Feb	Mar	Apr	May	Jun	Jul	Aug	Sep	Oct	Nov	Dec
1985	272.1	281.2	271.8	288.6	294.0	398.0	247.8	295.8	413.5	397.3	374.9	367.0
1986	213.9	352.8	217.5	397.7	403.0	238.6	247.5	239.9	233.4	236.5	231.1	224.6
1987	235.6	247.0	249.5	242.6	239.9	242.2	241.8	251.9	240.6	222.8	213.6	213.8
1988	229.0	237.8	235.1	229.6	237.5	246.2	249.6	261.0	259.9	258.6	259.0	258.2
1989	276.3	288.9	287.7	294.4	289.6	300.4	303.7	308.7	314.1	323.4	329.6	414.8
1990	404.0	393.5	392.5	385.8	406.8	397.5	395.0	414.9	420.8	419.6	405.0	393.9
1991	403.7	406.0	403.0	404.0	402.0	388.0	394.0	385.0	356.0	334.0	330.0	325.0
1992	403.7	386.0	381.2	383.9	393.2	389.2	372.8	382.7	382.1	375.1	378.6	401.1
1993[1]	406.9	345.9	345.7	346.0	340.5	351.8	342.1	341.6	333.6	326.4	319.9	321.4
1994[1]	331.1	315.0	318.8	313.0	311.8	320.8	308.4	329.5	324.7	309.5	304.3	

[1] Preliminary.   Source: International Rubber Study Group

Production of Synthetic Rubber in the United States   In Thousands of Metric Tons

Year	Jan	Feb	Mar	Apr	May	Jun	Jul	Aug	Sep	Oct	Nov	Dec	Total
1985	155.2	153.9	170.1	160.5	171.1	164.6	154.4	146.7	159.6	174.5	189.4	160.2	1,936
1986	183.3	173.0	190.3	193.2	191.4	183.7	166.7	178.4	173.0	179.7	158.3	147.5	2,156
1987	169.9	161.6	182.1	166.0	154.2	139.5	150.4	154.2	160.3	153.6	149.2	131.8	1,838
1988	166.5	156.7	189.1	178.6	167.8	164.9	155.3	170.5	178.6	186.7	145.6	174.7	2,335
1989	206.3	177.5	193.6	174.1	179.7	175.0	186.2	164.2	176.0	191.0	182.9	194.8	2,261
1990	173.5	180.1	182.5	187.8	174.6	172.0	171.9	180.9	180.4	190.3	167.4	153.1	2,115
1991	168.0	163.0	184.0	174.0	173.0	159.0	154.0	133.0	159.0	159.0	173.0	164.0	2,050
1992	180.0	190.0	200.0	210.0	200.0	190.0	190.0	200.0	210.0	200.0	195.0	175.0	2,300
1993[1]	120.0	160.0	220.0	190.0	200.0	180.0	190.0	180.0	180.0	180.0	190.0	180.0	2,170
1994[1]	180.0	180.0	210.0	200.0	210.0	200.0	200.0	210.0	190.0	210.0			

[1] Preliminary.   Source: International Rubber Study Group

Consumption of Synthetic Rubber in the United States   In Thousands of Metric Tons

Year	Jan	Feb	Mar	Apr	May	Jun	Jul	Aug	Sep	Oct	Nov	Dec	Total
1984	131.7	140.2	158.2	146.3	146.2	156.7	135.6	170.3	170.5	180.4	158.2	147.2	1,828
1985	177.5	175.4	180.5	166.7	167.1	171.0	147.1	173.9	151.5	184.1	166.3	147.2	2,062
1986	155.8	169.5	159.6	154.8	163.6	137.9	139.8	150.6	171.6	174.3	154.0	140.3	1,802
1987	160.7	145.0	175.7	157.6	163.9	148.0	151.5	168.5	160.6	177.5	145.8	155.7	2,020
1988	162.8	166.1	182.8	160.6	163.1	157.8	161.9	163.6	172.2	185.1	167.6	174.1	2,017
1989	158.5	166.8	186.8	163.1	172.1	166.3	160.9	171.1	162.5	170.6	180.5	150.5	2,051
1990	159.6	158.7	161.6	144.1	161.5	151.6	137.1	149.5	155.6	175.3	147.1	119.1	1,821
1991	145.0	140.0	160.0	150.0	160.0	135.0	140.0	140.0	160.0	140.0	150.0	149.0	1,768
1992	167.8	159.5	174.7	158.9	162.6	184.2	154.5	177.7	180.2	171.5	155.1	148.2	1,960
1993[1]	161.3	154.4	189.4	172.8	164.5	173.6	166.0	173.9	162.0	169.4	162.3	151.4	2,001
1994[1]	176.0	157.1	192.4	172.4	172.9	188.5	164.5	187.6	177.4	178.8			

[1] Preliminary.   Source: International Rubber Study Group

Exports of Synthetic Rubber in the United States   In Thousands of Metric Tons

Year	Jan	Feb	Mar	Apr	May	Jun	Jul	Aug	Sep	Oct	Nov	Dec	Total
1987	32.4	33.2	36.1	37.1	39.4	36.9	34.1	33.3	38.8	33.5	37.5	37.1	470.5
1988	39.7	37.4	41.8	41.7	40.4	41.1	29.8	44.0	38.6	37.2	36.3	32.1	514.0
1989	42.4	45.7	55.0	41.3	54.4	51.3	43.7	48.2	54.5	54.6	43.6	44.4	450.6
1990	45.6	39.0	50.2	42.6	42.7	41.0	37.4	43.1	42.0	50.8	50.3	39.0	523.7
1991	43.8	46.1	44.0	45.2	47.9	40.4	42.8	43.2	43.1	46.3	47.3	42.2	532.3
1992	52.3	55.1	51.3	59.1	58.2	51.6	46.5	52.8	58.0	51.4	48.1	39.7	624.1
1993[1]	47.1	34.1	57.7	47.4	52.4	46.9	46.9	43.8	48.8	46.6	49.0	41.9	562.6
1994[1]	48.8	46.4	55.4	57.0	52.4	49.6	50.2	62.8	60.7	59.9			

[1] Preliminary.   Source: International Rubber Study Group

Production of Tyres (Car and Truck) in the United States   In Thousands of Units

Year	Jan	Feb	Mar	Apr	May	Jun	Jul	Aug	Sep	Oct	Nov	Dec	Total
1984	16,749	17,498	19,122	16,988	18,043	18,557	15,546	18,078	17,333	19,136	16,645	15,682	209,375
1985	18,381	17,375	18,704	17,388	16,781	15,216	12,989	16,635	16,844	17,626	15,198	13,786	196,923
1986	16,306	15,966	16,968	16,037	15,003	14,647	14,203	16,112	16,540	18,180	15,144	15,183	190,289
1987	16,879	16,593	17,733	16,680	16,982	16,548	15,796	16,723	17,204	18,956	16,455	16,428	202,978
1988	17,345	18,027	19,305	17,642	17,403	17,941	15,022	18,058	18,115	19,138	17,253	16,102	211,351
1989	18,944	18,102	19,670	19,224	19,090	18,312	14,835	18,288	16,963	18,400	16,323	14,721	212,870
1990	19,017	17,376	19,522	17,680	17,990	18,186	14,996	18,555	17,612	19,965	16,077	13,687	210,663
1991	17,713	17,375	16,208	17,017	19,360	16,419	14,354	17,784	17,045	19,588	16,354	15,173	202,390
1992	18,772	18,762	20,356	19,065	18,874	19,380	17,273	20,306	19,975	21,602	18,384	17,501	230,250
1993[1]	----------61,809------------			----------60,752------------			----------57,702------------			----------57,184----------			237,447
1994[2]	----------63,586------------			----------63,331------------			----------57,018------------						

[1] Preliminary. [2] Estimate.   Source: International Rubber Study Group

Foreign Trade of Tyres (Car and Truck) in the United States   In Thousands of Units

Year	Imports 1st Quarter	2nd Quarter	3rd Quarter	4th Quarter	Total	Exports 1st Quarter	2nd Quarter	3rd Quarter	4th Quarter	Total
1986	9,346	10,148	11,458	10,215	41,167	1,268	1,146	1,267	1,474	5,223
1987	11,584	12,820	11,722	11,341	47,467	2,095	2,327	2,389	3,371	10,182
1988	11,383	12,059	12,383	12,783	48,608	4,203	4,120	3,712	4,034	16,069
1989	12,802	14,518	12,609	12,749	52,678	4,104	4,254	5,267	4,704	18,329
1990	13,713	13,564	11,951	11,633	50,861	5,453	5,532	6,031	6,730	23,746
1991	12,011	13,008	11,320	10,158	46,497	6,407	6,388	6,623	6,342	25,760
1992[1]	10,760	12,496	11,850	12,285	47,391	6,243	6,475	7,125	6,646	26,489
1993[2]	12,311	12,303	12,457	12,597	49,668	6,989	6,987	7,081	6,960	28,017

[1] Preliminary. [2] Estimate.   Source: International Rubber Study Group

Rye

U.S. rye production has been trending consistently lower for some time and rye might now be considered a minor crop. Imports, although small in quantity during the past two years, have nearly totaled half the crop size. Annual production in the 1990s has averaged about 10.5 million bushels, vs. an average during the 1980s of more than 20 million. The major producing states are Georgia and South Dakota. Production in 1994/95 was about 11.1 million bushels, compared to 10.3 million in 1993/94. The increase reflected an increase in acreage and small gain in average yield.

Rye is used as an animal feed and as an ingredient in bread and some whiskeys. In the U.S., nearly half of total supply is used as a feedstuff, a third as a foodstuff and the balance as seed and for whisky. Virtually no U.S. rye has been exported during the past three crop years.

Despite rye's declining use, the U.S. government maintains a price support program for the grain. The loan rate for producers in the 1994/95 marketing year was raised to $1.61 per bushel from $1.46 in the previous two seasons. The higher loan rate apparently encouraged the aforementioned increase in planted acreage, from 1.5 million acres in 1993/94 to 1.6 million for 1994/95.

On a world basis, production has fallen to an estimated 23.1 million tonnes in 1994/95 from 25.8 million in 1993/94. The downward trend shows little sign of reversing. World production in the mid-1980s averaged more than 30 million bushels. The reason for the slide is not adverse yield, but a steady decline in acreage.

Russia, the Ukraine and Poland accounted for more than 90 percent of total world output in 1994/95. Germany accounted for much of the balance. Almost all of the world's crop is consumed domestically, with the exception of Canada. Canada's output is only slightly larger than that of the U.S., but most of the crop is exported to the U.S.

World Production of Rye   In Thousands of Metric Tons

Crop Year	Argentina	Austria	Canada	Czech-oslovakia	Den-mark	France	Ger-many	Hungary	Nether-lands	Poland	Russia[4]	Spain	Turkey	Ukraine[4]	United States	World Total
1983-4	130	348	827	751	315	278	3,738	138	26	8,781	-----	253	380	14,000	689	31,407
1984-5	140	380	664	710	608	321	4,493	192	25	9,540	-----	325	360	13,400	827	33,398
1985-6	100	339	569	620	565	283	4,382	163	19	7,600	-----	295	360	15,700	524	32,217
1986-7	60	284	609	547	546	200	4,224	172	19	7,074	-----	220	350	15,248	496	30,782
1987-8	88	309	493	496	513	275	3,928	186	25	6,816	-----	320	350	18,055	503	33,034
1988-9	42	356	267	530	366	260	3,419	245	28	7,232	-----	357	360	18,517	373	32,989
1989-90	70	381	873	708	487	270	3,867	200	33	6,216	-----	336	320	18,288	347	33,412
1990-1	96	396	599	736	545	240	3,988	226	36	6,044	-----	267	240	21,193	258	36,861
1991-2	45	350	339	484	395	210	3,324	221	34	5,899	-----	242	240	14,061	248	27,319
1992-3[1]	45	315	275	380	400	230	3,000	200	25	5,200	13,890	220	240	1,160	254	27,931
1993-4[2]		290	320	300	320	190	2,980	110		5,000	9,150	300	230	1,200	260	26,060
1994-5[3]		280	390	350	380	180	3,500	200		5,300	6,000	220	250	700	280	22,160

[1] Preliminary. [2] Estimate. [3] Forecast. [4] Formerly part of the U.S.S.R.; data not reported separately until 1992. *Source: Foreign Agricultural Service, U.S. Department of Agriculture.*

Production of Rye in the United States   In Thousands of Bushels

Year	Georgia	Illinois	Indiana	Kansas	Michigan	Minne-sota	Nebraska	North Dakota	Ohio	Okla-homa	Penn-sylvania	South Carolina	South Dakota	Texas	Virginia	Wis-consin
1984	1,760	308	336	312	588	6,650	1,392	5,400	175	704	578	546	10,800	240	378	216
1985	2,070	256	308	300	651	3,300	1,242	2,640	172	828	470	532	4,440	400	312	234
1986	1,785	210	280	210	713	1,600	1,035	4,250	175	840	630	391	4,440	190	364	168
1987	1,540	144	162	270	640	1,200	1,150	5,115	180	360	525	528	5,040	150	435	100
1988	1,890	140	210	130	650	920	1,375	1,350	185	720	684	720	2,250	150	560	120
1989	1,610	312	204	80	825	1,088	600	1,064	155	532	576	644	3,240	126	264	360
1990	1,320	165	124	130	580	868	750	780	175	420	496	594	1,870	140	256	465
1991	1,300	162	100	115	360	648	1,000	992	155	665	297	630	1,152	228	264	435
1992	1,560	280	156	130	496	720	1,040	1,496	175	798	720	675	1,666	280	288	330
1993	1,380	224	150	693	420	667	500	1,050	150	660	340	380	1,600	363	165	260
1994[1]	1,890	144	120	325	442	810	546	722	170	900	320	600	1,305	435	252	875

[1] Preliminary. *Source: Agricultural Statistics Board, U.S. Department of Agriculture.*

WEEKLY NEAREST FUTURES
AS OF:05/12/95

RYE - WPG

CAN.$/
METRIC TON

Salient Statistics of Rye in the United States   In Thousands of Bushels

| Crop Year Beginning June 1 | Supply | | | | Disappearance | | | | | | Acreage | | Yield Per Harvested Acre Bushels |
| | Stocks June 1 | Pro- duction | Imports | Total Supply | Domestic Use | | | | | Exports | Total Disap- pearance | Planted | Harvested for Grain | |
					Food	Industry	Seed	Feed & Residual	Total			---- 1,000 Acres ----		
1983-4	5,822	27,008	1,600	34,430	3,500	2,100	4,700	11,919	22,219	1,000	23,219	2,707	892	30.3
1984-5	11,211	32,407	600	44,218	3,500	2,000	4,100	14,312	23,912	400	24,312	2,971	979	33.1
1985-6	19,906	20,373	2,200	42,479	3,500	2,100	3,800	11,010	20,410	200	20,610	2,543	708	28.8
1986-7	21,869	19,067	1,000	41,936	3,500	2,000	3,700	13,653	22,853	500	23,353	2,334	661	28.8
1987-8	18,583	19,526	1,204	39,313	3,500	2,000	3,800	10,601	19,901	500	20,401	2,428	671	29.1
1988-9	18,912	14,689	200	33,801	3,500	2,000	3,200	11,401	20,101	3,400	23,501	2,374	595	24.7
1989-90	10,300	13,647	30	23,977	3,500	2,000	3,000	9,035	17,535	800	18,335	2,014	484	28.2
1990-1	5,642	10,176	3,895	19,713	3,500	2,000	3,000	7,673	16,173	213	16,386	1,625	375	27.1
1991-2	3,327	9,761	4,500	17,588	3,500	2,000	3,000	7,512	16,012	53	16,065	1,671	396	24.6
1992-3[1]	1,523	11,952	3,500	16,975	3,500	2,000	3,000	6,950	15,450	25	15,475	1,582	406	29.4
1993-4[2]	1,555	10,340	4,600	16,495	3,600	2,000	3,000	6,900	15,500	0	15,500	1,493	381	27.1
1994-5[3]	971	11,138	4,500	16,609	3,600	2,000	3,000	7,000	15,600	0	15,600	1,603	406	27.4

[1] Preliminary.   [2] Estimate.   [3] Forecast.   *Source: Economic Research Service, U.S. Department of Agriculture.*

RYE

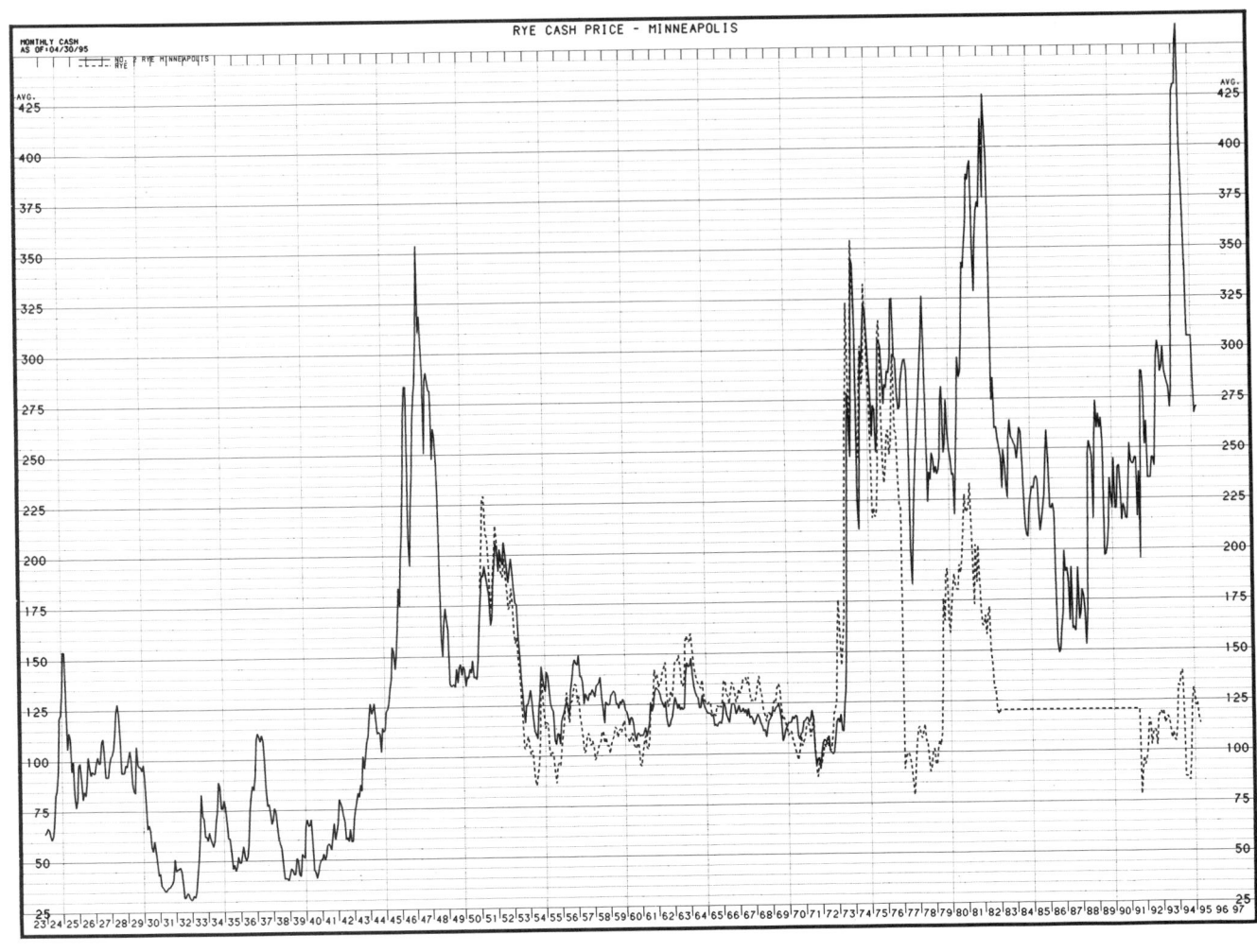

RYE CASH PRICE - MINNEAPOLIS

U.S. Rye Crop Production Reports and CCC Operations   In Thousands of Bushels

| Crop Year Beginning June 1 | Official Crop Reports | | | | Support Rate | | Under Loan Total | % of Production | Acquired by CCC |
	July 1	Aug. 1	Dec. 1	Final	$ Per Bushel	% of Parity			
1980-1	15,784	16,189	16,265	16,483	1.91	51	450	2.4	0
1981-2	16,743	17,083	18,621	18,822	2.04	48	500	2.6	0
1982-3	20,119	19,924	20,817	19,533	2.17	48	1,700	8.1	1,400
1983-4	26,058	25,698	28,152	27,008	2.25	47	5,300	19.6	1,400
1984-5	29,903	30,184	32,392	32,407	2.17	45	10,100	31.1	4,900
1985-6	19,255	19,298	20,637	20,373	2.17	47	4,100	19.9	9,900
1986-7	------	17,892	19,498	19,067	1.63	38	5,900	30.9	2,600
1987-8	------	19,098	19,718	19,526	1.55	38	8,600	44.1	1,600
1988-9	------	15,062	------	14,689	1.50	37	300	2.0	800
1989-90	------	13,610	------	13,647	1.40	32	600	4.4	0
1990-1	------	10,098	------	10,176	1.33	31	200	2.0	0
1991-2	------	9,761	------	9,761	1.38	32	100	1.0	0
1992-3[1]	------	11,952	------	11,952	1.46	34	200	1.7	0
1993-4[2]	------	10,340	------	10,340	1.46	34	100	1.0	0
1994-5[3]	------	11,138	------	11,138	1.61		100	1.0	0

[1] Preliminary. [2] Estimate. [3] Forecast.   *Source: National Agricultural Statistics Service, U.S. Department of Agriculture.*

Average Price of Cash Rye No. 2 at Minneapolis   In Cents Per Bushel

Year	July	Aug	Sept	Oct	Nov	Dec	Jan	Feb	Mar	Apr	May	June	Average
1982-3	342	276	286	260	261	256	251	246	231	250	244	232	261
1983-4	227	256	265	256	254	252	251	245	250	260	258	244	252
1984-5	227	209	207	206	221	227	231	230	235	236	235	248	226
1985-6	210	215	223	233	248	259	246	228	226	226	219	178	226
1986-7	156	151	160	168	173	202	195	185	185	173	196	163	176
1987-8	165	165	175	198	199	189	185	189	175	167	181	278	189
1988-9	266	264	264	247	269	280	268	268	264	270	257	201	260
1989-90	206	203	214	235	229	225	245	220	222	241	242	232	226
1990-1	215	222	220	220	190	245	252	243	242	242	245	245	232
1991-2	216	238	195	288	288	279	251	263	235	235	235	245	247
1992-3	245	241	267	295	303	298	288	290	300	289	285	282	282
1993-4	280	270	280	354	387	427	430	430	452	460	400	383	372
1994-5	360	336	305	305	305	305	285	267					309

Source: Agricultural Marketing Service, U.S. Department of Agriculture

Average Open Interest1 of Rye Futures in Winnipeg   In 20 Metric Ton Units

Year	Jan	Feb	Mar	Apr	May	June	July	Aug	Sept	Oct	Nov	Dec
1984	2,224	4,566	3,980	3,883	3,731	3,023	2,888	5,430	7,098	6,320	5,894	4,158
1985	4,267	4,826	4,175	4,227	3,893	3,919	4,031	5,022	4,872	5,478	4,289	3,786
1986	4,287	4,335	3,302	4,211	3,039	2,553	2,900	3,317	3,479	2,767	2,827	2,031
1987	2,128	2,406	1,892	2,813	3,778	4,427	2,866	3,167	4,209	3,228	3,211	2,494
1988	2,690	2,645	2,760	2,809	2,176	3,635	3,562	3,628	3,537	3,139	2,827	2,160
1989	2,382	2,556	1,768	1,586	1,666	1,963	1,990	3,027	3,004	2,954	3,434	2,537
1990	2,828	2,840	1,943	2,335	2,500	2,408	2,673	3,062	2,669	2,379	2,116	1,625
1991	1,713	1,834	1,765	1,685	1,165	1,078	1,017	1,447	1,724	1,842	1,630	1,168
1992	1,153	1,954	2,330	2,336	1,996	1,902	1,385	1,642	1,416	1,218	965	1,058
1993	935	1,053	785	860	792	760	644	623	558	461	476	476
1994	472	474	275	113	51	40	34	37	20	23	17	22

1 Data prior to 1986 are for end of month.   Source: Winnipeg Commodity Exchange

Rye Under Price Support Through the End of the Month
(Cumulative Total from Current Season's Crop)   In Thousands of Bushels

Year	July	Aug	Sept	Oct	Nov	Dec	Jan	Feb	Mar	Apr	May	June	Total
1983-4	83	1,819	2,228	3,533	3,885	4,199	4,577	4,862	5,141	5,228	5,254	5,256	5,256
1984-5	68	3,581	6,661	8,224	8,653	8,911	9,655	9,830	9,996	10,078	10,066	10,070	10,078
1985-6	567	1,769	2,836	3,516	3,728	3,816	3,955	3,996	4,012	4,060	4,074	4,078	4,078
1986-7	147	1,337	3,249	4,627	5,022	5,140	5,383	5,594	5,722	5,879	5,878	5,888	5,892
1987-8	------	1,237	4,472	5,621	6,498	6,690	7,282	8,164	8,485	8,579	8,605	8,607	8,604
1988-9	------	158	225	239	246	279	301	306	323	325	325	325	325
1989-90	------	352	490	516	523	535	558	558	563	563	563	563	563
1990-1	------	73	157	163	183	------	------	------	------	------	------	------	------
1991-2	------	51	70	227	79	80	83	83	83	83	83	83	227
1992-3	83	35	88	107	132	142	146	148	164	164	164	164	164
1993-4	164	30	70	81	83	83	83	85	93	93	93	93	93

Source: Agricultural Stabilization and Conservation Service, U.S. Department of Agriculture.

Salt

World salt resources are virtually unlimited. Almost every country has salt deposits or solar evaporation operations. In addition, the oceans have an inexhaustible supply of salt. Calcium chloride, calcium magnesium acetate, hydrochloric acid and potassium chloride are higher cost substitutes for salt in de-icing, chemical processing and food flavoring. Salt is the most important mineral feed stock used by the chemical industry. The U.S. Bureau of Mines estimates that given the multitude of applications, salt has approximately 14,000 different uses. While most associate salt with de-icing and food processing and flavoring, the largest end-use of salt is as a feed stock for chlorine and caustic soda manufacture.

The U.S. Bureau of Mines estimated world production, reserves and the reserve base of salt in 1993 at 186 million tonnes, up three percent. China has been increasing its synthetic soda ash output for domestic glass production, thereby contributing to higher quantities of salt produced.

The United States remains the world's leading salt-producing nation, with about one-fifth of the world total. The structure of the industry has changed. In 1970, there were 50 companies operating 95 plants in the U.S. Competition, cheap imports and excess production capacity resulted in downsizing. In 1993, there were 27 companies operating 67 plants.

In 1993, U.S. salt production was estimated at 39.7 million tonnes, up over 10 percent from the previous year. Salt sold or used by producers totaled 38.7 million tonnes, up 11 percent from 1992. U.S. exports of salt in 1993 were 688,000 tonnes, down over 30 percent from 1992. U.S. imports of salt for consumption were 5.87 million tonnes, up almost nine percent from the previous year. The primary import sources included Canada, Mexico, the Bahamas and Chile.

U.S. apparent consumption of salt in 1993 was 43.8 million tonnes, an increase of almost 12 percent from 1992. The chemical industry accounts for nearly one-half of total consumption.

World Production of All Salt — In Thousands of Metric Tons

Year	Australia	Canada	China	France	Germany	India	Italy	Japan	Mexico	Nether-lands	Poland	Spain	Ukraine[3]	United Kingdom	United States	World Total
1987[4]	7,150	11,165	19,800	8,642	18,299	10,915	4,702	1,540	7,047	4,386	6,807	3,522	16,976	7,806	36,943	197,010
1988	7,165	10,687	22,000	7,575	17,861	9,204	4,289	1,363	6,788	3,693	6,179	3,880	14,800	6,130	34,325	185,542
1989	7,069	11,021	28,000	8,267	17,129	9,603	4,186	1,367	6,703	3,756	4,670	3,090	15,000	6,720	35,251	191,660
1990	7,227	11,261	20,000	6,605	15,719	9,503	4,432	1,377	7,135	3,653	4,055	3,377	14,700	6,434	36,918	182,445
1991	7,791	11,993	24,100	6,500	14,979	9,503	3,954	1,380	7,533	3,417	3,840	3,400	14,000	6,828	35,902	188,265
1992	8,000	11,171	28,100	6,116	13,095	9,503	3,711	1,405	7,395	3,628	3,887	3,770	4,400	6,101	34,784	181,270
1993[1]	9,000	11,169	29,530	6,100	12,607	9,502	3,700	1,400	7,240	3,500	4,000	3,700	4,000	6,200	38,665	186,190
1994[2]	8,000	11,100	30,000	6,300	13,000	9,500	3,700		7,500		4,000	3,700	4,000	6,100	38,600	190,000

[1] Preliminary. [2] Estimate. [3] Formerly part of the U.S.S.R.; data not reported separately until 1992. [3] Reported in thousands of short tons prior to 1987.
Source: U.S. Bureau of Mines

Salient Statistics of the Salt Industry in the United States — In Thousands of Metric Tons

Year	Net Import Reliance as % of Apparent Consumption	Avg. Value F.O.B. Mine Vacuum & Open Pan $ Ton	Production Total	Production Open & Vacuum Pan	Production Solar	Production Rock	Production Brine	Sold or Used by Producers Open & Vacuum Pan	Sold or Used by Producers Rock Salt	Sold or Used by Producers Brine	Total Salt	Value/3 Million $	Imports for Consumption	Exports Total	Exports To Canada	Consumption
1987	11	94.21	36,943	3,776	3,120	12,230	17,817	3,776	11,965	18,124	36,493	684.2	5,716	541	477	41,668
1988[4]	11	97.71	35,534	3,469	3,065	11,567	17,434	3,467	11,703	17,782	35,326	699.3	4,966	802	650	39,490
1989	10	102.22	35,632	3,606	2,849	12,682	16,496	3,599	15,364	16,509	35,250	776.8	5,519	1,422	1,240	39,347
1990	9	110.58	36,794	3,662	2,985	12,772	17,374	3,655	13,056	17,724	36,916	826.7	5,969	2,266	2,087	40,619
1991	11	114.75	36,316	3,654	2,813	11,188	18,660	3,623	11,064	18,640	35,902	801.5	6,188	1,777	1,288	40,313
1992	11	113.20	36,016	3,811	3,221	11,411	17,574	3,763	10,910	34,784	34,784	802.6	5,394	992	718	39,186
1993[1]	12	111.99	39,694	3,864	3,541	14,253	18,036	3,850	13,401	38,665	38,665	893.0	5,868	688	499	43,845
1994[2]	19	112.00	39,500							38,600	38,600		9,500	700		47,400

[1] Preliminary. [2] Estimate. [3] Values are f.o.b. mine or refinery & they do not include cost of cooperage or containers. [4] Reported in thousands of short tons prior to 1988. *Source: U.S. Bureau of Mines.*

Salt Sold or Used by Producers in the U.S. by Classes & Consumers or Uses — In Thousands of Metric Tons

Year	Chemical[2]	Tanning Leather	Textile & Dyeing	Meat Packers	Canning	Baking	Agricultural Distribution	Feed Dealers	Feed Manufacturers	Rubber	Oil	Paper & Pulp	Metal Processing	Water Treatment	Grocery Stores	Water Conditioning Distrib.	Ice Control and/or Stabilization
1987	18,715	124	237	452	296	158	302	995	416	145	597	387	311	392	1,007	1,063	9,878
1988[3]	18,810	112	208	417	252	138	320	905	396	24	743	341	339	420	866	953	10,093
1989	18,105	105	211	394	263	152	530	810	363	31	653	338	363	469	880	880	10,397
1990	19,258	99	206	543	288	155	562	999	495	41	719	257	314	449	811	1,019	10,253
1991	20,014	76	232	370	255	142	546	1,097	335	138	554	237	293	432	897	889	9,360
1992	18,538	67	271	389	252	161	553	1,020	392	34	1,208	230	217	435	849	899	7,814
1993[1]	19,273	71	313	430	322	152	845	1,172	480	37	1,240	115	230	419	897	585	10,805

[1] Preliminary. [2] Chloralkali producers and other chemical. [3] Reported in thousands of short tons prior to 1988. *Source: U.S. Bureau of Mines*

Sheep & Lambs

On January 1, 1994, the U.S. inventory of sheep and lambs totaled a record low 9.6 million head, reflecting an 11percent reduction in the flock from 1992 to 1993. Contributing to the decline was the decision to phase out the U.S. wool program by 1996. The liquidation persisted through 1994 and was expected to carry into mid-1995 before some stabilization in flock numbers takes hold. The estimated January 1, 1995 sheep and lamb inventory was under 8.5 million head. Lower ewe lamb retention and a higher lambing rate during 1994 will contribute to increasing supplies of market lambs by late 1995. Commercial sheep slaughter in 1994 trailed 1993, but stock sheep slaughter through mid-1994 was running about 4 percent higher than a year earlier, and large numbers of cull ewes continued to move into Mexico.

U.S. lamb and mutton production fell 4 percent in 1993 to 152,000 tons. Production in 1994 was initially forecast up 2 percent to 155,000 tons, but the final totals are apt to prove closer to 1993, owing in part to lighter slaughter weights.

Lamb and mutton imports fell in 1994 from the previous year's 24,000 tons due partially to unfavorable exchange rates. Moderately higher shipments from Australia were more than offset by declining imports from New Zealand.

World Sheep and Goat Numbers in Specified Countries, January 1   In Thousands of Head

Year	Agrentina	Australia	China	France	Greece	India	Italy	Kazakhstan[4]	New Zealand	Romania	Russia[4]	South Africa	Spain	Turkey	United Kingdom	United States
1985	29,276	149,747	-----	11,580	10,029	52,770	11,098	-----	69,739	18,637	142,876	30,256	17,520	47,772	23,946	10,443
1986	29,243	155,561	-----	11,241	10,122	54,460	11,300	35,485	67,854	18,609	63,400	29,481	17,300	47,000	24,540	9,983
1987	28,998	158,800	166,220	10,580	10,000	55,482	11,451	36,408	69,204	18,762	64,100	29,753	17,600	43,500	25,976	10,334
1988	29,202	162,500	180,340	10,360	10,512	51,684	11,450	36,388	64,244	18,900	63,000	29,640	20,310	40,000	27,820	10,784
1989	29,345	171,292	201,527	11,495	10,694	155,204	11,623	36,498	64,600	16,210	62,700	30,935	23,797	45,700	29,045	10,858
1990	28,571	177,841	211,642	11,208	10,150	157,706	11,695	36,223	60,569	15,442	61,300	38,349	22,730	45,300	29,521	11,363
1991	27,552	173,982	210,021	11,071	9,759	160,207	10,848	35,700	57,852	14,062	58,200	37,585	24,037	45,000	30,147	11,200
1992	25,706	161,073	206,210	11,761	9,694	161,084	10,435	34,556	55,162	13,879	55,300	36,076	24,625	44,700	28,932	10,750
1993[1]	24,500	147,121	207,330	11,451	9,659	162,155	11,724	34,420	52,568	12,079	51,400	35,770	24,615	44,600	29,493	10,013
1994[2]	23,500	142,441	217,310	11,450	9,604	163,156	11,650	34,208	50,270	12,600	43,700	33,800	24,600	44,600	29,333	9,079
1995[3]	22,890	139,846	222,000	11,600	9,559	164,270	11,640	32,000	50,170	13,400	38,000	34,240	24,600	43,600	29,300	8,000

[1] Preliminary.   [2] Estimate.   [3] Forecast.   [4] Formerly part of the U.S.S.R.; data not reported separately until 1986.   Source: Foreign Agricultural Service, U.S. Department of Agriculture

Salient Statistics of Sheep & Lamb in the United States   In Thousands of Head

Year	Inventory, Jan. 1 Without New Crop Lambs	Inventory, Jan. 1 With New Crop Lambs	Lamb Crop	Total Supply	Marketings[3] Sheep	Marketings[3] Lambs	Slaughter Farm	Slaughter Commercial	Slaughter Total[4]	Net Exports	Total Disappearance	Production (Live Weight) Mil. Lbs.	Farm Value, Jan. 1 All Million $	Farm Value, Jan. 1 $ Per Hear
1985	10,716	11,519	7,412	18,931	1,653	6,593	136	6,165	6,300	338	10,908	704.1	654.1	61.1
1986	10,145	11,029	7,356	19,385	1,280	6,067	127	5,638	5,762	100	11,254	725.9	684.0	67.4
1987	10,572	11,417	7,190	18,607	1,195	6,194	111	5,200	5,312	15	12,085	733.1	799.3	75.7
1988	10,945	11,799	7,205	19,004	1,566	5,939	99	5,294	5,393	134	12,268	707.1	985.0	90.0
1989	10,858	11,674	7,721	19,395	1,058	6,492	98	5,466	5,563	188	12,412	775.6	894.9	82.4
1990	11,358	12,132	7,685	19,817	1,616	6,322	96	5,654	5,750	448	12,290	758.4	901.5	79.3
1991	11,174	11,930	7,651	19,581	1,777	6,566	92	5,722	5,813	787	11,763	762.8	734.9	65.6
1992	10,797	11,507	7,225	18,732	1,855	6,335	89	5,497	5,585	770	11,173	711.3	658.3	61.2
1993[1]	10,201	10,906	6,379	17,285			84	5,184	5,268	750	10,159		715.8	70.2
1994[2]	9,079	9,742	5,902	15,644			70	4,938	5,008	760	8,880		681.4	69.9

[1] Preliminary.   [2] Estimate.   [3] Excludes interfarm sales.   [4] Includes all commercial and farm.   Source: Economic Research Service, U.S. Department of Agriculture

Sheep and Lambs on Farms in the United States, January 1   In Thousands of Head

Year	California	Colorado	Idaho	Iowa	Minnesota	Missouri	Montana	New Mexico	Ohio	South Dakota	Texas	Utah	Wyoming	Total[3]
1985	1,065	675	313	360	255	123	515	538	265	639	1,810	515	860	10,443
1986	1,065	600	320	350	213	101	423	525	275	540	1,810	484	819	9,983
1987	980	690	314	375	237	110	523	480	300	605	1,930	464	775	10,334
1988	990	755	324	405	258	103	530	489	270	610	1,960	478	865	10,945
1989	940	825	287	420	290	125	600	516	246	590	1,870	503	837	10,858
1990	1,000	840	286	490	285	138	663	495	270	590	2,090	509	805	11,363
1991	1,015	710	272	465	300	134	683	462	305	640	2,000	508	830	11,200
1992	995	710	273	345	293	111	658	445	215	602	2,140	488	870	10,749
1993	995	685	250	320	245	97	554	405	190	591	2,000	490	885	10,500
1994[1]	1,120	647	266	267	231	91	534	340	198	550	1,895	442	813	9,742
1995[2]	1,060	545	270	294	190	88	490	315	162	530	1,700	445	790	8,895

[1] Preliminary.   [2] Estimate.   [3] Includes sheep & lambs on feed for market and stock sheep & lambs.   Source: Economic Research Service, U.S. Department of Agriculture

SHEEP AND LAMBS

Average Wholesale Price of Slaughter Lambs (Choice) at San Angelo, Texas — In Dollars Per 100 Pounds

Year	Jan.	Feb.	Mar.	Apr.	May	June	July	Aug.	Sept.	Oct.	Nov.	Dec.	Average
1986	65.81	67.50	63.58	74.22	81.25	77.36	73.84	68.12	66.38	59.65	65.42	73.33	69.71
1987	78.56	75.75	86.50	93.12	94.50	84.83	76.84	71.83	70.05	66.25	65.00	73.83	78.09
1988	83.53	77.25	83.75	76.50	72.67	59.38	59.00	56.19	59.50	63.94	65.55	68.83	68.84
1989	68.13	68.83	70.90	78.17	73.56	72.63	67.79	67.28	63.81	59.63	56.06	60.83	67.30
1990	54.80	60.38	63.69	63.13	62.25	53.56	53.25	51.20	51.75	52.50	50.42	48.08	55.42
1991	47.63	45.81	54.88	55.50	57.70	55.75	55.50	54.31	53.25	51.20	52.08	54.92	53.21
1992	58.56	57.69	66.55	74.63	68.88	64.50	58.17	52.38	53.61	52.81	56.93	67.25	61.00
1993	69.88	73.38	75.50	71.25	62.50	57.75	57.00	58.97	66.08	63.75	65.69	68.44	65.85
1994[1]	56.67	62.31	61.19	51.25	60.94	66.92	75.33	79.50	76.08	69.96	73.60	67.50	66.77

[1] Preliminary.   *Source: Economic Research Service, U.S. Department of Agriculture*

Federally Inspected Slaughter of Sheep & Lambs in the United States — In Thousands of Head

Year	Jan.	Feb.	Mar.	Apr.	May.	June	July	Aug.	Sept.	Oct.	Nov.	Dec.	Total
1986	507	441	524	477	417	406	432	426	495	495	401	442	5,464
1987	418	390	432	477	363	407	411	400	459	446	399	439	5,042
1988	380	408	535	388	414	413	387	442	452	437	418	447	5,122
1989	418	415	505	393	435	423	398	476	440	468	467	457	5,295
1990	479	431	481	466	465	426	430	463	422	490	465	449	5,469
1991	495	449	546	436	442	388	431	438	456	501	449	471	5,504
1992	468	422	481	503	374	419	427	400	470	452	413	460	5,290
1993	380	384	476	461	396	462	394	413	410	391	403	430	5,002
1994[1]	---------------------- 2,165 ----------------------						377	302	382	384	381	393	411	4,756

[1] Preliminary.   *Source: Economic Research Service, U.S. Department of Agriculture*

Cold Storage Holdings of Lamb and Mutton, on First of Month — In Thousands of Pounds

Year	Jan.	Feb.	Mar.	Apr.	May	June	July	Aug.	Sept.	Oct.	Nov.	Dec.
1986	12,765	11,615	13,813	11,811	12,754	12,742	14,068	14,318	15,459	14,450	14,641	13,843
1987	12,603	11,550	13,565	13,595	13,248	13,997	12,007	9,311	8,468	6,978	7,036	8,637
1988	7,949	8,069	6,190	7,056	7,639	8,018	8,738	8,537	7,253	6,827	6,396	6,001
1989	6,115	7,267	6,487	6,947	6,135	6,827	8,003	7,841	7,731	7,057	7,707	7,990
1990	7,625	7,844	8,468	7,905	8,390	8,052	9,685	10,107	9,144	8,929	8,458	8,099
1991	8,414	9,438	9,829	8,070	7,277	8,436	8,002	6,917	6,130	5,287	5,739	6,659
1992	6,296	7,255	6,670	8,455	8,580	9,870	10,968	11,711	9,314	8,751	8,520	8,406
1993	7,864	6,343	6,620	6,661	11,064	11,181	13,152	13,495	12,241	12,615	11,843	10,161
1994[1]	8,372	9,198	9,507	11,194	11,505	11,368	12,124	12,026	11,016	9,261	8,946	8,796

[1] Preliminary.   *Source: Economic Research Service, U.S. Department of Agriculture*

Average Price Received by Farmers for Sheep in the U.S. — In Dollars Per Hundred Pounds (Cwt.)

Year	Jan.	Feb.	Mar.	Apr.	May	June	July	Aug.	Sept.	Oct.	Nov.	Dec.	Average
1986	29.90	26.10	22.80	24.90	24.10	25.90	26.70	26.40	27.30	25.50	26.10	29.30	26.25
1987	31.60	32.20	30.70	28.60	28.30	25.70	28.50	32.00	32.50	31.50	30.90	32.30	30.40
1988	34.70	30.10	29.70	26.00	23.90	23.20	25.00	25.30	25.00	25.30	27.80	29.10	27.09
1989	34.20	35.70	30.30	25.40	21.60	22.20	24.60	23.40	23.10	22.70	29.50	31.10	26.98
1990	32.20	30.90	30.00	23.50	19.70	19.60	24.70	24.30	18.90	19.20	20.40	22.40	23.82
1991	23.50	19.90	21.50	21.30	18.30	21.00	20.30	19.20	18.90	18.20	19.80	22.60	20.38
1992	28.10	29.80	31.60	28.30	23.10	22.60	24.00	25.80	25.00	25.30	25.50	33.20	26.86
1993	33.10	35.20	36.10	27.30	29.10	28.90	29.00	28.50	25.80	24.60	25.70	30.30	29.47
1994[1]	33.40	35.20	34.60	29.60	29.30	33.50	30.50	29.70	28.90	27.20	30.60	34.00	31.38

[1] Preliminary.   *Source: Economic Research Service, U.S. Department of Agriculture*

Average Price Received by Farmers for Lambs in the U.S. — In Dollars Per Hundred Pounds (Cwt.)

Year	Jan.	Feb.	Mar.	Apr.	May	June	July	Aug.	Sept.	Oct.	Nov.	Dec.	Average
1986	63.90	67.00	64.90	69.10	76.30	74.00	71.90	69.50	67.60	62.50	69.30	73.20	69.10
1987	76.60	76.00	80.80	86.10	90.10	83.50	78.70	60.00	59.80	64.20	66.20	66.30	68.60
1988	80.70	80.40	80.20	74.80	72.60	60.20	60.00	59.80	66.60	65.90	62.00	58.70	59.00
1989	67.40	68.40	72.50	75.20	73.10	70.60	68.60	66.60	52.80	51.90	50.10	48.60	56.01
1990	56.40	59.80	66.00	62.90	59.80	55.40	54.40	54.00	52.80	51.70	50.70	52.00	52.49
1991	48.00	45.80	51.10	54.80	57.60	55.30	57.70	53.40	51.80	51.70	58.20	65.20	60.78
1992	53.50	55.20	63.40	69.30	68.80	65.60	62.20	55.90	56.70	55.40	58.20	65.20	60.78
1993	67.30	72.70	76.00	68.10	61.50	55.70	53.90	59.20	64.50	64.50	65.80	66.00	64.60
1994[1]	60.80	60.00	59.70	54.70	54.70	61.10	72.00	75.00	73.00	68.20	70.50	68.70	64.87

[1] Preliminary.   *Source: Economic Research Service, U.S. Department of Agriculture*

Silk

The U.S. Department of Agriculture reported that world production of silk in 1993 was 150 million pounds. This represented an increase of just over 1 percent from 1992. Since 1980, world silk production has averaged 137 million pounds. China produces approximately 68 percent of the world's silk, while India produces some 14 percent of the total. North Korea is also an important producer of silk. The world's largest importers of silk include Japan, Hong Kong and Italy.

In terms of production of all fibers, both natural and manmade, silk comprises only a very small share. In 1993, world silk production of 68,000 tonnes was less than 1 percent of the world total fiber production of 37.4 million tonnes.

U.S. fiber consumption, in 1994, according to the U.S. Bureau of the Census was 12.3 billion pounds. Mill consumption of silk (which for reporting purposes included flax) was 92.5 million pounds or 0.8 percent of the total. Imports were 572 million pounds while exports were nearly 79 million pounds. Per capita domestic consumption was 2.2 million pounds.

FUTURES MARKETS

Raw silk and dried cocoon futures are traded in Japan on the Kobe Raw Silk Exchange, the Maebashi Dried Cocoon Exchange, the Toyahashi Dried Cocoon Exchange and the Yokohama Raw Silk Exchange.

World Production of Silk   In Metric Tons

Year	Brazil	China	India	Iran	Japan	North Korea	South Korea	Kyrgyzstan[3]	Tajikistan[3]	Thailand	Turkey	Turkmenistan[3]	Uzbekistan[3]	Viet Nam	World Total
1985	1,200	38,956	7,029	280	9,591	3,500	1,436	-----	-----	1,300	80	-----	3,908	330	68,090
1986	1,200	39,098	9,300	280	8,336	3,600	1,342	-----	-----	1,400	85	-----	3,710	350	69,178
1987	1,800	40,940	9,498	900	7,864	3,700	1,413	-----	-----	1,200	216	-----	4,200	360	72,597
1988	1,900	42,041	10,255	900	6,862	3,800	1,355	-----	-----	1,250	251	-----	4,300	420	73,866
1989	1,697	50,244	10,500	537	6,078	4,000	1,400	-----	-----	1,250	250	-----	3,900	400	80,745
1990	1,693	55,003	11,000	537	6,000	4,200	971	-----	-----	1,250	290	-----	4,094	500	85,987
1991	2,077	60,002	14,000	537	5,527	4,400	837	-----	-----	1,300	180	-----	4,100	500	93,880
1992[1]	2,296	64,002	15,000	537	5,085	4,500	870	1,200	300	1,300	105	600	2,200	500	98,800
1993[2]	2,450	70,001	16,000	537	4,000	4,600	683	1,000	300	1,500	135	500	2,000	550	104,553

[1] Preliminary. [2] Estimate. [3] Formerly part of the U.S.S.R.; data not reported separately until 1992.   Source: Food and Agricultural Organization of the United Nations

World Trade of Silk by Selected Countries   In Metric Tons

Year	France	Hong Kong	India	Italy	Japan	South Korea	United States	World Total	Brazil	China	Hong Kong	Japan	North Korea	Russia[2]	World Total
1985	919	3,233	2,000	6,463	7,928	2,567	736	27,929	581	15,939	3,911	897	850	2,845	27,855
1986	572	3,179	2,100	7,133	8,943	3,747	475	29,835	692	16,349	4,115	586	1,060	2,816	27,931
1987	770	6,652	2,100	7,339	8,342	5,582	661	35,864	648	18,368	7,778	794	1,200	3,367	34,886
1988	771	7,489	1,411	8,094	10,259	4,851	435	39,216	670	20,168	8,553	442	1,200	4,432	37,276
1989	1,012	6,362	1,400	7,740	8,512	3,763	535	35,968	534	19,314	6,748	417	1,100	5,754	39,064
1990	796	3,928	1,647	4,775	7,111	3,204	326	27,322	1,064	13,066	4,102	380	1,200	1,703	27,977
1991	579	4,347	2,100	5,297	6,933	3,519	439	29,623	2,052	15,178	4,186	405	900	2,000	29,188
1992	693	4,400	2,843	4,337	5,137	3,627	288	28,233	1,552	13,474	4,358	701	800	410	26,435
1993[1]	960	5,475	4,700	5,634	5,982	4,494	375	35,391	1,495	15,652	7,204	904	350	166	34,799

[1] Preliminary. [2] Formerly part of the U.S.S.R.; data not reported separately until 1992.   Source: Food and Agricultural Organization of the United Nations

U.S. Raw Silk Deliveries   In Bales of 132-Pounds

Year	Jan.	Feb.	Mar.	Apr.	May	June	July	Aug.	Sept.	Oct.	Nov.	Dec.	Total
1984	715	537	455	315	636	655	229	672	532	562	391	538	6,237
1985	462	689	344	480	415	NA	NA	NA	NA	NA	NA	NA	4,813
1986	410	504	197	244	225	227	555	NA	NA	NA	NA	NA	4,272
1987	411	680	572	526	245	447	253	327	330	470	239	448	4,948
1988	292	430	559	317	302	189	203	613	310	126	367	108	3,816
1989	358	234	471	329	405	564	353	401	288	317	475	442	4,637
1990	455	352	387	158	342	150	248	53	49	103	152	139	2,588
1991	124	126	206	187	100	250	445	305	220	345	325	351	2,984
1992	145	192	425	209	122	459	173	166	146	223	249	132	2,641
1993	457	173	281	215	315	197	NA	NA	NA	NA	NA	NA	3,066
1994[1]	363	71	224	233	227	479	315	227	195	193	315	201	3,043

[1] Preliminary.   NA = Not available.   Source: Fiber Economics Bureau, Inc.

Silver

Silver prices during the first quarter of 1994 reached a five-year high, the advance carrying to almost $6 per ounce, basis December New York futures. At the contract's expiration prices were under $5 per ounce and near the year's low. Many variables impact silver's price with some rooted in basic and tangible supply/demand data, while others are intangible as inflation fears might be. Overshadowing these variables at times are computer/chart based signals in the futures market that can quickly trigger price swings in either direction, which are then rationalized as having viable supporting reasons. In 1994, silver prices were buoyed by expectations that the strengthening U.S. economy would increase demand for silver. Adding to the buoyancy was the persistent talk that inflationary pressures were building and in-turn buoyed gold, the traditional hedge against inflation, and silver—the poor man's gold—followed along. By year's end, the market attitude had changed. (1) The economy was strong, but its durability was suspect; (2) the Federal Reserve's half dozen increases in interest rates were seen as effectively blunting the more perceived than real inflationary pressures; and (3) the Fed's action also had the effect of making interest bearing assets more attractive than those offering little more than speculative appeal. Perhaps more importantly as 1994 drew to a close, the bulls in the silver market has lost their patience waiting for silver to recover its luster.

The world's mine production of silver in 1994 was estimated at 337 million troy ounces, up 6 million troy ounces from 1993. Mine production during 1990-92 averaged about 360 million troy ounces per year. Mexico is the world's largest producer, accounting for approximately 65 million troy ounces in 1994 versus 61 million troy ounces in 1993. Other large producers included Peru, Canada and Australia. The U.S. has been the second largest producer in recent years with an estimated 57 million troy ounces in 1994, up 1 million troy ounces from 1993. The recovery of silver from secondary supplies, such as scrap and old coinage, totaled about 142 million troy ounces in 1994 versus 140.6 million troy ounces in 1993. Thus, the world silver supply in 1994 totaled about 479 million troy ounces versus 471 million troy ounces in 1993, which was the low-est total supply since 1986. Significantly, the rise in silver's price from early-1993 and into 1994 apparently had little effect in stimulating any increase in secondary recovery, perhaps owing to the added costs of tighter environmental regulations in the retrieving and/or disposal of silver bearing materials.

World silver fabrication demand has increased steadily since the early 1980's, totaling an estimated 727 million troy ounces in 1994 versus 679 million troy ounces in 1993, and around a 400 million troy ounce annual average in the mid-1980s. The greatest growth has been in the jewelry and silverware sector with about 260 million troy ounces used in 1994, up nearly 40 million troy ounces from 1993. Silver's use in photography reached a record 204 million troy ounces in 1994 versus 196 million troy ounces in 1993, but a well entrenched fear lies over the market that someday the photographic industry will find a viable alternative for silver. The U.S. is a net silver importer and is the world's largest market for silver.

Based upon silver's apparent supply/demand, total use in 1994 will exceed new supply by almost 250 million troy ounces, up from a net deficit of 207 million troy ounces in 1993, and the fourth consecutive year in which demand has outdistanced supply. One enigma is the size of world silver stocks. An estimated 16.6 million troy ounces were officially drawndown in 1993 and unreported dealer and bank inventories in London were said to have been largely depleted by investors, but a sizeable speculative held inventory exists.

Silver's New York price averaged $4.26 per troy ounce in 1993, while the average for 1994 topped $5 per troy ounce. The monthly average of $5.45 per troy ounce was reached in March and dropped to under $5 per troy ounce during December.

Futures Markets

Silver futures and options are traded on the New York Commodity Exchange (COMEX) and the Chicago Board of Trade (CBOT). Cash and futures are also listed on the London Metals Exchange (LME).

World Mine Production of Silver, by Selected Countries — In Thousands of Kilograms (Metric Tons)

Year	Australia	Bolivia	Brazil	Canada[3]	Chile	China	Japan	Kazakhstan[4]	Rep. of Korea	Mexico	Peru	Poland	South Africa	Spain	Sweden	United States	World Total[2]
1980	767	190	24	1,037	298	78	268	1,431	71	1,557	1,381	766	222	141	166	1,005	10,661
1981	743	199	24	1,129	361	78	280	1,446	95	1,646	1,460	640	235	166	161	1,265	11,246
1982	907	170	24	1,314	382	78	306	1,459	101	1,840	1,305	657	216	118	168	1,252	11,543
1983	1,033	187	15	1,106	468	78	307	1,468	105	1,978	1,570	678	203	47	207	1,351	12,058
1984	972	142	26	1,327	490	78	324	1,474	117	2,343	1,651	744	218	290	239	1,387	13,064
1985	1,086	111	32	1,197	517	80	339	1,490	124	2,153	1,811	831	208	367	231	1,227	13,051
1986	1,023	95	58	1,088	500	90	351	1,500	157	2,303	1,926	829	222	327	263	1,074	13,034
1987	1,119	142	110	1,375	500	100	281	1,510	209	2,415	2,054	831	208	350	254	1,241	14,019
1988	1,118	232	124	1,443	507	110	252	2,500	227	2,359	1,552	1,063	200	353	208	1,661	15,484
1989	1,075	267	114	1,371	545	125	156	2,500	239	2,400	1,840	1,003	180	668	228	2,008	16,425
1990	1,173	311	171	1,501	655	130	150	2,500	238	2,425	1,762	832	161	500	243	2,121	16,489
1991	1,180	376	154	1,339	678	150	171	2,200	265	2,295	1,770	899	171	208	239	1,855	15,672
1992	1,248	282	155	1,214	1,029	170	178	900	333	2,098	1,573	798	183	160	281	1,804	14,737
1993[1]	1,100	300	155	901	940	200	136	900	330	2,128	1,573	800	193	150	280	1,645	14,089
1994[2]	1,200			900						2,200	1,600					1,400	14,000

[1] Preliminary. [2] Estimate. [3] Shipments. [4] Formerly part of the U.S.S.R.; data not reported separately until 1992. *Source: U.S. Bureau of Mines*

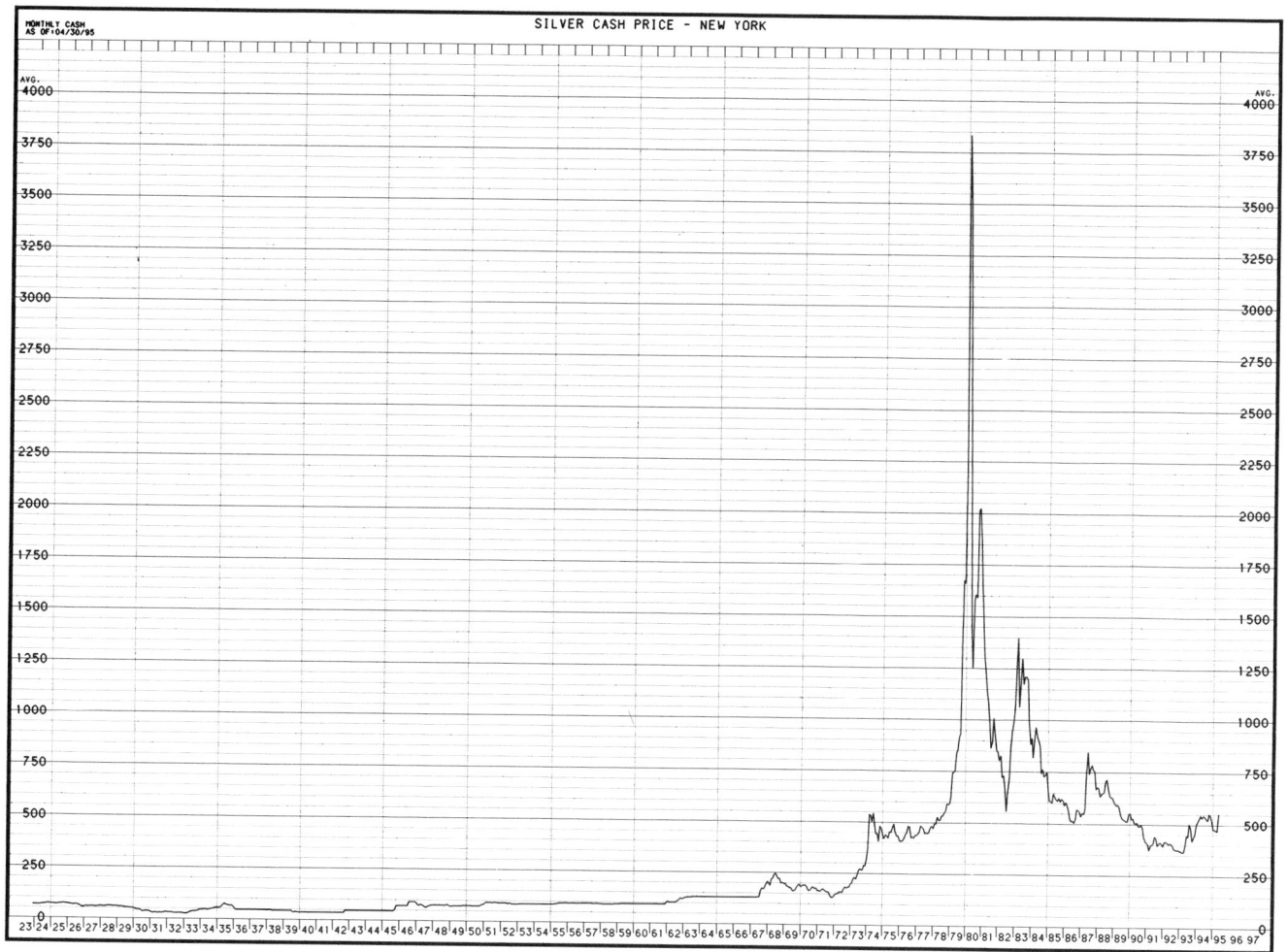

MONTHLY CASH
AS OF:04/30/95

SILVER CASH PRICE - NEW YORK

Average Price of Silver in New York (Handy & Harman)   In Cents Per Troy Ounce (.999 Fine)

Year	Jan.	Feb.	Mar.	Apr.	May	June	July	Aug.	Sept.	Oct.	Nov.	Dec.	Average
1972	147.31	150.36	153.64	157.20	158.30	156.90	173.58	184.61	177.67	181.06	183.25	197.60	168.45
1973	201.66	223.62	230.92	220.72	240.12	262.09	270.56	263.65	267.51	288.56	285.99	313.67	255.96
1974	363.70	535.90	532.55	503.60	543.18	489.61	441.55	443.14	404.88	482.98	469.39	439.13	470.80
1975	419.27	437.00	434.53	420.92	453.81	448.91	470.45	492.50	451.60	432.86	433.24	408.50	441.97
1976	406.27	408.64	418.91	435.05	448.85	481.17	477.95	423.70	429.52	422.51	437.27	434.68	435.38
1977	440.90	452.74	484.16	477.71	469.20	444.30	449.81	444.43	453.86	476.32	482.84	470.60	462.30
1978	493.40	493.57	526.80	511.59	511.95	531.59	533.07	549.50	557.48	591.79	586.49	592.95	540.02
1979	625.45	741.69	745.35	749.25	836.57	853.83	913.50	933.43	1,395.92	1,678.07	1,655.27	2,179.28	1,108.97
1980	3,827.21	3,508.50	2,413.33	1,384.09	1,253.29	1,574.76	1,605.97	1,589.71	2,014.38	2,018.14	1,864.82	1,639.33	2,063.29
1981	1,475.15	1,306.50	1,236.91	1,091.73	1,084.75	1,000.07	863.11	892.29	1,003.55	925.12	854.68	843.16	1,048.09
1982	803.05	826.79	721.30	731.07	667.35	557.79	649.67	713.61	872.52	946.75	991.83	1,058.63	795.03
1983	1,239.57	1,396.37	1,061.87	1,169.43	1,295.26	1,174.93	1,208.75	1,209.56	1,191.50	984.13	883.73	912.07	1,143.93
1984	818.24	912.65	965.11	922.05	897.20	874.38	741.57	761.30	726.34	731.68	748.89	669.42	814.07
1985	609.82	606.95	601.36	645.83	628.05	617.18	610.43	624.68	605.37	618.80	613.39	588.78	614.22
1986	605.30	587.37	563.93	522.91	511.48	515.26	504.93	521.83	568.29	566.69	559.56	536.40	547.00
1987	552.88	548.76	568.16	742.79	843.90	741.09	767.84	784.74	759.05	755.80	666.18	679.02	700.85
1988	673.25	632.48	641.28	647.83	654.26	703.68	714.65	670.80	636.48	628.45	627.53	610.83	653.46
1989	597.17	589.08	592.98	579.08	544.70	528.02	523.65	517.93	513.30	513.30	546.53	554.28	550.00
1990	524.30	527.84	505.82	504.58	507.39	490.60	485.90	498.15	479.03	436.59	416.90	406.84	482.00
1991	402.82	372.34	396.90	397.07	404.07	438.85	430.38	393.80	403.60	410.22	406.05	390.90	403.92
1992	412.08	413.71	410.36	403.00	406.83	405.64	394.89	379.67	376.33	373.66	376.32	370.98	393.62
1993	367.93	364.39	364.80	396.36	445.02	437.50	503.74	480.61	417.19	433.45	450.25	496.83	429.84
1994	513.14	527.24	545.11	530.87	543.64	539.34	528.65	519.54	552.88	544.10	519.60	476.88	528.42

Source: American Metal Market

SILVER

World Silver Consumption[1] In Millions of Troy Ounces

													——————— Coinage ———————						
			Ger-					**United**	**United**	**World**				**Ger-**		**Unites**	**World**	**World**
Year	Canada	France	many	India	Italy	Japan	Mexico	Kingdom	States	Total	Austria	Canada	France	many	Mexico	States	Total	Total
1973	10.4	22.5	60.0	13.0	41.5	69.0	16.5	31.0	196.4	522.5	6.3	6.6	.1	7.0	NA	.9	28.5	551.0
1974	10.3	21.0	55.0	15.0	38.6	46.5	10.2	25.0	176.0	470.0	5.7	9.0	3.6	7.6	NA	1.0	31.6	501.6
1975	10.3	21.0	38.9	13.0	28.9	46.4	8.8	28.0	157.7	407.7	9.1	10.4	1.8	5.4	NA	2.7	33.4	441.1
1976	9.3	31.8	52.9	18.0	32.1	60.7	10.2	28.0	170.6	484.7	6.9	8.4	6.2	1.8	NA	1.3	30.0	514.7
1977	9.1	32.6	48.1	17.6	33.8	63.2	8.6	32.2	153.6	459.9	8.9	.5	7.1	4.6	4.2	.1	34.5	494.4
1978	9.6	24.6	42.0	20.0	41.8	64.9	9.1	29.0	160.2	452.4	9.6	1.0	9.0	3.6	6.6	0	39.5	491.9
1979	7.3	24.1	39.8	19.0	33.3	68.8	8.6	27.6	157.3	448.2	4.0	.8	10.6	3.7	5.0	.2	31.0	479.2
1980	8.7	19.8	31.9	19.0	21.8	61.5	4.9	19.5	124.7	364.3	2.3	.2	.1	0	6.1	.1	15.0	379.3
1981	8.5	18.9	29.3	19.0	21.5	59.6	5.0	18.4	116.7	355.4	3.1	.3	.1	.5	0	.2	9.5	364.9
1982	9.0	17.1	32.7	16.1	20.8	63.2	5.7	18.1	118.8	361.4	4.5	.3	1.4	.3	0	1.8	12.0	373.4
1983	8.9	16.5	30.3	12.9	15.0	72.1	3.5	17.7	116.3	356.5	1.8	.4	2.2	0	0	2.1	10.2	366.7
1984	9.3	17.1	32.2	16.1	19.4	78.8	5.5	19.2	114.8	376.2	2.4	.3	3.9	0	2.5	2.0	13.7	389.9
1985	9.1	16.9	34.6	20.9	24.0	72.6	8.0	19.1	118.6	387.5	4.6	.3	2.2	0	3.5	.4	13.4	400.9
1986	9.6	17.0	36.3	22.5	33.5	78.6	7.7	19.1	118.9	409.7	1.1	1.3	2.2	0	2.0	10.3	26.8	436.5
1987	10.4	17.6	39.1	13.8	38.6	92.3	6.9	21.1	115.3	430.6	3.1	1.2	2.2	3.2	2.3	12.2	30.4	461.0
1988	11.0	21.3	44.1	16.0	37.9	102.0	7.1	22.7	112.0	450.8	2.0	1.1	2.2	3.2	2.0	7.9	25.3	476.1
1989	12.0	22.1	46.9	16.1	43.0	102.5	7.1	24.5	120.0	482.1	2.1	3.3	2.2	3.2	1.7	6.8	26.3	508.4
1990	12.5	22.4	48.4	22.5	47.9	106.9	7.2	24.4	125.3	514.3	.6	1.7	2.2	2.4	1.5	9.1	29.8	544.1
1991	13.1	21.9	52.3	25.7	53.0	108.9	11.7	21.7	118.7	548.5	.6	.8	1.8	5.5	1.5	9.1	27.7	576.2
1992	13.6	21.7	49.1	27.3	54.9	106.5	14.7	21.7	118.9	564.0	.5	.3	1.8	5.3	6.8	8.1	29.4	593.4
1993[2]	13.8	22.0	45.8	32.2	52.3	111.7	14.7	22.1	121.1	640.7	.6	1.0	1.8	4.5	15.0	8.9	38.0	678.7

[1] Non-communist areas only. [2] Preliminary. NA = Not available. *Source: The Silver Institute*

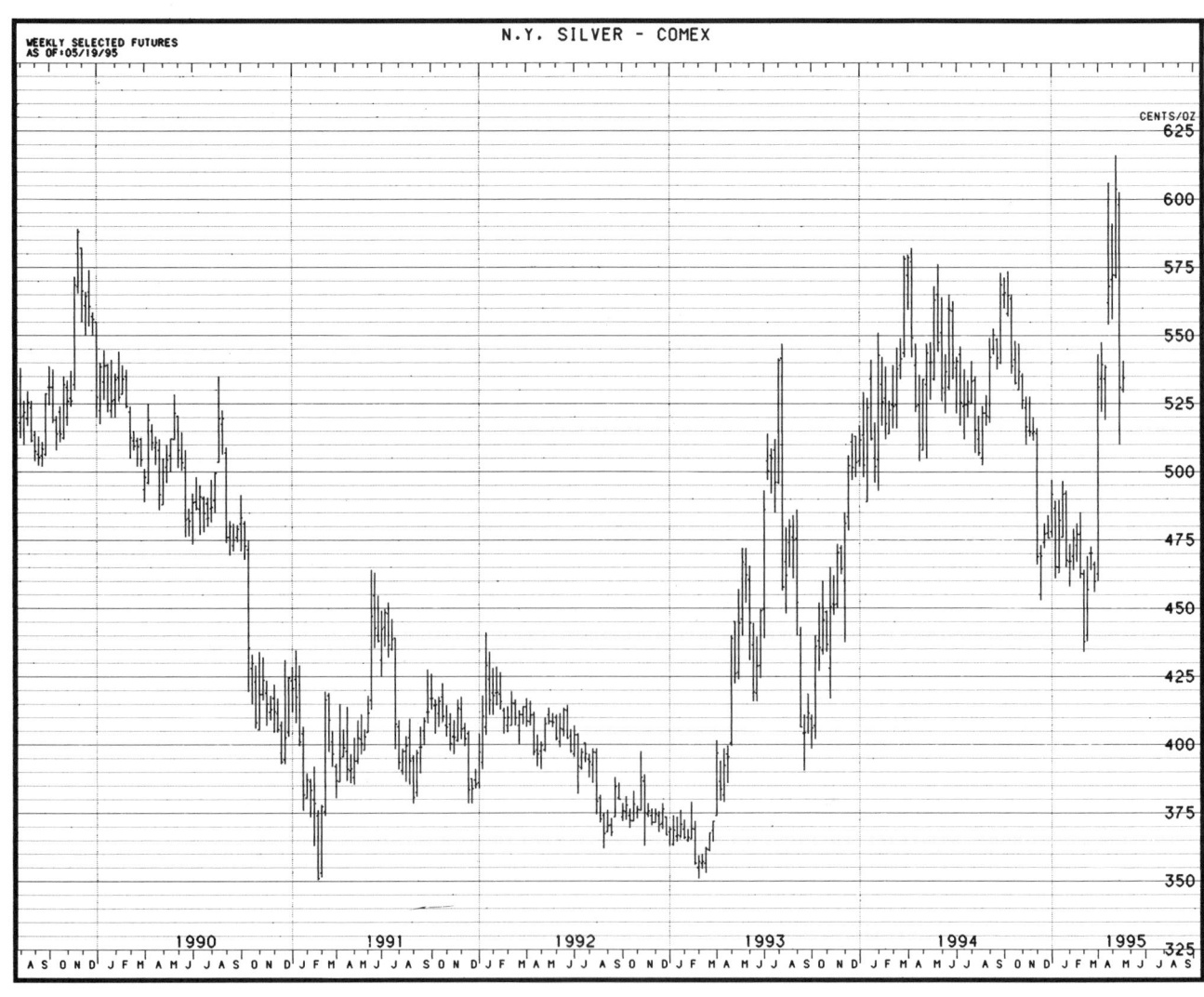

U.S. Mine Production of Recoverable Silver   In Metric Tons

Year	Arizona	Idaho	Montana	Nevada	Total	Year	Arizona	Idaho	Montana	Nevada	Total
1985	152	586	125	154	1,227	1990	173	442	220	646	2,125
1986	140	349	148	199	1,074	1991	148	337	222	578	1,848
1987	114	NA	185	379	1,241	1992	153	255	195	586	1,740
1988	152	340	192	608	1,661	1993[1]	157	190	125	713	1,604
1989	171	439	194	625	2,007	1994[2]	177	158	71	591	1,371

[1] Preliminary.   [2] Estimate.   NA = Not available.   *Source: U.S. Bureau of Mines*

U.S. Consumption of Silver, by End Use   In Millions of Troy Ounces

Year	Batteries	Brazing Alloys & Solders	Catalysts	Electrical Contacts & Conductors	Jewerly	Mirrors	Photo-graphic Materials	Sterling Ware	Silver-plate	Total Net Industrial Con-sumption	Coinage	Total Con-sumption
1978	6.0	11.0	8.2	30.8	6.8	1.9	64.3	17.9	7.3	160.2	0	160.2
1979	4.6	10.9	5.6	33.5	5.4	1.9	66.0	13.1	8.1	157.3	.2	157.4
1980	6.0	8.5	3.0	27.8	5.9	.7	49.8	9.1	4.4	124.7	.1	124.8
1981	3.8	7.7	3.8	26.4	5.4	.6	51.0	4.4	3.9	116.7	.2	116.8
1982	4.2	7.4	2.4	27.7	6.3	1.0	51.8	6.6	3.3	118.8	1.8	120.7
1983	2.6	5.8	2.4	26.3	6.9	1.0	51.8	7.0	3.2	116.3	2.1	118.4
1984	2.7	5.9	2.4	25.6	5.8	1.0	55.3	3.6	3.5	114.8	2.7	117.5
1985	2.5	5.6	2.4	27.5	5.8	1.0	57.9	3.5	3.7	118.6	.4	118.9
1986	3.7	6.4	2.3	27.4	4.6	1.0	55.4	3.9	3.7	118.9	10.3	129.2
1987	2.4	5.6	2.4	22.7	4.2	1.0	60.2	3.8	2.5	115.3	12.2	127.5
1988	2.5	NA	2.6	23.0	2.9	1.1	62.5	3.5	2.6	112.0	7.9	119.9
1989	2.8	NA	2.8	23.5	2.4	1.1	65.2	3.4	2.7	120.0	6.8	126.8
1990	3.0	NA	3.0	22.8	2.0	1.2	68.0	3.5	2.8	125.3	9.1	134.4
1991	3.1	NA	3.3	18.3	2.0	1.1	66.0	3.5	2.8	118.7	9.1	127.8
1992	3.1	NA	3.8	18.3	3.0	1.2	64.4	3.9	2.9	118.9	8.1	127.0
1993[1]	3.3	NA	4.0	18.8	3.3	1.3	65.0	4.0	3.0	121.1	8.9	130.0

[1] Preliminary.   NA = Not available.   *Source: The Silver Institute*

Commodity Exchange, Inc. (COMEX) Warehouse of Stocks of Silver   In Millions of Troy Ounces

Year	Jan. 1	Feb. 1	Mar. 1	Apr. 1	May 1	June 1	July 1	Aug. 1	Sept. 1	Oct. 1	Nov. 1	Dec. 1
1983	91.2	90.9	106.4	96.8	91.3	69.8	91.1	93.7	113.6	129.3	129.4	129.6
1984	127.4	123.7	116.8	117.2	115.3	114.3	121.8	120.3	116.2	115.0	113.4	115.4
1985	118.9	121.5	122.3	106.6	106.0	104.2	133.7	140.8	141	143.6	149.2	153.7
1986	155.2	142.3	145.9	151.3	154.9	144.6	151.9	150.7	158.6	156.8	138.1	145.1
1987	144.9	150.2	160.0	157.9	157.7	156.1	152.5	151.9	158.6	155.7	154.8	155.8
1988	156.3	156.3	156.9	155.8	161.3	164.3	167.1	169.7	175.6	178.8	175.3	178.5
1989	174.4	179.2	190.6	194.3	200.4	204.1	206.0	207.3	210.4	212.3	226.6	237.9
1990	238.8	240.8	243.4	252.1	253.8	255.4	251.6	251.5	255.8	260.2	258.6	257.7
1991	265.3	266.2	263.8	260.7	263.4	263.5	266.1	275.8	270.7	270.2	265.9	260.6
1992	270.7	270.0	279.6	269.6	262.3	268.0	268.4	271.8	274.7	278.6	278.6	280.7
1993	275.3	271.7	273.6	268.4	266.0	271.4	273.9	278.4	278.7	275.7	275.4	277.1
1994	263.5	252.9	250.8	239.4	241.4	233.8	237.4	246.9	250.0	254.0	259.2	265.1

Source: Commodity Exchange, Inc. of New York (COMEX)

United States Production[1] of Refined Silver from all Sources   In Metric Tons

Year	Jan.	Feb.	Mar.	Apr.	May	June	July	Aug.	Sept.	Oct.	Nov.	Dec.	Total
1983	9,121	8,533	9,063	9,653	7,663	10,210	8,579	8,342	7,886	8,738	9,880	12,058	112,200
1984	7,094	8,414	8,446	9,827	10,423	8,921	8,879	11,226	8,971	8,386	10,200	13,920	116,400
1985	8,414	7,930	8,645	9,238	9,344	9,850	8,578	9,885	8,191	8,429	8,987	11,467	109,000
1986	7,897	7,835	7,340	8,727	7,547	7,129	3,988	6,404	6,932	7,869	8,216	10,197	90,081
1987	8,170	6,098	7,047	7,946	8,473	7,839	8,777	7,731	7,703	6,692	6,955	9,024	92,455
1988	7,852	7,264	9,453	7,956	7,891	9,453	10,562	9,903	7,374	8,074	9,545	9,726	105,053
1989	10,025	9,488	9,883	9,650	12,006	8,956	7,722	9,337	7,978	7,901	10,099	8,999	112,044
1990	8,938	7,839	7,106	8,725	8,571	8,819	8,230	7,747	7,619	8,019	9,732	8,106	99,451
1991	8,767	6,715	7,378	7,334	9,162	7,579	7,070	8,165	8,444	8,335	8,023	8,614	95,586
1992[2]	---------- 1,064 ----------			---------- 1,031 ----------			---------- 933 ----------			---------- 557 ----------			3,921
1993	---------- 1,032 ----------			---------- 1,080 ----------			---------- 795 ----------			---------- 712 ----------			4,059
1994[3]	---------- 802 ----------			---------- 908 ----------			---------- 808 ----------			---------- 803 ----------			3,321

[1] Output of commercial bars .999 fine, including U.S. Mint purchases of crude. Production is from both foreign and domestic silver.   [2] Prior to 1992, shown in thousands of troy ounces.   [3] Preliminary.   *Source: U.S. Bureau of Mines*

SILVER

U.S. Exports of Refined Silver to Selected Countries   In Thousands of Troy Ounces

Year	Australia	Canada	France	Germany	Hong Kong	Japan	Singapore	South Korea	Switzer-land	United Arab Emirates	United Kingdom	Uruguay	Other Countries	Total
1987	NA	2,086	134	261	NA	5,426	NA	NA	NA	NA	2,568	NA	157	11,241
1988	NA	1,073	157	480	NA	6,030	NA	166	70	NA	4,894	NA	82	14,270
1989	NA	2,597	61	519	NA	5,997	NA	588	88	NA	3,722	NA	55	13,828
1990	NA	2,586	64	749	NA	16,568	1,005	298	74	NA	2,060	152	93	23,664
1991	NA	736	22	350	755	6,519	1,593	2,823	8	3,462	8,628	259	73	25,318
1992	593	2,177	44	140	497	4,554	2,126	NA	70	6,922	10,856	671	47	29,274
1993[1]	520	4,910	--	34	1,002	3,414	2,500	1,492	38	4,403	3,673	530	44	22,673

[1] Preliminary.   NA = Not available, included in "Other Countries," if any.   *Source: American Bureau of Metal Statistics*

U.S. Imports of Silver from Selected Countries   In Thousands of Troy Ounces

Year	Ores and Concentrates				Refined Bullion						
	Canada	Mexico	Other Countries	Total	Canada	Chile	Mexico	Peru	Uruguay	Other Countries	Total
1987	650	1,561	59	2,681	16,665	113	40,779	243	NA	71	67,959
1988	288	1,511	31	6,151	31,361	211	37,471	11	NA	139	72,663
1989	56	129	28	225	37,203	724	53,262	2,761	1,958	0	98,429
1990	12	189	2	203	33,518	1,671	40,204	8,141	2,265	165	86,741
1991	42	277	29	348	25,389	6,640	34,448	13,748	NA	17	81,198
1992	646	126	11	814	24,937	2,002	40,230	16,841	400	2	85,572
1993[1]	299	836	11	1,147	28,622	1,058	27,241	12,709	NA	28	70,189

[1] Preliminary.   NA = Not available, included in "Other Countries," if any.   *Source: American Bureau of Metal Statistics*

Average Open Interest of Silver Futures at New York (COMEX)   In Contracts

Year	Jan.	Feb.	Mar.	Apr.	May	June	July	Aug.	Sept.	Oct.	Nov.	Dec.
1983	39,122	49,642	45,929	49,603	51,481	50,738	42,589	48,332	49,920	51,782	54,999	59,067
1984	62,135	64,640	68,763	72,204	65,424	62,890	61,644	63,700	63,655	66,339	78,744	78,492
1985	82,285	83,773	74,987	75,583	74,587	76,985	71,610	73,325	71,100	81,987	87,775	86,249
1986	82,915	81,670	75,891	79,653	74,781	72,411	67,063	74,916	79,376	81,192	93,567	88,962
1987	93,442	94,823	94,366	114,498	98,917	91,469	82,200	87,131	79,747	84,420	78,669	71,204
1988	76,788	79,031	68,994	66,187	69,137	83,428	84,517	82,793	82,369	85,261	92,026	90,081
1989	93,582	95,876	93,953	99,598	90,996	86,804	83,466	88,886	85,248	88,406	91,459	93,606
1990	94,397	93,713	96,182	96,701	95,784	103,575	99,098	99,668	92,436	91,093	84,181	80,364
1991	91,685	101,352	99,564	99,791	94,921	105,646	97,554	95,536	87,079	90,791	89,765	91,390
1992	97,179	93,352	88,445	96,427	87,355	84,002	80,879	81,695	74,265	72,090	77,633	72,296
1993	80,155	86,241	87,127	100,985	105,931	102,539	107,537	109,427	93,891	93,316	101,576	110,029
1994	112,584	116,652	112,745	119,314	121,296	126,255	122,138	118,081	113,261	117,224	126,666	134,099

Source: Commodity Exchange, Inc. of New York (COMEX)

Volume of Trading of Silver Futures at New York (COMEX)   In Thousands of Contracts

Year	Jan.	Feb.	Mar.	Apr.	May	June	July	Aug.	Sept.	Oct.	Nov.	Dec.	Total
1983	502.7	601.4	446.6	452.9	516.1	623.7	454.3	656.5	492.0	569.0	596.9	512.7	6,433
1984	570.8	698.8	695.7	629.9	626.7	587.4	554.7	601.5	431.3	449.2	534.2	362.3	6,698
1985	531.8	488.0	518.4	449.8	424.8	377.9	377.7	388.5	267.7	314.0	332.8	349.9	4,821
1986	394.0	368.9	277.6	438.8	280.1	336.1	187.9	317.8	454.6	286.7	338.9	168.2	3,850
1987	247.3	248.0	343.2	932.7	438.6	486.4	378.7	502.7	390.3	468.1	355.9	263.7	5,056
1988	274.1	301.1	348.9	313.9	341.1	726.9	638.9	411.7	299.9	268.4	475.4	264.4	4,665
1989	317.2	408.5	447.3	354.2	278.5	484.7	272.3	360.4	224.9	261.1	622.1	345.4	4,377
1990	343.2	413.3	210.2	364.1	328.5	433.8	242.3	524.8	201.3	308.4	323.7	219.8	3,914
1991	309.8	420.1	446.5	396.0	255.5	547.5	344.7	320.6	268.7	253.0	349.7	242.6	3,801
1992	408.2	320.2	229.0	332.4	184.8	295.4	197.9	266.3	173.2	125.5	355.7	127.7	3,016
1993	167.2	332.5	243.0	453.9	433.5	523.9	503.9	531.8	428.4	338.2	520.6	373.0	4,856
1994	489.1	555.1	484.1	585.1	516.4	729.4	339.3	535.7	377.5	445.0	589.2	348.3	5,994

Source: Commodity Exchange, Inc. of New York (COMEX)

Soybean Meal

Soybean meal, of which the U.S. is the world's leading producer followed by Brazil and China, is a high protein feed used in formulating livestock and poultry rations and obtained from the processing (crush) of soybeans. It's also ranked as the world's top protein meal with about 60 percent of total production. Cottonseed and rapeseed meal account for a combined total of about 20 percent.

World soybean meal production in 1994/95 of a record high 82.3 million tonnes passed initial forecasts and came in about 3 million tonnes over 1993/94. Production averaged about 70 million tonnes in the early-1990s. The U.S. produces about one-third of total output. World 1994/95 consumption of 81.9 million tonnes, also a record high, compares with 78.8 million tonnes in 1993/94. The U.S. accounted for approximately 30 percent of that total. The increase in 1994/95 reflected higher domestic meal use in almost all consuming nations. World foreign trade has held around 28 million tonnes in recent years. In 1994/95, imports were forecast at a record high 29.1 million tonnes as growth in meal imports remains strong in Asia, the Middle East and European Union. Ending 1994/95 world stocks of 3.1 million tonnes were less than initially expected and compare with 3.6 million tonnes a year earlier, and over 4 million tonnes five years earlier.

U.S. soymeal production in 1994/95 reached a record large 32.2 million short tons, putting total supplies for the season (beginning October 1) at a record high 32.4 million tons including a 0.2 million ton carryover. Total supplies in the late-1980s averaged about 28 million tons. Domestic usage has climbed steadily since 1988/89 and was expected to total a record high 26.2 million tons in 1994/95, up nearly 1.6 million tons from 1993/94. Supporting the gain in meal use reflects the increases in poultry production.

Although production of beef and pork were expected to rise in 1994/95, these enterprises have more latitude to shift to other high protein meals and feeds. Cattle accounts for little soybean meal use.

U.S. soybean meal exports peaked in the 1970s with yearly totals often around 13 million tons. Exports in 1994/95 were forecast at 5.9 million tons, one-half million tons higher than 1993/94. The steady decline in the U.S. share of global meal trade is attributed largely to increased competition from South America and India. The decline may have been even greater were it not for U.S. export programs that underpinned meal exports. Future demand for meal exports are now strongly linked to developments in the former Soviet Union bloc as demand wanes from the traditional buyers in Western Europe.

If the 1994/95 supply/demand forecasts are realized, ending carryover on September 30, 1995 should total about 300,000 tons, twice the previous year total. Meal carryover has shown an irregular pattern since the early-1980s, hitting a low of 153,000 tons at the start of the 1988/89 season and a record high of 474,000 tons in the mid-1890s.

Soybean meal prices were expected to average between $150 per ton to $165 per ton in 1994/95, versus $193 per ton in 1993/94, basis 48 percent protein, Decatur, Illinois. If a mean average of $170 per ton is realized, it would be the lowest price since the 1985/86 average of $166.20 per ton.

Futures Markets

Soybean meal futures and options are traded on the Chicago Board of Trade (CBOT). A smaller futures contract is traded on the Mid-America Commodity Exchange (MidAm).

World Soybean Meal Supply & Demand   In Thousands of Metric Tons

Year Beginning Oct. 1	Production					Exports			Imports		Consumption			Ending Stocks		
	Brazil	China	EC-12	United States	Total	Brazil	United States	Total	France	Total	EC-12	United States	Total	Brazil	United States	Total
1985-6	9,690	2,190	10,220	22,635	61,060	7,380	5,476	23,140	3,670	23,950	18,730	17,318	61,790	610	192	2,860
1986-7	11,280	3,000	10,740	25,182	67,210	8,370	6,617	25,940	3,660	26,630	19,240	18,539	67,680	520	218	3,070
1987-8	10,130	3,980	10,400	25,460	67,555	7,350	6,191	24,560	3,110	25,310	18,930	19,344	67,660	970	140	3,720
1988-9	11,360	3,570	9,100	22,630	64,230	8,680	4,940	24,980	2,910	26,310	17,810	17,680	66,050	790	160	3,220
1989-90	12,350	3,020	10,580	25,150	70,089	9,430	4,830	26,010	3,480	25,730	19,900	20,220	68,950	1,114	290	4,070
1990-1	11,160	3,280	9,950	25,700	69,500	8,200	4,960	26,890	3,430	27,200	20,190	20,810	70,130	860	260	3,660
1991-2	11,740	2,750	10,400	27,060	73,080	8,780	6,300	28,670	3,550	28,430	20,490	20,870	73,380	520	210	3,100
1992-3	12,170	3,480	10,760	27,550	75,870	7,990	5,650	27,380	3,270	27,080	20,950	22,000	74,920	790	190	3,750
1993-4[1]	14,070	5,350	9,420	27,590	79,050	10,050	4,860	29,340	3,380	29,020	20,610	22,850	79,200	620	140	3,290
1994-5[2]	14,410	5,630	10,890	29,340	83,360	10,000	5,400	30,020	3,550	30,000	21,870	23,900	83,310	620	230	3,310

[1] Preliminary.   [2] Forecast.   Source: Foreign Agricultural Service, U.S. Department of Agriculture

SOYBEAN MEAL

Stocks (at Oil Mills)[2] of Soybean Cake & Meal in the United States   In Thousands of Short Tons

Year	Oct. 1	Nov. 1	Dec. 1	Jan. 1	Feb. 1	Mar. 1	Apr. 1	May 1	June 1	July 1	Aug. 1	Sept. 1
1976-7	354.9	423.5	427.7	353.9	384.7	429.9	412.6	449.0	408.3	390.7	399.0	270.4
1977-8	228.3	270.0	239.8	245.1	251.7	239.7	227.3	308.2	263.3	191.1	262.6	234.1
1978-9	242.9	210.4	178.2	260.5	215.1	198.7	210.4	231.6	207.4	205.3	232.2	140.3
1979-80	224.3	204.1	164.2	207.7	158.7	160.6	219.1	193.9	265.0	262.0	232.4	225.1
1980-1	189.7	211.1	350.0	221.8	209.7	214.4	232.2	184.4	254.0	209.7	156.1	199.7
1981-2	233.8	309.2	314.8	279.4	315.7	324.9	190.3	172.1	309.3	224.9	209.1	189.7
1982-3	175.2	342.8	349.6	332.3	400.2	422.8	341.0	356.1	341.5	272.3	365.2	378.5
1983-4	474.1	419.3	466.8	391.1	475.8	446.7	460.7	418.6	427.2	391.2	355.5	242.7
1984-5	255.4	236.1	285.7	336.8	319.6	334.1	444.6	429.8	495.8	569.6	562.5	458.0
1985-6	386.9	318.4	369.2	358.4	372.4	281.3	386.6	300.8	282.4	278.7	250.6	298.3
1986-7	211.7	218.0	387.3	240.3	311.2	277.5	235.8	244.0	321.7	261.3	292.9	301.3
1987-8	240.2	267.6	311.8	296.2	390.4	304.9	243.7	299.5	255.6	294.4	437.4	264.6
1988-9	153.5	267.8	295.6	353.6	442.3	395.7	237.9	296.8	260.4	218.0	264.9	152.0
1989-90	172.9	220.5	194.3	328.2	254.0	262.0	311.8	307.9	252.6	262.5	267.7	232.0
1990-1	318.3	290.9	313.6	------------ 455.8 ------------			------------ 527.8 ------------			------------ 425.0 ------------		
1991-2	------------ 285.0 ------------			281.0	258.3	291.3	315.6	310.4	310.2	274.7	260.5	209.9
1992-3	230.0	307.9	411.3	360.8	440.0	420.5	336.9	268.5	328.4	257.3	386.1	353.8
1993-4	204.4	375.1	282.3	290.1	230.0	283.1	277.3	333.0	325.2	254.3	267.5	140.0
1994-5[1]	149.6	240.9	231.6	240.0								

[1] Preliminary.   [2] Including millfeed and lecithin.   *Source: Economic Research Service, U.S. Department of Agriculture*

Supply and Distribution of Soybean Meal in the United States   In Thousands of Short Tons

Year Beginning Oct. 1	Supply			Distribution			$ Ton Decatur 48% Protein Solvent	$ Tonne		
	For Stocks Oct. 1	Pro-duction	Total Supply	Domestic	Exports	Total		Decatur 44% Solvent	Brazil FOB 45-46% Protein	Rotter-dam CIF
1987-8	240	28,060	28,300	21,323	6,824	28,147	239.35	245	239	254
1988-9	153	24,943	25,113	19,496	5,444	24,940	252.40	257	241	259
1989-90	173	27,719	27,928	22,291	5,319	27,610	186.48	192	181	204
1990-1	318	28,325	28,688	22,934	5,469	28,403	181.40	187	178	198
1991-2	285	29,831	30,183	23,008	6,945	29,953	189.20	194	184	203
1992-3[1]	230	30,364	30,687	24,251	6,232	30,483	193.75	201	185	207
1993-4[2]	204	30,417	30,691	25,185	5,356	30,541	192.86	199	182	202
1994-5[3]	150	32,340	32,550	26,500	5,600	32,300	145-165	164	161	178

[1] Preliminary.   [2] Estimate.   [3] Forecast.   *Source: Economic Research Service, U.S. Department of Agriculture*

U.S. Exports of Soybean Cake & Meal by Country of Destination   In Thousands of Metric Tons

Year	Algeria	Australia	Canada	Dominican Republic	Egypt	Ireland	Italy	Japan	Mexico	Nether-lands	Philip-pines	Russia[2]	Spain	United Kingdom	Vene-zuela	Total
1988	411.4	35.5	718.1	92.7	195.8	29.6	543.6	33.0	332.3	553.9	110.6	1,122.0	71.2	29.6	851.3	6,348
1989	389.1	7.7	569.2	66.2	165.9	5.7	188.6	10.8	269.5	269.0	59.1	1,417.9	44.2	29.6	283.8	4,712
1990	373.5	28.2	555.5	130.5	174.8	7.5	146.4	20.8	253.0	229.7	200.7	1,568.4	19.6	32.0	332.2	4,826
1991	323.5	99.4	651.2	142.6	118.6	7.5	33.5	24.1	303.6	339.8	150.4	2,271.0	5.5	29.6	405.9	5,536
1992	247.8	75.9	582.5	146.7	46.5	57.2	93.4	167.2	454.4	420.0	434.8	765.1	92.3	70.6	473.8	6,236
1993[1]	266.1	90.6	646.7	200.8	120.6	84.1	91.5	208.7	187.8	580.8	295.7	697.1	203.8	32.1	425.0	5,536

[1] Preliminary.   [2] Formerly part of the U.S.S.R.; data not reported separately until 1992.   *Source: The Oil World*

Production of Soybean Cake & Meal[2] in the U.S.   In Thousands of Short Tons

Crop Year	Production												Total	Yield of Meal from Soybeans in lbs.
	Oct.	Nov.	Dec.	Jan.	Feb.	Mar.	Apr.	May	June	July	Aug.	Sept.		
1987-8	2,439.4	2,667.8	2,649.3	2,554.4	2,377.1	2,572.8	2,449.9	2,339.9	2,129.0	2,110.3	1,872.5	1,897.8	28,060	47.76
1988-9	2,235.5	2,399.4	2,390.0	2,359.8	2,036.3	2,218.8	2,126.6	2,061.2	1,802.9	1,749.2	1,804.4	1,758.6	24,943	47.43
1989-90	2,246.2	2,492.5	2,519.6	2,548.6	2,187.2	2,432.3	2,263.7	2,224.2	2,183.4	2,196.6	2,237.1	2,187.3	27,718	47.63
1990-1	2,508.8	2,513.2	2,431.5	---------- 7,082.0 ----------			---------- 6,640.8 ----------			---------- 7,148.9 ----------			28,325	47.47
1991-2	---------- 7,920.4 ----------			2,665.5	2,393.8	2,544.4	2,411.3	2,262.5	2,372.4	2,434.2	2,429.0	2,397.3	29,831	47.51
1992-3	2,698.1	2,697.3	2,763.4	2,781.2	2,430.4	2,691.3	2,519.1	2,536.3	2,373.0	2,324.1	2,188.3	2,361.8	30,364	47.54
1993-4	2,707.1	2,714.8	2,696.7	2,620.9	2,447.4	2,684.6	2,499.0	2,435.8	2,320.6	2,387.6	2,396.2	2,506.3	30,417	47.60
1994-5[1]	2,800.2	2,890.9	3,014.7	2,995.9										47.29

[1] Preliminary.   [2] At oil mills; including millfeed and lecithin.   *Source: Economic Research Service, U.S. Department of Agriculture*

Average Open Interest of Soybean Futures at the Chicago Board of Trade   In Contracts

Year	Jan.	Feb.	Mar.	Apr.	May	June	July	Aug.	Sept.	Oct.	Nov.	Dec.
1987	60,584	67,643	65,842	67,193	65,323	66,752	52,442	48,901	52,914	65,831	74,924	75,468
1988	65,643	63,960	61,100	66,950	73,264	80,444	71,643	76,295	80,753	75,439	77,466	71,443
1989	71,792	71,599	67,542	58,923	58,794	64,212	59,547	60,925	59,271	60,038	63,552	57,219
1990	60,010	71,773	74,762	76,897	77,307	69,658	63,824	62,033	58,915	68,888	76,899	70,901
1991	62,172	60,017	56,179	59,107	49,973	57,068	55,629	54,342	67,765	68,627	68,263	71,900
1992	67,575	56,453	55,370	59,528	57,204	60,519	66,315	66,861	66,648	72,403	73,255	72,881
1993	63,178	70,384	64,550	66,121	78,386	74,191	91,435	73,770	75,267	77,065	83,802	85,039
1994	87,612	91,142	82,193	89,453	85,553	81,721	84,461	82,691	85,508	94,483	101,030	98,717

Source: Chicago Board of Trade

Volume of Trading of Soybean Meal Futures at the Chicago Board of Trade   In Thousands of Contracts

Year	Jan.	Feb.	Mar.	Apr.	May	June	July	Aug.	Sept.	Oct.	Nov.	Dec.	Total
1987	260.4	211.6	222.6	305.3	353.3	430.1	307.8	247.1	334.7	388.7	385.5	350.9	3,798
1988	393.7	371.5	350.4	396.3	497.3	584.3	482.0	427.7	449.6	446.3	533.1	424.0	5,313
1989	408.1	320.7	382.4	388.8	406.7	403.8	410.7	393.1	382.8	364.8	330.1	294.8	4,487
1990	308.6	276.4	400.2	428.4	421.0	398.3	460.2	435.3	401.6	476.3	448.7	448.5	4,904
1991	323.4	281.8	310.3	429.3	296.8	412.5	484.3	463.6	394.7	410.8	351.6	339.6	4,498
1992	368.7	290.5	312.6	312.2	388.1	381.0	426.0	333.6	327.6	320.2	327.9	357.1	4,146
1993	295.5	288.1	346.6	307.9	356.7	518.2	575.5	460.5	402.4	315.6	469.3	380.6	4,718
1994	405.6	339.8	330.7	380.7	467.2	456.3	384.5	354.4	366.3	317.4	370.4	420.5	4,594

Source: Chicago Board of Trade

SOYBEAN MEAL

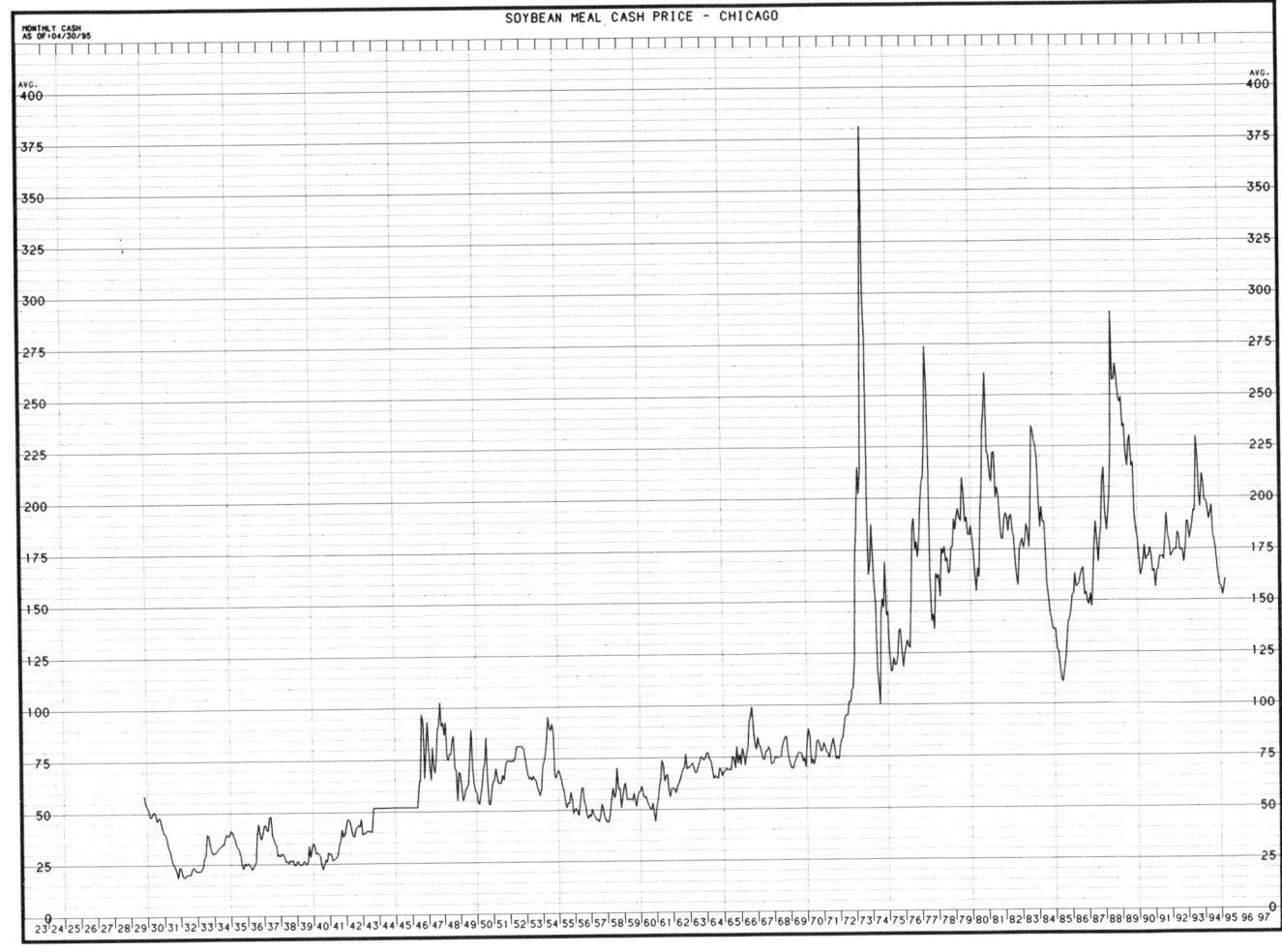

SOYBEAN MEAL CASH PRICE - CHICAGO

MONTHLY CASH AS OF: 04/30/95

Average Price of Soybean Meal (48% Solvent) at Decatur   In Dollars Per Short Ton--Bulk

Year	Oct.	Nov.	Dec.	Jan.	Feb.	Mar.	Apr.	May	June	July	Aug.	Sept.	Average
1984-5	156.50	150.00	150.50	146.80	137.40	137.50	128.60	120.75	119.40	122.75	128.75	137.90	136.40
1985-6	146.40	152.25	153.60	162.00	162.50	174.90	167.90	168.90	170.40	174.40	178.75	182.40	166.20
1986-7	165.40	167.40	164.30	158.00	169.25	161.20	173.40	190.00	200.70	196.50	186.40	195.20	177.31
1987-8	201.60	224.75	231.70	211.75	199.60	207.60	218.25	238.60	305.40	275.10	273.80	284.00	239.35
1988-9	280.10	268.90	266.90	270.10	252.10	254.00	238.00	232.30	246.25	251.00	234.30	234.90	252.40
1989-90	208.10	194.90	191.60	183.80	172.90	176.40	178.00	189.40	182.00	183.92	186.75	190.00	186.48
1990-1	185.40	174.25	175.90	167.00	174.50	177.60	182.50	182.10	183.25	181.00	188.75	204.25	181.38
1991-2	196.30	190.25	183.10	184.00	185.40	185.90	187.20	195.25	203.90	186.25	186.00	187.00	189.21
1992-3	180.60	181.90	187.60	188.75	179.90	183.60	187.40	193.25	193.10	229.90	219.10	199.90	193.75
1993-4	194.50	209.40	206.00	198.30	198.40	195.40	188.90	193.75	195.50	181.10	178.60	174.50	192.86
1994-5	168.50	161.30	156.90	156.40	152.00								159.02

Source: Economic Research Service, U.S. Department of Agriculture

Soybean Oil

World soybean oil production in 1994/95 of a record high 18.8 million tonnes compares with the previous high of 17.92 million tonnes in 1993/94. U.S. production is nearly twice that of Brazil, the world's second largest bean oil producer. Of the important vegetable oils, soyoil is the world's largest with palm oil second and rapeseed oil a distant third at about one-half that of soybean oil. World usage of soyoil in 1994/95 of about 18.6 million tonnes was a new high, as compared to 18.5 million tonnes consumed in 1993/94. World carryover stocks at the end of 1994/95 could fall to approximately 1.4 million tonnes, higher than initially expected and comparing with 1.3 million tonnes in the previous year.

Global exports, however, in 1994/95 are forecast to slip fractionally from the previous season's record high 4.8 million tonnes. Foreign trade in soyoil is quite diversified. Exports are concentrated among producing areas while imports are scattered. Argentina is the largest exporter with Brazil generally second, whose combined total about equals one-half of total exports. U.S. exports during the past few years have averaged about .65 million tonnes, one-half of Argentina's total. No single nation imports as much as one million tonnes per year, but on a bloc basis the Mideast is the largest importer, paced by Iran. U.S. soybean oil imports are insignificant.

A record crush and higher extraction rate pushed U.S. soybean oil production to a record high of about 15.2 million pounds, one million plus pounds higher than in 1993/94.

Even with tight carryin stocks on October 1, 1994 of about 1.1 million pounds, the total U.S. supply in 1994/95 of approximately 16.3 million pounds would reach a record high.

Domestic disappearance during 1994/95 was expected to reach a record high 13 million pounds, 1.5 percent above 1993/94. However, soybean oil exports may lag somewhat, 1.8 million pounds, if funding for the United States Department of Agriculture (USDA) export programs falls. U.S. oil exports in recent years have been disappointing at times, relative to the 1980s, during which the annual average exceeded 1.5 million pounds and competition from other oils, notably palm oil, was less intense. Total usage in 1994/95 of about 15 million pounds will be a record high, but trail total supplies by a comfortable margin. Carryover stocks as of September 30, 1995 are estimated at 1.3 million pounds, about 240 million pounds over a year earlier, but still well under the record large 2.1 million at the end of the 1987/88 season.

Soybean oil prices in 1994/95 were expected to range from 24.5¢ per pound to 27.5¢ per pound, versus the 27¢ per pound average in 1993/94.

Futures Markets

Soybean oil futures and options are traded on the Chicago Board of Trade (CBOT).

World Supply & Demand of Soybean Oil — In Thousands of Metric Tons

Year Beginning Oct. 1	Production — Brazil	EC-12	United States	Total	Exports — Brazil	United States	Total	Imports — India	Total	Consumption — Brazil	EC-12	India	United States	Total	Stocks[3] — United States	Total
1985-6	2,350	2,250	5,269	13,850	450	570	3,150	260	3,090	1,940	1,380	470	4,560	13,500	430	1,650
1986-7	2,730	2,360	5,798	15,200	950	538	3,900	360	3,790	1,930	1,460	450	4,915	14,760	782	1,990
1987-8	2,440	2,280	5,890	15,240	610	850	3,800	420	3,770	1,930	1,560	620	4,960	15,110	950	2,090
1988-9	2,740	2,010	5,320	14,630	700	750	3,710	30	3,490	2,140	1,590	410	4,800	14,870	780	1,660
1989-90	2,980	2,350	5,900	16,000	870	610	3,940	30	3,970	2,000	1,610	340	5,480	15,950	590	1,740
1990-1	2,679	2,243	6,082	15,909	686	356	3,635	20	3,587	2,136	1,661	370	5,515	15,886	810	1,988
1991-2	2,815	2,337	6,507	16,849	661	747	4,182	70	4,120	2,162	1,688	425	5,554	16,435	1,016	2,383
1992-3	2,918	2,469	6,259	17,123	805	700	4,365	50	4,370	2,243	1,877	540	5,776	17,407	800	2,104
1993-4[1]	3,400	2,200	6,310	17,910	1,340	690	4,960	50	4,870	2,320	1,670	640	5,850	18,360	500	1,470
1994-5[2]	3,470	2,510	6,880	19,020	1,050	930	5,040	80	4,950	2,500	1,770	630	5,900	18,760	560	1,640

[1] Preliminary. [2] Forecast. [3] End of season. *Source: Foreign Agricultural Service, U.S. Department of Agriculture*

Supply & Distribution of Soybean Oil in the U.S. — In Millions of Pounds

Year Beginning Oct. 1	Production	Imports	Stocks Oct. 1	Exports	Total Domestic	Food — Shortening	Margarine	Cooking & Salad Oils	Other Edible	Total Food	Non-Food — Paint & Varnish	Resins & Plastics	Total Non-Food	Total Disappearance
1985-6	11,617	9	632	1,257	10,053	3,440	1,735	4,686	138	10,004	60	99	280	11,310
1986-7	12,783	15	947	1,187	10,833	3,359	1,161	5,054	138	10,213	63	109	300	12,020
1987-8	12,974	194	1,725	1,873	10,930	3,627	1,629	5,043	130	10,429	54	106	285	12,803
1988-9	11,737	137	2,092	1,661	10,591	3,419	1,537	4,497	137	9,636	35	124	282	12,252
1989-90	13,004	22	1,715	1,353	12,083	3,934	1,754	4,726	124	10,537	38	112	272	13,436
1990-1	13,408	17	1,305	780	12,164	4,090	1,811	4,693	130	10,722	49	106	295	12,944
1991-2	14,345	1	1,786	1,648	12,245	4,091	1,911	4,961	148	11,112	46	98	301	13,893
1992-3	13,778	10	2,239	1,419	13,054	4,465	1,970	4,717	254	11,505	38	95	296	14,473
1993-4[1]	13,906	68	1,555	1,529	12,896	4,772	1,841	5,004	221	11,838	46	115	304	14,425
1994-5[2]	15,162		1,103	2,050	13,000									15,050

[1] Preliminary. [2] Forecast. *Source: Economic Research Service, U.S. Department of Agriculture*

243

SOYBEAN OIL

Crude and Refined Stocks of Soybean Oil in the U.S., at End of Month   In Millions of Pounds

Crop Year Beginning Oct.		Oct.	Nov.	Dec.	Jan.	Feb.	Mar.	Apr.	May	June	July	Aug.	Sept.
1990-1	Crude	1,019.1	1,109.8	1,227.7	-----------------------		1,629.0	-----------------------		1,616.5	-----------------------		1,518.4
	Refined	196.9	210.2	236.1			245.6			236.5			267.9
1991-2	Crude	-----------------------		1,955.9	1,915.8	2,156.8	2,175.8	2,211.3	2,213.9	2,216.8	2,205.0	2,126.8	2,026.2
	Refined			259.8	243.7	245.7	224.3	211.2	219.6	209.7	215.9	236.0	213.2
1992-3	Crude	1,856.1	1,885.0	2,041.5	2,177.8	2,110.4	2,029.0	2,068.9	2,006.4	1,967.0	1,848.8	1,518.6	1,352.9
	Refined	220.2	220.2	238.6	232.3	226.4	217.1	229.0	234.3	207.0	211.8	201.2	201.9
1993-4	Crude	1,239.6	1,209.9	1,189.3	1,184.2	1,184.0	1,192.3	1,329.8	1,346.2	1,330.0	1,352.6	1,124.0	904.7
	Refined	213.1	189.7	217.5	230.4	216.9	209.8	223.5	220.6	223.8	218.2	215.4	198.4
1994-5[1]	Crude	850.8	811.4	803.7									
	Refined	204.7	215.5	230.2									

[1] Preliminary.   *Source: Bureau of Census, U.S. Department of Commerce*

U.S. Exports of Soybean Oil[1], by Country of Destination   In Metric Tons

Year Beginning Oct. 1	Bolivia	Canada	Ecuador	Ethiopia	Haiti	India	Israel	Mexico	Morocco	Pakistan	Panama	Peru	Philippines	Turkey	Venezuela	Grand Total
1983-4	2,160	9,804	41,103	3,182	12,158	169,366	473	68,081		2,499	216,124	15,657	24,938	2,762	982	50,547	827,422
1984-5	2,691	12,915	44,721	23,966	16,110	62,805	874	45,422		3,758	168,437	8,034	11,399	2,822	0	51,882	752,918
1985-6	1,560	6,105	16,689	17,300	9,474	37,562	560	49,109		3,236	274,935	2,780	1,602	3,000	0	17,108	570,297
1986-7	2,293	6,940	18,814	561	6,940	47,098	560	21,883	59,547	146,663	2,975	1,292	5,926	0	18,652	538,466
1987-8	2,123	7,344	19,050	17,605	3,411	151,600	416	11,537	35,821	396,737	3,736	1,144	6,734	17,098	4,866	850,015
1988-9	998	5,364	30,930	8,960	2,846	28,127	454	17,730	80,023	453,067	6,695	5,778	3,657	0	29,055	753,576
1989-90	1,037	5,443	26,314	22,858	1,688	16,391	442	4,435	77,985	309,502	3,174	5,206	1,868	0	8,198	613,902
1990-1	1,549	3,790	20,832	14,948	4,946	13,544	321	11,087	73,255	66,209	8,123	6,566	3,006	16,460	0	353,959
1991-2	1,829	11,153	528	19,619	4,737	67,577	356	23,383	127,602	250	11,143	32,696	1,996	81,976	13	747,465
1992-3[2]	280	28,585	17	8,272	6,753	49,452	480	44,194	57,995	0	641	36,340	634	58,436	0	643,796
1993-4[2]		4,401		24,509	1,747	46,846		18,499	31,563	72,204		24,081		34,920		693,697

[1] Crude & refined oil combined as such.   [2] Preliminary.   *Source: Economic Research Service, U.S. Department of Agriculture*

U.S. Production of Crude Soybean Oil[2]   In Millions of Pounds

Year	Oct.	Nov.	Dec.	Jan.	Feb.	Mar.	Apr.	May	June	July	Aug.	Sept.	Total
1983-4	1,081	958	991	1,053	897	928	847	906	804	789	819	756	10,872
1984-5	996	1,072	1,096	1,027	879	946	918	983	919	913	869	853	11,468
1985-6	1,040	1,053	1,096	1,086	895	1,005	935	953	882	910	875	887	11,617
1986-7	1,163	1,172	1,152	1,186	1,110	1,149	1,047	1,038	981	1,014	891	881	12,783
1987-8	1,120	1,207	1,208	1,170	1,092	1,187	1,133	1,087	996	994	879	901	12,974
1988-9	1,047	1,109	1,110	1,106	952	1,041	1,010	977	856	836	855	843	11,737
1989-90	1,057	1,146	1,161	1,187	1,022	1,142	1,067	1,050	1,036	1,038	1,059	1,038	13,004
1990-1	1,188	1,168	1,138	------------	3,331	------------	------------	3,171	------------	------------	3,412	------------	13,408
1991-2	------------	3,772	------------	1,270	1,147	1,228	1,167	1,096	1,152	1,177	1,179	1,158	14,345
1992-3	1,238	1,200	1,239	1,247	1,102	1,216	1,148	1,152	1,083	1,070	1,006	1,078	13,778
1993-4	1,241	1,228	1,218	1,187	1,117	1,226	1,150	1,118	1,065	1,094	1,099	1,163	13,906
1994-5[1]	1,322	1,336	1,397	1,394									

[1] Preliminary.   [2] Not seasonally adjusted.   *Source: Economic Research Service, U.S. Department of Agriculture*

U.S. Production of Refined Soybean Oil   In Millions of Pounds

Year	Oct.	Nov.	Dec.	Jan.	Feb.	Mar.	Apr.	May	June	July	Aug.	Sept.	Total
1983-4	839.2	747.2	737.1	797.9	813.2	841.8	763.8	859.5	794.6	767.9	752.2	760.9	9,475
1984-5	907.6	835.5	821.2	838.7	796.1	835.5	865.0	899.5	773.1	763.9	806.2	794.4	9,937
1985-6	865.7	834.8	790.0	804.2	751.1	819.5	783.0	808.5	816.8	780.2	830.1	834.8	9,719
1986-7	911.3	848.1	850.0	790.2	763.6	900.7	871.2	826.9	871.3	921.8	898.6	946.5	10,400
1987-8	975.5	925.8	902.5	880.3	843.4	925.6	843.5	894.1	890.1	947.4	903.6	838.7	10,771
1988-9	867.1	826.9	800.8	776.7	709.6	830.1	800.6	867.4	801.4	791.4	866.6	866.6	9,805
1989-90	936.8	912.0	873.9	887.8	800.6	800.6	812.7	952.8	915.1	903.7	931.1	935.7	10,745
1990-1	1,028.0	980.6	934.7	------------	2,717.1	------------	------------	2,865.5	------------	------------	2,952.8	------------	11,479
1991-2	------------	2,918.1	------------	933.8	876.7	1,041.3	973.1	993.3	977.9	979.2	997.6	1,040.7	11,732
1992-3	1,095.6	999.4	951.0	960.1	935.4	1,054.9	1,039.7	950.6	1,042.8	978.2	1,066.7	1,109.7	12,184
1993-4	1,094.3	1,053.5	1,030.8	949.9	935.5	1,045.4	1,007.0	1,001.3	1,006.5	957.7	1,095.5	1,033.5	12,211
1994-5[1]	1,111.1	1,067.7	1,048.9										

[1] Preliminary.   *Source: Bureau of Census, U.S. Department of Commerce*

Soybean Oil Consumption in End Products in the U.S.   In Millions of Pounds

Year	Jan.	Feb.	Mar.	Apr.	May	June	July	Aug.	Sept.	Oct.	Nov.	Dec.	Total
1982	740.0	737.7	809.6	715.2	761.0	834.6	775.2	811.9	820.5	799.9	763.1	733.2	9,302
1983	761.6	702.2	827.3	765.9	814.9	830.3	745.1	847.0	894.3	812.7	711.4	705.2	9,418
1984	827.6	821.7	837.8	781.1	857.4	824.4	744.7	772.2	780.6	932.0	883.4	856.1	9,919
1985	989.0	804.0	867.1	885.9	940.8	810.5	825.9	856.1	863.7	922.4	864.2	851.6	10,481
1986	836.7	794.0	889.7	849.1	850.3	856.8	835.1	843.1	890.3	927.6	840.6	891.2	10,305
1987	800.9	799.4	862.0	869.6	824.4	918.9	932.7	902.9	949.6	961.4	876.0	891.5	10,589
1988	913.9	820.5	930.0	839.9	870.5	937.9	936.5	907.3	829.1	862.2	829.1	846.6	10,524
1989	780.8	729.5	834.7	800.8	851.9	854.2	774.7	876.9	876.2	923.2	889.7	887.0	10,080
1990	901.3	815.7	952.0	893.6	950.9	927.8	866.0	905.4	895.7	984.1	912.9	878.0	10,883
1991	----------	2,690.3	----------	----------	2,831.8	------------	----------	2,837.7	------------	----------	2,907.8	------------	11,268
1992	880.4	867.0	1,010.1	947.9	956.7	962.1	935.5	932.4	1,019.8	1,061.7	951.8	946.1	11,472
1993	934.5	942.2	1,092.6	1,044.6	981.2	1,036.0	1,019.3	1,097.3	1,103.3	1,123.6	1,092.1	1,029.2	12,496
1994[1]	909.2	924.3	1,067.8	1,024.1	986.3	1,007.9	960.3	1,101.5	1,059.1	1,106.3	1,086.3	1,047.9	12,281

[1] Preliminary.   Source: Bureau of Censue, U.S. Department of Commerce

U.S. Exports of Soybean Oil (Crude & Refined)   In Millions of Pounds

Year	Jan.	Feb.	Mar.	Apr.	May	June	July	Aug.	Sept.	Oct.	Nov.	Dec.	Total
1982	43.9	176.7	126.5	148.5	103.3	208.0	270.2	237.4	244.1	181.1	174.9	142.0	2,057
1983	124.0	225.9	90.4	305.7	127.5	94.1	208.9	125.1	225.1	55.1	54.7	95.5	1,732
1984	161.3	289.9	258.9	163.3	208.3	157.3	140.0	73.0	156.3	200.3	214.6	189.6	2,068
1985	66.7	198.3	184.9	66.9	52.4	138.8	174.4	70.1	102.8	125.4	38.1	74.3	1,293
1986	80.6	100.7	92.8	124.0	50.7	115.1	44.6	187.7	223.4	118.2	27.4	22.8	1,188
1987	67.9	74.0	52.1	28.2	47.4	85.0	175.6	261.0	224.8	100.1	139.0	134.0	1,389
1988	25.7	281.0	279.4	87.7	138.6	269.0	157.2	78.1	183.2	200.1	110.6	119.9	1,931
1989	104.5	65.8	112.4	105.5	161.4	72.1	159.3	181.1	265.6	116.2	82.5	113.4	1,540
1990	95.4	136.2	164.4	33.0	112.0	161.9	122.6	82.8	132.9	85.4	43.9	12.1	1,183
1991	----------	71.8	------------	----------	132.3	------------	----------	434.8	------------	----------	336.1	------------	975
1992	140.0	171.9	134.6	155.4	69.1	129.1	163.7	205.2	142.5	169.5	113.2	91.6	1,686
1993	146.8	188.0	143.3	61.1	154.8	75.4	59.9	116.0	99.7	190.4	88.6	200.2	1,524
1994[1]	120.4	144.6	94.4	46.1	111.6	36.1	57.7	184.6	254.0	154.8	303.2	305.9	1,813

[1] Preliminary.   Source: Economic Research Service, U.S. Department of Agriculture

SOYBEAN OIL

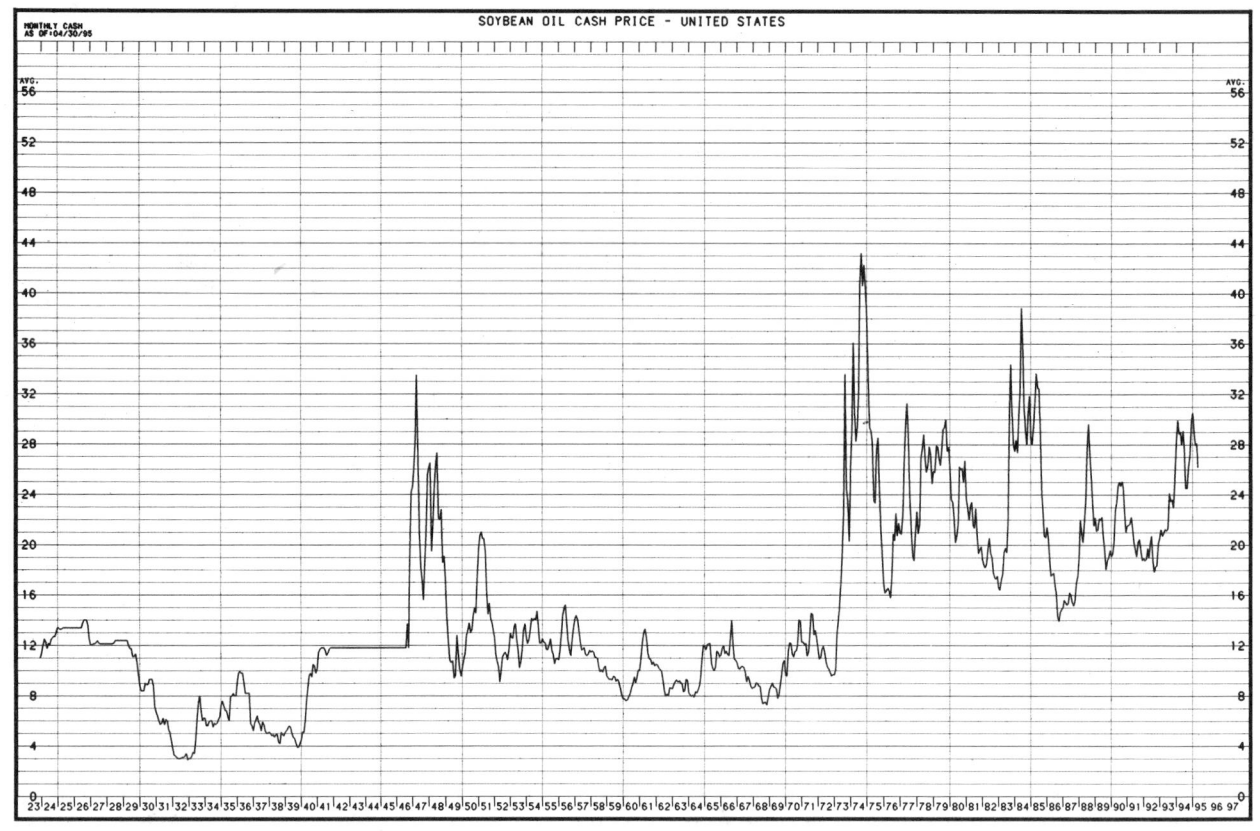

U.S. Stocks of Soybean Oil (Crude & Refined) at Factory & Warehouse   In Millions of Pounds

Year	Oct. 1	Nov. 1	Dec. 1	Jan. 1	Feb. 1	Mar. 1	Apr. 1	May 1	June 1	July 1	Aug. 1	Sept. 1
1982-3	1,103	1,208	1,305	1,587	1,713	1,700	1,842	1,600	1,552	1,546	1,411	1,408
1983-4	1,261	1,453	1,661	1,919	1,907	1,583	1,520	1,380	1,203	1,012	990	871
1984-5	721	597	580	777	884	724	716	666	707	732	724	716
1985-6	632	636	810	969	1,167	1,181	1,247	1,219	1,360	1,225	1,321	1,152
1986-7	947	964	1,269	1,507	1,837	2,017	2,352	2,344	2,416	2,339	2,184	1,979
1987-8	1,725	1,661	1,834	2,050	2,391	2,239	2,343	2,385	2,570	2,361	2,203	2,212
1988-9	2,092	2,046	2,303	2,540	2,703	2,902	2,893	2,759	2,743	2,683	2,427	2,070
1989-90	1,715	1,515	1,532	1,605	1,718	1,703	1,695	1,716	1,551	1,422	1,433	1,380
1990-1	1,305	1,216	1,320	----------- 1,464 -----------			----------- 1,875 -----------			----------- 1,853 -----------		
1991-2	----------- 1,786 -----------			2,217	2,159	2,402	2,400	2,423	2,433	2,427	2,421	2,363
1992-3	2,239	2,076	2,111	2,280	2,410	2,337	2,246	2,298	2,241	2,174	2,061	1,720
1993-4	1,555	1,453	1,400	1,407	1,415	1,401	1,402	1,553	1,567	1,554	1,571	1,339
1994-5[1]	1,103	1,056	1,027	1,055								

[1] Preliminary.   *Source: Economic Research Service, U.S. Department of Agriculture*

Average Prices of Crude Domestic Soybean Oil (in Tank Cars) F.O.B. Decatur   In Cents Per Pound

Year	Oct.	Nov.	Dec.	Jan.	Feb.	Mar.	Apr.	May	June	July	Aug.	Sept.	Average
1982-3	17.37	17.55	16.60	16.40	17.25	17.70	19.32	19.75	19.40	21.61	30.16	34.34	20.62
1983-4	30.66	28.06	27.32	28.32	27.23	30.14	32.08	39.00	33.87	30.96	29.01	27.97	30.55
1984-5	30.56	31.86	28.44	28.01	29.64	31.40	33.63	32.49	32.46	29.07	24.08	22.54	29.52
1985-6	20.71	20.62	21.39	20.63	18.64	17.56	17.65	17.79	16.80	16.22	14.28	13.94	18.02
1986-7	14.63	14.88	14.94	15.60	15.40	15.21	15.31	16.22	15.96	15.41	15.16	15.58	15.36
1987-8	17.03	17.55	19.00	21.98	20.94	20.22	21.67	23.56	27.68	29.65	27.16	25.55	22.67
1988-9	23.42	21.55	22.16	21.13	21.21	22.11	21.97	22.23	20.75	19.66	18.08	18.77	21.09
1989-90	19.02	19.57	19.11	19.28	20.27	22.80	23.35	24.72	25.03	24.69	25.05	24.45	22.28
1990-1	22.59	21.05	21.55	21.56	21.66	22.21	21.50	20.23	19.65	19.05	20.23	20.46	21.00
1991-2	19.57	18.78	18.99	18.77	18.88	19.74	19.00	20.15	20.71	18.82	17.87	18.28	19.10
1992-3	18.36	20.10	20.52	21.23	21.40	21.00	21.24	21.15	21.30	24.13	23.46	20.93	21.40
1993-4	22.98	25.37	28.09	29.91	26.84	29.03	27.94	29.10	27.60	24.53	24.51	26.11	27.00
1994-5[1]	27.06	29.84	30.61	29.01	28.15								

[1] Preliminary.   *Source: Economic Research Service, U.S. Department of Agriculture*

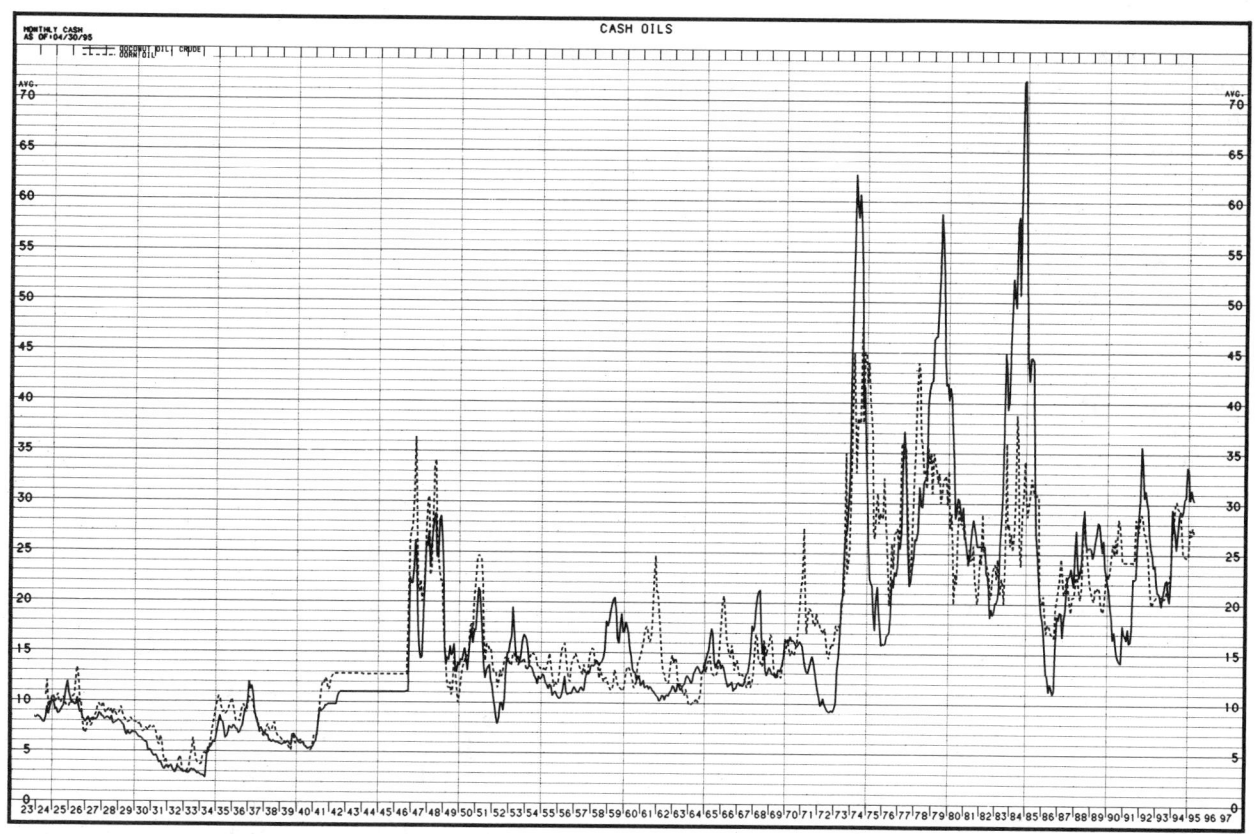

CASH OILS

Average Open Interest of Soybean Oil Futures at the Chicago Board of Trade   In Contracts

Year	Jan.	Feb.	Mar.	Apr.	May	June	July	Aug.	Sept.	Oct.	Nov.	Dec.
1982	50,210	53,926	50,108	51,762	54,572	55,441	55,869	53,243	46,052	43,332	41,425	23,823
1983	48,790	50,751	51,597	60,866	57,007	56,958	54,403	60,570	73,114	79,123	78,857	68,567
1984	61,271	59,187	53,640	57,139	65,025	61,391	54,517	47,204	45,349	40,365	43,138	42,943
1985	37,482	42,458	47,038	56,246	58,675	60,357	55,448	53,111	53,351	47,026	42,732	46,469
1986	48,384	52,875	55,877	56,114	53,063	60,035	63,034	60,095	54,905	57,256	69,227	67,871
1987	71,509	81,610	73,916	75,154	82,843	86,672	83,041	68,373	65,973	68,860	73,194	79,985
1988	85,953	88,260	86,472	85,712	87,253	94,791	95,931	87,566	86,994	82,541	82,477	75,688
1989	77,741	81,676	78,235	77,249	73,623	76,572	70,644	68,652	63,751	63,911	69,248	68,166
1990	73,368	80,842	87,615	92,845	103,116	103,747	88,763	81,310	73,841	78,548	86,786	75,995
1991	72,987	71,607	76,800	70,361	70,954	73,870	73,864	70,058	66,128	61,227	69,657	63,901
1992	68,619	73,919	75,508	68,749	65,084	71,507	64,450	72,569	70,228	65,243	76,168	76,908
1993	73,683	68,887	66,803	68,598	65,814	73,892	83,730	72,746	64,927	62,348	80,136	94,990
1994	97,198	99,640	100,334	98,659	97,595	83,165	93,994	88,196	81,735	86,901	108,327	114,928

Source: Chicago Board of Trade

Volume of Trading of Soybean Oil Futures at the Chicago Board of Trade   In Thousands of Contracts

Year	Jan.	Feb.	Mar.	Apr.	May	June	July	Aug.	Sept.	Oct.	Nov.	Dec.	Total
1982	219.1	245.6	239.8	272.2	277.7	270.7	264.5	294.9	260.5	195.4	307.4	221.6	3,049
1983	273.6	244.1	264.4	273.2	233.1	288.9	332.6	452.3	445.4	378.7	355.5	316.7	3,859
1984	358.3	346.5	337.7	360.0	513.7	436.7	353.6	280.8	244.2	269.5	288.0	220.5	4,010
1985	264.2	256.0	311.6	405.0	416.4	308.7	341.1	281.5	233.0	270.0	281.5	278.4	3,647
1986	263.1	235.9	254.0	311.7	273.8	262.0	296.0	237.9	202.7	324.8	261.4	259.6	3,183
1987	347.3	304.8	267.7	303.4	374.2	363.9	356.3	267.6	301.1	349.8	315.1	361.2	3,912
1988	437.0	390.7	346.8	442.7	399.2	580.2	461.4	403.6	390.0	303.1	377.3	364.2	4,896
1989	317.8	347.7	368.1	384.7	426.4	386.3	414.5	348.8	320.8	341.0	344.2	298.6	4,301
1990	294.1	397.1	413.9	447.7	488.8	441.5	462.3	405.6	319.2	344.1	370.2	266.3	4,651
1991	330.2	259.4	355.0	342.1	364.6	322.9	433.8	399.8	303.2	340.6	297.9	369.3	4,119
1992	344.2	293.1	400.0	255.8	381.8	352.3	413.1	298.0	425.9	346.8	365.8	405.5	4,283
1993	341.4	281.1	378.4	291.5	261.6	434.7	513.3	444.6	449.3	302.1	465.2	448.6	4,612
1994	442.0	401.6	366.0	391.2	442.4	378.2	397.5	357.9	415.4	476.9	516.7	477.4	5,063

Source: Chicago Board of Trade

Soybeans

In 1994, U.S. soybean production of a record high 2.5 billion bushels (63 million tonnes) accounted for approximately 50 percent of the world total 127.8 million tonnes. Global output was higher than initial estimates and more than 10 percent over the 1993/94 crop of 117 million tonnes. World production in the mid-1980s averaged under 100 million tonnes.

The U.S. is in no danger of losing its ranking as the world's largest soybean producer although, percentagewise, Brazil's and Argentina's production has nearly doubled since the mid-1980s. China, generally the world's third largest producer after Brazil, is in danger of losing its position to Argentina. Although the growth of China's economy is expected to maintain a strong domestic demand for soybean meal and provide farmers with enough incentive to maintain a large bean crop, its also expected that China's own needs will limit their soybean export potential perhaps by as much as 50 percent during 1994/95. Soybean production is estimated to reach 13.8 million tonnes in 1994/95, up from 11.6 million tonnes realized by Chinese farmers in 1993/94. Excessive rain caused a sharp reduction in India's 1994 production, while Brazil's prospects of about 24.3 million tonnes were hampered by lower producer prices that curtailed planted acreage. The marginal slack in foreign production, however, was more than offset by the hefty gain in U.S. production from 1993's flood ravaged 1.9 billion bushels.

Soybean world carryin stocks for the 1994/95 season of 17 million tonnes, coupled with the record crop, would place world supplies at a record large 150 million tonnes. However, lower world prices are expected to encourage a large crush and increase in foreign trade. The crush is estimated at 104 million tonnes versus 100 million tonnes in 1993/94, while world shipments are placed at over 32 million tonnes, compared to about 28 million tonnes in 1993/94. Still, total 1994/95 world usage will lag supplies and build the ending carryover to about 25.3 million tonnes. It should be noted that the soybean crop year varies. In the U.S. its runs from September to August; Brazil's season encompasses February to January and for Argentina its April to March.

U.S. farmers planted almost 62 million acres to soybeans in 1994, up 700,000 acres from the March stated intentions and 2.4 million acres above 1993, the largest acreage since 1985/86. Excellent planting conditions that accelerated Midwestern corn planting, weakened corn prices and helped shift more acreage to soybeans. In 1994, record or near record acreage was planted in a number of states, some of which along the northern and western fringes of the Midwest have doubled or tripled soybean acreage since the late-1970s. However, there has been some contraction in the Southern states in recent years. Yield far exceeded expectations, the record 1994 average of 41.5 bushels per acre compares with the 1993 average of 32.6 bushels pre acre, and the previous record of 37.6 bushels per acre in 1992.

U.S. soybean carryover stocks on August 31, 1994 totaled 209 million bushels. Total 1994/95 supplies of more than 2.7 billion bushels will exceed expected disappearance by perhaps 300 million bushels, and place carryin stocks for 1995/96 near 500 million bushels, the highest since 1987. The thriving domestic demand for oil and meal will keep a firm floor under crushing, estimated at a record large 1.35 billion bushels in 1994/95. Exports are forecast at 770 million bushels, up from 589 million bushels in 1993/94, but well under the pace seen at times in the early-1980s when more than 900 million bushels were exported. Lower world soybean prices are expected to maintain a stronger demand for beans relative to meal and oil. U.S. exports account for almost two-thirds of the world's exports, with Brazil and Argentina supplying much of the balance. Importing nations are numerous, the three biggest are usually Japan, Germany and the Netherlands.

The average price received by farmers in 1993/94 of $6.40 per bushel is well above the United States Department of Agriculture's (USDA) projected 1994/95 average of $4.80 per bushel to $5.50 per bushel, conformation of which may be seen in the plunge of more than $1.50 per bushel in 1994 crop futures values when the size of the new crop started to come into focus. The USDA initially believed it unlikely that the marketing loan will come into play in 1994/95, later beliefs were not as optimistic.

U.S. Farm Program

The effective marketing loan rate for the 1994 crop was $5.02 per bushel, versus the 1993 crop loan rate of $4.92 per bushel.

Futures Markets

Soybean futures and options are traded on the Chicago Board of Trade (CBOT). A smaller contract is traded on the Mid-America Commodity Exchange (MidAm).

World Production of Soybeans   In Thousands of Metric Tons

Crop Year[4]	Argen- tina	Bolivia	Brazil	Canada	China	India	Indo- nesia	Japan	Rep. of Korea	Meixco	Rom- ania	Para- guay	Thai- land	United States	former USSR	World Total
1985-6	7,300	81	14,100	1,063	9,500	1,100	825	228	234	750	270	600	240	57,127	465	94,699
1986-7	7,000	81	17,300	960	11,610	891	900	245	199	660	472	950	356	52,868	703	98,100
1987-8	9,700	158	18,020	1,267	12,470	980	950	287	203	750	350	1,100	338	52,746	712	103,810
1988-9	6,500	294	23,600	1,100	11,650	1,400	1,285	277	239	300	340	1,620	517	42,153	880	95,650
1989-90	10,750	173	20,340	1,219	10,227	1,806	1,315	272	252	984	304	1,575	672	52,354	956	107,367
1990-1	11,500	352	15,750	1,262	11,000	2,602	1,400	220	233	575	141	1,300	530	52,416	880	104,155
1991-2	11,114	384	19,456	1,460	9,713	2,492	1,555	197	183	719	179	1,352	436	54,065	830	107,847
1992-3[1]	11,250	470	22,400	1,455	10,304	3,106	1,620	188	176	594	126	1,850	422	59,546	700	117,434
1993-4[2]	12,000	520	24,500	1,850	15,310	3,900	1,700	100	170	500	150	1,800	450	49,220	650	116,980
1994-5[3]	12,500	550	24,000	2,000	13,800	4,200	1,720	110	170	600		1,850	500	62,120	740	127,750

[1] Preliminary.   [2] Estimate.   [3] Forecast.   [4] Split year includes Northern Hemisphere crops harvested in the late months of the first year shown combined with Southern Hemisphere crops harvested in the early months of the following year.   Source: Foreign Agricultural Service, U.S. Department of Agriculture

Supply and Distribution of Soybeans in the United States   In Millions of Bushels

Crop Year Beginning Sept. 1	Supply — Stocks, Sept. 1 — Farms	Mills, Elevators[2]	Total	Pro- duction	Total Supply	Distribution — Crushings	Exports	Seed, Feed & Residual	Total Distri- bution
1985-6	143.2	172.8	316	2,099	2,415	1,053	740	86	1,879
1986-7	167.1	369.3	536	1,943	2,479	1,179	757	106	2,042
1987-8	108.0	328.5	436	1,938	2,375	1,174	804	95	2,073
1988-9	105.1	197.4	302	1,549	1,855	1,058	527	87	1,673
1989-90	87.3	94.7	182	1,924	2,109	1,146	622	101	1,870
1990-1	86.0	153.1	239	1,926	2,169	1,187	557	95	1,840
1991-2	118.4	210.6	329	1,987	2,319	1,254	684	103	2,041
1992-3	105.0	173.4	278	2,190	2,471	1,279	770	130	2,179
1993-4[1]	125.0	167.3	292	1,871	2,170	1,272	589	100	1,961
1994-5[3]	59.1	150.0	209	2,558	2,775	1,365	785	115	2,265

[1] Preliminary.   [2] Also warehouses.   [3] Estimates.   Source: Economic Research Service, U.S. Department of Agriculture

U.S. Soybean Price Support Program & Official Crop Production Reports   In Millions of Bushels

Crop Year Beginning Sept.	Quantity Put Under Support	% of Pro- duction	Stocks Sept. 1	National - Average Support - % of Parity	$ Per Bu.	Crop Production Reports In Thousands of Bushels — Aug. 1	Sept. 1	Oct. 1	Nov. 1	Dec. 1	Final
1985	517.8	24.7	316.1	40	5.02	1,959,439	2,062,889	2,108,379	2,129,034	2,098,531	2,099,056
1986	327.6	16.9	536.4	39	4.77	1,979,773	1,979,773	1,991,763	2,009,333	2,007,033	1,942,558
1987	274.7	14.2	436.4	39	4.77	2,000,349	1,956,859	1,968,069	1,959,949	1,904,712	1,938,087
1988	120.1	7.8	302.5	40	4.77	1,473,986	1,472,376	1,501,381	1,511,876	----------	1,548,841
1989	208.9	10.9	182.0	37	4.53	1,905,300	1,889,265	1,926,385	1,936,545	----------	1,926,806
1990	241.4	12.5	239.1	36	4.50	1,836,017	1,834,602	1,823,462	1,903,832	----------	1,925,947
1991	152.8	8.0	329.0	40	5.02	1,868,825	1,816,825	1,933,570	1,961,840	----------	1,986,539
1992	182.1	8.3	278.4	41	5.02	2,079,487	NA	NA	NA	----------	2,190,354
1993	87.1	4.7	292.3		5.02	1,902,023	1,909,188	1,890,808	1,833,788	----------	1,870,958
1994[1]	338.6	13.2	209.1		4.92	2,282,367	2,316,077	2,458,087	2,522,527	----------	2,558,317

[1] Preliminary.   NA = Not available.   Source: National Agricultural Statistics Service, U.S. Department of Agriculture

Soybean Stocks in the United States   In Thousands of Bushels

Year	On Farms — Mar. 1	Jun. 1	Sept. 1	Dec. 1	Off Farms[1] — Mar. 1	Jun. 1	Sept. 1	Dec. 1	Total Stocks — Mar. 1	Jun. 1	Sept. 1	Dec. 1
1985	NA	326,596	143,221	NA	NA	281,821	172,836	NA	NA	608,417	316,057	NA
1986	NA	411,740	167,090	1,061,000	NA	437,186	369,275	895,637	NA	848,926	536,365	1,956,637
1987	589,000	282,100	107,950	865,300	749,958	554,654	328,497	889,981	1,338,958	836,754	436,447	1,755,281
1988	553,100	304,900	105,050	650,000	594,620	351,382	197,426	716,812	1,147,720	656,282	302,476	1,366,812
1989	415,000	229,200	87,320	793,400	475,246	235,311	94,709	816,583	890,246	464,511	182,029	1,609,983
1990	535,800	255,300	86,000	754,000	519,705	340,614	153,139	929,963	1,055,505	595,914	239,139	1,683,963
1991	555,500	336,500	118,400	810,000	634,619	387,022	210,642	968,957	1,190,119	723,522	329,042	1,778,957
1992	505,000	279,000	105,000	876,100	672,343	416,671	173,437	959,885	1,177,343	695,671	278,437	1,835,985
1993	576,900	319,800	124,970	697,400	638,667	363,613	167,314	876,220	1,215,567	683,413	292,284	1,573,620
1994	425,700	195,000	59,080	985,800	595,917	360,260	150,037	1,115,486	1,021,617	555,260	209,117	2,101,286

[1] Includes stocks at mills, elevators, warehouses, terminals and processors.   NA = Not available.   Source: National Agricultural Statistics Service, U.S. Department of Agriculture

SOYBEANS

U.S. Commercial Stocks of Soybeans on the First of the Month   In Millions of Bushels

Year	Jan.	Feb.	Mar.	Apr.	May	June	July	Aug.	Sept.	Oct.	Nov.	Dec.
1982	50.6	50.4	41.1	39.9	34.7	67.4	21.5	18.4	11.5	12.8	43.9	53.5
1983	53.6	58.2	57.5	55.7	55.9	44.7	34.9	35.8	42.5	47.0	78.8	83.0
1984	77.2	74.4	65.2	58.6	49.2	41.1	35.4	20.8	7.9	6.7	23.3	41.7
1985	41.1	44.0	38.2	33.3	22.8	14.7	12.7	11.3	6.9	9.6	47.6	60.9
1986	61.7	63.9	57.3	53.6	40.2	30.5	24.9	24.5	24.8	30.1	52.5	61.5
1987	62.0	61.4	56.9	52.5	49.4	46.3	38.4	26.0	16.6	21.3	56.5	57.1
1988	63.0	66.9	63.6	61.2	54.6	51.7	53.2	54.5	46.0	41.6	74.7	80.9
1989	81.3	75.6	63.8	53.4	35.8	31.2	21.1	18.6	14.1	11.4	62.1	71.3
1990	65.8	62.1	57.8	53.2	56.2	54.4	48.1	41.4	26.1	24.1	89.7	90.7
1991	90.2	78.1	70.5	56.2	43.5	35.5	33.3	25.5	25.3	29.7	80.6	84.0
1992	76.0	75.9	67.1	67.8	58.5	57.2	51.7	32.1	18.6	59.0	75.1	79.9
1993	71.5	63.5	54.5	48.5	44.0	32.1	26.6	24.4	15.8	9.6	52.3	60.2
1994	62.6	65.3	54.4	46.3	40.7	34.7	29.9	24.3	19.8	11.5	68.1	83.4

Source: Livestock Division, U.S. Department of Agriculture

Salient Statistics of Soybeans in the United States

Crop Year	Planted --- 1,000 Acres ---	Acreage Harvested --- 1,000 Acres ---	Yield Per Acre (Bu.)	Farm Price ($ Bu.)	Farm Value (Million Dollars)	Pounds Per Bushel Crushed — Yield of Oil	Pounds Per Bushel Crushed — Yield of Meal	Grand Total	Bel.-Luxem.	Canada	Germany	Japan	Netherlands	Spain	Taiwan	former USSR
1977-8	58,978	57,830	30.6	5.88	9,363	10.39	47.34	19,061	475	264	1,521	3,636	4,086	1,532	854	744
1978-9	64,708	63,663	29.4	6.66	12,450	11.07	47.63	20,117	420	352	1,486	3,865	4,012	1,475	1,271	1,178
1979-80	71,411	70,343	32.1	6.28	14,204	10.74	48.01	23,818	584	392	1,318	3,868	6,035	2,203	780	813
1980-1	60,930	67,813	26.5	7.57	13,601	11.09	47.93	19,712	670	345	1,791	3,816	3,839	1,383	1,063	NA
1981-2	67,543	66,163	30.1	6.07	12,005	10.72	47.86	25,285	1,404	310	2,135	4,196	5,349	3,855	1,059	683
1982-3	70,884	69,442	31.5	5.71	12,463	10.76	47.88	24,634	1,259	324	1,813	4,580	4,648	2,313	1,300	199
1983-4	63,779	62,525	26.2	7.83	12,775	11.26	47.36	20,215	882	248	967	4,394	2,988	1,800	1,382	408
1984-5	67,755	66,113	28.1	5.84	10,748	11.05	47.15	16,279	658	140	718	3,828	2,857	1,084	1,389	0
1985-6	63,145	61,599	34.1	5.05	10,571	11.01	47.27	20,158	784	114	934	4,293	3,056	1,519	1,506	1,519
1986-7	60,405	58,312	33.3	4.78	9,263	10.86	47.08	20,600	888	206	1,393	4,024	3,540	1,775	1,968	71
1987-8	58,180	57,172	33.9	5.88	11,391	11.04	47.76	21,870	825	154	1,416	3,914	4,267	1,593	1,857	831
1988-9	58,840	57,373	27.0	7.42	11,488	11.16	47.43	14,356	474	113	601	3,251	2,531	1,152	1,439	240
1989-90	60,820	59,538	32.3	5.69	10,916	11.17	47.63	16,933	666	276	818	3,480	2,721	1,565	2,016	342
1990-1	57,795	56,512	34.1	5.74	11,042	11.23	47.47	15,161	413	156	760	3,584	2,085	1,027	1,087	354
1991-2	59,180	58,011	34.2	5.58	11,092	11.42	47.51	19,277	797	76	814	3,891	3,167	1,459	2,034	543
1992-3	59,180	58,233	37.6	5.60	12,154	10.84	47.54	20,400	814	249	893	3,984	3,362	1,424	2,369	46
1993-4[1]	60,135	57,347	32.6	6.40	11,575	10.87	47.60	16,364	602	26	807	3,527	2,661	921	1,700	NA
1994-5[2]	61,940	61,129	41.9	5.20-.50	12,068	11.00	47.29									

[1] Preliminary.   [2] Forecast.   NA = Not available.   *Source: Economic Research Service, U.S. Department of Agriculture*

Production of Soybeans for Beans in the U.S., by Selected States   In Millions of Bushels

Year	Arkansas	Illinois	Indiana	Iowa	Kentucky	Louisiana	Michigan	Minnesota	Mississippi	Missouri	Nebraska	North Carolina	Ohio	South Carolina	Tennessee
1977	105.8	336.3	144.3	251.3	40.9	63.0	21.6	133.8	78.5	148.8	40.7	29.0	120.0	26.7	52.2
1978	115.2	309.5	144.2	283.1	40.8	76.0	21.6	146.2	81.7	155.0	42.5	40.3	127.7	32.3	56.9
1979	144.2	379.1	159.1	306.4	54.0	93.8	30.3	162.6	118.9	183.6	54.7	45.8	144.8	39.8	70.7
1980	65.3	309.9	157.7	318.4	36.0	67.0	30.4	149.9	61.6	135.5	53.1	34.7	135.4	20.8	45.9
1981	99.0	351.5	151.8	326.0	47.9	64.2	29.1	139.2	75.6	155.6	78.7	46.3	99.8	31.0	61.1
1982	105.6	354.2	173.3	306.6	51.3	75.4	35.3	169.1	92.3	171.0	78.8	52.5	133.2	39.6	61.0
1983	70.3	267.0	122.5	278.6	24.5	68.1	33.8	151.8	58.9	103.0	59.0	33.0	105.0	23.6	31.5
1984	101.4	284.1	150.1	264.6	42.3	66.8	32.1	172.9	76.8	108.7	66.3	46.5	137.6	29.8	48.1
1985	98.1	382.5	185.1	309.7	41.8	44.1	34.6	160.0	70.7	180.4	85.0	39.1	160.6	24.6	45.3
1986	66.0	360.0	157.3	350.7	35.8	35.0	28.8	162.8	41.7	170.6	93.1	36.7	146.6	13.7	35.5
1987	71.5	330.6	174.0	343.7	24.0	38.8	38.2	181.4	47.8	154.6	83.4	32.8	147.3	15.7	28.8
1988	83.2	234.9	115.5	251.1	24.1	56.6	35.1	124.8	49.5	112.1	70.8	35.4	99.9	18.6	32.0
1989	75.2	354.0	166.1	322.9	36.9	38.5	38.9	185.0	40.0	121.8	81.9	41.9	125.4	20.2	29.8
1990	90.5	354.9	171.4	327.9	39.0	42.0	43.3	179.4	39.9	124.5	81.4	32.4	135.7	13.9	33.8
1991	89.6	341.3	171.6	349.5	36.7	30.7	52.8	195.3	46.8	135.1	82.4	38.6	135.7	13.7	31.5
1992	104.3	405.5	194.4	359.5	42.2	35.1	47.5	172.8	59.5	161.5	103.3	36.5	147.2	14.7	33.3
1993	92.3	387.0	223.1	257.3	38.0	31.2	54.7	115.0	42.9	118.8	90.0	30.0	156.2	7.8	32.2
1994[1]	115.6	438.4	220.0	447.3	42.9	32.5	58.5	229.6	59.5	173.3	137.3	41.9	175.6	15.7	38.9

[1] Preliminary.   *Source: Agricultural Statistics Board, U.S. Department of Agriculture*

Soybean Stocks at U.S. Mills on First of Month   In Millions of Bushels

Crop Year	Sept.	Oct.	Nov.	Dec.	Jan.	Feb.	Mar.	Apr.	May	June	July	Aug.
1978-9	37.9	31.9	138.4	149.4	127.3	112.4	124.0	120.9	96.7	71.1	73.0	55.6
1979-80	37.5	39.2	166.5	184.5	163.3	145.4	130.7	118.6	95.8	79.7	75.7	73.9
1980-1	56.9	80.4	166.0	172.0	138.7	125.9	105.4	97.2	84.4	67.8	49.2	43.9
1981-2	33.4	31.5	105.8	135.2	114.5	99.8	84.6	79.2	72.2	60.8	51.2	43.6
1982-3	30.0	29.0	114.2	145.5	125.1	116.2	98.5	96.2	84.6	69.8	62.0	55.4
1983-4	58.6	63.9	124.5	142.3	124.0	125.3	114.8	105.3	94.2	101.7	83.4	57.7
1984-5	35.3	19.7	53.9	116.4	98.4	85.9	65.8	69.7	65.2	53.4	47.6	36.0
1985-6	26.7	25.7	92.8	113.4	119.9	124.6	97.5	84.9	67.6	53.2	40.7	40.2
1986-7	28.5	38.3	108.1	127.4	117.2	113.1	105.4	90.2	85.2	72.9	63.6	49.8
1987-8	31.2	65.7	158.5	155.5	145.0	141.8	139.3	133.8	113.9	95.4	90.1	66.2
1988-9	59.7	61.4	136.6	147.4	138.6	131.9	112.0	99.2	72.8	52.5	46.1	31.0
1989-90	23.8	24.5	96.3	108.5	89.7	93.6	91.4	83.5	73.0	67.5	58.8	46.9
1990-1	45.2	34.5	130.1	130.7	----------- 106.5 -----------			----------- 78.5 -----------			----------- 61.2	
1991-2	------	----------- 67.0 -----------			126.9	121.4	109.6	94.7	79.8	73.5	65.7	56.2
1992-3	43.8	46.3	132.3	137.4	119.1	111.2	97.2	90.1	83.6	67.7	67.1	55.3
1993-4	42.0	28.0	108.6	114.9	120.9	126.1	118.5	119.7	98.7	97.8	90.0	63.5
1994-5[1]	47.9	46.8	114.1	124.3	108.0							

[1] Preliminary.   *Source: Economic Research Service, U.S. Department of Agriculture*

Soybean Exports from the United States   In Millions of Bushels

Year	Sept.	Oct.	Nov.	Dec.	Jan.	Feb.	Mar.	Apr.	May	June	July	Aug.	Total
1980-1	41.4	60.3	75.0	74.5	71.7	55.5	103.2	60.0	69.6	41.8	29.6	41.8	724.3
1981-2	50.9	100.8	103.7	73.6	84.3	89.4	79.0	85.7	90.6	59.8	53.8	57.5	929.1
1982-3	58.0	94.4	93.6	90.1	86.3	87.2	84.4	73.3	58.5	67.7	51.6	60.2	905.2
1983-4	53.9	67.6	69.2	74.5	80.4	79.7	78.8	68.5	56.8	41.1	39.2	30.7	686.6
1984-5	19.0	40.9	93.5	84.8	70.3	72.6	59.8	60.4	33.1	18.2	19.2	26.3	598.2
1985-6	31.5	55.3	79.6	94.1	84.7	92.1	89.9	80.4	57.2	28.7	26.6	20.4	740.7
1986-7	30.2	89.7	96.6	89.0	71.7	73.8	67.8	53.9	37.6	37.9	54.3	54.5	756.9
1987-8	59.4	101.1	100.4	81.1	80.8	97.0	78.5	66.7	39.7	29.3	30.4	37.2	801.7
1988-9	26.7	50.2	61.3	69.3	66.3	56.1	66.8	40.8	23.2	31.2	16.4	18.3	526.5
1989-90	17.9	74.0	76.6	65.7	76.3	74.9	87.3	43.6	22.8	35.2	20.8	28.3	623.4
1990-1	27.9	29.8	62.8	55.8	----------- 190.1 -----------			----------- 117.7 -----------			73.9 -----------		557.9
1991-2	26.8	----------- 235.6 -----------			73.8	90.6	63.3	56.6	28.3	27.3	42.6	39.2	683.9
1992-3	50.1	98.0	84.2	73.6	89.1	104.7	79.7	48.7	34.6	39.4	42.7	24.6	769.5
1993-4	30.1	73.6	72.4	73.9	71.0	67.8	53.6	34.8	27.5	26.7	17.1	40.7	589.1
1994-5[1]	42.3	99.9	78.5	104.2									

[1] Preliminary.   *Source: Economic Research Service, U.S. Department of Agriculture*

Volume of Trading in Soybean Futures at the Chicago Board of Trade   In Millions of Bushels

Year	Jan.	Feb.	Mar.	Apr.	May	June	July	Aug.	Sept.	Oct.	Nov.	Dec.	Total
1982	3,120	3,497	4,478	4,484	3,517	4,245	4,017	3,822	3,197	4,014	4,282	3,198	45,828
1983	3,942	3,820	4,247	4,375	4,259	4,409	6,224	8,799	7,852	8,071	6,793	5,609	68,402
1984	5,550	5,247	6,008	4,945	7,300	6,323	5,314	4,045	2,505	3,687	3,427	2,463	56,813
1985	3,315	2,749	2,657	2,821	2,766	3,309	3,779	2,581	2,525	3,364	3,881	3,213	36,961
1986	3,692	2,484	2,435	2,976	2,546	2,199	2,925	2,049	1,812	3,266	2,473	1,811	30,668
1987	2,174	1,816	1,794	3,118	3,969	4,356	3,785	1,935	2,305	4,109	3,674	3,859	36,894
1988	4,436	4,252	4,284	4,822	6,339	7,975	5,574	5,214	4,516	5,235	5,001	4,777	62,485
1989	5,222	4,265	4,760	4,720	4,587	4,466	3,977	3,172	2,854	4,011	3,247	2,893	48,174
1990	3,278	2,673	4,133	4,422	5,630	5,209	5,188	4,528	3,214	5,660	4,299	3,275	67,887
1991	3,725	3,104	3,577	4,040	3,422	3,881	4,962	4,716	3,312	4,381	2,856	3,095	44,871
1992	4,022	3,692	3,440	2,794	4,369	5,273	4,666	3,154	2,861	4,337	3,066	3,327	45,001
1993	3,417	3,123	3,379	3,806	3,890	6,435	8,216	5,900	4,625	4,811	5,940	4,707	58,247
1994	5,673	4,493	4,610	4,597	5,792	5,985	4,462	3,442	3,113	4,285	4,129	3,166	53,745

Source: Chicago Board of Trade

SOYBEANS

Average Open Interest of Soybean Futures at Chicago Board of Trade   In Millions of Bushels

Year	Jan.	Feb.	Mar.	Apr.	May	June	July	Aug.	Sept.	Oct.	Nov.	Dec.
1980	542,923	555,696	506,850	512,455	501,404	544,760	669,411	716,959	836,481	994,450	1,069,985	1,083,919
1981	760,433	618,363	556,355	586,500	516,510	517,640	497,162	452,323	440,217	472,908	485,995	482,498
1982	404,223	406,528	393,035	460,729	418,686	391,052	374,053	380,213	355,169	397,810	425,089	438,322
1983	442,828	456,830	416,479	505,813	462,581	420,022	455,472	670,320	714,951	748,973	655,300	631,981
1984	558,727	544,108	564,202	535,411	546,508	495,022	360,313	286,738	270,991	326,171	353,568	356,011
1985	348,140	364,738	327,450	317,610	306,381	329,845	314,415	324,314	315,912	353,915	375,558	367,207
1986	377,175	375,378	374,277	382,321	342,736	333,767	303,102	290,679	298,112	366,628	410,962	405,791
1987	373,975	374,970	384,749	448,282	472,715	460,889	396,495	364,262	373,807	524,582	537,224	589,553
1988	592,560	617,929	609,312	692,576	763,473	849,772	644,812	574,151	598,951	607,404	558,608	603,549
1989	598,499	572,342	579,959	513,682	484,011	472,263	417,035	379,628	404,830	503,966	482,161	493,360
1990	478,591	496,834	556,976	615,027	655,864	590,047	483,946	458,531	489,646	599,204	625,678	617,759
1991	546,555	552,104	551,590	534,973	511,847	516,809	457,245	430,659	490,248	571,031	562,037	563,908
1992	574,356	591,586	663,193	605,856	606,990	689,478	581,040	534,148	520,573	628,670	594,385	571,307
1993	608,628	633,411	633,405	690,776	689,104	713,606	998,406	917,111	818,236	798,207	805,850	843,468
1994	888,241	836,087	780,293	737,844	728,991	751,017	660,050	605,630	634,736	735,989	685,934	681,753

Source: Chicago Board of Trade

Soybeans Under Price Support Through the End of the Month
(Cumulative Total from Current Season's Crop)   In Thousands of Bushels

Year	Sept.	Oct.	Nov.	Dec.	Jan.	Feb.	Mar.	Apr.	May	June	July	Aug.
1978-9	0	6,403	31,008	43,015	58,278	61,489	62,365	63,146	63,508	65,087	------	------
1979-80	11	9,507	39,559	67,372	101,052	106,135	113,638	119,860	121,684	122,013	------	------
1980-1	22	11,705	28,541	67,744	100,809	116,167	125,480	130,236	132,346	133,160	------	------
1981-2	1,044	26,019	81,377	138,202	191,386	208,285	216,412	219,743	144,165	221,303	------	------
1982-3	861	50,145	203,031	311,105	363,696	382,536	391,432	393,567	394,727	395,893	------	------
1983-4	0	9,098	32,869	62,736	84,526	92,974	98,945	100,030	100,656	100,817	------	------
1984-5	0	46,349	99,437	174,002	242,526	258,174	268,812	271,353	274,051	275,687	------	------
1985-6	1,056	86,633	265,929	408,793	482,658	499,223	506,818	511,462	513,089	513,954	------	------
1986-7	313	34,971	154,207	240,072	299,018	316,598	321,327	327,233	329,094	329,766	329,971	------
1987-8	4,383	58,666	165,997	209,121	259,010	211,856	272,632	274,046	274,774	274,952	274,929	------
1988-9	896	16,805	44,627	81,131	106,033	115,210	118,487	119,356	119,674	120,033	120,034	------
1989-90	294	35,539	119,734	159,422	195,471	201,659	207,676	208,359	208,715	208,835	208,897	------
1990-1	172	26,109	124,610	------	------	------	------	------	------	------	------	------
1991-2	1,954	34,505	101,580	125,302	154,149	156,853	157,968	158,606	158,791	158,845	158,849	0
1992-3	986	61,648	119,598	154,288	176,140	179,715	181,468	181,761	181,986	182,082	182,096	5
1993-4	69	22,123	54,798	74,433	83,454	85,312	86,518	86,882	87,084	87,143		

Source: U.S. Department of Agriculture

Soybean Crushed (Factory Consumption) in the U.S.   In Millions of Bushels--One Bushel=60 Pounds

Year	Sept.	Oct.	Nov.	Dec.	Jan.	Feb.	Mar.	Apr.	May	June	July	Aug.	Total
1978-9	71.4	89.3	89.6	96.4	90.6	81.5	89.0	83.3	86.9	82.8	80.6	76.4	1,018
1979-80	75.9	95.8	101.4	104.4	106.6	100.0	102.2	92.0	93.8	82.7	84.9	83.7	1,123
1980-1	81.0	97.8	98.5	94.1	92.2	79.6	88.7	85.4	82.3	73.4	72.3	74.6	1,020
1981-2	75.4	104.5	97.6	102.5	94.9	86.7	85.1	81.0	86.6	77.1	70.6	67.8	1,030
1982-3	76.0	100.2	108.1	111.9	110.0	93.0	94.6	81.8	83.7	81.5	81.6	85.7	1,108
1983-4	86.6	96.4	86.6	89.4	93.8	79.2	86.0	74.6	79.4	70.6	69.0	71.1	983
1984-5	65.5	89.2	98.9	101.1	94.5	80.8	85.6	83.2	89.3	82.7	82.0	77.5	1,030
1985-6	76.5	94.3	96.7	100.8	99.6	81.4	91.6	84.4	86.3	79.6	83.1	78.4	1,053
1986-7	79.4	107.0	109.4	107.6	110.3	102.3	106.0	95.9	95.3	90.6	92.6	82.4	1,179
1987-8	79.7	102.5	111.2	110.8	106.7	99.8	107.6	102.6	98.0	89.2	88.0	78.3	1,174
1988-9	79.9	94.4	101.0	100.7	99.8	85.8	93.5	89.6	87.0	76.0	74.0	75.9	1,058
1989-90	74.1	94.8	104.1	105.4	107.2	91.8	102.1	95.1	93.4	92.0	92.2	94.2	1,146
1990-1	92.1	106.1	106.0	102.7	----------- 297.9 -----------			----------- 280.1 -----------			202.5 -----------		1,187
1991-2	98.9	----------- 333.3 -----------			112.0	100.8	107.2	101.6	95.2	100.0	102.3	102.3	1,254
1992-3	101.2	113.9	113.1	116.2	116.8	102.2	113.0	105.9	106.5	99.9	98.0	92.2	1,279
1993-4	98.4	113.7	114.4	114.1	110.2	102.8	112.8	105.1	102.5	96.8	100.5	100.5	1,272
1994-5[1]	105.5	118.8	121.9	127.9	126.8								

[1] Preliminary.   *Source: Economic Research Service, U.S. Department of Agriculture*

Average Price Received by Farmers for Soybeans in the U.S.   In Cents Per Bushel

Year	Sept.	Oct.	Nov.	Dec.	Jan.	Feb.	Mar.	Apr.	May	June	July	Aug.	Average
1978-9	620	626	641	649	658	699	716	706	706	736	736	707	666
1979-80	681	635	630	627	639	620	594	563	576	591	675	718	628
1980-1	759	768	818	780	780	750	759	760	740	705	713	671	757
1981-2	621	606	603	600	613	604	604	617	627	612	599	559	604
1982-3	522	506	534	546	556	566	582	609	606	590	627	757	565
1983-4	828	796	780	774	785	728	768	783	812	799	695	650	783
1984-5	609	607	601	582	591	577	588	588	570	562	542	510	584
1985-6	499	485	492	501	516	518	523	523	525	519	511	499	505
1986-7	485	455	464	467	470	469	473	490	520	536	525	502	478
1987-8	502	504	536	563	573	596	605	639	698	818	850	833	588
1988-9	793	753	743	753	769	741	751	729	720	705	683	607	742
1989-90	570	554	566	564	565	556	565	582	597	588	597	600	570
1990-1	599	587	578	572	572	565	577	577	559	555	536	566	575
1991-2	564	549	548	545	554	559	567	566	587	594	559	540	560
1992-3	535	526	536	546	558	556	565	573	581	564	657	655	571
1993-4	621	601	632	664	672	670	674	657	677	672	592	558	641
1994-5[1]	547	530	536	541	536								538

[1] Preliminary.   *Source: Economic Research Service, U.S. Department of Agriculture*

SOYBEANS

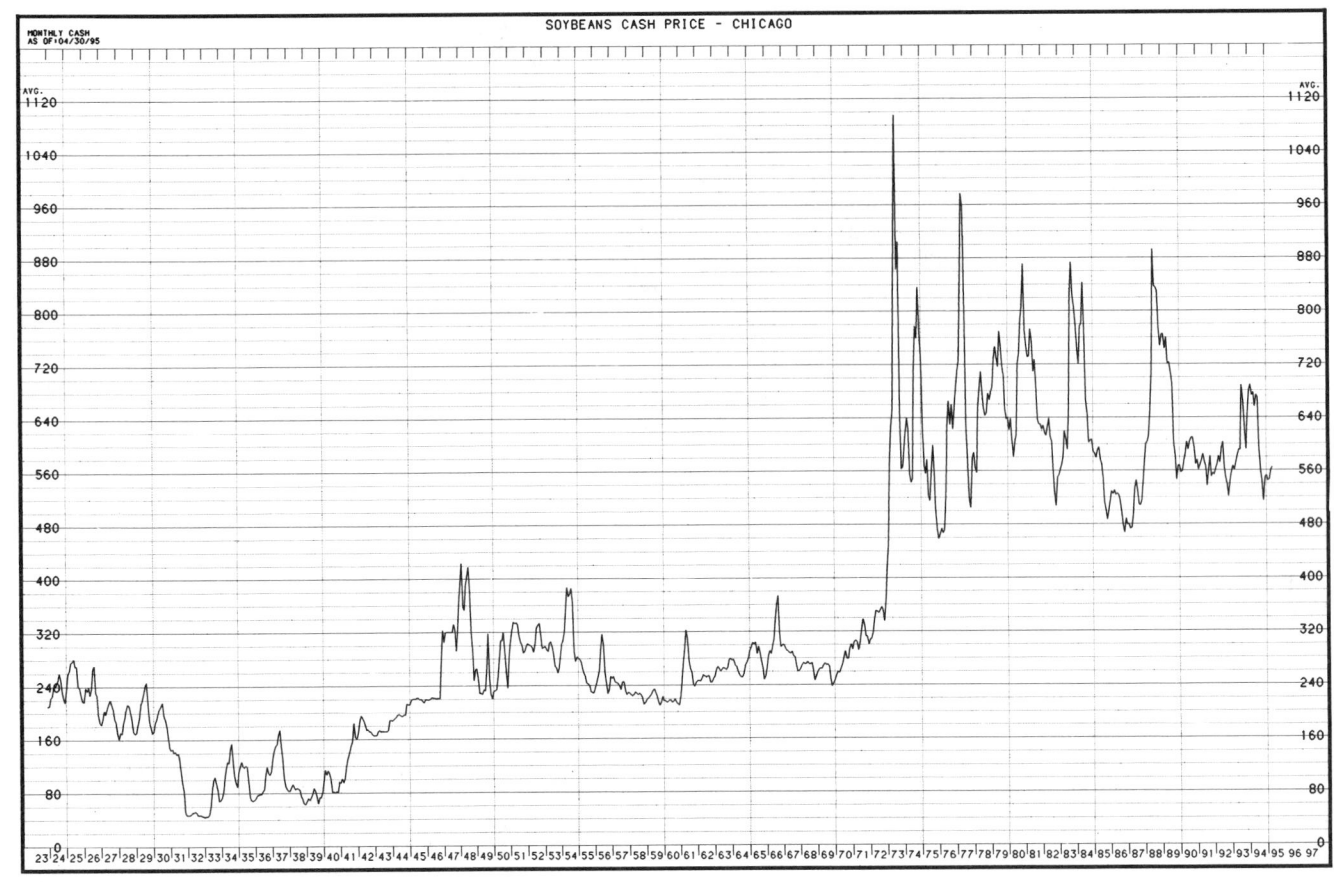

Average Cash Price of No. 1 Yellow Soybeans at Illinois Processor   In Cents Per Bushel

Year	Sept.	Oct.	Nov.	Dec.	Jan.	Feb.	Mar.	Apr.	May	June	July	Aug.	Average
1976-7	516	622	655	686	706	726	825	960	942	825	640	549	721
1977-8	642	507	584	594	573	565	658	681	701	676	662	647	624
1978-9	704	672	668	681	689	728	745	727	721	768	764	728	716
1979-80	813	656	652	653	636	642	607	580	604	610	722	745	660
1980-1	644	827	891	773	757	734	737	772	758	713	736	694	753
1981-2	540	630	628	623	630	624	616	642	656	631	620	573	618
1982-3	540	526	570	573	581	586	598	635	627	606	659	846	612
1983-4	893	846	820	777	767	737	797	798	861	791	685	663	786
1984-5	621	627	625	607	604	597	608	613	595	588	565	528	598
1985-6	519	505	519	532	545	538	547	540	544	543	533	500	530
1986-7	496	489	508	469	498	489	492	512	552	563	547	528	512
1987-8	527	532	564	594	617	621	630	671	731	913	859	852	676
1988-9	852	792	767	783	783	760	778	739	740	725	708	606	753
1989-90	600	564	570	582	572	585	600	600	620	609	619	626	596
1990-1	628	614	587	591	576	585	592	601	589	583	554	578	590
1991-2	598	568	571	568	577	581	593	585	609	619	580	564	584
1992-3	554	535	560	572	582	575	587	597	607	606	689	679	595
1993-4	643	606	664	694	701	686	692	670	689	685	603	576	659
1994-5[1]	557	531	566	567	558								556

[1] Preliminary.   Source: Economic Research Service, U.S. Department of Agriculture

254

Stock Index Futures, U.S.

The U.S. equity markets weathered a number of unsettling events during 1994, which from a traditional stance would have a bearish impact. The major negative factors were step ladder increases of short-term interest rates by the Federal Reserve, the effect of which would have normally triggered a movement of capital into higher yielding assets at the expense of equities if not also cut into corporate earnings as financing costs increased. Moreover, the Fed's actions raised fears as to the staying power of the U.S. economy's expansion. Another seemingly negative factor was Mexico's surprise devaluation of the peso, which helped to underscore the economic problems of many third world nations and the backlash it might have on U.S. exports.

On the other hand, the global economy's woes served as a reminder of the overall political and social stability of the United States. The same rationale also was seen as applicable to its economy. The latter undoubtedly contributed to the relative steadiness of the U.S. equity markets during the year, with trading volume at a record high.

The Dow Jones Industrial Average began 1994 at around 3820 and closed the year only about two percent higher. During the January-March quarter the Dow slipped about 200 points as the Fed's tightening unsettled the market, but a more positive psychology started to take root that slowly lifted the Dow into year-end and set the stage for a move that would carry the index to record highs in early 1995. The S & P 500 mirrored the Dow in that it was essentially flat during 1994, closing the year with about a one percent gain.

The smaller capitalized companies were hit harder than the larger companies. The NASDAQ index lost about four percent during 1994 while the Russell 2000 dropped more than 11 percent from its early 1994 high.

Indeed, for the stock value of small companies, 1994 was a difficult year, with many down 20 percent or more. The number of stocks that set new lows was the highest since 1990. Thus, the market action was skewed to the favor of blue chip stocks.

The outlook for 1995 suggested a more broadly based optimism towards equities, initially paced by the more well-known indices. Although the economy's real growth was likely to taper off from 1994, any recession fears were apt to remain on the back burner. Moreover, inflation was expected to be well contained. On balance, the marketplace perceives the Fed's stance geared to an economic policy that might be able to realize the best of all worlds: economic growth with minimal inflation. If that perception can take hold, as it seemed to be doing in early 1995, then by year-end the many U.S. stock indices were likely to be near or at record highs. The Fed holds the key. The risk focuses on whether monetary policy is tuned too finely, nudging the economy into a risk area as the 1996 presidential election bids begin to further cloud the outlook. Market psychology may prove as equally potent as corporate earnings in 1995.

Futures Markets

S & P 500 futures and options and the S & P MidCap 400 are traded on the Chicago Mercantile Exchange (CME). Options on the MidCap Index are traded on the American Stock Exchange (AMEX). A Major Market Index and Russell 2000 Index also are traded on the CME. The Kansas City Board of Trade has a Value line Index contract and a Mini-Value Line Index. A NYSE composite index is traded in New York.

Dow Jones Industrial Average (30 Stocks)

Year	Jan.	Feb.	Mar.	Apr.	May	June	July	Aug.	Sept.	Oct.	Nov.	Dec.	Average
1988	1,947.4	1,980.7	2,044.3	2,036.1	1,988.9	2,104.9	2,104.2	2,051.3	2,080.1	2,144.3	2,099.0	2,148.6	2,061.0
1989	2,234.7	2,304.3	2,283.1	2,348.9	2,439.6	2,494.9	2,554.0	2,691.1	2,693.4	2,692.0	2,642.5	2,728.5	2,508.9
1990	2,679.2	2,614.2	2,700.1	2,708.3	2,793.8	2,894.8	2,934.2	2,681.9	2,550.7	2,460.5	2,518.6	2,610.9	2,678.9
1991	2,587.6	2,863.0	2,920.1	2,925.5	2,928.4	2,968.1	2,978.2	3,006.1	3,010.4	3,019.7	2,986.1	2,958.6	2,929.3
1992	3,227.1	3,257.3	3,247.4	3,294.1	3,376.8	3,337.8	3,329.4	3,307.4	3,293.9	3,198.7	3,238.5	3,303.2	3,284.3
1993	3,277.7	3,367.3	3,440.7	3,423.6	3,478.2	3,513.8	3,529.4	3,597.0	3,592.3	3,625.8	3,674.7	3,744.1	3,522.1
1994	3,868.4	3,905.6	3,817.0	3,661.5	3,708.0	3,737.6	3,718.3	3,797.5	3,880.6	3,868.1	3,792.5	3,770.3	3,793.8

Source: Survey of Current Business

Dow Jones Transportation (20 Stocks)

Year	Jan.	Feb.	Mar.	Apr.	May	June	July	Aug.	Sept.	Oct.	Nov.	Dec.	Average
1988	756.0	790.1	861.3	853.7	820.2	873.1	881.2	856.1	879.5	923.1	916.2	955.4	863.8
1989	1,009.3	1,073.2	1,046.3	1,098.0	1,139.8	1,158.9	1,223.1	1,407.1	1,462.7	1,342.0	1,188.1	1,183.0	1,194.3
1990	1,139.8	1,083.4	1,160.3	1,164.8	1,163.1	1,181.9	1,150.0	951.1	881.3	850.8	848.1	908.4	1,040.3
1991	962.4	1,110.3	1,113.2	1,139.1	1,167.6	1,205.1	1,204.6	1,204.7	1,182.4	1,283.1	1,237.1	1,233.3	1,170.2
1992	1,378.7	1,412.2	969.9	1,356.9	1,380.4	1,333.3	1,303.1	1,254.6	1,275.2	1,286.2	1,375.9	1,430.1	1,349.6
1993	1,488.1	1,533.2	1,541.6	1,619.7	1,583.4	1,533.9	1,553.7	1,631.6	1,623.9	1,660.5	1,732.6	1,763.2	1,605.5
1994	1,812.1	1,810.4	1,719.9	1,614.7	1,602.2	1,619.2	1,596.2	1,602.8	1,553.7	1,485.8	1,473.7	1,415.3	1,608.8

Source: The Wall Street Journal

STOCK INDEX FUTURES

Dow Jones Public Utilities (15 Stocks)

Year	Jan.	Feb.	Mar.	Apr.	May	June	July	Aug.	Sept.	Oct.	Nov.	Dec.	Average
1988	182.2	185.0	177.7	171.4	169.3	180.0	178.7	178.6	179.9	185.0	184.1	185.2	179.8
1989	188.9	186.6	182.8	188.0	196.3	206.7	215.5	218.1	216.0	216.6	221.0	232.1	205.7
1990	223.2	221.2	217.0	210.7	212.4	211.2	205.0	210.1	199.8	207.2	210.3	210.6	210.8
1991	205.3	213.7	213.2	214.5	211.2	204.6	199.6	204.4	208.0	213.5	216.7	219.3	210.3
1992	215.7	206.8	204.4	206.1	213.2	212.5	219.1	220.2	220.0	217.2	217.7	220.2	214.4
1993	222.0	234.2	240.0	242.1	237.8	241.5	246.5	252.0	253.0	243.1	227.1	227.1	238.9
1994	222.3	215.6	207.0	196.5	185.5	182.9	181.8	188.9	179.6	179.9	177.7	181.0	191.6

Source: The Wall Street Journal

Standard & Poor's 500 Composite Price Index

Year	Jan.	Feb.	Mar.	Apr.	May	June	July	Aug.	Sept.	Oct.	Nov.	Dec.	Average
1988	250.5	258.1	265.7	262.6	256.1	270.7	269.1	263.7	268.0	277.4	271.0	276.5	265.8
1989	285.4	294.0	292.7	302.3	313.9	323.7	331.9	246.6	247.3	247.4	340.2	348.6	322.8
1990	340.0	330.5	338.5	338.2	350.3	360.4	360.0	330.8	315.4	307.1	315.3	328.8	334.6
1991	325.5	362.3	372.3	379.7	378.0	378.3	380.2	389.4	387.2	386.9	385.9	388.5	376.2
1992	416.1	412.6	407.4	407.4	414.8	408.3	415.1	417.9	418.5	412.5	422.8	435.6	415.8
1993	435.2	441.7	450.2	443.1	445.3	448.1	447.3	454.1	459.2	463.9	462.9	466.0	451.4
1994	473.0	471.6	463.8	447.2	451.0	454.8	451.4	464.2	467.0	463.8	461.0	455.2	460.3

Source: The Wall Street Journal

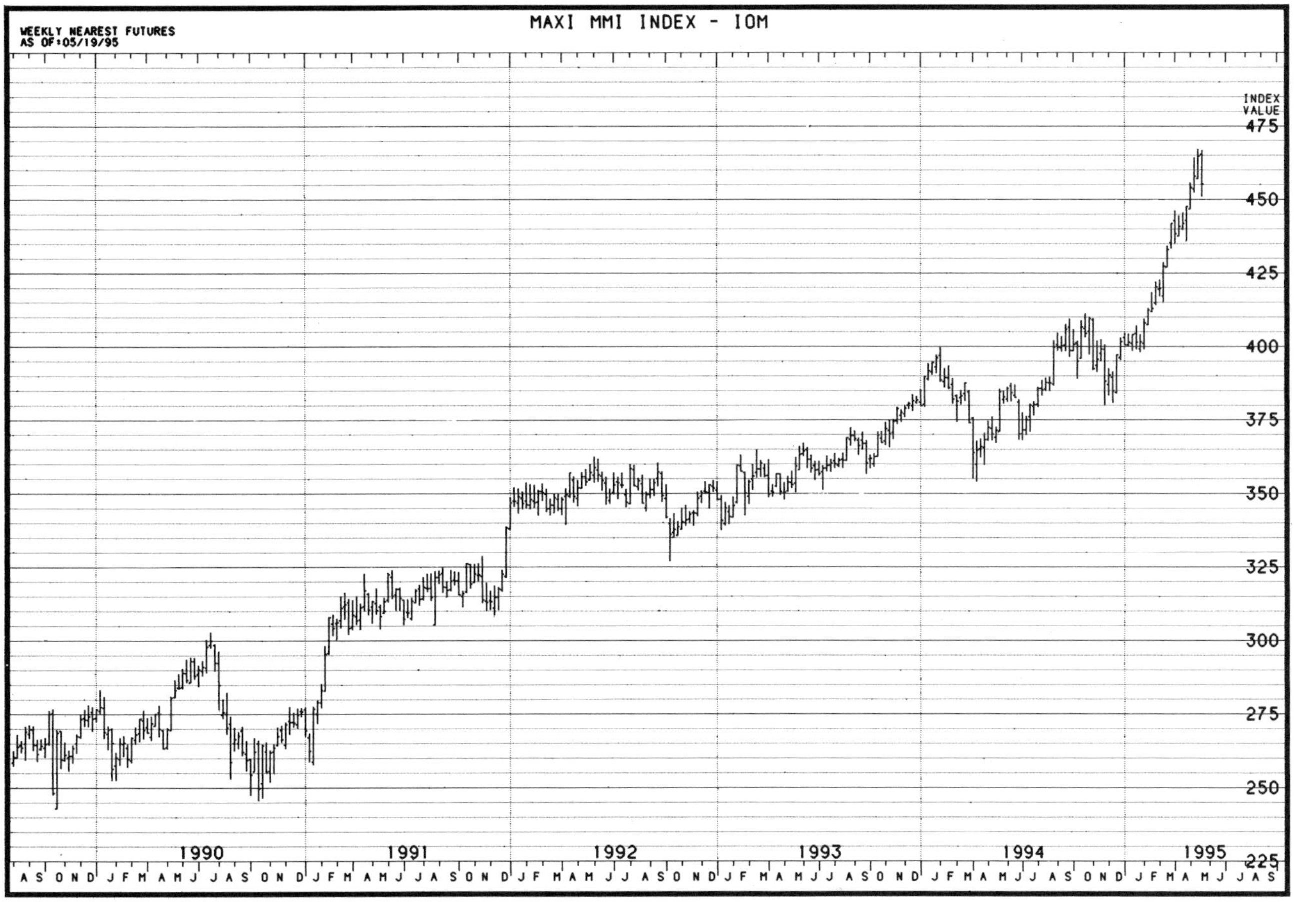

MAXI MMI INDEX - IOM

WEEKLY NEAREST FUTURES
AS OF:05/19/95

INDEX
VALUE

475

450

425

400

375

350

325

300

275

250

225

1990   1991   1992   1993   1994   1995

A S O N D J F M A M J J A S O N D J F M A M J J A S O N D J F M A M J J A S O N D J F M A M J J A S O N D J F M A M J J A S O N D J F M A M J J A S

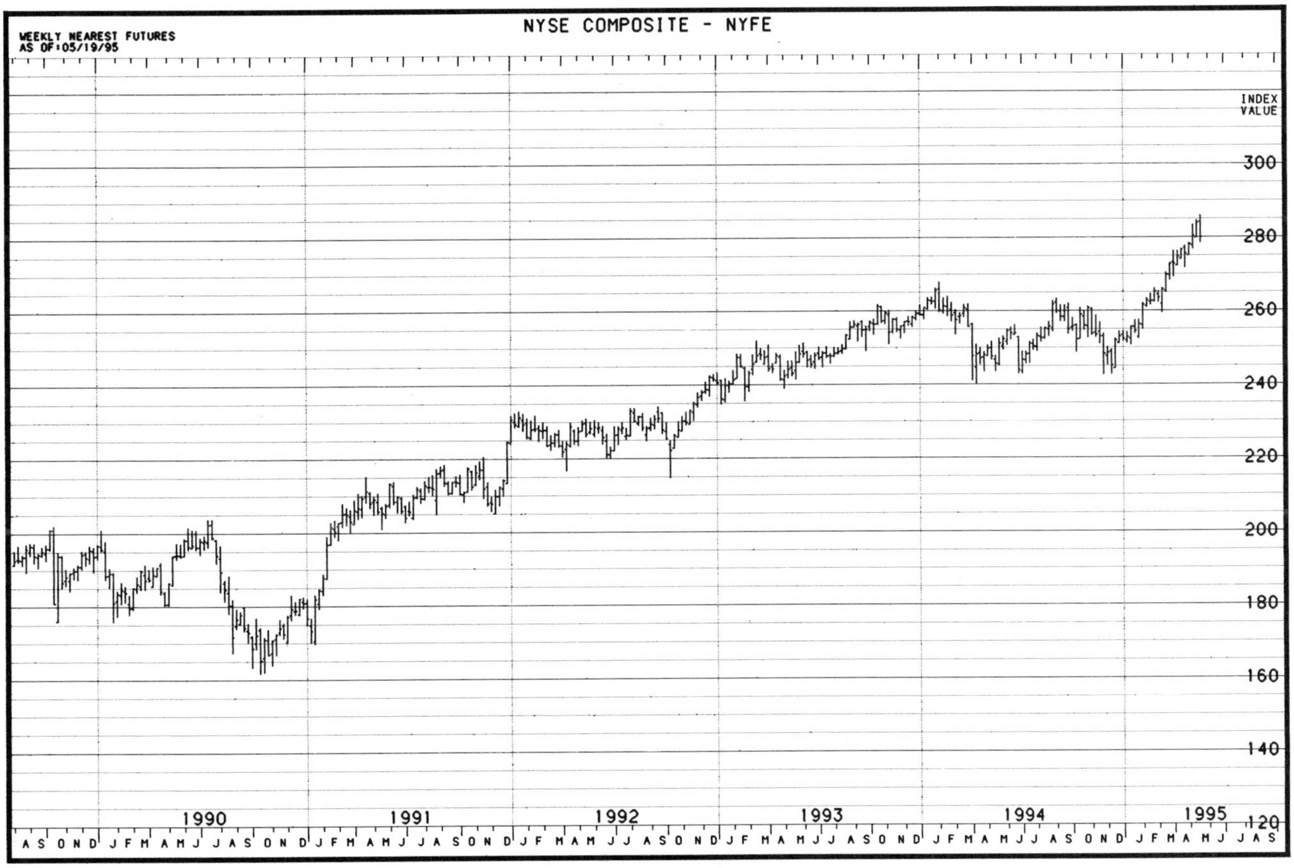

NYSE COMPOSITE - NYFE

WEEKLY NEAREST FUTURES
AS OF:05/19/95

INDEX
VALUE

300

280

260

240

220

200

180

160

140

120

1990   1991   1992   1993   1994   1995

A S O N D J F M A M J J A S O N D J F M A M J J A S O N D J F M A M J J A S O N D J F M A M J J A S O N D J F M A M J J A S O N D J F M A M J J A S

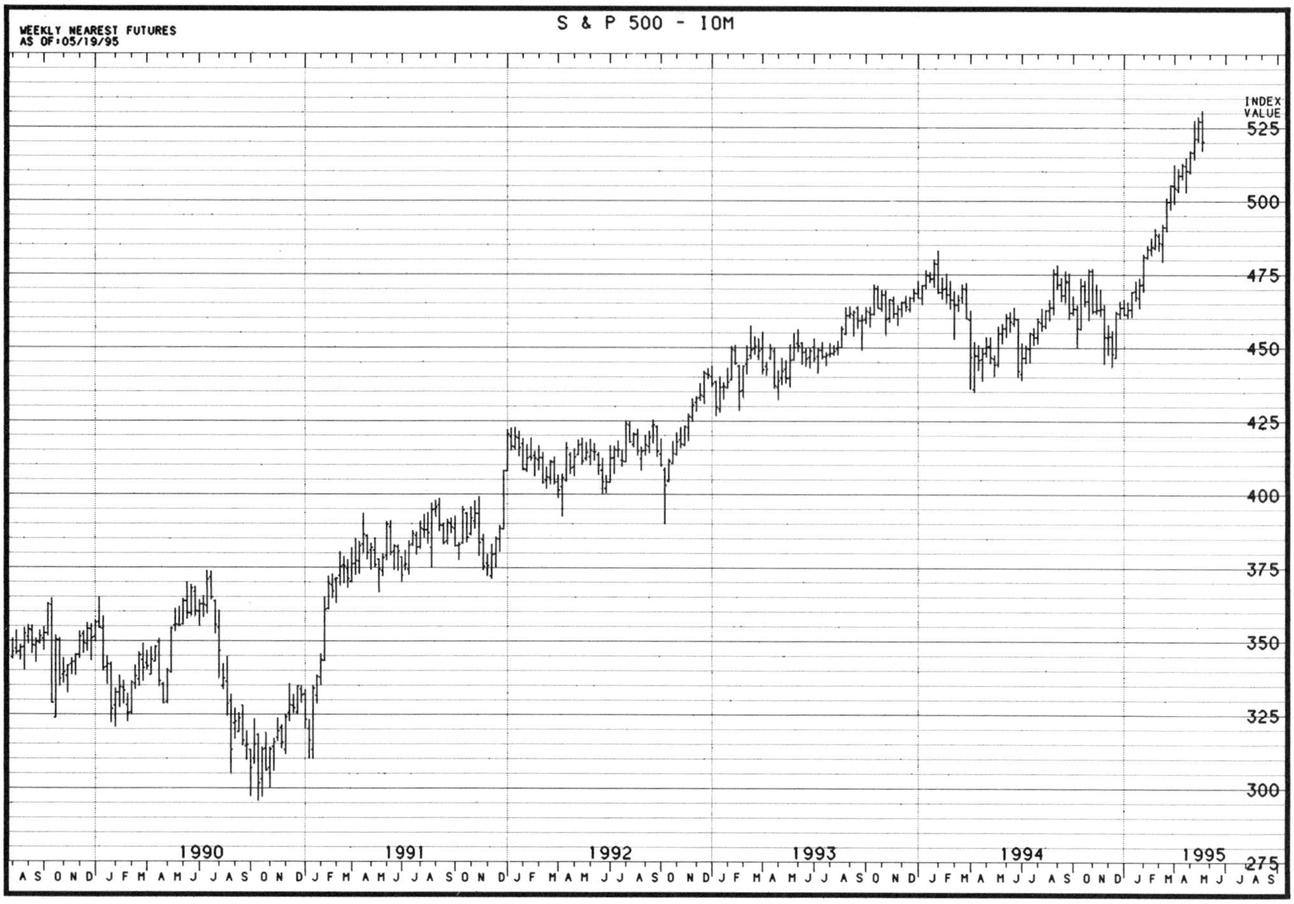

STOCK INDEX FUTURES

S & P 500 - IOM

INDEX VALUE

525
500
475
450
425
400
375
350
325
300
275

1990 1991 1992 1993 1994 1995

J A S O N D J F M A M J J A S O N D J F M A M J J A S O N D J F M A M J J A S O N D J F M A M J J A S O N D J F M A M J J A S O N D J F M A M J J A S

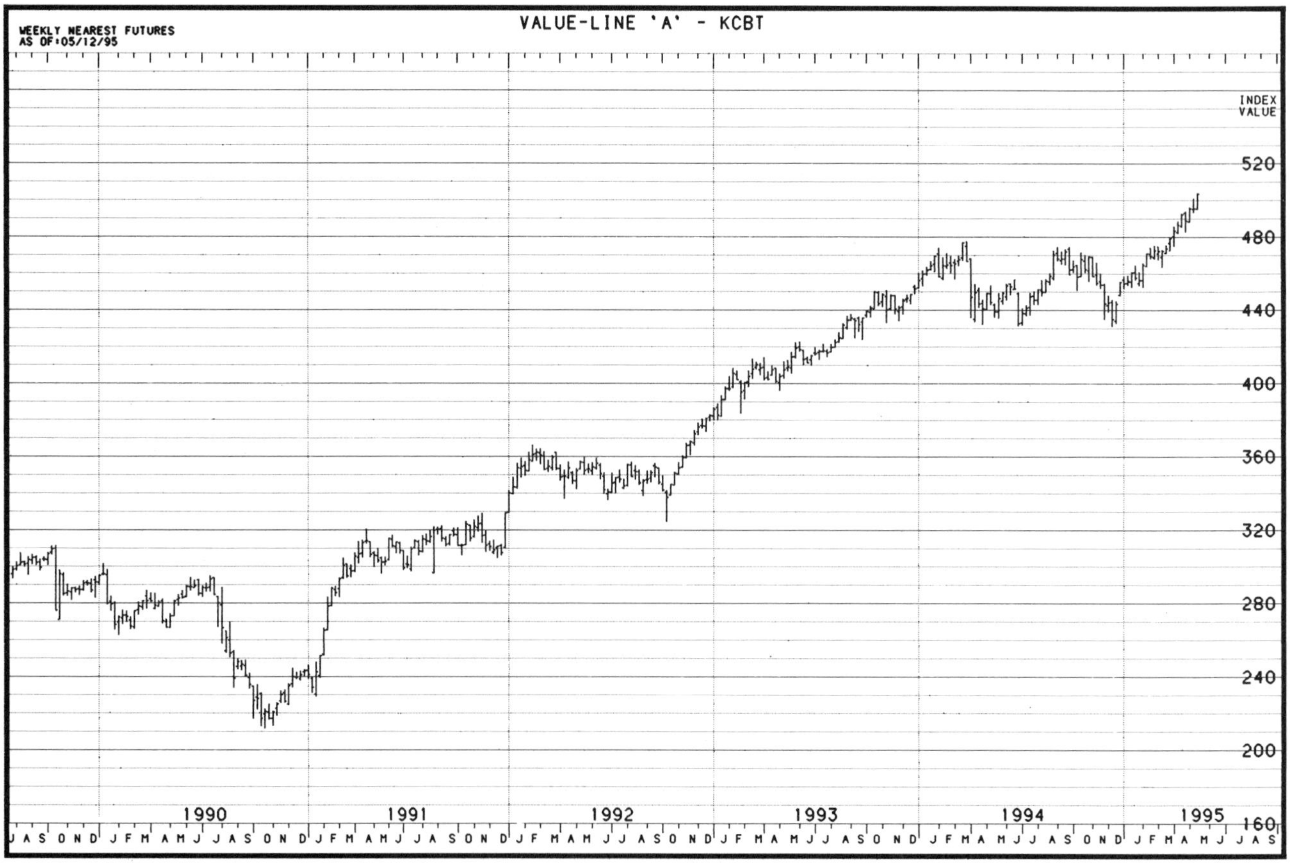

VALUE-LINE 'A' - KCBT

INDEX VALUE

520
480
440
400
360
320
280
240
200
160

1990 1991 1992 1993 1994 1995

J A S O N D J F M A M J J A S O N D J F M A M J J A S O N D J F M A M J J A S O N D J F M A M J J A S O N D J F M A M J J A S O N D J F M A M J J A S

258

Composite Index of Leading Indicators   (1987 = 100)

Year	Jan.	Feb.	Mar.	Apr.	May	June	July	Aug.	Sept.	Oct.	Nov.	Dec.	Average
1985	94.7	94.6	94.8	94.5	94.7	95.1	95.2	95.6	95.9	95.9	95.8	96.4	95.3
1986	96.6	96.8	97.1	97.5	97.4	97.6	97.7	97.7	97.7	98.2	98.5	99.2	97.7
1987	99.0	99.3	99.4	99.5	99.7	100.2	100.9	101.0	101.0	100.6	99.8	99.6	100.0
1988	99.4	100.0	100.0	100.0	99.9	100.6	100.0	100.2	100.1	100.1	100.0	100.5	100.1
1989	100.9	100.7	100.1	100.4	99.6	99.4	99.2	99.1	99.2	98.9	99.0	99.4	99.7
1990	99.4	98.9	99.4	99.2	99.4	99.3	99.1	98.4	97.8	97.2	96.5	96.5	98.4
1991	96.0	96.4	96.8	96.8	97.0	97.0	97.9	97.7	97.7	97.6	97.4	97.2	97.1
1992	97.5	97.8	98.1	98.1	98.3	98.2	98.1	97.9	97.8	98.0	98.2	99.2	98.1
1993[1]	98.9	99.1	98.4	98.4	98.1	98.1	97.9	98.3	98.7	99.2	99.6	100.3	98.8
1994[1]	100.5	110.7	101.3	101.4	101.5	101.7	101.7	102.3	102.3	102.2	102.5	102.6	101.7

[1]Preliminary.   *Source: Bureau of Economic Analysis, U.S. Department of Commerce*

Civilian Unemployment Rate   (1982=100)

Year	Jan.	Feb.	Mar.	Apr.	May	June	July	Aug.	Sept.	Oct.	Nov.	Dec.	Average
1988	5.7	5.7	5.7	5.5	5.6	5.4	5.5	5.6	5.4	5.3	5.3	5.3	5.5
1989	5.4	5.2	5.0	5.3	5.2	5.3	5.3	5.3	5.3	5.3	5.3	5.3	5.3
1990	5.3	5.3	5.3	5.4	5.3	5.3	5.5	5.6	5.7	5.7	5.9	6.1	5.5
1991	6.2	6.5	6.7	6.6	6.8	6.9	6.8	6.8	6.8	6.9	6.9	7.1	6.7
1992	7.1	7.3	7.3	7.2	7.5	7.7	7.6	7.6	7.5	7.4	7.3	7.3	7.4
1993[1]	7.1	7.0	7.0	7.0	6.9	7.0	6.8	6.7	6.7	6.7	6.5	6.4	6.8
1994[1]	6.7	6.6	6.5	6.4	6.1	6.1	6.1	6.0	5.8	5.7	5.6	5.4	6.1

[1]Preliminary.   *Source: Bureau of Economic Analysis, U.S. Department of Commerce*

Capacity Utilization Rates (Total Industry)   (Percent)

Year	Jan.	Feb.	Mar.	Apr.	May	June	July	Aug.	Sept.	Oct.	Nov.	Dec.	Average
1988	82.7	82.6	82.7	82.9	83.3	83.3	84.0	84.0	84.0	84.3	84.4	84.6	83.6
1989	84.8	84.0	83.7	84.2	83.8	83.6	83.7	83.9	83.6	83.5	83.3	82.3	83.7
1990	82.7	83.2	83.4	83.1	83.4	83.7	83.8	83.6	83.5	82.7	81.0	80.4	82.9
1991	80.0	79.1	78.4	78.6	79.1	79.6	80.0	79.8	79.9	79.8	79.3	78.8	79.4
1992	78.0	78.3	78.4	78.7	79.1	79.5	80.0	79.7	79.3	80.2	80.8	81.0	79.8
1993[1]	81.2	81.5	81.6	81.4	81.0	81.1	81.3	81.4	81.4	81.7	82.3	82.9	81.5
1994[1]	82.7	83.2	83.7	83.6	83.8	84.1	84.1	84.5	84.2	84.3	84.7	85.4	84.0

[1]Preliminary.   *Source: Bureau of Economic Analysis, U.S. Department of Commerce*

Manufacturers New Orders, Durable Goods   (In Billions of 1987 Dollars)

Year	Jan.	Feb.	Mar.	Apr.	May	June	July	Aug.	Sept.	Oct.	Nov.	Dec.	Total
1988	83.62	85.42	85.34	85.73	87.82	87.78	85.15	87.58	87.98	87.93	89.88	92.62	1,046.49
1989	90.82	89.12	86.34	89.73	87.85	86.77	82.76	90.45	87.84	87.60	109.02	110.41	1,098.71
1990	98.75	101.07	107.48	102.92	107.01	103.48	106.04	104.85	102.77	106.37	95.59	99.80	1,236.13
1991	96.39	96.04	91.52	94.81	96.68	95.46	106.62	102.27	94.89	97.83	87.76	92.39	1,145.58
1992[2]	95.63	95.19	96.92	98.62	96.46	99.55	96.42	96.39	96.80	100.85	98.63	107.31	1,182.69
1993[1]	114.64	116.99	112.96	112.61	109.77	114.50	111.08	113.68	115.01	117.87	120.10	122.20	1,381.61
1994[1]	126.86	124.58	125.24	125.61	126.94	128.04	122.78	130.42	130.95	129.76	133.26	134.58	1,539.02

[1]Preliminary. [2]Prior to 1993, shown in 1982 dollars.   *Source: Bureau of Economic Analysis, U.S. Department of Commerce*

STOCK INDEX FUTURES

New Plant and Equipment Expenditures -- Quarterly   (In Billions of Dollars)

Year	I	II	III	I	V	Average	Year	I	II	III	IV
1987	376.73	380.66	394.54	406.82	389.68	1991	496.29	487.06	491.95	529.87	528.39
1988	412.02	426.94	436.01	445.73	430.17	1992	535.72	540.91	547.63	560.16	546.60
1989	459.47	470.86	484.93	485.45	475.17	1993[1]	564.13	579.79	594.56	604.51	586.73
1990	524.07	527.06	520.80	516.54	522.12	1994[1]	619.34	637.08	651.92	645.13	638.37

[1]Preliminary.   Source: Bureau of Economic Analysis, U.S. Department of Commerce

Change in Manufacturing and Trade Inventories   (In Billions of Dollars)

Year	Jan.	Feb.	Mar.	Apr.	May	June	July	Aug.	Sept.	Oct.	Nov.	Dec.	Average
1988	39.3	46.2	36.6	43.8	47.0	72.1	63.3	91.5	78.6	-11.5	40.3	83.2	52.5
1989	82.9	34.1	29.4	70.0	81.0	32.5	81.4	33.4	2.4	31.0	43.1	-26.4	38.5
1990	21.4	-38.2	-4.2	28.6	52.2	-47.2	68.2	64.1	40.3	41.7	24.4	-65.9	15.5
1991	73.0	-38.9	-103.0	-32.7	-62.2	-55.3	-3.6	-1.8	32.8	27.0	10.0	32.1	-7.8
1992	-45.8	8.7	20.4	41.7	-1.4	51.0	36.5	23.5	-10.9	8.4	19.8	32.9	15.6
1993[1]	24.9	42.3	52.5	31.3	18.8	18.4	1.9	17.0	21.3	14.7	42.8	-7.9	23.2
1994[1]	25.3	49.8	-19.8	57.6	122.4	47.0	67.1	93.9	50.6	79.8	77.1		59.2

[1]Preliminary.   Source: Bureau of Economic Analysis, U.S. Department of Commerce

Corporate Profits After Tax -- Quarterly   (In Billions of Dollars)

Year	I	II	III	IV	Average	Year	I	II	III	IV	Average
1987	135.5	141.1	149.5	145.7	143.0	1991	189.7	182.7	189.6	207.4	210.7
1988	159.9	166.9	173.2	175.6	168.9	1992	229.7	272.3	274.3	295.9	275.4
1989	173.6	161.1	152.4	166.3	163.4	1993[1]	258.9	284.8	288.9	310.2	289.2
1990	167.1	166.1	179.4	N.A.	128.2	1994[1]	299.4	321.4	329.5		316.8

[1]Preliminary.   Source: Bureau of Economic Analysis, U.S. Department of Commerce

Productivity: Index of Output per Hour, All Persons, Nonfarm Business -- Quarterly   (1982 = 100)

Year	I	II	III	IV	Average	Year	I	II	III	IV	Average
1987	107.8	108.6	109.6	109.9	119.0	1991	107.9	108.4	108.6	109.6	108.7
1988	111.0	110.5	111.5	112.0	111.3	1992	110.6	111.1	114.3	115.3	113.7
1989	111.6	111.9	112.6	111.0	111.8	1993[1]	114.8	114.2	115.8	117.0	115.4
1990	110.7	110.7	110.8	N.A.	83.1	1994[1]	117.9	117.2	118.1		117.7

[1]Preliminary.   Source: Bureau of Economic Analysis, U.S. Department of Commerce

Consumer Confidence, The Conference Board   (1985 = 100)

Year	Jan.	Feb.	Mar.	Apr.	May	June	July	Aug.	Sept.	Oct.	Nov.	Dec.	Average
1988	90.8	91.6	94.6	91.2	94.8	94.7	93.4	97.4	97.3	94.1	93.0	91.9	93.7
1989	97.9	95.4	94.3	91.5	90.7	90.6	92.0	89.6	95.8	93.9	115.1	113.0	96.7
1990	106.5	106.7	110.6	107.3	107.3	102.4	101.7	84.7	85.6	62.6	61.7	61.3	61.2
1991	55.1	59.4	81.1	79.4	76.4	78.0	77.7	76.1	72.9	60.1	52.7	52.5	68.5
1992	50.2	47.3	56.5	65.1	71.9	72.6	61.2	59.0	57.3	54.6	65.6	78.1	61.6
1993[1]	76.7	68.5	63.2	67.6	61.9	58.6	59.2	59.3	63.8	60.5	71.9	79.8	65.9
1994[1]	82.6	79.9	86.7	92.1	88.9	92.5	91.3	90.4	89.5	89.1	100.4	103.4	90.6

[1]Preliminary.   Source: Bureau of Economic Analysis, U.S. Department of Commerce

Average Open Interest of NYSE Composite Stock Index Futures at New York   (In Contracts)

Year	Jan.	Feb.	Mar.	Apr.	May	June	July	Aug.	Sept.	Oct.	Nov.	Dec.
1988	5,530	5,760	6,013	6,785	8,372	7,400	7,003	7,668	6,689	6,816	7,600	6,419
1989	6,460	7,211	7,860	7,605	8,001	6,771	6,386	6,247	6,449	7,045	6,491	6,084
1990	6,350	6,098	5,443	4,925	5,129	5,160	4,732	6,079	6,003	5,272	4,983	4,554
1991	4,736	5,720	5,264	5,488	6,190	6,010	5,056	5,997	5,869	5,512	6,438	6,195
1992	5,216	5,290	5,469	4,575	4,867	5,858	6,491	7,049	6,647	6,034	6,430	5,890
1993	5,033	5,083	4,113	3,613	4,222	4,340	3,714	4,178	3,997	4,315	4,721	4,539
1994	4,653	4,471	4,823	3,720	3,839	3,969	3,903	3,982	4,142	4,494	4,244	4,617

Source: New York Futures Exchange

Average Open Interest of KC Value Line Stock Index Futures at Kansas City   (In Contracts)

Year	Jan.	Feb.	Mar.	Apr.	May	June	July	Aug.	Sept.	Oct.	Nov.	Dec.
1988	1,538	1,655	2,814	3,059	3,266	2,269	1,570	1,389	1,332	1,229	1,564	1,580
1989	1,394	1,189	1,288	1,262	1,421	1,513	1,615	1,710	1,522	1,250	1,200	1,182
1990	1,245	1,355	1,463	1,514	1,544	1,404	1,311	1,297	1,250	1,210	1,325	1,381
1991	1,534	2,211	2,107	2,326	2,384	2,138	1,860	1,884	1,764	1,509	1,857	2,100
1992	2,127	2,208	1,657	1,169	1,117	1,049	833	867	1,029	962	1,101	1,632
1993	1,999	1,822	1,356	934	1,188	1,118	1,100	1,181	1,039	1,057	1,302	1,461
1994	1,921	1,649	1,289	768	839	823	812	850	898	915	1,011	1,478

Source: Kansas City Board of Trade

Average Open Interest of Maxi Major Market Stock Index Futures at Chicago   (In Contracts)

Year	Jan.	Feb.	Mar.	Apr.	May	June	July	Aug.	Sept.	Oct.	Nov.	Dec.
1988	2,442	2,849	3,901	6,309	8,000	4,890	3,072	2,957	3,591	5,878	4,956	7,206
1989	7,060	6,421	5,554	6,335	6,280	4,130	6,213	5,235	4,043	7,169	4,835	5,552
1990	5,274	4,273	5,261	5,847	7,686	8,773	8,398	6,480	7,837	8,106	7,873	9,891
1991	9,705	9,856	7,894	7,739	7,715	7,130	5,519	5,501	5,042	4,296	3,877	5,118
1992	5,326	5,568	4,627	4,776	5,495	5,518	4,505	4,336	4,681	4,409	4,236	5,771
1993	5,880	5,122	3,730	3,137	3,116	2,913	2,033	1,903	1,849	2,040	2,867	3,699
1994	3,467	3,722	4,048	4,280	4,516	5,015	4,517	3,690	2,937	3,842	3,511	1,899

Source: Chicago Board of Trade

Average Open Interest of S & P 500 Stock Index Futures at Chicago   (In Contracts)

Year	Jan.	Feb.	Mar.	Apr.	May	June	July	Aug.	Sept.	Oct.	Nov.	Dec.
1987	107,367	116,765	119,444	110,154	127,090	131,406	115,722	127,385	128,930	139,741	141,059	130,387
1988	115,006	120,909	114,792	114,269	129,134	116,524	104,644	118,008	120,657	121,970	137,715	131,134
1989	129,453	136,285	137,068	136,664	140,627	128,578	116,935	129,989	129,949	126,039	126,444	117,875
1990	112,196	124,279	124,460	118,350	127,718	118,865	113,050	132,568	159,607	151,990	157,440	160,260
1991	148,112	168,803	158,994	148,106	157,103	154,848	142,665	152,067	151,609	144,279	153,898	145,324
1992	147,434	143,013	141,942	136,991	141,757	149,962	153,035	163,613	168,263	170,065	178,342	179,942
1993	164,614	173,691	178,939	174,277	182,896	190,053	182,189	191,311	208,390	195,109	201,374	196,175
1994	188,225	195,824	210,065	200,818	219,109	299,567	217,028	227,871	237,934	230,594	243,581	251,370

Source: International Monetary Market; Chicago Mercantile Exchange

STOCK INDEX FUTURES

DOW JONES 30 INDUSTRIALS INDEX
CASH

MONTHLY CASH
AS OF:04/30/95

INDEX VALUE

Stock Index Futures, Worldwide

Most of the world's equity markets during 1994 proved unexciting in dollar terms. The big loser was Mexico, down nearly 45 percent following the peso's surprise devaluation in late 1994. The major European markets posted lackluster results, reflecting relatively tight credit conditions. In the Pacific rim, the Hong Kong market was the major loser as values fell about 30 percent, reflecting uncertainties as to the nation's future if China opts to take control from the British in 1997.

However, when viewed in a longer term perspective, world equity markets have performed well since the late 1980's. Using 1988 as a base year (100), prices by year-end 1994 had almost doubled in the U.S. and Germany, and more than doubled in France. U.K values lagged but were still up about 75 percent, while Italy's and Canada's gained neared 50 percent. Significantly, Japan's equity values fell sharply in 1990-92 and the recovery since could be viewed as anemic.

In the U.S., stocks prices proved mixed in 1994 in that prices of the more seasoned, blue chip companies did reasonably well. The well publicized Dow Jones Industrial Average closed the year up 2.3 percent from 1993. However, the S & P 500 lost about 1.2 percent while the NASDAQ fell almost 4.5 percent. Trading volume reached record levels despite steadily rising interest rates during the year, which in the past would have typically siphoned traders enthusiasm away from equities and into higher yielding capital assets.

However, the rout in U.S. bond prices apparently proved too volatile for many market participants and they opted to remain in equities, especially those of seasoned corporations. Moreover, a sense of optimism prevailed towards the U.S. economy's growth despite the tightening monetary policy. Corporate downsizing was perceived as still in effect which could only enhance earnings and ultimately dividend payout.

Patience was apparently seen as necessary during 1994, and it proved rewarding as 1995 unfolded. Equities soared to record highs, paced by the blue chips, fostering expectations that the strength could easily be maintained across the equity market spectrum through the year. The Federal Reserve sees the U.S. economy slowly losing its momentum in 1995, but experiencing little more than a "soft landing" and minimal inflationary pressures; a positive setting for equity markets.

In Europe, the U.K.'s F-T (footsie) market lost nearly four percent in 1994, while French values fell nearly six percent. Germany's DAX index, however, rose nearly five percent, and Swiss prices gained nearly three percent. On a percentage basis, the Netherlands market featured nearly a 13 percent gain.

Despite Europe's mixed results in 1994, forecasts were generally positive for 1995. Most economies seemed to be on the right monetary and fiscal policy paths and inflation fears were generally subdued. Germany holds the key to Europe's recovery, perhaps to the chagrin of bordering nations, but if Germany's economic growth persists its apt to have a beneficial impact on most of Europe's equity markets in 1995.

Japan's Nikkei 225 index collapsed in early 1995, nearing its mid-1992 record low. The U.S. dollar's weakness against the J-yen is seen as cutting strongly into Japanese exports to the U.S., which may or may not happen. Contributing to the Nikkei weakness was the devastating earthquake in Kobe, Japan's 6th largest city, the recovery costs of which will run into the billions. Moreover, it could redirect Japan's economic powers to domestic needs at the expense of exports. It will take time for the jury (equity markets) to assess the longer term effect on the Nikkei.

Futures Markets

A number of stock index futures and options markets are traded in the world's major financial centers. The Chicago Mercantile Exchange CME) trades the S & P 500, the S & P MidCap 400, and the Major Market Index. The Nikkei 225 stock average is traded in Chicago, Tokyo, Osaka and Singapore. In New York, the NYSE composite index is traded. The Kansas City Board of Trade (KC) trades the Value Line index. The Canadian 25 stock index is traded on the Toronto Futures Exchange (TFE). The Sydney Futures Exchange (SFE) trades an Australian all Ordinaries share price index. In Europe, an FT-SE 100 index is traded on the London International Financial Futures Exchange (Liffe). In Paris, the CAC-40 stock index is traded on the MATIF.

STOCK INDEX FUTURES, WORLDWIDE

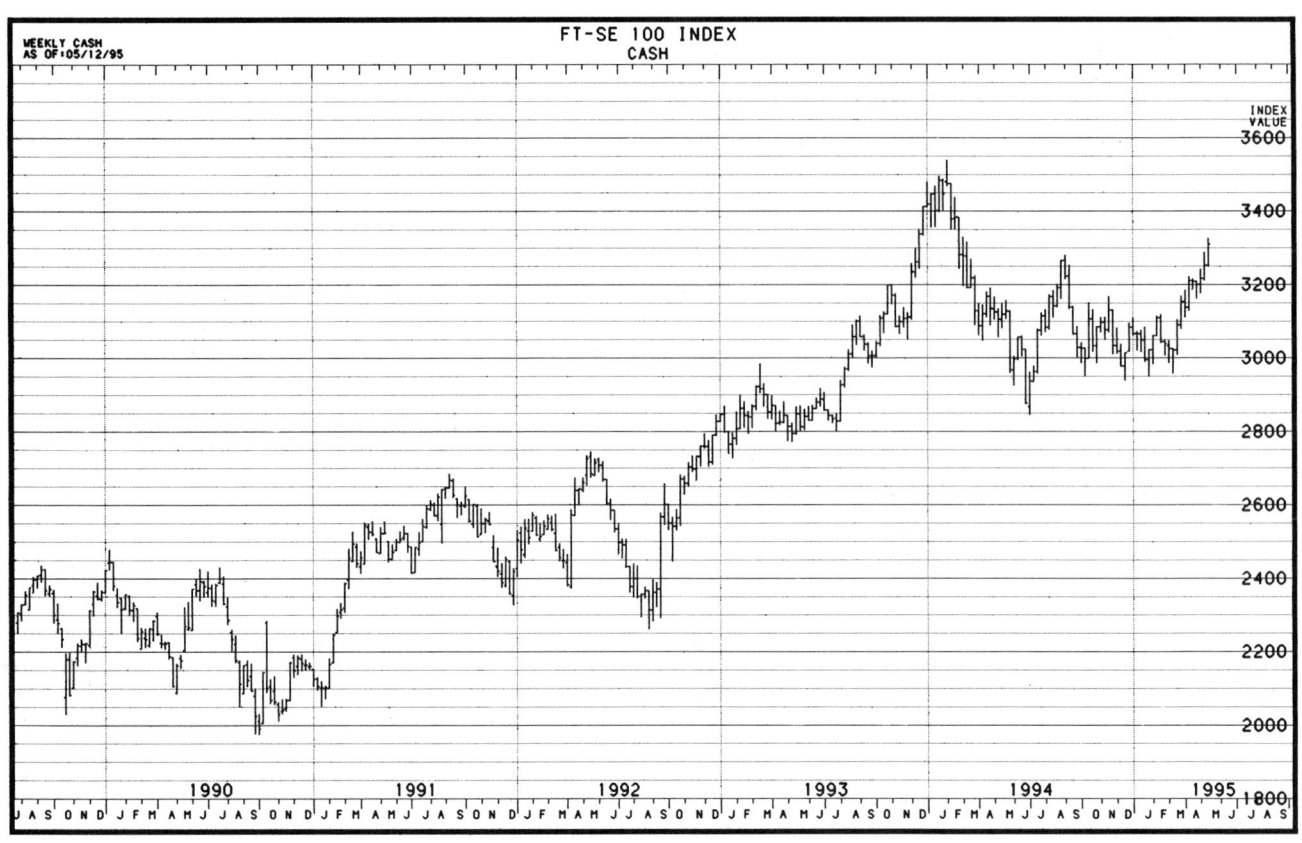

WEEKLY CASH
AS OF: 05/12/95
DTB GERMAN STOCK INDEX (DAX)
CASH

WEEKLY CASH
AS OF: 05/12/95
CAC 40 INDEX / CASH
CASH

WEEKLY CASH
AS OF: 05/12/95
TSE 300 INDEX / CASH
CASH

WEEKLY CASH
AS OF: 05/12/95
TOPIX INDEX / CASH
CASH

STOCK INDEX FUTURES, WORLDWIDE

Sugar

World sugar production and consumption in 1994/95 (September/August) were close to being in balance at 114 million tonnes (raw value). In each of the prior four crop years production either exceeded or lagged consumption by at least two million tonnes. In 1990/91 and 1991/92 world stocks increased about five million tonnes to a 23.5 million tonne carry-in for 1992/93. The buildup was then absorbed during the following two years as world usage reached a record high with carry-in stocks for 1994/95 falling back to 18 million tonnes, about the same as the projected carryover.

The stocks-to-use ratio for 1994/95 of 15.8 percent is down significantly from the early 1990s, and gives one reason for the firmness in world prices through the early months of 1994/95. However, there is a flip side to the price firmness in that it may contribute to slower world sugar use. From the mid-1970s and into the early 1990s usage grew about two percent annually, reflecting population growth, stability of the human diet and sugar's increasing role as a food staple in much of the world. Consumption may have since peaked. The less than one million tonnes gain in use during 1994/95 from 1993/94 partially reflects stagnant and even declining sugar use in the former Soviet Union and also in Western Europe, where use of alternative sweeteners is gaining. Still, these losses were offset by expanded use of sugar in the Western Hemisphere, and in Asia, which consumes about one-third of global use.

World production in 1994/95 was initially forecast at a near-record high 116 million tonnes, up 3.8 million from 1993/94. However, substantially lower production prospects for Cuba's cane crop because of the island's worsening economy, widespread drought across Europe, and a lowering of China's beet and cane prospects reduced the initial forecast by 2.3 million tonnes. India is the world's largest sugar producer with a 14.4 million tonnes crop for 1994/95, up from 11.6 million in 1993/94. India's crop is for domestic use, estimated at 14.3 million tonnes in 1994/95, suggesting a sharp reduction in imports during 1994/95.

Collectively, the EC is the largest producing region—all beet sugar—with an estimated 15.9 million tonnes in 1994/94, vs. the previous season's record high 17.4 million. France and Germany produce about half the total and vie for the top spot, but France usually has the edge. The Ukraine's 1994/95 crop fell to 3.8 million tonnes from 4.2 million a year earlier and well under the 4.4 million tonne goal the government sought. Sugar production in the Russian Federation continues to be disappointing, totaling only 2.1 million tonnes in 1994/95, vs. 2.7 million in 1993/94. Russia's beet sugar is apparently teetering on bankruptcy with low labor productivity and outmoded technology, while the government's program to renovate the processing industry lacks the finances to proceed. Russia relies heavily on imported sugar, estimated at 3.1 million tonnes in 1994/95, with Cuba still the leading supplier of raw sugar. Russia's consumption, meanwhile, continues to spiral downward, to an estimated 5.6 million tonnes in 1994/95, vs. 6.5 million a few years earlier as consumers have little purchasing power for staple foodstuffs.

In Cuba, once the world's largest producer (all cane), the 1994/95 harvested sugar crop may only total 3.5 million tonnes, half of what was produced five years earlier and the smallest crop since Castro came into power in 1959. With exports forecast at only 2.75 million tonnes from the 1994/95 crop, down 60 percent from 1990/91, Cuba will face another year of inadequate foreign exchange and the financial inability to rebuild its sugar industry in the foreseeable future.

U.S. sugar production of a record large 8.2 million short tons compared with 7.7 million in 1993/94. The beet crop reached a record large 4.8 million tons while cane totaled 3.3 million.

World sugar consumption continues to show its greatest growth in Latin America and Asia. In Western Europe and America, usage has stabilized, reflecting mature markets and the growing use of sugar substitutes. For fiscal 1995, U.S. consumption was placed at 9.28 million short tons, raw value, up 1.4 percent from 1994's 9.15 million tons and fractionally lower than the average growth rate of the past six years. On a per capita basis, U.S. refined sugar use has been stagnant at about 30 kg., vs. an EC average of about 35 kg. U.S. use has held owing to the growth in shipments to major industrial users in the baking and cereal sectors. Sugar will remain an integral ingredient in many processed food products, but HFCS use continues to gain ground, particularly in the non-alcoholic beverage industry.

About one-quarter of world production enters the export/import market. That total was 28-30 million tonnes in 1994/95, half of which was refined sugar. Six nations generally account for more than 70 percent of exports: Cuba, the EC, Ukraine, Australia, Thailand and Brazil. Global imports are less concentrated than exports. The top six importers—Russia, the EC, U.S., Japan, China and Canada—take nearly 40 percent of the total. Much of the balance goes to North Africa and the Middle East.

U.S. imports of foreign grown sugar are subject to a quota. For the period August 1, 1994 to September 30, 1995, the import quota was set by the USDA at 1,458,333 short tons. The top four exporters to the U.S. are Australia, Brazil, the Dominican Republic and the Philippines. The U.S. also imports products containing sugar that may not be subject to a quota.

World raw sugar prices firmed in 1994, averaging 11.3 cents per pound in the first half of the year, up 1.1 cents from a year earlier, basis N.Y. futures. As 1994 drew to a close, prices were at a four-year high, averaging close to 14 cents a pound, the strength reflecting in part prospects of larger imports by China and the lower Cuban and European crops.

Futures and Options Markets

World raw and white and domestic raw sugar futures are traded on the New York Coffee, Sugar and Cocoa Exchange (CSCE). World raw and white futures are listed on the London United Terminal Sugar Market. White sugar futures are also listed on the Paris International Sugar Market. Options on the No. 11 world sugar contract are traded on the CSCE and options are traded on the London FOX.

SUGAR

World Sugar Production, Supply & Stocks/Consumption Ratio   In Thousands of Metric Tons (Raw Value)

Marketing Year	Beginning Stocks	Pro-duction	Imports	Total Supply	Exports	Domestic Con-sumption	Ending Stocks	Stocks/ % Con-sumption
1987-8	23,117	103,786	27,076	153,979	27,076	106,554	20,349	19.4
1988-9	20,349	105,562	28,671	154,582	28,671	106,516	19,395	18.5
1989-90	19,395	108,805	33,167	161,367	33,167	108,746	19,454	18.0
1990-1	19,454	113,488	32,544	165,486	32,544	111,917	21,025	18.8
1991-2	21,025	116,446	30,770	168,241	30,770	113,896	23,575	20.7
1992-3	23,575	112,014	29,546	165,135	29,546	114,550	21,039	18.4
1993-4[1]	21,039	110,241	29,733	161,013	29,733	113,723	17,557	15.4
1994-5[2]	17,557	112,596	27,869	158,022	27,869	113,843	16,310	14.4

[1]Preliminary. [2]Forecast.   *Source: Foreign Agricultural Service, U.S. Department of Agriculture*

World Production of Sugar (Centrifugal Sugar - Raw Value)   In Thousands of Metric Tons

Year	Australia	Brazil	China	Cuba	France	Germany	India	Indonesia	Mexico	Philip-pines	Poland	South Africa	Thailand	United States	Ukraine[3]	World Total
1983-4	3,414	9,400	3,825	8,330	4,153	2,726	9,042	1,762	3,242	2,381	2,141	1,462	2,305	5,275	8,700	96,146
1984-5	3,548	9,300	4,627	8,100	4,301	3,146	7,071	1,709	3,436	1,767	1,878	2,514	2,533	5,289	8,587	100,267
1985-6	3,404	8,100	5,535	7,200	4,297	3,430	7,983	1,728	3,928	1,561	1,811	2,287	2,586	5,473	8,260	98,798
1986-7	3,457	8,650	5,774	7,220	3,707	3,469	9,474	2,024	3,970	1,350	1,891	2,289	2,639	6,246	8,700	103,951
1987-8	3,528	8,457	4,706	7,400	3,966	2,968	10,000	2,127	3,806	1,400	1,823	2,165	2,704	6,483	9,560	103,786
1988-9	3,680	8,582	5,312	8,100	4,372	3,003	10,150	1,889	3,678	1,600	1,825	2,240	4,055	6,089	8,900	105,562
1989-90	3,797	7,793	5,618	8,000	4,204	4,087	12,575	2,080	3,100	1,750	1,865	2,289	3,502	6,070	5,627	108,805
1990-1	3,637	7,900	6,765	7,620	4,736	4,675	13,707	2,120	3,900	1,718	2,214	2,152	3,954	6,330	5,369	113,488
1991-2	3,190	9,200	8,492	7,030	4,413	4,250	15,249	2,250	3,500	2,010	1,640	2,429	5,062	6,627	4,178	116,446
1992-3	4,367	9,800	8,300	4,280	4,723	4,401	12,470	2,300	4,330	2,060	1,567	1,600	3,750	7,109	3,965	112,014
1993-4[1]	4,460	9,930	6,505	4,000	4,772	4,750	11,730	2,480	3,780	1,809	2,270	1,244	3,975	6,963	4,190	110,241
1994-5[2]	4,987	10,500	6,200	3,200	4,288	4,000	14,835	2,500	4,044	2,000	1,700	1,750	4,700	7,430	3,800	112,596

[1]Preliminary. [2]Forecast. [3]Formerly part of the U.S.S.R.; data not reported separately until 1989.
Source: Foreign Agricultural Service, U.S. Department of Agriculture

World Stocks of Centrifugal Sugar at Beginning of Marketing Year   In Thousands of Tonnes (Raw Value)

Year	Australia	Brazil	China	Cuba	France	Germany	India	Iran	Italy	Japan	Mexico	Nether-lands	Philip-pines	Switzer-land	United Kingdom	United States	World Total
1986-7	348	981	2,057	550	1,042	692	2,166	296	256	227	1,620	270	283	246	420	1,499	25,636
1987-8	310	845	1,679	360	1,034	707	2,960	296	439	192	1,485	233	209	237	398	1,358	23,117
1988-9	236	771	2,575	460	710	432	2,700	246	479	180	577	223	160	205	338	1,194	20,349
1989-0	256	1,382	2,674	340	642	409	1,315	246	332	242	605	114	275	200	343	1,128	19,395
1990-1	256	1,164	1,350	475	434	330	2,376	220	425	192	750	58	308	197	300	1,111	19,454
1991-2	220	757	1,350	500	699	428	3,563	275	475	85	1,505	125	242	172	228	1,371	21,025
1992-3	192	950	2,002	500	599	340	5,245	300	333	110	910	137	515	149	281	1,332	23,575
1993-4[1]	154	925	905	150	684	358	3,515	300	375	144	1,040	147	679	144	416	1,534	21,039
1994-5[2]	170	604	335	200	644	376	2,295	300	180	100	641	85	503	139	450	1,209	17,557

[1]Preliminary. [2]Forecast.   *Source: Foreign Agricultural Service, U.S. Department of Agriculture*

Average Refined Beet Sugar1 (Wholesale) -- Midwest Market   In Cents Per Pound

Year	Jan	Feb	Mar	Apr	May	June	July	Aug	Sept	Oct	Nov	Dec	Average
1984	26.85	26.50	26.50	26.50	26.50	26.25	25.75	25.31	25.00	24.60	24.12	24.00	25.66
1985	23.50	23.42	23.00	23.12	23.55	23.12	23.25	23.50	23.44	23.13	22.50	22.62	23.18
1986	23.45	23.31	23.25	23.50	23.30	23.00	23.38	24.20	24.19	23.50	23.00	23.00	23.42
1987	23.30	23.50	23.50	23.50	24.15	24.44	24.50	24.50	24.00	22.85	22.50	22.50	23.60
1988	23.25	22.75	22.75	23.45	24.19	25.25	27.10	27.75	27.50	27.25	26.75	27.80	25.49
1989	28.75	29.00	29.50	29.50	29.50	29.50	29.38	29.25	29.06	28.20	29.50	31.38	29.38
1990	30.50	30.50	30.50	30.50	30.50	30.50	30.50	30.50	30.50	29.13	28.60	27.38	30.14
1991	26.88	26.50	26.50	26.13	26.00	25.75	25.50	25.50	25.00	24.94	24.60	24.50	26.57
1992	25.40	26.50	26.50	26.50	26.40	26.00	25.00	25.00	25.00	24.90	24.13	23.90	25.53
1993	23.25	23.00	23.00	23.50	23.50	23.50	25.50	27.75	27.50	27.50	27.25	26.50	24.45
1994[2]	25.75	25.50	25.50	24.50	24.75	25.25	25.00	25.00	24.70	25.00	25.38		25.12

[1]These are f.o.b. basis prices in bulk, not delivered prices. [2]Preliminary.   *Source: Economic Research Service, U.S. Department of Agriculture*

World Raw Sugar Price[1]   In Cents Per Pound

Year	Jan	Feb	Mar	Apr	May	June	July	Aug	Sept	Oct	Nov	Dec	Average
1983	5.98	6.40	6.18	6.71	9.27	10.80	10.53	10.52	9.46	9.67	8.52	7.82	8.49
1984	6.95	6.58	6.42	5.96	5.58	5.48	4.51	4.01	4.11	4.66	4.41	3.51	5.18
1985	3.59	3.66	3.78	3.37	2.77	2.74	3.15	4.35	5.14	5.01	5.53	5.37	4.04
1986	4.87	5.55	7.07	8.36	7.64	6.36	5.58	5.50	4.67	5.42	5.93	5.66	6.05
1987	6.47	7.32	7.51	6.64	6.71	6.40	6.03	5.57	5.79	6.60	7.28	8.25	6.71
1988	9.64	8.40	8.48	8.49	8.85	10.52	14.04	11.09	10.18	10.29	10.82	11.28	10.18
1989	6.69	10.49	11.54	12.14	11.93	12.63	14.01	13.96	14.13	14.42	15.02	13.52	12.79
1990	14.38	14.63	15.39	15.24	14.62	12.99	11.92	10.92	11.00	9.77	10.00	9.72	13.67
1991	8.88	8.57	9.22	8.55	7.88	9.37	10.26	9.45	9.39	9.10	8.79	9.03	9.26
1992	8.43	8.06	8.22	9.53	9.62	10.52	10.30	9.78	9.28	8.66	8.54	8.15	9.22
1993	8.27	8.61	10.75	11.30	11.87	10.35	9.60	9.30	9.52	10.27	10.10	10.47	9.58
1994[2]	10.29	10.80	11.71	11.10	11.79	12.04	11.73	12.05	12.62	12.75	13.88		11.25

[1]Contract No. 11, f.o.b. stowed Caribbean port, including Brazil, bulk spot price. [2]Preliminary.
Source: Economic Research Service, U.S. Department of Agriculture

Raw Sugar N.Y. Spot Price (C.I.F., Duty/Fee Paid, Contract #12 & #14)   In Cents Per Pound

Year	Jan	Feb	Mar	Apr	May	June	July	Aug	Sept	Oct	Nov	Dec	Average
1985	20.72	20.38	20.91	20.97	21.09	21.27	21.23	20.59	19.51	18.68	18.89	19.89	20.34
1986	20.67	21.01	20.95	20.85	20.88	20.99	20.97	20.87	20.87	21.08	21.17	21.12	20.95
1987	21.50	21.76	21.76	21.81	22.01	22.06	22.07	21.88	21.88	21.69	21.75	21.76	21.83
1988	21.83	22.11	22.16	22.16	22.13	22.54	23.43	21.90	21.77	21.74	21.70	21.99	22.12
1989	21.88	22.07	22.12	22.30	22.45	22.99	23.56	23.57	23.50	23.14	23.24	22.84	22.81
1990	23.11	22.93	23.58	23.81	23.58	23.33	23.42	23.27	23.23	23.29	23.15	22.47	23.29
1991	21.86	21.42	21.46	21.23	21.29	21.42	21.25	21.83	22.06	21.76	21.75	21.50	21.89
1992	21.38	21.56	21.36	21.38	21.04	20.92	21.10	21.34	21.55	21.61	21.39	21.11	21.39
1993	20.76	21.16	21.56	21.76	21.36	21.42	21.89	21.85	21.97	21.80	21.87	22.00	21.49
1994[1]	22.00	21.95	21.95	22.08	22.18	22.44	22.72	21.84	21.78	21.58	21.57		22.05

[1]Preliminary. *Source: Economic Research Service, U.S. Department of Agriculture*

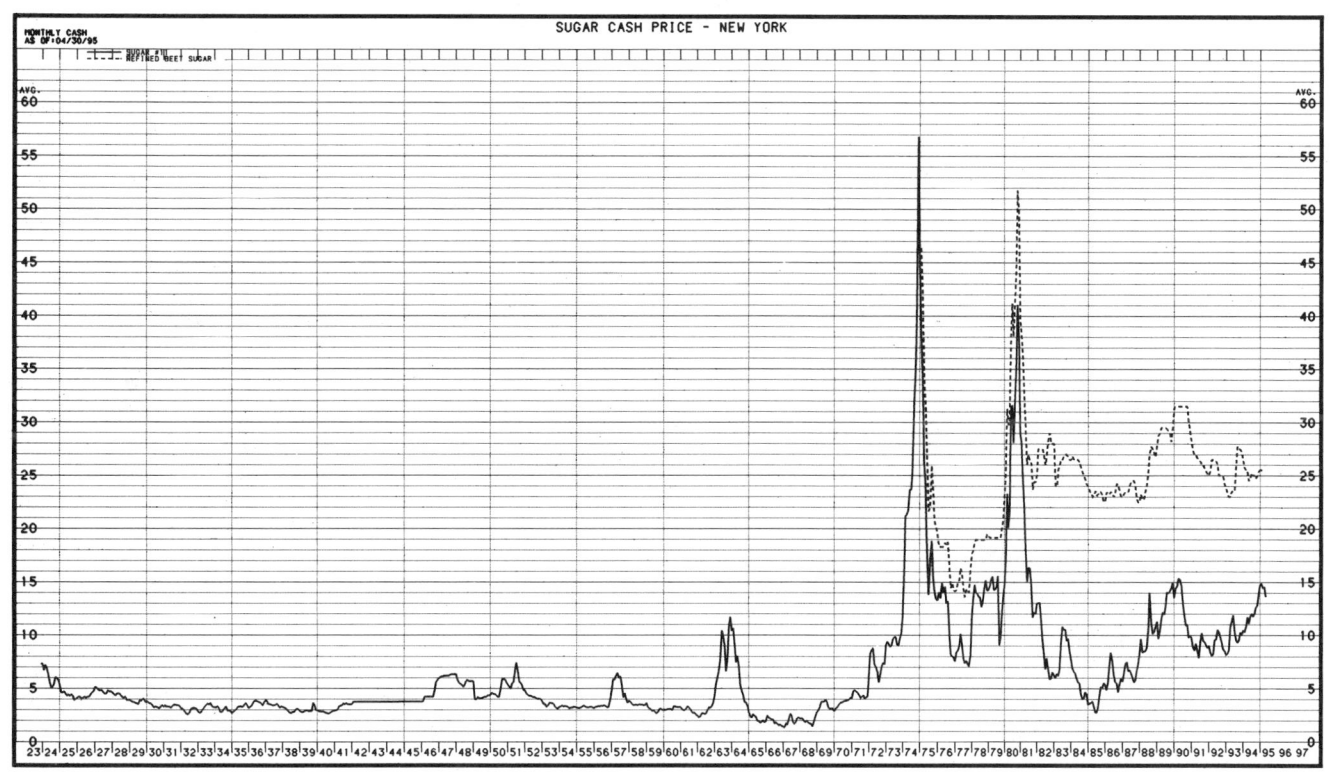

SUGAR

Centrifugal Sugar (Raw Value) Imported Into Selected Countries   In Thousands of Metric Tons

Year	Algeria	Canada	China	France	Germany	Iran	Israel	Rep. of Korea	Malaysia	Morocco	Nigeria	Russia/4	Peru	United Kingdom	United States	World Total
1986-7	680	1,119	1,507	367	161	750	229	973	661	297	578	5,057	341	1,235	1,503	27,458
1987-8	700	928	3,199	361	194	800	257	1,000	741	295	505	4,515	222	1,323	1,140	27,076
1988-9	650	711	2,462	382	630	650	-----	1,109	797	283	400	5,300	126	1,429	1,753	28,671
1989-0	840	824	1,132	357	482	774	260	1,110	841	276	396	4,550	130	1,350	2,351	33,167
1990-1	990	1,109	1,055	343	209	875	280	1,233	900	350	480	3,580	237	1,143	2,619	32,544
1991-2	980	961	1,230	398	173	825	290	1,258	921	380	560	3,850	267	1,442	2,071	30,770
1992-3[1]	980	1,095	506	487	154	780	300	1,233	900	408	430	3,500	305	1,352	1,832	29,546
1993-4[2]	990	1,205	675	439	153	950	300	1,258	920	354	510	3,150	249	1,363	1,597	29,733
1994-5[3]	1,000	1,211	1,500	486	153	820	300	1,240	1,000	350	380	3,100	240	1,405	1,838	27,869

[1]Preliminary. [2]Estimate. [3]Forecast. [4]Formerly part of the U.S.S.R.; data not reported separately until 1989-90.
Source: Foreign Agricultural Service, U.S. Department of Agriculture

Centrifugal Sugar (Raw Value) Exported From Selected Countries   In Thousands of Metric Tons

Year	Australia	Brazil	Czech Republic[4]	Cuba	Dominican Republic	France	Germany	Mauritius	Mexico	Netherlands	Philippines	South Africa	Swaziland	Thailand	United Kingdom	World Total
1986-7	2,658	2,086	240	6,630	587	1,917	1,891	691	505	666	197	875	506	1,960	366	27,458
1987-8	2,797	2,131	200	6,500	531	2,535	1,572	687	967	366	129	925	394	1,891	340	27,076
1988-9	2,860	1,371	140	7,420	550	2,804	1,264	690	410	446	210	900	428	3,004	366	28,671
1989-0	2,927	1,500	75	7,065	393	2,748	1,539	589	17	548	271	927	449	2,611	385	33,167
1990-1	2,819	1,300	133	6,800	328	2,751	1,857	621	285	538	286	757	469	2,741	255	32,544
1991-2	2,345	1,607	100	6,100	344	2,682	1,557	590	50	379	178	969	474	3,657	368	30,770
1992-3[1]	3,476	2,425	95	3,800	327	2,822	1,607	621	0	523	253	123	409	2,332	300	29,546
1993-4[2]	3,491	2,557	136	3,200	342	3,024	1,950	590	0	634	276	27	395	3,000	410	29,733
1994-5[3]	3,818	2,800	43	2,500	335	2,830	1,270	538	21	390	200	370	405	3,300	404	27,869

[1]Preliminary. [2]Estimate. [3]Forecast. [4]Formerly part of Czechoslovakia; data not reported separately until 1989-90.
Source: Foreign Agricultural Service, U.S. Department of Agriculture

United States Sugar (Cane & Beet) Supply and Utilization   In Thousands of Short Tons (Raw Value)

Year	Supply Production Cane	Beet	Total	Offshore Receipts Foreign	Territories	Total	Beginning Stocks	Total Supply	Total Use	Exports	Net Changes in Invisible Stocks	Refining Loss Adjustment	In Polyhydric Alcohol[4]	Total	Per Capita
1986-7	3,232	3,653	6,885	1,767	12	1,779	1,652	10,316	8,819	599	144	30	30	7,456	61.6
1987-8	3,324	3,822	7,146	1,272	19	1,291	1,497	9,934	8,618	440	-22	8	27	7,608	62.2
1988-9	3,316	3,396	6,712	2,025	12	2,037	1,316	10,065	8,841	516	8	53	9	7,689	63.7
1989-90	3,157	3,466	6,623	2,568	0	2,568	1,224	10,415	9,205	614	53	7	6	7,933	64.6
1990-1	3,124	3,854	6,978	2,825	0	2,825	1,224	11,027	9,503	627	-112	61	8	9,503	64.6
1991-2	3,461	3,845	7,306	2,194	0	2,194	1,524	11,024	9,547	554	-8	0	11	9,547	64.4
1992-3[1]	3,446	4,392	7,838	2,039	0	2,039	1,477	11,354	9,650	405	53	0	15	9,650	64.6
1993-4[2]	3,587	4,090	7,677	1,772	0	1,772	1,704	11,153	9,815	454	-119	0	16	9,815	65.0
1994-5[3]	3,540	4,700	8,240	1,989	0	1,989	1,338	11,567	9,975	495	0	0	15	9,975	65.2

[1]Preliminary. [2]Estimate. [3]Forecast. [4]Includes feed use.   *Source: Economic Research Service, U.S. Department of Agriculture*

Sugar Cane for Sugar & Seed and Production of Cane Sugar and Molasses in the United States

Year	Acreage Harvested 1,000 Acres	Yield of Cane Per Acre Harvested Net Tons	Production for Sugar 1,000 Tons	Production for Seed 1,000 Tons	Total 1,000 Tons	Sugar Yield Per Acre Short Tons	Farm Price $ Per Ton	Farm Value of Cane Used for Sugar — 1,000 Dollars —	of Cane Used for Sugar & Seed — 1,000 Dollars —	Sugar Production Raw Value Total 1,000 Tons	Per Ton of Cane Lbs.	Refined Basis 1,000 Tons	Molasses Made Edible 1,000 Gallons	Total[3] 1,000 Gallons
1986	796	38.1	28,936	1,375	30,311	4.37	27.3	788,678	824,724	3,281	227	3,066	1,700	185,970
1987	824	35.5	28,026	1,192	29,218	4.28	29.1	916,801	851,664	3,333	238	3,115	1,630	185,496
1988	845	35.4	28,479	1,425	29,904	4.28	29.4	836,810	877,817	3,398	239	3,176	1,925	191,208
1989	852	34.5	28,069	1,357	29,426	3.95	29.2	819,057	857,678	3,176	226	2,967	1,990	192,741
1990	794	35.4	26,475	1,661	28,136	4.07	30.8	815,630	863,497	3,152	238	2,945	1,405	178,273
1991	897	33.7	28,960	1,292	30,252	3.91	29.0	840,194	876,479	3,430	237	3,206	1,825	187,629
1992[1]	925	32.8	28,873	1,490	30,363	3.80				3,416		3,193	1,460	180,368
1993[1]	948	32.8	29,652	1,449	31,101	3.88				3,586		3,351		194,040
1994[2]	935	34.0	30,373	1,443	31,816	3.92				3,540		3,308		

[1]Preliminary. [2]Estimate. [3]Excludes edible molasses.   *Source: Economic Research Service, U.S. Department of Agriculture*

U.S. Sugar Beets, Beet Sugar, Pulp & Molasses Produced from Sugar Beets & Raw Sugar Spot Prices

Year of Harvest	Acreage Planted 1,000 Acres	Acreage Harvested 1,000 Acres	Yield Per Harvested Acre Tons	Production 1,000 Tons	Sugar Yield Per Acre Sh. Tons	Price[3] Dollars	Farm Value $1,000	Sugar Production Refined Basis 1,000 Sh. Tons	Sugar Production Equivalent Raw Value[4] 1,000 Sh. Tons	Raw Sugar Prices World[5] Refined #5 Cents Per Lb.	Raw Sugar Prices Cof., Sugar Exch. #11 World Cents Per Lb.	Raw Sugar Prices N.Y. Duty Paid Cents Per Lb.	Wholesale List Price HFCS (42%) Midwest
1985	1,125	1,103	20.4	22,529	2.72	33.80	761,236	3,033	2,835	6.79	4.04	20.34	17.75
1986	1,232	1,191	21.1	25,162	2.87	35.90	901,771	3,281	3,066	8.47	6.05	20.95	18.07
1987	1,267	1,252	22.4	28,072	3.19	38.20	1,073,584	3,998	3,736	8.75	6.71	21.83	16.50
1988	1,327	1,301	19.1	24,810	2.70	41.20	1,022,284	3,507	3,278	12.01	10.17	22.12	16.47
1989	1,324	1,295	19.4	25,131	2.66	42.10	1,058,298	3,442	3,217	17.15	12.79	22.81	19.24
1990	1,400	1,377	20.0	27,513	2.79	43.00	1,182,221	3,842	3,591	17.32	12.55	23.26	19.69
1991	1,427	1,412	20.3	28,203	2.68	38.50	1,085,728	3,729	3,485	13.41	9.04	21.57	20.93
1992[1]	1,437	1,412	20.6	29,143	3.10	41.40	1,206,000	4,114	3,845	12.39	9.09	21.31	20.70
1993[1]	1,438	1,409	18.6	26,249	2.87			4,699	4,392	12.79	10.03	21.62	18.83
1994[2]	1,476	1,443	22.2	32,008	3.12			4,376	4,090	15.12	11.57	22.10	21.05

[1]Preliminary. [2]Estimate. [3]Includes support payments, but excludes Gov't. sugar beet payments. [4]Refined sugar multiplies by factor of 1.07. [5]F.O.B. Europe. *Source: Economic Research Service, U.S. Department of Agriculture*

Sugar Deliveries and Stocks in the United States   In Thousands of Short Tons (Raw Value)

Year	Quota Allocation	Actual Imports	Deliveries by Primary Distributors Cane Sugar Refineries	Deliveries by Primary Distributors Beet Sugar Factories	Deliveries by Primary Distributors Importers of Direct Consumption Sugar	Deliveries by Primary Distributors Mainland Cane Sugar Mills[3]	Total Deliveries	Total Domestic Consumption	Stocks (January 1) Cane Sugar Refineries[4]	Stocks (January 1) Beet Sugar Factories	Stocks (January 1) Comm. Credit Corp.	Stocks (January 1) Refiners' Raw	Stocks (January 1) Mainland Cand Mills	Total
1986	1,849.9	1,845.7	4,594	3,077	28	3	7,702	8,422	197	1,189	220	523	834	2,964
1987	1,003.4	997.1	4,454	3,656	18	4	8,131	8,897	211	1,304	177	516	830	3,038
1988	1,056.7	1,024.8	4,290	3,832	20	5	8,147	8,557	184	1,546	0	401	996	3,128
1989	3,093.1	2,995.8	4,764	3,449	76	6	8,295	8,952	187	1,372	0	487	1,008	3,053
1990	2,314.9	2,242.8	4,998	3,570	39	8	8,615	9,309	155	1,412	0	381	899	2,947
1991	1,526.7	1,477.0	4,786	3,713	30	11	8,540	9,470	168	1,327	0	371	812	2,729
1992[1]	2,500.0	2,275.4	5,654	3,661	49	11	8,876	8,772	194	1,336	0	619	890	3,039
1993[1]	(5)	(5)			55		9,069	8,922	183	1,640	0	507	895	3,225
1994[2]	1,458.3	230.6			63		9,219	9,080	201	1,696	0	438	1,151	3,486

[1]Preliminary. [2]Estimate. [3]Sugar for direct consumption only. [4]Refined. [5]Combined with 1992.
Source: Economic Research Service, U.S. Depart,emt of Agriculture

Sugar, Refined -- Deliveries to End User in the U.S.   In Thousands of Short Tons

Year	Bakery & Cereal Products	Beverages	Confectionery[2]	Hotels, Restar. & Institutions	Ice Cream & Dairy Products	Canned, Bottled & Frozen Foods	All Other Food Uses	Retail Grocers[3]	Wholesale Grocers[4]	Non-food Uses	Non-Industrial Uses	Industrial Uses	Total Deliveries
1986	1,432	266	1,051	84	447	387	443	1,066	1,867	138	3,075	4,164	7,239
1987	1,513	212	1,146	91	449	398	534	996	2,040	149	3,199	4,400	7,599
1988	1,541	237	1,107	89	394	354	529	940	2,200	121	3,316	4,283	7,598
1989	1,532	215	1,187	106	426	342	637	1,026	2,051	126	3,259	4,465	7,723
1990	1,608	228	1,279	108	462	332	642	1,077	2,130	109	3,391	4,660	8,051
1991	1,632	204	1,277	100	439	331	623	1,182	2,079	88	3,469	4,594	8,063
1992	1,719	164	1,246	101	429	315	649	1,230	2,104	69	3,668	4,591	8,259
1993[1]	1,783	161	1,290	108	424	334	730	1,235	2,075	79	3,589	4,801	8,390

[1]Preliminary. [2]And related products. [3]Chain stores, supermarkets. [4]Jobbers, sugar dealers.
Source: Economic Research Service, U.S. Department of Agriculture

U.S. Deliveries[1] of All Sugar by Primary Distributors by Quarters   In Thousands of Short Tons (Raw Value)

Year	First Quarter	Second Quarter	Third Quarter	Fourth Quarter	Total	Year	First Quarter	Second Quarter	Third Quarter	Fourth Quarter	Total
1983	2,078	2,195	2,349	2,190	8,812	1989	1,923	2,051	2,181	2,185	8,340
1984	2,029	2,121	2,238	2,066	8,454	1990	1,837	1,911	2,154	2,149	8,051
1985	1,909	1,972	2,150	2,044	8,035	1991	1,878	1,955	2,173	2,057	8,063
1986	1,819	1,907	2,069	1,991	7,786	1992	1,842	2,050	2,256	2,112	8,251
1987	1,908	2,001	2,146	2,112	8,167	1993	1,913	2,044	2,328	2,105	8,390
1988	1,951	1,983	2,147	2,107	8,188	1994[2]	1,966	2,121	2,373		6,460

[1]Includes for domestic consumption and for export. [2]Preliminary.   *Source: Economic Research Service, U.S. Department of Agriculture*

SUGAR

Average Open Interest of World Sugar (#11) Futures at New York　In Contracts

Year	Jan	Feb	Mar	Apr	May	June	July	Aug	Sept	Oct	Nov	Dec
1983	71,695	82,030	81,988	88,663	89,703	98,999	93,593	94,514	88,524	80,498	83,762	84,159
1984	80,937	79,379	84,043	90,879	88,648	91,792	85,155	95,839	89,421	84,488	85,805	83,433
1985	88,595	88,208	81,731	84,538	86,437	90,837	84,727	91,241	92,998	79,755	92,348	98,473
1986	92,744	92,403	106,334	113,717	100,925	93,288	85,582	87,092	90,033	82,403	86,598	90,652
1987	98,697	103,115	95,910	93,886	96,153	98,463	97,889	98,401	100,395	99,286	103,205	126,916
1988	147,508	147,629	132,539	133,524	137,472	167,829	159,071	137,351	135,121	115,138	119,873	144,931
1989	123,554	126,504	146,798	157,254	146,878	162,097	186,211	179,077	168,840	152,276	171,354	164,757
1990	164,235	160,509	163,155	168,962	170,351	161,320	133,208	121,665	112,065	109,986	110,047	108,939
1991	124,637	129,361	114,432	115,704	110,142	105,607	106,406	107,852	102,546	91,649	90,976	93,827
1992	96,255	105,166	93,774	109,137	95,101	106,310	96,038	87,089	77,740	69,023	74,292	93,039
1993	91,426	105,147	123,023	115,400	112,085	101,843	94,296	94,932	91,312	92,832	96,246	99,592
1994[1]	108,936	123,148	137,582	115,060	117,030	126,843	106,749	118,057	141,361	140,011	171,843	191,801

Source: Coffee, Sugar & Cocoa Exchange, Inc. of New York

Volume of Trading of World Sugar (#11) Futures at New York　In Contracts

Year	Jan	Feb	Mar	Apr	May	June	July	Aug	Sept	Oct	Nov	Dec	Total
1983	207,678	249,392	198,034	261,939	396,435	396,267	272,150	329,129	283,827	214,897	231,757	160,436	3,201,941
1984	192,451	205,499	252,489	227,150	175,268	213,491	163,955	228,279	263,419	234,008	154,735	124,579	2,449,549
1985	273,316	265,967	215,540	210,046	193,527	237,904	263,842	338,816	323,387	224,856	216,340	249,398	3,012,929
1986	308,044	268,053	382,053	519,027	343,746	289,900	281,124	235,555	328,830	258,744	173,612	195,126	3,583,814
1987	387,630	381,393	323,047	381,972	278,857	313,001	248,133	235,263	367,074	331,052	268,226	337,851	3,853,499
1988	603,565	605,773	348,510	391,971	474,693	705,498	807,381	422,101	450,116	276,010	332,463	381,040	5,819,121
1989	499,199	520,018	575,486	600,852	557,386	660,521	624,969	517,295	526,834	328,469	456,485	375,927	6,243,361
1990	519,886	523,591	588,021	505,492	598,320	532,937	384,116	441,608	448,195	372,925	303,065	206,645	5,424,801
1991	313,915	510,163	388,672	477,954	286,120	534,639	309,836	352,351	366,007	240,812	253,201	234,876	4,268,546
1992	376,704	395,793	255,501	583,535	246,360	454,854	264,528	275,677	334,962	163,263	168,470	147,844	3,667,481
1993	330,474	481,506	507,370	518,292	415,283	390,261	255,581	307,181	368,194	222,082	272,579	217,142	4,285,945
1994[1]	289,593	486,222	360,787	472,388	407,343	443,002	252,012	349,079	471,899	316,330	484,943	387,620	4,719,218

Source: Coffee, Sugar & Cocoa Exchange, Inc. of New York

Sulfur

Elemental sulfur is used in the synthesis of sulfur compounds. It finds use in construction where it is added to concrete to aide in corrosion resistance. It is also an additive in asphalt for highway construction.

According to the U.S. Bureau of Mines, U.S. production of frasch sulfur for the first seven-months of 1994 was 1.595 million tonnes, up 27 percent from the same period of 1993. Sulfur recovered by petroleum refiners for the January-July 1994 period was 2.9 million tonnes, while that recovered by natural gas producers was 1.3 million tonnes. For the same period of 1993, petroleum recovered sulfur was 2.7 million tonnes, while natural gas recovered sulfur was 1.3 million tonnes. Total sulfur production reached 4.2 million tonnes, up 5 percent from 4 million tonnes in 1993.

Shipments of all sulfur during the January-July 1994 period were just over 6 million tonnes. This was an increase of over 50 percent from the like period of 1993. On July 31, 1994, stocks of all sulfur totaled 1.2 million tonnes. The previous July, sulfur stocks were only 172,000 tonnes.

Petroleum recovered sulfur stocks on July 31, 1994 were 441,000 tonnes, while natural gas recovered stocks were 190,000 tonnes.

U.S. imports of sulfur during the first six-months of 1994 were 646,000 tonnes. This represented a decline of 46 percent from the like period of 1993. Imports from Canada totaled 402,000 tonnes compared to 925,000 tonnes in 1993, while imports from Mexico were 241,000 tonnes, down slightly from 266,000 tonnes in the same period of 1993. U.S. exports of sulfur for the first half of 1994 totaled 368,000 tonnes compared to 347,000 tonnes for the January-June 1993 period.

U.S. consumption of sulfur for the first six-months of 1994 was 5.43 million tonnes, up almost 6 percent from the equivalent 1993 period. Consumption from domestic sources represented 88 percent of the total and imports accounting for the remainder. With the U.S. economy in an expansion phase, usage of sulfur should continue to increase.

World Production of Sulfur (All Forms)   In Thousands of Metric Tons

Year	Canada	China	Finland	France	Germany	Iraq	Italy	Japan	Mexico	Poland	Romania	Russia[3]	Saudi Arabia	Spain	Ukraine[3]	United States	World Total
1987	6,687	4,500	599	1,263	2,139	957	564	2,349	2,461	5,187	690	9,750	1,432	1,195	------	10,539	56,968
1988	6,908	4,750	600	1,181	2,153	1,185	618	2,432	2,378	5,200	750	10,765	1,378	1,177	------	10,746	59,160
1989	6,600	5,170	527	1,036	1,701	1,330	640	2,559	2,372	5,137	725	9,900	1,423	1,211	------	11,592	58,924
1990	6,790	5,370	636	1,049	1,550	1,180	587	2,657	2,413	4,902	660	9,025	1,435	1,147	------	11,560	58,026
1991	7,130	5,910	636	1,199	1,282	300	480	2,656	2,074	4,173	600	8,100	2,000	905	------	10,820	55,723
1992	7,487	5,470	607	1,150	1,164	600	470	2,631	2,302	3,152	585	2,150	1,630	860	1,200	10,663	52,740
1993[1]	8,247	6,030	607	1,050	1,100	800	475	2,669	1,635	2,135	580	2,100	1,600	687	1,000	10,959	52,270

[1] Preliminary.   [2] Estimate.   [3] Formerly part of the U.S.S.R.; data not reported separately until 1992.   *Source: U.S. Bureau of Mines*

Salient Statistics of Sulfur in the United States   In Thousands of Metric Tons (Sulfur Content)

Year	Native --Sulfur[3]-- Frasch	Recovered Petroleum & Coke	Recovered Natural Gas	Total	By-Product Sulfuric Acid[4]	Other Sulfuric Acid Compounds	Production (All Forms)	Imports Sulfuric Acid[4]	Exports Sulfuric Acid[4]	Producer Stocks, Dec. 31[5]	Apparent Consumption (All Forms)	Frasch	Recovered	Average
1987	3,202	3,622	2,539	6,161	1,003	173	10,539	1,599	97,954	2,316	11,323	107.15	79.63	89.78
1988	3,174	3,941	2,503	6,444	1,125	3	10,746	1,996	147,234	1,112	12,712	99.24	77.03	85.95
1989	3,888	3,971	2,539	6,510	1,190	4	11,592	2,260	145,629	1,301	12,685	100.18	78.70	86.62
1990	3,726	4,199	2,337	6,536	1,294	4	11,560	2,571	161,509	1,423	13,056	91.17	73.89	80.14
1991	2,869	4,243	2,402	6,645	1,302	4	10,820	3,020	148,872	1,194	12,932	87.05	64.17	71.45
1992	2,320	4,524	2,524	7,048	1,292	3	10,663	2,725	139,456	809	12,747	58.15	44.47	48.14
1993[1]	1,904	4,816	2,849	7,665	1,387	3	10,959	2,039	141,800	1,382	11,771	51.60	25.06	31.86
1994[2]	2,700			7,200	1,400		11,500	1,800		1,100	13,450			45.00

The "Sales Value of Shipments ------- F.O.B. Mine/Plant ------" header spans the Frasch, Recovered, and Average columns (in $ Per Tonne).

[1] Preliminary.   [2] Estimate.   [3] Or sulfur ore.   [4] Basis 100% H$_2$SO$_4$, sulfur equivalent.   [5] Frasch & recovered.   *Source: U.S. Bureau of Mines*

Sulfur Consumption & Foreign Trade of the United States   In Thousands of Metric Tons (Sulfur Content)

Year	Native Sulfur (Frasch)	Recovered Sulfur	Total Elemental Form	Total Sulfuric Acid	Pulpmills & Paper Products	Inorganic Chemicals[3]	Synthetic Rubber & Plastic	Phosphatic Fertilizers	Petroleum Refining[4]	Exports Frasch	Exports Recovered	Exports Value Thous. $	Imports Frasch	Imports Recovered	Imports Value
1987	3,938	6,209	10,147	11,092	262	412	253	7,556	793	465	777	139,431	793	806	152,096
1988	4,956	6,628	11,584	12,334	280	435	339	8,404	786	464	759	131,863	1,079	917	185,864
1989	4,536	6,955	11,491	12,563	320	423	383	8,642	683	330	694	107,126	1,086	1,174	209,465
1990	4,457	7,301	11,758	12,600	290	653	273	8,664	400	348	624	109,327	1,129	1,442	206,450
1991	3,931	7,694	11,625	12,842	279	901	272	8,311	383	448	748	119,713	1,259	1,760	241,749
1992	3,083	8,368	11,451	12,340	296	617	278	8,300	385	362	604	69,662	845	1,877	129,894
1993[1]	1,331	9,046	10,377	11,886	304	549	259	7,906	388	246	410	39,726	100	1,935	49,627

[1] Preliminary.   [2] Sulfur equivalent.   [3] Including inorganic pigments, paints & allied products, and other inorganic chemicals & products.   [4] Including other petroleum and coal products.   *Source: U.S. Bureau of Mines*

Sunflowerseed and Oil

The U.S. is not a large producer of sunflowerseed, but has a larger role in the world export market. Of the world's major oilseed crops, U.S. sunflowerseed production accounts for less than 10 percent. The world total of 22.8 million tonnes in 1994/95 was up about two million from 1993/94. World production so far in the 1990s has averaged near 22 million tonnes. The former USSR is the largest producer with about 25 percent of world output, followed by Argentina with nearly 20 percent. The world crush of sunflowerseed in 1994/95 was 19.4 million tonnes, compared to 17.7 million in 1993/94. However, unlike soybeans for which most of the crop is crushed for meal, sunflowerseed has nearly equal amounts of meal and oil produced. Sunflower meal production in 1994/95 of 8.86 million tonnes compared to 7.9 million in 1993/94. Sunflower oil production was 7.9 million tonnes in 1994/95, compared to 7.1 million in 1993/94.

Russia's 1994 sunflowerseed production of 3.1 million tonnes was about 100,000 more than expected as more acreage was planted. The additional production is expected to be exported to hard currency markets.

Planted acreage also increased in Western Europe. France expected a crop of 2.3 million tonnes, up 320,000 from 1993/94 with some of the increased acreage taken from corn. Germany's crop will also be larger by 130,000 tonnes. In Argentina, sunflower acreage has held fairly steady in recent years, but average yield appears to be on the rise with a near record large 1,786 tonnes per hectare

realized in 1994/95.

France is generally the world's largest sunflowerseed exporter with nearly 25 percent of the total. U.S. exports have fallen from the early 1980s, when levels over a millions tonnes per crop year were common. Exports in 1994/95 are forecast at only 159,000 tonnes, but still nearly 10 percent of production. U.S. exports of sunflowerseed oil, however, in 1994/95 were 200,000 tonnes, compared to 100,000 in 1993/94. The increase partially reflected the Sunflowerseed Oil Assistance Program (SOAP), under which some countries are targeted for sales. World sunflowerseed stocks are generally under one million tonnes, and the same applies to meal and oil.

U.S. sunflowerseed production in 1994/95 of 2.1 million tonnes compared to only 1.2 million in 1993/94. North Dakota, Minnesota and Kansas are major producing states. Although total U.S. usage may rise to 1.6 million tonnes from 1.2 million in 1993/94, the large crop will likely replenish carryover stocks on August 31, 1995 to 410,0000 tonnes, from the paltry 66,000 tonne carry-in a year earlier. Despite the stronger demand for the 1994/95 crop, its size and buildup of stock will likely put downward pressure on sunflowerseed prices received by farmers to a range of $8.20-$10.20 per cwt., from $13/cwt. in 1993/94. Sunflower oil prices were expected to range from 21.5 cents to 29.5 cents, vs. 30.5 cents in 1993/94. Meal prices were expected to range between $62-$82 per short ton, vs. $92.50 in 1993/94.

World Production of Sunflowerseed   In Thousands of Metric Tons

Crop Year	Argentina	Australia	Bulgaria	Burma (Myanmar)	China	France	Hungary	India	Romania	South Africa	Spain	Turkey	United States	Former U.S.S.R.	Yugoslavia	World Total
1990-1	4,027	186	389	96	1,339	2,413	684	889	556	628	1,312	860	1,032	6,559	418	23,010
1991-2	3,880	123	434	124	1,422	2,570	813	1,194	612	589	1,026	650	1,639	5,643	463	22,733
1992-3	3,100	74	578	109	1,450	2,110	765	1,185	774	205	1,343	950	1,181	5,570	412	21,442
1993-4[1]	3,850	105	442	90	1,282	1,640	702	1,280	696	362	1,215	650	1,178	5,320	435	20,865
1994-5[2]	3,700	159	520	110	1,270	2,100	730	1,380	740	438	1,100	830	1,700	5,500	440	22,675

[1] Preliminary. [2] Forecast. *Source: The Oil World*

Sunflowerseed Statistics in the United States

Crop Year Beginning Sept.	Acres Harvested In Thous.	Harvested Yield Per CWT	Farm Price $ Metric Ton	Value of Production Mil. $	Stocks, Sept. 1	Production	Imports	Total	Crush	Exports	Non-Oil Use & Seed	Total
1990-1	1,851	12.29	240	245.8	25	1,031	40	1,096	593	121	285	1,011
1991-2	2,673	13.52	192	316.8	85	1,639	75	1,800	952	163	422	1,537
1992-3	2,072	12.57	215	254.3	262	1,181	47	1,491	923	118	383	1,424
1993-4[1]	2,504	10.37	287	314.8	167	1,178	52	1,297	685	109	437	1,231
1994-5[2]	3,291	12.50	196-210		66	1,867	48	1,980	939	159	510	1,598

Supply — In Thousands of Metric Tons — Disappearance

[1] Preliminary. [2] Forecast. *Source: Economic Research Service, U.S. Department of Agriculture*

Sunflowerseed Product Statistics in the United States   In Thousands of Metric Tons

Crop Year Beginning Oct.	Stocks, Oct. 1	Production	Total[3]	Exports	Domestic	Total	Price $ Per Metric Ton (Crude Mpls.)	Stocks, Oct. 1	Production	Total[3]	Exports	Domestic	Total	Price $ Per Metric Ton 28%Protein
1990-1	17	243	275	163	91	254	520	5	293	316	5	306	311	97
1991-2	21	413	438	214	179	393	476	5	498	510	53	451	503	85
1992-3	45	331	376	266	85	351	558	6	440	451	48	401	449	98
1993-4[1]	25	274	305	210	68	278	672	2	340	345	32	308	340	102
1994-5[2]	27	376	406	250	102	352	540-584	5	463	472	36	431	467	70-90

Sunflower Oil — Supply — Disappearance / Sunflower Meal — Supply — Disappearance

[1] Preliminary. [2] Forecast. [3] Includes imports. *Source: Economic Research Bureau, U.S. Department of Agriculture*

Tall Oil

Tall oil is the major by-product of the kraft or sulfate processing of pinewood. After pulping, the resulting liquor concentrate is skimmed. Those skimmings are then acidified to produce crude tall oil.

Crude tall oil contains 40-60 percent resin acids, 40-55 percent fatty acids and 5-10 percent sterols, alcohols and other neutral components. When distilled, these resins and fatty acids are consumed in alkyd and synthetic resins, lubricants, adhesives, soaps and detergents, linoleum, flotation agents and waterproofing agents.

U.S. tall oil production during the October-December 1994 period was 320.3 million pounds, according to the U.S. Department of Commerce. For the same period of 1993, production was 457.4 million pounds. For all of the 1993-94 (October-September) crop year, U.S. production of tall oil was 1,265 billion pounds. Tall oil consumption in inedible products for calendar year 1994 was 1.044 billion pounds, some 17 percent more than in calendar year 1993. Over the last nine years, U.S. tall oil consumption in inedible products averaged 1.07 billion pounds per year. The inedible products tall oil is used in are resin and plastics, lubricants and fatty acids. The product tall oil finds the most use in is fatty acids, followed by resins and plastics and then lubricants.

Stocks of crude tall oil on December 31, 1993 were 103.7 million pounds with stocks of refined tall oil being 10.7 million pounds.

U.S. Tall Oil Consumption in Inedible Products   In Millions of Pounds

Year	Jan	Feb	Mar	Apr	May	June	July	Aug	Sept	Oct	Nov	Dec	Total
1987	109.2	107.9	104.5	100.1	100.1	112.1	109.9	99.3	104.8	111.4	94.8	87.6	1,243
1988	109.2	111.0	108.0	112.3	112.3	104.0	105.9	110.6	111.4	103.1	100.0	91.5	1,270
1989	111.5	107.7	107.3	102.9	102.9	105.0	101.6	111.9	88.8	88.8	84.3	82.8	1,196
1990	100.4	105.9	91.2	86.5	86.5	84.6	78.5	82.4	69.1	69.7	78.4	78.2	1,017
1991	---------	249.1	----------	-----------	237.3	-----------	------------	223.1	------------	------------	230.5	-----------	940
1992	77.8	77.5	73.2	67.6	77.8	74.8	71.5	78.4	77.1	78.9	63.8	69.2	884
1993	68.6	64.8	73.1	68.1	76.3	68.8	79.0	78.1	78.0	75.4	78.4	83.2	892
1994[1]	93.5	75.2	93.0	86.8	85.5	89.8	80.7	88.8	95.6	87.9	78.3	88.5	1,044

[1]Preliminary.   *Source: Bureau of Census, U.S. Department of Commerce*

Tall Oil Production in the United States   In Millions of Pounds

Crop Year		Oct	Nov	Dec	Jan	Feb	Mar	Apr	May	June	July	Aug	Sept	Total
1988-9	Crude	120.9	122.8	125.9	144.2	121.9	142.4	133.2	123.7	132.0	123.7	138.4	112.6	1,541.7
	Refined	9.8	8.7	8.0	9.5	7.5	9.4	9.1	8.0	9.5	8.6	8.3	7.0	103.4
1989-90	Crude	123.2	121.2	107.0	92.1	120.0	137.1	134.6	126.7	122.1	118.0	120.6	102.4	1,437.0
	Refined	9.3	8.1	6.6	6.0	5.2	4.8	5.5	4.7	4.8	5.3	3.3	5.7	69.3
1990-1	Crude	120.8	119.1	126.5	-----------	389.5	-----------	-----------	362.4	-----------	----------	375.0	-----------	1,469.6
	Refined	5.6	6.2	4.2	-----------	15.7	-----------	-----------	15.3	-----------	------------	17.6	-----------	64.6
1991-2	Crude	------------	342.7	------------	131.4	121.5	131.2	133.2	121.9	129.8	130.6	129.9	119.7	1,372.2
	Refined	------------	15.7	------------	5.4	5.6	6.2	W	W	W	W	W	W	W
1992-3	Crude	120.2	114.7	122.7	119.4	128.4	142.1	131.8	120.0	126.6	117.0	104.3	117.3	1,347.2
1993-4[1]	Crude	107.5	120.7	124.6	119.5	108.6	139.4	123.3	112.1	102.7	102.3	104.3	110.5	1,265.0
1994-5[1]	Crude	104.6	107.8	107.9										320.3

[1]Preliminary.   *Source: Bureau of the Census*

Tall Oil Stocks in the United States   In Millions of Pounds

Crop Year		Oct. 1	Nov. 1	Dec. 1	Jan. 1	Feb. 1	Mar. 1	Apr. 1	May 1	June 1	July 1	Aug. 1	Sept. 1
1988-9	Crude	109.7	107.6	103.1	106.4	120.1	122.5	125.9	127.7	134.1	127.9	133.4	125.0
	Refined	22.3	22.1	23.4	23.2	25.3	26.5	27.0	28.3	25.8	25.9	25.8	22.5
1989-90	Crude	112.7	130.4	145.2	133.9	114.0	112.6	106.6	114.1	106.9	103.5	108.3	104.8
	Refined	23.4	25.8	28.5	23.3	22.2	21.4	20.3	16.6	17.2	17.2	18.0	15.7
1990-1	Crude	101.5	83.1	76.6	-----------	144.5	-----------	-----------	119.8	-----------	-----------	140.4	-----------
	Refined	15.3	34.0	35.8	-----------	29.7	-----------	-----------	30.2	-----------	-----------	33.9	-----------
1991-2	Crude	-----------	139.1	-----------	188.9	153.9	163.1	163.2	156.9	158.4	161.0	190.7	186.1
	Refined	-----------	36.0	-----------	35.0	35.0	35.7	36.2	13.5	16.1	15.2	15.9	28.4
1992-3	Crude	173.3	167.5	143.7	137.8	162.5	170.8	184.7	187.3	165.3	179.2	173.1	149.9
	Refined	17.4	18.1	13.8	14.1	14.0	12.6	13.7	9.4	7.7	7.3	7.5	7.2
1993-4[1]	Crude	132.8	124.0	113.0	103.7	109.5	109.7	118.2	124.4	112.6	105.3	101.1	97.5
	Refined	7.0	7.5	8.5	10.7	13.7	13.5	13.5	12.0	10.2	9.7	11.5	10.9
1994-5[1]	Crude	86.3	82.6	94.1	103.5								
	Refined	12.0	14.4	16.3	13.5								

[1]Preliminary.   *Source: Bureau of Census, U.S. Department of Commerce*

Tallow and Greases

World production of tallow and greases in 1994 was forecast by the USDA at 6.44 million tonnes. This represented less than a one percent increase from 1993 output of 6.39 million. The U.S. is by far the world's largest producer of tallow and grease, with 1994 output forecast to be 3.27 million tonnes, marginally higher than the 1993 production of 3.25 million tonnes. Australia was the second largest producer of tallow and grease with 1994 output forecast at 470,000 tonnes. The large livestock producing countries of South America are also important producers. Brazilian production was estimated at 282,000 tonnes, up three percent. Argentine production was forecast at 276,000 tonnes, up two percent. Other important producers include the United Kingdom with expected output of 216,000 tonnes and Canada with 210,000 tonnes. Total European Union production was put at 1.21 million tonnes, about the same as in 1993.

The U.S. is the largest exporter of tallow and grease. U.S. exports in 1994 were forecast at 1.2 million tonnes, up two percent. Australian exports were forecast at 281,000 tonnes, down three percent. New Zealand exports virtually all of its production. Their 1994 exports were forecast at 120,000 tonnes. Canadian exports were predicted to increase close to 18 percent to 200,000 tonnes.

The major importer of tallow and grease is Mexico. Total imports in 1994 were forecast at 230,000 tonnes, up five percent. European Union exports, excluding intra-trade, were put at 422,000 tonnes, up two percent from 1993. South Korea was forecast to import 125,000 tonnes of tallow and grease in 1994 while Japanese import needs were estimated at 105,000 tonnes.

World consumption of tallow and grease in 1994 was forecast at 6.26 million tonnes, up less than one percent from 1993. The U.S. is the largest user with 1994 consumption forecast at 2.1 million tonnes. The European Union was forecast to consume 1.67 million tonnes. Other major users include Brazil, Argentina, Mexico, South Korea and Japan.

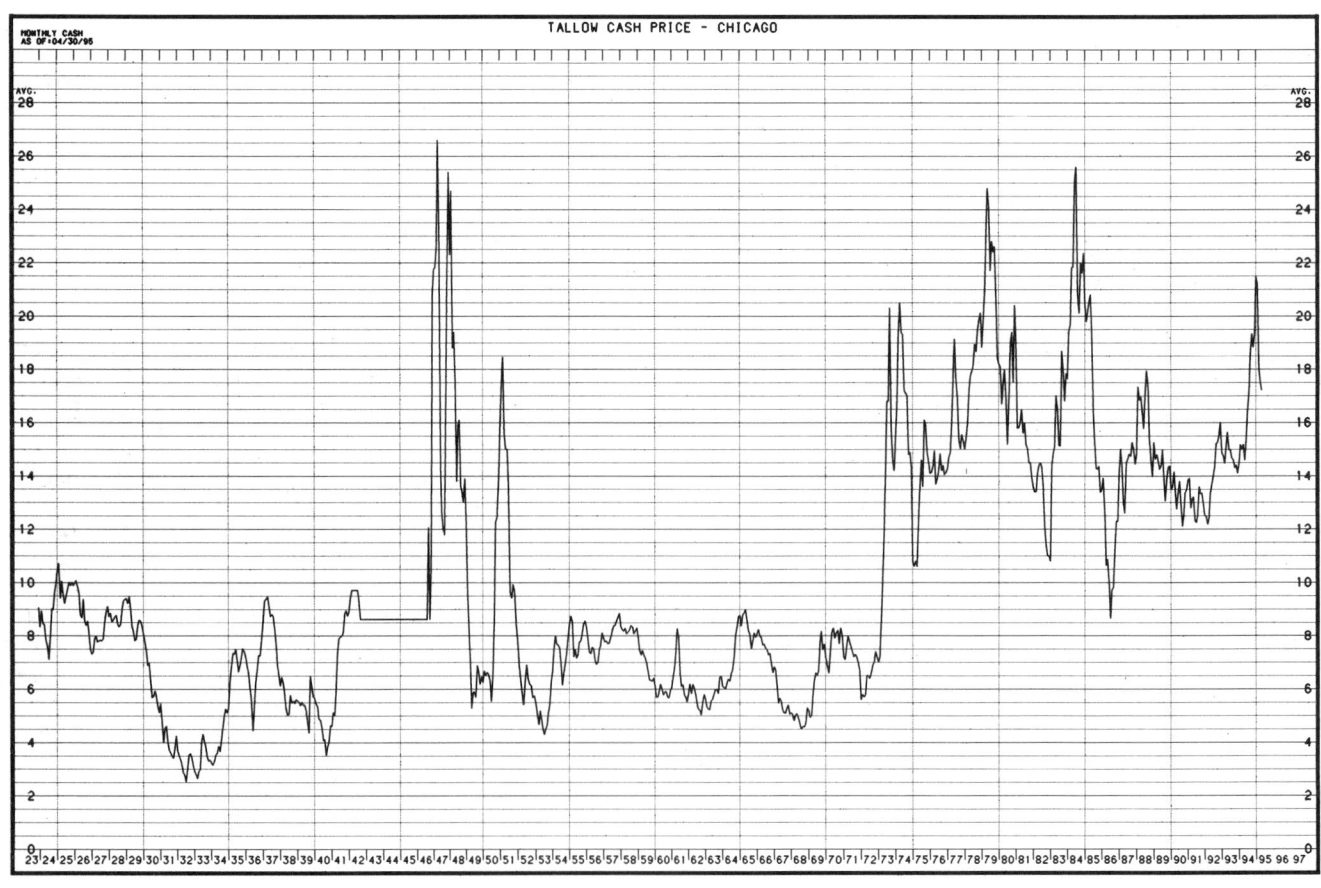

TALLOW CASH PRICE - CHICAGO

World Production of Tallow and Greases (Edible and Inedible)   In Thousands of Metric Tons

Year	Argen- tina	Aus- tralia	Brazil	Canada	Den- mark	France	Ger- many	Italy	Japan	Korea	Rep.of Mexico	Nether- lands	New Zealand	Russia[4]	United Kingdom	United States	World Total
1986	305	328	200	217	69	175	256	115	215	25	58	119	126	375	220	3,375	6,580
1987	289	350	170	205	70	182	282	110	219	46	43	127	132	380	233	3,190	6,420
1988	279	456	190	200	65	186	278	100	218	53	54	125	146	370	200	3,382	6,726
1989	278	489	272	203	83	179	280	90	168	60	65	125	133	400	207	3,212	6,614
1990	282	540	355	199	115	180	290	95	163	80	58	142	110	118	245	3,206	6,561
1991	285	530	348	193	122	185	270	96	164	85	55	150	132	108	230	3,242	6,608
1992	268	472	376	212	129	275	197	99	153	121	58	145	134	106	225	3,309	6,712
1993[1]	260	526	368	209	118	240	185	98	165	115	59	163	132	114	212	3,248	6,656
1994[2]	250	519	355	221	120	235	181	98	162	125	60	161	129	120	215	3,270	6,662
1995[3]	250	531	373	230	120	240	178	98	162	140	62	155	128	125	220	3,300	6,748

[1]Preliminary. [2]Estimate. [3]Forecast. [4]Formerly part of the U.S.S.R.; data not reported separately until 1990.
Source: Foreign Agricultural Service, U.S. Department of Agriculture

Salient Statistics of Tallow and Greases (Inedible) in the United States   In Millions of Pounds

Year	Supply Pro- duction	Supply Stocks Jan. 1	Supply Total	Exports	Consumption Soap	Consumption Feed	Consumption Total	Wholesale Prices, ¢ Per Lb. Edible, (Loose) Chicago	Wholesale Prices, ¢ Per Lb. Inedible, Chicago No. 1
1986	5,543	362	5,905	2,562	482	1,604	2,917	13.5	9.0
1987	5,602	316	5,918	2,491	571	1,727	3,082	15.6	14.9
1988	6,158	407	6,565	2,807	461	1,864	3,147	17.9	16.6
1989	5,848	399	6,247	2,679	368	1,919	3,194	15.8	14.4
1990	5,217	374	6,097	2,267	402	2,000	3,061	14.6	13.7
1991	5,759	357	6,116	1,936	392	1,748	2,949	14.3	13.3
1992[1]	5,768	349	6,117	2,276	334	1,954	3,050	15.5	14.3
1993[2]	6,621	309	6,930	2,117	300	1,995	3,018	16.2	14.9

[1]Preliminary. [2]Estimate. *Sources: Economic Research Service, U.S. Department of Agriculture; Bureau of Census, U.S. Department of Commerce*

Edible Tallow: Supply and Disappearance in the U.S.   In Millions of Pounds

Year	Supply Stocks Jan. 1	Supply Pro- duction	Supply Total	Disappearance Domestic	Disappearance Exports	Disappearance Total	Direct Use	Baking or Frying Fats	Per Capita (Lbs.)
1986	41	1,523	1,564	1,469	62	1,531	428	1,016	6
1987	33	1,258	1,291	1,186	65	1,251	220	905	5
1988	40	1,296	1,336	1,149	139	1,288	197	859	5
1989	48	1,167	1,215	975	202	1,177	273	774	5
1990	38	1,207	1,245	944	270	1,214	142	703	5
1991	37	1,251	1,299	975	285	1,261	353	498	4
1992	39	1,527	1,574	1,209	333	1,538	612	427	5
1993[1]	33	1,425	1,458	1,072	310	1,382	510	404	4

[1]Preliminary. *Source: Economic Research Service, U.S. Department of Agriculture; Bureau of Census, U.S. Department of Commerce*

Average Wholesale Price of Tallow, Inedible, No. 1 Packers (Prime), Delivered, Chicago   In Cents Per Lb.

Year	Jan	Feb	Mar	Apr	May	June	July	Aug	Sept	Oct	Nov	Dec	Average
1986	12.00	11.80	9.40	8.90	8.70	7.60	7.80	7.80	8.10	8.40	8.50	9.50	9.04
1987	15.84	15.15	13.03	12.98	15.42	14.73	15.17	14.50	15.53	15.23	15.17	15.56	14.86
1988	18.00	17.08	17.25	16.17	15.93	17.18	18.81	17.44	16.00	15.02	14.18	16.33	16.62
1989	14.90	16.00	14.86	14.60	14.70	15.10	14.48	13.52	14.13	15.25	15.50	15.50	14.88
1990	14.87	14.50	14.47	13.77	13.66	NA	13.50	10.12	12.00	13.42	14.09	14.75	13.56
1991	13.88	14.28	14.43	14.80	13.02	12.36	12.96	14.00	13.50	13.68	13.08	12.50	13.54
1992	12.25	12.63	12.68	13.25	13.75	13.98	14.75	15.42	15.25	15.73	16.75	16.00	14.37
1993	15.09	14.69	15.24	15.94	15.00	15.11	14.95	14.58	14.54	14.68	14.50	14.63	14.91
1994[1]	15.24	15.15	15.50	14.99	15.60	16.27							15.46

Source: Economic Research Service, U.S.D.A.

Tea

World tea production in 1993 reached 2.62 million tonnes, an eight percent increase from the 1992 total of 2.41 million. India was the largest producer with 758,100 tonnes, almost eight percent more than 1992. This represents an all time high and reflects favorable growing conditions in almost all producing regions, according to the USDA. North Indian production was six percent higher at 578,721 tonnes while South Indian production increased 13 percent to 179,342 tonnes. The Indian tea industry has set a production goal of 800,000 tonnes for 1995. India's domestic consumption accounts for about two-thirds of the crop. India exported about 180,000 tonnes of tea in 1993, a 6 percent increase from 1992. Of concern to the Indian tea industry are declining sales to Russia. Before the breakup of the Soviet Union, that country took well over half of India's tea exports under bilateral trade agreements. In 1992, Indian tea exports to Russia had fallen to 45,000 tonnes.

Chinese tea production in 1993 was estimated at 600,000 tonnes compared to 560,000 tonnes in 1992. Exports increased almost 15 percent to 201,454 tonnes. China is the principal supplier of tea to the U.S. with 28 percent of the market in 1993. The U.S. imported 24,035 tonnes of tea from China in 1993, about unchanged from 1992.

Sri Lanka's tea production in 1993 increased nearly 30 percent to 231,900 tonnes. The 1992 crop was damaged by drought. Part of the increase in production is attributable to the partial privatization of tea estates. Government-owned plantations have posted mounting losses due to corruption, waste and mismanagement. The government is making a strong effort to return the tea industry to the pri-

vate sector. Sri Lanka relies heavily on the export sector since domestic consumption accounts for about 10 percent of production. Tea exports in 1993 were 210,000 tonnes, almost 18 percent more than in 1992. There were increased sales to Russia, Syria and the United Kingdom. Shipments to Egypt, Iran and Saudi Arabia fell as buyers in those countries moved to lower-prices teas from India and Vietnam. The United Nation's embargo on sales to Iraq has had an adverse effect on Sri Lanka's exports. Prior to the embargo, Iraq was the second largest export market for Sri Lanka's tea.

U.S. per capita consumption of tea in 1993 was estimated at 6.9 gallons compared to 6.8 gallons in 1992. In 1985, per capita consumption was 7.3 gallons. U.S. retail food store tea sales in 1993 were estimated at $1.12 billion, up from 1992 sales of $1.04 billion. Liquid teas have become much more popular in recent years with their market share more than doubling in 1993. About 80 percent of U.S. consumption takes the form of iced tea. Efforts to increase tea drinking have been slowed by competition from beverages such as soft drinks, bottles water, fruit juices and alcoholic beverages. Liquid ready-to-drink teas have been successful in gaining market share in the cold beverage market.

World tea prices declined in 1993 due to large quantities of low-quality tea entering export markets. Average London auction prices for all teas in 1993 fell to 84.6 cents per pound from 91.3 cents in 1992. During January-May 1994, prices averaged 81.2 cents.

World Tea Production, in Major Producing Countries   In Thousands of Metric Tons

Year	Argentina	Bangla-desh	China	India	Indonesia	Iran	Japan	Kenya	Malawi	Mozam-bique	Sri Lanka	Taiwan	Tanzania	Turkey	Former USSR[2]	Grand Total
1983	45.0	43.7	401.0	581.5	111.5	25.0	102.7	119.7	32.0	14.0	180.0	24.3	15.6	101.0	145.6	2,035
1984	46.0	38.2	414.0	639.9	126.2	46.8	92.5	116.2	37.5	11.0	209.2	24.4	16.5	113.7	151.1	2,194
1985	35.0	43.3	432.0	656.2	132.3	41.5	95.5	147.1	40.0	7.0	215.3	23.2	16.5	137.1	152.1	2,292
1986	40.0	37.6	461.0	620.8	129.5	48.5	93.6	143.3	39.0	5.0	212.7	23.9	15.1	148.3	146.6	2,285
1987	43.0	40.6	508.0	665.3	126.1	45.6	96.3	155.8	31.9	3.0	214.6	25.6	14.5	140.7	120.0	2,356
1988	44.0	43.6	545.0	700.0	133.8	55.6	89.8	164.0	40.2	1.5	22.8	23.6	14.6	166.4	118.0	2,490
1989	48.0	39.1	535.0	688.1	141.4	46.0	90.5	180.6	39.5	1.8	208.0	22.1	17.0	141.6	119.2	2,444
1990	50.0	45.9	540.0	720.3	145.2	44.0	89.9	197.0	39.1	2.0	234.1	22.3	18.4	126.7	123.2	2,528
1991	40.0	45.2	542.0	741.7	133.4	45.0	87.9	203.6	40.5	2.0	241.6	21.4	19.3	135.3	110.0	2,541
1992	44.0	48.3	560.0	703.9	145.7	45.0	92.1	188.1	28.1	1.5	178.9	20.7	18.4	156.3	55.0	2,411
1993[1]	44.0	51.3	600.0	758.1	140.0	45.0	90.0	211.3	39.5	1.5	231.9	21.0	23.2	150.0	75.0	2,618

[1]Preliminary.   [2]Mostly Georgia and Azerbaijan.   *Source: Foreign Agricultural Service, U.S. Department of Agriculture*

World Tea Exports from Producing Countries   In Metric Tons

Year	Argentina	Bangla-desh	Brazil	China	India	Indonesia	Japan	Kenya	Malawi	Mozam-bique	New Guinea	Sri Lanka	Taiwan	Vietnam	Zimbabwe	Grand Total
1983	44,733	29,989	8,135	125,072	208,476	63,603	2,124	100,645	35,833	13,440	7,234	157,786	11,572	10,000	8,267	867,718
1984	42,102	23,100	9,301	145,346	217,400	85,664	2,787	91,198	37,208	7,550	7,530	204,226	11,862	11,000	9,835	942,733
1985	30,657	30,306	8,807	136,864	214,021	90,121	1,805	126,086	37,777	3,190	7,025	197,580	9,127	12,000	10,036	957,083
1986	36,279	27,675	10,851	172,028	203,149	78,957	1,261	116,456	40,189	1,820	5,213	207,567	9,011	12,500	11,819	997,534
1987	33,647	21,606	8,073	174,274	201,891	90,422	1,107	134,779	33,404	2,100	5,491	200,774	7,375	13,000	10,105	978,368
1988	34,258	26,187	9,686	198,289	200,956	92,687	1,260	138,201	36,961	830	5,834	219,710	7,631	14,800	14,190	1,039,313
1989	43,335	23,426	9,400	204,584	211,622	114,709	671	163,188	39,891	800	5,439	203,763	6,745	15,016	12,768	1,121,251
1990	45,966	26,970	7,976	195,471	209,085	110,964	322	169,586	43,039	700	5,375	215,251	5,853	24,698	11,507	1,141,026
1991	36,029	25,381	7,347	184,872	201,720	110,218	289	175,557	33,973	1,339	2,297	210,823	5,317	15,370	11,304	1,072,744
1992[1]	36,529	27,160	8,211	175,526	169,105	121,243	290	166,518	37,983	1,000	2,500	177,801	5,296	18,000	6,000	1,010,557
1993[2]				201,454	180,000		328	181,277				210,000				

[1]Preliminary.   [2]Estimate.   *Source: Foreign Agricultural Service, U.S. Department of Agriculture*

TEA

United States Imports of Tea   In Metric Tons

Year	Argentina	Brazil	China	Germany	India	Indonesia	Kenya	Malawi	Nether-lands	Papua New Guinea	Sri Lanka	Total	Black Teas	Green Teas	Oolong Teas	Mixed Teas	Total
1981	10,345	2,806	7,962	205	4,159	13,913	6,762	2,147	5,936	200	12,216	83,819	80,857	3,754	541	755	85,907
1982	10,011	3,537	7,143	289	4,724	14,676	5,498	2,356	7,668	56	12,991	86,299	78,273	3,290	541	768	82,872
1983	15,114	3,926	6,399	646	2,894	14,352	4,536	1,288	4,657	25	8,106	77,318	71,709	2,371	517	551	75,148
1984	18,142	3,611	9,622	1,161	3,758	15,501	3,932	915	4,792	76	9,383	88,256	82,486	5,385	646	634	89,151
1985	15,234	4,281	10,877	3,046	2,943	12,844	4,152	935	4,213	62	9,796	79,206	69,210	6,570	811	618	77,209
1986	16,367	5,554	16,925	2,535	3,884	16,270	4,330	1,205	4,053	14	7,756	90,549	81,036	5,543	722	471	87,772
1987	15,897	5,418	16,728	3,422	3,042	10,395	4,145	1,991	3,258	75	4,799	77,391	70,881	6,590	770	496	78,737
1988	13,815	4,147	22,950	5,198	3,625	14,380	6,198	1,645	3,843	321	5,919	90,144	79,430	4,547	689	572	85,238
1989	17,219	4,735	19,641	5,731	2,914	12,293	6,005	1,871	2,508	571	5,693	89,582	78,898	5,870	804	634	86,206
1990	17,100	3,882	19,579	4,931	2,565	10,650	3,996	1,585	2,633	822	3,762	76,997	70,885	5,183	845	534	77,447
1991	19,457	3,453	21,859	4,834	2,648	13,477	4,056	1,958	1,839	1,153	3,702	84,330	76,762	5,056	704	412	82,934
1992	22,879	3,679	24,026	4,408	2,893	16,350	4,357	2,650	811	831	3,907	91,365	83,510	5,551	788	526	90,375
1993[1]	21,268	2,684	24,035	3,961	2,912	13,247	3,938	3,146	937	1,126	3,750	84,893	77,796	4,470	768	538	83,572

[1]Preliminary. *Source: Foreign Agricultural Service, U.S. Department of Agriculture*

U.S. Per Capita Consumption of Specific Beverages and Tea Sales by U.S. Retail Stores

Year	Soft Drinks	Coffee[2]	Beer	Milk	Tea[2]	Bottled Water	Juices	Powdered Drinks	Wine[3]	Distilled Spirits	Tea Bags	Loose Tea	Instant Tea	Instant Mixes	Herbal	Total
1981	NA	NA	NA	NA	NA	NA	NA	NA	NA	NA	39,697	3,255	15,850	11,959	1,010	71,771
1982	35.6	26.6	24.4	19.7	7.5	3.3	6.8	6.0	2.2	1.9	40,638	3,023	14,905	11,742	1,875	72,183
1983	NA	NA	NA	NA	NA	NA	NA	NA	NA	NA	41,876	2,685	14,878	13,136	2,096	74,671
1984	38.8	26.4	23.9	19.7	7.2	4.0	6.6	6.4	2.3	1.9	40,685	2,329	13,287	12,192	2,109	70,602
1985	40.8	26.8	23.8	19.8	7.3	5.2	7.9	6.3	2.4	1.8	40,951	2,081	12,688	11,412	2,151	69,283
1986	42.1	25.8	24.1	19.9	7.3	5.7	7.3	6.0	2.4	1.7	40,410	1,816	12,065	10,573	2,350	67,214
1987	NA	NA	NA	NA	NA	NA	NA	NA	NA	NA	32,596	1,124	7,226	10,437	2,141	53,524
1988	46.0	25.4	23.7	19.3	7.4	7.2	7.1	5.2	2.2	1.6	31,924	939	6,521	10,589	2,191	52,164
1989	46.7	26.4	23.6	19.6	7.2	8.1	8.0	5.4	2.1	1.5	35,359	1,045	7,606	11,322	2,380	58,060
1990	47.7	26.4	24.1	19.4	7.0	9.2	7.1	5.7	2.0	1.5	34,806	972	6,858	11,659	2,458	57,153
1991	47.8	26.5	23.3	19.4	6.7	9.6	7.6	5.9	1.9	1.4	35,068	871	6,561	12,599	2,380	58,060
1992	48.0	26.1	23.0	19.1	6.8	9.9	7.1	6.1	2.0	1.3	35,025	749	5,761	12,846	2,477	57,607
1993[1]	48.9	25.9	22.8	18.9	6.9	10.5	7.0	6.0	1.7	1.3	34,534	730	5,239	13,283	2,581	57,697

[1]Preliminary. [2]Based on 3-year moving average. [3]Includes wine coolers beginning 1985. [4]Excludes sales by hotels, restaurants and institutional users.
NA = Not available. *Source: Foreign Agriculture Service, U.S. Department of Agriculture*

London Auction Tea Prices   In U.S. Cents Per Pound

Year	Jan	Feb	Mar	Apr	May	June	July	Aug	Sept	Oct	Nov	Dec	Average
1981	98.6	101.2	100.5	97.9	94.7	90.4	84.6	80.0	81.7	87.4	91.3	91.6	91.7
1982	92.0	94.2	88.5	84.7	84.8	83.3	79.9	80.8	86.7	91.4	89.8	96.1	87.7
1983	98.5	93.1	89.8	92.1	91.0	85.2	86.6	90.6	99.0	117.4	158.8	163.8	105.5
1984	194.2	169.0	166.7	160.4	161.3	144.8	130.3	133.2	154.1	164.2	155.2	147.9	156.8
1985	143.1	127.3	110.4	98.6	75.2	74.6	71.5	72.2	73.3	78.7	80.2	75.3	90.0
1986	82.1	85.7	91.5	91.3	85.9	79.7	79.8	86.5	91.6	94.1	93.6	88.6	87.5
1987	89.7	83.6	83.2	67.9	65.4	60.8	69.5	72.3	72.7	84.1	87.4	94.0	77.6
1988	96.1	88.0	87.2	83.6	77.3	75.3	66.4	67.2	74.7	82.5	87.4	89.4	81.3
1989	87.5	82.4	80.6	77.3	76.7	80.4	88.1	83.2	97.7	118.4	106.7	115.5	91.2
1990	114.7	95.9	87.3	88.5	84.8	82.6	86.3	79.2	84.1	100.0	103.8	99.6	92.2
1991	107.2	90.2	83.6	84.3	78.7	73.8	70.4	73.5	79.6	84.4	89.4	89.7	83.7
1992	78.7	73.8	76.1	89.6	98.2	95.7	93.7	100.6	99.2	91.4	93.7	105.4	91.3
1993	108.6	92.5	86.9	80.6	78.3	75.9	74.7	75.8	82.4	90.9	84.3	84.4	84.6
1994[1]	74.7	78.9	84.7	84.3	83.4	90.2	82.4	83.3	91.2	86.5	81.4		

[1]Preliminary. *Source: Foreign Agricultural Service, U.S. Department of Agriculture*

Tin

Tin prices moved higher during 1994, reflecting the general rise in base metals that has occurred for most of the year. Strong economic growth, particularly in the U.S., and drawdowns in stocks on the London Metals Exchange have contributed to the increase in prices. By mid-September 1994, Platt's Metals Week reported that the composite price of tin was $3.56 per pound. In June 1994, the price had reached $3.726 per pound, while for all of 1993, the average composite price of tin was $3.498 per pound.

The rate of U.S. consumption of primary tin for the first seven-months of 1994 was very similar to 1993. For January-July 1994, primary tin consumption was 19,600 tonnes, for an average monthly rate of use of 2,800 tonnes. If this rate continues, total use for 1994 will be about 33,600 tonnes. This would compare to the 1993 consumption total of 33,700 tonnes. U.S. consumption of secondary tin during January-July 1994 was 5,400 tonnes or about 770 tonnes per month. At the current rate of use , secondary tin consumption could reach over 9,200 tonnes for the year. That would represent an increase of about 7 percent from the 1993 total of 8,600 tonnes.

Tin is manufactured into a coating for steel containers used to preserve foods and beverages. In addition, it is utilized in solder alloys, electroplating, ceramics and plastic. According to the U.S. Bureau of Mine, U.S. consumption of tin over the first seven-months of 1994 reached 17,294 tonnes. Among the distributed consumption by finished product: tin solder took 5,719 tonnes; tinplate (which includes secondary pig tin and tin acquired in chemicals) took 5,551 tonnes; chemicals 3,144 tonnes; bronze and brass 1,143 tonnes; tinning, 436 tonnes; tin powder 253 tonnes; and babbitt 102 tonnes. Estimated undistributed consumption, which is the estimated consumption of plants reporting data on an annual basis, during January-July 1994 was 7,700 tonnes. For all of 1993, tin consumed by finished products was 29,061 tonnes, while estimated undistributed consumption was 13,200 tonnes for total consumption of 42,300 tonnes.

Tinplate (all forms) production over the January-July 1994 period was 930,817 tonnes (gross weight). Tin content of this production was 5,551 tonnes. For all of 1993, tinplate production was 1.626 million tonnes, with a tin content of 9,945 tonnes.

Tin recovered from scrap processed in the U.S. in July 1994 totaled 359 tonnes. Tin recovered from bronze and brass, including tin recovered from copper, lead and tin base scrap, totaled 308 tonnes in July 1994. Minor amounts were recovered from tin metal. Data on recovery from lead and tin alloys was mostly withheld to avoid disclosing company proprietary data. For all of 1993, tin recovered from scrap was 7,564 tonnes.

U.S. imports of unwrought tin metal during January-June 1994 were 17,041 tonnes. The primary supplier was Brazil with 5,334 tonnes; Bolivia provided 4,074 tonnes; and Indonesia 3,388 tonnes. China has also become an important source of unwrought tin metal with shipments of 1,937 tonnes. During 1993, U.S. imports of unwrought tin metal were 33,682 tonnes. Imports of other tin products over the first half of 1994 totaled 4,827 tonnes. Imports of tin alloys made up over 60 percent of the total, while waste and scrap comprised 23 percent of the total. For all of 1993, imports of other tin products were 12,214 tonnes. The U.S. exports small amounts of tin metal. During the January-June 1994 period, exports were 1,345 tonnes. For all of 1993, exports were 2,598 tonnes.

U.S. industry stocks of tin on July 31, 1994 were 3,034 tonnes, down over 20 percent from stocks on June 30, 1994. Stocks of pig tin were 2,515 tonnes.

The Defense Logistics Agency (DLA) has tried to accelerate the disposal of many metals due to reduced world military tensions. For 1993, the disposal limit was set at 12,000 tonnes, a significant increase from 7,000 tonnes in 1992. This plan has been opposed by tin producers who feel that it will depress prices. In 1993, DLA disposals of stockpile tin were 6,022 tonnes. During January-August 1994, DLA disposals had reached 3,545 tonnes.

FUTURES MARKETS

Tin futures are traded on the London Metals Exchange (LME) and in Kuala Lumpur.

World Mine Production of Tin — In Metric Tons (Contained Tin)

Year	Australia	Bolivia	Brazil	China	Indonesia	Malaysia	Nigeria	Peru	Portugal	Russia[3]	South Africa	Thailand	United Kingdom	Zaire	Zimbabwe	World Total
1989	7,709	15,849	50,232	40,000	31,263	32,034	217	5,082	63	16,000	1,306	14,922	3,846	2,346	1,130	232,857
1990	7,377	17,249	39,149	42,000	30,200	28,468	192	5,134	1,300	15,000	1,140	14,635	3,400	2,221	1,120	218,057
1991	5,700	16,830	29,253	42,100	30,061	20,710	217	6,559	3,100	13,500	1,042	14,937	2,326	1,522	1,060	196,272
1992	6,400	16,516	27,500	43,000	29,400	14,339	186	10,195	3,000	6,000	582	11,484	2,000	1,020	950	178,365
1993[1]	8,042	18,634	25,900	46,000	29,000	10,384	186	13,700	5,300	5,000	600	7,000	1,500	700	800	178,207
1994[2]	8,000	20,000	25,000	45,000	29,000	9,000		15,000	6,000	5,000		7,000		1,000		180,000

[1] Preliminary. [2] Estimate. [3] Formerly part of the U.S.S.R.; data not reported separately until 1992. *Source: U.S. Bureau of Mines*

World Smelter Primary Production of Tin — In Metric Tons

Year	Australia	Bolivia	Brazil	China	Indonesia	Japan	Malaysia	Mexico	Russia[2]	South Africa	Spain	Thailand	United Kingdom	Zimbabwe	World Total
1988	439	5,373	41,857	29,500	28,365	846	49,945	1,812	18,500	1,377	806	14,675	9,014	855	215,163
1989	424	9,448	44,240	29,500	29,916	808	50,874	4,752	18,000	1,306	1,767	14,571	3,584	848	221,569
1990	312	12,567	37,580	35,000	30,389	816	49,067	5,004	16,000	1,140	600	15,512	6,100	838	223,310
1991	268	14,663	25,776	36,400	30,415	716	42,722	2,262	13,000	1,042	600	11,255	1,661	796	190,107
1992	250	14,393	30,000	39,600	31,915	821	45,598	1,907	6,000	592	600	10,679		716	186,585
1993[1]	250	16,700	30,000	43,000	30,000	800	42,000	2,000	5,000	450	500	9,000		657	183,822

[1] Preliminary. [2] Formerly part of the U.S.S.R.; data not reported separately until 1992. *Source: U.S. Bureau of Mines*

Tin Foreign Trade of the United States   In Metric Tons

						Imports for Consumption										
		---- Concentrates³ (Ore) ----								Unwrought Tin Metal						
Year	Exports (Metal²)	Total All Ore	Bolivia	Peru	Total All Metal	Aus-tralia	Belgium	Bolivia	Brazil	China	Indo-nesia	Malaysia	Nigeria	Singa-pore	Thailand	United Kingdom
1979	569	4,529	3,745	-----	48,355	-----	100	5,387	933	185	5,429	23,448	-----	1,070	10,440	550
1980	595	840	528	-----	45,982	145	190	5,597	2,031	858	6,477	15,548	770	864	12,414	416
1981	2,361	232	-----	232	45,874	552	-----	8,277	1,129	2,032	7,096	13,163	520	656	11,967	46
1982	5,769	1,961	192	1,416	27,939	334	10	4,340	2,409	2,632	5,744	2,364	124	600	9,116	55
1983	1,340	969	257	341	34,048	390	45	5,739	5,604	1,938	6,004	4,704	265	1,029	7,436	18
1984	1,429	3,272	271	2,502	41,224	288	137	5,438	10,220	1,640	4,985	6,622	60	781	9,531	583
1985	1,478	1,616	22	1,506	33,830	266	-----	1,815	11,021	4,513	4,586	379	-----	1,886	6,373	48
1986	1,547	3,936	259	3,676	35,768	94	-----	4,893	9,456	2,955	4,149	6,230	-----	691	1,901	730
1987	1,318	2,953	732	2,165	41,150	1,406	302	3,476	13,089	8,044	4,001	4,959	79	743	1,460	467
1988	1,209	2,837	923	1,914	43,493	1,342	-----	3,926	16,213	6,223	5,334	5,317	41	1,342	670	1,354
1989	904	216	-----	149	33,988	1,420	-----	4,795	10,572	4,793	5,162	2,392	-----	456	180	391
1990	658	-----	-----	-----	33,810	1,660	-----	8,472	6,535	4,339	4,695	3,873	-----	40	60	227
1991	970	1	1	-----	29,102	1,105	221	8,912	4,489	5,281	4,425	1,751	-----	100	-----	344
1992	1,888	-----	-----	-----	27,314	300	1	4,623	8,167	5,389	3,854	2,799	------	320	427	-----
1993¹	2,598	-----	-----	-----	33,682	-----	1	8,027	11,366	4,202	5,678	846	-----	220	-----	6

¹ Preliminary.   ² Excludes re-exports from 1979.   ³ Tin content.   *Source: U.S. Bureau of Mines*

United States Tin (Pig) Consumption (Total)   In Metric Tons

Year	Jan.	Feb.	Mar.	Apr.	May	June	July	Aug.	Sept.	Oct.	Nov.	Dec.	Total
1979	5,400	5,500	6,400	5,400	5,400	5,300	4,900	4,900	5,000	5,500	5,000	4,600	62,465
1980	5,500	5,300	5,750	5,300	4,600	4,100	3,700	3,900	4,150	4,300	4,050	3,750	56,362
1981	4,300	4,400	4,100	4,600	4,400	4,350	3,900	4,200	3,950	3,900	3,400	2,950	54,373
1982	3,400	3,300	3,750	5,100	5,000	5,100	4,900	4,700	4,700	4,600	4,500	4,400	53,450
1983	4,400	4,700	4,900	4,700	4,700	4,800	4,300	4,600	4,700	4,800	4,400	4,800	55,800
1984	4,600	4,300	5,300	3,900	4,500	4,400	4,100	4,400	4,100	4,000	3,300	3,500	50,400
1985	4,000	3,900	4,600	4,500	4,600	4,400	4,200	4,400	4,300	4,500	4,200	4,000	51,600
1986	4,300	4,000	4,200	4,500	4,400	4,400	4,100	4,100	4,000	4,300	3,900	3,900	50,100
1987	4,100	3,900	4,200	4,700	4,300	4,200	4,400	4,400	4,400	4,300	4,600	4,400	44,219
1988	4,600	4,700	4,800	4,700	5,300	5,600	5,300	5,300	5,500	5,600	4,900	4,900	45,073
1989	4,800	4,700	4,300	4,500	4,500	4,100	4,000	4,200	4,100	4,300	4,000	3,300	46,371
1990	4,000	4,000	4,200	4,100	4,200	4,100	4,100	4,300	4,100	4,100	4,200	3,900	44,363
1991	4,100	3,900	4,100	4,300	4,100	4,200	3,900	4,100	4,000	4,300	4,100	4,000	49,000
1992	3,800	3,800	3,800	3,800	3,700	3,800	3,800	3,500	3,600	3,600	3,400	3,300	45,090
1993¹	3,400	3,500	3,600	3,600	3,500	3,600	3,500	3,600	3,500	3,500	3,500	3,400	47,107
1994¹	3,500	3,700	3,700	3,600	3,600	3,700	3,500	3,400	2,500	3,600	3,600	3,400	42,500

¹ Preliminary.   *Source: U.S Bureau of Mines*

United States Tin Stocks (Pig -- Industrial)   In Metric Tons

Year	Jan. 1	Feb. 1	Mar. 1	Apr. 1	May 1	June 1	July 1	Aug. 1	Sept. 1	Oct. 1	Nov. 1	Dec. 1
1979	5,040	4,594	4,254	5,891	6,097	5,938	6,317	6,270	6,096	5,058	4,901	4,244
1980	4,238	7,720	6,882	7,527	5,443	7,263	6,592	6,544	6,051	5,180	5,208	5,086
1981	5,504	5,968	5,745	5,229	5,725	5,978	6,227	6,465	5,663	5,710	5,325	5,563
1982	5,988	3,872	3,490	3,829	5,222	4,953	4,653	3,888	2,910	2,940	2,970	3,437
1983	3,152	4,609	3,513	3,815	4,026	3,527	3,634	3,931	4,091	3,604	3,074	3,180
1984	3,020	2,968	2,268	2,840	2,646	3,119	2,795	2,688	2,837	2,495	2,512	2,326
1985	2,592	2,766	2,283	2,407	2,228	2,853	3,042	2,762	2,663	2,985	4,121	4,913
1986	5,665	5,310	4,692	3,097	4,127	3,987	4,032	4,166	4,246	3,497	3,554	4,681
1987	4,802	5,232	6,394	6,321	7,263	8,087	6,663	4,288	5,373	5,533	6,402	5,460
1988	4,428	4,490	5,989	5,631	5,868	6,128	6,456	5,665	4,350	4,171	4,371	4,781
1989	4,943	4,242	3,894	4,320	3,717	4,945	4,912	5,597	5,872	6,241	5,313	5,530
1990	6,072	5,975	5,824	6,401	4,959	3,298	3,792	3,592	3,836	4,762	4,819	4,829
1991	6,337	6,677	6,688	6,177	5,993	5,991	6,348	6,739	6,544	8,544	6,616	6,347
1992	3,024	3,022	3,369	2,844	2,877	2,901	2,651	3,111	3,321	3,454	3,654	3,178
1993¹	3,221	3,368	3,429	3,607	3,704	3,423	4,003	4,464	4,349	3,709	3,262	3,535
1994¹	3,553	4,635	3,775	3,975	3,471	3,470	3,825	3,027	2,893	2,980	2,844	2,908

¹ Preliminary.   *Source: U.S. Bureau of Mines*

TIN

TIN CASH PRICE - NEW YORK

MONTHLY CASH
AS OF 04/30/95

Average Price of Ex-Dock Tin in New York[1]   In Cents Per Pound

Year	Jan.	Feb.	Mar.	Apr.	May	June	July	Aug.	Sept.	Oct.	Nov.	Dec.	Average
1978	591.19	595.93	557.48	537.85	570.58	600.95	606.21	641.80	679.66	739.69	758.84	695.86	631.34
1979	684.56	724.57	746.14	740.06	745.18	760.14	712.31	739.93	762.03	785.54	801.23	830.88	756.87
1980	836.46	866.39	900.23	872.21	861.84	845.19	836.95	834.61	861.92	832.92	788.67	751.36	840.73
1981	739.94	705.76	691.70	677.38	652.07	652.77	680.22	746.06	777.36	798.70	813.00	801.59	728.05
1982	787.41	749.93	669.51	649.58	662.35	643.00	638.00	636.33	644.33	627.94	627.93	630.18	663.88
1983	648.90	653.89	669.18	692.29	683.36	670.54	663.13	653.10	649.31	650.65	653.02	636.71	660.34
1984	590.60	592.10	603.40	605.10	601.70	602.20	593.50	594.70	590.20	578.60	574.40	566.10	591.05
1985	542.10	532.00	533.80	559.10	557.70	576.30	594.90	593.80	578.60	580.50	NQ	NQ	564.88
1986	NQ	NQ	350.64	274.98	265.04	260.28	261.51	261.26	260.69	267.48	292.84	308.26	280.30
1987	321.56	320.39	317.66	320.98	323.60	316.96	307.59	314.63	321.86	324.81	332.21	327.65	320.83
1988	326.68	321.12	324.79	323.85	325.28	337.37	342.18	351.14	355.20	347.84	351.10	352.42	338.25
1989	355.80	377.77	419.64	486.72	484.42	474.15	458.64	415.80	395.99	379.67	329.10	324.79	408.54
1990	317.89	296.28	302.41	308.97	307.02	295.86	288.09	287.48	279.20	296.11	292.27	261.82	295.41
1991	269.97	268.00	264.51	265.78	271.78	272.30	270.55	269.02	265.86	264.50	262.26	262.05	267.21
1992	261.30	267.79	267.52	277.20	290.05	313.07	331.10	322.19	315.66	291.60	268.54	271.76	289.81
1993	280.40	280.91	277.43	275.67	269.62	255.35	252.31	230.17	213.22	220.02	224.88	236.90	251.41
1994	249.55	267.55	261.20	258.49	277.79	282.43	276.11	265.35	279.39	292.17	325.83	346.21	281.84

[1] Data prior to 1984 are for Straits (Alloyer Price).   NQ = No quote.   *Source: American Metal Market*

Tin Plate Production & Tin Recovered in the United States   In Metric Tons

| | | -------------- Tin Content of Tinplate Produced -------------- | | | | | | | | | | | |
| | | ------------- Tinplate (All Forms) ---------- | | | ------------------------- Tin Recovered from Scrap by Form of Recovery ------------------------- | | | | | | | | |
Year	Tinplate Waste -------- Gross Weight ---------	Tinplate	Tin Content (Tonne)	Tin per Tonne of Plate (Kilograms)	Tin Metal	Bronze & Brass	Solder	Type Metal	Babbitt	Antimonial Lead	Chemical Compounds	Misc.[2]	Grand Total
1979	360,582	4,236,578	17,929	4.2	1,767	12,090	5,282	584	441	867	433	29	21,493
1980	311,770	3,699,920	16,346	4.4	1,703	10,402	4,423	525	378	856	321	30	18,638
1981	284,505	3,288,662	13,306	4.0	1,587	8,894	3,035	576	261	791	265	29	15,438
1982	208,074	2,712,678	10,936	4.0	1,067	6,971	2,723	222	237	1,015	447	101	12,783
1983	166,186	2,586,810	9,328	3.6	1,180	8,517	3,072	172	185	803	182	94	14,205
1984	151,540	2,409,399	8,659	3.6	1,107	9,146	3,653	142	123	894	301	51	15,417
1985	146,041	2,215,042	9,321	4.2	1,302	8,045	3,565	122	88	791	186	10	14,109
1986	120,186	2,068,246	8,660	4.2	1,134	7,996	3,676	197	66	891	W	17	13,977
1987	141,842	2,302,173	10,357	4.5	1,353	10,245	3,765	66	77	623	W	30	16,159
1988	149,054	2,375,809	11,582	4.9	578	9,939	3,619	70	112	902	W	29	15,249
1989	153,542	2,263,769	11,764	5.2	569	10,305	3,225	46	116	952	W	W	15,213
1990	156,419	2,467,205	11,750	4.8	186	13,312	2,876	46	28	739	W	4	17,187
1991	166,647	2,468,769	11,482	4.7	234	11,719	W	44	24	928	W	2,705	12,949
1992	195,760	1,620,007	9,821	6.1	137	12,761	W	47	78	704	W	181	13,727
1993[1]	196,874	1,625,132	9,945	6.0	W	4,891	W	15	W	333	W	2,325	7,564

[1] Preliminary.   [2] Includes foil, terne metal, cable lead, and items indicated by symbol "W".   W = Withheld proprietary data.   *Source: U.S. Bureau of Mines*

U.S. Consumption of Primary and Secondary Tin   In Metric Tons

Year	Net Import Reliance as a % of Apparent Consumption	Industry Stocks Jan. 1[2]	Net Receipts — Primary	Secondary	Scrap	Total	Available Supply	Stocks Dec. 31 (Total Available Less Total Processed)	Total Processed	Consumed in Manufacturing Products
1980	79	7,075	43,545	2,461	7,709	53,715	60,790	3,593	57,197	56,362
1981	77	8,835	41,162	5,692	8,050	54,904	63,739	8,640	55,099	54,373
1982	68	8,717	35,843	6,507	7,830	50,180	58,897	12,328	46,569	46,295
1983	73	7,549	36,494	5,412	7,435	49,341	56,890	11,098	45,792	45,547
1984	74	8,063	38,813	6,110	6,791	51,714	59,777	11,145	48,632	48,315
1985	72	8,430	38,006	8,904	7,471	54,381	62,811	13,928	48,883	48,669
1986	74	9,336	35,475	11,636	6,346	53,457	62,793	18,915	43,878	43,524
1987	74	9,876	38,401	11,707	6,635	56,743	66,619	21,887	44,731	44,219
1988	78	10,217	39,421	12,472	6,707	58,600	68,817	23,586	46,232	45,602
1989	77	9,242	37,760	10,901	8,168	56,829	66,071	19,184	46,887	46,463
1990	71	13,551	38,473	9,501	6,534	54,508	68,059	22,578	45,481	45,165
1991	74	12,502	36,126	1,622	8,370	46,118	58,620	13,540	45,080	44,805
1992	80	12,038	34,327	2,279	8,412	45,018	57,056	11,669	45,387	45,120
1993[1]	84	8,556	38,044	3,470	8,768	50,282	58,838	11,566	47,272	47,107

[1] Preliminary.   [2] Includes tin in transit to the U.S.   *Source: U.S. Bureau of Mines*

Consumption of Tin in the United States by Finished Products   In Metric Tons (Contained Tin)

Year	Tinplate[2]	Solder	Babbitt	Bronze & Brass	Tinning	Chemicals[3]	Tin Powder	Bar Tin & Anodes	White Metal	Other	Total	Total — Primary	Secondary
1980	16,346	15,618	2,380	7,478	2,577	W	1,109	486	914	8,794	56,362	44,342	12,020
1981	13,306	15,799	3,844	7,041	2,491	4,417	983	455	1,201	1,788	54,373	40,229	14,144
1982	11,134	13,142	1,915	4,400	1,887	W	906	509	1,177	11,225	46,295	33,019	13,276
1983	9,462	14,120	2,881	4,583	1,759	W	793	654	937	10,358	45,547	34,301	11,246
1984	8,825	17,249	2,684	4,998	1,748	W	1,057	526	958	11,396	48,315	37,201	11,114
1985	9,321	18,621	1,488	4,330	1,511	W	976	466	937	12,100	48,669	36,524	12,145
1986	8,660	15,810	1,324	3,502	1,437	W	1,002	449	1,134	10,204	43,522	33,324	10,198
1987	10,357	15,240	1,060	3,559	1,398	W	W	703	1,175	10,704	44,219	35,620	8,599
1988	11,582	15,288	926	3,934	1,406	W	W	557	1,131	10,777	45,601	37,529	8,072
1989	11,764	16,370	794	3,693	1,505	W	711	619	1,074	9,926	46,456	36,603	9,853
1990	11,750	16,443	763	3,166	1,707	6,275	563	603	1,045	2,850	45,165	36,770	8,395
1991	11,482	16,296	941	2,896	1,465	6,564	539	436	868	3,318	44,805	35,138	9,667
1992	9,821	18,461	916	2,916	1,275	6,301	573	919	974	2,964	45,120	34,983	10,137
1993[1]	9,765	19,461	823	3,093	1,249	6,446	608	946	789	3,927	47,107	34,973	12,134

[1] Preliminary.   [2] Includes small quantity of secondary pig tin and tin acquired in chemicals.   [3] Including tin oxide.   W = Withheld proprietary data.
Source: U.S. Bureau of Mines

Titanium

Titanium's unique properties of having one-half the density of steel, excellent strength and immunity for corrosion, make it an ideal construction material for engines and airframes. Pure titanium metal is called "sponge" because of its porous cellular form. The sponge is processed to form an ingot, and the ingot is processed by mills to make plate sheet tubing. There are titanium sponge plants in the U.S., Japan, Britain, China and, and the former Soviet Union. Numerous titanium mill products are used outside the aerospace industry in pollution control devices, desalination plants, chemical processing, and in tubing for power plants and oil refineries. Titanium dioxide finds use as a white pigment for exterior paints, paper production, and pigment for ink and porcelain enamels.

According to the United States Bureau of Mines, U.S. titanium ingot production for the first half of 1994 was 14,047 tonnes. For all of 1993, ingot production was 27,900 tonnes. Production of mill products during the same period was 9,149 tonnes, compared to 18,871 for 1993 as a whole.

Consumption of titanium sponge during the January-

June 1994 period was 8,345 tonnes, which compares with 15,140 tonnes for 1993 as a whole. Consumption of titanium scrap was 7,856 tonnes, while for calendar 1993 it ran 15,300 tonnes. Titanium ingot use was 12,730 tonnes in the first half of 1994, while in 1993 it was 25,665 tonnes.

U.S. exports of products like sponge, scrap, ingot, sheet bar, rods and wire totaled 3,568 tonnes in the first half of 1994. Exports of titanium oxide for January-May 1994 were 14,853, ores and concentrate were 6,121 tonnes, and pigments were 122,073 tonnes.

In the second quarter of 1994, the Defense National Stockpile Center awarded 5,147 short dry tons of rutile ore in the government stockpile under invitation for bids. Rutile is offered for sale each month from the Defense National Stockpile on a competitive sealed bid basis.

According to industry reports, Boeing Company qualified the Russian titanium ingot and mill product producer Verkhnaya Salda Metallurgical Production Association as a supplier of a specific grade of 6-4 ingot used in airframes. The Russian firm is estimated to be the largest producer of titanium mill products in the world.

Average Titanium Prices in the United States

Year	Ilmenite F.O.B. Australian Ports[2] $ Tonne[4]	Slag, 85% TiO$_2$ F.O.B. Richards Bay, South Africa $ Tonne[4]	Rutile Large Lots Bulk, F.O.B. U.S. East Coast[3] $ Tonne[5]	Rutile Bagged F.O.B. Australian Ports $ Tonne[5]	Avg. Price of Grade A Titanium Sponge, F.O.B. Shipping Point	Titanium Metal Sponge	Titanium Dioxide Pigments, F.O.B. U.S. Plants — Anatase	Rutile
					Dollars Per Pound			
1983	70-75	187-198	400-430	267-284	6.30	5.55	.69	.75
1984	36-38	200	320-340	339-359	5.70	5.55	.69	.75
1985	38-42	212	350-360	371-386	5.70	3.50-4.00	.72-.73	.78
1986	47-53	225-230	355-375	398-422	4.32	3.90-4.30	.75-.77	.80-.82
1987	46-52	235-245	355-375	398-418	4.06	4.00-4.20	.75-.77	.80-.82
1988	64-77	250-275	NA	547-572	4.21	4.25-4.75	.92-.95	.95-.97
1989	67-75	275-300	540-550	553-632	5.11	4.80-5.30	1.01-1.02	1.04-1.05
1990	69-77	285-310	550-580	693-770	5.31	4.75	.99	1.01
1991	68-76	295-325	606-650	515-545	5.25	4.75	.99	.99
1992	58-62	310	510-520	380-414	3.96	3.50-4.00	.99	.92-.95
1993[1]	61-64	330	NA	370-400	3.75	3.50-4.00	.99	.92-.95
1994[6]	68-72	320	351-372	358-375		3.75-4.25	.94-.99	.92-.94

[1] Preliminary.   [2] Prior to 1984 prices are for TiO$_2$ F.O.B. Atlanta Seaboard.   [3] Prior to 1984 prices are for F.O.B. Eastern Ports.   [4] Prices prior to 1984 are

Salient Statistics of Titanium in the United States   In Metric Tons

Year	Titanium Dioxide Pigment — Production	Imports[3]	Apparent Consumption	Ilmenite — Imports[3]	Consumption	Titanium Slag — Imports[3]	Consumption	Rutile[4] — Imports[3]	Consumption	Exports of Titanium Products — Ores & Concentrates	Scrap	Dioxide & Pigments	Ingots, Billets, Etc.
1983	659,710	138,922	741,065	348,366	583,250	247,845	225,541	163,325	238,937	4,391	5,379	91,702	1,371
1984	834,889	193,501	916,198	409,605	783,391	209,839	200,858	180,508	317,902	8,651	4,109	106,124	2,071
1985[5]	783,393	178,001	893,195	459,765	685,896	264,742	228,635	162,988	276,944	25,183	6,133	93,624	2,039
1986	844,274	183,862	908,055	422,401	731,436	328,285	250,677	158,595	298,601	4,821	5,809	104,734	1,922
1987	878,558	174,219	966,169	307,515	744,266	408,785	251,423	197,937	320,505	4,023	5,083	108,889	2,467
1988	926,746	185,468	991,536	394,170	679,008	434,641	300,013	231,124	352,356	9,368	5,939	118,422	2,083
1989	1,006,581	166,346	947,259	411,751	659,584	386,146	414,830	264,895	366,143	19,832	5,474	212,197	2,702
1990	978,659	147,592	925,447	345,907	688,948	373,623	390,537	274,605	369,454	18,765	5,487	202,288	2,371
1991	991,976	166,094	935,829	213,886	738,089	408,302	341,379	240,120	368,643	26,912	4,568	211,854	1,700
1992	1,137,038	169,260	999,930	294,585	684,882	537,118	539,323	317,399	460,969	34,665	2,770	270,422	1,455
1993[1]	1,161,469	171,939	1,028,311	299,204	693,940	475,522	545,809	371,481	464,825	15,202	3,893	290,192	856
1994[2]	1,250,000	177,000	1,110,000	334,749		384,402		307,913		18,255	3,761	328,344	1,057

[1] Preliminary.   [2] Estimate.   [3] For consumption.   [4] Natural and synthetic.   [5] Data shown in short tons prior to 1985.   *Source: U.S. Bureau of Mines*

World Production of Titanium Ilmenite Concentrates In Thousands of Metric Tons

Year	Aus-tralia[2]	Brazil	China	India	Malaysia	Norway	Sierra Leone	Sri Lanka	Thailand	Ukraine[3]	World Total	-- Titaniferous Slag[4] -- Canada	South Africa
1979	1,327	14.5	NA	161.9	220.3	903.7	NA	61.0	NA	450	4,752	526	316
1980	1,553	18.6	NA	185.1	208.3	912.5	NA	37.4	NA	460	5,420	934	379
1981	1,478	17.5	150.0	179.1	190.4	727.1	NA	88.2	NA	470	5,266	837	408
1982	1,289	12.5	150.0	168.6	111.6	608.2	NA	75.3	NA	475	4,496	737	420
1983	1,003	33.6	154.0	148.2	245.5	612.8	NA	90.1	NA	480	4,108	700	460
1984[5]	1,681	45.1	154.0	154.3	296.0	718.5	NA	112.5	NA	485	5,091	800	460
1985	1,433	76.4	140.0	143.0	314.7	735.8	NA	114.9	1.0	445	4,737	845	435
1986	1,252	75.5	140.0	140.0	414.9	803.6	NA	129.9	13.5	450	4,705	850	435
1987	1,509	169.3	140.0	140.0	509.2	852.3	5.6	128.5	27.1	455	3,937	925	650
1988	1,622	142.2	150.0	229.7	486.3	898.0	42.1	74.3	18.3	460	4,033	1,025	400
1989	1,714	144.2	150.0	240.7	533.7	929.8	62.3	101.4	17.0	460	4,353	1,040	725
1990	1,621	114.1	150.0	280.0	530.2	814.5	54.6	66.4	10.7	430	4,072	1,046	840
1991	1,381	69.1	150.0	311.5	336.3	625.0	60.4	60.9	17.1	400	3,411	701	808
1992	1,522	70.0	150.0	300.0	337.7	708.0	60.3	33.3	2.9	200	3,384	753	884
1993[1]	1,783	70.0	155.0	320.0	210.0	700.0	62.9	76.9	20.7	180	3,579	653	892

[1] Preliminary. [2] Includes leucoxene. [3] Formerly part of the U.S.S.R.; data not reported separately until 1992. [4] Approximately 10% of total production is ilmenite. Beginning in 1988, 25% of Norway's ilmenite production was used to produce slag containing 75% TiO_2. [5] Data prior to 1985 are shown in thousands of short tons. NA = Not available. *Source: U.S. Bureau of Mines*

World Production of Titanium Rutile Concentrates In Metric Tons

Year	Australia	Brazil	India	Sierre Leone	South Africa	Sri Lanka	Thailand	Ukraine[2]	World Total
1979	302,620	484	5,445	8,267	46,000	16,176	NA	11,000	389,992
1980	343,639	472	5,908	52,356	53,000	14,097	NA	11,000	480,472
1981	254,432	190	7,397	55,992	55,000	14,662	NA	11,000	398,673
1982	243,277	258	6,374	52,590	52,000	7,950	NA	11,000	373,449
1983	180,089	510	6,100	79,146	62,000	8,921	NA	11,000	347,766
1984[3]	187,860	454	6,600	100,641	62,000	7,129	NA	11,000	375,684
1985	211,615	713	6,800	80,611	55,000	8,558	110	10,000	373,407
1986	215,774	495	7,000	97,100	55,000	8,443	48	10,000	393,860
1987	246,263	324	7,000	113,300	55,000	7,200	92	10,000	439,179
1988	230,637	1,514	5,000	126,358	55,000	5,255	128	10,000	433,892
1989	243,000	2,613	9,931	128,198	60,000	5,589	150	10,000	459,331
1990	245,000	1,814	11,000	144,284	64,056	5,460	NA	9,500	481,114
1991	201,000	1,094	13,635	154,800	75,000	3,085	76	9,000	457,690
1992	190,000	1,100	10,000	148,990	95,000	2,741	281	5,000	453,112
1993[1]	190,000	1,100	13,900	152,000	100,000	2,643	300	4,000	463,943

[1] Preliminary. [2] Formerly part of the U.S.S.R.; data not reported separately until 1992. [3] Data prior to 1985 are shown in short tons. NA = Not available. *Source: U.S. Bureau of Mines*

World Production of Titanium Sponge Metal & U.S. Consumption of Titanium Concentrates

	Production of Titanium (In Metric Tons) -- Sponge Metal[2]						-- U.S. Consumption of Titanium Concentrates, by Products (In Metric Tons) -- Ilmenite (TiO_2 Content)			Rutile (TiO_2 Content)			
Year	China	Japan	Russia[3]	United Kingdom	United States	Total	Pigments	Misc.	Total	Welding Rod Coatings	Pigments	Misc.	Total
1979	NA	14,000	43,000	2,600	NA	NA	475,342	11,886	487,228	9,947	230,776	52,189	292,912
1980	NA	21,257	45,000	2,600	NA	NA	502,108	11,207	513,315	6,876	211,599	59,407	277,882
1981	2,000	27,500	42,000	2,600	26,419	100,519	501,301	9,721	511,022	6,944	192,779	66,873	266,596
1982	1,500	18,600	44,000	2,600	15,600	82,300	345,618	6,775	35,293	5,275	184,403	35,435	225,113
1983	2,000	11,600	45,000	2,000	13,966	74,000	468,279	6,006	474,285	3,649	210,949	35,820	250,418
1984	2,000	16,938	46,000	2,500	24,326	92,000	492,658	6,319	498,977	3,911	231,808	62,920	298,639
1985	2,000	16,938	47,000	1,500	23,257	91,000	474,561	6,450	481,011	4,881	239,893	41,714	286,488
1986	2,000	18,000	48,000	1,500	17,500	87,000	511,070	1,655	512,725	7,667	244,178	57,539	309,384
1987[4]	2,000	11,105	49,000	1,500	19,675	83,000	463,072	1,817	510,449	4,168	271,658	56,558	332,384
1988	2,000	16,500	46,000	1,500	24,000	88,000	429,736	590	429,737	3,737	262,998	64,641	331,376
1989	2,000	21,000	46,000	1,500	25,225	95,725	419,329	414	419,743	3,603	271,208	71,178	345,989
1990	2,000	25,630	47,000	1,500	24,679	101,000	445,502	726	446,228	4,047	271,637	71,373	347,057
1991	2,000	18,945	20,000	2,000	13,366	56,000	476,145	495	476,640	6,931	286,741	42,200	335,872
1992	2,000	14,554	20,000	2,000	W	38,554	425,876	647	426,523	W	405,875	32,553	438,428
1993[1]	2,000	14,400	35,000	1,000	W	37,000	434,097	451	434,548	W	405,784	30,223	436,007

[1] Preliminary. [2] Unconsolidated metal in various forms. [3] Formerly part of the U.S.S.R.; data not reported separately until 1993. [4] Data prior to 1988 are shown in short tons. NA = Not available. W = Withheld proprietary data. *Source: U.S. Bureau of Mines*

Tobacco

The U.S. Department of Agriculture (USDA) forecast U.S. tobacco production to decline to 1.54 billion pounds. This represents a decline of four percent from the 1993 crop of 1.61 billion pounds. While the growing season was excellent, the decline was due solely to less harvested acreage. For 1994, tobacco producers harvested 676,000 acres, the lowest since 1988 when 634,000 acres were harvested. The national average yield jumped almost six percent to 2,280 pounds per acre. With larger beginning stocks, total supplies of U.S. tobacco will be higher.

Major producing states include North Carolina, South Carolina and Kentucky. the U.S.-grown tobacco supply (types 11-72) for 1994/95 is forecast to increase with more burley and flue-cured tobacco. Stocks entering the new marketing year were likely to reach 2.48 billion pounds, eight percent more than a year earlier. Stocks of imported leaf fell three percent from the record high level of a year earlier.

U.S. cigarette consumption continued to trend lower in 1994. This represented the tenth consecutive year of declining cigarette use. The decline stems from the increasing number of prohibitions and restriction on where people can smoke, and continued anti-smoking activity such as advertisements showing the relationship between smoking and health. Social acceptance of cigarette smoking has also declined markedly.

For the 1993/94 (July-June) year, 484 billion cigarettes were smoked, 10 billion less that the year before. In 1985, 598 billion cigarettes were smoked. The market share of discount-brand cigarettes fell to about 33 percent during 1993/94, compared with 36 percent in the prior year. Per capita consumption of cigarettes during 1994 (persons 18 and older) is forecast by USDA to be 125 packs of 20 cigarettes each. This represents a decline of two percent from 1993 and the lowest number since 1941.

Cigarette exports continue to increase and represent a growing segment of the market for American tobacco companies. For the first six months of 1994, U.S. cigarette exports were 198.4 billion units. For the first half of 1994, cigarette exports to Japan were 26.6 billion units, an increase of almost five percent from 1993. Exports to Belgium-Luxembourg (a point of entry and distribution for other European countries) rose 15 percent to 19.6 billion units. Exports to the countries that formerly made up the Soviet Union jumped over 100 percent to six billion units.

Retail prices of tobacco products were over five percent lower in July 1994 than a year earlier. Tobacco manufac-turers sharply lowered prices in August 1993 but increased prices somewhat in November 1993. In August 1993, cigarette manufacturers lowered prices of premium-brand cigarettes more than 25 percent to slow the gains in market share being made by discount brand cigarettes.

Seven states and the District of Columbia enacted or imposed tax hikes in 1994 that averaged 12 cents for a pack of 20. The weighted average state tax on cigarettes was 29.1 cents per pack of 20 in April 1994. The tax rates range from 2.5 cents in Virginia to 75 cents in Michigan. Taxes are also imposed by many cities and local governments. Some 43 states now impose sales taxes on cigarettes. The Federal excise tax remains at 24 cents per pack. Under the Clinton Administration's health care reform plan, the excise tax would increase 75 cents to 99 cents. An alternative tax plan would increase it 45 cents to 69 cents. Three senate subcommittees have proposed tax increases of $1.00, $1.50 and $1.76 per pack.

From April to June there were several Congressional hearings concerning cigarette nicotine levels, additives, advertising and other issues. Some of the hearings were concerned with whether nicotine levels in cigarettes are manipulated. The Food and Drug Administration (FDA) contends that nicotine levels are manipulated while cigarette manufacturers indicate they are not. A FDA panel met in August 1994 to discuss the effect of nicotine on smokers. The panel concluded that nicotine is an additive drug and smoking cigarettes causes addiction.

Consumption of large cigars (including cigarillos) in 1994 was expected to increase from the previous year's 2.19 billion. Cigarillos, which are less than half the weight of cigars, had 1993 sales of 813 million. Consumption of smoking tobacco was expected to continue its decline but chewing tobacco production in 1994 was expected to increase to 64.4 million pounds. This represents the first increase in a decade and is a result of changing consumer tastes and product advertising. Consumption of snuff was expected to increase in 1994 for the seventh year in a row. This is attributable to smoking restrictions and product advertising.

U.S. exports of unmanufactured tobacco during 1993/94 (July-June) fell to 442 million pounds. The reduction occurred primarily because lower-priced tobacco is in ample supply in other countries. Flue-cured tobacco and barley tobacco exports during July-June 1993/94 were down 15 percent.

World Production of Leaf Tobacco   In Thousands of Metric Tons

Year	Brazil	Canada	China	France	Greece	India	Indonesia	Italy	Japan	Kyrgy-zstan[3]	Pakistan	Philip-pines	Turkey	United States	Zimb-abwe	World Total
1985	411.0	85.9	3,425	34.9	148.5	472.8	172.5	166.5	116.2	381.0	87.4	75.9	170.5	686.9	108.7	6,993
1986	385.0	70.1	1,707	38.6	148.8	439.4	154.1	145.5	118.2	321.0	78.3	72.8	161.5	528.0	117.0	6,005
1987	410.0	61.4	1,945	33.9	144.0	460.2	154.0	162.1	104.4	296.0	69.0	79.4	184.7	539.3	131.5	6,160
1988	419.0	69.8	2,732	29.4	134.8	367.4	137.8	184.4	85.8	242.0	69.5	68.8	218.8	621.2	123.7	6,840
1989	462.0	75.6	2,830	29.2	115.8	492.8	146.9	197.3	74.4	239.0	71.1	73.3	269.5	620.2	135.2	7,110
1990	435.0	63.1	2,628	28.3	134.4	564.4	158.9	214.8	80.5	292.7	68.0	70.1	295.6	737.7	139.8	7,106
1991	422.0	78.7	3,031	29.5	165.7	555.9	164.9	193.8	69.9	250.5	80.8	82.3	239.4	754.9	178.1	7,607
1992	577.0	71.8	3,499	23.1	196.5	584.4	145.4	150.8	79.4	18.2	108.0	114.9	331.8	780.9	211.4	8,293
1993[1]	608.0	83.8	3,451	25.8	148.0	580.6	152.8	132.3	67.4	55.6	106.0	102.5	326.3	731.9	235.3	8,289
1994[2]	442.0	68.9	3,020	26.5	140.9	528.0	162.1	130.4	81.9	55.6	104.1	54.0	213.1	714.8	177.8	7,242

[1]Preliminary.   [2]Estimate.   *Source: Foreign Agricultural Service, U.S. Department of Agriculture*

Production and Consumption of Tobacco Products in the United States

Year	Cigar-ettes -Billions-	Cigars[3] -Millions-	Chewing Tobacco — Plug Million Pounds	Twist	Loose-leaf	Total	Smoking Tobacco	Snuff[4]	Cigar-ettes — Number —	Cigars[3]	Cigar-ettes	Consumption[5] of Per Capita[6] Cigars[3] Pounds	Smoking Tobacco	Chewing Tobacco	Total Products
1986	658.0	2,932	10.4	1.4	69.6	81.4	19.4	47.5	3,274.0	35.8	5.7	.59	.29	.93	6.56
1987	689.4	2,133	9.9	1.4	67.3	78.7	18.0	46.2	3,197.0	31.7	5.5	.52	.27	.89	6.30
1988	694.5	1,980	8.9	1.4	65.6	75.9	17.8	48.6	3,096.0	29.1	5.4	.47	.25	.86	6.11
1989	677.2	2,010	8.3	1.3	64.9	74.5	17.0	49.7	2,926.0	27.9	4.9	.46	.22	.82	5.67
1990	709.7	1,896	7.4	1.3	64.3	72.9	16.4	53.1	2,817.0	26.2	4.8	.43	.20	.79	5.48
1991	694.5	1,740	6.7	1.2	64.3	72.2	15.7	54.3	2,713.0	24.9	4.7	.41	.19	.79	5.41
1992	718.5	1,741	5.9	1.2	61.6	69.7	14.9	57.5	2,640.0	24.1	4.7	.40	.17	.74	5.38
1993[1]	661.0	1,750	5.3	1.1	58.0	64.4	13.7	59.1	2,539.0	23.9	4.5	.39	.17	.70	5.12
1994[2]	685.0	1,770	4.5	1.1	58.0	63.6	13.4	58.8	2,493.0	24.3	4.6	.40	.16	.71	5.30

[1]Preliminary. [2]Estimate. [3]Large cigars and cigarillos. [4]Includes loose-leaf. [5]Consumption of tax-paid tobacco products. Unstemmed processing weight. [6]18 years and older. *Source: Economic Research Service, U.S. Department of Agriculture*

Production of Tobacco in the United States   In Thousands of Pounds

Year	Connect-icut	Florida	Georgia	Indiana	Ken-tucky	Maryland	Massach-usetts	Missouri	North Carolina	Ohio	Pennsyl-vania	South Carolina	Tenn-essee	Virginia	West Virginia	Wis-consin
1986	3,062	13,303	67,890	12,095	314,940	21,120	622	4,389	444,790	13,574	21,830	75,480	82,821	73,524	2,640	11,860
1987	2,716	13,804	72,160	11,070	304,845	13,338	653	3,519	466,592	12,044	20,700	94,080	87,291	76,900	2,592	8,370
1988	2,971	17,152	85,880	10,945	355,024	11,970	767	4,422	552,627	14,497	18,175	100,125	93,142	92,177	2,720	6,906
1989	2,793	17,755	87,200	13,237	366,551	8,103	746	5,450	541,056	15,925	17,925	103,680	79,820	93,814	1,885	11,248
1990	3,007	19,044	103,845	15,050	442,253	9,656	805	5,928	639,639	18,915	19,780	109,905	112,218	110,269	2,720	13,346
1991	2,831	15,312	80,600	18,920	479,794	12,900	830	6,825	634,655	22,776	20,765	111,180	121,524	116,849	3,420	15,191
1992	2,258	19,575	100,980	18,900	524,378	11,931	740	3,298	609,873	21,840	20,840	112,320	146,556	111,459	3,623	13,100
1993	2,533	18,673	96,320	17,415	455,080	13,300	738	4,760	608,415	18,900	18,260	110,760	139,423	99,544	3,600	6,643
1994[1]	2,625	16,575	80,660	15,265	458,075	12,750	803	8,190	597,525	19,295	18,360	110,450	134,672	108,752	3,600	5,800

[1]Preliminary. *Source: Agricultural Statistics Board, U.S. Department of Agriculture*

Salient Statistics of Tobacco in the United States

Year	Acres Harvested 1,000 Acres	Yield Per Acre Pounds	Pro-duction Million Pounds	Farm Price ¢ Lb.	Farm Value Million $	Tobacco (July-June) Exports[2] - Million Pounds -	Imports[3]	Cigar-ettes Millions	U.S. Exports of Cigars & Cheroots	All Tobacco	Smoking Tobacco[4]	Stocks of Tobacco[5] Various Types All Tobacco Million Pounds	Fire Cured[6]	Cigar Filler[7]	Mary-land
1986	581.6	1,998	1,163	152.2	1,771	533.6	487.1	63,945	62	591	41.8	3,815	94.4	54.8	45.6
1987	586.3	2,028	1,191	157.1	1,871	500.0	480.3	100,246	145	573	43.3	3,406	93.0	43.3	42.0
1988	634.0	2,160	1,370	164.6	2,254	476.7	394.6	118,499	87	555	43.9	2,909	79.2	35.1	37.6
1989	678.4	2,016	1,367	170.8	2,335	485.9	365.0	141,782	78	582	46.6	2,714	75.9	31.8	27.0
1990	732.3	2,218	1,625	173.8	2,827	487.4	415.0	164,301	72	631	58.0	2,401	70.2	26.9	19.3
1991	763.4	2,179	1,664	177.3	2,951	511.0	502.2	179,200	70	640	63.2	2,232	66.7	25.6	12.1
1992	784.4	2,195	1,722	177.7	3,059	528.8	881.0	205,600	76	630	59.1	2,280	61.6	26.7	9.4
1993	746.4	2,163	1,614	175.2	2,827	529.7	707.8	195,476	67	538	62.5	2,412	64.0	26.7	7.5
1994[1]	672.9	2,368	1,593	177.0	2,800	442.1		200,000	62		77.0	2,588	69.6	24.1	8.4

[1]Preliminary. [2]Domestic. [3]For consumption. [4]In bulk. [5]Flue-cured and cigar wrapper, year beginning July 1; for all other types, October 1. [6]Kentucky-Tennessee types 22-23. [7]Types 41-46. *Source: Economic Research Service, U.S. Department of Agriculture*

Tobacco Production in the U.S., by Types   In Millions of Pounds (Farm-Sale Weight)

Types	11-14	21	22	23	31	32	35-36	37	41	41-61	51	54	55	61
1986	644.6	3.5	26.6	11.2	407.9	27.8	10.9	.2	15.2	30.4	2.0	4.7	6.4	1.7
1987	690.9	2.6	17.5	7.5	419.4	20.7	6.8	.1	13.3	25.3	1.9	5.7	2.7	1.6
1988	813.2	2.9	19.8	8.0	477.2	18.4	7.4	.1	11.7	22.5	1.6	5.0	1.9	2.1
1989	808.4	2.5	18.5	8.0	482.6	17.8	6.4	.1	10.7	25.7	1.3	7.8	3.6	2.3
1990	939.2	2.8	22.9	9.3	597.9	16.3	7.5	.1	13.1	30.3	1.2	9.6	4.0	2.7
1991	911.9	3.6	20.6	8.7	658.2	19.9	8.7	.2	13.7	32.6	1.4	9.3	5.1	2.2
1992	906.0	2.6	23.7	10.5	719.6	18.8	10.3	.1	14.0	30.1	1.5	8.5	4.6	1.5
1993	886.9	1.9	27.0	12.1	633.8	19.4	11.1	.1	12.2	22.1	1.7	4.7	2.0	1.6
1994[1]	869.6	2.2	29.8	12.1	628.5	19.8	10.8	.1	11.3	20.6	1.7	4.2	1.6	1.8

[1]Preliminary. *Source: Agricultural Statistics Board, U.S. Department of Agriculture*

TOBACCO

U.S. Exports of Unmanufactured Tobacco   In Millions of Pounds (Declared Weight)

Year	Australia	Belgium-Luxem.	Denmark	Egypt	France	Germany	Ireland	Italy	Japan	Nether-lands	Norway	Sweden	Switzer-land	Thailand	United Kingdom	Total U.S. Exports
1984	8.2	9.4	19.8	37.4	5.1	66.0	8.0	31.3	92.1	22.3	4.7	11.5	25.3	14.6	31.8	542.7
1985	7.3	11.5	16.2	41.2	9.9	76.7	7.3	28.7	102.0	20.9	3.3	15.8	23.9	17.8	18.4	548.9
1986	11.7	10.1	14.5	46.5	8.4	82.7	3.4	22.5	83.2	31.2	4.3	10.2	11.5	13.0	21.8	477.5
1987	8.5	8.2	15.6	11.0	6.7	69.3	1.2	22.4	105.4	32.1	3.3	8.0	12.6	7.5	16.7	430.0
1988	9.0	9.7	16.4	15.7	5.7	87.2	2.0	32.4	70.4	41.0	3.7	12.0	15.5	13.5	19.6	481.8
1989	6.2	12.3	13.8	.4	4.8	75.4	1.3	17.1	105.3	43.2	3.6	8.3	10.4	15.7	18.4	485.9
1990	8.3	12.4	15.1	.5	5.7	75.9	1.6	19.3	106.5	45.3	3.4	9.5	13.3	22.2	20.5	492.5
1991	7.7	11.0	14.8	4.6	6.5	82.8	4.3	19.9	83.1	42.8	3.5	8.3	14.8	19.5	18.9	499.3
1992	6.9	21.3	15.6	.2	4.2	93.3	2.5	19.0	131.0	49.9	3.4	8.8	7.5	16.9	24.3	574.4
1993	5.7	12.8	15.5	7.8	4.3	52.1	2.4	7.3	124.7	38.1	3.8	8.1	6.1	17.8	20.8	458.0
1994[1]	6.4	12.3	14.9		3.1	54.1	1.3	11.3	126.2	30.9		7.3	6.0	19.0	14.7	433.8

[1] Preliminary.   *Source: Economic Research Service, U.S. Department of Agriculture*

U.S. Salient Statistics for Flue-Cured Tobacco (Types 11-14)   In Millions of Pounds

Year	Acres Harvested 1,000	Yield Per Acre Pounds	Mar-ketings	Stocks July 1	Total Supply	Exports	Domestic Disap-pearance	Total Disap-pearance	Farm Price ¢ Lb.	Placed Under Gov't Loan Mil. Lb.	Price Support Level ¢ Lb.	Loan Stocks Nov. 30	Loan Stocks Uncom-mitted
1984-5	392.0	2,206	850	2,165	3,015	481	454	935	181.1	159.0	169.9	927.4	664.8
1985-6	357.1	2,241	789	2,080	2,870	435	477	912	171.9	132.2	169.9	922.4	767.7
1986-7	308.3	2,099	667	1,958	2,625	393	480	873	152.7	55.5	143.8	752.9	475.9
1987-8	324.6	2,129	683	1,752	2,435	385	537	922	158.7	24.8	143.5	630.4	397.7
1988-9	366.4	2,219	796	1,513	2,309	363	522	885	161.3	15.2	144.2	421.9	328.4
1989-90	390.7	2,069	838	1,424	2,262	387	567	954	167.4	28.4	146.8	314.5	218.2
1990-1	416.9	2,253	920	1,308	2,228	403	609	1,012	167.3	74.4	148.8	226.4	223.8
1991-2	402.6	2,265	882	1,216	2,098	403	472	875	172.3	49.9	152.8	153.7	174.5
1992-3	401.5	2,257	901	1,223	2,124	420	509	929	172.6	81.8	156.0	223.6	129.0
1993-4[1]	400.1	2,217	892	1,195	2,087	359	433	792	168.1	204.9	157.7	330.5	317.5
1994-5[2]	359.5	2,419	807	1,295	2,102	335	485	820	170.3	98.3	158.3	300.9	396.5

[1] Preliminary.   [2] Estimate.   *Source: Economic Research Service, U.S. Department of Agriculture*

U.S. Salient Statistics for Burley Tobacco (Type 31)   In Millions of Pounds

Year	Acres Harvested 1,000	Yield Per Acre Pounds	Mar-ketings	Stocks Oct. 1	Total Supply	Exports	Domestic Disap-pearance	Total Disap-pearance	Farm Price ¢ Lb.	Gross Sales[3]	Price Support Level ¢ Lb.	Loan Stocks Nov. 30	Loan Stocks Uncom-mitted
1984-5	315.7	2,256	674	1,344	2,018	154	403	556	187.6	479.0	175.1	426.7	376.0
1985-6	255.1	2,247	542	1,462	2,004	151	425	576	159.7	494.0	148.8	570.3	566.0
1986-7	210.7	1,936	420	1,426	1,846	165	402	567	156.5	409.9	148.8	544.0	479.6
1987-8	215.9	1,943	428	1,279	1,706	157	478	635	156.3	374.2	148.8	332.9	231.0
1988-9	226.4	2,109	468	1,073	1,541	164	414	578	161.0	351.5	150.0	243.4	117.7
1989-90	244.4	1,975	498	963	1,461	169	446	614	167.2	398.1	153.2	314.5	91.6
1990-1	270.6	2,204	592	847	1,439	199	475	674	175.3	467.8	155.8	226.4	52.0
1991-2	312.0	2,110	657	765	1,422	209	407	616	178.8	501.5	158.4	62.3	32.8
1992-3	332.7	2,163	700	807	1,507	183	385	568	181.5	502.4	164.9	131.2	129.0
1993-4[1]	299.7	2,115	627	939	1,566	152	400	552	181.6	492.4	168.3	178.8	317.5
1994-5[2]	268.6	2,340	580	1,014	1,594	145	450	595		455.7	171.4	380.8	396.5

[1] Preliminary.   [2] Estimate.   [3] Before Christmas holidays.   *Source: Economic Research Service, U.S. Department of Agriculture*

Exports of Tobacco from the United States (Quantity and Value)   In Metric Tons

Year	Unmanufactured Flue-Cured	Value $1,000	Burley	Value $1,000	Total	Value $1,000	Manu-factured	Value $1,000
1991	115,481	776,654	61,852	441,223	226,463	1,427,630	NA	4,574,086
1992	146,100	983,478	64,481	483,743	260,526	1,650,559	58,115	4,509,395
1993	111,636	752,646	51,892	389,964	207,747	1,306,067	49,669	4,253,286
1994[1]	107,411	749,305	49,859	380,993	196,792	1,302,744	63,837	5,367,220

[1] Preliminary.   NA = Not available.   *Source: Foreign Agricultural Service, U.S. Department of Agriculture*

Tung Oil

Tung oil is derived from the seeds of the tung tree, and is used as an industrial lubricant and drying agent. The tung tree is found mainly in China, which is the leading producer and exporter of tung oil.

The Food and Agricultural Organization (FAO) of the United Nations estimates that world production of tung oil in 1993 was 83,000 tonnes, a decline of 9 percent from 1992. Over the period of 1979 to 1981, world tung oil production averaged 79,000 tonnes. By far, the largest producer of tung oil is China with 1993 production forecast at 61,000 tonnes, or nearly three-quarters of total world output. There are a number of other countries which are smaller producers. The next largest producer is Argentina with output forecast at 11,000 tonnes. This is the same output as in the previous two seasons but down from the average production of 1979-81 of 13,000 tonnes. Paraguay is also a tung oil producer with 1993 output estimated by the FAO at 8,000 tonnes. This also represents a decline from the 1979-81 average of 13,000 tonnes.

The U.S. is an importer of tung oil of around 3,000 tonnes per year. Over the first six months of 1994, the average price per pound of imported tung oil in New York, f.o.b., was $129.50.

World Tung Oil Trade   In Metric Tons

Year	Germany	Hong Kong	Italy	Japan	Nether-lands	South Korea	Taiwan	United Kingdom	United States	World Total	Argentina	China	EC-12	Hong Kong	Paraguay	World Total
					Imports								Exports			
1987	1,426	5,197	506	14,794	881	2,426	-----	1,198	5,894	48,873	5,660	30,570	984	4,768	7,741	50,245
1988	341	7,118	699	10,688	585	2,234	-----	848	6,407	43,639	5,061	26,933	1,097	7,343	5,213	46,201
1989	263	4,119	541	13,137	631	2,533	1,538	1,037	6,474	45,469	9,506	24,248	637	4,085	8,296	47,373
1990	239	4,176	319	12,424	1,212	3,249	3,152	924	4,046	37,820	8,557	16,069	662	4,454	8,347	38,741
1991	407	6,476	411	11,890	553	3,035	4,957	862	5,646	41,274	8,522	14,485	620	7,182	9,039	40,684
1992[1]	242	8,509	439	13,326	812	3,722	6,676	893	4,996	45,523	5,808	20,867	467	8,174	4,221	40,290
1993[2]	226	5,222	399	6,549	1,330	3,490	3,595	717	4,270	31,776	5,400	18,000	1,228	6,004	2,850	34,166

[1]Preliminary. [2]Estimate. *Source: The Oil World*

U.S. Consumption of Tung Oil in Inedible Products   In Thousands of Pounds

Year	Jan	Feb	Mar	Apr	May	June	July	Aug	Sept	Oct	Nov	Dec	Total
1988	2,169	1,143	988	1,117	1,072	878	713	1,148	1,276	2,751	2,509	4,317	20,081
1989	4,106	3,360	3,074	2,717	2,313	2,508	2,511	2,512	2,541	2,845	2,668	2,510	33,665
1990	2,573	646	680	823	795	923	712	738	607	626	472	611	10,206
1991	-----------1,953 -----------			-----------1,555 -----------			-----------1,334 -----------			-----------1,100 -----------			5,942
1992	435	459	574	498	502	694	572	705	674	873	530	790	7,306
1993	958	966	693	1,041	833	1,022	867	1,427	1,354	860	585	593	11,199
1994[1]	608	592	635	1,408	1,558	840	861	910	480	392	660	384	9,328

[1]Preliminary. *Source: Bureau of Census, U.S. Department of Commerce*

U.S. Stocks of Tung Oil at Factories & Warehouses   In Thousands of Pounds

Year	Jan. 1	Feb. 1	Mar. 1	Apr. 1	May 1	June 1	July 1	Aug. 1	Sept. 1	Oct. 1	Nov. 1	Dec. 1
1988	3,224	4,501	5,296	4,374	4,304	3,500	3,913	3,797	3,422	4,999	3,821	3,498
1989	3,739	3,012	3,867	3,526	3,225	3,216	4,836	3,860	3,640	5,450	4,649	5,037
1990	5,448	4,648	2,744	2,529	3,164	2,859	2,003	1,553	1,880	1,018	1,913	2,374
1991	1,829	-----------------------		2,997	-----------------------		1,379	-----------------------		963	-----------------------	
1992	1,608	2,421	2,439	1,605	1,323	1,540	847	1,348	2,162	1,724	2,560	3,545
1993	3,122	2,038	2,390	2,120	2,966	1,773	866	815	1,596	1,217	1,635	1,752
1994[1]	1,551	2,053	1,507	2,049	2,091	2,591	2,148	1,562	820	2,455	1,712	1,909

[1]Preliminary. *Source: Bureau of Census, U.S. Department of Commerce*

Average Price of Tung Oil (Imported, Drums) F.O.B. New York   In Cents Per Pound

Year	Jan	Feb	Mar	Apr	May	June	July	Aug	Sept	Oct	Nov	Dec	Average
1987	33.20	44.50	50.50	59.50	57.25	56.38	56.50	56.50	56.50	56.50	56.50	56.50	53.36
1988	57.63	58.00	58.00	56.88	53.50	52.00	51.00	49.80	49.00	48.25	44.75	44.00	51.90
1989	41.00	41.00	41.00	41.00	41.00	41.00	41.00	41.00	41.00	41.00	41.00	41.00	41.00
1990	41.00	41.00	41.00	59.00	59.00	58.25	58.00	58.00	58.00	55.50	62.00	70.00	55.06
1991	70.00	63.00	61.50	63.00	63.00	61.50	61.00	61.00	61.00	61.00	61.00	70.00	63.08
1992	70.00	70.00	70.00	76.00	82.00	130.00	130.00	130.00	132.00	131.50	132.00	130.00	106.96
1993	130.00	130.00	130.00	130.00	117.00	130.00	130.00	130.00	130.00	130.00	130.00	130.00	128.92
1994[1]	130.00	130.00	130.00	129.00	129.00	129.00							129.50

[1]Preliminary. *Source: Economic Research Service, U.S. Department of Agriculture*

Tungsten

Tungsten finds its major use in the production of cutting and wear-resistant materials. Nearly 60 percent of tungsten is used to produce tungsten carbide. Tungsten carbide is used for cutting tools, mining and drilling tools, dies, bearings and armor-piercing projectiles. Nearly 25 percent of tungsten use is in unalloyed tungsten, which is formed into wire and employed in filaments for incandescent and fluorescent lamps. Tungsten also finds use as a fireproofing material.

U.S. consumption of tungsten concentrate in the second quarter of 1994 was 1,116 (tungsten content). Data for the first quarter of 1994 was withheld to avoid disclosing company proprietary data. Imports for consumption over the January-May 1994 period totaled 481 tonnes. For 1993, imports for consumption were 1,721 tonnes. Tungsten scrap consumption for the first six-months of 1994 was 997 tonnes. Stocks of tungsten concentrate on June 30, 1994 were 535 tonnes.

U.S. consumption of ammonium paratungstate for the first half of 1994 was 3,118 tonnes, compared to 6,695 tonnes in 1993. Stocks on June 30, 1994 were 251 tonnes.

Production of tungsten metal powder for the January-June 1994 period was 1,836 tonnes. For all of 1993, metal powder production was 4,811 tonnes. Tungsten carbide powder production for January-June 1994 was 2,077 tonnes. During 1993, production was 4,150 tonnes. Production data for tungsten cast and crystalline carbide powder and chemical was withheld to avoid disclosing company proprietary data. Stocks of tungsten products on June 30, 1994 were 1,239 tonnes. December 31, 1993 stocks were 1,482 tonnes.

U.S. exports of tungsten for January-May 1994 were 997 tonnes. Major destinations included Canada, Germany, Israel and Japan.

World Concentrate Production of Tungsten — In Metric Tons (Contained Tungsten[3])

Year	Australia	Austria	Bolivia	Brazil	Burma	China	Kazakhstan[4]	Mongolia	Peru	Portugal	Rep. of Korea	Russia[4]	World Total
1986	1,600	1,387	1,095	875	715	15,000	------	1,500	742	1,637	2,455	9,200	43,480
1987	1,150	1,250	638	800	493	21,000	------	1,500	205	1,207	2,375	9,200	42,474
1988	1,261	1,235	900	738	307	30,000	------	1,000	432	1,382	2,029	9,200	50,869
1989	1,371	1,517	1,118	679	233	30,200	------	600	970	1,376	1,701	9,300	51,038
1990	1,086	1,378	1,014	316	351	32,000	------	500	1,536	1,400	1,361	8,800	51,805
1991	237	1,314	1,065	223	275	31,800	------	300	1,232	1,400	780	8,000	48,567
1992	160	1,500	851	205	375	25,000	500	260	802	1,200	247	4,000	37,452
1993[1]	100	300	320	250	270	20,000	500	250	800	1,000	200	3,500	29,509
1994[2]	100		800	100	100	15,000					200	2,000	21,000

[1] Preliminary. [2] Estimate. [3] Conversion factors: WO₃ to W, multiply by 0.7931; 60% WO₃ to W, multiply by 0.4758. [4] Formerly part of the U.S.S.R.; data not reported separately until 1992. *Source: U.S. Bureau of Mines*

Salient Statistics of Tungsten in the U.S. — In Metric Tons (Contained Tungsten)

Year	Net Import Reliance as a % Apparent Consumption	Total Consumption	Tool	Stainless & Heat Assisting	Alloy Steel[3]	Superalloys	Cutting & Wear Resistant Materials	Products Made from Metal Powder	Miscellaneous	Chemical and Ceramic	Exports	Imports for Consumption	Consumers	Producers
1987	79	5,506	306	68	28	212	3,911	W	2,662	41	2	4,414	329	21
1988	86	7,832	317	73	77	279	4,651	2,066	748	84	172	8,045	499	21
1989	84	7,725	258	62	W	258	5,018	1,828	476	52	203	7,896	1,261	10
1990	81	5,878	342	64	74	325	4,985	2,181	464	50	139	6,420	1,077	16
1991	91	5,309	243	44	W	287	4,801	1,941	614	44	21	7,837	1,778	26
1992	86	4,313	407	52	66	25	4,211	1,309	828	W	38	2,477	702	44
1993[1]	82	2,866	388	43	40	282	5,064	1,434	2	37	63	1,721	702	44
1994[2]	94	4,000										3,600	------- 400 -------	

Consumption of Tungsten Products by End Uses. Steel headings: Tool, Stainless & Heat Assisting, Alloy Steel[3]. Stocks at End of Year — Concentrates — Consumers, Producers.

[1] Preliminary. [2] Estimate. [3] Other than tool. W = Withheld proprietary data. *Source: U.S. Bureau of Mines*

Tungsten Prices (Monthly Average) — In U.S. Dollars

Year	Jan.	Feb.	Mar.	Apr.	May	June	July	Aug.	Sept.	Oct.	Nov.	Dec.	Average
European Market (London), 65% WO3 Basis, C.I.F.[1] -- $ Per Metric Ton
1990	50.75	48.57	47.83	48.25	50.00	48.44	46.28	45.00	43.81	42.56	42.50	43.00	46.42
1991	44.16	47.75	48.54	53.69	56.38	57.00	57.89	61.25	63.00	63.00	63.00	63.00	56.56
1992	61.50	61.00	61.00	61.00	60.57	59.21	57.50	57.50	55.75	51.67	50.00	45.00	56.81
1993	45.00	42.63	37.50	36.38	33.94	33.00	32.44	27.75	27.89	32.13	33.00	33.00	34.56
U.S. Spot Quotations, 65% WO3, Basis C.I.F., U.S. Ports (Including Duty) -- $ Per Short Ton
1990	43.73	41.89	43.54	46.57	45.06	43.82	41.34	41.34	38.77	38.58	38.58	39.13	41.86
1991	39.80	46.00	47.63	57.00	58.00	59.38	61.00	61.70	62.50	62.13	57.00	57.00	55.76
1992	57.00	57.00	56.25	54.40	52.50	50.88	49.50	49.00	49.00	48.10	43.75	43.50	50.91
1993	43.50	43.50	42.00	40.50	40.50	40.50	40.50	35.63	34.00	34.00	34.00	34.00	38.55

[1] Combined wolframite and scheelite quoations. *Source: U.S. Bureau of Mines*

U.S. Basis of Turkey-Feed Price Ration   In Pounds[1]

Year	Jan	Feb	Mar	Apr	May	June	July	Aug	Sept	Oct	Nov	Dec	Average
1984	3.6	3.2	3.3	3.3	3.3	3.3	3.6	3.8	3.9	4.4	5.0	5.5	3.9
1985	4.7	3.8	3.7	3.7	3.7	3.9	4.2	4.5	5.0	5.5	5.5	5.6	4.5
1986	3.4	3.4	3.5	3.5	3.8	4.3	4.5	4.6	4.7	4.9	4.8	4.0	4.1
1987	3.3	3.4	3.4	3.5	3.4	3.3	3.1	3.0	2.9	2.8	3.1	3.6	3.2
1988	2.9	2.6	2.5	2.7	2.8	3.0	3.0	3.1	3.4	3.6	3.6	2.9	3.0
1989	2.7	2.9	3.1	3.3	3.5	3.5	3.3	3.3	3.0	3.2	3.4	3.3	3.2
1990	3.0	2.8	3.1	3.1	3.2	3.2	3.3	3.4	3.4	3.6	3.6	3.1	3.2
1991	2.9	3.0	3.1	3.2	3.2	3.3	3.4	3.5	3.5	3.1	3.1	3.2	3.2
1992	3.0	3.0	3.1	3.1	3.1	3.2	3.2	3.1	3.1	3.2	3.3	3.2	3.1
1993	2.9	2.9	3.1	3.0	3.0	3.0	3.1	3.2	3.3	3.4	3.4	3.3	3.1
1994[2]	2.9	2.9	3.0	3.0	3.1	3.1	3.2	3.2	3.3	3.5	3.5	3.3	3.2

[1]Pounds of feed equal in value to one pound of turkey, liveweight.   [2]Preliminary.   *Source: Economic Research Service, U.S. Department of Agriculture*

Average Price Received by Farmers for Turkeys in the United States (Liveweight)   In Cents Per Pound

Year	Jan	Feb	Mar	Apr	May	June	July	Aug	Sept	Oct	Nov	Dec	Average
1984	46.50	40.80	41.20	42.90	42.30	42.00	43.70	45.40	46.70	51.30	56.30	60.00	46.59
1985	50.30	40.50	39.50	39.20	38.50	40.60	44.00	47.50	51.80	56.90	58.40	59.10	47.19
1986	35.60	36.30	36.90	38.10	40.90	45.90	49.30	50.90	51.40	53.00	51.50	43.00	44.40
1987	35.10	35.80	35.70	36.30	35.50	34.10	33.50	32.10	31.30	30.20	34.00	38.40	34.33
1988	32.30	29.70	28.40	28.40	29.80	32.10	40.40	42.00	45.40	48.40	47.90	38.30	36.93
1989	35.50	38.40	40.30	42.00	43.60	43.80	41.20	40.80	36.40	38.20	40.70	39.30	40.02
1990	35.40	33.70	36.40	36.60	38.30	38.70	39.10	40.20	40.30	42.50	42.30	36.90	38.37
1991	33.60	35.10	37.00	37.60	38.30	38.70	39.10	40.10	40.20	37.00	37.00	38.10	37.65
1992	36.30	35.50	37.00	37.00	37.70	37.70	37.90	37.80	37.50	38.50	39.40	39.30	37.63
1993	35.60	35.70	37.60	37.60	37.70	37.60	38.70	39.60	41.10	43.20	42.70	40.80	38.99
1994[1]	36.80	37.10	38.40	39.10	39.50	40.00	41.20	41.70	42.60	44.30	44.80	42.30	40.65

[1]Preliminary.   *Source: Economic Research Service, U.S. Department of Agriculture*

Wholesale Price of Turkeys[1] (Hens, 8-16 Lbs.) N.Y.   In Cents Per Pound

Year	Jan	Feb	Mar	Apr	May	June	July	Aug	Sept	Oct	Nov	Dec	Average
1984	72.19	64.72	66.08	66.95	66.85	67.00	68.57	72.42	76.24	82.61	91.49	97.31	74.37
1985	74.05	65.62	67.04	64.62	62.64	68.13	72.84	78.37	82.37	90.20	93.11	86.88	75.49
1986	60.25	61.67	63.94	64.61	67.08	73.83	77.85	80.46	81.21	83.17	80.68	71.11	72.16
1987	55.25	58.47	60.34	58.33	55.26	55.72	56.30	56.14	56.14	54.73	60.73	66.45	57.82
1988	52.79	47.09	47.01	46.90	49.29	57.14	70.82	70.46	76.02	79.64	75.97	61.59	61.23
1989	59.03	62.17	65.71	68.33	72.08	72.98	66.40	62.61	57.88	67.61	72.45	72.70	66.66
1990	55.55	55.16	58.86	59.62	61.27	62.88	63.37	66.57	68.99	76.15	73.70	56.05	63.18
1991	53.49	55.76	59.10	60.32	62.32	62.68	63.41	64.66	64.38	60.52	63.07	65.18	61.24
1992	58.74	55.00	58.77	60.00	60.03	59.46	57.02	57.80	61.02	63.92	65.57	65.14	60.21
1993	58.05	56.83	58.41	58.98	58.81	58.35	59.76	63.43	66.73	71.28	71.76	68.20	62.55
1994[2]	60.09	59.32	60.98	61.58	63.14	64.61	65.26	66.39	68.98	73.13	74.01	70.35	65.65

[1]Ready-to-cook.   [2]Preliminary.   *Source: Economic Research Service, U.S. Department of Agriculture*

Certified Federally Inspected Turkey Slaughter in the U.S. (Ready-to-Cook Weights)   In Millions of Pounds

Year	Jan	Feb	Mar	Apr	May	June	July	Aug	Sept	Oct	Nov	Dec	Total
1984	138.1	139.0	155.1	163.1	202.6	223.6	242.3	279.6	255.4	320.8	271.7	182.8	2,574
1985	157.7	148.0	176.4	177.3	212.5	238.5	271.1	295.2	288.3	341.5	282.5	210.7	2,800
1986	187.5	175.0	193.6	205.2	236.4	275.8	307.6	299.4	331.4	365.8	307.1	248.2	3,133
1987	215.4	212.8	241.9	255.0	274.1	335.8	358.8	357.4	383.9	411.4	373.5	297.0	3,717
1988	255.7	266.9	314.0	276.6	331.3	373.2	322.4	377.3	365.8	395.7	371.7	272.8	3,923
1989	254.1	248.1	301.3	268.8	356.9	388.6	360.4	430.3	385.7	422.6	423.1	334.9	4,175
1990	334.0	298.3	351.1	328.4	384.1	389.2	395.7	444.0	382.9	478.4	446.2	328.6	4,561
1991	365.6	322.0	329.7	375.8	398.2	380.7	402.2	421.8	404.8	482.0	419.2	349.9	4,652
1992	362.9	331.7	361.3	385.2	374.2	435.0	451.8	411.9	431.3	467.6	423.0	393.1	4,829
1993	354.1	322.7	382.9	391.9	378.7	446.7	419.3	426.9	436.0	451.4	461.8	375.3	4,848
1994[1]	347.8	342.0	400.9	380.6	415.6	457.9	405.6	483.6	447.7	453.6	453.9	397.5	4,992

[1]Preliminary.   *Source: Economic Research Service, U.S. Department of Agriculture*

TURKEYS

U.S. Basis of Turkey-Feed Price Ration   In Pounds[1]

Year	Jan	Feb	Mar	Apr	May	June	July	Aug	Sept	Oct	Nov	Dec	Average
1984	3.6	3.2	3.3	3.3	3.3	3.3	3.6	3.8	3.9	4.4	5.0	5.5	3.9
1985	4.7	3.8	3.7	3.7	3.7	3.9	4.2	4.5	5.0	5.5	5.5	5.6	4.5
1986	3.4	3.4	3.5	3.5	3.8	4.3	4.5	4.6	4.7	4.9	4.8	4.0	4.1
1987	3.3	3.4	3.4	3.5	3.4	3.3	3.1	3.0	2.9	2.8	3.1	3.6	3.2
1988	2.9	2.6	2.5	2.7	2.8	3.0	3.0	3.1	3.4	3.6	3.6	2.9	3.0
1989	2.7	2.9	3.1	3.3	3.5	3.5	3.3	3.3	3.0	3.2	3.4	3.3	3.2
1990	3.0	2.8	3.1	3.1	3.2	3.2	3.3	3.4	3.4	3.6	3.6	3.1	3.2
1991	2.9	3.0	3.1	3.2	3.2	3.3	3.4	3.5	3.5	3.1	3.1	3.2	3.2
1992	3.0	3.0	3.1	3.1	3.1	3.2	3.2	3.1	3.1	3.2	3.3	3.2	3.1
1993	2.9	2.9	3.1	3.0	3.0	3.0	3.1	3.2	3.3	3.4	3.4	3.3	3.1
1994[2]	2.9	2.9	3.0	3.0	3.1	3.1	3.2	3.2	3.3	3.5	3.5	3.3	3.2

[1]Pounds of feed equal in value to one pound of turkey, liveweight.   [2]Preliminary.   *Source: Economic Research Service, U.S. Department of Agriculture*

Average Price Received by Farmers for Turkeys in the United States (Liveweight)   In Cents Per Pound

Year	Jan	Feb	Mar	Apr	May	June	July	Aug	Sept	Oct	Nov	Dec	Average
1984	46.50	40.80	41.20	42.90	42.30	42.00	43.70	45.40	46.70	51.30	56.30	60.00	46.59
1985	50.30	40.50	39.50	39.20	38.50	40.60	44.00	47.50	51.80	56.90	58.40	59.10	47.19
1986	35.60	36.30	36.90	38.10	40.90	45.90	49.30	50.90	51.40	53.00	51.50	43.00	44.40
1987	35.10	35.80	35.70	36.30	35.50	34.10	33.50	32.10	31.30	30.20	34.00	38.40	34.33
1988	32.30	29.70	28.40	28.40	29.80	32.10	40.40	42.00	45.40	48.40	47.90	38.30	36.93
1989	35.50	38.40	40.30	42.00	43.60	43.80	41.20	40.80	36.40	38.20	40.70	39.30	40.02
1990	35.40	33.70	36.40	36.60	38.30	38.70	39.10	40.20	40.30	42.50	42.30	36.90	38.37
1991	33.60	35.10	37.00	37.60	38.30	38.70	39.10	40.10	40.20	37.00	37.00	38.10	37.65
1992	36.30	35.50	37.00	37.00	37.70	37.70	37.90	37.80	37.50	38.50	39.40	39.30	37.63
1993	35.60	35.70	37.60	37.60	37.70	37.60	38.70	39.60	41.10	43.20	42.70	40.80	38.99
1994[1]	36.80	37.10	38.40	39.10	39.50	40.00	41.20	41.70	42.60	44.30	44.80	42.30	40.65

[1]Preliminary.   *Source: Economic Research Service, U.S. Department of Agriculture*

Wholesale Price of Turkeys[1] (Hens, 8-16 Lbs.) N.Y.   In Cents Per Pound

Year	Jan	Feb	Mar	Apr	May	June	July	Aug	Sept	Oct	Nov	Dec	Average
1984	72.19	64.72	66.08	66.95	66.85	67.00	68.57	72.42	76.24	82.61	91.49	97.31	74.37
1985	74.05	65.62	67.04	64.62	62.64	68.13	72.84	78.37	82.37	90.20	93.11	86.88	75.49
1986	60.25	61.67	63.94	64.61	67.08	73.83	77.85	80.46	81.21	83.17	80.68	71.11	72.16
1987	55.25	58.47	60.34	58.33	55.26	55.72	56.30	56.14	56.14	54.73	60.73	66.45	57.82
1988	52.79	47.09	47.01	46.90	49.29	57.14	70.82	70.46	76.02	79.64	75.97	61.59	61.23
1989	59.03	62.17	65.71	68.33	72.08	72.98	66.40	62.61	57.88	67.61	72.45	72.70	66.66
1990	55.55	55.16	58.86	59.62	61.27	62.88	63.37	66.57	68.99	76.15	73.70	56.05	63.18
1991	53.49	55.76	59.10	60.32	62.32	62.68	63.41	64.66	64.38	60.52	63.07	65.18	61.24
1992	58.74	55.00	58.77	60.00	60.03	59.46	57.02	57.80	61.02	63.92	65.57	65.14	60.21
1993	58.05	56.83	58.41	58.98	58.81	58.35	59.76	63.43	66.73	71.28	71.76	68.20	62.55
1994[2]	60.09	59.32	60.98	61.58	63.14	64.61	65.26	66.39	68.98	73.13	74.01	70.35	65.65

[1]Ready-to-cook.   [2]Preliminary.   *Source: Economic Research Service, U.S. Department of Agriculture*

Certified Federally Inspected Turkey Slaughter in the U.S. (Ready-to-Cook Weights)   In Millions of Pounds

Year	Jan	Feb	Mar	Apr	May	June	July	Aug	Sept	Oct	Nov	Dec	Total
1984	138.1	139.0	155.1	163.1	202.6	223.6	242.3	279.6	255.4	320.8	271.7	182.8	2,574
1985	157.7	148.0	176.4	177.3	212.5	238.5	271.1	295.2	288.3	341.5	282.5	210.7	2,800
1986	187.5	175.0	193.6	205.2	236.4	275.8	307.6	299.4	331.4	365.8	307.1	248.2	3,133
1987	215.4	212.8	241.9	255.0	274.1	335.8	358.8	357.4	383.9	411.4	373.5	297.0	3,717
1988	255.7	266.9	314.0	276.6	331.3	373.2	322.4	377.3	365.8	395.7	371.7	272.8	3,923
1989	254.1	248.1	301.3	268.8	356.9	388.6	360.4	430.3	385.7	422.6	423.1	334.9	4,175
1990	334.0	298.3	351.1	328.4	384.1	389.2	395.7	444.0	382.9	478.4	446.2	328.6	4,561
1991	365.6	322.0	329.7	375.8	398.2	380.7	402.2	421.8	404.8	482.0	419.2	349.9	4,652
1992	362.9	331.7	361.3	385.2	374.2	435.0	451.8	411.9	431.3	467.6	423.0	393.1	4,829
1993	354.1	322.7	382.9	391.9	378.7	446.7	419.3	426.9	436.0	451.4	461.8	375.3	4,848
1994[1]	347.8	342.0	400.9	380.6	415.6	457.9	405.6	483.6	447.7	453.6	453.9	397.5	4,992

[1]Preliminary.   *Source: Economic Research Service, U.S. Department of Agriculture*

Turkey Per Capita Consumption in the U.S.   In Pounds

Year	Jan	Feb	Mar	Apr	May	June	July	Aug	Sept	Oct	Nov	Dec	Total
1983	0.7	0.6	0.8	0.7	0.7	0.8	0.7	0.9	0.9	1.1	2.1	1.2	11.0
1984	0.6	0.7	0.7	0.7	0.7	0.8	0.8	1.0	0.8	1.3	2.1	1.1	11.0
1985	0.7	0.6	0.7	0.6	0.8	0.8	0.9	0.9	1.0	1.3	2.3	1.1	11.6
1986	0.7	0.7	0.9	0.7	0.8	0.9	0.9	1.0	1.1	1.4	2.5	1.3	12.9
1987	0.8	0.8	0.9	0.9	0.9	1.0	1.1	1.1	1.3	1.7	2.8	1.3	14.7
1988	1.0	0.9	1.2	0.9	1.2	1.3	1.1	1.3	1.4	1.5	2.6	1.3	15.7
1989	1.0	1.0	1.2	0.9	1.2	1.1	1.3	1.4	1.5	1.7	2.9	1.4	16.6
1990	1.2	1.1	1.2	1.1	1.3	1.2	1.3	1.5	1.4	1.9	2.9	1.4	17.6
1991	1.4	1.1	1.2	1.3	1.4	1.3	1.4	1.4	1.4	1.8	3.0	1.5	18.0
1992	1.1	1.1	1.2	1.3	1.2	1.3	1.4	1.4	1.4	1.8	3.1	1.6	18.0
1993	1.2	1.0	1.4	1.2	1.2	1.3	1.2	1.3	1.4	1.8	3.2	1.5	17.8
1994[1]	----------- 3.6		-----------	----------- 3.8		-----------	----------- 4.5		-----------	-----------	6.2	-----------	18.0

[1]Preliminary. Source: Economic Research Service, U.S. Department of Agriculture

Storage Stocks of Turkeys (Frozen) in the United States   In Millions of Pounds

Year	Jan. 1	Feb. 1	Mar. 1	Apr. 1	May 1	June 1	July 1	Aug. 1	Sept. 1	Oct. 1	Nov. 1	Dec. 1
1984	161.8	161.5	145.8	144.4	142.2	180.9	226.3	278.2	331.3	390.6	415.4	195.7
1985	125.3	124.1	129.5	131.1	157.0	183.7	243.3	304.7	387.8	444.5	484.1	208.2
1986	150.2	159.2	163.6	150.5	188.9	229.5	297.8	388.1	449.3	511.6	543.2	249.0
1987	178.2	198.1	211.4	226.0	250.8	298.1	381.6	472.7	560.0	640.8	629.9	321.5
1988	282.4	281.8	321.5	339.0	370.7	410.1	456.8	496.2	551.9	572.8	583.3	303.5
1989	249.7	262.5	263.1	269.2	298.7	355.6	454.6	496.9	574.3	569.3	571.8	258.6
1990	235.9	268.4	276.3	317.9	354.9	405.6	481.3	541.7	593.1	623.6	625.1	338.4
1991	306.4	302.5	342.2	370.0	408.5	453.4	503.1	571.3	625.8	667.2	653.0	305.5
1992	264.1	325.5	354.1	392.3	430.2	486.8	580.1	662.1	684.2	734.4	714.7	320.5
1993	271.7	314.7	359.8	359.2	424.4	474.0	556.1	624.2	678.6	713.8	683.6	290.6
1994[1]	249.1	279.8	304.8	346.5	399.1	463.7	545.3	598.2	623.4	648.6	636.2	280.7

[1]Preliminary. Source: Economic Research Service, U.S. Department of Agriculture

Turkey (Whole) Costs to Selected Retailers in the U.S.   In Cents Per Pound

Year	Jan	Feb	Mar	Apr	May	June	July	Aug	Sept	Oct	Nov	Dec	Average
1983	61.40	61.50	62.30	62.60	63.80	68.80	67.40	67.70	70.40	71.00	72.50	80.40	67.48
1984	78.40	73.70	74.80	75.20	75.60	75.90	77.00	79.80	83.50	89.30	97.70	104.50	82.12
1985	84.00	75.30	75.90	73.30	71.80	75.90	80.40	84.30	89.50	97.00	99.80	95.90	83.59
1986	72.60	71.10	72.30	72.90	76.30	83.30	86.30	90.00	90.20	92.70	91.90	80.30	81.66
1987	63.80	65.80	67.60	67.00	65.50	65.00	64.70	63.30	64.30	64.30	68.00	75.70	66.25
1988	63.30	58.00	57.60	56.40	57.80	68.30	72.30	78.50	83.30	87.50	79.80	79.60	74.02
1989	67.60	66.90	71.90	75.10	79.40	80.60	74.40	71.80	76.60	81.90	82.30	66.40	71.35
1990	65.20	64.60	67.30	69.40	70.10	70.10	68.70	73.60	72.80	69.10	70.80	73.90	68.96
1991	62.30	63.06	66.61	66.78	69.70	70.00	70.30	72.20	72.80	69.10	74.00	74.90	69.45
1992	67.90	65.80	68.10	68.70	69.24	69.04	65.70	68.10	69.60	72.30	74.00	74.90	69.45
1993	67.85	67.22	67.94	68.80	68.40	68.19	67.08	72.07	74.91	78.37	80.08	75.03	71.33
1994[1]	70.30	69.40	70.60	70.90	72.00	72.58	72.77	74.75	77.32	79.89	83.33	77.34	74.27

[1]Preliminary. Source: Economic Research Service, U.S. Department of Agriculture

Turkey (Whole) Retail-to-Consumer Price Spread in the U.S.   In Cents Per Pound

Year	Jan	Feb	Mar	Apr	May	June	July	Aug	Sept	Oct	Nov	Dec	Average
1983	30.0	30.9	29.5	30.0	29.0	23.5	25.6	23.7	20.0	24.3	15.2	9.0	24.2
1984	14.3	20.6	20.8	19.1	21.7	23.2	24.3	20.9	18.8	14.5	-0.4	1.5	16.6
1985	25.1	32.0	29.4	31.1	31.2	27.0	23.6	20.1	17.8	10.5	4.4	7.2	21.6
1986	33.7	36.7	32.5	31.3	27.1	19.0	19.3	19.5	21.7	20.2	16.2	21.8	34.9
1987	39.8	37.4	35.4	33.4	37.3	40.1	41.1	41.8	39.0	38.3	22.0	13.6	34.9
1988	29.8	34.9	33.4	33.0	35.1	24.6	23.7	21.0	17.3	16.5	14.7	26.7	25.9
1989	29.8	29.9	25.7	23.2	20.7	20.7	30.2	32.3	34.2	28.9	13.4	15.4	25.4
1990	33.7	33.7	32.1	27.7	29.8	29.7	32.1	27.8	26.7	23.7	8.8	29.6	27.9
1991	37.1	38.1	31.2	33.7	30.9	32.0	32.6	31.2	30.3	34.9	20.8	17.5	30.9
1992	28.2	29.2	27.0	29.4	29.6	29.5	33.3	32.5	31.4	27.2	15.4	18.1	27.5
1993	30.0	31.7	32.6	31.9	32.3	34.5	35.8	29.7	27.7	25.0	13.6	20.4	28.8
1994[1]	27.5	29.7	28.1	25.1	27.1	28.8	28.7	27.6	27.1	25.5	13.9	20.3	25.8

[1]Preliminary. Source: Economic Research Service, U.S. Department of Agriculture

Uranium

The future of uranium oxide use in the U.S. continues to be muddled by public resistance to nuclear power for the generation of electricity. For the U.S., data from the Energy Information Administration indicated that electricity generated by nuclear power in 1994 was 298 trillion kilowatthours, down almost 2 percent from 1993. Nuclear power's share of electricity generation in 1994 was 20.9 percent, compared to 21.8 percent in 1993. This compares with other power sources for electricity generation. Coal's share of electricity generation in 1994 was 57 percent, up from 56.4 percent in 1993. Petroleum's share of U.S. net electricity generation was 4 percent, compared to 3 percent in 1993. Natural gas's share in 1994 was 8.5 percent compared to 7.7 percent.

The dismantlement of nuclear weapons, both in the U.S. and the former Soviet Union is indicative of the trend to lower use of uranium. The dismantlement process, which is technically difficult and enormously expensive appears to be going forward. Russia is to take highly enriched uranium removed from nuclear weapons and dilute it to produce low-enriched uranium for use by American nuclear power plants. The drive to reduce availability of nuclear material such as uranium and plutonium has been marred by reports of smuggling of these materials out of the former Soviet bloc. In late-1994, several hundred pounds of nuclear grade uranium was moved to the U.S. from a former Soviet republic in a sign of cooperation in the control of this material.

Prices of uranium have been declining for many years. In January 1980, uranium prices were about $42 per pound. Recently they have declined to around $7 per pound. There is some indication that the long downtrend in prices may be about to change. One reason is that production has declined. As prices moved lower, mining concerns shut down. This in turn reduced the output of uranium ore.

The reduction in world production is expected to ultimately result in higher uranium prices. While the nuclear power industry in the U.S. has been under fire, other countries have looked to build nuclear generation capacity. This new demand for uranium by foreign electric concerns is now more than offsetting the declining demand by nuclear weapons contractors. Most of the new nuclear power plant construction is taking place in the Pacific Rim, which is undergoing rapid economic growth. The Uranium Institute reported that in the early-1980s, stockpiles of uranium in Western industrialized markets were enough to supply more than seven year's worth of consumption. Stockpiles have now shrunk to about 290 million pounds, which is roughly equivalent to 2.5 years of consumption. The Uranium Institute estimates that the Russian Federation's stockpiles contain between 275 and 420 million pounds of uranium, but noted that those inventories were difficult to verify. The U.S. allows Russia to sell its low-cost uranium to U.S. utilities, but limits those export sales to 6.6 million pounds a year and requires the utilities to buy equal amounts of uranium from domestic producers. Russian shipments under the agreement have been minimal so far but are expected to pick up.

A major issue facing various countries is how to dispose of spent radioactive fuel. A Canadian study has found that the safest way to store spent fuel is deep underground in the granite rock that extends under much of that country. This bed of rock has been unaffected by earthquakes. If the plan is approved, bundles of uranium fuel rods from Canada's 22 nuclear reactors will be placed in titanium casks and sealed with clay inside granite caverns bored two-thirds of a mile deep in the rock.

World Production of Uranium Oxide (U₃O₈) Concentrate   In Short Tons (Uranium Content)

Year	Australia	Canada	China	Czech Rep. & Slovakia	France	Gabon	Germany	India	Namibia	Niger	South Africa	Spain	United States	Former U.S.S.R.	World Total
1985	4,200	14,150	NA	NA	4,150	1,200	NA	NA	4,400	4,150	6,350	NA	5,550	NA	45,150
1986	5,400	15,250	NA	NA	4,250	1,100	NA	NA	4,500	4,100	6,000	NA	6,550	NA	48,200
1987	4,902	16,127	NA	NA	4,377	1,030	26	164	4,590	3,848	5,219	322	6,500	NA	47,745
1988	4,580	15,646	NA	NA	4,377	1,194	58	194	4,551	3,845	5,039	348	6,500	NA	46,846
1989	4,752	14,855	1,039	2,989	4,183	1,157	4,961	273	4,000	3,874	3,810	229	6,919	18,849	75,264
1990	4,589	11,400	1,039	2,600	3,661	922	3,864	273	4,030	3,682	3,169	213	4,443	18,199	64,604
1991	4,909	10,609	1,039	2,340	3,204	882	1,569	260	3,185	3,853	2,248	254	3,976	13,650	53,420
1992[1]	3,032	12,087	1,039	2,040	2,755	702	325	299	2,199	3,855	2,449	241	2,823	10,789	45,719
1993[2]	3,021	11,990			2,220								1,534		

[1] Preliminary. [2] Estimate. NA = Not available. *Source: American Bureau of Metal Statistics, Inc.*

Month-End Uranium (U₃O₈) Transaction Values[1]   In Dollars Per Pound

Year	Jan.	Feb.	Mar.	Apr.	May	June	July	Aug.	Sept.	Oct.	Nov.	Dec.	Average
1985	16.20	15.70	15.05	14.90	14.45	14.60	14.75	15.10	15.10	15.75	15.80	16.55	15.33
1986	16.55	16.70	16.70	17.10	17.15	17.20	17.50	17.45	17.35	17.25	17.30	17.35	17.13
1987	17.35	16.90	16.95	17.00	17.20	17.10	17.30	17.55	18.20	18.05	17.80	17.20	17.38
1988	16.85	16.65	16.55	16.45	16.10	15.80	15.45	15.00	14.50	14.40	13.30	12.50	15.30
1989	12.25	12.00	11.25	11.00	10.75	10.45	9.95	9.80	9.80	9.65	9.55	9.40	10.49
1990	9.25	9.05	8.75	8.65	8.55	8.80	9.75	10.80	11.40	10.10	9.30	9.15	9.46
1991	9.40	9.45	9.35	9.30	9.30	9.20	9.15	8.95	8.70	8.35	7.45	7.50	8.84
1992	7.55	7.80	7.95	7.90	7.85	7.80	7.75	7.85	7.95	8.40	8.55	8.75	8.01
1993	8.80	8.60	8.80	9.20	8.70	8.90	8.20	8.80	9.05	8.45	8.60	-----	8.74

[1] Transaction value is a weighted average price of recent natural uranium sales transactions, based on prices paid on transactions closed within the previous 3-month period for which delivery is scheduled within one year of the transaction date; at least 10 transactions involving a sum total of at least 2 million pounds of U₃O₈ equivalent. *Source: American Metal Market*

Vanadium

Vanadium is commercially important as an oxidation catalyst. It is used in the production of carbon and alloy steels and plates, structural bar, and pipe steels. Vanadium also finds use in ceramics as a coloring agent, enhances strength and toughness, and can be used in tools. Ferrovanadium is an iron alloy used in steel. Vanadium pentoxide usage includes dyeing and printing applications. Vanadium is critical in the production of aerospace titanium alloys, and as a catalyst in the production of maleic anhydride and sulfuric acid.

Consumption of vanadium by end use is in transportation, machinery and tools, and building and heavy construction. U.S. consumption of ferrovanadium for the January-July 1994 period totaled over 2.097 million kilograms. Consumption of other vanadium products including vanadium alloys, chlorides, vanadates, vanadium metal, and specialty chemicals totaled 189,679 kilograms over the same period.

By end use, steel consumption accounted for over 90 percent of total vanadium consumed. Carbon steel was the largest component of use with 35 percent consumed or 810,617 kilograms. Full-alloy steel took 19 percent, while high-strength, low-alloy steel used 24 percent of the total. Tool steel accounted for 11 percent of total U.S. vanadium consumption.

Exports of ferrovanadium during the January-June 1994 period were 164,834 kilograms (vanadium content). Over the same period, exports of vanadium pentoxide were 212,778 kilograms, while other oxides and hydroxides were 460,348 kilograms (vanadium content). Exports of ferrovanadium go primarily to Canada while vanadium pentoxide exports are shipped mostly to Belgium.

Imports of ferrovanadium over the January-June 1994 period were over 1.07 million kilograms. Primary sources included Russia and Canada. Imports of vanadium pentoxide for the same period were 134,109 kilograms, supplied primarily by South Africa and Russia. Imports of vanadium metal, including waste and scrap, were 282,244 kilograms (vanadium content). South Africa supplied 98 percent of this material.

World Production of Vanadium by Country In Metric Tons (Contained Vanadium)

| | | | From Ores, Concentrates and Slag | | | | From Petroleum Residues, Ash, Spent Catalysts | | | |
| | | | Republic of South Africa | | | | | | | |
Year	China[3]	Russia[4]	Content of Pentoxide & Vanadate Products	Content of Vanadiferous Slag Product	Total	Total[5]	Japan[6]	United States[7]	Total	World Grand Total
1986	4,500	9,600	5,761	9,600	15,361	29,461	843	2,114	2,957	32,418
1987	4,500	9,600	5,842	10,100	15,942	30,042	728	2,275	3,003	33,045
1988	4,500	9,600	6,330	11,300	17,631	31,731	728	2,950	3,678	35,409
1989	4,500	9,600	7,270	11,300	18,567	32,967	868	2,389	3,257	36,224
1990	4,500	9,000	7,100	10,000	17,106	30,906	700	2,308	3,008	33,914
1991	4,500	8,500	6,500	8,460	14,962	28,162	889	2,250	3,139	31,301
1992	4,700	7,000	6,300	7,730	14,033	25,933	870	1,347	2,217	28,150
1993[1]	5,000	6,000	6,500	7,500	14,000	25,200	870	2,867	3,737	28,937
1994[2]	5,500	7,500			13,000	26,000				

[1] Preliminary. [2] Estimate. [3] In vanadiferous slag product. [4] Formerly part of the U.S.S.R.; data not reported separately until 1992. [5] Excludes U.S. production. [6] In vanadium pentoxide products. [7] In vandium pentoxide and ferrovandium products. *Source: U.S. Bureau of Mines*

Salient Statistics of Vanadium   In Metric Tons (Contained Vanadium)

| | Consumer & Producer Stocks, Dec. 31 | Vanadium Consumption by Uses In U.S. | | | | | | | | Exports | | | | Imports | | | |
Year		Tool Steel	Cast Irons	High Strength, Low Alloy	Stainless & Heat Resisting	Superalloys	Carbon	Full Alloy	Total	Average $ Per Lb. V2O5	Vanadium Pentoxide Anhydride	Oxides & Hydr-oxides	Ferro-Vanadium	Ores, Slag, Residues	Vanadium Pentoxide, Anhydride	Oxides & Hydr-oxides	Ferro-Vanadium
1987	2,057	422	23	1,212	59	9	1,086	740	4,221	3.50	742	-----	311	2,054	207	-----	310
1988	1,266	481	20	1,339	41	9	1,259	887	4,834	3.40	620	-----	462	2,025	219	-----	108
1989	1,736	420	18	1,225	96	38	1,103	898	4,646	6.17	1,171	1,080	399	4,210	133	106	527
1990	1,082	421	18	1,122	38	42	994	814	4,081	4.21	819	976	271	3,826	83	217	262
1991	935	242	15	919	37	14	919	739	3,293	2.85	700	1,110	94	882	145	110	428
1992	1,084	453	17	989	28	13	1,262	828	4,079	2.28	26	1,113	213	838	253	103	603
1993[1]	900	373	21	981	33	13	1,413	789	3,973	1.45	126	895	219	1,454	70	19	1,649
1994[2]	1,000	320	W	975	25	13	1,477	759	3,939	1.55	150	800	230	1,000	50	21	800

[1] Preliminary. [2] Estimate. W = Withheld proprietary data. *Source: U.S. Bureau of Mines*

Vegetables

In 1993, U.S. vegetable production, including potatoes, sweetpotatoes and dry beans,declined 1 percent from the previous year according to the United States Department of Agriculture (USDA). Output of processing vegetables was up 1 percent, but was more than outweighed by lower potato production, fresh market vegetables, and dry edible beans. Poor weather in Florida caused fresh market tomato production to decline 8 percent in 1993.

U.S. production of the 13 major vegetable for processing rose 1 percent in 1993 to 15.1 million short tons. In 1994, contract area is expected to increase 12 percent for the five major vegetables for processing. Acreage of cucumbers for pickles is expected to remain unchanged, while increases are expected for each of the other four commodities. Due to low stocks, processors increased green pea acreage the most. The first estimate of 1994 contract production for green peas rose 42 percent, to 474,490 short tons, as harvested acreage rose 30 percent and per acre yields increased 6 percent. Contract tomato production was forecast to rise 14 percent as acreage and per acre yields rose.

U.S. sweetpotato production for 1993 totaled 11.1 million hundredweights, down 8 percent. Shipments of fresh sweetpotatoes in 1993 fell 7 percent to 3.7 million hundred-weights. In 1994, harvested acreage was expected to increase 1 percent in 1994 to 81,200 acres. U.S. dry edible bean production fell 3 percent in 1993 due to flooding and frosts in the upper Midwest. Harvested acreage in 1994 was expected to increase 21 percent to 1.9 million acres.

U.S. fresh tomato production in 1994 was forecast to be 3.62 billion pounds, up almost 3 percent. Imports of fresh tomatoes in 1994 were 895 million pounds, down 3 percent. Exports were forecast at 355 million pounds with domestic utilization at 4.17 billion pounds, up almost 2 percent. Per capita use was estimated at 16 pounds, the highest level since 1989.

U.S. fresh head lettuce production in 1994 was forecast at 6.95 billion pounds, up over 2 percent. Imports are minimal at 25 million pounds. Exports were forecast at 475 million pounds with domestic utilization at 6.5 billion pounds, up 2 percent. Per capita use was forecast at 24.9 pounds.

U.S. fresh onion production in 1994 was forecast at 5.2 billion pounds, up 10 percent. Imports were put at 490 million pounds. Exports were forecast at 466 million pounds, while domestic use was put at 4.23 billion pounds. Per capita use of fresh onions in 1994 was estimated at 16.2 pounds.

Commercial and Fresh Vegetables: Index of Prices Received by U.S. Growers   1977 = 100

Year	Jan.	Feb.	Mar.	Apr.	May	June	July	Aug.	Sept.	Oct.	Nov.	Dec.	Annual
Commercial[1]													
1989	177	159	145	160	144	143	160	135	127	136	118	133	145
1990	210	187	131	113	116	113	126	131	139	148	155	133	142
1991	132	120	147	149	195	153	122	113	116	116	149	113	136
1992	148	182	211	152	124	120	142	155	161	175	144	162	156
1993	163	179	153	239	178	126	144	149	147	124	139	168	159
1994[2]	169	157	136	117	124	136	134	141	144	143			
Fresh													
1989	186	161	145	164	143	143	166	132	122	132	109	128	144
1990	240	208	130	106	110	104	122	128	139	152	162	130	144
1991	132	117	158	162	226	167	122	108	112	113	158	107	140
1992	142	180	219	152	118	111	138	159	166	177	140	166	156
1993	170	193	159	275	192	120	146	146	151	120	141	179	166
1994[2]	177	161	134	109	128	133	136	139	144	143			

Indexes are not seasonally adjusted.   [1] Includes fresh and processing vegetable.   [2] Preliminary.   *Source: National Agricultural Statistics Service, U.S. Department of Agriculture*

U.S. Processed Vegetables: Monthly Producer Price Index   1982 = 100

Year	Jan.	Feb.	Mar.	Apr.	May	June	July	Aug.	Sept.	Oct.	Nov.	Dec.	Annual
Canned[1] (0244)													
1989	118.7	119.7	119.8	119.4	119.1	118.6	118.9	118.8	118.9	118.0	117.8	118.0	118.8
1990	117.9	117.8	118.0	118.8	118.2	118.5	116.5	115.2	115.4	114.4	114.9	114.0	116.6
1991	114.8	114.8	115.1	113.8	114.0	113.3	114.0	112.2	110.9	111.2	110.1	109.8	112.8
1992	110.3	109.7	109.3	108.9	109.8	109.4	109.5	109.6	109.2	109.1	109.5	109.8	109.5
1993	110.1	109.8	109.3	108.7	108.8	109.5	111.1	109.6	110.4	111.5	112.3	112.6	110.3
1994[2]	113.1	116.1	116.8	116.5	117.9	118.0	118.9	121.4	116.2	115.7	114.0		
Frozen (0245)													
1989	113.1	114.3	114.8	115.3	115.3	115.7	115.5	116.2	116.2	115.3	116.4	117.0	115.4
1990	117.6	117.9	118.4	118.9	120.1	117.6	118.1	118.3	118.5	118.6	118.6	119.0	118.5
1991	118.4	118.5	118.3	117.9	118.1	117.5	117.8	117.2	117.4	116.6	116.5	116.8	117.6
1992	116.6	116.1	116.2	116.4	116.3	115.5	115.4	115.4	116.7	116.3	117.5	118.0	116.4
1993	118.0	118.0	117.9	118.7	119.9	121.1	121.3	122.1	122.6	123.2	123.7	124.7	120.9
1994[2]	125.5	126.1	126.1	126.4	126.9	127.0	126.4	126.9	126.7	125.6	125.5		

[1] Includes canned vegetables and juices, including hominy and mushrooms.   [2] Preliminary.   *Source: Bureau of Labor Statistics, U.S. Department of Labor*

U.S. Per Capita Use of Selected Commercially Produced Fresh and Processing Vegetables
Pounds, Farm Weight Basis

Crop	1984	1985	1986	1987	1988	1989	1990	1991	1992	1993[9]	1994[10]
Asparagus, all	.8	.9	1.0	1.0	1.0	1.0	1.0	1.0	1.0	1.0	1.0
Fresh	.3	.3	.3	.3	.3	.3	.3	.3	.3	.3	.3
Canning	.3	.3	.3	.3	.3	.3	.3	.3	.3	.3	.3
Freezing	.1	.1	.1	.1	.1	.1	.1	.1	.1	.1	.1
Snap Beans, all	6.8	7.0	6.7	6.7	6.7	7.1	6.8	7.0	7.1	7.4	6.9
Fresh	1.3	1.3	1.3	1.2	1.2	1.2	1.1	1.1	1.4	1.6	1.4
Canning	3.7	3.8	3.9	3.8	3.8	3.9	3.7	4.1	4.0	4.0	3.7
Freezing	1.8	1.9	1.5	1.7	1.7	2.0	2.0	1.8	1.7	1.8	1.8
Broccoli, all[1]	4.3	4.5	4.7	5.3	6.2	6.0	5.6	5.4	5.8	5.1	5.4
Fresh	2.5	2.6	3.0	3.1	3.8	3.8	3.4	3.1	3.4	2.8	3.1
Freezing	1.8	1.9	1.7	2.2	2.4	2.2	2.2	2.3	2.4	2.3	2.3
Carrots, all[2]	10.7	9.7	9.5	11.4	10.6	11.5	11.3	11.2	12.2	12.5	11.8
Fresh	6.7	6.5	6.5	8.3	7.2	7.9	8.0	7.5	8.6	8.4	8.0
Canning	1.1	.9	.8	.8	.9	1.0	.9	1.0	1.0	1.1	1.0
Freezing	2.9	2.3	2.2	2.3	2.5	2.6	2.4	2.7	2.6	3.0	2.8
Cauliflower, all[1]	2.7	2.7	3.1	3.0	3.2	3.1	3.0	2.6	2.6	2.4	2.5
Fresh	1.8	1.8	2.2	2.1	2.2	2.3	2.2	2.0	1.9	1.7	1.8
Freezing	.9	.9	.9	.9	1.0	.8	.8	.6	.7	.7	.7
Celery, fresh	7.3	7.0	6.6	6.7	7.2	7.5	7.2	6.8	6.7	6.2	6.4
Sweet Corn, all[3]	24.6	26.2	25.8	24.7	24.8	24.3	26.1	26.2	27.6	27.3	26.1
Fresh	6.4	6.4	6.1	6.3	5.7	6.4	6.5	5.7	6.7	6.3	6.2
Canning	10.2	11.9	12.1	10.6	10.4	9.5	11.0	11.1	11.9	11.2	10.7
Freezing	8.0	7.9	7.6	7.8	8.7	8.4	8.6	9.4	9.0	9.8	9.2
Cucumbers, all	9.9	10.2	9.9	10.3	10.1	10.0	9.9	9.5	9.5	10.0	9.9
Fresh	4.7	4.4	4.6	5.1	4.8	4.8	4.7	4.6	5.2	5.5	5.4
Pickles	5.2	5.8	5.3	5.2	5.3	5.2	5.2	4.9	4.3	4.5	4.5
Melons	23.9	24.1	24.6	24.3	23.7	26.5	24.6	23.4	24.5	24.3	24.4
Watermelon	14.4	13.5	12.8	13.0	13.5	13.6	13.3	12.8	14.2	14.2	14.3
Cantaloupe	7.7	8.5	9.4	9.1	7.9	10.4	9.2	8.7	8.3	8.5	8.3
Honeydew	1.8	2.1	2.4	2.2	2.3	2.5	2.1	1.9	2.0	1.6	1.8
Lettuce, Head	24.9	23.7	21.9	25.7	27.0	28.8	27.8	26.1	25.9	24.6	24.9
Onions, all	14.6	15.2	15.6	14.9	16.2	16.4	17.1	17.3	17.5	17.8	18.0
Fresh	13.1	13.6	13.7	13.4	14.5	14.8	15.1	15.7	16.1	15.7	16.2
Green peas, all[4]	4.0	4.2	4.1	3.7	3.7	3.7	4.2	4.2	4.1	3.5	3.3
Canning	2.0	2.1	2.2	2.0	1.8	1.7	2.0	1.9	2.1	1.6	1.5
Freezing	2.0	2.1	1.9	1.7	1.9	2.0	2.2	2.3	2.0	1.9	1.8
Tomatoes, all	82.8	78.2	79.5	81.0	78.1	86.2	90.9	92.8	89.0	92.2	89.0
Fresh	14.3	15.0	15.9	15.8	16.8	16.8	15.5	15.4	15.2	15.9	16.0
Canning	68.5	63.2	63.6	65.2	61.3	69.4	75.4	77.4	73.8	76.3	73.0
Subtotal, all[5]	242.8	242.9	241.3	247.3	248.4	262.9	266.7	265.7	268.0	270.0	263.5
Fresh	123.1	126.4	125.2	131.3	134.3	141.5	137.0	132.9	138.5	137.3	137.3
Canning	98.3	95.3	95.6	95.2	91.2	98.9	107.2	109.4	107.2	107.9	103.3
Freezing	19.9	19.6	18.6	19.3	21.2	20.9	20.5	21.8	20.9	22.7	21.1
Potatoes, all	122.1	122.4	126.0	126.0	122.4	127.1	127.7	130.4	132.4	135.7	133.9
Fresh	48.3	46.3	48.8	47.9	49.6	50.0	45.8	46.4	48.9	51.9	49.1
Processing	73.8	76.1	77.2	78.1	72.8	77.1	81.9	84.0	83.5	83.8	84.8
Sweet Potatoes, all	4.9	5.4	4.4	4.4	4.1	4.1	4.6	4.0	4.3	3.9	4.0
Total, all items	378.9	381.9	382.8	386.9	385.9	403.9	410.1	411.8	416.1	420.8	412.7

[1] All production for processing broccoli and cauliflower is for freezing. [2] Industry allocation suggests that 27% of processing carrot production is for canning and 73% is for freezing. [3] On-cob basis. [4] In-shell basis. [5] Includes artichokes, brussel sprouts, eggplant, endive/excarole, garlic, radishes and spinach. [6] Includes beets, chile peppers and spinach. [7] Includes green lima beans, spinach and miscellaneous freezing vegetables. [8] Fresch, canning and freezing data do not add to the total because onions are for dehydrating are included in total. [9] Preliminary. [10] Forecast. *Source: Economic Research Service, U.S. Department of Agriculture*

VEGETABLES

Fresh Vegetables: Average Prices Received by U.S. Growers   Dollars Per Cwt.

Year	Jan.	Feb.	Mar.	Apr.	May	June	July	Aug.	Sept.	Oct.	Nov.	Dec.	Season Average
Broccoli													
1992	17.50	14.30	27.60	16.70	22.00	26.30	23.60	27.40	24.00	24.70	30.50	32.80	23.50
1993	32.60	28.10	28.60	23.70	22.30	26.80	24.50	20.00	36.60	22.40	24.20	30.00	26.60
1994[1]	23.50	21.40	19.50	21.80	27.10	21.10	21.60	18.50	38.60	36.10			31.60
Carrots													
1992	18.90	17.10	13.20	12.80	11.70	10.80	16.90	16.60	14.40	12.80	12.00	13.80	14.50
1993	18.00	13.10	11.10	12.60	11.10	10.20	9.02	9.98	10.10	10.20	11.00	11.10	11.90
1994[1]	10.70	10.50	11.50	10.30	12.20	12.10	13.60	16.50	15.40	15.50			13.20
Cauliflower													
1992	23.70	19.60	21.90	25.00	33.90	37.80	23.20	43.50	26.60	27.80	37.90	40.30	29.10
1993	34.30	29.10	24.70	44.90	26.90	37.00	28.90	31.10	39.50	28.50	21.60	30.90	31.20
1994[1]	24.80	24.90	23.10	20.80	32.30	29.10	30.20	24.40	33.80	30.70			29.60
Celery													
1992	8.81	7.77	10.40	15.20	16.00	12.20	11.50	14.90	16.10	13.10	12.40	15.30	12.30
1993	24.00	35.50	27.40	16.50	14.50	9.62	9.52	12.00	14.20	13.30	11.40	11.80	14.80
1994[1]	11.90	9.29	8.40	8.31	13.20	9.06	13.00	14.90	12.70	10.80			11.80
Corn, Sweet													
1992	26.30	21.90	28.20	16.20	14.70	12.00	14.90	14.80	13.80	16.90	20.40	22.60	14.60
1993	20.90	36.80	22.80	21.90	19.10	17.10	18.90	17.10	14.90	15.60	16.90	22.50	17.80
1994[1]	26.40	21.70	25.90	16.60	18.00	18.90	19.80	14.20	15.30	20.00			17.70
Lettuce, Head													
1992	7.23	6.75	11.90	9.91	11.20	9.84	13.00	19.90	21.00	13.60	9.63	16.30	12.50
1993	10.80	18.80	14.30	38.00	12.60	11.50	18.80	14.90	16.80	12.20	10.70	8.93	16.00
1994[1]	8.03	11.80	9.90	11.70	11.30	13.80	10.40	10.90	17.10	16.10			13.00
Tomatoes													
1992	40.50	76.00	80.70	32.40	16.70	21.90	28.30	23.50	29.30	60.10	39.00	34.30	35.80
1993	38.30	21.90	21.20	45.20	57.80	23.50	23.30	32.70	29.80	20.20	32.30	57.50	31.70
1994[1]	41.10	18.80	24.20	16.50	20.60	29.10	27.50	33.50	22.70	22.60			27.20

[1] Preliminary.   Source: National Agricultural Statistics Service, U.S. Department of Agriculture

Frozen Vegetables: January 1 & July 1 Cold Storage Holdings   In Thousands of Pounds

Crop	1990 July 1	1991 Jan. 1	1991 July 1	1992 Jan. 1	1992 July 1	1993 Jan. 1	1993 July 1	1994 Jan. 1	1994 July 1	1995[1] Jan. 1
Asparagus	18,662	11,486	19,990	9,673	17,597	7,791	22,307	14,782	19,175	9,888
Lima Beans	27,222	91,248	60,760	100,392	49,264	65,047	26,164	49,594	24,093	58,969
Snap Beans	85,694	253,184	113,486	248,737	116,360	190,465	73,907	184,418	71,457	222,109
Broccoli	196,395	113,014	137,670	88,286	150,460	143,486	194,061	134,774	152,312	108,499
Brussels Sprouts	19,714	30,691	20,856	22,216	13,000	26,467	12,029	34,338	20,166	31,258
Carrots	138,266	224,533	109,649	203,637	99,743	254,040	176,830	260,993	165,748	272,158
Cauliflower	45,003	91,414	56,277	88,234	40,636	71,135	32,461	60,683	40,077	80,848
Corn, Sweet[2]	139,146	436,794	233,433	470,816	285,023	489,019	239,379	493,411	119,206	331,359
Mixed Vegetables	62,226	61,408	59,383	57,422	53,945	47,721	42,013	44,916	51,737	57,371
Okra	24,571	43,073	21,087	51,643	33,548	44,679	18,387	16,341	31,799	62,479
Onions	32,014	34,421	31,049	32,137	27,829	34,230	24,787	36,101	31,296	49,902
Black-Eyed Peas	6,695	23,878	13,449	19,416	7,323	12,559	4,636	9,605	3,159	13,329
Green Peas	218,958	282,118	220,022	272,691	229,461	305,164	177,245	261,338	218,032	259,544
Peas and Carrots	7,685	7,805	6,730	6,583	8,228	6,921	7,506	15,363	14,063	9,375
Spinach	110,326	90,923	107,268	53,293	83,863	56,182	79,337	47,159	120,542	67,467
Squash	44,978	65,537	48,804	50,618	43,597	54,708	40,941	61,679	53,763	64,791
Southern Greens	21,751	29,940	31,462	27,496	21,458	27,173	22,251	31,786	29,194	30,005
Other Vegetables	207,724	269,029	192,357	274,768	216,709	295,028	211,523	258,611	238,554	258,728
Total	1,404,030	2,303,101	1,483,732	2,243,853	1,498,044	2,300,040	1,405,764	2,015,892	1,404,373	2,288,079
Potatoes	977,585	975,754	1,213,532	970,012	1,131,381	963,167	989,818	1,006,416	1,099,850	1,083,747
Grand Total	2,381,615	3,278,855	2,697,264	3,213,865	2,629,425	3,263,207	2,395,582	3,022,308	2,504,223	3,371,826

[1] Preliminary.   [2] Cut-basis with cob corn converted to cut-basis using a factor of 0.4706.   Source: National Agricultural Statistics Service, U.S. Department of Agriculture

Wheat

World wheat production in 1994/95 of about 527 million tonnes lagged initial forecasts and fell to the lowest total since 1988/89. Production in 1993/94 totaled 559 million tonnes. Although output was down in many countries, much of the decline in 1994 reflected a 17 percent drop in the former Soviet Union and a 47 percent drop in Australia's crop. World consumption was forecast to slip in 1994/95 to about 552 million tonnes, from the record large 564 million tonnes in 1993/94. If the 1994/95 supply/demand totals are realized, world stocks at the end of the season would fall to 117 million tonnes, the lowest since 1981/82 versus nearly 143 million tonnes a year earlier. The former Soviet Union accounts for more than one-third of the decline in carryover, but stocks held by major exporters are also down by almost 20 percent. The drop in exporter stocks has the greatest impact on world prices, as these stocks are the major source for meeting unexpected production shortfalls and increases in demand. Availability of exportable supplies was expected to play a major role in determining the source of 1994/95 exports. Australia's exports may fall to 7.5 million tonnes from nearly 13 million tonnes in 1993/94, which is expected to benefit foreign demand for U.S., Canadian and Argentine wheat.

China, the world's largest wheat producer with about 20 percent of total production, 103 million tonnes in 1994/95, is also the biggest enigma in respect to the world's wheat trade. China's 1994/95 wheat consumption is placed at a record high 114 million tonnes, which if realized is thought to require imports of approximately 10 million tonnes, more than double the 1993/94 season. However, just how much China will import is uncertain as China's stock of wheat is unknown, as is the government's willingness to utilize their carryover supplies. In the fall of 1994, China negotiated for wheat with several exporting nations, but the actual purchases proved minimal. China's import needs are very price sensitive and the U.S. market tends to respond quickly when Chinese purchases are rumored. Early 1994/95 U.S. exports to China of nearly one million tonnes were nearly three times ahead of the previous year's pace.

The Russian Federation, the world's largest importer until 1993/94, now trails a number of countries. Russia's 1994/95 imports of 5.5 million tonnes are almost one-half that of China, and moderately below Japan, Brazil and Egypt. Russia's lack of foreign exchange and/or credit accounts can be attributed for the drop in imports, which in the early-1990s averaged about 12 million tonnes.

The U.S. is the world's largest wheat exporter, shipping on average about one-third of the total global trade. In 1994/95, the U.S. was forecast to deliver 34 million tonnes of expected world exports of nearly 110 million tonnes. In the previous year, the totals were 33 million tonnes and 117 million tonnes, respectively. The European Community (EC-12) and Canadian 1994/95 exports were forecast at 18 million tonnes and 20.5 million tonnes, respectively, with the former unchanged from 1993/94 and Canada up one million tonnes. Generally, four regions account for the bulk of world wheat exports, while importing nations are well scattered if the Former Soviet Union needs are excluded.

The U.S. 1994 wheat crop of 2.32 billion bushels, down 3.5 percent from 1993, reflected a smaller harvested acreage and lower yields. For the second consecutive year, farmers were not required to idle any wheat base to participate in the wheat program. Nevertheless, plantings fell nearly 1.7 million acres, owing largely to weather related problems. Winter wheat production totalled 1.7 billion bushels, down 6 percent from 1993, as yields fell 3 bushels or more per acre in seven of the largest 10 winter wheat producing states. However, Kansas, the largest producing state, realized a 433 million bushel crop, the largest since 1990 and up nearly 50 million bushels from 1993. In Oklahoma, the second largest producing state, the crop was down 12 percent from 1993. Spring wheat production of about 561 million bushels was fractionally under 1993. North Dakota is the largest spring wheat producing state. Durum wheat production totaled 94 million bushels, up 33 percent from 1993. Most durum wheat is produced in North Dakota and Minnesota.

The U.S. imports some wheat, about 85 million bushels in 1994/95 versus 109 million bushels in 1993/94. Canada is the largest source of U.S. imports. Carryin stocks as of June 1, 1994 of 570 million bushels compared with 529 million bushels a year earlier, and average carryin from 1989/90-1992/93 of 644 million bushels. The domestic wheat supply for 1994/95 of nearly 3 billion bushels is about 70 million bushels under 1993/94.

U.S. wheat usage in 1994/95 of about 2.45 billion bushels was fractionally lower than in the previous two seasons. Exports account for more than one-half the total disappearance, whereas in 1993/94 exports marginally trailed domestic use. Food use takes about two-thirds of domestic usage, feed about 25 percent and seed the balance. If the 1994/95 supply/demand estimates are realized, ending stocks on May 31, 1995 would total about 518 million bushels, one-fourth of which would be Commodity Credit Corporation (CCC) owned. In the mid-1980s, the carryover averaged nearly three time higher than the expected 1994/95 carryover, dropping the stock-to-use ratio to about 20.9 percent versus 23.1 percent for 1993/94. This ratio is often used to forecast prices, the higher it is the greater the likelihood for lower prices as the crop year progresses.

The tightening global supply buoyed prices early in the 1994/95 crop year, but about one-half the gain was lost towards the end of calendar year 1994. The 1994/95 season average price received by farmers is expected to range from $3.25 per bushel to $3.65 per bushel. The low end of this range is higher than the season average price for the previous five-years, except for the 1993/94 average of $3.26 per bushel.

U.S. Farm Program

The 1994 target price for wheat was $4.00 per bushel, unchanged from 1993. The price support rate was lifted to $2.58 per bushel from $2.45. per bushel

Futures Markets

Wheat futures and options are traded on the Chicago Board of Trade (CBOT), the Kansas City Board of Trade (KCBT) and the Minneapolis Grain Exchange (MGE). Feed wheat futures are traded on the Winnipeg Commodity Exchange (WCE).

WHEAT

World Production of Wheat   In Thousands of Metric Tons

Crop Year	Argentina	Australia	Canada	China	France	Germany	India	Italy	Pakistan	Russia[4]	Spain	Turkey	United Kingdom	United States	World Total
1983-4	12,760	22,016	26,505	81,390	24,785	8,998	42,502	8,514	12,414	78,000	4,330	13,300	10,800	65,857	489,454
1984-5	13,200	18,666	21,199	87,820	33,241	10,223	45,476	10,057	10,882	68,600	5,800	13,300	14,957	70,618	511,463
1985-6	8,500	16,127	24,252	85,810	29,262	9,866	44,069	8,516	11,703	78,100	5,326	12,700	12,045	66,001	498,810
1986-7	9,000	16,700	31,850	90,295	26,500	10,406	46,885	9,070	13,922	92,306	4,292	14,000	13,900	56,793	529,419
1987-8	8,800	12,442	25,950	85,840	27,234	9,932	44,323	9,381	12,020	83,312	5,768	13,000	11,940	57,362	502,300
1988-9	8,400	14,060	15,995	85,432	29,660	11,922	46,169	7,952	12,675	84,445	6,173	16,000	11,750	49,320	500,300
1989-90	10,150	14,214	24,796	90,807	32,100	14,482	54,110	7,413	14,419	87,151	5,200	12,500	14,030	55,428	533,001
1990-1	10,900	15,066	32,098	98,229	33,600	15,242	49,850	8,108	14,429	49,596	4,759	16,000	14,000	74,292	587,995
1991-2	9,880	10,557	31,946	96,000	34,590	16,610	55,134	9,416	14,565	38,900	5,000	16,500	14,400	53,891	542,558
1992-3[1]	9,800	16,184	29,871	101,590	32,780	15,540	55,690	8,800	15,684	46,170	4,600	15,500	15,540	67,135	561,871
1993-4[2]	9,400	16,900	27,232	106,390	29,630	15,770	56,760		16,157	43,500		16,500	15,770	65,220	558,927
1994-5[3]	10,500	8,600	23,350	103,000	30,900	16,500	57,800		15,100	35,000		14,000	16,500	63,157	527,496

[1] Preliminary. [2] Estimate. [3] Forecast. [4] Formerly part of the U.S.S.R.; data not reported separately until 1990-91. *Source: Foreign Agricultural Service, U.S. Department of Agriculture*

World Wheat Supply & Demand   In Millions of Metric Tons/Hectares

Crop Year	Area Harvested	Yield	Production	World Trade	Utilization Total	Ending Stocks	Stocks as % of Utilization
1987-8	219.7	2.26	496.0	112.2	525.3	149.8	28.5
1988-9	217.4	2.28	495.0	102.4	524.3	120.5	23.0
1989-90	225.8	2.36	533.2	102.8	532.2	121.5	22.8
1990-1	231.4	2.54	588.0	101.2	563.2	146.3	26.0
1991-2	222.4	2.44	542.6	109.3	558.5	130.3	23.3
1992-3[1]	222.9	2.52	561.9	112.5	543.9	148.3	27.3
1993-4[2]	222.0	2.52	558.9	99.5	563.9	143.4	25.4
1994-5[3]	215.4	2.45	527.5	96.5	553.0	117.9	21.3

[1] Preliminary. [2] Estimate. [3] Forecast. *Source: Foreign Agricultural Service, U.S. Department of Agriculture*

Salient Statistics of Wheat in the United States

Crop Year	Planting Intentions	Acreage Harvested — Winter	Acreage Harvested — Spring	Acreage Harvested — All	Average--All Yield Per Acre in Bushels	Value of Production $1,000	Foreign Trade[5] Domestic Exports[2]	Foreign Trade[5] Imports[3]	Per Capita[4] Consumption Flour	Per Capita[4] Consumption Cereal
		1,000 Acres					Millions of Bushels		In Pounds	
1987-8	65,829	39,332	16,613	55,945	37.7	5,497,712	1,587.9	16.1	130.0	3.7
1988-9	65,529	39,800	13,389	53,189	34.1	6,683,999	1,414.9	22.7	130.0	3.8
1989-90	76,615	41,509	20,680	62,189	32.7	7,542,464	1,232.0	22.5	129.6	4.0
1990-1	77,041	49,721	19,382	69,103	39.5	7,184,427	1,069.5	36.4	135.8	4.3
1991-2	69,881	39,506	18,297	57,803	34.3	5,956,642	1,282.3	40.7	136.5	4.5
1992-3	72,219	42,123	20,638	62,761	39.3	7,978,911	1,353.6	70.0	138.3	4.7
1993-4[1]	72,168	43,811	18,901	62,712	38.2	7,204,000	1,227.8	108.8		
1994-5[1]	70,421	41,335	20,436	61,771	37.6					

[1] Preliminary. [2] Includes flour milled from imported wheat. [3] Total wheat, flour & other products. [4] Civilian only. [5] Year beginning June.
Source: Economic Research Service, U.S. Department of Agriculture

Supply and Distribution of Wheat in the United States   In Millions of Bushels

Crop Year Beginning June	Supply — Stocks, June 1 — On Farms	Supply — Stocks, June 1 — Mills, Elevators[3]	Supply — Total Stocks	Supply — Production	Supply — Imports[4]	Supply — Total Supply	Domestic Disappearance — Food	Domestic Disappearance — Seed	Domestic Disappearance — Feed & Residual[5]	Domestic Disappearance — Total	Domestic Disappearance — Exports[4]	Total Disappearance
1987-8	560.0	1,260.9	1,820.9	2,107.7	16.1	3,945	720.7	85.0	290.2	1,096.0	1,587.9	2,684
1988-9	525.0	735.8	1,260.8	1,812.2	22.7	3,096	725.8	103.0	150.5	979.2	1,414.9	2,394
1989-90	289.0	412.6	701.6	2,036.6	22.5	2,761	748.9	104.3	139.1	992.3	1,232.0	2,224
1990-1	212.5	324.0	536.5	2,729.8	36.4	3,303	789.8	92.9	482.1	1,365.1	1,069.5	2,435
1991-2	341.2	524.7	868.1	1,980.1	40.7	2,889	789.5	97.7	244.5	1,131.6	1,282.3	2,414
1992-3	144.6	327.2	475.0	2,466.8	70.0	3,012	834.3	99.1	194.2	1,127.6	1,353.6	2,481
1993-4[1]	183.8	345.3	529.2	2,396.4	108.8	3,036	869.3	96.3	274.1	1,239.7	1,227.8	2,467
1994-5[2]	177.3	393.2	570.5	2,320.6	90.0	2,979	875.0	98.0	250.0	1,223.0	1,300.0	2,523

[1] Preliminary. [2] Estimate. [3] Also warehouses and all off-farm storage not otherwise disignated, including flour mills. [4] Imports & exports are for wheat, including flour & other products in terms of wheat. [5] Mostly feed use. *Source: Economic Research Service, U.S. Department of Agriculture*

Stocks, Production and Exports of Wheat by Class   In Millions of Bushels

Year Beginning June	Hard Spring June 1 Stocks	Hard Spring Pro-duction	Hard Spring Exports[3]	Durum[2] June 1 Stocks	Durum[2] Pro-duction	Durum[2] Exports[3]	Hard Winter June 1 Stocks	Hard Winter Pro-duction	Hard Winter Exports[3]	Soft Red Winter June 1 Stocks	Soft Red Winter Pro-duction	Soft Red Winter Exports[3]	White June 1 Stocks	White Pro-duction	White Exports[3]
1987-8	490	431	255	95	93	62	973	1,019	901	77	349	160	185	216	210
1988-9	402	181	194	83	45	20	567	882	639	75	473	315	135	232	247
1989-90	219	433	280	60	92	55	302	711	359	39	549	345	81	251	193
1990-1	155	555	201	50	122	53	215	1,196	369	32	344	230	85	313	216
1991-2	279	431	380	62	104	45	360	901	559	80	325	105	87	219	193
1992-3	131	707	438	55	100	47	194	967	464	41	427	210	54	266	195
1993-4[1]	171	512	266	49	70	54	204	1,066	486	43	401	173	64	347	249
1994-5[4]	201	515	310	28	97	35	227	971	490	45	433	225	67	303	240

[1] Preliminary.   [2] Includes "Red Durum."   [3] Includes flour made from U.S. wheat & shipments to territories.   [4] Estimate.

Seeded Acerage, Yield and Production of Wheat in the United States

Year	Seeded Acreage (1,000 Acres) Winter	Other Spring	Durum	All	Yield Per Harvested Acre (Bushels) Winter	Other Spring	Durum	All	Production (1,000,000 Bushels) Winter	Other Spring	Durum	All
1988	48,800	13,393	3,336	65,529	39.2	19.5	15.7	34.1	1,561.9	205.5	44.8	1,812.2
1989	55,091	17,733	3,791	76,615	35.0	28.8	25.1	32.7	1,454.6	489.7	92.2	2,036.6
1990	56,748	16,723	3,570	77,041	40.7	36.7	34.9	39.5	2,024.2	583.1	122.4	2,729.8
1991	51,024	15,604	3,253	69,881	34.7	33.4	32.5	34.3	1,371.6	504.6	104.0	1,980.1
1992	50,922	18,750	2,547	72,219	38.2	41.8	39.7	39.3	1,609.3	757.6	99.9	2,466.8
1993	51,587	18,340	2,241	72,168	40.2	33.7	33.6	38.2	1,760.1	565.8	70.5	2,396.4
1994[1]	49,247	18,324	2,850	70,421	40.2	31.8	35.5	37.6	1,661.0	562.2	97.3	2,320.6

[1] Preliminary.   Source: Economic Research Service, U.S. Department of Agriculture

Production of Winter Wheat in the United States   In Thousands of Bushels

Year	Colorado	Idaho	Illinois	Indiana	Kansas	Mich-igan	Missouri	Mon-tana	Nebraska	Ohio	Okla-homa	Oregon	South Dakota	Tenn-essee	Texas	Wash-ington
1983	117.0	55.6	64.4	49.5	448.2	35.8	70.3	79.1	98.9	58.8	150.5	62.0	51.3	19.8	161.0	162.5
1984	110.4	56.7	70.4	48.3	431.2	45.6	84.1	67.0	81.0	48.4	190.8	66.2	61.2	21.4	150.0	148.8
1985	134.6	46.1	36.8	37.1	433.2	45.0	49.9	22.4	89.7	58.9	165.0	51.8	44.1	8.0	187.2	115.2
1986	92.8	51.9	36.1	30.1	336.6	30.6	18.8	64.0	76.0	48.3	150.8	53.9	57.6	10.7	120.0	102.9
1987	93.8	60.0	56.1	34.8	366.3	19.2	35.4	79.2	85.8	46.4	129.6	49.5	55.1	14.0	100.8	104.0
1988	75.9	50.8	67.5	35.0	323.0	26.0	76.0	39.9	72.0	46.0	172.8	46.9	21.6	21.5	89.6	108.5
1989	57.2	56.7	105.0	51.9	213.6	33.9	87.0	54.0	55.4	62.7	153.9	48.9	35.1	18.9	60.0	68.9
1990	84.2	69.0	88.8	50.4	472.0	41.3	76.0	87.5	85.5	79.7	201.6	54.6	57.6	17.6	130.2	138.6
1991	71.3	49.0	44.8	28.8	363.0	24.1	48.0	72.0	67.2	52.9	140.0	41.6	45.5	7.7	84.0	40.6
1992	70.5	55.3	62.1	25.0	363.8	35.3	64.8	65.3	55.5	59.1	168.2	42.9	33.6	13.4	129.2	102.0
1993	94.4	67.2	68.2	34.8	388.5	22.1	53.2	102.9	73.5	52.5	156.6	61.1	56.6	13.9	118.4	162.5
1994[1]	76.5	56.9	50.4	38.4	433.2	30.7	49.5	64.8	71.4	68.4	143.1	55.7	43.2	15.0	75.4	124.2

[1] Preliminary.   Source: Crop Reporting Board, U.S. Department of Agriculture

United States Official Winter Wheat Crop Production Reports   In Thousands of Bushels

Crop Year	May 1	June 1	July 1	August 1	September 1	Current December	Final
1983-4	1,893,241	1,882,916	1,937,388	1,963,243	1,976,843	1,993,888	1,988,304
1984-5	1,979,366	1,972,776	2,021,918	2,045,088	2,036,028	2,060,646	2,060,266
1985-6	1,974,228	1,892,438	1,854,254	1,842,884	1,839,284	1,827,195	1,826,625
1986-7	1,603,127	1,578,277	1,553,026	1,532,526	1,532,526	1,519,143	1,520,433
1987-8	1,549,344	1,577,489	1,574,439	2,125,097	2,114,492	1,565,176	1,565,381
1988-9	1,620,257	1,570,417	1,568,052	1,554,812	1,560,970	1,561,145	1,561,910
1989-90	1,430,148	1,407,898	1,461,924	1,466,049	1,451,746	1,453,842	1,454,642
1990-1	2,091,614	2,089,234	2,035,087	2,054,287	2,036,059	----------	2,030,874
1991-2	1,495,943	1,449,418	1,361,316	1,371,946	1,372,182	----------	1,372,617
1992-3	1,618,017	1,618,017	1,573,901	1,600,931	NA	----------	1,609,284
1993-4	1,807,657	1,824,062	1,821,345	1,788,005	1,788,005	----------	1,760,143
1994-5[1]	1,657,938	1,674,563	1,658,426	1,670,436	1,670,436	----------	1,661,043

[1] Preliminary.   NA = Not available.   Source: Crop Reporting Board, U.S. Department of Agriculture

Wheat

Production of All Spring Wheat in the United States   In Millions of Bushels

				---- Durum Wheat ----							---- Other Spring Wheat ----							
Year	Arizona	Cali-fornia	Minne-sota	Mon-tana	North Dakota	South Dakota	Total Durum	Colo-rado	Idaho	Minne-sota	Mon-tana	North Dakota	Oregon	South Dakota	Utah	Wash-ington	Total
1985	3.9	7.4	1.7	1.4	95.5	2.6	112.5	4.8	25.9	130.4	26.4	212.0	4.2	64.5	1.6	13.1	485.0
1986	4.2	6.5	1.3	4.3	80.0	1.6	97.9	3.6	29.9	98.1	70.2	198.4	4.5	49.5	1.7	14.0	472.2
1987	3.8	5.1	1.2	5.3	74.1	3.0	92.6	3.6	25.5	98.4	66.7	189.1	3.4	48.6	1.7	10.3	449.7
1988	4.3	5.6	.8	2.1	31.2	.8	44.8	3.6	24.7	49.5	18.0	70.5	4.9	15.6	1.2	16.1	205.5
1989	7.6	8.7	1.0	6.0	66.0	2.9	92.2	4.9	34.7	96.9	85.0	174.0	4.9	45.1	1.0	41.7	489.7
1990	4.1	5.6	1.3	4.5	103.7	3.2	122.4	2.8	30.6	134.8	23.9	277.2	3.1	67.2	1.2	11.5	583.1
1991	3.7	3.4	1.0	5.9	88.4	1.7	104.0	2.7	32.7	64.2	81.6	212.4	2.3	49.0	1.1	58.0	504.6
1992	3.7	5.1	.5	4.9	84.7	1.0	99.9	3.6	44.8	137.5	79.1	382.2	4.9	85.0	1.1	17.6	757.6
1993	4.5	3.8	.2	3.5	58.0	.4	70.5	2.6	43.2	69.8	99.9	274.4	3.9	54.5	1.2	15.1	565.8
1994[1]	8.6	5.6	.9	5.3	76.4	.6	97.3	3.2	43.4	70.0	100.5	278.8	2.9	51.5	1.0	9.8	562.2

[1] Preliminary.   Source: Crop Reporting Board, U.S. Department of Agriculture

Wheat Under Price Support Through the End of the Month
(Cumulative total from Current Season's Crop)   In Thousands of Bushels

Year	July	Aug.	Sept.	Oct.	Nov.	Dec.	Jan.	Feb.	Mar.	Apr.	May	June
1984-5	48.8	104.9	195.5	213.4	225.6	237.7	263.5	270.2	275.7	279.7	280.1	280.8
1985-6	269.5	414.2	567.7	679.0	714.3	740.7	786.2	803.8	813.5	825.0	827.3	828.1
1986-7	81.7	155.7	274.6	400.5	441.6	456.0	487.9	500.7	505.6	512.6	513.5	513.4
1987-8	-----	105.1	259.6	350.4	396.7	418.2	442.8	460.2	466.5	470.7	472.0	472.1
1988-9	-----	60.0	85.9	91.3	94.1	99.3	103.6	104.7	105.7	106.2	106.3	106.3
1989-90	-----	42.7	69.7	82.1	89.7	97.6	104.6	107.5	111.7	113.3	113.4	113.4
1990-1	36.7	113.0	219.8	254.7	277.1	293.4	-----	401.6	404.5	405.1	405.1	405.1
1991-2	405.1	67.4	114.1	125.8	132.0	135.3	140.7	141.5	142.9	143.2	143.2	143.2
1992-3	143.2	74.2	140.4	190.6	208.4	220.6	234.0	236.5	239.9	240.2	240.3	240.3
1993-4	240.3	94.7	169.9	207.4	222.4	230.3	241.4	245.4	256.5	258.2	258.3	258.3

Source: Economic Research Service , U.S. Department of Agriculture

United States Grindings of Wheat by Mills   In Millions of Bushels (60 Pounds Each)

Year	July	Aug.	Sept.	Oct.	Nov.	Dec.	Jan.	Feb.	Mar.	Apr.	May	June	Total
1985-6	54.6	60.9	59.5	65.1	63.7	56.0	60.0	59.2	54.6	57.0	58.6	57.6	706.8
1986-7	60.0	65.4	65.9	69.2	65.8	64.1	59.3	60.2	62.7	62.8	66.1	64.2	765.7
1987-8	62.3	66.3	65.8	69.5	66.7	62.5	59.6	58.4	61.2	58.0	65.7	63.8	759.8
1988-9	63.6	70.0	66.0	70.0	69.7	63.8	65.0	60.8	60.4	60.7	64.7	59.6	773.3
1989-90	58.5	70.6	63.6	67.4	65.1	58.7	63.4	64.0	66.7	61.6	63.6	60.6	763.8
1990-1	62.3	73.2	65.7	74.9	73.9	64.3	66.7	65.2	63.2	67.6	69.9	60.9	807.8
1991-2	65.3	71.2	67.7	72.2	73.5	65.6	65.7	66.0	65.6	67.3	67.0	67.2	814.3
1992-3	70.0	77.3	71.9	77.9	71.9	65.5	68.1	70.0	76.2	72.0	69.6	67.9	858.2
1993-4	69.2	75.2	74.1	75.8	77.0	76.3	69.7	67.9	80.8	72.6	72.6	70.2	881.5
1994-5[1]	68.5	78.2	75.9	77.5	75.5	70.7							446.3

[1] Preliminary.   Source: Bureau of Census, U.S. Department of Commerce

Comparative Average Cash Wheat Prices   In Dollars Per Bushel

						--- Minneapolis ---				----- Export Prices[2] (U.S. $ Per Metric Tons) -----				
Crop Year Beginning June	Received by U.S. Farmers	No. 2 Soft Red Winter Chicago	No. 1 Hard Red Ordinary Protein Kansas City	No. 2 Soft Red Winter St. Louis	No. 1 Dark Northern Spring 14%	No. 1 Hard Amber Durum	No. 1 Soft Portland Oregon	No. 2 Western White Pacific N.W.	No. 2 Soft White Toledo	Aust-ralia Standard White	Canada Vancouver No. 1 CWRS 13½%	Argentina F.O.B. B.A.	U.S. Gulf No. 2 H.W.	Rotter-dam C.I.F. U.S. No. 2 Hard Winter
1985-6	3.08	3.22	3.28	3.26	3.94	4.07	3.72	3.34	3.12	141	173	106	137	169
1986-7	2.42	2.76	2.72	2.87	3.07	3.57	2.90	2.59	2.66	120	161	88	117	148
1987-8	2.57	2.89	2.96	2.95	3.15	4.13	3.06	2.74	2.94	115	134	89	114	141
1988-9	3.72	4.00	4.17	4.08	4.36	5.53	4.53	4.13	3.90	150	177	125	146	176
1989-90	3.72	3.92	4.22	3.94	4.16	4.25	4.28	3.88	3.80	176	202	151	171	190
1990-1	2.61	2.74	2.94	2.81	3.06	3.48	3.16	2.75	2.59	144	158	107	137	164
1991-2	3.00	3.49	3.77	3.32	3.82	3.61	4.11	3.66	3.41	137	141	99	129	154
1992-3	3.24	3.49	3.67	3.54	3.91	3.88	4.11	3.73	3.18	165	177	122	152	173
1993-4[1]	3.26	3.20	3.60	3.23	5.02	5.76	3.53	NA	3.16	153	192	131	141	200

[1] Preliminary.   [2] Calendar year.   NA = Not available.   Source: Economic Research Service, U.S. Department of Agriculture

Wheat Government Loan Program Data in the United States   Loan Rates (Cents Per Bushel)

Crop Year Beginning June	National Average[3]	Target Rate	Corn Belt (Soft Red Winter)	Central & Southern Plains (Hard Winter)	Northern Plains (Spring & Durum)	Pacific Northwest (White)	Placed Under Loan	% of Production	Acquired by CCC Under Program	Total Stocks	Total CCC Stocks	CCC Loans	Farmer-Owned Reserve	"Free"
										Millions of Bushels				
1986-7	240	438	236	237	240	250	514	24.6	473	1,905	602	678	463	528
1987-8	228	438	235	226	228	239	472	22.4	147	1,821	830	237	467	511
1988-9	221	423	233	221	221	232	106	5.8	45	1,261	283	178	287	225
1989-90	206	410	214	204	206	217	113	5.6	62	702	191	19	144	275
1990-1	195	400	200	194	195	206	405	14.8	90	536	117	144	14	691
1991-2	204	400	209	200	204	214	143	7.2	1	868	163	14	50	273
1992-3[1]	221	400	232	220	221	237	240	9.8	.1	475	152	50	28	353
1993-4[2]	245	400	251	243	245	269	258	14.7	.3	531	150	28	6	412
1994-5[2]	258	400					207	12.4	0	569	150	6	0	314

[1] Preliminary.   [2] Estimate.   [3] The national average loan rate at the farm as a percentage of the parity-priced wheat at the beginning of the marketing year.
Source: Agricultural Marketing Service, U.S. Department of Agriculture

Exports of Wheat (Only)[2] from the United States   In Thousands of Bushels

Year	June	July	Aug.	Sept.	Oct.	Nov.	Dec.	Jan.	Feb.	Mar.	Apr.	May	Total
1986-7	79,497	104,677	114,853	98,234	84,769	59,182	53,837	65,047	67,764	65,529	65,426	64,603	923,419
1987-8	119,769	157,706	112,758	119,945	101,680	71,166	113,609	140,228	143,959	149,146	152,830	147,667	1,530,46
1988-9	121,842	111,498	107,562	127,564	93,153	93,309	100,149	115,846	127,060	141,780	115,916	90,658	1,346,33
1989-90	90,490	137,933	131,176	150,697	89,336	68,664	81,813	78,343	87,647	104,903	84,576	71,572	1,177,15
1990-1	88,235	80,831	93,617	107,786	84,488	76,800	56,444	66,473	91,313	112,809	88,526	81,760	1,029,07
1991-2	59,167	79,319	97,794	94,991	124,155	136,385	112,771	132,413	115,126	103,024	116,850	59,764	1,231,75
1992-3	75,045	96,382	99,290	92,723	132,232	108,235	111,389	111,584	118,607	118,782	126,845	104,540	1,295,65
1993-4	85,874	103,836	100,516	104,732	100,618	112,667	121,900	109,389	87,250	96,873	71,575	82,838	1,178,06
1994-5[1]	73,364	66,314	103,941	117,555	101,450	107,549	104,139						674,312

[1] Preliminary..   [2] Grains.   *Source: Economic Research Service, U.S. Department of Agriculture*

United States Wheat and Flour Imports and Exports   In Thousands of Bushels

Year Beginning June	Imports — Wheat — Suitable for Milling	Unfit for Human Consumption	Grain	Flour & Products[2]	Total	P.L. 480	Foreign Donations Sec. 416	Aid[3]	Total Concessional	CCC Export Credit	Export Enhancement Program	Total U.S. Wheat Exports
			--- Wheat Equivalent ---						In Thousands of Metric Tons			
1985-6	11,340	71	11,412	4,875	16,287	4,685	76	513	5,274	7,740	4,916	24,626
1986-7	14,837	984	15,821	5,430	21,250	3,927	406	1	4,334	8,125	12,214	28,204
1987-8	9,020	969	9,989	6,097	16,086	3,321	1,186	292	4,800	9,273	26,679	40,523
1988-9	15,870	NA	15,870	6,798	22,668	3,020	138	806	3,964	8,897	17,906	37,774
1989-90	13,548	NA	12,583	9,884	22,467	2,985	0	28	3,065	7,759	12,806	27,999
1990-1	25,540	NA	25,574	10,832	36,407	2,975	0	0	3,067	8,339	15,150	26,792
1991-2	31,615	NA	31,019	9,675	40,694	2,286	0	0	2,416	13,334	21,111	34,322
1992-3[1]			56,859	13,142	70,001	2,704	1,681	0	5,828	8,538	21,832	36,039

[1] Preliminary.   [2] Includes macaroni, semolina & similar products.   [3] Shipments mostly under the Commodity Import Program, financed with foreign aid funds.   NA = Not available.   *Source: Economic Research Service, U.S. Department of Agriculture*

Wheat Stocks in the United States   In Millions of Bushels

Year	On Farms Mar. 1	June 1	Sept. 1	Dec. 1	Off Farms Mar. 1	June 1	Sept. 1	Dec. 1	Total Stocks Mar. 1	June 1	Sept. 1	Dec. 1
1986	NA	681.1	1,293.0	1,063.0	NA	1,223.9	1,861.6	1,610.5	2,255.8	1,905.0	3,154.6	2,673.5
1987	794.0	560.0	1,168.0	971.0	1,456.4	1,260.9	1,820.5	1,534.3	2,250.4	1,820.9	2,988.5	2,505.3
1988	748.0	525.0	798.0	620.0	1,175.5	735.8	1,455.6	1,095.9	1,923.5	1,260.8	2,253.6	1,715.9
1989	463.0	289.0	832.0	592.0	764.7	412.6	1,086.0	830.5	1,227.7	701.6	1,918.0	1,422.5
1990	376.0	212.5	1,000.0	763.2	567.1	324.0	1,409.5	1,144.8	943.1	536.5	2,409.5	1,909.5
1991	532.9	341.2	828.0	564.8	863.3	524.7	1,212.7	877.3	1,396.3	865.9	2,040.7	1,442.1
1992	275.6	144.6	979.4	672.0	611.7	327.2	1,128.2	918.5	887.2	471.9	2,107.6	1,590.5
1993	378.0	183.8	987.0	653.1	670.3	346.8	1,145.6	932.6	1,048.3	530.7	2,132.6	1,585.7
1994[1]	363.2	175.3	859.8	575.6	664.8	393.2	1,209.7	919.7	1,028.0	568.5	2,069.5	1,495.2

[1] Preliminary.   NA = Not available.   *Source: Crop Reporting Board, U.S. Department of Agriculture*

WHEAT

Wheat Supply and Distribution in Canada, Australia and Agrentina   In Millions of Metric Tons

| | --------- Canada (Year Beginning Aug. 1) --------- | | | | | --------- Australia (Year Beginning Oct. 1) --------- | | | | | --------- Agrentina (Year Beginning Dec. 1) --------- | | | | |
| | ------------- Supply ------------- | | | -- Disappearance -- | | ------------- Supply ------------- | | | -- Disappearance -- | | ------------- Supply ------------- | | | -- Disappearance -- | |
Crop Year	Stocks Aug. 1	New Crop	Total Supply	Domestic	Exports[3]	Stocks Oct. 1	New Crop	Total Supply	Domestic	Exports[3]	Stocks Dec. 1	New Crop	Total Supply	Domestic	Exports[3]
1983-4	10.0	26.5	36.5	5.5	21.8	2.3	22.0	24.3	3.4	13.3	1.1	12.8	13.9	4.7	7.8
1984-5	9.2	21.2	30.2	5.2	17.5	7.5	18.7	26.2	2.9	15.8	1.3	13.2	14.5	4.6	9.4
1985-6	7.6	24.3	31.9	5.6	17.7	8.6	16.2	24.8	2.9	16.0	.5	8.5	9.0	4.4	4.3
1986-7	8.6	31.4	40.0	6.4	20.8	5.9	16.1	22.0	2.7	15.6	.3	8.9	9.2	4.5	4.4
1987-8	12.7	25.9	38.7	7.9	23.5	3.8	12.4	16.1	3.5	9.9	.2	8.8	9.0	4.5	3.7
1988-9	7.3	15.9	23.2	5.8	12.4	2.8	14.1	16.8	2.9	11.3	.8	8.4	9.2	4.7	4.0
1989-90	5.0	24.8	29.8	6.5	16.9	2.6	14.2	16.8	3.0	10.8	.5	10.2	10.7	4.5	6.1
1990-1	6.4	32.1	38.5	6.5	20.5	3.0	15.1	18.1	3.5	11.7	0	10.9	10.9	4.5	4.8
1991-2	10.3	31.9	42.2	7.7	24.3	2.8	10.6	13.4	3.4	8.2	.8	9.9	10.7	4.6	5.7
1992-3[1]	10.1	29.9	40.0	7.9	21.7	2.9	16.2	19.1	4.2	9.5	.3	9.8	10.1	4.3	7.3
1993-4[1]	12.4	27.2	39.6	9.4	18.7	5.0	16.9	21.9	4.1	12.8	0	9.4	9.4	4.6	4.5
1994-5[2]	11.2	23.4	34.6	6.7	20.5	4.1	8.6	12.7	4.8	6.8	.2	10.5	10.7	4.6	5.6

[1] Preliminary.   [2] Forecast.   [3] Including flour.   Source: Foreign Agricultural Service, U.S. Department of Agriculture

United States Wheat Quarterly Supply and Disappearance   In Millions of Bushels

| | --------------------- Supply --------------------- | | | | ------------------------------- Disappearance ------------------------------- | | | | | | --------- Ending Stocks --------- | | |
| | | | | | ----------------- Domestic Use ----------------- | | | | | Total Disap- | | | |
Year Beginning June 1	Beginning Stocks	Pro- duction	Imports[3]	Total Supply	Food	Seed	Feed & Residual[6]	Total	Exports[3]	pearance	Gov't. Owned[4]	Privately Owned[5]	Total Stocks
1987-8	1,821.0	2,107.7	16.1	3,945	720.7	85.0	290.2	1,096.0	1,587.9	2,683.8	283.0	977.8	1,260.8
June-Aug.	1,821.0	2,107.7	2.7	3,931	181.0	1.0	363.8	545.8	409.0	954.8	798.8	2,189.7	2,976.5
Sept.-Nov.	2,977.0	---------	4.5	2,981	193.0	58.0	-79.1	172.0	308.5	480.4	755.4	1,750.5	2,500.6
Dec.-Feb.	2,501.0	---------	3.7	2,504	172.1	3.0	-7.3	167.7	413.0	580.8	450.1	1,473.4	1,923.5
Mar.-May	1,924.0	---------	5.1	1,929	174.6	23.0	12.8	210.4	547.4	667.8	283.0	977.8	1,260.8
1988-9	1,261.0	1,812.2	22.6	3,096	725.8	103.0	150.5	979.2	1,414.9	2,394.1	190.5	511.1	701.6
June-Aug.	1,261.0	1,812.2	8.6	3,082	183.3	1.0	282.2	466.4	361.6	828.1	250.0	2,003.6	2,253.6
Sept.-Nov.	2,254.0	---------	6.3	2,260	197.3	67.0	-49.4	214.9	329.0	543.9	213.0	1,502.9	1,715.9
Dec.-Feb.	1,716.0	---------	3.7	1,720	173.4	3.0	-44.5	131.9	360.0	491.9	203.2	1,024.5	1,227.7
Mar.-May	1,228.0	---------	4.1	1,232	171.8	32.0	-37.8	166.0	364.2	530.2	190.5	511.1	701.6
1989-90	701.6	2,036.6	23.4	2,761	748.9	104.3	139.1	992.3	1,232.0	2,224.3	116.6	419.9	536.5
June-Aug.	701.6	2,036.6	5.9	2,744	190.7	1.7	264.9	457.4	368.7	826.1	167.9	1,750.1	1,918.0
Sept.-Nov.	1,918.0	---------	7.1	1,925	191.7	70.3	-87.8	174.1	328.6	502.7	154.5	1,268.0	1,422.5
Dec.-Feb.	1,423.0	---------	4.7	1,427	184.3	2.7	37.4	224.4	259.6	484.0	136.5	806.6	943.1
Mar.-May	943.1	---------	5.8	948	182.2	29.6	-75.4	136.4	275.1	411.5	116.6	419.9	536.5
1990-1	536.5	2,729.8	36.4	3,303	789.8	92.9	482.4	1,365.1	1,069.5	2,434.5	162.7	705.4	868.1
June-Aug.	536.5	2,729.8	8.0	3,274	194.1	1.7	399.7	595.5	267.7	863.1	104.6	2,306.5	2,411.1
Sept.-Nov.	2,409.5	---------	13.4	2,425	210.6	62.9	-38.3	235.2	279.4	514.5	129.9	1,780.0	1,909.9
Dec.-Feb.	1,908.0	---------	7.8	1,918	191.0	2.1	101.5	294.6	225.5	520.0	152.5	1,245.2	1,397.7
Mar.-May	1,396.0	---------	7.2	1,405	194.1	26.3	19.5	239.9	296.9	536.8	162.7	705.4	868.1
1991-2	868.1	1,980.1	40.7	2,889	789.5	97.2	244.5	1,131.6	1,282.3	2,413.9	152.0	323.0	475.0
June-Aug.	868.1	1,980.1	7.8	2,856	189.4	1.2	359.1	549.6	251.7	801.3	162.8	1,891.9	2,054.7
Sept.-Nov.	2,054.7	---------	7.3	2,062	213.0	62.2	-26.9	248.3	365.9	614.2	160.7	1,287.1	1,447.8
Dec.-Feb.	1,447.8	---------	10.7	1,459	192.9	2.4	-0.5	194.8	371.7	566.5	156.9	735.1	892.0
Mar.-May	892.0	---------	14.9	907	194.2	31.9	-87.3	138.9	293.0	431.9	152.0	323.0	475.0
1992-3[1]	475.0	2,466.8	70.0	3,012	834.3	99.1	194.2	1,127.6	1,353.6	2,481.2	150.0	380.7	530.7
June-Aug.	475.0	2,466.8	20.1	2,962	212.1	1.4	345.3	558.8	282.6	841.4	151.6	1,969.0	2,120.6
Sept.-Nov.	2,120.6	---------	16.4	2,137	218.8	63.4	-81.9	200.3	345.0	545.3	151.1	1,440.6	1,591.7
Dec.-Feb.	1,591.7	---------	17.4	1,609	196.7	2.6	5.2	204.5	356.3	560.8	150.4	897.9	1,048.3
Mar.-May	1,048.3	---------	16.1	1,064	206.7	31.7	-74.4	164.0	369.7	533.7	150.0	380.7	530.7
1993-4[1]	530.7	2,396.4	108.8	3,036	869.3	96.3	274.1	1,239.7	1,227.8	2,467.4	150.3	418.2	568.5
June-Aug.	530.7	2,396.4	14.6	2,942	211.3	1.3	295.8	508.4	300.7	809.1	149.9	1,982.7	2,132.6
Sept.-Nov.	2,132.6	---------	30.1	2,163	225.3	60.9	-38.5	247.7	329.2	577.0	150.3	1,435.4	1,585.7
Dec.-Feb.	1,585.7	---------	26.9	1,613	210.1	2.3	39.9	252.3	332.3	584.6	150.4	877.6	1,028.0
Mar.-May	1,028.0	---------	37.2	1,065	222.6	31.8	-23.2	231.2	265.5	496.7	150.3	418.2	568.5
1994-5[2]	568.5	2,320.6	90.0	2,979	875.0	98.0	250.0	1,223.0	1,300.0	2,523.0	142.0	314.1	456.1
June-Aug.	568.5	2,320.6	30.7	2,920	212.3	1.6	376.7	590.7	259.6	850.3	146.4	1,923.1	2,069.5
Sept.-Nov.	2,069.5	---------	21.4	2,091	228.2	61.9	-32.6	257.5	338.2	595.7	142.8	1,350.2	1,495.2

[1] Preliminary.   [2] Forecast.   [3] Imports & exports include flour and other products expressed in wheat equivalent.   [4] Uncommitted, Government only.
[5] Includes total loans.   [6] Includes alcoholic beverages.   Source: Economic Research Service, U.S. Department of Agriculture

Average Price of No. 2 Soft Red Winter (30 Days) Wheat at Chicago   In Dollars Per Bushel

Year	June	July	Aug.	Sept.	Oct.	Nov.	Dec.	Jan.	Feb.	Mar.	Apr.	May	Average
1982-3	3.31	3.36	3.35	3.18	2.98	3.33	3.23	3.32	3.40	3.36	3.51	3.55	3.32
1983-4	3.53	3.59	3.71	3.62	3.56	3.42	3.55	3.47	3.34	3.57	3.65	3.65	3.56
1984-5	3.51	3.44	3.49	3.47	3.51	3.62	3.49	3.51	3.55	3.58	3.63	3.34	3.51
1985-6	3.27	3.09	2.87	2.83	3.04	3.33	3.46	3.34	3.37	3.40	3.39	3.25	3.22
1986-7	2.52	2.58	2.44	2.36	2.57	2.73	2.76	2.87	2.91	3.11	3.16	3.08	2.76
1987-8	2.63	2.54	2.61	2.77	2.82	2.80	3.00	3.23	3.23	2.94	3.02	3.13	2.89
1988-9	3.56	3.52	3.61	3.84	4.07	4.09	4.25	4.39	4.30	4.31	4.04	4.07	4.00
1989-90	3.87	3.92	3.94	3.93	4.07	4.07	4.13	4.03	3.92	3.61	3.83	3.71	3.92
1990-1	3.26	3.04	2.83	2.62	2.62	2.41	2.52	2.50	2.53	2.76	2.80	2.83	2.73
1991-2	2.86	2.79	2.97	3.24	3.50	3.57	3.79	4.12	4.15	3.71	3.53	3.68	3.49
1992-3	3.60	3.39	3.09	3.24	3.39	3.60	3.59	3.77	3.67	3.58	3.72	3.19	3.49
1993-4	2.82	3.03	3.12	2.99	3.02	3.29	3.53	3.67	3.48	3.20	3.15	3.15	3.20
1994-5	3.21	3.14	3.34	3.63	3.97	3.85	3.99	3.88					3.63

Source: Agricultural Marketing Service, U.S. Department of Agriculture

Stocks of Wheat Flour Held by Mills in the United States   In Thousands of Sacks (100 Pounds Each)

Year	Jan. 1	April 1	July 1	Oct. 1	Year	Jan. 1	April 1	July 1	Oct. 1
1984	3,805	3,780	3,763	3,833	1990	5,207	5,072	5,818	7,980
1985	4,230	4,363	5,040	5,052	1991	8,051	5,474	8,115	6,336
1986	4,847	4,740	5,141	5,101	1992	5,660	5,210	5,841	5,864
1987	5,228	4,900	5,581	5,258	1993	5,487	4,863	6,197	5,882
1988	5,858	4,508	4,822	5,303	1994[1]	5,611	6,232	6,091	6,295
1989	4,800	4,423	5,116	5,489	1995[1]	7,627			

[1] *Preliminary.*   *Source: U.S. Department of Commerce*

WHEAT

Commercial Stocks of Domestic Wheat[1] in the United States, at First of Month   In Millions of Bushels

Year	July	Aug.	Sept.	Oct.	Nov.	Dec.	Jan.	Feb.	Mar.	Apr.	May	June
1984-5	265.2	423.0	413.7	409.4	387.8	352.8	309.9	268.0	248.5	239.8	215.1	221.4
1985-6	312.5	434.8	474.8	510.9	504.2	473.9	446.3	435.7	413.0	400.3	399.0	407.2
1986-7	437.5	483.7	494.7	475.9	472.7	445.0	435.0	420.0	410.1	393.3	381.1	366.8
1987-8	417.8	436.5	443.7	451.9	439.9	421.4	387.1	361.1	302.6	261.2	235.6	203.7
1988-9	291.6	334.2	342.4	340.8	331.1	297.2	293.7	266.5	213.3	181.1	150.1	114.4
1989-90	130.5	171.6	211.7	211.8	196.0	180.2	164.2	150.4	127.9	109.7	87.2	77.8
1990-1	121.8	212.7	289.7	290.2	284.6	264.8	243.7	237.7	------	------	174.5	174.5
1991-2	244.8	275.5	296.9	308.2	271.0	264.8	249.8	227.0	205.2	180.7	170.9	209.1
1992-3	269.6	290.5	202.5	228.2	231.9	202.7	185.5	169.5	153.3	132.6	112.9	87.0
1993-4	102.9	145.1	171.8	194.9	199.3	174.9	169.5	168.3	162.2	143.8	127.3	111.4
1994-5	145.7	203.9	243.1	269.7	268.6	238.2	199.5	181.0				

[1] Domestic wheat in storage in public and private elevators in 39 markets and wheat afloat in vessels or barges at lake and seaboard ports, the first Saturday of the month.   *Source: Livestock Division, U.S. Department of Agriculture*

Average Open Interest of All Wheat Futures Contracts at Chicago & Kansas City   In Thousands of Bushels

Year	Jan.	Feb.	Mar.	Apr.	May	June	July	Aug.	Sept.	Oct.	Nov.	Dec.	Kansas City[2] Jan.
1985	206,892	191,587	173,737	190,077	194,039	197,308	186,000	196,731	170,237	169,586	149,812	152,746	95,317
1986	165,634	160,985	162,241	176,466	178,596	187,200	177,405	173,918	173,247	183,853	152,193	125,838	71,056
1987	128,805	137,113	147,187	154,030	160,892	175,160	176,293	200,085	199,244	194,362	163,349	152,801	66,850
1988	192,824	209,322	206,533	217,011	209,546	283,122	283,710	280,121	342,077	372,677	348,955	313,480	112,972
1989	334,519	315,770	323,343	308,643	301,955	349,492	335,590	327,315	307,555	261,229	260,113	270,586	156,530
1990	271,124	281,973	284,920	257,741	283,120	319,096	322,882	298,960	286,186	291,155	279,248	235,303	142,888
1991	242,983	257,602	279,608	268,339	265,149	294,983	274,730	261,417	276,101	306,286	288,394	259,224	128,872
1992	307,419	350,761	294,787	268,528	254,891	251,702	300,579	310,357	250,467	272,821	288,463	246,317	177,990
1993	251,644	239,291	224,427	241,772	256,763	279,143	293,523	321,674	293,017	307,481	314,383	252,615	148,971
1994	269,558	240,064	225,548	237,148	222,762	273,110	285,754	326,938	365,999	392,094	354,076	335,752	196,237

[1] Chicago Board of Trade.   [2] Kansas City Board of Trade.   *Source: Commodity Futures Trading Commission*

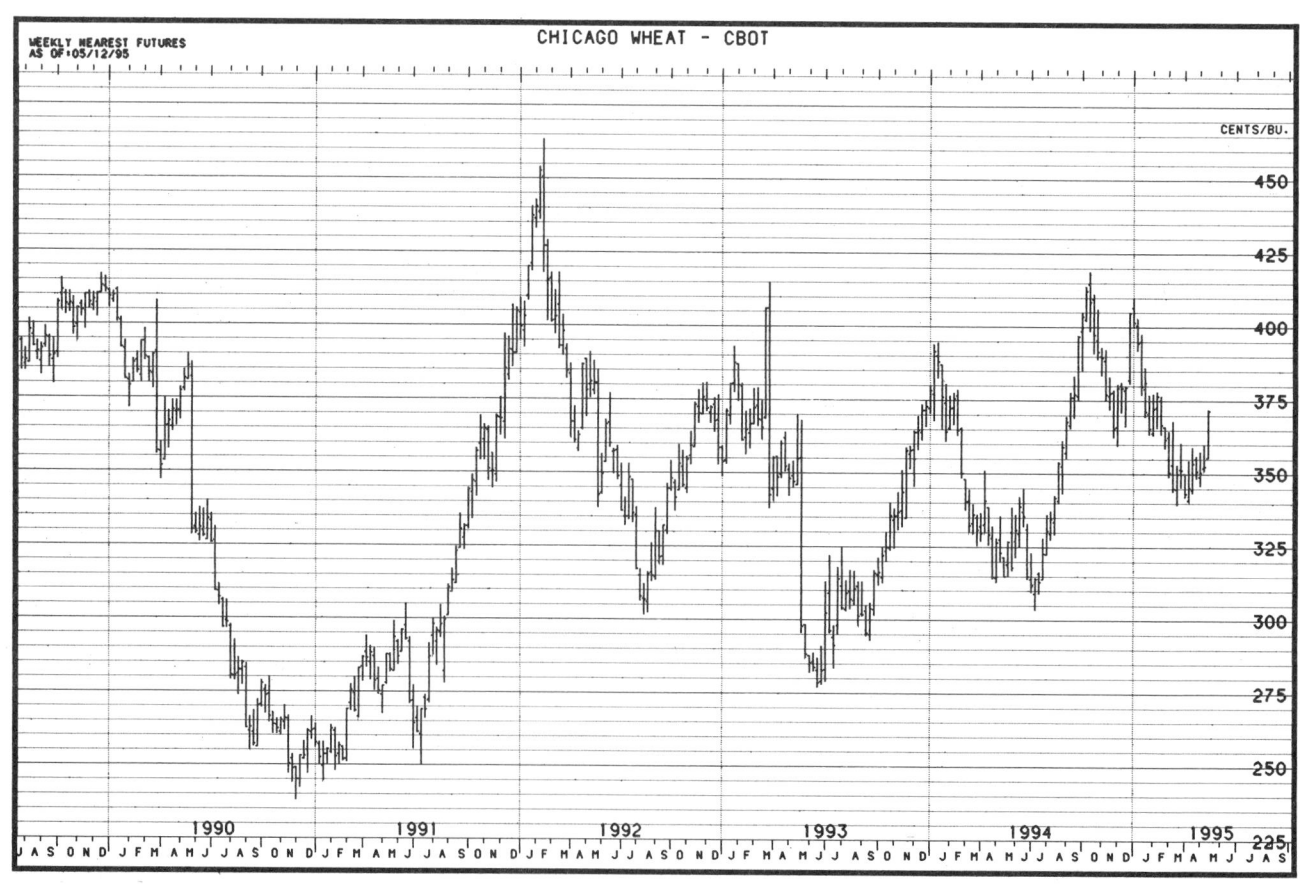

Average Price of No. 1 Hard Red Winter (Ordinary Protein) Wheat, at Kansas City   In Cents Per Bushel

Year	June	July	Aug.	Sept.	Oct.	Nov.	Dec.	Jan.	Feb.	Mar.	Apr.	May	Average
1987-8	270	259	265	278	290	290	310	320	328	310	314	320	296
1988-9	379	377	378	403	413	418	425	440	437	432	446	455	417
1989-90	444	428	424	418	428	436	439	430	413	404	413	391	422
1990-1	360	311	289	282	281	278	278	271	277	294	298	304	294
1991-2	299	291	310	331	364	376	406	466	451	433	402	390	377
1992-3	391	352	327	356	360	378	381	397	375	374	359	351	367
1993-4	333	338	334	337	352	339	415	400	380	364	363	365	360
1994-5	360	348	370	405	431	424	427	406					396

Source: Economic Research Service, U.S. Department of Agriculture

Average Price of No. 1 Dark Northern Spring Wheat at Minneapolis (14% Protein)   In Cents Per Bushel

Year	June	July	Aug.	Sept.	Oct.	Nov.	Dec.	Jan.	Feb.	Mar.	Apr.	May	Average
1987-8	307	294	294	304	315	311	313	324	332	315	330	342	315
1988-9	432	423	424	432	433	422	426	444	440	456	447	455	436
1989-90	441	436	418	408	411	412	423	421	406	396	408	409	416
1990-1	396	356	305	284	285	280	282	283	285	300	307	310	306
1991-2	304	294	310	321	368	378	411	436	456	436	428	444	382
1992-3	442	404	365	379	385	394	388	405	387	387	380	371	391
1993-4	396	480	488	490	517	550	545	532	529	494	499	505	502
1994-5	420	414	400	427	440	441	437	421					425

Source: Economic Research Service, U.S. Department of Agriculture

Average Price[1] Received by Farmers for Wheat in the U.S.   In Cents Per Bushel

Year	June	July	Aug.	Sept.	Oct.	Nov.	Dec.	Jan.	Feb.	Mar.	Apr.	May	Average[2]
1987-8	244	232	236	253	262	269	270	275	279	274	279	297	257
1988-9	337	350	361	374	384	388	394	402	403	407	403	401	372
1989-90	385	378	374	372	375	372	379	371	356	348	349	340	372
1990-1	308	279	258	246	243	239	240	242	243	253	260	264	255
1991-2	255	250	263	280	307	325	344	354	378	372	365	364	300
1992-3	343	315	301	320	321	329	331	337	333	330	326	311	324
1993-4	284	285	296	310	325	347	363	358	360	370	356	343	326
1994-5	321	304	324	356	377	376	373	360					349

[1] Weighted average by sales. [2] Includes an allowance for unredeemed loans at average loan value.   *Source: Economic Research Service, U.S. Department of Agriculture*

Average Producer Price Index of Wheat Flour (Spring[1])   June 1983 = 100

Year	July	Aug.	Sept.	Oct.	Nov.	Dec.	Jan.	Feb.	Mar.	Apr.	May	June	Average
1987-8	88.4	88.0	90.1	91.3	90.1	90.0	91.2	94.4	90.6	93.5	93.9	107.0	92.4
1988-9	107.0	107.7	110.0	110.5	109.0	109.1	110.7	110.0	112.4	109.5	112.0	112.7	110.5
1989-90	112.1	110.7	109.5	108.5	108.7	109.6	109.4	109.0	106.9	108.8	107.9	106.0	100.2
1990-1	99.7	93.4	92.0	91.2	89.4	89.8	88.7	90.2	92.0	93.0	94.0	93.0	94.5
1991-2	91.3	94.1	96.3	100.1	97.5	102.7	109.7	116.4	111.5	110.3	109.2	111.0	107.3
1992-3	104.9	99.6	104.1	104.4	104.7	103.5	107.5	108.1	107.2	108.4	105.2	104.7	105.2
1993-4	103.7	107.2	102.1	107.3	108.4	112.5	111.8	110.5	109.9	107.9	109.0	106.4	108.1
1994-5	100.8	101.2	109.2	112.8	111.2	112.0							107.9

[1] Standard patent.   *Source: Bureau of Labor Statistics, U.S. Department of Commerce (0212-0301)*

World Wheat Flour Production (Monthly Average)   In Thousands of Metric Tons

Year	Australia[3]	France	Germany	Hungary	India	Japan	Kazakhstan	Rep. of Korea	Mexico	Poland	Russia	Sweden	Turkey	United Kingdom	Yugoslavia
1987	101.4	418.4	273.0	99.7	293.8	374.7	161.2	134.4	188.0	226.9	NA	38.1	133.0	319.1	190.2
1988	105.5	433.6	282.0	98.0	363.3	372.1	159.1	141.0	198.6	236.3	NA	38.4	111.2	333.0	183.8
1989	109.0	435.6	280.0	102.2	391.3	378.4	164.0	134.5	207.0	241.1	NA	40.1	136.4	333.0	193.4
1990	114.9	442.7	218.1	102.4	394.3	374.3	163.5	134.7	209.4	150.6	NA	41.0	112.9	328.0	175.5
1991	112.7	464.8	341.1	97.7	398.0	390.3	167.8	130.4	207.3	128.6	NA	47.7	111.1	326.0	160.4
1992	113.9	465.2	327.0	106.9	400.0	NA	161.0	129.4	223.3	167.1	NA	44.6	112.2	NA	NA
1993[1]	120.8	480.6	336.4	75.0	399.4	367.6	155.3	129.5	214.0	113.4	449.5	44.8	122.1	327.3	82.0
1994[2]	123.0	463.5	330.5	59.2	314.0	378.5	150.6	132.7	220.6	97.6	323.6	47.2	102.9	324.4	62.5

[1] Preliminary. [2] Estimate. [3] Average of twelve months ending June 30.   NA = Not available.   *Source: United Nations*

WHEAT

United States Wheat Flour Production   In Millions of Sacks (100 Pounds Each)

Year	July	Aug.	Sept.	Oct.	Nov.	Dec.	Jan.	Feb.	Mar.	Apr.	May	June	Total
1986-7	26.4	28.9	29.1	30.4	28.9	28.2	26.3	26.6	28.0	26.9	29.2	28.7	241.0
1987-8	27.6	30.1	29.3	31.3	29.8	28.0	26.5	26.5	27.1	26.0	29.2	28.6	340.0
1988-9	28.5	31.4	29.4	31.3	31.1	28.5	29.1	27.1	27.0	27.2	28.6	26.6	345.8
1989-90	26.6	32.3	29.8	31.8	30.0	27.8	27.9	28.0	29.2	27.0	27.6	26.7	354.3
1990-1	27.7	33.7	29.9	32.2	32.7	29.1	29.4	29.5	29.5	29.4	29.2	29.1	362.3
1991-2	29.2	31.8	30.1	32.2	32.7	29.2	29.3	29.3	29.4	30.0	29.8	29.8	363.0
1992-3	31.1	34.2	31.9	34.6	32.2	29.2	30.6	31.3	34.1	32.0	31.0	30.3	382.4
1993-4	30.7	33.3	32.9	33.5	34.0	33.8	30.7	29.9	35.7	32.1	32.0	30.9	389.6
1994-5[1]	30.3	34.7	33.9	34.8	33.5	31.5							198.6

[1] Preliminary.   Source: Bureau of Census, U.S. Department of Commerce

United States Wheat Flour Exports (Grain Equivalent[2])   In Thousands of Bushels

Year	June	July	Aug.	Sept.	Oct.	Nov.	Dec.	Jan.	Feb.	Mar.	Apr.	May	Total
1986-7	5,104	4,795	6,675	4,731	5,999	2,332	6,664	6,681	3,676	6,173	6,722	6,365	65,918
1987-8	5,450	6,816	4,749	3,999	3,418	6,746	4,316	6,934	2,556	823	2,463	2,520	50,790
1988-9	7,036	6,400	6,002	2,402	7,908	3,368	6,086	4,108	6,040	3,974	6,469	5,205	64,998
1989-90	907	1,897	5,775	8,917	3,579	6,817	3,606	4,943	3,124	4,466	6,132	3,287	53,450
1990-1	1,035	2,207	2,785	1,464	3,303	3,407	4,480	2,698	3,809	6,301	3,719	3,525	38,733
1991-2	5,582	5,362	4,207	3,743	1,179	2,222	3,140	2,549	5,549	4,630	3,771	4,579	46,514
1992-3	3,257	5,284	2,856	2,325	3,840	4,641	3,903	2,325	7,744	5,832	7,499	5,285	54,789
1993-4	4,408	3,793	1,811	3,642	3,840	3,416	3,170	5,838	4,390	6,099	4,198	3,368	47,972
1994-5[1]	2,922	6,824	5,636	3,407	3,105	4,721	4,734						31,349

[1] Preliminary.   [2] Includes meal, groats and durum.   Source: Economic Research Service, U.S. Department of Agriculture

Supply and Distribution of Wheat Flour in the United States

Year	Wheat Ground 1,000 Bu.	Millfeed Production 1,000 Tons	Flour Production[3]	Flour & Product Imports[2]	Total Supply	Exports Flour	Exports Products[2]	Domestic Disappearance	Total Population July 1 Millions	Per Capita Disappearance Pounds
					1,000 Cwt.					
1986	737,537	5,799	326,316	2,252	328,568	26,160	124	302,283	240.7	126
1987	767,507	6,260	341,565	2,663	344,228	28,880	144	315,204	242.8	130
1988	769,699	6,163	344,154	2,727	346,881	24,097	185	322,599	245.0	132
1989	761,021	6,072	342,762	3,337	346,099	25,265	180	320,654	247.3	130
1990	788,186	6,109	354,348	3,623	357,971	18,872	273	338,826	249.9	136
1991	808,966	6,436	362,311	4,070	366,381	20,044	440	345,897	252.6	137
1992	833,339	6,707	370,829	5,037	375,866	20,711	619	354,536	255.4	139
1993	871,408	6,963	387,419	6,233	393,652	23,241	548	369,863	258.1	143
1994[1]	880,130	7,179	390,017	9,048	399,065	24,234	734	374,097	260.7	144

[1] Preliminary.   [2] Import and exports of macaroni and noodle products (flour equivalent), reporting methods changed in 1990.   [3] Commercial production of wheat flour, whole wheat, industrial and durum flour and farina reported by Bureau of Census.   Source: Economic Research Service, U.S. Department of Agriculture

Wheat and Flour -- Price Relationship at Milling Centers   In Dollars

Crop Year (June-May)	At Kansas City Cost of Wheat to Produce 100 lb. Flour[1]	At Kansas City Bakery Flour Per 100 lb.[2]	At Kansas City By-Products Obtained 100 lb. Flour[3]	At Kansas City Total Products Actual	At Kansas City Total Products Over Cost of Wheat	At Minneapolis Cost of Wheat to Produce 100 lb. Flour[1]	At Minneapolis Bakery Flour Per 100 lb.[2]	At Minneapolis By-Products Obtained 100 lb. Flour[3]	At Minneapolis Total Products Actual	At Minneapolis Total Products Over Cost of Wheat
1989-90	9.58	10.41	1.45	11.86	2.28	9.48	10.00	1.36	11.36	1.89
1990-1	6.86	7.78	1.29	9.07	2.21	6.98	7.73	1.21	8.94	1.96
1991-2	8.58	9.53	1.26	10.79	2.21	8.71	9.39	1.16	10.55	1.84
1992-3	8.53	9.65	1.28	10.93	2.40	8.91	10.12	1.15	11.27	2.37
1993-4	10.03	10.34	1.46	11.79	1.77	11.45	12.50	1.28	13.77	2.33
1994-5 I	8.56	9.72	1.27	10.99	2.43	9.38	10.82	1.14	11.95	2.57
II	9.73	10.80	1.29	12.09	2.36	9.94	11.13	1.11	12.24	2.30
Dec.[4]	9.85	10.95	1.31	12.26	2.41	9.96	11.10	1.06	12.16	2.19
Jan.[4]	9.28	10.50	1.10	11.60	2.32	9.60	10.70	.87	11.57	1.97

[1] Based on 73% extraction rate, cost of 2.28 bushels: at Kansas City, No. 1 hard winter, 13 % protein; and at Minneapolis, No. 1 dark northern spring, 14% protein.   [2] Quoted as mid-month bakers' standard patent at Kansas City and spring standard patent at Minneapolis, bulk basis.   [3] Assumed 50-50 millfeed distribution between bran and shorts or middlings, bulk basis.   Source: Agricultural Marketing Service, U.S. Department of Agriculture

Wool

Global year-to-year world wool production has been declining since 1989/90 when 7.4 billion pounds (greasy) were produced (equivalent to four billion pounds clean). The reason is lower sheep numbers, down from 1,154 million head in 1989/90 to 1,053 million in 1993/94. More than 10 percent of the world's sheep is in Australia. Clean wool production in 1993/94 of 3.6 billion pounds compares with 3.7 billion in 1992/93. World consumption slipped moderately in 1993/94 to 3.6 billion from 1992/93, and compares with 3.8 billion five years earlier. There are signs, however, that global use could stabilize if the strong demand from the Far East and Europe persists. World stocks have increased sharply during the past few years, to an estimated 1.4 billion (clean) at the beginning of 1993/94 from 0.3 billion for the 1989/90 season.

Global wool foreign trade during the past few years showed an irregular trend. Exports (greasy) in 1993/94 of nearly 2.3 billion pounds were up from 2.1 billion in 1992/93, but down from over 2.4 billion in 1991/92. Australia exports about two-thirds of the world's wool, with New Zealand much of the balance followed by Argentina and South Africa. Importing nations are numerous, but the leaders include China, whose imports have increased sharply in the 1990s, Japan, the United Kingdom and Italy. U.S. imports have averaged about 115 million pounds (greasy) during the past few years, equal to about 90 million pounds clean.

Australian wool accounts for more than 80 percent of U.S. imports. The U.S. exports a small amount of wool, mostly to Korea and China. Global wool prices are a function of origin and grade. South African wool is generally more than twice Australian prices, while the latter are somewhat higher than New Zealand's prices.

The total 1994 U.S. supply of raw wool was about 192 million pounds, clean. That was two percent below 1993 and so far the lowest supply of the 1990s. Stocks have also declined sharply, to 34 million pounds at year-end 1994 from 89 million five years earlier. Imports in 1994 were placed at 100 million pounds. Mill use, however, has held steady since 1991 at about 152 million pounds, necessitating a draw upon stocks and some increase in imports.

Wool prices in the U.S. in the first half of 1994 were considerably higher than in 1993, basis Australian grade 64's, type 62. Towards the end of the year, finer grade Australian wool was showing more price strength, while the 64's appeared to have stabilized. The USDA's Commodity Credit Corporation set the wool support price for the 1994 marketing year at $2.09 per pound. 1994 marked the first year of a two-year phaseout of the wool program.

Futures Markets

Greasy wool futures are traded on the Sydney Futures Exchange (SFE).

World Production of Wool   In Metric Tons (Degreased)

Year	Argentina	Australia	China	Kazak-hstan[3]	New Zealand	Pakistan	Romania	Russia[3]	South Africa	United Kingdom	United States	Uruguay	World Total
1986	92,000	505,000	109,800	------	268,000	29,700	25,655	281,400	48,500	42,130	21,400	59,000	1,822,602
1987	73,311	573,200	124,800	------	308,400	31,400	25,640	273,000	45,000	44,466	20,560	55,000	1,932,887
1988	81,200	546,585	112,000	------	310,100	32,450	28,000	286,800	46,200	47,000	21,660	54,000	1,931,251
1989	87,600	622,000	120,111	------	302,800	34,800	20,900	284,400	46,500	52,765	21,665	60,000	2,011,693
1990	85,800	724,000	122,400	64,750	233,000	28,200	26,500	136,050	49,500	53,358	21,140	58,100	2,029,209
1991	75,400	699,000	123,000	62,640	227,000	28,900	19,196	122,700	51,000	51,055	20,830	56,500	1,953,339
1992[1]	74,200	574,000	121,500	22,200	221,000	29,600	18,900	107,400	48,500	50,876	19,980	50,700	1,786,344
1993[2]	58,000	557,000	122,000	21,000	200,000	30,400	24,000	108,000	45,000	48,693	20,220	49,410	1,719,217

[1]Preliminary. [2]Estimate. [3]Formerly part of the U.S.S.R.; data not reported separately until 1990.
Source: Food and Agriculture Organization of the United Nations

Wool Goods1 Production in the United States   In Millions of Yards

Year	First Quarter	Second Quarter	Third Quarter	Fourth Quarter	Total Year	Year	First Quarter	Second Quarter	Third Quarter	Fourth Quarter	Total Year
1985	40.6	39.5	24.3	34.0	138.3	1990	38.0	38.7	32.6	31.4	140.7
1986	37.7	38.8	27.3	30.2	134.1	1991	38.0	48.7	41.4	41.5	169.6
1987	48.0	45.9	36.0	40.9	168.9	1992	45.7	47.2	43.9	39.5	176.3
1988	50.6	53.0	43.0	43.9	190.5	1993[2]	48.4	48.9	43.9	42.8	184.0
1989	48.3	50.9	40.1	37.0	176.3	1994[2]	49.1	51.0	39.4	38.9	178.4

[1]Woolen and worsted woven goods, except woven felts. [2]Preliminary. *Source: Bureau of Census, U.S. Department of Commerce*

Price Received by Farmers for Shorn Wool (Greasy Basis) in the U.S.   In Cents Per Pound

Year	Jan.	Feb.	Mar.	Apr.	May	June	July	Aug.	Sept.	Oct.	Nov.	Dec.	Average[1]
1988	84.8	109.0	140.0	153.0	166.0	161.0	134.0	122.0	113.0	123.0	119.0	116.0	138.0
1989	109.0	131.0	133.0	135.0	136.0	134.0	121.0	112.0	115.0	147.0	102.0	94.0	124.0
1990	68.5	74.4	81.8	87.6	93.9	90.7	75.6	71.0	53.2	74.2	55.9	47.6	80.0
1991	42.0	46.0	50.0	55.0	61.0	63.0	57.0	47.0	47.0	59.0	49.0	39.0	55.0
1992	46.0	61.0	73.0	81.0	85.0	81.0	72.0	62.0	59.0	71.0	60.0	55.0	74.0
1993[2]	43.3	43.7	45.5	45.5	55.0	55.1	48.6	38.8	37.8	51.6	50.6	38.1	50.0

[1]Weighted average. [2]Price quotes discontinued in 1994. *Source: Economic Research Service, U.S. Department of Agriculture*

WOOL

Salient Statistics of Wool in the United States

Year	Sheep & Lambs Shorn[4] 1,000s	Weight per Fleece Lbs.	Shorn Wool Production 1,000 Lbs.	Price per Lb.	Value of Production 1,000 $	Shorn Wool — Support $ Per Lb.	Shorn Wool — Payment Rate $ Per Lb.	Total Wool Production	Domestic Production	Exports Domestic Wool	Dutiable Imports for Consumption[3] (48's & Finer)	Total New Supply[2]	Duty Free Raw Imports (Not Finer than 46's)	Mill Consumption – Apparel	Mill Consumption – Carpet
1984	12,322	7.77	95,670	79.5	75,988	165	107.5	95,670	50,514	488	63,271	144,202	30,905	128,982	13,088
1985	11,247	7.88	88,055	63.3	55,732	165	160.7	88,055	46,493	1,415	50,164	124,550	29,308	106,051	10,562
1986	10,827	7.82	84,372	66.8	56,331	178	166.5	84,372	44,548	788	66,090	140,751	30,901	126,768	9,960
1987	10,922	7.75	84,450	91.7	77,009	181	97.4	84,450	44,590	1,037	74,054	148,673	31,066	129,677	13,092
1988	11,531	7.76	89,482	138.0	124,993	178	29.0	89,482	47,246	1,247	72,324	142,740	24,417	117,069	15,633
1989	11,314	7.89	89,220	124.0	110,537	177	42.7	89,220	47,108	1,188	77,003	152,860	29,937	120,534	14,122
1990	11,222	7.84	88,033	80.0	69,534	182	127.5	88,033	46,481	2,736	50,328	115,461	21,388	120,622	12,124
1991	11,009	7.97	87,740	55.0	47,178	188	241.8	87,740	46,327	3,867	68,242	128,916	18,214	137,187	14,352
1992[1]	10,568	7.89	83,411	74.0	60,473	197	166.2	83,411	44,041	3,413	65,457	129,912	23,827	136,143	14,695

[1]Preliminary. [2]Production minus exports plus imports; stocks not taken into consideration. [3]Apparel wool includes all dutiable wool; carpet wool includes all duty-free wool. [4]Includes sheep shorn at commercial feeding yards. *Source: Economics Service, U.S. Department of Agriculture*

Consumption of Apparel Wool in the United States — In Millions of Pounds – Clean Basis

Year	Jan.	Feb.	Mar.	Apr.	May	June	July	Aug.	Sept.	Oct.	Nov.	Dec.	Total
1984	10.6	12.0	14.0	11.3	11.9	13.0	8.2	9.9	11.2	8.5	8.9	9.4	129.0
1985	9.1	8.1	9.6	8.4	9.0	10.5	6.5	8.1	10.4	8.6	8.8	8.9	106.1
1986	11.9	10.6	10.0	12.7	10.2	10.8	11.3	9.4	9.4	11.1	9.3	10.1	126.8
1987	9.9	11.0	12.9	10.9	10.6	12.7	9.0	9.4	11.7	10.9	9.6	11.2	129.7
1988	9.1	9.2	12.6	9.3	8.7	12.1	9.1	8.8	9.5	9.2	8.3	11.2	117.1
1989	10.6	11.1	13.7	10.4	8.7	11.9	9.3	9.7	10.8	9.4	7.8	9.1	113.0
1990	-------	31.5	-------	-------	31.7	-------	-------	26.9	-------	-------	30.5	-------	120.6
1991	-------	31.6	-------	-------	37.1	-------	-------	34.6	-------	-------	33.9	-------	137.2
1992	-------	36.4	-------	-------	35.1	-------	-------	33.6	-------	-------	31.1	-------	136.2
1993	-------	35.5	-------	-------	35.9	-------	-------	35.5	-------	-------	34.4	-------	141.3
1994[1]	-------	36.5	-------	-------	35.6	-------	-------	32.6	-------	-------	33.9	-------	138.6

[1]Preliminary. *Source: Bureau of Census, U.S. Department of Commerce*

Average Wool Prices[1] – Australian – 64's, Type 62, Duty Paid – U.S. Mills — In Cents Per Pound

Year	Jan.	Feb.	Mar.	Apr.	May	June	July	Aug.	Sept.	Oct.	Nov.	Dec.	Average
1985	246	233	236	227	234	229	230	226	224	224	217	222	229
1986	231	229	231	238	252	242	NA	229	224	230	240	250	236
1987	252	259	288	325	327	335	332	373	341	348	347	356	324
1988	391	468	496	564	564	513	489	467	461	488	472	475	487
1989	511	484	454	429	414	403	405	410	414	417	417	420	431
1990	417	404	403	414	406	342	338	352	355	343	332	332	370
1991	334	335	209	221	271	286	NA	248	229	215	274	270	242
1992	259	270	277	264	268	246	NA	224	210	192	195	193	236
1993	186	176	170	158	179	169	167	154	153	171	175	176	170
1994	204	216	205	223	249	258	243	248	259	256	273	281	243

[1]Raw, clean basis. *Source: Economic Research Service, U.S. Department of Agriculture*

Average Wool Prices – Domestic[1] – Graded Territory, 64's, Staple 2 3/4 & Up – U.S. Mills — In Cents Per Lb.

Year	Jan.	Feb.	Mar.	Apr.	May	June	July	Aug.	Sept.	Oct.	Nov.	Dec.	Average
1985	205	195	185	182	191	193	193	193	193	193	193	193	192
1986	193	189	180	188	198	198	193	190	190	190	190	190	191
1987	193	202	216	260	270	270	270	300	295	300	300	300	265
1988	315	397	435	453	463	460	450	450	450	463	475	450	438
1989	450	438	410	375	375	365	350	350	350	350	333	300	370
1990	294	287	287	284	275	257	242	235	235	235	225	220	256
1991	217	210	163	167	203	230	230	167	156	148	148	155	158
1992	163	203	195	196	199	218	210	188	210	193	168	168	193
1993	158	148	132	127	135	140	138	140	130	129	133	133	124
1994	140	150	170	201	226	230	230	235	250	238	238	238	212

[1]Raw, shorn, clean basis. *Source: U.S. Department of Agriculture*

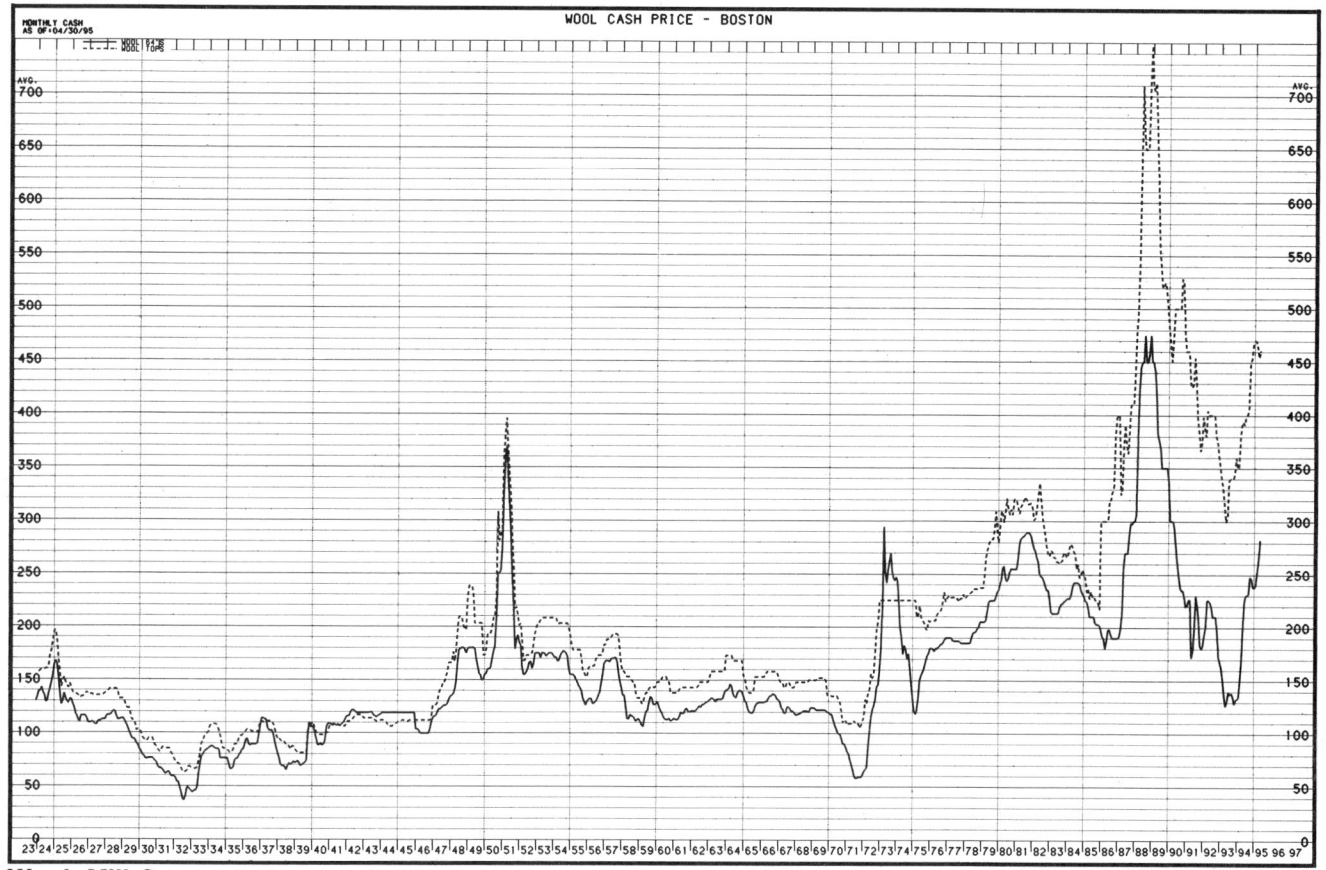

WOOL CASH PRICE - BOSTON

Wool: Mill Consumption, by Grades in the U.S., Scoured Basis   In Millions of Pounds

| | Apparel Wool[1] | | | | | | | |
| | Woolen System | | | Worsted System | | | | |
Year	60's & Finer	50's Up to 60's	Total	60's & Finer	Coarser Than 60's	Total	All Total	Carpet Wool[2]
1983	30.5	30.2	60.7	42.4	23.6	66.0	126.7	13.9
1984	32.9	32.3	65.2	39.7	24.1	63.8	129.0	13.1
1985	28.0	27.7	55.7	33.6	16.7	50.3	106.0	10.6
1986	34.1	32.2	66.3	41.7	18.8	60.5	126.8	10.0
1987	32.4	28.6	61.0	53.8	14.8	68.7	129.7	13.1
1988	23.8	20.9	44.7	54.5	17.9	72.4	117.1	15.6
1989	24.1	21.8	45.9	56.1	18.5	74.6	120.5	14.1
1990	26.2	24.9	51.1	50.6	18.9	69.5	120.6	12.1
1991	32.0	26.6	58.6	56.5	22.1	78.6	137.2	14.4
1992[3]	33.9	25.6	59.5	58.5	18.1	76.7	136.1	14.7
1993[4]	40.9	26.6	67.5			73.9	141.4	15.4

[1]Domestic & duty-paid foreign. [2]Duty-free foreign. [3]Preliminary. [4]Estimate. *Source: Economic Research Service, U.S. Department of Agriculture*

United States Imports[1] of Unmanufactured Wool (Clean Yield)   In Millions of Pounds

Year	Jan.	Feb.	Mar.	Apr.	May	June	July	Aug.	Sept.	Oct.	Nov.	Dec.	Total
1984	11.2	9.0	7.8	7.8	10.4	6.7	9.6	6.4	6.0	6.9	5.6	6.8	94.2
1985	10.7	5.8	6.0	5.7	7.1	4.9	7.3	4.5	6.9	7.1	5.5	8.0	79.5
1986	10.2	8.8	7.6	7.5	8.0	8.6	7.8	6.3	7.0	5.0	9.2	10.8	97.0
1987	8.6	8.2	9.5	8.7	13.4	8.9	8.6	8.4	6.7	7.0	8.2	9.0	105.1
1988	12.0	12.7	8.8	9.1	8.6	7.4	7.7	5.0	3.3	6.7	8.6	6.7	96.7
1989	8.7	11.3	9.0	13.1	10.3	8.3	10.0	6.9	3.9	10.4	5.1	9.8	106.9
1990	7.3	9.2	4.7	8.2	5.0	4.8	3.4	5.5	5.0	6.9	7.5	4.2	71.7
1991	10.7	6.9	5.4	5.5	7.3	8.1	9.2	7.0	4.4	7.8	5.1	9.0	86.5
1992	10.2	8.1	7.3	10.6	8.8	6.2	6.9	5.0	3.9	5.5	9.1	7.8	89.3
1993	7.8	8.7	8.5	9.3	11.0	9.6	9.7	8.7	5.7	5.9	7.7	7.2	100.3
1994[2]	8.4	10.0	7.4	12.7	7.5	7.7	6.9	6.5	4.1		5.7	8.1	

[1]Data are imports for consumption. [2]Preliminary. *Source: Economic Research Service, U.S. Department of Agriculture*

Zinc

Zinc is utilized as a protective coating on other metals, such as iron or steel, in a process known as galvanizing. Zinc also has use as an alloy with copper to make brass, and as an alloying compound with aluminum and magnesium.

For the January-June 1994 period, U.S. mine production of recoverable zinc was 270,056 tonnes, compared with 1993 production of 488,374 tonnes. Smelter production of slab zinc for the first half of 1994 was 205,800 tonnes. For all of 1993, smelter production of zinc was 398,900 tonnes. Zinc oxide production was put at 63,689 tonnes compared with 126,859 tonnes for 1993 as a whole.

In October 1994, the International Lead and Zinc Study Group (ILZSG) forecast that western world production of zinc metal in 1994 was expected to fall one percent below the 1993 level of 5.38 million tonnes, with output in Europe forecast down three percent to 2.1 million tonnes.

Consumption was expected to increase significantly by four percent to 5.76 million tonnes. Strong growth was expected in the U.S., and Europe was expected to recover from declines in 1992 and 1993. Mine output in the western world in 1994 was forecast to fall two percent to 5.13 million tonnes due to declines in Canada and a sharp fall in Australian output. Exports from Eastern countries, particularly China, have been increasing, noted the ILZSG. For 1995, the ILZSG saw a further increase in consumption of almost four percent to 5.97 million tonnes. U.S. consumption was seen as more limited as was Japan. Mine output in 1995 was expected to increase 5 percent to 5.42 million tonnes, due to increased production in Canada and Australia. Zinc metal production was forecast to show a more limited increase of 1.5 percent to 5.45 million tonnes. Exports from Eastern countries were expected to remain substantial.

For the January-June 1994 period, according to the United States Bureau of Mines, U.S. consumption of zinc was 458,700 tonnes. For all of 1993 it was 851,800 tonnes. Consumption of slab zinc over the first half of 1994 was 331,045 tonnes, while for all of 1993 it was 617,835 tonnes. Consumption of base scrap zinc was 60,000 tonnes. In 1993 it was 110,000 tonnes. Copper-base scrap consumption was 66,000 tonnes compared with 121,000 tonnes in 1993. Stocks of slab zinc on June 30, 1994 were 57,000 tonnes. Producers held 19 percent of stocks, consumers held 71 percent and merchants held over 9 percent. Slab zinc is used by various industries. Over the January-June 1994 period, sheet and strip galvanizing used 37 percent, brass and bronze took 14 percent, and zinc-base alloy consumed 21 percent.

U.S. imports of slab zinc over the January-May 1994 period were 303,911 tonnes. In 1993, they were 723,563 tonnes. Canada supplied almost 67 percent of the total while Mexico, Peru, Spain and Australia were less important suppliers. Imports of zinc ore and concentrate had zinc content of 10,581 tonnes over the same period. Mexico and Peru were the major suppliers. Imports of waste and scrap (gross weight) were 18,835 tonnes in the first five months of 1994 while imports of zinc oxide (gross weight) were 18,142 tonnes. Canada supplied 61 percent of the zinc oxide while Mexico shipped almost 18 percent.

U.S. exports of zinc ore are much less than imports. For the first five months of 1994, exports of slab zinc were 5,312 tonnes; ore and concentrate (zinc content) were 36,394 tonnes; waste and scrap (zinc content) 16,141 tonnes; zinc oxide (gross weight) 4,272 tonnes; and zinc sulfate 1,252 tonnes.

Futures Market

Zinc futures are traded on the London Metal Exchange (LME).

U.S. Historical Salient Zinc Statistics   In Metric Tons

Year	Slab Zinc Production Primary	Slab Zinc Production Secondary	Mine Production (Recovered)	Imports for Consumption Slab Zinc	Imports for Consumption Ore (Zinc Content)	Exports Ore Slab Zinc	Exports (Zinc Content)	Consumption Slab Zinc[3]	Consumption Consumed as Ore	Consumption All Classes[4]	Net Import as % of Consumption	High-Grade Price Cents/Lb.
1979	472,481	53,212	267,341	524,130	87,499	279	20,095	1,000,606	79,710	1,394,314	63	37.30
1980	340,456	29,396	317,103	410,163	182,370	302	54,457	811,146	58,986	1,142,409	60	37.43
1981	346,563	50,192	312,418	612,007	245,710	323	54,232	840,875	60,643	1,189,369	65	44.56
1982	228,176	74,288	303,160	456,233	66,809	341	77,289	795,000	35,515	1,038,600	58	38.47
1983	235,694	69,390	275,294	617,679	63,156	427	60,168	933,000	36,912	1,246,300	65	41.39
1984	253,432	78,113	252,768	639,228	86,172	760	30,579	980,000	45,487	1,344,000	68	48.60
1985	261,209	72,563	226,545	610,900	90,186	1,011	23,264	961,000	39,886	1,257,000	70	40.37
1986	253,369	62,912	202,983	665,126	75,786	1,938	3,269	999,000	19,236	1,274,000	73	38.00
1987	261,345	82,589	216,327	705,985	46,464	1,082	16,921	1,052,000	2,536	1,324,000	69	41.92
1988	241,294	88,492	244,314	748,130	62,966	482	33,590	1,089,000	2,412	1,340,000	70	60.20
1989	260,305	97,904	275,883	711,554	40,974	5,532	78,877	1,060,000	2,107	1,311,000	61	82.02
1990	262,704	95,708	515,355	631,742	46,684	1,238	220,446	992,000	2,178	1,240,000	41	74.59
1991	253,276	124,078	517,804	549,137	45,419	1,253	381,416	933,000	2,098	1,165,000	24	52.77
1992[1]	272,000	128,000	523,430	644,482	44,523	5,886	307,114	1,035,000	2,400	1,276,000	30	58.38
1993[2]	255,000	120,000	488,374	723,563	33,093	8,765	311,278	1,035,000	2,200	1,360,000	45	46.15
1994[2]	240,000	140,000	556,580	707,954	27,374	13,220	386,578	1,134,000	2,400	1,350,000	41	46.40

[1]Preliminary. [2]Estimate. [3]Data through 1981 are reported consumption of slab zinc; 1982 forward, data are apparent consumption of slab zinc. [4]Based on apparent consumption of slab zinc plus zinc content or ores and concentrates and secondary materials used to make zinc dust and chemicals.
Source: U.S. Bureau of Mines

World Production of Zinc[3]   In Thousands of Metric Tons

Year	Australia	Belgium	Canada	France	Germany	Italy	Japan	Kazak-hstan[4]	Mexico	Norway	Peru	Poland	Spain	United Kingdom	United State	World Total
1988	307.0	298.1	703.2	274.1	376.3	242.1	678.2	963.0	192.5	121.2	123.1	174.0	256.0	76.0	329.8	7,163
1989	296.5	306.0	669.7	265.8	372.0	259.5	714.7	977.0	193.3	120.4	126.7	163.7	246.4	79.8	358.2	7,245
1990	308.5	356.5	591.8	263.1	350.3	264.4	731.6	890.0	199.3	125.1	120.6	132.2	252.7	93.3	358.4	7,178
1991	326.5	385.1	660.6	299.6	345.7	263.8	778.7	800.0	189.1	124.9	154.6	126.0	262.2	100.7	375.8	7,311
1992[1]	333.5	310.6	671.7	305.0	383.1	253.0	780.6	250.0	151.6	127.6	124.4	134.6	365.9	96.8	399.5	7,136
1993[2]	314.5	300.8	60.0	336.0	380.0	270.0	696.0	250.0	209.9	127.5	124.0	130.0	258.0	105.0	381.8	7,177

[1]Preliminary. [2]Estimated. [3]Secondary metal included. [4]Formerly part of the U.S.S.R.;data not reported separately until 1992. *Source: U.S. Bureau of Mines*

Consumption (Reported) of Slab Zinc in the United States, by Industries and Grades   In Metric Tons

Year	Total	By Industries — Gal-vanizers	Brass Products	Zinc-Base Alloy[3]	Zinc Oxide	Other	By Grades — Special High Grade	High Grade	Remelt and Other	Prime Western
1988	832,425	406,541	89,995	205,566	61,367	68,956	412,417	104,235	93,852	221,921
1989	884,655	444,603	95,798	189,690	70,417	84,147	458,020	120,433	94,340	214,410
1990	801,969	388,421	104,276	171,771	67,532	69,969	445,427	92,424	78,265	210,373
1991[1]	764,038	364,629	97,952	169,883	64,035	67,539	421,316	91,468	57,786	189,930
1992[2]	814,228	396,480	112,990	165,598	71,224	67,936	414,661	119,660	56,185	223,723
1993[2]	773,709	372,279	107,137	157,676	63,448	73,169	403,696	116,500	71,202	182,309

[1]Preliminary. [2]Estimated. [3]Die casters. *Source: U.S. Bureau of Mines*

Zinc Foreign Trade of the United States   In Metric Tons

Year	Ores[1]	Imported for Consumption — Blocks, Pigs, Slabs	Sheets, Plates, Other	Waste & Scrap	Dross, Ashes, Fume	Dust, Powder & Flakes	Total Value $1,000	Zinc Ore & Manufactures Exported — Blocks, Pigs, Anodes, etc. Un-wrought	Un-wrought Alloys	Wrought & Alloys Sheets, Plates & Strips	Angles, Bars, Rods, etc.	Waste & Scrap	Dust (Blue Powder)	Zinc Ore & Con-centrates
1987	46,464	705,985	960	4,025	6,727	7,001	608,256	1,082	5,825	1,732	1,271	90,204	1,927	16,921
1988	62,699	749,133	4,100	5,727	6,346	7,652	884,524	482	5,748	3,814	2,016	103,732	2,221	33,590
1989	40,974	711,554	3,066	9,367	9,031	7,253	1,241,659	5,532	2,423	16,515	2,653	108,086	8,137	78,877
1990	46,684	631,742	929	31,720	6,411	8,834	1,049,940	1,238	4,566	11,881	3,731	109,316	8,701	220,446
1991	45,419	549,137	539	31,596	6,483	15,424	687,879	1,253	4,224	10,385	6,151	96,314	5,737	381,416
1992	44,523	644,482	171	31,176	11,813	17,051	910,289	---- 5,886 ----		NA	NA	82,088	5,889	307,114
1993[2]	33,093	723,563	136	38,079	11,862	16,218	799,999	---- 8,765 ----		NA	NA	46,385	6,727	311,278
1994[3]	27,374	793,482	475	51,676	12,152	11,954	871,200	--- 14,351 ---		NA	NA	58,297	7,200	389,488

[1]Zinc content. [2]Preliminary. [3]Estimate. NA = Not available. *Source: U.S. Bureau of Mines*

U.S. Mine Production of Recoverable Zinc   In Thousands of Metric Tons

Year	Jan.	Feb.	Mar.	Apr.	May	June	July	Aug.	Sept.	Oct.	Nov.	Dec.	Total
1987	17.8	17.8	19.0	18.0	17.8	18.1	17.8	19.1	18.5	18.5	16.1	18.5	216.3
1988	16.8	18.2	22.3	21.9	22.0	22.4	18.8	21.5	19.9	19.9	19.9	19.3	244.3
1989	22.2	20.8	22.9	22.4	23.4	24.3	20.8	25.3	23.1	25.1	22.8	20.9	275.9
1990	26.9	24.8	26.4	26.2	27.9	45.6	50.7	57.1	44.7	42.7	40.4	43.6	515.4
1991	45.5	41.9	43.8	45.5	49.4	36.9	43.0	47.4	49.5	39.0	33.4	38.0	517.8
1992	41.5	48.8	47.7	40.3	40.7	40.4	46.2	49.1	47.6	36.2	40.4	42.2	520.1
1993[1]	48.0	42.5	46.4	39.5	43.0	40.7	33.5	32.1	35.9	41.8	41.4	43.4	488.3
1994[1]	43.2	40.2	48.4	48.3	47.9	47.1	52.5	49.5	50.1	41.6	46.0	48.0	556.6
1994[1]	43.2	40.2	48.4	48.3	47.9	47.1	52.5	49.5	50.1	41.6	46.0	48.0	556.6

[1]Preliminary. *Source: U.S. Bureau of Mines*

U.S. Consumption of Slab Zinc by Fabricators   In Thousands of Metric Tons

Year	Jan.	Feb.	Mar.	Apr.	May	June	July	Aug.	Sept.	Oct.	Nov.	Dec.	Total
1987	66.2	78.9	101.0	87.0	81.2	86.9	87.2	98.3	93.0	96.1	95.5	84.4	1,052.0
1988	79.5	76.4	110.3	97.9	110.7	84.6	73.9	111.8	100.0	97.5	87.2	88.1	1,089.0
1989	90.0	81.4	96.0	81.6	97.0	82.1	76.1	101.2	81.2	92.0	92.7	78.0	1,060.0
1990	82.4	79.2	88.0	74.0	79.4	91.0	102.8	100.0	73.0	86.0	73.0	67.1	826.5
1991	80.0	69.0	65.9	67.8	68.3	68.8	73.6	78.0	79.3	85.9	84.2	82.0	764.0
1992	93.8	77.2	85.0	89.9	76.0	76.9	47.2	53.8	52.2	53.5	50.3	47.6	814.2
1993[1]	50.9	49.2	55.8	59.2	60.8	55.7	44.6	49.1	47.0	52.7	50.9	51.0	774.0
1994[1]	50.8	53.7	55.7	58.5	58.7	52.7	48.0	53.2	53.6	53.9	52.5	45.0	623.0

[1]Preliminary. *Source: U.S. Bureau of Mines*

ZINC

Average Price of Zinc, Prime Western Slab (Delivered U.S. Basis)   In Cents Per Pound)

Year	Jan.	Feb.	Mar.	Apr.	May	June	July	Aug.	Sept.	Oct.	Nov.	Dec.	Average
1987	43.33	41.38	41.38	41.38	44.15	46.92	48.00	48.00	44.87	43.38	44.10	45.38	44.36
1988	45.90	46.93	49.36	54.14	57.74	65.08	68.38	68.38	69.88	71.07	72.54	75.37	62.07
1989	81.58	89.01	95.38	87.76	85.38	81.06	80.38	83.26	81.88	80.31	76.57	73.38	83.00
1990	71.33	66.47	77.37	83.12	87.38	87.38	86.54	82.45	81.00	72.30	70.00	70.00	77.95
1991	70.00	64.53	62.00	62.00	62.00	62.00	62.00	N.Q.	N.Q.	50.44	54.85	59.22	60.90
1992	57.62	56.40	60.19	64.12	66.83	67.29	64.57	66.47	67.12	57.84	52.16	52.71	61.11
1993	52.70	53.18	49.72	50.07	49.27	46.75	46.90	45.08	44.54	46.21	46.54	48.69	48.30
1994	49.64	48.29	46.70	46.16	47.66	48.42	48.81	48.26	50.55	53.81	58.64	57.41	50.36

Source: American Metal Market